T0188818

# Lecture Notes in Computer Science　　10892

*Commenced Publication in 1973*
Founding and Former Series Editors:
Gerhard Goos, Juris Hartmanis, and Jan van Leeuwen

## Editorial Board

David Hutchison
　*Lancaster University, Lancaster, UK*
Takeo Kanade
　*Carnegie Mellon University, Pittsburgh, PA, USA*
Josef Kittler
　*University of Surrey, Guildford, UK*
Jon M. Kleinberg
　*Cornell University, Ithaca, NY, USA*
Friedemann Mattern
　*ETH Zurich, Zurich, Switzerland*
John C. Mitchell
　*Stanford University, Stanford, CA, USA*
Moni Naor
　*Weizmann Institute of Science, Rehovot, Israel*
C. Pandu Rangan
　*Indian Institute of Technology Madras, Chennai, India*
Bernhard Steffen
　*TU Dortmund University, Dortmund, Germany*
Demetri Terzopoulos
　*University of California, Los Angeles, CA, USA*
Doug Tygar
　*University of California, Berkeley, CA, USA*
Gerhard Weikum
　*Max Planck Institute for Informatics, Saarbrücken, Germany*

More information about this series at http://www.springer.com/series/7410

Bart Preneel · Frederik Vercauteren (Eds.)

# Applied Cryptography and Network Security

16th International Conference, ACNS 2018
Leuven, Belgium, July 2–4, 2018
Proceedings

 Springer

*Editors*
Bart Preneel 🆔
imec-COSIC
KU Leuven
Heverlee
Belgium

Frederik Vercauteren 🆔
imec-COSIC
KU Leuven
Heverlee
Belgium

ISSN 0302-9743          ISSN 1611-3349 (electronic)
Lecture Notes in Computer Science
ISBN 978-3-319-93386-3          ISBN 978-3-319-93387-0 (eBook)
https://doi.org/10.1007/978-3-319-93387-0

Library of Congress Control Number: 2018944429

LNCS Sublibrary: SL4 – Security and Cryptology

Printed on acid-free paper

This Springer imprint is published by the registered company Springer International Publishing AG
part of Springer Nature
The registered company address is: Gewerbestrasse 11, 6330 Cham, Switzerland

# Preface

ACNS 2018, the 16th International Conference on Applied Cryptography and Network Security, was held during July 2–4, 2018, at KU Leuven, Belgium. The local organization was in the capable hands of the COSIC team at KU Leuven and we are deeply indebted to them for their support and smooth collaboration.

We received 173 paper submissions, out of which 36 were accepted, resulting in an acceptance rate of 20%. These proceedings contain revised versions of all the papers. The invited keynotes were delivered by Gilles Barthe, who spoke on formal verification of side-channel resistance and Haya Shulman who shared with the audience her perspective on RPKI's Deployment and Security of BGP.

The Program Committee consisted of 52 members with diverse backgrounds and broad research interests. The review process was double-blind. Each paper received at least three reviews; for submissions by Program Committee members, this was increased to five. During the discussion phase, additional reviews were solicited when necessary. An intensive discussion was held to clarify issues and to converge toward decisions. The selection of the program was challenging; in the end some high-quality papers had to be rejected owing to lack of space. The committee decided to give the Best Student Paper Award to the paper "Non-interactive zaps of knowledge" by Georg Fuchsbauer and Michele Orrù.

We would like to sincerely thank the authors of all submissions for contributing high-quality submissions and giving us the opportunity to compile a strong and diverse program. We know that the Program Committee's decisions can be very disappointing, especially rejections of good papers that did not find a slot in the sparse number of accepted papers.

Special thanks go to the Program Committee members; we value their hard work and dedication to write careful and detailed reviews and to engage in interesting discussions. A few Program Committee members, whom we asked to serve as shepherds, spent additional time in order to help the authors improve their works. More than 160 external reviewers contributed to the review process; we would like to thank them for their efforts.

Finally, we thank everyone else — speakers and session chairs — for their contribution to the program of ACNS 2018. We would also like to thank the sponsors for their generous support.

We hope that the papers in this volume prove valuable for your research and professional activities and that ACNS will continue to play its unique role in bringing together researchers and practitioners in the area of cryptography and network security.

April 2018

Bart Preneel
Frederik Vercauteren

# ACNS 2018

# Applied Cryptography and Network Security 2018

KU Leuven, Belgium
July 2–4, 2018

## General Chair

Bart Preneel          KU Leuven, Belgium

## Program Chairs

Bart Preneel          KU Leuven, Belgium
Frederik Vercauteren  KU Leuven, Belgium

## Program Committee

Michel Abdalla        ENS and CNRS, France
Masayuki Abe          NTT, Japan
Elli Androulaki       IBM Research, Switzerland
Alex Biryukov         University of Luxembourg, Luxembourg
Marina Blanton        University at Buffalo, The State University of New York,
                          USA
Jan Camenisch         IBM Research, Switzerland
Liqun Chen            University of Surrey, UK
Chen-Mou Cheng        National Taiwan University, Taiwan
Naccache David        ENS, France
Dieter Gollmann       Hamburg University of Technology, Germany
Peter Gutmann         University of Auckland, New Zealand
Shai Halevi           IBM Research, USA
Goichiro Hanaoka      AIST, Japan
Amir Herzberg         University of Connecticut, USA
Tibor Jager           Paderborn University, Germany
Marc Joye             NXP Semiconductors, USA
Aniket Kate           Purdue University, USA
Stefan Katzenbeisser  TU Darmstadt, Germany
Florian Kerschbaum    University of Waterloo, Canada
Aggelos Kiayias       University of Edinburgh, UK
Kwangjo Kim           KAIST, Korea
Kaoru Kurosawa        Ibaraki University, Japan
Ralf Kusters          University of Stuttgart, Germany

Xuejia Lai                    Shanghai Jiaotong University, China
Benoit Libert                 CNRS and ENS de Lyon, France
Dongdai Lin                   SKLOIS, Chinese Academy of Sciences, China
Michael Locasto               SRI International, USA
Javier Lopez                  University of Malaga, Spain
Mark Manulis                  University of Surrey, UK
Atefeh Mashatan               Ryerson University, Canada
Bart Mennink                  Radboud University, The Netherlands
Atsuko Miyaji                 JAIST, Japan
Refik Molva                   Eurecom, France
Michael Naehrig               Microsoft Research, USA
Miyako Ohkubo                 NICT, Japan
Panos Papadimitratos          KTH Royal Institute of Technology, Sweden
Thomas Peyrin                 Nanyang Technological University, Singapore
Josef Pieprzyk                QUT, Australia
Benny Pinkas                  Bar-Ilan University, Israel
Bart Preneel                  KU Leuven, Belgium
Christian Rechberger          TU Graz, Austria
Matt Robshaw                  Impinj, USA
Ahmad Sadeghi                 TU Darmstadt, Germany
Yu Sasaki                     NTT Secure Platform Laboratories, Japan
Willy Susilo                  University of Wollongong, Australia
Mehdi Tibouchi                NTT Secure Platform Laboratories, Japan
Damien Vergnaud               ENS, France
Ivan Visconti                 University of Salerno, Italy
Frederik Vercauteren          KU Leuven, Belgium
Avishai Wool                  Tel Aviv University, Israel
Moti Yung                     Colombia University, USA
Jianying Zhou                 Singapore University of Technology and Design,
                                  Singapore

## Additional Reviewers

| | | |
|---|---|---|
| Aydin Abadi | Pascal Bemmann | Jiageng Chen |
| Mai Ben Adar-Bessos | Fabrice Benhamouda | Rongmao Chen |
| Megha Agrawal | Cecilia Boschini | Yu Chen |
| Hyeongcheol Ahn | Florian Bourse | Céline Chevalier |
| Muhamad Erza Aminanto | Ferdinand Brasser | Rakyong Choi |
| Hassan Asghar | Niklas Büscher | Tung Chou |
| Nuttapong Attrapadung | Seyit Camtepe | Sherman S. M. Chow |
| Joonsang Baek | Luigi Catuogno | Peter Chvojka |
| Anubhab Baksi | Avik Chakraborti | Michele Ciampi |
| Josep Balasch | Jagmohan Chauhan | Craig Costello |
| Harry Barlett | Hao Chen | Angelo De Caro |

Yi Deng
David Derler
Christoph Dobraunig
Manu Drijvers
Li Duan
Maria Eichlseder
Kaoutar Elkhiyaoui
Keita Emura
Oguzhan Ersoy
Thomas Espitau
Gerardo Fenandez
Carmen Fernandez
Daniel Fett
Dario Fiore
Steven Galbraith
Adria Gascon
Romain Gay
Kai Gellert
Junqing Gong
Zheng Gong
Alonso Gonzalez
Lorenzo Grassi
Clémentine Gritti
Jian Guo
Jinguang Han
Yoshikazu Hanatani
Lin Hou
Guifang Huang
Jialin Huang
Ilia Iliashenko
Vincenzo Iovino
Ai Ishida
Dirmanto Jap
Saqib Kakvi
Daniel Kales
Jean-Gabriel Kammerer
Julien Keuffer
Jongkil Kim
Markulf Kohlweiss
Florian Kohnhäuser
Takeshi Koshiba
Hugo Krawczyk
Po-Chun Kuo
Rafael Kurek
Jianchang Lai

Qiqi Lai
Ben Lapid
Jeeun Lee
Qi Li
Christopher Liebchen
Tingting Lin
Helger Lipmaa
Patrick Longa
Xiapu Luo
Yiyuan Luo
Xuecheng Ma
Takahiro Matsuda
Matthew McKague
Siang Meng Sim Meng
Weizhi Meng
Markus Miettinen
Takaaki Mizuki
Kirill Morozov
Fabrice Mouhartem
Johannes Mueller
Zakaria Najm
Toru Nakanishi
Surya Nepal
Khoa Nguyen
David Niehues
Ana Nieto
Ariel Nof
David Nuñez
Kazuma Ohara
Shinya Okumura
Kazumasa Omote
Melek Önen
Leo Perrin
Thomas Peters
Le Trieu Phong
Tran Viet Xuan Phuong
Thomas Pöppelmann
Jeyavijayan Rajendran
Sebastian Ramacher
Somindu Ramanna
Daniel Rausch
Joost Renes
Sietse Ringers
Ruben Rios
Rodrigo Roman

Yusuke Sakai
Katerina Samari
John Schanck
Guido Schmitz
Jacob Schuldt
Hwajeong Seo
Mike Simon
Luisa Siniscalchi
Chunhua Su
Koutarou Suzuki
Akira Takahashi
Katsuyuki Takashima
Harry Chandra
  Tanuwidjaja
Tadanori Teruya
Yosuke Todo
Junichi Tomida
Patrick Towa
Yiannis Tselekounis
Ida Tucker
Aleksei Udovenko
Cédric Van Rompay
Dimitrios Vasilopoulos
Vesselin Velichkov
Nikita Veshchikov
Haoyang Wang
Qingju Wang
Yohei Watanabe
Keita Xagawa
Weijia Xue
Shota Yamada
Takashi Yamakawa
Hailun Yan
Guomin Yang
Kazuki Yoneyama
Hirotaka Yoshida
Hongbo Yu
Zheng Yuan
Thomas Zacharias
Rina Zeitoun
Bingsheng Zhang
Lei Zhang
Tao Zhang
Vincent Zucca

# Contents

**Privacy Preserving Computation**

**Multi-party Computation**

**Symmetric Key Primitives**

## Symmetric Key Cryptanalysis

## Public Key Encryption

## Authentication and Biometrics

**Cloud and Peer-to-Peer Security**

# Cryptographic Protocols

# A Cryptographic Analysis of the WireGuard Protocol

Benjamin Dowling$^{(\boxtimes)}$ and Kenneth G. Paterson

Information Security Group, Royal Holloway, University of London, Egham, UK
{benjamin.dowling,kenny.paterson}@rhul.ac.uk

**Abstract.** WireGuard (Donenfeld, NDSS 2017) is a recently proposed secure network tunnel operating at layer 3. WireGuard aims to replace existing tunnelling solutions like IPsec and OpenVPN, while requiring less code, being more secure, more performant, and easier to use. The cryptographic design of WireGuard is based on the Noise framework. It makes use of a key exchange component which combines long-term and ephemeral Diffie-Hellman values (along with optional preshared keys). This is followed by the use of the established keys in an AEAD construction to encapsulate IP packets in UDP. To date, WireGuard has received no rigorous security analysis. In this paper, we, rectify this. We first observe that, in order to prevent Key Compromise Impersonation (KCI) attacks, any analysis of WireGuard's key exchange component must take into account the first AEAD ciphertext from initiator to responder. This message effectively acts as a key confirmation and makes the key exchange component of WireGuard a 1.5 RTT protocol. However, the fact that this ciphertext is computed using the established session key rules out a proof of session key indistinguishability for WireGuard's key exchange component, limiting the degree of modularity that is achievable when analysing the protocol's security. To overcome this proof barrier, and as an alternative to performing a monolithic analysis of the entire WireGuard protocol, we add an extra message to the protocol. This is done in a minimally invasive way that does not increase the number of round trips needed by the overall WireGuard protocol. This change enables us to prove strong authentication and key indistinguishability properties for the key exchange component of WireGuard under standard cryptographic assumptions.

**Keywords:** Authenticated key exchange · Cryptographic protocols
Formal analysis · WireGuard

## 1 Introduction

**WireGuard:** WireGuard [11] was recently proposed by Donenfeld as a replacement for existing secure communications protocols like IPsec and OpenVPN. It has numerous benefits, not least its simplicity and ease of configuration, high performance in software, and small codebase. Indeed, the protocol is implemented

© Springer International Publishing AG, part of Springer Nature 2018
B. Preneel and F. Vercauteren (Eds.): ACNS 2018, LNCS 10892, pp. 3–21, 2018.
https://doi.org/10.1007/978-3-319-93387-0_1

in less than 4,000 lines of code, making it relatively easy to audit compared to large, complex and buggy code-bases typically encountered with IPsec and SSL/TLS (on which OpenVPN is based).

From a networking perspective, WireGuard encapsulates IP packets in UDP packets, which are then further encapsulated in IP packets. This is done carefully so as to avoid too much packet overhead. WireGuard also offers a highly simplified version of IPsec's approach to managing which security transforms get applied to which packets: essentially, WireGuard matches on IP address ranges and associates IP addresses with static Diffie-Hellman keys. This avoids much of the complexity associated with IPsec's Security Associations/Security Policy Database mechanisms.

From a cryptographic perspective, WireGuard presents an interesting design. It is highly modular, with a key exchange phase, called the handshake, that is presented as being clearly separated from the subsequent use of the keys in a data transport protocol. A key feature is the one-round (or 1-RTT) nature of the key exchange phase. The key exchange phase runs between an initiator and a responder. It combines long-term and ephemeral Diffie-Hellman values, exclusively using Curve25519 [3], and is built from the Noise protocol framework [23]. In fact, every possible pairwise combination of long-term and ephemeral values is involved in the key computations, presumably in an effort to strengthen security in the face of various combinations of long-term and ephemeral private key compromise. The long-term keys are not supported by a PKI, but are instead assumed to be pre-configured and known to the communicating parties (or trusted on first use, as per SSH). The protocol specification includes an option for using preshared keys between pairs of parties, to augment the DH-based exchange and as a hedge against quantum adversaries. The key exchange phase relies on the BLAKE2s hash function [2] for hashing parts of the transcript, to build HMAC (a hash-based MAC algorithm), and for HKDF (an HMAC-based key derivation function). The data transport protocol uses solely ChaCha20-Poly1305 as specified in RFC 7539 [22] as an AEAD scheme in a lightweight packet format. The AEAD processing incorporates explicit sequence numbers and the receiver uses a standard sliding window technique to deal with packet delays and reorderings.

**Security of WireGuard:** To the best of our knowledge, with the exception of an initial and high-level symbolic analysis,[1] WireGuard has received no rigorous security analysis. In particular, it has not benefitted from any computational (as opposed to symbolic) proofs. In this paper, we provide such an analysis.

We cannot prove the handshake protocol (as presented in [11]) secure because of an unfortunate reliance on the first message sent in the subsequent data transport protocol to provide entity authentication of the initiator to the responder. Without this extra message, there is a simple Key Compromise Impersonation (KCI) attack, violating a desirable authentication goal of the protocol. This attack was already pointed out by Donenfeld in [11]. Strictly speaking, it means that the key exchange phase is not 1-RTT (as the responder cannot safely send

---

[1] https://www.wireguard.com/papers/wireguard-formal-verification.pdf.

data to the initiator until it has received a verified data transport message from the initiator). We show that there is also an attack on the forward secrecy of the protocol in the same KCI setting, similar to observations made by Krawczyk in [18]. Such an attack recovers session keys rather than breaking authentication properties, and is arguably more serious. However, the attack requires a particular set of compromise capabilities on the part of the attacker, so we regard it more as a barrier to obtaining strong security proofs than as a practical attack.

On the other hand, if we take the extra message required to prevent the KCI attack of [11] and our new attack into account, it becomes impossible to prove the usual key indistinguishability (KI) property desired of a key exchange protocol (and which, broadly speaking, guarantees that it can be securely composed with subsequent use of the keys [9]). This is because the data transport protocol uses the very keys that we would desire to prove indistinguishable from random to AEAD-protect potentially known plaintexts. Such issues are well-known in the analysis of real-world secure communications protocols – they are endemic, for example, in the analysis of SSL/TLS prior to version 1.3 [16,19,21].

There are two basic approaches to solving this problem: analyse the entire protocol (handshake and data transport) as a monolithic entity, or modify the protocol to provide a proper key separation between keys used in the handshake to provide authentication and keys used in the data transport layer. The former approach has been successfully applied (see for example the ACCE framework of [16]) but is complex, requires models highly tuned to the protocol, and results in quite unwieldy proofs. The latter approach makes for easier analysis and highlights better what needs to be considered to be part of the key exchange protocol in order to establish its security, but necessitates changes to the protocol.

**Our Contributions:** In this paper, we adopt the latter approach, making minimally invasive changes to WireGuard to enable us to prove its security. In more detail, we work with a security model for key exchange based on that of Cremers and Feltz [10] but extended to take into account WireGuard's preshared key option. The model allows us to handle a full range of security properties in one clean sweep, including authentication, regular key indistinguishability, forward security, and KCI attacks (including advanced forms in which key security is considered). The model considers a powerful adversary who is permitted to make every combination of ephemeral and honestly-generated long-term key compromise bar those allowing trivial attacks, and who is able to interact with multiple parties in arbitrary numbers of protocol runs.

We build a description of WireGuard's key exchange phase that takes into account all of its main cryptographic features, including the fine details of its many key derivation and (partial) transcript hashing steps. However, in-line with our choice of how to handle the KI/modularity problem, we make a small modification to the handshake protocol, adding an extra flow from initiator to responder which explicitly authenticates one party to the other. This job is currently fulfilled by the first packet from initiator to responder in the data transport protocol. With this modification in place, we are then able to prove the security of WireGuard's key exchange protocol under fairly standard cryptographic assumptions, in the standard model. Specifically, our proof relies on a PRFODH assumption [8,16] (alternatively, we could have chosen to work with gap-DH and the Random Oracle Model).

**Roadmap:** Section 2 provides preliminary definitions, mostly focussed on security notions for the base primitives used in WireGuard. Section 3 describes the WireGuard handshake protocol. Section 4 presents the security model for key exchange that we use in Sect. 5, where our main security result, Theorem 1, can be found. We wrap up with conclusion and future work in Sect. 6.

## 2    Preliminaries

Here we formalise the security assumptions that we will be using in our analysis of WireGuard, specifically the security assumptions for pseudo-random function (PRF) security, for Authenticated-Encryption with Associated Data (AEAD) schemes (due to space constraints, these can be found in the full version [14]). We use an asymptotic approach, relying on primitives that are parameterised with a security parameter $\lambda$; all our definitions and results can be made concrete at the expense of using extended notation. In later sections, we will suppress all dependence on $\lambda$ in our naming of primitives to ease the notation.

We let $\mathbb{G} = \langle g \rangle$ denote a finite cyclic group of prime order $q$ that is generated by $g$. We utilise different typefaces to represent distinct objects: algorithms (such as an adversary $\mathcal{A}$ and a challenger $\mathcal{C}$ in a security game), adversarial Queries (such as Test or Reveal), protocol and per-session *variables* (such as a public-key/secret-key pair $(pk, sk)$), definitions for security notions (such as coll or aead), and `constant` protocol values (such as `InitiatorHello` and `ResponderHello`).

We now introduce the PRFODH assumption that will be needed for our analysis of WireGuard. The first version of this assumption was introduced by [16] in order to prove the TLS-DHE handshake secure in the standard model. This was subsequently modified in later works analysing real-world protocols, such as TLS-RSA [19], the in-development TLS 1.3 [12,13], and the Extended Access Control Protocol [7]. This assumption was generalised in [8] in order to capture the different variants of PRFODH in a parameterised way. We give the formulation from [8] verbatim in the full version [14].

We extend the definition from [8] similarly to [12]: compared to [8] we allow the adversary access to $\mathsf{ODH}_u$ and $\mathsf{ODH}_v$ oracles *before* the adversary issues the challenge query $x^*$. This generalisation is necessary in our analysis of WireGuard, because public ephemeral DH values are used to compute a salt value that is used as an input to a PRF during the key computations. We refer to our extension as the *symmetric generic* PRFODH *assumption*.

**Definition 1 (Symmetric Generic PRFODH Assumption).** *Let $\mathbb{G}$ be a cyclic group of order $q$ with generator $g$ (where $\mathbb{G}$, $q$ and $g$ all implicitly depend on $\lambda$). Let $\mathsf{PRF}_\lambda : \mathbb{G} \times \mathcal{M} \to \mathcal{K}$ be a function from a pseudo-random function family that takes a group element $k \in \mathbb{G}$ and a salt value $m \in \mathcal{M}$ as input, and outputs a value $y \in \mathcal{K}$. We define a security notion, sym-lr-PRFODH security,* *which is parameterised by:* $l, r \in \{n, s, m\}$ *indicating how often the adversary is allowed to query "left" and "right" oracles (*$\mathsf{ODH}_u$ *and* $\mathsf{ODH}_v$*), where* $n$ *indicates that no query is allowed,* $s$ *that a single query is allowed, and* $m$ *that multiple (polynomially many) queries are allowed to the respective oracle. Consider the following security game* $\mathsf{G}^{\mathsf{sym\text{-}lr\text{-}PRFODH}}_{\mathsf{PRF}, \mathcal{A}}$ *between a challenger* $\mathcal{C}$ *and a PPT adversary* $\mathcal{A}$*, both running on input* $\lambda$*.*

1. *The challenger* $\mathcal{C}$ *samples* $u, v \xleftarrow{\$} \mathbb{Z}_q$ *and provides* $\mathbb{G}, g, g^u, g^v$ *to* $\mathcal{A}$*.*
2. *If* $l = m$*,* $\mathcal{A}$ *can issue arbitrarily many queries to oracle* $\mathsf{ODH}_u$*, and if* $r = m$ *and* $\mathsf{sym} = Y$ *to the oracle* $\mathsf{ODH}_v$*. These are implemented as follows:*
   - $\mathsf{ODH}_u$*: on a query of the form* $(S, x)$*, the challenger first checks if* $S \notin \mathbb{G}$ *and returns* $\perp$ *if this is the case. Otherwise, it computes* $y \leftarrow \mathsf{PRF}_\lambda(S^u, x)$ *and returns* $y$*.*
   - $\mathsf{ODH}_v$*: on a query of the form* $(T, x)$*, the challenger first checks if* $T \notin \mathbb{G}$ *and returns* $\perp$ *if this is the case. Otherwise, it computes* $y \leftarrow \mathsf{PRF}_\lambda(T^v, x)$ *and returns* $y$*.*
3. *Eventually,* $\mathcal{A}$ *issues a challenge query* $x^*$*. It is required that, for all queries* $(S, x)$ *to* $\mathsf{ODH}_u$ *made previously, if* $S = g^v$*, then* $x \neq x^*$*. Likewise, it is required that, for all queries* $(T, x)$ *to* $\mathsf{ODH}_v$ *made previously, if* $T = g^u$*, then* $x \neq x^*$*. This is to prevent trivial wins by* $\mathcal{A}$*.* $\mathcal{C}$ *samples a bit* $b \xleftarrow{\$} \{0, 1\}$ *uniformly at random, computes* $y_0 = \mathsf{PRF}_\lambda(g^{uv}, x^*)$*, and samples* $y_1 \xleftarrow{\$} \{0, 1\}^\lambda$ *uniformly at random. The challenger returns* $y_b$ *to* $\mathcal{A}$*.*
4. *Next,* $\mathcal{A}$ *may issue (arbitrarily interleaved) queries to oracles* $\mathsf{ODH}_u$ *and* $\mathsf{ODH}_v$*. These are handled as follows:*
   - $\mathsf{ODH}_u$*: on a query of the form* $(S, x)$*, the challenger first checks if* $S \notin \mathbb{G}$ *or if* $(S, x) = (g^v, x^*)$ *and returns* $\perp$ *if either holds. Otherwise, it returns* $y \leftarrow \mathsf{PRF}_\lambda(S^u, x)$*.*
   - $\mathsf{ODH}_v$*: on a query of the form* $(T, x)$*, the challenger first checks if* $T \notin \mathbb{G}$ *or if* $(T, x) = (g^u, x^*)$ *and returns* $\perp$ *if either holds. Otherwise, it returns* $y \leftarrow \mathsf{PRF}_\lambda(T^v, x)$*.*
5. *At some point,* $\mathcal{A}$ *outputs a guess bit* $b' \in \{0, 1\}$*.*

*We say that the adversary wins the* $\mathsf{sym\text{-}lr\text{-}PRFODH}$ *game if* $b' = b$ *and define the advantage function*

$$\mathsf{Adv}^{\mathsf{sym\text{-}lr\text{-}PRFODH}}_{\mathsf{PRF}, \mathbb{G}, q, \mathcal{A}}(\lambda) = |2 \cdot \Pr(b' = b) - 1|.$$

*We say that the* $\mathsf{sym\text{-}lr\text{-}PRFODH}$ *assumption holds if the advantage* $\mathsf{Adv}^{\mathsf{sym\text{-}lr\text{-}PRFODH}}_{\mathsf{PRF}, \mathbb{G}, q, \mathcal{A}}(\lambda)$ *of any PPT adversary* $\mathcal{A}$ *is negligible.*

## 3   The WireGuard Protocol

The WireGuard protocol is, as presented in [11][2], cleanly separated into two distinct phases:

---

[2] And in the updated version at https://www.wireguard.com/papers/wireguard.pdf that we rely on hereafter.

- A *key exchange* or *handshake* phase, where users exchange ephemeral elliptic-curve Diffie-Hellman values, as well as encrypted long-term Diffie-Hellman values and compute AEAD keys; and
- A *data transport* phase, where users may send authenticated and confidential transport data under the previously computed AEAD keys.

The handshake phase is a 1-RTT protocol in which users maintain the following set of variables:

- A randomly-sampled session identifier $ID_\rho$ for each user in the session (i.e we use $ID_i$ to refer to the session identifier of the initiator and for the responder we refer to $ID_r$).
- An updating seed value $C_k$, is used to seed the key-derivation function at various points during the key-exchange.
- An updating hash value $H_k$, is used to hash subsets of the transcript together, to bind the computed AEAD keys to the initial key-exchange.
- A tuple of AEAD keys that are used for confidentiality of the long-term key of the initiator, and to authenticate hash values.
- Long-term elliptic-curve Diffie-Hellman keys $g^u, g^v$ of initiator and responder, respectively.
- Ephemeral elliptic-curve Diffie-Hellman keys $g^x, g^y$ of initiator and responder, respectively.
- Optional long-term preshared key $psk$.

In Fig. 1 we describe the computations required to construct the key exchange messages, which we refer to as `InitiatorHello` and `ResponderHello`. For conciseness, we do not include the chaining steps required to compute the various $C_k$ and $H_k$ values throughout the protocol (we instead list them in Table 1). Nor do we make explicit the verification of the `mac1`, `mac2` MAC values nor the `time`, `zero` AEAD values, but assume that they are correctly verified before deriving the session keys $tk_i$ and $tk_r$.

## 3.1 Remarks on the Protocol

As noted in the introduction (and noted by Donenfeld [11]), it is clear that WireGuard's 1-RTT handshake taken in isolation is not secure in the KCI setting. This is because an attacker in possession of the responder's long-term private DH value $v$ can construct the first protocol message and thence impersonate the initiator *to* the responder. Our attack in Sect. 5.1 extends this authentication attack to a session key recovery attack. WireGuard protects against this kind of KCI attack by requiring the first data transport message to be sent by the initiator and the responder to check the integrity of this message. Strictly speaking, then, the first data transport message should be regarded as part of the handshake, making it no longer 1-RTT.

An attractive aspect of WireGuard (from a provable security standpoint) is that it is "cryptographically opinionated", meaning that the protocol has no algorithm negotiation functionality—all WireGuard sessions will use Curve25519

| Initiator | | Responder |
|-----------|--|-----------|

$(x, g^x) \overset{\$}{\leftarrow} \mathsf{DHGen}, \mathsf{epk}_i \leftarrow g^x, \mathsf{sid}_i = ID_i \overset{\$}{\leftarrow} \{0,1\}^{32}$

$\mathtt{ltk} = \mathsf{AEAD}(\kappa_3, 0, g^u, H_3)$

$now \leftarrow \mathsf{Timestamp}()$

$\mathtt{time} \leftarrow \mathsf{AEAD.Enc}(\kappa_4, 0, H_4, now)$

$\mathtt{mac1} \leftarrow \mathsf{MAC}(\mathsf{H}(\mathtt{label3}\|g^v), \mathtt{type}\|0^3\|\mathsf{sid}_i\|\mathsf{epk}_i\|\mathtt{ltk}\|\mathtt{time})$

$\mathtt{mac2} \leftarrow \mathsf{MAC}(cookie, \mathtt{type}\|0^3\|\mathsf{sid}_i\|\mathsf{epk}_i\|\mathtt{ltk}\|\mathtt{time}\|\mathtt{mac1})$

$\mathtt{InitiatorHello} \leftarrow \mathtt{type}\|0^3\|\mathsf{sid}_i\|\mathsf{epk}_i\|\mathtt{ltk}\|\mathtt{time}\|\mathtt{mac1}\|\mathtt{mac2}$

$$\xrightarrow{\quad\quad\quad\quad\quad\quad \mathtt{InitiatorHello} \quad\quad\quad\quad\quad\quad}$$

$(y, g^y) \overset{\$}{\leftarrow} \mathsf{DHGen}, \mathsf{epk}_r \leftarrow g^y, \mathsf{sid}_r = ID_r \overset{\$}{\leftarrow} \{0,1\}^{32}$

$\mathtt{zero} \leftarrow \mathsf{AEAD.Enc}(\kappa_9, 0, H_9, \emptyset)$

$\mathtt{mac1} \leftarrow \mathsf{MAC}(\mathsf{H}(\mathtt{label3}\|g^u), \mathtt{type}\|0^3\|\mathsf{sid}_r\|\mathsf{sid}_i\|\mathsf{epk}_r\|\mathtt{zero})$

$\mathtt{mac2} \leftarrow \mathsf{MAC}(cookie, \mathtt{type}\|0^3\|\mathsf{sid}_r\|\mathsf{sid}_i\|\mathsf{epk}_r\|\mathtt{zero}\|\mathtt{mac1})$

$\mathtt{ResponderHello} \leftarrow \mathtt{type}\|0^3\|\mathsf{sid}_r\|\mathsf{sid}_i\|\mathsf{epk}_r\|\mathtt{zero}\|\mathtt{mac1}\|\mathtt{mac2}$

$$\xleftarrow{\quad\quad\quad\quad\quad\quad \mathtt{ResponderHello} \quad\quad\quad\quad\quad\quad}$$

$tk_i \leftarrow \mathsf{KDF}(C_9, \emptyset, 1)$

$tk_r \leftarrow \mathsf{KDF}(C_9, \emptyset, 2)$

**Fig. 1.** A brief overview of the WireGuard Key-Exchange Protocol. For more details on the computation of the chaining seed $(C_k)$, hash $(H_k)$ and intermediate key $(\kappa_k)$ values, refer to Table 1. Note that all verifications of MAC and AEAD values are left implicit, but are obviously crucial to security.

for ECDH key exchange, BLAKE2 as the underlying hash function that builds both HMAC and HKDF, and ChaCha20-Poly1305 as the AEAD encryption scheme. As is known from the analysis of SSL/TLS, [1,4,5,15] and more generally [17], such negotiation mechanisms can lead to downgrade attacks that can fatally undermine security especially if a protocol supports both weak and strong cryptographic options. This decision to avoid ciphersuite negotiation simplifies the analysis of WireGuard.

Surprisingly, the full key exchange transcript is not authenticated by either party—the mac1 and mac2 values are keyed with public values $H(\mathtt{label3}\|g^v)$ and *cookie* and thus can be computed by an adversary. While the hash values $H_3$, $H_4$ and $H_9$ are headers in AEAD ciphertexts, these $H$ values do not contain all of the transcript information—the session identifiers $\mathsf{sid}_i$ and $\mathsf{sid}_r$ are not involved in either the seed or hash chains. This then limits the options for analysing WireGuard, as we cannot hope to show full transcript authentication properties. It would be a straightforward modification to include the session identifiers in the derivation of the session keys and thus bind the session identifiers to the session keys themselves. One could argue that the lack of binding between transcripts and output session keys has facilitated attacks on SSL/TLS, such as the Triple

**Table 1.** A detailed look at the computation of the chaining seed $(C_k)$ and hash $(H_k)$ values, as well as the intermediate AEAD keys $(\kappa_k)$ used in the WireGuard Key-Exchange protocol. Note that unless otherwise specified, the triples $(X, Y, Z)$ in the table are used in that order as the inputs to a key-derivation function $\mathsf{KDF}(X, Y, Z)$ (so $X$ is used as the keying material, $Y$ is the salt value and $Z$ the index of the output key) to compute the relevant values. Finally, we denote with $\emptyset$ values that are not used during protocol execution.

| k | Seed value $C_k$ | Key $\kappa_k$ | Hash value $H_k$ |
|---|---|---|---|
| 1 | $\mathsf{H}(\mathtt{label}_1)$ | $\emptyset$ | $\mathsf{H}(C_1 \| \mathtt{label}_2)$ |
| 2 | $(C_1, g^x, 1)$ | $\emptyset$ | $\mathsf{H}(H_1 \| g^v)$ |
| 3 | $(C_2, g^{xv}, 1)$ | $(C_2, g^{xv}, 2)$ | $\mathsf{H}(H_2 \| g^x)$ |
| 4 | $(C_3, g^{uv}, 1)$ | $(C_3, g^{uv}, 2)$ | $\mathsf{H}(H_3 \| \mathtt{ltk})$ |
| 5 | $\emptyset$ | $\emptyset$ | $\mathsf{H}(H_4 \| \mathtt{time})$ |
| 6 | $(C_4, g^y, 1)$ | $\emptyset$ | $\mathsf{H}(H_5 \| g^y)$ |
| 7 | $(C_6, g^{xy}, 1)$ | $\emptyset$ | $\emptyset$ |
| 8 | $(C_7, g^{uy}, 1)$ | $\emptyset$ | $\emptyset$ |
| 9 | $(C_8, psk, 1)$ | $(C_8, psk, 3)$ | $\mathsf{H}(H_6 \| \mathsf{KDF}(C_8, psk, 2))$ |
| 10 | $\emptyset$ | $\emptyset$ | $\mathsf{H}(H_9 \| \mathtt{zero})$ |

Handshake attack [6], and so a small modification to the inputs of the chaining values $C$ and hash values $H$ would strengthen the security of the protocol.

# 4   Security Model

We propose a modification to the eCK-PFS security model introduced by Cremers and Feltz [10] that incorporates preshared keys and strengthens the security definitions accordingly. We explain the framework and give an algorithmic description of the security model in Sect. 4.1, and describe the corruption abilities of the adversary in Sect. 4.2. We then describe the modifications necessary to capture the exact security guarantees that WireGuard attempts to achieve by explaining the differences between our partnering definitions and traditional notions of partnering in Sect. 4.3. We then give our modified cleanness definitions in Sect. 4.4. Given that WireGuard uses a mix of long-term identity keys, ephemeral keys and preshared secrets in its key exchange protocol, it is appropriate to use an extended-Canetti-Krawcyzk model (as introduced in [20]), wherein the adversary is allowed to reveal subsets of these secrets. It is claimed in [11] that WireGuard "achieves the requirements of authenticated key exchange (AKE) security, avoids key-compromise impersonation, avoids replay attacks, provides perfect forward secrecy," [11]. These are all notions captured by our extended eCK-PFS model, so our subsequent security proof will formally establish that WireGuard meets its goals.

## 4.1  Execution Environment

Consider an experiment $\mathsf{Exp}_{\mathsf{KE},n_P,n_S,\mathcal{A}}^{\mathsf{eCK\text{-}PFS\text{-}PSK}}(\lambda)$ played between a challenger $\mathcal{C}$ and an adversary $\mathcal{A}$. $\mathcal{C}$ maintains a set of $n_P$ parties $P_1, \ldots, P_{n_P}$ (representing users interacting with each other via the protocol), each capable of running up to $n_S$ sessions of a probabilistic key-exchange protocol $\mathsf{KE}$, represented as a tuple of algorithms $\mathsf{KE} = (f, \mathsf{ASKeyGen}, \mathsf{PSKeyGen}, \mathsf{EPKeyGen})$. We use $\pi_i^s$ to refer to both the identifier of the $s$-th instance of the $\mathsf{KE}$ being run by party $P_i$ and the collection of per-session variables maintained for the $s$-th instance of $\mathsf{KE}$ run by $P_i$. We describe the algorithms below:

$\mathsf{KE}.f(\lambda, pk_i, sk_i, \pi, m) \xrightarrow{\$} (m', \pi')$ is a (potentially) probabilistic algorithm that takes a security parameter $\lambda$, the long-term asymmetric key pair $pk_i, sk_i$ of the party $P_i$, a collection of per-session variables $\pi$ and an arbitrary bit string $m \in \{0,1\}^* \cup \{\emptyset\}$, and outputs a response $m' \in \{0,1\}^* \cup \{\emptyset\}$ and an updated per-session state $\pi'$, acting in accordance with an honest protocol implementation.

$\mathsf{KE}.\mathsf{ASKeyGen}(\lambda) \xrightarrow{\$} (pk, sk)$ is a probabilistic asymmetric-key generation algorithm taking as input a security parameter $\lambda$ and outputting a public-key/secret-key pair $(pk, sk)$.

$\mathsf{KE}.\mathsf{PSKeyGen}(\lambda) \xrightarrow{\$} (psk, pskid)$ is a probabilistic symmetric-key generation algorithm that also takes as input a security parameter $\lambda$ and outputs a symmetric preshared secret key $psk$ and (potentially) a preshared secret key identifier $pskid$.

$\mathsf{KE}.\mathsf{EPKeyGen}(\lambda) \xrightarrow{\$} (ek, epk)$ is a probabilistic ephemeral-key generation algorithm that also takes as input a security parameter $\lambda$ and outputs an asymmetric public-key/secret-key pair $(ek, epk)$.

$\mathcal{C}$ runs $\mathsf{KE}.\mathsf{ASKeyGen}(\lambda)$ $n_P$ times to generate a public-key/secret-key pair $(pk_i, sk_i)$ for each party $P_i \in \{P_1, \ldots, P_{n_P}\}$ and delivers all public-keys $pk_i$ for $i \in \{1, \ldots, n_P\}$ to $\mathcal{A}$. The challenger $\mathcal{C}$ then randomly samples a bit $b \xleftarrow{\$} \{0,1\}$ and interacts with the adversary via the queries listed in Sect. 4.2. Eventually, $\mathcal{A}$ terminates and outputs a guess $b'$ of the challenger bit $b$. The adversary wins the eCK-PFS-PSK key-indistinguishability experiment if $b' = b$, and additionally if the session $\pi_i^s$ such that $\mathsf{Test}(i, s)$ was issued satisfies a cleanness predicate clean, which we discuss in more detail in Sect. 4.4. We give an algorithmic description of this experiment in Fig. 2.

Each session maintains the following set of per-session variables:

- $\rho \in \{\texttt{init}, \texttt{resp}\}$ – the role of the party in the current session. Note that parties can be directed to act as $\texttt{init}$ or $\texttt{resp}$ in concurrent or subsequent sessions.
- $pid \in \{1, \ldots, n_P, \star\}$ – the intended communication partner, represented with $\star$ if unspecified. Note that the identity of the partner session may be set during the protocol execution, in which case $pid$ can be updated once.
- $m_s \in \{0,1\}^* \cup \{\perp\}$ – the concatenation of messages sent by the session, initialised by $\perp$.
- $m_r \in \{0,1\}^* \cup \{\perp\}$ – the concatenation of messages received by the session, initialised by $\perp$.

$\mathsf{Exp}_{\mathsf{KE},\mathsf{clean},n_P,n_S,\mathcal{A}}^{\mathsf{eCK\text{-}PFS\text{-}PSK\text{-}ind}}(\lambda):$

1: $b \xleftarrow{\$} \{0,1\}$
2: tested ← false
3: **for** $i = 1$ **to** $n_P$ **do**
4:    $(pk_i, sk_i) \xleftarrow{\$} \mathsf{ASKeyGen}(\lambda)$
5:    $\mathsf{ASKflag}_i \leftarrow$ clean
6:    $\mathbf{PSK}_i[1, \ldots, n_P] \leftarrow \bot$
7:    $\mathbf{PSKflag}_i[1, \ldots, n_P] \leftarrow \bot$
8:    $\mathbf{EPKflag}_i[1, \ldots, n_S] \leftarrow \bot$
9:    $\mathbf{RSKflag}_i[1, \ldots, n_S] \leftarrow \bot$
10:   $ctr_i \leftarrow 0$
11: **end for**
12: $b' \xleftarrow{\$} \mathcal{A}^{\mathsf{Create}*,\mathsf{Send},\cdots}(pk_1, \ldots, pk_{n_P})$
13: **if** $\mathsf{clean}(\pi_i^s)$ **then**
14:   **return** $(b' = b)$
15: **else**
16:   **return** $b' \xleftarrow{\$} \{0,1\}$
17: **end if**

---

$\mathsf{Create}(i, j, role):$

1: $ctr_i \leftarrow ctr_i + 1$
2: $s \leftarrow ctr_i$
3: $\pi_i^s.pid \leftarrow j$
4: $\pi_i^s.\rho \leftarrow role$
5: $\pi_i^s.ek \leftarrow \mathsf{KE}.\mathsf{EPKeyGen}(\lambda)$
6: $\pi_i^s.psk \leftarrow \mathbf{PSK}_i[j]$
7: **return** $(i, s)$

---

$\mathsf{Send}(i, s, m):$

1: **if** $\pi_i^s = \bot$ **then**
2:   **return** $\bot$
3: **else**
4:   $\pi_i^s.m_r \leftarrow \pi_i^s.m_r \| m$
5:   $(\pi_i^s, m') \leftarrow \mathsf{KE}.f(\lambda, pk_i, sk_i, \pi_i^s, m)$
6:   $\pi_i^s.m_s \leftarrow \pi_i^s.m_s \| m'$
7:   $\pi_i^s.T \leftarrow \pi_i^s.T \| m \| m'$
8:   **return** $m'$
9: **end if**

---

$\mathsf{Reveal}(i, s):$

1: **if** $(\pi_i^s.\alpha \neq$ accept$)$ **then**
2:   **return** $\bot$
3: **else**
4:   $\mathbf{RSKflag}_i[s] \leftarrow$ corrupt
5:   **return** $\pi_i^s.k$
6: **end if**

---

$\mathsf{CreatePSK}(i, j):$

1: **if** $(i = j) \vee (\mathbf{PSKflag}_i[j] \neq \bot)$ **then**
2:   **return** $\bot$
3: **end if**
4: $(psk, pskid) \leftarrow \mathsf{KE}.\mathsf{PSKeyGen}(\lambda)$
5: $\mathbf{PSK}_i[j] \leftarrow (psk, pskid)$
6: $\mathbf{PSK}_j[i] \leftarrow (psk, pskid)$
7: $\mathbf{PSKflag}_i[j], \mathbf{PSKflag}_j[i] \leftarrow$ clean
8: **if** $pskid \neq \emptyset$ **then**
9:   **return** $pskid$
10: **else**
11:   **return** $\top$
12: **end if**

---

$\mathsf{CorruptPSK}(i, j):$

1: **if** $\mathbf{PSK}_i[j] = \bot$ **then**
2:   **return** $\bot$
3: **end if**
4: **if** $\mathbf{PSKflag}_i[j] \neq$ clean **then**
5:   **return** $\bot$
6: **else**
7:   $\mathbf{PSKflag}_i[j] \leftarrow$ corrupt
8:   $\mathbf{PSKflag}_j[i] \leftarrow$ corrupt
9:   **return** $\mathbf{PSK}_i[j]$
10: **end if**

---

$\mathsf{CorruptEPK}(i, s):$

1: $\mathbf{EKflag}_i[s] \leftarrow$ corrupt
2: **return** $\pi_i^s.ek$

---

$\mathsf{CorruptASK}(i):$

1: $\mathsf{ASKflag}_i \leftarrow$ corrupt
2: **return** $sk_i$

---

$\mathsf{Test}(i, s):$

1: **if** (tested $=$ true) $\vee$ $(\pi_i^s.\alpha \neq$ accept$) \vee (\pi_i^s = \bot)$ **then**
2:   **return** $\bot$
3: **end if**
4: tested ← true
5: **if** $b = 0$ **then**
6:   **return** $\pi_i^s.k$
7: **else**
8:   **return** $k \xleftarrow{\$} \mathcal{K}$
9: **end if**

**Fig. 2.** eCK-PFS-PSK experiment for adversary $\mathcal{A}$ against the key-indistinguishability security of protocol KE.

- $kid \in \{0,1\}^* \cup \{\perp\}$ – the concatenation of public keyshare information received by the session, initialised by $\perp$.
- $\alpha \in \{\texttt{active}, \texttt{accept}, \texttt{reject}, \perp\}$ – the current status of the session, initialised with $\perp$.
- $k \in \{0,1\}^* \cup \{\perp\}$ – the computed session key, or $\perp$ if no session key has yet been computed.
- $ek \in \{0,1\}^* \times \{0,1\}^* \cup \{\perp\}$ – the ephemeral key pair used by the session during protocol execution, initialised as $\perp$.
- $psk \in \{0,1\}^* \times \{0,1\}^* \cup \{\perp\}$ – the preshared secret and identifier used by the session during protocol execution, initialised as $\perp$.
- $st \in \{0,1\}^*$ – any additional state used by the session during protocol execution.

Finally, the challenger manages the following set of corruption registers, which hold the leakage of secrets that $\mathcal{A}$ has revealed.

- preshared keys $\{\mathsf{PSKflag}_1, \mathsf{PSKflag}_2, \dots, \mathsf{PSKflag}_{n_P}\}$ where for each element $\mathsf{PSKflag}_i[j] \in \mathsf{PSKflag}_i$, $\mathsf{PSKflag}_i[j] \in \{\texttt{corrupt}, \texttt{clean}, \perp\} \ \forall \ i, j \in [n_P]$ and $\mathsf{PSKflag}_i[j] = \perp$ for $i = j$.
- long-term keys $\{\mathsf{ASKflag}_1, \dots, \mathsf{ASKflag}_{n_P}\}$, where $\mathsf{ASKflag}_i \in \{\texttt{corrupt}, \texttt{clean}, \perp\} \ \forall \ i \in [n_P]$.
- ephemeral keys $\{\mathsf{EPKflag}_1, \dots, \mathsf{EPKflag}_{n_P}\}$, where $\mathsf{EPKflag}_i[s] \in \{\texttt{corrupt}, \texttt{clean}, \perp\} \ \forall \ i \in [n_P]$ and $s \in [n_S]$.
- session keys $\{\mathsf{RSKflag}_1, \dots, \mathsf{RSKflag}_{n_P}\}$, where $\mathsf{RSKflag}_i[s] \in \{\texttt{corrupt}, \texttt{clean}, \perp\} \ \forall \ i \in [n_P]$ and $s \in [n_S]$.

We formalise the advantage of a PPT algorithm $\mathcal{A}$ in winning the eCK-PFS-PSK key indistinguishability experiment in the following way:

**Definition 2 (eCK-PFS-PSK Key Indistinguishability).** *Let* KE *be a key-exchange protocol, and* $n_P$, $n_S \in \mathbb{N}$. *For a particular given predicate* clean, *and a PPT algorithm* $\mathcal{A}$, *we define the advantage of* $\mathcal{A}$ *in the* eCK-PFS-PSK *key-indistinguishability game to be:*

$$\mathsf{Adv}_{\mathsf{KE}, n_P, n_S, \mathcal{A}}^{\mathsf{eCK\text{-}PFS\text{-}PSK}, \mathsf{clean}}(\lambda) = |\Pr[\mathsf{Exp}_{\mathsf{KE}, n_P, n_S, \mathcal{A}}^{\mathsf{eCK\text{-}PFS\text{-}PSK}, \mathsf{clean}}(\lambda) = 1] - \frac{1}{2}|.$$

*We say that* KE *is* eCK-PFS-PSK-*secure if, for all* $\mathcal{A}$, $\mathsf{Adv}_{\mathsf{KE}, n_P, n_S, \mathcal{A}}^{\mathsf{eCK\text{-}PFS\text{-}PSK}, \mathsf{clean}}(\lambda)$ *is negligible in the security parameter* $\lambda$.

### 4.2    Adversarial Interaction

Our security model is intended to be as generic as possible, in order to capture eCK-like security notions, but to also include long-term preshared keys. This would allow our model to be used in analysing (for example) the Signal protocol, where users exchange both long-term Diffie-Hellman keyshares used in many protocol executions, but also many ephemeral Diffie-Hellman keyshares that are only used within a single session. Another example would be TLS 1.3, where users may have established preshared keys to reduce the protocol's computational overheads, or to enable 0-RTT confidential data transmission.

Our attacker is a standard key-exchange model adversary, in complete control of the communication network, able to modify, inject, delete or delay messages. They can also compromise several layers of secrets:

- long-term private keys, modelling the misuse or corruption of long-term secrets in other sessions, and additionally allowing our model to capture forward-secrecy notions.
- ephemeral private keys, modelling the use of bad randomness generators.
- preshared symmetric keys, modelling the leakage of shared secrets, potentially due to the misuse of the preshared secret by the partner, or the forced later revelation of these keys.
- session keys, modelling the leakage of keys by their use in bad cryptographic algorithms.

The adversary interacts with the challenger via the queries below. An algorithmic description of how the challenger responds is in Fig. 2.

- Create$(i, j, role) \rightarrow \{(i, s), \bot\}$: allows the adversary to begin new sessions.
- CreatePSK$(i, j) \rightarrow \{pskid, \top, \bot\}$: allows the adversary to direct parties to generate a preshared key for use in future protocol executions.
- Reveal$(i, s)$: allows the adversary access to the secret session key computed by a session during protocol execution.
- CorruptPSK$(i) \rightarrow \{psk, \bot\}$: allows the adversary access to the secret pre-shared key jointly shared by parties prior to protocol execution.
- CorruptASK$(i) \rightarrow \{sk_i, \bot\}$: allows the adversary access to the secret long-term key generated by a party prior to protocol execution.
- CorruptEPK$(i, s) \rightarrow \{ek, \bot\}$: allows the adversary access to the secret ephemeral key generated by a session during protocol execution.
- Send$(i, s, m) \rightarrow \{m', \bot\}$: allows the adversary to send messages to sessions for protocol execution and receive their output.
- Test$(i, s) \rightarrow \{k, \bot\}$: sends the adversary a real-or-random session key used in determining the success of $\mathcal{A}$ in the key-indistinguishability game.

## 4.3   Partnering Definitions

In order to evaluate which secrets the adversary is able to reveal without trivially breaking the security of the protocol, key-exchange models must define how sessions are *partnered*. Otherwise, an adversary would simply run a protocol between two sessions, faithfully delivering all messages, Test the first session to receive the real-or-random key, and Reveal the session partner's key. If the keys are equal, then the Test key is real, and otherwise the session key has been sampled randomly. BR-style key-exchange models traditionally use *matching conversations* in order to do this. When introducing the eCK-PFS model, Cremers and Feltz [10] used the relaxed notion of *origin sessions*.

However, both of these are still too restrictive for analysing WireGuard, because this protocol does not explicitly authenticate the full transcript. Instead, for WireGuard, we are concerned matching only on a subset of the transcript information – the honest contributions of the keyshare and key-derivation materials. We introduce the notion of *contributive keyshares* to capture this intuition.

**Definition 3 (Contributive Keyshares).** *Recall that $\pi_i^s.kid$ is the concatenation of all keyshare material sent by the session $\pi_i^s$ during protocol execution. We say that $\pi_j^t$ is a contributive keyshare session for $\pi_i^s$ if $\pi_j^t.kid$ is a substring of $\pi_i^s.m_r$.*

This definition is protocol specific because $\pi_i^s.kid$ is: in WireGuard $\pi_i^s.kid$ consists only of the long-term public Diffie-Hellman value and the ephemeral public Diffie-Hellman value provided by the initiator and responder; in TLS 1.3 (for example) it would consist of the long-term public keys, the ephemeral public Diffie-Hellman values and any preshared key identifiers provided by the client and selected by the server.

### 4.4   Cleanness Predicates

We now define the exact combinations of secrets that an adversary is allowed to leak without trivially breaking the protocol. The original cleanness predicate of Cremers and Feltz [10] allows the reveal of long-term secrets for the test session's party $P_i$ at any time, which places us firmly in the setting where the adversary has key-compromise-impersonation abilities, but only allowed the reveal of long-term secrets of the intended peer after the test session has established a secure session, which captures perfect forward secrecy.

We now turn to modifying the cleanness predicate $\mathsf{clean_{eCK\text{-}PFS\text{-}PSK}}$ for the preshared secret setting.

**Definition 4 ($\mathsf{clean_{eCK\text{-}PFS\text{-}PSK}}$).** *A session $\pi_i^s$ such that $\pi_i^s.\alpha = \mathsf{accept}$ in the security experiment defined in Fig. 2 is $\mathsf{clean_{eCK\text{-}PFS\text{-}PSK}}$ if all of the following conditions hold:*

1. *The query $\mathsf{Reveal}(i, s)$ has not been issued.*
2. *For all $(j, t) \in n_P \times n_S$ such that $\pi_i^s$ is a contributive keyshare session for $\pi_j^t$, the query $\mathsf{Reveal}(j, t)$ has not been issued.*
3. *If $\mathbf{PSKflag}_i[\pi_i^s.pid] = \mathsf{corrupt}$ or $\pi_i^s.psk = \bot$, the queries $\mathsf{CorruptASK}(i)$ and $\mathsf{CorruptEPK}(i, s)$ have not both been issued.*
4. *If $\mathbf{PSKflag}_i[\pi_i^s.pid] = \mathsf{corrupt}$ or $\pi_i^s.psk = \bot$, and for all $(j, t) \in n_P \times n_S$ such that $\pi_j^t$ is a contributive keyshare session for $\pi_i^s$, then $\mathsf{CorruptASK}(j, t)$ and $\mathsf{CorruptEPK}(j, t)$ have not both been issued.*
5. *If there exists no $(j, t) \in n_P \times n_S$ such that $\pi_j^t$ is a contributive keyshare session for $\pi_i^s$, $\mathsf{CorruptASK}(j)$ has not been issued before $\pi_i^s.\alpha \leftarrow \mathsf{accept}$.*

We specifically forbid the adversary from revealing the long-term and ephemeral secrets if the preshared secret between the test session and its intended partner has already been revealed. Since preshared keys are optional in our framework, we also must consider the scenario where a preshared secret does not exist between the test session $\pi_i^s$ and its intended partner. Similarly, we forbid the adversary from revealing the long-term and ephemeral secrets if there exists no preshared secret between the two parties. Finally, since WireGuard does not authenticate the full transcript, but relies instead on implicit authentication of derived session keys based on secret information, we must use our contributive keyshare partnering definition instead of the origin sessions of [10]. Like eCK-PFS, we capture perfect forward secrecy under key-compromise-impersonation attack in condition 5, where the long-term secret of the test session's intended partner is allowed to be revealed only after the test session has accepted. Additionally, we allow for the optional incorporation of preshared secrets in conditions 3 and 4, where the adversary falls back to eCK-PFS leakage paradigm if the preshared secret between the test session and its peer either does not already exist, or has been already revealed.

# 5    Security Analysis

In this section we examine the security implications of modelling the WireGuard handshake as a 1-RTT key exchange protocol. We have already noted that this results in a KCI attack on the protocol, also observed in [11]. However, we note an arguably more serious attack on session key security in our eCK-PFS-PSK security model that results from this modelling. We discuss the implications of this attack in Sect. 5.1. Making minor modifications to the WireGuard handshake protocol will allow us to prove key-indistinguishability security in the strong eCK-PFS-PSK model. Specifically, we will add a key-confirmation message generated by the initiator. We describe the modified WireGuard handshake protocol in Sect. 5.2 and prove it secure in Sect. 5.3.

## 5.1    Attack on Forward-Secrecy Notions

We briefly describe an attack on WireGuard as a 1-RTT protocol that is allowable within the eCK-PFS-PSK security model. It uses the ability of the adversary to target perfect forward secrecy combined with key-compromise-impersonation and results in full session key recovery. Specifically, it allows the adversary to corrupt the long-term key of a responder session, and thus impersonate any party initiating a session to the corrupted party. Since we model WireGuard as a 1-RTT key exchange protocol, we do not include the data transport message that would otherwise authenticate the initiator to a responder session, and thus the responder has to accept the session as soon as the responder has sent the ResponderHello message (this being the last message in the 1-RTT version of the protocol). Afterwards, the adversary is permitted to corrupt the long-term key of the party that it is impersonating. This enables it to compute the session key, and thus distinguish real session keys from random ones, breaking eCK-PFS-PSK key indistinguishability. The exact details of this attack within the eCK-PFS-PSK security model can be found in the full version [14].

Readers may argue that this attack is implausible in a real-world setting, and is entirely artificial, allowable only because of the severe key compromises permitted in the security model. We tend to agree, and present the attack here only as a means of illustrating that the WireGuard handshake protocol, as originally presented in its 1-RTT form, is not only vulnerable to standard KCI attacks, but also to key recovery attacks, and therefore not directly amenable to strong security proofs without incorporating additional messages as part of the handshake.

## 5.2   The Modified WireGuard Handshake

We note that in [11], the protection for a responder against KCI attacks is to wait for authenticated data transport messages to arrive from the initiator. Incorporating this into the WireGuard handshake would make it impossible to prove it secure with respect to a key indistinguishability security notion, however, because the session keys, being used in the data transport protocol, would no longer remain indistinguishable from random when the subject of a Test query.

As explained in the introduction, there are two basic ways of surmounting this obstacle: consider the protocol (handshake and data transport) as a monolithic whole, or modify the protocol. We adopt the latter approach, and present a modification to the WireGuard handshake protocol that allows us to prove notions of perfect forward secrecy and defence against key-compromise impersonation attacks. Figure 3 shows the modified protocol, denoted mWG. It adds a key-confirmation message sent from the initiator to the responder, computed using an extra derived key $\kappa_{10}$ used solely for this purpose.

Our modifications are minor (involving at most 5 extra symmetric key operations) and do not require an additional round trip before either party can begin sending transport data, as the responder was already required to wait for initiator-sent data before it was able to begin safely sending its own.

## 5.3   Security of the Modified WireGuard Handshake

This section is dedicated to proving our main result:

**Theorem 1.** *The modified WireGuard handshake protocol* mWG *is* eCK-PFS-PSK-*secure with cleanness predicate* clean$_{eCK-PFS-PSK}$ *(capturing perfect forward secrecy and resilience to KCI attacks). That is, for any PPT algorithm* $\mathcal{A}$ *against the* eCK-PFS-PSK *key-indistinguishability game (defined in Fig. 2)* Adv$_{mWG,clean_{eCK-PFS-PSK},n_P,n_S,\mathcal{A}}^{eCK-PFS-PSK}(\lambda)$ *is negligible under the* prf, auth-aead, sym-ms-PRFODH, sym-mm-PRFODH *and* ddh *assumptions.*

Due to space constraints, we point readers to the full version of this work [14] for a more detailed security statement, as well as full details of the proof.

| Initiator | | Responder |
|---|---|---|

$(x, g^x) \xleftarrow{\$} \mathsf{DHGen}$, $\mathsf{epk}_i \leftarrow g^x$, $\mathsf{sid}_i = ID_i \xleftarrow{\$} \{0,1\}^{32}$
$\mathtt{ltk} = \mathsf{AEAD}(\kappa_3, 0, g^u, H_3)$
$now \leftarrow \mathsf{Timestamp}()$
$\mathtt{time} \leftarrow \mathsf{AEAD.Enc}(\kappa_4, 0, H_4, now)$
$\mathtt{InitiatorHello}$: $\mathtt{type}\|0^3\|\mathtt{sid}_i\|\mathtt{epk}_i\|\mathtt{ltk}\|\mathtt{time}\|\mathtt{mac1}\|\mathtt{mac2}$

$$\xrightarrow{\hspace{3cm} \mathtt{InitiatorHello} \hspace{3cm}}$$

$(y, g^y) \xleftarrow{\$} \mathsf{DHGen}$, $\mathsf{epk}_r \leftarrow g^y$, $\mathsf{sid}_r = ID_r \xleftarrow{\$} \{0,1\}^{32}$
$\mathtt{zero} \leftarrow \mathsf{AEAD.Enc}(\kappa_9, 0, H_9, \emptyset)$
$\mathtt{ResponderHello} \leftarrow \mathtt{type}\|0^3\|\mathtt{sid}_r\|\mathtt{sid}_i\|\mathtt{epk}_r\|\mathtt{zero}\|\mathtt{mac1}\|\mathtt{mac2}$

$$\xleftarrow{\hspace{3cm} \mathtt{ResponderHello} \hspace{3cm}}$$

$C_{10}, \kappa_{10} \leftarrow \mathsf{KDF}(C_9, \emptyset)$
$\mathtt{conf} \leftarrow \mathsf{AEAD.Enc}(\kappa_{10}, 0, H_{10}, \emptyset)$
$\mathtt{mac1} \leftarrow \mathsf{MAC}(\mathsf{H}(\mathtt{label}_3\|g^v), \mathtt{type}\|0^3\|\mathtt{sid}_i\|\mathtt{sid}_r\|\mathtt{conf})$
$\mathtt{mac2} \leftarrow \mathsf{MAC}(cookie, \mathtt{type}\|0^3\|\mathtt{sid}_i\|\mathtt{sid}_r\|\mathtt{conf}\|\mathtt{mac1})$
$\mathtt{SenderConf} \leftarrow \mathtt{type}\|0^3\|\mathtt{sid}_i\|\mathtt{sid}_r\|\mathtt{conf}\|\mathtt{mac1}\|\mathtt{mac2}$

$$\xrightarrow{\hspace{3cm} \mathtt{SenderConf} \hspace{3cm}}$$

$tk_i \leftarrow \mathsf{KDF}(C_{10}, \emptyset, 1)$
$tk_r \leftarrow \mathsf{KDF}(C_{10}, \emptyset, 2)$

**Fig. 3.** The modification to the WireGuard handshake that allows eCK-PFS-PSK security. The change is limited to an additional $\mathtt{SenderConf}$ message that contains the value $\mathtt{conf} \leftarrow \mathsf{AEAD}(\kappa_{10}, 0, H_{10}, \emptyset)$. Except for the computation of the new $C_{10}, \kappa_{10}$ values, all values are computed as in the original WireGuard handshake protocol, and can be found in Table 1.

## 6   Conclusions and Future Work

We gave a description of the WireGuard protocol, and demonstrated that it has an implicit entanglement of its data transport phase and its key exchange (or handshake) phase. This is needed to ensure protection against KCI attacks. In turn this means that WireGuard either cannot be proven secure as a key exchange protocol using standard key-indistinguishability notions, or it is vulnerable to key-recovery attacks in the KCI setting. Despite this issue, we believe that the design of WireGuard protocol is an interesting one, and our attack is intended more to make a subtle point about the need to cleanly separate a key exchange protocol and the usage of its session keys in subsequent protocols.

We presented the eCK-PFS-PSK security model. This amends the previous eCK-PFS model of [10] to cover key exchange protocols such as WireGuard that combine preshared keys with long-term and ephemeral keys. We then made a minimal set of modifications to the WireGuard handshake protocol, and proved that the modified WireGuard protocol achieves key-indistinguishability security in our new (and strong) eCK-PFS-PSK model.

Other approaches to analysing WireGuard may also be rewarding. Instead of separately establishing the security of the handshake and assuming it securely composes with the data transport phase, one could imagine making a monolithic analysis similar to the ACCE approach introduced in [16]. However, this would require a different "record layer" modelling from that used for TLS in [16] to allow for packet loss and packet reordering. One could also implement our modification and measure its effect on the performance of WireGuard, but we expect it to be very small.

Finally, we made certain simplifications to simplify our analysis of Wire-Guard. For instance we did not model the Cookie Reply messages that are designed to protect peers that are under load, nor did we analyse WireGuard's key rotation mechanisms. Given its several attractive properties, WireGuard is certainly deserving of further formal security analysis.

**Acknowledgements.** Dowling was supported by EPSRC grant EP/L018543/1. Paterson was supported in part by a research programme funded by Huawei Technologies and delivered through the Institute for Cyber Security Innovation at Royal Holloway, University of London, and in part by EPSRC grants EP/M013472/1 and EP/L018543/1. We are grateful to Håkon Jacobsen and Benjamin Lipp as well as the anonymous reviewers for feedback on our work.

# References

1. Adrian, D., Bhargavan, K., Durumeric, Z., Gaudry, P., Green, M., Halderman, J.A., Heninger, N., Springall, D., Thomé, E., Valenta, L., VanderSloot, B., Wustrow, E., Béguelin, S.Z., Zimmermann, P.: Imperfect forward secrecy: how Diffie-Hellman fails in practice. In: 22nd ACM SIGSAC Conference on Computer and Communications Security, CCS 2015 Denver, Colorado, USA, pp. 5–17 (2015)
2. Aumasson, J.-P., Meier, W., Phan, R.C.-W., Henzen, L.: The Hash Function BLAKE. ISC. Springer, Heidelberg (2014). https://doi.org/10.1007/978-3-662-44757-4
3. Bernstein, D.J.: Curve25519: new Diffie-Hellman speed records. In: Yung, M., Dodis, Y., Kiayias, A., Malkin, T. (eds.) PKC 2006. LNCS, vol. 3958, pp. 207–228. Springer, Heidelberg (2006). https://doi.org/10.1007/11745853_14
4. Beurdouche, B., Bhargavan, K., Delignat-Lavaud, A., Fournet, C., Kohlweiss, M., Pironti, A., Strub, P.-Y., Zinzindohoue, J.K.: A messy state of the union: taming the composite state machines of TLS. In: 2015 IEEE Symposium on Security and Privacy, pp. 535–552. IEEE Computer Society Press, May 2015
5. Bhargavan, K., Brzuska, C., Fournet, C., Green, M., Kohlweiss, M., Béguelin, S.Z.: Downgrade resilience in key-exchange protocols. In: 2016 IEEE Symposium on Security and Privacy, pp. 506–525. IEEE Computer Society Press, May 2016
6. Bhargavan, K., Delignat-Lavaud, A., Fournet, C., Pironti, A., Strub, P.-Y.: Triple handshakes and cookie cutters: breaking and fixing authentication over TLS. In: 2014 IEEE Symposium on Security and Privacy, pp. 98–113. IEEE Computer Society Press, May 2014

7. Brendel, J., Fischlin, M.: Zero round-trip time for the extended access control protocol. In: Foley, S.N., Gollmann, D., Snekkenes, E. (eds.) ESORICS 2017. LNCS, vol. 10492, pp. 297–314. Springer, Cham (2017). https://doi.org/10.1007/978-3-319-66402-6_18

8. Brendel, J., Fischlin, M., Günther, F., Janson, C.: PRF-ODH: relations, instantiations, and impossibility results. In: Katz, J., Shacham, H. (eds.) CRYPTO 2017. LNCS, vol. 10403, pp. 651–681. Springer, Cham (2017). https://doi.org/10.1007/978-3-319-63697-9_22

9. Brzuska, C., Fischlin, M., Warinschi, B., Williams, S.C.: Composability of Bellare-Rogaway key exchange protocols. In: Chen, Y., Danezis, G., Shmatikov, V. (eds.) ACM CCS 11, pp. 51–62. ACM Press, October 2011

10. Cremers, C., Feltz, M.: Beyond eCK: perfect forward secrecy under actor compromise and ephemeral-key reveal. In: Foresti, S., Yung, M., Martinelli, F. (eds.) ESORICS 2012. LNCS, vol. 7459, pp. 734–751. Springer, Heidelberg (2012). https://doi.org/10.1007/978-3-642-33167-1_42

11. Donenfeld, J., WireGuard: next generation kernel network tunnel. In: 24th Annual Network and Distributed System Security Symposium, NDSS 2017, San Diego, California, USA (2017)

12. Dowling, B., Fischlin, M., Günther, F., Stebila, D.: A cryptographic analysis of the TLS 1.3 handshake protocol candidates. In: Ray, I., Li, N., Kruegel, C. (eds.) ACM CCS 2015, pp. 1197–1210. ACM Press, October 2015

13. Dowling, B., Fischlin, M., Günther, F., Stebila, D.: A cryptographic analysis of the TLS 1.3 draft-10 full and pre-shared key handshake protocol. Cryptology ePrint Archive, Report 2016/081 (2016). http://eprint.iacr.org/2016/081

14. Dowling, B., Paterson, K.G.: A Cryptographic Analysis of the WireGuard Protocol. Cryptology ePrint Archive, Report 2018/080, January 2018. https://eprint.iacr.org/2018/080

15. Dowling, B., Stebila, D.: Modelling ciphersuite and version negotiation in the TLS protocol. In: Foo, E., Stebila, D. (eds.) ACISP 2015. LNCS, vol. 9144, pp. 270–288. Springer, Cham (2015). https://doi.org/10.1007/978-3-319-19962-7_16

16. Jager, T., Kohlar, F., Schäge, S., Schwenk, J.: On the security of TLS-DHE in the standard model. In: Safavi-Naini, R., Canetti, R. (eds.) CRYPTO 2012. LNCS, vol. 7417, pp. 273–293. Springer, Heidelberg (2012). https://doi.org/10.1007/978-3-642-32009-5_17

17. Jager, T., Paterson, K.G., Somorovsky, J.: One bad apple: backwards compatibility attacks on state-of-the-art cryptography. In: NDSS 2013. The Internet Society, February 2013

18. Krawczyk, H.: HMQV: a high-performance secure Diffie-Hellman protocol. In: Shoup, V. (ed.) CRYPTO 2005. LNCS, vol. 3621, pp. 546–566. Springer, Heidelberg (2005). https://doi.org/10.1007/11535218_33

19. Krawczyk, H., Paterson, K.G., Wee, H.: On the security of the TLS protocol: a systematic analysis. In: Canetti, R., Garay, J.A. (eds.) CRYPTO 2013. LNCS, vol. 8042, pp. 429–448. Springer, Heidelberg (2013). https://doi.org/10.1007/978-3-642-40041-4_24

20. LaMacchia, B.A., Lauter, K., Mityagin, A.: Stronger security of authenticated key exchange. In: Susilo, W., Liu, J.K., Mu, Y. (eds.) ProvSec 2007. LNCS, vol. 4784, pp. 1–16. Springer, Heidelberg (2007). https://doi.org/10.1007/978-3-540-75670-5_1

21. Morrissey, P., Smart, N.P., Warinschi, B.: A modular security analysis of the TLS handshake protocol. In: Pieprzyk, J. (ed.) ASIACRYPT 2008. LNCS, vol. 5350, pp. 55–73. Springer, Heidelberg (2008). https://doi.org/10.1007/978-3-540-89255-7_5
22. Nir, Y., Langley, A.: ChaCha20 and Poly1305 for IETF Protocols. RFC 7539 (Informational), May 2015
23. Perrin, T.: The Noise Protocol Framework, October 2017. http://noiseprotocol.org/noise.html

# Distributed SSH Key Management with Proactive RSA Threshold Signatures

Yotam Harchol[1]([✉]), Ittai Abraham[2], and Benny Pinkas[2,3]

[1] UC Berkeley, Berkeley, USA
yotamhc@berkeley.edu
[2] VMware Research, Palo Alto, USA
[3] Bar-Ilan University, Ramat Gan, Israel

**Abstract.** SSH is a security network protocol that uses public key cryptography for client authentication. SSH connections are designed to be run between a client and a server and therefore in enterprise networks there is no centralized monitoring of all SSH connections. An attractive method for enforcing such centralized control, audit or even revocation is to require all clients to access a centralized service in order to obtain their SSH keys. The benefits of centralized control come with new challenges in security and availability.

In this paper we present ESKM - a *distributed enterprise SSH key manager*. ESKM is a secure and fault-tolerant logically-centralized SSH key manager. ESKM leverages $k$-out-of-$n$ threshold security to provide a high level of security. SSH private keys are never stored *at any single node*, not even when they are used for signing. On a technical level, the system uses $k$-out-of-$n$ threshold RSA signatures, which are enforced with new methods that refresh the shares in order to achieve proactive security and prevent many side-channel attacks. In addition, we support password-based user authentication with security against offline dictionary attacks, that is achieved using threshold oblivious pseudo-random evaluation.

ESKM does not require modification in the server side or of the SSH protocol. We implemented the ESKM system, and a patch for OpenSSL libcrypto for client side services. We show that the system is scalable and that the overhead in the client connection setup time is marginal.

## 1 Introduction

SSH (Secure Shell) is a cryptographic network protocol for establishing a secure and authenticated channel between a client and a server. SSH is extensively used for connecting to virtual machines, managing routers and virtualization infrastructure in data centers, providing remote support and maintenance, and also for automated machine-to-machine interactions.

This work describes a key manager for SSH. Client authentication in SSH is typically based on RSA signatures. We designed and implemented a system called ESKM – a distributed Enterprise SSH Key Manager, which implements and manages client authentication using threshold proactive RSA signatures.

© Springer International Publishing AG, part of Springer Nature 2018
B. Preneel and F. Vercauteren (Eds.): ACNS 2018, LNCS 10892, pp. 22–43, 2018.
https://doi.org/10.1007/978-3-319-93387-0_2

Our work focuses on SSH but has implications beyond SSH key management. Enterprise-level management of SSH connections is a known to be a critical problem which is hard to solve (see Sect. 1.1). The solution that we describe is based on threshold cryptography, and must be compliant with the SSH protocol. As such, it needs to compute RSA signatures. Unfortunately, existing constructions for threshold computation of RSA signatures with proactive security, such as [20–22], do not tolerate temporary unavailability of key servers (which is a common feature). We therefore designed a new threshold RSA signature protocol with proactive security, and implemented it in our system. This protocol should be of independent interest.

*Technical Contributions.* In addition to designing and implementing a solution for SSH key management, this work introduces the following novel techniques:

- **Threshold proactive RSA signatures with graceful handling of non-cooperating servers:** Threshold cryptography divides a secret key between several servers, such that a threshold number of servers is required to compute cryptographic operations, and a smaller number of servers learns nothing about the key. Threshold RSA signatures are well known [27]. There are also known constructions of RSA threshold signatures with proactive security [20–22]. However, these constructions require all key servers to participate in each signature. If a key server does not participate in computing a signature then its key-share is reconstructed and exposed to all other servers. This constraint is a major liveness problem and is unacceptable in any large scale system.

  This feature of previous protocols is due to the fact that the shares of threshold RSA signatures must be refreshed modulo $\phi(N)$ (for a public modulus $N$), but individual key servers cannot know $\phi(N)$ since knowledge of this value is equivalent to learning the private signature key.

  ESKM solves this problem by refreshing the shares over the integers, rather than modulo $\phi(N)$. We show that, although secret sharing over the integers is generally insecure, it is secure for proactive share refresh of RSA keys.
- **Dynamic addition of servers:** ESKM can also securely add key servers or recover failed servers, without exposing to any key server any share except its own. (This was known for secret sharing, but not for threshold RSA signatures.)
- **Client authentication:** Clients identify themselves to the ESKM system using low-entropy secrets such as passwords. We enable authentication based on threshold oblivious pseudo-random function protocols [19] (as far as we know, we are the first to implement that construction). The authentication method is secure against offline dictionary attacks even if the attacker has access to the memory of the clients and of less than $k$ of the key servers.

## 1.1   Current SSH Situation

*SSH as a Security Risk.* Multiple security auditing companies report that many large scale enterprises have challenges in managing the complexity of SSH keys.

SSH communication security [5] "analyzed 500 business applications, 15,000 servers, and found three million SSH keys that granted access to live production servers. Of those, 90% were no longer used. Root access was granted by 10% of the keys". Ponemon Institute study [4] in 2014 "of more than 2,100 systems administrators at Global 2000 companies found that three out of the four enterprises were vulnerable to root-level attacks against their systems because of failure to secure SSH keys, and more than half admitted to SSH-key-related compromises." It has even been suggested by security analysts at Venafi [6] that one of the ways Edward Snowden was able to access NSA files is by creating and manipulating SSH keys. Recent analysis [33] by Tatu Ylonen, one of the authors of the SSH protocol, based on Wikileaks reports, shows how the CIA used the BothanSpy and Gyrfalcon hacking tools to steal SSH private keys from client machines.

The risk of not having an enterprise level solution for managing SSH keys is staggering. In a typical kill chain the attacker begins by compromising one machine, from there she can start a devastating lateral movement attack. SSH private keys are either stored in the clear or protected by a pass-phrase that is typically no match for an offline dictionary attack. This allows an attacker to gain new SSH keys that enable elevating the breach and reaching more machines. Moreover, since many SSH keys provide root access, this allows the attacker to launch other attacks and to hide its tracks by deleting auditing controls. Finally, since SSH uses state-of-of-the-art cryptography it prevents the defender from having visibility to the attackers actions.

*Motivation.* A centralized system for storing and managing SSH secret keys has major advantages:

- A centralized security manager can observe, approve and log all SSH connections. This is in contrast to the peer-to-peer nature of plain SSH, which enables clients to connect to arbitrary servers without any control by a centralized authority. A centralized security manager can enforce policies and identify suspicious SSH connections that are typical of intrusions.
- Clients do not need to store keys, which otherwise can be compromised if a client is breached. Rather, in a centralized system clients store no secrets and instead only need to authenticate themselves to the system (in ESKM this is done using passwords and an authentication mechanism that is secure against offline dictionary attacks).

In contrast to the advantages of a central key server, it is also a single point of failure, in terms of both availability and security. In particular, it is obviously insecure to store all secret keys of an organization on a single server. We therefore deploy $n$ servers (also known as "control cluster nodes" – CC nodes) and use $k$-out-of-$n$ threshold security techniques to ensure that a client can obtain from any $k$ CC nodes the information needed for computing signatures, while any subset of fewer than $k$ CC nodes cannot learn anything useful about the keys. Even though computing signatures is possible with the cooperation of $k$ CC nodes, the private key itself is never reconstructed. Security is enhanced by proactive refresh of the CC nodes: every few seconds the keys stored on the

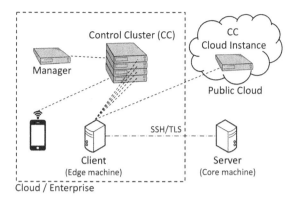

**Fig. 1.** General system architecture

nodes are changed, while the signature keys remain the same. An attacker who wishes to learn a signature key needs to compromise at least $k$ CC nodes in the short period before a key refresh is performed.

*Secret Key Leakage.* There are many side-channel attack vectors that can be used to steal keys from servers (e.g., [2,23,30]). Typically, side-channel attacks steal a key by repeatedly leaking little parts of the secret information. Such attacks are one of the main reasons for using HSMs (Hardware Secure Modules). Proactive security reduces the vulnerability to side-channel attacks by replacing the secret key used in each server after a very small number of invocations, or after a short timeout. It cab therefore be used as an alternative to HSMs. We discuss proactive security and our solutions is Sects. 2.2 and 3.2. (It is also possible to use both threshold security and HSMs, by having some CC nodes use HSMs for their secret storage.)

*Securing SSH.* The focus of this work is on securing client keys that are used in SSH connections. Section 2.1 describes the basics of the handshake protocol used by SSH. We use Shamir's secret sharing to secure the storage of keys. The secret sharing scheme of Shamir is described in Sect. 2.2. We also ensure security in the face of actively corrupt servers which send incorrect secret shares to other servers. This is done using verifiable secret sharing which is described in Sect. 2.2. The main technical difficulty is in computing signatures using shared keys, so that no server has access to a key neither in computation nor in storage. This is achieved by using Shoup's threshold RSA signatures (Sect. 2.2). We also achieve proactive security, meaning that an attacker needs to break into a large subset of the servers in a single time frame. This is enabled by a new cryptographic construction that is described in Sect. 3.

## 1.2   ESKM

ESKM (Enterprise SSH Key Manager) is a system for secure and fault-tolerant management of SSH private keys. ESKM provides a separation between the security control plane, and the data plane. The logically-centralized control plane is in charge of managing and storing private keys in a secure and fault-tolerant manner, so that keys are never stored in any single node at any given time. The control plane also provides centralized management services, such as auditing and logging for network-wide usage of secrets, and key revocation.

The general architecture of ESKM is presented in Fig. 1. The control plane is composed of a *security manager* (SM) and a *control cluster* (CC). The ESKM CC is a set of servers that provide the actual cryptographic services to data plane clients. These servers can be located in the same physical site (e.g., a datacenter), in multiple sites, or even in multiple public clouds. These servers can be run in a separate hardened machine or as VMs or a container. They do not require any specialized hardware but can be configured to utilize secure hardware as a secondary security layer.

*Threshold Cryptography.* The ESKM control plane leverages $k$-out-of-$n$ *threshold* security techniques to provide guarantees for both a high level of security and for strong liveliness. Secrets are split into $n$ shares, where each share is stored on a different control plane node. In order to retrieve a secret or to use it, at least $k$ shares are required ($k < n$). Specifically, in order to sign using a private key, $k$ out of $n$ shares of the private key are used, but the private key itself is never reconstructed, not even in memory, in cache, or in the CPU of any machine. Instead, we use a threshold signature scheme where each node uses its share of the private key to provide a signature fragment to the client. Any $k$ of these fragments are then transformed by the client to a standard RSA signature. Any smaller number of these fragments is useless for an attacker, and in any case, the shares, or the private key, cannot be derived from these fragments.

*Proactive Security.* ESKM also provides a novel proactive security protocol that refreshes the shares stored on each CC node, such that the shares are randomly changed, but the secret they hide remains the same. This protects against a mobile adversary and side-channel attacks, since keys are refreshed very frequently while on the other hand any successful attack must compromise at least $k$ servers *before* the key is refreshed. Known constructions of proactive refreshing of threshold RSA signatures are inadequate for our application:

- In principle, proactive refreshing can be computed using generic secure multi-party computation (MPC) protocols. However, this requires quite heavy machinery (since operations over a secret modulus need to be computed in the MPC by a circuit).
- There are known constructions of RSA threshold signatures with proactive security [20–22], but these constructions require all key servers to participate in each signature. If a key server does not participate in computing a signature then its key-share is reconstructed by the other servers and is exposed, and therefore this key server is essentially removed from the system. This constraint is a major liveness problem and is unacceptable in any large scale system.

Given these constraints of the existing solutions for proactively secure threshold RSA, we use a novel, simple and lightweight multi-party computation protocol for share refresh, which is based on secret sharing over the integers.

While secret sharing over the integers is generally insecure, we show that under certain conditions, when the secret is a random integer in the range $[0 \ldots R)$ and the number $n$ of servers is small ($n^n \ll R$), then such a scheme is statistically hiding in the sense that it leaks very little information about the secret key. In our application $|R|$ is the length of an RSA key, and the number $n$ of servers is at most a double-digit number. (The full version of this paper [16] contains a proof of security for the case where the threshold is 2, and a conjecture and a proof sketch for the general case.) Our implementation of proactive secret sharing between all or part of the CC nodes, takes less than a second, and can be performed every few seconds.

*Provisioning New Servers.* Using a similar mechanism, ESKM also allows distributed provisioning of new CC nodes, and recovery of failed CC nodes, without ever reconstructing or revealing the key share of one node.

*Minimal Modifications to the SSH Infrastructure.* As with many new solutions, there is always the tension between clean-slate and evolution. With so much legacy systems running SSH servers, it is quite clear that a clean-slate solution is problematic. In our solution there is *no modification* to the server or to the SSH protocol. The only change is in a very small and restricted part of the client implementation. The ESKM system can be viewed as a virtual security layer on top of client machines (whether these are workstations, laptops, or servers). This security layer manages secret keys on behalf of the client and releases the client from the liability of holding, storing, and using multiple unmanaged secret keys. In fact, even if an attacker takes full control over a client machine, it will not be able to obtain the secret keys that are associated with this client.

Abstractly, our solution implements the concept of *algorithmic virtualization*: The server believes that a common legacy single-client is signing the authentication message while in fact the RSA signature is generated via a threshold mechanism involving the client and multiple servers.

*Implementation and Experiments.* We fully implemented the ESKM system: a security manager and a CC node, and a patch for the OpenSSL libcrypto for client side services. Applying this patch makes the OpenSSH client, as well as other software that uses it such as `scp`, `rsync`, and `git`, use our service where the private key is not supplied directly but is rather shared between CC nodes. We also implemented a sample phone application for two-factor human authentication, as discussed in Sect. 4.2.

We deployed our implementation of the ESKM system in a private cloud and on Amazon AWS. We show by experiments that the system is scalable and that the overhead in the client connection setup time is up to 100 ms. We show that the control cluster is able to perform proactive share refresh in less than 500 ms, between the 12 nodes we tested.

*Summary of Contributions:*

1. A system for secure and fault-tolerant management of secrets and private keys of an organization. ESKM provides a distributed, yet logically-centralized control plane that is in charge of managing and storing the secrets in a secure and fault-tolerant manner using $k$-out-of-$n$ threshold signatures.
2. Our main technical contribution is a lightweight proactive secret sharing protocol for threshold RSA signatures. Our solution is based on a novel utilization of secret sharing over the integers.
3. The system also supports password-based user authentication with security against offline dictionary attacks, which is achieved by using threshold oblivious pseudo-random evaluation (as is described in Sect. 3.4).
4. We implemented the ESKM system to manage SSH client authentication using the standard OpenSSH client, with no modification to the SSH protocol or the SSH server.
5. Our experiments show that ESKM has good performance and that the system is scalable. A single ESKM CC node running on a small AWS VM instance can handle up to 10K requests per second, and the latency overhead for the SSH connection time is marginal.

# 2    Background

## 2.1    SSH Cryptography

The SSH key exchange protocol is run at the beginning of a new SSH connection, and lets the parties agree on the keys that are used in the later stages of the SSH protocol. The key exchange protocol is specified in [32] and analyzed in [7,28]. The session key is decided by having the two parties run a Diffie-Hellman key exchange. Since a plain Diffie-Hellman key exchange is insecure against active man-in-the-middle attacks the parties must authenticate themselves to each other. The server confirms its identity to the client by sending its public key, verified by a certificate authority, and using the corresponding private key to sign and send a signature of a hash computed over all messages sent in the key exchange, as well as over the exchanged key. This hash value is denoted as the "session identifier".[1]

Client authentication to the server is described in [31]. The methods that are supported are password based authentication, host based authentication, and authentication based on a public key signature. We focus on public key authentication since it is the most secure authentication method. In this method the client uses its private key to sign the session identifier (the same hash value signed by the server). If the client private key is compromised, then an adversary with knowledge of that key is able to connect to the server while impersonating

---

[1] Security cannot be proved under the sole assumption that the hash function is collision-resistant, since the input to the function contains the exchanged key. In [28] the security of SSH is analyzed under the assumption that the hash function is a random oracle. In [7] it was analyzed under the assumption that the function essentially implements a PRF.

as the client. Since the client key is the only long-lived secret that the client must keep, we focus on securing this key.

## 2.2  Cryptographic Background

**Shamir's Secret Sharing.** The basic service provided by ESKM is a secure storage service. This is done by applying Shamir's polynomial secret sharing [26] on secrets and storing each share on a different nodes. Specifically, given a secret $d$ in some finite field, the system chooses a random polynomial $s$ of degree $k-1$ in that field, such that $s(0) = d$. Each node $1 \leq i \leq n$ stores the share $s(i)$. $k$ shares are sufficient and necessary in order to reconstruct the secret $d$.

**Proactive Secret Sharing.** One disadvantage of secret sharing is that the secret values stored at each node are fixed. This creates two vulnerabilities: (1) an attacker may, over a long period of time, compromise more than $k-1$ nodes, (2) since the same shares are used over and over, an attacker might be able to retrieve them by exploiting even a side channel that leaks very little information by using de-noising and signal amplification techniques.

The first vulnerability is captured by the *mobile adversary model*, in this model the adversary is allowed to move from one node to another as long as at most $k-1$ nodes are compromised at any given two-round period [24]. For example, for $k = 2$, the adversary can compromise any single node and in order to move from this node to another node the adversary must have one round in between were no node is compromised.

Secret sharing solutions that are resilient to mobile adversaries are called *proactive secret sharing* schemes [18,34]. The core idea is to constantly replace the polynomial that is used for sharing a secret with a new polynomial which shared the same secret. This way, knowing $k-1$ values from each of two different polynomials does not give the mobile attacker any advantage in learning the secret that is shared by these polynomials.

Proactive secret sharing is particularly effective against side-channel attacks: Many side-channel attacks are based on observing multiple instances in which the same secret key is used in order to de-noise the data from the side channel. By employing proactive secret sharing one can limit the number of times each single key is used, as well as limit the duration of time in which the key is used (for example, our system is configured to refresh each key every 5 s or after the key is used 10 times).

**Feldman's Verifiable Secret Sharing.** Shamir's secret sharing is not resilient to a misbehaving dealer. Feldman [11] provides a non-interactive way for the dealer to prove that the shares that are delivered are induced by a degree $k$ polynomial. In this scheme, all arithmetic is done in a group in which the discrete logarithm problem is hard, for example in $Z_p^*$ where $p$ is a large prime.

To share a random secret $d$ the dealer creates a random degree $k$ polynomial $s(x) = \sum_{0 \leq i \leq k} a_i x^i$ where $a_0 = d$ is the secret. In addition, a public generator $g$

is provided. The dealer broadcasts the values $g^{a_0}, \ldots, g^{a_k}$ and in addition sends to each node $i$ the share $s(i)$. Upon receiving $s(i), g^{a_0}, \ldots, g^{a_k}$, node $i$ can verify that $g^{s(i)} = \prod_{0 \leq j \leq k} (g^{a_j})^{i^j}$. If this does not hold then node $i$ publicly complains and the dealer announces $s(i)$. If more than $k$ nodes complain, or if the public shares are not verified, the dealer is disqualified.

**Shoup's Threshold RSA Signatures.** The core idea of threshold RSA signature schemes is to spread the private RSA key among multiple servers [8,12]. The private key is never revealed, and instead the servers collectively sign the requested messages, essentially implementing a secure multi-party computation of RSA signatures.

Recall that an RSA signature scheme has a public key $(N, e)$ and a private key $d$, such that $e \cdot d = 1 \mod \phi(N)$. A signature of a message $m$ is computed as $(H(m))^d \mod N$, where $H()$ is an appropriate hash function.

An $n$-out-of-$n$ threshold RSA scheme can be easily implemented by giving each server a key-share, such that the sum of all shares (over the integers) is equal to $d$ [8,12]. Such schemes, however, require all parties to participate in each signature. This issue can be handled using interactive protocols [13], some with potentially exponential worst case costs [25,34]. These protocols essentially recover the shares of non-cooperating servers and reveal them to all other servers, and are therefore not suitable for a system that needs to operate even if some servers might be periodically offline.

To overcome these availability drawbacks, Shoup [27] suggested a threshold RSA signing protocol based on secret sharing, which provides $k$-out-of-$n$ reconstruction (and can therefore handle $n - k$ servers being offline). Shoup's scheme is highly practical, does not have any exponential costs, is non-interactive, and provides a public signature verification. (However, it does not provide proactive security.)

We elaborate more on the details of the threshold RSA signature scheme suggested by Shoup: The main technical difficulty in computing threshold RSA is that polynomial interpolation is essentially done in the exponent, namely modulo $\phi(N)$. Polynomial interpolation requires multiplying points of the polynomial by Lagrange coefficients: given the pairs $\{(x_i, s(x_i))\}_{i=1,\ldots,k}$ for a polynomial $s()$ of degree $k - 1$, there are known Lagrange coefficients $\lambda_1, \ldots, \lambda_k$ such that $s(0) = \sum_{i=1,\ldots,k} \lambda_i s(x_i)$. The problem is that computing these Lagrange coefficients requires the computation of an inverse modulo $\phi(N)$. However, the value $\phi(N)$ must be kept hidden (since knowledge of $\phi(N)$ discloses the secret key $d$). Shoup overcomes this difficulty by observing that all inverses used in the computation of the Lagrange coefficients are of integers in the range $[1, n]$, where $n$ is the range from which the indexes $x_i$ are taken. Therefore, replacing each Lagrange coefficient $\lambda_i$ with $\Delta \cdot \lambda_i$, where $\Delta = n!$, converts each coefficient to an integer number, and thus no division is required.

We follow Shoup's scheme [27] to provide a distributed non-interactive verifiable RSA threshold signature scheme. Each private key $d$ is split by the system manager into $n$ shares using a random polynomial $s$ of degree $k - 1$, such that $s(0) = d$. Each node $i$ of the system receives $s(i)$.

Given some client message $m$ to be signed (e.g., a SSH authentication string), node $i$ returns to the client the value

$$x_i = H(m)^{2 \cdot \Delta \cdot s(i)} \mod N,$$

where $H$ is a hash function, $\Delta = n!$, and $N$ is the public key modulus.

The client waits for responses from a set $S$ of at least $k$ servers, and performs a Lagrange interpolation on the exponents as defined in [27], computing

$$w = \prod_i x_i^{2 \cdot \lambda_i^S}$$

where $\lambda_i^S$ is defined as the Lagrange interpolation coefficient applied to index $i$ in the set $S$ in order to compute the free coefficient of $s()$, multiplied by $\Delta$ to keep the value an integer. Namely,

$$\lambda_i^S = \Delta \cdot \frac{\prod_{j \in S \setminus \{i\}} j}{\prod_{j \in S \setminus \{i\}} (j - i)} \in Z$$

The multiplication by $\Delta$ is performed in order to cancel out all items in the denominator, so that the computation of $\lambda_i^S$ involves only multiplications and no divisions.

The result of the interpolation is $w = (H(m))^{4\Delta^2 \cdot d}$. Then, since $e$ is relatively prime to $\Delta$, the client uses the extended Euclidean algorithm to find integers $a, b$ such that $4\Delta^2 a + eb = 1$. The final signature $(H(m))^d$ is computed as $y = w^a \cdot H(m)^b = (H(m)^d)^{4\Delta^2 a} \cdot (H(m)^{de})^b = (H(m)^d)^{4\Delta^2 a + eb} = (H(m))^d$. The client then verifies the signature by verifying that $H(m) = y^e$ (where $e$ is the public key).

**Share Verification:** Shoup's scheme also includes an elegant non-interactive verification algorithm for each share. This means that the client can quickly detect invalid shares that might be sent by a malicious adversary which controls a minority of the nodes, and use the remaining honest majority of shares to interpolate the required signature. We only describe the highlights of the verification procedure. Recall that an honest server must return $x_i = H(m)^{2 \cdot \Delta \cdot s(i)}$, where only $s(i)$ is unknown to the client. The protocol requires the server to initially publish a value $v_i = v^{s(i)}$, where $v$ is a publicly known value. The verification is based on well known techniques for proving the equality of discrete logarithms: The server proves that the discrete log of $(x_i)^2$ to the base $(H(m))^{4\Delta}$, is equal to the discrete log of $v_i$ to the base $v$. (The discrete log of $(x_i)^2$ is used due to technicalities of the group $Z_N^*$.) The proof is done using a known protocol of of Chaum and Pedersen [9], see Shoup's paper [27] for details. The important issue for our system is that whenever the shares $s(i)$ are changed by the proactive refresh procedure, the servers' verification values, $v^{s(i)}$, must be updated as well.

Using polynomial secret sharing for RSA threshold signatures gives very good liveliness and performance guarantees that are often not obtainable using comparable $n$-out-of-$n$ RSA threshold signatures. The main drawback of Shoup's scheme, as well as of all other known polynomial secret sharing schemes for RSA, is that they do not provide an obvious way to implement *proactive security*, which will redistribute the servers shares such that (1) the new shares still reconstruct the original signature (2) the old shares of the servers contain no information that can help in recovering the secret key from the new shares. Proactive security gives guarantees against a mobile adversary and against side channel attacks as discussed in the introduction. We address this drawback and provide a novel proactive scheme for Shoup's threshold signatures in Sect. 3.

# 3   ESKM Cryptography

In this section we describe the cryptographic novelties behind the ESKM system, for cryptographic signing and for storage services for secret keys. We focus on RSA private keys as secrets, as they are the most interesting use case of ESKM. However, the same techniques can be applied to other secrets as well. ESKM uses Shamir's secret sharing in order to securely split secrets, such that each share is stored on a different CC node. Given a secret $d$, the ESKM manager creates a random polynomial $s$ over $\phi(N)$ such that $s(0) = d$. It then provides each node $i$ with the value of $s(i)$.

Threshold signatures are computed according to Shoup's protocol. We focus in this section on the new cryptographic components of our construction, which support three new features:

1. Proactive refresh of the shares of the secret key.
2. Recovery and provisioning of new servers (this is done by the existing servers, without the help of any trusted manager).
3. Support for password-based user authentication (with security against offline dictionary attacks).

## 3.1   Security Model

The only entity in the ESKM system that is assumed to be fully trusted is the system manager, which is the root of trust for the system. However, this manager has no active role in the system other than initializing secrets and providing centralized administrative features. In particular, the manager does not store any secrets.

For the ESKM control cluster nodes (CC) we consider both the semi-honest and malicious models and we provide algorithms for both. In the semi-honest model, up to $f = k - 1$ CC nodes can be subject to offline attacks, side-channel attacks, or to simply fail, and the system will continue to operate securely. In the malicious model we also consider the case of malicious CC nodes that intentionally lie or do not follow the protocol. Note that our semi-honest model is also malicious-abortable. That is, a node which deviates from the protocol (i.e., behaves maliciously) will be detected and the refresh and recovery processes will be aborted, so the system can continue to operate, although without share refreshing and node recovery.

Clients are considered trusted to access the ESKM service, based on the policy associated with their identity. Clients have to authenticate with the ESKM CC nodes. Each authenticated client has a policy associated with its identity. This policy defines what keys this client can use and what secrets it may access. We discuss the client authentication issue in Sect. 3.4.

### 3.2 Proactive Threshold Signatures

In order to protect CC nodes against side-channel and offline attacks, we use a proactive security approach to refresh the shares stored on each CC node. The basic common approach to proactive security is to add, at each refresh round, a set of random *zero-polynomials*. A zero-polynomial is a polynomial $z$ of degree $k - 1$ such that $z(0) = 0$ and all other coefficients are random. Ideally, each CC node chooses a uniformly random zero-polynomial, and sends the shares of this polynomial to all other participating nodes. If only a subset of the nodes participate in the refresh protocol, the value that the zero-polynomial assigns for the indexes of non-participating nodes must be zero. All participating nodes verify the shares they receive and add them, along with the share they produce for themselves, to their original shares. The secret is therefore now shared by a new polynomial which is the sum of the original polynomial $s()$ and the $z()$ polynomials that were sent by the servers. The value of this new polynomial at 0 is equal to $s(0) + z(0) = s(0) + 0 = d$, which is the original secret. This way, while the shares change randomly, the secret does not change as we always add zero to it.

As is common in the threshold cryptography literature, a mobile adversary which controls $k - 1$ nodes at a specific round and then moves to controlling $\ell > 0$ new nodes (as well $k - \ell - 1$ of nodes that it previously controlled), must have a transition round, between leaving the current nodes and controlling the new nodes, where she compromises at most $k - \ell - 1$ nodes. Even for $\ell = 1$ this means that the adversary has at most $k - 2$ linear equations of the $k - 1$ non-zero coefficients of $z$. This observation is used to prove security against a mobile adversary.

**The Difficulty in Proactive Refresh for RSA:** The proactive refresh algorithm is typically used with polynomials that are defined over a finite field. The challenge in our setting is that the obvious way of defining the polynomial $z$ is over the secret modulus $\phi(N) = (p - 1)(q - 1)$. On the other hand, security demands that $\phi(N)$ must not be known to the CC nodes, and therefore they cannot create a $z$ polynomial modulo $\phi(N)$. In order not to expose $\phi(N)$ we take an alternative approach: Each server chooses a zero polynomial $z$ over the *integers* with very large random positive coefficients (specifically, the coefficients are chosen in the range $[0, N - 1]$). We show that the result is correct, and that the usage of polynomials over the integers does not reduce security.

With respect to correctness, recall that for all integers $x, s, j$ it holds that $x^s = x^{s + j \cdot \phi(N)} \mod N$. The secret polynomial $s()$ satisfies $s(0) = d \mod \phi(N)$. In other words, interpolation of this polynomial over the *integers* results in a value $s(0) = d + j\phi(N)$ for some integer $j$. The polynomial $z()$ is interpolated over the integers to $z(0) = 0$. Therefore, $x^{s(0)+z(0)} = x^{d+j\cdot\phi(N)+0} = x^d \mod N$.

With regards to security, while polynomial secret sharing over a finite field is perfectly hiding, this is not the case over the integers. For example, if a polynomial $p()$ is defined over the positive integers then we know that $p(0) < p(1)$, and therefore if $p(1)$ happens to be very small (smaller than $N$) than we gain information about the secret $p(0)$. Nevertheless, since the coefficients of the polynomial are chosen at random, we show in [16, Appendix B] that with all but negligible probability, the secret will have very high entropy. To the best of our knowledge, this is the first such analysis for polynomial secret sharing over the integers.

**The Refresh Protocol for Proactive Security.** Algorithm 1 presents our share refresh algorithm for the malicious model. This is a synchronous distributed algorithm for $n$ nodes, with up to $f = k - 1$ malicious or faulty nodes, where $n = 2f + 1$. The dealer provides the initial input parameters to all nodes. Note that verification is done over some random prime field $v_p$ and not over the RSA modulus $N$ $(v_p > N)$.

For the semi-honest-malicious-abortable CC nodes model, Round 3 of the algorithm is not necessary anymore, as well as signature validation for verification values (lines 4, 9) and the completion of missing information in line 21.

**Proactive Refresh of Verification Information:** Secret sharing over the integers allows to refresh the secret shares, but this is not enough. To obtain *verifiable* RSA threshold signatures we also need to refresh the verification information to work with the new shares, as is done in line 19 of the protocol.

**Security:** The security analysis of the proactive share refresh appears in the full version of our paper [16]. Unlike secret sharing over a finite field, secret sharing over the integers does not provide perfect security. Yet, since in our application the shares are used to hide long keys (e.g., 4096 bits long), then revealing a small number of bits about a key should be harmless: in the worst case, leaking $\sigma$ bits of information about the secret key can only speed up attacks on the system by a factor of $2^\sigma$ (any algorithm $A$ that breaks the system in time $T$ given $\sigma$ bits about the secret key can be replaced by an algorithm $A'$ that breaks the system in time $2^\sigma T$ given only public information, by going over all options for the leaked bits and running $A$ for each option).

The degradation of security that is caused by leaking $\sigma$ bits can therefore be mitigated by replacing the key length $|N|$ that was used in the original system (with no leakage), by a slightly longer key length which is sufficiently long to ensure that the best known attacks against the new key length are at least $2^\sigma$ times slower than the attacks against the original shorter key length.

In the full version of the paper [16] we prove an upper bound on the amount of information that is leaked about the secret key in 2-out-of-$n$ proactive secret sharing, and state a conjecture about the case of $k$-out-of-$n$ proactive secret sharing, for $k > 2$. (The exact analysis of the latter case seems rather technical,

---

**Algorithm 1.** Malicious Model Share Refresh Algorithm for Node $i$

---

Input parameters:

$s_i$ - current share of node $i$; $N$ - public key modulus;

$p$ - an upper bound on the coefficients of the zero polynomial(typically, $p = N$);

$n$ - number of nodes; $f$ - maximal number of faulty nodes ($f = k - 1$)

$v$ - used as the base for verification of exponents; $v^{s_1}, \ldots, v^{s_n}$ - verification values;

$v_p$ - verification field; $\mathcal{H}$ - hash function for message signing

(Note: computations mod $N$, unless noted otherwise)

*Round 1:*

1: Choose $\alpha_1^i, \ldots, \alpha_{k-1}^i \sim U([0, p))$ to create a zero-polynomial $z^i(x) = \sum_{q=1}^{k-1} \alpha_q^i \cdot x^q$
   over the integers.

2: Compute shares $z_1^i = z^i(1), \ldots, z_n^i = z^i(n)$

3: Compute $v^{\alpha_1^i}, \ldots, v^{\alpha_{k-1}^i}$ over $v_p$

4: Compute $Sig_i \leftarrow \mathcal{H}(v^{\alpha_1^i}, \ldots, v^{\alpha_{k-1}^i})$

5: **for each** node $\ell \neq i$ Send $z_\ell^i, (v^{\alpha_1^i}, \ldots, v^{\alpha_{k-1}^i}), Sig_i$ to node $\ell$

   *Round 2:*

6: **for each** received share $z_i^\ell$ from node $\ell$ **do**

7:      Verify that $\mathcal{H}(v^{\alpha_1^\ell}, \ldots, v^{\alpha_{k-1}^\ell}) = Sig_\ell$

8:      Verify that $v^{z_i^\ell} = \prod_{q=1}^{k-1} \left( v^{\alpha_q^\ell} \right)^{i^q} \mod v_p$

9:      **If** verification failed **then** Report node $\ell$

10: **end for**

11: **if** verified at least $f + 1$ shares **then**

12:      Let $s_i^* = s_i + \left( \sum_{\text{verified shares } \ell} z_i^\ell \right)$. (Summation is over the integers)

13:      For each $j$, compute $v^{s_j^*} = v^{s_j} \prod_{\ell=1}^{n} \prod_{q=1}^{k-1} v^{\alpha_q^\ell \cdot j^q} = v^{s_j} \prod_\ell v^{z_j^\ell} \mod v_p$.

14:      Send **OK** messages to everyone with $Sig_\ell$ of each verified sender $\ell$,
    $(v^{s_1^*}, \ldots, v^{s_n^*})$, and with a report of missing or invalid shares.

15: **else** Abort

16: **end if**

   *Round 3:*

17: Compare signatures in all received OKs

18: Publicly announce everything known by node $i$ on disputed and missing shares to
    everyone (there are up to $f$ such shares)

   *Round 4:*

19: Complete missing information using information sent in Round 3: Update $s_i^*$,
    Update $v^{s_1^*}, \ldots, v^{s_n^*}$, Ignore OKs and shares of identified malicious nodes.

20: **if** received at least $f + 1$ valid OKs **then**

21:      Commit new share: $s_i \leftarrow s_i^*$

22:      Commit $v^{s_1^*}, \ldots, v^{s_n^*}$

23: **else** Abort

24: **end if**

---

and we leave it as an open question.) For the case of $n = 16$ servers and $k = 2$,
the upper bound implies that, except with probability $2^{-40}$, an adversary learns
at most 22 bits of knowledge about the secret key.

### 3.3   Recovery and Provisioning of CC Nodes

Using a slight variation of the refresh protocol, ESKM is also able to securely recover CC nodes that have failed, or to provision new CC nodes that are added to the system (and by that increase reliability). The process is done without exposing existing shares to the new or recovered nodes, and without any existing node knowing the share of the newly provisioned node.

The basic idea behind this mechanism is as follows: A new node $r$ starts without any shares in its memory. It contacts at least $k$ existing CC nodes. Each one of these existing nodes creates a random polynomial $z()$ such that $z(r) = 0$ and sends to each node $i$ the value $z(i)$ (we highlight again that these polynomials evaluate to 0 for an input $r$). If all nodes are honest, each node should simply add its original share $s(i)$ to the sum of all $z(i)$ shares it received, and compute $s^*(i) = s(i) + \sum z(i)$. The result of this computation, $s^*()$, is a polynomial which is random except for the constraint $s^*(r) = s(r)$. Node $i$ then sends $s^*(i)$ to the new node $r$, which then interpolates the values it received and finds $s^*(r) = s(r)$. Since we assume that nodes may be malicious, the algorithm uses verifiable secret sharing to verify the behavior of each node.

The pseudo-code for the recovery process is presented in [16]. Algorithm 2 in [16] presents the pseudo-code for each existing CC node participating in the recovery process. Algorithm 3 in [16] presents the logic of the recovered node.

We note that if this mechanism is used to provision an additional node (as opposed to recovery of a failed node), it changes the threshold to $k$-out-of-$n + 1$. The security implication of this should be taken into account when doing so.

### 3.4   Threshold-Based Client Authentication

ESKM CC nodes need to verify their clients' identity in order to securely serve them and associate their corresponding policies and keys. However, in order to be authenticated clients must hold some secret that represents their identity, and hence we have a chicken-and-egg problem: Where would this secret be stored?

The adversary model assumes that an adversary might control some CC nodes (but less than $k$ CC nodes), and might have access to the client machine. The adversary must also be prevented from launching an offline dictionary attack against the password.

*Human Authentication:* A straightforward authentication solution could be to encrypt the private key using a password and store it at the client or in the CC nodes, but since the password might have low entropy this approach is insecure against offline dictionary attacks on the encrypted file. In addition, passwords or hashes of passwords must not be recoverable by small server coalitions.

A much preferable option for password-based authentication is to use a threshold oblivious pseudo-random function protocol (T-OPRF), as suggested in [19]. A T-OPRF is a threshold modification to the concept of an OPRF. An OPRF is a two-party protocol for obliviously computing a pseudo-random function $F_K(x)$, where one party knows the key $K$ and the second party knows $x$.

At the end the protocol the second party learns $F_K(x)$ and the first party learns nothing. (At an intuitive level, one can think of the pseudo-random function as the equivalent of AES encryption. The protocol enables to compute the encryption using a key known to one party and a plaintext known to the other party.) A T-OPRF is an OPRF where the key is distributed between multiple servers. Namely $K$ is shared between these servers using a polynomial $p$ such that $p(0) = K$. The client runs a secure protocol with each of the members of a threshold subset of the servers, where it learns $F_{p(i)}(x)$ from each participating server $i$. The protocol enables the client to use this data to compute $F_K(x)$. The details of the T-OPRF protocol, as well as its security proof and its usage for password-based threshold authentication, are detailed in [19]. (In terms of availability, the protocol enables the client to authenticate itself after successfully communicating with any subset of the servers whose size is equal to the threshold.)

The T-OPRF protocol is used for secure human authentication as follows: The T-OPRF protocol is run with the client providing a password $pwd$ and the CC nodes holding shares of a master key $K$. The client uses the protocol to compute $F_K(pwd)$. Note that the password is not disclosed to any node, and the client must run an online protocol, rather than an offline process, to compute $F_K(pwd)$. The value of $F_K(pwd)$ can then be used as the private key of the client (or for generating a private key), and support strong authentication in a standard way. For example, the client can derive a public key from this private key and provide it to the ESKM system (this process can be done automatically upon initialization or password reset). Thus, using this scheme, the client does not store any private information, and solely relies on the password, as memorized by the human user. Any attempt to guess the password requires running an online protocol with the CC nodes. This approach can be further combined with a private key that is stored locally on the client machine or on a different device such as a USB drive, in order to reduce the risk from password theft.

*Machine Authentication:* For automated systems (e.g., scripts running on servers), a client machine must locally store a single private key which authenticates it to the ESKM system. This key can be stored either in main memory or on secure hardware (e.g., Amazon KMS). In terms of costs, this is of course better than storing a massive number of client-server keys in such costly services. In addition, any usage of this single private key is fully and securely audited by the ESKM CC nodes. In an unfortunate case of theft, the key can be immediately revoked without having to log into multiple destination server machines and revoke the key separately on each one of them.

## 4   ESKM System Design

In this section we describe the design details of the ESKM system, which is presented in Fig. 1. The system includes a logically-centralized control plane, which provides security services, and a data plane, which consumes these services.

### 4.1 ESKM Control Plane

The ESKM control plane provides security services for network users, whether these are humans or machines. It manages identities, access policies, private keys and secret storage. It also provides centralized auditing and logging capabilities. The control plane is divided into two key parts: the *security manager* (SM) and the *control cluster* (CC).

**ESKM Security Manager.** The ESKM security manager (SM) is a single (possibly replicated) node that serves as the entry point for all administrative and configuration requests from the system. It manages CC nodes with regards to policy enforcement, storage of secrets, revocation of keys and policies, etc. It is also a central access point for administrators for the purpose of auditing and logging. The SM gives privileged admins the right to read audit logs, but not to delete or prune them (this can be done at each CC node separately).

The SM provides a service for key generation.[2] Upon request, given some key specification, the SM can generate a private key for an identity, and immediately share it with the CC nodes. It then returns the *public key* to the user who requested the generation of the key, but the private key and its shares are deleted from the SM memory. The private key is never revealed or stored on disk.

**ESKM Control Cluster.** The ESKM control cluster (CC) is a set of servers, referred to as "CC nodes". These servers are not replicas. Each CC node implements the CC node specification with regards to the communication protocol. However, each CC node stores different shares of the secrets they protect. In order to add robustness, each CC node can be implemented by a different vendor, run on a different operating system, or a different cryptography library.

A CC node provides two main services: signing, and secret storage and retrieval. The signing service is based on the threshold signatures discussed in Sects. 2 and 3. The storage and retrieval service is based on secret sharing as discussed in Sect. 2.

*Proactive Share Refresh.* The CC nodes have a module that is responsible for executing the share refresh algorithm presented in Sect. 3.2. A refresh policy has a future start date, duration of a single refresh round, and an interval between each two successive rounds. A refresh policy also specifies what to do in case of a failure on a refresh round. A failure can be caused by a malicious or faulty node, or by some misconfiguration such as unsynchronized clocks. The available options are to ignore the failure as possible, report the failure and try to continue, report and abort the ongoing round, report and abort all future refresh rounds of this policy, or report and abort the CC node completely.

---

[2] The only way to prevent key generation by a single entity is by running a secure multi-party protocol for RSA key generation. However, such protocols, e.g., [17], are too slow to be practical, especially when run between more than two servers, and therefore we did not implement them.

*Secure Recovery and Provisioning.* The CC nodes also have a module that is responsible for receiving and responding to recovery requests. Upon receiving such a request, the CC node executes the recovery algorithm described in Sect. 3.3. In addition, each CC node web server can initialize a recovery request and send it to the active CC nodes.

*Auditing.* One important feature of ESKM is the ability to provide fault-tolerant network-wide auditing of private key usage. Each CC node keeps track of the requests it handles and the signatures it produces, in a local log system.

In order to provide fault-tolerance of up to $f = k - 1$ failures, the SM is allowed to query CC nodes for log entries in order to compose audit reports. Deletion or pruning of CC node logs can only be done by the administrator of a CC node. Thus, even if $f$ nodes are compromised, an attacker cannot wipe their traces by deleting the logs.

This centralized and robust auditing service provides two powerful features. The first feature is the ability to have a system wide view of all SSH sessions, and thus a centralized control and option of activating immediate system-wide user revocation. The second feature is fault-tolerance and threshold security that are provided by implementing the distributed auditing over the CC nodes.

## 4.2   ESKM Data Plane

The only modification in the data plane that is required in order to incorporate ESKM is in the SSH client. In particular, we implemented ESKM in the client by adding a patch to the libcrypto library of OpenSSL.

**Authentication to ESKM CC Nodes.** A client connects to a CC node over a secure channel. The CC node authenticates itself using a certificate. Client authentication depends on the type of the client: a human or an automated machine: *Client edge machines* are operated by humans, while *client core machines* are automated. When using ESKM, a human infiltrator must authenticate to ESKM from an edge machine in order to log into a core machine, and by that to perform a lateral movement to other machines. Thus, by hardening the authentication for edge machines we protect the entire network.

*Machine-to-Machine Authentication.* Automated clients (core machines) use SSH client private key authentication in order to authenticate with CC nodes.

*Human Authentication.* We employ two-factor authentication for human clients to authenticate with CC nodes. We use password authentication as *something-you-know*, and a private key as *something-you-have*.

Our preferred password authentication method is using threshold OPRF, as discussed in Sect. 3.4. However, we also support two weaker methods: SSH/HTTPS password-based authentication, and authentication using a private key that is stored encrypted by the user's password. We give users the ability to configure their installation of ESKM with their preferred method.

For the "something you have" authentication, we use RSA private keys that can be installed on the client machine, a secure USB device, or on the user's smartphone. In the latter case, when the phone is notified when an authentication request arrives, and the user is asked to enter a password or use her thumbprint in order to authorize the smartphone to perform the RSA signing. The signature is tunneled through a special CC node back to the client machine to complete the authentication.

## 5   Experimental Results

The implementation of the ESKM system is described in [16, Appendix A].

We evaluated our implementation of the ESKM system by deploying it in VMs in a private cloud. Our setup includes 14 VMs: One VM runs the ESKM security manager, twelve VMs serve as ESKM CC nodes, and one VM serves as a local client. Each VM on the private cloud is allocated a single CPU core of type Intel Xeon E5-2680, with clock speed of 2.70 GHz. Most VMs do not share their physical host. We also deploy one CC node on an AWS t2.micro VM.

The client agent performance experiment tests the latency overhead introduced by our client agent, for the execution of the RSA_sign function in libcrypto, compared to a standard execution of this function using a locally stored private key. Another measurement we provide is the throughput of the client agent.

**ESKM Client Performance in a Private Cloud.** We first use the twelve CC nodes that are deployed in our private cloud. We measure client agent performance as a function of $k$ - the minimal number of CC nodes replies required to construct the signed authentication message. The figure in [16, Fig. 3] shows the results of this experiment. Even when $k$ is high, the latency overhead does not exceed 100 ms, and the throughput of the client agent does not drop below 19 requests per second. We note that the throughput can be greatly improved using batching techniques, when request frequency is high.

**Client Performance with a Public Cloud CC Node.** As mentioned in Sect. 4.1, for enhanced security, CC nodes may also be placed in a public cloud, and one share from these remote CC nodes must be used in order to make a progress. We repeated the previous experiments with a CC node deployed in AWS (t2.micro instance). The additional latency was 103 ms on average.

**Client Performance with Failing CC Nodes.** The figure in [16, Fig. 4] shows the throughput and latency of the client agent every second over time, when during this time more and more CC nodes fail. After each failure there is a slight degradation in performance. However, these changes are insignificant and the performance remains similar even when most CC nodes fail.

**ESKM CC Node Performance.** We evaluated the performance of an AWS CC node by measuring the CPU utilization and memory usage of the process, as a function of the number of sign requests it processed per second. The figure in [16, Fig. 5] presents the results of these measurements: our CC node is deployed on a single-core low-end VM, and is able to handle thousands of sign requests per second without saturating the CPU.

**Proactive Share Refresh.** We tested our proactive share refresh algorithm implementation to find how fast all 12 CC nodes can be refreshed. Usually, the algorithm requires less than 500 ms to complete successfully. However, in some rare cases this is not enough due to message delays. We set the refresh to be done at least every two seconds, and to limit the length of a single refresh round to at least one second.

**CC Node Recovery.** We also tested our node recovery algorithm implementation and found that it provides similar performance as the refresh algorithm. In all our tests, the recovery process required less than 500 ms in order to complete successfully. As for the refresh algorithm, we recommend to use a duration of at least one second to avoid failures that may occur due to message delays.

## 6 Related Work

Polynomial secret sharing was first suggested by Shamir [26]. Linear $k$-out-of-$k$ sharing of RSA signatures was suggested by Boyd [8], Frankel [12]. Desmedt and Frankel [10] observed that RSA $k$-out-of-$n$ threshold signatures is challenging because the interpolation of the shares is over $\phi(n)$. Frankel et al. [13] provided methods to move from polynomial to linear sharing and back. This technique is interactive and not practical.

Rabin [25] provided a simpler proactive RSA signature scheme, using a two layer approach (top is linear, bottom uses secret sharing). This protocol is used in Zhou et al. [34] use in COCA. The scheme leaks information publicly when there is a failure and hence does not seem suitable against a mobile adversary. It also can incur exponential costs in the worst case.

Wu et al. [29] proposed a library for threshold security that provides encryption, decryption, signing, and key generation services. Their scheme is based on additive RSA signatures, and in order to provide threshold properties they use exponential number of shares as in previous additive schemes.

Shoup [27] suggested a scheme that overcomes the interpolation problem, and provides non-interactive verification, that is resilient to an adversary controlling a minority. Gennaro et al. [14] improve Shoup's scheme to deal with large dynamic groups. Gennaro et al. [15] provide constructions for verifiable RSA signatures that are secure in standard models, but require interaction.

Centralized management of SSH keys has recently been the focus of several open source projects: BLESS by Netflix [3], and Vault by Hashicorp [1]. They do not provide threshold signature functionality, but instead resort to the more traditional single node approach.

## 7 Conclusion

We presented *ESKM*: an Enterprise SSH Key Manager. ESKM advocates a logically-centralized and software-defined security plane that is decoupled from the data plane. By separating the security functionality we can incorporate cutting-edge cryptography in a software defined manner.

Our implementation shows that with minimal changes to the OpenSSL library in the client, one can significantly increase the security of enterprise SSH key management without making any changes to the server SSH deployment. In this sense, ESKM provides a virtual layer of security on top of any existing legacy SSH server implementation. Our experiments show that ESKM incurs a modest performance overhead on the client side. Our implementation of the ESKM control plane is scalable and fault-tolerant, and is able to proactively refresh the shares of CC nodes in a distributed way every few seconds.

# References

1. Hashicorp Vault. https://github.com/hashicorp/vault
2. Heartbleed bug. http://heartbleed.com
3. Netflix Bless. https://github.com/Netflix/bless
4. Ponemon report. https://www.venafi.com/assets/pdf/Ponemon_2014_SSH_Security_Vulnerability_Report.pdf
5. SSH report. https://www.ssh.com/iam/ssh-key-management/
6. Venafi report. https://www.venafi.com/blog/deciphering-how-edward-snowden-breached-the-nsa
7. Bergsma, F., Dowling, B., Kohlar, F., Schwenk, J., Stebila, D.: Multi-ciphersuite security of the secure shell (SSH) protocol. In: Proceedings of the 2014 ACM Conference on Computer and Communications Security, pp. 369–381 (2014)
8. Boyd, C.: Digital multisignatures. In: Cryptography and Coding (1986)
9. Chaum, D., Pedersen, T.P.: Wallet databases with observers. In: Brickell, E.F. (ed.) CRYPTO 1992. LNCS, vol. 740, pp. 89–105. Springer, Heidelberg (1993). https://doi.org/10.1007/3-540-48071-4_7
10. Desmedt, Y., Frankel, Y.: Threshold cryptosystems. In: Brassard, G. (ed.) CRYPTO 1989. LNCS, vol. 435, pp. 307–315. Springer, New York (1990). https://doi.org/10.1007/0-387-34805-0_28
11. Feldman, P.: A practical scheme for non-interactive verifiable secret sharing. In: FOCS 1987, pp. 427–438 (1987)
12. Frankel, Y.: A practical protocol for large group oriented networks. In: Quisquater, J.-J., Vandewalle, J. (eds.) EUROCRYPT 1989. LNCS, vol. 434, pp. 56–61. Springer, Heidelberg (1990). https://doi.org/10.1007/3-540-46885-4_8
13. Frankel, Y., Gemmell, P., MacKenzie, P.D., Yung, M.: Optimal resilience proactive public-key cryptosystems. In: FOCS 1997, pp. 384–393 (1997)
14. Gennaro, R., Halevi, S., Krawczyk, H., Rabin, T.: Threshold RSA for dynamic and Ad-Hoc groups. In: Smart, N. (ed.) EUROCRYPT 2008. LNCS, vol. 4965, pp. 88–107. Springer, Heidelberg (2008). https://doi.org/10.1007/978-3-540-78967-3_6
15. Gennaro, R., Rabin, T., Jarecki, S., Krawczyk, H.: Robust and efficient sharing of RSA functions. J. Cryptol. **20**(3), 393 (2007)
16. Harchol, Y., Abraham, I., Pinkas, B.: Distributed SSH key management with proactive RSA threshold signature. Cryptology ePrint Archive (2018)
17. Hazay, C., Mikkelsen, G.L., Rabin, T., Toft, T.: Efficient RSA key generation and threshold paillier in the two-party setting. In: Dunkelman, O. (ed.) CT-RSA 2012. LNCS, vol. 7178, pp. 313–331. Springer, Heidelberg (2012). https://doi.org/10.1007/978-3-642-27954-6_20

18. Herzberg, A., Jarecki, S., Krawczyk, H., Yung, M.: Proactive secret sharing or: how to cope with perpetual leakage. In: Coppersmith, D. (ed.) CRYPTO 1995. LNCS, vol. 963, pp. 339–352. Springer, Heidelberg (1995). https://doi.org/10.1007/3-540-44750-4_27

19. Jarecki, S., Kiayias, A., Krawczyk, H., Xu, J.: TOPPSS: cost-minimal password-protected secret sharing based on threshold OPRF. Cryptology ePrint Archive, Report 2017/363 (2017). http://eprint.iacr.org/2017/363

20. Jarecki, S., Saxena, N.: Further simplifications in proactive RSA signatures. In: Kilian, J. (ed.) TCC 2005. LNCS, vol. 3378, pp. 510–528. Springer, Heidelberg (2005). https://doi.org/10.1007/978-3-540-30576-7_28

21. Jarecki, S., Saxena, N., Yi, J.H.: An attack on the proactive RSA signature scheme in the URSA ad hoc network access control protocol. In: Proceedings of the 2nd ACM Workshop on Security of ad hoc and Sensor Networks, SASN, pp. 1–9 (2004)

22. Kong, J., Zerfos, P., Luo, H., Lu, S., Zhang, L.: Providing robust and ubiquitous security support for MANET. In: ICNP (2001)

23. Liu, F., Yarom, Y., Ge, Q., Heiser, G., Lee, R.B.: Last-level cache side-channel attacks are practical. In: 2015 IEEE Symposium on Security and Privacy, SP 2015, pp. 605–622. IEEE Computer Society (2015)

24. Ostrovsky, R., Yung, M.: How to withstand mobile virus attacks (extended abstract). In: PODC 1991, pp. 51–59. ACM, New York (1991)

25. Rabin, T.: A simplified approach to threshold and proactive RSA. In: Krawczyk, H. (ed.) CRYPTO 1998. LNCS, vol. 1462, pp. 89–104. Springer, Heidelberg (1998). https://doi.org/10.1007/BFb0055722

26. Shamir, A.: How to share a secret. Commun. ACM **22**(11), 612–613 (1979)

27. Shoup, V.: Practical threshold signatures. In: Preneel, B. (ed.) EUROCRYPT 2000. LNCS, vol. 1807, pp. 207–220. Springer, Heidelberg (2000). https://doi.org/10.1007/3-540-45539-6_15

28. Williams, S.C.: Analysis of the SSH key exchange protocol. In: Chen, L. (ed.) IMACC 2011. LNCS, vol. 7089, pp. 356–374. Springer, Heidelberg (2011). https://doi.org/10.1007/978-3-642-25516-8_22

29. Wu, T.D., Malkin, M., Boneh, D.: Building intrusion-tolerant applications. In: USENIX Security (1999)

30. Yarom, Y., Falkner, K.: FLUSH+RELOAD: a high resolution, low noise, L3 cache side-channel attack. In: 23rd USENIX Conference on Security Symposium, SEC 2014, pp. 719–732. USENIX Association, Berkeley (2014)

31. Ylonen, T., Lonvick, C.: The Secure Shell (SSH) Authentication Protocol. Internet Requests for Comments, RFC 4252 (2004)

32. Ylonen, T., Lonvick, C.: The Secure Shell (SSH) Transport Layer Protocol. Internet Requests for Comments, RFC 4253 (2004)

33. Ylonen, T.: Bothanspy & Gyrfalcon - analysis of CIA hacking tools for SSH, August 2017. https://www.ssh.com/ssh/cia-bothanspy-gyrfalcon

34. Zhou, L., Schneider, F.B., Van Renesse, R.: COCA: a secure distributed online certification authority. ACM Trans. Comput. Syst. **20**(4), 329–368 (2002)

# Non-interactive Zaps of Knowledge

Georg Fuchsbauer[1,2]([✉]) and Michele Orrù[1,2]([✉])

[1] Inria, Paris, France
[2] École normale supérieure, CNRS, PSL University, Paris, France
{georg.fuchsbauer,michele.orru}@ens.fr

**Abstract.** While non-interactive zero-knowledge (NIZK) proofs require trusted parameters, Groth, Ostrovsky and Sahai constructed non-interactive witness-indistinguishable (NIWI) proofs without any setup; they called their scheme a non-interactive zap. More recently, Bellare, Fuchsbauer and Scafuro investigated the security of NIZK in the face of parameter subversion and observe that NI zaps provide subversion-resistant soundness and WI.

Arguments of knowledge prove that not only the statement is true, but also that the prover knows a witness for it, which is essential for anonymous identification. We present the first NIWI argument of knowledge *without* parameters, i.e., a NI zap of knowledge. Consequently, our scheme is also the first subversion-resistant knowledge-sound proof system, a notion recently proposed by Fuchsbauer.

**Keywords:** Non-interactive proofs · Argument of knowledge
Subversion resistance

## 1 Introduction

The concept of zero-knowledge proof systems, first proposed by Goldwasser et al. [GMR89], is a central tool in modern cryptography. Consider an NP relation $R$ which defines the language of all statements $x$ for which there exists a witness $w$ so that $R(x, w) = \mathbf{true}$. In a zero-knowledge proof for $R$ a prover, knowing a witness, wants to convince a verifier that $x$ is in the language. The protocol must be *complete*, that is, if the prover knows a witness for $x$ then it can convince the verifier; it should be *sound*, in that no malicious prover can convince the verifier of a false statement, and *zero-knowledge*: the execution of the protocol reveals no information to the verifier (beyond the fact that $x$ is in the language).

Feige and Shamir [FS90] proposed a relaxation of zero-knowledge called *witness indistinguishability*, which only requires that it is indistinguishable which witness was used to compute a proof. This notion turns out to be sufficient in many contexts. *Non-interactive* zero-knowledge proofs (NIZK) [BFM88] allow the prover to convince the verifier by only sending a single message. However, they rely on the existence of a common-reference string (CRS) to which prover and verifier have access. The CRS is assumed to have been set up by some

B. Preneel and F. Vercauteren (Eds.): ACNS 2018, LNCS 10892, pp. 44–62, 2018.
https://doi.org/10.1007/978-3-319-93387-0_3

trusted party, which represents a serious limitation for all applications of NIZK in scenarios where parties mutually distrust each other.

Dwork and Naor [DN00] constructed a two-round witness-indistinguishable proof system for NP in the plain model, that is, where no trusted CRS is assumed. In their protocol the first message (sent from the verifier to the prover) can be fixed once and for all, and the second one provides the actual proof. They called such protocols *zaps*. Barak et al. [BOV03] introduced the concept of *non-interactive* zaps, where the prover sends a single message to deliver the proof. Non-interactive zaps are thus non-interactive proof systems *without* a CRS. Since in this scenario it is impossible to achieve zero-knowledge [GO94], witness indistinguishability (WI) is the best one can hope for. Groth, Ostrovsky, and Sahai constructed the first non-interactive zaps from standard assumptions [GOS06a]. Subsequently [GOS06a], there have been many works extending this line of research [BW06, BW07, Gro06].

All aforementioned schemes guarantee that proofs can only be computed for valid statements. Arguments of knowledge are proof systems that satisfy a stronger notion of soundness. They require the prover to *know* a witness for the proved statement. This is formalized via the notion of knowledge soundness that demands that for each prover there exists an efficient extractor which can extract a witness from the prover whenever the latter outputs a valid proof. (When this holds for computationally bounded provers only, we speak of *arguments* rather than proofs.) Since, by definition, false statements have no witnesses, knowledge soundness implies the standard notion of (computational) soundness.

Succinct non-interactive arguments of knowledge (SNARKs) are non-interactive proof systems with short (that is, independent of the size of the statement or the witness) efficiently verifiable proofs that satisfy knowledge soundness. SNARKs were initially introduced for verifiable computation and are now the most widely deployed proof systems in the real world. They are used in cryptocurrencies such as Zcash [BCG+14], which guarantees anonymity via zero-knowledge SNARKs. As for all NIZK systems, a drawback of SNARKs is that they require a CRS, that is, they require a one-time trusted setup of public parameters. Since for SNARKs every CRS has a simulation trapdoor, subversion of these parameters leads to full compromise of soundness.

**Subversion Resistance.** Motivated by the subversion of trusted public parameters in standardized cryptographic protocols led by mass-surveillance activities, Bellare et al. [BFS16] investigate what security properties can be maintained for NIZK when its trusted parameters are subverted. CRS's for NIZK are especially easy to subvert, since they must be subvertible by design: zero knowledge requires that an honest CRS must be indistinguishable from a backdoored one, where the backdoor is the trapdoor used to simulate proofs.

Bellare et al. defined multiple security properties that protect against parameter subversion: subversion soundness (S-SND) means that no adversary can generate a malicious CRS together with a valid proof for a false statement; subversion zero knowledge (S-ZK) requires that even if the adversary sets up the CRS, there exists a simulator able to produce its full view; and subversion witness indistinguishability (S-WI) formalizes that even for proofs that were made under a subverted CRS, it is still infeasible to tell which of two witnesses was used.

Following Goldreich and Oren [GO94], Bellare et al. [BFS16] also showed that it is impossible to achieve subversion soundness and (standard) zero-knowledge simultaneously. For subversion-sound proof systems, subversion witness indistinguishability is thus the best one can hope for. The authors [BFS16] observe that since proof systems that do not rely on a CRS cannot succumb to CRS-subversion attacks, non-interactive zaps [GOS06a] achieve both S-SND and S-WI.

Bellare et al. did not consider the stronger notion of knowledge soundness, which is the notion achieved by SNARKs, and which in many applications is the required notion for the used proof systems. For example, for all kinds of anonymous authentication, users prove knowledge of signatures (often called *certificates* or *credentials*, depending on the context); in this case soundness is not sufficient, as signatures always exist, but in the security proof they must actually be extracted in order to rely on their unforgeability. Fuchsbauer [Fuc18] has recently defined a subversion-resistant notion of knowledge soundness but left it open to give a scheme that achieves it. Such a scheme would protect against possible parameter subversion in any context where proving knowledge of a witness is required.

**Our Contribution.** Our result can be summarized as follows:

(i) We provide the first non-interactive zap with knowledge soundness; that is, a witness-indistinguishable proof system without parameters for which there exists an extractor that recovers a witness from every valid proof.
(ii) Our zap is also the first fully subversion-resistant WI argument-of-knowledge system. In particular, it satisfies the recently defined notion of subversion knowledge soundness [Fuc18], as well as subversion witness indistinguishability [BFS16] (the strongest notion compatible with S-SND).

Bellare et al. [BFS16] introduce a new type of knowledge-of-exponent assumption, which they call DH-KE. They prove (standard) soundness and subversion zero knowledge of their main construction under DH-KE and the decision linear assumption (DLin) [BBS04]. Our construction builds on the DLin-based non-interactive zap from [GOS06a], whose soundness we upgrade to knowledge soundness, assuming DH-KE. As for this zap, the language of our proof system is circuit satisfiability and thus universal. Groth et al. [GOS06a] starting point is a "dual-mode" [GOS06b, PVW08] non-interactive proof system, for which there are two indistinguishable types of CRS: one leading to proofs that are perfectly sound and the other leading to proofs that are perfectly WI. To construct a non-interactive zap, they let the prover choose the CRS. As the prover could choose a CRS that leads to "unsound" proofs, the prover must actually choose two CRS's that are related in a way that guarantees that at least one of them is of the "sound" type. It must then provide a proof of the statement under both of them. The authors [GOS06a] then show that this protocol still achieves computational WI.

We turn their construction into a proof of knowledge by again doubling the proof, thereby forcing the prover to prove knowledge of a trapdoor which allows to extract the witness from one of the sound proofs. We prove our non-interactive zap of knowledge secure under the same assumptions as Bellare et al.'s S-ZK+SND scheme. Our result is summarized in the following theorem.

**Theorem 1.** *Assuming DLin and DH-KE, there exists a non-interactive zap for circuit satisfiability that satisfies knowledge soundness. The proof size is $O(\lambda k)$, where $\lambda$ is the security parameter and $k$ is the size of the circuit.*

Let us finally note that our system also implies a proof system which achieves (standard) knowledge soundness, (standard) zero knowledge and *subversion* witness indistinguishability. This is obtained by plugging our zap of knowledge into the construction by Bellare et al. [BFS16] that achieves SND, ZK and S-WI.

Their scheme uses a length-doubling pseudorandom generator (PRG) and a CRS contains a random bit string $\sigma$ of length $2\lambda$ (where $\lambda$ is the security parameter). A proof for statement $x$ is a zap for the following statement: either $x$ is a valid statement or $\sigma$ is in the range of the PRG. Using a zap of knowledge (ZaK), knowledge soundness follows from knowledge soundness of the ZaK since with overwhelming probability $\sigma$ is *not* in the range of the PRG. (The extractor must thus extract a witness for $x$.) Zero knowledge follows from WI of the zap, as after replacing $\sigma$ with an element in the range of the PRG, proofs can be simulated using a preimage of $\sigma$. Finally, S-WI follows from S-WI of the zap.

**Related Work.** Since the introduction of non-interactive zaps [BOV03, GOS06a], a number of papers have studied and provided different (and more efficient) implementations of zaps. Groth and Sahai [GS08] provided a more general framework for NIWI and NIZK proofs, which leads to more efficient proofs for concrete languages (instead of circuit satisfiability). Furthermore, their proof system can also be based on other assumptions apart from DLin, such as SXDH, allowing for shorter proofs.

Bitanski and Paneth [BP15] presented a different approach to constructing zaps and WI proofs based on indistinguishability obfuscation (iO), but constructions using iO are only of theoretical interest. Ràfols [Ràf15] showed how to base non-interactive zaps on Groth-Sahai proofs, thereby achieving an improvement in efficiency (by a constant factor) over the original construction [GOS06a]. Her construction can be implemented in asymmetric ("Type-1") pairing groups.

Her scheme can also serve as the starting point for a scheme achieving knowledge soundness and we explore this in the full version [FO18]. (See Table 1 for an overview.) Although this scheme is more efficient, we decided to concentrate on building a scheme from [GOS06a], as we can prove it secure under the assumptions that underlie Bellare et al.'s [BFS16] SND+S-ZK scheme; in contrast, a scheme built on asymmetric bilinear groups would require an analogue of the DH-KE assumption in such groups (we refer to it as ADH-KE in [FO18]). This is a qualitatively different assumption, as without a symmetric pairing it cannot be checked whether the triple returned by the adversary is of the right form (see Fig. 3); it would thus not be efficiently decidable if an adversary has won

**Table 1.** Efficiency and security of the original zaps and our constructions of zaps of knowledge, where $w$ is the number of wires, $g$ the number of gates and $|\mathbb{G}|$ is the size of an element of a group $\mathbb{G}$.

| Protocol | Efficiency | Assumptions |
|---|---|---|
| Zap [GOS06a] | $(18w + 12g + 5)\,|\mathbb{G}|$ | DLin |
| Zap of knwlg, Sect. 5 | $(36w + 24g + 14)\,|\mathbb{G}|$ | DLin, DH-KE |
| Zap [Ràf15] (of knwlg; [FO18]) | $(12w + 8g + 3)\,(|\mathbb{G}_1|+|\mathbb{G}_2|)$ | SXDH (ADH-KE) |

the game. Finally, our main scheme achieves *tight* security, whereas our proof of knowledge soundness with asymmetric pairings (which we present in the full version [FO18]) has a security loss that is linear in the circuit size.

## 2   Preliminaries

**Notation.** Let $\lambda$ be the security parameter. We let $\mathsf{M.rl}(\lambda)$ be a *length function* in $\lambda$ defining the length of the randomness for a probabilistic machine $\mathsf{M}$. When sampling the value $a$ uniformly at random from the set $S$, we write $a \leftarrow_{\$} S$. When sampling the value $a$ from the probabilistic algorithm $\mathsf{M}$, we write $a \leftarrow \mathsf{M}$. We use $:=$ to denote assignment. Elements of $\mathbb{Z}_p$ are denoted in lower case, group elements are denoted with capital letters. We employ additive notation for groups. Let $\mathsf{R}$ be a relation between statements denoted by $\phi$ and witnesses denoted by $w$. By $\mathsf{R}(\phi)$ we denote the set of possible witnesses for the statement $\phi$ in $\mathsf{R}$. We let $\mathcal{L}(\mathsf{R}) := \{\phi : \mathsf{R}(\phi) \neq \emptyset\}$ be the *language* associated to $\mathsf{R}$.

We consider the language of circuit satisfiability, which is NP-complete. For a binary circuit $\mathsf{C}$, the set $\mathsf{R}(\mathsf{C})$ is the set of inputs $w$ that satisfy $\mathsf{C}(w) = 1$. Without loss of generality, we assume that circuits consist solely of NAND gates. Unless otherwise specified, all following algorithms are assumed to be randomized and to run in time $\mathsf{poly}(\lambda)$. As Bellare et al. [BFS16], who follow [Gol93], we only consider uniform machines to model the adversary $\mathsf{A}$ and the extractor $\mathsf{Ext}$. (See [BFS16, Fuc18] for discussions on how this choice affects the hardness assumptions and security guarantees.)

**Bilinear Groups.** Throughout this work, we make use of prime-order abelian groups equipped with a (symmetric) bilinear map. Concretely, we assume the existence of groups $\mathbb{G}, \mathbb{G}_T$ of odd prime order $p$ of length $\lambda$ and an efficiently computable non-degenerate bilinear map $e\colon \mathbb{G} \times \mathbb{G} \to \mathbb{G}_T$. That is, the map $e$ is such that for all $U, V \in \mathbb{G}$ and $a, b \in \mathbb{Z}_p : e(aU, bV) = ab \cdot e(U, V)$, and if $U$ is a generator of $\mathbb{G}$, then $e(U, U)$ is a generator of $\mathbb{G}_T$. We say that a bilinear group is *verifiable* if there exists an efficient verification algorithm that outputs **true** if and only if $\Gamma = (p, \mathbb{G}, \mathbb{G}_T, e)$ is the description of a bilinear group. For instance, the elliptic-curve group of [BBS04] equipped with the Weil pairing is publicly verifiable. In most practical scenarios, the group description is embedded as a part of the protocol specification and agreed upon in advance; in these cases there is no need for verification.

Throughout this paper, we assume the existence of a deterministic algorithm G that, given as input the security parameter in unary $1^\lambda$, outputs a bilinear group description $\Gamma$. The same assumption was already employed by Bellare et al. [BFS16]. The main advantage in choosing G to be deterministic is that every entity in the scheme can (re)compute the group from the security parameter, and no party must be trusted with generating the group. Moreover, real-world pairing schemes are defined for groups that are fixed for some $\lambda$. For the sake of simplicity, we define all our schemes w.r.t. a group description $\Gamma$ and assume that the security parameter ($\lambda \in \mathbb{N}$ such that $\Gamma := \mathsf{G}(1^\lambda)$) can be derived from $\Gamma$.

**Extractable Commitment Schemes.** A commitment scheme Com consists of the following three algorithms:

- $(\sigma, \tau) \leftarrow \mathsf{Com.K}(\Gamma)$, the key generation algorithm, outputs a CRS $\sigma$ together with the trapdoor information $\tau$.
- $(C, r) \leftarrow \mathsf{Com.C}(\sigma, v)$, the commitment algorithm, outputs a commitment $C$ to the given value $v$ together with the *opening information $r$*.
- $bool \leftarrow \mathsf{Com.O}(\sigma, C, v, r)$, the opening algorithm, outputs **true** if $C$ is a commitment to $v$ witnessed by $r$, and **false** otherwise.

In our case, Com.C returns the used randomness and Com.O simply recomputes the commitment and checks that $C = \mathsf{Com.C}(V; r)$. Consequently, *correctness* of the scheme is trivial. To ease notation for commitments and openings, we will always assume that the group description $\Gamma$ can be deduced from $\sigma$, and omit the opening information from the returned value.

Generally, we require commitment schemes to be *hiding* and *binding*. Loosely speaking, a scheme is *hiding* if the commitment $C$ reveals no information about $v$. A scheme is *binding* if a cheating committer cannot change its mind about the value it committed to. Formally, it is hard to find $C, v, r, v'$ and $r'$ such that $v \neq v'$ and $\mathsf{Com.O}(\sigma, C, v, r) = \textbf{true} = \mathsf{Com.O}(\sigma, C, v', r')$.

We also require a perfectly binding commitment scheme to be *extractable*, that is, Com is equipped with an efficient extraction algorithm Com.E that, given as input the trapdoor information $\tau$, recovers the value $v$ to which $C$ is bound.

**Proof Systems.** A non-interactive proof system $\Pi$ for a relation R consists of the following three algorithms:

- $(\sigma, \tau) \leftarrow \Pi.\mathsf{K}(\Gamma)$, the CRS generation algorithm that outputs a CRS $\sigma$ (and possibly some trapdoor information $\tau$). Since we are dealing with *publicly verifiable protocols*, the trapdoor information $\tau$ will be omitted in most cases and used solely in the proofs or when combining protocols.
- $\pi \leftarrow \Pi.\mathsf{P}(\sigma, \phi, w)$, a prover which takes as input some $(\phi, w) \in \mathsf{R}$ and a CRS $\sigma$, and outputs a proof $\pi$.
- $bool \leftarrow \Pi.\mathsf{V}(\sigma, \phi, \pi)$ a verifier that, given as input a statement $\phi$ together with a proof $\pi$ outputs **true** or **false**, indicating acceptance of the proof.

| Game $\mathrm{WI}_{\Pi,R,A}(\lambda)$ | Oracle $\mathrm{PROVE}(\phi, w_0, w_1)$ |
|---|---|
| $b \leftarrow_\$ \{0,1\}$; $\Gamma := G(1^\lambda)$ | if $R(\phi, w_0) = \mathbf{false} \vee R(\phi, w_1) = \mathbf{false}$ |
| $(\sigma, \tau) \leftarrow \Pi.K(\Gamma)$ | return $\perp$ |
| $b' \leftarrow A^{\mathrm{PROVE}}(\sigma)$ | $\pi \leftarrow \Pi.P(\sigma, \phi, w_b)$ |
| return $(b = b')$ | return $\pi$ |

**Fig. 1.** Witness indistinguishability (WI) game.

A proof is complete if every correctly generated proof verifies. If the CRS is clear from the context, we omit $\sigma$ from the arguments of $\Pi.P$ or $\Pi.V$.

**Zaps.** A zap is a two-round, *witness-indistinguishable* proof system where the first-round message is fixed "once and for all" [DN00] for all future instances of the protocol. The notion of *witness-indistinguishability* [FLS90] informally states that no PPT adversary can tell which of two possible witnesses has been used to construct a proof.

**Definition 2.** *A proof system* $\Pi$ *is witness-indistinguishable (WI) for relation* R *if* $\mathsf{Adv}^{\mathrm{wi}}_{\Pi,R,A}(\lambda)$ *is negligible in* $\lambda$ *for any PPT adversary* A, *where* $\mathsf{Adv}^{\mathrm{wi}}_{\Pi,R,A}(\lambda) :=$ $\Pr[\mathrm{WI}_{\Pi,R,A}(\lambda)] - 1/2$ *and* $\mathrm{WI}_{\Pi,R,A}(\lambda)$ *is depicted in Fig. 1.*

A zap is *non-interactive* if there is no first-round message from the verifier to the prover: the prover simply sends a single message. The proof system thus reduces to a pair $(P, V)$ or can be considered as defined above, but with a CRS generation algorithm that always outputs $\perp$. We next define the soundness notion for *non-interactive arguments of knowledge*.

*Knowledge soundness* [BG93] means that for any prover able to produce a valid proof there exists an efficient algorithm, which has access to the prover's random coins, capable of extracting a witness for the given statement.

**Definition 3.** *A proof system* $\Pi$ *is* knowledge-sound *for* R *if for any PPT adversary* A *there exists a PPT extractor* Ext *such that* $\mathsf{Adv}^{\mathrm{ksnd}}_{A,\mathrm{Ext},R,\Pi}(\lambda)$ *is negligible in* $\lambda$, *where* $\mathsf{Adv}^{\mathrm{ksnd}}_{\Pi,R,A,\mathrm{Ext}}(\lambda) := \Pr[\mathrm{KSND}_{\Pi,R,A,\mathrm{Ext}}(\lambda)]$ *and* $\mathrm{KSND}_{A,\mathrm{Ext},R,\Pi}(\lambda)$ *is defined in Fig. 2. An* argument of knowledge *is a knowledge-sound proof system.*

Variations of this argument are often found in the literature. Most of them allow the extractor to rewind the adversary for interactive proof systems in

| Game $\mathrm{KSND}_{\Pi,R,A,\mathrm{Ext}}(\lambda)$ |
|---|
| $\Gamma := G(1^\lambda)$; $(\sigma, \tau) \leftarrow \Pi.K(\Gamma)$ |
| $r \leftarrow_\$ \{0,1\}^{A.\mathrm{rl}(\lambda)}$; $(\phi, \pi) := A(\sigma; r)$ |
| $w \leftarrow \mathrm{Ext}(\sigma, r)$ |
| return $(\Pi.V(\sigma, \phi, \pi)$ **and** $R(\phi, w) = \mathbf{false})$ |

**Fig. 2.** Game for knowledge soundness.

| Game $\text{DLin}_{\mathsf{G},\mathsf{A}}(\lambda)$ | Game $\text{DH-KE}_{\mathsf{G},\mathsf{A},\mathsf{Ext}}(\lambda)$ |
|---|---|
| $b \leftarrow_{\$} \{0,1\}\,;\ \Gamma := (p, \mathbb{G}, \mathbb{G}_T, e, G) := \mathsf{G}(1^\lambda)$ | $\Gamma := (p, \mathbb{G}, \mathbb{G}_T, e, G) := \mathsf{G}(1^\lambda)$ |
| $u, v, r, s \leftarrow_{\$} \mathbb{Z}_p$ | $r \leftarrow_{\$} \{0,1\}^{\mathsf{A}.\mathsf{rl}(\lambda)}$ |
| if $b = 1$ then $H := (r + s)G$ | $(X, Y, Z) := \mathsf{A}(\Gamma; r)$ |
| else $H \leftarrow_{\$} \mathbb{G}$ | $s \leftarrow \mathsf{Ext}(\Gamma, r)$ |
| $b' \leftarrow \mathsf{A}(\Gamma, uG, vG, urG, vsG, H)$ | if $sG = X \vee sG = Y$ then return 0 |
| return $(b = b')$ | return $(e(X, Y) = e(Z, G))$ |

**Fig. 3.** Games for Assumptions 1 (DLin) and 2 (DH-KE).

addition to black-box access, most notably for $\Sigma$-protocols. In case of non-interactive provers the extractor is provided with the adversary's random coins.

**Assumptions.** Our protocol is based on the DH-KE assumption and the existence of a homomorphic extractable commitment scheme. Such schemes have been widely studied and there are constructions from standard assumptions such as the subgroup decision assumption or the decisional linear (DLin) assumption [BBS04]. For this work, we rely on the latter, which is also used in [GOS06a].

The DLin assumption [BBS04] for an abelian group $\mathbb{G} = \langle G \rangle$ of order $p$ states that it is computationally difficult to distinguish $(uG, vG, urG, vsG, (r + s)G)$ with $u, v, r, s \leftarrow_{\$} \mathbb{Z}_p$ from a uniformly random 5-tuple in $\mathbb{G}$.

**Assumption 1 (DLin).** *We say that the Decisional Linear assumption holds for the group generator $\mathsf{G}$ if for all PPT adversaries $\mathsf{A}$ we have:*

$$\mathsf{Adv}^{\text{dlin}}_{\mathsf{G},\mathsf{A}}(\lambda) := \Pr\left[\text{DLin}_{\mathsf{G},\mathsf{A}}(\lambda)\right] - 1/2 = \mathsf{negl}(\lambda)\,,$$

*where the game $\text{DLin}_{\mathsf{G},\mathsf{A}}(\lambda)$ is defined in Fig. 3.*

The intuition behind DH-KE [BFS16] is that it is difficult for some machine to produce a (Diffie-Hellman) DH triple $(xG, yG, xyG)$ in $\mathbb{G}$ without knowing at least $x$ or $y$. The assumption is in the spirit of earlier knowledge-of-exponent assumptions [Gro10, BCI+10], whose simplest form states that given $(G, xG) \in \mathbb{G}^2$ it is hard to return $(yG, xyG)$ without knowing $y$.

**Assumption 2 (DH-KE).** *The Diffie-Hellman Knowledge of Exponent assumption holds for the bilinear group generator $\mathsf{G}$ if for any PPT adversary $\mathsf{A}$ there exists a PPT extractor $\mathsf{Ext}$ such that:*

$$\mathsf{Adv}^{\text{dhke}}_{\mathsf{G},\mathsf{A},\mathsf{Ext}}(\lambda) := \Pr\left[\text{DH-KE}_{\mathsf{G},\mathsf{A},\mathsf{Ext}}(\lambda)\right] = \mathsf{negl}(\lambda)\,,$$

*where the game $\text{DH-KE}_{\mathsf{G},\mathsf{A},\mathsf{Ext}}(\lambda)$ is defined in Fig. 3.*

In other variants of knowledge of exponent assumptions the adversary is provided with some auxiliary information, which amounts to a stronger assumption. This is typically required as in the security proofs the reduction obtains a challenge which it needs to embed in the input to the adversary. In our specific case, all the proof material is generated by the prover itself, including the CRS. Consequently, the game DH-KE considers an adversary that simply takes as input a group description, without any auxiliary information. Compared to [BFS16], where the adversary is provided with additional information, our variant is thus weaker.

## 3   An Extractable Commitment Scheme from DLin

We recall the homomorphic commitment scheme based on linear encryption [BBS04] by Groth et al. [GOS06a]. It defines two types of key generation: a perfectly hiding and perfectly binding one. Given a bilinear group $\Gamma := (p, \mathbb{G}, \mathbb{G}_T, e, G)$, it defines two key-generation algorithms $\mathsf{Com.K}^{(b)}$ and $\mathsf{Com.K}^{(h)}$ producing binding and hiding keys, respectively:

| $\mathsf{Com.K}^{(h)}$ | $\mathsf{Com.K}^{(b)}$ |
|---|---|
| $\tau := (r_u, s_v) \leftarrow_\$ (\mathbb{Z}_p^*)^2; \ (x, y) \leftarrow_\$ (\mathbb{Z}_p^*)^2$ | $\tau := (x, y, z) \leftarrow_\$ (\mathbb{Z}_p^*)^3; \ (r_u, s_v) \leftarrow_\$ (\mathbb{Z}_p^*)^2$ |
| $F := xG, \ \ H := yG$ | $F := xG, \ \ H := yG$ |
| $(U, V, W) := (r_u F, s_v H, (r_u + s_v)G)$ | $(U, V, W) := (r_u F, s_v H, (r_u + s_v + z)G)$ |
| $\sigma := (F, H, U, V, W)$ | $\sigma := (F, H, U, V, W)$ |
| **return** $(\sigma, \tau)$ | **return** $(\sigma, \tau)$ |

In order to commit to a value $m \in \mathbb{Z}_p$, one samples $r, s \leftarrow_\$ \mathbb{Z}_p$ and returns:

$$C = \mathsf{Com.C}(m; r, s) = \big(mU + rF, mV + sH, mW + (r + s)G\big).$$

Since $\mathsf{Com.C}(m_0; r_0, s_0) + \mathsf{Com.C}(m_1; r_1, s_1) = \mathsf{Com.C}(m_0 + m_1; r_0 + r_1, s_0 + s_1)$, commitments are additively homomorphic. A committed value is opened by providing the randomness $(r, s)$. Under a perfectly hiding key, a commitment to $m$ can be opened to any value $m'$, given trapdoor information $\tau = (r_u, s_v)$:

$$\begin{aligned} \mathsf{Com.C}(m; r, s) &= \big((mr_u + r)F, (ms_v + s)V, (mr_u + r + ms_v + s)G\big) \\ &= \mathsf{Com.C}\big(m'; r - (m' - m)r_u, s - (m' - m)s_v\big). \end{aligned} \tag{1}$$

Under the DLin assumption, keys output by the perfectly hiding setup are computationally indistinguishable from ones output by the perfectly binding setup. For this reason, the perfectly hiding setup leads to computationally binding commitments and vice versa.

We say that a triple of group elements is *linear* w.r.t. $(F, H, G)$ if it is of the form $(rF, sH, (r + s)G)$ for some $r, s \in \mathbb{Z}_p$. Commitments to 0 are linear triples and every commitment under a *hiding* key is also a linear. Under a *binding* key we have:

$$\mathsf{Com.C}(m; r, s) = \big((mr_u + r)F, (ms_v + s)H, mzG + (mr_u + r + ms_v + s)G\big).$$

A commitment to $m$ is thus a *linear encryption* [BBS04] of $mzG \in \mathbb{G}_1$ under randomness $(mr_u + r, ms_v + s)$. Given a commitment $C$ and the trapdoor information $\tau = (x, y, z)$, one can *extract* the committed message. The extraction algorithm $\mathsf{Com.E}$ is defined as:

$$\mathsf{Com.E}\big(\tau,\,(C_0, C_1, C_2)\big) := \mathsf{dLog}\big(z^{-1}(C_2 - x^{-1}C_0 - y^{-1}C_1)\big), \qquad (2)$$

where $\mathsf{dLog}$ can be efficiently computed if the message space is of logarithmic size; for instance, assuming $m \in \{0,1\}$, we define $\mathsf{Com.E}$ to return 0 if $(C_2 - x^{-1}C_0 - y^{-1}C_1)$ is the identity element, and 1 otherwise.

**Theorem 4 ([GOS06a]).** *Assuming DLin, $\mathsf{Com}$, as defined above, is an extractable homomorphic commitment scheme that is:*

- *perfectly binding, computationally hiding when instantiated with $\mathsf{Com.K}^{(b)}$;*
- *computationally binding, perfectly hiding when instantiated with $\mathsf{Com.K}^{(h)}$.*

The "parameter switching" technique, which defines different types of keys that are computationally indistinguishable, has proved very useful and also applies to encryption schemes. The idea has been defined (and named) several times. "Parameter switching" [GOS06a] is also called "meaningful/meaningless encryption" [KN08], "dual-mode encryption" [PVW08] and "lossy encryption" [BHY09].

**Proofs of Binarity.** As a building block for their zaps Groth et al. [GOS06a] first construct a witness-indistinguishable non-interactive proof system $\mathsf{Bin}$. Given a commitment key $\sigma = (F, H, U, V, W)$ and a commitment $C \in \mathbb{G}^3$, it allows to prove that $C$ commits to a value in $\{0,1\}$ under $\sigma$. The proof is perfectly sound and perfectly witness-indistinguishable. (We recall their scheme in the full version [FO18].)

## 4    Non-interactive Zaps

To construct a non-interactive zap (i.e., a WI proof system without a CRS), Groth et al. [GOS06a] first construct a proof system for circuit satisfiability *with* a CRS, based on the commitment scheme from Sect. 3 and their proof of binarity. Then, in order to make their scheme CRS-less, they define the prover to pick two CRS's that are correlated in a way that makes it impossible for the adversary to cheat under both of them.

As the commitment scheme described in Sect. 3 is homomorphic, it is possible to perform linear operations on commitments, and in particular prove logical relations between them.

First, proving that either $C$ or $C' := C - (U, V, W)$ is linear proves that $C$ is a commitment to a bit. In order to prove that committed values satisfy wire assignments of a NAND gate, Groth et al. [GOS06b] observe that if $a, b \in \{0,1\}$ then $c := \neg(a \wedge b)$ iff $t := a + b + 2c - 2 \in \{0,1\}$. Reasoning with homomorphic commitments, we have that three commitments $A := (A_0, A_1, A_2)$, $B := (B_0, B_1, B_2)$, and $C := (C_0, C_1, C_2)$ are bound respectively to the values $a, b, c$, such that $c = \neg(a \wedge b)$, if and only if

$$T := A + B + 2 \cdot C - 2 \cdot (U, V, W) \qquad (3)$$

| $\mathsf{ZAP.P}(1^\lambda, \phi, w)$ | $\mathsf{ZAP.V}(\phi, (\sigma_0, \pi_0, \pi_1))$ |
|---|---|
| $\Gamma := \mathsf{G}(1^\lambda); \ (\sigma_0, \tau) \leftarrow \mathsf{Circ.K}(\Gamma)$ | $\sigma_1 := \sigma_0 + (0, 0, 0, 0, G)$ |
| $\sigma_1 := \sigma_0 + (0, 0, 0, 0, G)$ | $\mathbf{return} \ \left( \bigwedge_{i \in \{0,1\}} \mathsf{Circ.V}(\sigma_i, \phi, \pi_i) \right)$ |
| $\pi_0 \leftarrow \mathsf{Circ.P}(\sigma_0, \phi, w); \ \pi_1 \leftarrow \mathsf{Circ.P}(\sigma_1, \phi, w)$ | |
| $\mathbf{return} \ (\sigma_0, \pi_0, \pi_1)$ | |

**Fig. 4.** The (non-interactive) ZAP protocol of [GOS06a].

is a commitment to either 0 or 1. Thus, to prove that $A, B, C$ are commitments to values in $\{0, 1\}$ and that $C$ is a commitment to the NAND of the values in $A$ and $B$, it is sufficient to prove that $A$, $B$, $C$ and $T$ are all bit commitments. With these observations, GOS construct a perfectly witness-indistinguishable proof system Circ for circuit satisfiability as follows:

The key generation algorithm Circ.K simply emulates $\mathsf{Com.K}^{(h)}$, that is, it generates a hiding commitment key. The prover $\mathsf{Circ.P}(\sigma, \mathsf{C}, w)$ takes as input a circuit $\mathsf{C}$ and a witness $w$ satisfying $\mathsf{C}(w) = 1$, and does the following: represent the circuit evaluation $\mathsf{C}(w)$ in such a way that $w_k$ is the value running in the $k$-th wire. For each $w_k$, produce a commitment $C_k \leftarrow \mathsf{Com.C}(\sigma, w_k)$ to $w_k$ and prove it is to a bit under $\sigma$ using proof system Bin. For each gate, construct $T$ from the commitments corresponding to the ingoing and outgoing wires as above and prove that it too is a commitment to 0 or 1. For the output commitment, create a commitment $C_{\mathrm{out}}$ to 1 that can be easily reproduced and checked by the verifier: $C_{\mathrm{out}} := \mathsf{Com.C}(\sigma, 1; (0, 0))$. Let $\Pi$ be the collection of all other commitments together with the respective proofs of binarity generated. Return $\Pi$.

The verifier $\mathsf{Circ.V}(\sigma, \mathsf{C}, \Pi)$, computes $C_{\mathrm{out}} := \mathsf{Com.C}(\sigma, 1; (0, 0))$ and for every gate the value $T$ as in Eq. (3); using Bin.V, it checks that all the wire commitments are to values in $\{0, 1\}$ and respect the gates (by checking the values $T$); if all verifications succeed, return **true**. Otherwise, return **false**.

**Theorem 5** ([GOS06a]). *Assuming DLin, Circ is a non-interactive, perfectly sound computationally witness-indistinguishable proof system.*

The reason why we cannot let the prover choose the CRS in Circ is that it could chose it as a perfectly hiding CRS and then simulate proofs. However, if the prover must construct two proofs under two different CRS's which are related in such a way that at least one of them is not linear (and thus binding), then the prover cannot cheat. In particular, note that given a 5-tuple $\sigma_0 \in \mathbb{G}^5$, and defining $\sigma_1 := \sigma_0 + (0, 0, 0, 0, G)$ then at *most* one of $\sigma_0, \sigma_1$ is linear. At the same time, both of them are valid CRS's. With this last trick, it is straightforward to construct the zap scheme ZAP, as illustrated in Fig. 4.

**Theorem 6** ([GOS06a]). *Assuming DLin, ZAP is a non-interactive zap with perfect soundness and computational witness indistinguishability.*

*Remark 7.* We note that soundness of ZAP relies only on the fact that $\Gamma$ is a bilinear group. In [GOS06a] the prover is allowed to generate $\Gamma$ and it is required

| $\mathsf{ZAK.P}(1^\lambda, \phi, w)$ | $\mathsf{ZAK.V}(\phi, (\Sigma, \Delta, \Pi))$ |
|---|---|
| $\Gamma := \mathsf{G}(1^\lambda)$ | // Check if $\Delta$ is consistent with $\Sigma$ |
| **for** $i = 0, 1$ **do** | **if not** $\mathsf{DH}(\Delta, \Sigma)$ **return false** |
| $\quad (\sigma_{i,0}, \tau_i) \leftarrow \mathsf{Circ.K}(\Gamma)$ | **for** $i$ **in** $\{0,1\}$ **do** |
| $\quad \sigma_{i,1} := \sigma_{i,0} + (0,0,0,0,G)$ | $\quad \sigma_{i,1} := \sigma_0 + (0,0,0,0,G)$ |
| $\quad \pi_{i,0} \leftarrow \mathsf{Circ.P}(\sigma_{i,0}, \phi, w)$ | **return** $\left( \bigwedge_{i,j \in \{0,1\}} \mathsf{Circ.V}(\sigma_{i,j}, \phi, \pi_{i,j}) \right)$ |
| $\quad \pi_{i,1} \leftarrow \mathsf{Circ.P}(\sigma_{i,1}, \phi, w)$ | |
| Compute $\Delta$ from $\tau_0, \tau_1$ as in Eq. (4). | |
| $\Sigma := [\sigma_{i,0}]_{i \in \{0,1\}},\ \Pi = [\pi_{i,j}]_{i,j \in \{0,1\}}$ | |
| **return** $(\Sigma, \Delta, \Pi)$ | |

**Fig. 5.** The ZAK protocol.

that $\Gamma$ is verifiable. We presented a zap for deterministically generated groups, as considered by Bellare et al. [BFS16], which is also required for our construction of non-interactive zaps of knowledge in the next section.

## 5   ZAK: A Non-interactive Zap of Knowledge

We now present our NIWI argument of knowledge for circuit satisfiability. The high-level idea of our protocol is to double the ZAP proof of [GOS06a] and link the two CRS's so the prover must know the extraction trapdoor for one of them. Whereas the protocol ZAP used two Circ proofs to construct a zap from a proof that requires a CRS, we will use two zap proofs to not only prove circuit satisfiability, but to prove *knowledge* of a satisfying assignment. More specifically, knowledge soundness is obtained by generating two independent zap proofs, and then linking the respective trapdoor information with multiple DH in a matrix of group elements $\Delta$. This additional matrix $\Delta$, that we call *linking element*, is constructed in such a way that (under DH-KE) it is possible to recover the trapdoor from one of the two zap proofs, and use it to extract the witness from the commitments contained in a valid zap proof. Witness indistinguishability of the single proofs follows immediately from [GOS06a], but our proofs also contain the linking element $\Delta$, which depend on the randomness of the CRS's. We thus have to argue that these additional elements do not harm witness indistinguishability.

Bellare et al. [BFS16] also used an extractor to recover the trapdoor hidden in an adversarially generated CRS to construct a scheme satisfying subversion-zero knowledge. Our protocol is detailed in Fig. 5, where by DH we denote the algorithm that checks that $\delta_{i,j}$ is the CDH of $(\sigma_{0,0})_i$ and $(\sigma_{1,0})_j$ (see below).

The trapdoor information $\tau_0 = (x_0, y_0)$ and $\tau_1 = (x_1, y_1)$ is correlated in $\Delta$ to form the following products:

$$\Delta := [\delta_{i,j}]_{i,j \in \{0,1\}} = \begin{bmatrix} x_0 x_1 G & x_0 y_1 G \\ y_0 x_1 G & y_0 y_1 G \end{bmatrix} \tag{4}$$

Correctness of $\Delta$ can be checked by the verification algorithm using the bilinear map. For $i = 0, 1$, let the CRS be $\sigma_i = (F_i, H_i, U_i, V_i, W_i)$, and let $x_i, y_i$ be such that:

$$F_i := x_i G, \qquad H_i := y_i G,$$

in which case $\Delta$ is constructed as in Eq. (4). The verifier checks that the following holds:

$$\begin{aligned}
e(\delta_{0,0}, G) &= e(F_0, F_1), \quad e(\delta_{0,1}, G) = e(F_0, H_1), \\
e(\delta_{1,0}, G) &= e(H_0, F_1), \quad e(\delta_{1,1}, G) = e(H_0, H_1).
\end{aligned} \tag{5}$$

Let us denote by DH the algorithm that, given as input $\Sigma$ and $\Delta$ returns **true** if all equalities of Eq. (5) are satisfied, and **false** otherwise. This procedure is used by the verification equation, as detailed in Fig. 5.

We now proceed with the proof of our main result, Theorem 1, which we rephrase here for completeness:

**Theorem 1.** *Assume that DLin and DH-KE hold for G. Then ZAK as defined in Fig. 5 is a non-interactive zap that satisfies knowledge soundness and witness indistinguishability. In particular, we have*

$$\mathsf{Adv}_{\mathsf{ZAK}}^{\mathrm{ksnd}}(\lambda) \leq 4 \cdot \mathsf{Adv}^{\mathrm{dh\text{-}ke}}(\lambda) \quad and \quad \mathsf{Adv}_{\mathsf{ZAK}}^{\mathrm{wi}}(\lambda) \leq 8 \cdot \mathsf{Adv}^{\mathrm{dlin}}(\lambda).$$

Completeness of the protocol is trivial: the prover (respectively, the verifier) simply performs 4 iterations of Circ proofs (respectively, verifications), and therefore correctness is implied by Theorem 5 and the fact that $\Delta$ as in Eq. 4 satisfies Eq. 5. We now prove knowledge soundness and witness indistinguishability.

*Proof (of computational knowledge soundness).* We show that for any adversary able to produce a valid proof we can construct a PPT extractor that can extract a witness from such a proof with overwhelming probability.

Let A be an adversarial prover in game $\mathrm{KSND}(\lambda)$ (Fig. 2, with $\Pi.\mathsf{K}$ void). On input $1^\lambda$, A returns a proof consisting of $\sigma_{i,0} = (F_i, H_i, U_i, V_i, W_i)$ for $i \in \{0, 1\}$, of $\Delta = [\delta_{i,j}]_{i,j \in \{0,1\}}$ and $\Pi = [\pi_{i,j}]_{i,j \in \{0,1\}}$. From A we construct four adversaries $\mathsf{A}_{i,j}$ (for $i, j \in \{0, 1\}$) that execute A and output some components of the proof produced by A, namely

$$\begin{aligned}
(F_0, F_1, \delta_{0,0}) &= (x_0 G, x_1 G, x_0 x_1 G), && \text{(for } \mathsf{A}_{0,0}) \\
(F_0, H_1, \delta_{0,1}) &= (x_0 G, y_1 G, x_0 y_1 G), && \text{(for } \mathsf{A}_{0,1}) \\
(H_0, F_1, \delta_{1,0}) &= (y_0 G, x_1 G, y_0 x_1 G), && \text{(for } \mathsf{A}_{1,0}) \\
(H_0, H_1, \delta_{1,1}) &= (y_0 G, y_1 G, y_0 y_1 G), && \text{(for } \mathsf{A}_{1,1})
\end{aligned}$$

where $x_i, y_i$ are such that $F_i = x_i G$, $H_i = y_i G$, and these four equations hold if $\mathsf{ZAK.V}(\mathsf{C}, (\Sigma, \Delta, \Pi))$ returns **true**. By the DH-KE assumption there exist extractors $\mathsf{Ext}_{i,j}$ for each of the adversaries $\mathsf{A}_{i,j}$ that given its coins outputs:

$$\begin{aligned}
x_0 \text{ or } x_1, && x_0 \text{ or } y_1, && \text{(for } \mathsf{Ext}_{0,0}, \mathsf{Ext}_{0,1}) \\
y_0 \text{ or } x_1, && y_0 \text{ or } y_1 && \text{(for } \mathsf{Ext}_{1,0}, \mathsf{Ext}_{1,1})
\end{aligned}$$

if the above equations hold. The statement $(x_0 \vee x_1) \wedge (y_0 \vee x_1) \wedge (x_0 \vee y_1) \wedge (y_0 \vee y_1)$ is logically equivalent to $(x_0 \wedge y_0) \vee (x_1 \wedge y_1)$. This means that together, these four extractors allow to recover either $(x_0, y_0)$ or $(x_1, y_1)$, that is, the extraction trapdoor for one of the CRS's. Let $i^*$ be such that $(x_{i^*}, y_{i^*})$ is the extracted pair.

For $j \in \{0, 1\}$, let $F_{i^*}, H_{i^*}, U_{i^*}, V_{i^*}, W_{i^*} \in \mathbb{G}$ be such that $\sigma_{i^*, j} = (F_{i^*}, H_{i^*}, U_{i^*}, V_{i^*}, W_{i^*} + jG)$. Let $j^* \in \{0, 1\}$ be the smallest integer satisfying:

$$x_{i^*}^{-1} U_{i^*} + y_{i^*}^{-1} V_{i^*} - (W_{i^*} + j^* G) \neq 0G.$$

The above implies that $\sigma_{i^*, j^*}$ is not a linear tuple, which means that it is a binding CRS. Let $C_{(i^*, j^*), k}$ denote the commitment to the $k$-th wire contained in $\pi_{i^*, j^*}$. Using the extraction algorithm described in Eq. (2) we can recover this witness:

$$w_k = \mathsf{Com.E}\big((x_{i^*}, y_{i^*}),\ C_{(i^*, j^*), k}\big).$$

It remains to prove that the extracted witness is indeed correct. Upon receiving a valid proof from adversary $\mathsf{A}$, we know from the verification equation (the subroutine $\mathsf{DH}$) that each $\mathsf{A}_{i,j}$ will output a DH triple. Therefore, extractors $\mathsf{Ext}_{i,j}$ together recover $\tau_{i^*} = (x_{i^*}, y_{j^*})$ with probability at least $1 - \sum_{i,j \in \{0,1\}} \mathsf{Adv}^{\mathrm{dhke}}_{\mathsf{G}, \mathsf{A}_{i,j}, \mathsf{Ext}_{i,j}}(\lambda)$, that is, by DH-KE, with overwhelming probability. Since the commitment scheme $\mathsf{Com}$ is perfectly binding if the CRS is not a linear tuple (Theorem 4), a message $w_k$ is always successfully extracted. Correctness of $w_k$ follows from the underlying proof system: by perfect soundness of $\mathsf{Bin}$ we are guaranteed that $w_k \in \{0, 1\}$; by perfect soundness of $\mathsf{Circ}$ (Theorem 5) that each gate evaluation is correct. The bound in the construction of the extractor is tight: we have $\mathsf{Adv}^{\mathrm{ksnd}}(\lambda) \leq 4 \cdot \mathsf{Adv}^{\mathrm{dhke}}(\lambda)$. $\qquad\square$

*Proof (of computational witness indistinguishability).* Consider an adversary in the WI game (Fig. 1, where $\Pi.\mathsf{K}$ is void) that makes $q = q(\lambda)$ queries to the PROVE oracle, each of the form $(\mathsf{C}^{(k)}, w_0^{(k)}, w_1^{(k)})$, for $0 \leq k < q$. Consider the following sequence of hybrid games where $\mathsf{H}_0$ corresponds to $\mathsf{WI}_{\mathsf{ZAK}, \mathsf{CIRC\text{-}SAT}, \mathsf{A}}(\lambda)$ with $b = 0$ and $\mathsf{H}_{12}$ corresponds to $\mathsf{WI}_{\mathsf{ZAK}, \mathsf{CIRC\text{-}SAT}, \mathsf{A}}(\lambda)$ with $b = 1$. The games differ in how the PROVE oracle is implemented, which is specified in Fig. 6 for the first half of the hybrids (the second half is analogous). We give an overview of all hybrids in Table 2 below.

$\mathsf{H}_0$ The challenger simulates an honest PROVE oracle, using (for every $k < q$) the first witness $w_0^{(k)}$ supplied by the adversary. It outputs $(\Sigma^{(k)}, \Delta^{(k)}, \Pi^{(k)})$, where in particular we recall:

$$\Sigma^{(k)} = \begin{bmatrix} \sigma_{0,0}^{(k)} = (F_0^{(k)}, H_0^{(k)}, U_0^{(k)}, V_0^{(k)}, W_0^{(k)}) \\ \sigma_{1,0}^{(k)} = (F_1^{(k)}, H_1^{(k)}, U_1^{(k)}, V_1^{(k)}, W_1^{(k)}) \end{bmatrix} \quad \text{and} \quad \Pi^{(k)} = \begin{bmatrix} \pi_{0,0}^{(k)} & \pi_{0,1}^{(k)} \\ \pi_{1,0}^{(k)} & \pi_{1,1}^{(k)} \end{bmatrix}.$$

Recall that the two rows of $[\Sigma^{(k)} | \Pi^{(k)}]$ are independent zaps and that $\sigma_{0,0}^{(k)}$ and $\sigma_{1,0}^{(k)}$ are chosen to be *hiding*. The PROVE oracle computes $\sigma_{i,j}^{(k)}$ which

| Oracle PROVE in $H_1$, $\boxed{H_2}$, and $\boxed{H_3}$ | Oracle PROVE in $H_4$ and $\boxed{H_5}$ |
|---|---|
| $\Gamma := G(1^\lambda)$ | $\Gamma := G(1^\lambda)$ |
| $(\sigma_{0,0}, \tau_i) \leftarrow \text{Circ.K}(\Gamma)$ | $(\sigma_{0,1}, \tau_i) \leftarrow \text{Circ.K}(\Gamma)$ |
| $\boxed{(\sigma_{0,0}, \tau_i) \leftarrow \text{Com.K}^{(b)}(\Gamma)}$ | $\sigma_{0,0} := \sigma_{0,1} - (0,0,0,0,G)$ |
| $\sigma_{0,1} := \sigma_{0,0} + (0,0,0,0,G)$ | $\boxed{(\sigma_{0,1}, \tau_i) \leftarrow \text{Com.K}^{(b)}(\Gamma)}$ |
| $\boxed{\begin{array}{l}(\sigma_{0,1}, \tau_i) \leftarrow \text{Circ.K}(\Gamma) \\ \sigma_{0,0} := \sigma_{0,1} - (0,0,0,0,G)\end{array}}$ | $\pi_{0,0} \leftarrow \text{Circ.P}(\sigma_{0,0}, \text{C}, w_1)$ |
| | $\pi_{0,1} \leftarrow \text{Circ.P}(\sigma_{0,1}, \text{C}, w_1)$ |
| $\pi_{0,0} \leftarrow \text{Circ.P}(\sigma_{0,0}, \text{C}, w_1)$ | // The second zap is as in ZAK.P using $w_0$. |
| $\pi_{0,1} \leftarrow \text{Circ.P}(\sigma_{0,1}, \text{C}, w_0)$ | $(\sigma_{1,0}, \pi_{1,0}, \pi_{1,1}) \leftarrow \text{ZAP.P}(1^\lambda, \text{C}, w_0)$ |
| // The second zap is as in ZAK.P using $w_0$. | Compute $\Delta$ as in Eq. (4). |
| $(\sigma_{1,0}, \pi_{1,0}, \pi_{1,1}) \leftarrow \text{ZAP.P}(1^\lambda, \text{C}, w_0)$ | **return** $(\Sigma, \Delta, \Pi)$ |
| Compute $\Delta$ as in Eq. (4). | |
| **return** $(\Sigma, \Delta, \Pi)$ | |

**Fig. 6.** Overview of the simulations of the prove oracle in the first hybrid games for the proof of WI. Hybrids $H_1$ and $H_4$ are defined by ignoring all boxes (the light gray highlights the differences with respect to the previous hybrids), whereas $\boxed{H_2}$ and $\boxed{H_5}$ include the light boxes but not the gray one and $\boxed{H_3}$ includes all boxes.

is of the form $\sigma_{i,j}^{(k)} = \left(F_i^{(k)}, H_i^{(k)}, U_i^{(k)}, V_i^{(k)}, W_i^{(k)} + jG\right)$, for $i, j \in \{0, 1\}$. Furthermore, $\pi_{i,j}^{(k)}$ is a Circ proof using $w_0^{(k)}$ under the CRS $\sigma_{i,j}^{(k)}$.

$H_1$ For every PROVE query, the simulator uses witness $w_1^{(k)}$ (instead of $w_0^{(k)}$) to produce $\pi_{0,0}^{(k)}$. As the respective CRS $\sigma_{0,0}^{(k)}$ was generated using the perfectly hiding commitment setup Circ.K, the two hybrids are distributed equivalently (any commitment under a hiding key is a random linear triple; cf. Eq. (1)).

$H_2$ For every PROVE query, the simulator now generates CRS $\sigma_{0,0}^{(k)}$ as a *binding* key via Com.K$^{(b)}$; $\sigma_{0,1}^{(k)}$ is generated as before (adding $(0,0,0,0,G)$), and so are all proofs. Note that the linking elements $\Delta^{(k)}$ can be constructed knowing only the trapdoor $(x_1^{(k)}, y_1^{(k)})$ of the CRS $\sigma_{1,0}^{(k)}$, which remained unchanged:

$$\Delta^{(k)} = \begin{bmatrix} y_1^{(k)} H_0^{(k)} & y_1^{(k)} F_0^{(k)} \\ x_1^{(k)} H_0^{(k)} & x_1^{(k)} F_0^{(k)} \end{bmatrix}. \qquad (6)$$

$H_1$ and $H_2$ are computationally indistinguishable under the DLin assumption: given a DLin challenge $(F, H, U, V, W)$, the reduction can exploit the random self-reducibility property of DLin to construct $q$ instances of the DLin challenge: $\forall k < q$ select $\bar{x}^{(k)}, \bar{y}^{(k)}, \bar{r}^{(k)}, \bar{s}^{(k)}, \bar{z}^{(k)} \leftarrow_{\$} \mathbb{Z}_p$ and compute $\sigma_{0,0}^{(k)}$ as $\left(\bar{x}^{(k)} F, \ \bar{y}^{(k)} H, \ \bar{r}^{(k)} \bar{x}^{(k)} F + \bar{z}^{(k)} \bar{x}^{(k)} U, \ \bar{s}^{(k)} \bar{y}^{(k)} H + \bar{z}^{(k)} \bar{y}^{(k)} V, \ (\bar{r}^{(k)} + \bar{s}^{(k)})G + \bar{z}^{(k)} W\right)$.
Each $\sigma_{0,0}^{(k)}$ is a random linear tuple if and only if the DLin challenge is, and it is a uniformly random tuple if the DLin challenge is, as shown in [BFS16].

**Table 2.** Overview of changes throughout the hybrids: (h) denotes hiding setup; (b) denotes binding setup; $w_b$ identifies the witness used to produce the proof.

| Hybrid | $\sigma_{0,0}^{(k)}$ | $\pi_{0,0}^{(k)}$ | $\sigma_{0,1}^{(k)}$ | $\pi_{0,1}^{(k)}$ | $\sigma_{1,0}^{(k)}$ | $\pi_{1,0}^{(k)}$ | $\sigma_{1,1}^{(k)}$ | $\pi_{1,1}^{(k)}$ |
|---|---|---|---|---|---|---|---|---|
| $H_0$ | (h) | $w_0$ | (b) | $w_0$ | (h) | $w_0$ | (b) | $w_0$ |
| $H_1$ | | $w_1$ | | | | | | |
| $H_2$ | (b) | | | | | | | |
| $H_3$ | | | (h) | | | | | |
| $H_4$ | | | | $w_1$ | | | | |
| $H_5$ | | | (b) | | | | | |
| $H_6$ | (h) | | | | | | | |
| $H_7$ | | | | | | $w_1$ | | |
| $H_8$ | | | | | (b) | | | |
| $H_9$ | | | | | | | (h) | |
| $H_{10}$ | | | | | | | | $w_1$ |
| $H_{11}$ | | | | | | | (b) | |
| $H_{12}$ | (h) | $w_1$ | (b) | $w_1$ | (h) | $w_1$ | (b) | $w_1$ |

Computing $\sigma_{1,0}^{(k)}$ as in $H_1$ (hiding) and defining $\Delta$ as in Eq. 6, the simulator generates the rest of the game as defined. It returns the adversary's guess and thus breaks DLin whenever the adversary distinguishes $H_1$ and $H_2$.

$H_3$  The simulator replaces each CRS $\sigma_{0,1}^{(k)}$ for all $k < q$ with a *hiding* commitment and defines $\sigma_{0,0}^{(k)} := \sigma_{0,1}^{(k)} - (0,0,0,0,G)$, which is therefore (once again) binding. More specifically, the simulator creates a linear tuple invoking Circ.K:

$$\sigma_{0,1}^{(k)} = \left( x_0^{(k)} G, \ y_0^{(k)} G, \ x_0^{(k)} r^{(k)} G, \ y_0^{(k)} s^{(k)} G, \ (r^{(k)} + s^{(k)}) G \right)$$

where $x_0^{(k)}, y_0^{(k)}, r^{(k)}, s^{(k)} \leftarrow_\$ \mathbb{Z}_p$.

The two distributions are proven computationally indistinguishable under DLin by an argument analogous to the one for $H_1 \to H_2$. This time the challenger constructs all the instances of the DLin challenge for $\sigma_{0,1}^{(k)}$, while $\sigma_{0,0}^{(k)}$ is derived. From there, the proof proceeds identically.

$H_4$  The simulator replaces each proof $\pi_{0,1}^{(k)}$ by using $w_1^{(k)}$ instead of $w_0^{(k)}$ ($\forall k < q$). This hybrid is equivalently distributed as the previous one; this is proved via the same argument as for $H_0 \to H_1$.

$H_5$  The simulator switches $\sigma_{0,1}^{(k)}$ from a hiding to a binding key. This game hop is analogous to the hop $H_1 \to H_2$ (which switched $\sigma_{0,0}^{(k)}$ from hiding to binding).

$H_6$  The simulator switches $\sigma_{0,0}^{(k)}$ from binding to hiding. Indistinguishability from the previous hybrid is shown analogously to the hop $H_2 \to H_3$. Note that in this hybrid the first zap $(\sigma_{0,0}^{(k)}, \pi_{0,0}^{(k)}, \pi_{0,1}^{(k)})$ is distributed according to the protocol specification, but using witness $w_1^{(k)}$.

Hybrids $H_7$ to $H_{12}$ are now defined analogously to hybrids $H_1$ to $H_6$, except for applying all changes to $\sigma_1^{(k)}$ and $\pi_{1,0}^{(k)}$ and $\pi_{1,1}^{(k)}$. In hybrid $H_{12}$ the adversary is then given arguments of knowledge for witness $w_1$.

As the difference between hybrids $H_1$ and $H_{12}$ is bounded by 8 times the advantage of a DLin distinguisher, the adversary has total advantage

$$\mathsf{Adv}_{\mathsf{ZAK},\mathsf{C},\mathsf{A}}^{\mathsf{wi}}(\lambda) \leq 8 \cdot \mathsf{Adv}_{\mathsf{ZAK},\mathsf{C},\mathsf{A}}^{\mathsf{dlin}}(\lambda) = \mathsf{negl}(\lambda)\,.$$

The bound is thus tight. □

**Acknowledgements.** The authors would like to thank the anonymous reviewers of PKC 2018 and ACNS 2018 for their helpful comments. The first author is supported by the French ANR EfTrEC project (ANR-16-CE39-0002). The second author is supported by ERC grant 639554 (project aSCEND).

# References

[BBS04] Boneh, D., Boyen, X., Shacham, H.: Short group signatures. In: Franklin, M. (ed.) CRYPTO 2004. LNCS, vol. 3152, pp. 41–55. Springer, Heidelberg (2004). https://doi.org/10.1007/978-3-540-28628-8_3

[BCG+14] Ben-Sasson, E., Chiesa, A., Garman, C., Green, M., Miers, I., Tromer, E., Virza, M.: Zerocash: decentralized anonymous payments from bitcoin. In: 2014 IEEE Symposium on Security and Privacy, pp. 459–474. IEEE Computer Society Press, May 2014

[BCI+10] Brier, E., Coron, J.-S., Icart, T., Madore, D., Randriam, H., Tibouchi, M.: Efficient indifferentiable hashing into ordinary elliptic curves. In: Rabin, T. (ed.) CRYPTO 2010. LNCS, vol. 6223, pp. 237–254. Springer, Heidelberg (2010). https://doi.org/10.1007/978-3-642-14623-7_13

[BFM88] Blum, M., Feldman, P., Micali, S.: Non-interactive zero-knowledge and its applications (extended abstract). In: 20th ACM STOC, pp. 103–112. ACM Press, May 1988

[BFS16] Bellare, M., Fuchsbauer, G., Scafuro, A.: NIZKs with an untrusted CRS: security in the face of parameter subversion. In: Cheon, J.H., Takagi, T. (eds.) ASIACRYPT 2016. LNCS, vol. 10032, pp. 777–804. Springer, Heidelberg (2016). https://doi.org/10.1007/978-3-662-53890-6_26

[BG93] Bellare, M., Goldreich, O.: On defining proofs of knowledge. In: Brickell, E.F. (ed.) CRYPTO 1992. LNCS, vol. 740, pp. 390–420. Springer, Heidelberg (1993). https://doi.org/10.1007/3-540-48071-4_28

[BHY09] Bellare, M., Hofheinz, D., Yilek, S.: Possibility and impossibility results for encryption and commitment secure under selective opening. In: Joux, A. (ed.) EUROCRYPT 2009. LNCS, vol. 5479, pp. 1–35. Springer, Heidelberg (2009). https://doi.org/10.1007/978-3-642-01001-9_1

[BOV03] Barak, B., Ong, S.J., Vadhan, S.: Derandomization in cryptography. In: Boneh, D. (ed.) CRYPTO 2003. LNCS, vol. 2729, pp. 299–315. Springer, Heidelberg (2003). https://doi.org/10.1007/978-3-540-45146-4_18

[BP15] Bitansky, N., Paneth, O.: ZAPs and non-interactive witness indistinguishability from indistinguishability obfuscation. In: Dodis, Y., Nielsen, J.B. (eds.) TCC 2015. LNCS, vol. 9015, pp. 401–427. Springer, Heidelberg (2015). https://doi.org/10.1007/978-3-662-46497-7_16

[BW06]  Boyen, X., Waters, B.: Compact group signatures without random oracles. In: Vaudenay, S. (ed.) EUROCRYPT 2006. LNCS, vol. 4004, pp. 427–444. Springer, Heidelberg (2006). https://doi.org/10.1007/11761679_26

[BW07]  Boyen, X., Waters, B.: Full-domain subgroup hiding and constant-size group signatures. In: Okamoto, T., Wang, X. (eds.) PKC 2007. LNCS, vol. 4450, pp. 1–15. Springer, Heidelberg (2007). https://doi.org/10.1007/978-3-540-71677-8_1

[DN00]  Dwork, C., Naor, M.: Zaps and their applications. In: 41st FOCS, pp. 283–293. IEEE Computer Society Press, November 2000

[FLS90]  Feige, U., Lapidot, D., Shamir, A.: Multiple non-interactive zero knowledge proofs based on a single random string (extended abstract). In: 31st FOCS, pp. 308–317. IEEE Computer Society Press, October 1990

[FO18]  Fuchsbauer, G., Orrú, M.: Non-interactive zaps of knowledge. Cryptology ePrint Archive, Report 2018/228 (2018)

[FS90]  Feige, U., Shamir, A.: Witness indistinguishable and witness hiding protocols. In: 22nd ACM STOC, pp. 416–426. ACM Press, May 1990

[Fuc18]  Fuchsbauer, G.: Subversion-zero-knowledge SNARKs. In: Abdalla, M., Dahab, R. (eds.) PKC 2018. LNCS, vol. 10769, pp. 315–347. Springer, Cham (2018). https://doi.org/10.1007/978-3-319-76578-5_11

[GMR89]  Goldwasser, S., Micali, S., Rackoff, C.: The knowledge complexity of interactive proof systems. SIAM J. Comput. 18(1), 186–208 (1989)

[GO94]  Goldreich, O., Oren, Y.: Definitions and properties of zero-knowledge proof systems. J. Cryptol. 7(1), 1–32 (1994)

[GOS06a]  Groth, J., Ostrovsky, R., Sahai, A.: Non-interactive zaps and new techniques for NIZK. In: Dwork, C. (ed.) CRYPTO 2006. LNCS, vol. 4117, pp. 97–111. Springer, Heidelberg (2006). https://doi.org/10.1007/11818175_6

[GOS06b]  Groth, J., Ostrovsky, R., Sahai, A.: Perfect non-interactive zero knowledge for NP. In: Vaudenay, S. (ed.) EUROCRYPT 2006. LNCS, vol. 4004, pp. 339–358. Springer, Heidelberg (2006). https://doi.org/10.1007/11761679_21

[GS08]  Groth, J., Sahai, A.: Efficient non-interactive proof systems for bilinear groups. In: Smart, N. (ed.) EUROCRYPT 2008. LNCS, vol. 4965, pp. 415–432. Springer, Heidelberg (2008). https://doi.org/10.1007/978-3-540-78967-3_24

[Gol93]  Goldreich, O.: A uniform-complexity treatment of encryption and zero-knowledge. J. Cryptol. 6(1), 21–53 (1993)

[Gro06]  Groth, J.: Simulation-sound NIZK proofs for a practical language and constant size group signatures. In: Lai, X., Chen, K. (eds.) ASIACRYPT 2006. LNCS, vol. 4284, pp. 444–459. Springer, Heidelberg (2006). https://doi.org/10.1007/11935230_29

[Gro10]  Groth, J.: Short pairing-based non-interactive zero-knowledge arguments. In: Abe, M. (ed.) ASIACRYPT 2010. LNCS, vol. 6477, pp. 321–340. Springer, Heidelberg (2010). https://doi.org/10.1007/978-3-642-17373-8_19

[KN08]  Kol, G., Naor, M.: Cryptography and game theory: designing protocols for exchanging information. In: Canetti, R. (ed.) TCC 2008. LNCS, vol. 4948, pp. 320–339. Springer, Heidelberg (2008). https://doi.org/10.1007/978-3-540-78524-8_18

[PVW08] Peikert, C., Vaikuntanathan, V., Waters, B.: A framework for efficient and composable oblivious transfer. In: Wagner, D. (ed.) CRYPTO 2008. LNCS, vol. 5157, pp. 554–571. Springer, Heidelberg (2008). https://doi.org/10.1007/978-3-540-85174-5_31

[Ràf15] Ràfols, C.: Stretching groth-sahai: NIZK proofs of partial satisfiability. In: Dodis, Y., Nielsen, J.B. (eds.) TCC 2015. LNCS, vol. 9015, pp. 247–276. Springer, Heidelberg (2015). https://doi.org/10.1007/978-3-662-46497-7_10

# Side Channel Attacks and Tamper Resistance

# Formal Verification of Side-Channel Countermeasures via Elementary Circuit Transformations

Jean-Sébastien Coron[✉]

University of Luxembourg, Luxembourg City, Luxembourg
`jean-sebastien.coron@uni.lu`

**Abstract.** We describe a technique to formally verify the security of masked implementations against side-channel attacks, based on elementary circuit transforms. We describe two complementary approaches: a generic approach for the formal verification of any circuit, but for small attack orders only, and a specialized approach for the verification of specific circuits, but at any order. We also show how to generate security proofs automatically, for simple circuits. We describe the implementation of CheckMasks, a formal verification tool for side-channel countermeasures. Using this tool, we formally verify the security of the Rivain-Prouff countermeasure for AES, and also the recent Boolean to arithmetic conversion algorithms from CHES 2017.

**Keywords:** Side-channel attacks and countermeasures
High-order masking · Security proof · Automated security analysis

## 1 Introduction

**The Masking Countermeasure.** Masking is the most widely used countermeasure against side-channel attacks for block-ciphers and symmetric-key algorithms. In a first-order countermeasure, all intermediate variables $x$ are masked into $x' = x \oplus r$ where $r$ is a randomly generated value. For such countermeasure, it is usually straightforward to verify its security against first-order attacks; namely it suffices to check that all intermediate variables have the uniform distribution, or at least that their distribution is independent from the key; therefore an attacker processing the side-channel leakage of intermediate variables separately (as in a first-order attack) does not get useful information.

However second-order attacks combining the leakage on $x'$ and $r$ can be mounted in practice, so it makes sense to design masking algorithms resisting higher-order attacks. This is done by extending Boolean masking to $n$ shares with $x = x_1 \oplus \cdots \oplus x_n$; in that case an implementation should be resistant against $t$-th order attacks, in which the adversary combines leakage information from at most $t < n$ intermediate variables.

© Springer International Publishing AG, part of Springer Nature 2018
B. Preneel and F. Vercauteren (Eds.): ACNS 2018, LNCS 10892, pp. 65–82, 2018.
https://doi.org/10.1007/978-3-319-93387-0_4

**Security Proofs.** In principle any countermeasure against high-order attacks should have a security proof, but such proof can be either missing, incomplete, or incorrect. In this paper we describe the construction of a tool, called CheckMasks, to automatically verify the security of high-order masking schemes.

The first step is to specify what it means for a masking countermeasure to be secure, *i.e.* what is the security model. Such formalization was initiated by Ishai et al. in [ISW03]. In this model, the adversary can probe at most $t$ wires in the circuit, but he should not learn anything about the secret key. The approach for proving security is based on simulation: one must show that any set of $t$ wires probed by the adversary can be perfectly simulated without the knowledge of the secret-key. This shows that the $t$ probes do not bring any useful information to the attacker, since he could run this simulation by himself.

More precisely, the simulation technique consists in showing that any set of $t$ probes can be perfectly simulated by the knowledge of only a proper subset of the input shares $x_i$. At the beginning of the algorithm an original variable $x$ is shared into $n$ shares $x_i$. When $x$ is part of the secret-key, this pre-sharing cannot be probed by the adversary. Since any subset of at most $n-1$ input shares $x_i$ are uniformly and independently distributed, the simulation of the probed variables can be performed without knowing the secret-key.

The main result in [ISW03] is to show that any circuit $C$ can be transformed into a new circuit $C'$ of size $\mathcal{O}(t^2 \cdot |C|)$ that is resistant against an adversary probing at most $t$ wires in the circuit. The construction is based on secret-sharing every variable $x$ into $n$ shares with $x = x_1 \oplus \cdots \oplus x_n$, and processing the shares in a way that prevents a $t$-limited adversary from leaning any information about the initial variable $x$, using $n \geq 2t + 1$ shares.

**Formal Verification of Masking.** The formal verification of the masking countermeasure was initiated by Barthe *et al.* in [BBD+15]. The authors describe an automated method to prove the security of masked implementation against $t$-th order attacks, for small values of $t$ (in practice, $t < 5$). The method only works for small values of $t$ because the number of possible $t$-tuples of intermediate variables grows exponentially with $t$. To formally prove the security of a masking algorithm, the authors describe an algorithm to construct a bijection between the observations of the adversary (corresponding to a $t$-tuple of intermediate variables) and a distribution that is syntactically independent from the secret inputs; this implies that the adversary learns nothing from this particular $t$-tuple of intermediate variables. All possible $t$-tuples of intermediates variables are then examined by exhaustive search.

The authors obtain a formal verification of various masked implementations, up to second order masked implementation of AES, and up to 5-th order for the masked Rivain-Prouff multiplication [RP10]. In particular, the authors were able to rediscover some known attacks and discover new ways of attacking already broken schemes. Their approach is implemented in the framework of EasyCrypt [BDG+14], and relies on its internal representations of programs and expressions.

The main drawback of the previous approach is that it can only work for small orders $t$, since the running time is exponential in $t$. To overcome this problem, in a follow-up work [BBD+16], Barthe *et al.* studied the composition property of masked algorithms. In particular, the authors introduce the notion of *strong simulatability*, a stronger property which requires that the number of input shares necessary to simulate the observations of the adversary in a given gadget is independent from the number of observations made on output wires. This ensures some separation between the input and the output wires: no matter how many output wires must be simulated (to ensure the composition of gadgets), the number of input wires that must be known to perform the simulation only depends on the number of internal probes within the gadget.

The paper [BBD+16] has a number of important contributions that we summarize below. Firstly, the authors introduce the $t$-NI and $t$-SNI definitions. The $t$-NI security notion corresponds to the original security definition in the ISW probing model [ISW03]; it requires that any $t_c \leq t$ probes of the gadget circuit can be simulated from at most $t_c$ of its input shares. The stronger $t$-SNI notion corresponds to the strong simulatability property mentioned above, in which the number of input shares required for the simulation is upper bounded by the number of probes $t_c$ in the circuit, and is independent from the number of output variables $|\mathcal{O}|$ that must be simulated (as long as the condition $t_c + |\mathcal{O}| < t$ is satisfied). We recall these definitions in Sect. 2, as they are fundamental in our paper.

The authors show that the $t$-SNI definition allows for securely composing masked algorithms; *i.e.* for a construction involving many gadgets, one can prove that the full construction is $t$-SNI secure, based on the $t$-SNI security of its components. The advantages are twofold: firstly the proof becomes modular and much easier to describe. Secondly as opposed to [ISW03] the masking order does not need to be doubled throughout the circuit, as one can work with $n \geq t + 1$ shares, instead of $n \geq 2t + 1$ shares. Since most gadgets have complexity $\mathcal{O}(n^2)$, this usually gives a factor 4 improvement in efficiency. In [BBD+16], the authors prove the $t$-SNI property of several useful gadgets: the multiplication of Rivain-Prouff [RP10], the mask refreshing based on the same multiplication algorithm, and the multiplication between linearly dependent inputs from [CPRR13].

Moreover, in [BBD+16] the authors also machine-checked the multiplication of Rivain-Prouff and the multiplication-based mask refreshing in the EasyCrypt framework [BDG+14]. The main point is that their machine verification works for any order, whereas in [BBD+15] the formal verification could only be performed at small orders $t$. However, the approach seems difficult to understand (at least for a non-expert in formal methods), and when reading [BBD+16] it is far from obvious how the automated verification of the countermeasure can be implemented concretely; this seems to require a deep knowledge of the EasyCrypt framework.

Finally, the authors built an automated approach for verifying that an algorithm constructed by composing provably secure gadgets is itself secure. They also implemented an algorithm for transforming an input program $P$ into a program $P'$ secure at order $t$; their algorithm automatically inserts mask refreshing gadgets whenever required.

**Our Contributions.** Our main goal in this paper is to simplify and extend the formal verification results from [BBD+15, BBD+16]. We describe two complementary approaches: a generic approach for the formal verification of any circuit, but for small attack orders only (as in [BBD+15]), and a specialized approach for the verification of specific circuits, but at any order (as in [BBD+16]).

For the generic verification of countermeasures at small orders, we use a different formal language from [BBD+15]. In particular we represent the underlying circuit as nested lists, which leads to a simple and concise implementation in Common Lisp, a programming language well suited to formal manipulations. We are then able to formally verify the security of the Rivain-Prouff countermeasure with very few lines of code. Our running times for formal verification are similar to those in [BBD+15]. Thanks to this simpler approach, we could also extend [BBD+15] to handle a combination of arithmetic and Boolean operations, and we have formally verified the security of the recent Boolean to arithmetic conversion algorithm from [Cor17c]. To perform these formal verifications we describe the implementation of CheckMasks, our formal verification tool for side-channel countermeasures.

For the verification of specific gadgets at any order (instead of small orders only with the generic approach), our technique is quite different from [BBD+16] and consists in applying elementary transforms to the circuit, until the $t$-NI or $t$-SNI properties become straightforward to verify. We show that for a set of well-chosen elementary transforms, the formal verification time becomes polynomial in $t$ (instead of exponential with the generic approach); this implies that the formal verification can be performed at any order. Using our CheckMasks tool, we provide a formally verified proof of the $t$-SNI property of the multiplication algorithm in the Rivain-Prouff countermeasure, and of the mask refreshing based on the same multiplication algorithm; in both cases the running time of the formal verification is polynomial in the number of shares $n$.

Finally, we show how to get the best of both worlds, at least for simple circuits: we show how to automatically apply the circuit transforms that lead to a polynomial time verification, based on a limited set of generic rules. Namely we identify a set of three simple rules that enable to automatically prove the $t$-SNI property of the multiplication based mask refreshing, and also two security properties of mask refreshing considered in [Cor17c].

**Source Code.** The source code of our CheckMasks verification tool is publicly available at [Cor17a], under the GPL v2.0 license.

## 2   Security Properties

In this section we recall the $t$-NI and $t$-SNI security definitions from [BBD+16]. For simplicity we only provide the definitions for a simple gadget taking as input a single variable $x$ (given by $n$ shares $x_i$) and outputting a single variable $y$ (given by $n$ shares $y_i$). Given a vector of $n$ shares $(x_i)_{1 \leq i \leq n}$, we denote by $x_{|I} := (x_i)_{i \in I}$ the sub-vector of shares $x_i$ with $i \in I$. In general we wish to simulate any subset of intermediate variables of a gadget from the knowledge of as few $x_i$'s as possible.

**Definition 1 ($t$-NI security).** *Let $G$ be a gadget taking as input $(x_i)_{1 \leq i \leq n}$ and outputting the vector $(y_i)_{1 \leq i \leq n}$. The gadget $G$ is said $t$-NI secure if for any set of $t_c \leq t$ intermediate variables, there exists a subset $I$ of input indices with $|I| \leq t_c$, such that the $t_c$ intermediate variables can be perfectly simulated from $x_{|I}$.*

**Definition 2 ($t$-SNI security).** *Let $G$ be a gadget taking as input $(x_i)_{1 \leq i \leq n}$ and outputting $(y_i)_{1 \leq i \leq n}$. The gadget $G$ is said $t$-SNI secure if for any set of $t_c$ intermediate variables and any subset $\mathcal{O}$ of output indices such that $t_c + |\mathcal{O}| \leq t$, there exists a subset $I$ of input indices with $|I| \leq t_c$, such that the $t_c$ intermediate variables and the output variables $y_{|\mathcal{O}}$ can be perfectly simulated from $x_{|I}$.*

The $t$-NI security notion corresponds to the original security definition in the ISW probing model, in which $n \geq 2t + 1$ shares are required. The stronger $t$-SNI notion allows for securely composing masked algorithms, and allows to prove the security with $n \geq t + 1$ shares only [BBD+16]. The difference between the two notions is as follows: in the stronger $t$-SNI notion, the size of the input shares subset $I$ can only depend on the number of internal probes $t_c$ and is independent of the number of output variables $|\mathcal{O}|$ that must be simulated (as long as the condition $t_c + |\mathcal{O}| \leq t$ is satisfied). The $t$-SNI security notion is very convenient for proving the security of complex constructions, as one can prove that the $t$-SNI security of a full construction based on the $t$-SNI security of its components.

# 3    Formal Verification of Generic Circuits for Small Order

In this section, we show that the $t$-NI and $t$-SNI properties can be easily verified formally for any Boolean circuit, using a generic approach. As in [BBD+15] the complexity of the formal verification is exponential in the number of shares $n$, so this can only work for small $n$.

## 3.1    The RefreshMasks Algorithm

To illustrate our approach we first consider the RefreshMasks algorithm below from [RP10]; see Fig. 1 for an illustration.

We first recall a straightforward property of the RefreshMasks algorithm: when the intermediate variables of the algorithm are not probed, any subset of $n - 1$ output shares $y_i$ of RefreshMasks is uniformly and independently distributed. In the next section, we show how to formally verify this property.

**Lemma 1.** *Let $(y_i)_{1 \leq i \leq n}$ be the output of RefreshMasks. Any subset of $n - 1$ output shares $y_i$ is uniformly and independently distributed.*

**Algorithm 1.** RefreshMasks

**Input:** $x_1, \ldots, x_n$, where $x_i \in \{0,1\}^k$
**Output:** $y_1, \ldots, y_n$ such that $y_1 \oplus \cdots \oplus y_n = x_1 \oplus \cdots \oplus x_n$
1: $y_n \leftarrow x_n$
2: **for** $i = 1$ to $n - 1$ **do**
3:     $r_i \leftarrow \{0,1\}^k$
4:     $y_i \leftarrow x_i \oplus r_i$
5:     $y_n \leftarrow y_n \oplus r_i$          $\triangleright$ $y_{n,i} = x_n \oplus \bigoplus_{j=1}^{i} r_j$
6: **end for**
7: **return** $y_1, \ldots, y_n$

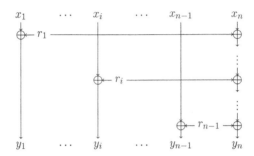

**Fig. 1.** The RefreshMasks algorithm, with the randoms $r_i$ accumulated on the last column.

### 3.2   Formal Verification of Circuits

**Circuit Representation.** We represent a circuit with nested lists, using the prefix notation. Consider for example the circuit taking as input $x$ and $y$ and outputting $x \oplus y$; we represent it as (+ X Y). Similarly the circuit computing $x \cdot y$ is represented as (* X Y). To represent more complex circuits the lists are recursively nested. For example, to represent the circuit $x \cdot (y \oplus z)$, we write (* X (+ Y Z)). If a circuit has many outputs, we represent the list of outputs without any prefix operator; for example, the circuit outputting $(x \oplus y, x \cdot y)$ can be represented as ((+ X Y) (* X Y)).

It is easy to write a program in Common Lisp that generates the circuit corresponding to RefreshMasks; we refer to [Cor17a] for the source code. For example, we obtain for $n = 3$ input shares:

```
> (RefreshMasks '(X1 X2 X3))
((+ R1 X1) (+ R2 X2) (+ R2 (+ R1 X3)))
```

which corresponds to $y_1 = r_1 \oplus x_1$, $y_2 = r_2 \oplus x_2$ and $y_3 = r_2 \oplus (r_1 \oplus x_3)$. Note that the above RefreshMasks function in Common Lisp takes as input a list of $n$ shares (here $n = 3$) and outputs a list of $n$ shares; therefore it can be easily composed with other such Common Lisp functions to create more complex circuits.

**List Substitutions.** We now explain how to formally verify Lemma 1. Consider for example the two output variables (+ R1 X1) and (+ R2 (+ R1 X3)) from above. We would like to show that these two variables are uniformly and independently distributed. Since the random R2 is used only once in those two outputs, it can play the role of a one-time pad, and we can perform the following substitution in the second output:

$$(+ \text{ R2 } (+ \text{ R1 X3})) \longrightarrow \text{R2}$$

Namely, since R2 is used only once, the distribution of (+ R2 (+ R1 X3)) is the same as the distribution of R2. Starting with the above list of two output variables, we can perform the following sequence of elementary substitutions:

$$((+ \text{ R1 X1}) (+ \text{ R2 } (+ \text{ R1 X3}))) \longrightarrow ((+ \text{ R1 X1}) \text{ R2}) \longrightarrow (\text{R1 R2})$$

The first substitution is possible because R2 is used only once, and the second substitution is possible because R1 is used only once after the first substitution. Since we have obtained two distinct randoms (R1 R2) at the end, the two output variables are uniformly and independently distributed, as required.

**Formal Verification.** To formally verify Lemma 1, it suffices to consider all possible subsets of $n - 1$ output shares $y_i$ among $n$, and check that for every subset, we obtain after a series of elementary substitutions a list of $n - 1$ distinct randoms. These substitutions are easy to implement in Common Lisp. Namely it suffices to perform a tree search to count the number of times a given random R is used, and if a random R is used only once, we can then perform the substitution:

$$(+ \text{ R X}) \longrightarrow \text{R} \tag{1}$$

In the particular case of Lemma 1, there are only $n$ subsets to consider, so the formal verification is performed in polynomial time. We obtain for example for $n = 3$:

```
> (Check−RefreshMasks−Uni  3)
Input:  (X0 X1 X2)
Output: ((+ R1 X0) (+ R2 X1) (+ R2 (+ R1 X2)))
Case  0: ((+ R2 X1) (+ R2 (+ R1 X2))) => ((+ R2 X1) (+ R2 R1))
         => ((+ R2 X1) R1) => (R2 R1)
Case  1: ((+ R1 X0) (+ R2 (+ R1 X2))) => ((+ R1 X0) R2)
         => (R1 R2)
Case  2: ((+ R1 X0) (+ R2 X1)) => ((+ R1 X0) R2) => (R1 R2)
```

The above transcript shows that Lemma 1 is formally verified for $n = 3$; namely in all 3 possible cases, after a sequence of elementary substitutions, we obtain a list of 2 distinct randoms, showing that the two output variables are uniformly and independently distributed; see [Cor17a] for the source code.

### 3.3   Security Properties of RefreshMasks

In this section we show how to formally verify some existing properties of Refresh-Masks. We first consider the straightforward $t$-NI property, for $t = n - 1$.

**Lemma 2 ($t$-NI of RefreshMasks).** *Let $(x_i)_{1 \leq i \leq n}$ be the input of* Refresh-Masks *and let $(y_i)_{1 \leq i \leq n}$ be the output. For any set of $t_c \leq n - 1$ intermediate variables, there exists a subset $I$ of input indices such that the $t_c$ intermediate variables can be perfectly simulated from $x_{|I}$, with $|I| \leq t_c$.*

**Formal Verification of the $t$-NI Property of** RefreshMasks. The $t$-NI property of RefreshMasks is straightforward because in the definition of RefreshMasks, any intermediate variable depends on at most one input $x_i$; therefore any subset of $t_c$ probes can be perfectly simulated from the knowledge of at most $t_c$ inputs $x_i$. Consider for example RefreshMasks with $n = 3$ as previously:

```
> (RefreshMasks '(X1 X2 X3))
((+ R1 X1) (+ R2 X2) (+ R2 (+ R1 X3)))
```

If we probe the two intermediate variables (+ R1 X1) and (+ R1 X3), then the knowledge of the two inputs X1 and X2 is sufficient for the simulation; moreover we cannot perform any substitution because the random R1 is used twice. On the other hand if we probe the two variables (+ R2 X2) and (+ R1 X3), we can perform the substitution:

$$((+ \text{ R2 X2}) (+ \text{ R1 X3})) \to (\text{R2} (+ \text{ R1 X3})) \to (\text{R2 R1})$$

showing that the knowledge of the input variables X2 and X3 is not required for that simulation.

More generally, to verify the $t$-NI property of any circuit, it suffices to exhaustively consider all possible $t_c$-tuples of intermediate variables for all $t_c \leq t$, and verify that after a set of elementary substitutions the knowledge of at most $t_c$ input variables is needed for the simulation of the $t_c$-tuple.

**Other Security Properties of** RefreshMasks. We perform a formal verification of several non-trivial properties of RefreshMasks that were used to prove the security of the Boolean to arithmetic conversion algorithm from [Cor17c]; the full version of this paper [Cor17b]. The first property is the following: if the output $y_n$ is among the $t_c$ probed variables, then we can simulate those $t_c$ probed variables with $t_c - 1$ input shares $x_i$ only, instead of $t_c$ as in Lemma 2. This property was crucial for obtaining a provably secure Boolean to arithmetic conversion algorithm in [Cor17c].

**Lemma 3 (**RefreshMasks **[Cor17c]).** *Let $x_1, \ldots, x_n$ be the input of a* Refresh-Masks *where the randoms are accumulated on $x_n$, and let $y_1, \ldots, y_n$ be the output. Let $t_c$ be the number of probed variables, with $t_c < n$. If $y_n$ is among the probed variables, then there exists a subset $I$ such that all probed variables can be perfectly simulated from $x_{|I}$, with $|I| \leq t_c - 1$.*

As previously, to perform a formal verification of Lemma 3, it suffices to consider all possible $t_c$-tuples of intermediate variables (where $y_n$ is part of the $t_c$-tuple) and show that after a sequence of elementary substitutions, there remains at most $t_c - 1$ input variables. In the full version of this paper [Cor17b], we argue that it is actually sufficient to perform such verification for $t_c = n - 1$ only, instead of all $1 \leq t_c \leq n - 1$. The timings of formal verification are summarized in Table 1. Although we are only able to verify Lemma 3 for small values of $n$, this still provides some confidence in the correctness of Lemma 3 for any $n$. We refer to the full version of this paper [Cor17b] for some other properties of RefreshMasks and their formal verification for small values of $n$.

Table 1. Formal verification of Lemma 3, for small values of $n$.

| $n$ | #variables | #tuples | Security | Time |
|---|---|---|---|---|
| 3 | 9 | 36 | ✓ | $\varepsilon$ |
| 4 | 13 | 286 | ✓ | $\varepsilon$ |
| 5 | 17 | 2,380 | ✓ | $\varepsilon$ |
| 6 | 21 | 20,349 | ✓ | 0.2 s |
| 7 | 25 | 177,100 | ✓ | 1.5 s |
| 8 | 29 | 1,560,780 | ✓ | 17 s |
| 9 | 33 | 13,884,156 | ✓ | 195 s |

## 3.4 Formal Verification of $t$-SNI Properties: The FullRefresh and SecMult Algorithms

It is easy to see that that the RefreshMasks algorithm from the previous section does not achieve the stronger $t$-SNI property, as already observed in [BBD+16]. Namely one can probe the output $y_1 = r_1 \oplus x_1$ and the internal variable $y_{n,1} = r_1 \oplus x_n$. This gives $y_1 \oplus y_{n,1} = x_1 \oplus x_n$ and therefore the knowledge of both inputs $x_1$ and $x_n$ is required for the simulation, whereas only $t_c = 1$ internal variable has been probed.

**The FullRefresh Algorithm.** We recall below an improved mask refreshing algorithm that does satisfy the $t$-SNI property for $t = n - 1$, as shown in [BBD+16]. The algorithm FullRefresh is based on the masked multiplication from [ISW03] and was already used in [ISW03, DDF14]. Note that the algorithm has complexity $\mathcal{O}(n^2)$ instead of $\mathcal{O}(n)$ for RefreshMasks.

**Lemma 4 ($t$-SNI of FullRefresh [BBD+16]).** *Let $(x_i)_{1 \leq i \leq n}$ be the input shares of the FullRefresh operation, and let $(y_i)_{1 \leq i \leq n}$ be the output shares. For any set of $t_c$ intermediate variables and any subset $\mathcal{O}$ of output shares such that $t_c + |\mathcal{O}| < n$, there exists a subset $I$ of indices with $|I| \leq t_c$, such that the $t_c$ intermediate variables as well as the output shares $y_{|\mathcal{O}}$ can be perfectly simulated from $x_{|I}$.*

---

**Algorithm 2.** FullRefresh

---

**Input:** $x_1, \ldots, x_n$
**Output:** $y_1, \ldots, y_n$ such that $\bigoplus_{i=1}^{n} y_i = \bigoplus_{i=1}^{n} x_i$
1: **for** $i = 1$ **to** $n$ **do** $y_i \leftarrow x_i$
2: **for** $i = 1$ **to** $n$ **do**
3:      **for** $j = i+1$ **to** $n$ **do**
4:          $r \leftarrow \{0,1\}^k$                              ▷ Referred by $r_{i,j}$
5:          $y_i \leftarrow y_i \oplus r$                          ▷ Referred by $y_{i,j}$
6:          $y_j \leftarrow y_j \oplus r$                          ▷ Referred by $y_{j,i}$
7:      **end for**
8: **end for**
9: **return** $y_1, \ldots, y_n$

---

**Formal Verification of** FullRefresh. In the following, we describe the formal verification of Lemma 4 using our CheckMasks tool. As previously we first implement the FullRefresh algorithm in Common Lisp; for example, we get the following output for $n = 3$ shares:

```
> (FullRefresh '(X1 X2 X3))
((+ R2 (+ R1 X1)) (+ R3 (+ R1 X2)) (+ R3 (+ R2 X3)))
```

Using our CheckMasks tool, the $(n-1)$-SNI property in Lemma 4 can be easily verified for small values of $n$. Namely it suffices to compute the list of all $(n-1)$-tuples of intermediate variables (including the outputs $y_i$) and check that every such $(n-1)$-tuple can be perfectly simulated from the knowledge of at most $t_c$ inputs $x_i$, where $t_c$ is the number of non-output variables in the $(n-1)$-tuple. Consider for example the two variables $(+ R2 (+ R1 X1))$ and $(+ R1 X2)$ in the circuit above for $n = 3$; since $(+ R2 (+ R1 X1))$ is an output variable, the simulation must be performed using at most a single input $x_i$. We obtain using elementary substitutions:

$$((+ R2 (+ R1 X1)) (+ R1 X2)) \rightarrow (R2 (+ R1 X2)) \rightarrow (R2 R1)$$

and therefore no input $x_i$ is actually needed to simulate those two variables. However if we probe the two variables $(+ R2 (+ R1 X1))$ and X2, we can perform the substitutions:

$$((+ R2 (+ R1 X1)) X2) \rightarrow (R2 X2)$$

and therefore the knowledge of X2 is required for the simulation.[1] Note that the running time to consider all possible $(n-1)$-tuples of intermediate variables is exponential in $n$. We summarize in Table 2 the running time of the formal verification of FullRefresh, up to $n = 6$. In Sect. 5 we will show how to formally verify Lemma 4 in time polynomial in $n$, so that the formal verification can be performed for any number of shares $n$ used in practice.

---

[1] This is still according to the $t$-SNI property, because $(+ R2 (+ R1 X1))$ is an output variable and therefore $t_c = 1$.

**Table 2.** Formal verification of the $t$-SNI property of FullRefresh for $t = n - 1$, for small values of $n$.

| $n$ | #variables | #tuples | Security | Time |
|---|---|---|---|---|
| 3 | 12 | 66 | ✓ | $\varepsilon$ |
| 4 | 22 | 1,540 | ✓ | 0.02 s |
| 5 | 35 | 52,360 | ✓ | 0.6 s |
| 6 | 51 | 2,349,060 | ✓ | 46 s |

**The Rivain-Prouff Countermeasure.** The Rivain-Prouff countermeasure for AES is based on an extension over $\mathbb{F}_{2^k}$ of the masked AND gate from [ISW03]. It enables to securely compute a $n$-sharing of the product $c = a \cdot b$ over $\mathbb{F}_{2^k}$, from an $n$-sharing of $a$ and $b$. The algorithm was proven $t$-SNI in [BBD+16]. In the full version of this paper [Cor17b], we recall the corresponding SecMult algorithm, and we show how to formally verify its $t$-SNI property for small values of $n$, for $t = n - 1$.

## 4 Formal Verification of Boolean to Arithmetic Conversion

In this section we show how to extend [BBD+15] to handle a combination of arithmetic and Boolean operations. This enables to formally verify the security of the high-order Boolean to arithmetic conversion algorithm recently described at CHES 2017 [Cor17c], with a $t$-SNI security proof for $n \geq t + 1$. The algorithm can be seen as a generalization of Goubin's algorithm [Gou01] to any order, still with a complexity independent of the register size $k$. Although the algorithm has complexity $\mathcal{O}(2^n)$, instead of $\mathcal{O}(n^2 \cdot k)$ in [CGV14], for small values of $n$ it is an order of magnitude more efficient. The algorithm takes as input $n$ Boolean shares $x_i$ such that

$$x = x_1 \oplus \cdots \oplus x_n$$

and using a recursive algorithm computes $n$ arithmetic shares $D_i$ such that

$$x = D_1 + \cdots + D_n \pmod{2^k}$$

**Boolean to Arithmetic Conversion.** The algorithm from [Cor17c] is based on the affine property of the function $\Psi(x, r) := (x \oplus r) - r \pmod{2^k}$. As illustrated in Fig. 2 the algorithm is recursive and makes two recursive calls to the same algorithm $C$ with $n - 1$ inputs. For $n = 2$ one uses a $t$-SNI variant of Goubin's algorithm:

$$D_1 = \big((x_1 \oplus r_1) \oplus \Psi(x_1 \oplus r_1, r_2 \oplus (x_2 \oplus r_1))\big) \oplus \Psi(x_1 \oplus r_1, r_2) \tag{2}$$

$$D_2 = x_2 \oplus r_1 \tag{3}$$

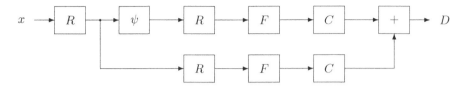

**Fig. 2.** Sequence of operations in the Boolean to arithmetic conversion algorithm from [Cor17c].

For $n \geq 3$ the algorithm works as follows. One first performs a mask refreshing $R$, while expanding the $x_i$'s to $n + 1$ shares. One obtains, from the definition of the $\Psi$ function:

$$x = x_1 \oplus x_2 \oplus \cdots \oplus x_{n+1}$$
$$= (x_1 \oplus \cdots \oplus x_{n+1} - x_2 \oplus \cdots \oplus x_{n+1}) + x_2 \oplus \cdots \oplus x_{n+1}$$
$$= \Psi(x_1, x_2 \oplus \cdots \oplus x_{n+1}) + x_2 \oplus \cdots \oplus x_{n+1}$$

From the affine property of the $\Psi$ function, the left term can be decomposed into the xor of $n$ shares $\Psi(x_1, x_i)$ for $2 \leq i \leq n + 1$, where the first share is $(\overline{n \wedge 1}) \cdot x_1 \oplus \Psi(x_1, x_2)$:

$$x = (\overline{n \wedge 1}) \cdot x_1 \oplus \Psi(x_1, x_2) \oplus \Psi(x_1, x_3) \oplus \cdots \oplus \Psi(x_1, x_{n+1}) + x_2 \oplus \cdots \oplus x_{n+1}$$

We obtain that $x$ is the arithmetic sum of two terms, each with $n$ Boolean shares; this corresponds to the two branches in Fig. 2. One then performs a mask refreshing $R$ on both branches, and then a compression function $F$ that simply xors the last two shares, so there remains only $n - 1$ shares on both branches. One can then apply the Boolean to arithmetic conversion $C$ recursively on both branches, taking as input $n - 1$ Boolean shares (instead of $n$), and outputting $n - 1$ arithmetic shares; we obtain:

$$x = (A_1 + \cdots + A_{n-1}) + (B_1 + \cdots + B_{n-1}) \pmod{2^k}$$

Eventually it suffices to do some additive grouping to obtain $n$ arithmetic shares as output, as required:

$$x = D_1 + \cdots + D_n \pmod{2^k}$$

We refer to [Cor17c] for the details of the algorithm. The algorithm is proven $t$-SNI secure with $n \geq t + 1$ shares in [Cor17c].

**Algorithm Representation.** In Sect. 3.3 we have described a formal verification of the security properties of RefreshMasks that are required for the security proof of the above Boolean to arithmetic conversion algorithm in [Cor17c]. However this provides only a *partial* verification of the algorithm, since in that case the adversary is restricted to only probing the Boolean operations performed within the RefreshMasks. To obtain a *full* verification, we must consider an adversary who can probe any variable in the Boolean to arithmetic algorithm. In that case the formal verification becomes more complex as we must handle both Boolean and arithmetic operations.

Since in our nested list representation we have already using the + operator for the xor, we use the ADD keyword to denote the arithmetic sum. For example, the final additive grouping can be represented as:

```
> (additive-grouping '(A1 A2) '(B1 B2))
((ADD A1 B1) A2 B2)
```

which corresponds to the three arithmetic shares $D_1 = A_1 + B_1 \pmod{2^k}$, $D_2 = A_2$ and $D_3 = B_2$. We also use the PSI operator to denote the application of the $\Psi$ function. For example, the Boolean to arithmetic conversion algorithm for $n = 2$ gives from (2) and (3):

```
> (convba '(X1 X2))
((+ (+ (+ X1 R1) (PSI (+ X1 R1) (+ R2 (+ X2 R1))))
    (PSI (+ X1 R1) R2))
 (+ X2 R1))
```

**Simplification Rules.** Given a list of intermediate variables that must be simulated, as previously we must use a set of simplification rules to determine how many inputs $x_i$ are required for the simulation. For the verification of Boolean circuits in the previous section, this was relatively straightforward as we had essentially a single simplification rule, namely replacing $x \oplus r$ by $r$ when the random $r$ appears only once in the intermediate variables. However when combining arithmetic and Boolean operations the formal verification becomes more complex and we used the following simplification rules. We illustrate every rule by an example that can be run from the source code [Cor17a].

- Rule 1: when $\omega = x_1 + x_2 \bmod 2^k$ must be simulated, simulate both $x_1$ and $x_2$.

```
> (prop-add '((ADD X1 X2)))
(X1 X2)
```

- Rule 2: from the affine property of the function $\Psi$, replace $\Psi(x,y) \oplus \Psi(x,z)$ by $x \oplus \Psi(x, y \oplus z)$.

```
> (replace-psi '(+ (PSI A B) (PSI A C)))
(+ A (PSI A (+ B C)))
```

- Rule 3: from the definition of $\Psi$, replace $\Psi(x,y)$ by $(x \oplus y) - y \bmod 2^k$; we denote by SUB the arithmetic subtraction.

```
> (replace-psi-sub '(PSI A B)
(SUB (+ A B) B)
```

- Rule 4: when a random $r$ is used only once, replace $x \oplus r$ by $r$, and similarly for $x + r \bmod 2^k$ and $x - r \bmod 2^k$. This is an extension of the rule given by (1).

```
> (iter−simplify '((+ X1 R1) (ADD X2 R2) (SUB X3 R3)))
(R1 R2 R3)
```

- Rule 5: when a random $r$ is not used in two intermediate variables $e_1$ and $e_2$, replace the simulation of $(e_1 \oplus r, e_2 \oplus r)$ by the simulation of $(r, (e_1 \oplus r) \oplus e_2)$; this corresponds to the change of variable $r' = e_1 \oplus r$.

```
> (simplify−x '((+ R1 X1) (+ R1 X2)))
(R1 (+ (+ R1 X1) X2))
```

- Rule 6: when $\Psi(x_1, x_2)$ must be simulated, simulate both $x_1$ and $x_2$.

```
> (prop−psi '((PSI A B)))
(A B)
```

We note that the order in which the rules are applied matters. For example, once Rule 3 has been applied, Rule 2 cannot be applied to the same expression, because the PSI operator has been replaced by SUB. One must therefore use the right strategy for the application of the rules; an overview is provided in Fig. 3. In particular, we only apply Rule 3 if subsequently applying Rule 4 enables to eliminate the SUB operator, and Rule 6 is only applied as a last resort, when other rules have failed.

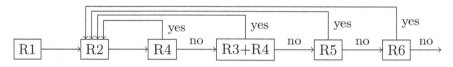

**Fig. 3.** The rule application strategy for the formal verification of Boolean to arithmetic conversion.

**Formal Verification.** In order to verify the $t$-SNI property of the Boolean to arithmetic algorithm, as previously we must check that for all possible $(n-1)$-tuples of intermediate variables (including the outputs $D_i$), the number of input variables $x_i$'s that remain after the application of the above rules is always $\leq t_c$, where $t_c$ is the number of non-output variables in the $(n-1)$-tuple.

We summarize in Table 3 the timings of formal verification for the algorithm in [Cor17c]. Note that the Boolean to arithmetic conversion algorithm has complexity $\mathcal{O}(2^n)$, and therefore the number of possible $(n-1)$-tuples of intermediate variables is $\mathcal{O}(2^{n^2})$; that is why we could only perform the formal verification up to $n = 5$.

**Table 3.** Formal verification of the $t$-SNI property of the Boolean to arithmetic conversion algorithm from [Cor17c].

| $n$ | #variables | #tuples | Security | Time |
|---|---|---|---|---|
| 2 | 11 | 11 | ✓ | $\varepsilon$ |
| 3 | 48 | 1,128 | ✓ | 0.08 s |
| 4 | 133 | 383,306 | ✓ | 85 s |
| 5 | 312 | 387,278,970 | ✓ | 88 h |

# 5 Formal Verification in Polynomial Time

The main drawback of the previous approach is that it has exponential complexity in the number of shares $n$, because the number of $t$-tuples to consider grows exponentially with $n$. In this section we describe a new approach for proving the security of a side-channel countermeasure. Instead of performing a simulation of the probed variables as in [ISW03], our approach consists in applying a sequence of elementary circuit transforms, until the transformed circuit becomes so simple that the security property becomes straightforward to verify. The main advantage is that in the context of formal verification, our new approach seems much easier to verify formally than the classical simulation-based approach from [ISW03]. For Boolean circuits our technique is based on the following two elementary transforms:

- The Random-zero transform: we set to 0 a subset of the randoms $r_i$ used in the circuit.
- The One-time-pad transform: if a random $r$ appears only once in a circuit, and moreover $r$ is not probed, we can replace any variable $x \oplus r$ by $r$.

**The Random-Zero Transform.** Our first circuit transformation consists in setting to 0 a subset of the randoms $r_i$ used in the circuit. The transform only applies to *additively masked* circuits.

**Definition 3 (Additive masking).** *Let $C$ be a circuit taking as input $x_1, \ldots, x_n$. We say that $C$ is additively masked if every intermediate variable $y$ in the circuit can be written as $y = f(x_1, \ldots, x_n) + g(r_1, \ldots, r_n)$, where $g$ is a linear function.*

For example, the circuit computing $y = x_1 \cdot x_2 + r_1 + r_2$ is additively masked, while the circuit computing $y = x_1 \cdot r_1$ is not. Most side-channel countermeasures for block-ciphers are additively masked. In particular, this holds for the RefreshMasks, FullRefresh and SecMult algorithms considered in the previous sections. The following lemma shows that it is sufficient to consider the security of a simpler circuit $C_0$ where a subset of the randoms are fixed to 0. Namely if there is an attack against the original circuit $C$, then the same attack applies against $C_0$; see the full version of this paper [Cor17b] for the proof.

**Lemma 5 (Random-zero transform).** *Let $C$ be an additively masked circuit and let $C_0$ be the same circuit as $C$ but with a subset of the randoms fixed to 0. Anything an adversary can compute from a set of probes in $C$, he can compute from the same set of probes in the circuit $C_0$.*

*Remark 1.* Lemma 5 does not hold for general circuits; consider for example the circuit taking as input $sk$ and outputting $(sk \cdot r, r)$; when considering the output only, the circuit would be secure when $r$ is fixed to 0, but the output leaks the secret $sk$ whenever $r \neq 0$.

**Application: $t$-NI of** RefreshMasks. The $t$-NI property of RefreshMasks, as stated in Lemma 2, is easily verified formally using the Random-zero transform. Namely, if we fix all randoms of RefreshMasks to 0, we obtain the identity function, which is trivially $t$-NI. For example, we obtain for $n = 4$:

```
> (check-refreshmasks-tni-poly 4)
Input: (X1 X2 X3 X4)
Output: ((+ R1 X1) (+ R2 X2) (+ R3 X3) (+ R3 (+ R2 (+ R1 X4))))
Random zero => (X1 X2 X3 X4)
Identity function: T
```

Note that the verification is performed in polynomial time in $n$, while in the generic approach the complexity would be exponential in $n$ when examining all possible $t$-tuples.

**The One-Time Pad Transform.** The One-time Pad transform is defined as follows: if a random $r$ is used only once in a circuit, and moreover $r$ is not probed, then we can replace the variable $x \oplus r$ by $r$. Note that in principle the variable $x$ can still be probed, so it must not be removed from the circuit.

We can assume that a certain random $r$ has not been probed when we have an upper bound on the number of probes in the circuit, as it is the case for the $t$-NI and $t$-SNI properties. For example, if a circuit contains $n$ randoms $r_i$ but the adversary has only access to $t = n - 1$ probes, then we are guaranteed that at least one of the random $r_i$ has not been probed, and we can apply the One-time Pad transform on this random. The proof technique then consists in considering all possible $n$ cases separately (corresponding to the non-probed $r_i$, for $1 \leq i \leq n$), and then applying the admissible One-time Pad transform in each case.

**Formal Verification in Polynomial-Time.** More generally, the proof strategy is to perform a sequence of elementary circuit transforms until we obtain a simple circuit $C$ for which the $t$-NI or $t$-SNI properties is straightforward to verify. In the full version of this paper [Cor17b] we illustrate this approach by providing a formal verification of the same security properties of the Refresh-Masks, FullRefresh and SecMult algorithms as considered in Sect. 3, but this time with complexity polynomial in $n$, instead of exponential. This implies that the security of these algorithms can be formally verified for any value of $n$ for which the countermeasure would be used in practice. We refer to [Cor17a] for the source code of the formal verification.

## 6  Towards Automatic Generation of Security Proofs

The drawback of the previous approach is that for the security verification to happen in polynomial time, we must select ourselves the right sequence of circuit transforms. Instead we would like to have the circuit transforms being selected automatically by our verification tool, based on a limited set of elementary rules, and still in polynomial-time.

In the following, we show that this can be achieved for simple circuits based on the three following rules. We denote by $P$ the property that must be checked; for example, for $t$-NI security, the property $P$ would require that any $t$-tuple of intermediate variables is simulatable from a subset of the inputs $x_{|I}$, with $|I| \leq t$. Below we denote by $C_{otp}$ the circuit $y_i = x_i \oplus r_i$ for $1 \leq i \leq n$ (see the full version of this paper [Cor17b]). We assume that the property $P$ is already verified by $C_{otp}$, so that $P$ does not need to be verified explicitly for $C_{otp}$.

(R1) Perform a loop to select and remove the subset of the circuit that is unprobed.

(R2) Apply the random-zero transform, except on randoms used only once in the circuit.

(R3) Check whether the resulting circuit is equal to $C_{otp}$. Otherwise check the property $P$ for all possible $t$-tuple of probes.

We show in the full version of this paper [Cor17b] that from the three above rules, we can formally verify in polynomial time the main properties of Refresh-Masks and FullRefresh considered in this paper.

## References

[BBD+15] Barthe, G., Belaïd, S., Dupressoir, F., Fouque, P.-A., Grégoire, B., Strub, P.-Y.: Verified proofs of higher-order masking. In: Oswald, E., Fischlin, M. (eds.) EUROCRYPT 2015. LNCS, vol. 9056, pp. 457–485. Springer, Heidelberg (2015). https://doi.org/10.1007/978-3-662-46800-5_18. https://eprint.iacr.org/2015/060

[BBD+16] Barthe, G., Belaïd, S., Dupressoir, F., Fouque, P.-A., Grégoire, B., Strub, P.-Y., Zucchini, R.: Strong non-interference and type-directed higher-order masking. In: Proceedings of the 2016 ACM SIGSAC Conference on Computer and Communications Security, Vienna, Austria, 24–28 October 2016, pp. 116–129 (2016). Publicly available at https://eprint.iacr.org/2015/506.pdf. See also a preliminary version, under the title "Compositional Verification of Higher-Order Masking: Application to a Verifying Masking Compiler", publicly available at https://eprint.iacr.org/2015/506/20150527:192221

[BDG+14] Barthe, G., Dupressoir, F., Grégoire, B., Kunz, C., Schmidt, B., Strub, P.-Y.: EasyCrypt: a tutorial. In: Aldini, A., Lopez, J., Martinelli, F. (eds.) FOSAD 2012-2013. LNCS, vol. 8604, pp. 146–166. Springer, Cham (2014). https://doi.org/10.1007/978-3-319-10082-1_6

[CGV14] Coron, J.-S., Großschädl, J., Vadnala, P.K.: Secure conversion between boolean and arithmetic masking of any order. In: Batina, L., Robshaw, M. (eds.) CHES 2014. LNCS, vol. 8731, pp. 188–205. Springer, Heidelberg (2014). https://doi.org/10.1007/978-3-662-44709-3_11

[Cor17a] Coron, J.-S.: CheckMasks: formal verification of side-channel countermeasures (2017). Publicly available at https://github.com/coron/checkmasks

[Cor17b] Coron, J.-S.: Formal verification of side-channel countermeasures via elementary circuit transformations. Cryptology ePrint Archive, Report 2017/879 (2017). https://eprint.iacr.org/2017/879

[Cor17c] Coron, J.-S.: High-order conversion from Boolean to arithmetic masking. In: Fischer, W., Homma, N. (eds.) CHES 2017. LNCS, vol. 10529, pp. 93–114. Springer, Cham (2017). https://doi.org/10.1007/978-3-319-66787-4_5

[CPRR13] Coron, J.-S., Prouff, E., Rivain, M., Roche, T.: Higher-order side channel security and mask refreshing. In: Moriai, S. (ed.) FSE 2013. LNCS, vol. 8424, pp. 410–424. Springer, Heidelberg (2014). https://doi.org/10.1007/978-3-662-43933-3_21

[DDF14] Duc, A., Dziembowski, S., Faust, S.: Unifying leakage models: from probing attacks to noisy leakage. In: Nguyen, P.Q., Oswald, E. (eds.) EUROCRYPT 2014. LNCS, vol. 8441, pp. 423–440. Springer, Heidelberg (2014). https://doi.org/10.1007/978-3-642-55220-5_24

[Gou01] Goubin, L.: A sound method for switching between boolean and arithmetic masking. In: Koç, Ç.K., Naccache, D., Paar, C. (eds.) CHES 2001. LNCS, vol. 2162, pp. 3–15. Springer, Heidelberg (2001). https://doi.org/10.1007/3-540-44709-1_2

[ISW03] Ishai, Y., Sahai, A., Wagner, D.: Private circuits: securing hardware against probing attacks. In: Boneh, D. (ed.) CRYPTO 2003. LNCS, vol. 2729, pp. 463–481. Springer, Heidelberg (2003). https://doi.org/10.1007/978-3-540-45146-4_27

[RP10] Rivain, M., Prouff, E.: Provably secure higher-order masking of AES. In: Mangard, S., Standaert, F.-X. (eds.) CHES 2010. LNCS, vol. 6225, pp. 413–427. Springer, Heidelberg (2010). https://doi.org/10.1007/978-3-642-15031-9_28

# Drive-By Key-Extraction Cache Attacks
# from Portable Code

Daniel Genkin[1,2], Lev Pachmanov[3], Eran Tromer[3,4(✉)], and Yuval Yarom[5,6]

[1] University of Pennsylvania, Philadelphia, PA, USA
danielg3@cis.upenn.edu
[2] University of Maryland, College Park, MD, USA
[3] Tel Aviv University, Tel Aviv, Israel
{levp,tromer}@tau.ac.il
[4] Columbia University, New York, NY, USA
[5] University of Adelaide, Adelaide, Australia
yval@cs.adelaide.edu.au
[6] Data61, Sydney, Australia

**Abstract.** We show how malicious web content can extract cryptographic secret keys from the user's computer. The attack uses portable scripting languages supported by modern browsers to induce contention for CPU cache resources, and thereby gleans information about the memory accesses of other programs running on the user's computer. We show how this side-channel attack can be realized in WebAssembly and PNaCl; how to attain fine-grained measurements; and how to extract ElGamal, ECDH and RSA decryption keys from various cryptographic libraries.

The attack does not rely on bugs in the browser's nominal sandboxing mechanisms, or on fooling users. It applies even to locked-down platforms with strong confinement mechanisms and browser-only functionality, such as Chromebook devices.

Moreover, on browser-based platforms the attacked software too may be written in portable JavaScript; and we show that in this case even implementations of supposedly-secure constant-time algorithms, such as Curve25519's, are vulnerable to our attack.

## 1 Introduction

Since their introduction [5, 29, 30, 36], microarchitectural side channel attacks have become a serious security concern. Contrary to physical side channels, which require physical proximity for exploitation, microarchitectural attacks only require the attacker to execute code on the target machine. Even without special privileges, such code can contend with concurrently-executing target code for the use of low-level microarchitectural resources; and by measuring the thus-induced timing variability, an attacker can glean information from the target code. Many such resources have been analyzed and exploited, including branch predictors and arithmetic units, but contention for cache resources has been

© Springer International Publishing AG, part of Springer Nature 2018
B. Preneel and F. Vercauteren (Eds.): ACNS 2018, LNCS 10892, pp. 83–102, 2018.
https://doi.org/10.1007/978-3-319-93387-0_5

proven to be particularly devastating. Cache attacks allow fine grained monitoring of memory access patterns, and can extract cryptographic keys [5,29,30], website fingerprints [28], and keystrokes [15]; see [11] for a survey.

Less is known, however, about realistic attack vectors by which cache attacks (and other microarchitectural attacks) be deployed in practice. Most research has assumed that the attacker has the ability to run native code on the target machine. This makes sense for scenarios such as attacks across virtual machines [17,31,37], especially in public compute clouds, or attacks between different users sharing the same PC. But in the typical end-user setting, hardware devices are not shared by multiple mistrusting users. Moreover, native code, run locally by a user, usually executes in a security context that allows access to that user's data, making security-savvy users reluctant to run such untrusted code.

Recent works [13,28] made progress towards effective cache attacks on end-user devices, using JavaScript code running in the target's browser and without requiring native code execution. However, since JavaScript is far-removed from the native platform, the information obtained by a JavaScript attacker is severely degraded. Indeed compared to attacks which are based on native-code execution, those works were only able to detected coarse-scale events (distinguishing between websites loaded in another browser tab or ASLR de-randomization), leaving open the feasibility of monitoring and exploiting fine-grained events.

Thus, in this work we focus on the following question: (a) **Are there practical deployment vectors for microarchitectural attacks on single-user devices, that are capable of extracting fine-grained information (such as cryptographic keys), and do not require privileged user operations (such as software installation or native code execution)?** In particular, do such attacks apply to locked-down platforms, such as Chromebook running Chrome OS, where functionality is restricted to sandboxed web browsing?

Even when microarchitectural information leakage occurs, its exploitability depends on the implementation of the attacked software. Modern cryptographic software is often designed with side channels in mind, employing mitigation techniques that require low-level details of the executed code—first and foremost, to make it constant-time. This picture changes when cryptographic software is deployed as portable high-level code, where the final code and memory layout are left to the whims of a just-in-time compiler. On the one hand, defensively exercising the requisite control becomes more difficult. On the other hand, the attacker too has to cope with increased variability and uncertainty, so it is not obvious that leakage (if any) is at all exploitable. We thus ask: (b) **Do portable program representations compromise the side-channel resilience of (supposedly) constant-time algorithms?**

## 1.1  Our Results

We answer both questions in the affirmative. (a) We present cache side-channel attacks which can be executed from a web page loaded in a sandboxed browser

**Fig. 1.** Attack scenario screenshot. The targeted user opens an online streaming website in Tab 2. Clicking within this tab (e.g., to start a movie) causes a pop-under to open up as Tab 3. The malicious advertisement in Tab 3 then monitors the cache activity on the target machine. When an encrypted email is received and decrypted using Google's encrypted email extension (in Tab 1), the malicious advertisement in Tab 3 learns information about the user's secret key.

environment, and are capable of extracting keys from ElGamal and RSA implementations. (b) We demonstrate key extraction even from an implementation of Curve25519 ECDH, which was explicitly designed to minimize side channel leakage, but becomes susceptible due to use of high-level JavaScript.

Our attacks do not require installing any software on the target machine, and do not rely on vulnerabilities in the browser's nominal isolation mechanisms (e.g., they work even if Same Origin Policy and Strict Site Isolation are perfectly enforced). Rather, they glean information from outside the browser's sandbox purely by inducing and measuring timing variability related to memory accesses outside its sandbox. All the target user has to do in order to trigger the attack is to have its browser execute malicious code embedded in a comprised website.

**Drive-By Attack.** The main attack scenario we investigate is a "drive-by" web attack, where the attacker's code is embedded in a web page and is automatically activated when it is rendered by the user's browser. This can happen when the user explicitly visits the attacker's web page (e.g., enticed by phishing), or a page into which the attacker can inject HTML code (e.g., by a cross-site scripting attack). Most deviously, the attack may be automatically triggered when the user visits unrelated third-party web sites, if those sites display ads from web ad services that support non-static ads (JavaScript, pop-under or IFRAME ads).

Concretely, we embedded the attack code in an advertisement, which we submitted to a commercial web ad service. Whenever a user navigated to a site that uses that service, and our ad was selected for display, the attack code was triggered (see Fig. 1). This code measured the memory access patterns on the user's machine, and sent it to our server for analysis. When the targeted cryptographic software happens to be repeatedly invoked using some secret key during the time when the ad was shown in some browser tab (even in the background), our code extracted the secret key in as little as 3 min. This works even across processes and browsers (e.g., JavaScript ad in Firefox attacking cryptographic code running in Chrome).

**Attacking Curve25519.** One of our attacks targets a JavaScript implementation of Curve25519 Elliptic Curve Diffie-Hellman (ECDH) [6]. The implementation attempts to mitigate side-channel leakage by using a nearly constant-time Montgomery-ladder scalar-by-point multiplication, but the in-browser compilation from JavaScript introduces key-dependent control flow, which we can detect and exploit by a portable code-cache side-channel attack.

**Measurement Technique.** We implement the cache measurement procedure using portable code running within the browser. To achieve the measurement resolution required to mount an attack on ElGamal and ECDH, we used PNaCl or WebAssembly. These are architecture-independent code representations which browsers execute in a sandbox—analogously to JavaScript, but lower-level and more efficient. PNaCl is supported by desktop versions of the Chrome and Chromium browsers since 2013, and automatically executed by the browser without user involvement. WebAssembly is the standardization of the idea behind PNaCl. It is supported by all major browsers and enabled by default since 2017.

Like JavaScript, PNaCl and WebAssembly are sandboxed, subject to Same Origin Policy, and isolated from host resources such as the filesystem and other processes. However, the portable code (inevitably) uses the underlying microarchitectural resources of the CPU it is executing on, and in particular the data cache. Thus, it can induce the memory-contention effects required for cache side-channel attacks. Using this, and additional techniques, the portable code can execute a variant of the Prime+Probe attack of [29], to detect which memory addresses are accessed by other processes.

Compared to the two prior works on portable-code cache attacks (see Sect. 1.3), our use of a portable but low-level program representation, as opposed to JavaScript in [28], reduces measurement overheads and provides better timing sources on modern browsers; and by using a precise eviction set construction algorithm (adapting the approach of [23] to the portable setting) we moreover reduce the eviction sets' size by ×64 compared to [13]. Taken together, these attain the requisite temporal resolution for several cryptanalytic attacks.

**Challenges.** Launching cache attacks involves numerous challenges, such as recovering the mapping between the memory and the cache, and identifying cache sets corresponding to security-critical accesses (see [23] for a detailed list). Mounting the attack from portable code introduces several additional challenges:

1. *Emulated environment:* Both PNaCl and WebAssembly modules run inside an emulated 32-bit environment, preventing access to useful host platform services such as huge pages, `mlock()` and `posix_memalign()`.

2. *Slower memory access:* memory accesses using (current implementations of) portable architectures incur an overhead compared to native execution, reducing the measurements' temporal resolution.
3. *Inability to flush the CPU pipeline and cache:* PNaCl and WebAssembly do not support instructions for flushing the CPU pipeline, the cache or avoiding out-of-order execution, as needed by many native-code attacks.
4. *Inaccurate time source:* Architecture independence forces PNaCl applications to only use generic interfaces or indirect measurements to measure time. WebAssembly modules can interact with external APIs only using JavaScript, hence they are limited to the time sources available to JavaScript code.

   Moreover, the cryptographic software we attack is implemented in JavaScript, which introduces yet more challenges:
5. *Unpredictable memory layout:* The target's JavaScript code is compiled anew at every page load, and moreover, its memory allocations are done in an unpredictable way at every invocation.
6. *No shared memory:* Many prior cache attacks relied on the attacker code and target code having some shared memory (e.g., AES S-tables or code), due to shared libraries or memory deduplication, not unavailable here.

## 1.2   Targeted Hardware and Software

**Chromebook.** We demonstrate the attacks on a Chromebook device (Samsung XE550C22) which is tailored for running Chrome OS 58.0.3029.112 (a locked-down version of Linux running the Chrome web browser), including all of its security measures. It is equipped with an Intel Celeron 867 Sandy-bridge 1.3 GHz CPU featuring a 2048 KB L3 cache divided into 4096 sets and 8 ways.

**HP Laptop.** The attacks are mostly independent of the operating system, and of the precise CPU model (within a CPU family). To demonstrate this, we also execute the attacks on an HP EliteBook 8760w laptop, running Kubuntu 14.04 with Linux kernel 3.19.0-80, with an Intel i7-2820QM Sandy Bridge 2.3 GHz CPU featuring a 8192KB L3 cache divided into 8192 sets and 16 ways.

**Elliptic.** Elliptic [18] is an open-source JavaScript cryptographic library, providing efficient implementations of elliptic-curve cryptographic primitives such as Elliptic Curve Diffie-Hellman (ECDH). Elliptic is widely used (over 20M downloads), and underlies more than a hundred dependent projects including crypto-currency wallets. Elliptic supports state-of-the-art elliptic curve constructions such as Curve25519 [6], which was designed to offer increased resistance to side channel attacks. We show that while Elliptic's implementation does use the Montgomery-ladder method with apparently constant execution time, memory access leakage induced by the JavaScript routines does allow for key extraction.

**Google's End-to-End Library.** End-to-End is an open-source JavaScript cryptographic library developed by Google for use by websites and browser plug-ins. To facilitate email encryption and signing directly inside the user's browser, End-to-End supports the OpenPGP standard, as documented in RFC 4880. End-to-End is the cryptographic engine for many browser plugins such as E2EMail, Google encrypted email extension, and Yahoo's fork of EndToEnd.

**OpenPGP.js.** OpenPGP.js is a popular open-source library for browser-based cryptographic operations, and in particular encrypted email. Similarly to End-to-End, OpenPGP.js implements the OpenPGP standard and is widely deployed in web applications and browser plug-ins. These include password managers, encrypted mail clients and other applications. To create seamless user experience, some of those plug-ins (e.g., ProtonMail and CryptUp) automatically decrypt received content upon opening the received email.

## 1.3 Related Work

**Cache Attacks.** Cache attacks were introduced over a decade ago [5,29,30, 36]. Initial attacks exploited the L1 and L2 data caches [29,35], however later attacks targeted other caches, such as the L1 instruction cache [1,4] the shared last level cache [16,23] and specialized caches including the branch prediction unit [2,3,10] and the return stack buffer [7]. Recent works [13,34] were able to extract information without using huge pages. See [11] for a survey.

**Cache Attacks from Portable Code.** The first published browser-based cache attack was shown by [28]. Using JavaScript, they detected coarse cache access patterns and used them to classify web sites rendered in other tabs. They did not demonstrate attacks that use fine-grain cache monitoring (such as key extraction attacks). Moreover, following [28] web browsers nowadays provide reduced timer precision, making the techniques of [28] inapplicable.

Recently, [13] achieved higher cache-line accuracy, and used it to derandomize the target's ASLR from within it's browser. They relied on constructing very large eviction sets, resulting in low temporal resolution of the memory access detection, well below what is required for key extraction attacks (see Sect. 3).

The Rowhammer attack [20] was also implemented in JavaScript by [14].

**Speculative Execution Attacks.** Going beyond cryptographic keys, cache attacks can be also leveraged to read memory contents across security domains. The Meltdown [22] and Spectre [21] attacks exploit the CPU's speculative execution to let a process glean memory content to which it does not have access permissions, by accessing that memory directly (Meltdown) or by inducing the valid owner of that memory to access it within a mispredicted branch (Spectre). In both attacks, the read is invalid and the architectural state will eventually be rewound, but the carefully-crafted side effects on the cache can be observed.

These attacks rely on cache covert channels, for which very coarse cache measurements suffice, as opposed to our side-channel setting, which necessitates fine-grained cache measurements. Meltdown further requires the attacker to access a protected memory that is mapped into its own address space; this is inapplicable to portable code. Web-based Spectre does not work across browser processes (of different browsers or tabs).

**Side-Channel Attacks on ElGamal Encryption.** Several works show side-channel attacks on implementations of ElGamal encryption. [39] show a cross-VM attack on ElGamal that exploits the L1 data cache and the hypervisor's scheduler. Our attack is loosely modeled after [23], who implemented a Prime+Probe attack [29] targeting an implementation of ElGamal. Recently, [12] show a physical (electromagnetic) side-channel attack on ElGamal running on PCs.

## 2   Preliminaries

### 2.1   Portable Code Execution

JavaScript is the oldest and most common portable programing language that can be executed inside the web browser. For intensive computational tasks, JavaScript is much slower than native applications; NaCl, PNaCl and WebAssembly are alternative, more efficient solutions.

**PNaCl.** Modern Chrome browser support Google Native Client (NaCl) [38]. This is a sandboxing technology which enables secure execution of native code as part of untrusted web applications, which can run compiled code at near-native speeds and fine-grained control over the memory usage. While NaCl deploys architecture-dependent (through OS-independent) code, the subsequent Portable Native Client (PNaCl) achieves full cross-platform portability by splitting the compilation process into two parts. First, the developer compiles the source code into an intermediate representation, called a *bitcode executable*. Next, as part of loading the code to the host browser, the bitcode executable is automatically translated to the host-specific machine language. PNaCl is enabled by default on Chrome browsers and does not require user interaction.

**WebAssembly.** WebAssembly is the standardized successor of PNaCl, standardized by the World Wide Web Consortium (W3C), and supported by all major web browsers on all operating systems, including mobile platforms. Similarly to PNaCl, WebAssembly defines a binary format which can be executed in a sandboxed environment inside the browser. Code is represented in simple stack machine, with a limited set of operations (mostly arithmetical and memory accesses). This is translated, by the browser, to the host's native instruction set, allowing it to be executed in near-native speed.

The simple abstract machine severely limits the environment observable to WebAssembly code. As oppose to PNaCl, the limited instruction set of WebAssembly does not directly expose any of the system's APIs; functionality beyond simple computation is exposed only via call-outs to interpreted JavaScript code, which are relatively slow.

**Web Workers and JavaScript's `SharedArrayBuffer`.** Web Workers is an API designed to allow JavaScript code to run heavy computational tasks in a separate context, without interfering with the user interface, using multiple threads. The communication between the main JavaScript context and Web Workers threads can be done using an asynchronous messaging system, or via the `SharedArrayBuffer` API which can allocate a shared memory buffer and coordinate access to it using synchronization primitives.

## 3   Constructing Eviction Sets

The Prime+Probe attack relies on having an eviction set for every targeted cache set. The main obstacle to constructing these sets is the requirement of finding the mapping between the internal addresses used in the attacker's program and the cache sets they map to In the case of both PNaCl and WebAssembly, the mapping from memory addresses to cache sets consists of multiple abstraction layers, as follows. The portable runtime emulates a 32-bit execution environment, which is mapped (by the browser) into the hosting process's virtual address space, which is in turn mapped (by the operating system) into physical memory. Neither mapping is made available to the portable code. Lastly, physical memory addresses are mapped (by the CPU) to cache sets; Intel does not disclose this mapping, but it has been reverse-engineered. Despite two levels of indirections with unknown mapping, and complications introduced by the third one, we can find the mapping of memory blocks to sets.

**Past Approaches.** Several prior works [14,23,24] describe techniques for creating the eviction sets using *huge pages*: a CPU feature that allows pages in the page table to have a very large size (typically 2 MB instead of 4 KB), for improved address translation efficiency (e.g., reduced TLB thrashing).

Because both the physical and the virtual starting addresses of a huge page must be a multiple of a huge page size, the virtual address and its corresponding physical address share the least significant 21 bits. In particular, that means that given a virtual address in a huge page, we know bits 0–20 of the physical address and consequently we know the index within a slice of the cache set that the virtual address maps to.

**Avoiding Huge Pages.** Recent attacks [13,34] were able to avoid huge pages, at the cost of imposing other limitations. The attack of [34] assumes consecutive physical memory allocation and deterministic heap behavior. Those assumptions allows the attacker to find the cache set index up to a fixed offset, providing as much information as using huge pages. Unfortunately, they are generally inapplicable, and for JavaScript code running in a browser environment, due to its complex garbage collection pattern, we empirically did not observe any allocation pattern between different execution of the decryption operations.

Next, the work of [13] avoided huge pages by only using the 6 bits shared between the virtual address and physical address to construct the eviction-sets. In this approach, all cache-sets sharing the 6 least significant bits are mapped to a single large eviction set. However, using such large eviction sets increases probing time by a factor of ×64 (compared to smaller eviction sets which are designed to only evict a single cache set) thus reducing the channel's bandwidth. Large eviction sets also induce higher measurement noise due to unrelated memory accesses. While that method suffices to derandomize ASLR, key extraction attacks requires fine-grained, low-noise measurements of the target's memory access, with temporal resolution on the order of a big-integer multiplication.

### 3.1   Methodology

We now describe our methodology of constructing eviction sets by recovering the mapping from memory blocks to cache sets. As described above, the mapping consists of several layers. The work of [23] introduced an algorithm for uncovering the mapping between the physical address and cache slices, without the knowledge of the CPU's internals. However, the algorithm assumed knowledge of the cache set index, acquired by using huge pages. This assumption does not hold for PNaCl and WebAssembly since they do not provide access to huge pages. Instead we generalize this algorithm to the portable environment.

**Constructing Eviction Sets from Portable Environment.** Portable code only has access to the 12 least significant bits of the physical address, due to the fact that "page offset" goes through the mapping between portable environment and physical address space. Thus, the portable code knows the 6 least significant bits of the cache set index, but is missing the 4 or 5 most significant bits.

To overcome this, we first find eviction sets for all of the cache sets that have indices with 6 least significant bits being zero. To that end, we create a large pool of memory address whose least significant 12 bits are zero. Applying the algorithm of [23] on the pool results in initial eviction set for each cache set index with 6 least significant bits equal to 0. Then, by enumerating each of the possible values for the 6 least significant bits, we extend each initial eviction set to 64 eviction sets, each corresponding to a single cache set.

However, for the algorithm to work, we need to modify the eviction testing procedure. This is since when running on a system configured with regular-size memory pages, performing eviction testing as described accesses a large number of memory pages. This stresses the address translation mechanism, and in particular causes evictions from the Translation Lookaside Buffer (TLB), which is a specialized cache used for storing the results of recent address translations.

These TLB evictions causes delays in memory accesses even when the accessed memory block is cached. In particular, this introduces noise when checking if the witness block is successfully evicted.

**Handling TLB Noise.** *Eviction testing* finds whether accessing a list of memory blocks forces a cache eviction of a specific, *witness*, memory block. To address the TLB noise, we modify the eviction testing approach, ensuring that the TLB entry for the witness block is updated before we measure the access time. We achieve this by accessing another memory block in the same page as the witness. Thus the *eviction testing* algorithm becomes: access the witness to ensure it is in the cache; access each memory block in the list of memory blocks; access a memory block in the same page as the witness (to ensure the TLB entry for the page is updated); and finally measure the access time to the witness (which will be short if the witness is in the cache or long if accessing the list of memory blocks evicts the witness from the cache).

**Handling Additional Noise.** Even after handling the noise from the TLB, the increased footprint of our methodology and the overhead of the portable environment causes high measurement noise. We handle this noise by repeating the contracting stage, randomizing the order of the tested elements each time, and calculating the intersection between the constructed eviction sets.

## 3.2   Implementation

**PNaCl Implementation.** The above approach requires several capabilities. In order to distinguish between slow memory accesses (corresponding to cache misses) and fast memory accesses (corresponding to cache hits) the attack code must gain accesses to a timing source of sufficient resolution. Conveniently, PNaCl provides a `clock_gettime()` function which provides time at nanosecond accuracy (when called with `clock_realtime` parameter). Next, in order to construct the eviction sets in PNaCl's execution environment we allocate a sufficiently large contiguous buffer (approximately 4 times larger than the size of the LLC). Using this buffer and the aforementioned timing source, we performed the phases outlined above for the construction of the eviction sets.

**WebAssembly Implementation.** As discussed in Sect. 2.1, PNaCl has been available for a few years, but only on Chrome browser. Using the newer WebAssembly standard, along with Web Workers and `SharedArrayBuffers` allowed us to reimplement the approach without using browser-specific features. Similarly to PNaCl, in order to construct eviction sets we obtain a high-precision timer, and a contiguous allocated memory buffer.

The work of [28] prompted the web browser developers to reduce the precision of the time source available to JavaScript code. Unlike PNaCl, WebAssembly does not have access to system's APIs like `clock_gettime()`. Thus, we use an alternative technique, based on an intentional inter-thread race condition (see [33] for a recent survey of JavaScript timing sources, including this one).

In this approach, we allocate a `SharedArrayBuffer` array within the main JavaScript context, and pass it to a "Timer" Web Worker which iteratively increments the value in the first cell of the array in a tight loop. To learn the current time, the main context reads that cell. The naive implementation, accessing the array directly, did not work due to runtime optimization of supposedly-redundant reads. To overcome this, we used the `Atomics` API to force reading from the array (with sufficiently small performance penalty).

Next, we construct our eviction sets using `WebAssembly.Memory` contiguous buffer accessible both for JavaScript and WebAssembly. Accessing to this buffer from WebAssembly, and using the time source described above, allows us to identify cache misses using the above techniques.

**Exprimental Results.** On the Chromebook machine described in Sect. 1.2 we used the PNaCl implementation. Out of the 4096 sets, withing less then a minute we were able to construct 4032–4160 eviction sets (some duplicate eviction set was not removed during the collect phase). For the HP EliteBook 8760w laptop equipped with 8192 cache set, constructing the eviction sets took 11 min using the PNaCl and resulted in 7680–8320 eviction sets (with some duplicates as well). Using the WebAssembly implementation we were able to construct eviction sets on Chrome and Firefox as well. Constructing the eviction sets took 60–70 min and yield 7040–7680 eviction sets.

## 4  Attacking Elliptic

This section shows that even highly regular algorithms, which do not perform key-dependent operations or memory accesses, can produce exploitable side channel leakage when implemented in high-level programming languages such as JavaScript. We empirically demonstrate this on Elliptic's Curve25519-based ECDH implementation, which uses the Montgomery ladder method.

### 4.1  Deployment

Our attack scenario is based on running cache-monitoring portable code, using either of PNaCl or WebAssembly, inside the target's browser. We now describe a specific attack scenario which does not require the user to install any malicious application or even actively browse to the attacker's website.

**Pop-Under Advertisement.** Pop-Under advertisement is a common technique to circumvent pop-up protection used in modern web browsers. Once the user clicks anywhere inside the web page, a new browser tab containing the requested web page is shown with while the previous tab (which is now hidden) is redirected to an advertisement loaded from the attacker's website.

**Attack Scenario.** We created an advertisement leading to a web page containing our portable attack code and submitted it to a web ad service. The targeted user opened a web browser (either Chrome or Firefox, and on either the Chromebook or HP laptops described in Sect. 1.2), accessed a third party web page which uses the ad service, and clicked anywhere within the page. Consequentially (courtesy of the ad service), our advertisement was opened in a background tab and started monitoring the cache access patterns on the target machine. Concurrently, the user opened a third tab, in the Chrome browser, which performed ECDH key-exchange operations using Ellipstic's Curve25519. Neither the website used to trigger the attack, nor the ad service, were controlled by the attacker; and the user never typed or followed a link to an attacker-controlled website.

### 4.2   Key Extraction

**ECDH.** Elliptic curve Diffie Hellman (ECDH) is a variant of the Diffie-Hellman key exchange protocol [8] performed over suitable elliptic curves. Given a curve over a finite field $\mathbb{F}$ and a generator point $G \in (\mathbb{F} \times \mathbb{F})$, in order to generate a key Alice chooses a random scalar $k$ as a private key and computed the public key by $[k]G$ (here and onward, we use additive group notation with and $[k]G$ denoting scalar-by-point multiplication of $k$ and $G$). In order to compute the shared secret, Bob sends his public key $G' = [k']G$ to Alice (where $k'$ is Bob's secret key). Alice and Bob then recover the shared secret by computing $[k]G'$ and $[k']G$, respectively. Notice that $[k]G' = [k]([k']G) = [k']([k]G) = [k']G$.

**Curve25519.** Curve25519 is an elliptic curve introduced by [6] and standardized by RFC 7748. Curve25519 was specifically designed to increase resistance to side channel attacks and other common implementation issues.

**Scalar-By-Point Multiplication.** In order to increase side channel resistance, implementations of Curve25519-based ECDH often use the Montgomery ladder [26] to perform the scalar-by-point multiplication operation. See Algorithm 1. Notice that the algorithm performs the same number and order of addition and double operations, regardless of the value of $k_i$, making it more side channel resistant compared to other multiplication algorithms [19,27].

**Inapplicability of Data Cache Leakage.** The Montgomery ladder scalar-by-point multiplication routine attempts to achieve side channel resistance by being highly regular. Each iteration of the main loop of Algorithm 1 accesses both of the internal variables ($a$ and $b$) and performs a single elliptic curve add operation followed by a single elliptic curve double operation. In particular, both operations are performed, in the same order, irrespective of the value of the current secret key bit ($k_i$). Thus, the Montgomery powering ladder does not leak the secret key via key-dependent sequences of double and add operations, or key-dependent memory accesses to a table of precomputed values. As we

**Algorithm 1.** Elliptic's Point Multiplication (simplified).

**Input:** A scalar $k$ and a point $P$ where the $k = \sum_{i=0}^{n-1} k_i 2^i$.
**Output:** $b = [k]P$.

```
1:  procedure SCALAR_BY_POINT_MULTIPLICATION(k, P)
2:      a ← P, b ← O                                              ▷ O is the point of infinity
3:      for i ← n to 1 do
4:          if k_i = 0 then
5:              a ← a.ADD(b)                                      ▷ a + b
6:              b ← b.DOUBLE()                                    ▷ [2]b
7:          else
8:              b ← a.ADD(b)                                      ▷ a + b
9:              a ← a.DOUBLE()                                    ▷ [2]a
10:     return b
```

have empirically validated, Elliptic's implementation of Algorithm 1, running on Chrome, is almost constant time, without key-dependent timing deviations.

While Algorithm 1 does leak the secret key via memory accesses performed to the operand of the elliptic curve double operation (Lines 6 and 9) as well as the memory accesses to the result of the elliptic curve add operation (Lines 5 and 8), this leakage is hard to exploit due to JavaScript's memory allocation mechanism. Concretely, since each iteration of the main loop always updates both variables, Elliptic's implementation always allocates new objects for the updated values, at different and changing memory addresses. As we empirically verified, the addresses of $a$ and $b$ change with each iteration of the main loop, without any obvious patterns. This makes monitoring memory accesses to $a$ and $b$ difficult, since the attacker has to predict and monitor a different cache set at every iteration of the main loop.

While the memory re-allocation countermeasure was probably unintentional, this countermeasure combined with the inherent regularity of the Montgomery ladder scalar by point multiplication routine prevent the use of the data cache as a source of side channel leakage.

**Finding a Leakage Source.** We choose, instead, to conduct a code-cache side-channel attack. In this approach we identify a key-dependent change in the target's control flow. During the ECDH operation, we monitor the code cache accesses via PNaCl or WebAssembly, deduce control flow changes, and from these, recover the key.

An immediate candidate for such key-dependent control flow would be the if-else statement in Line 4 of Algorithm 1. However, distinguishing between different cases of the if-else statement in Line 4 appears to be difficult, since both case are very similar, call the same functions in the same order, have the same length and are relatively small (each consisting of only two code lines).

While a high-level examination of Algorithm 1 does not reveal any additional key-dependent control flow, we do observe that Algorithm 1 invokes the double operation in Line 6 on variable $b$, while in Line 9 it is invoked on object $a$. While

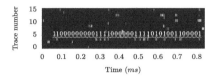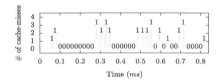

**Fig. 2.** Cache accesses as detected by the attacker during ECDH key exchange over Curve25519 by Elliptic. Trace 3 (left) contains cache misses observed by the attacker during the scalar-by-point multiplication. On the right, which only shows Trace 3, it can clearly be noticed that the cache-misses corresponds to key bits of 1, while sequence without cache-misses of 20 μs corresponds to bits of 0.

in a low-level programing language the execution of different code paths is usually explicit, in a high-level language such as JavaScript, the compiler/interpreter is at liberty to select different execution paths for performing identical operations on different data. Empirically, this indeed occurs here. We were able to empirically distinguish, using code cache leakage, between the double operation performed in Line 6 (on variable $b$) from the double operation in Line 9 (performed on $a$)—thus attaining key extraction.

**Monitoring Elliptic's Side Channel Leakage with WebAssembly.** We demonstrated our WebAssembly attack in a cross-browser, cross-process scenario. We used the HP laptop to launch two separate web browser instances: Chrome, running a page that uses Elliptic's implementation of Curve25519-based ECDH, and Firefox, running a third-party web site presenting advertisements from our advertisement provider. After clicking inside the third-party web site, our WebAssembly attack code was loaded as a pop-under ad, and automatically started the eviction-set construction procedure described in Sect. 3. The CPU of this HP laptop has 8192 cache sets, and each Curve25519 ECDH key exchange lasts 2.5 ms. Hence, after the construction procedure, our code sampled each of the 8192 eviction sets, performing Prime+Probe cycle every 380 μs for a duration of 22 ms, for a total sampling time of about 3 min.

**Monitoring Elliptic's Side Channel Leakage with PNaCl.** Alternatively, we opened two tabs in the Chromebook's browser: one tab running our PNaCl attack code, and the other running Elliptic's implementation of Curve25519-based ECDH, with each key exchange lasting 4.5 ms. Next, we sampled each of the 4096 eviction sets, performing Prime+Probe cycle every 3 μs for a duration of 35 ms, totally sampling for less than 3 min.

**Leakage Analysis.** Out of the acquired traces, for each of the sampling methods we identified 5 as containing the side channel leakage described above. Figure 2 shows some out of the acquired traces using PNaCl on the Chromebook machine, Trace 3 (left) contains the information regarding the secret key.

As can be seen from the right part of Fig. 2, showing only Trace 3, a sequence of $10\,\mu s$ of cache-misses cache-misses followed by $5\,\mu s$ of cache-hits in the monitored set corresponds to a bit of 1, while $20\,\mu s$ of cache-hits corresponds to 0 bit.

Using this, we automated the extraction of keys from traces, yielding correct extraction of up to 236 (out of 252) bits of the secret key from *individual* traces. Combining 4 traces of key-exchange operations we were able to extract all the 252 bits of the secret key. For the WebAssembly attacks, the acquired traces and automated algorithm are very similar, and likewise result in full key extraction.

## 5 Attacking ElGamal

### 5.1 Attacking End-to-End

ElGamal [9] is a public-key crptosystem based on hardness of computing discrete logarithms. In a nutshell, to decrypt a ciphertext $(c_1, c_2)$, one has to compute the shared secret $s = c_1^x \bmod p$ and then recovers the message by computing $m' = c_2 \cdot s^{-1} \bmod p$. To compute the modular exponentiation during decryption, End-to-End uses a variant of the fixed-window ($m$-ary) exponentiation algorithm [25, Algorithm 14.109]. The algorithm divides the secret exponent into equal-sized groups of bits called windows, performing a single multiplication for each window using a precomputed value for every possible windows value.

Our attack largely follows the technique of [23] and consists of two phases. In the *online phase* we collect many memory access traces, with the aim of capturing enough samples of accesses to memory locations that store the table of pre-computed multipliers. In the *offline phase* we analyse the collected traces to identify the traces that correspond to memory locations that store pre-computed multipliers. From these, we recover information on the operands of the multiplications, from which we deduce bits of the exponent and then recover the key.

**Monitoring End-to-End's Side Channel Leakage.** Following Sect. 4 we opened two tabs in the Chromebook's browser: one running our PNaCl attack code, and the other running End-to-End's ElGamal, where each decryption operation lasts 1.58 s on the Chromebook device. Next, we selected 8 random cache sets and monitored them in parallel, performing a Prime+Probe cycle on each of the cache sets once every $31.5\,\mu s$ for a duration of 5 s. We repeated this process sequentially for about 74 min, acquiring 7100 traces.

**Leakage Analysis.** Figure 3 shows the side channel leakage from an End-to-End ElGamal decryption. Traces 3 and 19 contains cache misses observed during the multiplication operations used by the exponentiation algorithm. To extract the key, we applied offline processing: denoising, clustering, merging, conflict resolution and key recovery. This took 90 min (cost: under \$6 on Amazon EC2). We ran our attack on several random ElGamal keys with 3072-bit public primes, both on the Chromebook and the HP laptop, successfully extracting the entire secret exponent in every trial.

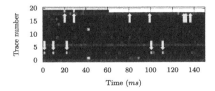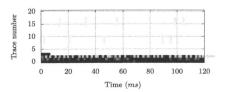

**Fig. 3.** Cache accesses as detected by the attacker during ElGamal decryption by End-to-End (left) and OpenPGP.js (right). Intensity represents the number of cache misses. Traces 3 and 19 on the left, and trace 11 and 19 on the right, contain cache misses observed by the attacker during the multiplication operations used by the exponentiation algorithm. Trace 2 (right) shows code-cache misses in the execution of the modular multiplication code during an OpenPGP.js decryption operation; the different intervals between the multiplications leak the location of sequences of zero bits.

End-to-End's implementation of RSA [32] decryption operations uses the same fixed-window routine to perform modular exponentiation. Thus, our attack is applicable for extracting RSA keys, even tough End-to-End implemented ciphertext blinding countermeasure against side-channel attacks.

### 5.2   Attacking OpenPGP.js

OpenPGP.js implements ElGamal decryption using sliding-window exponentiation [25, Algorithm 14.85]. Similarly to fixed-window exponentiation, the sliding window algorithm also use indexes a table of precomputed multipliers, on every multiplication operation. However, for speed, sequences of 0-bits are handled by simply performing corresponding squaring operations. Thus, the sliding-window algorithm leaks the location and length of zero sequences, and has been proven less resistant to side-channel attacks [23].

To measure the leakage we used an analogous setup to the one used in Sect. 5.1. Using the Chromebook, we opened two browser tabs with one tab running our PNaCl attack code while the other tab was performing ElGamal decryption operations using the OpenPGP.js. We monitored random cache sets, performing a Prime+Probe cycle on each set every $20\,\mu s$ for a period of $0.62\,s$. The cache access patterns observed by the attacker reveal when a specific window value is used during the multiplication operations, Fig. 3 (right) shows the side channel leakage from one ElGamal decryption operation. Finally, the squaring operations performed by the sliding-window algorithm reveal long sequences of zero exponent bits This additional source leakage in Trace 2 of Fig. 3 (right) by monitoring the executions of the modular multiplication code.

## 6   Conclusion

In this paper we present a method for implementing an LLC-based Prime+Probe attack on an multiple cryptographic libraries ranging from ElGamal to state-of-the-art Curve25519-based ECDH using portable code executing inside a sandboxed web browser. We successfully deployed the attack using a commercial ad service that triggers the attack code from third-party websites, and automatically starts monitoring the memory access patterns when users navigate to the ad. To our knowledge, this is the first demonstration of a drive-by cache attack, and the first portable cryptographic side channel attack.

Unlike prior works, our attack target is implemented using a portable code. Yet, even without the knowledge of the target's memory layout, the attack successfully extracts the target's ElGamal and ECDH keys. Finally, we show that in spite of their secure design, Chromebooks are vulnerable to cache based attacks.

**Countermeasures.** Side-channel resistant code requires constant-time implementation and avoiding secret dependent branches and memory accesses. These approaches are very delicate, and may fail when on different hardware or with different compilers. Using these techniques in JIT-compiled environments is an unexplored area that we leave for future work. Meanwhile, cryptographic operations in JavaScript should to delegated to suitable native implementations, such as (extensions of) WebCrypto API.

**Limitations.** Constructing eviction sets as described in Sect. 3 depends on the cache structure and eviction policy: in particular, an inclusive LLC, and an LRU (or similar) eviction policy. While both assumptions hold for modern Intel CPUs, other vendors may differ. Some of our attacks (Sect. 4) requires only a few minutes of sampling time (corresponding to about a thousand decryptions), and suggest a realistic threat to affected systems that conduct frequent decryptions. Others (Sect. 5) requires over an hour of sampling time, but should none the less indicate that observable leakage is prevalent across diverse cryptographic algorithms and implementations, and is expoitable by portable code.

Thus, the threat of cache timing side-channel attacks from sandboxed portable code must be considered, and mitigated, in the design of modern systems where such code is trivially controlled by attackers.

**Acknowledgments.** This work was partially inspired by unpublished work on portable cache attacks done jointly with Ethan Heilman, Perry Hung, Taesoo Kim and Andrew Meyer.

Daniel Genkin, Lev Pachmanov and Eran Tromer are members of the Check Point Institute for Information Security. Yuval Yarom performed part of this work as a visiting scholar at the University of Pennsylvania.

This work was supported by the Australian Department of Education and Training through an Endeavour Research Fellowship; by the Blavatnik Interdisciplinary Cyber Research Center (ICRC); by the Check Point Institute for Information Security; by the Defense Advanced Research Project Agency (DARPA) and Army Research Office (ARO) under Contract #W911NF-15-C-0236; by the Israeli Ministry of Science and Technology; by the Israeli Centers of Research Excellence I-CORE program (center 4/11); by the Leona M. & Harry B. Helmsley Charitable Trust; by NSF awards #CNS-1445424 and #CCF-1423306; by the 2017–2018 Rothschild Postdoctoral Fellowship; by the Warren Center for Network and Data Sciences; by the financial assistance award 70NANB15H328 from the U.S. Department of Commerce, National Institute of Standards and Technology; and by the Defense Advanced Research Project Agency (DARPA) under Contract #FA8650-16-C-7622. Any opinions, findings, and conclusions or recommendations expressed are those of the authors and do not necessarily reflect the views of ARO, DARPA, NSF, the U.S. Government or other sponsors.

# References

1. Acıiçmez, O., Brumley, B.B., Grabher, P.: New results on instruction cache attacks. In: Mangard, S., Standaert, F.-X. (eds.) CHES 2010. LNCS, vol. 6225, pp. 110–124. Springer, Heidelberg (2010). https://doi.org/10.1007/978-3-642-15031-9_8
2. Acıiçmez, O., Gueron, S., Seifert, J.-P.: New branch prediction vulnerabilities in OpenSSL and necessary software countermeasures. In: Galbraith, S.D. (ed.) Cryptography and Coding 2007. LNCS, vol. 4887, pp. 185–203. Springer, Heidelberg (2007). https://doi.org/10.1007/978-3-540-77272-9_12
3. Acıiçmez, O., Koç, Ç.K., Seifert, J.-P.: Predicting secret keys via branch prediction. In: Abe, M. (ed.) CT-RSA 2007. LNCS, vol. 4377, pp. 225–242. Springer, Heidelberg (2006). https://doi.org/10.1007/11967668_15
4. Acıiçmez, O., Schindler, W.: A vulnerability in RSA implementations due to instruction cache analysis and its demonstration on OpenSSL. In: Malkin, T. (ed.) CT-RSA 2008. LNCS, vol. 4964, pp. 256–273. Springer, Heidelberg (2008). https://doi.org/10.1007/978-3-540-79263-5_16
5. Bernstein, D.J.: Cache-timing attacks on AES (2005). http://cr.yp.to/papers.html#cachetiming
6. Bernstein, D.J.: Curve25519: new Diffie-Hellman speed records. In: Yung, M., Dodis, Y., Kiayias, A., Malkin, T. (eds.) PKC 2006. LNCS, vol. 3958, pp. 207–228. Springer, Heidelberg (2006). https://doi.org/10.1007/11745853_14
7. Bulygin, Y.: CPU side-channels vs. virtualization malware: the good, the bad or the ugly. In: ToorCon (2008)
8. Diffie, W., Hellman, M.E.: New directions in cryptography. IEEE Trans. Inf. Theory 22(6), 644–654 (1976)
9. ElGamal, T.: A public key cryptosystem and a signature scheme based on discrete logarithms. IEEE Trans. Inf. Theory 31(4), 469–472 (1985)
10. Evtyushkin, D., Ponomarev, D., Abu-Ghazaleh, N.B.: Understanding and mitigating covert channels through branch predictors. TACO 13(1), 10:1–10:23 (2016)
11. Ge, Q., Yarom, Y., Cock, D., Heiser, G.: A survey of microarchitectural timing attacks and countermeasures on contemporary hardware. J. Cryptograph. Eng. 8(1), 1–27 (2018)
12. Genkin, D., Pachmanov, L., Pipman, I., Tromer, E.: Stealing keys from PCs using a radio: cheap electromagnetic attacks on windowed exponentiation. In: Güneysu, T., Handschuh, H. (eds.) CHES 2015. LNCS, vol. 9293, pp. 207–228. Springer, Heidelberg (2015). https://doi.org/10.1007/978-3-662-48324-4_11
13. Gras, B., Razavi, K., Bosman, E., Bos, H., Giuffrida, C.: ASLR on the line: practical cache attacks on the MMU. In: NDSS (2017)
14. Gruss, D., Maurice, C., Mangard, S.: Rowhammer.js: a remote software-induced fault attack in JavaScript. In: Caballero, J., Zurutuza, U., Rodríguez, R.J. (eds.) DIMVA 2016. LNCS, vol. 9721, pp. 300–321. Springer, Cham (2016). https://doi.org/10.1007/978-3-319-40667-1_15
15. Gruss, D., Spreitzer, R., Mangard, S.: Cache template attacks: automating attacks on inclusive last-level caches. In: USENIX, pp. 897–912 (2015)

16. İnci, M.S., Gulmezoglu, B., Irazoqui, G., Eisenbarth, T., Sunar, B.: Cache attacks enable bulk key recovery on the cloud. In: Gierlichs, B., Poschmann, A.Y. (eds.) CHES 2016. LNCS, vol. 9813, pp. 368–388. Springer, Heidelberg (2016). https://doi.org/10.1007/978-3-662-53140-2_18

17. Inci, M.S., Gülmezoglu, B., Apecechea, G.I., Eisenbarth, T., Sunar, B.: Seriously, get off my cloud! cross-VM RSA key recovery in a public cloud. IACR Cryptology ePrint Archive, p. 898 (2015)

18. Indutny, F.: Fast elliptic curve cryptography in plain JavaScript (2017). https://github.com/indutny/elliptic

19. Joye, M., Yen, S.-M.: The montgomery powering ladder. In: Kaliski, B.S., Koç, K., Paar, C. (eds.) CHES 2002. LNCS, vol. 2523, pp. 291–302. Springer, Heidelberg (2003). https://doi.org/10.1007/3-540-36400-5_22

20. Kim, Y., Daly, R., Kim, J., Fallin, C., Lee, J., Lee, D., Wilkerson, C., Lai, K., Mutlu, O.: Flipping bits in memory without accessing them: an experimental study of DRAM disturbance errors. In: ISCA, pp. 361–372 (2014)

21. Kocher, P., Genkin, D., Gruss, D., Haas, W., Hamburg, M., Lipp, M., Mangard, S., Prescher, T., Schwarz, M., Yarom, Y.: Spectre attacks: exploiting speculative execution. ArXiv e-prints (2018)

22. Lipp, M., Schwarz, M., Gruss, D., Prescher, T., Haas, W., Mangard, S., Kocher, P., Genkin, D., Yarom, Y., Hamburg, M.: Meltdown. ArXiv e-prints (2018)

23. Liu, F., Yarom, Y., Ge, Q., Heiser, G., Lee, R.B.: Last-level cache side-channel attacks are practical. In: Symposium on Security and Privacy, pp. 605–622 (2015)

24. Maurice, C., Weber, M., Schwartz, M., Giner, L., Gruss, D., Boano, C.A., Römer, K., Mangard, S.: Hello from the other side: SSH over robust cache covert channels in the cloud. In: NDSS (2017)

25. Menezes, A.J., Vanstone, S.A., Oorschot, P.C.V.: Handbook of Applied Cryptography, 1st edn. CRC Press, Boca Raton (1996)

26. Montgomery, P.L.: Speeding the Pollard and elliptic curve methods of factorization. Math. Comput. **48**(177), 243 (1987)

27. Okeya, K., Kurumatani, H., Sakurai, K.: Elliptic curves with the montgomery-form and their cryptographic applications. In: Imai, H., Zheng, Y. (eds.) PKC 2000. LNCS, vol. 1751, pp. 238–257. Springer, Heidelberg (2000). https://doi.org/10.1007/978-3-540-46588-1_17

28. Oren, Y., Kemerlis, V.P., Sethumadhavan, S., Keromytis, A.D.: The spy in the sandbox: practical cache attacks in JavaScript and their implications. In: ACM SIGSAC, pp. 1406–1418 (2015)

29. Osvik, D.A., Shamir, A., Tromer, E.: Cache attacks and countermeasures: the case of AES. In: Pointcheval, D. (ed.) CT-RSA 2006. LNCS, vol. 3860, pp. 1–20. Springer, Heidelberg (2006). https://doi.org/10.1007/11605805_1

30. Percival, C.: Cache missing for fun and profit. In: Presented at BSDCan (2005). http://www.daemonology.net/hyperthreading-considered-harmful

31. Ristenpart, T., Tromer, E., Shacham, H., Savage, S.: Hey, you, get off of my cloud! Exploring information leakage in third-party compute clouds. In: CCS, pp. 199–212 (2009)

32. Rivest, R.L., Shamir, A., Adleman, L.M.: A method for obtaining digital signatures and public-key cryptosystems. Commun. ACM **21**(2), 120–126 (1978)

33. Schwarz, M., Maurice, C., Gruss, D., Mangard, S.: Fantastic timers and where to find them: high-resolution microarchitectural attacks in JavaScript. In: Kiayias, A. (ed.) FC 2017. LNCS, vol. 10322, pp. 247–267. Springer, Cham (2017). https://doi.org/10.1007/978-3-319-70972-7_13

34. Schwarz, M., Weiser, S., Gruss, D., Maurice, C., Mangard, S.: Malware guard extension: using SGX to conceal cache attacks. In: Polychronakis, M., Meier, M. (eds.) DIMVA 2017. LNCS, vol. 10327, pp. 3–24. Springer, Cham (2017). https:// doi.org/10.1007/978-3-319-60876-1_1
35. Tromer, E., Osvik, D.A., Shamir, A.: Efficient cache attacks on AES, and counter-measures. J. Cryptol. **23**(1), 37–71 (2010)
36. Tsunoo, Y., Saito, T., Suzaki, T., Shigeri, M., Miyauchi, H.: Cryptanalysis of DES implemented on computers with cache. In: Walter, C.D., Koç, Ç.K., Paar, C. (eds.) CHES 2003. LNCS, vol. 2779, pp. 62–76. Springer, Heidelberg (2003). https://doi.org/10.1007/978-3-540-45238-6_6
37. Yarom, Y., Falkner, K.: FLUSH+RELOAD: a high resolution, low noise, L3 cache side-channel attack. In: USENIX, pp. 719–732 (2014)
38. Yee, B., Sehr, D., Dardyk, G., Chen, J.B., Muth, R., Ormandy, T., Okasaka, S., Narula, N., Fullagar, N.: Native client: a sandbox for portable, untrusted x86 native code. In: IEEE Symposium on Security and Privacy, pp. 79–93 (2009)
39. Zhang, Y., Juels, A., Reiter, M.K., Ristenpart, T.: Cross-VM side channels and their use to extract private keys. In: CCS, pp. 305–316 (2012)

# On the Ineffectiveness of Internal Encodings - Revisiting the DCA Attack on White-Box Cryptography

Estuardo Alpirez Bock[1,2(✉)], Chris Brzuska[1,2], Wil Michiels[3,4], and Alexander Treff[1]

[1] Hamburg University of Technology, Hamburg, Germany
{estuardo.alpirezbock,brzuska,alexander.treff}@tuhh.de
[2] Aalto University, Espoo, Finland
[3] NXP Semiconductors, Eindhoven, The Netherlands
wil.michiels@nxp.com
[4] Technische Universiteit Eindhoven, Eindhoven, The Netherlands

**Abstract.** The goal of white-box cryptography is to implement cryptographic algorithms securely in software in the presence of an adversary that has complete access to the software's program code and execution environment. In particular, white-box cryptography needs to protect the embedded secret key from being extracted. Bos et al. (CHES 2016) introduced differential computational analysis (DCA), the first automated attack on white-box cryptography. The DCA attack performs a statistical analysis on execution traces. These traces contain information such as memory addresses or register values, that is collected via binary instrumentation tooling during the encryption process. The white-box implementations that were attacked by Bos et al., as well as white-box implementations that have been described in the literature, protect the embedded key by using internal encodings techniques introduced by Chow et al. (SAC 2002). Thereby, a combination of linear and non-liner nibble encodings is used to protect the secret key. In this paper we analyse the use of such internal encodings and prove rigorously that they are too weak to protect against DCA. We prove that the use of non-linear nibble encodings does not hide key dependent correlations, such that a DCA attack succeeds with high probability.

**Keywords:** White-box cryptography
Differential computational analysis · Software execution traces
Mixing bijections

## 1 Introduction

When an application for mobile payment runs in software on Android or other open platforms, it needs to protect itself as it cannot rely on platform security. In particular, the cryptographic algorithms used within an application need to

© Springer International Publishing AG, part of Springer Nature 2018
B. Preneel and F. Vercauteren (Eds.): ACNS 2018, LNCS 10892, pp. 103–120, 2018.
https://doi.org/10.1007/978-3-319-93387-0_6

be secured against adversaries who have a high degree of control over the environment. In 2002, Chow et al. [9,10] introduced *white-box cryptography*, which aims at remaining secure even when the adversary has full control over the execution environment. As mobile payment became widely used and as its security nowadays often relies on software security only, Visa and Mastercard made the use of white-box cryptography for mobile payment applications mandatory [15].

A necessary requirement for secure white-box cryptography is that an adversary cannot extract the embedded secret key from the implementation. However, hiding the secret key is not always enough to achieve security in the white-box attack scenario. For example, if a mobile payment application uses a secret key for authentication by encrypting a challenge, then an adversary may simply try to copy the white-box program performing the encryption and run it on another device. The adversary could successfully use the functionality of the white-box program without knowing the value of its embedded secret key.

While it seems clear that a white-box program needs to achieve more than just security against key extraction, hiding the secret key remains a difficult task to achieve for real-life applications. Chow et al. [9,10] suggest to implement a symmetric cipher with a fixed key as a network of look-up tables (LUT). The key is compiled into a table instead of being stored in plain in the implementation. To achieve robustness against reverse-engineering, Chow et al. propose to obfuscate the lookup tables and the intermediate results via a combination of linear and non-linear encodings. The idea of implementing symmetric ciphers as such an obfuscated network of LUTs has caught on in the white-box community since then, see, e.g., [7,11]. While the LUT-based white-box designs only store the keys obfuscated in lookup tables, all aforementioned LUT-based designs turn out to be susceptible to key extraction attacks performed via differential and algebraic cryptanalysis (see [4,14,16,17]). Specifically, these attacks invert the obfuscation process by deriving the applied encoding functions after which the key can easily be recovered.

In real-life applications, mounting cryptanalysis and reverse engineering attacks requires abundant skills and time from an adversary. Thus, Bos et al. [6] and Sanfelix et al. [20] introduced *automated* key extraction attacks that are substantially simpler and faster to carry out. The authors call their method differential computational analysis (DCA) and describe it as the software counterpart of the differential power analysis (DPA), a method for attacking cryptographic hardware implementations [13]. Bos et al. [6] monitor the memory addresses accessed by a program during the encryption process and display them in the form of *software execution traces*. These software execution traces can also include other information that can be monitored using binary instrumentation, such as stack reads or register values. These traces serve the following three goals. (1) They can help to determine which cryptographic algorithms was implemented. (2) The traces provide hints to determine where roughly the cryptographic algorithm is located in the software implementation. (3) Finally and most importantly, the traces can be statistically analyzed to extract the secret key. The automated DCA attack turned out to be successful against a large number of publicly available white-box implementations. It has since then become a popular method for the evaluation of newly proposed white-box implementations [5] and software countermeasures for white-box cryptography [2].

In this paper, we analyze why step (3) of the attack by Bos et al. [6] actually works and show which types of encodings are susceptible to the DCA attack. The work of Sasdrich et al. [21] takes a first step towards this understanding. They use the Walsh transform to show that the encodings used by their white-box AES design are not balanced correlation immune and thus are susceptible to the DCA attack. In this paper, we aim at giving a structured exposition to improve our understanding of the power of the DCA attack.

*Our Contribution.* In this paper we provide an annotated step-by-step graphical presentation of the key-extraction step of the DCA attack, which relies on a difference of means distinguisher, and explain how to interpret the results. Our presentation follows the style that Kocher [12] and Messerges [18] used for the (analogous) differential power analysis on hardware implementations.

Further, we analyse how the presence of internal encodings on white-box implementations affects the effectiveness of the DCA attack. Here, we focus on the encodings suggested by Chow et al. [9,10], which are a combination of linear and non-linear transformations. We start by studying the effects of a single linear transformation. We show that the DCA attack can successfully extract the key from a look-up table when it only uses linear or affine encodings. Next, we consider the effect of non-linear nibble encodings and prove that the use of nibble encodings provides conditions so that the DCA attack succeeds. Namely, when we attack a key-dependent look-up table encoded via non-linear nibble encodings, we always obtain a difference of means curve with values equal to either 0, 0.25, 0.5, 0.75 or 1 for the correct key guess. The results obtained from these analyses help us determine why the DCA attack also works in the presence of both linear and non-linear nibble encodings as we discuss shortly in the end of the paper and in more detail in the extended version [1]. Throughout the paper, we also present experimental results of the DCA attack when performed on single key-dependent look-up tables and on complete white-box implementations. In all cases, the experimental results align with the theoretical observations.

## 2    White-Box Cryptography Implementations

White-box cryptography can be seen as special-purpose obfuscation, but is usually not discussed in this way. In particular, *general*-purpose obfuscation with perfect security is known to be impossible [3] and the hope is that achieving perfect security or at least a good level of security for a *specific* algorithm is still feasible. The most popular approach in academic literature (and perhaps also beyond) for white-box implementations of symmetric encryption is to encode the underlying symmetric cipher with a fixed key as a networks of look-up tables (LUT). In particular, the LUTs depend on the secret key used in the cipher. An additional protection technique is to apply linear and non-liner *internal* encodings which are used to encode the intermediate state between LUTs. Another popular technique are *external* encodings which are applied on the outside of the cipher and help to bind the white-box to an application. In this paper, we focus solely on internal encodings, because, as Bos et al. point out in [6], applying external input and output encodings yields an implementation of a function that is not functionally equivalent to AES anymore and thus, some of its security can be shifted to other programs. Moreover, this paper focusses on using internal encodings for LUT-based white-box constructions of AES. We will focus on the encodings and refer to the LUT-based construction as an abstract design. The interested reader may find the work by Muir [19] a useful read for a more detailed description on how to construct an LUT-based white-box AES implementation. In the following, we introduce the concept of internal encodings.

Consider an LUT-based white-box implementation of AES, where the LUTs depend on the secret key. Internal encodings can now help to re-randomize those LUTs to make it harder to recover secret-key information based on the LUTs. Such internal encodings were first suggested by Chow et al. [9,10]. We now discuss two types of encodings.

**Non-linear Encodings.** Recall that the secret key is hard-coded in the LUTs. When non-linear encodings are applied, each LUT in the construction becomes statistically independent from the key and thus, attacks need to exploit key dependency across several LUTs. A table $T$ can be transformed into a table $T'$ by using the input bijections $I$ and output bijections $O$ as follows:

$$T' = O \circ T \circ I^{-1}.$$

As a result, we obtain a new table $T'$ which maps encoded inputs to encoded outputs. Note that no information is lost as the encodings are bijective. If table $T'$ is followed by another table $R'$, their corresponding output and input encodings can be chosen such that they cancel out each other. Considering a complex network of LUTs of an AES implementation, we have input- and output encodings on almost all look-up tables. The only exceptions are the very first and the very last tables of the AES implementation, which take the input of the algorithm and correspondingly return the output data. The first tables omit the input encodings and the last tables omit the output encodings. As the internal encodings cancel each other out, the encodings do not affect the input-output behaviour of the AES implementation.

*Size Requirements.* Descriptions of uniformly random bijections (which are non-linear with overwhelming probability) are exponential in the input size of the bijection. Therefore, a uniformly random encoding of the 8-bit S-box requires a storage of $2^8$ bytes. Although this may still be acceptable, the problem arises when two values with a byte encoding need to be XORed. An encoded XOR has a storage requirement of $2^{16}$ nibbles. As we need many of them, this becomes an issue. Therefore, one usually splits longer values in nibbles of 4 bits. When XORing those, we only need a lookup table of $2^8$ nibbles. However, by moving to a split non-linear encoding we introduce a vulnerability since a bit in one nibble does no longer influence the encoded value of another nibble in the same encoded word. To (partly) compensate for this, Chow et al. propose to apply linear encodings whose size is merely quadratic in the input size and thus, they can be implemented on larger words.

**Linear Encodings.** Chow et al. suggest to apply linear encodings to words that are input or output of an XOR-network. These linear encodings have as width the complete word and are applied before the non-linear encodings discussed above. While the non-linear encodings need to be removed before performing an XOR-operation, one can perform the XOR on linearly encoded values (due to commutativity). Therefore, one usually refers to linear encodings as *mixing bijections.*

The linear encodings are invertible and selected uniformly at random. For example, we can select $L$ and $A$ as a mixing bijections for inputs and outputs of table $T$ respectively:

$$A \circ T \circ L^{-1}.$$

As stated above, it is not necessary to cancel the effect of the linear encodings before an XOR-operation. However, after the XOR-operation we obtain an output which is still dependent on the linear function $A$ and the effect of $A$ needs to be eventually removed, e.g. at the end of an AES round. In this case, dedicated tables in the form of $L_n \circ A^{-1}$ are introduced, where $L_n$ is the corresponding linear encoding needed for the next LUT. In the white-box designs of Chow et al. we have 8-bit and 32-bit mixing bijections. The former encode the 8-bit S-box inputs, while the latter obfuscate the MixColumns outputs.

## 3    Differential Computational Analysis

We now revisit the DCA attack on white-box implementations, which aims at finding key dependent correlations by analysing memory access information recorded during the encryption process. To display the tracked memory-information in so called *software execution traces*, one proceeds as follows: one fixes one bit of information of the bit string that describes the memory address and displays whether the bit was 0 or 1 at each memory access performed during the execution. For more details on the acquisition of software traces, see the original DCA paper by Bos et al. [6]. In this section we provide a detailed description of one statistical method to analyse such software execution traces, namely the *difference of means* method. Note that this method corresponds 1-to-1 to the difference of means method as presented by Kocher using power traces [12]. Nevertheless we now show the results obtained from a difference of means analysis when performed using a group of software traces. The two attack capabilities required to perform the DCA attack are as follows:

– execute the white-box program under attack several times in a controlled environment with different input messages.
– knowledge of the plaintext[1] values given to the program as input.

---

[1] The attack works analogously when having access to the ciphertexts. The attacker needs access to either plaintexts or ciphertexts.

The goal of the attack is to determine the first-round key of AES as it allows to recover the entire key. The first-round key of AES is 128 bits long and the attack aims to recover it byte-by-byte. For the remainder of this section, we focus on recovering the first byte of the first-round key, as the recovery attack for the other bytes of the first round key proceeds analogously. For the first key byte, the attacker tries out all possible 256 key byte hypotheses $k^h$, with $1 \leq h \leq 256$, uses the traces to test how good a key byte hypothesis is, and eventually returns the key hypothesis that performs best according to a metric that we specify shortly. For sake of exposition, we focus on one particular key-byte hypothesis $k^h$. The analysis steps on a DCA attack are performed as follows.

**1. Collecting Traces:** We first execute the white-box program $n$ times, each time using a different plaintext $p_e$, $1 \leq e \leq n$ as input. For each execution, one software trace $s_e$ is recorded during the first round of AES. Figure 1 shows a single software trace consisting of 300 samples. Each sample corresponds to one bit of the memory addresses accessed during execution.

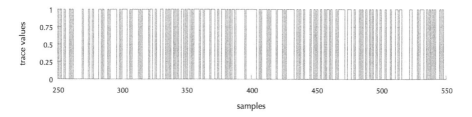

**Fig. 1.** Single software trace consisting of 300 samples

**2. Selection Function:** We define a selection function for calculating an intermediate state-byte $z$ of the calculation process of AES. More precisely, we calculate a state-byte which depends on the key-byte we are analysing in the actual iteration of the attack. The selection function returns only one bit of $z$, which we refer to as our *target bit*. The value of our target bit will be used as a distinguisher in the following steps. In this work, our selection function $\mathtt{Sel}(p_e, k^h, j)$ calculates the state $z$ after the $\mathtt{SBox}$ substitution in the first round. The index $j$ indicates *which* bit of $z$ is returned, with $1 \leq j \leq 8$.

$$\mathtt{Sel}(p_e, k^h, j) := \mathtt{SBox}(p_e \oplus k^h)[j] = b \in \{0, 1\}. \tag{1}$$

Depending on the white-box implementation being analysed, it may be the case that strong correlations between $b$ and the software traces are only observable for some bits of $z$, i.e. depending on which $j$ we choose to focus on. Thereby, we perform the following Steps 3, 4 and 5 for each bit $j$ of $z$.

**3. Sorting of Traces:** We sort each trace $s_e$ into one of the two sets $A_0$ or $A_1$ according to the value of $\mathtt{Sel}(p_e, k^h, j) = b$:

$$\text{For } b \in \{0, 1\} \ A_b := \{s_e | 1 \leq e \leq n, \ \mathtt{Sel}(p_e, k^h, j) = b\}. \tag{2}$$

**4. Mean Trace:** We now take the two sets of traces obtained in the previous step and calculate a *mean trace* for each set. We add all traces of one set sample wise and divide them by the total number of traces in the set. For $b \in \{0, 1\}$, we define

$$\bar{A}_b := \frac{\sum_{s \in A_b} s}{|A_b|}. \tag{3}$$

**5. Difference of Means:** We now calculate the difference between the two previously obtained mean traces sample wise. Figure 2 shows the resulting difference of means trace:

$$\Delta = |\bar{A}_0 - \bar{A}_1|. \tag{4}$$

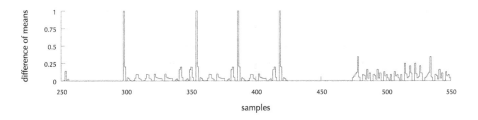

**Fig. 2.** Difference of means trace for correct key guess

**6. Best Target Bit:** We now compare the difference of means traces obtained for all target bits $j$ for a given key hypothesis $k^h$. Let $\Delta^j$ be the difference of means trace obtained for target bit $j$, and let $H(\Delta^j)$ be the highest peak in the trace $\Delta^j$. Then, we select $\Delta^j$ as the best difference of means trace for $k^h$, such that $H(\Delta^j)$ is maximal amongst the highest peaks of all other difference of means traces, i.e. $\forall\, 1 \leq j' \leq 8,\ H(\Delta^{j'}) \leq H(\Delta^j)$.

In other words, we look for the highest peak obtained from any difference of means trace. The difference of means trace with the highest peak $H(\Delta^j)$ is assigned as the difference of means obtained for the key hypothesis $k^h$ analysed in the actual iteration of the attack, such that $\Delta^h := \Delta^j$. We explain this reasoning in the analysis provided after Step 7.

**7. Best Key Byte Hypothesis:** Let $\Delta^h$ be the difference of means trace for key hypothesis $h$, and let $H(\Delta^h)$ be the highest peak in the trace $\Delta^h$. Then, we select $k^h$ such that $H(\Delta^h)$ is maximal amongst all other difference of means traces $\Delta^h$, i.e. $\forall\, 1 \leq h' \leq 256,\ H(\Delta^{h'}) \leq H(\Delta^h)$.

*Analysis.* The higher $H(\Delta^h)$, the more likely it is that this key-hypothesis is the correct one, which can be explained as follows. The attack partitions the traces in sets $A_0$ and $A_1$ based on whether a bit in $z$ is set to 0 or 1. First, suppose that the key hypothesis is correct and consider a region $R$ in the traces where (an encoded version of) $z$ is processed. Then, we expect that the memory accesses in $R$ for $A_0$ are slightly different than for $A_1$. After all, if they would be the same, the computations would be the same too. We know that the computations are different because the value of the target bit is different. Hence, it may be expected that this difference is reflected in the mean traces for $A_0$ and $A_1$, which results in a peak in the difference of means trace. Next, suppose that the key hypothesis is not correct. Then, the sets $A_0$ and $A_1$ can rather be seen as a random partition of the traces, which implies that $z$ can take any arbitrary value in both $A_0$ and $A_1$. Hence, we do not expect big differences between the executions traces from $A_0$ and $A_1$ in region $R$, which results in a rather flat difference of means trace.

To illustrate this, consider the difference of means trace depicted in Fig. 2. This difference of means trace corresponds to the analysis performed on a white-box implementation obtained from the hack.lu challenge [8]. This is a public table-based implementation of AES-128, which does not make any use of internal encodings. For analysing it, a total of 100 traces were recorded. The trace in Fig. 2 shows four spikes which reach the maximum value of 1 (note that the sample points have a value of either 0 or 1). Let $\ell$ be one of the four sample points in which we have a spike. Then, having a maximum value of 1 means that for all traces in $A_0$, the bit of the memory address considered in $\ell$ is 0 and that this bit is 1 for all traces in $A_1$ (or vice versa). In other words, the target bit $z[j]$ is either directly or in its negated form present in the memory address accessed in the implementation. This can happen if $z$ is used in non-encoded form as input to a lookup table or if it is only XORed with a constant mask. For sake of completeness, Fig. 3 shows a difference of means trace obtained for an incorrect key-hypothesis. No sample has a value higher than 0.3.

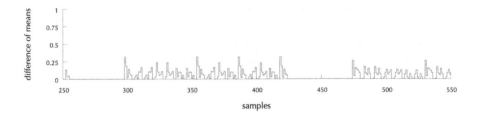

**Fig. 3.** Difference of means trace for incorrect key guess

The results of the DCA attack shown in this section correspond to the attack performed using software traces which consist of the memory addresses accessed during the encryption process. The attack can also be performed using software traces which consist of other type of information, e.g., the stack writes and/or reads performed during encryption. In all cases, the analysis is performed in an analogous way as explained in this section.

**Successful Attack.** Throughout this paper, considering the implementation of a cipher, we refer to the DCA attack as being *successful for a given key $k$*, if this key is ranked number 1 among all possible keys for a large enough number of traces. It may be the case that multiple keys have this same rank. If DCA is not successful for $k$, then it is called *unsuccessful for key $k$*. Remark that in practice, an attack is usually considered successful as long as the correct key guess is ranked as one of the best key candidates. We use a stronger definition as we require the correct key guess to be ranked as the best key candidate.

Alternatively when attacking a single $n$-bit to $n$-bit key dependent look-up table, we consider the DCA attack as being *successful for a given key $k$*, if this key is ranked number 1 among all possible keys for exactly $2^n$ traces. Thereby, each trace is generated by giving exactly $2^n$ different inputs to the look-up table, i.e. all possible inputs that the look-up table can obtain. To get the correlation between a look-up table output and our selection function, the correlation we obtain by evaluating all $2^n$ possible inputs is exactly equal to the correlation we obtain by generating a large enough number of traces for inputs chosen uniformly at random. We use this property for the experiments we perform in the following section.

## 4   Effect of the Encodings

Chow et al. [9] recommend a combination of linear and non-linear encodings as means to protect key dependent look-up tables in a white-box implementation. These types of encodings are the methods usually applied in the literature and in several publicly available white-box implementations. In this section we analyse how these types of encodings affect the effectiveness of the DCA attack. Namely, if intermediate values in an implementation are encoded, it becomes more difficult to re-calculate such values using a selection function as defined in Step 2 of the DCA, as this selection function does not consider any encodings (see Sect. 3). For our analyses in this section, we first build single look-up tables which map an 8-bit long input to an 8-bit long output. More precisely, these look-up tables correspond to the key addition operation merged with the S-box substitution step performed on AES. As common in the literature, we refer to such look-up tables as *T-boxes*. We apply the different encoding methods to the outputs of the look-up tables and obtain encoded T-boxes. Note that Chow et al. merge the T-box and the MixColumns operation into one 8-to-32 bit look-up table and encode the look-up table output via a 32-bit linear transformation. However, an 8-to-32 bit look-up table can be split into four 8-to-8 bit lookup tables, which correspond to the look-up tables used for our analyses.[2]

Following our definition for a successful DCA attack on an $n$-to-$n$ look-up table given in Sect. 3, we generate exactly 256 different software traces for attacking a T-box. Our selection function is defined the same way as in Step 2 of Sect. 3 and calculates the output of the T-boxes *before* it is encoded. The output of the T-box is a typical vulnerable spot for performing the DCA on white-box implementations as this output can be calculated based on a known plaintext and a key guess. As we will see in this section, internal encodings as suggested by

---

[2] It can be the case that the four lookup tables are, in isolation, not bijective. In that case, our results do not apply directly. It is left as an exercise to adapt them to this setting.

Chow et al. cannot effectively add a masking countermeasure to the outputs of the S-box.

## 4.1   Linear Encodings

The outputs of a T-box can be *linearly* encoded by applying linear transformations. To do this, we randomly generate an 8-to-8 invertible matrix $A$. For each output $y$ of a T-box $T$, we perform a matrix multiplication $A \cdot y$ and obtain an encoded output $m$. We obtain a new look-up table $lT$, which maps each input $x$ to a linearly encoded output $m$. Figure 4 displays this behaviour.

**Fig. 4.** An lT-box maps each input $x$ to a linearly encoded output $m$.

We now compute the DCA on the outputs of an $lT$, constructed with a randomly generated invertible matrix $A$. Figure 5 shows the results of the analysis when using the correct key guess. Since we are attacking only an $8 \times 8$ look-up table, the generated software traces consist only of 24 samples. No high peaks can be seen in the difference of means trace, i.e., no correlations can be identified and thus, the analysis is not successful if the output of the original T-box is encoded using the matrix $A$.

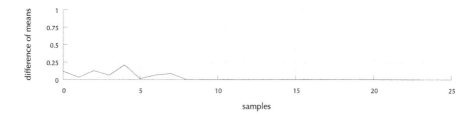

**Fig. 5.** Difference of means trace for the lT-box

The results shown in Fig. 5 correspond to the DCA performed on a look-up table constructed using one particular linear transformation to encode the output of one look-up table. We observe that the DCA as described in Sect. 3 is not effective in the presence of this particular transformation. The theorem below gives a necessary and sufficient condition under which linear transformations provide protection against the DCA attack.

**Theorem 1.** *Given a T-box encoded via an invertible matrix A. The difference of means curve obtained for the correct key hypothesis returns a peak value equal to 1 if and only if the matrix A has at least one row i with Hamming weight (HW) = 1. Otherwise, the difference of means curve obtained for the correct key hypothesis returns peak values equal to 0.*

*Proof.* For all $1 \leq j \leq 8$ let $y[j]$ be the $j$th bit of the output $y$ of a T-box. Let $a_{ij} \in GF(2)$ be the entries of an $8 \times 8$ matrix $A$, where $i$ denotes the row and $j$ denotes the column of the entry. We obtain each encoded bit $m[i]$ of the lT-box via

$$m[i] = \sum_j a_{ij} \cdot y[j] = \sum_{j:a_{ij}=1} y[j]. \tag{5}$$

Suppose that row $i$ of $A$ has $HW(i) = 1$. Let $j$ be such that $a_{ij} = 1$. It follows from Eq. (5) that $m[i] = y[j]$. Let $k^h$ be the correct key hypothesis and let bit $y[j]$ be our target bit. With our selection function $\mathtt{Sel}(p_e, k^h, j)$ we calculate the value for $y[j]$ and sort the corresponding trace in the set $A_0$ or $A_1$. We refer to these sets as sets consisting of encoded values $m$, since a software trace is a representation of the encoded values. Recall now that $y[j] = m[i]$. It follows that $m[i] = 0$ for all $m \in A_0$ and $m[i] = 1$ for all $m \in A_1$. Thus, when calculating the averages of both sets, for $\bar{A}[i]$, we obtain $\bar{A}_0[i] = 0$ and $\bar{A}_1[i] = 1$. Subsequently, we obtain a difference of means curve with $\Delta[i] = 1$, which leads us to a successful DCA attack.

What's left to prove is that if row $i$ has $HW(i) > 1$, then the value of bit $y[j]$ is masked via the linear transformation such that the difference of means curve obtained for $\Delta[i]$ has a value equal to zero. Suppose that row $i$ of $A$ has $HW(i) = l > 1$. Let $j$ be such that $a_{ij} = 1$ and let $y[j']$ denote one bit of $y$, such that $a_{ij'} = 1$. It follows from Eq. (5) that the value of $m[i]$ is equal to the sum of at least two bits $y[j]$ and $y[j']$. Let $k^h$ be the correct key hypothesis and let $y[j']$ be our target bit. Let $\vec{v}$ be a vector consisting of the bits of $y$, for which $a_{ij} = 1$, excluding bit $y[j']$. Since row $i$ has $HW(i) = l$, vector $\vec{v}$ consists of $l - 1$ bits. This means that $\vec{v}$ can have up to $2^{l-1}$ possible values. Recall that each non-encoded T-box output value $y$ occurs with an equal probability of $1/256$ over the inputs of the T-box. Thus, all $2^{l-1}$ possible values of $\vec{v}$ occur with the same probability over the inputs of the T-box. The sum of the $l-1$ bits in $\vec{v}$ is equal to 0 or 1 with a probability of 50%, independently of the value of $y[j']$. Therefore, our target bit $y[j']$ is masked via $\sum_{j:a_{ij}=1, j \neq j'} y[j]$ and our calculations obtained with $\mathtt{Sel}(p_e, k^h, j')$ only match 50% of the time with the value of $m[i]$. Each set $A_b$ consists thus of an equal number of values $m[i] = 0$ and $m[i] = 1$ and the difference between the averages of both sets is equal to zero. □

One could be tempted to believe that using a matrix which does not have any identity row serves as a good countermeasure against the DCA. However, we could easily adapt the DCA attack such that it is also successful in the presence of a matrix without any identity row. In Step 2, we just need to define our selection function such that, after calculating an 8-bit long output state $z$, we calculate all possible linear combinations $LC$ of the bits in $z$. Thereby, in Step 3 we sort according to the result obtained for an $LC$. This means that we perform Steps 3 to 5 for each possible $LC$ ($2^8 = 256$ times per key guess). For at least one of those cases, we will obtain a difference of means curve with peak values equal to 1 for the correct key guess as our $LC$ will be equal to the $LC$ defined by row $i$ of matrix $A$. Our selection function calculates thus a value equal to the encoded value $m[i]$ and we obtain perfect correlations.

Note that Theorem 1 also applies in the presence of affine encodings. In case we add a 0 to a target bit, traces $\bar{A}_0$ and $\bar{A}_1$ do not change and in case we add a 1 the entries in $\bar{A}_0$ and $\bar{A}_1$ that relate to the target bit change to 1 minus their value. In both cases, the difference of means value does not change.

To illustrate how the effect of linear encodings is shown on complete white-box implementations, we now perform the DCA attack on our white-box implementation of AES which only makes use of linear encodings. This is a table based implementation which follows the design strategy proposed by Chow et al., but only uses linear encodings. We collect 200 software traces, which consist of the memory addresses accessed during the encryption process. We use our selection function $\mathtt{Sel}(p_e, k^h, j) = z[j]$. Figure 6 shows the difference of means trace obtained for the correct key guess.

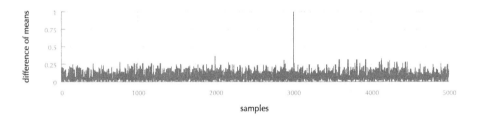

**Fig. 6.** DCA results for our white-box implementation with linear encodings

Figure 6 shows one peak reaching a value of 1 (see sample 3001). Since the peak reaches the value of 1, we can again say that our selection function is perfectly correlated with the targeted bit $z[j]$, even though the output $z$ was encoded using a linear transformation. Since our partition was done with our selection function calculating the output of the T-box, our results tell us that the matrix used to encode the T-box outputs contains at least one identity row.

## 4.2  Non-linear Encodings

Next, we consider the effect that non-linear encodings have on the outputs of a T-box. For this purpose, we randomly generate bijections, which map each output value $y$ of the T-box to a different value $f$ and thus obtain a non-linearly encoded T-box, which we call OT-box. Recall that a T-box is a bijective function. If we encode each possible output of a T-box $T$ with a randomly generated byte function $O$ and obtain the OT-box $OT$, then $OT$ does not leak any information about $T$. Namely, given $OT$, *any* other T-box $T'$ could be a candidate for constructing the same OT-box $OT$, since there always exists a corresponding function $O'$ which could give us $OT'$ such that $OT' = OT$. Chow et al. refer to this property as *local security* [10]. Based on this property, we could expect resistance against the DCA attack for a non-linearly encoded T-box. For practical implementations, unfortunately, using an 8-to-8 bit encoding for each key dependent look-up table is not realistic in terms of code size (see Sect. 4.1 of [19] for more details). Therefore, non-linear *nibble encodings* are typically used to encode the outputs of a T-box. The output of a T-box is 8-bits long and each half of the output is encoded by a different 4-to-4 bit transformation and both results are concatenated. Figure 7 displays the behaviour of an OT-box constructed using two nibble encodings.

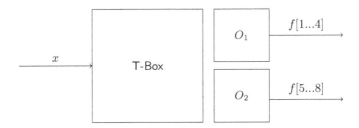

**Fig. 7.** Non-linear encodings of the T-Box outputs

Encoding the outputs of a T-box via non-linear nibble encodings does not hide correlations between the secret key of the T-box and its output bits as proved in the theorem below. When collecting the traces of an OT-box to perform a DCA using the correct key hypothesis, each (encoded) nibble value is returned a total of 16 times. Thereby, all encoded nibbles that have the same value are always grouped under the same set $A_b$ in Step 3. Therefore, we always obtain a difference of means curve which consists of only 5 possible correlation values.

**Theorem 2.** *Given an OT-box which makes use of nibble encodings, the difference of means curve obtained for the correct key hypothesis $k^h$ consists only of values equal to 0, 0.25, 0.5, 0.75 or 1.*

*Proof.* We first prove that the mean value of the set $A_0$ is always a fraction of 8 when we sort the sets according to the correct key hypothesis. The same applies for the set $A_1$ and the proof is analogous. For all $1 \leq j \leq 8$ let $y_d[j]$ be the $j$th bit of the output $y$ of a T-box, where $d \in \{1, 2\}$ refers to the nibble of $y$ where bit $j$ is located. Let $k^h$ be the correct key hypothesis. With our selection function $\mathtt{Sel}(p_e, k^h, j)$ we calculate a total of 128 nibble values $y_d$, for which $y_d[j] = 0$.

As there exist only 8 possible nibble values $y_d$ for which $y_d[j] = 0$ holds, we obtain each value $y_d$ a total of 16 times. Each time we obtain a value $y_d$, we group its corresponding encoded value $f_d$ under the set $A_0$. Recall that an OT-box uses one bijective function to encode each nibble $y_d$. Thus, when we calculate the mean trace $\bar{A}_0$ and focus on its region corresponding to $f_d$, we do the following:

$$\bar{A}_0[f_d] = \frac{16 f_d}{128} + \cdots + \frac{16 f_d'}{128} = \frac{f_d}{8} + \cdots + \frac{f_d'}{8},$$

with $f_d \neq f_d'$. We now prove that the difference between the means of sets $A_0$ and $A_1$ is always equal to the values 0, 0.25, 0.5, 0.75 or 1. Let $f_d[j]$ be one bit of an encoded nibble $f_d$.

- If $f_d[j] = 0$ is true for all nibbles in set $A_0$, then this implies that $f_d[j] = 1$ is true for all nibbles in set $A_1$, that is $\bar{A}_0[j] = \frac{8}{8}$ and $\bar{A}_1[j] = \frac{0}{8}$. The difference between the means of both sets is thus $\Delta[j] = |\frac{0}{8} - \frac{8}{8}| = |0 - 1| = 1$.
- If $f_d[j] = 1$ is true for 1 nibble in set $A_0$, then $f_d[j] = 1$ is true for 7 nibbles in set $A_1$, that is, the difference between both means is $\Delta[j] = |\frac{1}{8} - \frac{7}{8}| = |\frac{6}{8}| = 0.75$.
- If $f_d[j] = 1$ is true for 2 nibbles in set $A_0$, then $f_d[j] = 1$ is true for 6 nibbles in set $A_1$, that is, the difference between both means is $\Delta[j] = |\frac{2}{8} - \frac{6}{8}| = |\frac{4}{8}| = 0.5$.
- If $f_d[j] = 1$ is true for 3 nibbles in set $A_0$, then $f_d[j] = 1$ is true for 5 nibbles in set $A_1$, that is, the difference between both means is $\Delta[j] = |\frac{3}{8} - \frac{5}{8}| = |\frac{2}{8}| = 0.25$.
- If $f_d[j] = 1$ is true for 4 nibbles in set $A_0$, then $f_d[j] = 1$ is true for 4 nibbles in set $A_1$, that is, the difference between both means is $\Delta[j] = |\frac{4}{8} - \frac{4}{8}| = |\frac{0}{8}| = 0$.

The remaining 4 cases follow analogously and thus, all difference of means traces consist of only the values 0, 0.25, 0.5, 0.75 or 1.  $\square$

A peak value of 0.5, 0.75 or 1 is high enough to ensure that its corresponding key candidate will be ranked as the correct one. We now argue that, when we use an incorrect key guess, nibbles with the same value may be grouped in different sets. If we partition according to an incorrect key hypothesis $k^h$, the value we calculate for $y_d[j]$ does not always match with what is calculated by the T-box and afterwards encoded by the non-linear function. It is not the case that for each nibble value $y_d$ for which $y_d[j] = 0$, we group its corresponding encoded value $f_d$ in the same set. Therefore, our sets $A_b$ consist of up to 16 different encoded nibbles, whereby each nibble value is repeated a different number of times. This applies for both sets $A_0$ and $A_1$ and therefore, both sets have similar mean values, such that the difference between both means is a value closer to zero.

To get practical results corresponding to Theorem 2, we now construct 10 000 different OT-boxes. Thereby, each OT-box is based on a different T-box, i.e. each one depends on a different key, and is encoded with a different pair of functions $O_1$ and $O_2$. We now perform the DCA attack on each OT-box. The DCA attack is successful on almost all of the 10 000 OT-boxes with the exception of three. In all cases, the difference of means curves obtained when using the correct key hypotheses return a highest peak value of 0.25, 0.5, 0.75 or 1. The three OT-boxes which cannot be successfully attacked return peak values of 0.25 for the correct key guess. For each of the three cases, the correct key guess is not ranked as the best key candidate because there exists at least one other key candidate with a peak value slightly higher or with the same value of 0.25. The table below summarizes how many OT-boxes return each peak value for the correct key hypotheses.

| Peak value for correct key | Nr. of OT-boxes |
|---|---|
| 1 | 55 |
| 0.75 | 2804 |
| 0.5 | 7107 |
| 0.25 | 34 |

We now perform the DCA attack on our table-based white-box implementation of AES which only makes use of non-linear nibble encodings. We collect 2000 software traces, which consist of the memory addresses accessed during the encryption process. Figure 8 shows the difference of means trace obtained when using the correct key byte with our selection function.

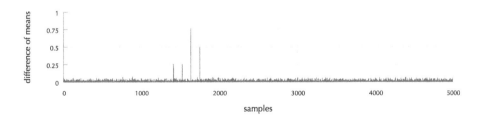

**Fig. 8.** DCA results for our white-box implementation with non-linear encodings

Figure 8 is flat with one peak with a value very close to 0.75 (see sample 1640), another peak with a value very close to 0.5 (see sample 1750). Additionally, the value of two peaks is very close to 0.25. This result corresponds to the difference of means results obtained with our OT-box examples and to Theorem 2. Based on the results shown in this section we can conclude that randomly generated nibble encodings do not effectively work as a countermeasure for hiding key dependent correlations when performing the difference of means test. Additionally, we learn one way to increase our success probabilities when performing the DCA: when ranking the key hypotheses, if no key candidate returns a peak value which really stands out (0.5 or higher), we could rank our key candidates according to the convergence of their peaks to the values 0.25 or 0. In the extended version of this paper, we describe this generalization of the DCA attack in more detail [1].

### 4.3   Combination of Linear and Non-linear Encodings

We now discuss shortly the effectiveness of the DCA when performed on white-box implementations that make use of both linear and non-linear encodings to protect their key-dependent look-up tables. For a more detailed description of the effect of this type of encodings, we refer the reader to the extended version of this paper [1]. The combination of both encodings is the approach proposed by Chow et al. in order to protect the content of the look-up tables from reverse engineering attempts. The output of each key-dependent look-up table, such as a T-box, is first encoded by a linear transformation and afterwards by the combination of two non-linear functions.

We now perform the DCA attack on the OpenWhiteBox challenge by Chow.[3] This AES implementation was designed based on the work described in [9,19]. We collect 2000 software traces which consist of values read *and* written to the stack during the first round. We define our selection function the same way as in Sect. 3, $\text{Sel}(p_e, k^h, j) = z[j]$. For the correct key byte 0x69 we obtain the difference of means trace shown in Fig. 9.

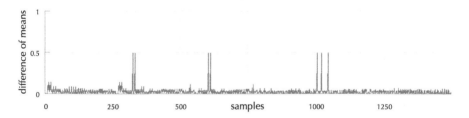

**Fig. 9.** Difference of means results for the OpenWhiteBox Challenge when using the correct key guess and targeting bit $z[2]$

Figure 9 shows a flat trace with 7 peaks reaching a value of almost 0.5 (see e.g. sample 327). Due to this trace, the key byte 0x69 is ranked as the best key candidate and the DCA attack is successful. The peak values shown in Fig. 9 correspond to those described in Theorem 2. We discuss these results shortly based on Theorems 1 and 2. From Theorem 1 we can conclude that, when considering an output bit of a T-box, it is important that all bits can still be transformed in all possible values (i.e., 0 and 1) for achieving resistance against the DCA. When a white-box uses the combination of linear and non-linear encodings and we target an output bit, we need to consider the output of a T-box as two individual

---

[3] https://github.com/OpenWhiteBox/AES/tree/master/constructions/chow.

nibbles. Thereby, it is important that each nibble can be transformed into each possible value in $GF(2^4)$. If that is the case, we can avoid correlation values such as those mentioned in Theorem 2 caused by the use of non-linear nibble encodings.

## 5  Conclusions

As automated attacks on white-box implementations become more popular, it is important to understand the experimental success of the original DCA attack in order to aim for resistance against such attacks. Internal encodings as suggested by Chow et al. do not effectively hide information regarding the outputs of a key dependent look-up table. Therefore, the use of such encodings makes a white-box implementation very vulnerable against DCA. In this work we focused on analysing these types of encodings due to their popularity amongst the white-box community and hope that our results motivate the further research on efficient alternatives for internal encodings in white-box cryptographic designs.

**Acknowledgments.** The authors would like to thank the anonymous referee for his/her helpful comments. The authors would like to acknowledge the contribution of the COST Action IC1306. Chris Brzuska is grateful to NXP for supporting his chair for IT Security Analysis.

## References

1. Alpirez Bock, E., Brzuska, C., Michiels, W., Treff, A.: On the ineffectiveness of internal encodings - revisiting the DCA attack on white-box cryptography (2018). https://eprint.iacr.org/2018/301
2. Banik, S., Bogdanov, A., Isobe, T., Jepsen, M.: Analysis of software countermeasures for whitebox encryption. IACR Trans. Symmetric Cryptol. **2017**(1), 307–328 (2017)
3. Barak, B., Goldreich, O., Impagliazzo, R., Rudich, S., Sahai, A., Vadhan, S., Yang, K.: On the (im)possibility of obfuscating programs. In: Kilian, J. (ed.) CRYPTO 2001. LNCS, vol. 2139, pp. 1–18. Springer, Heidelberg (2001). https://doi.org/10.1007/3-540-44647-8_1
4. Billet, O., Gilbert, H., Ech-Chatbi, C.: Cryptanalysis of a white box AES implementation. In: Handschuh, H., Hasan, M.A. (eds.) SAC 2004. LNCS, vol. 3357, pp. 227–240. Springer, Heidelberg (2004). https://doi.org/10.1007/978-3-540-30564-4_16
5. Bogdanov, A., Isobe, T., Tischhauser, E.: Towards practical whitebox cryptography: optimizing efficiency and space hardness. In: Cheon, J.H., Takagi, T. (eds.) ASIACRYPT 2016. LNCS, vol. 10031, pp. 126–158. Springer, Heidelberg (2016). https://doi.org/10.1007/978-3-662-53887-6_5
6. Bos, J.W., Hubain, C., Michiels, W., Teuwen, P.: Differential computation analysis: hiding your white-box designs is not enough. In: Gierlichs, B., Poschmann, A.Y. (eds.) CHES 2016. LNCS, vol. 9813, pp. 215–236. Springer, Heidelberg (2016). https://doi.org/10.1007/978-3-662-53140-2_11

7. Bringer, J., Chabanne, H., Dottax, E.: White box cryptography: another attempt. Cryptology ePrint Archive, Report 2006/468 (2006). http://eprint.iacr.org/2006/468

8. Bédrune, J.-B.: Hack.lu 2009 reverse challenge 1 (2009). https://2017.hack.lu/

9. Chow, S., Eisen, P., Johnson, H., Van Oorschot, P.C.: White-box cryptography and an AES implementation. In: Nyberg, K., Heys, H. (eds.) SAC 2002. LNCS, vol. 2595, pp. 250–270. Springer, Heidelberg (2003). https://doi.org/10.1007/3-540-36492-7_17

10. Chow, S., Eisen, P., Johnson, H., van Oorschot, P.C.: A white-box DES implementation for DRM applications. In: Feigenbaum, J. (ed.) DRM 2002. LNCS, vol. 2696, pp. 1–15. Springer, Heidelberg (2003). https://doi.org/10.1007/978-3-540-44993-5_1

11. Karroumi, M.: Protecting white-box AES with dual ciphers. In: Rhee, K.-H., Nyang, D.H. (eds.) ICISC 2010. LNCS, vol. 6829, pp. 278–291. Springer, Heidelberg (2011). https://doi.org/10.1007/978-3-642-24209-0_19

12. Kocher, P., Jaffe, J., Jun, B., Rohatgi, P.: Introduction to differential power analysis. J. Cryptogr. Eng. **1**, 5–27 (2011)

13. Kocher, P., Jaffe, J., Jun, B.: Differential power analysis. In: Wiener, M. (ed.) CRYPTO 1999. LNCS, vol. 1666, pp. 388–397. Springer, Heidelberg (1999). https://doi.org/10.1007/3-540-48405-1_25

14. Lepoint, T., Rivain, M., De Mulder, Y., Roelse, P., Preneel, B.: Two attacks on a white-box AES implementation. In: Lange, T., Lauter, K., Lisoněk, P. (eds.) SAC 2013. LNCS, vol. 8282, pp. 265–285. Springer, Heidelberg (2014). https://doi.org/10.1007/978-3-662-43414-7_14

15. Mastercard Mobile Payment SDK: Security guide for MP SDK v1.0.6. White paper (2017). https://developer.mastercard.com/media/32/b3/b6a8b4134e50bfe53590c128085e/mastercard-mobile-payment-sdk-security-guide-v2.0.pdf

16. De Mulder, Y., Roelse, P., Preneel, B.: Cryptanalysis of the Xiao – Lai white-box AES implementation. In: Knudsen, L.R., Wu, H. (eds.) SAC 2012. LNCS, vol. 7707, pp. 34–49. Springer, Heidelberg (2013). https://doi.org/10.1007/978-3-642-35999-6_3

17. De Mulder, Y., Wyseur, B., Preneel, B.: Cryptanalysis of a perturbated white-box AES implementation. In: Gong, G., Gupta, K.C. (eds.) INDOCRYPT 2010. LNCS, vol. 6498, pp. 292–310. Springer, Heidelberg (2010). https://doi.org/10.1007/978-3-642-17401-8_21

18. Messerges, T.S., Dabbish, E.A., Sloan, R.H.: Investigations of power analysis attacks on smartcards. In: Proceedings of the USENIX Workshop on Smartcard Technology, WOST 1999, Berkeley, CA, USA, p. 17. USENIX Association (1999)

19. Muir, J.A.: A tutorial on white-box AES (2013). https://eprint.iacr.org/2013/104.pdf

20. Sanfelix, E., de Haas, J., Mune, C.: Unboxing the white-box: practical attacks against obfuscated ciphers. In: Presentation at BlackHat Europe 2015 (2015). https://www.blackhat.com/eu-15/briefings.html

21. Sasdrich, P., Moradi, A., Güneysu, T.: White-box cryptography in the gray box. In: Peyrin, T. (ed.) FSE 2016. LNCS, vol. 9783, pp. 185–203. Springer, Heidelberg (2016). https://doi.org/10.1007/978-3-662-52993-5_10

# Continuously Non-malleable Codes
# with Split-State Refresh

Antonio Faonio[1]([✉]), Jesper Buus Nielsen[2], Mark Simkin[2],
and Daniele Venturi[3]

[1] IMDEA Software Institute, Madrid, Spain
antonio.faonio@imdea.org
[2] Aarhus University, Aarhus, Denmark
[3] Sapienza University of Rome, Rome, Italy

**Abstract.** Non-malleable codes for the split-state model allow to encode a message into two parts, such that arbitrary independent tampering on each part, and subsequent decoding of the corresponding modified codeword, yields either the same as the original message, or a completely unrelated value. Continuously non-malleable codes further allow to tolerate an unbounded (polynomial) number of tampering attempts, until a decoding error happens. The drawback is that, after an error happens, the system must self-destruct and stop working, otherwise generic attacks become possible.

In this paper we propose a solution to this limitation, by leveraging a split-state refreshing procedure. Namely, whenever a decoding error happens, the two parts of an encoding can be locally refreshed (i.e., without any interaction), which allows to avoid the self-destruct mechanism. An additional feature of our security model is that it captures directly security against continual leakage attacks. We give an abstract framework for building such codes in the common reference string model, and provide a concrete instantiation based on the external Diffie-Hellman assumption.

Finally, we explore applications in which our notion turns out to be essential. The first application is a signature scheme tolerating an arbitrary polynomial number of split-state tampering attempts, without requiring a self-destruct capability, and in a model where refreshing of the memory happens only after an invalid output is produced. This circumvents an impossibility result from a recent work by Fuijisaki and Xagawa (Asiacrypt 2016). The second application is a compiler for tamper-resilient RAM programs. In comparison to other tamper-resilient compilers, ours has several advantages, among which the fact that, for the first time, it does not rely on the self-destruct feature.

**Keywords:** Non-malleable codes · Tamper-resilient cryptography

# 1 Introduction

Tampering attacks are subtle attacks that undermine the security of cryptographic implementations by exploiting physical phenomena that allow to modify the underlying secrets. Indeed, a long line of works (see, e.g., [3,4,16,18])

© Springer International Publishing AG, part of Springer Nature 2018
B. Preneel and F. Vercauteren (Eds.): ACNS 2018, LNCS 10892, pp. 121–139, 2018.
https://doi.org/10.1007/978-3-319-93387-0_7

has established that black-box interaction with a tampered implementation can potentially expose the entire content of the secret memory. Given this state of affairs, protecting cryptographic schemes against tampering attacks has become an important goal for modern cryptographers.

An elegant solution to the threat of tampering attacks against the memory comes from the notion of non-malleable codes (NMCs), put forward by Dziembowski et al. [10]. Intuitively, a non-malleable encoding (Encode, Decode) allows to encode a value $M$ into a codeword $C \leftarrow_\$ \mathsf{Encode}(M)$, with the guarantee that a modified codeword $\widetilde{C} = f(C)$ w.r.t. a tampering function $f \in \mathcal{F}$, when decoded, yields either $M$ itself, or a completely unrelated value. An important parameter for characterizing the security guarantee offered by NMCs is the class of modifications $\mathcal{F}$ that are supported by the scheme. Since non-malleability is impossible to obtain for arbitrary (albeit efficient) modifications,[1] research on NMCs has focused on constructing such schemes in somewhat restricted, yet interesting, models. One such model that has been the focus of intensive research (see, e.g., [1,2,12,17]) is the split-state model, where the codeword $C$ consists of two parts $(C_0, C_1)$ that can be modified independently (yet arbitrarily). This setting is also the focus of this paper.

Unfortunately, standard NMCs protect only against a single tampering attack,[2] To overcome this limitation, Faust *et al.* [12] introduced *continuously* non-malleable codes (CNMCs for short), where the attacker can tamper for an unbounded (polynomial) number of times with the codeword, until a decoding error happens which triggers the self-destruction of the device. As argued in [12], the self-destruct capability is necessary, as each decoding error might be used to signal one bit of information about the target codeword.

Another desirable feature of non-malleable codes is their ability to additionally tolerate leakage attacks, by which the adversary can obtain partial information on the codeword while performing a tampering attack. Note that in the split-state model this means that the adversary can leak independently from the two parts $C_0$ and $C_1$. All previous constructions of leakage-resilient NMCs either achieve security in the so-called bounded-leakage model [1,12,17], where the total amount of leakage (from each part) is upper-bounded by a value $\ell$ that is a parameter of the scheme, or only satisfy non-continuous non-malleability [11].

**Our Contributions.** We introduce a new form of CNMCs (dubbed R-CNMCs) that include a split-state algorithm for refreshing a valid codeword. The refresh procedure is invoked either after a decoding error happens, or in order to amplify resilience to leakage, and takes place *directly* on the memory and without the

---

[1] As it can be seen by considering the tampering function that first decodes the codeword, flips one bit of the message, and then encodes the result.

[2] When using NMCs to obtain security against memory tampering, one can still obtain security against continuous attacks by enforcing a re-encoding of the secret key after each invocation; however, this comes with several disadvantages [11], among which the fact that the encoding process is considerably more complex than the decoding process.

need of a central unit. Our new model has a number of attractive features, which we emphasize below.

- It captures security in the so-called noisy-leakage model, where between each refresh the adversary can leak an arbitrary (yet independent) amount of information on the two parts $C_0, C_1$, as long as the leakage does not reveal (information-theoretically) more than $\ell$ bits of information. Importantly, this restriction is well-known to better capture realistic leakage attacks.
- It avoids the need for the self-destruct capability in some applications. Besides mitigating simple denial-of-service attacks, this feature is useful in situations where a device (storing an encoding of the secret state) is not in the hands of the adversary (e.g., because it has been infected by a malware), as it still allows to (non-interactively) refresh the secret state and continue to safely use the device in the wild.

Our first contribution is an abstract framework for constructing R-CNMCs, which we are able to instantiate under the external Diffie-Hellman assumption. This constitutes the first NMC that achieves at the same time continuous non-malleability and security under continual noisy leakage, in the split-state model (assuming an untamperable common reference string).

Next, we explore applications of R-CNMCs. As second contribution, we show how to construct a split-state[3] signature scheme resilient to continuous (non-persistent) tampering and leakage attacks, without relying on the self-destruct capability, and where the memory content is refreshed in case a decoding error is triggered. Interestingly, Fujisaki and Xagawa [13] recently showed that such a notion is impossible to achieve for standard (i.e., non split-state) signature schemes, even if the self-destruct capability is available; hence, our approach can be interpreted as a possible way to circumvent the impossibility result in [13].

Our third contribution consists of two generic compilers for protecting random access machine (RAM) computations against tampering attacks. Here, we build on the important work of Dachman-Soled *et al.* [7], who showed how to compile any RAM to be resilient to continual tampering and leakage attacks, by relying both on an update and a self-destruct mechanism. We refer the reader to Sect. 5 for further details on our RAM compilers. Below, we highlight the main technical ideas behind our code construction.

**Code Construction.** The starting point of our code construction is the recent work of Faonio and Nielsen [11]. The scheme built in [11] follows a template that originates in the work of Liu and Lysyanskaya [17], in which the left side of the encoding stores the secret key $sk$ of a PKE scheme, whereas the right side of the encoding stores a ciphertext $c$, encrypting the encoded message $M$, plus a non-interactive zero-knowledge (NIZK) argument that proves knowledge of the secret key under the label $c$; the PKE scheme is chosen to be a continual-leakage resilient storage friendly PKE (CLRS friendly PKE for short) scheme

---

[3] This means that the signing key is made of two shares that are stored in two separate parts of the memory, and need to be combined upon signing.

(see Dodis *et al.* [9]), whereas the NIZK is chosen to be a malleable NIZK argument of knowledge (see Chase *et al.* [5]). Such a code was shown to admit a split-state refresh procedure, and, at the same time, to achieve *bounded-time* non-malleability.

The NM code of [11] does not satisfy security against continuous attacks. In fact, an attacker can create two valid codewords $(C_0, C_1)$ and $(C_0, C_1')$ such that $\mathsf{Decode}(C_0, C_1) \neq \mathsf{Decode}(C_0, C_1')$. Given this, the adversary can tamper the left side to $C_0$ and the right side to either $C_1$ or $C_1'$ according to the bits of the right side of the target encoding. In a non-persistent model, the adversary can leak all the bits of $C_1$ without activating the self-destruct mechanism. More in general, for any R-CNMC it should be hard to find two valid codewords $(C_0, C_1)$ and $(C_0, C_1')$ such that $\mathsf{Decode}(C_0, C_1) \neq \mathsf{Decode}(C_0, C_1')$. This property, which we call "message uniqueness", was originally defined in [12].[4]

Going back to the described code construction, an attacker can sample a secret key $sk$ and create two ciphertexts, $c_0$ for $M$ and $c'$ for $M'$, where $M \neq M'$, together with the corresponding honestly computed NIZKs, and thus break message uniqueness. We fix this issue by further binding the right and the left side of an encoding. To do so, while still be able to refresh the two parts independently, we keep untouched the structure of the right side of the codeword, but we change the message that it carries. Specifically, the ciphertext $c$ in our code encrypts the message $M$ concatenated with the randomness $r$ for a commitment $\gamma$ that is stored in the left side of the codeword together with the secret key for the PKE scheme. Observe that "message uniqueness" is now guaranteed by the binding property of the commitment scheme. Our construction additionally includes another NIZK for proving knowledge of the committed value under the label $sk$, in order to further link together the left and the right side of the codeword.

*Proof Strategy.* Although our construction shares similarities with previous work, our proof techniques diverge significantly from the ones in [11,12]. The main trick of [12] is to show that given one half of the codeword it is possible to fully simulate the view of the adversary in the tampering experiment, until a decoding error happens. To catch when a decoding error happens, [12] carries on two independent simulators in an interleaved fashion; as they prove, a decoding error happens exactly when the outputs of the two simulations diverge. The main obstacle they faced is how to succinctly compute the index where the two simulations diverge so that they can reduce to the security of the inner leakage-resilient scheme storage (see Daví *et al.* [8]) they rely on. To solve this, [12] employs an elegant dichotomic search-by-hash strategy over the partial views produced by the two simulators. At this point the experiment can terminate,

---

[4] Faust *et al.* also consider "codeword uniqueness", where the fact that $\mathsf{Decode}(C_0, C_1) \neq \mathsf{Decode}(C_0, C_1')$ is not required. However, this flavor of uniqueness only allows to rule-out so-called *super* continuous non-malleability, where one asks that not only the decoded value, but the entire modified codeword, be independent of the message. It is easy to see that no R-CNMC can satisfy "codeword uniqueness", as for instance $C_1'$ could be obtained as a valid refresh of $C_1$.

and thanks to a specific property of the leakage-resilient storage scheme, the simulator can "extract" the view.

Unfortunately, we cannot generalize the above proof strategy to multiple rounds. In fact, the specific property of the leakage-resilient storage scheme they make use of is inherently one shot. Specifically, the property allows the adversary to get an half of the leakage-resilient codeword. However, to allow this the adversary must lose leakage oracle access to the other half of the codeword. In our case, we would need to repeat the above trick again and again, after a decoding error and a subsequent refresh of the target encoding happens; however, once we ask for an entire half of the codeword, even if we refreshed the codeword, we cannot regain access to the leakage oracles[5]. We give a solution to this problem by relying on a simple information-theoretic observation.

Let $(X_0, X_1)$ be two random variables, and consider a process that interleaves the computation of a sequence of leakage functions $g^1, g^2, g^3, \ldots$ from $X_0$ and from $X_1$. The process continues until, for some index $i \in \mathbb{N}$, we have that $g^i(X_0) \neq g^i(X_1)$. We claim that $\bar{g}^i(X_0) := g^1(X_0), g^2(X_0), \cdots, g^{i-1}(X_0)$ do not reveal more information about $X_0$ than what $X_1$ and the index $i$ already reveal. To see this, consider $\widetilde{\mathbb{H}}_\infty(X_0 \mid \bar{g}^i(X_0))$ to be the average conditional min-entropy of $X_0$, which is, roughly speaking, the amount (in average) of the uncertainty of $X_0$ given $\bar{g}^i(X_0)$ as side information. Now, since $\bar{g}^i(X_0)$ and $\bar{g}^i(X_1)$ are exactly the same random variables we can derive[6]:

$$\widetilde{\mathbb{H}}_\infty(X_0 \mid \bar{g}^i(X_0)) = \widetilde{\mathbb{H}}_\infty(X_0 \mid \bar{g}^i(X_1)) \geq \widetilde{\mathbb{H}}_\infty(X_0 \mid X_1, \ i).$$

The above observation implies that the size of the view of the adversary, although much larger than the leakage bound, does reveal only little information.

We can already give a different proof of security for the scheme in [12] where the reduction to the inner-product leakage-resilient storage loses only a factor $O(\kappa)$ in the leakage bound (instead of $O(\kappa \log \kappa)$). Briefly, the idea is to carries on two independent simulators in an interleaved fashion (as in [12]) and, at each invocation, outputting first the hashes[7] of the simulated tampered codeword, then, if the hashes match, leak the full simulated tampered codeword avoiding, in this way, the dichotomic search-by-hash strategy. The information-theoretic observation above guarantees that only the last hashes (which will be different) reveals information. The latter implies that the amount of leakage is bounded by $O(\kappa)$.

## 2   Preliminaries and Building Blocks

We introduce the cryptographic primitives on which we build. For space reasons, standard notation and formal definitions are deferred to the full version of the paper.

---

[5] In particular, this property does not hold for a CLRS friendly PKE scheme.

[6] In the last equation, we also use that the output of a function is at most as informative as the input.

[7] By collision resistance of the hash function, if the two hashes match then the simulated tampered codewords are the same for both the simulators.

*Oracle Machines.* Given a pair of strings $X = (X_0, X_1) \in (\{0,1\}^*)^2$ define the oracle $\mathcal{O}_\infty(X)$ to be the *split-state leakage oracle* that takes as input tuples of the form $(\beta, g)$, where $\beta \in \{0,1\}$ is an index and $g$ is a function described as a circuit, and outputs $g(X_\beta)$. An adversary A with oracle access to $\mathcal{O}_\infty(X)$ is called $\ell$-*valid*, for some $\ell \in \mathbb{N}$, if for all $\beta \in \{0,1\}$ the concatenation of the leakage functions sent by A is an $\ell$-leaky function of $X_\beta$ (i.e., the total amount of leakage does not reduce the entropy of $X_\beta$ by too much).

Given two PPT interactive algorithms A and B we write $(y_\mathsf{A}; y_\mathsf{B}) \leftarrow (\mathsf{A}(x_\mathsf{A}) \leftrightarrows \mathsf{B}(x_\mathsf{B}))$ to denote the execution of algorithm A (with input $x_\mathsf{A}$) and algorithm B (with input $x_\mathsf{B}$). The string $y_\mathsf{A}$ (resp. $y_\mathsf{B}$) is the output of A (resp. B) at the end of such interaction. In particular, we write $\mathsf{A} \leftrightarrows \mathcal{O}_\infty(X)$ to denote A having oracle access to the leakage oracle with input $X$. Moreover, we write $\mathsf{A} \leftrightarrows \mathsf{B}, \mathsf{C}$ to denote A interacting in an interleaved fashion both with B and with C.

*Non-interactive Zero-Knowledge.* Let $\mathcal{R} \subseteq \{0,1\}^* \times \{0,1\}^*$ be an NP-relation; the language associated with $\mathcal{R}$ is $\mathcal{L}_\mathcal{R} := \{x : \exists w \text{ s.t. } (x, w) \in \mathcal{R}\}$. We typically assume that given a pair $(x, w)$ it is possible to efficiently verify whether $(x, w) \in \mathcal{R}$ or not. Roughly, a non-interactive argument (NIA) for an NP-relation $\mathcal{R}$ allows to create non-interactive proofs for statements $x \in \mathcal{L}$, when additionally given a valid witness $w$ corresponding to $x$. More formally, a NIA $\mathcal{NIA} :=$ (CRSGen, Prove, Ver) for $\mathcal{R}$, with label space $\Lambda$, is a tuple of PPT algorithms specified as follows (1) The (randomized) initialization algorithm CRSGen takes as input the security parameter $1^\kappa$, and creates a common reference string (CRS) $\omega \in \{0,1\}^*$; (2) The (randomized) prover algorithm Prove takes as input the CRS $\omega$, a label $\lambda \in \Lambda$, and a pair $(x, w)$ such that $(x, w) \in \mathcal{R}$, and produces a proof $\pi \leftarrow_\$ \mathsf{Prove}^\lambda(\omega, x, w)$; (3) The (deterministic) verifier algorithm Ver takes as input the CRS $\omega$, a label $\lambda \in \Lambda$, and a pair $(x, \pi)$, and outputs a decision bit $\mathsf{Ver}^\lambda(\omega, x, \pi)$.

Completeness means that for all CRSs $\omega$ output by $\mathsf{CRSGen}(1^\kappa)$, for all labels $\lambda \in \Lambda$, and for all pairs $(x, w) \in \mathcal{R}$, we have that $\mathsf{Ver}^\lambda(\omega, x, \mathsf{Prove}^\lambda(\omega, x, w)) = 1$ with all but a negligible probability. As for security, we require the following properties.

- **Adaptive multi-theorem zero-knowledge:** Honestly computed proofs do not reveal anything beyond the validity of the statement, and, as such, can be simulated given only the statement itself.
- **$\Phi$-Malleable label simulation extractability:** Our construction will be based on a so-called label-malleable NIA, parametrized by a set of label transformations $\Phi$, where for any $\phi \in \Phi$, the co-domain of $\phi$ is a subset of $\Lambda$. For such NIAs, given a proof $\pi$ under some label $\lambda \in \Lambda$, one can efficiently generate new proofs $\pi'$ for the same statement under a different label $\phi(\lambda)$, for any $\phi \in \Phi$ (without knowing a witness); this is formalized via an additional (randomized) label-derivation algorithm LEval, which takes as input the CRS $\omega$, a transformation $\phi \in \Phi$, a label $\lambda \in \Lambda$, and a pair $(x, \pi)$, and outputs a new proof $\pi'$. The property we need intuitively says that a NIA satisfies knowledge soundness, except that labels are malleable w.r.t. $\Phi$. More in details,

there exists a knowledge extractor K that for any adversary which can query polynomially many simulated proofs of false statements and then it produces a tuple $(x, \lambda, \pi)$ where $\pi$ is a valid NIZK proof for $(x, \lambda)$ can extract either (1) the witness for $x$ or (2) a transformation $\phi \in \Lambda$ which maps $\phi(\lambda') = \lambda$ and $(x, \lambda')$ was precedently queried by the adversary.

– **Label derivation privacy:** It is hard to distinguish a fresh proof for some statement $x$ (with witness $w$) under label $\lambda$, from a proof re-randomized using algorithm LEval w.r.t. some function $\phi \in \Phi$; moreover, the latter should hold even if $(x, w, \lambda, \phi)$ are chosen adversarially (possibly depending on the CRS).

*Public-Key Encryption.* A public-key encryption (PKE) scheme is a tuple of algorithms $\mathcal{PKE} = (\mathsf{Setup}, \mathsf{KGen}, \mathsf{Enc}, \mathsf{Dec})$ with the usual syntax. We will require two additional algorithms, the first one to re-randomize a given ciphertext, and the second one for re-randomizing the secret key (without changing the corresponding public key). More formally: The (randomized) algorithm UpdateC takes as input a ciphertext $c$, and outputs a new ciphertext $c'$; The (randomized) algorithm UpdateS takes as input a secret key $sk$, and outputs a new secret key $sk'$.

As for security, we require the following properties.

– **CLRS friendly PKE security:** This property is essentially a strengthening of semantic security, where the adversary can additionally observe noisy independent leakages from $S_0 = sk$ and $S_1 = c$ ($c$ is the challenge ciphertext).
– **Ciphertext-update privacy:** The distributions of fresh and updated ciphertexts are the same.
– **Secret-key-update privacy:** The distributions of fresh and updated keys are the same.

Additionally, we make use of a (non-interactive) commitment scheme $\mathcal{COM} = (\mathsf{CRSGen}, \mathsf{Commit})$ with statistical hiding and computationally binding and of an authenticated encryption scheme $\mathcal{SKE} := (\mathsf{KGen}, \mathsf{Enc}, \mathsf{Dec})$. This notions are standard therefore we defer the definitions to the full version of the paper.

# 3   Non-malleability with Refresh

A coding scheme in the CRS model is a tuple of polynomial-time algorithms $\mathcal{CS} = (\mathsf{Init}, \mathsf{Encode}, \mathsf{Decode})$ with the following syntax: (1) The (randomized) initialization algorithm Init takes as input the security parameter $1^\kappa$, and outputs a CRS $\omega \in \{0, 1\}^*$; (2) The (randomized) encoding algorithm Encode takes as input the CRS $\omega$ and a message $M \in \mathcal{M}$, and outputs a codeword $C \in \mathcal{C}$; (3) The (deterministic) decoding algorithm Decode takes as input the CRS $\omega$ and a codeword $C \in \mathcal{C}$, and outputs a value $M \in \mathcal{M} \cup \{\bot\}$ (where $\bot$ denotes an invalid codeword). A coding scheme is correct if for all $\omega$ output by $\mathsf{Init}(1^\kappa)$, and any $M \in \mathcal{M}$, we have $\mathbb{P}[\mathsf{Decode}(\omega, \mathsf{Encode}(\omega, M)) = M] = 1$, where the probability is taken over the randomness of the encoding algorithm.

We consider coding schemes with an efficient *refreshing algorithm*. Specifically, for a coding scheme $\mathcal{CS}$ we assume there exists a randomized algorithm Rfrsh that, upon input the CRS $\omega$ and a codeword $C \in \mathcal{C}$, outputs a codeword $C' \in \mathcal{C}$. For correctness we require that for all $\omega$ output by $\mathsf{Init}(1^\kappa)$, we have $\mathbb{P}[\mathsf{Decode}(\omega, \mathsf{Rfrsh}(\omega, C)) = \mathsf{Decode}(\omega, C)] = 1$, where the probability is over the randomness used by the encoding and refreshing algorithms.

*Split-State Model.* In this paper we are interested in coding schemes in the split-state model, where a codeword consists of two parts that can be refreshed independently and without the need of any interaction. More precisely, given a codeword $C := (C_0, C_1)$, the refresh procedure $\mathsf{Rfrsh}(\omega, (\beta, C_\beta))$, for $\beta \in \{0, 1\}$, takes as input either the left or the right part of the codeword, and updates it. Sometimes we also write $\mathsf{Rfrsh}(\omega, C)$ as a shorthand for the algorithm that independently executes $\mathsf{Rfrsh}(\omega, (0, C_0))$ and $\mathsf{Rfrsh}(\omega, (1, C_1))$.

Correctness here means that for all $\omega$ output by $\mathsf{Init}(1^\kappa)$, for all $C \in \mathcal{C}$, and for any $\beta \in \{0, 1\}$, if we let $C' = (C_0', C_1')$ be such that $C_\beta' \leftarrow_{\$} \mathsf{Rfrsh}(\omega, (\beta, C_\beta))$ and $C_{1-\beta}' = C_{1-\beta}$, then $\mathbb{P}[\mathsf{Decode}(\omega, C') = \mathsf{Decode}(\omega, C)] = 1$.

### 3.1   The Definition

We give the security definition for continuously non-malleable codes with split-state refresh (R-CNMCs for short). Our notion compares two experiments, which we denote by **Tamper** and **SimTamper** (cf. Fig. 1). Intuitively, in the experiment **Tamper** we consider an adversary continuously tampering with, and leaking from, a target encoding $C = (C_0, C_1)$ of a message $M \in \mathcal{M}$ (the message can be chosen adaptively, depending on the CRS). For each tampering attempt $(f_0, f_1)$, the adversary gets to see the output $\widetilde{M}$ of the decoding corresponding to the modified codeword $\widetilde{C} = (f_0(C_0), f_1(C_1))$. Tampering is non-persistent, meaning that each tampering function is applied to the original codeword $C$, until, eventually, a decoding error happens; at this point the adversary is allowed to make one extra tampering query $(f_0^*, f_1^*)$, and, if the corresponding tampered codeword $\widetilde{C}^*$ is valid and is not an encoding of the original message $M$, it receives a refresh of $\widetilde{C}^*$ (otherwise the adversary receives $M$ or $\bot$). After that, the target encoding $C$ is refreshed, and the adversary can start tampering with, and leaking from, the refreshed codeword. (Below we explain why this extra feature is useful.)

In the experiment **SimTamper**, we consider a simulator $\mathsf{S} = (\mathsf{S}_0, \mathsf{S}_1)$, where $\mathsf{S}_0$ outputs a simulated CRS, while $\mathsf{S}_1$'s goal is to simulate the view of the adversary in the real experiment; the simulator $\mathsf{S}_1$, in faking a tampering query $(f_0, f_1)$, is allowed to output a special value $\diamond$, signaling that (it believes) the adversary did not change the encoded message, in which case the experiment replaces $\diamond$ with $M$; We stress that the simulator $\mathsf{S}$ is stateful; in particular algorithms $\mathsf{S}_0, \mathsf{S}_1$ implicitly share a state.

---

**Tamper$_{CS,A}(\kappa, \ell, q)$:**

$i \leftarrow 0$; err, stop $\leftarrow 0$
$\omega \leftarrow \mathsf{Init}(1^\kappa)$
$(M, s_0) \leftarrow \mathsf{A}_0(\omega)$
$C_0 := (C_0^0, C_1^0) \leftarrow_\$ \mathsf{Encode}(\omega, M)$
For all $i \in [0, q]$:
$\quad s_{i+1} \leftarrow (\mathsf{A}_1(s_i) \leftrightarrows \mathcal{O}_\infty(C_i), \mathcal{O}_{\mathsf{tamp}}(C_i))$
$\quad C_{i+1} \leftarrow_\$ \mathsf{Rfrsh}(\omega, C_i)$
$\quad i \leftarrow i + 1$; err, stop $\leftarrow 0$
Return $\mathsf{A}_2(s_q)$.

**SimTamper$_{A,S}(\kappa, \ell, q)$:**

$i \leftarrow 0$
$\omega \leftarrow_\$ \mathsf{S}_0(1^\kappa)$
$(M, s_0) \leftarrow \mathsf{A}_0(\omega)$
For all $i \in [0, q]$:
$\quad s_{i+1} \leftarrow (\mathsf{A}_1(s_i) \leftrightarrows \mathsf{S}_1(\mathsf{Leak}, \cdot), \mathcal{O}^{\mathsf{S}_1}_{\mathsf{sim\_tamp}}(\cdot))$
$\quad i \leftarrow i + 1$
Return $\mathsf{A}_2(s_q)$.

Oracle $\mathcal{O}_{\mathsf{tamp}}(C_i, (f_0, f_1))$:

Upon $(\mathsf{Tamp}, f_0, f_1)$:
$\quad \widetilde{M} = \mathsf{Decode}(\omega, f_0(C_0^i), f_1(C_1^i))$
$\quad$ If $(\widetilde{M} = \bot)$ then err $\leftarrow 1$
$\quad$ If $((\mathsf{err} = 1) \vee (\mathsf{stop} = 1))$
$\quad\quad \widetilde{M} \leftarrow \bot$
$\quad$ Return $\widetilde{M}$
Upon $(\mathsf{Final}, f_0^*, f_1^*)$:
$\quad$ stop $\leftarrow 1$
$\quad \widetilde{C}^* = (f_0^*(C_0^i), f_1^*(C_1^i))$
$\quad \widetilde{M}^* = \mathsf{Decode}(\omega, \widetilde{C}^*)$
$\quad$ If $(\widetilde{M}^* \in \{\bot, M\})$ then $\widetilde{C}' \leftarrow \widetilde{M}^*$
$\quad$ Else $\widetilde{C}' \leftarrow_\$ \mathsf{Rfrsh}(\omega, \widetilde{C}^*)$
$\quad$ Return $\widetilde{C}'$.

Oracle $\mathcal{O}^{\mathsf{S}_1}_{\mathsf{sim\_tamp}}(\cdot)$:

Upon $(\mathsf{Tamp}, f_0, f_1)$:
$\quad \widetilde{M} \leftarrow_\$ \mathsf{S}_1(\mathsf{Tamp}, f_0, f_1)$
$\quad$ If $(\widetilde{M} = \diamond)$ then $\widetilde{M} \leftarrow M$
$\quad$ Return $\widetilde{M}$
Upon $(\mathsf{Final}, f_0^*, f_1^*)$:
$\quad \widetilde{C}' \leftarrow_\$ \mathsf{S}_1(\mathsf{Final}, f_0^*, f_1^*)$
$\quad$ If $((\widetilde{C}' = \diamond) \vee (\mathsf{Decode}(\omega, \widetilde{C}') = M))$
$\quad\quad \widetilde{C}' \leftarrow M$
$\quad$ Return $\widetilde{C}'$

---

**Fig. 1.** Experiments defining continuously non-malleable codes with split-state refresh.

**Definition 1 (Continuous non-malleability with split-state refresh).**
*For $\kappa \in \mathbb{N}$, let $\ell = \ell(\kappa)$ be a parameter. We say that a coding scheme $\mathcal{CS}$ is an $\ell$-leakage-resilient and continuously non-malleable code with split-state refresh (R-CNMC for short) if for all adversaries $\mathsf{A} := (\mathsf{A}_0, \mathsf{A}_1, \mathsf{A}_2)$, where $\mathsf{A}_0$ and $\mathsf{A}_2$ are PPT algorithms and $\mathsf{A}_1$ is an $\ell$-valid deterministic polynomial-time algorithm, there exists a PPT simulator $\mathsf{S} = (\mathsf{S}_0, \mathsf{S}_1)$ and a negligible function $\nu : \mathbb{N} \to [0, 1]$ such that, for any polynomial $q(\kappa)$, the following holds:*

$$\left| \mathbb{P}\left[ \mathbf{Tamper}_{CS,A}(\kappa, \ell, q) = 1 \right] - \mathbb{P}\left[ \mathbf{SimTamper}_{A,S}(\kappa, \ell, q) = 1 \right] \right| \leq \nu(\kappa),$$

*where the experiments $\mathbf{Tamper}_{CS,A}(\kappa, \ell, q)$ and $\mathbf{SimTamper}_{A,S}(\kappa, \ell, q)$ are defined in Fig. 1.*

We give some intuitions on why the extra tampering query is meaningful. First, observe that for (standard) continuously non-malleable codes, the notion of non-persistent tampering is strictly stronger than the notion of persistent tampering. This is because the effect of any sequence of persistent tampering functions

$f^1, f^2, f^3, \cdots$ can be simulated in the non-persistent setting by the sequence of tampering functions $f^1, f^2 \circ f^1, f^3 \circ f_2 \circ f_1, \cdots$. For R-CNMCs, instead, we cannot simulate persistent tampering, as in such a setting the refreshing procedure can be invoked on invalid codewords. The extra tampering query in our definition allows for some flavor of persistent tampering, in that the adversary gets to see a refresh of the tampered codeword, as long as the codeword is valid[8]. Unfortunately, it is impossible to further generalize our definition to handle the refreshing of invalid codewords.[9]

As additional remark, we notice that in the **Tamper** security game the adversary does not have a "direct" access to a refresh oracle (namely, an oracle that, under request of the adversary, would refresh the codeword). We skim this extra detail to not overload the (already heavy) notation. However, the choice comes without loss of any generality. In fact, we can simulate an adversary that makes explicit call to a refreshing oracle by an adversary stop, and return its state (this would indeed trigger a refresh in the experiment), and restart again in the next iteration of the **Tamper** experiment.

# 4   Code Construction

Let $\mathcal{PKE} = (\mathsf{Setup}, \mathsf{KGen}, \mathsf{Enc}, \mathsf{Dec}, \mathsf{UpdateC}, \mathsf{UpdateS})$ be a CLRS friendly PKE scheme, with secret-key space $\mathcal{SK}$. We assume there exists an efficient polynomial-time function $\mathsf{PK}$ that maps a secret key to the corresponding public key. Let $\mathcal{COM} = (\mathsf{CRSGen}, \mathsf{Commit})$ be a commitment scheme in the CRS model. Consider the following NP-relations, parametrized by the PKE and the commitment scheme, respectively:

$$\mathcal{R}_0 := \{(pk, sk) : \; pk = \mathsf{PK}(sk), sk \in \mathcal{SK}\},$$
$$\mathcal{R}_1 := \{((\omega, \gamma), (M, r)) : \; \gamma = \mathsf{Commit}(\omega, M; r)\}.$$

Let $\Phi_0$ and $\Phi_1$ be two sets of label transformations defined below:

$$\Phi_0 := \{\phi : \; \exists pk, sk \text{ s.t. } (\forall m, r) \; \mathsf{Dec}(sk, \phi(\mathsf{Enc}(pk, m; r))) = m, pk = \mathsf{PK}(sk)\}$$
$$\Phi_1 := \{\phi : \; (\forall sk) \; \mathsf{PK}(sk) = \mathsf{PK}(\phi(sk))\}.$$

---

[8] A sequence of persistent tampering functions $f^1, f^2, \cdots, f^q$ followed by a refreshing (on tampered codeword) can be simulated in the non-persistent setting by the sequence of concatenation of tampering functions (as described above) and then invoking a final tampering query with tampering function set to $f^1 \circ f^2 \circ \ldots \circ f^q$.

[9] This can be seen by the following attack. Consider an attacker that computes offline a valid codeword $(\overline{C}_0, \overline{C}_1)$, and then makes two extra tampering queries (in two subsequent rounds, say, $i$ and $i+1$) such that the first query overwrites $(C_0^i, C_1^i)$ with $(C_0^i, \overline{C}_1)$, and the second query overwrites $(C_0^{i+1}, C_1^{i+1})$ with $(\overline{C}_0, C_1^{i+1})$; by combining the refreshed codewords obtained as output, the adversary gets a refresh of the original codeword, which cannot be simulated in the ideal experiment (recall that the refresh algorithm updates the two shares independently).

Notice that $\mathcal{R}_0, \mathcal{R}_1, \Phi_0$ and $\Phi_1$ are implicitly parametrized by the public parameters $\rho \in \{0,1\}^*$ of the PKE scheme. Finally, let $\mathcal{U}^0$ and $\mathcal{U}^1$ be the following sets of label transformations:

$$\mathcal{U}^0 := \{\mathsf{UpdateC}(\,\cdot\,;r_u) : \ r_u \in \{0,1\}^*\}$$
$$\mathcal{U}^1 := \{\mathsf{UpdateS}(\,\cdot\,;r_u) : \ r_u \in \{0,1\}^*\}.$$

It is easy to verify that $\mathcal{U}_\beta \subseteq \Phi_\beta$, for $\beta \in \{0,1\}$. In fact, for $\beta = 0$, by the correctness of the PKE scheme, there exists $sk$ such that $\mathbb{P}[\mathsf{Dec}(sk, \mathsf{UpdateC}(\mathsf{Enc}(pk,m))) = m] = 1$ and $pk = \mathsf{PK}(sk)$; similarly, for $\beta = 1$, again by correctness of the PKE scheme, for any $sk' \leftarrow\!\!\text{\tiny\$}\ \mathsf{UpdateS}(pk, sk)$ we have that $\mathsf{PK}(sk) = \mathsf{PK}(sk')$.

*Scheme Description.* Let $\mathcal{NIA}_0 = (\mathsf{CRSGen}_0, \mathsf{Prove}_0, \mathsf{Vrfy}_0, \mathsf{LEval}_0)$ and $\mathcal{NIA}_1 = (\mathsf{CRSGen}_1, \mathsf{Prove}_1, \mathsf{Vrfy}_1, \mathsf{LEval}_1)$ be NIAs for the above defined relations $\mathcal{R}_0$ and $\mathcal{R}_1$. Our code $\mathcal{CS} = (\mathsf{Init}, \mathsf{Encode}, \mathsf{Decode})$ works as follows.

- $\mathsf{Init}(1^\kappa)$: For $\beta \in \{0,1\}$, sample $\omega_\beta \leftarrow\!\!\text{\tiny\$}\ \mathsf{CRSGen}_\beta(1^\kappa)$, $\omega \leftarrow \mathsf{CRSGen}(1^\kappa)$, and $\rho \leftarrow \mathsf{Setup}(1^\kappa)$. Return $\overline{\omega} = (\omega_0, \omega_1, \omega, \rho)$.
- $\mathsf{Encode}(\overline{\omega}, M)$: Parse $\overline{\omega} := (\omega_0, \omega_1, \omega, \rho)$, sample $(pk, sk) \leftarrow\!\!\text{\tiny\$}\ \mathsf{KGen}(\rho)$, and $r \leftarrow\!\!\text{\tiny\$}\ \{0,1\}^*$. Compute $c \leftarrow\!\!\text{\tiny\$}\ \mathsf{Enc}(pk, M||r)$, $\gamma = \mathsf{Commit}(\omega, M; r)$, and $\pi_0 \leftarrow\!\!\text{\tiny\$}\ \mathsf{Prove}_0^c(\omega_0, pk, sk)$, and $\pi_1 \leftarrow\!\!\text{\tiny\$}\ \mathsf{Prove}_1^{sk}(\omega_1, (\omega, \gamma), (M, r))$. Set $C_0 := (pk, c, \pi_0)$ and $C_1 := (sk, \gamma, \pi_1)$, and return $C := (C_0, C_1)$.
- $\mathsf{Decode}(\overline{\omega}, C)$: Parse $\overline{\omega} := (\omega_0, \omega_1, \omega, \rho)$ and $C := (C_0, C_1)$, where $C_1 := (sk, \gamma, \pi_1)$ and $C_0 = (pk, c, \pi_0)$. Compute $M||r := \mathsf{Dec}(sk, c)$, and if the following conditions hold return $M$ else return $\perp$:
    I. Left check: $\mathsf{Ver}_0^c(\omega_0, pk, \pi_0) = 1$.
    II. Right check: $\mathsf{Ver}_1^{sk}(\omega_1, (\omega, \gamma), \pi_1) = 1$.
    III. Cross check: $\mathsf{Commit}(\omega, M; r) = \gamma$.
- $\mathsf{Rfrsh}(\overline{\omega}, (\beta, C_\beta))$: Parse $\overline{\omega} := (\omega_0, \omega_1, \omega, \rho), C_0 := (pk, c, \pi_0)$, and $C_1 = (sk, \gamma, \pi_1)$. Hence:
    • For $\beta = 0$, pick $r_{\mathsf{upd}}^0 \leftarrow\!\!\text{\tiny\$}\ \{0,1\}^*$, let $c' := \mathsf{UpdateC}(c; r_{\mathsf{upd}}^0)$ and $\pi_0' \leftarrow\!\!\text{\tiny\$}\ \mathsf{LEval}_0(\omega_0, \mathsf{UpdateC}(\cdot; r_{\mathsf{upd}}^0), (pk, c, \pi_0))$, and return $C_0' := (pk, c', \pi_0')$.
    • For $\beta = 1$, pick $r_{\mathsf{upd}}^1 \leftarrow\!\!\text{\tiny\$}\ \{0,1\}^*$, let $sk' := \mathsf{UpdateS}(sk; r_{\mathsf{upd}}^1)$, and $\pi_1' \leftarrow\!\!\text{\tiny\$}\ \mathsf{LEval}_1(\omega_1, \mathsf{UpdateS}(\cdot; r_{\mathsf{upd}}^1), ((\gamma, \omega), sk, \pi_1))$, and return $C_1' := (\gamma, sk', \pi_1')$.

We show the following result. In the full version we provide a concrete instantiation of our code, based on fairly standard computational assumptions.

**Theorem 1.** *Let $\mathcal{PKE}$ be a PKE scheme with message space $\mathcal{M}_{\mathrm{pke}}$ and public-key space $\mathcal{PK}$, let $\mathcal{COM}$ be a commitment scheme with message space $\mathcal{M}$, and let $\mathcal{NIA}_0$ (resp. $\mathcal{NIA}_1$) be a NIA w.r.t. the relations $\mathcal{R}_0$ (resp. $\mathcal{R}_1$). Define $\mu(\kappa) := \log|\mathcal{M}|, \mu_{\mathrm{pke}}(\kappa) := \log|\mathcal{M}_{\mathrm{pke}}|$, and $\delta(\kappa) := \log|\mathcal{PK}|$.*

*For any $\ell \in \mathbb{N}$, assuming that $\mathcal{PKE}$ is an $(\ell + 3\mu + 2\kappa + \max\{\delta, \mu_{\mathrm{pke}}\})$-noisy CLRS-friendly PKE scheme, that $\mathcal{COM}$ is a non-interactive statistically binding commitment scheme, and that $\mathcal{NIA}_0$ (resp. $\mathcal{NIA}_1$) satisfies adaptive multi-theorem zero-knowledge, $\Phi_0$-malleable (resp. $\Phi_1$-malleable) label simulation* *extractability, and label derivation privacy, then the coding scheme $\mathcal{CS}$ described above is an $\ell$-leakage-resilient continuously non-malleable code with split-state refresh.*

*Proof Intuition.* The proof of the above theorem is quite involved. We provide some highlights here. We defer the formal proof to the full version of the paper. Consider a simulator $(S_0, S_1)$, where $S_0$ simulates a fake CRS $\overline{\omega} = (\omega_0, \omega_1, \omega, \rho)$ by additionally sampling the corresponding zero-knowledge and extraction trapdoors for the NIAs (which are then passed to $S_1$). At the core of our simulation strategy are two algorithms $T^0$ and $T^1$, whose goal is essentially to emulate the outcome of the real tampering experiment, with the important difference that $T^0$ is only given the left part of a (simulated) codeword $C_0$ and the left tampering function $f_0$, whereas $T^1$ is given $(C_1, f_1)$.

The simulator $S_1$ then works as follows. Initially, it samples a fresh encoding $(C_0, C_1)$ of $0^\mu$. More in details, the fresh encoding comes from the (computationally close) distribution where the proofs $\pi_0$ and $\pi_1$ are simulated proofs. At the beginning of each round, it runs a simulated refresh procedure in which the ciphertext $c$ is updated via UpdateC (and the simulated proof $\pi_0$ is re-computed using fresh randomness), and similarly the secret key $sk$ is updated via UpdateS (and the simulated proof $\pi_1$ is re-computed using fresh randomness). Hence, for each tampering query $(f_0, f_1)$, the simulator $S_1$ runs $\widetilde{M}_0 := T^0(C_0, f_0)$, $\widetilde{M}_1 := T^1(C_1, f_1)$, and it returns $\widetilde{M}_0$ as long as $\bot \neq \widetilde{M}_0 = \widetilde{M}_1 \neq \bot$ (and $\bot$ otherwise). The extra tampering query $(f_0^*, f_1^*)$ is simulated similarly, based on the outcome of the tampering simulators $(T^0, T^1)$. We briefly describe the tampering simulators $T^0$ and $T^1$:

- Algorithm $T^0$ lets $f_0(C_0) := (\widetilde{pk}, \widetilde{c}, \widetilde{\pi}_0)$. If the proof $\widetilde{\pi}_0$ does not verify, it returns $\bot$. Else, if $(\widetilde{pk}, \widetilde{c}, \widetilde{\pi}_0) = (pk, c, \pi_0)$, it returns $\diamond$. Else, it extracts the proof $\widetilde{\pi}_0$, this leads to two possible outcomes[10]:
  - (a) The extractor outputs a secret key $\widehat{sk}$ which is used to decrypt $\widetilde{c}$, and the tampering simulator returns the corresponding plaintext $\widetilde{M}$.
  - (b) The extractor outputs a transformation $\phi$ which maps the label of the simulated proof $\pi_0$, namely the encryption of $0^\mu$, to $\widetilde{c}$. In this case the tampering function $f_0$ has modified the original ciphertext $c$ to the mauled ciphertext $\widetilde{c}$ which is an encryption of the same message, so we can safely output $\diamond$.
- Algorithm $T^1$ lets $f_1(C_1) := (\widetilde{\gamma}, \widetilde{sk}, \widetilde{\pi}_1)$. If the proof $\widetilde{\pi}_1$ does not verify, it returns $\bot$. Else, if $(\widetilde{\gamma}, \widetilde{sk}, \widetilde{\pi}_1) = (\gamma, sk, \pi_1)$, it returns $\diamond$. Else, it extracts the proof $\widetilde{\pi}_1$, again, this leads to two possible outcomes:
  - (a) the extractor outputs the committed message $\widetilde{M}$ (along with the randomness of the commitment), so the tampering simulator can simply return $\widetilde{M}$.

---

[10] The above description is simplified, in that extraction could potentially fail, however, this happens only with negligible probability when the proof verifies correctly.

(b) The extractor outputs a transformation $\phi$ which maps the label of the simulated proof $\pi_1$, namely the original secret key $sk$, to the mauled secret key $\widetilde{sk}$. In this case, the mauled proof $\widetilde{\pi^1}$ must be a valid proof which instance is the original commitment, so, again, we can safely output $\diamond$.

To show that the above simulator indeed works, we use a hybrid argument where we incrementally change the distribution of the ideal tampering experiment until we reach the distribution of the real tampering experiment. Each step introduces a negligible error, thanks to the security properties of the underlying building blocks. Perhaps, the most interesting step is the one where we switch the ciphertext $c$ from an encryption of zero to an encryption of the real message (to which we always have to append the randomness of the commitment); in order to show that this change is unnoticeable, we rely on the CLRS storage friendly security of the PKE scheme. In particular, this step of the proof is based on the following observations:

- The reduction can perfectly emulate the distribution of the CRS $\overline{\omega}$, and of all the elements $(pk, \pi_0, \gamma, \pi_1)$, except for $(c, sk)$. However, by outputting $(0^\mu \| r, M \| r)$ as challenge plaintexts—where $r \in \{0,1\}^*$ is the randomness for the commitment—the reduction can obtain independent leakages from $C_0$ and $C_1$ with the right distribution.
- Refresh of codewords can also be emulated by exploiting the fact that the reduction is allowed to update the challenge secret key and ciphertext.
- The reduction can answer tampering queries from the adversary by using $\mathsf{T}^0$ and $\mathsf{T}^1$ as leakage functions. The main obstacle is to ensure that $\mathsf{T}^0$ and $\mathsf{T}^1$ are $\ell$-leaky, where $\ell \in \mathbb{N}$ is the leakage bound tolerated by the PKE scheme. Luckily, by using carefully the information-theoretic argument explained in the Introduction, we can show that this is indeed the case, which allows simulation to go through. In particular, between each refresh the reduction needs to interleave the executions of $\mathsf{T}^0$ and $\mathsf{T}^1$ until their outputs diverge. So let $q$ be the number of tampering queries that the simulator performs until triggering a decoding error. The leakage that the reduction needs to perform during this stage (namely, between two consecutive refresh) is $\mathsf{T}^0(C_0, f_0^0), \mathsf{T}^1(C_1, f_1^0), \dots, \mathsf{T}^0(C_0, f_0^q), \mathsf{T}^1(C_1, f_1^q)$ where $(f_0^0, f_1^0), \dots, (f_0^q, f_1^q)$ is the list of tampering functions applied. By the information-theoretic argument:

$$\widetilde{\mathbb{H}}_\infty(C_0 \mid \mathsf{T}^0(C_0, f_0^0), \dots, \mathsf{T}^0(C_0, f_0^q))$$
$$= \widetilde{\mathbb{H}}_\infty(C_0 \mid \mathsf{T}^1(C_1, f_1^0), \dots, \mathsf{T}^0(C_1, f_1^{q-1}), \mathsf{T}^0(C_0, f_0^q)).$$

In fact, the outputs of the $\mathsf{T}^0(C_0, f_0^i)$ and $\mathsf{T}^0(C_0, f_0^i)$ is exactly the same when $i < q$. Moreover:

$$\widetilde{\mathbb{H}}_\infty(C_0 \mid \mathsf{T}^1(C_1, f_1^0), \dots, \mathsf{T}^0(C_1, f_1^{q-1}), \mathsf{T}^0(C_0, f_0^q))$$
$$\geq \widetilde{\mathbb{H}}_\infty(C_0 \mid C_1, q, \mathsf{T}^0(C_0, f_0^q)).$$

Because the output of a function cannot be more informative than the inputs of the function itself. Lastly, we can notice that $C_1$ gives little information about $C_0$ and that $q$ and $T^0(C_0, f_0^q)$ can decrease the min-entropy of $C_0$ of at most their size which is $O(\kappa)$. The reduction, therefore, is a valid adversary against for the CLRS storage-friendly security experiment of the PKE.

*Remark 1 (On the refresh procedures).* The notion of split-state refresh does not imply that a refreshed codeword is indistinguishable from a freshly sampled one. And indeed the codeword of our CNMC-R is not, as the public key *pk* (resp. the commitment $\gamma$) do not change after the refresh algorithms are executed. However, the latter is not required for our proof, as the only thing that matters is that the information about the target codeword that the adversary gathers before a refresh takes place will not be useful after the refresh. Put differently, the adversary could potentially leak the entire values *pk* and $\gamma$, but this information would not be useful for breaking the security of the scheme.

## 5    Applications

**Tamper-Resilient Signatures Without Self-destruct.** Consider a signature scheme $\mathcal{SS}$. We would like to protect $\mathcal{SS}$ against tampering attacks with the memory, storing the signing key *sk*. As observed originally by Gennaro *et al.* [14], however, without further assumptions, this goal is too ambitious. Their attack can be circumvented by either assuming the self-destruct capability, or a key-update mechanism.

Interestingly, Fujisaki and Xagawa [13] observed that, whenever the key-update mechanism is invoked only after an invalid output is generated, the goal of constructing tamper-resilient signature is impossible, even assuming the self-destruct capability. The idea behind the attack is to generate two valid pairs of independent signing/verification keys, and thus to overwrite the original secret key with either of the two sampled signing keys in order to signal one bit of the original key. Note that such an attack never generates invalid signatures, thus rendering both the self-destruct capability and a key-update mechanism useless.

In the full version of the paper we show that it is possible to avoid self-destruct and obtain tamper-resilient signatures against arbitrary attacks in the split-state model.

**RAM Compilers.** Consider a RAM machine, where both the data and the program to be executed are stored in the random access memory. Such a RAM program is modeled as a tuple consisting of a CPU and its memory. At each clock cycle the CPU fetches a memory location and performs some computation. We focus on read-only RAM programs that do not change the content of the memory after the computation is performed. More in details, a read-only RAM program $\Lambda = (\Pi, \mathcal{D})$ consists of a next instruction function $\Pi$, a state state stored in a non-tamperable but non-persistent register, and some database $\mathcal{D}$. The next instruction function $\Pi$ takes as input the current state state and input inp, and outputs an instruction I and a new state state$'$. The initial state is set to (start, $\star$).

A RAM compiler is a tuple of algorithms $\Sigma =$ (Setup, CompMem, CompNext). Algorithm Setup takes as input the security parameter $1^\kappa$, and outputs an untamperable CRS $\omega$. The memory compiler CompMem takes as input the CRS $\omega$, and a database $\mathcal{D}$, and outputs a database $\widehat{\mathcal{D}}$ along with an initial internal state state. The next instruction function $\Pi$ is compiled to $\widehat{\Pi}$ using CompNext and the CRS. To define security, we compare two experiments (cf. Fig. 2). The real experiment features an adversary A that is allowed, via the interface doNext, to execute RAM programs on chosen inputs *step-by-step*; upon input $x$, oracle doNext($x$) outputs the result of a single step of the computation, as well as the memory location that is accessed during that step. Additionally, adversary A can also apply tampering attacks that are parametrized by two families of functions $\mathcal{F}_{mem}$ and $\mathcal{F}_{bus}$, where: (1) Each function $f \in \mathcal{F}_{mem}$ is applied to the compiled memory. (2) Each function $f \in \mathcal{F}_{bus}$ is applied to the data in transit on the bus.

The ideal experiment features a simulator S that is allowed, via the interface Execute, to execute RAM programs on chosen inputs in one g;. Upon input $x$, oracle Execute($x$) outputs the result of the entire computation and the list of all the memory locations that were accessed during that computation. Briefly, a RAM compiler is tamper-resilient if for all possible logics $\Pi$, and all efficient adversaries A, there exists a simulator S such that the real and ideal experiment are computationally indistinguishable. A formal definition follows.

**Definition 2 (Tamper simulatability).** *A compiler $\Sigma =$ (Setup, CompMem, CompNext) is tamper simulatable w.r.t. $(\mathcal{F}_{bus}, \mathcal{F}_{mem})$ if for every next instruction function $\Pi$, and for every PPT adversary A, there exists a PPT simulator S and a negligible function $\nu : \mathbb{N} \to [0, 1]$ such that, for all PPT distinguishers D and any database $\mathcal{D}$, we have that:*

$$\left| \mathbb{P}\left[ \mathsf{D}(\mathbf{TamperExec}_{\mathsf{A},\Sigma,\Lambda}^{\mathcal{F}_{bus},\mathcal{F}_{mem}}(\kappa)) = 1 \right] - \mathbb{P}\left[ \mathsf{D}(\mathbf{IdealExec}_{\mathsf{S},\Lambda}(\kappa)) = 1 \right] \right| \leq \mathrm{negl}(\kappa)$$

*with $\Lambda := (\Pi, \mathcal{D})$, and where the experiments $\mathbf{TamperExec}_{\mathsf{A},\Sigma,\Lambda}^{\mathcal{F}_{bus},\mathcal{F}_{mem}}$ and $\mathbf{IdealExec}_{\mathsf{S},\Lambda}(\kappa)$ are defined in Fig. 2.*

We propose two compilers for protecting arbitrary RAM computations against tampering attacks.

*First Compiler.* The first compiler achieves security in a model where only non-persistent tampering on the buses is allowed. The compiler encodes a random secret key $k$ for an authenticated encryption scheme using a R-CNMC; let $(K_0, K_1)$ be the corresponding codeword. Then, the compiler encrypts each data block in the original memory $\mathcal{D}$, along with its index, under the key $k$; let $\mathcal{E}$ be the encrypted memory. The encoded memory is made of two parts $\mathcal{D}_0 := (K_0, \mathcal{E})$ and $\mathcal{D}_1 := (K_1, \mathcal{E})$. When fetching the location $j$, the compiled RAM program first reads and decodes $(K_0, K_1)$, and stores $k$ in the untamperable register; then, it loads $\mathcal{E}[j]$ from both $\mathcal{D}_0$ and $\mathcal{D}_1$ and checks that, indeed, they are the same

Experiment **TamperExec**$_{\mathsf{A},\varSigma,\varLambda}^{\mathcal{F}_{\mathsf{bus}},\mathcal{F}_{\mathsf{mem}}}(k)$:

---

$\omega \leftarrow \mathsf{Setup}(1^\kappa)$;
Parse $\varLambda$ as $(\bar{\mathcal{D}}, \bar{\Pi})$; $\mathcal{Q} \leftarrow \emptyset$;
$\mathcal{D} \leftarrow \mathsf{CompMem}(\omega, \bar{\mathcal{D}})$, $\mathcal{D}' \leftarrow \mathcal{D}$;
$\Pi \leftarrow \mathsf{CompNext}(\omega, \bar{\Pi})$;
$b \leftarrow \big(\mathsf{A}(\omega) \leftrightarrows \mathsf{doNext}((\mathcal{D}', \Pi), \cdot), \mathcal{O}_{\mathsf{tamp}}(\cdot)\big)$;
Return $(b, \mathcal{Q})$.

Experiment **IdealExec**$_{\mathsf{S},\varLambda}(\kappa)$:

---

$\mathcal{Q} \leftarrow \emptyset$;
$b \leftarrow \big(\mathsf{S}(1^\kappa) \leftrightarrows \mathsf{Execute}(\varLambda, \cdot), \mathsf{Add}(\cdot)\big)$;
Return $(b, \mathcal{Q})$.

Oracle $\mathsf{Add}(x)$:

---

$\mathcal{Q} \leftarrow \mathcal{Q} \cup \{x\}$;

Oracle $\mathcal{O}_{\mathsf{tamp}}$:

---

Upon $(\mathtt{TampMem}, f)$:
    If $f \in \mathcal{F}_{\mathsf{mem}}$, then set $\mathcal{D} \leftarrow f(\mathcal{D})$.
Upon $(\mathtt{TampBus}, f)$:
    If $f \in \mathcal{F}_{\mathsf{bus}}$, then set $\mathcal{D}' \leftarrow f(\mathcal{D})$.

Oracle $\mathsf{doNext}((\mathcal{D}, \Pi), x)$:

---

If state $= (\mathsf{start}, \star)$
    inp $\leftarrow x$; $\mathcal{Q} \leftarrow \mathcal{Q} \cup \{x\}$
$(\mathsf{I}, \mathsf{state}') \leftarrow \Pi(\mathsf{state}, \mathsf{inp})$
If $\mathsf{I} = (\mathsf{read}, v)$
    inp $\leftarrow \mathcal{D}[v]$; state $:=$ state$'$
If $\mathsf{I} = (\mathsf{stop}, z)$, then state $\leftarrow (\mathsf{start}, \star)$
Else, state $:=$ state$'$
Output $\mathsf{I}$.

Oracle $\mathsf{Execute}((\mathcal{D}, \Pi), x)$:

---

state $\leftarrow (\mathsf{start}, \star)$, $\mathcal{I} \leftarrow \emptyset$;
repeat $\mathsf{I}' \leftarrow \mathsf{doNext}((\mathcal{D}, \Pi), x)$; $\mathcal{I} \leftarrow \mathcal{I} \| \mathsf{I}'$;
until $\mathsf{I}' = (\mathsf{stop}, v)$;
Output $\mathcal{I}$.

**Fig. 2.** Experiments defining security of a RAM compiler.

ciphertext, which is then decrypted.[11] If an error happens, the compiled RAM invokes the refresh mechanism.

The reason behind the redundant encoding of $\mathcal{E}$ can be explained using the information-theoretic observation described in the introduction of the paper. In fact, the mauled ciphertexts from $\mathcal{D}_0$ (resp. $\mathcal{D}_1$) can be arbitrary functions of the non-malleable encoding $K_0$ (resp. $K_1$). However, as long as the mauled ciphertexts from $\mathcal{D}_0$ are equal to the mauled ciphertexts from $\mathcal{D}_1$, the amount of information they carry about $K_0$ is bounded by the amount of information that $K_1$ reveals about $K_0$. If the two ciphertexts are not equal, some information about $K_0$ may be leaked, but in this case the codeword is refreshed and the leaked information becomes useless.

In the full version of the paper we prove the following theorem and give the details of the construction.

**Theorem 2 (Informal).** *Let $n, \kappa \in \mathbb{N}$ be parameters. Assume there exists a coding scheme that is $\mathrm{poly}(\kappa, \log n)$-leakage-resilient R-CNMC and assume there exists an authenticated encryption scheme with ciphertext space of length at least $\mathrm{poly}(\log n)$. Then there exists a tamper-resilient RAM compiler w.r.t. $(\mathcal{F}_{\mathsf{bus}}, \emptyset)$ for RAM programs with database of length $n$, where $\mathcal{F}_{\mathsf{bus}}$ is the family of split-state tampering functions.*

---

[11] The compiled RAM program additionally needs to check that the encrypted index is equal to $j$, in order to avoid shuffling attacks.

*Tamper-Resilient for Persistent Tampering.* The above compiler is not secure against adversaries that can tamper persistently with the memory. In fact, such attackers can "copy-paste" the value $K_0$ (resp. $K_1$) in a part of the memory $\mathcal{D}_0$ (resp. $\mathcal{D}_1$) that is not refreshed, and restore these values at a later point, bypassing the refreshing procedure.

To partially overcome this problem we assume that, once a decoding error is triggered, the system can switch in a *safe mode* where the communication between CPU and memory is tamper free. While in safe mode, the system will perform a consistency check. To minimize the dependency on the assumption we constraint the consistency check to be succinct, meaning that its complexity depends only on the security parameter and not on the size of the RAM program. Finally, if the consistency check passes, the refresh procedure will be executed otherwise the self-destruct is triggered. In the full version of the paper we prove the following theorem and give the details of the construction.

**Theorem 3 (Informal).** *Let $n, \kappa \in \mathbb{N}$ be parameters. Assume there exists a coding scheme that is $\mathrm{poly}(\kappa, \log n)$-leakage-resilient R-CNMC and assume there exists an authenticated encryption scheme with ciphertext space of length at least $\mathrm{poly}(\log n)$. Moreover, assume the system can switch in safe mode for $\mathrm{poly}(\kappa)$ number of operations and self destruct, then there exists a tamper-resilient RAM compiler w.r.t. $(\mathcal{F}_{\mathsf{bus}}, \mathcal{F}_{\mathsf{mem}})$ for RAM programs with database of length $n$, where both $\mathcal{F}_{\mathsf{bus}}$ and $\mathcal{F}_{\mathsf{mem}}$ are the family of split-state tampering functions.*

*The Compiler of* [7]. In order to better compare our RAM compilers with previous work, we first describe the compiler of Dachman-Soled *et al.* [7] in some details. The starting point is a RAM program $\Lambda = (\Pi, \mathcal{D})$ that is previously compiled using an Oblivious RAM [15], and later encoded using a (split-state) locally-updatable and locally-decodable non-malleable code (LULD-NMC)[12]. In particular, one first samples a random key $k$ for an authenticated encryption scheme, encrypts all the locations $\mathcal{D}[i]$ block by block, and finally computes a Merkle tree of the encrypted blocks. A non-malleable encoding $(K_0, K_1)$ of $k$ together with the root of the Merkle tree is computed and the resulting codeword is composed of $(K_0, K_1)$, the encrypted memory $\mathcal{D}'$, and the merkle tree $T$. Since the encoded memory $\mathcal{D}'$ is encrypted block-by-block, it is possible to locally decode it and update it using $\Omega(\log n)$ operations,[13] where $n$ is the number of blocks in $\mathcal{D}$.

The security model in [7] is a flavour of the standard 2-split-state model tampering model, where the adversary can choose tampering functions $f = (f_1, f_2)$. Tampering function $f_1$ is any tampering function supported by the underlying 2-split-state NMC that was used to compute $(K_0, K_1)$ and the function can depend on the encrypted memory blocks $\mathcal{D}'$, and the merkle tree $T$. Tampering function $f_2$ enables the adversary to tamper with the memory and the merkle tree, but the function *does not* depend on the codeword $(K_0, K_1)$.

---

[12] The compiler, more generally, can be instantiated with any kind of (standard) NMC, for concreteness we consider only the instantiation based on split-state NMC.

[13] In a subsequent work, Dachman-Soled et al. [6] showed that, in order to have security against "reset attacks", the overhead of $\Omega(\log n)$ is necessary.

*Comparison.* Finally, let us review the main differences between our RAM compilers and the one by Dachman-Soled *et al.* [7]. First, the compiler of [7] can handle very general RAM programs that can also write on the memory. Our compilers, instead, are specifically tuned for RAMs that make only read operations (recall that we want to avoid write-back operations); this feature allows us to exploit the non-interactive refresh procedure of the underlying R-CNMC. The read-only model is strictly weaker than the model that is considered in [7] and reset attacks cannot exist in our model. This enables us to avoid the use of a Merkle tree and obtain a construction similar to the one given in [7], thus reducing the overhead from $\Omega(\log n)$ to $O(1)$.

Second, the compiler of [7] only achieves security in a variant of the regular split-state model (as described above), whereas both our compilers are secure in the standard split-state model. On the downside, we require an untamperable CRS, which is not needed in [7].

Third, we do not aim to hide the access pattern of the RAM machine. Notice that the latter can be avoided using ORAMs (as done in [7]). However, we think of this as an orthogonal problem. In fact, in some cases, ORAMs could be, more efficiently, replaced by constant-time implementations, or by fixed-pattern ones (for example when hardening cryptographic primitives).

Lastly, our first compiler is the first RAM compiler that achieves security against continuous attacks without relying on the self-destruct capability. This feature allows us also to tolerate non-malicious hardware faults that may affect the data of the bus accidentally, while at the same time maintaining security against malicious tampering attacks. We notice that a similar property could be achieved in the scheme of [7] by applying a layer of error-correcting code over the non-malleable encoding. This allows to transparently correct the hardware faults as long as these faults are supported by the capability of the error correcting code and otherwise self destruct. On the other hand, our compiler cannot correct such hardware faults, but it can detect them (without any bound on their nature) and trigger a refresh before safely continuing the computations.

# References

1. Aggarwal, D., Dodis, Y., Kazana, T., Obremski, M.: Non-malleable reductions and applications. In: STOC, pp. 459–468 (2015)
2. Aggarwal, D., Dodis, Y., Lovett, S.: Non-malleable codes from additive combinatorics. In: STOC, pp. 774–783 (2014)
3. Biham, E., Shamir, A.: Differential fault analysis of secret key cryptosystems. In: Kaliski, B.S. (ed.) CRYPTO 1997. LNCS, vol. 1294, pp. 513–525. Springer, Heidelberg (1997). https://doi.org/10.1007/BFb0052259
4. Boneh, D., DeMillo, R.A., Lipton, R.J.: On the importance of checking cryptographic protocols for faults. In: Fumy, W. (ed.) EUROCRYPT 1997. LNCS, vol. 1233, pp. 37–51. Springer, Heidelberg (1997). https://doi.org/10.1007/3-540-69053-0_4

5. Chase, M., Kohlweiss, M., Lysyanskaya, A., Meiklejohn, S.: Malleable proof systems and applications. In: Pointcheval, D., Johansson, T. (eds.) EUROCRYPT 2012. LNCS, vol. 7237, pp. 281–300. Springer, Heidelberg (2012). https://doi.org/10.1007/978-3-642-29011-4_18

6. Dachman-Soled, D., Kulkarni, M., Shahverdi, A.: Tight upper and lower bounds for leakage-resilient, locally decodable and updatable non-malleable codes. In: Fehr, S. (ed.) PKC 2017. LNCS, vol. 10174, pp. 310–332. Springer, Heidelberg (2017). https://doi.org/10.1007/978-3-662-54365-8_13

7. Dachman-Soled, D., Liu, F.-H., Shi, E., Zhou, H.-S.: Locally decodable and updatable non-malleable codes and their applications. In: Dodis, Y., Nielsen, J.B. (eds.) TCC 2015. LNCS, vol. 9014, pp. 427–450. Springer, Heidelberg (2015). https://doi.org/10.1007/978-3-662-46494-6_18

8. Davì, F., Dziembowski, S., Venturi, D.: Leakage-resilient storage. In: Garay, J.A., De Prisco, R. (eds.) SCN 2010. LNCS, vol. 6280, pp. 121–137. Springer, Heidelberg (2010). https://doi.org/10.1007/978-3-642-15317-4_9

9. Dodis, Y., Lewko, A.B., Waters, B., Wichs, D.: Storing secrets on continually leaky devices. In: FOCS, pp. 688–697 (2011)

10. Dziembowski, S., Pietrzak, K., Wichs, D.: Non-malleable codes. In: Innovations in Computer Science, pp. 434–452 (2010)

11. Faonio, A., Nielsen, J.B.: Non-malleable codes with split-state refresh. In: Fehr, S. (ed.) PKC 2017. LNCS, vol. 10174, pp. 279–309. Springer, Heidelberg (2017). https://doi.org/10.1007/978-3-662-54365-8_12

12. Faust, S., Mukherjee, P., Nielsen, J.B., Venturi, D.: Continuous non-malleable codes. In: Lindell, Y. (ed.) TCC 2014. LNCS, vol. 8349, pp. 465–488. Springer, Heidelberg (2014). https://doi.org/10.1007/978-3-642-54242-8_20

13. Fujisaki, E., Xagawa, K.: Public-key cryptosystems resilient to continuous tampering and leakage of arbitrary functions. In: Cheon, J.H., Takagi, T. (eds.) ASIACRYPT 2016. LNCS, vol. 10031, pp. 908–938. Springer, Heidelberg (2016). https://doi.org/10.1007/978-3-662-53887-6_33

14. Gennaro, R., Lysyanskaya, A., Malkin, T., Micali, S., Rabin, T.: Algorithmic tamper-proof (ATP) security: theoretical foundations for security against hardware tampering. In: Naor, M. (ed.) TCC 2004. LNCS, vol. 2951, pp. 258–277. Springer, Heidelberg (2004). https://doi.org/10.1007/978-3-540-24638-1_15

15. Goldreich, O.: Towards a theory of software protection and simulation by oblivious RAMs. In: STOC (1987)

16. Govindavajhala, S., Appel, A.W.: Using memory errors to attack a virtual machine. In: IEEE Symposium on Security and Privacy, pp. 154–165 (2003)

17. Liu, F.-H., Lysyanskaya, A.: Tamper and leakage resilience in the split-state model. In: Safavi-Naini, R., Canetti, R. (eds.) CRYPTO 2012. LNCS, vol. 7417, pp. 517–532. Springer, Heidelberg (2012). https://doi.org/10.1007/978-3-642-32009-5_30

18. Otto, M.: Fault attacks and countermeasures. Ph.D. thesis, University of Paderborn, Germany (2006)

# Digital Signatures

# Efficient Unconditionally Secure Signatures Using Universal Hashing

Ryan Amiri[1], Aysajan Abidin[2(⊠)], Petros Wallden[3], and Erika Andersson[1]

[1] SUPA, Institute of Photonics and Quantum Sciences, Heriot-Watt University,
Edinburgh EH14 4AS, UK
{ra2,e.andersson}@hw.ac.uk
[2] imec-COSIC, KU Leuven, Leuven, Belgium
aysajan.abidin@esat.kuleuven.be
[3] LFCS, School of Informatics, University of Edinburgh, 10 Crichton Street,
Edinburgh EH8 9AB, UK
petros.wallden@ed.ac.uk

**Abstract.** Digital signatures are one of the most important cryptographic primitives. In this work we construct an information-theoretically secure signature scheme which, unlike prior schemes, enjoys a number of advantageous properties such as short signature length and high generation efficiency, to name two. In particular, we extend symmetric-key message authentication codes (MACs) based on universal hashing to make them transferable, a property absent from traditional MAC schemes. Our main results are summarised as follows.

- We construct an unconditionally secure signature scheme which, unlike prior schemes, does not rely on a trusted third party or anonymous channels.
- We prove information-theoretic security of our scheme against forging, repudiation, and non-transferability.
- We compare our scheme with existing both "classical" (not employing quantum mechanics) and quantum unconditionally secure signature schemes. The comparison shows that our new scheme, despite requiring fewer resources, is much more efficient than all previous schemes.
- Finally, although our scheme does not rely on trusted third parties, we discuss this, showing that having a trusted third party makes our scheme even more attractive.

**Keywords:** Digital signatures · Information-theoretic security
Transferable MAC · Universal hashing

## 1 Introduction

Digital signatures are one of the most widely used cryptographic primitives and are indispensable for information and communications security. Secure digital

© Springer International Publishing AG, part of Springer Nature 2018
B. Preneel and F. Vercauteren (Eds.): ACNS 2018, LNCS 10892, pp. 143–162, 2018.
https://doi.org/10.1007/978-3-319-93387-0_8

signature schemes offer authenticity and integrity, non-repudiation, and transferability of digital content. However, the public-key digital signature schemes that are currently in use, such as RSA [1], ElGamal DSA [2] and ECDSA [3], provide only computational security, and rely on unproven hardness assumptions in number theory. This implies that algorithmic breakthrough and/or the advancement in computing technologies may one day render such digital signature schemes totally insecure. Another emerging threat to the security of these schemes is from quantum computers, which can use Shor's algorithm [4] to efficiently solve the underlying "hard" problems and break all pre-quantum public-key cryptosystems. In response to this threat, the field of post-quantum cryptography is being developed. One can argue and ask whether quantum computers will ever be built. Large companies such as Google, Microsoft and IBM certainly seem to think it's possible, and are allocating significant resources to research in this area. Furthermore, the National Security Agency (NSA) in the USA is also taking the threat from quantum computers very seriously, and in August 2015, the NSA recommended a transition to post-quantum secure algorithms [5].

In post-quantum cryptography, there exist "quantum-safe" public-key cryptosystems which are not *yet* known to be vulnerable to quantum attacks. Such schemes range from the historical McEliece cryptosystem [6], which is based on error-correcting codes, to more recent ones based on hash functions, lattices and multivariate polynomials. The security of these "quantum-safe" alternatives is based upon (again unproven) hard problems, some of which have not yet stood the test of time[1]. We stress again that even if the underlying problems were proven to be hard to solve, the security of such schemes is still only computational, and relies on the adversary having bounded computational resources. If we want signature schemes with "everlasting" security or are unsure of the resources available to our adversary, computational security may not be sufficient.

An alternative to "quantum-safe" public key signature schemes are unconditionally secure signature (USS) schemes, where security does not rely on any unproven assumptions, nor on bounds placed on the adversary's computational resources. Instead, these schemes provide information-theoretic security. Such a high level of security, however, comes at a cost. So far, all USS schemes have been significantly less efficient than their quantum-safe competitors in terms of signature length, re-usability and key sizes. A more restrictive disadvantage however, is that all USS schemes use secret keys, rather than public keys.

USS schemes require a setup phase in which secret keys are distributed among participants before messages can be signed or verified. Therefore, they do not have the universal verifiability property inherent to standard public-key digital signature schemes. Due to this restriction, it is clear that USS schemes are not a suitable replacement for many core applications where digital signatures are used. Nevertheless, there may still be applications where USS schemes are useful for particularly important communications, for example in high-value banking

---

[1] In lattice-based cryptography [7] for example, it is not quite clear anymore whether all such protocols are truly quantum resistant [8,9].

transactions, when signing important legal documents, or securing sensitive government communications. Due to the requirement of distributing secret shared keys between participants, USS schemes should not be viewed as a standalone product. Instead, it should be viewed as a complement to existing QKD systems in fixed networks environments.

In this work, we propose a new USS scheme based on universal hashing. Compared to the previous USS schemes in the literature, our scheme enjoys a number of favourable properties such as short secret key lengths, short signature length, and high efficiency. Before we proceed, we first briefly survey the USS schemes which are already proposed in the literature. For a detailed overview, we refer the interested reader to [10] and the references therein.

## 1.1   Related Works

There are two lines of work on USS schemes: one on "classical" schemes (not employing quantum mechanics), and the other taking advantage of quantum-mechanical features. Although our scheme is entirely classical, it is similar to the quantum USS scheme proposed in Ref. [11].

**Classical USS Schemes.** The first attempt to construct an USS scheme was suggested by Chaum and Roijakkers [12], using authenticated broadcast channels, secret authenticated channels and also using untraceable sending protocols. Their scheme, however, only allows users to sign single-bit messages, and is therefore impractical. Moreover, the Chaum-Roijakkers scheme does not offer adequate transferability, which is crucial for a signature scheme, because the security is weakened as the message-signature pair is transferred among recipients. Pfitzmann and Waidner [13] also considered USS schemes (which they called pseudo-signatures) and constructed a scheme, somewhat related to ours, which could be used to generate information-theoretically secure Byzantine agreement. Their scheme built upon the protocol by Chaum and Roijakkers, but allowed longer messages to be signed and verified, though the scheme still required authenticated broadcast channels and untraceable sending protocols for implementation. Our scheme removes the requirement of authenticated broadcast channels by employing a method similar to secret sharing techniques [14].

Later, Hanaoka et al. [15] proposed an USS scheme relying on a trusted authority for key distribution, the existence of which allowed improvements both in efficiency and security over the scheme by Chaum and Roijakkers, at the cost of introducing this additional trust assumption. This scheme further improved all existing USS protocols by making the signature scheme re-usable. Nevertheless, the lengths of both the signature and the secret keys needed to generate signing/verification algorithms were still rather long, severely limiting its use in practice. A later variation of this scheme was proposed by Hanaoka et al. in [16]. This scheme sacrificed the re-usability of the previous scheme to achieve a reduction in the size of the secret keys needed to generate signing/verification algorithms by approximately a factor of 10.

Security notions of classical USS schemes are proposed and analysed in Shikata *et al.* [17] as well as Swanson and Stinson [18].

**Quantum USS Schemes.** There are also quantum USS schemes, first proposed by Gottesman and Chuang [19], in which security is derived from the laws of quantum physics. Lu and Feng [20] proposed a quantum USS scheme using quantum one-way functions, though it required a trusted authority (which they called an arbiter) to resolve disputes. Quantum USS schemes were first experimentally demonstrated by Clarke *et al.* [21]. While these early quantum schemes require long-term quantum memories (which are highly impractical to realise, effectively rendering these schemes unusable), the more recently proposed schemes do not [11,22,23]. Quantum USS schemes without quantum memories have also been experimentally demonstrated [24,25]. Furthermore, these recent schemes and their experimental demonstrations use the already ripe technologies required for quantum key distribution [26].

## 1.2    Contributions

In this work, we propose an USS scheme which naturally extends unconditionally secure message authentication schemes. The main difference between an unconditionally secure message authentication code and an USS scheme is that signature schemes ensure the transferability of signed content, while authentication codes do not. We propose a simple method, similar to secret sharing [14], allowing unconditionally secure authentication codes to be transformed into USS schemes. Our method requires only minimal trust assumptions and fewer resources than previous USS schemes. We do not assume a trusted authority, nor the existence anonymous channels or authenticated broadcast channels. Instead, we only require participants to share short secret keys pairwise, and that the majority of participants are honest. Our contributions can be summarised as follows.

1. We construct an USS scheme that, unlike prior schemes, does not rely on a trusted authority, anonymous channels or broadcast channels (Sect. 3).
2. We prove information-theoretic security of our scheme against forging, repudiation, and non-transferability (Sect. 4).
3. We compare our scheme with existing both classical and quantum USS schemes. The comparison shows that our new scheme has a number of unparalleled advantages over the previous schemes (Sect. 5).

The distribution stage of our scheme derives from the Generalised P2 protocol described in Ref. [27]. However, instead of participants distributing bits, in our scheme a sender shares with each of the remaining protocol participants (or recipients) a set of keys (hash functions) from a family of universal hash functions. This conceptual difference leads to vast efficiency improvements (see Sect. 5) as it allows the distribution stage to be performed only once for all possible future messages, as opposed to Generalised P2 in which the distribution stage is performed independently *for each* future message. This is because, in our scheme, a signature for a message is a vector of tags generated by applying the hash functions to the message. Our scheme can be viewed as an extension of MAC schemes, and therefore its practical implementation is straightforward and efficient.

## 2 Preliminaries

We begin by formally defining an USS scheme.

**Definition 1** ([27]). *An USS scheme $\mathcal{Q}$ is an ordered set $\{\mathcal{P}, \mathcal{M}, \Sigma, L,$ Gen, Sign, Ver$\}$ where*

- *The set $\mathcal{P} = \{P_0, P_1, \ldots, P_N\}$, is the set containing the signer, $P_0$, and the $N$ potential receivers.*
- *$\mathcal{M}$ is the set of possible messages.*
- *$\Sigma$ is the set of possible signatures.*
- *Gen is the generation algorithm that gives rise to the functions Sign and Ver, used respectively to generate a signature and verify its validity. More precisely, the generation algorithm specifies the instructions for the communication that takes place in the distribution stage of the protocol. Based on the data obtained during the distribution stage, the generation algorithm instructs how to construct the functions Sign and Ver. The generation algorithm includes the option of outputting an instruction to abort the protocol.*
- *Sign: $\mathcal{M} \rightarrow \Sigma$ is a deterministic function that takes a message $m \in \mathcal{M}$ and outputs a signature $\sigma \in \Sigma$.*
- *$L = \{-1, 0, 1, \ldots, l_{max}\}$ is the set of possible verification levels of a signed message. A verification level $l$ corresponds to the minimum number of times that a signed message can be transferred sequentially to other recipients. For a given protocol, the maximum number of sequential transfers that can be guaranteed is denoted by $l_{max} \leq N$.*
- *Ver: $\mathcal{M} \times \Sigma \times \mathcal{P} \times L \rightarrow \{$True, False$\}$ is a deterministic function that takes a message $m$, a signature $\sigma$, a participant $P_i$ and a level $l$, and gives a boolean value depending on whether participant $P_i$ accepts the signature as valid at the verification level $l$.*

**Definition 2.** *For a fixed participant, $P_i$, at a fixed verification level, $l$, we denote the verification function as $\mathrm{Ver}_{i,l}(m, \sigma) := \mathrm{Ver}(m, \sigma, i, l)$.*

**Definition 3.** *A signature $\sigma$ on a message $m$ is $i$-acceptable if $\mathrm{Ver}_{i,0}(m, \sigma) =$ True.*

The meaning of this definition is that participant $P_i$ will accept $(m, \sigma)$ as a valid message-signature pair at the lowest verification level, $l = 0$.

**Definition 4.** *An USS protocol $\mathcal{Q}$ is correct if $\mathrm{Ver}_{i,l}(m, \mathrm{Sign}(m)) =$ True for all $m \in \mathcal{M}$, $i \in \{1, \ldots, N\}$, and $l \in L$.*

The signature protocol presented in this paper uses almost strongly universal hash function families.

**Definition 5** ([28]). *Let $\mathcal{F} = \{f : \mathcal{M} \to \mathcal{T}\}$ be a set of functions such that*

1. *For any $m \in \mathcal{M}$, $t \in \mathcal{T}$, $|\{f \in \mathcal{F} : f(m) = t\}| = |\mathcal{F}|/|\mathcal{T}|$.*
2. *For any $m_1, m_2 \in \mathcal{M}$, $t_1, t_2 \in \mathcal{T}$, such that $m_1 \neq m_2$, $|\{f \in \mathcal{F} : f(m_1) = t_1$ and $f(m_2) = t_2\}| \leq \epsilon \frac{|\mathcal{F}|}{|\mathcal{T}|}$.*

*Then we say $\mathcal{F}$ is $\epsilon$-$ASU_2$. The domain of each function in $\mathcal{F}$ is the message set, $\mathcal{M}$, and the range is the set of tags, $\mathcal{T}$.*

The efficiency of our protocol relies on the ability to find an $\epsilon$-$ASU_2$ set which is "small".

**Proposition 1** ([29]). *Let $a := \log |\mathcal{M}|$ and $b := \log |\mathcal{T}|$, be the size (in bits) of the message and tag respectively[2]. Let $\mathcal{F}$ be an $\epsilon$-$ASU_2$ set with $\epsilon = 2/|\mathcal{T}|$. It is possible to specify an element of $\mathcal{F}$ using $y$ bits of data, where $y = 3b + 2s$ and $s$ is such that $a = (b + s)(1 + 2^s)$.*

## 3    The Protocol

The protocol contains $N + 1$ participants: a sender $P_0$ and $N$ receivers, $P_1, \ldots, P_N$. Before the protocol, all participants agree on an $\epsilon$-$ASU_2$ family of functions, $\mathcal{F}$, where $\epsilon = 2/|\mathcal{T}|$. The basic idea is for the sender to give each recipient a number of keys (hash functions) which will be used in future to authenticate a message by appending tags (hash values) to the message being sent. To check the signature, participants will apply their hash functions to the message, and check that the outcome matches the tags appended to the message by the sender. They will count the number of mismatches between their hash values and the appended tags, and only accept the message if they find less than a threshold amount of mismatches. However, if the sender were to know which hash functions are held by which participant, she could choose to append appropriate tags such that one recipient accepts the message while another does not, thereby breaking transferability of the scheme. To ensure transferability then, each recipient will group the hash functions received from the sender into $N$ equally sized sets (of size $k$), and send one set (using secret channels) to each other recipient, keeping one for himself. The recipients test each of the $N$ sets independently.

**Transferability Levels.** The situation is further complicated if the sender is in collusion with some of the recipients. In that case, the sender can have partial knowledge on who holds which keys, which forces us to define levels of transferability. Levels of transferability are perhaps confusing, so here we will try to highlight the need for such levels. Imagine that a sender is in collusion with

---

[2] In this paper all logarithms are taken to base 2.

a single recipient. In this case, the sender knows $k$ of the keys held by honest recipient $H_1$, and $k$ of the keys held by honest recipient $H_2$ - namely he knows the keys that were forwarded by his dishonest partner. For these known keys, the sender can attach tags that are correct for $H_1$, and are incorrect for $H_2$. Therefore, based on the number of colluding adversaries, the sender is able to bias the number of mismatches and the number of incorrect sets found between each honest party. To ensure transferability then, we require that the second verifier accepts a message as authentic even if each set contains a higher number of mismatches, and there are more invalid sets than found by the first verifier. Of course, to ensure security against forging, we cannot allow message-signature pairs containing too many errors to be accepted, and so there must be a cap on the highest level of mismatches acceptable by anyone. This leads to levels of verification, and a limit on the number of times a message is guaranteed to be transferable in sequence. For clarity, suppose then there are three levels of verification, $l_0$, $l_1$ and $l_2$. Accepting a message at any of these levels means the message is guaranteed to have originated with the claimed sender. If $H_1$ accepts a message at level $l_2$ (the highest verification level, i.e. the level with the fewest errors in the signature), then he can forward it to $H_2$, who will first try to accept the message at level $l_2$. If he finds too many mismatches for the message to be accepted at level $l_2$, he will instead try to verify at level $l_1$. The protocol ensures that if $H_1$ found the message to be valid at level $l_2$, then $H_2$ will find the message to be valid at level $l_1$ with high probability. Therefore, with three verification levels, accepting the message at level $l_2$ guarantees that the message can be transferred at least twice more. In practice, the message may be transferred many more times, since with honest participants it is highly likely that $H_2$ will also find the message valid at level $l_2$ and they will not need to move to the next verification level.

With this in mind, to begin the protocol we must first decide the maximum number of dishonest participants we want our protocol to be able to tolerate (which, as per the proceeding paragraph, will impact our verification levels). We set this to be $\omega$ such that $\omega < (N+1)/2$, since the protocol cannot be made secure using the majority vote dispute resolution process if more than half of the participants are dishonest. We also define the notation $d_R := (\omega - 1)/N$, where $d_R$ is the maximum fraction of dishonest *recipients* possible when the sender is part of the coalition. As in previous protocols, there are two stages – the distribution stage and the messaging stage.

### 3.1   Distribution Stage

1. The sender independently and uniformly at random selects (with replacement) $N^2k$ functions from the set $\mathcal{F}$, where $k$ is a security parameter. We denote these by $(f_1, \ldots, f_{N^2k})$ and refer to them as the *signature functions*.
2. To each recipient, $P_i$, the sender uses secret classical channels to transmit the functions $(f_{(i-1)Nk+1}, \ldots, f_{iNk})$. This requires the sender to share $Nky$ secret bits with each recipient.

3. Each recipient $P_i$ randomly splits the set $\{(i-1)Nk+1, \ldots, iNk\}$ into $N$ disjoint subsets of size $k$, which we denote $R_{i \to 1}, \ldots, R_{i \to N}$. He then uses the secret classical channels to send $R_{i \to j}$ and $F_{i \to j} := \{f_r : r \in R_{i \to j}\}$ to recipient $P_j$. To securely transmit the signature functions and their positions requires each pair of participants to share $ky + k \log(Nk)$ secret bits. Following this symmetrisation, participant $P_i$ holds the $Nk$ functions given by $F_i := \bigcup_{j=1}^{N} F_{j \to i}$ and their positions given by $R_i := \bigcup_{j=1}^{N} R_{j \to i}$. We refer to these as the *key functions* and *function positions* of participant $P_i$. The participants will use these to check a future signature declaration.

## 3.2  Messaging Stage

1. To send message $m \in \mathcal{M}$ to $P_i$, the sender sends $(m, \mathsf{Sig}_m)$, where

$$\mathsf{Sig}_m := (f_1(m), f_2(m), \ldots, f_{N^2k}(m)) = (t_1, \ldots, t_{N^2k}).$$

   Since the tags have size $b$, the signature is $N^2kb$ bits in size.
2. For message $m$ and the signature elements $t_r$ such that $r \in R_{j \to i}$, participant $P_i$ defines the following test

$$T_{i,j,l}^m = \begin{cases} 1 & \text{if } \sum_{r \in R_{j \to i}} g(t_r, f_r(m)) < s_l k \\ 0 & \text{otherwise} \end{cases} \tag{1}$$

   where $s_l$ is a fraction defined by the protocol, such that $1/2 > s_{-1} > s_0 > \ldots > s_{l_{max}}$, and $g(.,.)$ is a function of two inputs which returns 0 if the inputs are equal, and 1 if the inputs are different. For each fixed $l$, if the outcome of the test is 1, we say that that test is passed at level $l$. Essentially, this test checks whether the signature matches what the recipient expects to receive, but allows for a certain number, $s_l k$, of errors. For any verification level, the recipient will perform $N$ such tests, one for each $j = 1, \ldots, N$. Note that participant $P_i$ knows all of the signature functions $f_{i'}$ with $i' \in R_i$ and so can perform all tests *without* interaction with any other participant.
3. Participant $P_i$ will accept $(m, \mathsf{Sig}_m)$ as valid at level $l$ if

$$\sum_{j=1}^{N} T_{i,j,l}^m > N\delta_l \tag{2}$$

   That is, participant $P_i$ accepts the signature at level $l$ if more than a fraction of $\delta_l$ of the tests are passed, where $\delta_l$ is a threshold given by $\delta_l = 1/2 + (l+1)d_R$. Therefore, we see that each participant can accept/reject a message without interacting with any other recipient in the messaging stage.
4. To forward a message, $P_i$ simply forwards $(m, \mathsf{Sig}_m)$ to the desired recipient.

Note that the number of dishonest participants the protocol is able to tolerate is directly related to the number of allowed transferability levels, according to the parameter $\delta_l = 1/2 + (l+1)d_R$. Specifically, the maximum transferability level for a given number of dishonest participants is set by $(l_{\max} + 1)d_R < 1/2$.

# 4  Security

Informally, USS schemes must provide the following security guarantees [18]:

1. Unforgeability: Except with negligible probability, it should not be possible for an adversary to create a valid signature.
2. Transferability: If a verifier accepts a signature, he should be confident that any other verifier would also accept the signature.
3. Non-repudiation: Except with negligible probability, a signer should be unable to repudiate a legitimate signature that he has created.

Formal security definitions covering both quantum and classical USS schemes were first provided in Ref. [27]. For completeness, the definitions are reproduced in Appendix A. Below we prove that the scheme presented in Sect. 3 is secure against each type of dishonest behaviour. The security analysis for transferability and non-repudiation is similar to the one provided in Ref. [27], and as such it is presented in Appendix B.

**Theorem 1.** *The protocol defined in Sect. 3 is secure against forging attempts. Letting $H_2$ denote the binary entropy, we find*

$$\mathbb{P}(Forge) \leq (N - \omega)^2 \, 2^{-k(1-H_2(s_0))}. \tag{3}$$

*Proof.* In order to forge, a coalition, $C$ (which does not include the signer), with access to a single message-signature pair $(m, \mathrm{Sig}_m)$, must output a distinct message-signature pair $(m', \mathrm{Sig}_{m'})$ that will be accepted (at any level $l \geq 0$) by a participant $P_i \notin C$. We consider forging to be successful if the coalition can deceive any (i.e. at least one) honest participant.

It is easiest for the coalition to forge a message at the lowest verification level $l = 0$, so we consider this case in what follows. We assume that the coalition hold a valid message-signature pair $(m, \mathrm{Sig}_m)$. We first restrict our attention to the coalition trying to deceive a fixed participant, and we will prove that this probability decays exponentially fast with the parameter $k$. We then use this to bound the general case where the target is not a fixed participant. Therefore, for now, we fix the recipient that the coalition wants to deceive to be $P_i \notin C$.

To successfully forge, the coalition should output a message-signature pair, $(m', \mathrm{Sig}_{m'})$, that passes at least $N\delta_0 + 1$ of the $N$ tests that $P_i$ performs in step 2 of the messaging stage, where $m' \neq m$ and $\delta_0 = 1/2 + d_R$, meaning $N\delta_0 + 1 = N/2 + \omega$. By the definition of the protocol, the number of members in a coalition is at most $\omega$. The coalition knows $F_{j \to i}$ and $R_{j \to i}$ for all $P_j \in C$, so they can use this knowledge to trivially ensure that $P_i$ passes $\omega$ of the $N$ tests performed at level $l = 0$. To pass the required $N\delta_0 + 1$ tests, the coalition must pass a further $N/2$ tests out of the $N - \omega$ remaining tests. The first step in computing this probability is to calculate the probability of the coalition being able to create a signature such that, for a single $P_j \notin C$, $T_{i,j,0}^{m'} = 1$, i.e. the probability that the coalition can guess the tags forwarded from a single honest recipient $P_j$ to $P_i$.

Let $p_t$ denote the probability that the coalition can force $T_{i,j,0}^{m'} = 1$, when they have no access to $(F_{j \to i}, R_{j \to i})$, i.e. $p_t$ is the probability that the coalition can create a message-signature pair that will pass the test performed by $P_i$ for the functions received from $P_j \notin C$. As per the protocol, $P_j$ sent $(F_{j \to i}, R_{j \to i})$ to $P_i$ using secure channels and therefore $F_{j \to i}$ and $R_{j \to i}$ are unknown to the coalition. However, we assume the coalition possess a valid message-signature pair $(m, \text{Sig}_m)$, from which they can gain partial information on $(F_{j \to i}, R_{j \to i})$. Let us denote the $k$ unknown functions in $F_{j \to i}$ by $u_1, \ldots, u_k$, and consider how the coalition might try to guess the value of $t_1' := u_1(m')$, given $t_1 := u_1(m)$, where $m' \neq m$.

Since $\mathcal{F}$ is $\epsilon$-ASU$_2$, using Definition 5 the coalition immediately knows $u_1$ is in a set $\mathcal{F}_1 \subset \mathcal{F}$ which has size $|\mathcal{F}|/|\mathcal{T}|$. Upon receiving message $m'$, $P_i$ will be expecting to find tag $t_1'$ in the signature. The coalition does not know $t_1'$ though, so the best they can do is to pick a random function in $\mathcal{F}_1$, and hope that this function also maps $m'$ to the unknown $t_1'$. Again by Definition 5, the fraction of functions in $\mathcal{F}_1$ that map $m'$ to $t_1'$ is at most $2/|\mathcal{T}|$. Therefore, the probability that the coalition chooses a function that gives the correct tag for message $m'$ is $2/|\mathcal{T}|$. This is independently true for each of the $k$ unknown functions.

Let $X$ be the random variable that counts how many incorrect tags the coalition declares. Then $X$ follows a binomial distribution and we have

$$p_t = \mathbb{P}(X < ks_0) = \sum_{v=0}^{ks_0-1} \binom{k}{v} \left(\frac{2}{|\mathcal{T}|}\right)^{k-v} \left(1 - \frac{2}{|\mathcal{T}|}\right)^v. \tag{4}$$

This decays exponentially fast with the parameter $k$. For example, it may be desirable to choose a small tag length in order to minimise the length of the signature. For $|\mathcal{T}| = 4$ the signature is $2N^2k$ bits in size and we have

$$p_t = \sum_{v=0}^{ks_0-1} \binom{k}{v} \left(\frac{1}{2}\right)^k \approx 2^{-k(1-H_2(s_0))}. \tag{5}$$

Of course, choosing a larger tag size will increase security against forging. We will now give an upper bound for the probability of forging against a fixed participant. We start by computing the probability of passing at least one of the unknown $N - \omega$ tests, which is given by

$$P(\text{FixedForge}) \leq 1 - (1 - p_t)^{N-\omega} \approx (N - \omega)p_t, \tag{6}$$

where we have used the fact that $p_t \ll 1$ in the approximation.

The total number of honest recipients is $N - \omega$ and for successful forging we only require that any one of them is deceived. Using the probability of forging against a fixed participant, we can bound the probability of deceiving any honest participant as

$$P(\text{Forge}) = 1 - (1 - P(\text{FixedForge}))^{N-\omega} \approx (N - \omega)^2 p_t, \tag{7}$$

where we have used the fact that $P(\text{FixedForge}) \ll 1$ in the approximation. We again note that this probability decays exponentially fast with parameter $k$, and thus the protocol is secure against forging attempts.

**Theorem 2.** *The protocol defined in Sect. 3 is secure against non-transferability attempts. Defining $N_p := [(N(1 - d_R)][N(1 - d_R) - 1]/2$, we find*

$$\mathbb{P}(\textit{Non-Transferability}) \leq N_p(N(\delta_l - d_R) + 1)\exp\left(-\frac{(s_{l-1} - s_l)^2}{2}k\right). \qquad (8)$$

*Proof.* See Appendix B.

**Theorem 3.** *The protocol defined in Sect. 3 is secure against repudiation attempts. We find*

$$\mathbb{P}(\textit{Rep}) \leq N_p(N(\delta_l - d_R) + 1)\exp\left(-\frac{(s_{-1} - s_0)^2}{2}k\right). \qquad (9)$$

*Proof.* See Appendix B.

We note here that Eqs. (3), (8) and (9) are independent of the message size, meaning the signature size will be constant with respect to the size of the message being sent.

## 5     Comparisons

### 5.1     Classical USS Schemes

In this section we compare the performance of our protocol to the one proposed in [15] constructed using polynomials over a finite field. We will refer to this protocol as the HSZI scheme. Since the HSZI scheme allows all participants to send multiple messages, we extend our protocol to facilitate a comparison.

Consider the protocol described in Sect. 3, except that now each participant performs the distribution stage $\psi$ times in the role of the sender. Trivially, this extended distribution stage allows all participants in the scheme to send up to $\psi$ messages securely in the role of sender. We call this the *extended protocol* and all comparisons are made with reference to this scheme.

This extended scheme still enjoys a number of advantages when compared to the HSZI scheme. Namely,

1. We require fewer trust assumptions – our scheme does not require any trusted authority.
2. Security in our scheme can be tuned independently of message size, resulting in shorter signature lengths.
3. Our scheme scales more efficiently (with respect to message size) in terms of the number of secret shared bits required by participants.

We will look at the second and third advantages in more detail. According to Theorem 3 of [15] (translated to our notation) the HSZI scheme has

$$|\Sigma| = q^{(\omega+1)}, \quad |\mathcal{S}| = q^{(\omega+1)(\psi+1)}, \quad |\mathcal{V}| = q^{\omega+(N+1)(\psi+1)}, \qquad (10)$$

where $\Sigma$ is the set containing all possible signatures, $\mathcal{S}$ is the set containing all possible signing algorithms, $\mathcal{V}$ is the set containing all possible verification algorithms, $q$ is the number of elements in the chosen finite field and $\psi$ is the number of times the keys can be reused.

**Signature Length.** Let us first consider the size of the signature. Since the signature must be transmitted with the message, it is desirable to have as small a signature as possible. In the HSZI scheme the message $m$ is an element of the finite field, meaning the size of the finite field must be at least as big as the size of the message set, i.e. $q \geq |\mathcal{M}|$. Accordingly, in what follows we set $q = |\mathcal{M}|$. Equation (10) implies that $(\omega + 1)\log(|\mathcal{M}|)$ is the bit-length of the signature. The authors also show that the HSZI scheme provides security proportional to $1/|\mathcal{M}|$.

Immediately we see that both the size of the signature and the security level depend on the size of the message to be sent. On the other hand, in our scheme the signature length is $2N^2k$ bits, regardless of the message length. The security level of our scheme depends on the parameter $k$, but is independent of the length of the message being signed. This allows our scheme to bypass the optimality results presented in Ref. [15]. Specifically, the authors show that the signature generated by the HSZI scheme is optimally small *for a given security level*. By decoupling the security level from the size of the message being sent, we are able to generate smaller signatures while maintaining security.

**Secret Key Requirements.** We now consider the number of secret shared bits required to securely distribute the signing/verification keys. In the HSZI scheme, to secretly send the signing and verification keys to all participants, the trusted authority must hold

$$\left[(\omega + 1)(\psi + 1) + \omega + (N + 1)(\psi + 1)\right]\log(|\mathcal{M}|) = O(N\psi \log |\mathcal{M}|) \qquad (11)$$

secret shared bits with each participant (as implied by Eq. (10)).

For the hash scheme, each recipient must share $Nky$ secret bits with the sender (to receive the signature functions), and $ky + k\log(Nk)$ with every other recipient (to forward on a selection of the key functions and their positions). For the extended protocol, where the distribution stage is performed $\psi$ times for each participant acting as sender, each participant must share: (i) $Nky$ secret bits with each of the $N$ recipients for the $\psi$ rounds in which he is the sender; and (ii) $Nky$ bits with the sender and $ky + k\log(Nk))$ secret bits with each of the $(N - 1)$ other recipients for each of the $N\psi$ rounds when he is not the sender. This is a total of

$$\begin{aligned}
N^2k\psi y + N\psi\big[Nky &+ k(N - 1)(y + \log(Nk))\big] \\
&= Nk\psi(3N - 1)y + N(N - 1)k\psi \log(Nk) \\
&= Nk\psi(3N - 1)(6 + 2s) + N(N - 1)k\psi \log(Nk) \\
&= O\big(N^2k\psi(\log\log|\mathcal{M}| + \log Nk)\big)
\end{aligned} \qquad (12)$$

secret shared bits per recipient. The second equality follows using Proposition 1 with $b = 2$. The last equality follows using the Lambert W function to find a leading order approximation for $s$ when $s$ is large [30]. The results are summarised in Table 1 below.

The table shows that the signature length in our scheme is constant with respect to the size of the message to be signed. On the other hand, the signature length in the HSZI scheme increases linearly with the bit-length of the message to be signed. Similarly, the secret shared key required by our scheme increases logarithmically with the bit-length of the message, whereas the increase in the HSZI scheme is linear in the bit-length of the message.

The fact that our scheme scales unfavourably with respect to the number of participants is due to the lack of a trusted authority, meaning participants must perform the pairwise exchange process. As discussed below, this $N^2$ scaling can be removed from the hash scheme by introducing a trusted authority.

**Table 1.** Comparison of the signature length and secret shared keys required for various signature protocols. Our scheme scales favourably with respect to the message length, $a = \log|\mathcal{M}|$, both in terms of signature length and required secret shared key. The "Quantum" column refers to the two most efficient quantum USS schemes at present, described in [23, 27].

|            | Hash scheme                       | HSZI            | Quantum                       |
| ---------- | --------------------------------- | --------------- | ----------------------------- |
| Signature  | $2N^2k$                           | $(\omega + 1)a$ | $O(N^2a)$                     |
| Secret key | $O\big(N^2\psi(\log a + \log N)\big)$ | $O(N\psi a)$    | $O\big(N^2\psi(a + \log N)\big)$ |

**Disadvantages.** Due to the inclusion of a trusted authority, the HSZI scheme enjoys a number of advantages over our scheme. These are:

1. Pairwise secret shared keys between all participants are not required by the HSZI scheme. Instead, each participant only needs a shared secret key with the trusted authority. This means that the HSZI scheme scales favourably with respect to the number of protocol participants.
2. Participants in the HSZI scheme are able to enter the protocol even after the distribution stage. The new participant only needs to communicate with the trusted authority to join.
3. The HSZI protocol has unlimited transferability, whereas our scheme can only guarantee transferability a finite number of times.

While these advantages are significant, they are only possible due to the existence of a trusted authority – an additional trust assumption not present in our scheme. Our scheme could easily be modified to include a trusted authority, in which case it would achieve the same three benefits above, as well as being significantly more efficient.

A trusted authority could be included into our scheme as follows. In the distribution stage, the signer would send $Nk$ functions to the trusted authority, where $N$ is an arbitrarily large number chosen to be the maximum number of participants able to verify the senders signature. When the sender wants to send a signed message, the trusted authority randomly (and secretly) sends $k$ of the $Nk$ functions to the recipient. Recipients could either obtain their $k$

functions at the start of the protocol (i.e. have a distribution stage), or simply request the functions from the trusted authority as and when needed. Security against forging would follow as before from the properties of $\epsilon$-ASU$_2$ sets, while security against repudiation would come from the fact that the trusted authority distributes the functions out at random, so each honest participant would have the same expected number of mismatches with any signature declaration.

### 5.2   Quantum USS Schemes

A central motivating factor in the study of quantum USS schemes was that they seemed to require fewer resources than classical USS schemes. This benefit came at a cost, and all quantum USS schemes proposed have been much less efficient than classical USS schemes[3].

Until now, this decrease in efficiency had been justified by the fact that quantum protocols do not require broadcast channels, anonymous channels, or a trusted authority. Instead, the only assumption is that a limited number of the participants are dishonest, and that the participants all share a number of secret bits, which could be expanded via QKD.

However, the classical scheme presented in this paper makes *the same* trust assumptions as quantum USS schemes, and still achieves two key advantages. Namely, our scheme generates much shorter signatures and requires significantly fewer secret shared bits. One of the reasons for the increase in efficiency is that, so far, all quantum USS schemes have been of the Lamport-type, in which the distribution stage must be performed for every possible future message. On the other hand, our scheme does not follow this blueprint, and instead requires users to share hash functions in the distribution stage, which can be used to sign any future message (up to some chosen size).

**Efficiency.** Here we consider the signature length and secret shared bit requirements of our scheme, and compare it to Generalised P2, the most efficient realisable quantum USS scheme. We assume that a group of $N + 1 = 51$ participants are trying to sign a 1Mb message to a security level of $10^{-10}$. For comparing to quantum USS schemes, rather than considering the extended protocol, we assume the participants perform the regular distribution stage as specified in Sect. 3, i.e. there is a designated sender and only one message to be sent. In order to have $l_{max} = 1$, we assume that at most $\omega = 13$ participants are dishonest meaning $d_R = 0.24$. We also choose $s_{-1} = 0.41$, $s_0 = 0.21$ and $s_1 = 0.01$ so as to have even gaps between the verification levels[4].

---

[3] Although it may appear from Table 1 that quantum USS schemes scale comparably to the HSZI scheme, in fact the constant of proportionality for the quantum schemes is very large, meaning that for all practical purposes the HSZI scheme is far more efficient.

[4] This choice is somewhat arbitrary, but is chosen to minimise the required signature lengths.

With these parameters, Eqs. (3), (8) and (9) show that $k = 1700$ is necessary for the message to be secure to a level of $10^{-10}$. Given this value of $k$, the signature length is $8.50 \times 10^6$ bits and each recipient must hold a total of $7.69 \times 10^6$ secret shared bits (shared over the different participants).

When considering Generalised P2, we assume the sender signs the 1 Mb message bit-by-bit, each to a level of $10^{-10}$. Overall this gives a lower security level than signing the message as a whole, but makes the protocol significantly more efficient[5]. Equations (24), (29) and (31) of Ref. [27] can be used to show that the resulting signature length is $4.25 \times 10^{12}$, and that each recipient must hold a total of $5.96 \times 10^{12}$ secret shared bits (shared over the different participants).

This example shows just how powerful our new scheme is when compared to existing quantum schemes – even for a relatively small message, our scheme is 6 orders of magnitude more efficient both in terms of signature size and secret shared bit requirements. Our results show that quantum USS schemes must either be drastically improved, or find a new source of motivation if they are to remain competitive.

# A    Security Definitions

In this section we formally define security in USS protocols. We begin by defining the notion of a dispute resolution process.

In the messaging stage of the protocol all participants are able to check the validity of a message-signature pair without communicating with any other participant. Nevertheless, there may still be scenarios in which disagreements arise regarding whether a message is valid or not. For example, the sender may deny having ever sent a message, even though a recipient who (allegedly) followed the correct procedure found the message to be valid. In these cases, the participants need a method of deciding who is telling the truth. This is done via the dispute resolution process.

**Definition 6.** *When the validity of a message-signature pair $(m, \sigma)$ is in dispute, we invoke a majority vote dispute resolution method $\mathrm{MV}(m, \sigma)$, defined by the following rule:*

*1. $\mathrm{MV}(m, \sigma) = \mathrm{Valid}$ if $\mathrm{Ver}_{(i,-1)}(m, \sigma) = \mathrm{True}$ for more than half of the users.*
*2. $\mathrm{MV}(m, \sigma) = \mathrm{Invalid}$ otherwise*

*where $\mathrm{Ver}_{(i,-1)}(m, \sigma)$ is the verification function at level $l = -1$.*

Essentially, all participants check the message-signature pair at level $-1$ and the majority decision prevails. The $l = -1$ verification level is only used in dispute resolution, and not in normal runs of the protocol. The dispute resolution process is expensive, as it requires all participants to communicate to decide

---

[5] Signing the message as a whole would require participants to share secret keys of size $O(2^{|\mathcal{M}|}) = O(2^{10^6})$, which is clearly impossible.

whether the message is valid or not. It is expected that even dishonest participants would not try to force dispute resolution, since losing would come with consequences and the procedure ensures that honest participants prevail as long as they are in the majority. Dispute resolution should be thought of as akin to taking legal action; in the vast majority of cases it does not happen, but its existence is necessary to prevent dishonesty.

Signature schemes must be secure against three types of security threat – forging, repudiation and non-transferability.

**Definition 7** (Forging). *Let $\mathcal{Q}$ be an USS protocol and let $C \subset \mathcal{P}$ be a coalition of malevolent parties, not including the signer $P_0$. Suppose that the coalition holds any valid message-signature pair $(m, \sigma)$ and can use this to output a message-signature pair $(m', \sigma')$ with $m' \neq m$. We define* Forging *to be the function:*

$$Forg_C(\mathcal{Q}, m', \sigma') = \begin{cases} 1 & \text{if } (m', \sigma') \text{ is } i\text{-acceptable for some } P_i \notin C \\ 0 & \text{otherwise.} \end{cases} \quad (13)$$

**Definition 8** (Non-Transferability). *Let $\mathcal{Q}$ be an USS protocol and $C \subset \mathcal{P}$ a coalition of malevolent participants including the signer $P_0$. Suppose that $C$ outputs a message-signature pair $(m, \sigma)$ and a verification level $l$. We define* Non-Transferability *to be the function:*

$$NonTrans_C(\mathcal{Q}, m, \sigma, l) = \begin{cases} 1 & \text{if } \mathrm{Ver}_{(i,l)}(m, \sigma) = \text{True for some } P_i \notin C \text{ and} \\ & \mathrm{Ver}_{(j,l')}(m, \sigma) = \text{False for some } 0 \leq l' < l \\ & \text{and some } j \neq i, P_j \notin C \\ 0 & \text{otherwise.} \end{cases}$$
$$(14)$$

**Definition 9** (Repudiation). *Let $\mathcal{Q}$ be an USS protocol and $C \subset \mathcal{P}$ a coalition of malevolent participants including the signer $P_0$. Suppose that $C$ outputs a message-signature pair $(m, \sigma)$ and a verification level $l$. We define* Repudiation *to be the function:*

$$Rep_C(\mathcal{Q}, \mathrm{MV}, m, \sigma) = \begin{cases} 1 & \text{if } (m, \sigma) \text{ is } i\text{-acceptable for some } P_i \notin C \text{ and} \\ & \mathrm{MV}(m, \sigma) = \text{Invalid} \\ 0 & \text{otherwise.} \end{cases}$$
$$(15)$$

We say that the protocol is secure against forging/non-transferability/repudiation if the probability of a dishonest coalition being successful decays exponentially fast with respect to some security parameter.

## B    Security Proofs

In this section we prove Theorems 2 and 3 stated in Sect. 4.

## B.1    Proof of Theorem 2

In order to break the transferability of the protocol, a coalition $C$ (which includes the signer $P_0$) must generate a signature that is accepted by recipient $P_i \notin C$ at level $l$, while also being rejected by another recipient $P_j \notin C$ at a level $l' < l$.

The task of the coalition is easiest if $l' = l - 1$ and so we consider this case in what follows. To provide an upper bound, we allow for the biggest coalition $C$ that includes $Nd_R$ recipients and the sender, i.e. all the dishonest participants. For simplicity, again we will fix the participants whom the coalition is trying to deceive to be the honest participants $P_i$ and $P_j$, while all other honest participants are labelled with the index $h$. In general, transferability fails if the coalition forms a signature that is not transferable for at least one pair of honest participants $(P_i, P_j)$. Therefore, we should take into account all possible pairs of honest participants. We begin by focusing on the case of a fixed pair of participants, and at the end we give the more general expressions.

The first step is to compute $p_{m_{l,l-1}}$, which is the probability that: (i) test $T^m_{i,h,l}$ is passed (i.e. the tags sent from honest participant $P_h$ to recipient $P_i$ are accepted at level $l$); and (ii), the test $T^m_{j,h,l-1}$ fails (i.e. the tags sent from honest participant $P_h$ to recipient $P_j$ are rejected at level $l-1$). Since the sender $P_0$ is dishonest, it can be assumed that the coalition know all the signature functions. However, they are unaware of the sets $R_{h \to i}$ and $R_{h \to j}$. Therefore, the coalition can control the number of mismatches the signature will make with the signature functions originally sent to $P_h$, but they cannot separately bias the number of mismatches the signature will make with the functions in $F_{h \to i}$ and $F_{h \to j}$. Therefore, when participants $P_i$ and $P_j$ test the functions sent to them by an honest participant $P_h$, they will both have the same expected fraction of mismatches; we call this fraction $p_e$.

It is helpful to use the following bound

$$p_{m_{l,l-1}} = \mathbb{P}(P_i \text{ passes test at level } l \text{ AND } P_j \text{ fails test at level } l - 1)$$
$$\leq \min\{\mathbb{P}(P_i \text{ passes test at level } l), \mathbb{P}(P_j \text{ fails test at level } l - 1)\}. \tag{16}$$

The probability of passing the test at level $l$ when $p_e > s_l$ can be bounded using Hoeffding's inequalities to be below $\exp(-2(p_e - s_l)^2 k)$. The probability of failing the test at level $l - 1$ when $p_e < s_{l-1}$ can similarly be bounded to be smaller than $\exp(-2(s_{l-1} - p_e)^2 k)$. Note that $s_{l-1} > s_l$ and so the above two cases cover all possible values for $p_e$. Since we are taking the minimum over both cases, the optimal choice for the coalition is to have these probabilities equal to each other. This is achieved by choosing $p_e = (s_l + s_{l-1})/2$. In this case we obtain the bound $p_{m_{l,l-1}} \leq \exp\left(-\frac{(s_{l-1} - s_l)^2}{2}k\right)$, which decays exponentially with $k$.

For a test that involves a member of $C$ it is trivial for the coalition to make two recipients disagree in any way they wish, i.e. they can make $T^m_{i,c,l}$ and $T^m_{j,c,l-1}$ take any values they wish. However, the number of those tests is at most $Nd_R$, which is the maximum number of recipients in the coalition. For the participant $P_i$ to accept a message at level $l$, he needs strictly greater than $N\delta_l$ of the tests to pass at this level. On the other hand, for the participant $P_j$ to reject the message at level $l-1$, less than or equal to $N\delta_{l-1}$ of tests must pass at this level. Therefore, since it holds that $\delta_l = \delta_{l-1} + d_R$, in order for the coalition to be successful, the honest participants $P_i$ and $P_j$ need to disagree on at least $Nd_R+1$ tests. As we saw, the coalition can easily make them disagree on the $Nd_R$ tests originating from coalition members, but they still have to disagree on at least one more test originating from an honest recipient. There are $N(\delta_l - d_R) + 1$ such tests (tests originating from an honest recipient that were passed by $P_i$), and the $P_j$ need only reject one of them for the coalition to succeed. Therefore, we have

$$\mathbb{P}(\text{Fixed Non-Transferability}) \leq 1 - (1 - p_{m_{l,l-1}})^{N(\delta_l - d_R)+1}$$
$$\approx (N(\delta_l - d_R) + 1)p_{m_{l,l-1}}. \tag{17}$$

Lastly, we consider the general case, where the participants $P_i$ and $P_j$ are not fixed. We find

$$\mathbb{P}(\text{Non-Transferability}) \leq 1 - (1 - \mathbb{P}(\text{Fixed Non-Transferability}))^{N_p}$$
$$\approx N_p(N(\delta_l - d_R) + 1)p_{m_{l,l-1}}, \tag{18}$$

where $N_p := [(N(1 - d_R)][N(1 - d_R) - 1]/2$. Again, this decays exponentially with $k$, and thus the protocol is secure against non-transferability.

### B.2    Proof of Theorem 3

The proof is a special case of non-transferability, see Sect. 5 A of [27]. We find

$$\mathbb{P}(\text{Rep}) \leq N_p(N(\delta_0 - d_R) + 1)p_{m_{0,-1}}. \tag{19}$$

As for non-transferability, this goes to zero exponentially fast with $k$, and thus the protocol is secure against repudiation.

# References

1. Rivest, R.L., Shamir, A., Adleman, L.: A method for obtaining digital signatures and public-key cryptosystems. Commun. ACM **21**(2), 120–126 (1978)
2. ElGamal, T.: A public key cryptosystem and a signature scheme based on discrete logarithms. In: Blakley, G.R., Chaum, D. (eds.) CRYPTO 1984. LNCS, vol. 196, pp. 10–18. Springer, Heidelberg (1985). https://doi.org/10.1007/3-540-39568-7_2
3. Johnson, D., Menezes, A., Vanstone, S.: The elliptic curve digital signature algorithm (ECDSA). Int. J. Inf. Secur. **1**(1), 36–63 (2001)
4. Shor, P.W.: Algorithms for quantum computation: discrete logarithms and factoring. In: Goldwasser, S., (ed.) Proceedings 35th Annual Symposium on Foundations of Computer Science. SFCS 1994, vol. 35, pp. 124–134. IEEE Computer Society (1994)
5. National Security Agency: Cryptography Today, August 2015. https://www.nsa.gov/ia/programs/suiteb_cryptography/
6. McEliece, R.J.: A public-key cryptosystem based on algebraic coding theory (1978)

7. Micciancio, D.: Lattice-based cryptography. In: van Tilborg, H.C.A., Jajodia, S. (eds.) Encyclopedia of Cryptography and Security. Springer, Boston (2011). https://doi.org/10.1007/978-1-4419-5906-5_417

8. Song, F.: A note on quantum security for post-quantum cryptography. In: Mosca, M. (ed.) PQCrypto 2014. LNCS, vol. 8772, pp. 246–265. Springer, Cham (2014). https://doi.org/10.1007/978-3-319-11659-4_15

9. Biasse, J.F., Song, F.: On the quantum attacks against schemes relying on the hardness of finding a short generator of an ideal in $Q(\zeta pn)$ (2015)

10. Amiri, R., Andersson, E.: Unconditionally secure quantum signatures. Entropy **17**(8), 5635–5659 (2015)

11. Wallden, P., Dunjko, V., Kent, A., Andersson, E.: Quantum digital signatures with quantum-key-distribution components. Phys. Rev. A **91**(4), 042304 (2015)

12. Chaum, D., Roijakkers, S.: Unconditionally-secure digital signatures. In: Menezes, A.J., Vanstone, S.A. (eds.) CRYPTO 1990. LNCS, vol. 537, pp. 206–214. Springer, Heidelberg (1991). https://doi.org/10.1007/3-540-38424-3_15

13. Pfitzmann, B., Waidner, M.: Information-theoretic pseudosignatures and byzantine agreement for $t \geq n/3$. IBM (1996)

14. Shamir, A.: How to share a secret. Commun. ACM **22**(11), 612–613 (1979)

15. Hanaoka, G., Shikata, J., Zheng, Y., Imai, H.: Unconditionally secure digital signature schemes admitting transferability. In: Okamoto, T. (ed.) ASIACRYPT 2000. LNCS, vol. 1976, pp. 130–142. Springer, Heidelberg (2000). https://doi.org/10.1007/3-540-44448-3_11

16. Hanaoka, G., Shikata, J., Zheng, Y.: Efficient unconditionally secure digital signatures. IEICE Trans. Fundam. Electron. Commun. Comput. Sci. **87**(1), 120–130 (2004)

17. Shikata, J., Hanaoka, G., Zheng, Y., Imai, H.: Security notions for unconditionally secure signature schemes. In: Knudsen, L.R. (ed.) EUROCRYPT 2002. LNCS, vol. 2332, pp. 434–449. Springer, Heidelberg (2002). https://doi.org/10.1007/3-540-46035-7_29

18. Swanson, C.M., Stinson, D.R.: Unconditionally secure signature schemes revisited. In: Fehr, S. (ed.) ICITS 2011. LNCS, vol. 6673, pp. 100–116. Springer, Heidelberg (2011). https://doi.org/10.1007/978-3-642-20728-0_10

19. Gottesman, D., Chuang, I.: Quantum digital signatures. arXiv preprint quant-ph/0105032 (2001)

20. Lu, X., Feng, D.: Quantum digital signature based on quantum one-way functions. In: ICACT 2005, vol. 1, pp. 514–517. IEEE (2005)

21. Clarke, P.J., Collins, R.J., Dunjko, V., Andersson, E., Jeffers, J., Buller, G.S.: Experimental demonstration of quantum digital signatures using phase-encoded coherent states of light. Nat. Commun. **3**, 1174 (2012)

22. Dunjko, V., Wallden, P., Andersson, E.: Quantum digital signatures without quantum memory. Phys. Rev. Lett. **112**(4), 040502 (2014)

23. Amiri, R., Wallden, P., Kent, A., Andersson, E.: Secure quantum signatures using insecure quantum channels. Phys. Rev. A **93**(3), 032325 (2016). https://doi.org/10.1103/PhysRevA.93.032325

24. Collins, R.J., Donaldson, R.J., Dunjko, V., Wallden, P., Clarke, P.J., Andersson, E., Jeffers, J., Buller, G.S.: Realization of quantum digital signatures without the requirement of quantum memory. Phys. Rev. Lett. **113**(4), 040502 (2014)

25. Donaldson, R.J., Collins, R.J., Kleczkowska, K., Amiri, R., Wallden, P., Dunjko, V., Jeffers, J., Andersson, E., Buller, G.S.: Experimental demonstration of kilometer-range quantum digital signatures. Phys. Rev. A **93**(1), 012329 (2016)

26. Scarani, V., Bechmann-Pasquinucci, H., Cerf, N.J., Dušek, M., Lütkenhaus, N., Peev, M.: The security of practical quantum key distribution. Rev. Mod. Phys. **81**(3), 1301 (2009)
27. Arrazola, J.M., Wallden, P., Andersson, E.: Multiparty quantum signature schemes. Quantum Inf. Comput. **16**, 435–464 (2016)
28. Carter, L., Wegman, M.N.: Universal classes of hash functions. J. Comput. Syst. Sci. **18**, 143–154 (1979)
29. Bierbrauer, J., Johansson, T., Kabatianskii, G., Smeets, B.: On families of hash functions via geometric codes and concatenation. In: Stinson, D.R. (ed.) CRYPTO 1993. LNCS, vol. 773, pp. 331–342. Springer, Heidelberg (1994). https://doi.org/10.1007/3-540-48329-2_28
30. Abidin, A., Larsson, J.Å.: New universal hash functions. In: Armknecht, F., Lucks, S. (eds.) WEWoRC 2011. LNCS, vol. 7242, pp. 99–108. Springer, Heidelberg (2012). https://doi.org/10.1007/978-3-642-34159-5_7

# Floppy-Sized Group Signatures
# from Lattices

Cecilia Boschini[1,2]([✉]), Jan Camenisch[1], and Gregory Neven[1]

[1] IBM Research, Zurich, Switzerland
{bos,jca,nev}@zurich.ibm.com
[2] Università della Svizzera Italiana, Lugano, Switzerland

**Abstract.** We present the first lattice-based group signature scheme whose cryptographic artifacts are of size small enough to be usable in practice: for a group of $2^{25}$ users, signatures take 910 kB and public keys are 501 kB. Our scheme builds upon two recently proposed lattice-based primitives: the verifiable encryption scheme by Lyubashevsky and Neven (Eurocrypt 2017) and the signature scheme by Boschini, Camenisch, and Neven (IACR ePrint 2017). To achieve such short signatures and keys, we first re-define verifiable encryption to allow one to encrypt a function of the witness, rather than the full witness. This definition enables more efficient realizations of verifiable encryption and is of independent interest. Second, to minimize the size of the signatures and public keys of our group signature scheme, we revisit the proof of knowledge of a signature and the proofs in the verifiable encryption scheme provided in the respective papers.

**Keywords:** Lattices · Group signature · Verifiable encryption

## 1 Introduction

Lattice-based cryptography has made substantial advances and now includes public-key encryption schemes [30,31] and digital signature schemes [14,15,27] that are essentially as practical as those based on traditional number-theoretic assumptions: all keys and outputs are less than 1 kB for 128 bits of security. Somewhat more complex primitives such as identity-based encryption [15,19] can be implemented with keys and ciphertexts being around 4 kB, and the best blind signature scheme [35] has artifacts of around 100 kB. For group signatures [13], however, the lattice-based schemes known are much less efficient than their traditional counterparts, despite the attention they have recently received.

In a group signature scheme, the group manager provides distinct secret keys to each user, who is then able to sign messages anonymously on behalf of the group. While anyone can check that a message was signed by a group member, only the opener is able to recover the identity of the originator of a signature. Group signatures are particularly useful in scenarios where remote devices need to be authenticated as valid devices, but privacy imposes that individual devices

© Springer International Publishing AG, part of Springer Nature 2018
B. Preneel and F. Vercauteren (Eds.): ACNS 2018, LNCS 10892, pp. 163–182, 2018.
https://doi.org/10.1007/978-3-319-93387-0_9

can only be identified by a designated authority. Examples include government-issued electronic identity (eID) cards, where each issued smart card creates identity claims as signed statements about its attributes, without needing to fully identify its owner [6], or remote anonymous attestation of computing platforms, where devices prove which software they execute [9].

A typical approach to construct a group signature scheme is to use a signature scheme, an encryption scheme, and a non-interactive zero-knowledge proof of knowledge (NIZK PoK) [1,5,12] as follows. The group public key consists of the group manager's signature public key and the opener's encryption public key. A user's secret key is a signature by the group manager on the identity of the user. To sign a message, the user encrypts her identity under the opener's public key and creates a NIZK PoK of a signature on the encrypted value.

The main obstacle in achieving an efficient scheme with this approach is the efficiency of the NIZK PoK and the choice of signature and encryption schemes that allow for an efficient NIZK PoK. In this paper, we build a dynamic group signature scheme by combining the recent signature scheme with protocols by Boschini et al. [8] and the recent (verifiable) encryption scheme by Lyubashevsky and Neven [29]. Both these schemes already come with NIZK proofs of knowledge of a signature and of a plaintext, but their straightforward combination results in a group signature scheme that is not practical due to its large signature size.

*Our Techniques and Results.* Boschini et al. [8] presented a (relaxed) signature scheme allowing for efficient zero-knowledge proofs of knowledge of a signature on a hidden message, where a signature on a polynomial with small coefficients $\mathbf{m}$ is a vector $\mathbf{S}$ of small-coefficient polynomials (or "short" vector) such that $[\mathbf{A}|\mathbf{B}|\mathbf{C}+\mathbf{m}\mathbf{G}|\mathbf{1}]\mathbf{S} = \mathbf{u}$, where the public key contains row vectors $\mathbf{A},\mathbf{B},\mathbf{C},\mathbf{G}$ and a polynomial $\mathbf{u}$. To prove knowledge of a signature on a hidden message, the prover first generates a commitment $\mathbf{F} = \mathbf{b}^{-1}(\mathbf{C}+\mathbf{m}\mathbf{G}+\mathbf{E})$ to $\mathbf{m}$, where $\mathbf{b}$ is a random small-coefficient polynomial and $\mathbf{E}$ is an error vector. The commitment $\mathbf{F}$ can be plugged into the verification equation by computing a short vector $\mathbf{S}'$ such that $[\mathbf{A}|\mathbf{B}|\mathbf{F}|\mathbf{1}]\mathbf{S}' = \mathbf{u}$. The prover can then use Lyubashevsky's Fiat-Shamir with aborts technique [27] to prove knowledge of

$$\text{(I) } [\mathbf{A}|\mathbf{B}|\mathbf{F}|\mathbf{1}]\bar{\mathbf{S}} = \bar{\mathbf{c}}\mathbf{u} \qquad \text{(II) } [\mathbf{F}^T|\mathbf{G}^T|\mathbf{1}]\begin{bmatrix}\bar{\mathbf{b}}\\\bar{\mathbf{m}}\\\bar{\mathbf{E}}\end{bmatrix} = \bar{\mathbf{c}}'\mathbf{C}.$$

The relaxed verifiable encryption scheme of Lyubashevsky and Neven [29] can encrypt a witness $\mathbf{x}$ to a relation $\mathbf{M}\mathbf{x} = \mathbf{y}$ so that decryption is guaranteed to yield $(\bar{\mathbf{x}},\bar{\mathbf{c}})$ such that $\mathbf{M}\bar{\mathbf{x}} = \bar{\mathbf{c}}\mathbf{y}$. The most straightforward way to build a group signature scheme would be to combine it with the above building blocks, letting a user's signing key be given by a signature $\mathbf{S}$ by the group manager on the user's identity $\mathbf{m}$, and letting a group signature be a non-interactive proof of relations (I) and (II), combined with a verifiable encryption to allow the opener to recover the user's identity $\mathbf{m}$.

The problem with this approach is that the Lyubashevsky-Neven verifiable encryption scheme encrypts the full witness $[\mathbf{S} ; \bar{\mathbf{b}} ; \bar{\mathbf{m}} ; \bar{\mathbf{E}}^T$, rather than just the witness $\mathbf{m}$, resulting in a very long signature size. In this paper, we define a variant of relaxed verifiable encryption that encrypts only part of the witness, resulting in a much shorter signature size. In this way, given $\mathbf{F}$ as before, it is possible to encrypt the message $\mathbf{m}$ and still prove that it was used to construct $\mathbf{F}$, without having to also encrypt $\mathbf{S}$, $\mathbf{b}$, and $\mathbf{E}$. Moreover, we prove relations (I) and (II) in two separate proofs, resulting in better parameters.

Our group signature scheme satisfies anonymity and traceability as defined by Bellare et al. [4] in the random-oracle model. Analogously to the non-lattice-based world, where schemes under weak assumptions do exist [3,4] but truly practical schemes typically require stronger assumptions [1,7], we also prove our scheme secure under relatively strong assumptions. Namely, we follow the approach by Boschini et al. [8] and use two interactive assumptions that can be interpreted in two different ways. One can either believe the interactive assumptions as stated, in which case we obtain a tight security reduction and the most efficient parameters for our scheme, resulting in signatures of 910 kB for a group of $2^{25}$ users and 80 bits of security. Alternatively, one can see our assumptions as being implied by the standard Ring-SIS and Ring-LWE assumptions through a complexity leveraging argument. To compensate for the loose reduction, the parameters increase, resulting in signatures of 1.72 MB.

*Related Work.* The early lattice-based group signature schemes [10,20] have signature sizes that are linear in the number of group members and are therefore mainly proofs of concepts, unsuitable for any practical application. Later schemes [21,25,34] are asymptotically more efficient with signature sizes being logarithmic in the number of users.

Making use of the advances in lattice-based signature schemes, a number of group signature schemes were proposed following the general construction approach we have outlined earlier [21,23–26,37]. These schemes use as proof of knowledge protocols either an adaptation of Stern's protocol [36] or the "single-bit-challenge" version of the lattice-based Fiat-Shamir protocol by Lyubashevsky [27]. As these proofs have soundness error 2/3 and 1/2, respectively, they need to be repeated sufficiently many times in parallel, resulting in group signature schemes that can hardly be considered practical. None of these scheme give concrete parameters, providing asymptotic efficiency analyses instead. The only exception is the scheme by Libert et al. [23] which is the most efficient scheme prior to ours, with signatures over 60 MB and public keys of 4.9 MB for a group size of only $2^{10}$ users for 80 bits of security – still much less efficient than ours.

## 2 Prerequisites

We denote vectors and matrices with upper-case letters. Column vectors are denoted as $V = [v_1 ; \ldots ; v_n]$ and row vectors as $V = [v_1 \ldots v_n]$. Sampling and element $x$ from a distribution $\mathcal{D}$ will be denoted as $x \xleftarrow{\$} \mathcal{D}$. If $x$ is sampled from a uniform over a set $A$, we will abuse the notation and write $x \xleftarrow{\$} A$. With $x \leftarrow a$ we will denote that $x$ is assigned the value $a$. When necessary, we will denote the uniform distribution over a set $S$ as $U(S)$.

## 2.1 Polynomial Rings

Consider the polynomial ring $\mathcal{R}_q = \mathbb{Z}_q/\langle \mathbf{x}^n + 1 \rangle$ for a prime $q \equiv 5 \bmod 8$. Elements in the ring are polynomials of degree at most $n - 1$ with coefficients in $[-(q-1)/2, (q-1)/2]$ and operations between ring elements are done modulo $q$. Let $\deg(\mathbf{a})$ be the degree of the polynomial $\mathbf{a}$. For an element $\mathbf{a} = \sum_{i=0}^{n-1} a_i \mathbf{x}^i$ in $\mathcal{R}_q$, the standard norms are computed as $\|\mathbf{a}\|_1 = \sum_i |a_i|$, $\|\mathbf{a}\| = \sqrt{\sum_i a_i^2}$ and $\|\mathbf{a}\|_\infty = \max |a_i|$. For any $K|n$, we can construct a subring $\mathcal{R}_q^{(K)}$ of $\mathcal{R}_q$ as the subset of elements $\mathbf{a} \in \mathcal{R}_q$ such that $\mathbf{a} = \sum_{i=0}^{K-1} a_i \mathbf{x}^{in/K}$. For integer $p$, $\mathcal{R}_p$ (resp., $\mathcal{R}_p^{(K)}$) is the subset of $\mathcal{R}_q$ (resp., $\mathcal{R}_q^{(K)}$) that contains polynomials with coefficients in $[-(p-1)/2, (p-1)/2]$. Lemma 1 shows that the ring $\mathcal{R}_q$ has a large set of invertible elements that are easy to identify.

**Lemma 1** ([29, Lemma 2.2]). *Let $\mathcal{R}_q = \mathbb{Z}_q[\mathbf{x}]/\langle \mathbf{x}^n + 1 \rangle$ where $n > 1$ is a power of 2 and $q$ is a prime congruent to 5 mod 8. This ring has exactly $2q^{n/2} - 1$ elements without an inverse. Moreover, every non-zero polynomial $\mathbf{a}$ in $\mathcal{R}_q$ with $\|\mathbf{a}\|_\infty < \sqrt{q/2}$ has an inverse.*

There are some easy bounds on the norm of the product of polynomials.

**Lemma 2.** *For $\mathbf{a}, \mathbf{b} \in \mathcal{R}_q$ it holds: $\|\mathbf{ab}\|_\infty \leq \min\{\|\mathbf{a}\|_\infty\|\mathbf{b}\|_1, (q-1)/2\}$. Moreover, let $\mathbf{a}, \mathbf{b} \in \mathcal{R}_q$ be such that $n\|\mathbf{a}\|_\infty \cdot \|\mathbf{b}\|_\infty \leq (q-1)/2$. Then we have that $\|\mathbf{ab}\| \leq \|\mathbf{a}\|\|\mathbf{b}\|\sqrt{n}$ and $\|\mathbf{ab}\|_\infty \leq \|\mathbf{a}\|_\infty\|\mathbf{b}\|_\infty n \leq \frac{q-1}{2}$.*

## 2.2 Lattices

An integer lattice is an additive subgroup of $\mathbb{Z}^n$. Every lattice $\Lambda$ is generated by a basis $\mathbf{B} = \{\mathbf{b}_1, \ldots, \mathbf{b}_k\} \in \mathbb{Z}^{n \times m}$, where $m$ is called *dimension* of the lattice. Such lattice is denoted by $\Lambda = \mathcal{L}(\mathbf{B})$. If $k = n$ and the vectors in the basis are linearly independent the lattice is a *full-rank* lattice. The Gram-Schmidt orthogonalization of a full-rank basis $\mathbf{B}$ is denoted by $\tilde{\mathbf{B}} = \{\tilde{\mathbf{b}}_1, \ldots \tilde{\mathbf{b}}_n\}$. Let $\tilde{\lambda}(\mathcal{L}(\mathbf{B})) = \min_{\mathbf{B}' \text{s.t.} \mathcal{L}(\mathbf{B}')=\mathcal{L}(\mathbf{B})} \|\tilde{\mathbf{B}}'\|$. For a matrix $\mathbf{A} \in \mathbb{Z}^{n \times m}$, $\Lambda^\perp$ is the lattice: $\Lambda^\perp = \mathcal{L}^\perp(\mathbf{A}) = \{\mathbf{x} \in \mathbb{Z}^m \mid \mathbf{Ax} = \mathbf{0} \bmod q\} \subseteq \mathbb{Z}^m$. We define the *discrete Gaussian distribution* centered in $\mathbf{c}$ with standard deviation $\sigma$ on a full-rank lattice $\Lambda$ as $\mathcal{D}_{\Lambda,\mathbf{c},\sigma}(\mathbf{v}) = e^{-\frac{\pi\|\mathbf{v}-\mathbf{c}\|^2}{\sigma^2}} / \sum_{\mathbf{u} \in \Lambda} e^{-\frac{\pi\|\mathbf{u}-\mathbf{c}\|^2}{\sigma^2}}$ for all $\mathbf{v} \in \Lambda$, and 0 on all the other points in the space. Let $\mathcal{D}_{\mathbf{A},\mathbf{u},\sigma}^\perp$ be the distribution of the vectors $\mathbf{s}$ such that $\mathbf{s} \sim \mathcal{D}_{\mathbb{Z}^n,\mathbf{0},\sigma}$ conditioned on $\mathbf{As} = \mathbf{u} \bmod q$.

**Lemma 3** (cf. [2, Lemma 1.5], [27, Lemma 4.4]). *Let $\mathbf{A} \in \mathbb{Z}^{n \times m}$ with $2^{11} < m$ and $\mathbf{u} \in \mathbb{Z}_q^n$. For $\sigma \geq \tilde{\lambda}(\mathcal{L}^\perp(\mathbf{A}))$ it holds:*

$$\Pr_{\mathbf{s} \xleftarrow{\$} \mathcal{D}_{\mathbf{A},\mathbf{u},\sigma}^\perp} (\|\mathbf{s}\| > 1.05\sigma\sqrt{m}) < 2^{-5} \quad \text{and} \quad \Pr_{\mathbf{s} \xleftarrow{\$} \mathcal{D}_{\mathbf{A},\mathbf{u},\sigma}^\perp} (\|\mathbf{s}\|_\infty > 8\sigma) < m2^{-46}.$$

*In particular, the inequalities hold also when $\mathbf{s} \xleftarrow{\$} \mathcal{D}_{\mathbb{Z}^m,\mathbf{u},\sigma}$.*

## 2.3   Lattices over Rings

Lattices over the polynomial ring $\mathcal{R}_q$ can be defined similarly to lattices over $\mathbb{Z}_q$. Indeed, given $\mathbf{A} \in \mathcal{R}_q^{1 \times m}$ we can construct $m$-dimensional lattice $\mathcal{L}^\perp(\mathbf{A})$ as $\Lambda^\perp = \mathcal{L}^\perp(\mathbf{A}) = \{\mathbf{V} \in (\mathbb{Z}[\mathbf{x}]/\langle \mathbf{x}^n + 1\rangle)^m \mid \mathbf{AV} = \mathbf{0} \bmod q\} \subseteq \mathcal{R}_q^m$. Consider the obvious embedding that maps a polynomial to the vector of its coefficients. Then $\Lambda^\perp$ can be also seen as a $nm$-dimensional integer lattice over $\mathbb{Z}$. With a slight abuse of notation, we will write $\mathbf{y} \xleftarrow{\$} \mathcal{D}_{\mathcal{R}_q, \mathbf{u}, \sigma}$ to indicate that $\mathbf{y}$ was sampled from $\mathcal{D}_{\mathbb{Z}^n, \mathbf{u}, \sigma}$ and then mapped to $\mathcal{R}_q$. Similarly, we omit the $\mathbf{0}$ and write $[\mathbf{y}_1 \dots \mathbf{y}_k] \xleftarrow{\$} \mathcal{D}_{\mathcal{R}_q, \sigma}^k$ to mean that a vector $\mathbf{y}$ is generated according to $\mathcal{D}_{\mathbb{Z}^{kn}, \mathbf{0}, \sigma}$ and then gets interpreted as $k$ polynomials $\mathbf{y}_i$.

We recall some results about sampling an element from a Gaussian distribution over a lattice given some trapdoor.

**Theorem 1 (adapted from [32]).** *Let $\mathbf{A}$ be a vector in $\mathcal{R}_q^{1 \times \ell}$ and $\mathbf{X}$ be a matrix in $\mathcal{R}_q^{\ell \times m}$. Also define the gadget matrix $\mathbf{G} = \begin{bmatrix} 1 & \lceil q^{1/m} \rceil & \dots & \lceil q^{(m-1)/m} \rceil \end{bmatrix}$. Then for any invertible $\mathbf{m} \in \mathcal{R}_q$, there is an algorithm that can sample from the distribution $\mathcal{D}_{[\mathbf{A} \ \mathbf{AX} + \mathbf{mG}], \mathbf{u}, \sigma}^\perp$ for any $\sigma \sim q^{\frac{1}{m}} s_1(\mathbf{X}) > \tilde{\lambda}(\Lambda^\perp([\mathbf{A} \ \mathbf{AX} + \mathbf{mG}]))$ for any $\mathbf{u} \in \mathcal{R}_q$.*

**Lemma 4.** *Suppose $\mathbf{U} \in \mathcal{R}_q^{1 \times k}$ and $\mathbf{V} \in \mathcal{R}_q^{1 \times m}$ are polynomial vectors, and $\mathbf{B}_U, \mathbf{B}_{(U,V)}$ are bases of $\Lambda^\perp(\mathbf{U})$ and $\Lambda^\perp([\mathbf{U} \ \mathbf{V}])$ respectively such that $\|\tilde{\mathbf{B}}_U\|, \|\tilde{\mathbf{B}}_{(U,V)}\| < \sigma \sqrt{\pi/\ln(2n+4)}$. Then, there exists an algorithm $\mathsf{SampleD}(\mathbf{U}, \mathbf{V}, \mathbf{B}, \mathbf{u}, \sigma)$, where $\mathbf{B}$ is either $\mathbf{B}_U$ or $\mathbf{B}_{(U,V)}$, that can efficiently sample from the distribution $D_{[\mathbf{U} \ \mathbf{V}], \mathbf{u}, \sigma}^\perp$ for any $\mathbf{u} \in \mathcal{R}_q$.*

## 2.4   Hardness Assumptions

We recall two well-studied lattice problems over rings: Ring-SIS and Ring-LWE.

**Definition 1 (Ring-SIS$_{m,q,\beta}$ problem).** *The Ring-SIS$_{m,q,\beta}$ problem is given a vector $\mathbf{A} \in \mathcal{R}_q^{1 \times (m-1)}$ to find a vector $\mathbf{S} \in \mathcal{R}_q^m$ such that $[\mathbf{A} \ 1]\mathbf{S} = \mathbf{0}$ and $\|\mathbf{S}\| \leq \beta$.*

**Definition 2.** *The Ring-LWE$_D$ distribution outputs pairs $(\mathbf{a}, \mathbf{b}) \in \mathcal{R}_q \times \mathcal{R}_q$ such that $\mathbf{b} = \mathbf{as} + \mathbf{e}$ for a uniformly random $\mathbf{a}$ from $\mathcal{R}_q$ and $\mathbf{s}, \mathbf{e}$ sampled from distribution $D$. The Ring-LWE$_{k,D}$ decisional problem on ring $\mathcal{R}_q$ with distribution $D$ is to distinguish whether $k$ pairs $(\mathbf{a}_1, \mathbf{b}_1), \dots, (\mathbf{a}_k, \mathbf{b}_k)$ were sampled from the Ring-LWE$_D$ distribution or from the uniform distribution over $\mathcal{R}_q^2$.*

There is a polynomial-time reduction from solving the shortest vector problem over rings to Ring-SIS [28, Theorem 5.1] and a polynomial-time quantum reduction from solving the shortest vector problem over rings to Ring-LWE with Gaussian error distribution (cf. [30]). The root Hermite factor $\delta$ introduced by Gama and Nguyen [18] is used to estimate the hardness of the lattice problems for given parameters in the security reductions.

Boschini et al. [8] introduce new hardness assumptions to be able to prove their schemes secure with or without complexity leveraging. The idea is to state the assumptions in two forms, selective and adaptive. The schemes are proved secure assuming the adaptive variants of the assumptions. Then, a reduction from adaptive to selective is proved using complexity leveraging, and Ring-SIS and Ring-LWE are reduced to the selective version. Hence, allowing the use of complexity leveraging it is possible to base the security of the schemes on Ring-SIS and Ring-LWE, otherwise security is guaranteed under the adaptive version of the new hardness assumptions (cf. Assumptions 1 and 3).

**Assumption 1.** *Consider the following game between an adversary* A *and a challenger for fixed* $m \in \mathbb{N}$ *and distribution* $D$:

1. *The challenger outputs a uniformly random* $\mathbf{C} \xleftarrow{\$} \mathcal{R}_q^{1 \times m}$ *to* A.
2. A *sends back* $\mathbf{m} \in \mathcal{U}$.
3. *The challenger picks a uniformly random bit* $b \xleftarrow{\$} \{0,1\}$. *If* $b = 1$, *it samples an error vector* $\mathbf{E} \xleftarrow{\$} D^m$ *and* $\mathbf{s} \xleftarrow{\$} D$, *and sends* $\mathbf{F} = (\mathbf{C} + \mathbf{mG} - \mathbf{E})\mathbf{s}^{-1}$ *to* A. *Otherwise, it sends a uniform* $\mathbf{F} \xleftarrow{\$} \mathcal{R}_q^{1 \times m}$ *to* A.
4. A *sends a bit* $b'$ *to the challenger.*

*The advantage of* A *in winning the game is* $\left| \Pr(b = b') - \frac{1}{2} \right|$. *The assumption states that no PPT* A *can win the previous game with non-negligible advantage.*

**Assumption 2 (Selective variant of Assumption 1).** *Consider the game of Assumption 1, but with steps 1 and 2 switched, meaning,* A *outputs* $\mathbf{m} \in \mathcal{U}$ *before being given* $\mathbf{C}$. *The assumption states that no PPT adversary can win this previous game with non-negligible advantage.*

Boschini et al. proved that Assumption 2 is at least as hard as Ring-LWE with $m$ samples and distribution $D$. It is possible to reduce Assumption 2 to 1 with a complexity leveraging argument by guessing the value of $\mathbf{m} \in \mathcal{U}$.

**Assumption 3.** *Let* $\bar{\Sigma} = \{(\mathbf{c}_1, \mathbf{S}, \mathbf{c}_2) \in \bar{\mathcal{C}} \times \mathcal{R}_q^{3+2m} \times \mathcal{R}_q : \|\mathbf{S}\| \leq N' \wedge \|\mathbf{c}_2\| \leq C'\}$ *for some fixed parameters. Consider the following game between an adversary* A *and a challenger for fixed* $m \in \mathbb{N}$ *and distribution* $D$:

1. *The challenger chooses* $\mathbf{a} \xleftarrow{\$} \mathcal{R}_q$, $\mathbf{C} \xleftarrow{\$} \mathcal{R}_q^{1 \times m}$, *and* $\mathbf{X} \xleftarrow{\$} \mathcal{D}_{\mathcal{R}_q, \sigma_t}^{2 \times m}$. *It sets* $\mathbf{A} = [\mathbf{a}|\mathbf{1}]$ *and* $\mathbf{B} = \mathbf{A}\mathbf{X} + \mathbf{G}$, *where* $\mathbf{G} = [\mathbf{1} \lceil q^{1/m} \rceil \ldots \lceil q^{(m-1)/m} \rceil]$.
2. *The challenger runs* A *on input* $[\mathbf{A}\ \mathbf{B}\ \mathbf{C}\ \mathbf{1}]$, *giving it access to a random oracle* $\mathcal{H} : \{0,1\}^* \to \mathcal{R}_q$ *and an oracle* $\mathcal{O}_S$ *that on input* $\mathbf{m} \in \mathcal{U}$ *and a string* $\alpha \in \{0,1\}^*$ *outputs a small vector* $[\mathbf{S}\,;\mathbf{0}]$ *in the coset* $\mathcal{L}^{\perp}([\mathbf{A}\ \mathbf{B}\ \mathbf{C} + \mathbf{mG}\ \mathbf{1}]) + \mathcal{H}(\alpha)$ *such that* $\|\mathbf{S}\| \leq N_S$.
3. *Algorithm* A *outputs* $\bar{\mathbf{m}} \in \bar{\mathcal{U}}$, $\bar{\alpha} \in \{0,1\}^*$, $\bar{\mathbf{c}}_1 \in \bar{\mathcal{C}}$, *a ring element* $\bar{\mathbf{c}}_2$ *and a vector* $\bar{\mathbf{S}}$. *Algorithm* A *wins the game if* $(\bar{\mathbf{c}}_1, \bar{\mathbf{S}}, \bar{\mathbf{c}}_2) \in \bar{\Sigma}$, $\bar{\mathbf{m}} \in \bar{\mathcal{U}}$, *such that* $\mathbf{S}$ *is a short vector of the coset* $\mathcal{L}^{\perp}([\mathbf{A}\ \mathbf{B}\ \bar{\mathbf{C}}\ \mathbf{1}]) + \mathbf{c}_2 \mathcal{H}(\bar{\alpha})$ *where* $\bar{\mathbf{C}} = \bar{\mathbf{c}}_1 \mathbf{C} - \bar{\mathbf{m}}\mathbf{G}$, *and* $(\bar{\mathbf{m}}\bar{\mathbf{c}}_1^{-1}, \bar{\alpha})$ *was not queried to the* $\mathcal{O}_S$ *oracle.*

*The assumption states that no PPT algorithm* A *can win the game with non-negligible probability.*

**Assumption 4 (Selective variant of Assumption 3).** *Consider the game of Assumption 3, but where step 1 is preceded with a step where* A, *on input only the security parameter* $\lambda$, *outputs the message* $\bar{\mathsf{m}} \in \bar{\mathcal{U}}$, *and in step 3 outputs the remaining items* $\bar{a}$, $\bar{c}_1, \bar{c}_2 \in \bar{\mathcal{C}}$, *and* $\bar{\mathbf{S}}$. *The assumption states that no PPT adversary can win this previous game with non-negligible advantage.*

**Theorem 2 (Hardness of Assumption 4).** *Let* A *be a probabilistic algorithm that breaks Assumption 4 in time* $t$ *with probability* $\epsilon_A$. *Then there exists a probabilistic algorithm* B *that either breaks Ring-LWE$_{m,\mathcal{D}_\sigma}$ in time* $t$ *with probability* $\epsilon_A$ *or Ring-SIS$_{3+m,q,\beta_s}$ in time* $t$ *with probability* $\epsilon_B \geq (\epsilon_A - \epsilon_{\mathrm{LWE}})/(2 \cdot |\bar{\mathcal{C}}|)$, *where* $\beta_s = N'^2 + \frac{\sigma_t^2}{\pi} n^2 (\sqrt{2} + \sqrt{m} + \log n)^2 (2\sqrt{2^{K_c}})^2 N'^2 + \frac{\sigma^2}{\pi} n (1 + \sqrt{2} + \log n)^2 (C'^2 + (1.05\sigma_t\sqrt{n})^2)$, $\epsilon_{\mathrm{LWE}}$ *is the probability of breaking the Ring-LWE problem over* $\mathcal{R}_q$ *in time* $t$, *in the Random Oracle Model.*

The bound $\beta_s$ is different from the original result, as we choose larger message and challenge spaces. From complexity leveraging (guessing $\bar{\mathsf{m}}$ in $\bar{\mathcal{U}}$ and $\bar{c}_1$ in $\bar{\mathcal{C}}$) it follows that breaking Assumption 4 implies breaking Assumption 3.

## 2.5    Group Signature

A group signature is a set of algorithms (GPGen, GKGen, UKGen, OKGen, GSign, GVerify, GOpen) run by a group manager, an opener and users. The group signature parameters *gpar* are generated via GPGen$(1^\lambda)$ (where $\lambda$ is the security parameter). The group manager and the opener generate their keys running $(gpk, gsk) \leftarrow$ GKGen$(gpar)$ and $(opk, osk) \leftarrow$ OKGen$(gpk)$ respectively. If a user wants to join, she sends her identity to the group manager and obtains back her user secret key $usk \leftarrow$ UKGen$(gsk, id)$. The user can sign a message $M$ on behalf of the group using her secret key with the algorithm GSign$(usk, gpk, opk, M)$. A signature *sig* on a message $M$ can be verified with the algorithm $\{1, 0\} \leftarrow$ GVerify$(M, sig, gpk, opk)$. Finally, the opener can recover the identity of the group member that signed a message $M$ running $id \leftarrow$ GOpen$(M, sig, osk)$. We require the scheme to be correct (honestly generated signatures satisfy verification and can be opened to the identity of the signer), traceable (the group manager should be able to link every signature to the user who produced it) and anonymous (signatures produced by different users should be indistinguishable).

## 2.6    One-Time Signature

A One-Time Signature (OTS) scheme for message set $\mathcal{M}$ is a triple (OTSGen, OTSSign, OTSVf), where $(sk, vk) \leftarrow$ OTSGen$(1^\lambda)$ is the key generation algorithm, $ots \leftarrow$ OTSSign$(sk, msg)$ is the signing algorithm and $0/1 \leftarrow$ OTSVf$(vk, msg, ots)$ is the verification algorithm. Correctness requires that for all security parameters $\lambda \in \mathbb{N}$ the verification of a honestly generated signature always outputs 1. An OTS is unforgeable if, given $sk, vk$, no adversary can come up with a signature on a message $msg'$ w.r.t. $vk$ after seeing a signature on $msg$ generated using *sk*. In particular, the Lamport signature [22] is quantum-secure, thus it can be used with the relaxed $\Sigma$-protocol.

## 2.7    Relaxed ZK Proofs

Given two NP-languages $L \subseteq \bar{L}$ defined by the relations $R \subseteq \bar{R}$ respectively, a relaxed $\Sigma$-protocol for $L, \bar{L}$ is a three-rounds two-party protocol between PPT algorithms $(\mathcal{P}, \mathcal{V})$ that satisfies standard completeness and zero-knowledge, but where extraction is only guaranteed to output a witness $w$ such that $(x, w) \in \bar{R}$. A protocol can be made non-interactive using Fiat-Shamir transform [17]. Simulation-soundness of the transform can be ensured (cf. [16]) by a property called "quasi-unique responses": it should be impossible for an adversary to create two valid transcripts that differ only in the responses. Applying the Fiat-Shamir transform to a relaxed $\Sigma$-protocol with quasi-unique responses results in a relaxed NIZK proof, i.e., a non-interactive protocol that satisfies classical completeness, unbounded non-interactive zero-knowledge and the following relaxed definition of simulation soundness:

**Definition 3 (Relaxed unbounded simulation soundness).** *There exists a PPT simulator* S *such that for all PPT adversaries* A,

$$\Pr\left[\mathcal{V}^{S_1}(x^*, \pi^*) = 1 \wedge x^* \notin \bar{L} \wedge (x^*, \pi^*) \notin Q \; : \; (x^*, \pi^*) \leftarrow A^{S_1, S_2'}(1^\lambda)\right]$$

*is negligible, where* $Q$ *is the set of tuples* $(x, \pi)$ *where* A *made a query* $S_2(x)$ *and obtained response* $\pi$.

It is also possible to obtain relaxed unbounded simulation soundness using an OTS scheme with the Fiat-Shamir transform. A formal description and full proof of the construction can be found in the work by Boschini et al. [8].

To instantiate such protocols over lattices, consider the languages $(L, \bar{L})$ associated with the following relations:

$$R = \left\{ ((\mathbf{A}, \mathbf{U}), (\mathbf{S}, \mathbf{1})) \in \mathcal{R}_q^{\ell \times m} \times \mathcal{R}_q^{1 \times \ell} \times \mathcal{R}_q^m \times \{1\} : \mathbf{AS} = \mathbf{U}, \|\mathbf{S}\| \leq N \right\}$$

$$\bar{R} = \left\{ ((\mathbf{A}, \mathbf{U}), (\bar{\mathbf{S}}, \bar{\mathbf{c}})) \in \mathcal{R}_q^{\ell \times m} \times \mathcal{R}_q^{1 \times \ell} \times \mathcal{R}_q^m \times \bar{\mathcal{C}} : \mathbf{A}\bar{\mathbf{S}} = \bar{\mathbf{c}}\mathbf{U}, \|\mathbf{S}\| \leq \bar{N}_2, \|\mathbf{S}\|_\infty \leq \bar{N}_\infty \right\}$$

where $0 < N \leq \bar{N}_2$, $0 < \bar{N}_\infty$ and, if the set of the challenges used in the protocol is $\mathcal{C}$, the set of relaxed challenges is $\bar{\mathcal{C}} = \{\mathbf{c} - \mathbf{c}' \; : \; \mathbf{c}, \mathbf{c}' \in \mathcal{C}\}$. Finding a witness $(\mathbf{S}, \mathbf{c})$ for an element $(\mathbf{A}, \mathbf{U})$ of the language $\bar{L}$ is hard under the computational assumption that Ring-SIS$_{\bar{N}}$ is hard. In the relaxed $\Sigma$-protocol for $L, \bar{L}$, the prover $\mathcal{P}$ samples a masking vector $\mathbf{Y} \xleftarrow{\$} \mathcal{D}_\sigma^m$ and sends $\mathbf{T} = \mathbf{AY}$ to the verifier $\mathcal{V}$. Next, $\mathcal{V}$ samples a challenge $\mathbf{c} \in \mathcal{C}$ and sends it back to $\mathcal{P}$. The prover constructs $\mathbf{Z} = \mathbf{Y} + \mathbf{cS}$ and, depending on rejection sampling (see [27, Theorem 4.6]), either aborts or sends it to $\mathcal{V}$. The verifier accepts if $\mathbf{AZ} - \mathbf{cU} = \mathbf{T}$ and $\|\mathbf{Z}\| \leq 1.05\sigma\sqrt{mn} =: N_2$, $\|\mathbf{Z}\|_\infty \leq 8\sigma =: N_\infty$. The zero-knowledge property is guaranteed by rejection sampling. A standard deviation $\sigma = 12T$, where $T$ is a bound on the norm of $\mathbf{cS}$ obtained from $N$, guarantees that the prover outputs something with probability greater than $(1 - -2^{100})/e$ (cf. [27, Theorem 4.6]). Setting $\bar{N}_2 = 2N_2 = 2.1\sigma\sqrt{mn}$ and $\bar{N}_\infty = 2N_\infty = 16\sigma$ allows to prove that this is a relaxed $\Sigma$-protocol.

The proof-system we introduced can be adapted to prove that a component $\mathbf{s}_i$ of $\mathbf{S}$ is in a subring $\mathcal{R}_q^{(2^{K_m})}$ by using as challenge space $\mathcal{C} = \mathcal{R}_3^{(2^{K_c})}$, that is a subset of $\mathcal{R}_q^{(2^{K_m})}$ when $K_m \geq K_c$ and sampling the $i$-th element of the "masking" vector $\mathbf{Y}$ from $\mathcal{R}_q^{(2^{K_m})}$. Hence the output vector $\mathbf{Z} = \mathbf{Sc} + \mathbf{Y}$ is such that $\mathbf{z}_i \in \mathcal{R}_q^{(2^{K_m})}$. The verifier has to check also this latter condition before accepting.

## 2.8   Relaxed Signatures

Boschini et at. [8] introduced a new lattice-based relaxed signature scheme, i.e., a signature (SParGen, SKeyGen, Sign, SVerify) where the verification algorithm is relaxed to accept signature on messages coming from a set $\bar{\mathcal{M}}$ larger than the set $\mathcal{M}$ of signed messages. The signature is proved unforgeable under a relaxed notion of unforgeability under chosen-message attacks that includes as a forgery a signature on a message in $\bar{\mathcal{M}}$ that is the image of a message in $\mathcal{M}$ through some function $f$ that was not signed by the signing oracle. The relaxation in the definition is necessary in order to combine the signature with the relaxed $\Sigma$-protocol (see Sect. 2.7).

Given that we reduce the unforgeability of the group signature directly to the hardness of Assumption 1, we do not discuss security of the signature here. We only remark that we use a different set of messages, namely $\mathcal{U} = \mathcal{R}_3^{(16)}$, while the original lattice instantiation signs messages composed by a small polynomial and a bit-string. When using it in the group signature, the small polynomial $\mathbf{m} \in \mathcal{U}$ encodes a user's identity, but there is no need for the bit string. Therefore, we substitute the output of the hash of the bit-string with a constant polynomial $\mathbf{u}$ chosen uniformly at random in $\mathcal{R}_q$ during the key generation and sign only messages in $\mathcal{M} = \mathcal{U}$. The modified scheme is trivially still unforgeable under Assumption 3 in the Random Oracle Model.

*Parameters Generation.* The parameters *spar* are generated by SParGen$(1^\lambda)$ and include $(n, q, m, \sigma_t, \sigma, r, N, N', C', \mathbf{C})$ where: $n$ is a power of 2, $q$ is a prime, $q \equiv 5 \bmod 8$, $m$ determines the gadget vector $\mathbf{G}$ in Theorem 1, $\sigma_t$ is standard deviation of the distribution of the trapdoor, $\sigma = q^{1/m}\frac{\sigma_t}{\sqrt{\pi}}\sqrt{n}\cdot(\sqrt{2}+\sqrt{m}+\log(n))$ is the standard deviation of the Gaussian from which signatures are sampled, $r$ bounds the norm of the polynomial part of the messages in $\bar{\mathcal{U}} = \mathcal{R}_r^{(16)}$, $N = 1.05\sigma\sqrt{n(2m+2)}$ bounds the norm of a signature output by Sign, $N' > N$ and $C' \geq 1$ define the set of valid signatures $\bar{\Sigma}$, and $\mathbf{C}$ is uniformly random matrix in $\mathcal{R}_q^{1\times m}$.

*Key generation.* The signer selects a uniformly random matrix $\mathbf{A} = \begin{bmatrix} \mathbf{a}\ 1 \end{bmatrix}$ in $\mathcal{R}_q^{1\times 2}$ and an element $\mathbf{u} \xleftarrow{\$} \mathcal{R}_q$ as verification key and a matrix with small coefficients $\mathbf{X} \stackrel{\$}{\leftarrow} \mathcal{D}^{2 \times m}_{\mathcal{R}_q, \sigma_t}$ as secret signing key. The public verification key is the vector $\mathbf{V} = \begin{bmatrix} \mathbf{A} \ \mathbf{B} \ \mathbf{C} \end{bmatrix} = \begin{bmatrix} \mathbf{A} \ \mathbf{AX} + \mathbf{G} \ \mathbf{C} \end{bmatrix} \in \mathcal{R}_q^{1 \times (2+2m)}$.

*Signing.* If $M = \mathbf{m} \notin \mathcal{M}$ abort. Otherwise, the signer computes $\mathbf{S} \leftarrow \mathsf{SampleD}$ $\left( \begin{bmatrix} \mathbf{A} \ \mathbf{B} \ \mathbf{C} + \mathbf{mG} \end{bmatrix}, \mathbf{u}, \sigma \right)$ (see Lemma 4) and outputs a signature $sig = (1, \begin{bmatrix} \mathbf{S} ; \mathbf{0} \end{bmatrix}, 1)$. The entry $(\mathbf{m}, sig)$ is stored so that if a signature on $\mathbf{m}$ is queried twice, the algorithm outputs always $sig$.

*Verification.* Verification of a signature $sig = (\mathbf{c}_1, \mathbf{S}, \mathbf{c}_2)$ on message $M = \mathbf{m}$ returns 1 if $\begin{bmatrix} \mathbf{A} \ \mathbf{B} \ \mathbf{c}_1 \mathbf{C} + \mathbf{mG} \ 1 \end{bmatrix} \mathbf{S} = \mathbf{c}_2 \mathbf{u}$, if the message $M \in \bar{\mathcal{M}}$, and if the signature $sig \in \bar{\Sigma} = \{ (\mathbf{c}_1, \mathbf{S}, \mathbf{c}_2) \in \bar{\mathcal{C}} \times \mathcal{R}_q^{3+2m} \times \mathcal{R}_q : \|\mathbf{S}\| \leq N' \wedge \|\mathbf{c}_2\| \leq C' \}$. Otherwise, it returns 0.

The relaxed signature scheme is $f$-uf-cma secure w.r.t. the message relaxation function $f(\mathbf{m}) = \{ (\mathbf{mc}) : \mathbf{c} \in \bar{\mathcal{C}} \}$.

**Theorem 3.** *An algorithm* A *that breaks the $f$-uf-cma unforgeability of the relaxed signature scheme in time $t$ and probability $\epsilon_A$ can break the Assumption 3 in time $t$ with probability $\epsilon_A$ in the Random Oracle Model.*

To prove knowledge of a signature on a message $\mathbf{m}$ without revealing $\mathbf{m}$, Boschini et al. combine the relaxed signature, a relaxed commitment and the relaxed $\Sigma$-protocol, where the commitment is used to hide the part of the verification key of the signature that depends on $\mathbf{m}$. Let $\mathbf{S} = \begin{bmatrix} \mathbf{S}_1 ; \mathbf{S}_2 ; \mathbf{S}_3 ; 1 \end{bmatrix}$ be a signature on $\mathbf{m}$ w.r.t. the public key $spk = \begin{bmatrix} \mathbf{A} \ \mathbf{B} \ \mathbf{C} \end{bmatrix}$. To hide the part of the verification equation of the signature that depends on $\mathbf{m}$, Boschini et al. present the following trick. First, construct $\mathbf{F} = \mathbf{b}^{-1}(\mathbf{C} + \mathbf{mG} + \mathbf{E})$ choosing random $\mathbf{E} \stackrel{\$}{\leftarrow} \mathcal{R}_3^{1 \times m}$ and $\mathbf{b} \stackrel{\$}{\leftarrow} \mathcal{R}_3$. Assuming Assumption 1 is hard or using complexity leveraging and assuming the hardness of Ring-LWE (cf. Sect. 2.4), we have that $\mathbf{F}$ hides $\mathbf{m}^1$ then, set $\mathbf{S}_s$ to be $\mathbf{S}_s = \begin{bmatrix} \mathbf{S}_1 ; \mathbf{S}_2 ; \mathbf{bS}_3 ; -\mathbf{ES}_3 \end{bmatrix}$. It is easy to see that $\mathbf{s}_s$ satisfies $\begin{bmatrix} \mathbf{A} \ \mathbf{B} \ \mathbf{F} \ 1 \end{bmatrix} \mathbf{S}_s = \mathbf{u}$.

## 3  Relaxed Partial Verifiable Encryption

Lyubashevsky and Neven [29] defined a relaxed verifiable encryption as a scheme to encrypt a witness $w$ of $x \in L$ such that decryption of a valid ciphertext is guaranteed to yield a witness $\bar{w}$ in the relaxed language such that $(x, \bar{w}) \in \bar{R}$.

The straightforward combination with the relaxed signature and commitment scheme of Boschini et al. [8] does not yield a particularly efficient group signature scheme, however, because the Lyubashevsky-Neven verifiable encryption scheme encrypts and recovers the *full* witness. A group signature typically consists of a verifiable encryption of the user's identity together with a proof that the user knows a valid signature on the encrypted identity by the group manager.

---

[1] Boschini et al. proved that, for $\mathcal{U} \subset \mathcal{R}_3^{(16)}$, this is actually a relaxed commitment scheme. We do not need the relaxed binding property, hence we can choose a larger set of messages (as long as it still guarantees the hiding property).

The verifiable encryption as defined by Lyubashevsky and Neven would therefore encrypt both the user's identity and the signature on it, which unnecessarily blows up the size of the verifiable ciphertext. Even when using a commitment to the user's identity to separate the proof of knowledge of the signature from the verifiable encryption, the ciphertext will encrypt the user's identity as well as the opening information to the commitment.

We therefore introduce a variant of the Lyubashevsky-Neven relaxed verifiable encryption scheme called relaxed *partial* verifiable encryption that, rather than decrypting the full witness $\bar{w}$, recovers only a function of that witness $g(\bar{w})$ while proving knowledge of the full witness $\bar{w}$. When constructing a group signature case, we will use a function $g$ that outputs just the user's identity.

### 3.1 Definition of Relaxed Partial Verifiable Encryption

Our general definition of relaxed partial verifiable encryption are inspired by the definition of relaxed verifiable encryption by Lyubashevsky and Neven [29] and of verifiable encryption by Camenisch and Shoup [11]. Let $L$ be a language with witness relation $R$ and let $\bar{L} \supseteq L$ be a relaxed language with relaxed relation $\bar{R} \supseteq R$. Let $\bar{R} \subseteq \bar{L} \times \bar{W}$ and let $g : \bar{W} \to D$ be a function.

Given relations $R$, $\bar{R}$ and function $g$, a *relaxed partial verifiable encryption scheme* is composed by four algorithms (EKeyGen, Enc, EVerify, Dec). The key generation algorithm $\mathsf{EKeyGen}(1^\lambda)$ outputs a pair of keys $(epk, esk)$. The encryption algorithm $\mathsf{Enc}(epk, x, w, \ell)$, where $(x, w) \in R$ and $\ell \in \{0,1\}^*$ is an encryption label, returns a ciphertext $t$ and a proof $\pi = (\alpha, \beta, \gamma)$. Verification $\mathsf{EVerify}(epk, x, t, \pi, \ell)$ returns 1 if $\pi$ shows that $t$ is a valid ciphertext w.r.t. $x$ and $epk$ with label $\ell$, and returns 0 otherwise. Finally, the decryption algorithm $\mathsf{Dec}(esk, x, t, \pi, \ell)$ returns a value $M$ or a failure symbol $\bot$.

**Correctness.** The scheme is correct if $\Pr\left[\mathsf{Dec}(esk, x, \mathsf{Enc}(epk, x, w, \ell)) = g(w)\right]$ $= 1$ for all keys $(epk, esk) \leftarrow \mathsf{EKeyGen}(1^\lambda)$, all $(x, w) \in R$, and all $\ell \in \{0,1\}^*$.

**Completeness.** The scheme satisfies completeness if $\Pr[\mathsf{EVerify}(epk, \mathsf{Enc}(epk, x, w, \ell), \ell) = 1] = 1$ for all keys $(epk, esk) \leftarrow \mathsf{EKeyGen}(1^\lambda)$, all $(x, w) \in R$, and all $\ell \in \{0,1\}^*$.

**Special soundness.** Special soundness implies that a valid proof $\pi$ is a proof of knowledge of a valid witness $\bar{w}$ for the relation $\bar{R}$ and that decryption of the ciphertext $t$ returns $g(\bar{w})$. More specifically, for all PPT adversaries $\mathsf{A}$ there exists a PPT extractor $\mathsf{E}$ such that the following probability is negligible:

$$\Pr\left[\begin{array}{c} b = b' = 1 \ \wedge \ \beta \neq \beta' \ \wedge \\ (\ \mathsf{Dec}(esk, x, t, \ell) \neq g(\bar{w}) \\ \vee \ (x, \bar{w}) \notin \bar{R}\ ) \end{array} : \begin{array}{l} (epk, esk) \leftarrow \mathsf{EKeyGen}(1^\lambda), \\ (x, t, (\alpha, \beta, \gamma, \beta', \gamma'), \ell) \leftarrow \mathsf{A}(epk, esk), \\ b \leftarrow \mathsf{EVerify}(epk, x, t, (\alpha, \beta, \gamma), \ell), \\ b' \leftarrow \mathsf{EVerify}(epk, x, t, (\alpha, \beta', \gamma'), \ell)), \\ \bar{w} \leftarrow \mathsf{E}(epk, esk, x, t, (\alpha, \beta, \gamma, \beta', \gamma'), \ell) \end{array}\right].$$

**Chosen-ciphertext simulatability.** There exists a simulator $\mathsf{S}$ that outputs ciphertexts indistinguishable from honestly generated ones, i.e., the following probability is negligible:

$$\left| \Pr \left[ b = b' \; : \; \begin{array}{l} b \xleftarrow{\$} \{0,1\}, \; (epk, esk) \leftarrow \mathsf{EKeyGen}(1^\lambda), \\ (,x,w,\ell) \leftarrow \mathsf{A}^{\mathsf{Dec}(esk,\cdot,\cdot,\cdot,\cdot)}(epk), \\ (t_0, \pi_0) \leftarrow \mathsf{Enc}(epk, x, w), \; (t_1, \pi_1) \leftarrow \mathsf{S}(epk, x, \ell), \\ b' \leftarrow \mathsf{A}^{\mathsf{Dec}(esk,\cdot,\cdot,\cdot,\cdot)}(,t_b, \pi_b) \end{array} \right] - \frac{1}{2} \right| ,$$

where A cannot query its Dec oracle on $(x, t_b, \pi_b, \ell)$.

Observe that our definition of Special Soundness hardwires the use of Fiat-Shamir in the general construction. It is possible to give a more general definition of Special Soundness adapting the definition of weak simulation extractability By Faust et al. [16], but such a definition would be beyond the scope of this paper.

### 3.2    Relaxed Partial Verifiable Encryption over Lattices

Let $L$ and $\bar{L}$ be a language and its relaxed version defined w.r.t. the following relations

$$R_{\mathrm{ve}} = \left\{ \begin{array}{c} ((\mathbf{A}, \mathbf{U}), (\mathbf{m}, \mathbf{S}, 1)) \in \\ (\mathcal{R}_q^{\ell_1 \times (\ell_2+1)} \times \mathcal{R}_q^{\ell_1}) \times (\mathcal{U} \times \mathcal{R}_q^{\ell_2} \times \{1\}) \end{array} \; : \; \mathbf{A} \begin{bmatrix} \mathbf{m} \\ \mathbf{S} \end{bmatrix} = \mathbf{U} \bmod q \wedge \|\mathbf{S}\| \le N \right\}$$

$$\bar{R}_{\mathrm{ve}} = \left\{ \begin{array}{c} ((\mathbf{A}, \mathbf{U}), (\bar{\mathbf{m}}, \bar{\mathbf{S}}, \bar{\mathbf{c}})) \in \\ (\mathcal{R}_q^{\ell_1 \times (\ell_2+1)} \times \mathcal{R}_q^{\ell_1}) \times (\bar{\mathcal{U}} \times \mathcal{R}_q^{\ell_2} \times \bar{\mathcal{C}}) \end{array} \; : \; \mathbf{A} \begin{bmatrix} \bar{\mathbf{m}} \\ \bar{\mathbf{S}} \end{bmatrix} = \bar{\mathbf{c}} \mathbf{U} \bmod q \wedge \|\bar{\mathbf{S}}\| \le \bar{N} \right\}$$

for some sets $\mathcal{U}, \bar{\mathcal{U}}, \bar{\mathcal{C}} \subseteq \mathcal{R}_q$ and some integers $\ell_1, \ell_2, N, \bar{N} > 0$.

We will construct a relaxed partial verifiable encryption scheme for relations $R_{\mathrm{ve}}$ and $\bar{R}_{\mathrm{ve}}$ and function $g((\bar{\mathbf{m}}, \bar{\mathbf{S}}, \bar{\mathbf{c}})) = \bar{\mathbf{m}}/\bar{\mathbf{c}} \bmod q$. Our scheme is a modified version of the "multi-shot" chosen-ciphertext secure verifiable encryption scheme of Lyubashevsky-Neven. The multi-shot scheme involves multiple parallel repetitions of the proof with sub-exponential challenge set sizes, and decryption takes strictly sub exponential time (as opposed to expected polynomial time for the one-shot scheme).

Rather than producing one big proof of knowledge of the terms in relation $R_{\mathrm{ve}}$, we split it into two proofs, one for each term. The first proof only contains the ciphertext equations and is repeated multiple times with a sub-exponential challenge set to enable efficient decryption. The second includes the relation equation as well as the ciphertext, proving that the encrypted plaintext is derived from a valid witness. The latter proof uses an exponential-size challenge set, so that it doesn't need to be repeated. Let $p$ and $q$ be two public primes with $p > 2$.

*Key Generation.* The recipient generates two key pairs for Ring-LWE encryption [30], but discards the secret key of the second pair. It samples $\mathbf{s}_1, \mathbf{d}_1, \mathbf{s}_2, \mathbf{d}_2 \xleftarrow{\$} \mathcal{R}_3$ and $\mathbf{a} \xleftarrow{\$} \mathcal{R}_q$, and computes $\mathbf{t}_1 = \mathbf{a}\mathbf{s}_1 + \mathbf{d}_1 \bmod q$ and $\mathbf{t}_2 = \mathbf{a}\mathbf{s}_2 + \mathbf{d}_2 \bmod q$. The public key is $epk = (p, q, \mathbf{a}, \mathbf{t}_1, \mathbf{t}_2)$, the secret key is $esk = \mathbf{s}_1$.

*Encryption.* Given a witness $(\mathbf{m}, \mathbf{S}, 1)$ for language member $(\mathbf{A}, \mathbf{U})$ in the relation $R_{\mathrm{ve}}$, the algorithm Enc uses the Naor-Yung technique [33] by encrypting $\mathbf{m}$ twice using standard Ring-LWE encryption under public keys $\mathbf{t}_1$ and $\mathbf{t}_2$. More precisely, it samples $\mathbf{r}, \mathbf{e}_1, \mathbf{e}_2, \mathbf{f}_1, \mathbf{f}_2 \xleftarrow{\$} \mathcal{R}_3$ and sets $\mathbf{v}_1 = p(\mathbf{ar} + \mathbf{e}_1) \bmod q$, $\mathbf{w}_1 = p(\mathbf{t}_1\mathbf{r} + \mathbf{f}_1) + \mathbf{m} \bmod q$, $\mathbf{v}_2 = p(\mathbf{ar} + \mathbf{e}_2) \bmod q$, and $\mathbf{w}_2 = p(\mathbf{t}_2\mathbf{r} + \mathbf{f}_2) + \mathbf{m} \bmod q$.

Then, letting $\mathbf{A}_1$ be the first column of the matrix $\mathbf{A} = \begin{bmatrix} \mathbf{A}_1 & \mathbf{A}_2 \end{bmatrix}$ in relation $R_{\mathrm{ve}}$, it constructs a NIZK proof $\Pi_1$ using the scheme from Sect. 2.7 for the relation

$$
\begin{bmatrix}
0 & pa & p & 0 & 0 & 0 & \mathbf{0}^{1\times\ell_2} \\
1 & pt_1 & 0 & p & 0 & 0 & \mathbf{0}^{1\times\ell_2} \\
0 & pa & 0 & 0 & p & 0 & \mathbf{0}^{1\times\ell_2} \\
1 & pt_2 & 0 & 0 & 0 & p & \mathbf{0}^{1\times\ell_2} \\
\mathbf{A}_1 & \mathbf{0}^{\ell_1\times 1} & \mathbf{0}^{\ell_1\times 1} & \mathbf{0}^{\ell_1\times 1} & \mathbf{0}^{\ell_1\times 1} & \mathbf{0}^{\ell_1\times 1} & \mathbf{A}_2
\end{bmatrix}
\begin{bmatrix}
\mathbf{m} \\ \mathbf{r} \\ \mathbf{e}_1 \\ \mathbf{f}_1 \\ \mathbf{e}_2 \\ \mathbf{f}_2 \\ \mathbf{S}
\end{bmatrix}
=
\begin{bmatrix}
\mathbf{v}_1 \\ \mathbf{w}_1 \\ \mathbf{v}_2 \\ \mathbf{w}_2 \\ \mathbf{U}
\end{bmatrix},
\tag{1}
$$

whereby it uses the challenge set $\mathcal{C}_1 = \{\mathbf{c} \in \mathcal{R}_3 \mid \|\mathbf{c}\|_1 \leq 32\}$.

To enable Lyubashevsky-Neven's multi-shot decryption technique without having to repeat the above proof multiple times, the encryptor again uses the relaxed NIZK proof of Sect. 2.7 to construct a separate proof $\Pi_2$ for the relation

$$
\begin{bmatrix}
0 & pa & p & 0 & 0 & 0 \\
1 & pt_1 & 0 & p & 0 & 0 \\
0 & pa & 1 & 0 & p & 0 \\
1 & pt_2 & 0 & 0 & 0 & p
\end{bmatrix}
\begin{bmatrix}
\mathbf{m} \\ \mathbf{r} \\ \mathbf{e}_1 \\ \mathbf{f}_1 \\ \mathbf{e}_2 \\ \mathbf{f}_2
\end{bmatrix}
=
\begin{bmatrix}
\mathbf{v}_1 \\ \mathbf{w}_1 \\ \mathbf{v}_2 \\ \mathbf{w}_2
\end{bmatrix},
\tag{2}
$$

whereby it includes $epk, (\mathbf{A}, \mathbf{U}), (\mathbf{v}_1, \mathbf{w}_1, \mathbf{v}_2, \mathbf{w}_2), \Pi_1, \ell$ in the Fiat-Shamir hash. To obtain efficient decryption but keep the soundness error negligible, this proof is repeated $l = 11$ times with challenge set $\mathcal{C}_2 = \mathcal{R}_3^{(16)}$. The algorithm outputs ciphertext $(\mathbf{v}_1, \mathbf{w}_1, \mathbf{v}_2, \mathbf{w}_2)$ and proof $(\Pi_1, \Pi_2)$.

*Verification.* The verification algorithm $\mathsf{EVerify}((p, q, \mathbf{a}, \mathbf{t}_1, \mathbf{t}_2), (\mathbf{A}, \mathbf{U}), (\mathbf{v}_1, \mathbf{w}_1, \mathbf{v}_2, \mathbf{w}_2, \Pi_1, \Pi_2), \ell)$ checks that $\Pi_1$ and $\Pi_2$ are valid relaxed NIZK proofs for the relations of Eqs. (1) and (2), including the correct arguments $epk, (\mathbf{A}, \mathbf{U}), (\mathbf{v}_1, \mathbf{w}_1, \mathbf{v}_2, \mathbf{w}_2), \Pi_1, \ell$ in the Fiat-Shamir hash of $\Pi_2$.

*Decryption.* The decryption algorithm $\mathsf{Dec}(\mathbf{s}_1, (\mathbf{A}, \mathbf{U}), (\mathbf{v}_1, \mathbf{w}_1, \mathbf{v}_2, \mathbf{w}_2), (\Pi_1, \Pi_2), \ell)$ first checks that the proofs are valid using the verification algorithm above, returning $\perp$ if it is not valid. It then decrypts the cihpertext by applying the Lyubashevsky-Neven multi-shot decryption on proof $\Pi_2 = (\mathbf{Y}^{(1)}, \mathbf{c}^{(1)}, \mathbf{Z}^{(1)}, \ldots, \mathbf{Y}^{(l)}, \mathbf{c}^{(l)}, \mathbf{Z}^{(l)})$ by, for $i = 1, \ldots, l$, going over all challenges $\mathbf{c}' \in \mathcal{C}_2$ to try to decrypt $(\bar{\mathbf{c}}\mathbf{v}, \bar{\mathbf{c}}\mathbf{w}_1)$ as a Ring-LWE ciphertext, where $\bar{\mathbf{c}} = \mathbf{c}^{(i)} - \mathbf{c}'$. It does so by computing $\bar{\mathbf{m}}' = (\mathbf{w}_1 - \mathbf{v}_1\mathbf{s}_1)\bar{\mathbf{c}} \bmod q$, checking that $\|\bar{\mathbf{m}}'\|_\infty < q/2C$ where $C$ is as defined in Lemma 5, and if so, compute $\bar{\mathbf{m}} = \bar{\mathbf{m}}' \bmod p$ and return $\bar{\mathbf{m}}/\bar{\mathbf{c}} \bmod q$; otherwise, it returns $\perp$.

*Decryption Runtime.* Decryption terminates in time at most $2^{26}$. Indeed, if the ciphertext is honestly generated the algorithm needs to guess the challenge only once. On the other hand, for a dishonestly generated ciphertext the probability that verification succeeds and still decryption fails is negligible. Indeed, if the adversary could answer only one challenge $\mathbf{c}$, when making the random oracle queries the probability of hitting always $\mathbf{c}$ would be $1/(\ell \cdot |\mathcal{C}_2|)$. Hence, a second challenge exists w.h.p. and decryption requires to guess a challenge $\mathbf{c}'$ at most $|\mathcal{C}_2| \leq 2^{26}$ times.

Remark that the decryption does not recover the full witness: the algorithm decrypts the ciphertext, but it does not recover the randomness used to generate it or the vector $\mathbf{S}$. Moreover, differently from Lyubashevsky-Neven construction, in our case the relation $\mathbf{A}\begin{bmatrix}\mathbf{m}\\\mathbf{S}\end{bmatrix} = \mathbf{U}$ holds modulo $q$, while in the original scheme it has to hold modulo $p$. We show the correctness of the scheme using Lemma 5, which is a variant of a result by Lyubashevsky and Neven [29, Lemma 3.1]. In this lemma we show that, for some choice of the parameters, the decryption always return the same value $\bar{\mathbf{m}}/\bar{\mathbf{c}}$ over the ring $\mathcal{R}_q$. This is slightly different from the original decryption algorithm, as in the original scheme it was enough for decryption to return the same $\bar{\mathbf{m}}/\bar{\mathbf{c}}$ modulo $p$.

**Lemma 5.** *Let* $\mathbf{a} \xleftarrow{\$} \mathcal{R}_q$, *and* $\mathbf{t} = \mathbf{a}\mathbf{s} + \mathbf{d}$ *where* $\mathbf{s}, \mathbf{d} \xleftarrow{\$} \mathcal{R}_3$. *If there exist* $\bar{\mathbf{r}}, \bar{\mathbf{e}}, \bar{\mathbf{f}}$, $\bar{\mathbf{m}}, \bar{\mathbf{c}}$ *such that*

$$p(\mathbf{a}\bar{\mathbf{r}} + \bar{\mathbf{e}}) = \bar{\mathbf{c}}\mathbf{v} \bmod q \quad and \quad p(\mathbf{t}\bar{\mathbf{r}} + \bar{\mathbf{f}}) + \bar{\mathbf{m}} = \bar{\mathbf{c}}\mathbf{w} \bmod q \quad (3)$$

*and* $\|p(\bar{\mathbf{r}}\mathbf{d} + \bar{\mathbf{f}} - \bar{\mathbf{e}}\mathbf{s}) + \bar{\mathbf{m}}\|_\infty < q/2C$ *and* $\|\bar{\mathbf{m}}\|_\infty < p/2C$, *where* $C = \max_{\bar{\mathbf{c}} \in \bar{\mathcal{C}}} \|\bar{\mathbf{c}}\|_1$ $= \max_{\bar{\mathbf{c}}, \bar{\mathbf{c}}' \in \mathcal{C}} \|\bar{\mathbf{c}} - \bar{\mathbf{c}}'\|_1$, *then*

1. $\|(\mathbf{w} - \mathbf{v}\mathbf{s})\mathbf{c}' \bmod q\|_\infty < q/2C$ *and* $\|(\mathbf{w} - \mathbf{v}\mathbf{s})\mathbf{c}' \bmod q \bmod p\|_\infty < p/2C$
2. *for any* $\bar{\mathbf{c}}' \in \bar{\mathcal{C}}$ *such that* $\|(\mathbf{w} - \mathbf{v}\mathbf{s})\mathbf{c}' \bmod q\|_\infty < q/2C$ *and* $\|(\mathbf{w} - \mathbf{v}\mathbf{s})\mathbf{c}' \bmod q \bmod p\|_\infty < p/2C$ *we have* $(\mathbf{w} - \mathbf{v}\mathbf{s})\bar{\mathbf{c}}' \bmod q \bmod p/\bar{\mathbf{c}}' = \bar{\mathbf{m}}/\bar{\mathbf{c}}$.

*Proof.* The proof is a simple verification of the claims and it is very similar to the proof of Lemma 3.1 in [29], hence we omit it. ∎

Hence, for decryption to be correct, we must choose parameters that guarantee that the values decrypted from $\Pi_2$ using $\mathbf{s}_i$ for $i = 1, 2$ satisfy $\|p(\bar{\mathbf{r}}_i\mathbf{d}_i + \bar{\mathbf{f}}_i - \bar{\mathbf{e}}_i\mathbf{s}_i) + \bar{\mathbf{m}}\|_\infty < q/2C$ and $\|\bar{\mathbf{m}}_i\|_\infty < p/2C$, i.e., $p$, $q$ and $n$ should be such that $16\sigma_2(2np + p + 1) < q/2C$ and $16\sigma_2 < p/2C$, where $C \leq 64$ as challenges come from $\mathcal{R}_3^{(16)}$. We enforce this condition on both ciphertexts to guarantee decryption to work using either $\mathbf{s}_1$ or $\mathbf{s}_2$. This allows to prove CCA simulatability following the Naor-Young paradigm [33].

In the next lemma, we prove that with high probability the $\bar{\mathbf{m}}/\bar{\mathbf{c}}$ returned by decryption is equal to the polynomial $\bar{\mathbf{m}}'/\bar{\mathbf{c}}'$ returned from an extractor for $\Pi_2$. The proof of this lemma consists only of a plain computation of the probability, and can be found in the full version of the paper.

**Lemma 6.** *Let* $\bar{\mathbf{m}}$ *and* $\bar{\mathbf{c}}$ *be the output of the decryption and* $\bar{\mathbf{m}}', \bar{\mathbf{c}}'$ *be the values extracted from* $\Pi_1$. *Then with probability at least* $1 - 2^{-35928}$, *over the choice of the opening key* $\mathbf{t}$, $\bar{\mathbf{m}}/\bar{\mathbf{c}} = \bar{\mathbf{m}}'/\bar{\mathbf{c}}'$ *(where parameters are set as in Table 1).*

Finally, for the CCA simulatability the proofs that we use in the scheme need to be unbounded simulation soundness. Following the same reasoning used in Lyubashevsky and Neven, we prove that $\Pi_2$ has quasi-unique responses, hence simulation soundness. Indeed, breaking quasi-uniqueness means finding $\mathbf{z} \neq \mathbf{z}'$ with $\ell_\infty$ norm less than $8\sigma_2$ such that $\mathbf{Mz} = \mathbf{Mz}' \bmod q$, where with $\mathbf{M}$ we mean the matrix in 2. Thus, either there is a non-zero tuple $(\mathbf{y}_1, \mathbf{y}_2) \in \mathcal{R}_q$ with $\ell_\infty$ norm less than $16\sigma_2$ such that $p(\mathbf{ay}_1 + \mathbf{y}_2) = 0 \bmod q$ or $p\mathbf{y}_1 + \mathbf{y}_2 = 0 \bmod q$. Imposing $p > 16\sigma_2$ and $16\sigma_2 p + 16\sigma_2 < q$ implies that the second equality is not possible. Also, setting $(32\sigma_2)^2 < q$, we can use a standard probabilistic argument to show that for all $\mathbf{y}_1, \mathbf{y}_2$ of $\ell_\infty$ norm less than $16\sigma_2$,

$$\mathsf{Pr}_{\mathbf{a} \in \mathcal{R}_q}\left[\mathbf{ay}_1 + p\mathbf{y}_2 = 0 \bmod q\right] = 2^{-\Omega(n)}.$$

Therefore for almost all $\mathbf{a}$, there will not be a short solution $(\mathbf{y}_1, \mathbf{y}_2)$ that satisfies $\mathbf{ay}_1 + p\mathbf{y}_2 = 0$. Observe that the same argument works for $\Pi_1$. Hence imposing the same inequalities on $\sigma_1$ yields simulation soundness also for $\Pi_1$, thus for the protocol $(\Pi_1, \Pi_2)$.

**Theorem 4.** *If Ring-LWE$_{U(\mathcal{R}_q)}$ is hard and the relaxed NIZK proof system is unbounded non-interactive zero-knowledge and unbounded simulation soundness, the scheme* (EKeyGen, Enc, EVerify, Dec) *is a relaxed partial verifiable encryption scheme w.r.t. the function $g$.*

# 4 Group Signature Scheme

The combination of Boschini et al.'s relaxed signature scheme [8] with our relaxed partial verifiable encryption scheme yields an efficient group signature with practical parameters (see Sect. 4.2). Although the building blocks are "relaxed" schemes, the resulting group signature enjoys non-relaxed traceability. Indeed, the correctness of the verifiable encryption guarantees that when opening a signature, the recovered identity is in the original set of group members id (and not in the relaxed one).

## 4.1 A Lattice-Based Group Signature

Let $\mathcal{U} = \mathcal{R}_3^{(16)}$ be the set of possible user identities.

*Parameters Generation.* On input the security parameter $\lambda$, the algorithm runs the parameter generator of the signature scheme $par \leftarrow \mathsf{SParGen}(1^\lambda)$ and chooses integer $p, q, n$ where $p$ and $q$ are prime and $p < q$. It outputs $gpar := (par, p, q, n)$.

*Group Manager Key Generation.* The group manager generates the keys $gsk = \mathbf{X}$ and $gpk = (\begin{bmatrix} \mathbf{A} \ \mathbf{B} \ \mathbf{C} \ \mathbf{1} \end{bmatrix}, \mathbf{u})$ by running SKeyGen and choosing a random ring element $\mathbf{u} \xleftarrow{\$} \mathcal{R}_q$.

*Opener Key Generation.* The opener runs the key generation algorithm of the verifiable encryption scheme $\mathsf{EKeyGen}(1^\lambda)$ and returns the resulting key pair $(opk = epk, osk = esk)$.

*User Key Generation.* The group manager generates a signing key user identity $id = \mathbf{m} \in \mathcal{U} = \mathcal{R}_3^{(16)}$ by running $\mathsf{Sign}(gsk, \mathbf{m})$ to yield $(1, [\mathbf{S} \, ; \, \mathbf{0}], 1)$ as described in Sect. 2.8. Recall that $\mathbf{S}$ is a short vector so that $[\mathbf{A} \, \mathbf{B} \, \mathbf{C} + \mathbf{m}\mathbf{G}] \, \mathbf{S} = \mathbf{u} \bmod q$. It then returns $usk := \mathbf{S}$.

*Signing Algorithm.* The user first generates a key one-time signature key pair $(sk, vk) \leftarrow \mathsf{OTSGen}(1^\lambda)$. The user then blinds her identity $\mathbf{m}$ using the technique from Sect. 2.8 by choosing random $\mathbf{E} \overset{\$}{\leftarrow} \mathcal{R}_3^{1 \times m}$ and $\mathbf{b} \overset{\$}{\leftarrow} \mathcal{R}_3$, and computing $\mathbf{F} = \mathbf{b}^{-1}(\mathbf{C} + \mathbf{m}\mathbf{G} + \mathbf{E})$. If $\mathbf{S} = [\mathbf{S}_1 \, ; \, \mathbf{S}_2 \, ; \, \mathbf{S}_3]$ with $\mathbf{S}_1 \in \mathcal{R}_q^{2 \times 1}$ and $\mathbf{S}_2, \mathbf{S}_3 \in \mathcal{R}_q^{m \times 1}$, then we have that $[\mathbf{A} \, \mathbf{B} \, \mathbf{F} \, 1] \, [\mathbf{S}_1 \, ; \, \mathbf{S}_2 \, ; \, \mathbf{b}\mathbf{S}_3 \, ; \, -\mathbf{E}\mathbf{S}_3] = \mathbf{u} \bmod q$. The user can therefore create a relaxed NIZK proof $\Pi_0$ for the relation

$$
\begin{aligned}
R_0 &= \left\{ (([\mathbf{A} \, \mathbf{B} \, \mathbf{F} \, 1], \mathbf{u}), (\mathbf{T}_0, 1)) \; : \; [\mathbf{A} \, \mathbf{B} \, \mathbf{F} \, 1] \, \mathbf{T}_0 = \mathbf{u} \; \wedge \; \|\mathbf{T}_0\| \leq N_0 \right\} \\
\bar{R}_0 &= \left\{ (([\mathbf{A} \, \mathbf{B} \, \mathbf{F} \, 1], \mathbf{u}), (\bar{\mathbf{T}}_0, \bar{c})) \; : \; [\mathbf{A} \, \mathbf{B} \, \mathbf{F} \, 1] \, \bar{\mathbf{T}}_0 = \bar{c}\mathbf{u} \wedge \; \bar{c} \in \bar{\mathcal{C}}_0 \; \wedge \; \|\bar{\mathbf{T}}_0\| \leq \bar{N}_0 \right\}
\end{aligned}
\tag{4}
$$

where she includes $vk$ in the Fiat-Shamir hash. The parameters follow from rejection sampling (see Sect. 2.7): the noise vector is sampled from a Gaussian with standard deviation $\sigma_0 = 12 T_0$, where $T_0$ is obtained from $N_0$ as a bound on the norm of $\mathbf{c}\mathbf{T}_0$ for $\mathbf{c} \in \mathcal{C}_0$, and $\bar{N}_0 = 2.1\sigma_0\sqrt{n(3 + 2m)}$. The challenge space is set to $\mathcal{C}_0 = \{\mathbf{c} \in \mathcal{R}_3 \; : \; \|\mathbf{c}\|_1 \leq 32\}$ so that the proof only needs to be repeated once, as indeed $|\mathcal{C}_0| > 2^{256}$.

Next, from the way $\mathbf{F}$ was computed, we have that $[\mathbf{G}^\mathsf{T} \, \mathbf{F}^\mathsf{T} \, \mathbb{I}_m] \, [\mathbf{m} \, ; \, -\mathbf{b} \, ; \, \mathbf{E}^\mathsf{T}] = -\mathbf{C}^\mathsf{T}$. Setting $\mathbf{T}_{\mathrm{ve}} = [-\mathbf{b} \, ; \, \mathbf{E}^\mathsf{T}]$ the prover can therefore use the verifiable encryption scheme to encrypt a witness of the languages with relations

$$
R_{\mathrm{ve}} = \left\{
\begin{aligned}
&(([\mathbf{G}^\mathsf{T} \, \mathbf{F}^\mathsf{T} \, \mathbb{I}_m], -\mathbf{C}^\mathsf{T}), (\mathbf{m}, \mathbf{T}_{\mathrm{ve}}, 1)) \in (\mathcal{R}_q^{m \times (m+2)} \times \mathcal{R}_q^m) \times (\mathcal{U} \times \mathcal{R}_q^{m+1} \times \{1\}) \\
&\qquad : \quad [\mathbf{G}^\mathsf{T} \, \mathbf{F}^\mathsf{T} \, \mathbb{I}_m] \begin{bmatrix} \mathbf{m} \\ \mathbf{T}_{\mathrm{ve}} \end{bmatrix} = -\mathbf{C}^\mathsf{T} \bmod q \; \wedge \; \|\mathbf{T}_{\mathrm{ve}}\| \leq N_{\mathrm{ve}}
\end{aligned}
\right\}
$$

$$
\bar{R}_{\mathrm{ve}} = \left\{
\begin{aligned}
&(([\mathbf{G}^\mathsf{T} \, \mathbf{F}^\mathsf{T} \, \mathbb{I}_m], -\mathbf{C}^\mathsf{T}), (\bar{\mathbf{m}}, \bar{\mathbf{T}}_{\mathrm{ve}}, \bar{c})) \in (\mathcal{R}_q^{m \times (m+2)} \times \mathcal{R}_q^m) \times (\bar{\mathcal{U}} \times \mathcal{R}_q^{m+1} \times \bar{\mathcal{C}}_{\mathrm{ve}}) \\
&\qquad : \quad [\mathbf{G}^\mathsf{T} \, \mathbf{F}^\mathsf{T} \, \mathbb{I}_m] \begin{bmatrix} \bar{\mathbf{m}} \\ \bar{\mathbf{T}}_{\mathrm{ve}} \end{bmatrix} = -\bar{c}\mathbf{C}^\mathsf{T} \bmod q \; \wedge \; \|\bar{\mathbf{T}}_{\mathrm{ve}}\| \leq \bar{N}_{\mathrm{ve}}
\end{aligned}
\right\}
$$

The user runs the encryption algorithm $\mathsf{Enc}(opk, x, w, vk)$ with language member $x = ([\mathbf{G}^\mathsf{T} \, \mathbf{F}^\mathsf{T} \, \mathbb{I}_m], -\mathbf{C}^\mathsf{T})$, witness $w = (\mathbf{m}, [-\mathbf{b} \, ; \, \mathbf{E}^\mathsf{T}], 1)$, and the verification key $vk$ as the encryption label, to generate a ciphertext $t = (\mathbf{v}_1, \mathbf{w}_1, \mathbf{v}_2, \mathbf{w}_2)$ and proof $\pi = (\Pi_1, \Pi_2)$. The user then computes the one-time signature $ots \leftarrow \mathsf{OTSSign}(sk, (\mathbf{A}, \mathbf{B}, \mathbf{F}, \mathbf{u}, \Pi_0, t, \pi, M))$ and returns the group signature $sig = (\mathbf{F}, \Pi_0, t, \pi, vk, ots)$.

*Verification Algorithm.* The verifier checks the one-time signature by running $\mathsf{OTSVf}(vk, (\mathbf{A}, \mathbf{B}, \mathbf{F}, \mathbf{u}, \Pi_0, t, \pi, M), ots)$, checks the NIZK proof $\Pi_0$ in the group signature $sig = (\mathbf{F}, \Pi_0, t, \pi)$, making sure that $vk$ is included in the Fiat-Shamir hash, and checks the encryption proof by running $\mathsf{EVerify}(opk, x, t, \pi, vk)$ with $x = \left( \begin{bmatrix} \mathbf{G}^\mathsf{T} & \mathbf{F}^\mathsf{T} & \mathbb{I}_m \end{bmatrix}, -\mathbf{C}^\mathsf{T} \right)$ and with $vk$ as the encryption label. If all tests succeed then he outputs 1, else he outputs 0.

*Opening Algorithm.* The opener first verifies the group signature by running the $\mathsf{GVerify}$ algorithm above. If it is invalid, then the opener returns $\bot$, else it decrypts $\mathbf{m} \leftarrow \mathsf{Dec}(esk, x, t, \pi, vk)$ with $x$ as above and returns $id = \mathbf{m}$.

To guarantee the correctness of the scheme, the norm bounds $N_0$, $N_{\mathrm{ve}}$ and $\bar{N}_{\mathrm{ve}}$ should be chosen carefully. First, as observed in Sect. 2.8, a honest $\mathbf{T}$ is generated as $\mathbf{T} = \begin{bmatrix} \mathbf{S}_1 & \mathbf{S}_2 & b\mathbf{S}_3 & -\mathbf{E}\mathbf{S}_3 \end{bmatrix}$, where the vector $\mathbf{S} = \begin{bmatrix} \mathbf{S}_1 & \mathbf{S}_2 & \mathbf{S}_3 \end{bmatrix} \in \mathcal{R}_q^{1 \times (2+2m)}$ is sampled from a Gaussian with standard deviation $\sigma$. Hence it each of its components has norm bounded by $1.05\sigma\sqrt{n}$. Moreover, using the bounds in Lemma 2, it holds $\|b\mathbf{S}_3\| \leq 8\sigma n\sqrt{m}$ and $\| - \mathbf{E}\mathbf{S}_3\| \leq \sqrt{\sum_{i=1}^m \|\mathbf{E}_i\mathbf{S}_{3,i}\|_2^2} \leq 8\sigma n\sqrt{m}$. Hence we can set the bound $N_0$ to be:

$$N_0 = \sqrt{(2 + m)(1.05\sigma\sqrt{n})^2 + m(8\sigma n)^2 + m(8\sigma n)^2}.$$

The value $N_{\mathrm{ve}}$ in $R_{\mathrm{ve}}$ bounds the norm of a vector of polynomials with coefficients in $\{0, 1\}$ one of which is in $\mathcal{R}_3^{(16)}$, hence $N_{\mathrm{ve}} := \sqrt{256 + n(m^2 + 1)}$. Finally, the parameter $\bar{N}_{\mathrm{ve}}$ bounds the norm of what is returned extracting from the NIZK proof, hence it is computed from the standard deviation of the Gaussian distribution used in rejection sampling as explained in Sect. 2.7.

**Theorem 5 (Traceability).** *Our group signature scheme is traceable in the random-oracle model if Assumption 3 holds and the relaxed partial verifiable encryption scheme of Sect. 3 satisfies special soundness.*

**Theorem 6 (CCA-Anonymity).** *Our group signature scheme is CCA-anonymous in the random-oracle model if Assumption 1 holds, if the NIZK proof is statistical zero-knowledge and if the relaxed partial verifiable encryption scheme of Sect. 3 is chosen-ciphertext simulatable.*

As stated in Sect. 2.4, there are two ways to interpret Assumption 3 and Assumption 1, either as a quite strong interactive assumption, or as implied through a complexity leveraging argument by the Ring-LWE and the Ring-SIS assumptions, and by the Ring-LWE$_{m,D}$ assumption, respectively.

### 4.2 Practical Parameters and Storage Requirement

In Table 1 we give a set of practical parameters for different security requirements and all guaranteeing $\lambda = 80$ bits of security against quantum adversaries. Following the approach in Boschini et al. [8], we give the possibility to choose whether to base the security of the scheme on complexity leveraging or not. All parameters are computed w.r.t. fixed $n = 2^{11}$, $\sigma_t = 4$ and $p$ a prime such that $\log p \leq 2^{50}$. The second column contains the maximum value of the Hermite root factor computed for the Ring-SIS instance in Theorem 2. Given that not only Assumption 4, but also the hardness of finding a witness for an element of $L$ in

**Table 1.** Table of parameters for $n = 2^{11}$, $\sigma_t = 4$ and $p \sim 2^{50}$ for $2^{25}$ users.

| Compl. lev. | $\delta_s$ | Parameters | | | | | Sizes | | | |
|---|---|---|---|---|---|---|---|---|---|---|
| | | $m$ | $q$ | $\sigma_0$ | $\sigma_1$ | $\sigma_2$ | $gpk$(MB) | $usk$(kB) | $opk$(kB) | $sig$(MB) |
| NO | 1.00352 | 7 | $\sim 2^{115}$ | $2.891 \cdot 10^{17}$ | $6.51 \cdot 10^4$ | $2.13 \cdot 10^4$ | 0.501 | 122.95 | 88.32 | 0.91 |
| YES | 1.0014 | 22 | $\sim 2^{116}$ | $4.325 \cdot 10^{14}$ | $9.36 \cdot 10^4$ | $2.13 \cdot 10^4$ | 1.396 | 224.26 | 89.1 | 1.72 |

Sect. 2.7 is based on that, we decided to use it to have a hardness estimate even when relying only on the hardness of Assumption 3. The only difference with the other case (and the reason for which $\delta_s$ is different) is that when assuming complexity leveraging we need to compensate also for the tightness loss of the reductions in Sect. 2.4, while in the other case it is only necessary to compensate for the tightness loss in the proofs of Theorems 5 and 6. We recall that the most efficient scheme prior to ours [23] has signatures over 60 MB and public keys of 4.9 MB for a group size of only $2^{10}$ users for 80 bits of security. While they still have to deal with big lattices (dimensions: $n = 2^8$, $m = 2^{12}$), their coefficients are smaller than ours (bounded by $q = 2^8$), and this allow for more efficient computations.

**Acknowledgements.** The authors thank Vadim Lyubashevsky for many helpful discussions and the anonymous reviewers for the useful comments. This work was supported by the ERC under grant #321310 PERCY) and the SNF under grant #200021_157080 (Efficient Lattice-Based Cryptographic Protocols).

# References

1. Ateniese, G., Camenisch, J., Joye, M., Tsudik, G.: A practical and provably secure coalition-resistant group signature scheme. In: Bellare, M. (ed.) CRYPTO 2000. LNCS, vol. 1880, pp. 255–270. Springer, Heidelberg (2000). https://doi.org/10.1007/3-540-44598-6_16
2. Banaszczyk, W.: New bounds in some transference theorems in the geometry of numbers. Math. Ann. **296**(1), 625–635 (1993)
3. Bellare, M., Micciancio, D., Warinschi, B.: Foundations of group signatures: formal definitions, simplified requirements, and a construction based on general assumptions. In: Biham, E. (ed.) EUROCRYPT 2003. LNCS, vol. 2656, pp. 614–629. Springer, Heidelberg (2003). https://doi.org/10.1007/3-540-39200-9_38
4. Bellare, M., Shi, H., Zhang, C.: Foundations of group signatures: the case of dynamic groups. In: Menezes, A. (ed.) CT-RSA 2005. LNCS, vol. 3376, pp. 136–153. Springer, Heidelberg (2005). https://doi.org/10.1007/978-3-540-30574-3_11
5. Benhamouda, F., Camenisch, J., Krenn, S., Lyubashevsky, V., Neven, G.: Better zero-knowledge proofs for lattice encryption and their application to group signatures. In: Sarkar, P., Iwata, T. (eds.) ASIACRYPT 2014. LNCS, vol. 8873, pp. 551–572. Springer, Heidelberg (2014). https://doi.org/10.1007/978-3-662-45611-8_29
6. Bichsel, P., Camenisch, J., Groß, T., Shoup, V.: Anonymous credentials on a standard Java card. In: ACM CCS (2009)

7. Boneh, D., Boyen, X., Goh, E.-J.: Hierarchical identity based encryption with constant size ciphertext. In: Cramer, R. (ed.) EUROCRYPT 2005. LNCS, vol. 3494, pp. 440–456. Springer, Heidelberg (2005). https://doi.org/10.1007/11426639_26

8. Boschini, C., Camenisch, J., Neven, G.: Relaxed lattice-based signatures with short zero-knowledge proofs. Cryptology ePrint Archive, Report 2017/1123 (2017)

9. Brickell, E.F., Camenisch, J., Chen, L.: Direct anonymous attestation. In: ACM CCS (2004)

10. Camenisch, J., Neven, G., Rückert, M.: Fully anonymous attribute tokens from lattices. In: Visconti, I., De Prisco, R. (eds.) SCN 2012. LNCS, vol. 7485, pp. 57–75. Springer, Heidelberg (2012). https://doi.org/10.1007/978-3-642-32928-9_4

11. Camenisch, J., Shoup, V.: Practical verifiable encryption and decryption of discrete logarithms. In: Boneh, D. (ed.) CRYPTO 2003. LNCS, vol. 2729, pp. 126–144. Springer, Heidelberg (2003). https://doi.org/10.1007/978-3-540-45146-4_8

12. Chase, M., Lysyanskaya, A.: On signatures of knowledge. In: Dwork, C. (ed.) CRYPTO 2006. LNCS, vol. 4117, pp. 78–96. Springer, Heidelberg (2006). https://doi.org/10.1007/11818175_5

13. Chaum, D., van Heyst, E.: Group signatures. In: Davies, D.W. (ed.) EUROCRYPT 1991. LNCS, vol. 547, pp. 257–265. Springer, Heidelberg (1991). https://doi.org/10.1007/3-540-46416-6_22

14. Ducas, L., Durmus, A., Lepoint, T., Lyubashevsky, V.: Lattice signatures and bimodal Gaussians. In: Canetti, R., Garay, J.A. (eds.) CRYPTO 2013. LNCS, vol. 8042, pp. 40–56. Springer, Heidelberg (2013). https://doi.org/10.1007/978-3-642-40041-4_3

15. Ducas, L., Lyubashevsky, V., Prest, T.: Efficient identity-based encryption over NTRU lattices. In: Sarkar, P., Iwata, T. (eds.) ASIACRYPT 2014. LNCS, vol. 8874, pp. 22–41. Springer, Heidelberg (2014). https://doi.org/10.1007/978-3-662-45608-8_2

16. Faust, S., Kohlweiss, M., Marson, G.A., Venturi, D.: On the non-malleability of the Fiat-Shamir transform. In: Galbraith, S., Nandi, M. (eds.) INDOCRYPT 2012. LNCS, vol. 7668, pp. 60–79. Springer, Heidelberg (2012). https://doi.org/10.1007/978-3-642-34931-7_5

17. Fiat, A., Shamir, A.: How to prove yourself: practical solutions to identification and signature problems. In: Odlyzko, A.M. (ed.) CRYPTO 1986. LNCS, vol. 263, pp. 186–194. Springer, Heidelberg (1987). https://doi.org/10.1007/3-540-47721-7_12

18. Gama, N., Nguyen, P.Q.: Predicting lattice reduction. In: Smart, N. (ed.) EUROCRYPT 2008. LNCS, vol. 4965, pp. 31–51. Springer, Heidelberg (2008). https://doi.org/10.1007/978-3-540-78967-3_3

19. Gentry, C., Peikert, C., Vaikuntanathan, V.: Trapdoors for hard lattices and new cryptographic constructions. In: ACM STOC (2008)

20. Gordon, S.D., Katz, J., Vaikuntanathan, V.: A group signature scheme from lattice assumptions. In: Abe, M. (ed.) ASIACRYPT 2010. LNCS, vol. 6477, pp. 395–412. Springer, Heidelberg (2010). https://doi.org/10.1007/978-3-642-17373-8_23

21. Laguillaumie, F., Langlois, A., Libert, B., Stehlé, D.: Lattice-based group signatures with logarithmic signature size. In: Sako, K., Sarkar, P. (eds.) ASIACRYPT 2013. LNCS, vol. 8270, pp. 41–61. Springer, Heidelberg (2013). https://doi.org/10.1007/978-3-642-42045-0_3

22. Lamport, L.: Constructing digital signatures from a one-way function. Technical report SRI-CSL-98, SRI International Computer Science Laboratory (1979)

23. Libert, B., Ling, S., Nguyen, K., Wang, H.: Zero-knowledge arguments for lattice-based accumulators: logarithmic-size ring signatures and group signatures without trapdoors. In: Fischlin, M., Coron, J.-S. (eds.) EUROCRYPT 2016. LNCS, vol. 9666, pp. 1–31. Springer, Heidelberg (2016). https://doi.org/10.1007/978-3-662-49896-5_1

24. Libert, B., Mouhartem, F., Nguyen, K.: A lattice-based group signature scheme with message-dependent opening. In: Manulis, M., Sadeghi, A.-R., Schneider, S. (eds.) ACNS 2016. LNCS, vol. 9696, pp. 137–155. Springer, Cham (2016). https://doi.org/10.1007/978-3-319-39555-5_8

25. Ling, S., Nguyen, K., Wang, H.: Group signatures from lattices: simpler, tighter, shorter, ring-based. In: Katz, J. (ed.) PKC 2015. LNCS, vol. 9020, pp. 427–449. Springer, Heidelberg (2015). https://doi.org/10.1007/978-3-662-46447-2_19

26. Ling, S., Nguyen, K., Wang, H., Xu, Y.: Lattice-based group signatures: achieving full dynamicity with ease. Cryptology ePrint Archive, Report 2017/353 (2017)

27. Lyubashevsky, V.: Lattice signatures without trapdoors. In: Pointcheval, D., Johansson, T. (eds.) EUROCRYPT 2012. LNCS, vol. 7237, pp. 738–755. Springer, Heidelberg (2012). https://doi.org/10.1007/978-3-642-29011-4_43

28. Lyubashevsky, V., Micciancio, D.: Generalized compact knapsacks are collision resistant. In: Bugliesi, M., Preneel, B., Sassone, V., Wegener, I. (eds.) ICALP 2006. LNCS, vol. 4052, pp. 144–155. Springer, Heidelberg (2006). https://doi.org/10.1007/11787006_13

29. Lyubashevsky, V., Neven, G.: One-shot verifiable encryption from lattices. In: Coron, J.-S., Nielsen, J.B. (eds.) EUROCRYPT 2017. LNCS, vol. 10210, pp. 293–323. Springer, Cham (2017). https://doi.org/10.1007/978-3-319-56620-7_11

30. Lyubashevsky, V., Peikert, C., Regev, O.: On ideal lattices and learning with errors over rings. In: Gilbert, H. (ed.) EUROCRYPT 2010. LNCS, vol. 6110, pp. 1–23. Springer, Heidelberg (2010). https://doi.org/10.1007/978-3-642-13190-5_1

31. Lyubashevsky, V., Peikert, C., Regev, O.: A toolkit for ring-LWE cryptography. In: Johansson, T., Nguyen, P.Q. (eds.) EUROCRYPT 2013. LNCS, vol. 7881, pp. 35–54. Springer, Heidelberg (2013). https://doi.org/10.1007/978-3-642-38348-9_3

32. Micciancio, D., Peikert, C.: Trapdoors for lattices: simpler, tighter, faster, smaller. In: Pointcheval, D., Johansson, T. (eds.) EUROCRYPT 2012. LNCS, vol. 7237, pp. 700–718. Springer, Heidelberg (2012). https://doi.org/10.1007/978-3-642-29011-4_41

33. Naor, M., Yung, M.: Public-key cryptosystems provably secure against chosen ciphertext attacks. In: ACM STOC (1990)

34. Nguyen, P.Q., Zhang, J., Zhang, Z.: Simpler efficient group signatures from lattices. In: Katz, J. (ed.) PKC 2015. LNCS, vol. 9020, pp. 401–426. Springer, Heidelberg (2015). https://doi.org/10.1007/978-3-662-46447-2_18

35. Rückert, M.: Lattice-based blind signatures. In: Abe, M. (ed.) ASIACRYPT 2010. LNCS, vol. 6477, pp. 413–430. Springer, Heidelberg (2010). https://doi.org/10.1007/978-3-642-17373-8_24

36. Stern, J.: A new identification scheme based on syndrome decoding. In: Stinson, D.R. (ed.) CRYPTO 1993. LNCS, vol. 773, pp. 13–21. Springer, Heidelberg (1994). https://doi.org/10.1007/3-540-48329-2_2

37. Xagawa, K., Tanaka, K.: Zero-knowledge protocols for NTRU: application to identification and proof of plaintext knowledge. In: Pieprzyk, J., Zhang, F. (eds.) ProvSec 2009. LNCS, vol. 5848, pp. 198–213. Springer, Heidelberg (2009). https://doi.org/10.1007/978-3-642-04642-1_17

# On the Security Notions for Homomorphic Signatures

Dario Catalano[1], Dario Fiore[2], and Luca Nizzardo[2(✉)]

[1] Dipartimento di Matematica e Informatica, Università di Catania, Catania, Italy
catalano@dmi.unict.it
[2] IMDEA Software Institute, Madrid, Spain
{dario.fiore,luca.nizzardo}@imdea.org

**Abstract.** Homomorphic signature schemes allow anyone to perform computation on signed data in such a way that the correctness of computation's results is publicly certified. In this work we analyze the security notions for this powerful primitive considered in previous work, with a special focus on adaptive security. Motivated by the complications of existing security models in the adaptive setting, we consider a simpler and (at the same time) stronger security definition inspired to that proposed by Gennaro and Wichs (ASIACRYPT'13) for homomorphic MACs. In addition to strength and simplicity, this definition has the advantage to enable the adoption of homomorphic signatures in dynamic data outsourcing scenarios, such as delegation of computation on data streams. Then, since no existing homomorphic signature satisfies this stronger notion, our main technical contribution are general compilers which turn a homomorphic signature scheme secure under a weak definition into one secure under the new stronger notion. Our compilers are totally generic with respect to the underlying scheme. Moreover, they preserve three important properties of homomorphic signatures: composability, context-hiding (i.e. signatures on computation's output do not reveal information about the input) and efficient verification (i.e. verifying a signature against a program $\mathcal{P}$ can be made faster, in an amortized, asymptotic sense, than recomputing $\mathcal{P}$ from scratch).

## 1 Introduction

Digital signatures are a fundamental cryptographic primitive for guaranteeing the authenticity of digital information. In a digital signature scheme, a user Alice can use her secret key $sk$ to generate a signature $\sigma_m$ on a message $m$, and a user Bob can use Alice's public key $pk$ to check the authenticity of $(m, \sigma_m)$. The standard security notion of digital signatures, unforgeability against chosen message attacks, says that an attacker who has access to a collection of signatures on messages of his choice cannot produce a signature on a new message. This notion essentially means that signatures must be *non-malleable* in the sense that, from a signature on $m$ one cannot derive a signature on some $m' \neq m$.

Even if in the most popular applications one wishes such a strong notion of non-malleability, there are application scenarios where some form of malleability

© Springer International Publishing AG, part of Springer Nature 2018
B. Preneel and F. Vercauteren (Eds.): ACNS 2018, LNCS 10892, pp. 183–201, 2018.
https://doi.org/10.1007/978-3-319-93387-0_10

can become very useful, paradoxically even for signature schemes. A notable example is that of homomorphic signatures, a notion first proposed by Desmedt [19] and Johnson et al. [26], defined in the context of linear network coding by Boneh et al. [6] and later properly formalized by Boneh and Freeman [7]. This is what we study in this work.

**Homomorphic Signatures.** In homomorphic signatures, a user Alice can use her secret key $sk$ to generate signatures $\sigma_1, \ldots, \sigma_n$ on a collection of messages $(m_1, \ldots, m_n)$ – a so-called dataset. Then the interesting feature of this primitive is a (publicly computable) Eval algorithm that takes the signatures $\sigma_1, \ldots, \sigma_n$ and a program $\mathcal{P}$, and outputs a signature $\sigma_{\mathcal{P},m}$ on the message $m = \mathcal{P}(m_1, \ldots, m_n)$ *as the output of* $\mathcal{P}$. It is crucial that $\sigma_{\mathcal{P},m}$ is not a signature on just $m$, but on $m$ as output of the program $\mathcal{P}$. The latter observation indeed makes sure that signatures are not "too malleable", but they rather have a controlled malleability. This means that a user Bob will use Alice's public key $pk$ to check the triple $(\mathcal{P}, m, \sigma_{\mathcal{P},m})$ and get convinced of whether $m$ is the correct output of $\mathcal{P}$ on messages previously signed by Alice.

In addition to this interesting functionality, what makes this primitive attractive is the following set of features. First, homomorphic signatures must be *succinct*, meaning that their size must be significantly smaller than the size of the input dataset.[1] Second, Bob can verify computation's outputs without needing to know the original dataset, a very appealing feature when considering computations on very large datasets that could not be stored locally by verifiers. Third, homomorphic signatures are *composable*, in the sense that signatures obtained from Eval can be fed as inputs to new computations. Using composability, one can, for example, distribute different subtasks to several untrusted workers, ask each of them to produce a proof of its local task, and use these proofs to create another unique proof for the final job (as in the MapReduce approach). All these features make homomorphic signatures an interesting candidate to be used for securely delegating computation on previously outsourced data.

If the functionality of homomorphic signatures can be explained as above, defining the security notion of this primitive is a more delicate task. The following paragraphs provide an explanation of the security notions and then give an overview of our results. We warn the reader that the explanations in the introduction intentionally hide some details of the model for ease of exposition. A detailed formalization appears in Sect. 2.

**Security of Homomorphic Signatures.** Properly defining security for homomorphic signatures is tricky. Clearly, an homomorphic signature cannot meet the usual unforgeability requirement [24] as the primitive does allow the adversary to come up (honestly) with new signatures. The first satisfactory security definition was proposed by Boneh and Freeman in [7]. Intuitively, a homomorphic

---

[1] Without the succinctness requirement homomorphic signatures are trivial to realize as one can simply set $\sigma = (\mathcal{P}, (m_1, \sigma_1), \ldots, (m_\ell, \sigma_\ell))$.

signature is secure if an adversary who knows the public key can only come up with signatures that are either obtained from the legitimate signer Alice, or they are obtained by running Eval on the signatures obtained by Alice. In other words, the adversary can only do what is in the scope of the public evaluation algorithm. Slightly more in detail, this new unforgeability game can be explained as follows. During a training phase the adversary $\mathcal{A}$ is allowed to see the signatures of messages belonging to different datasets. The adversary then wins the game if she can produce either (1) a signature on a message $m$ belonging to some previously unseen dataset (this is called a *Type 1* forgery), or (2) for some previously seen dataset $\Delta = \{m_1, \ldots, m_n\}$, she manages to produce a triplet $(\mathcal{P}, \sigma, m)$, such that $\sigma$ verifies correctly but $m \neq \mathcal{P}(m_1, \ldots, m_n)$ (this is called a *Type 2* forgery). Again explained in words, this definition means that the adversary can cheat either by claiming an output on a dataset that she never saw/queried, or by claiming an incorrect output of a given program $\mathcal{P}$, executed on a collection of messages for which she saw signatures.

A noteworthy caveat of the Boneh and Freeman [7] definition is the requirement that the adversary submits *all* the messages belonging to each queried dataset. Namely, for each queried dataset $\Delta$, $\mathcal{A}$ has to ask *exactly* $n$ signing queries.[2] In this work, because of this limitation, we call this notion *semi-adaptive security*.[3]

To overcome this limitation, Freeman [21] later proposed a stronger notion where the adversary is allowed to adaptively query messages one by one, and even to sprinkle queries from different datasets. In this work, because of its increased adaptivity, we call the notion in [21] *adaptive security*.

**The Shortcomings of Adaptive Security.** Adaptive security, while very natural, has a dark side. Loosening the query-all requirement implies that the adversary might provide a forgery $(\mathcal{P}, \sigma, m)$ that corresponds to a previously seen dataset $\Delta$, but for which $\mathcal{A}$ did not ask signing queries on all the inputs of $\mathcal{P}$. For instance, $\mathcal{A}$ might pretend to have a signature on $m \neq \mathcal{P}(m_1, m_2)$ without having ever made a query on $m_2$. The issue in this case is that it is not even possible to define what is the correct output of $\mathcal{P}$ in order to say whether the adversary has cheated (i.e., if $m$ is a correct output or not). To deal with this issue, Freeman proposed a notion of "well-defined program" which characterizes when the output of $\mathcal{P}$ can be defined in spite of missing inputs. The idea is simple and intuitively says that a program is well defined if the missing inputs do not change its outcome (e.g., $\mathcal{P}(m_1, \cdot)$ is constant). Freeman's definition then considered a forgery also one that passes verification for a $\mathcal{P}$ not well-defined, and called such a forgery *Type 3*.

Type 3 forgeries are however nasty animals. Not only they are very hard to work with (as the security definition turns complicated), but they also make

---

[2] We remark that the original Boneh-Freeman definition imposes the even stronger restriction that these $n$ messages are queried all at once.

[3] We stress that semi-adaptive security *does not* limit the way the adversary is allowed to choose its signing queries. It only restricts the *number* of signing queries permitted.

the outcome of the security experiment not efficiently computable. In fact, when considering general functions it may not be possible to check the well-definedness of $\mathcal{P}$ in polynomial time. This can be solved when $\mathcal{P}$ is a linear [21] or a low degree polynomial [9,17], but the issue remains for the more general case, e.g., polynomial size circuits. In particular, this issue can generate troubles when proving the security of homomorphic signatures as well as when using them in larger protocols (as simply testing whether an adversary returned a forgery may not be doable in polynomial time).

## 1.1 Our Contribution

The state of the art of security notions for homomorphic signatures, as discussed above, seems quite unsatisfactory. Having expressive, yet easy to use, definitions is indeed a fundamental step towards a better understanding of cryptographic primitives.

**A Stronger and Simpler Security Notion.** To address the issues of adaptive security, we consider a new security notion that is both simpler and stronger than the one in [21]. This notion, that we call *strong adaptive security*, is the public key version of the one proposed by Gennaro and Wichs [23] for homomorphic message authenticators (the secret key equivalent of homomorphic signatures).[4] Strong adaptive security deals with the case of programs with missing inputs in a simple way: if the triplet $(\mathcal{P}, m, \sigma)$ returned by the adversary verifies correctly and some inputs of $\mathcal{P}$ were not queried during the experiment, then it is considered a forgery (we call it a *Type 3 Strong* forgery).

Compared to previous notions, strong adaptive security has several advantages. First, the winning condition of the experiment is efficiently computable, thus avoiding the issues that may arise when proving and using homomorphic signatures. Second, the new forgery definition is arguably much simpler to state and work with. Finally, being a strengthening of adaptive security, homomorphic signature schemes that are strongly adaptive secure can be used in more application scenarios as discussed before.

**Realizing Strong Adaptive Security, Generically.** If we aim for strong adaptive security to be the "right" strong notion to use for homomorphic signatures, then we face the problem that virtually all existing schemes are not secure under this strong notion. This is the case for those schemes that support linear or low-degree polynomials and were proven secure under the adaptive notion of [21], as well as for the recently proposed leveled homomorphic scheme for circuits [25] which is only semi-adaptive secure. Notably, all these constructions break down in the new security experiment as they do not tolerate adversaries that issue Type 3 Strong forgeries. The only scheme which stands security in

---

[4] With some adaptations to deal with multiple datasets which was not considered in [23].

this stronger model is a recent proposal of Elkhiyaoui et al. [20] which supports constant-degree polynomials and relies on multilinear maps in the random oracle model. To remedy this situation, our main contribution is to show that strong adaptive security can be easily achieved without additional assumptions and in the standard model. Specifically, our main result is a generic compiler that, starting from an homomorphic signature scheme $\Sigma$ satisfying semi-adaptive security, converts $\Sigma$ into a strongly adaptive secure scheme that supports the same class of functions.

The compiler uses, as additional building block, a semi-adaptive secure signature scheme $\Sigma_{OR}$ that supports OR operations over $\mathbb{Z}_2$. Clearly, if $\Sigma$ supports arbitrary boolean circuits, then $\Sigma_{OR}$ can be instantiated using $\Sigma$ itself. In such a case, our result is thus providing a transformation that "bootstraps" semi-adaptive security to strong adaptive security. If, on the other hand, $\Sigma_{OR}$ cannot be instantiated using $\Sigma$, our result still provides a way to get strong adaptive security, under the additional assumption that semi-adaptive secure OR-homomorphic signatures exist. Nevertheless, since very few concrete examples of OR-homomorphic signatures are known (essentially, only one [25]), even if we think that this is not a limitation by itself, we asked whether a similar result could be obtained out of some more widely studied primitive. Along this direction, our second result is another compiler that combines a semi-adaptive secure scheme $\Sigma$ together with a semi-adaptive secure *linearly-homomorphic* signature $\Sigma_{LH}$ that works for messages over a large ring, say $\mathbb{Z}_p$. This combination yields a homomorphic signature scheme that is strongly adaptive secure and supports the same class of functions supported by $\Sigma$. A limitation of this second transformation is that it applies only to schemes that are leveled homomorphic (i.e., for circuits of bounded depth). As an interesting feature, however, this result shows that strong adaptive security can be obtained from linearly-homomorphic schemes, a class of constructions for which many constructions are known (most of which are also way more efficient in practice than [25]).

Both our transformations hold in the standard model, and they preserve three properties of homomorphic signatures: composability, context-hiding and efficient-verification (so, security can be upgraded without penalties). Context hiding deals with privacy and informally says that signatures on computation's outputs do not reveal information on the inputs. The latter instead fully enables the use of homomorphic signatures for verifiable delegation of computation, by requiring that verifying a signature for a program $\mathcal{P}$ is asymptotically faster (in an amortized, offline-online sense) than recomputing $\mathcal{P}$ from scratch (for the formal definitions of both context hiding and efficient verification we refer to [14]). We point out that our compilers are completely generic with respect to the semi adaptive secure scheme. This means, for instance, that when applied to the recent (leveled) fully homomorphic solution of [25] they lead to homomorphic signature schemes for general circuits achieving strong adaptive security.

**On the Importance of Strong Adaptive Security.** As an important application of (strong) adaptive secure homomorphic signatures, we mention *certified* *computation on streaming data.* Consider a scenario where a user Alice outsources a stream of data $m_1, m_2, \ldots$ to an untrusted Cloud, so that the Cloud can compute a program $\mathcal{P}$ on the current snapshot $(m_1, \ldots, m_i)$ and post the result publicly (e.g., on a third party website). Using homomorphic signatures, Alice can sign each element of the data stream, while the Cloud can compute a homomorphic signature $\sigma_{\mathcal{P}, y_i}$ on every computed result $y_i = \mathcal{P}(m_1, \ldots, m_i)$ and post $(y_i, \sigma_{\mathcal{P}, y_i})$. This way, anyone with the only knowledge of Alice's public key is able to check the results validity. Notably, the Cloud can produce the certified results in a completely non-interactive fashion, and no communication between Alice and the verifiers is needed (except, of course, for sending the public key). In such a scenario, where datasets grow dynamically and one performs computations on their current version, (strong) adaptive security is fundamental as it prevents the cloud from claiming to have results computed on dataset elements that it did not receive (yet). This is particularly relevant in scenarios where there is no communication between the signer and the verifiers, who may not be aware of the current status of the outsourced stream. Furthermore, strong adaptive security is important in the case of very large, potentially unbounded, datasets (as in the streaming case) as one cannot assume that the adversary queries the whole dataset. This actually shows an inherent limitation of semi-adaptive security, which cannot cope with datasets of arbitrarily large, unbounded, size. Indeed, to fit the requirements of the definition, adversaries would be required to ask signing queries on the whole dataset. However, if datasets are unbounded either the notion of whole dataset does not exist, or it can be approximated by configuring the scheme to work on a dataset of exponential size, which could not be queried in full by a polynomially bounded adversary.

As a final note, we remark that, in settings where the messages $m_1, \ldots, m_i$ are signed sequentially, one at a time, it might be tempting to address the limitations of semi-adaptive security via (standard) signatures as follows. One simply includes a signature of the largest index $i$ signed so far. When verifying an homomorphic signature for $\mathcal{P}(m_1, \ldots, m_k)$, where $k$ is the largest index touched by $\mathcal{P}$, one also requires a (standard) signature on $k$. This solution has the drawback of requiring an ordering of indexes. More seriously, it only works in contexts where messages are signed in index-increasing order. Our solution, on the other hand, encompasses the more general case where messages are signed in completely arbitrary order (and without imposing additional constraints on the underlying indexes).

**Other Related Work.** The notion of homomorphic signature was (informally) suggested by Desmedt [19] and later more formally introduced by Johnson *et al.* [26]. The special case of linearly homomorphic signatures was first considered by Boneh *et al.* [6] as a key tool to prevent pollution attacks in network coding routing mechanisms. Following this work, several papers further studied this primitive both in the random oracle [7,8,11,22], and in the standard model [3–5,13,15,16,21]. In the symmetric setting realizations of linearly homomorphic MACs have been proposed by Agrawal and Boneh in [1].

Several recent works also considered the question of constructing homomorphic authenticators (i.e., signatures and/or MACs) supporting more expressive functionalities. Boneh and Freeman in [7] proposed an homomorphic signature scheme for constant degree polynomials, in the random oracle model. Gennaro and Wichs [23] presented a construction of fully homomorphic MACs based on fully homomorphic encryption in a restricted adversarial model where no verification queries are allowed. Catalano and Fiore [9] proposed a much more efficient homomorphic MAC solution that, while capturing a less expressive class of functionalities (i.e. arithmetic circuits of polynomially bounded degree), allows for verification queries. This latter result was further generalized in [10]. All these constructions of homomorphic MACs achieve adaptive security.

In the asymmetric setting, Catalano, Fiore and Warinschi [17] proposed a homomorphic signature that achieves adaptive security in the standard model, works for constant degree polynomials and is based on multilinear maps. Moreover, Gorbunov, Vaikuntanathan and Wichs [25] recently proposed the first homomorphic signature construction that can handle boolean circuits of bounded polynomial depth; their scheme is secure in the semi-adaptive model, and is based on standard lattices.

Finally, we notice that Ahn et al. [2] and Chase et al. [18] worked on malleable signatures. In particular, [18] considered a problem similar to the one addressed in this work, i.e., elaborating a definition that allows one to establish, in an efficient way, when the signature produced by the adversary is a valid forgery. They deal with this problem by formalizing the idea that the adversary "must know" the function and the input that were used to obtain the forgery. To formalize this idea, their definition asks for the existence of a black-box extractor that must extract this information from what is in the view of the game and the output of the adversary. Unfortunately, this type of definition is impossible to achieve when one considers the case of *succinct* homomorphic signatures for $n$-ary functions, as we do in our paper. The reason is simply that the extractor should extract an amount of information (such as the function input) that is much larger than what is in its input.

## 1.2   An Overview of Our Compiler

To obtain strongly-adaptive secure homomorphic signatures from semi-adaptive secure ones, we propose a compiler that takes a semi-adaptive secure scheme $\Sigma$ and upgrades its security with the help of an additional building block: an homomorphic signature scheme $\Sigma_{OR}$ that supports OR operations over $\mathbb{Z}_2$. The basic idea of our compiler is to use $\Sigma_{OR}$ to additionally sign a bit '0' for every dataset input. The homomorphic properties of this scheme then guarantee that the resulting bit remains 0 if and only if one properly operates on '0' bits. This can be achieved either directly, by employing an or-homomorphic scheme, or indirectly, via an homomorphic signature for additions (over a sufficiently large ring $\mathbb{Z}_p$). This latter construction is more efficient, but it comes with restrictions. Indeed, to avoid false positives (i.e., invalid signatures that are interpreted as correct ones), $p$ should be large, i.e., larger than $c^d$, where $c$ is the (constant) fan-in and $d$ the maximum depth of the supported circuits.

More in detail, the compiler works as follows. For every dataset input $m$, in addition to signing $m$ using the scheme $\Sigma$, we also sign the bit '0' using $\Sigma_{OR}$. So, every signature now consists of a pair $(\sigma_m, \sigma_b)$, where $\sigma_m$ is a signature with the scheme $\Sigma$ on some message $m$, and $\sigma_b$ is a signature of a bit $b$ with the scheme $\Sigma_{OR}$. Next, at every gate $g$ we compute $g$ homomorphically on the $\sigma_m$'s components, and we compute OR homomorphically on the $\sigma_b$'s. Finally, signature verification consists into the usual verification of $\sigma_m$ (for a program $\mathcal{P}$), plus checking that $\sigma_b$ verifies for 0 for a computation that is simply an OR of all the dataset input bits. The reason why this makes the scheme resistant to strong Type-3 forgeries is that when the adversary does not ask all the dataset inputs (and thus misses a signature of '0' on the missing inputs) it is forced to create a forgery for the $\sigma_b$ component. The latter must verify for '0' by construction. However, one of the missing bits could be set to be '1' (notice indeed that the adversary does not see it), thus making the correct output of the OR computation '1'. Hence the signature returned by the adversary must verify for an incorrect output, i.e., it is a forgery for $\Sigma_{OR}$.

**Notation.** We denote with $\lambda \in \mathbb{N}$ a security parameter. A *probabilistic polynomial time* (PPT) algorithm $\mathcal{A}$ is a randomized algorithm for which there exists a polynomial $p(\cdot)$ such that for every input $x$ the running time of $\mathcal{A}(x)$ is bounded by $p(|x|)$. We say that a function $\epsilon : \mathbb{N} \to \mathbb{R}^+$ is *negligible* if for every positive polynomial $p(\lambda)$ there exists $\lambda_0 \in \mathbb{N}$ such that for all $\lambda > \lambda_0$: $\epsilon(\lambda) < 1/p(\lambda)$. If $S$ is a set, $x \xleftarrow{\$} S$ denotes the process of selecting $x$ uniformly at random in $S$. If $\mathcal{A}$ is a probabilistic algorithm, $y \xleftarrow{\$} \mathcal{A}(\cdot)$ denotes the process of running $\mathcal{A}$ on some appropriate input and assigning its output to $y$. For a positive integer $n$, we denote by $[n]$ the set $\{1, \ldots, n\}$.

## 2    Homomorphic Signatures

In this section we recall the definition of homomorphic signatures. This definition extends the one by Freeman in [21] in order to work with the general notion of labeled programs [23].

**Labeled Programs** [23]. A *labeled program* $\mathcal{P}$ is a tuple $(f, \tau_1, \ldots, \tau_n)$ such that $f : \mathcal{M}^n \to \mathcal{M}$ is a function of $n$ variables (e.g., a circuit) and $\tau_i \in \{0, 1\}^*$ is a label of the $i$-th input of $f$. Labeled programs can be composed as follows: given $\mathcal{P}_1, \ldots, \mathcal{P}_t$ and a function $g : \mathcal{M}^t \to \mathcal{M}$, the composed program $\mathcal{P}^*$ is the one obtained by evaluating $g$ on the outputs of $\mathcal{P}_1, \ldots, \mathcal{P}_t$, and it is denoted as $\mathcal{P}^* = g(\mathcal{P}_1, \ldots, \mathcal{P}_t)$. The labeled inputs of $\mathcal{P}^*$ are all the distinct labeled inputs of $\mathcal{P}_1, \ldots, \mathcal{P}_t$ (all the inputs with the same label are grouped together and considered as a unique input of $\mathcal{P}^*$).

Let $f_{id} : \mathcal{M} \to \mathcal{M}$ be the identity function and $\tau \in \{0, 1\}^*$ be any label. We refer to $\mathcal{I}_\tau = (f_{id}, \tau)$ as the identity program with label $\tau$. Note that a program $\mathcal{P} = (f, \tau_1, \cdots, \tau_n)$ can be expressed as the composition of $n$ identity programs $\mathcal{P} = f(\mathcal{I}_{\tau_1}, \cdots, \mathcal{I}_{\tau_n})$.

**Definition 1 (Homomorphic Signature).** *A homomorphic signature scheme* HSig *consists of a tuple of PPT algorithms* (KeyGen, Sign, Ver, Eval) *with the following syntax:*

KeyGen($1^\lambda, \mathcal{L}$) *the key generation algorithm takes as input a security parameter* $\lambda$, *a description of the label space* $\mathcal{L}$ *(which fixes the maximum data set size* $N$*), and outputs a public key* vk *and a secret key* sk. *The public key* vk *contains a description of the message space* $\mathcal{M}$ *and the set* $\mathcal{F}$ *of admissible functions.*

Sign(sk, $\Delta, \tau, m$) *the signing algorithm takes as input a secret key* sk, *a data set identifier* $\Delta \in \{0, 1\}^*$, *a label* $\tau \in \mathcal{L}$, *a message* $m \in \mathcal{M}$, *and it outputs a signature* $\sigma$.

Eval(vk, $f, \sigma_1, \ldots, \sigma_n$) *the evaluation algorithm takes as input a public key* vk, *a function* $f \in \mathcal{F}$ *and a tuple of signatures* $\{\sigma_i\}_{i=1}^n$ *(assuming that* $f$ *takes* $n$ *inputs). It outputs a new signature* $\sigma$.

Ver(vk, $\mathcal{P}, \Delta, m, \sigma$) *the verification algorithm takes as input a public key* vk, *a labeled program* $\mathcal{P} = (f, \tau_1, \ldots, \tau_n)$ *with* $f \in \mathcal{F}$, *a dataset identifier* $\Delta$, *a message* $m \in \mathcal{M}$, *and a signature* $\sigma$. *It outputs either 0 (reject) or 1 (accept).*

A homomorphic signature scheme is required to satisfy the properties of *authentication correctness*, *evaluation correctness* and *succinctness* that we describe below. The security property is discussed slightly later in Sect. 2.1.

**Authentication Correctness.** Intuitively, a homomorphic signature scheme has authentication correctness if the signature generated by Sign(sk, $\Delta, \tau, m$) verifies correctly for $m$ as the output of the identity program $\mathcal{I}_\tau$ on a dataset with identifier $\Delta$. More formally, a scheme HSig satisfies the authentication correctness property if for a given label space $\mathcal{L}$, all key pairs (sk, vk) $\leftarrow$ KeyGen($1^\lambda, \mathcal{L}$), any label $\tau \in \mathcal{L}$, dataset identifier $\Delta \in \{0, 1\}^*$, and any signature $\sigma \leftarrow$ Sign(sk, $\Delta, \tau$, $m$), Ver(vk, $\mathcal{I}_\tau, \Delta, m, \sigma$) outputs 1 with all but negligible probability.

**Evaluation Correctness.** Intuitively, this property says that running the evaluation algorithm on signatures $(\sigma_1, \ldots, \sigma_t)$ such that each $\sigma_i$ verifies for $m_i$ as the output of a labeled program $\mathcal{P}_i$ and a dataset with identifier $\Delta$, produces a signature $\sigma$ which verifies for $g(m_1, \ldots, m_t)$ as the output of the composed program $g(\mathcal{P}_1, \ldots, \mathcal{P}_t)$ and same dataset $\Delta$. More formally, fix a key pair (vk, sk) $\xleftarrow{\$}$ KeyGen($1^\lambda, \mathcal{L}$), a function $g : \mathcal{M}^t \to \mathcal{M}$, and any set of program/message/signature triples $\{(\mathcal{P}_i, m_i, \sigma_i)\}_{i=1}^t$ such that Ver(vk, $\mathcal{P}_i, \Delta, m_i$, $\sigma_i$) = 1. If $m^* = g(m_1, \ldots, m_t)$, $\mathcal{P}^* = g(\mathcal{P}_1, \ldots, \mathcal{P}_t)$, and $\sigma^* =$ Eval(vk, $g, \sigma_1, \ldots$, $\sigma_t$), then Ver(vk, $\mathcal{P}^*, \Delta, m^*, \sigma^*$) = 1 holds with all but negligible probability.

**Succinctness.** A homomorphic signature scheme is said to be *succinct* if, for a fixed security parameter $\lambda$, the size of signatures depends at most logarithmically on the size of the input dataset. More formally, HSig satisfies succinctness if there exists a polynomial $p(\lambda)$ such that for all $(\mathsf{vk}, \mathsf{sk}) \overset{\$}{\leftarrow} \mathsf{KeyGen}(1^\lambda, \mathcal{L})$, all $(m_1, \ldots, m_t) \in \mathcal{M}^t$, all $(\tau_1, \ldots, \tau_t) \in \mathcal{L}^t$, any $\Delta \in \{0, 1\}^*$, and all functions $f \in \mathcal{F}$, if $\sigma_i \overset{\$}{\leftarrow} \mathsf{Sign}(\mathsf{sk}, \Delta, \tau_i, m_i)$ and $\sigma \leftarrow \mathsf{Eval}(\mathsf{vk}, f, \sigma_1, \ldots, \sigma_t)$, then $|\sigma| \leq p(\lambda) \cdot \log t$.

## 2.1  Security

At an intuitive level, a homomorphic signature is secure if an adversary, without knowledge of the secret key, can only come up with signatures that it obtained from the signer, or signatures that are obtained by running the Eval algorithm on signatures obtained from the legitimate signer. Formalizing this intuition turns out to be tricky and leaves space to different possibilities.

In what follows we present three different security notions for homomorphic signatures that we call *semi-adaptive*, *adaptive*, and *strong adaptive*, respectively. These notions share the same security experiment between an adversary $\mathcal{A}$ and a challenger, and the only difference lies in what is considered a forgery. The security experiment, denoted $\mathbf{Exp}^{\mathsf{UF}}_{\mathcal{A}, \mathsf{HSig}}(\lambda)$, proceeds as described below:

**Key Generation.** The challenger runs $(\mathsf{vk}, \mathsf{sk}) \overset{\$}{\leftarrow} \mathsf{KeyGen}(1^\lambda, \mathcal{L})$ and gives $\mathsf{vk}$ to $\mathcal{A}$.

**Signing Queries.** $\mathcal{A}$ can adaptively submit queries of the form $(\Delta, \tau, m)$, where $\Delta$ is a data set identifier, $\tau \in \mathcal{L}$, and $m \in \mathcal{M}$. The challenger proceeds as follows:
- if $(\Delta, \tau, m)$ is the first query with the data set identifier $\Delta$, the challenger initializes an empty list $T_\Delta = \emptyset$ for $\Delta$.
- If $T_\Delta$ does not already contain a tuple $(\tau, \cdot)$ (i.e., $\mathcal{A}$ never asked for a query $(\Delta, \tau, \cdot)$), the challenger computes $\sigma \overset{\$}{\leftarrow} \mathsf{Sign}(\mathsf{sk}, \Delta, \tau, m)$, returns $\sigma$ to $\mathcal{A}$ and updates the list $T_\Delta \leftarrow T_\Delta \cup (\tau, m)$.
- If $(\tau, m) \in T_\Delta$ (i.e., the adversary had already queried the tuple $(\Delta, \tau, m)$), the challenger replies with the same signature generated before.
- If $T_\Delta$ contains a tuple $(\tau, m')$ for some message $m' \neq m$, then the challenger ignores the query. Note that this means that a tuple $(\Delta, \tau, \cdot)$ can be queried only once.

**Forgery.** The previous stage is executed until the adversary $\mathcal{A}$ outputs a tuple $(\mathcal{P}^*, \Delta^*, m^*, \sigma^*)$. The experiments outputs 1 if the tuple returned by $\mathcal{A}$ is a forgery, and 0 otherwise.

To complete the description of the experiment, it remains to define when a tuple $(\mathcal{P}^*, \Delta^*, m^*, \sigma^*)$ is considered a forgery. We give below three different forgery definitions; each of them yields a corresponding security notion for the homomorphic signature scheme.

**Semi-adaptive Secure Homomorphic Signatures.** Informally speaking, in the semi-adaptive security game a forgery is one where either (1) the dataset $\Delta^*$ is "new" (i.e., no signing query $(\Delta^*, \cdot, \cdot)$ was ever made during the game), or (2) the claimed output $m^*$ of $\mathcal{P}^*$ is not the correct one. The crucial aspect of this definition is that to identify what is a correct output, one assumes that the adversary has fully specified the inputs of $\mathcal{P}^*$, namely $\mathcal{A}$ has asked for signatures on $(\Delta^*, \tau_i^*, m_i)$, for all $i = 1$ to $n$. More formally,

**Definition 2 (Semi-adaptive Security).** *We define* $\mathbf{Exp}^{\text{semi-Ad-UF}}_{\mathcal{A},\text{HSig}}(\lambda)$ *as the security experiment which proceeds as* $\mathbf{Exp}^{\text{UF}}_{\mathcal{A},\text{HSig}}(\lambda)$ *with the addition that the tuple* $(\mathcal{P}^* := (f^*, \tau_1^*, \dots, \tau_n^*), \Delta^*, m^*, \sigma^*)$ *returned by the adversary* $\mathcal{A}$ *is considered a forgery if* $\text{Ver}(\text{vk}, \mathcal{P}^*, \Delta^*, m^*, \sigma^*) = 1$ *and either one of the following conditions hold:*

**Type 1:** *The list $T_{\Delta^*}$ has not been initialised during the game.*
**Type 2:** *For all $i \in [n]$, $\exists (\tau_i, m_i) \in T_{\Delta^*}$ and $m^* \neq f^*(m_1, \dots, m_n)$.*

*Let* $\mathbf{Adv}^{\text{semi-Ad-UF}}_{\mathcal{A},\text{HSig}}(\lambda) = \Pr[\mathbf{Exp}^{\text{semi-Ad-UF}}_{\mathcal{A},\text{HSig}}(\lambda) = 1]$ *be the advantage of* $\mathcal{A}$ *against the semi-adaptive security of scheme* HSig. *We say that a homomorphic signature scheme* HSig *is semi-adaptive secure (or simply secure) if for every PPT adversary* $\mathcal{A}$ *there exists a negligible function $\epsilon(\lambda)$ such that* $\mathbf{Adv}^{\text{semi-Ad-UF}}_{\mathcal{A},\text{HSig}}(\lambda) \leq \epsilon(\lambda)$.

We stress that in the above security experiment the adversary $\mathcal{A}$ is restricted to produce Type 2 forgeries where *all* the inputs of the labeled program have been queried during the experiment. This notion works well for applications where the dataset is signed in one shot (as in the earlier proposals of homomorphic signatures [7]), or where one computes on the signed data only *after* the whole dataset has been filled up. In contrast, in those applications where the dataset is signed incrementally and one performs computations in between (e.g., in streaming applications), semi-adaptive security falls short of providing good guarantees. The issue is that in such a dynamic setting the adversary may claim a forgery with a labeled program containing a label $\tau^*$ that was not queried during the game. In this case, the input of $\mathcal{P}^*$ is no longer specified and defining whether the adversary's output is a forgery is not captured by Definition 2. From the literature, we note that the schemes in [6,7,22,25] are proven under a weaker version of semi-adaptive security where the messages of every dataset have to be queried all at once.[5]

**Adaptive Secure Homomorphic Signatures.** The issue of adversaries who claim programs in which some of the inputs are missing in the forgery stage was recognized earlier on by Freeman [21]. To deal with this issue, he proposed a notion of "well-defined programs" which characterizes when the output of a program can be defined in spite of missing inputs. Intuitively, the idea is that a program is well-defined if the missing inputs do not change its outcome.

---

[5] Actually, the authors of [25] mention that the proof of their scheme can be modified to hold under a definition with adaptive queries to data items, corresponding to the semi-adaptive security presented in this paper.

**Definition 3 (Well-Defined Labeled Program** [21]**).** *A labeled program*
$\mathcal{P}^* = (f^*, \tau_1^*, \ldots, \tau_n^*)$ *is well-defined with respect to a list* $T = \{(\tau_i, m_i)\}_{i \in I}$
*if one of the two following cases holds:*

- $\forall i = 1, \ldots, n : (\tau_i^*, m_i) \in T$.
- $\exists\, j \in [n]$ *s.t.* $(\tau_j, \cdot) \notin T$, *and for all possible choices of* $\tilde{m}_j \in \mathcal{M}$ *such that*
  $(\tau_j, \cdot) \notin T$ $f^*(m_1', \ldots, m_n')$ *is the same, where* $m_i' = m_i$ *for all* $i$ *s.t.* $(\tau_i, m_i) \in$
  $T$ *and* $m_i' = \tilde{m}_i$ *otherwise.*

With the notion of well-defined programs, adaptive security can be defined
as follows.

**Definition 4 (Adaptive Security** [21]**).** *We define* $\mathbf{Exp}_{\mathcal{A},\mathsf{HSig}}^{\mathsf{Ad\text{-}UF}}(\lambda)$ *as the secu-*
*rity experiment which proceeds as* $\mathbf{Exp}_{\mathcal{A},\mathsf{HSig}}^{\mathsf{UF}}(\lambda)$ *with the addition that the tuple*
$(\mathcal{P}^* := (f^*, \tau_1^*, \ldots, \tau_n^*), \Delta^*, m^*, \sigma^*)$ *returned by the adversary* $\mathcal{A}$ *is considered a*
*forgery if* $\mathsf{Ver}(\mathsf{vk}, \mathcal{P}^*, \Delta^*, m^*, \sigma^*) = 1$ *and either one of the following conditions*
*hold:*

**Type 1:** *The list* $T_{\Delta^*}$ *has not been initialized during the game.*
**Type 2:** $\mathcal{P}^*$ *is well-defined with respect to* $T_{\Delta^*}$, *and* $m^* \neq f^*(m_1', \ldots, m_n')$
   *where* $m_i' = m_i$ *for all* $i$ *s.t.* $(\tau_i, m_i) \in T_{\Delta^*}$ *and* $m_i' = \tilde{m}$ *(for some arbi-*
   *trary* $\tilde{m} \in \mathcal{M}$*), otherwise.*
**Type 3:** $\mathcal{P}^*$ *is* not *well-defined with respect to* $T_{\Delta^*}$.

*Let* $\mathbf{Adv}_{\mathcal{A},\mathsf{HSig}}^{\mathsf{Ad\text{-}UF}}(\lambda) = \Pr[\mathbf{Exp}_{\mathcal{A},\mathsf{HSig}}^{\mathsf{Ad\text{-}UF}}(\lambda) = 1]$ *be the advantage of* $\mathcal{A}$ *against the*
*adaptive security of scheme* $\mathsf{HSig}$. *We say that a homomorphic signature scheme*
$\mathsf{HSig}$ *is* adaptive secure *if for every PPT adversary* $\mathcal{A}$ *there exists a negligible*
*function* $\epsilon(\lambda)$ *such that* $\mathbf{Adv}_{\mathcal{A},\mathsf{HSig}}^{\mathsf{Ad\text{-}UF}}(\lambda) \leq \epsilon(\lambda)$.

Comparing the above definition of adaptive security with the semi-adaptive
definition presented earlier, we note the following: Type 1 forgeries are identical
in both definitions. Type 2 forgeries are similar: intuitively, they both capture
the case when the adversary cheats on the result of $\mathcal{P}^*$, except that Definition 4
addresses the case of missing inputs by defining what is, in this case, a correct
output (using the notion of well-defined program). Finally, Type 3 forgeries are
introduced in Definition 4 to address the remaining case in which $\mathcal{P}^*$ may have
different outputs, yet the forgery verifies correctly.

From the literature, the schemes in [3,11,13,15–17,21] are proven under the
adaptive security notion presented above.

**Strongly Adaptive Secure Homomorphic Signatures.** The good of the
adaptive definition given above is that it addresses the issue of labeled programs
with unspecified inputs by modeling when an adversary is cheating. The modeling of Definition 4 however comes at the price of a rather cumbersome security
definition. Well-defined programs are certainly not the most intuitive notion to
work with. In addition, besides simplicity, the main issue with the above notion
is that deciding whether the tuple returned by the adversary is a forgery may

not be doable in polynomial time. Indeed, making this test would require to execute $f^*$ on all possible values of the missing inputs (that may be exponentially many). In the case when admissible functions are low-degree arithmetic circuits over a large field, it has been shown that well-defined programs can be tested probabilistically, and that Type 3 forgeries can be reduced to Type 2 ones [10]. However, for general circuits the inefficient test issue remains and can generate troubles when proving the security of homomorphic signature schemes as well as when using them in larger protocols (as simply testing whether an adversary returned a forgery – wins – may not be doable in polynomial time).

To address this issue, in what follows we consider a stronger and much simpler security definition. This notion is obtained by extending the notion of semi-adaptive security (Definition 2) with a very simple notion of Type 3 forgeries. The latter are just forgeries where the labeled program contains a "new" label. The formal definition follows.

**Definition 5 (Strong Adaptive Security).** *We define* $\mathbf{Exp}_{\mathcal{A},\mathsf{HSig}}^{\mathsf{strong}\text{-}\mathsf{Ad}\text{-}\mathsf{UF}}(\lambda)$ *as the security experiment which proceeds as* $\mathbf{Exp}_{\mathcal{A},\mathsf{HSig}}^{\mathsf{UF}}(\lambda)$ *except that the tuple* $(\mathcal{P}^* := (f^*, \tau_1^*, \ldots, \tau_n^*), \Delta^*, m^*, \sigma^*)$ *returned by the adversary* $\mathcal{A}$ *is considered a forgery if* $\mathsf{Ver}(\mathsf{vk}, \mathcal{P}_{\Delta^*}^*, m^*, \sigma^*) = 1$ *and either one of the following conditions hold:*

**Type 1:** *The list* $T_{\Delta^*}$ *has not been initialized during the game.*
**Type 2:** *For all* $i \in [n]$, $\exists (\tau_i, m_i) \in T_{\Delta^*}$ *and* $m^* \neq f^*(m_1, \ldots, m_n)$.
**Type 3 Strong:** *there exists* $j \in [n]$ *such that* $(\tau_j^*, \cdot) \notin T_{\Delta^*}$.

*Let* $\mathbf{Adv}_{\mathcal{A},\mathsf{HSig}}^{\mathsf{strong}\text{-}\mathsf{Ad}\text{-}\mathsf{UF}}(\lambda) = \Pr[\mathbf{Exp}_{\mathcal{A},\mathsf{HSig}}^{\mathsf{strong}\text{-}\mathsf{Ad}\text{-}\mathsf{UF}}(\lambda) = 1]$ *be the advantage of* $\mathcal{A}$ *against the strong adaptive security of scheme* $\mathsf{HSig}$. *We say that a homomorphic signature scheme* $\mathsf{HSig}$ *is* strongly adaptive secure *if for every PPT adversary* $\mathcal{A}$ *there exists a negligible function* $\epsilon(\lambda)$ *such that* $\mathbf{Adv}_{\mathcal{A},\mathsf{HSig}}^{\mathsf{strong}\text{-}\mathsf{Ad}\text{-}\mathsf{UF}}(\lambda) \leq \epsilon(\lambda)$.

The security notion of Definition 5 now allows to detect forgeries in polynomial time, and is without doubt much simpler than Definition 4. Basically, this notion is the public-key equivalent of the security notion proposed by Gennaro and Wichs [23] for fully-homomorphic MACs (with some cosmetic changes due to the handling of multiple datasets).

**Relation Between Security Notions.** We note that the three security definitions presented in this Section are increasingly strong. Definition 4 is strictly stronger than Definition 2: while all forgeries in $\mathbf{Exp}_{\mathcal{A},\mathsf{HSig}}^{\mathsf{semi}\text{-}\mathsf{Ad}\text{-}\mathsf{UF}}(\lambda)$ are also forgeries in $\mathbf{Exp}_{\mathcal{A},\mathsf{HSig}}^{\mathsf{Ad}\text{-}\mathsf{UF}}(\lambda)$, the converse is not true as any forgery in $\mathbf{Exp}_{\mathcal{A},\mathsf{HSig}}^{\mathsf{Ad}\text{-}\mathsf{UF}}(\lambda)$ where the labeled program $\mathcal{P}^*$ contains an unqueried label is not considered a forgery in $\mathbf{Exp}_{\mathcal{A},\mathsf{HSig}}^{\mathsf{semi}\text{-}\mathsf{Ad}\text{-}\mathsf{UF}}(\lambda)$.

Definition 5 is strictly stronger than Definition 4. In one direction, any Type 1 and Type 3 forgery in $\mathbf{Exp}_{\mathcal{A},\mathsf{HSig}}^{\mathsf{Ad}\text{-}\mathsf{UF}}(\lambda)$ yields, respectively, a Type 1 and a Type 3 Strong forgery in $\mathbf{Exp}_{\mathcal{A},\mathsf{HSig}}^{\mathsf{strong}\text{-}\mathsf{Ad}\text{-}\mathsf{UF}}(\lambda)$, and a Type 2 forgery in $\mathbf{Exp}_{\mathcal{A},\mathsf{HSig}}^{\mathsf{Ad}\text{-}\mathsf{UF}}(\lambda)$ becomes either a Type 2 forgery or a Type 3 Strong forgery in $\mathbf{Exp}_{\mathcal{A},\mathsf{HSig}}^{\mathsf{strong}\text{-}\mathsf{Ad}\text{-}\mathsf{UF}}(\lambda)$.

In the other direction, there exist forgeries in experiment $\mathbf{Exp}_{\mathcal{A},\mathsf{HSig}}^{\mathsf{strong}\text{-}\mathsf{Ad}\text{-}\mathsf{UF}}(\lambda)$ that are not considered so in $\mathbf{Exp}_{\mathcal{A},\mathsf{HSig}}^{\mathsf{Ad}\text{-}\mathsf{UF}}(\lambda)$. We show this by considering the following adversary $\mathcal{A}$. $\mathcal{A}$ asks signing queries $(\Delta, \tau_1, m_1), (\Delta, \tau_2, m_2)$ and obtains signatures $\sigma_1, \sigma_2$; it computes $\sigma^* \leftarrow \mathsf{Eval}(\mathsf{vk}, \times, \sigma_1, \sigma_2)$, and outputs $(\mathcal{P}^* :=  (f, \tau_1, \tau_2, \tau_3), \Delta, m_1 \cdot m_2)$, where $f$ is the function $f(x, y, z) = x(y + z) - xz.$ [6] As one can see, the output of $\mathcal{A}$ is a Type 3 Strong forgery, since $\tau_3$ is a label which has never been queried, while it is not a forgery in $\mathbf{Exp}_{\mathcal{A},\mathsf{HSig}}^{\mathsf{Ad}\text{-}\mathsf{UF}}(\lambda)$, since $\mathcal{P}^* := (f, \tau_1, \tau_2, \tau_3)$ is well-defined with respect to the set of queries $T_\Delta = \{(\tau_1, m_1), (\tau_2, m_2)\}$, and $m_1 \cdot m_2$ is the correct output.

In addition to the fact that the security notions are strictly separated, we also note that by using a counterexample such as the one above it is possible to show that previously proposed homomorphic signatures (e.g., [7, 17, 25] are *not* strong adaptive secure.

## 3  A Generic Transformation from Semi-adaptive to Strong Adaptive Security

In this Section we show a technique that allows one to turn a semi-adaptive unforgeable homomorphic signature into one that satisfies strong adaptive security. Specifically, our main result is stated in the following theorem:

**Theorem 1.** *If $\Sigma$ is a semi-adaptive unforgeable fully (resp. leveled) homomorphic signature scheme for boolean circuits, then there exists a strong adaptive unforgeable homomorphic signature scheme $\widehat{\Sigma}$ that supports the same class of functions. Furthermore, if $\Sigma$ satisfies context-hiding (resp. efficient verification, composability) so does $\widehat{\Sigma}$.*

The core of our result is a general transformation which shows how to combine a semi-adaptive secure scheme $\Sigma$ together with a semi-adaptive secure scheme $\Sigma_{\mathsf{OR}}$ that supports only OR operations over $\mathbb{Z}_2$. This combination yields a homomorphic signature scheme that is strong adaptive secure and supports the same class of functions supported by $\Sigma$.

Clearly, if $\Sigma$ supports the evaluation of boolean circuits, then $\Sigma_{\mathsf{OR}}$ can be instantiated using $\Sigma$. In this case, our result provides a way to bootstrap the security of $\Sigma$ from semi-adaptive to strong adaptive. This yields our main result above.

In the case where $\Sigma_{\mathsf{OR}}$ cannot be instantiated using $\Sigma$ (e.g., $\Sigma$ is not expressive enough), our transformation still provides a recipe to obtain strong adaptive security using a separate OR-homomorphic scheme. However, motivated by the lack of many candidates of OR-homomorphic signature schemes (concretely, [25] is the only available one), we investigated how to obtain a similar transformation by using schemes that have been studied more widely. Our second result is

---

[6] Any other function where the third input cancels out would work. Furthermore, although in the given example it is trivial to recognize that $\mathcal{P}$ is well-defined, this may not be the case for general functions.

a transformation which can combine a semi-adaptive secure scheme $\Sigma$ together with a semi-adaptive secure *linearly-homomophic* signature $\Sigma_{\mathsf{LH}}$ that works for scalar messages[7] over a large ring, say $\mathbb{Z}_p$. This combination yields a homomorphic signature scheme that is strong adaptive secure and supports the same class of functions supported by $\Sigma$. A limitation of this second transformation is that it applies only to schemes that are leveled homomorphic (i.e., for circuits of bounded depth) as it requires to set $p > 2^d$ where $d = poly(\lambda)$ is the bound on circuits depth. On the other hand, the advantage is that strong adaptive security can be obtained by using linearly-homomorphic schemes, a class of constructions that has received significant attention, of which we know many constructions from several assumptions [3–5,11,13,15,16,21], most of which are way more efficient in practice than [25]. As for the efficiency of the scheme resulting from our transformations, it basically depends on the efficiency of the scheme one starts from. In the worst case, however, the efficiency loss is comparable to executing the original algorithms twice.

### 3.1   Strong Adaptive Security from OR-Homomorphic Signatures

Here we present our first transformation. The tools we start from are a homomorphic signature scheme $\Sigma := (\Sigma.\mathsf{KeyGen}, \Sigma.\mathsf{Sign}, \Sigma.\mathsf{Ver}, \Sigma.\mathsf{Eval})$ for a class $\mathcal{C}$ of (boolean or arithmetic) circuits, and a homomorphic signature $\Sigma_{\mathsf{OR}} := (\Sigma_{\mathsf{OR}}.\mathsf{KeyGen}, \Sigma_{\mathsf{OR}}.\mathsf{Sign}, \Sigma_{\mathsf{OR}}.\mathsf{Ver}, \Sigma_{\mathsf{OR}}.\mathsf{Eval})$ that works over message space $\mathbb{Z}_2$ and supports homomorphic OR operations. More precisely, $\Sigma_{\mathsf{OR}}$ must support circuits that are composed only of OR gates and have the same depth as those in $\mathcal{C}$.

Using $\Sigma$ and $\Sigma_{\mathsf{OR}}$ in a black box way, we build a scheme $\widehat{\Sigma}$ which supports evaluation of circuits in $\mathcal{C}$. Moreover, assuming only semi-adaptive security of both $\Sigma$ and $\Sigma_{\mathsf{OR}}$, we show that $\widehat{\Sigma}$ is strong adaptive secure.

$\widehat{\Sigma}.\mathsf{KeyGen}(1^\lambda, \mathcal{L})$. Run the key generation algorithms $(\mathsf{vk}, \mathsf{sk}) \leftarrow \mathsf{KeyGen}(1^\lambda, \mathcal{L})$ and $(\mathsf{vk}_{\mathsf{OR}}, \mathsf{sk}_{\mathsf{OR}}) \leftarrow \Sigma_{\mathsf{OR}}.\mathsf{KeyGen}(1^\lambda, \mathcal{L})$, and output $(\hat{\mathsf{vk}}, \hat{\mathsf{sk}}) := ((\mathsf{vk}, \mathsf{vk}_{\mathsf{OR}}), (\mathsf{sk}, \mathsf{sk}_{\mathsf{OR}}))$.

$\widehat{\Sigma}.\mathsf{Sign}(\hat{\mathsf{sk}}, \Delta, \tau, m)$. The signing algorithm uses the secret key to compute $\sigma \leftarrow \mathsf{Sign}(\mathsf{sk}, \Delta, \tau, m)$ and $\sigma_{\mathsf{OR}} \leftarrow \Sigma_{\mathsf{OR}}.\mathsf{Sign}(\mathsf{sk}_{\mathsf{OR}}, \Delta, \tau, 0)$, and outputs $\hat{\sigma} := (\sigma, \sigma_{\mathsf{OR}})$.

   Note that the OR-homomorphic component $\sigma_{\mathsf{OR}}$ of the signature signs the bit 0. Although the usefulness of this component will become more clear in the security proof, the intuition is that this component keeps track of those labels that are used throughout the computation.

$\widehat{\Sigma}.\mathsf{Eval}(\hat{\mathsf{vk}}, f, \hat{\sigma}_1, \ldots, \hat{\sigma}_n)$. We describe the homomorphic evaluation of $f$ in a gate-by-gate fashion, distinguishing the cases of unary and binary gates. One can easily see that the construction generalizes to $n$-ary gates. Describing the evaluation gate-by-gate is also useful to clearly see that *our transformation*

---

[7] Namely, we do not need to work with vectors as most linearly-homomorphic signatures do.

*allows for arbitrary composition* of signatures (i.e., running $\widehat{\Sigma}$.Eval on outputs of $\widehat{\Sigma}$.Eval). At every gate $g$, one proceeds as follows.

**Unary Gates.** Let $g$ be an unary gate and let $\hat{\sigma}_1 := (\sigma_1, \sigma_{\mathsf{OR},1})$ be the input. We compute the output signature $\hat{\sigma}_{\mathsf{out}} := (\sigma_{\mathsf{out}}, \sigma_{\mathsf{OR},\mathsf{out}})$ by computing $\sigma_{\mathsf{out}} \leftarrow \Sigma$.Eval$(\mathsf{vk}, g, \sigma_1)$ and $\sigma_{\mathsf{OR},\mathsf{out}} \leftarrow \sigma_{\mathsf{OR},1}$. Basically, we evaluate $g$ over the $\Sigma$ component, while for the OR-homomorphic component we simply evaluate an identity function.

**Binary Gates.** Let $g$ be a binary gate and let $\hat{\sigma}_1 := (\sigma_1, \sigma_{\mathsf{OR},1})$ and $\hat{\sigma}_2 := (\sigma_2, \sigma_{\mathsf{OR},2})$ be its two inputs. We compute the output signature $\hat{\sigma}_{\mathsf{out}} := (\sigma_{\mathsf{out}}, \sigma_{\mathsf{OR},\mathsf{out}})$ by first evaluating $\sigma_{\mathsf{out}} \leftarrow \Sigma$.Eval$(\mathsf{vk}, g, \sigma_1, \sigma_2)$ and then evaluating $\sigma_{\mathsf{OR},\mathsf{out}} \leftarrow \Sigma_{\mathsf{OR}}$.Eval$(\mathsf{vk}_{\mathsf{OR}}, \mathsf{OR}, \sigma_{\mathsf{OR},1}, \sigma_{\mathsf{OR},2})$. Basically, we evaluate the binary $g$ over the $\Sigma$ components, while for the OR-homomorphic components we perform their homomorphic OR.

By proceeding over $f$ in a gate-by-gate fashion, eventually we obtain a signature $\hat{\sigma} := (\sigma, \sigma_{\mathsf{OR}})$, and $\widehat{\Sigma}$.Eval returns $\hat{\sigma}$.

At this point, it is worth mentioning that the evaluation algorithm of our transformation generates $(\sigma, \sigma_{\mathsf{OR}})$ such that $\sigma = \Sigma$.Eval$(\mathsf{vk}, f, \sigma_1, \ldots, \sigma_n)$ and $\sigma_{\mathsf{OR}} = \Sigma_{\mathsf{OR}}$.Eval$(\mathsf{vk}_{\mathsf{OR}}, f_{\mathsf{OR}}, \sigma_{\mathsf{OR},1}, \ldots, \sigma_{\mathsf{OR},n})$, where $f_{\mathsf{OR}}$ is an "OR version" of the circuit $f$ obtained by changing any unary gate with an identity gate and any binary gate with an OR gate.

$\widehat{\Sigma}$.Ver$(\mathsf{vk}, \mathcal{P}, \Delta, m, \hat{\sigma})$. Parse $\mathcal{P} = (f, \tau_1, \ldots, \tau_n)$ and $\hat{\sigma} := (\sigma, \sigma_{\mathsf{OR}})$. Next, define $\mathcal{P}_{\mathsf{OR}} := (f_{\mathsf{OR}}, \tau_1, \ldots, \tau_n)$, where $f_{\mathsf{OR}}$ is the circuit composed only of OR (and identity) gates, obtained from $f$ as described above. Then check if $\Sigma$.Ver$(\mathsf{vk}, \mathcal{P}, \Delta, m, \sigma) = 1$ and $\Sigma_{\mathsf{OR}}$.Ver$(\mathsf{vk}_{\mathsf{OR}}, \mathcal{P}_{\mathsf{OR}}, \Delta, 0, \sigma_{\mathsf{OR}}) = 1$. If both the verification runs output 1, then output 1, otherwise output 0.

In the following theorem we show that our generic scheme $\widehat{\Sigma}$ satisfies strong adaptive security, as long as the schemes $\Sigma$ and $\Sigma_{\mathsf{OR}}$ are only semi-adaptive secure (proof is given in the full version of the paper [12].

**Theorem 2.** *Assume that $\Sigma$ is a semi-adaptive secure homomorphic signature scheme for a class of circuits $\mathcal{C}$, and that $\Sigma_{\mathsf{OR}}$ is a semi-adaptive secure homomorphic signature with message space $\mathbb{Z}_2$ and supporting OR circuits. Then the scheme $\widehat{\Sigma}$ described above is a strong-adaptive secure homomorphic signature for $\mathcal{C}$. Furthermore, if both $\Sigma$ and $\Sigma_{\mathsf{OR}}$ satisfy context-hiding (resp. efficient verification, composability), then so does $\widehat{\Sigma}$.*

### 3.2 Strong Adaptive Security from Linearly-Homomorphic Signatures

Here we present our second transformation. This transformation is similar to the one of Sect. 3.1: it incorporates signatures from a second homomorphic signature scheme in order to handle Type 3 forgeries. However, instead of a OR-homomorphic scheme, here we use a linearly-homomorphic one. More in detail, our constructions takes in a homomorphic signature scheme $\Sigma := (\Sigma.\mathsf{KeyGen}, \Sigma.\mathsf{Sign}, \Sigma.\mathsf{Ver}, \Sigma.\mathsf{Eval})$ that supports circuits of polynomial depth at most $d$

and fan-in 2,[8] and an additive-homomorphic signature $\Sigma_{LH} := (\Sigma_{LH}.\mathsf{KeyGen},$ $\Sigma_{LH}.\mathsf{Sign}, \Sigma_{LH}.\mathsf{Ver}, \Sigma_{LH}.\mathsf{Eval})$ that works over message space $\mathbb{Z}_p$, where $p > 2^d$. Using $\Sigma$ and $\Sigma_{LH}$ in a black box way, we build a scheme $\Sigma'$ which supports the same circuits as $\Sigma$, and assuming only semi-adaptive security of $\Sigma$ and $\Sigma_{LH}$, we show that $\Sigma'$ is strong adaptive secure. The scheme $\Sigma'$ is defined as follows:

$\Sigma'.\mathsf{KeyGen}(1^\lambda, \mathcal{L})$. Run both $(\mathsf{vk}, \mathsf{sk}) \leftarrow \Sigma.\mathsf{KeyGen}(1^\lambda, \mathcal{L})$ and $(\mathsf{vk}_{LH}, \mathsf{sk}_{LH}) \leftarrow$ $\Sigma_{LH}.\mathsf{KeyGen}(1^\lambda, \mathcal{L})$, and output $(\mathsf{vk}', \mathsf{sk}') := ((\mathsf{vk}, \mathsf{vk}_{LH}), (\mathsf{sk}, \mathsf{sk}_{LH}))$.

$\Sigma'.\mathsf{Sign}(\mathsf{sk}', \Delta, \tau, m)$. The signing algorithm uses $\mathsf{sk}'$ to compute $\sigma \leftarrow \mathsf{Sign}(\mathsf{sk}, \Delta, \tau, m)$ and $\sigma_{LH} \leftarrow \Sigma_{LH}.\mathsf{Sign}(\mathsf{sk}_{LH}, \Delta, \tau, 0)$, and outputs $\sigma' := (\sigma, \sigma_{LH})$.

$\Sigma'.\mathsf{Eval}(\mathsf{vk}', f, \sigma'_1, \ldots, \sigma'_n)$. As in the previous section, we describe the homomorphic evaluation of $f$ in a gate-by-gate fashion, distinguishing the cases of unary and binary gates. At every gate $g$, one proceeds as follows.

**Unary Gates.** Let $g$ be an unary gate and let $\sigma'_1 := (\sigma_1, \sigma_{LH,1})$ be the input. We compute the output signature $\sigma'_{out} := (\sigma_{out}, \sigma_{LH,out})$ by computing $\sigma_{out} \leftarrow \Sigma.\mathsf{Eval}(\mathsf{vk}, g, \sigma_1)$ and $\sigma_{LH,out} \leftarrow \sigma_{LH,1}$.

**Binary Gates.** Let $g$ be a binary gate and let $\sigma'_1 := (\sigma_1, \sigma_{LH,1})$ and $\sigma'_2 := (\sigma_2, \sigma_{LH,2})$ be its two inputs. We compute the output signature $\sigma'_{out} := (\sigma_{out}, \sigma_{LH,out})$ by first evaluating $\sigma_{out} \leftarrow \Sigma.\mathsf{Eval}(\mathsf{vk}, g, \sigma_1, \sigma_2)$ and then evaluating $\sigma_{LH,out} \leftarrow \Sigma_{LH}.\mathsf{Eval}(\mathsf{vk}_{LH}, +, \sigma_{LH,1}, \sigma_{LH,2})$.

By proceeding over $f$ in a gate-by-gate fashion, eventually we obtain a signature $\sigma' := (\sigma, \sigma_{LH})$, and $\Sigma'.\mathsf{Eval}$ returns $\sigma'$. We note that the evaluation algorithm of our transformation generates $(\sigma, \sigma_{LH})$ such that $\sigma = \Sigma.\mathsf{Eval}(\mathsf{vk}, f, \sigma_1, \ldots, \sigma_n)$ and $\sigma_{LH} = \Sigma_{LH}.\mathsf{Eval}(\mathsf{vk}_{LH}, f_+, \sigma_{LH,1}, \ldots, \sigma_{LH,n})$, where $f_+$ is an "additive version" of the circuit $f$ obtained by changing any unary gate with an identity gate and any binary gate with an additive gate.

$\Sigma'.\mathsf{Ver}(\mathsf{vk}, \mathcal{P}, \Delta, m, \sigma')$. Parse $\mathcal{P} = (f, \tau_1, \ldots, \tau_n)$ and $\sigma' := (\sigma, \sigma_{LH})$. Next, define $\mathcal{P}_+ := (f_+, \tau_1, \ldots, \tau_n)$, where $f_+$ is the additive circuit obtained from $f$ as described above. Then check if $\Sigma.\mathsf{Ver}(\mathsf{vk}, \mathcal{P}, \Delta, m, \sigma) = 1$ and $\Sigma_{LH}.\mathsf{Ver}(\mathsf{vk}_{LH}, \mathcal{P}_+, \Delta, 0, \sigma_{LH}) = 1$. If both the verification runs output 1, then output 1, otherwise output 0.

In the following theorem we show that our generic scheme $\Sigma'$ satisfies strong adaptive security, as long as the schemes $\Sigma$ and $\Sigma_{LH}$ are only semi-adaptive secure (proof is given in the full version of the paper [12]).

**Theorem 3.** *Assume that $\Sigma$ is a semi-adaptive secure homomorphic signature scheme for circuits of polynomial depth at least $d$ and fan-in 2, and that $\Sigma_{LH}$ is a semi-adaptive secure linearly-homomorphic signature scheme whose message space is $\mathbb{Z}_p$, with $p > 2^d$. Then the scheme $\Sigma'$ described above is a strong-adaptive secure homomorphic signature. Furthermore, if both $\Sigma$ and $\Sigma_{LH}$ satisfy context-hiding (resp. efficient verification), then so does $\Sigma'$.*

---

[8] We describe the transformation for fan-in 2 only for ease of exposition. It is easy to see that the same technique would work for constant fan-in $c$ setting up $p > c^d$.

**Acknowledgements.** The work of Dario Fiore and Luca Nizzardo was partially supported by the Spanish Ministry of Economy under project references TIN2015-70713-R (DEDETIS), RTC-2016-4930-7 (DataMantium), and under a Juan de la Cierva fellowship to Dario Fiore, and by the Madrid Regional Government under project N-Greens (ref. S2013/ICE-2731).

# References

1. Agrawal, S., Boneh, D.: Homomorphic MACs: MAC-based integrity for network coding. In: Abdalla, M., Pointcheval, D., Fouque, P.-A., Vergnaud, D. (eds.) ACNS 2009. LNCS, vol. 5536, pp. 292–305. Springer, Heidelberg (2009). https://doi.org/10.1007/978-3-642-01957-9_18

2. Ahn, J.H., Boneh, D., Camenisch, J., Hohenberger, S., Shelat, A., Waters, B.: Computing on authenticated data. In: Cramer, R. (ed.) TCC 2012. LNCS, vol. 7194, pp. 1–20. Springer, Heidelberg (2012). https://doi.org/10.1007/978-3-642-28914-9_1

3. Attrapadung, N., Libert, B.: Homomorphic network coding signatures in the standard model. In: Catalano, D., Fazio, N., Gennaro, R., Nicolosi, A. (eds.) PKC 2011. LNCS, vol. 6571, pp. 17–34. Springer, Heidelberg (2011). https://doi.org/10.1007/978-3-642-19379-8_2

4. Attrapadung, N., Libert, B., Peters, T.: Computing on authenticated data: new privacy definitions and constructions. In: Wang, X., Sako, K. (eds.) ASIACRYPT 2012. LNCS, vol. 7658, pp. 367–385. Springer, Heidelberg (2012). https://doi.org/10.1007/978-3-642-34961-4_23

5. Attrapadung, N., Libert, B., Peters, T.: Efficient completely context-hiding quotable and linearly homomorphic signatures. In: Kurosawa, K., Hanaoka, G. (eds.) PKC 2013. LNCS, vol. 7778, pp. 386–404. Springer, Heidelberg (2013). https://doi.org/10.1007/978-3-642-36362-7_24

6. Boneh, D., Freeman, D., Katz, J., Waters, B.: Signing a linear subspace: signature schemes for network coding. In: Jarecki, S., Tsudik, G. (eds.) PKC 2009. LNCS, vol. 5443, pp. 68–87. Springer, Heidelberg (2009). https://doi.org/10.1007/978-3-642-00468-1_5

7. Boneh, D., Freeman, D.M.: Homomorphic signatures for polynomial functions. In: Paterson, K.G. (ed.) EUROCRYPT 2011. LNCS, vol. 6632, pp. 149–168. Springer, Heidelberg (2011). https://doi.org/10.1007/978-3-642-20465-4_10

8. Boneh, D., Freeman, D.M.: Linearly homomorphic signatures over binary fields and new tools for lattice-based signatures. In: Catalano, D., Fazio, N., Gennaro, R., Nicolosi, A. (eds.) PKC 2011. LNCS, vol. 6571, pp. 1–16. Springer, Heidelberg (2011). https://doi.org/10.1007/978-3-642-19379-8_1

9. Catalano, D., Fiore, D.: Practical homomorphic MACs for arithmetic circuits. In: Johansson, T., Nguyen, P.Q. (eds.) EUROCRYPT 2013. LNCS, vol. 7881, pp. 336–352. Springer, Heidelberg (2013). https://doi.org/10.1007/978-3-642-38348-9_21

10. Catalano, D., Fiore, D., Gennaro, R., Nizzardo, L.: Generalizing homomorphic MACs for arithmetic circuits. In: Krawczyk, H. (ed.) PKC 2014. LNCS, vol. 8383, pp. 538–555. Springer, Heidelberg (2014). https://doi.org/10.1007/978-3-642-54631-0_31

11. Catalano, D., Fiore, D., Gennaro, R., Vamvourellis, K.: Algebraic (trapdoor) one-way functions and their applications. In: Sahai, A. (ed.) TCC 2013. LNCS, vol. 7785, pp. 680–699. Springer, Heidelberg (2013). https://doi.org/10.1007/978-3-642-36594-2_38

12. Catalano, D., Fiore, D., Nizzardo, L.: On the security notions for homomorphic signatures. Full Version: Cryptology ePrint Archive. https://eprint.iacr.org/2016/1175.pdf

13. Catalano, D., Fiore, D., Nizzardo, L.: Programmable hash functions go private: constructions and applications to (homomorphic) signatures with shorter public keys. In: Gennaro, R., Robshaw, M. (eds.) CRYPTO 2015. LNCS, vol. 9216, pp. 254–274. Springer, Heidelberg (2015). https://doi.org/10.1007/978-3-662-48000-7_13

14. Catalano, D., Fiore, D., Nizzardo, L.: Homomorphic signatures with sublinear public keys via asymmetric programmable hash functions. Des. Codes Cryptogr. (2017). https://doi.org/10.1007/s10623-017-0444-3

15. Catalano, D., Fiore, D., Warinschi, B.: Adaptive pseudo-free groups and applications. In: Paterson, K.G. (ed.) EUROCRYPT 2011. LNCS, vol. 6632, pp. 207–223. Springer, Heidelberg (2011). https://doi.org/10.1007/978-3-642-20465-4_13

16. Catalano, D., Fiore, D., Warinschi, B.: Efficient network coding signatures in the standard model. In: Fischlin, M., Buchmann, J., Manulis, M. (eds.) PKC 2012. LNCS, vol. 7293, pp. 680–696. Springer, Heidelberg (2012). https://doi.org/10.1007/978-3-642-30057-8_40

17. Catalano, D., Fiore, D., Warinschi, B.: Homomorphic signatures with efficient verification for polynomial functions. In: Garay, J.A., Gennaro, R. (eds.) CRYPTO 2014. LNCS, vol. 8616, pp. 371–389. Springer, Heidelberg (2014). https://doi.org/10.1007/978-3-662-44371-2_21

18. Chase, M., Kohlweiss, M., Lysyanskaya, A., Meiklejohn, S.: Malleable signatures: new definitions and delegatable anonymous credentials. In: 2014 IEEE 27th Computer Security Foundations Symposium, pp. 199–213. IEEE (2014)

19. Desmedt, Y.: Computer security by redefining what a computer is. In: NSPW (1993)

20. Elkhiyaoui, K., Önen, M., Molva, R.: Online-offline homomorphic signatures for polynomial functions. Cryptology ePrint Archive, Report 2015/954 (2015). http://eprint.iacr.org/

21. Freeman, D.M.: Improved security for linearly homomorphic signatures: a generic framework. In: Fischlin, M., Buchmann, J., Manulis, M. (eds.) PKC 2012. LNCS, vol. 7293, pp. 697–714. Springer, Heidelberg (2012). https://doi.org/10.1007/978-3-642-30057-8_41

22. Gennaro, R., Katz, J., Krawczyk, H., Rabin, T.: Secure network coding over the integers. In: Nguyen, P.Q., Pointcheval, D. (eds.) PKC 2010. LNCS, vol. 6056, pp. 142–160. Springer, Heidelberg (2010). https://doi.org/10.1007/978-3-642-13013-7_9

23. Gennaro, R., Wichs, D.: Fully homomorphic message authenticators. In: Sako, K., Sarkar, P. (eds.) ASIACRYPT 2013. LNCS, vol. 8270, pp. 301–320. Springer, Heidelberg (2013). https://doi.org/10.1007/978-3-642-42045-0_16

24. Goldwasser, S., Micali, S., Rivest, R.L.: A digital signature scheme secure against adaptive chosen-message attacks. SIAM J. Comput. **17**(2), 281–308 (1988)

25. Gorbunov, S., Vaikuntanathan, V., Wichs, D.: Leveled fully homomorphic signatures from standard lattices. In: 47th ACM STOC. ACM Press (2015)

26. Johnson, R., Molnar, D., Song, D., Wagner, D.: Homomorphic signature schemes. In: Preneel, B. (ed.) CT-RSA 2002. LNCS, vol. 2271, pp. 244–262. Springer, Heidelberg (2002). https://doi.org/10.1007/3-540-45760-7_17

# Invisible Sanitizable Signatures and Public-Key Encryption are Equivalent

Marc Fischlin and Patrick Harasser[✉]

Cryptoplexity, Technische Universität Darmstadt, Darmstadt, Germany
{marc.fischlin,patrick.harasser}@cryptoplexity.de
http://www.cryptoplexity.de

**Abstract.** Sanitizable signature schemes are signature schemes which support the delegation of modification rights. The signer can allow a sanitizer to perform a set of admissible operations on the original message and then to update the signature, in such a way that basic security properties like unforgeability or accountability are preserved. Recently, Camenisch *et al.* (PKC 2017) devised new schemes with the previously unattained invisibility property. This property says that the set of admissible operations for the sanitizer remains hidden from outsiders. Subsequently, Beck *et al.* (ACISP 2017) gave an even stronger version of this notion and constructions achieving it. Here we characterize the invisibility property in both forms by showing that invisible sanitizable signatures are equivalent to $\mathsf{IND-CPA}$-secure encryption schemes, and strongly invisible signatures are equivalent to $\mathsf{IND-CCA2}$-secure encryption schemes. The equivalence is established by proving that invisible (resp. strongly invisible) sanitizable signature schemes yield $\mathsf{IND-CPA}$-secure (resp. $\mathsf{IND-CCA2}$-secure) public-key encryption schemes and that, vice versa, we can build (strongly) invisible sanitizable signatures given a corresponding public-key encryption scheme.

**Keywords:** Sanitizable signatures · Digital signatures · Invisibility
Public-key encryption · One-way functions

## 1 Introduction

Sanitizable signature schemes enable the signer of a document to declare certain sections of the message as admissible for modification, so that another designated party (the sanitizer) can modify them and update the signature without affecting the authenticity and integrity of the immutable parts. The main motivation is to balance out the verifier's wish to check authenticity of parts of the original document and the signer's desire for privacy of the sanitized data. The idea of sanitizable signature schemes dates back to a work by Ateniese *et al.* [2].

In [2], the authors introduced several security properties for sanitizable signature schemes. Besides unforgeability against outsiders, a desirable property is immutability, which demands that even a malicious sanitizer can only alter

© Springer International Publishing AG, part of Springer Nature 2018
B. Preneel and F. Vercauteren (Eds.): ACNS 2018, LNCS 10892, pp. 202–220, 2018.
https://doi.org/10.1007/978-3-319-93387-0_11

admissible parts. Privacy asks that one cannot reconstruct the original document given only the sanitized version and signature, and its strengthening called unlinkability [7] says that one cannot determine the origin to a sanitized document among several known possibilities. Signer and sanitizer accountability ensure that in case of a dispute the parties can give a convincing proof of who created a signature, the signer or the sanitizer. A less common property is transparency, which should hide who created a signature, in case neither of the parties helps to determine the originator—this stands in contrast to public accountability, where no additional help is required to determine who signed the document.

### 1.1  Invisible Sanitizable Signatures

Recently, Camenisch *et al.* [10] formalized the notion of invisibility of sanitizable signatures. This property, formerly called strong transparency in [2], should hide which modifications a sanitizer is allowed to perform. In previous constructions the description of admissible operations, denoted ADM, had usually been attached in clear to the signature. Gong *et al.* [25] were the first to argue that this information can be of value, and later Camenisch *et al.* showed that hiding it may be a desirable goal. They also revised the theoretical framework of sanitizable signatures in order to capture the invisibility property, and gave constructions achieving it based on a new type of chameleon hash functions with ephemeral trapdoors. Soon after, Beck *et al.* [3] further strengthened the notion of invisibility.

In its basic form, invisibility protects against leakage of ADM if the sanitizer public key is only used in connection with a single signer. In applications this means that the sanitizer must create a fresh key pair for each user. Strong invisibility, on the other hand, allows to use the same sanitizer key pair with multiple signers. Beck *et al.* use unique signatures, $\mathsf{IND-CCA2}$-secure encryption, and collision-resistant chameleon hash functions to achieve strong invisibility.

Technically, the difference between the two invisibility notions lies in the capabilities of an adversary trying to establish which of two potential operation sets, $\mathrm{ADM}_0$ or $\mathrm{ADM}_1$, has been encoded as admissible into the signature. Given a challenge signature, the adversary may query a sanitizing oracle on it as long as the requested modification does not allow to distinguish the two cases trivially (this happens e.g. if the modification is admissible for one of the two sets but not for the other). For the basic invisibility notion the adversary can ask for sanitizations only in connection with the public key $\mathsf{pk}_{\mathsf{Sig}}$ of the genuine signer. In the stronger notion, the adversary can also request sanitizations of messages signed with other, possibly maliciously chosen signer keys $\mathsf{pk}'_{\mathsf{Sig}}$.

### 1.2  Our Contributions

In this work we show that invisible sanitizable signature schemes and public-key encryption schemes are equivalent. Our equivalence proof consists of four parts.

*Invisibility Implies* IND−CPA-*Secure Encryption.* Our first result is to show that an invisible sanitizable signature scheme yields an IND−CPA-secure bit-encryption scheme. An invisible scheme hides the actual admissible operations for a signature; we can use this property to securely embed a message bit $b$ by using one of two fixed and distinct admissible operation descriptions ($ADM_0$ or $ADM_1$) to build a signature $\sigma$ under a fresh signer key pair. The ciphertext consists of the signature $\sigma$ and the signer public key $pk_{Sig}$. Invisibility now guarantees that no outsider is able to distinguish the two cases.

The trapdoor information for decryption is the sanitizer secret key; his public key acts as the public key of the encryption scheme. With his secret key, the sanitizer can run the sanitization process and check via a distinguishing modification which operation $ADM_b$ has been embedded: Only the admissible one ($ADM_b$) will result in a valid new signature. For the other operation ($ADM_{1-b}$), the modification should fail by the immutability property of the sanitizable scheme. Note that we obviously need some other security property besides invisibility, because it is easy to devise invisible signature schemes without any other security property, e.g. with constant signatures.

*Strong Invisibility Implies* IND−CCA2-*Secure Encryption.* While the construction of an IND−CPA-secure scheme via the embedding of the hidden ADM may be expected, we argue next that the same construction yields an IND−CCA2-secure encryption scheme if the underlying sanitizable signature scheme is strongly invisible. This result is less conventional, since it links the sanitization for different signer keys with the ability to securely decrypt different ciphertexts.

The proof idea is to note that ciphertexts in our encryption system are of the form $(\sigma, pk_{Sig})$. Given a challenge ciphertext $(\sigma, pk_{Sig})$, recall that for IND−CCA2-security we must allow for oracle decryptions of ciphertexts $(\sigma', pk'_{Sig}) \neq (\sigma, pk_{Sig})$. Since decryption is performed via sanitization, and strong invisibility allows us to call the sanitizer for different keys $pk'_{Sig}$, we can easily decrypt ciphertexts of the form $(\sigma', pk'_{Sig})$ with $pk'_{Sig} \neq pk_{Sig}$. To handle ciphertexts $(\sigma', pk_{Sig})$ under the original signer key we rely on the strong unforgeability property of the signature scheme: it says that one cannot create fresh signatures $\sigma'$ under $pk_{Sig}$, and therefore an IND−CCA2-adversary cannot submit valid oracle queries of this form.

In a sense, this result warrants the deployment of an IND−CCA2-secure encryption scheme in the strongly invisible construction of Beck *et al.* [3]: Any strongly invisible sanitizable signature scheme already implies IND−CCA2-secure encryption systems. Note that we construct an IND−CCA2-secure *bit* encryption scheme, but this is sufficient to derive an IND−CCA2-secure *string* encryption scheme [14,26,31,32].

IND−CPA-*Secure Encryption Implies Invisibility.* Next we establish the converse implication, i.e. from IND−CPA-secure public-key encryption schemes to invisible sanitizable signatures. Note that the existence of the former primitive also implies the existence of one-way functions (the argument is identical to the one in [35, Lemma 1]), and thus of secure digital signature schemes [33,35], so that we can use this building block in our construction as well. Besides invisibility, the derived sanitizable signature scheme has all the common properties, like unforgeablility, immutability, privacy, and accountability.

The construction idea is to have the signer sign every message block of the message with a different, ephemeral key, and then to protect this tuple of signatures with an additional signature under his secret key. This "message" part of the signature ensures unforgeability, privacy, and accountability. To enable the sanitizer to modify the admissible blocks, the signer appends another "administrative" signature over the description ADM and the tuple of secret keys used to sign the admissible blocks, both encrypted under the sanitizer public encryption key to allow for invisibility. If some admissible block has to be modified, the sanitizer can retrieve the corresponding ephemeral key via decryption, change the message block and then update the relevant signatures in the "message" part. Immutability (i.e., protection against inadmissible modifications from a malicious sanitizer) then follows from the unforgeability of the underlying digital signature scheme: It is ensured by the fact that the sanitizer only receives the signing keys for the blocks he is allowed to modify.

We stress here that our construction does not achieve some less common properties, in particular transparency and unlinkability, and that our security reduction is non-tight. On the other hand, we regard our work as being above all a feasibility result, so that tightness—even though desirable—should not be viewed as essential, and we believe that invisible, non-transparent sanitizable signatures can have interesting applications: One can envision scenarios where it should be impossible to learn which (if any) message blocks have the potential to be altered, but on the other hand it should be clear who signed the document (e.g., for legal and accountability reasons).

IND−CCA2-*Secure Encryption Implies Strong Invisibility.* The noteworthy property of the above construction is that IND−CPA-security suffices to achieve (ordinary) invisibility. With a slight technical twist, we interestingly achieve strong invisibility if we now have an IND−CCA2-secure encryption scheme: Namely, we include the signer public key in the encryption of ADM and the trapdoor information for the sanitizer. Hence, together with our converse construction of IND−CCA2-secure encryption from strong invisibility, we also characterize this form of invisibility through public-key encryption.

In light of the strongly invisible construction of Beck *et al.* [3], which besides an IND−CCA2-secure encryption scheme also relies on signature schemes and collision-resistant chameleon hash functions, our solution shows that the former (together with a regular signature scheme) suffices. Of course, the solution by Beck *et al.* is significantly more efficient.

### 1.3 Related Work

As mentioned above, sanitizable signature schemes were introduced by Ateniese *et al.* in their foundational work [2]. The first, and to this date widely adopted security model describing this primitive is due to Brzuska *et al.* [5], where the authors formalized the unforgeability, immutability, privacy, transparency, and accountability properties of a sanitizable signature scheme with game-based security definitions. Later on, Brzuska *et al.* added the important unlinkability property [7,9], as well as non-interactive public accountability [8,9], to the picture of security notions—see Appendix C in the full version [21] for all the definitions.

Subsequently, the formal framework introduced in [5] came under scrutiny by Gong *et al.* [25], who pointed out that sanitizable signatures formalized as above were vulnerable to so-called rights-forge attacks. Their solution was to introduce stronger versions of unforgeability, immutability and accountability, which also consider the admissible blocks in the security experiments. Even stronger variants of unforgeability, privacy, transparency, and accountability were later provided by Krenn *et al.* [30], who decided to also track the signatures in the definitions (in much the same way as for regular signature schemes, when upgrading from "ordinary" to strong unforgeability). Finally, the invisibility property was formalized by Camenisch *et al.* [10], following ideas already discussed in [2], and recently further strengthened by Beck *et al.* [3].

The above literature deals with sanitizable signature schemes as they are intended here. On the other hand, we point out that there are many other primitives and extensions that are closely related to, but slightly different from sanitizable signature schemes as treated in this work. Among these there are redactable signatures [4,16,18,28], sanitizable signatures where sanitizer modifications are limited to certain values [11,19,29,34] or where the signer is allowed to add sanitizers after having signed the message [13,36], sanitizable signatures supporting a multi-signer, multi-sanitizer paradigm [6,9,12], or allowing for sanitization of signed, encrypted data [15,20]. More generally, we note that this whole body of literature falls under the broad category of computing on authenticated data [4,23,24]. We refer to the extensive overviews of Ahn *et al.* [1] and Demirel *et al.* [17] for further information.

We conclude the related work overview by mentioning that our work also continues a line of research started in [6], where the authors showed that it is possible to construct a sanitizable signature scheme achieving unforgeability, immutability, privacy, and accountability only assuming that arbitrary secure signature schemes exist, i.e. only assuming that one-way functions exist. In this regard, and in light of known separation results of public-key cryptography and one-wayness [27], our work proves that the same does most likely not hold for (strongly) invisible sanitizable signature schemes.

## 1.4   Organization

In Sect. 2 we outline the syntax of sanitizable signature schemes (and the corresponding specific notation), give an overview of the correctness and security notions, and discuss the invisibility property. In Sect. 3 we show how to construct a public-key bit-encryption scheme from an invisible sanitizable signature scheme, and we prove the corresponding security results, whereas Sect. 4 is devoted to the converse implication. Finally, we draw some conclusions in Sect. 5.

## 2 Definition of Sanitizable Signatures

### 2.1 Notation

The starting point of our theoretical discussion on sanitizable signatures is the security model introduced by Brzuska et al. in [5]. However, since invisibility will play a crucial role in our work, their framework has to be slightly adapted. Their approach often relies on the fact that the description ADM of admissible parts is recoverable from signatures, in direct contrast to the invisibility property which aims to hide this information. Thus, before we can actually start with the definition of sanitizable signatures, we need to introduce some preliminary notation. In doing so we mainly follow the work of Camenisch et al. [10].

Messages $m \in \mathcal{M}$ are assumed to consist of a finite number of *blocks*, each block being an element from a set $\mathcal{B}$ (usually $\mathcal{B} \subseteq \{0,1\}^*$). The message space $\mathcal{M}$ is thus a subset of $\mathcal{B}^*$. We use the notation $m[i]$ to refer to the $i$-th block and write $m = (m[1], \ldots, m[\ell])$ to stress that the message $m$ consists of $\ell$ blocks.

Admissible blocks in a message $m = (m[1], \ldots, m[\ell]) \in \mathcal{M}$ are identified by means of the parameter $\mathrm{ADM} = (A, l) \in \mathcal{P}(\mathbb{N}) \times \mathbb{N}$ (also called *sanitizing rights*), where $l \in \mathbb{N}$ denotes the total number of blocks a message must have, while $A := \{a_1, \ldots, a_j\}$ is the set containing the indices of the blocks the sanitizer is allowed to modify. Of course, here we need $1 \le a_1, \ldots, a_j \le l$, a condition that we will always assume to be satisfied. We then say that ADM *matches* $m$ if $\ell = l$, in which case we write $\mathrm{ADM}(m) = \top$ (otherwise $\mathrm{ADM}(m) = \bot$). If $\mathrm{ADM}_0 = (A_0, l)$ and $\mathrm{ADM}_1 = (A_1, l)$ are two sanitizing rights matching $m$, we define $\mathrm{ADM}_0 \cap \mathrm{ADM}_1 := (A_0 \cap A_1, l)$. Similarly, to identify admissible block indices, we write $a \in \mathrm{ADM} = (A, l)$ if $1 \le a \le l$ and $a \in A$.

If $m = (m[1], \ldots, m[\ell]) \in \mathcal{M}$ is a message, the actual modifications to certain blocks made by the sanitizer (i.e., the *sanitizing instructions*) are identified by means of the parameter $\mathrm{MOD} = (M, l) \in \mathcal{P}(\mathbb{N} \times \mathcal{B}) \times \mathbb{N}$, where $l \in \mathbb{N}$ denotes the total number of blocks in a message and $M := \{(i_1, \bar{m}_1), \ldots, (i_k, \bar{m}_k)\}$ denotes the set of changes made by the sanitizer. Here $(i, \bar{m}) \in M$ is intended to mean that the sanitizer will replace block $m[i]$ with $\bar{m}$. Again, here we need $1 \le i_1, \ldots, i_k \le l$, which we will assume throughout. We then say that MOD *matches* $m$ if $\ell = l$, in which case we write $\mathrm{MOD}(m)$ for the message $m'$ obtained by modifying $m$ according to MOD, i.e. $m' = \mathrm{MOD}(m)$ if and only if $m' = (m'[1], \ldots m'[\ell]) \in \mathcal{M}$ and, for every $1 \le i \le \ell$, $m'[i] = \bar{m}_i$ if $i \in \{i_1, \ldots, i_k\}$, and $m'[i] = m[i]$ otherwise. We write $\mathrm{MOD}(m) = \bot$ if MOD does not match $m$.

Finally, recall that the sanitizer is supposed to modify only message blocks declared as admissible by the signer. In this regard, the following notation will be useful: If $\mathrm{ADM} = (A, l_{\mathrm{ADM}})$ and $\mathrm{MOD} = (M, l_{\mathrm{MOD}})$ are as above, we say that MOD *matches* (or *is valid w.r.t.*) ADM if $l_{\mathrm{ADM}} = l_{\mathrm{MOD}}$ and $\widetilde{M} \subseteq A$, where $\widetilde{M} := \{i_1, \ldots, i_k\}$ is the set of indices of the blocks which the sanitizer intends to modify (as specified by $M$). In this case we write $\mathrm{MOD}(\mathrm{ADM}) = \top$, otherwise $\mathrm{MOD}(\mathrm{ADM}) = \bot$.

## 2.2  Definition of Sanitizable Signature Schemes

With the notation introduced above we are now ready to define sanitizable signature schemes. The definition is based on the one given by Brzuska *et al.* in [5] but takes into account that the sanitizing rights are no longer publicly recoverable from a valid message-signature pair. We remark here that, nonetheless, the sanitizer is always able to learn which message blocks he can modify by trying to sanitize them singularly and checking if the resulting signature is valid, an operation linear in the number of blocks of the message. This is the reason why we do not include ADM as an additional input to the Sanit algorithm: Either it is implicitly in the signatures or it must be communicated out-of-band.

Since our definition is similar to the one in [10], we give here only a schematic overview of the algorithms comprising a sanitizable signature scheme and their syntax. The complete definition can be found in the full version [21].

**Definition 1.** *A* sanitizable signature scheme SSS *is a tuple of eight probabilistic polynomial-time algorithms* $\mathsf{SSS} := (\mathsf{PGen}, \mathsf{KGen}_{\mathsf{Sig}}, \mathsf{KGen}_{\mathsf{San}}, \mathsf{Sign}, \mathsf{Sanit}, \mathsf{Verify}, \mathsf{Proof}, \mathsf{Judge})$, *whose syntax is as follows:*

- $\mathsf{pp} \leftarrow_\$ \mathsf{PGen}(1^\lambda)$, *to generate public parameters;*
- $(\mathsf{pk}_{\mathsf{Sig}}, \mathsf{sk}_{\mathsf{Sig}}) \leftarrow_\$ \mathsf{KGen}_{\mathsf{Sig}}(\mathsf{pp})$, *to generate signing keys;*
- $(\mathsf{pk}_{\mathsf{San}}, \mathsf{sk}_{\mathsf{San}}) \leftarrow_\$ \mathsf{KGen}_{\mathsf{San}}(\mathsf{pp})$, *to generate sanitization keys;*
- $\sigma \leftarrow_\$ \mathsf{Sign}(\mathsf{pp}, m, \mathsf{sk}_{\mathsf{Sig}}, \mathsf{pk}_{\mathsf{Sig}}, \mathsf{pk}_{\mathsf{San}}, \mathrm{ADM})$, *for signatures;*
- $\sigma' \leftarrow_\$ \mathsf{Sanit}(\mathsf{pp}, m, \sigma, \mathsf{sk}_{\mathsf{San}}, \mathsf{pk}_{\mathsf{Sig}}, \mathsf{pk}_{\mathsf{San}}, \mathrm{MOD})$, *for sanitized signatures;*
- $d \leftarrow \mathsf{Verify}(\mathsf{pp}, m, \sigma, \mathsf{pk}_{\mathsf{Sig}}, \mathsf{pk}_{\mathsf{San}})$, *for verification;*
- $\pi \leftarrow_\$ \mathsf{Proof}(\mathsf{pp}, m, \sigma, \{(m_i, \sigma_i)\}_{i=1}^k, \mathsf{sk}_{\mathsf{Sig}}, \mathsf{pk}_{\mathsf{Sig}}, \mathsf{pk}_{\mathsf{San}})$, *to generate proofs;*
- $d \leftarrow \mathsf{Judge}(\mathsf{pp}, m, \sigma, \mathsf{pk}_{\mathsf{Sig}}, \mathsf{pk}_{\mathsf{San}}, \pi)$, *to determine who signed the document.*

## 2.3  Correctness and Security Properties of Sanitizable Signature Schemes

We now turn to the definition of correctness and the statement of security properties of a sanitizable signature scheme SSS. As for correctness, we follow Brzuska *et al.* [5] and subsequent work and require that the following three properties hold. We give only an informal description here and refer to Appendix B in the full version [21] for complete definitions, as adapted to our framework.

- *Signing Correctness*: Every time an honest signer signs a message $m \in \mathcal{M}$ with sanitizing rights matching $m$, he produces a valid signature $\sigma \neq \bot$ such that $(m, \sigma)$ verifies under the corresponding public keys;
- *Sanitizing Correctness*: Every time the intended sanitizer honestly sanitizes a valid message-signature pair $(m, \sigma) \in \mathcal{M} \times \mathcal{S}$ with sanitizing instructions MOD matching the sanitizing rights given to him by the signer, he produces a valid signature $\sigma' \neq \bot$ such that $(\mathrm{MOD}(m), \sigma')$ verifies under the corresponding public keys;
- *Proof Correctness*: Every time an honest signer generates a proof regarding a valid message-signature pair, Judge identifies the correct accountable party.

Next we discuss the relevant security properties of a sanitizable signature scheme SSS. Most of these properties were introduced in their basic form by Brzuska *et al.* in [5] and later in [7,8]. We will be mainly concerned with their "strong" counterparts as formalized by Krenn *et al.* in [30] and later adopted by Camenisch *et al.* [10] and Beck *et al.* [3]. The definitions we adopt take into account that the sanitizing rights ADM (which are no longer assumed to be publicly recoverable from a valid message-signature pair) are an information which needs protection, as work by Gong *et al.* [25] has shown. In particular, by requiring a sanitizable signature scheme to satisfy the "strong" versions of the unforgeability, signer- and sanitizer-accountability properties, we mostly avoid so-called *rights forge attacks* as discussed in [25] (for immutability the matter is more delicate—see Appendix C in the full version [21] for further discussions).

We again give only a brief and intuitive description of the security properties here and refer the interested reader to Appendix C in the full version [21] for complete definitions and the corresponding security experiments. Only the notion of invisibility, central to our work, will be discussed here in detail.

- *Unforgeability*: No adversary should be able to produce a valid message-signature pair never seen before;
- *Immutability*: The sanitizer should be able to modify only message blocks previously declared as admissible by the signer;
- *Privacy*: Given a valid, sanitized message-signature pair, no adversary should be able to recover any information about the original content of the sanitized blocks;
- *Transparency*: Given a valid message-signature pair, no adversary should be able to determine whether it was the signer or the sanitizer who produced the signature;
- *Signer-Accountability*: A malicious signer should not be able to produce a valid message-signature pair $(m, \sigma) \in \mathcal{M} \times \mathcal{S}$ and a proof which induces Judge into erroneously blaming the sanitizer for $(m, \sigma)$;
- *Sanitizer-Accountability*: A malicious sanitizer should not be able to produce a valid message-signature pair $(m', \sigma') \in \mathcal{M} \times \mathcal{S}$ such that legitimate proofs generated by the signer induce Judge into blaming the signer for $(m', \sigma')$;
- *Unlinkability*: Given a valid message-signature pair $(m', \sigma') \in \mathcal{M} \times \mathcal{S}$ that has been sanitized, no adversary should be able to decide from which known pair $(m, \sigma) \in \mathcal{M} \times \mathcal{S}$ it originated from;
- *Non-Interactive Public Accountability*: The party accountable for a valid message-signature pair can be determined publicly, without the need of any further information. In particular, the Proof algorithm is trivial.

### 2.4   (Strong) Invisibility

Loosely speaking, a sanitizable signature scheme is *invisible* if, given a valid message-signature pair $(m, \sigma) \in \mathcal{M} \times \mathcal{S}$, no adversary is able to decide if any specific message block is admissible (i.e., can be modified by the sanitizer) or immutable. This property was first introduced by Ateniese *et al.* in their foundational work [2] under the name "strong transparency" (an expression later fallen into disuse, not to be confused with the notion of transparency defined in the literature). However, they did not provide any formal definition or construction achieving it. It was later abandoned by Brzuska *et al.* [5] on the grounds that it appeared to be too strong. Indeed, since they worked under the assumption that ADM is always publicly recoverable from a valid signature $\sigma \neq \perp$ (in obvious conflict with the invisibility notion), it was in fact unachievable. Later on, the invisibility property was considered by Camenisch *et al.* [10], who defined it formally and gave the first provably secure construction of an invisible sanitizable signature scheme. A stronger version of invisibility was later defined by Beck *et al.* in [3], where the sanitizer may use his public key with multiple signers.

In the invisibility security experiment, a signer and a sanitizer key pair are generated and a bit $b \leftarrow_{\$} \{0, 1\}$ is chosen uniformly at random and kept secret. An adversary $\mathcal{A}$ is given access to an oracle $\mathcal{O}^{\mathsf{LoR}}$ which, on input a message and two sanitizing rights $\mathrm{ADM}_0$, $\mathrm{ADM}_1$, produces a signature $\sigma$ (under the signer secret key and the sanitizer public key) making $\mathrm{ADM}_b$ admissible. In addition, $\mathcal{A}$ has adaptive access to restricted signing, sanitizing, and proof oracles.

We remark that, in the above experiment, a restricted signing oracle (with fixed sanitizer public key $\mathsf{pk}_{\mathsf{San}}$) can be simulated by querying $\mathcal{O}^{\mathsf{LoR}}$ and putting $\mathrm{ADM}_0 = \mathrm{ADM}_1$. Furthermore, for sanitization requests of any message-signature pair $(m, \sigma) \in \mathcal{M} \times \mathcal{S}$ with $\sigma \leftarrow_{\$} \mathcal{O}^{\mathsf{LoR}}(m, \mathrm{ADM}_0, \mathrm{ADM}_1)$, $\mathcal{A}$ must be limited to modifications matching $\mathrm{ADM}_0 \cap \mathrm{ADM}_1$ in order to avoid trivial attacks exposing $b$. This is why all queries to and answers from $\mathcal{O}^{\mathsf{LoR}}$, together with the allowed sanitizing rights $\mathrm{ADM}_0 \cap \mathrm{ADM}_1$, are recorded in a "whitelist" $W$: Whenever $\mathcal{A}$ queries $\mathcal{O}^{\mathsf{Sanit}}$, the oracle goes through the list $W$ of previously signed messages, to see which blocks the adversary is indeed allowed to modify. If the query is accepted, the whitelist has to be updated to also include the new (sanitized) message-signature pair, with the same sanitizing rights as the original pair (this has to be done because a sanitized message could be sanitized again). In the basic invisibility property the answers are only computed for the given key $\mathsf{pk}_{\mathsf{Sig}}$.

The adversary's goal is to guess $b$, i.e., to decide which set of blocks the oracle $\mathcal{O}^{\mathsf{LoR}}$ has made admissible. The scheme $\mathsf{SSS}$ is invisible if no efficient adversary as above succeeds in doing so with probability significantly greater than $1/2$.

We observe that the definition of invisibility already has the flavor of the "strong" variant of the definitions given in [10,30], in that we always keep track of the signatures in the whitelist $W$. On the other hand, the main drawback of this definition is that it is not possible to query the sanitization oracle for keys different from the challenge ones. As remarked by Beck *et al.* [3], this may have undesirable consequences: $\mathcal{A}$ could pose as another signer and, as soon as he gets access to a sanitization oracle, could potentially learn the bit $b$.

To address these concerns (and to give a definition of invisibility that also protects against dishonest signers), one can allow queries to the sanitization oracle with public keys chosen by the adversary $\mathcal{A}$. This approach leads to the definition of strong invisibility. The main difference between the invisibility and the strong invisibility experiments is that the adversary is allowed oracle queries to $\tilde{\mathcal{O}}^{\mathsf{LoR}}$ and $\tilde{\mathcal{O}}^{\mathsf{Sanit}}$ with adversarially chosen public keys. A sanitizable signature scheme secure in this stronger sense does not suffer from the flaw mentioned above. As a side effect, the signing oracle derived from $\tilde{\mathcal{O}}^{\mathsf{LoR}}$ is no longer restricted. The formal definition of (strong) invisibility is given in the full version [21].

# 3   Invisible Sanitizable Signatures Imply Public-Key Encryption Schemes

In this section we show how to construct a public-key bit-encryption scheme from an invisible sanitizable signature scheme.

## 3.1   Construction

Suppose that Alice wants to send a secret bit $b \in \{0,1\}$ to Bob, without an adversary $\mathcal{A}$ being able to learn it. To do so, Bob publicly chooses a sanitizable signature scheme SSS and a security parameter $\lambda \in \mathbb{N}$, and generates a tuple of public parameters $\mathsf{pp} \leftarrow_{\$} \mathsf{PGen}(1^{\lambda})$. Observe that the block set $\mathcal{B}$ defined by $\mathsf{pp}$ clearly must contain at least two elements—we will assume that $\{0,1\} \subseteq \mathcal{B}$, but for other block sets the adjustment is straightforward. Moreover, we assume that the two-block-messages $(0,0), (1,0), (0,1)$ belong to the message space $\mathcal{M}$, but again our construction can be easily modified should this not be the case.

Bob then generates a sanitizer key pair $(\mathsf{pk}_{\mathsf{San}}, \mathsf{sk}_{\mathsf{San}}) \leftarrow_{\$} \mathsf{KGen}_{\mathsf{San}}(\mathsf{pp})$, and chooses a message $m \in \mathcal{M}$ consisting of two blocks, e.g. $m = (0,0)$. He sends $(\mathsf{pp}, m, \mathsf{pk}_{\mathsf{San}})$ to Alice over an unprotected channel, while $\mathsf{sk}_{\mathsf{San}}$ is kept secret.

Upon receiving $(\mathsf{pp}, m, \mathsf{pk}_{\mathsf{San}})$, Alice runs $(\mathsf{pk}_{\mathsf{Sig}}, \mathsf{sk}_{\mathsf{Sig}}) \leftarrow_{\$} \mathsf{KGen}_{\mathsf{Sig}}(\mathsf{pp})$ to generate a signer key pair. Now, depending on whether she wants to encrypt $b = 0$ or $b = 1$, she signs the message $m$ declaring as admissible the first or the second block, respectively. She then sends the signature $\sigma$ and her public key $\mathsf{pk}_{\mathsf{Sig}}$ to Bob, while $\mathsf{sk}_{\mathsf{Sig}}$ is kept secret.

Upon receiving $(\sigma, \mathsf{pk}_{\mathsf{Sig}})$, Bob tries to separately modify the first and the second message block by replacing it with '1'. He thus sets $\mathrm{MOD}_0 \leftarrow (\{(1,1)\}, 2)$ and $\mathrm{MOD}_1 \leftarrow (\{(2,1)\}, 2)$ and then computes $\sigma'_0 \leftarrow_{\$} \mathsf{Sanit}(\mathsf{pp}, m, \sigma, \mathsf{sk}_{\mathsf{San}}, \mathsf{pk}_{\mathsf{Sig}}, \mathsf{pk}_{\mathsf{San}}, \mathrm{MOD}_0)$ and $\sigma'_1 \leftarrow_{\$} \mathsf{Sanit}(\mathsf{pp}, m, \sigma, \mathsf{sk}_{\mathsf{San}}, \mathsf{pk}_{\mathsf{Sig}}, \mathsf{pk}_{\mathsf{San}}, \mathrm{MOD}_1)$.

Now, assuming that SSS is sanitizing correct and immutable, exactly one of the two signatures computed by Bob will be valid. If Alice has encrypted $b = 0$, then $\sigma'_0$ will be valid with overwhelming probability (because of the sanitizing correctness property), while $\sigma'_1$ will be either invalid or equal to $\bot$ with very high probability (because SSS is immutable). On the other hand, if Alice has chosen $b = 1$, then $\sigma'_1$ will be valid and $\sigma'_0$ not by the same argument. In the unlikely event that both signatures are valid or both are invalid, Bob cannot decrypt the message sent by Alice.

We thus conclude that Bob is able to correctly decrypt the bit encrypted by Alice with very high probability by sanitizing $m$ twice and checking the signatures (or error messages). Moreover, if we also assume SSS to be invisible, then any adversary $\mathcal{A}$ will be able to learn $b$ only with negligible probability. In fact, from an outsider's perspective learning $b$ is equivalent to establishing which message block is admissible, which is highly unlikely by the invisibility assumption.

We now turn to a more rigorous definition of our public-key bit-encryption scheme, as well as to the statement of the correctness and security properties.

**Construction 1.** *Let* SSS := (PGen, KGen$_{Sig}$, KGen$_{San}$, Sign, Sanit, Verify, Proof, Judge) *be a sanitizable signature scheme. We define a public-key bit-encryption scheme $\Pi$ as in Fig. 1.*

---

$\Pi$.PGen($1^\lambda$):

1. pp$_{SSS}$ ←$_\$$ SSS.PGen($1^\lambda$)
2. $\mathcal{M}_\Pi$ ← {0,1}, $\mathcal{C}_\Pi$ ← $\mathcal{S}_{Sig} \times \mathcal{K}_{Sig,pk}$, $\mathcal{K}_\Pi$ ← $\mathcal{K}_{San}$
3. $m$ ← (0,0)
4. pp$_\Pi$ ← (pp$_{SSS}$, $\mathcal{M}_\Pi$, $\mathcal{C}_\Pi$, $\mathcal{K}_\Pi$, $m$)
5. return pp$_\Pi$

$\Pi$.KGen(pp$_\Pi$):

1. parse pp$_\Pi$ = (pp$_{SSS}$, $\mathcal{M}_\Pi$, $\mathcal{C}_\Pi$, $\mathcal{K}_\Pi$, $m$)
2. (pk$_{San}$, sk$_{San}$) ←$_\$$ SSS.KGen$_{San}$(pp$_{SSS}$)
3. pk$_\Pi$ ← pk$_{San}$, sk$_\Pi$ ← sk$_{San}$
4. return (pk$_\Pi$, sk$_\Pi$)

$\Pi$.Enc(pp$_\Pi$, $b$, pk$_\Pi$):

1. parse pp$_\Pi$ = (pp$_{SSS}$, $\mathcal{M}_\Pi$, $\mathcal{C}_\Pi$, $\mathcal{K}_\Pi$, $m$), pk$_\Pi$ = pk$_{San}$
2. (pk$_{Sig}$, sk$_{Sig}$) ←$_\$$ SSS.KGen$_{Sig}$(pp$_{SSS}$)
3. ADM$_0$ ← ({1}, 2)
4. ADM$_1$ ← ({2}, 2)
5. $\sigma$ ←$_\$$ SSS.Sign(pp$_{SSS}$, $m$, sk$_{Sig}$, pk$_{Sig}$, pk$_{San}$, ADM$_b$)
6. return ($\sigma$, pk$_{Sig}$)

$\Pi$.Dec(pp$_\Pi$, $c$, pk$_\Pi$, sk$_\Pi$):

1. parse pp$_\Pi$ = (pp$_{SSS}$, $\mathcal{M}_\Pi$, $\mathcal{C}_\Pi$, $\mathcal{K}_\Pi$, $m$), $c$ = ($\sigma$, pk$_{Sig}$), pk$_\Pi$ = pk$_{San}$, sk$_\Pi$ = sk$_{San}$
2. $d$ ← SSS.Verify(pp$_{SSS}$, $m$, $\sigma$, pk$_{Sig}$, pk$_{San}$)
3. if $d$ = $\bot$ then
4.     return $\bot$
5. MOD$_0$ ← ({(1,1)}, 2)
6. MOD$_1$ ← ({(2,1)}, 2)
7. $m'_0$ ← MOD$_0$($m$), $m'_1$ ← MOD$_1$($m$)
8. $\sigma'_0$ ←$_\$$ SSS.Sanit(pp$_{SSS}$, $m$, $\sigma$, sk$_{San}$, pk$_{Sig}$, pk$_{San}$, MOD$_0$)
9. $\sigma'_1$ ←$_\$$ SSS.Sanit(pp$_{SSS}$, $m$, $\sigma$, sk$_{San}$, pk$_{Sig}$, pk$_{San}$, MOD$_1$)
10. $d_0$ ← SSS.Verify(pp$_{SSS}$, $m'_0$, $\sigma'_0$, pk$_{Sig}$, pk$_{San}$)
11. $d_1$ ← SSS.Verify(pp$_{SSS}$, $m'_1$, $\sigma'_1$, pk$_{Sig}$, pk$_{San}$)
12. if $d_0$ = $\top$ ∧ $d_1$ = $\bot$ then
13.     return 0
14. if $d_0$ = $\bot$ ∧ $d_1$ = $\top$ then
15.     return 1
16. return $\bot$

---

**Fig. 1.** Public-key bit-encryption scheme from an invisible sanitizable signature scheme

## 3.2  IND−CPA-Security

We now formally state our security results about the public-key bit encryption scheme in Construction 1.

**Theorem 2.** *Let* SSS := (PGen, KGen$_{Sig}$, KGen$_{San}$, Sign, Sanit, Verify, Proof, Judge) *be a sanitizable signature scheme, and let $\Pi$ := (PGen, KGen, Enc, Dec) be the public-key bit-encryption scheme defined in Construction 1. If SSS is sanitizing correct, immutable and invisible, then $\Pi$ is correct and IND−CPA-secure.*

The proof gives a tight reduction in terms of the advantages: For any adversary $\mathcal{A}$ playing the $\mathsf{IND-CPA}$-game we construct an adversary $\mathcal{B}$ against the invisibility game with roughly the same running time as $\mathcal{A}$, such that

$$\mathbf{Adv}_{\mathcal{A},\Pi}^{\mathsf{IND-CPA}}(\lambda) = \mathbf{Adv}_{\mathcal{B},\mathsf{SSS}}^{\mathsf{Inv}}(\lambda).$$

Note that we need the immutability property only to bound the correctness error by $2 \cdot \mathbf{Adv}_{\mathcal{C},\mathsf{SSS}}^{\mathsf{Imm}}(\lambda)$ for some efficient adversary $\mathcal{C}$ against the immutability game. The proof of Theorem 2 can be found in the full version [21].

### 3.3  IND−CCA2-Security

We next argue that the scheme above achieves $\mathsf{IND-CCA2}$-security if SSS is assumed to be strongly invisible. Recall that the difference to regular invisibility is that now the adversary against strong invisibility can also make left-or-right signature requests for $(m, \mathsf{pk}'_{\mathsf{San}}, \mathrm{ADM}_0, \mathrm{ADM}_1)$ with different sanitizer public keys $\mathsf{pk}'_{\mathsf{San}} \neq \mathsf{pk}_{\mathsf{San}}$, and sanitization requests for $(m, \sigma, \mathsf{pk}'_{\mathsf{Sig}}, \mathrm{MOD})$ with different signer public keys $\mathsf{pk}'_{\mathsf{Sig}} \neq \mathsf{pk}_{\mathsf{Sig}}$. Interestingly, for our construction and proof we only rely on the latter property.

For the security proof we also need strong unforgeability of the sanitizable signature scheme. The reason is that ciphertexts are of the form $(\sigma, \mathsf{pk}_{\mathsf{Sig}})$, and the $\mathsf{IND-CCA2}$-adversary may ask for decryptions of the form $(\sigma', \mathsf{pk}_{\mathsf{Sig}})$ where it alters the signature component for the same message. This would allow to break the security of the encryption scheme easily.

**Theorem 3.** *Let* SSS $:= (\mathsf{PGen}, \mathsf{KGen}_{\mathsf{Sig}}, \mathsf{KGen}_{\mathsf{San}}, \mathsf{Sign}, \mathsf{Sanit}, \mathsf{Verify}, \mathsf{Proof}, \mathsf{Judge})$ *be a sanitizable signature scheme, and let* $\Pi := (\mathsf{PGen}, \mathsf{KGen}, \mathsf{Enc}, \mathsf{Dec})$ *be the public-key bit-encryption scheme defined in Construction 1. If* SSS *is sanitizing correct, strongly unforgeable, immutable and strongly invisible, then* $\Pi$ *is correct and* $\mathsf{IND-CCA2}$-*secure.*

The proof also gives a tight reduction in terms of the advantages: For any adversary $\mathcal{A}$ playing the $\mathsf{IND-CCA2}$-game we construct adversaries $\mathcal{B}$ and $\mathcal{C}$ with roughly the same running time as $\mathcal{A}$, such that

$$\mathbf{Adv}_{\mathcal{A},\Pi}^{\mathsf{IND-CCA2}}(\lambda) \leq \mathbf{Adv}_{\mathcal{B},\mathsf{SSS}}^{\mathsf{SInv}}(\lambda) + 2 \cdot \mathbf{Adv}_{\mathcal{C},\mathsf{SSS}}^{\mathsf{SUnf}}(\lambda).$$

In fact, for $\mathsf{IND-CCA1}$-security regular unforgeability is sufficient. Once more, we need immutability only to bound the correctness error. The proof of Theorem 3 can be found in the full version [21].

## 4  Public-Key Encryption Implies Invisible Sanitizable Signatures

In this section we present our construction of an invisible sanitizable signature scheme, starting from a secure public-key encryption scheme.

### 4.1 Construction

Our construction based on public-key encryption follows the established encode-and-sign paradigm and exploits the idea of using chameleon hash functions and signing the hash values with a regular signature scheme $\Sigma$ (see, e.g., [2,5]). The sanitizer can then find collisions for the hashes with the help of his trapdoor key, allowing him to modify the message. Here, instead of chameleon hashes we use the signature scheme $\Sigma$ itself.

In our scheme, signatures consist of two parts: the "message" part ensures the basic unforgeability and accountability properties, and can be created by either of the two parties. In contrast, the "administrative" part contains the information needed by the sanitizer to perform modifications, and can be created only by the signer. Parts of the administrative information are encrypted under an encryption scheme $\Pi$ under the sanitizer's public key, to ensure invisibility.

To begin with, the signer generates a key pair $(\mathsf{pk}_\Sigma, \mathsf{sk}_\Sigma)$ for $\Sigma$, while the sanitizer creates keys $(\mathsf{pk}'_\Sigma, \mathsf{sk}'_\Sigma)$ and $(\mathsf{pk}_\Pi, \mathsf{sk}_\Pi)$ for $\Sigma$ and $\Pi$, respectively. To sign a message $m = (m[1], \dots, m[\ell])$, the signer generates a new key pair $(\mathsf{pk}^i_\Sigma, \mathsf{sk}^i_\Sigma)$ $(1 \le i \le \ell)$ for each block of $m$, signs every block with the corresponding key, and creates a tuple of signatures $S := (\sigma^1, \dots, \sigma^\ell)$. He then generates a signature $\sigma_{\mathrm{MSG}}$ of the message $(0, m, S, \mathsf{pk}_{\mathsf{Sig}}, \mathsf{pk}_{\mathsf{San}})$ under $\mathsf{sk}_\Sigma$. Here, $m$ and $S$ are signed so that they are protected from modification by outsiders, whereas $\mathsf{pk}_{\mathsf{Sig}}, \mathsf{pk}_{\mathsf{San}}$ and the initial bit '0' are included for technical reasons (namely, domain separation). The "message" part of the final signature $\sigma$ then consists of $(S, \sigma_{\mathrm{MSG}})$.

The first part of the signature must now be complemented with the information required to sanitize the admissible parts of the message, and to verify the signature. To this end, the signer generates the tuple $K_{\mathrm{ADM}} = (\mathsf{sk}^{i_1}_\Sigma, \mathsf{sk}^{i_2}_\Sigma, \dots)$ containing the secret keys of the admissible blocks $i_j \in \mathrm{ADM}$ (properly padded to ensure a length-invariant encoding), and encloses it for the sanitizing party via encryption under $\mathsf{pk}_\Pi$. In addition, we also hide the parameter ADM (to ensure invisibility) and the signer public key (in foresight of the strongly invisible version of our result) in this encryption. In summary, the signer creates an encryption $C$ of $(\mathsf{pk}_{\mathsf{San}}, K_{\mathrm{ADM}}, \mathrm{ADM})$ under $\mathsf{pk}_\Pi$ and then, in order to prevent changes in these administrative data, creates a (regular) signature $\sigma_{\mathrm{ADM}}$ of the message $(1, \mathsf{pk}_{\mathsf{San}}, V, C)$. Here, $V := (\mathsf{pk}^1_\Sigma, \dots, \mathsf{pk}^\ell_\Sigma)$ contains the verification keys for the single blocks, and again the initial bit '1' is included for domain separation reasons. The "administrative" part of the signature is then $(V, C, \sigma_{\mathrm{ADM}})$, and the final signature is $\sigma := (S, \sigma_{\mathrm{MSG}}, V, C, \sigma_{\mathrm{ADM}})$.

If the sanitizer receives a signature $\sigma$ for a message $m$, he first checks the validity of the signatures $S$, $\sigma_{\mathrm{MSG}}$ and $\sigma_{\mathrm{ADM}}$, and recovers ADM and the corresponding signing keys $K_{\mathrm{ADM}}$ by decrypting $C$. Then, given valid sanitizing instructions $m' = \mathrm{MOD}(m)$, he can update the "message" part of $\sigma$, leaving the "administrative" part unchanged. He obtains $S'$ by substituting the relevant entries in $S$ with new signatures of the modified blocks under the corresponding keys $K_{\mathrm{ADM}}$, and updates $\sigma_{\mathrm{MSG}}$ by re-signing $(0, m', S', \mathsf{pk}_{\mathsf{Sig}}, \mathsf{pk}_{\mathsf{San}})$ under $\mathsf{sk}'_\Sigma$. Finally, the sanitized signature for $m'$ is given by $\sigma' = (S', \sigma'_{\mathrm{MSG}}, V, C, \sigma_{\mathrm{ADM}})$.

Immutability of the scheme is achieved by the fact that the sanitizer does not know the secret keys for the blocks he is not supposed to modify, and therefore cannot obtain suitable replacements for signatures in $S$. Observe that the signature $\sigma_{MSG}$ immediately ensures public accountability, since it serves as a proof of who put the overall signature. This also implies that our scheme does not achieve transparency. For technical reasons it neither supports unlinkability.

*Remark 1.* The above discussion presumes that some mild assumptions on $\Sigma$ and $\Pi$ are satisfied, which we will henceforth assume to be in place. In particular, all signature keys must be of fixed length $L$ (this can be achieved via padding of the keys), and the message blocks, as well as the tuples of the form $(0, m, S, \mathsf{pk}_{Sig}, \mathsf{pk}_{San})$ and $(1, \mathsf{pk}_{San}, V, C)$, must lie in the message space of $\Sigma$ (this is no restriction, because the signatures constructed in [33,35] support messages of arbitrary polynomial length). Also, ADM must be encoded in a length-invariant manner, and tuples of the form $(\mathsf{pk}_{San}, K_{ADM}, ADM)$ must lie in the message space of $\Pi$ (which can be achieved through hybrid encryption).

We now turn to a more rigorous definition of our sanitizable signature scheme, as well as to the statement of the correctness and security results.

---

SSS.PGen($1^\lambda$):

1. $\mathsf{pp}_\Pi \leftarrow_\$ \Pi.\mathsf{PGen}(1^\lambda)$
2. $\mathsf{pp}_\Sigma \leftarrow_\$ \Sigma.\mathsf{PGen}(1^\lambda)$
3. $\mathcal{M} \leftarrow \mathcal{M}_\Sigma^l$
4. $\mathsf{pp}_{SSS} \leftarrow (\mathsf{pp}_\Pi, \mathsf{pp}_\Sigma, \mathcal{M})$
5. return $\mathsf{pp}_{SSS}$

SSS.KGen$_{Sig}$($\mathsf{pp}_{SSS}$):

1. parse $\mathsf{pp}_{SSS} = (\mathsf{pp}_\Pi, \mathsf{pp}_\Sigma, \mathcal{M})$
2. $(\mathsf{pk}_\Sigma, \mathsf{sk}_\Sigma) \leftarrow_\$ \Sigma.\mathsf{KGen}(\mathsf{pp}_\Sigma)$
3. $\mathsf{pk}_{Sig} \leftarrow \mathsf{pk}_\Sigma, \mathsf{sk}_{Sig} \leftarrow \mathsf{sk}_\Sigma$
4. return $(\mathsf{pk}_{Sig}, \mathsf{sk}_{Sig})$

SSS.KGen$_{San}$($\mathsf{pp}_{SSS}$):

1. parse $\mathsf{pp}_{SSS} = (\mathsf{pp}_\Pi, \mathsf{pp}_\Sigma, \mathcal{M})$
2. $(\mathsf{pk}_\Pi, \mathsf{sk}_\Pi) \leftarrow_\$ \Pi.\mathsf{KGen}(\mathsf{pp}_\Pi)$
3. $(\mathsf{pk}'_\Sigma, \mathsf{sk}'_\Sigma) \leftarrow_\$ \Sigma.\mathsf{KGen}(\mathsf{pp}_\Sigma)$
4. $\mathsf{pk}_{San} \leftarrow (\mathsf{pk}_\Pi, \mathsf{pk}'_\Sigma)$
5. $\mathsf{sk}_{San} \leftarrow (\mathsf{sk}_\Pi, \mathsf{sk}'_\Sigma)$
6. return $(\mathsf{pk}_{San}, \mathsf{sk}_{San})$

SSS.Sign($\mathsf{pp}_{SSS}, m, \mathsf{sk}_{Sig}, \mathsf{pk}_{Sig}, \mathsf{pk}_{San}, ADM$):

1. if $ADM(m) = \bot$ then return $\bot$
2. parse $\mathsf{pp}_{SSS} = (\mathsf{pp}_\Pi, \mathsf{pp}_\Sigma, \mathcal{M})$, $\mathsf{sk}_{Sig} = \mathsf{sk}_\Sigma$, $m = (m[1], \ldots, m[l])$, $\mathsf{pk}_{Sig} = \mathsf{pk}_\Sigma$, $\mathsf{pk}_{San} = (\mathsf{pk}_\Pi, \mathsf{pk}'_\Sigma)$, $ADM = (A, l)$
3. $V \leftarrow \emptyset, S \leftarrow \emptyset, K_{ADM} \leftarrow \emptyset$
4. for $1 \leq i \leq l$ do
5. $\quad (\mathsf{pk}_\Sigma^i, \mathsf{sk}_\Sigma^i) \leftarrow_\$ \Sigma.\mathsf{KGen}(\mathsf{pp}_\Sigma)$
6. $\quad V \leftarrow V \cup \{(i, \mathsf{pk}_\Sigma^i)\}$
7. $\quad \sigma^i \leftarrow_\$ \Sigma.\mathsf{Sign}(\mathsf{pp}_\Sigma, m[i], \mathsf{sk}_\Sigma^i, \mathsf{pk}_\Sigma^i)$
8. $\quad S \leftarrow S \cup \{(i, \sigma^i)\}$
9. $\quad K_{ADM} \leftarrow K_{ADM} \cup \begin{cases} \{(i, \mathsf{sk}_\Sigma^i)\} & i \in A \\ \{(i, 0^L)\} & \text{else} \end{cases}$
10. parse $V = (\mathsf{pk}_\Sigma^1, \ldots, \mathsf{pk}_\Sigma^l), S = (\sigma^1, \ldots, \sigma^l)$, $K_{ADM} = (K_{ADM}^1, \ldots, K_{ADM}^l)$
11. $t \leftarrow (0, m, S, \mathsf{pk}_{Sig}, \mathsf{pk}_{San})$
12. $\sigma_{MSG} \leftarrow_\$ \Sigma.\mathsf{Sign}(\mathsf{pp}_\Sigma, t, \mathsf{sk}_\Sigma, \mathsf{pk}_\Sigma)$
13. $C \leftarrow_\$ \Pi.\mathsf{Enc}(\mathsf{pp}_\Pi, (\mathsf{pk}_{Sig}, K_{ADM}, ADM), \mathsf{pk}_\Pi)$
14. $u \leftarrow (1, \mathsf{pk}_{San}, V, C)$
15. $\sigma_{ADM} \leftarrow_\$ \Sigma.\mathsf{Sign}(\mathsf{pp}_\Sigma, u, \mathsf{sk}_\Sigma, \mathsf{pk}_\Sigma)$
16. $\sigma \leftarrow (S, \sigma_{MSG}, V, C, \sigma_{ADM})$
17. return $\sigma$

**Fig. 2.** Invisible sanitizable signature scheme from a public-key encryption scheme: parameter generation, signer and sanitizer key generation, and signing algorithms.

SSS.Verify($\mathsf{pp_{SSS}}, m, \sigma, \mathsf{pk_{Sig}}, \mathsf{pk_{San}}$):

1. parse $\mathsf{pp_{SSS}} = (\mathsf{pp}_\Pi, \mathsf{pp}_\Sigma, \mathcal{M})$,
   $m = (m[1], \dots, m[l])$,
   $\sigma = (S, \sigma_{\mathrm{MSG}}, V, C, \sigma_{\mathrm{ADM}})$,
   $S = (\sigma^1, \dots, \sigma^l)$,
   $V = (\mathsf{pk}_\Sigma^1, \dots, \mathsf{pk}_\Sigma^l)$,
   $\mathsf{pk_{Sig}} = \mathsf{pk}_\Sigma$,
   $\mathsf{pk_{San}} = (\mathsf{pk}_\Pi, \mathsf{pk}_\Sigma')$
2. $t \leftarrow (0, m, S, \mathsf{pk_{Sig}}, \mathsf{pk_{San}})$
3. $d_1 \leftarrow \Sigma.\mathsf{Verify}(\mathsf{pp}_\Sigma, t, \sigma_{\mathrm{MSG}}, \mathsf{pk}_\Sigma)$
4. $d_2 \leftarrow \Sigma.\mathsf{Verify}(\mathsf{pp}_\Sigma, t, \sigma_{\mathrm{MSG}}, \mathsf{pk}_\Sigma')$
5. $u \leftarrow (1, \mathsf{pk_{San}}, V, C)$
6. $d_3 \leftarrow \Sigma.\mathsf{Verify}(\mathsf{pp}_\Sigma, u, \sigma_{\mathrm{ADM}}, \mathsf{pk}_\Sigma)$
7. if $(d_1 = \bot \wedge d_2 = \bot) \vee$
   $d_3 = \bot \vee \Sigma.\mathsf{Verify}(\mathsf{pp}_\Sigma, m[i],$
   $\sigma^i, \mathsf{pk}_\Sigma^i) = \bot$ for some $1 \leq i \leq l$
   then
8.     return $\bot$
9. return $\top$


SSS.Judge($\mathsf{pp_{SSS}}, m, \sigma, \mathsf{pk_{Sig}}, \mathsf{pk_{San}}, \pi$):

1. parse $\mathsf{pp_{SSS}} = (\mathsf{pp}_\Pi, \mathsf{pp}_\Sigma, \mathcal{M})$,
   $\sigma = (S, \sigma_{\mathrm{MSG}}, V, C, \sigma_{\mathrm{ADM}})$,
   $\mathsf{pk_{Sig}} = \mathsf{pk}_\Sigma$,
   $\mathsf{pk_{San}} = (\mathsf{pk}_\Pi, \mathsf{pk}_\Sigma')$
2. $t \leftarrow (0, m, S, \mathsf{pk_{Sig}}, \mathsf{pk_{San}})$
3. $d_1 \leftarrow \Sigma.\mathsf{Verify}(\mathsf{pp}_\Sigma, t, \sigma_{\mathrm{MSG}}, \mathsf{pk}_\Sigma)$
4. $d_2 \leftarrow \Sigma.\mathsf{Verify}(\mathsf{pp}_\Sigma, t, \sigma_{\mathrm{MSG}}, \mathsf{pk}_\Sigma')$
5. if $d_1 = \top \wedge d_2 = \bot$ then
6.     return $\mathsf{Sig}$
7. if $d_1 = \bot \wedge d_2 = \top$ then
8.     return $\mathsf{San}$
9. return $\bot$


SSS.Sanit($\mathsf{pp_{SSS}}, m, \sigma, \mathsf{sk_{San}}, \mathsf{pk_{Sig}},$
$\mathsf{pk_{San}}, \mathrm{MOD}$):

1. if $\mathrm{MOD}(m) = \bot$ then return $\bot$
2. parse $\mathsf{pp_{SSS}} = (\mathsf{pp}_\Pi, \mathsf{pp}_\Sigma, \mathcal{M})$,
   $m = (m[1], \dots, m[l])$,
   $\sigma = (S, \sigma_{\mathrm{MSG}}, V, C, \sigma_{\mathrm{ADM}})$,
   $V = (\mathsf{pk}_\Sigma^1, \dots, \mathsf{pk}_\Sigma^l)$,
   $\mathsf{sk_{San}} = (\mathsf{sk}_\Pi, \mathsf{sk}_\Sigma')$, $\mathsf{pk_{Sig}} = \mathsf{pk}_\Sigma$,
   $\mathsf{pk_{San}} = (\mathsf{pk}_\Pi, \mathsf{pk}_\Sigma')$,
   $\mathrm{MOD} = (M, l)$,
   $M = \{(i_1, m_1), \dots, (i_k, m_k)\}$
3. $t \leftarrow \Pi.\mathsf{Dec}(\mathsf{pp}_\Pi, C, \mathsf{pk}_\Pi, \mathsf{sk}_\Pi)$
4. parse $t = (\mathsf{pk}_{\mathrm{Sig}}', K_{\mathrm{ADM}}, \mathrm{ADM})$,
   $K_{\mathrm{ADM}} = (K_{\mathrm{ADM}}^1, \dots, K_{\mathrm{ADM}}^l)$,
   with $K_{\mathrm{ADM}}^i = \mathsf{sk}_\Sigma^i$ for $i \in \mathrm{ADM}$
5. $d_1 \leftarrow \mathsf{SSS.Verify}(\mathsf{pp_{SSS}}, m, \sigma, \mathsf{pk_{Sig}}, \mathsf{pk_{San}})$
6. if $d_1 = \bot \vee \mathrm{MOD}(\mathrm{ADM}) = \bot \vee$
   $\mathsf{pk}_{\mathrm{Sig}}' \neq \mathsf{pk_{Sig}}$ then
7.     return $\bot$
8. $m' \leftarrow \mathrm{MOD}(m)$
9. for $1 \leq j \leq k$ do
10.    $\sigma^{i_j} \leftarrow_\$ \Sigma.\mathsf{Sign}(\mathsf{pp}_\Sigma, m_j, \mathsf{sk}_\Sigma^{i_j}, \mathsf{pk}_\Sigma^{i_j})$
11. $S' \leftarrow (\sigma^1, \dots, \sigma^l)$
12. $u \leftarrow (0, m', S', \mathsf{pk_{Sig}}, \mathsf{pk_{San}})$
13. $\sigma_{\mathrm{MSG}}' \leftarrow_\$ \Sigma.\mathsf{Sign}(\mathsf{pp}_\Sigma, u, \mathsf{sk}_\Sigma', \mathsf{pk}_\Sigma')$
14. $\sigma' \leftarrow (S', \sigma_{\mathrm{MSG}}', V, C, \sigma_{\mathrm{ADM}})$
15. $d_2 \leftarrow \mathsf{SSS.Verify}(\mathsf{pp_{SSS}}, m', \sigma', \mathsf{pk_{Sig}}, \mathsf{pk_{San}})$
16. if $d_2 = \bot$ then
17.    return $\bot$
18. return $\sigma'$


SSS.Proof($\mathsf{pp_{SSS}}, m, \sigma, \{(m_i, \sigma_i)\}_{i=1}^k, \mathsf{sk_{Sig}},$
$\mathsf{pk_{Sig}}, \mathsf{pk_{San}}$):

1. return $\bot$

**Fig. 3.** Invisible sanitizable signature scheme from a public-key encryption scheme: verification, sanitization, judge and proof algorithms.

**Construction 4.** *Let* $\Sigma := (\mathsf{PGen}, \mathsf{KGen}, \mathsf{Sign}, \mathsf{Verify})$ *be a signature scheme and* $\Pi := (\mathsf{PGen}, \mathsf{KGen}, \mathsf{Enc}, \mathsf{Dec})$ *a public-key encryption scheme. We define a sanitizable signature scheme* SSS *as in Figs. 2 and 3 above.*

### 4.2 Security

The formal security statement for our construction is given in Theorem 5. Its proof can be found in the full version [21].

**Theorem 5.** *If the signature scheme $\Sigma$ is correct and unforgeable, and the encryption scheme $\Pi$ is correct, then the sanitizable signature scheme* SSS *in Construction 4 is correct. If $\Sigma$ is unforgeable and $\Pi$ is* IND$-$CPA*-secure, then* SSS *is unforgeable, immutable, private, publicly accountable, and invisible.*

### 4.3  Achieving Strong Invisibility

In the previous sections we have shown that invisibility is equivalent to IND$-$CPA-secure encryption, and that strong invisibility implies IND$-$CCA2-secure encryption. Here we show that the latter implication also holds in the other direction: If we use an IND$-$CCA2-secure encryption scheme in our construction, then we get a strongly invisible sanitizable signature scheme.

**Theorem 6.** *If the signature scheme $\Sigma$ is correct and unforgeable, and the encryption scheme $\Pi$ is correct, then the sanitizable signature scheme* SSS *in Construction 4 is correct. If $\Sigma$ is unforgeable and $\Pi$ is* IND$-$CCA2*-secure, then* SSS *is unforgeable, immutable, private, publicly accountable, and strongly invisible.*

The proof of Theorem 6 can be found in the full version [21].

## 5  Conclusions

Our results show that building invisible sanitizable signature schemes from one-way functions alone is presumably hard, since deriving public-key encryption from one-wayness in a black-box way is infeasible [27]. This is in contrast to sanitizable schemes without the invisibility and transparency properties. Namely, Brzuska *et al.* [6] gave a simple construction of a non-invisible, non-transparent scheme based on regular signature schemes only.

An interesting open question concerns the minimal assumptions required to achieve *transparency* for sanitizable signatures, independently of the question regarding invisibility. It is possible to achieve all the common security properties, except for transparency (and except for invisibility, of course), using one-way functions alone [6,9]. Current constructions achieving transparency are based on assumptions seemingly stronger than one-way functions, such as group signature schemes [7], zero-knowledge proofs [22], or (chameleon) hash functions [3,10]. Finally, for a sanitizable signature scheme to be both transparent and invisible, public-key encryption is at least necessary, as discussed here.

**Acknowledgments.** We thank the anonymous reviewers for their valuable comments and suggestions. This work has been co-funded by the DFG as part of project P2 within the CRC 1119 CROSSING.

# References

1. Ahn, J.H., Boneh, D., Camenisch, J., Hohenberger, S., Shelat, A., Waters, B.: Computing on authenticated data. In: Cramer, R. (ed.) TCC 2012. LNCS, vol. 7194, pp. 1–20. Springer, Heidelberg (2012). https://doi.org/10.1007/978-3-642-28914-9_1
2. Ateniese, G., Chou, D.H., de Medeiros, B., Tsudik, G.: Sanitizable signatures. In: De Capitani di Vimercati, S., Syverson, P., Gollmann, D. (eds.) ESORICS 2005. LNCS, vol. 3679, pp. 159–177. Springer, Heidelberg (2005). https://doi.org/10.1007/11555827_10
3. Beck, M.T., Camenisch, J., Derler, D., Krenn, S., Pöhls, H.C., Samelin, K., Slamanig, D.: Practical strongly invisible and strongly accountable sanitizable signatures. In: Pieprzyk, J., Suriadi, S. (eds.) ACISP 2017. LNCS, vol. 10342, pp. 437–452. Springer, Cham (2017). https://doi.org/10.1007/978-3-319-60055-0_23
4. Brzuska, C., et al.: Redactable signatures for tree-structured data: definitions and constructions. In: Zhou, J., Yung, M. (eds.) ACNS 2010. LNCS, vol. 6123, pp. 87–104. Springer, Heidelberg (2010). https://doi.org/10.1007/978-3-642-13708-2_6
5. Brzuska, C., Fischlin, M., Freudenreich, T., Lehmann, A., Page, M., Schelbert, J., Schröder, D., Volk, F.: Security of sanitizable signatures revisited. In: Jarecki, S., Tsudik, G. (eds.) PKC 2009. LNCS, vol. 5443, pp. 317–336. Springer, Heidelberg (2009). https://doi.org/10.1007/978-3-642-00468-1_18
6. Brzuska, C., Fischlin, M., Lehmann, A., Schröder, D.: Santizable signatures: how to partially delegate control for authenticated data. In: BIOSIG 2009, pp. 117–128 (2009)
7. Brzuska, C., Fischlin, M., Lehmann, A., Schröder, D.: Unlinkability of sanitizable signatures. In: Nguyen, P.Q., Pointcheval, D. (eds.) PKC 2010. LNCS, vol. 6056, pp. 444–461. Springer, Heidelberg (2010). https://doi.org/10.1007/978-3-642-13013-7_26
8. Brzuska, C., Pöhls, H.C., Samelin, K.: Non-interactive public accountability for sanitizable signatures. In: De Capitani di Vimercati, S., Mitchell, C. (eds.) EuroPKI 2012. LNCS, vol. 7868, pp. 178–193. Springer, Heidelberg (2013). https://doi.org/10.1007/978-3-642-40012-4_12
9. Brzuska, C., Pöhls, H.C., Samelin, K.: Efficient and perfectly unlinkable sanitizable signatures without group signatures. In: Katsikas, S., Agudo, I. (eds.) EuroPKI 2013. LNCS, vol. 8341, pp. 12–30. Springer, Heidelberg (2014). https://doi.org/10.1007/978-3-642-53997-8_2
10. Camenisch, J., Derler, D., Krenn, S., Pöhls, H.C., Samelin, K., Slamanig, D.: Chameleon-hashes with ephemeral trapdoors. In: Fehr, S. (ed.) PKC 2017. LNCS, vol. 10175, pp. 152–182. Springer, Heidelberg (2017). https://doi.org/10.1007/978-3-662-54388-7_6
11. Canard, S., Jambert, A.: On extended sanitizable signature schemes. In: Pieprzyk, J. (ed.) CT-RSA 2010. LNCS, vol. 5985, pp. 179–194. Springer, Heidelberg (2010). https://doi.org/10.1007/978-3-642-11925-5_13
12. Canard, S., Jambert, A., Lescuyer, R.: Sanitizable signatures with several signers and sanitizers. In: Mitrokotsa, A., Vaudenay, S. (eds.) AFRICACRYPT 2012. LNCS, vol. 7374, pp. 35–52. Springer, Heidelberg (2012). https://doi.org/10.1007/978-3-642-31410-0_3
13. Canard, S., Laguillaumie, F., Milhau, M.: *Trapdoor* sanitizable signatures and their application to content protection. In: Bellovin, S.M., Gennaro, R., Keromytis, A., Yung, M. (eds.) ACNS 2008. LNCS, vol. 5037, pp. 258–276. Springer, Heidelberg (2008). https://doi.org/10.1007/978-3-540-68914-0_16

14. Coretti, S., Maurer, U., Tackmann, B., Venturi, D.: From single-bit to multi-bit public-key encryption via non-malleable codes. In: Dodis, Y., Nielsen, J.B. (eds.) TCC 2015. LNCS, vol. 9014, pp. 532–560. Springer, Heidelberg (2015). https://doi.org/10.1007/978-3-662-46494-6_22

15. Damgård, I., Haagh, H., Orlandi, C.: Access control encryption: enforcing information flow with cryptography. In: Hirt, M., Smith, A. (eds.) TCC 2016. LNCS, vol. 9986, pp. 547–576. Springer, Heidelberg (2016). https://doi.org/10.1007/978-3-662-53644-5_21

16. de Meer, H., Pöhls, H.C., Posegga, J., Samelin, K.: On the relation between redactable and sanitizable signature schemes. In: Jürjens, J., Piessens, F., Bielova, N. (eds.) ESSoS 2014. LNCS, vol. 8364, pp. 113–130. Springer, Cham (2014). https://doi.org/10.1007/978-3-319-04897-0_8

17. Demirel, D., Derler, D., Hanser, C., Pöhls, H.C., Slamanig, D., Traverso, G.: Overview of functional and malleable signature schemes (PRISMACLOUD deliverable d4.4). Technical report (2015)

18. Derler, D., Pöhls, H.C., Samelin, K., Slamanig, D.: A general framework for redactable signatures and new constructions. In: Kwon, S., Yun, A. (eds.) ICISC 2015. LNCS, vol. 9558, pp. 3–19. Springer, Cham (2016). https://doi.org/10.1007/978-3-319-30840-1_1

19. Derler, D., Slamanig, D.: Rethinking privacy for extended sanitizable signatures and a black-box construction of strongly private schemes. In: Au, M.-H., Miyaji, A. (eds.) ProvSec 2015. LNCS, vol. 9451, pp. 455–474. Springer, Cham (2015). https://doi.org/10.1007/978-3-319-26059-4_25

20. Fehr, V., Fischlin, M.: Sanitizable signcryption: sanitization over encrypted data (full version). Cryptology ePrint Archive, Report 2015/765 (2015). http://eprint.iacr.org/2015/765

21. Fischlin, M., Harasser, P.: Invisible sanitizable signatures and public-key encryption are equivalent. Cryptology ePrint Archive, Report 2018/337 (2018). https://eprint.iacr.org/2018/337

22. Fleischhacker, N., Krupp, J., Malavolta, G., Schneider, J., Schröder, D., Simkin, M.: Efficient unlinkable sanitizable signatures from signatures with rerandomizable keys. In: Cheng, C.-M., Chung, K.-M., Persiano, G., Yang, B.-Y. (eds.) PKC 2016. LNCS, vol. 9614, pp. 301–330. Springer, Heidelberg (2016). https://doi.org/10.1007/978-3-662-49384-7_12

23. Ghosh, E., Goodrich, M.T., Ohrimenko, O., Tamassia, R.: Fully-dynamic verifiable zero-knowledge order queries for network data. Cryptology ePrint Archive, Report 2015/283 (2015). http://eprint.iacr.org/2015/283

24. Ghosh, E., Ohrimenko, O., Tamassia, R.: Zero-knowledge authenticated order queries and order statistics on a list. In: Malkin, T., Kolesnikov, V., Lewko, A.B., Polychronakis, M. (eds.) ACNS 2015. LNCS, vol. 9092, pp. 149–171. Springer, Cham (2015). https://doi.org/10.1007/978-3-319-28166-7_8

25. Gong, J., Qian, H., Zhou, Y.: Fully-secure and practical sanitizable signatures. In: Lai, X., Yung, M., Lin, D. (eds.) Inscrypt 2010. LNCS, vol. 6584, pp. 300–317. Springer, Heidelberg (2011). https://doi.org/10.1007/978-3-642-21518-6_21

26. Hohenberger, S., Lewko, A., Waters, B.: Detecting dangerous queries: a new approach for chosen ciphertext security. In: Pointcheval, D., Johansson, T. (eds.) EUROCRYPT 2012. LNCS, vol. 7237, pp. 663–681. Springer, Heidelberg (2012). https://doi.org/10.1007/978-3-642-29011-4_39

27. Impagliazzo, R., Rudich, S.: Limits on the provable consequences of one-way permutations. In: 21st ACM STOC, pp. 44–61 (1989)

28. Johnson, R., Molnar, D., Song, D., Wagner, D.: Homomorphic signature schemes. In: Preneel, B. (ed.) CT-RSA 2002. LNCS, vol. 2271, pp. 244–262. Springer, Heidelberg (2002). https://doi.org/10.1007/3-540-45760-7_17

29. Klonowski, M., Lauks, A.: Extended sanitizable signatures. In: Rhee, M.S., Lee, B. (eds.) ICISC 2006. LNCS, vol. 4296, pp. 343–355. Springer, Heidelberg (2006). https://doi.org/10.1007/11927587_28

30. Krenn, S., Samelin, K., Sommer, D.: Stronger security for sanitizable signatures. In: Garcia-Alfaro, J., Navarro-Arribas, G., Aldini, A., Martinelli, F., Suri, N. (eds.) DPM/QASA -2015. LNCS, vol. 9481, pp. 100–117. Springer, Cham (2016). https://doi.org/10.1007/978-3-319-29883-2_7

31. Matsuda, T., Hanaoka, G.: An asymptotically optimal method for converting bit encryption to multi-bit encryption. In: Iwata, T., Cheon, J.H. (eds.) ASIACRYPT 2015. LNCS, vol. 9452, pp. 415–442. Springer, Heidelberg (2015). https://doi.org/10.1007/978-3-662-48797-6_18

32. Myers, S., Shelat, A.: Bit encryption is complete. In: 50th FOCS, pp. 607–616 (2009)

33. Naor, M., Yung, M.: Universal one-way hash functions and their cryptographic applications. In: 21st ACM STOC, pp. 33–43 (1989)

34. Pöhls, H.C., Samelin, K., Posegga, J.: Sanitizable signatures in XML signature — performance, mixing properties, and revisiting the property of transparency. In: Lopez, J., Tsudik, G. (eds.) ACNS 2011. LNCS, vol. 6715, pp. 166–182. Springer, Heidelberg (2011). https://doi.org/10.1007/978-3-642-21554-4_10

35. Rompel, J.: One-way functions are necessary and sufficient for secure signatures. In: 22nd ACM STOC, pp. 387–394 (1990)

36. Yum, D.H., Seo, J.W., Lee, P.J.: Trapdoor sanitizable signatures made easy. In: Zhou, J., Yung, M. (eds.) ACNS 2010. LNCS, vol. 6123, pp. 53–68. Springer, Heidelberg (2010). https://doi.org/10.1007/978-3-642-13708-2_4

# Delegatable Attribute-Based Anonymous Credentials from Dynamically Malleable Signatures

Johannes Blömer and Jan Bobolz[✉]

Paderborn University, Paderborn, Germany
`jan.bobolz@uni-paderborn.de`

**Abstract.** We introduce the notion of *delegatable attribute-based anonymous credentials* (DAAC). Such systems offer fine-grained anonymous access control and they give the credential holder the ability to issue more restricted credentials to other users. In our model, credentials are parameterized with attributes that (1) express what the credential holder himself has been certified and (2) define which attributes he may issue to others. Furthermore, we present a practical construction of DAAC. For this construction, we deviate from the usual approach of embedding a certificate chain in the credential. Instead, we introduce a novel approach for which we identify a new primitive we call *dynamically malleable signatures* (DMS) as the main ingredient. This primitive may be of independent interest. We also give a first instantiation of DMS with efficient protocols.

**Keywords:** Delegatable credentials · Anonymous credentials
Malleable signatures · Attribute-based credentials · Authentication

## 1 Introduction

In this paper, we construct delegatable attribute-based anonymous credentials (DAAC) that offer fine-grained anonymous access control for many typical scenarios. For example, consider a company with the usual hierarchical organization structure. We want the company owner to be able to grant appropriate access rights to department managers. For this, he issues each of them a *credential* with certain attributes encoding what rights the department manager has. The department managers, in turn, should be able to grant appropriate subsets of their rights to their staff by *delegating* a (weaker) version of their credential to them. Then a staff member may want to grant access rights to her interns, etc.

This scenario could be trivially realized using certificate chains (similar to the ones used in TLS): the company owner signs the public key of a department manager alongside some string that encodes which attributes the manager has

This work was partially supported by the German Research Foundation (DFG) within the Collaborative Research Center "On-The-Fly Computing"(SFB 901).

B. Preneel and F. Vercauteren (Eds.): ACNS 2018, LNCS 10892, pp. 221–239, 2018.
https://doi.org/10.1007/978-3-319-93387-0_12

and which ones he may delegate to his staff. Then the department manager can extend the chain by signing a staff member's public key, and so on.

However, our goal is to enable *anonymity* for authentication: An authorized user requesting access to a resource should be indistinguishable from *all other users who have access to it*. Still, the verifier, who is executing the authentication checks, should be assured that only authorized users can pass them. Overall, we have the following requirements:

R1. The verifier must not learn the sequence of delegations a user's credential went through.
R2. The verifier must only learn as much as necessary about the attributes of the authenticating user or of any users involved in the delegation.
R3. A user must not be able to grant other users more rights/attributes than he is allowed to.
R4. A user should not be able to pass the authentication checks without being given an appropriate credential.
R5. Users shall remain anonymous while delegating and receiving a credential.

Most previous constructions of delegatable credentials [1,4,14] fulfill R1, R3, R4 and R5. However, in those constructions the attributes of all users in the chain are presented in plain to the verifier. This violates R2. A more recent scheme [6] supports R1, R3, R4 and R2. However, in their construction, credential holders see all attributes of the users in the delegation chain. This violates R5. In this paper, we introduce the first construction of practical delegatable attribute-based anonymous credentials that supports all five requirements.

*Our Model of Delegatable Attribute-Based Anonymous Credentials.* In DAAC, users have a single secret key and can derive an arbitrary number of unlinkable public keys (usually called *pseudonyms*). Users can issue credentials to other users (also anonymously, if desired). A credential is parameterized with a delegation flag $d \in \{0, 1\}$, which determines whether or not the credential is delegatable, and an attribute vector $(A_1, \ldots, A_n) \in (\mathbb{A} \cup \{\star\})^n$ for some set $\mathbb{A}$ (e.g., $\mathbb{A} = \mathbb{Z}_p$). Each $A_i$ in the attribute vector either takes on a concrete value from $\mathbb{A}$, or the special value $\star$, which can be interpreted as a placeholder that can be replaced with an arbitrary $\mathbb{A}$-value.

We define the *covers* relation on attribute vectors that will determine what attributes the user can delegate and show. A vector $(A_1, \ldots, A_n)$ covers another vector $(A'_1, \ldots, A'_n)$ (we write $\vec{A} \succeq \vec{A'}$) if and only if $(A_i \neq \star) \Rightarrow (A'_i = A_i)$ for all $i$. This means that the placeholder $\star$ can be replaced with any concrete $\mathbb{A}$ value (or $\star$ again), whereas concrete values from $\mathbb{A}$ cannot be changed.

Given a credential with delegation flag $d = 1$ and attribute-vector $\vec{A}$, a user is able to issue a credential with any delegation flag $d^* \in \{0, 1\}$ and any attributes $\vec{A^*}$ as long as $\vec{A} \succeq \vec{A^*}$. A credential with delegation flag $d = 0$ cannot be delegated any further. When *showing* a credential for an access policy $\phi$ (e.g., a Boolean formula over statements like "$A_2 = 13$"), the user proves that his attributes cover some concrete $\vec{A'} \in \mathbb{A}^n$ for which $\phi(\vec{A'}) = 1$. Note that it is natural that whatever users can delegate, they can also show.

In the simplest case, each attribute $A_i$ may just encode a Boolean access right and users can delegate subsets of their access rights. In the concrete instantiation based on Construction 11 in our paper, you can encode arbitrary elements of $\mathbb{A} = \mathbb{Z}_p$ (e.g., short strings) into credentials, hence our scheme can realize more elaborate authentication scenarios. As a small example for this, the state of California may issue San Francisco a delegatable credential like $\vec{A} = (\star, \star, \text{San Francisco})$. This allows the city to delegate credentials with attributes $\vec{A}^* = (\text{John}, \text{Doe}, \text{San Francisco})$ to its citizens, but prohibits issuing credentials encoding other cities.

When authenticating with a credential, the only information revealed to the verifier is the root of the delegation chain (e.g., the company owner or the state), a pseudonym of the authenticating user, and the fact that the credential's attributes fulfill some predicate.

*Idea of Our Construction.* We deviate from the usual way of constructing delegatable credentials and instead follow a novel approach. We identify a new primitive we call *dynamically malleable signatures* (DMS) as the main ingredient. DMS are similar to usual malleable signatures, but the set of allowed transformations is specific to each signature and can be incrementally restricted over time (*"dynamic"* refers to the fact that the set of allowed transformations is not static but can be changed "at runtime" for each signature). More specifically, the Sign algorithm takes some vector of messages $(m_1, \ldots, m_n)$ and an index set $I \subseteq \{1, \ldots, n\}$ as input and produces a signature $\sigma$ and a *malleability key* $mk$. The index set $I$ determines which of the positions in the vector are malleable, i.e. given $\sigma$ and $mk$, anyone can derive a signature $\sigma'$ on any message $(m_1', \ldots, m_n')$ as long as $m_i' = m_i$ for all $i \notin I$. This process also yields a malleability key $mk'$ for $\sigma'$, which can be restricted to allow further modification of $\sigma'$ only on some (smaller) index set $I' \subseteq I$. In Sect. 5, we give an efficient construction of DMS with supporting protocols. Our construction is based on the Pointcheval-Sanders signature scheme [17] and it can be proven secure in the generic group model.

Using any secure DMS scheme with an efficient protocol to derive a signature on a committed value, we generically implement a DAAC as follows: With some details omitted, a credential for a user with secret $usk$ and attributes $\vec{A} = (15, 7, \star, \star)$ is a dynamically malleable signature on $usk$ and $\vec{A}$. For each $\star$ in $\vec{A}$, we instead sign 0. More formally, in this example we would sign $(m_1, \ldots, m_5) := (usk, 15, 7, 0, 0)$ and allow the receiver to use malleability on the first index (to change $usk$ when delegating) and the last two indices (to model the $\star$), i.e. $I = \{1, 4, 5\}$. Unforgeability of the signature scheme then guarantees that this user cannot produce a credential whose first two attributes are not 15 and 7 (cf. requirement R3). If he wants to delegate attributes $\vec{A}' = (15, 7, 13, \star)$ to another user with secret key $usk'$, the two parties engage in a protocol to derive a signature on $(usk', 15, 7, 13, 0)$ such that only the first and the last message can be changed further, i.e. $I' = \{1, 5\} \subset I$. Note that the issuer's $usk$ or his exact attributes are not part of the derived credential, immediately implying R1. Our delegation protocol will also ensure R5. To mark the credential non-delegatable ($d = 0$), the delegator can remove the first index from the index set, which precludes the receiver from changing the signature to any other secret key $usk'' \neq usk'$. Showing the credential to a verifier follows standard procedure [15], i.e. the user runs a zero-knowledge protocol to prove knowledge of a signature on his user secret and on attributes fulfilling some policy (and that his user secret is consistent with his pseudonym). The zero-knowledge property ensures requirement R2 while the proof of knowledge property and the unforgeability of the signature scheme ensures R4.

*Related Work on Delegatable Credentials.* Chase and Lysyanskaya introduced the first anonymous delegatable credential system [8], which extended the idea of anonymous credentials [9] to enable delegation. Later, Belenkiy et al. published an elegant construction of delegatable credentials [4] and introduced formal security requirements. In their paper, delegatable credentials are defined through *levels*. Any user can publish a pseudonym $pk_{\text{root}}$ and issue a level $L = 1$ credential to another user. Then, a level $L$ credential can be used to derive a level $L + 1$ credential for another user. When showing a credential, the verifier learns the root pseudonym $pk_{\text{root}}$ of the credential, the prover's pseudonym $pk_L$, and the credential's level $L$.

The construction of [4] allows users to attach public attributes to a credential when delegating, meaning that a level $L$ credential is parameterized with $L$ attribute descriptions $(A_1, \ldots, A_L) \in (\{0,1\}^*)^L$, where the issuer of the level $\ell \leq L$ credential chooses $A_\ell$. However, they do not describe a way to hide the attributes of any user in the delegation chain, which weakens anonymity considerably (cf. our requirement R2). Furthermore, there are no restrictions on the attribute strings a delegator can add when delegating a credential (cf. requirement R3). Hence the burden of verifying plausibility of delegated attributes lies with the verifier.

If we instantiate our generic construction of DAAC with our concrete DMS scheme (Sect. 5), a credential with $n$ attributes consists of at most $n + 3$ group elements. In particular, the credential size is independent of the delegation chain length. Using standard variants of Schnorr's protocol, showing the credential can be done very efficiently compared to [4], whose credentials are Groth-Sahai proofs with size linear in the chain length. As a trade-off, we reach this level of efficiency mainly by (1) not encoding the delegation chain into credentials (which also precludes the feature of tracing the sequence of credential owners using a trapdoor), and (2) leveraging a new ad-hoc algebraic assumption for the construction of our concrete DMS scheme (there *are* delegatable credentials that are secure under standard assumptions, e.g., DLIN [7]).

Most other constructions [1,7,14] also follow roughly the same techniques as [4], i.e. using malleable proof systems (like Groth-Sahai) as a building block, improving upon and generalizing the original idea. However, there do not seem to be any constructions that improve upon their handling of (public) attributes.

More recently, Camenisch et al. published a delegatable credential system [6]. Their construction is very efficient and practical. They achieve this by allowing credential holders to see all attributes on all levels in plain, i.e. not offering anonymity for delegators. In many contexts, this is not a problem. However, consider the example of a distributed car sharing scenario where the car owner is issued a credential for his car. In a car-sharing fashion, he can delegate his access rights to any other person. In this scenario, the car owner has no reason to reveal his identity. Our construction shows that one does not have to sacrifice support for such scenarios to achieve practicality: Namely, our scheme's efficiency is comparable to [6] while offering anonymity for delegators (R5).

*Related Work on Malleable Signatures.* Malleable signature schemes allow anyone to transform a signature on a message $m$ to be valid for a different message $m'$ for a well-defined set $\mathcal{T}$ of allowed transformations on $m$ (e.g., [7]).

In contrast, our notion of DMS allows signers to choose transformation sets $\mathcal{T}_\sigma$ on a per-signature basis, which can be further restricted to some subset $\mathcal{T}_{\sigma'}$ when transforming $\sigma$ to $\sigma'$.

The general idea for DMS is similar to homomorphic signatures like [2,3,5,13]. In these constructions (mostly designed for network coding), a signer effectively signs a vector space by signing its base vectors with a homomorphic signature scheme. This allows computing signatures on any vector in the vector space. Like DMS, homomorphic signature schemes allow to derive signatures on related messages. However, the main feature of DMS is that one can derive signatures that are *more restricted* than the original. Furthermore, one cannot combine two restricted signatures to produce a signature on a message not covered by either of them.

## 2 Basics and Notation

For a random variable $X$, $[X] := \{x \mid \Pr[X = x] > 0\}$ is the *support* of $X$. With $X \leftarrow S$, we denote that $X$ is chosen uniformly at random from the set $S$. If $X$ and $Y$ are identically distributed random variables, we write $X \approx Y$. With $X \leftarrow A(y)$ we denote that $X$ is generated by running the probabilistic algorithm $A$ on input $y$. The notation $\Pr[X_1 \leftarrow S, X_2 \leftarrow A(y, X_1); \phi(X_1, X_2)]$ denotes the probability that the predicate $\phi(X_1, X_2)$ holds in the probability space described by $X_1, X_2$. For a prime number $p$, $\mathbb{Z}_p$ is the field of order $p$ and $\mathbb{Z}_p^* = \mathbb{Z}_p \backslash \{0\}$.

**Definition 1.** Let $A, B$ be probabilistic interactive algorithms that halt on every input. We write $y_A \leftarrow A(x_A) \leftrightarrow B(x_B) \rightarrow y_B$ to denote that $A$ on input $x_A$ interacts with $B$ on input $x_B$; then $A$ outputs $y_A$ and $B$ outputs $y_B$. Furthermore, we define output$_A[A(x_A) \leftrightarrow B(x_B)]$ to be the random variable taking on $y_A$, i.e. the output of $A$ after interacting with $B$.                    ⋄

**Definition 2 (Protocols and signatures of knowledge).** The expression $ZKAK[(w); (x, w) \in \Psi]$ denotes a zero-knowledge argument of knowledge for the relation $\Psi$. $NIZK[(w); (x, w) \in \Psi](m)$ denotes a *signature of knowledge* on message $m$ for the relation $\Psi$.                    ⋄

Zero-knowledge arguments of knowledge can be implemented, for example, using Damgård's technique [12] on Schnorr-like $\Sigma$ protocols. Signatures of knowledge can be implemented, for example, using the Fiat-Shamir heuristic.

# 3    Delegatable Attribute-Based Anonymous Credentials

In this section, we define DAAC. Each credential is parameterized with a vector $\vec{A} = (A_1, \ldots, A_n) \in (\mathbb{A} \cup \{\star\})^n$, a delegation flag $d$, and the root authority's pseudonym $pk_{\text{root}}$.

To define what a user may do with his credential, we need the relation "*covers*". An attribute vector $\vec{A} = (A_1, \ldots, A_n) \in (\mathbb{A} \cup \{\star\})^n$ *covers* another attribute vector $\vec{A}' = (A_1', \ldots, A_n') \in (\mathbb{A} \cup \{\star\})^n$ if $(A_i \neq \star) \Rightarrow (A_i' = A_i)$ for all $1 \leq i \leq n$. In this case we write $\vec{A} \succeq \vec{A}'$. Furthermore, we say that an attribute vector $\vec{A} \in (\mathbb{A} \cup \{\star\})^n$ *covers* a predicate $\phi : \mathbb{A}^n \to \{0, 1\}$ if it covers some vector without $\star$ fulfilling $\phi$, i.e. $\exists \vec{A}' \in \mathbb{A}^n : \vec{A} \succeq \vec{A}' \wedge \phi(\vec{A}') = 1$. We write $\vec{A} \succeq \phi$.

Let $cred$ be a credential with attributes $\vec{A}$, delegation flag $d$, and root authority's pseudonym $pk_{\text{root}}$ (we say that $cred$ is *rooted* at $pk_{\text{root}}$). With $cred$, the user can do the following: (1) Prove possession of a $pk_{\text{root}}$-rooted credential that covers some predicate $\phi$, and (2) if $d = 1$, he can issue a derived credential still rooted at $pk_{\text{root}}$ with attributes $\vec{A}' \in (\mathbb{A} \cup \{\star\})^n$ iff $\vec{A} \succeq \vec{A}'$.

## 3.1    Formal Definition

**Definition 3.** A DAAC system consists of the following ppt algorithms:

$\mathrm{Setup}(1^\lambda) \to (pp, osk)$ generates public parameters $pp$ and an opening key $osk$. We assume an attribute universe $\mathbb{A}$ be to be encoded in $pp$.

$\mathrm{KeyGen}(pp) \to (usk, id)$ generates a user secret $usk$ and an identity $id$.

$\mathrm{FormNym}(pp, usk, 1^n) \to (pk, sk)$ generates a pseudonym $pk$ and a pseudonym secret $sk$ such that credentials rooted at $pk$ support $n$ attributes.

$\mathrm{Open}(pp, osk, pk) = id$ is a deterministic algorithm that extracts an identity $id$ from the pseudonym $pk$.

$\mathrm{CreateCred}(pp, pk, sk) \to cred$ creates a root credential, i.e. a delegatable credential with attributes $(\star, \ldots, \star)$ and delegation flag $d = 1$, rooted at $pk$.

$\mathrm{DelegIssue}(pp, pk_{\text{root}}, usk, cred, \vec{A}^*, d^*, pk^*)$
$\leftrightarrow \mathrm{DelegRcv}(pp, pk_{\text{root}}, \vec{A}^*, d^*, pk^*, sk^*, usk^*) \to cred^*$ is an interactive protocol with common input the root's pseudonym $pk_{\text{root}}$, the receiver's pseudonym $pk^*$, the attributes to be issued $\vec{A}^*$, and the delegation flag $d^* \in \{0, 1\}$. Additionally, the issuer gets his user secret $usk$ as private input, as well as his credential $cred$. Finally, the receiver gets his pseudonym secret $sk^*$ and user secret $usk^*$ as private input. After the protocol, the receiver side outputs a credential $cred^*$ or the failure symbol $\bot$.

$\mathrm{ShowProve}(pp, pk_{\text{root}}, pk, \phi, sk, usk, cred) \leftrightarrow \mathrm{ShowVrfy}(pp, pk_{\text{root}}, pk, \phi) \to b$ is an interactive protocol with common input the root's pseudonym $pk_{\text{root}}$, the prover's pseudonym $pk$, and a statement over attributes $\phi : \mathbb{A}^n \to \{0, 1\}$. The prover gets his pseudonym secret $sk$, his user secret $usk$, and his credential $cred$ as private input. The verifier outputs a bit $b$.

Furthermore, we require three helper predicates that enable simpler correctness and security definitions: CheckPseud($pp, pk, sk, usk$), CheckShow ($pp, pk_{\text{root}}, pk, \phi, sk, usk, cred$), and CheckDeleg($pp, pk_{\text{root}}, usk, cred, \vec{A}^*$).

For correctness, we require that

- All pseudonyms $(pk, sk)$ generated by FormNym($pp, usk, 1^n$) pass the check CheckPseud. We call $(pk, sk)$ that pass CheckPseud *valid*.
- For all $(usk, id) \in [\text{KeyGen}(pp)]$ and valid $(pk, sk)$: Open($pp, osk, pk$) = $id$.
- ShowVrfy $\leftrightarrow$ ShowProve succeeds if its input passes CheckShow and also CheckPseud.
- In DelegIssue $\leftrightarrow$ DelegRcv, if the protocols' inputs pass CheckDeleg for the issuer's credential and CheckPseud for the receiver's pseudonym, then DelegRcv does not output the error symbol $\perp$.
- Any output of DelegRcv($pp, pk_{\text{root}}, \vec{A}^*, d^*, pk^*, sk^*, usk^*$) is either $\perp$ or a credential $cred^*$ that passes CheckShow($pp, pk_{\text{root}}, pk', \phi, sk', usk^*, cred^*$) for all $\vec{A}^* \succeq \phi$. If $d^* = 1$, it also passes CheckDeleg($pp, pk_{\text{root}}, usk^*, cred^*, \vec{A}'$) for all $\vec{A}^* \succeq \vec{A}'$.
- Root credentials $cred \in [\text{CreateCred}(pp, pk_{\text{root}}, sk_{\text{root}})]$ are universal, i.e. if $(pk, sk)$ are valid, then CheckShow($pp, pk_{\text{root}}, pk, \phi, sk, usk, cred$) = 1 for all satisfiable $\phi$. Furthermore, CheckDeleg($pp, pk_{\text{root}}, usk, cred, \vec{A}^*$) = 1 for all $\vec{A}^* \in (\mathbb{A} \cup \{\star\})^n$. $\diamond$

A more formal version of correctness can be found in the full version of this paper.

The system is set up using Setup, and the special opener secret $osk$ is given to a trusted authority. Any user can join the system by simply calling KeyGen to generate their own user secret $usk$ and identity $id$. With the user secret, one can generate any number of pseudonyms $pk$ using FormNym. A user can declare himself a credential-issuing authority by publishing one of his pseudonyms $pk_{\text{root}}$ and creating a root credential with CreateCred which allows him to delegate arbitrary credentials rooted at $pk_{\text{root}}$. To delegate a credential, the delegator runs DelegIssue while the receiver runs DelegRcv. To show a credential, a user runs ShowProve while the verifier runs ShowVrfy. In case of abuse, the opener secret $osk$ can be used to extract the identity of a user from one of his pseudonyms.

Note the omission of a registration mechanism that prevents users from repeatedly generating ephemeral identities to circumvent persecution by the opener. A registration mechanism can be generically constructed from the credential system itself. We explain this in Sect. 3.2.

For security, we expect anonymity (users cannot be traced when showing, delegating, or receiving credentials) and soundness (users cannot impersonate other users or show credentials they have not been issued).

**Definition 4 (Anonymity).** A DAAC system $\Pi$ has *anonymity* if there is an ppt algorithm $(pp, osk, td) \leftarrow \mathfrak{S}^{pp}(1^\lambda)$ whose output is such that $(pp, osk)$ is distributed exactly like Setup($1^\lambda$). Furthermore, there are ppt simulators $\mathfrak{S}_{\text{ShowProve}}, \mathfrak{S}_{\text{DelegIssue}}, \mathfrak{S}_{\text{DelegRcv}}$ such that no (unrestricted) $\mathcal{A}$ can distinguish between interacting

- with ShowProve($pp, pk_{\text{root}}, pk, \phi, sk, usk, cred$) or with $\mathfrak{S}_{\text{ShowProve}}(td, pk_{\text{root}}, pk, \phi$)
- with DelegIssue($pp, pk_{\text{root}}, usk, cred, \vec{A}^*, d^*, pk^*$) or $\mathfrak{S}_{\text{DelegIssue}}(td, pk_{\text{root}}, \vec{A}^*, d^*, pk^*, usk_{\text{alt}}, cred_{\text{alt}}$) for *any* $usk_{\text{alt}}, cred_{\text{alt}}$ that pass the CheckDeleg ($pp, pk_{\text{root}}, usk_{\text{alt}}, cred_{\text{alt}}, \vec{A}^*$) check.
- with DelegRcv($pp, pk_{\text{root}}, \vec{A}^*, d^*, pk^*, sk^*, usk^*$) or $\mathfrak{S}_{\text{DelegRcv}}(td, pk_{\text{root}}, \vec{A}^*, d^*, pk^*$).

Furthermore, for all ppt $\mathcal{A}$ there is a negligible function *negl* s.t. for all $\lambda \in \mathbb{N}$,

$$\Pr[(pp, osk, td) \leftarrow \mathfrak{S}^{pp}(1^\lambda), (usk_0, id_0), (usk_1, id_1) \leftarrow \text{KeyGen}(pp), b \leftarrow \{0,1\},$$

$$b' \leftarrow \mathcal{A}^{\mathcal{O}_{\text{FormNym}}(\cdot), \mathcal{O}_{\text{Open}}(\cdot)}(1^\lambda, pp, td, usk_0, id_0, usk_1, id_1); b = b'] \leq 1/2 + negl(\lambda)$$

where $\mathcal{O}_{\text{FormNym}}(1^n)$ returns pseudonyms of $usk_b$, it runs $(pk, sk) \leftarrow$ FormNym($pp, usk_b, 1^n$) and returns $pk$. $\mathcal{O}_{\text{Open}}(pk)$ returns $\bot$ if $pk$ was previously output by $\mathcal{O}_{\text{FormNym}}(\cdot)$, otherwise returns Open($pp, osk, pk$). ◇

A more formally rigorous definition can be found in the full version of this paper. Our simulators get as input the simulation trapdoor $td$ and the common public input of the simulated protocol. In addition, $\mathfrak{S}_{\text{DelegIssue}}$ gets *any* $usk_{\text{alt}}, cred_{\text{alt}}$ (which can be completely uncorrelated to the actual delegator's $usk, cred$) as input to help with the simulation. The experiment in the last part of the definition models a situation where the ppt algorithm $\mathcal{A}$ knows all secrets except the opener's $osk$. He interacts with one of two possible honest users (who generated their $usk$ honestly) and may request additional pseudonyms from that unknown user. Additionally, $\mathcal{A}$ may use $usk_0, usk_1$ to create any situation it wants for the two users. We allow $\mathcal{A}$ to query FormNym and Open oracles (with the usual constraints) to try to learn information about the unknown user from his pseudonyms. All other actions that $\mathcal{A}$ may want to make the unknown user do (issue credentials, etc.), can be perfectly simulated by $\mathcal{A}$ without knowledge of $b$. For this, we supply $\mathcal{A}$ with the simulation trapdoor $td$.

**Definition 5 (Soundness).** In the soundness experiment $\text{Exp}_{\Pi,\mathcal{A}}^{\text{soundness}}(\lambda)$, the challenger plays the role of an arbitrary number of honest users. The adversary may internally set up any number of corrupted users.

The experiment begins with handing $pp, osk$ to the adversary $\mathcal{A}$. We allow $\mathcal{A}$ to make honest users run FormNym and CreateCred, and to interact with honest users running DelegIssue, DelegRcv, or ShowProve. Furthermore, $\mathcal{A}$ can make honest users delegate credentials among themselves.

Eventually, $\mathcal{A}$ outputs a challenge ($pk_{\text{root}}, pk, \phi$). The experiment runs the protocol ShowVrfy($pp, pk_{\text{root}}, pk, \phi$) interacting with $\mathcal{A}$. The experiment outputs 1 if ShowVrfy accepts and one of the following is true:

- *The user or root issuer's identity cannot be traced*: Open($pp, osk, pk$) $=\bot$ or Open($pp, osk, pk_{\text{root}}$) $=\bot$.
- *$\mathcal{A}$ was able to impersonate some honest user*: Open($pp, osk, pk$) $= id'$ for some honest user's identity $id'$.

– $\mathcal{A}$ *was able to show a credential he did not receive*: $\text{Open}(pp, osk, pk_{\text{root}}) = id'$
   for some honest user's $id'$ and $\mathcal{A}$ never queried to receive a credential $cred^*$
   on a pseudonym $pk^*$ such that: (1) $cred^*$ is rooted at $pk_{\text{root}}$, (2) $cred^*$ has
   attributes $\vec{A}^* \succeq \phi$, and (3) $cred^*$ is marked delegatable or $\text{Open}(pp, osk, pk) = \text{Open}(pp, osk, pk^*)$.

A DAAC system $\Pi$ is *sound* if for all ppt adversaries $\mathcal{A}$ there exists a negligible function $negl$ with $\Pr[\text{Exp}_{\Pi,\mathcal{A}}^{\text{soundness}}(\lambda) = 1] \leq negl(\lambda)$ for all $\lambda \in \mathbb{N}$.    ◇

The complete experiment can be found in the full version of this paper.

The adversary's win conditions imply that a credential with delegation flag $d = 0$ can only be shown with a pseudonym that opens to the same identity as the pseudonym used when receiving the credential. Note that even if $d = 0$, it is *always* possible for a credential holder $A$ to reveal his credential *and* his user secret $usk_A$ to another user $B$ (who can then show the credential somewhere and gain access). However, users are discouraged from doing this because after revealing $usk_A$ to $B$, $B$ can perform (malicious) activities, which the opener will then trace back to $A$. Hence $A$ bears the risk of being made responsible for $B$'s actions. For more details of how we propose applications use the security guarantees of Definition 5 to enforce accountability, we refer to Sect. 3.2.

## 3.2 How to Deploy Delegatable Attribute-Based Anonymous Credential Systems in Practice

In the following, we describe an example how an application would utilize DAAC in practice. The system should be set up by a trusted authority (TA). The TA runs $(pp, osk) \leftarrow \text{Setup}(1^\lambda)$, $(usk_{\text{TA}}, id_{\text{TA}}) \leftarrow \text{KeyGen}(pp)$, $(pk_{\text{TA}}, sk_{\text{TA}}) \leftarrow \text{FormNym}(pp, usk_{\text{TA}}, 1^0)$. He then publishes $pp$ and $pk_{\text{TA}}$.

In order to join the system, a user generates $(usk, id) \leftarrow \text{KeyGen}(pp)$. He then approaches the TA to register in the system. For this, he sends one of his pseudonyms $pk$ to the TA and uses some mechanism to authenticate with his real identity (e.g., physically showing a passport). The TA computes the user's $id$ using $\text{Open}(pp, osk, pk)$ and stores $id$ alongside the user's real identity information. Then the TA uses the user's $pk$ to issue a non-delegatable ($d = 0$) "master" credential $cred_{\text{master}}$.

Whenever the user introduces a new pseudonym $pk'$ to some verifier, he first shows the master credential by running $\text{ShowProve}(pp, pk_{\text{TA}}, pk', \phi, sk', usk, cred_{\text{master}})$ with the verifier. This ensures that the user indeed registered with the TA and hence the TA will be able to trace his pseudonyms to his real identity. If at some point the user breaks some rule within the application, the verifier can approach the TA with $pk'$, which the TA can trace to the user's identity by computing $\text{Open}(pp, osk, pk')$. This is because the soundness property (Definition 5) ensures that the non-delegatable credential $cred_{\text{master}}$, which was issued to $pk$, can be successfully shown *only* for $pk'$ where $\text{Open}(pp, osk, pk') = \text{Open}(pp, osk, pk)$.

Of course, you may also want to ensure that users cannot be *falsely* accused by verifiers for (malicious) actions they never committed. The application can enforce this by logging relevant actions and making a user certify each log entry by issuing a credential to the verifier whose attributes encode the log entry. This credential (rooted at the user's pseudonym $pk'$) can be used by the verifier to prove to the TA that $pk'$ indeed executed the logged action. Honest users cannot be falsely accused anymore because the soundness property (Definition 5) prohibits forging/showing a credential rooted at a pseudonym that traces to an honest user. The user's privacy when issuing the credential to the verifier is still guaranteed because the anonymity property (Definition 4) guarantees anonymity not only for the receiver of a credential, but also for the issuer. Note that the TA may still lie about the identity that $\mathrm{Open}(pp, osk, pk')$ outputs. This can be prevented with standard techniques, e.g., by making the TA prove non-interactively that the claimed identity is indeed output by Open.

# 4    Dynamically Malleable Signatures with Efficient Protocols

For our construction of DAAC, we introduce *dynamically malleable signatures* (DMS) as a building block. As explained in the introduction, a DMS is a malleable signature where the set of allowed transformations on the signed message can be incrementally restricted. We first define DMS, then define related protocols that are used in our DAAC construction.

## 4.1    Definition

A DMS is accompanied by a *malleability key* $mk$ and parameterized with an *index set* $I$. We describe malleability through a relation $\equiv_I$, which depends on $I$. Namely, using $mk$, a message $\vec{m}$ can be changed into a message $\vec{m}'$ iff $\vec{m} \equiv_I \vec{m}'$. We remark that our definitions (syntax and security) for DMS apply to arbitrary equivalence relations $\equiv_I$ and arbitrary index sets $I$ satisfying $I' \subseteq I \Rightarrow \equiv_{I'} \subseteq \equiv_I$, i.e. restricting $I$ restricts the malleability relation. However, in this paper, we are going to use the following concrete relation $\equiv_I$.

**Definition 6.** Let $I \subseteq \{1, \ldots, n\}$ be an index set. We define $\equiv_I$ by

$$(m_1, \ldots, m_n) \equiv_I (m'_1, \ldots, m'_n) \Leftrightarrow \forall i \notin I : m_i = m'_i \ .$$

$\diamond$

This means that malleability of DMS is restricted so that exactly the messages at indices present in $I$ can be modified. A DMS is called *dynamically* malleable because given any signature $\sigma$ and malleability key $mk$ with index set $I$, one can efficiently compute $\sigma', mk'$ with index set $I' \subseteq I$. We now formally define DMS.

**Definition 7 (Dynamically malleable signatures).** A DMS scheme consists of the following (probabilistic) polynomial-time algorithms:

Setup($1^\lambda$) $\rightarrow pp$ for security parameter $\lambda$ outputs public parameters $pp$. We
assume that the message space $M$ can be inferred from $pp$ and that $|pp| \geq \lambda$.

KeyGen($pp, 1^n$) $\rightarrow (pk, sk)$ for $n \in \mathbb{N}$ outputs a key pair $(pk, sk)$.

Sign($pp, sk, \vec{m}, I$) $\rightarrow (\sigma, mk)$ for a message vector $\vec{m} \in M^n$ and an index set $I$
outputs a signature $\sigma$ and a malleability key $mk$.

Transform($pp, \vec{m}, \vec{m}', \sigma, mk, I'$) $\rightarrow (\sigma', mk')$ on input a signature $\sigma$ on $\vec{m}$ outputs
a signature $\sigma'$ and a malleability key $mk'$ for $\vec{m}', I'$.

Vrfy($pp, pk, \vec{m}, \sigma$) $= b$ is a deterministic algorithm that outputs a bit.

VrfyMk($pp, pk, \vec{m}, \sigma, mk, I$) $= b$ is a deterministic algorithm that outputs a bit.

A DMS scheme is *correct* if for all $\lambda, n \in \mathbb{N}$, all $pp \in [\text{Setup}(1^\lambda)]$, all $(pk, sk) \in$
[KeyGen($pp, 1^n$)], all $\vec{m} \in M^n$ and index sets $I \subseteq \{1, \ldots, n\}$:

- $\Pr[(\sigma, mk) \leftarrow \text{Sign}(pp, sk, \vec{m}, I); \text{Vrfy}(pp, pk, \vec{m}, \sigma) = \text{VrfyMk}(pp, pk, \vec{m}, \sigma,$ $mk, I) = 1] = 1$ (signatures and malleability keys from Sign are accepted by the verification algorithms)

- $\Pr[(\sigma', mk') \leftarrow \text{Transform}(\vec{m}, \vec{m}', \sigma, mk, I'); \text{Vrfy}(pp, pk, \vec{m}', \sigma') = \text{VrfyMk}$ $(pp, pk, \vec{m}', \sigma', mk', I') = 1] = 1$ for all $\vec{m}' \equiv_I \vec{m}$, $I' \subseteq I$, and all $(\sigma, mk)$ with VrfyMk($pp, pk, \vec{m}, \sigma, mk, I) = 1$. (signatures and malleability keys derived from Transform are accepted by the verification algorithms). $\diamond$

Note that our definition implies that any signature/malleability key created with Transform can again be input to Transform to further change the message or weaken the malleability key. Also note that we model both Vrfy and VrfyMk as the former may be more efficient.

We now define security for DMS. We expect (1) derivation privacy: signatures derived with $mk$ are indistinguishable from signatures freshly created with $sk$ and (2) unforgeability: an adversary cannot produce a signature that cannot be legally derived from oracle-queried signatures. For derivation privacy, we demand *perfect* derivation privacy for simplicity.

**Definition 8 (Perfect derivation privacy).** A DMS scheme $\mathcal{S}$ is *perfectly derivation private* if for all $\lambda, n \in \mathbb{N}$, all $pp \in [\text{Setup}(1^\lambda)]$, all $pk, \sigma, mk$, all $\vec{m}, \vec{m}' \in M^n$, and all index sets $I, I'$ with $\vec{m}' \equiv_I \vec{m}$, $I' \subseteq I$, and VrfyMk($pp, pk, \vec{m}, \sigma, mk, I$) $= 1$, it holds that (1) $\exists sk$ with $(pk, sk) \in$ [KeyGen($pp, 1^n$)], and (2) for all $sk$ such that $(pk, sk) \in$ [KeyGen($pp, 1^n$)], Transform($\vec{m}, \vec{m}', \sigma, mk, I'$) $\approx$ Sign($pp, sk, \vec{m}', I'$) $\diamond$

The first item (that for each $pk$ accepted by VrfyMk, there exists a corresponding $sk$) is a somewhat technical requirement. Without this requirement, it may happen that someone receives valid $\sigma, mk$ from an untrusted source for a public key $pk$ for which there exists no corresponding $sk$. In this case the premise $(pk, sk) \in$ [KeyGen($pp, 1^n$)] of the second item does not apply and hence any signatures $\sigma'$ derived from $\sigma, mk$ would be allowed to be easily traced back to $\sigma$.

For the second property, unforgeability, we simply weaken the standard EUF-CMA definition for digital signatures such that signatures that can be legally derived using Transform are not considered forgeries anymore. Note that for simplicity, we only define unforgeability for perfectly derivation private schemes.

**Definition 9 (Unforgeability).** Consider the experiment $\texttt{SigForge}_{\Pi,\mathcal{A}}(\lambda, n)$ for a DMS scheme $\Pi$ and an adversary $\mathcal{A}$:

- $pp \leftarrow \text{Setup}(1^\lambda)$, $(pk, sk) \leftarrow \text{KeyGen}(pp, 1^n)$. $\mathcal{A}$ is given $pp, pk$ and oracle access to $\text{Sign}(pp, sk, \cdot, \cdot)$.
- Eventually $\mathcal{A}$ outputs $\vec{m}^*, \sigma^*$. The experiment outputs 1 iff $\text{Vrfy}(pp, pk, \vec{m}^*, \sigma^*) = 1$ and $\mathcal{A}$ never made a query $\text{Sign}(pp, sk, \vec{m}', I')$ where $\vec{m}^* \equiv_{I'} \vec{m}'$.

A perfectly derivation private DMS scheme $\Pi$ is *unforgeable* if for all polynomials $p$ and all ppt $\mathcal{A}$ there is a negligible function *negl* such that for all $\lambda \in \mathbb{N}$ and $n \leq p(\lambda)$, $\Pr[\texttt{SigForge}_{\Pi,\mathcal{A}}(1^\lambda, 1^n) = 1] \leq negl(\lambda)$.    ◇

For perfectly derivation private schemes, the output of Transform is distributed the same as the output of Sign. Hence there is no need to give $\mathcal{A}$ explicit access to a Transform oracle. Furthermore, note that the definition can be fulfilled by schemes where a signature $\sigma$ can be modified even without a corresponding malleability key $mk$. Consequently, the distinction between $\sigma$ and $mk$ is somewhat arbitrary – one may just as well merge $mk$ into $\sigma$. However, note that $mk$ is not required as input to Vrfy; hence we keep the distinction for the sake of intuition and potential efficiency gains.

### 4.2 Deriving a Signature on a Committed Message

For our construction of DAAC, we will require a protocol for deriving a signature on a hidden committed message. The setting for the protocol is the following: The *issuer* holds a signature $\sigma$ on a message $\vec{m} = (m_1, \ldots, m_n)$ and corresponding malleability key $mk$ for index set $I$. For $i \in I$ and $I^* \subseteq I$ and a message $m^*$, the *receiver* wants to obtain the output of $\text{Transform}(pp, \vec{m}, (m_1, \ldots, m_{i-1}, m^*, m_{i+1}, \ldots, m_n), \sigma, mk, I^*)$ without revealing his $m^*$. For this, the receiver commits to $m^*$, then both parties engage in a protocol to jointly compute Transform.

**Definition 10 (Deriving a signature on a committed value).** A scheme for deriving a signature on a committed value consists of two ppt algorithms and two interacting algorithms:

$\text{BlindInit}(\sigma, mk, \vec{m}, i) \rightarrow (K, k)$ on input a signature $\sigma$ on $\vec{m}$, an index $i$, and a corresponding malleability key $mk$, outputs a key $K$ for the commitment scheme and some secret information $k$.

$\text{Commit}(K, m^*, r) \rightarrow C$ takes as input a key $K$, a message $m^*$ and some randomness $r$, and outputs a commitment $C$.

$\text{BlindIssue}(\sigma, mk, \vec{m}, i, I^*, k, C)$ on input a signature $\sigma$ on $\vec{m}$, an index set $I^*$, a malleability key $mk$, a commitment $C$, an index $i$, and the secret $k$, interacts with BlindRcv.

$\text{BlindRcv}(m^*, i, I^*, K, C, r) \rightarrow (\sigma^*, mk^*)$ on input a message $m^*$, an index $i$, an index set $I^*$, a commitment $C$ for key $K$ and its randomness $r$, interacts with BlindIssue and outputs a signature $\sigma^*$ and a malleability key $mk^*$.

The public parameters $pp$ and the public key under which the issuer's signature is valid are considered implicit input to all the algorithms above.

Such a protocol is *correct* if for all $m^* \in M$, all $\sigma, mk$ valid on $\vec{m}$ with index set $I$, all $i \in I$, and all $I^* \subseteq I$, the result $(\sigma^*, mk^*)$ of BlindRcv$(m^*, i, I^*, K, C, r) \leftrightarrow$ BlindIssue$(\sigma, mk, \vec{m}, i, I^*, k)$, where $C = \text{Commit}(K, m^*, r)$, is a valid signature (and malleability key) on $(m_1, \ldots, m_{i-1}, m^*, m_{i+1}, \ldots, m_n)$.    ⋄

In this scenario, the issuer would use BlindInit to create a commitment key $K$. He then sends $K$ to the receiver, who uses it to commit to his message $m^*$. Then both parties engage in the BlindIssue $\leftrightarrow$ BlindRcv protocol, which yields the signature and malleability key for the receiver.

In our credential system construction, we are going to make the receiver prove something about the message $m^*$ that he committed to. For this reason, the commitment process is made explicit in this definition as opposed to hiding it in the implementation details of the BlindRcv $\leftrightarrow$ BlindIssue protocol.

For the security of such a protocol, we require security for the receiver and for the issuer. Security for the receiver requires that (1) the commitment scheme is perfectly hiding, and (2) runs of BlindRcv for two distinct committed messages are perfectly indistinguishable for the issuer. Security for the issuer requires that (1) the distribution of the commitment key $K$ is independent of the issuer's concrete $\sigma, mk$ and $\vec{m}$, and (2) the receiver only learns a single signature. We detail these requirements formally in the full version of this paper.

## 5    Construction of Dynamically Malleable Signatures Based on Pointcheval-Sanders Signatures

Our construction is an extension of Pointcheval-Sanders signatures [17].

The Setup, KeyGen, Vrfy algorithms below are exactly the same as in the original Pointcheval-Sanders signature scheme, as are the signatures produced by Sign. We extend the Sign algorithm to output a malleability key and we add the VrfyMk and Transform algorithms. The main observation for our construction is that a signature $(h, h^{x+\sum y_i m_i})$ on $(m_1, \ldots, m_n)$ can be made malleable at position $i$ by adding $h^{y_i}$ to the malleability key.

**Construction 11 (DMS scheme).**

Setup$(1^\lambda)$ generates a bilinear group $\mathbb{G} = (\mathbb{G}_1, \mathbb{G}_2, \mathbb{G}_T, e, p)$ of prime order $p \geq 2^\lambda$. It outputs $pp = \mathbb{G}$. The message space is $M = \mathbb{Z}_p$.

KeyGen$(pp, 1^n)$ chooses random generator $\tilde{g} \leftarrow \mathbb{G}_2$. It then chooses random $x, y_1, \ldots, y_n \leftarrow \mathbb{Z}_p$. The secret key is $sk = (x, y_1, \ldots, y_n)$ and the public key is $pk = (\tilde{g}, \tilde{g}^x, \tilde{g}^{y_1}, \ldots, \tilde{g}^{y_n})$. It outputs $(pk, sk)$.

Sign$(pp, sk, m_1, \ldots, m_n, I)$ chooses $h \leftarrow \mathbb{G}_1 \backslash \{1\}$. It then computes $\sigma = (h, h^{x+\sum_i y_i m_i})$ and $mk = (h^{y_i})_{i \in I}$. It outputs $(\sigma, mk)$.

Vrfy$(pp, pk, \vec{m}, \sigma)$ parses $\sigma$ as $(h, \sigma_2)$, $pk$ as $(\tilde{g}, \tilde{g}^x, \tilde{g}^{y_1}, \ldots, \tilde{g}^{y_n})$, and returns 1 iff $h \neq 1$ and $e(h, \tilde{g}^x \cdot \prod_{i=1}^n (\tilde{g}^{y_i})^{m_i}) = e(\sigma_2, \tilde{g})$.

$\mathrm{VrfyMk}(pp, pk, \vec{m}, \sigma, mk, I)$ checks $\mathrm{Vrfy}(pp, pk, \vec{m}, \sigma) \overset{!}{=} 1$ and outputs 0 if the check does not pass. It parses $\sigma$ as $(h, \sigma_2)$ and $mk$ as $(h_i)_{i \in I}$. Then it returns 1 iff $e(h_i, \tilde{g}) = e(h, \tilde{g}^{y_i})$ for all $i \in I$.

$\mathrm{Transform}(\vec{m}, \vec{m}', \sigma, mk, I')$ parses $\sigma$ as $(h, h^{x + \sum_i y_i m_i})$ and $mk$ as $(h^{y_i})_{i \in I}$[1]. It aborts if $\mathrm{VrfyMk}(pp, pk, \vec{m}, \sigma, mk, I) \neq 1$ or $I' \not\subseteq I$ or $\vec{m} \not\equiv_I \vec{m}'$. Otherwise it chooses $r \leftarrow \mathbb{Z}_p^*$ and computes

$$\sigma' = (h^r, (h^{x + \sum_i y_i m_i} \cdot \prod_{i \in I} (h^{y_i})^{m_i' - m_i})^r) \text{ and } mk' = ((h^{y_i})^r)_{i \in I'}.$$

It outputs $(\sigma', mk')$.    ◇

One can easily check that our scheme fulfills the correctness requirements (Definition 7). Furthermore, Transform clearly produces signatures with the same distribution as Sign since $h^r$ is uniformly distributed over $\mathbb{G}_1 \backslash \{1\}$ and the second signature component as well as $mk$ are uniquely determined by that choice. Consequently, the scheme is perfectly derivation private (Definition 8). The scheme can be proven unforgeable in the generic group model.

**Theorem 12 (Unforgeability).** *Construction 11 is unforgeable in the generic group model for type-3 bilinear groups.*

The proof is straight-forward and very similar to other generic group model proofs (e.g., [17]). It can be found in the full version of this paper.

As noted above, for our construction of DAAC, we need an efficient protocol for deriving a signature on a committed value (cf. Definition 10). A protocol for *signing* a committed value for the original signature scheme was given in [17]. Our protocol is similar, with some changes to account for transforming an existing signature instead of creating new one, and to account for privacy of the issuer (which was not a requirement before). The commitment scheme we use is essentially Pedersen's commitment [16], but we derive the commitment key from the issuer's signature.

**Construction 13 (Deriving a signature on a committed value).**

$\mathrm{BlindInit}(\sigma, mk, \vec{m}, i)$ parses $\sigma$ as $(h, \sigma_2) \in (\mathbb{G}_1 \backslash \{1\}) \times \mathbb{G}_1$ and $mk = (h^{y_j})_{j \in I}$. It chooses $k \leftarrow \mathbb{Z}_p^*$. It sets $K = ((h^{y_i})^k, h^k)$ and outputs $(K, k)$.

$\mathrm{Commit}(K, m, r)$ parses $K$ as $(h^{y_i k}, h^k) \in \mathbb{G}_1 \times (\mathbb{G}_1 \backslash \{1\})$ and interprets $r$ as an element of $\mathbb{Z}_p$. It outputs the commitment $C = (h^{y_i k})^m \cdot (h^k)^r$.

$\mathrm{BlindRcv}(m^*, i, I^*, K, C, r) \leftrightarrow \mathrm{BlindIssue}(\sigma, mk, \vec{m}, i, I^*, k, C)$ works as follows: BlindIssue parses $\sigma$ as $(h, \sigma_2)$ and $mk$ as $(h^{y_i})_{i \in I}$, chooses a random $u \leftarrow \mathbb{Z}_p^*$ and computes $(\sigma_1', \sigma_2') = (h^{ku}, (\sigma_2^k \cdot (h^{y_i})^{-km_i} \cdot C)^u)$. It sends $(\sigma_1', \sigma_2')$ together with $mk' = ((h^{y_j})^{ku})_{j \in I^*}$ to the receiver. BlindRcv then unblinds $(\sigma_1', \sigma_2')$ as $\sigma^* = (\sigma_1^*, \sigma_2^*) = (\sigma_1', \sigma_2' \cdot (\sigma_1')^{-r})$. BlindRcv outputs $(\sigma^*, mk')$.    ◇

The proof of security for this construction is straight-forward and can be found in the full version of this paper.

---

[1] VrfyMk guarantees that the signature and the malleability key have this specific form.

# 6    Constructing Delegatable Attribute-Based Anonymous Credentials from Dynamically Malleable Signatures with Efficient Protocols

We now construct DAAC from a DMS scheme with efficient protocols. The general construction idea is similar to the generic construction of (attribute-based) credential systems *without* delegation [15], but using DMS instead of standard signatures essentially allows adding the delegation feature. We define the following notation:

**Definition 14.** Let $\mathcal{H}$ be a hash function. For $\vec{A} \in (\mathbb{A} \cup \{\star\})^n$, $d \in \{0,1\}$, $usk$, and $pk_{\mathrm{root}}$, we define

– $\vec{m}^{(\vec{A}, usk, pk_{\mathrm{root}})} := (m_1, \ldots, m_n, usk, \mathcal{H}(pk_{\mathrm{root}}))$, where $m_i = A_i$ if $m_i \in \mathbb{A}$, and $m_i = 0$ if $A_i = \star$ (where $0 \in M$ denotes some constant).
– $I^{(d, \vec{A})} := \{i \mid A_i = \star \vee (i = n + 1 \wedge d = 1)\} \subseteq \{1, \ldots, n + 2\}$    ⋄

We will also use the special case $\vec{m}^{(\vec{A}, 0, pk_{\mathrm{root}})}$, which is the same as above but with the user secret set to the constant $0 \in M$. In our construction, the predicates CheckPseud, CheckShow, and CheckDeleg from Definition 3 can be evaluated in polynomial time and we are going to use them in the algorithm descriptions.

With some details omitted, our construction is going to work as follows: A credential for user $usk$ rooted at $pk_{\mathrm{root}}$ with attribute vector $\vec{A}$ and delegation flag $d$ will be a dynamically malleable signature on $\vec{m}^{(\vec{A}, usk, pk_{\mathrm{root}})}$ with index set $I^{(d, \vec{A})}$. To delegate a credential, the issuer needs to derive a signature on the receiver's $usk$ without being given $usk$ itself. For this, we use a protocol for deriving a signature on a committed value (cf. Definition 10). Showing the credential consists of the user proving possession of $usk$ and a signature with attributes fulfilling some predicate $\phi$, such that $usk$ is both within his pseudonym and the signature. The identity of a user with key $usk$ will be $id = f(usk)$ for some one-way function $f$. Then, following standard techniques, a user's pseudonym is an encryption $c$ of $id$. For issuing credentials, each pseudonym also contains a signature scheme key $pk_{\mathcal{S}}$ and a signature of knowledge binding the encryption $c$ and $pk_{\mathcal{S}}$ together.

**Construction 15 (Generic construction of delegatable attribute-based anonymous credentials).** Let $\mathcal{S} = (\mathrm{Setup}_{\mathcal{S}}, \mathrm{KeyGen}_{\mathcal{S}}, \mathrm{Sign}_{\mathcal{S}}, \mathrm{Transform}_{\mathcal{S}}, \mathrm{Vrfy}_{\mathcal{S}})$ be a DMS scheme with $(\mathrm{BlindInit}_{\mathcal{S}}, \mathrm{BlindIssue}_{\mathcal{S}}, \mathrm{BlindRcv}_{\mathcal{S}}, \mathrm{Commit}_{\mathcal{S}})$ for deriving a signature on a committed value. Let $\mathcal{E} = (\mathrm{Setup}_{\mathcal{E}}, \mathrm{KeyGen}_{\mathcal{E}}, \mathrm{Encrypt}_{\mathcal{E}}, \mathrm{Decrypt}_{\mathcal{E}})$ be a public-key encryption scheme. Let $\mathcal{OW} = (\mathrm{Setup}_{\mathcal{OW}}, \mathrm{GenFnct}_{\mathcal{OW}})$ be a one-way function scheme. Let $\mathcal{H}$ be a (collision-resistant) hash function (usage hidden within the $\vec{m}^{(\cdots)}$ notation, cf. Definition 14).

We require that $\mathrm{Setup}_{\mathcal{S}} = \mathrm{Setup}_{\mathcal{E}} = \mathrm{Setup}_{\mathcal{OW}} =: \mathrm{Setup}$. We denote the (finite) message spaces of $\mathcal{S}$ and $\mathcal{E}$ as $M_{\mathcal{S}}$ and $M_{\mathcal{E}}$, respectively (they may depend on the output of Setup) and require that functions $f \in [\mathrm{GenFnct}_{\mathcal{OW}}(pp)]$ bijectively map between the message spaces for the signature and encryption scheme, i.e. $f : M_S \to M_\mathcal{E}$. Furthermore, the hash function must hash to $M_S$, i.e. $\mathcal{H} : \{0,1\}^* \to M_S$. The scheme consists of the following algorithms:

Setup($1^\lambda$) runs $pp_{S,\mathcal{E},\mathcal{OW}} \leftarrow$ Setup($1^\lambda$), $(pk_\mathcal{E}, sk_\mathcal{E}) \leftarrow$ KeyGen$_\mathcal{E}(pp_{S,\mathcal{E},\mathcal{OW}})$, and $f \leftarrow$ GenFnct$_{\mathcal{OW}}(pp_{S,\mathcal{E},\mathcal{OW}})$. It outputs $pp = (pp_{S,\mathcal{E},\mathcal{OW}}, pk_\mathcal{E}, f)$ and the opening key $osk = sk_\mathcal{E}$. The attribute universe $\mathbb{A}$ is $M_S$.

KeyGen($pp$) chooses $usk \leftarrow M_S$ and sets $id = f(usk)$. It returns $(usk, id)$.

FormNym($pp, usk, 1^n$) generates keys $(pk_S, sk_S) \leftarrow$ KeyGen$_S(pp_{S,\mathcal{E},\mathcal{OW}}, 1^{n+2})$. It encrypts $usk$ as $c = $ Encrypt$_\mathcal{E}(pk_\mathcal{E}, f(usk); r')$ using fresh randomness $r'$. It then creates a signature of knowledge on $pk_S$ and $c$ proving that it can open $c$: $\gamma = NIZK[(usk, r'); c = $ Encrypt$_\mathcal{E}(pk_\mathcal{E}, f(usk); r')](pk_S, c)$. The pseudonym is $pk = (pk_S, c, \gamma)$ and the secret is $sk = (sk_S, r', usk)$. It outputs $(pk, sk)$.

Open($pp, osk, pk$) parses $pk$ as $(pk_S, c, \gamma)$, checks $\gamma$ (outputs $\perp$ and aborts if the check fails), then it runs and outputs Decrypt$_\mathcal{E}(sk_\mathcal{E}, c)$.

CreateCred($pp, pk, sk$) runs $(\sigma, mk) \leftarrow$ Sign$_S(sk_S, \vec{m}^{((\star,\dots,\star),usk,pk)}, I^{(1,(\star,\dots,\star))})$. It outputs $cred = (\sigma, mk, (\star,\dots,\star), d = 1)$

DelegIssue($pp, pk_{\mathrm{root}}, usk, cred, \vec{A}^*, d^*, pk^*$) $\leftrightarrow$ DelegRcv($pp, pk_{\mathrm{root}}, \vec{A}^*, d^*, pk^*$, $sk^*, usk^*$) works as follows:

1. The issuer checks CheckDeleg($pp, pk_{\mathrm{root}}, usk, cred, \vec{A}^*$) $\overset{!}{=} 1$ and parses $cred$ as $(\sigma, mk, \vec{A}, d)$.

2. The receiver checks CheckPseud($pp, pk^*, sk^*, usk^*$) $\overset{!}{=} 1$.

3. The issuer prepares an anonymized delegatable credential by running $(\sigma', mk') \leftarrow$ Transform($pp, \vec{m}^{(\vec{A},usk,pk_{\mathrm{root}})}, \vec{m}^{(\vec{A}^*,0,pk_{\mathrm{root}})}, \sigma, mk, I^{(1,\vec{A}^*)}$).

4. If $d^* = 1$, the issuer simply hands $(\sigma', mk')$ to the receiver. Then the receiver changes the signature to his user secret by running $(\sigma^*, mk^*) \leftarrow$ Transform($pp, \vec{m}^{(\vec{A}^*,0,pk_{\mathrm{root}})}, \vec{m}^{(\vec{A}^*,usk^*,pk_{\mathrm{root}})}, \sigma', mk', I^{(d^*,\vec{A}^*)}$)

5. If $d^* = 0$, we write $pk_{\mathrm{root}} = (pk_{S,\mathrm{root}}, c_{\mathrm{root}}, \gamma_{\mathrm{root}})$. Then

   (a) the issuer runs $(K, k) \leftarrow$ BlindInit$_S(\sigma', mk', \vec{m}^{(\vec{A}^*,0,pk_{\mathrm{root}})}, n+1)$, sends $K$ to the receiver.

   (b) the receiver computes $C \leftarrow$ Commit$_S(K, usk^*, r)$ for some random $r$, sends $C$ to the issuer, and then runs a zero knowledge argument of knowledge with the issuer, proving he can open the commitment and his pseudonym $pk^* = (pk_S^*, c^*, \gamma^*)$ to his user secret (using $r'$ and $usk^*$ from $sk^* = (sk_S^*, r', usk^*)$):

$$ZKAK[(usk^*, r, r'); C = \text{Commit}_S(K, usk^*, r)$$
$$\wedge\, c^* = \text{Encrypt}_\mathcal{E}(pk_\mathcal{E}, f(usk^*); r')]$$

   (c) if the $ZKAK$ protocol accepts, then the issuer runs the protocol BlindIssue$_S(\sigma', mk', \vec{m}^{(\vec{A}^*,0,pk_{\mathrm{root}})}, n+1, I^{(d^*,\vec{A}^*)}, k, C)$, while the receiver runs $(\sigma^*, mk^*) \leftarrow$ BlindRcv$_S(usk^*, n+1, I^{(d^*,\vec{A}^*)}, K, C, r)$.

6. The receiver checks VrfyMk$_S(pk_{S,\mathrm{root}}, \vec{m}^{(\vec{A}^*,usk^*,pk_{\mathrm{root}})}, \sigma^*, mk^*, I^{(d^*,\vec{A}^*)})$ $\overset{!}{=} 1$. If the check fails, it outputs $\perp$, otherwise it outputs $cred^* := (\sigma^*, mk^*, \vec{A}^*, d^*)$.

ShowVrfy$(pp, pk_{\text{root}}, pk, \phi) \leftrightarrow$ ShowProve$(pp, pk_{\text{root}}, pk, \phi, sk, usk, cred)$ : Parse $pk_{\text{root}} = (pk_{\mathcal{S},\text{root}}, \cdot, \cdot)$, $pk = (\cdot, c, \cdot)$ and $sk = (sk_{\mathcal{S}}, r', usk)$.

1. The prover checks CheckShow$(pp, pk_{\text{root}}, pk, \phi, sk, usk, cred) \overset{!}{=} 1$.
2. The prover parses $cred = (\sigma, mk, \vec{A}, d)$ and computes some $\vec{A}' \in \mathbb{A}^n$ with $\vec{A}' \preceq \vec{A}$ and $\phi(\vec{A}') = 1$.[2]
3. Prover runs $(\sigma', mk') \leftarrow$ Transform$(pp, \vec{m}^{(\vec{A}, usk, pk_{\text{root}})}, \vec{m}^{(\vec{A}', usk, pk_{\text{root}})},$ $\sigma, mk, I)$ with $I = \emptyset$.
4. The prover runs the following black-box zero-knowledge argument of knowledge protocol with the verifier:

$$ZKAK[(usk, r', \sigma', \vec{A}'); \text{Vrfy}_{\mathcal{S}}(pk_{\mathcal{S},\text{root}}, \vec{m}^{(\vec{A}', usk, pk_{\mathcal{S},\text{root}})}, \sigma') = 1$$
$$\wedge \phi(\vec{A}') = 1 \wedge c = \text{Encrypt}_{\mathcal{E}}(pk_{\mathcal{E}}, f(usk); r')]$$

The checker predicates required by Definition 3 are as follows. We denote them as algorithms because in our case the predicates are polynomial-time computable.

CheckPseud$(pp, pk, sk, usk)$ outputs 1 if and only if $pk = (pk_{\mathcal{S}}, c, \gamma)$ and $sk = (sk_{\mathcal{S}}, r', usk)$ such that $c = \text{Encrypt}_{\mathcal{E}}(pk_{\mathcal{E}}, f(usk); r')$ and $\gamma$ is valid signature of knowledge for $NIZK[(usk, r'); c = \text{Encrypt}_{\mathcal{E}}(pk_{\mathcal{E}}, f(usk); r')](pk_{\mathcal{S}}, c)$.

CheckShow$(pp, pk_{\text{root}}, pk, \phi, sk, usk, cred)$ outputs 1 iff CheckPseud$(pp, pk, sk, usk) = 1$, and $pk_{\text{root}} = (pk_{\mathcal{S},\text{root}}, c_{\text{root}}, \gamma_{\text{root}})$, $cred = (\sigma, mk, \vec{A}, d)$ such that $\vec{A} \succeq \phi$, VrfyMk$_{\mathcal{S}}(pk_{\mathcal{S},\text{root}}, \vec{m}^{(\vec{A}, usk, pk_{\text{root}})}, \sigma, mk, I^{(d, \vec{A})}) = 1$, and $\gamma_{\text{root}}$ is a valid signature of knowledge $NIZK[(usk_{\text{root}}, r_{\text{root}}); c_{\text{root}} = \text{Encrypt}_{\mathcal{E}}$ $(pk_{\mathcal{E}}, f(usk_{\text{root}}); r_{\text{root}})](pk_{\mathcal{S},\text{root}}, c_{\text{root}})$

CheckDeleg$(pp, pk_{\text{root}}, usk, cred, \vec{A}^*)$ outputs 1 if and only if $pk_{\text{root}} = (pk_{\mathcal{S},\text{root}}, c_{\text{root}}, \gamma_{\text{root}})$, and $cred = (\sigma, mk, \vec{A}, d)$ such that $\gamma_{\text{root}}$ is a valid signature of knowledge with respect to $NIZK[(usk_{\text{root}}, r_{\text{root}}); c_{\text{root}} = \text{Encrypt}_{\mathcal{E}}(pk_{\mathcal{E}}, f(usk_{\text{root}}); r_{\text{root}})](pk_{\mathcal{S},\text{root}}, c_{\text{root}})$, and $d = 1$, $\vec{A} \succeq \vec{A}^*$, and VrfyMk$_{\mathcal{S}}(pk_{\mathcal{S},\text{root}}, \vec{m}^{(\vec{A}, usk, pk_{\text{root}})}, \sigma, mk, I^{(d, \vec{A})}) = 1$                                       ⬦

Note that parameters for the argument of knowledge, signature of knowledge, and the hash function $\mathcal{H}$ also need to be part of the public parameters $pp$, but we abstract from the details here.

One can instantiate this construction in a type-3 bilinear group setting, i.e. Setup generates a bilinear group $\mathbb{G} = (\mathbb{G}_1, \mathbb{G}_2, \mathbb{G}_T, e, p)$ of prime order $p$. You can use the DMS scheme and its protocol from Sect. 5 for $\mathcal{S}$, and Cramer-Shoup encryption [11] in $\mathbb{G}_1$ for $\mathcal{E}$. Then $M_{\mathcal{S}} = \mathbb{Z}_p$ and $M_{\mathcal{E}} = \mathbb{G}_1$, so the bijective one-way function $\mathcal{OW}$ can simply be $x \mapsto g^x$. In this setting, the statements in the zero-knowledge arguments of knowledge fall into the *prove knowledge of exponents* category. Hence they can be easily constructed from Schnorr-like $\Sigma$ protocols together with Damgård's technique [12] (using Pedersen's commitment)

---

[2] We assume that the set of valid $\phi$ allows an efficient computation of such an $\vec{A}'$, e.g,. $\phi$ is given in disjunctive normal form, or $n$ is upper-bounded by some constant $n_{\max}$.

to make it concurrent black-box zero-knowledge. To enable arbitrary Boolean formulas for policies $\phi$, one can combine the $\Sigma$ protocol with proofs of partial knowledge [10]. For the signatures of knowledge, you can use Schnorr-like protocols with the Fiat-Shamir heuristic.

**Theorem 16 (Security of the generic construction).** *If $\mathcal{E}$ is correct and CCA-secure, $\mathcal{S}$ is correct (Definition 7), unforgeable (Definition 9) and perfectly derivation private (Definition 8) with secure protocol for deriving a signature on a committed value, $\mathcal{OW}$ is a secure one-way function scheme, and $\mathcal{H}$ is a collision-resistant hash function, then Construction 15 is correct (Definition 3), anonymous (Definition 4), and sound (Definition 5).*

A sketch of the proof can be found in the full version of this paper.

# References

1. Acar, T., Nguyen, L.: Revocation for delegatable anonymous credentials. In: Catalano, D., Fazio, N., Gennaro, R., Nicolosi, A. (eds.) PKC 2011. LNCS, vol. 6571, pp. 423–440. Springer, Heidelberg (2011). https://doi.org/10.1007/978-3-642-19379-8_26
2. Ahn, J.H., Boneh, D., Camenisch, J., Hohenberger, S., Shelat, A., Waters, B.: Computing on authenticated data. J. Cryptol. **28**(2), 351–395 (2015)
3. Attrapadung, N., Libert, B.: Homomorphic network coding signatures in the standard model. In: Catalano, D., Fazio, N., Gennaro, R., Nicolosi, A. (eds.) PKC 2011. LNCS, vol. 6571, pp. 17–34. Springer, Heidelberg (2011). https://doi.org/10.1007/978-3-642-19379-8_2
4. Belenkiy, M., Camenisch, J., Chase, M., Kohlweiss, M., Lysyanskaya, A., Shacham, H.: Randomizable proofs and delegatable anonymous credentials. In: Halevi, S. (ed.) CRYPTO 2009. LNCS, vol. 5677, pp. 108–125. Springer, Heidelberg (2009). https://doi.org/10.1007/978-3-642-03356-8_7
5. Boneh, D., Freeman, D., Katz, J., Waters, B.: Signing a linear subspace: signature schemes for network coding. In: Jarecki, S., Tsudik, G. (eds.) PKC 2009. LNCS, vol. 5443, pp. 68–87. Springer, Heidelberg (2009). https://doi.org/10.1007/978-3-642-00468-1_5
6. Camenisch, J., Drijvers, M., Dubovitskaya, M.: Practical UC-secure delegatable credentials with attributes and their application to blockchain. In: CCS, pp. 683–699. ACM (2017)
7. Chase, M., Kohlweiss, M., Lysyanskaya, A., Meiklejohn, S.: Malleable signatures: new definitions and delegatable anonymous credentials. In: CSF 2014, pp. 199–213. IEEE (2014)
8. Chase, M., Lysyanskaya, A.: On signatures of knowledge. In: Dwork, C. (ed.) CRYPTO 2006. LNCS, vol. 4117, pp. 78–96. Springer, Heidelberg (2006). https://doi.org/10.1007/11818175_5
9. Chaum, D.: Security without identification: transaction systems to make big brother obsolete. Commun. ACM **28**(10), 1030–1044 (1985)
10. Cramer, R., Damgård, I., Schoenmakers, B.: Proofs of partial knowledge and simplified design of witness hiding protocols. In: Desmedt, Y.G. (ed.) CRYPTO 1994. LNCS, vol. 839, pp. 174–187. Springer, Heidelberg (1994). https://doi.org/10.1007/3-540-48658-5_19

11. Cramer, R., Shoup, V.: A practical public key cryptosystem provably secure against adaptive chosen ciphertext attack. In: Krawczyk, H. (ed.) CRYPTO 1998. LNCS, vol. 1462, pp. 13–25. Springer, Heidelberg (1998). https://doi.org/10.1007/BFb0055717
12. Damgård, I.: Efficient concurrent zero-knowledge in the auxiliary string model. In: Preneel, B. (ed.) EUROCRYPT 2000. LNCS, vol. 1807, pp. 418–430. Springer, Heidelberg (2000). https://doi.org/10.1007/3-540-45539-6_30
13. Freeman, D.M.: Improved security for linearly homomorphic signatures: a generic framework. In: Fischlin, M., Buchmann, J., Manulis, M. (eds.) PKC 2012. LNCS, vol. 7293, pp. 697–714. Springer, Heidelberg (2012). https://doi.org/10.1007/978-3-642-30057-8_41
14. Fuchsbauer, G.: Commuting signatures and verifiable encryption and an application to non-interactively delegatable credentials. IACR Cryptology ePrint Archive 2010/233 (2010). http://eprint.iacr.org/2010/233
15. Lysyanskaya, A.: Signature schemes and applications to cryptographic protocol design. Ph.D. thesis, Massachusetts Institute of Technology (2002). http://groups.csail.mit.edu/cis/theses/anna-phd.pdf
16. Pedersen, T.P.: Non-interactive and information-theoretic secure verifiable secret sharing. In: Feigenbaum, J. (ed.) CRYPTO 1991. LNCS, vol. 576, pp. 129–140. Springer, Heidelberg (1992). https://doi.org/10.1007/3-540-46766-1_9
17. Pointcheval, D., Sanders, O.: Short randomizable signatures. In: Sako, K. (ed.) CT-RSA 2016. LNCS, vol. 9610, pp. 111–126. Springer, Cham (2016). https://doi.org/10.1007/978-3-319-29485-8_7

# Privacy Preserving Computation

# Privacy-Preserving Ridge Regression with only Linearly-Homomorphic Encryption

Irene Giacomelli[1]([✉]), Somesh Jha[1], Marc Joye[2], C. David Page[1], and Kyonghwan Yoon[1]

[1] University of Wisconsin-Madison, Madison, WI, USA
irene.giacomelli29@gmail.com
[2] NXP Semiconductors, San Jose, CA, USA

**Abstract.** Linear regression with 2-norm regularization (*i.e.,* ridge regression) is an important statistical technique that models the relationship between some explanatory values and an outcome value using a linear function. In many applications (*e.g.,* predictive modeling in personalized health-care), these values represent sensitive data owned by several different parties who are unwilling to share them. In this setting, training a linear regression model becomes challenging and needs specific cryptographic solutions. This problem was elegantly addressed by Nikolaenko *et al.* in S&P (Oakland) 2013. They suggested a two-server system that uses linearly-homomorphic encryption (LHE) and Yao's two-party protocol (garbled circuits). In this work, we propose a novel system that can train a ridge linear regression model using only LHE (*i.e.,* without using Yao's protocol). This greatly improves the overall performance (both in computation and communication) as Yao's protocol was the main bottleneck in the previous solution. The efficiency of the proposed system is validated both on synthetically-generated and real-world datasets.

**Keywords:** Ridge regression · Linear regression · Privacy
Homomorphic encryption

## 1 Introduction

Linear regression is an important statistical tool that models the relationship between some explanatory values (features) and an outcome value using a linear function. Despite its simple definition, a linear regression model is very useful. Indeed, it can be used to quantitatively relate the features and the outcome (*e.g.,* identify which features influence more directly the outcome) and for future prediction (*e.g.,* if a new vector of features with no known outcome is given, the model can be used to make a prediction about it). *Ridge regression* is one of the most widely-used forms of regression; see the survey in [21]. It lessens the overfitting of ordinary least squares regression without adding computational cost. In practice, this is achieved giving preference to models with small Euclidean norm. To enhance the efficacy of the learned model, prior experience in model

© Springer International Publishing AG, part of Springer Nature 2018
B. Preneel and F. Vercauteren (Eds.): ACNS 2018, LNCS 10892, pp. 243–261, 2018.
https://doi.org/10.1007/978-3-319-93387-0_13

training suggests using training data from a large and diverse set. Indeed, it is known that having more data (more relevant features and/or more data points) typically improves the ability to learn a reliable model. A simple way to obtain such training dataset is to merge data contained in "data silos" collected by different entities. However, in many applications (*e.g.*, personalized medicine [28]) the data points encode *sensitive* information and are collected by possibly mutually distrustful entities. Often, these entities will not (or cannot) share the private data contained in their silos, making collaborative analysis on joint data impossible.

Consider the following example: We would like to use a given linear regression method in order to predict the weight of a baby at birth on the basis of some ultrasound measurements made during the last month of pregnancy (*e.g.*, head circumference, femur length,...). On one hand, in order to avoid computing a biased model, we would like to run the selected learning algorithm on data points collected in different hospitals in various locations. On the other hand, each hospital legally cannot share (in the clear) patients' sensitive data (the measurements) with other hospitals or with a third party (*e.g.*, a cloud-computing server). This real-life case exemplifies the challenge on which we focus on: *training a linear regression model on joint data that must be kept confidential and/or are owned by multiple parties.* Moreover, we want to run such collaborative analysis without exposing an entity's sensitive data to any other party in the system (*i.e.*, no entity in the system is trusted to handle the data in the clear).

Our paper takes up the above challenge and proposes an efficient solution in the *two-server model* [16], commonly used by previous works on privacy-preserving machine learning (*e.g.*, see [12,22,23]), where no party needs to be trusted to handle the data in the clear. In this setting, the computation of the model from the merged data is outsourced to two *non-colluding* (but not necessarily trusted) third-parties. After a first phase of collecting private data *in encrypted form* from possibly many data-owners, the two third parties then engage in a second phase for the computation of the model itself. The system is designed in such a way that no extra information (beside that released by the model itself) is revealed to these two parties if they do not collude (condition that can, for example, be enforced by law). Our solution is based only on a simple cryptographic primitive that can be implemented via efficient constructions. Indeed, our system is designed using just a *linearly-homomorphic encryption* (LHE) scheme, that is, an encryption scheme that enables computing the sum of encrypted messages. Previous solutions to the problem considered here are based on multi-party computation protocols (*e.g.*, secret-sharing based protocols like BGW [6] or the 2-party protocol by Yao [29]) or on somewhat-homomorphic encryption (*i.e.*, encryption schemes that support a limited number of arithmetic operations on encrypted messages). A hybrid approach that uses both homomorphic encryption and Yao's scheme was presented in [23]. In this work, *we present the first approach to privacy-preserving ridge regression that uses only linearly-homomorphic encryption.* We believe that this result is interesting both from the theoretical and the practical points of view. Indeed our system can be seen as a new black-box application of LHE and shows that this basic crypto-primitive can be used alone to handle involved tasks (*i.e.,* ridge regression over distributed data). Furthermore, our system achieves practical performances when implemented using a standard encryption scheme like Paillier's cipher [24]. We show this via an evaluation of our system that uses synthetically-generated and real-world data. Overall, our experiments demonstrate that, for many real scenarios, LHE is all you need to *privately* yet efficiently train a ridge regression model on *distributed* data. As an illustrative example, consider the following existing medical scenario: the *Warfarin dosing model*. Warfarin is a popular anticoagulant for which the International Warfarin Pharmacogenetics Consortium proposed an accurate dosing model trained using linear regression on a medical database that was the merge of the data silos collected by 21 research groups. Using a commodity machine, our system can compute the same model in less than 3 min with the guarantee of confidentiality for the data silos of each research group involved.

*Related Work.* The question of privacy-preserving machine learning was introduced in 2000 by two pioneering works [1, 20]. Later on, privacy-preserving linear regression was considered in a number of different works (*e.g.,* [2,8,10,15,17–19,25]). In 2013, Nikolaenko *et al.* [23] introduced the scenario we consider in this paper: privacy-preserving linear regression protocol in the two-server model. The solution in [23] considers ridge regression on a *horizontally-partitioned* dataset in which each party has some of the data points that form the training set (*e.g.,* two or more hospitals, each of which collects the same medical data on different sets of patients). Their solution is based on LHE and Yao's protocol. The latter is a two-party protocol that allows the evaluation of a circuit $C$ on a pair of inputs $(a, b)$ such that one party knows only $a$ and the other party knows only $b$. At the end of the protocol, the value $C(a, b)$ is revealed but no party learns extra information beyond what is revealed by this value. In [23], the ridge regression model is computed using Yao's protocol to compute the solution of a linear system of the form $A\boldsymbol{w} = \boldsymbol{b}$ where the entries of matrix $A$ and vector $\boldsymbol{b}$ are encrypted (and must be kept private). The solution $\boldsymbol{w}^*$ is the model. The circuit $C$ is the one that solves a linear system computing the Cholesky decomposition of the coefficient matrix. Recently, in [12], the system presented in [23] was extended to *vertically-partitioned* datasets in which the features in the training dataset are distributed among different parties (*e.g.,* two or more hospitals, each of which collects different medical data on the same set of patients). Gascón *et al.* [12] achieve this result using multiparty-computation techniques to allow the data-owners to distribute shares of the merged datasets to the two parties active in the second phase. Moreover, Gascón *et al.* also improve the running time of the second phase of the protocol presented in [23] by designing a new conjugate gradient descent algorithm that is used as circuit $C$ in the place of Cholesky decomposition. This approach was subsequently further improved by Mohassel and Zhang [22] using mini-batch stochastic gradient descent, and extended to logistic regression and neural networks on arbitrarily partitioned datasets.

*Our Contribution.* Our paper follows this line of work and presents a novel system for ridge regression in the two-server model. For the first phase, we extend the approach used by Nikolaenko *et al.* to datasets that are arbitrarily partitioned using the techniques of labeled-homomorphic encryption [4] to support multiplications among pairs of ciphertexts encrypted via an LHE scheme. In this way we show that a solution based only on LHE can handle scenarios more complicated than the horizontally-partitioned case. For the second phase, we avoid Yao's protocol by designing an ad-hoc two-party protocol that solves $A\boldsymbol{w} = \boldsymbol{b}$ using only the linear homomorphic property of the underlying encryption scheme. This allows to boost the overall performance and, in particular, to considerably reduce the communication overhead.[1] As a highlight, if we horizontally partition (into ten equal-sized parts) a dataset of 10 millions instances and 20 features, our privacy-preserving regression method runs in under 2 min[2] and produces a communication overhead of 1.3 MB. The system presented in [23] needs more than 50 min and 270 MB exchanged data to perform a similar computation.[3] Finally, we notice that gradient descent based solutions (*e.g.*, [12,22]) use iterative algorithms and present the problem of estimating the number of iterations $t$. Either $t$ is fixed to a high value that ensures finding a good approximation of the model, which incurs higher complexity for the protocol; either $t$ is chosen adaptively based on the dataset, which can be infeasible in the privacy-preserving setting. Our solution for solving $A\boldsymbol{w} = \boldsymbol{b}$ does not present this problem.

## 2   Background

**Linear Regression.** A linear regression learning algorithm is a procedure that on input $n$ points $\{(\boldsymbol{x}_1, y_1), \ldots, (\boldsymbol{x}_n, y_n)\}$ (where $\boldsymbol{x}_i \in \mathbb{R}^d$ and $y_i \in \mathbb{R}$) outputs a vector $\boldsymbol{w}^* \in \mathbb{R}^d$ such that $\boldsymbol{w}^{*\mathsf{T}} \boldsymbol{x}_i \approx y_i$ for all $i = 1, \ldots, n$. One common way to compute such a model $\boldsymbol{w}^*$ is to use the squared-loss function and the associated empirical error function (mean squared error): $f_{X,y}(\boldsymbol{w}) = \|X\boldsymbol{w} - \boldsymbol{y}\|_2^2$. Here $X \in \mathbb{R}^{n \times d}$ is the matrix with the vector $\boldsymbol{x}_i^\mathsf{T}$ as $i^{\text{th}}$ row and $\boldsymbol{y} \in \mathbb{R}^n$ is the vector with the value $y_i$ as $i^{\text{th}}$ component. We assume that $X$ is always full-rank (*i.e.*, $\text{rk}(X) = d$). Specifically, $\boldsymbol{w}^*$ is computed by minimizing a linear combination of the aforementioned error function and a regularization term, that is, $\boldsymbol{w}^* \in \text{argmin}_{\boldsymbol{w} \in \mathbb{R}^d} f_{X,y}(\boldsymbol{w}) + \lambda R(\boldsymbol{w})$ where $\lambda \geq 0$ is fixed. The regularization term is added to avoid over-fitting the training dataset and to bias toward simpler models. In practice, one of the most common regularization terms is the 2-norm ($R(\boldsymbol{w}) = \|\boldsymbol{w}\|_2^2$), which generates a model with overall smaller components. In this case (called *ridge regression*), the model $\boldsymbol{w}^*$ is computed by minimizing the function $F_{\text{ridge}}(\boldsymbol{w}) = \|X\boldsymbol{w} - \boldsymbol{y}\|_2^2 + \lambda \|\boldsymbol{w}\|_2^2$. Since, $\nabla F_{\text{ridge}}(\boldsymbol{w}) = 2X^\mathsf{T}(X\boldsymbol{w} - \boldsymbol{y}) + 2\lambda\boldsymbol{w}$, we have that $\boldsymbol{w}^*$ is computed solving the linear system

$$A\boldsymbol{w} = \boldsymbol{b} \qquad (1)$$

---

[1] Size of the messages exchanged among the parties running the system.
[2] Timing on a 2.6 GHz 8 GB RAM machine running Linux 16.04; 80-bit security.
[3] Timing on a 1.9 GHz 64 GB RAM machine running Linux 12.04; 80-bit security.

where $A = X^\mathsf{T}X + \lambda I$ (symmetric $d \times d$ matrix) and $\boldsymbol{b} = X^\mathsf{T}\boldsymbol{y}$ (vector of $d$ components). Notice that since $X$ is full-rank, $A$ is positive definite and therefore $\det(A) > 0$ (in particular $A$ is invertible).

**Cryptographic Tools.** To design our privacy-preserving system, we utilize homomorphic encryption. Let $(\mathcal{M}, +)$ be a finite group. A *linearly-homomorphic encryption* (LHE) scheme for messages in $\mathcal{M}$ is defined by three algorithms:

1. The key-generation algorithm Gen takes as input the security parameter $\kappa$ and outputs a matching pair of secret and public keys, $(sk, pk) \leftarrow \mathsf{Gen}(\kappa)$.
2. The encryption algorithm Enc is a randomized algorithm that uses the public key $pk$ to transform a message $m$ from $\mathcal{M}$ (plaintext space) into a ciphertext, $c \leftarrow \mathsf{Enc}_{pk}(m)$.
3. The decryption algorithm Dec is a deterministic function that uses the secret key $sk$ to recover the original plaintext from a ciphertext $c$.

The standard security property (semantic security) says that it is infeasible for any computationally bounded algorithm to gain extra information about a plaintext when given only its ciphertext and the public key $pk$. Moreover, we have the homomorphic property: Let $\mathcal{C}$ be the set of all possible ciphertexts, then there exists an operation $\odot$ on $\mathcal{C}$ such that for any $a$-tuple of ciphertexts $c_1 \leftarrow \mathsf{Enc}_{pk}(m_1), \ldots, c_a \leftarrow \mathsf{Enc}_{pk}(m_a)$ ($a$ positive integer), it holds that $\Pr[\mathsf{Dec}_{sk}(c_1 \odot \cdots \odot c_a) = m_1 + \cdots + m_a] = 1$. This implies that, if $c = \mathsf{Enc}_{pk}(m)$, $\mathsf{Dec}_{sk}(\mathsf{cMult}(a, c)) = am$, where $\mathsf{cMult}(a, c) = c \odot \cdots \odot c$ ($a$ times).

In some cases being able to perform only linear operations on encrypted messages is not sufficient. For example, when considering arbitrarily partitioned datasets, we will need to be able to compute the encryption of the product of *two* messages given the encryptions of the individual messages. An LHE scheme cannot directly handle such an operation. On the other hand, a general solution to the problem of computing on encrypted data can be obtained via the use of fully-homomorphic encryption [13]. Since full fledged constructions of fully-homomorphic encryption are still inefficient, more efficient solutions have been designed for evaluating low-degree polynomials over encrypted data functionalities (somewhat-homomorphic encryption). In a recent work, Barbosa *et al.* [4] introduce the concept of *labeled-homomorphic encryption* (labHE); this new primitive significantly accelerates homomorphic computation over encrypted data when the function that is being computed is known to the party that decrypts the result. Since in this paper we consider that the machine-learning algorithm and the data distribution among the participants is publicly known, the previous assumption is satisfied and we can make use of labHE. In particular, Barbosa *et al.* show how to design an homomorphic encryption scheme that supports the evaluation of degree-two polynomials using only an LHE and a pseudo-random function. The new scheme is public-key and works in the multi-user setting: two or more users encrypt different messages, an encryption of the evaluation of a degree-two polynomial on these messages can be constructed by any party having access to the public key and the ciphertexts. Then the party holding the secret key can decrypt and reveal the result of the evaluation (the polynomial is public, the correspondence user-ciphertext is known). We briefly recall here their construction [4, Sect. 5] in the case that the polynomial is evaluated on messages encrypted only by two different users.

Let $(\mathsf{Gen}, \mathsf{Enc}, \mathsf{Dec})$ be an LHE scheme with security parameter $\kappa$ and message space $\mathcal{M}$. Assume that a multiplication operation is given in $\mathcal{M}$; i.e., $(\mathcal{M}, +, \cdot)$ is a finite ring. Let also $F \colon \{0, 1\}^s \times \mathcal{L} \to \mathcal{M}$ be a pseudo-random function with seed space $\{0, 1\}^s$ $(s = \mathrm{poly}(\kappa))$ and label space $\mathcal{L}$. Define:

- $\mathsf{labGen}(\kappa)$: On input $\kappa$, it runs $\mathsf{Gen}(\kappa)$ and outputs $(sk, pk)$.
- $\mathsf{localGen}(pk)$: For each user $i$ and with the public key as input, it samples a random seed $\sigma_i$ in $\{0, 1\}^s$ and computes $pk_i = \mathsf{Enc}_{pk}(\underline{\sigma_i})$ where $\underline{\sigma_i}$ is an encoding of $\sigma_i$ as an element of $\mathcal{M}$. It outputs $(\sigma_i, pk_i)$.
- $\mathsf{labEnc}_{pk}(\sigma_i, m, \tau)$: On input a message $m \in \mathcal{M}$ with label $\tau \in \mathcal{L}$ from the user $i$, it computes $b = F(\sigma_i, \tau)$ and outputs the labeled ciphertext $\boldsymbol{c} = (a, c) \in \mathcal{M} \times \mathcal{C}$ with $a = m - b$ in $\mathcal{M}$ and $c = \mathsf{Enc}_{pk}(b)$.
- $\mathsf{labMult}(\boldsymbol{c}, \boldsymbol{c}')$: On input two labeled ciphertexts, $\boldsymbol{c} = (a, c)$ and $\boldsymbol{c}' = (a', c')$, it computes a "multiplication" ciphertext $d = \mathsf{labMult}(\boldsymbol{c}, \boldsymbol{c}')$ as $d = \mathsf{Enc}_{pk}(a \cdot a') \odot \mathsf{cMult}(a, c') \odot \mathsf{cMult}(a', c)$.

  Observe that $\mathsf{Dec}_{sk}(d) = m \cdot m' - b \cdot b'$. Moreover, notice that given two or more multiplication ciphertexts $d_1, \ldots, d_n$, they can be "added" using the operation of the underlying LHE scheme: $d_1 \odot \cdots \odot d_n$. Assume that user $i$ and user $j$ have both encrypted $n$ messages, $m_1, \ldots, m_n$ and $m'_1, \ldots, m'_n$, respectively. Let $\tilde{c} \in \mathcal{C}$ be the ciphertext obtained as

$$\bigodot_{t=1}^{n} \mathsf{labMult}\big(\mathsf{labEnc}_{pk}(\sigma_i, m_t, \tau_t), \mathsf{labEnc}_{pk}(\sigma_j, m'_t, \tau'_t)\big).$$

- $\mathsf{labDec}_{sk}(pk_i, pk_j, \tilde{c})$: On input $\tilde{c}$, it first recovers $\sigma_i$ and $\sigma_j$ from $\mathsf{Dec}_{sk}(pk_i)$ and $\mathsf{Dec}_{sk}(pk_j)$. Next, it computes $b_t = F(\sigma_i, \tau_t)$ and $b'_t = F(\sigma_j, \tau'_t)$ for all $t = 1, \ldots, n$. Finally, it computes $\tilde{b} = \sum_{t=1}^{n} b_t \cdot b'_t$ and $\tilde{m} = \mathsf{Dec}_{sk}(\tilde{c}) - \tilde{b}$. It is easy to verify that $\tilde{m} = \sum_{t=1}^{n} m_t \cdot m'_t$.

**Data Representation.** In order to use the cryptographic tools described in the former section, we need to represent the real values that form the input datasets as elements in the finite set $\mathcal{M}$ (the message space). Without loss of generality, we assume that $\mathcal{M} = \mathbb{Z}_N$ for some big integer $N$ and that the entries of $X$ and $\boldsymbol{y}$ are numbers from the real interval $[-\delta, \delta]$ (with $\delta > 0$)[4] with at most $\ell$ digits in their fractional part. In this case, the conversion from real values to elements in $\mathcal{M}$ can be easily done by rescaling all the entries of $X$ and $\boldsymbol{y}$ and then mapping the integers in $\mathbb{Z}_N$ using the modular operation. For this reason, from now on we consider that the entries of $X$ and $\boldsymbol{y}$ are integers from 0 to $N - 1$. This implies that we consider the matrix $A$ and the vector $\boldsymbol{b}$ having positive integer entries[5]

---

[4] In other words, $\delta = \max\{\|X\|_\infty, \|\boldsymbol{y}\|_\infty\}$ for the original $X$ and $\boldsymbol{y}$.
[5] We assume that $\lambda \in \mathbb{R}$ has at most $2\ell$ digits in the fractional part.

and, finally, that we assume that the model $\boldsymbol{w}^*$ is a vector in $\mathbb{Q}^d$. Notice that for the integer representation of $A$ and $\boldsymbol{b}$ it holds that $\|A\|_\infty, \|\boldsymbol{b}\|_\infty \leq 10^{2\ell}(n\delta^2 + \lambda)$. Therefore, if $10^{2\ell}(n\delta^2 + \lambda) \leq \frac{N-1}{2}$, then $A$ and $\boldsymbol{b}$ are embedded in $\mathbb{Z}_N$ without overflow for their entries. However, if the linear system (1) is now solved over $\mathbb{Z}_N$, then clearly the entries of the solution are given as modular residues of $\mathbb{Z}_N$ and may be different from the entries of the desired model $\boldsymbol{w}^*$ in $\mathbb{Q}^d$. In order to solve this problem and recover the model in $\mathbb{Q}^d$ from the model computed over $\mathbb{Z}_N$, we can apply the *rational reconstruction* technique component-wise. With rational reconstruction [11,27] we mean the application of the Lagrange-Gauss algorithm to recover a rational $t = r/s$ from its representation in $\mathbb{Z}_N$ as $t' = r\,s^{-1} \bmod N$, for $N$ big enough (see (4) in Sect. 4).

## 3   Threat Model and System Overview

We consider the setting where the training dataset is not available in the clear to the entity that wants to train the ridge regression model. Instead, the latter can access encrypted copies of the data and, for this reason, needs the help of the party handling the cryptographic keys in order to learn the desired model. More precisely, protocols in this paper are designed for the following parties:

- The *Data-Owners*: There are $m$ data-owners $DO_1, \ldots, DO_m$; each data-owner $DO_i$ has a private dataset $\mathcal{D}_i$ and is willing to share it only if encrypted.
- The *Machine-Learning Engine* (MLE): This is the party that wants to run a linear regression algorithm on the dataset $\mathcal{D}$ obtained by merging the local datasets $\mathcal{D}_1, \ldots, \mathcal{D}_m$, but has access only to the encrypted copies of them. For this reason, MLE needs the help of the Crypto Service Provider.
- The *Crypto Service Provider* (CSP) takes care of initializing the encryption scheme used in the system and interacts with MLE to help it in achieving its task (computing the linear regression model). CSP manages the cryptographic keys and is the only entity capable of decrypting.

We assume that MLE and CSP do not collude and that all the parties involved are honest-but-curious. That is, they always follow the instructions of the protocol but try to learn extra information about the dataset from the messages received during the execution of the protocol (*i.e., passive security*). Moreover, we assume that for each pair of parties involved in the protocol there exists a private and authenticated peer-to-peer channel. In particular, communications between any two players cannot be eavesdropped.

The goal is to ensure that MLE obtains the model while both MLE and CSP do not learn any other information about the private datasets $\mathcal{D}_i$ beyond what is revealed by the model itself. Even in the case that one of the two servers (MLE or CSP) colludes with some of the data-owners, they should learn no extra information about the data held by the honest data-owners. In order to achieve this goal we design a system that can be seen as multi-party protocol run by the $m + 2$ parties mentioned before and specified by a sequence of steps. This system (described in Sect. 4) has the following two-phase architecture:

**Phase 1 (merging the local datasets):** CSP generates the key pair $(sk, pk)$, stores $sk$ and makes $pk$ public; each $DO_i$ sends to MLE specific ciphertexts computed using $pk$ and the values in $\mathcal{D}_i$. MLE uses the ciphertexts received and the homomorphic property of the underling encryption scheme in order to obtain encryptions of $A$ and $\boldsymbol{b}$ (coefficient matrix and vector in (1)).

**Phase 2 (computing the model):** MLE uses the ciphertexts $\mathsf{Enc}_{pk}(A)$ and $\mathsf{Enc}_{pk}(\boldsymbol{b})$ and private random values in order to obtain encryptions of new values that we call "masked data"; these encryptions are sent to the CSP; the latter decrypts and runs a given algorithm on the masked data. The output of this computation ("masked model") is a vector $\tilde{\boldsymbol{w}}$ that is sent back from the CSP to the MLE. The latter computes the output $\boldsymbol{w}^*$ from $\tilde{\boldsymbol{w}}$.

Informally, we say that the system is *correct* if the model computed by the MLE is equal to the model computed by the learning algorithm in the clear using $\mathcal{D}$ as training data. And we say that the system is *private* if the distribution of the masked data sent by the MLE to the CSP is independent of the distribution of the local inputs. Thus, no information about $\mathcal{D}_1, \ldots, \mathcal{D}_m$ is revealed by the messages exchanged during Phase 2.

As we will see in Sect. 4, the specific design of the protocol realizing Phase 1 depends on the distributed setting: horizontally- or arbitrarily-partitioned datasets. However, in both cases, the data-owners input encryptions of local values and the MLE gets the encryptions of $A$ and $\boldsymbol{b}$. The CSP simply takes care of initializing the cryptographic primitive and generates the relative keys. Phase 2 is realized by an interactive protocol between the MLE and the CSP. CSP takes on input the encryptions of $A$ and $\boldsymbol{b}$ from the MLE and returns the solution of the system $A\boldsymbol{w} = \boldsymbol{b}$ following this pattern (we refer to this as the *"masking trick"*):

- The MLE samples a random invertible matrix[6] $R \in \mathrm{GL}(d, \mathcal{M})$ and a random vector $\boldsymbol{r} \in \mathcal{M}$ and it uses the linear homomorphic property of the underlying encryption scheme to compute $C' = \mathsf{Enc}_{pk}(AR)$ and $\boldsymbol{d}' = \mathsf{Enc}_{pk}(\boldsymbol{b} + A\boldsymbol{r})$. The values $C = AR$ and $\boldsymbol{d} = \boldsymbol{b} + A\boldsymbol{r}$ are the "masked data." We slightly abuse notation here; $\mathsf{Enc}_{pk}(\cdot)$ is applied component-wise in the computation of $C$ and of $\boldsymbol{d}'$.
- The CSP decrypts $C'$ and $\boldsymbol{d}'$ and computes $\tilde{\boldsymbol{w}} = C^{-1}\boldsymbol{d}$. The vector $\tilde{\boldsymbol{w}}$ is the "masked model" sent back to the MLE.
- The MLE computes the desired model as $\boldsymbol{w}^* = R\tilde{\boldsymbol{w}} - \boldsymbol{r}$. Indeed, it is easy to verify that $R\tilde{\boldsymbol{w}} - \boldsymbol{r} = R(AR)^{-1}(\boldsymbol{b} + A\boldsymbol{r}) - \boldsymbol{r} = A^{-1}\boldsymbol{b}$.

Informally, the security of the encryption scheme assures privacy against an honest-but-curious MLE. On the other hand, if $R$ and $\boldsymbol{r}$ are sampled uniformly at random, then the distribution of the masked data is independent of $A$ and $\boldsymbol{b}$. This guarantees privacy against an honest-but-curious CSP. Similar masking tricks have been previously used in different settings. In [3], a similar method is

---

[6] $\mathrm{GL}(d, \mathcal{M})$ denotes the general linear group of degree $d$ over the ring $\mathcal{M}$; namely, the group of $d \times d$ invertible matrices with entries from $\mathcal{M}$.

used to design a secret-shared based MPC protocol for the evaluation of general functions. In this work, we tailor the masking trick for the goal of solving the linear system $A\boldsymbol{w} = \boldsymbol{b}$ gaining in efficiency. In [26], masking with random values is used to outsource a large-scale linear system to an untrusted "cloud server". They assume that the coefficient matrix $A$ and vector $\boldsymbol{b}$ of the linear system are known to a "cloud customer" seeking the solution $\boldsymbol{w}$. In this work, $A$ and $\boldsymbol{b}$ are encrypted and the masking is applied "inside the encryption"; to make the masking trick, which works in $\mathbb{Q}$, compatible with the encryption and the modular arithmetic used for it, we make use of rational reconstruction.[7]

Notice that the two-server model allows for different implementations in practice. If we consider applications in which the majority of data-owners are willing to help to run collaborative analysis but don't want to (or cannot) spend to much resources to execute it, then the role of MLE and CSP can be taken by two semi-trusted[8] third-parties (*e.g.*, two independent research institutions). This setting offers the practical advantage that the involvement of all data-owners is minimal. Otherwise, since CSP and MLE are only required to be non-colluding, their role can be taken by two disjoint subsets of data-owners (*e.g.*, for $m \geq 2$, we can have $DO_1$ and $DO_2$ playing the role of MLE and CSP, respectively). In this case, no third-parties are required to implement the system.

## 4    Protocols Description

In this section we describe how to implement Phase 1 and Phase 2. Let (Gen, Enc, Dec) be an LHE scheme with security parameter $\kappa$ and message space $\mathcal{M} = \mathbb{Z}_N$.

### 4.1    Phase 1: Merging the Dataset

*Horizontally-Partitioned Setting.* Assume that the dataset represented by the matrix $X$ and the vector $\boldsymbol{y}$ is horizontally-partitioned in $m$ datasets. That is, the data-owner $DO_k$ holds

$$\mathcal{D}_k = \left\{ (\boldsymbol{x}_{n_{k-1}+1}, y_{n_{k-1}+1}), \ldots, (\boldsymbol{x}_{n_k}, y_{n_k}) \right\}, \tag{2}$$

for $k = 1, \ldots, m$ $(0 = n_0 < n_1 < \cdots < n_m = n)$. In this case, as already noticed in [23], defining $A_k = \sum_{i=n_{k-1}+1}^{n_k} \boldsymbol{x}_i \boldsymbol{x}_i^{\mathsf{T}}$ and $\boldsymbol{b}_k = \sum_{i=n_{k-1}+1}^{n_k} y_i \boldsymbol{x}_i$, we have that $A = \sum_{k=1}^m A_k + \lambda I$ and $\boldsymbol{b} = \sum_{k=1}^m \boldsymbol{b}_i$. In Protocol $\Pi_{1,\text{hor}}$, each data-owner $DO_k$ computes and sends to MLE encryptions of the entries of $A_k$ and $\boldsymbol{b}_k$; then MLE computes encryptions of the entries of $A$ and $\boldsymbol{b}$ using the above formulas and the operation $\odot$ (details in Protocol 1).

---

[7] Notice that the system presented in [26] fails because no techniques are used to make the arithmetic over $\mathbb{Q}$ compatible with the modular arithmetic used by the underling LHE (*i.e.*, Paillier's scheme). See [7] for more details on this.

[8] That is, trusted to be non-colluding.

**Protocol 1.** $\Pi_{1,\text{hor}}$: Phase 1 in the horizontally-partitioned setting.

---

- *Parties*: CSP, MLE, and $DO_k$ with input $\mathcal{D}_k$ (as defined in (2)) for all $k = 1, \dots, m$.
- *Output*: MLE gets $A'$ and $\boldsymbol{b}'$ (*i.e.*, encryptions of $A$ and $\boldsymbol{b}$, respectively).

*Step 1*: (*key-generation*)   CSP runs $(sk, pk) \leftarrow \mathsf{Gen}(\kappa)$ and makes $pk$ public, while it keeps $sk$ secret.

*Step 2*: (*local computation*)   For all $k = 1, \dots, m$, $DO_k$ computes $A_k = \sum_i \boldsymbol{x}_i \boldsymbol{x}_i^\mathsf{T}$ and $\boldsymbol{b}_k = \sum_i y_i \boldsymbol{x}_i$ with $n_{k-1} + 1 \le i \le n_k$; next, $DO_k$ encrypts them, $A_k'[i,j] = \mathsf{Enc}_{pk}(A_k[i,j])$, $\boldsymbol{b}_k'[i] = \mathsf{Enc}_{pk}(\boldsymbol{b}_k[i])$ for all $i, j = 1, \dots, d$ and $j \ge i$; finally, $DO_k$ sends all $A_k'$ and $\boldsymbol{b}_k'$ to MLE.

*Step 3*: (*datasets merge*)   For all $i, j = 1, \dots, d$ and $j \ge i$, MLE computes

$$
A'[i,j] = \begin{cases} \left(\bigodot_{k=1}^m A_k'[i,i]\right) \odot \mathsf{Enc}_{pk}(\lambda) & \text{if } j = i \\ \bigodot_{k=1}^m A_k'[i,j] & \text{if } j > i \end{cases}, \quad \boldsymbol{b}'[i] = \bigodot_{k=1}^m \boldsymbol{b}_k'[i].
$$

---

*Arbitrarily-Partitioned Setting.*   Assume that each $DO_k$ holds some elements of $X$ and $\boldsymbol{y}$. That is, $DO_k$ holds

$$
\mathcal{D}_k = \left\{ X[i,j] = \boldsymbol{x}_i[j] \mid (i,j) \in D_k \right\} \cup \left\{ \boldsymbol{y}[i] = y_i \mid (i,0) \in D_k \right\}, \tag{3}
$$

where $D_k \subseteq \{1, \dots, n\} \times \{0, 1, \dots, d\}$. Assume that each data-owner sends encryptions of the elements it knows to MLE. Then, in order to compute encryptions of the entries of $A$ and $\boldsymbol{b}$, MLE needs to multiply two ciphertexts. Indeed, we have $\boldsymbol{b}[i] = \sum_{t=1}^n \boldsymbol{x}_t[i] \boldsymbol{y}[t]$ and $A[i,j] = \sum_{t=1}^n \boldsymbol{x}_t[i] \boldsymbol{x}_t[j]$ if $j \ne i$, otherwise $A[i,i] = \sum_{t=1}^n \boldsymbol{x}_t[i] \boldsymbol{x}_t[i] + \lambda$. To allow this, we use labeled-homomorphic encryption. As we recalled in Sect. 2, the latter can be constructed on top of any LHE scheme and it enhances the underlying scheme with the multiplication command $\mathsf{labMult}$. In particular, after having received labeled-encryptions of the input from the data-owners,[9] MLE can compute the encryptions of the entries of $A$ and $\boldsymbol{b}$ using formulas of the form $\bigodot_{t=1}^n \mathsf{labMult}(\mathsf{labEnc}(\boldsymbol{x}_t[i]), \mathsf{labEnc}(\boldsymbol{x}_t[j]))$. Remember that the output of the command $\mathsf{labMult}$ used to compute the encryption of the product of two messages, $m_1$ and $m_2$, is in fact an encryption of $m_1 m_2 - b_1 b_2$ where $b_1, b_2$ are two random values used to compute the labeled-encryptions of the values $m_1$ and $m_2$. For this reason, at the end of the procedure described before, MLE obtains encryptions of $A - B$ and $\boldsymbol{b} - \boldsymbol{c}$, instead of encryption of $A$ and $\boldsymbol{b}$, where $B$ and $\boldsymbol{c}$ depend on the random values used to encrypt the entries of the local datasets using the labeled-homomorphic scheme. The matrix $B$ and the vector $\boldsymbol{c}$ can be reconstructed by the party handling the decryption key (*i.e.*, CSP). The decryption procedure of the labeled-homomorphic scheme, $\mathsf{labDec}$, accounts for this. However, in the application we consider here (training a ridge

---

[9] If $\boldsymbol{x}_t[i]$ and $\boldsymbol{x}_t[j]$ are both held by one $DO_k$, then the former can send $\mathsf{Enc}_{pk}(\boldsymbol{x}_t[i]\boldsymbol{x}_t[j])$ to MLE, who updates the formulas in Step 3 of $\Pi_{1,\text{arb}}$ accordingly.

**Protocol 2.** $\Pi_{1,\mathrm{arb}}$: Phase 1 in the arbitrarily-partitioned setting.

---

– *Parties*: CSP, MLE, and $\mathrm{DO}_k$ with input $\mathcal{D}_k$ (as defined in (3)) for all $k = 1, \ldots, m$.
– *Output*: MLE gets $A'$ and $\boldsymbol{b}'$ (*i.e.*, encryptions of $A$ and $\boldsymbol{b}$, respectively).

*Step 1*: (*key-generation*)  CSP runs $(sk, pk) \leftarrow \mathsf{labGen}(\kappa)$ and makes $pk$ public, while it keeps $sk$ secret. For $k = 1, \ldots, m$, $\mathrm{DO}_k$ runs $(\sigma_k, pk_k) \leftarrow \mathsf{localGen}(pk)$ and makes $pk_k$ public, while it keeps $\sigma_k$ secret.

(*setup*)  For $k = 1, \ldots, m$, CSP recovers $\sigma_k$ from $\mathsf{Dec}_{sk}(pk_k)$ and computes $b_{ij} = F(\sigma_k, (i, j))$ with $(i, j) \in D_k$. For $i, j = 1, \ldots, d$ and $j \geq i$, CSP computes $B'[i, j] = \mathsf{Enc}_{pk}(\sum_{t=1}^{n} b_{ti} b_{tj})$ and $\boldsymbol{c}'[i] = \mathsf{Enc}_{pk}(\sum_{t=1}^{n} b_{ti} b_{t0})$. These are sent to MLE.

*Step 2*: (*local computation*)  For $k = 1, \ldots, m$, $\mathrm{DO}_k$ computes labeled-encryptions of the known entries of $X$ and $\boldsymbol{y}$. That is, for all $(i, j) \in D_k$, $\mathrm{DO}_k$ computes $c_{ij} = (a_{ij}, c_{ij}) = \mathsf{labEnc}_{pk}(\sigma_k, \boldsymbol{x}_i[j], (i, j))$ when $j > 0$ and $c_{i0} = (a_{i0}, c_{i0}) = \mathsf{labEnc}_{pk}(\sigma_k, \boldsymbol{y}[i], (i, 0))$.

For all $k = 1, \ldots, m$, $\mathrm{DO}_k$ sends all labeled-ciphertexts $c_{ij}$ to MLE.

*Step 3*: (*datasets merge*)  For all $i, j = 1, \ldots, d$ and $j \geq i$, MLE computes

$$A'[i, j] = \begin{cases} \left( \bigodot_{t=1}^{n} \mathsf{labMult}(c_{ti}, c_{ti}) \right) \odot B'[i, i] \odot \mathsf{Enc}_{pk}(\lambda) & \text{if } j = i \\ \left( \bigodot_{t=1}^{n} \mathsf{labMult}(c_{ti}, c_{tj}) \right) \odot B'[i, j] & \text{if } j > i \end{cases},$$

$$\boldsymbol{b}'[i] = \left( \bigodot_{t=1}^{n} \mathsf{labMult}(c_{ti}, c_{t0}) \right) \odot \boldsymbol{c}'[i].$$

---

regression model) it is necessary that at the end of Phase 1 the MLE has proper encryptions for $A$ and $\boldsymbol{b}$. Indeed, only in this case we can proceed to Phase 2 and use the masking trick (using the masking trick with labeled-encryptions of $A$ and $\boldsymbol{b}$ doesn't work). For this reason, we need to add one round of communication where CSP sends to MLE encryptions of the entries of $B$ and $\boldsymbol{c}$. This can be done before the beginning of the actual computation (Step 1 of Phase 1) since $B$ and $\boldsymbol{c}$ do not depend on the actual data used to train the regression model. In this way, the MLE can finally gets encryptions of $A$ and $\boldsymbol{b}$. Protocol $\Pi_{1,\mathrm{arb}}$ in Protocol 2 describes this in detail.

## 4.2   Phase 2: Computing the Model

At the end of Phase 1, MLE knows component-wise encryption of the matrix $A$ and the vector $\boldsymbol{b}$ (both with entries represented in $\mathbb{Z}_N$, the message space of the LHE scheme used in Phase 1). Recall that the final goal of our system is computing $\boldsymbol{w}^* \in \mathbb{Q}^d$ solution of (1). In order to do this in a privacy-preserving manner, in Phase 2 we implement the masking trick described in Sect. 3 and compute $\tilde{\boldsymbol{w}}^*$ that solves (1) in $\mathbb{Z}_N$. Then we use rational reconstruction to find $\boldsymbol{w}^*$. All the details of this are reported in Protocol $\Pi_2$ (Protocol 3). The correctness is easy to

**Protocol 3.** $\Pi_2$: Phase 2.

---

- *Parties*: CSP knows $sk$, MLE knows $A' = \mathsf{Enc}_{pk}(A)$ and $b' = \mathsf{Enc}_{pk}(b)$.
- *Output*: MLE gets $w^*$.

*Step 1*: (*data masking*)  MLE samples $R \leftarrow \mathrm{GL}(d, \mathbb{Z}_N)$ and $r \leftarrow \mathbb{Z}_N^d$ and computes

$$C'[i,j] = \bigodot_{k=1}^d \mathsf{cMult}(R[k,j], A'[i,k])$$
$$d'[i] = b'[i] \odot \left( \bigodot_{k=1}^d \mathsf{cMult}(r[k], A'[i,k]) \right)$$

for all $i, j = 1, \ldots, d$; next, MLE sends $C'$ and $d'$ to CSP.

*Step 2*: (*masked model computation*)  CSP first decrypts $C'$ and $d'$ obtaining $C$ and $d$ ($C[i,j] = \mathsf{Dec}_{sk}(C'[i,j])$, $d[i] = \mathsf{Dec}_{sk}(d'[i])$ for all $i, j = 1, \ldots, d$); then it computes $\tilde{w} \equiv C^{-1}d \bmod N$ and sends it $\tilde{w}$ to MLE.

*Step 3*: (*model reconstruction*)  MLE computes $\tilde{w}^* \equiv R\tilde{w} - r \bmod N$ and uses rational reconstruction on each component of $\tilde{w}^*$ to compute $w^* \in \mathbb{Q}^d$.

---

verify, indeed we have $R\tilde{w} - r \equiv R(AR)^{-1}(b + Ar) - r \equiv A^{-1}b \pmod{N}$. Security is also straightforward: Protocol $\Pi_2$ is secure against a honest-but-curious CSP because the values seen by it (the masked data $AR \bmod N$ and $b + Ar$ $\bmod N$) have a distribution that is unrelated with the input datasets. Moreover, Protocol $\Pi_2$ is secure against a honest-but-curious MLE because of the security of the underlying encryption scheme. Indeed, the MLE sees only an encrypted version of $A$ and $b$. See [14, Appendix A.6] for the formal security proof.

In some applications, a desirable property is that the model is delivered only to the data-owners. If the role of MLE and CSP is taken by third-parties, this can be achieved using a standard tool like threshold encryption [9]. In this case, the key generation step of Phase 1 is enhanced with the sharing of $sk$ (*i.e.*, CSP knows $sk$ and each $DO_i$ knows a share for $sk$). Then, Step 2 of Protocol $\Pi_2$ is modified in such a way that CSP sends to MLE the value $\mathsf{Enc}_{pk}(\tilde{w})$, instead of the vector $\tilde{w}$ in the clear. MLE computes $\mathsf{Enc}_{pk}(\tilde{w}^*)$ and broadcasts it to all data-owners. Finally, the $DO_i$ collaborates to jointly decrypt and compute $w^*$.

**Choice of Parameters.** In the last step of $\Pi_2$ we use rational reconstruction to recover the components of $w^* \in \mathbb{Q}^d$ from the solution of $Aw = b$ computed in $\mathbb{Z}_N$. According to [11,27] if a rational $t = r/s$ with $-R \leq r \leq R$, $0 < s \leq S$ and $\gcd(s, N) = 1$ is represented as $t' = rs^{-1} \bmod N$ in $\mathbb{Z}_N$, then the Lagrange-Gauss algorithm uniquely recovers $r$ and $s$ provided that $2RS < N$. Since $w^* = A^{-1}b = \frac{1}{\det(A)} \mathrm{adj}(A)b \in \mathbb{Q}^d$, in order to choose $N$ that satisfies the condition stated before, we need to bound the $\det(A)$ and the entries of the vector $\mathrm{adj}(A)b$. Let $\alpha = \max\{\|A\|_\infty, \|b\|_\infty\}$, using the Hadamard's inequality, we have that $0 < \det(A) \leq \alpha^d$ ($A$ is a positive definite matrix) and $\|\mathrm{adj}(A)b\|_\infty \leq d(d-1)^{\frac{d-1}{2}}\alpha^d$.

Using the same assumptions of Sect. 2 on the entries of $X$ and $y$ (that is, the entries of $X$ and $y$ are real number in $[-\delta, \delta]$ with at most $\ell$ digits in the fractional part), we have that $\alpha \leq 10^{2\ell}(n\delta^2 + \lambda)$. It follows that the condition $2RS < N$ is fulfilled when

$$2d(d-1)^{\frac{d-1}{2}} 10^{4\ell d} (n\delta^2 + \lambda)^{2d} < N. \tag{4}$$

**Communication Complexity.** The messages sent during Protocol $\Pi_{1,\text{hor}}$ and Protocol $\Pi_2$ contain $\Theta(d^2)$ elements from $\mathbb{Z}_N$, while the ones in Protocol $\Pi_{1,\text{arb}}$ contain $\Theta(dn)$ elements. This implies a communication cost of $O(d^3 \log(nd))$ bits for $\Pi_{1,\text{hor}}$ and $\Pi_2$, and of $O((nd^2 + d^3)\log(nd))$ bits for $\Pi_{1,\text{arb}}$ (details in [14, Appendix A.3]). In particular, our approach significantly improves the communication complexity compared to the previous solutions that use Yao's scheme [12, 23]. Indeed, the latter requires CSP send-

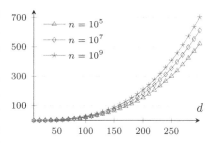

**Fig. 1.** Communication overhead in MB of $\Pi_2$ ($\delta = 1$, 80-bit security, $\ell = 3$, Paillier's scheme, $\lambda = 0$).

ing the garbled representation of a boolean circuit of millions of gates (see [23, Fig. 5] and [12, Fig. 7]) to MLE. In [23] the authors show that the garbled representation of one gate is a lookup table of around 30 bytes (80-bit security). This means that a privacy-preserving system based on Yao's scheme, only for sending the garbled circuit and without considering the other steps needs at least hundreds of megabytes. On the other hand, even for large values of $n$ and $d$, the communication complexity of $\Pi_2$ is much smaller than 100 MB (see Fig. 1). For example, in the horizontally-partitioned setting [23] uses same techniques we deploy in $\Pi_{1,\text{hor}}$ and Yao's protocol. In particular, [23] reports that the garbled representation of the circuit that solves (1) with $d = 20$ using Cholesky decomposition (24-bit integer representation) has size 270 MB. On the other hand, for a dataset with 10 millions instances and $d = 20$, the *overall* overhead[10] of $\Pi_{1,\text{hor}} + \Pi_2$ is less than 1.3 MB. In the arbitrarily-partitioned setting, the communication overheard of our system is dominated by the cost of Phase 1 (Protocol $\Pi_{1,\text{arb}}$) because of its linear dependency on the number of instances $n$. However, this seems to be the case also in other approaches. For example, in [12], a secure inner-product protocol based on additive secret-sharing and Beaver's triples [5] is used to compute the inner product of the columns of the matrix $X$ vertically-partitioned among two or more users. The complexity of this approach for Phase 1 is $\Theta(nd^2 \log(n))$ bits (comparable with the complexity of $\Pi_{1,\text{arb}}$). In Phase 2, [12] use Yao's protocol and conjugate gradient descent (CGD) algorithm to solve (1). They do not report the concrete size of the circuit, but they show the number of gates. For $d = 100$ and 5 iterations of the CGD, more than $10^8$ gates are used: this gives an overhead of at least 3 GB only for sending the garbled

---

[10] In this section, for our system we assume $\ell = 3$ and Paillier's scheme with 80-bit security as underlying LHE.

circuit during Phase 2 (assuming a garbled gate is 30 bytes). On the other hand, the *overall* overhead of $\Pi_{1,\mathrm{arb}} + \Pi_2$ when $d = 100$ for a dataset of 5 thousands instances is less than 1.3 GB.

The SecureML paper [22] uses only additive secret-sharing and Beaver's triples to design a system that assumes an arbitrary partitioning of the dataset. When the pre-processing needed for the triples is implemented via LHE, the linear regression training system proposed in [22] has complexity $\Theta(nd + n)$. Thus, in terms of communication complexity, [22] performs better than our solution in the arbitrarily-partitioned case. Our system, however, is preferable if the training dataset is horizontally-partitioned and $n \gg d$ (*e.g.*, $n = \Theta(d^{2.5})$). For example, if $d = 100$ and $n = 10^5$ the system in [22] has an overheard of 200 MB for the pre-processing phase only (see [22, Table II]), while the total cost of $\Pi_{1,\mathrm{hor}} + \Pi_2$ is less than 120 MB.

## 5    Implementation

In this section we describe our implementation case study of the system described in Sect. 4. Our goal is to evaluate the effect of the public parameters on the system's accuracy and efficiency, and to test our system on real-world datasets. In particular, the experiments we run are designed to answer the following questions:

1. *Evaluating accuracy*: How does the system parameter $\ell$ (number of digits in the fractional part of the input data) influence the accuracy of the output model $\boldsymbol{w}^*$? Recall that we assume that the values in $X$ and $\boldsymbol{y}$ are real number with at most $\ell$ digits in the fractional part. In practice, this means that each user must truncate all the entries in the local dataset after the $\ell^{\mathrm{th}}$ digit in the fractional part. This is done before inputting the values in the privacy-preserving system. On the other hand, in the standard machine learning-setting this requirement is not necessary, and the model is computed using floating point arithmetic on values with more than $\ell$ digits in the fractional part. For this reason, the model $\boldsymbol{w}^*$, which is trained using our privacy-preserving system, can differ from the model $\bar{\boldsymbol{w}}^*$ learned in the clear (same regularization parameter $\lambda$ is used). To evaluate this difference we use

$$R_{\mathrm{MSE}} = \left| \frac{\mathrm{MSE}(\boldsymbol{w}^*) - \mathrm{MSE}(\bar{\boldsymbol{w}}^*)}{\mathrm{MSE}(\bar{\boldsymbol{w}}^*)} \right|$$

   where MSE is the mean squared error of the model computed on a test dataset (this is a common measure of model accuracy in the machine learning setting). The value $R_{\mathrm{MSE}}$ tells the loss in accuracy caused by using the vector $\boldsymbol{w}^*$ instead of $\bar{\boldsymbol{w}}^*$ as model.
2. *Evaluating running-time*: How do the data parameters $n$ and $d$ influence in practice the running time of each step in our privacy-preserving system? In [14, Appendix A.3], we report the number of different elementary operations (*e.g.*, encryptions, modular additions, etc.) for each step in the system, while in this section we report the total running time of each step.

3. *Evaluating efficiency in practice*: How does our system behave when is run on real-world data? In particular, we run our system on datasets downloaded from the UCI repository,[11] which is commonly used for evaluating new machine-learning algorithms in the standard setting (*i.e.*, with no privacy guarantees).

**Setup.** We implemented our system using Paillier's scheme with message space $\mathcal{M} = \mathbb{Z}_N$. In order to assure a security level of at least 100 bits,[12] decrease the running time and the communication overhead, and satisfy (4), we choose $N$ such that $\log_2(N) = \max\{2048, \lfloor \beta \rfloor + 1\}$ where $\beta$ is the logarithm in base 2 of the left-hand side of (4). We wrote our software in Python 3 5.2 using the `phe 1.3` library[13] to for Paillier encryption/decryption and operations on cipher-

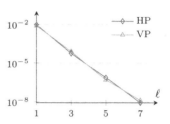

**Fig. 2.** Error rate $R_{\mathrm{MSE}}$ (log scale) in function of $\ell$ ($n = 10^3, d = 10$).

texts, and the `gmpy2` library[14] for arithmetic operations with large integers. Gaussian elimination was used to compute determinants and linear systems.

To test the system composed by $\Pi_{1,\mathrm{hor}} + \Pi_2$, we run experiments in the *horizontally-partitioned* (HP) setting, splitting $n$ data points evenly among 10 data-owners. To test the system $\Pi_{1,\mathrm{arb}} + \Pi_2$, we run experiments in the *vertically-partitioned* (VP) setting, where we assume that $d$ features are evenly split among 3 data-owners and $DO_3$ also has $\boldsymbol{y}$.

**Numerical Results.** All experiments were run on a machine with the following specifics. OS: Scientific Linux 7.4, CPU: 40 core (Intel(R) Xeon(R) CPU E5-2660 v2 2.20 GHz), Memory: 500 GB. All the timings are reported in seconds, all the values are averaged on 5 repetitions of the same experiment.

To answer Question 1, we measure the $R_{\mathrm{MSE}}$ for different values of $\ell$ for synthetically-generated data in both the HP and VP settings (see Fig. 2). With the increasing of $\ell$, regardless of the values of $n$ and $d$, the value of $R_{\mathrm{MSE}}$ decreases very rapidly, while the efficiency degrades. Indeed, because of (4), the value of $\ell$ has effect on the bit-length of the plaintexts and ciphertexts. For this reason, we recommend to choose $\ell$ equal to a small integer (*e.g.*, $\ell = 3$). This choice allows to have a negligible error rate (*e.g.*, $R_{\mathrm{MSE}}$ of order $10^{-4}$) without degrading the system efficiency.

To answer Question 2 and assess the effect of parameters $n$ and $d$ on our system's performance, we report in Table 1 the running time of each step of the system when it is run on synthetic data. The advantage of this approach is

---

[11] https://archive.ics.uci.edu/ml/datasets.html.
[12] According to NIST standard, an RSA modulus of 2048 bits gives 112-bit security.
[13] http://python-paillier.readthedocs.io.
[14] https://pypi.python.org/pypi/gmpy2.

**Table 1.** Running times (secs) for synthetic data in the HP and VP settings ($\ell = 3$).

| | $n$ | $d$ | $\log_2(N)$ | $R_{\mathrm{MSE}}$ | Phase 1 | | | Phase 2 | | |
|---|---|---|---|---|---|---|---|---|---|---|
| | | | | | Step 1 | Step 2 | Step 3 | Step 1 | Step 2 | Step 3 |
| HP setting | 1000 | 10 | 2048 | 7.21E−05 | 0.21 | 1.10 | 0.03 | 1.21 | 0.56 | 0.04 |
| | | 20 | 2048 | 1.54E−04 | 0.32 | 3.88 | 0.12 | 7.96 | 2.15 | 0.14 |
| | | 30 | 2048 | 1.58E−04 | 0.18 | 8.34 | 0.26 | 24.76 | 4.80 | 0.29 |
| | | 40 | 2504 | 2.01E−04 | 0.38 | 26.13 | 0.62 | 100.94 | 14.72 | 0.67 |
| | 10000 | 10 | 2048 | 5.45E−05 | 0.16 | 1.11 | 0.03 | 1.21 | 0.57 | 0.04 |
| | | 20 | 2048 | 1.29E−04 | 0.09 | 3.93 | 0.12 | 7.99 | 2.14 | 0.15 |
| | | 30 | 2072 | 1.90E−04 | 0.36 | 8.83 | 0.26 | 25.96 | 5.17 | 0.32 |
| | | 40 | 2768 | 1.84E−04 | 0.39 | 29.81 | 0.72 | 120.43 | 19.34 | 0.86 |
| | 100000 | 10 | 2048 | 1.05E−04 | 0.13 | 1.17 | 0.03 | 1.22 | 0.57 | 0.05 |
| | | 20 | 2048 | 1.08E−04 | 0.20 | 4.13 | 0.12 | 7.99 | 2.15 | 0.16 |
| | | 30 | 2270 | 1.38E−04 | 0.23 | 11.65 | 0.31 | 33.19 | 6.26 | 0.40 |
| | | 40 | 3034 | 1.76E−04 | 0.61 | 38.38 | 0.86 | 151.37 | 24.82 | 1.08 |
| VP setting | 1000 | 10 | 2048 | 1.50E−04 | 1.41 | 62.06 | 135.09 | 1.22 | 0.56 | 0.04 |
| | | 15 | 2048 | 8.90E−05 | 2.52 | 90.36 | 220.32 | 3.51 | 1.22 | 0.08 |
| | | 20 | 2048 | 1.78E−04 | 4.08 | 118.73 | 327.48 | 8.10 | 2.16 | 0.14 |
| | 2000 | 10 | 2048 | 1.08E−04 | 1.92 | 124.35 | 276.13 | 1.23 | 0.59 | 0.04 |
| | | 15 | 2048 | 6.64E−05 | 3.54 | 181.09 | 443.78 | 3.56 | 1.31 | 0.09 |
| | | 20 | 2048 | 1.67E−04 | 5.62 | 236.54 | 653.06 | 8.03 | 2.17 | 0.14 |
| | 3000 | 10 | 2048 | 6.46E−05 | 2.31 | 185.89 | 402.53 | 1.21 | 0.57 | 0.04 |
| | | 15 | 2048 | 1.06E−04 | 4.38 | 270.12 | 659.67 | 3.52 | 1.22 | 0.08 |
| | | 20 | 2048 | 1.36E−04 | 7.00 | 355.12 | 979.89 | 8.12 | 2.14 | 0.14 |

that we can run experiments for a wide range of parameters values. For Step 2 in Phase 1 (Protocol $\Pi_{1,\mathrm{hor}}$ in the HP setting, Protocol $\Pi_{1,\mathrm{arb}}$ in the VP setting) we report the average running time for one data-owner. In Protocol $\Pi_{1,\mathrm{hor}}$, Step 2 is the most expensive one. Here, the data-owner $\mathrm{DO}_k$ computes the $d \times d$ matrix $A_k$ and encrypts its entries. In our setting ($n$ data points evenly split among the ten data-owners), this costs $\Theta(nd^2)$ arithmetic operations on plaintext values and $\Theta(d^2)$ encryptions for one data-owner. We verified that the costs of the encryptions is dominant for all values of $n$ considered here.[15] In Step 3 of $\Pi_{1,\mathrm{hor}}$, the MLE computes the encryption of $A$ and $\boldsymbol{b}$ using approximately $\Theta(d^2)$ ciphertexts additions (*i.e.*, multiplications modulo $N$), which turns out to be fast. In $\Pi_{1,\mathrm{arb}}$, Step 3 is the most expensive step, here the MLE performs $\Theta(nd^2)$ ciphertexts operation to compute $\mathsf{Enc}_{pk}(A)$ and $\mathsf{Enc}_{pk}(\boldsymbol{b})$. In particular, the running time of $\Pi_{1,\mathrm{arb}}$ is more influenced by the value of $n$ than that of $\Pi_{1,\mathrm{hor}}$ and $\Pi_2$. Finally, for $\Pi_2$ the results in Table 1 show that Step 1 requires longer time compared to the other two steps because of the $\Theta(d^3)$ operations done on ciphertexts. Step 2 and 3 require $\Theta(d^2)$ decryptions and $\Theta(d^2)$ operations on plaintexts and therefore are faster (*e.g.*, less then 27 s for both the steps for a dataset of one hundred thousands instances with 40 features).

---

[15] For larger values of $n$ and $d$, using Damgård and Jurik's scheme instead of Paillier's scheme reduces the running time of operations on ciphertexts. See [14, Appendix A.5].

**Table 2.** Running times (secs) for UCI datasets in the HP and VP settings.

| | Dataset | $n$ | $d$ | $\ell$ | $\log_2(N)$ | $R_{MSE}$ | Phase 1 | | Phase 2 | |
|---|---|---|---|---|---|---|---|---|---|---|
| | | | | | | | Time | kB | Time | kB |
| HP | Air | 6252 | 13 | 1 | 2048 | 4.15E−09 | 1.99 | 53.24 | 3.65 | 96.51 |
| | Beijing | 37582 | 14 | 2 | 2048 | 5.29E−07 | 2.37 | 60.93 | 4.26 | 110.10 |
| | Boston | 456 | 13 | 4 | 2048 | 2.34E−06 | 2.00 | 53.24 | 3.76 | 96.51 |
| | Energy | 17762 | 25 | 3 | 2724 | 5.63E−07 | 12.99 | 238.26 | 37.73 | 451 |
| | Forest | 466 | 12 | 3 | 2048 | 3.57E−09 | 1.66 | 46.08 | 2.81 | 82.94 |
| | Student | 356 | 30 | 1 | 2048 | 4.63E−07 | 9.36 | 253.44 | 30.40 | 483.84 |
| | Wine | 4409 | 11 | 4 | 2048 | 2.62E−05 | 1.71 | 39.42 | 2.38 | 70.40 |
| VP | Boston | 456 | 13 | 4 | 2048 | 2.34E−06 | 123.76 | $1.5\,10^3$ | 3.73 | 96.51 |
| | Forest | 466 | 12 | 3 | 2048 | 3.57E−09 | 115.04 | $1.4\,10^3$ | 2.92 | 82.94 |
| | Student | 356 | 30 | 1 | 2048 | 4.63E−07 | 297.52 | $2.7\,10^3$ | 30.54 | 483.84 |

To answer Question 3 and show the practicality of our system we report in Table 2 the total running time and communication overhead for seven different UCI datasets (references in [14, Appendix A.4]). Some of these datasets were used also in [12,23]. For example, [23] reports a running time of 45 s and a communication overhead of 83 MB (69 MB, resp.) for the Phase 2 of their system run on the dataset "forest" ("wine", resp.) ([23, Table I]). Our protocol $\Pi_2$ for the same datasets takes about 3 s with less then 83 kB sent. Phase 2 of the system presented in [12] runs on the dataset "student" in 19 s ([12, Table 3]) and we estimate an overhead of 3 GB (20 CGD iterations). Protocol $\Pi_2$ on the same dataset runs in about 40 s with 484 kB of overhead.

**Acknowledgments.** This work was partially supported by the Clinical and Translational Science Award (CTSA) program, through the NIH National Center for Advancing Translational Sciences (NCATS) grant UL1TR002373, and by the NIH BD2K Initiative grant U54 AI117924.

# References

1. Agrawal, R., Srikant, R.: Privacy-preserving data mining. In: 2000 ACM SIGMOD International Conference on Management of Data, pp. 439–450. ACM Press (2000)
2. Aono, Y., Hayashi, T., Phong, L.T., Wang, L.: Fast and secure linear regression and biometric authentication with security update. Cryptology ePrint Archive, Report 2015/692 (2015)
3. Bar-Ilan, J., Beaver, D.: Non-cryptographic fault-tolerant computing in constant number of rounds of interaction. In: Eighth Annual ACM Symposium on Principles of Distributed Computing, pp. 201–209. ACM Press (1989)
4. Barbosa, M., Catalano, D., Fiore, D.: Labeled homomorphic encryption: scalable and privacy-preserving processing of outsourced data. In: Foley, S.N., Gollmann, D., Snekkenes, E. (eds.) ESORICS 2017. LNCS, vol. 10492, pp. 146–166. Springer, Cham (2017). https://doi.org/10.1007/978-3-319-66402-6_10

5. Beaver, D.: Efficient multiparty protocols using circuit randomization. In: Feigenbaum, J. (ed.) CRYPTO 1991. LNCS, vol. 576, pp. 420–432. Springer, Heidelberg (1992). https://doi.org/10.1007/3-540-46766-1_34
6. Ben-Or, M., Goldwasser, S., Wigderson, A.: Completeness theorems for noncryptographic fault-tolerant distributed computation. In: 20th Annual ACM Symposium on Theory of Computing, STOC, pp. 1–10. ACM Press (1988)
7. Cao, Z., Liu, L.: Comment on "harnessing the cloud for securely outsourcing large-scale systems of linear equations". IEEE Trans. Parallel Distrib. Syst. **27**(5), 1551–1552 (2016)
8. Cock, M.D., Dowsley, R., Nascimento, A.C.A., Newman, S.C.: Fast, privacy preserving linear regression over distributed datasets based on pre-distributed data. In: 8th ACM Workshop on Artificial Intelligence and Security, pp. 3–14. ACM Press (2015)
9. Damgård, I., Jurik, M.: A generalisation, a simplification and some applications of Paillier's probabilistic public-key system. In: Kim, K. (ed.) PKC 2001. LNCS, vol. 1992, pp. 119–136. Springer, Heidelberg (2001). https://doi.org/10.1007/3-540-44586-2_9
10. Du, W., Han, Y.S., Chen, S.: Privacy-preserving multivariate statistical analysis: linear regression and classification. In: Fourth SIAM International Conference on Data Mining, pp. 222–233. SIAM (2004)
11. Fouque, P.-A., Stern, J., Wackers, G.-J.: CryptoComputing with rationals. In: Blaze, M. (ed.) FC 2002. LNCS, vol. 2357, pp. 136–146. Springer, Heidelberg (2003). https://doi.org/10.1007/3-540-36504-4_10
12. Gascón, A., Schoppmann, P., Balle, B., Raykova, M., Doerner, J., Zahur, S., Evans, D.: Privacy-preserving distributed linear regression on high-dimensional data. PoPETS **2017**(4), 248–267 (2017)
13. Gentry, C.: Fully homomorphic encryption using ideal lattices. In: 41st Annual ACM Symposium on Theory of Computing, STOC, pp. 169–178. ACM Press (2009)
14. Giacomelli, I., Jha, S., Joye, M., Page, C.D., Yoon, K.: Privacy-preserving ridge regression with only linearly-homomorphic encryption. Cryptology ePrint Archive, Report 2017/979 (2017)
15. Hall, R., Fienberg, S.E., Nardi, Y.: Secure multiple linear regression based on homomorphic encryption. J. Off. Stat. **27**(4), 669–691 (2011)
16. Kamara, S., Mohassel, P., Raykova, M.: Outsourcing multi-party computation. Cryptology ePrint Archive, Report 2011/272 (2011)
17. Karr, A.F., Lin, X., Sanil, A.P., Reiter, J.P.: Regression on distributed databases via secure multi-party computation. In: 2004 Annual National Conference on Digital Government Research, pp. 108:1–108:2 (2004)
18. Karr, A.F., Lin, X., Sanil, A.P., Reiter, J.P.: Secure regression on distributed databases. J. Comput. Graph. Stat. **14**(2), 263–279 (2005)
19. Karr, A.F., Lin, X., Sanil, A.P., Reiter, J.P.: Privacy-preserving analysis of vertically partitioned data using secure matrix products. J. Off. Stat. **25**(1), 125–138 (2009)
20. Lindell, Y., Pinkas, B.: Privacy preserving data mining. In: Bellare, M. (ed.) CRYPTO 2000. LNCS, vol. 1880, pp. 36–54. Springer, Heidelberg (2000). https://doi.org/10.1007/3-540-44598-6_3
21. McDonald, G.C.: Ridge regression. Wiley Interdiscip. Rev.: Comput. Stat. **1**(1), 93–100 (2009)
22. Mohassel, P., Zhang, Y.: SecureML: a system for scalable privacy-preserving machine learning. In: 2017 IEEE Symposium on Security and Privacy, pp. 19–38. IEEE Computer Society (2017)

23. Nikolaenko, V., Weinsberg, U., Ioannidis, S., Joye, M., Boneh, D., Taft, N.: Privacy-preserving ridge regression on hundreds of millions of records. In: 2013 IEEE Symposium on Security and Privacy, pp. 334–348. IEEE Computer Society (2013)
24. Paillier, P.: Public-key cryptosystems based on composite degree residuosity classes. In: Stern, J. (ed.) EUROCRYPT 1999. LNCS, vol. 1592, pp. 223–238. Springer, Heidelberg (1999). https://doi.org/10.1007/3-540-48910-X_16
25. Sanil, A.P., Karr, A.F., Lin, X., Reiter, J.P.: Privacy preserving regression modelling via distributed computation. In: Tenth ACM SIGKDD International Conference on Knowledge Discovery and Data Mining, pp. 677–682. ACM Press (2004)
26. Wang, C., Ren, K., Wang, J., Wang, Q.: Harnessing the cloud for securely outsourcing large-scale systems of linear equations. IEEE Trans. Parallel Distrib. Syst. **24**(6), 1172–1181 (2013)
27. Wang, P.S., Guy, M.J.T., Davenport, J.H.: $P$-adic reconstruction of rational numbers. ACM SIGSAM Bull. **16**(2), 2–3 (1982)
28. The International Warfarin Pharmacogenetics Consortium: Estimation of the Warfarin dose with clinical and pharmacogenetic data. N. Engl. J. Med. **360**(8), 753–764 (2009)
29. Yao, A.C.C.: How to generate and exchange secrets. In: 27th Annual Symposium on Foundations of Computer Science, FOCS, pp. 162–167. IEEE Computer Society (1986)

# Privacy-Preserving Plaintext-Equality of Low-Entropy Inputs

Sébastien Canard[1], David Pointcheval[2,3], Quentin Santos[1,2,3(✉)], and Jacques Traoré[1]

[1] Orange Labs, Applied Crypto Group, Caen, France
quentin.santos@orange.com
[2] DIENS, CNRS École normale supérieure, PSL University, Paris, France
[3] INRIA, Paris, France

**Abstract.** Confidentiality requires to keep information away from the eyes of non-legitimate users, while practicality necessitates to make information usable for authorized users. The former issue is addressed with cryptography, and encryption schemes. The combination of both has been shown to be possible with advanced techniques that permit to perform computations on encrypted data. Searchable encryption concentrates on the problem of extracting specific information from a ciphertext.

In this paper, we focus on a concrete use-case where sensitive tokens (medical records) allow third parties to find matching properties (compatible organ donor) without revealing more information than necessary (contact information).

We reduce such case to the plaintext-equality problem. But in our particular application, the message-space is of limited size or, equivalently, the entropy of the plaintexts is small: public-key existing solutions are not fully satisfactory. We then propose a suitable security model, and give an instantiation with an appropriate security analysis.

## 1 Introduction

With the advance of computing and networking, cryptography has evolved from providing straightforward guarantees such as confidentiality, integrity and authenticity to providing many complex features. In particular, much research has been done on the task of performing various kinds of operations on encrypted data. The most well-known topics include fully homomorphic encryption and garbled circuits, whose practical realization would bring into the realm of possibility many applications that would have deemed as magical and unlikely a few decades ago.

A simpler but still useful problem is that of extracting information from a ciphertext. This can include allowing the testing of a single bit of a ciphertext, testing whether a ciphertext contains a particular value or not, whether it includes this value as a substring or not. Searchable encryption already allows

© Springer International Publishing AG, part of Springer Nature 2018
B. Preneel and F. Vercauteren (Eds.): ACNS 2018, LNCS 10892, pp. 262–279, 2018.
https://doi.org/10.1007/978-3-319-93387-0_14

many practical uses, such as spam filtering or threat detection in encrypted traffic, but has the advantage over more generic cryptocomputing techniques to have much more efficient instantiations.

## 1.1 Motivation: Organ Donation

In this paper, we take the specific use case of organ donation as a motivation and derive our constraints from issues related to the actual realization of a solution. With this approach, we devise a method to solve the problem using a new kind of cryptographic primitive. This work is connected to the Kidner Project[1] which aims at providing a solution for kidney donation matching using a blockchain.

**Organ Donation.** Organ transplant requires the donor and the recipient to be compatible, so as to reduce the risks of a graft rejection. In practice, this means that they must be of similar age, have compatible antigens (blood type and human leukocyte antigen (HLA) system), etc. This also means that a list of donors and a list of recipients must be maintained: when a new donor (respectively recipient) enters the system, the new entry should be checked against existing recipients (respectively donors).

Donors are usually willing to give an organ only to a close relative; this means that the pool for potential matches is very restricted. To lift this constraint, the common approach is to pair a willing donor with a recipient, disregarding medical incompatibility. Then, the problem consists in finding two pairs that are mutually compatible (the donor of a pair is compatible with the recipient of the other pair), so that each donor accepts to give their organ to the other recipient.

To enlarge the pool of potential matches further, we can consider the directed graph over donor-recipient pairs, and draw an edge from a donor to a compatible recipient. The general problem is that of finding simple cycles in this graph; the simplest version is a cycle of length 2, involving two donor-recipient pairs, but longer cycles allow more compatibility solutions.

Confidential information on donors and recipients is usually managed by non-profit entities (e.g., Organ Procurement Organizations) who exchange information in order to find matching pairs. Optimizing the number of matches requires merging information from as many sources as possible, but threatens the confidentiality of patient records.

In this paper, we explore a method to encrypt such records in order to obtain both data confidentiality and the ability to test for compatibility.

**Compatibility Matching by Equality Check.** We show how to reduce this problem to that of testing for equality.

*Blood Type.* First, consider compatibility on blood type alone. Donor and recipient can each be O, A, B or AB. The compatibilities are shown on Fig. 1. The recipient will generate a record for each of the compatible donors: for instance,

---

[1] https://www.kidner-project.com.

a recipient of blood type A will generate a record whose field `Blood Type` is set to O, and another where this field is set to A.

|           |    | Donor |   |   |    |
|-----------|----|-------|---|---|----|
|           |    | O | A | B | AB |
|           | O  | ✓ |   |   |    |
| Recipient | A  | ✓ | ✓ |   |    |
|           | B  | ✓ |   | ✓ |    |
|           | AB | ✓ | ✓ | ✓ | ✓  |

**Fig. 1.** Blood compatibility

*Remark 1.* Records should not be linkable one to another; however, if they are, the number of compatible blood types can be hidden by padding with filler values. This can be done by constant incompatible values between donors and receivers.

*Age Group.* Second, consider compatibility on age alone. This criterion is soft: individuals of similar ages should match, but we do not want to discriminate them into separate age groups. Instead, we use overlapping age groups by letting the recipient list acceptable age groups for the donor. For instance, a 19-year-old recipient would list age groups $[12 - 19]$ and $[20 - 39]$.

*Human Leukocyte Antigens (HLA).* Each individual is associated with six variables HLA-{A,B,C,E,F,G}. Two individuals are considered to be HLA-wise compatible when at least three of these variables match. This time, the recipient and the donor each generate a record for each of the 20 combinations of three HLAs (binomial of 3 out of 6).

*All Together.* By combining these brute-force-inspired solutions, we expect an individual to generate on average less than 200 records. The overhead is non-negligible but overcomes complex matching procedures.

We now consider an encrypted version of an individual's record, called a "fingerprint", and we want to test whether two fingerprints are equal or not.

## 1.2   Related Work

Testing whether two ciphertexts hold the same value can be easily done in some contexts. For instance, when all the relevant ciphertexts are encrypted under the same key, and when a deterministic encryption scheme is used, it is sufficient to compare the two outputs [BBO06]. It is also possible to allow testing a ciphertext against a plaintext value by simply using deterministic public key encryption or a one-way function (optionally along with a classical encryption of the message, if decryption is needed).

Public Key Encryption with Equality Test (PKEET) allows testing plaintext-equality between two ciphertexts [YTHW10], while encryption can be done by anyone. One may think of deterministic public key encryption schemes as a subset of PKEET schemes.

In other contexts, more elaborate schemes are needed. In searchable encryption [SWP00,BDOP04], each word $w$ from the input message $m$ is encrypted separately as $s = \mathsf{PEKS}(w)$. The $\mathsf{PEKS}$ scheme then allows other participants to search for a keyword $w'$ in $m$ simply by testing whether $w = w'$ given $s$, as well as a trapdoor value $T_{w'}$. Another variant allows testing between a ciphertext and a plaintext, without a trapdoor [CFGL12]. In different settings, it is possible to use interactive protocols, such as for private matching and set intersection [FNP04].

### 1.3  Our Contribution

**Fingerprinting and Testing Keys.** It is important to note that PKEETs rely on the high min-entropy of the message distribution [LZL13]. Indeed, an attacker may test a target ciphertext against arbitrary messages to conduct a brute-force search over the message space, since encryption is public. We thus have to exclude this approach.

We introduce the notion of fingerprint, a kind of probabilistic ciphertext that allows plaintext-equality testing. Private fingerprinting (generation of fingerprint) allows us to provide semantic security [GM84] (a.k.a. indistinguishability or polynomial security). Alternatively (or additionally), it is possible to make the testing private. We consider all scenarios in our generic model but, since legitimate users need to run many more plaintext-equality testings than fingerprintings (contrary to an adversary), we are interested in a mechanism where testing is public and fingerprinting is private.

Finally, we would prefer non-interactive matching protocols: in our motivation, searching for a cycle requires many compatibility tests; using an interactive protocol would incur an important communication cost and make the system less robust to network hazards.

**Blind and Threshold Fingerprinting.** We could entrust the fingerprinting key to a trusted third party (TTP) to control the number of queries but we want the fingerprints to be generated without seeing the input messages. Thus, we will use blind fingerprinting, which is similar to blind signing [Cha82], but we do not require unlinkability.

This is not enough for privacy: the fingerprinter can still generate and test for plaintext-equality as many fingerprints as they want (assuming public-key testing). To actually achieve a decent level of privacy, we therefore split them into several fingerprinters: without collusions above some threshold, no information is leaked about the input message (blindness) and no brute-force attack is possible.

### 1.4    Organization

In Sect. 2, we first draw a generic model for fingerprinting under the constraints listed above; in particular, we take into consideration both public and private fingerprinting and both public and private testing. Then, in Sect. 3, we introduce the two assumptions which our construction relies on, one of which is new to this paper, and holds in the generic bilinear group model. Finally, we propose a construction for our new scheme in Sect. 4, show its security, and present the blind and threshold variants which extend the privacy of the user.

The proof for the new assumption in the generic bilinear group model is postponed to Appendix A, and the proofs of security of our construction can be found in Subsect. 4.3.

## 2    Fingerprinting Scheme

In this section, we first define a more general fingerprinting mechanism, where the generation of fingerprints and the testing algorithm require keys that can be either private or public. We will later focus on our concrete scenario, with private fingerprint generation and public testing.

### 2.1    Description

We consider three kinds of players:

- the **fingerprinter** who generates the fingerprints of messages using the fingerprinting key. We consider this operation in the honest-but-curious framework, since we eventually split the fingerprinter into several parties, each holding a share of the fingerprinting key;
- the **tester** who checks whether two fingerprints correspond to the same message or not, using the testing key;
- the **users** who have access to the list of fingerprints, and who may query for new fingerprints (through the fingerprinter) and compare fingerprints (through the tester).

We stress however that the fingerprinting and testing keys may be either public or private. When a key is secret, the users have to interact with the owner of the key to benefit from the corresponding functionality; when it is public, the users can act on behalf of the fingerprinter or the tester. The choice of publishing a key or keeping it private will depend on the scenario under consideration.

Finally, we eventually choose to take advantage of the asymmetric nature of our use case: bipartite matching, between people from two different groups (donors and receivers). So, we will manipulate two kinds of fingerprints: "left" and "right" fingerprints in this generic specification.

We thus define four protocols:

- KeyGen($1^k$) creates the global parameters and the left and right fingerprinting keys lk and rk as well as the testing key tk, for security parameter $k$;

- LFingerprint(lk, $m$), given a left-fingerprinting key lk and a message $m$, outputs a left-fingerprint $f_L$;
- RFingerprint(rk, $m$), given a right-fingerprinting key rk and a message $m$, outputs a right-fingerprint $f_R$;
- Test(tk, $f_L$, $f_R$), given a testing key tk, a left-fingerprint $f_L$ and a right-fingerprint $f_R$, reveals whether they correspond to the same message or not.

As already noted above, these procedures can be either private or public, and they can be algorithms to be run offline, or interactive protocols. Various situations can be envisioned according to the secrecy of the fingerprinting and testing keys.

- Testing and fingerprinting keys public: security solely rely on the high entropy of the inputs (message-locked encryption, as in PKEETs);
- Fingerprinting keys private only: our use case, where we want to limit the generation of fingerprints, but allow anyone to test freely for compatibility;
- Testing key private only: this can be relevant if the message space is very constrained, when even a few tests could leak too much information;
- Testing and fingerprinting keys private: this has the highest security guarantee, but is usually impractical unless performing very few queries is enough.

*Remark 2.* We can choose to have one of the fingerprinting keys private, and the other public. This setup can give some flexibility for specific use cases.

## 2.2 Security Model

Let us now make more precise the security notions we want to achieve. Since secret information can include the fingerprinting keys lk and rk, the testing key tk, and the users' input messages, we consider the following security properties:

1. unforgeability of fingerprinting (even against the tester[2]);
2. one-more indistinguishability of testing (even against the fingerprinter[3]);
3. privacy of the user w.r.t. the tester;
4. privacy of the user w.r.t. the fingerprinter.

*Authentication of the Fingerprinter.* The *raison d'être* of the fingerprinter is to generate fingerprints, so unforgeability guarantees that no one else can do so: even a collusion between the tester (access to the testing key) and users (queries to the fingerprinter) should be unable to generate a valid fingerprint that was not provided by the fingerprinter. This implies that the fingerprinting key is not leaked during this game. We formally define Fingerprint-Unforgeability (FP−UF).

---

[2] Even the testing key should give no advantage to anybody in generating fingerprints.
[3] Even the fingerprinting key should give no advantage to anybody in making tests.

**Definition 1 (FP–UF).** *Let* $\Pi = (KeyGen, LFingerprint, RFingerprint, Test)$ *be the scheme presented above, and let* $\mathcal{A}$ *be a polynomial-time adversary. Let*

$$Adv_{\Pi,L}^{FP-UF}(\mathcal{A}) = \Pr \left( \begin{array}{l} (lk, rk, tk) \stackrel{\$}{\leftarrow} KeyGen(1^k), (m^\star, f_L^\star) \leftarrow \mathcal{A}^{\mathcal{L}}(rk, tk), \\ f_R \leftarrow RFingerprint(rk, m^\star) : Test(tk, f_L^\star, f_R) = 1 \end{array} \right)$$

*where* $\mathcal{L}$ *refers to the left-fingerprinting oracle, which answers to queries on message* $m_i$ *with* $f_{L,i} = LFingerprint(lk, m_i)$. *We insist that* $m^\star$ *is distinct from any queried* $m_i$.

*We similarly define* $Adv_{\Pi,R}^{FP-UF}$, *with the left-fingerprinting key but access to the right-fingerprinting oracle. We say that* $\Pi$ *is* $(t, \varepsilon) - FP-UF$-*secure when both* $Adv_{\Pi,L}^{FP-UF}(\mathcal{A}) \leq \varepsilon$ *and* $Adv_{\Pi,R}^{FP-UF}(\mathcal{A}) \leq \varepsilon$ *for any* $\mathcal{A}$ *running within time* $t$.

*Authentication of the Tester.* The purpose of the tester is to help the user to test plaintext equality between fingerprints. But even a collision between the fingerprinter (access to the fingerprinting key) and users (queries to the tester), should be unable to guess the result of another test. This implies that the testing key is not leaked. We formally define Testing-Indistinguishability (T–IND).

**Definition 2 (T–IND).** *Let* $\Pi = (KeyGen, LFingerprint, RFingerprint, Test)$ *be the scheme presented above, and* $\mathcal{A} = (\mathcal{A}_1, \mathcal{A}_2)$ *a polynomial-time adversary. Let*

$$Adv_{\Pi,L}^{T-IND}(\mathcal{A}) = \left| \Pr \left( \begin{array}{l} (lk, rk, tk) \stackrel{\$}{\leftarrow} KeyGen(1^k), \\ (m_0, m_1, s) \leftarrow \mathcal{A}_1^{\mathcal{T}}(lk, rk), f_L \leftarrow LFingerprint(lk, m_0), \\ b \stackrel{\$}{\leftarrow} \{0,1\}, f_R \leftarrow RFingerprint(rk, m_b), \\ b' \leftarrow \mathcal{A}_2^{\mathcal{T}}(s, f_L, f_R) : b' = b \end{array} \right) - \frac{1}{2} \right|$$

*where* $\mathcal{T}$ *refers to the testing oracle, who answers to queries on fingerprints* $f_L, f_R$ *with* $\mathcal{T}(f_L, f_R) = Test(tk, f_L, f_R)$. *We require that the attacker does not submit the challenge fingerprint* $f_R$ *to the testing-oracle.*

*We define* $Adv_{\Pi,R}^{T-IND}(\mathcal{A})$ *in a similar fashion. We say that* $\Pi$ *is* $(t, \varepsilon) - T-IND$-*secure if both* $Adv_{\Pi,L}^{T-IND}(\mathcal{A}) \leq \varepsilon$ *and* $Adv_{\Pi,R}^{T-IND}(\mathcal{A}) \leq \varepsilon$ *for any adversary* $\mathcal{A}$ *running within time* $t$.

One can note that for such a strong notion of indistinguishability, which only excludes the challenge fingerprints from being queried to the testing-oracle, the fingerprints must be non-malleable.

*Privacy of the User.* This security notion adapts semantic security to our scheme: given access to the even a collusion between the tester (access to the testing key) and users (queries to the fingerprinter) should not be able to distinguish a fingerprint of a message $m_0$ from a fingerprint of a message $m_1$ (unless they know a fingerprint of $m_0$ or of $m_1$). Furthermore, the collusion could include one of the two fingerprinting keys (but not both): give the left-fingerprinting key when proving the semantic security of left-fingerprinting, and the right-fingerprinting key when proving the semantic security of right-fingerprinting. We formally define Fingerprint-Indistinguishability (FP–IND).

**Definition 3 (FP–IND).** *Let $\Pi = (KeyGen, LFingerprint, RFingerprint, Test)$ be the scheme presented above, and let $\mathcal{A} = (\mathcal{A}_1, \mathcal{A}_2)$ be a polynomial-time adversary. Let*

$$
Adv_{\Pi,L}^{FP-IND}(\mathcal{A}) = \left| \Pr \left( \begin{array}{l} (lk, rk, tk) \xleftarrow{\$} KeyGen(1^k), (m_0, m_1, s) \leftarrow \mathcal{A}_1^{\mathcal{R}}(lk, tk), \\ b \xleftarrow{\$} \{0,1\}, f_L \leftarrow LFingerprint(lk, m_b), \\ b' \leftarrow \mathcal{A}_2^{\mathcal{R}}(s, f_L) : b' = b \end{array} \right) - \frac{1}{2} \right|
$$

*where $\mathcal{R}$ refers to the right-fingerprinting oracle, which answers to queries on message $m_i'$ with $\mathcal{R}(m_i') = RFingerprint(rk, m_i')$. We insist that $m_i' \notin \{m_0, m_1\}$ for any queries to $\mathcal{R}$.*

*We define $Adv_{\Pi,R}^{FP-IND}(\mathcal{A})$ similarly. We say that $\Pi$ is $(t, \varepsilon) - FP–IND$-secure if both $Adv_{\Pi,L}^{FP-IND}(\mathcal{A}) \leq \varepsilon$ and $Adv_{\Pi,R}^{FP-IND}(\mathcal{A}) \leq \varepsilon$ for any adversary $\mathcal{A}$ running within time $t$.*

Note that fingerprinting generation itself should not reveal anything about the message that is being fingerprinted: the view of the fingerprinter should be the same regardless of the message. Like in blind signatures [Cha82], no adversary playing the role of fingerprinter should be able to distinguish a fingerprinting of $m_0$ from a fingerprinting of $m_1$. However, if the fingerprinter sees the resulting fingerprint and locally generates a fingerprint for $m_0$, they could easily distinguish between the two cases. To avoid this, the fingerprinter should be split into several parties that need to cooperate to create a new fingerprint. This last security notion thus suggest the use of a blind protocol and a threshold scheme.

*Remark 3.* Contrary to blind signatures, user anonymity is not required; in our use-case, contact information must be joined with the final published fingerprint.

## 3   Assumptions

Our construction adapts the randomizable signature proposed by Pointcheval and Sanders [PS16], which relies on $q$-MSDH-1 [PS18]. Our scheme additionally requires indistinguishability, which implies another assumption; for this, we introduce $q$-DMSDH-1, which is decisional variant of $q$-MSDH-1, and prove it to hold in the generic bilinear group model.

**Definition 4 ($q$-MSDH-1).** *Let $(p, \mathbb{G}_1, \mathbb{G}_2, \mathbb{G}_T, e)$ be a bilinear group setting of type 3, with $g$ (respectively $\tilde{g}$) a generator of $\mathbb{G}_1$ (respectively $\mathbb{G}_2$). Given $(g^{x^i}, \tilde{g}^{x^i})_{0 \leq i \leq q}$ along with $(g^a, \tilde{g}^a, \tilde{g}^{a \cdot x})$ for $a, x \xleftarrow{\$} \mathbb{Z}_p^*$, no adversary can output a tuple $(w, P, h^{\frac{1}{x+w}}, h^{\frac{a}{P(x)}})$ for some $h \in \mathbb{G}_1^*$ where $P$ is a polynomial of degree at most $q$ and $w$ is a scalar such that $(X + w)$ and $P(X)$ are relatively prime.*

**Definition 5 ($q$-DMSDH-1).** *Let $(p, \mathbb{G}_1, \mathbb{G}_2, \mathbb{G}_T, e)$ be a bilinear group setting of type 3, with $g$ (respectively $\tilde{g}$) a generator of $\mathbb{G}_1$ (respectively $\mathbb{G}_2$). Given $(g^{x^i}, \tilde{g}^{x^i})_{0 \leq i < q}$ along with $(g^a, g^{a \cdot x}, \tilde{g}^a)$ for $a, x \xleftarrow{\$} \mathbb{Z}_p^*$, and for any $(w, P)$ where*

*P is a polynomial of degree at most q and w is a scalar such that $(X + w)$ and $P(X)$ are relatively prime, no adversary can distinguish $(h^{\frac{1}{x+w}}, h^{\frac{a}{P(x)}})$ for some $h \in \mathbb{G}_1^*$ from a random pair of elements of $\mathbb{G}_1$.*

**Theorem 1.** *q-DMSDH-1 holds in the generic bilinear group model.*

*Proof.* The computational assumption $q$-MSDH-1 from [PS18] gives $\tilde{g}^{a \cdot x} \in \mathbb{G}_2$ and expects the forged pair in $\mathbb{G}_1$, whereas the decisional version $q$-DMSDH-1 gives $g^{a \cdot x} \in \mathbb{G}_1$ and the challenge pair in $\mathbb{G}_1$. So, the group the pair belongs to determines what security guarantee we obtain (either unforgeability from $q$-MSDH-1 or indistinguishability from $q$-DMSDH-1). Thus, the reasoning for $q$-DMSDH-1 is very similar to that for $q$-MSDH-1. The full proof can be found in Appendix A.

# 4   Fingerprinting from Pointcheval-Sanders Signatures

In the following, we focus on our initial scenario with secret fingerprinting and public testing of plaintext-equality, for low-entropy messages. Our construction is heavily influenced by the assumption that it is possible to efficiently enumerate all the valid messages.

## 4.1   The Pointcheval-Sanders Signature Scheme

Our construction derives from Pointcheval-Sanders signatures [PS16,PS18]. We reproduce here the definition for the single-message version. Let $e : \mathbb{G}_1 \times \mathbb{G}_2 \to \mathbb{G}_T$ be a type-3 pairing with $\mathbb{G}_1, \mathbb{G}_2, \mathbb{G}_T$ of prime order $p$, and $\mathbb{G}_1^* = \mathbb{G}_1 \backslash \{1_{\mathbb{G}_1}\}$. Then, we define the following procedures.

- KeyGen($1^k$): $(\tilde{g}, x, y) \xleftarrow{\$} \mathbb{G}_2 \times \mathbb{Z}_p^2$, sk $= (x, y)$ and pk $= (\tilde{g}, \tilde{X} = \tilde{g}^x, \tilde{Y} = \tilde{g}^y)$.
- Sign(sk, $m$): draw $h \xleftarrow{\$} \mathbb{G}_1^*$ and return $\sigma = (h, h^{x+ym})$.
- Verify(pk, $m$, $\sigma$): return 1 if $\sigma_1 \neq 1_{\mathbb{G}_1}$ and $e(\sigma_1, \tilde{X}\tilde{Y}^m) = e(\sigma_2, \tilde{g})$, else 0.

This signature scheme has been shown unforgeable in the sense of EUF–CMA under the interactive PS assumption [PS16], and in the sense of EUF–wCMA (non-adaptive) under the $q$-MSDH-1 assumption (where $q$ is the bound on signing requests asked before the setup) [PS18]. The same levels of security are achieved when elements $g \in \mathbb{G}_1$ and $Y = g^y$ are included in the public key pk, as long as $X = g^x$ is kept private.

## 4.2   Fingerprinting Scheme with Public Plaintext-Equality Testing

Let $\mathcal{H}$ be a random oracle. We now propose a fingerprinting scheme where the fingerprinting procedure requires a secret key lk or rk, while testing is a public process (there is no testing key tk, or alternatively it is public).

- KeyGen($1^k$): randomly draw $(g, \tilde{g}, x, y) \xleftarrow{\$} \mathbb{G}_1 \times \mathbb{G}_2 \times \mathbb{Z}_p^2$, set $(X, \tilde{X}, Y, \tilde{Y}) \leftarrow (g^x, \tilde{g}^x, g^y, \tilde{g}^y)$, return lk $= X$, rk $= \tilde{X}$, and pk $= (g, Y, \tilde{g}, \tilde{Y})$.

- LFingerprint($\mathsf{lk}, m$): draw $u \xleftarrow{\$} \mathbb{Z}_p^*$, return $f_L = (g^u, (XY^{\mathcal{H}(m)})^u)$.
- RFingerprint($\mathsf{rk}, m$): draw $u \xleftarrow{\$} \mathbb{Z}_p^*$, return $f_R = (\tilde{g}^u, (\tilde{X}\tilde{Y}^{\mathcal{H}(m)})^u)$.
- Test($f_L, f_R$): return 1 if $f_{L,1}, f_{R,1} \neq 1_{\mathbb{G}_1}$ and $e(f_{L,1}, f_{R,2}) = e(f_{L,2}, f_{R,1})$, else 0.

## 4.3   Security of the Basic Scheme

**Theorem 2.** *Our fingerprinting scheme is FP−UF under q-MSDH-1 in the random oracle model, where q corresponds to the number of queries to the random oracle or to the fingerprinting oracles.*

*Proof.* We define the extended Pointcheval-Sanders signature scheme (EPS) as a variant of the PS signature scheme where $\mathsf{pk}$ includes $Y$, i.e. $\mathsf{pk} = (Y, \tilde{g}, \tilde{X}, \tilde{Y})$. We argue that EPS is EUF–wCMA secure under $q$-MSDH-1 in Lemma 1, and reduce the FP−UF security of our fingerprinting scheme to the EUF–wCMA security of EPS in Lemma 2.

**Lemma 1.** *If q-MSDH-1 holds, then EPS is EUF–wCMA where q is the number of queries to the signing oracle.*

*Proof.* We refer to the proof of theorem 10 from [PS18, Sect. 5.1, p. 330] where the challenger is given $(g^{x^i})_i$, $(\tilde{g}^{x^i})_i$ and $(g^a, \tilde{g}^a, \tilde{g}^{a \cdot x})$ and feeds the challenger with $\tilde{Y}_1 \leftarrow \tilde{g}^a$ and $\tilde{Y}_i \leftarrow \tilde{Y}_1^{u_i}$. To prove the EUF–wCMA security of the signature scheme when $\mathsf{pk}$ includes $(Y_i)_i$, it suffices to have the challenger also offer $Y_1 \leftarrow g^a$ and $Y_i \leftarrow Y_1^{u_i}$.

**Lemma 2.** *If EPS is EUF–wCMA, then our fingerprinting scheme is FP−UF. The number of queries to the signing oracle in EPS maps to the number of queries to the random oracle or to the fingerprinting oracles in our scheme.*

*Proof.* Let $\mathcal{A}$ be an adversary that breaks the FP−UF security of our scheme. Then, we create an adversary $\mathcal{B}$ that breaks the EUF–wCMA security of EPS. By symmetry of the left and right games, we assume that $\mathsf{Adv}_{\Pi,L}^{FP-IND}(\mathcal{A})$ is non-negligible without loss of generality.

We will use $\mathcal{H}$ to "redirect" the queries from $\mathcal{A}$ towards predetermined values: $\mathcal{B}$ first draws $(m_i)_i \xleftarrow{\$} \mathbb{Z}_p^q$, submits the list of messages $(m_i)_i$ to the signing challenger, and will answer to the $i$-th original query to $\mathcal{H}$ (for some message $M_i$) with $m_i$.

In return, our adversary $\mathcal{B}$ is given $\mathsf{pk} = (Y, \tilde{g}, \tilde{X}, \tilde{Y})$ as well as signatures $(\sigma_i)_i$ for $(m_i)_i$, i.e. values such that $e(\sigma_{i,1}, \tilde{X}\tilde{Y}^{m_i}) = e(\sigma_{i,2}, \tilde{g})$ We need to output $(m^\star, \sigma^\star)$ such that $e(\sigma_1^\star, \tilde{X}\tilde{Y}^{m^\star}) = e(\sigma_2^\star, \tilde{g})$ where $m^\star$ is distinct from any queried $m_i$.

For this, we simulate the FP−UF game for $\mathcal{A}$ with $\mathsf{pk}' \leftarrow (g, Y, \tilde{g}, \tilde{Y})$, $\mathsf{rk} \leftarrow \tilde{X}$ as well as access to an oracle $\mathcal{L}$ which answer to queries $M_i$ with $\sigma_i$. Then, $\mathcal{A}$ should output $(M^\star, f_L^\star)$ where $M^\star$ is distinct from any queried $M_i$. We also require that $\mathsf{Test}(\mathsf{tk}, f_L^*, f_R)$ for some $f_R \leftarrow \mathsf{RFingerprint}(\mathsf{rk}, m^*) = 1$, i.e. such that $f_{L,1} \neq 1_{\mathbb{G}_1}$ and:

$$e\left(f_{L,1}, \left(\tilde{X}\tilde{Y}^{\mathcal{H}(M^*)}\right)^u\right) = e\left(f_{L,2}, \tilde{g}^u\right)$$

for some $u$. Thus, $\sigma^* = f_L^*$ is a valid PS signature for $m^* = \mathcal{H}(M^*)$ with $m^*$ distinct from any queried $m_i$.

**Theorem 3.** *Our fingerprinting scheme is* FP–IND *under* q-DMSDH-1 *in the random oracle model, where* q *corresponds to the number of queries to the random oracle or to the fingerprinting oracles.*

*Proof.* Let $\mathcal{A}$ be an adversary against FP–IND, then we provide an adversary $\mathcal{B}$ against q-DMSDH-1. We assume that $\mathsf{Adv}_{\Pi,L}^{\mathsf{FP-IND}}(\mathcal{A})$ is non-negligible. Since the roles of $\mathbb{G}_1$ and $\mathbb{G}_2$ are symmetric, the same reasoning applies when $\mathsf{Adv}_{\Pi,R}^{\mathsf{FP-IND}}(\mathcal{A})$.

First, $\mathcal{B}$ is given $(g^{x^i})_{0 \leq i \leq q}$, $(g^a, g^{a \cdot x}, \tilde{g}^a)$. Then, it draws $(m_i) \xleftarrow{\$} \mathbb{Z}_p^q$, $m \xleftarrow{\$} \mathbb{Z}_p$, sets $P = \prod_i (X + m_i)$, and submits $(m, P)$ to the challenger, which answers with a pair $\sigma$ which is either random or of the form $(h^{\frac{1}{x+m}}, h^{\frac{a}{P(x)}})$ for some $h \in \mathbb{G}_1$.

Now, $\mathcal{B}$ should be able to distinguish between these two cases. For this, $\mathcal{B}$ will run $\mathcal{A}$ while simulating the game for FP–IND by setting $g' \leftarrow g^{\prod_i (x+m_i)}$ and $\tilde{g}' \leftarrow \tilde{g}^{\prod_i (x+m_i)}$, using $(g^{x^i})_i$ and $(\tilde{g}^{x^i})_i$, as well as $X \leftarrow g^{a \cdot x}$, $Y \leftarrow g^a$, and $\tilde{Y} \leftarrow \tilde{g}^a$ to define the public key $\mathsf{pk} = (g', Y, \tilde{g}', \tilde{Y})$ and the left-fingerprinting key $\mathsf{lk} = X$. This implicitly sets $x' = \frac{a \cdot x}{\prod_i (x+m_i)}$ and $y' = \frac{a}{\prod_i (x+m_i)}$.

To generate fingerprints for the $q$ queried fingerprints, $\mathcal{B}$ sets the random oracle $\mathcal{H}$ to map the $j$-th original query $M_j$ to $m_j$, and the right-fingerprinting oracle $\mathcal{R}$ to return $((\tilde{g}'^{\prod_{i \neq j}(x+m_i)})^{u_j}, (\tilde{g}'^a)^{u_j})$. One may verify that this is a valid right-fingerprint for $M_j$.

Finally, $\mathcal{A}$ outputs $(M_0', M_1')$, and $\mathcal{B}$ draws $b \leftarrow \{0,1\}$. We would now like to set $\mathcal{H}(M_b')$ to $m$, but $\mathcal{A}$ may have queried the random oracle on this value before. Thus, on any query $M_j$, $\mathcal{H}$ will additionally guess with probability $\frac{1}{q}$ that $M_j = M_b'$ and accordingly set $\mathcal{H}(M_j)$ to $m$ instead of $m_j$. $\mathcal{B}$ can then check its guess when $\mathcal{A}$ outputs $(M_0', M_1')$, and abort if it was incorrect; this implies a penalty of a factor $q$ to the probability that $\mathcal{B}$ wins the q-DMSDH-1 game.

Now, since $\mathcal{H}(M_b') = m$, if $\sigma$ is of the form $(h^{\frac{1}{x+m}}, h^{\frac{a}{P(x)}})$, then it is a valid left-fingerprint for $M_b$. Otherwise, it provides no information about $b$ to the adversary. Thus, $\mathcal{B}$ answers the final request of $\mathcal{A}$ with $\sigma$, and, if $\mathcal{A}$ guesses $b$ correctly, then $\mathcal{B}$ guesses that $\sigma$ is of the form $(h^{\frac{1}{x+m}}, h^{\frac{a}{P(x)}})$; otherwise, that it is a random pair.

## 4.4    Improving the Privacy of the User

Since the left and right fingerprintings work in similar ways, we will only present the protocols for left fingerprinting.

**Against the Fingerprinter Without the Final Fingerprint.** In the naive construction above, the user sends the message in the clear to get back the fingerprint. In order to extend user privacy to the fingerprinters, we propose a blinded version, as in [PS16]:

1. the user draws $r \xleftarrow{\$} \mathbb{Z}_p$ and sends $C \leftarrow Y^m g^r$;
2. the user runs a Zero-Knowledge Proof of Knowledge (ZKPoK) of $m, r$ such that $C = Y^m g^r$;
3. the fingerprinter draws $u \xleftarrow{\$} \mathbb{Z}_p$ and sends back $\alpha \leftarrow (g^u, (XC)^u)$;
4. the user sets $f_1 \leftarrow \alpha_1$, $f_2 \leftarrow \alpha_2 \cdot \alpha_1^{-r}$.

This protocol is perfectly blind to the fingerprinter, since his view is just the perfectly hiding Pedersen commitment [Ped92] and a ZK protocol, which do not leak any information about $m$. Hence the privacy of the user. With an extractable ZKPoK, it is possible to prove the security of this blinded version, as in [PS16].

**Against the Fingerprinter with the Final Fingerprint.** With the protocol presented above, if the fingerprinter gains access to the final fingerprint $f$, their ability to create fingerprints for arbitrary messages and the publicness of the testing key let them retrieve the message. In order to block exhaustive searches, we amend the protocol by splitting the fingerprinter into $n$ parties, using secret sharing of the fingerprinting key. For some threshold $k$, no collusion of less than $k$ parties can generate fingerprints; equivalently, having access to up to $k - 1$ shares of the fingerprinting key does not reveal more than being a common user.

The threshold version makes use of Shamir's secret sharing [Sha79] to split the secret scalar $x$ into $n$ shares $x_i$ (for each sub-fingerprinter $\mathsf{F}_i$), and we note $X_i = g^{x_i}$. This way, for any qualified subset of $\mathsf{F}_i$ (with at least $k$ shares), there are public coefficients $\lambda_i$ (Lagrange coefficients) such that $x = \sum \lambda_i x_i$, and then $\prod X_i^{\lambda_i} = X$. A group of $k$ sub-fingerprinters interacts as follows with the user:

1. the user draws $r \xleftarrow{\$} \mathbb{Z}_p$ and broadcasts $C \leftarrow Y^m g^r$;
2. the user sends a NIZKPoK of $m, r$ such that $C = Y^m g^r$;
3. each $\mathsf{F}_i$ draws $u_i \xleftarrow{\$} \mathbb{Z}_p$ and broadcasts $\alpha_{i,1} \leftarrow g^{u_i}$;
4. each $\mathsf{F}_i$ computes $G \leftarrow \prod \alpha_{j,1}^{\lambda_j}$, and sends back $\alpha_{i,2} \leftarrow G^{x_i} C^{u_i}$;
5. the user sets

$$f_1 \leftarrow G = g^u \qquad\qquad f_2 \leftarrow G^{-r} \prod \alpha_{i,2}^{\lambda_i} = (XY^m)^u$$

which implicitly defines $u = \sum \lambda_i u_i$.

First, one can easily see that this still preserves the privacy of the user, since, as before, $C$ does not contain any information about $m$; neither does the NIZK. The final fingerprint $f$ traces back to the user but the anonymity is not required: in our use case, it must be possible to contact the appropriate hospital when a match is found. The important property is the privacy of $m$: no subset of less than $k$ sub-fingerprinters can guess the conduct an exhaustive search.

Of course, we have to prove this still preserves fingerprinter privacy, or more precisely this does not leak private information of honest sub-fingerprinters to corrupted ones. To this aim, we show that the view of any (static) subset of corrupted sub-fingerprinters can be simulated from the same information $\alpha = (\alpha_1, \alpha_2)$ as the one output by the fingerprinter in the centralized protocol.

Let us assume that the corrupted sub-fingerprinters are $\mathsf{F}_1, \ldots, \mathsf{F}_c$, and the honest ones are $\mathsf{F}_{c+1}, \ldots, \mathsf{F}_k$ (where $c < k$), and the simulator has drawn $v_i \xleftarrow{\$} \mathbb{Z}_p$ for $i = c+1, \ldots, k$: the corrupted players send $\alpha_{i,1}$ for $i = 1, \ldots, c$, and the simulator draws $u_i \xleftarrow{\$} \mathbb{Z}_p$ and generates $\alpha_{i,1} \leftarrow g^{u_i}$ for $i = c+1, \ldots, k-1$, while $\alpha_{k,1} \leftarrow (\alpha_1 / \prod_{i=1}^{k-1} \alpha_{i,1}^{\lambda_i})^{1/\lambda_k}$. The simulator also sets $G \leftarrow \alpha_1$, and computes $\alpha_{i,2} \leftarrow G^{v_i} C^{u_i}$ for $i = c+1, \ldots, k-1$, while $\alpha_{k,2} \leftarrow (\alpha_2 / \prod_{i=1}^{k-1} \alpha_{i,2}^{\lambda_i})^{1/\lambda_k}$.

Since no information is known about the actual secret values $x_i$, and the values $v_i$ are indistinguishable from the real secret, all the simulated elements are perfectly indistinguishable from a real execution, under the condition that the corrupted sub-fingerprinters are honest-but-curious (and the subset of honest players remains the same: static corruptions). Indeed, in this protocol, no verifiability is required about the sub-fingerprinters: they are trusted to compute correctly, even if they try to learn more information.

### 4.5  Verifiability

If one wants to consider malicious sub-fingerprinters, verifiability is required for the user (private verifiability). An additional improvement can be reached: one could avoid fake or copies of fingerprints posted by malicious users in the database, by using a proof of knowledge of the fingerprinted message (public verifiability). To achieve this, sub-fingerprinters first need to publish a commitment $C_i = g^{x_i} Y^{t_i}$ of their secret shares $x_i$ during key generation. This is a perfectly hiding commitment, and the binding property relies on secrecy of the discrete logarithm of $Y$ in basis $g$.

**Private Verifiability.** For the former case, verifiability can be enforced during the original process of creating the fingerprint, with the additional verification of a NIZK Proof of Existence of $u_i$ and a NIZK Proof of Knowledge of $x_i$ and $t_i$ such that $\alpha_{i,1} = g^{u_i}$ and $\alpha_{i,2} = G^{x_i} C^{u_i}$. The proofs can be efficiently done with Schnorr-like proofs.

**Public Verifiability.** In order to avoid fake fingerprints or copies, the user should prove their validity (to avoid fake ones) and freshness (to avoid copies). A non-malleable NIZK could solve this challenge: in addition to $f = (f_1, f_2)$, and the NIZKs provided by the sub-fingerprinters, the user sends a NIZK Proof of Knowledge of $m$ and $r$ such that $\alpha_2 / f_2 = \alpha_1^r$ and $C = Y^m g^r$. In order to guarantee non-malleability or replay attacks, the user includes his own identity in the challenge computation (signature of knowledge).

## 4.6   Full Protocol

Let us now fully describe the resulting protocol, with an optimized NIZK for the public verifiability: the fingerprinters $F_i$, for $i = 1, \ldots, n$, jointly generate a Shamir's secret sharing of a random scalar secret $x$. They each own a share $x_i$, and publish a commitment $C_i = g^{x_i} Y^{t_i}$, for a random scalar $t_i$. In order to get a fingerprint on a message $m$, the user (with identity Id) contacts a subset of $k$ sub-fingerprinters:

1. the user draws $r \xleftarrow{\$} \mathbb{Z}_p$ and broadcasts $C \leftarrow Y^m g^r$;
2. the user sends an (extractable) NIZKPoK of $m, r$ such that $C = Y^m g^r$;
3. each $F_i$ draws $u_i \xleftarrow{\$} \mathbb{Z}_p$ and sends back $\alpha_{i,1} \leftarrow g^{u_i}$;
4. each $F_i$ computes $G \leftarrow \prod \alpha_{j,1}^{\lambda_j}$, and sends back $\alpha_{i,2} \leftarrow G^{x_i} C^{u_i}$;
5. each $F_i$ starts a NIZK for $u_i$, $x_i$ and $t_i$ such that

$$\alpha_{i,1} = g^{u_i} \qquad\qquad \alpha_{i,2} = G^{x_i} C^{u_i}.$$

   More precisely, it draws $u_i', x_i', t_i' \xleftarrow{\$} \mathbb{Z}_p$ and sends

$$A_{i,1} = g^{u_i'} \qquad\qquad A_{i,2} = G^{x_i'} C^{u_i'};$$

6. the user generates

$$\alpha_1 \leftarrow G = \prod \alpha_{i,1}^{\lambda_i} = g^u \qquad\qquad \alpha_2 \leftarrow \prod \alpha_{i,2}^{\lambda_i} = (XC)^u$$

$$A_1 \leftarrow \prod A_{i,1}^{\lambda_i} = g^{u'} \qquad\qquad A_2 \leftarrow \prod A_{i,2}^{\lambda_i} = (XC)^{u'},$$

   where $u = \sum \lambda_i u_i$ and $u' = \sum \lambda_i u_i'$, as well as

$$f_1 \leftarrow \alpha_1 \qquad\qquad f_2 \leftarrow G^{-r} \alpha_2$$

   and starts the NIZK for $m$ and $r$ such that $\alpha_2 / f_2 = \alpha_1^r$ and $C = Y^m g^r$, with random $r'$ and $m'$:

$$B_1 \leftarrow \alpha_1^{r'} \qquad\qquad B_2 \leftarrow Y^{m'} g^{r'}$$

   and publishes the challenge $e = \mathcal{H}(\mathsf{Id}, C, f_1, f_2, A_1, A_2, B_1, B_2)$;
7. each $F_i$ completes the NIZK with

$$u_i'' \leftarrow u_i' - e u_i \qquad\qquad x_i'' \leftarrow x_i' - e x_i$$

8. the user sets

$$u'' \leftarrow \sum \lambda_i u_i'' \qquad\qquad x'' \leftarrow \sum \lambda_i x_i''$$

   which satisfy

$$g^{u''} = A_1 \alpha_1^{-e} \qquad\qquad G^{x''} C^{u''} = A_2 \alpha_2^{-e}$$

   and completes his NIZK with

$$m'' \leftarrow m' - em \qquad\qquad r'' \leftarrow r' - er$$

   which satisfy

$$\alpha_1^{r''} = B_1 (\alpha_2 / f_2)^{-e} \qquad\qquad Y^{m''} g^{r''} = B_2 C^{-e}.$$

The final fingerprint $f = (f_1, f_2)$ is published along with the intermediate values $(\alpha_2, C)$, the challenge $e$ and the exponents $(u'', x'', m'', r'')$, which constitute a proof that can be verified by checking that $e = \mathcal{H}(\mathsf{Id}, C, f_1, f_2, A_1, A_2, B_1, B_2)$, where the missing elements can be recomputed as

$$A_1 \leftarrow g^{u''} f_1^e \qquad\qquad A_2 \leftarrow f_1^{x''} C^{u''} \alpha_2^e$$
$$B_1 \leftarrow f_1^{r''} (\alpha_2/f_2)^e \qquad\qquad B_2 \leftarrow Y^{m''} g^{r''} C^e$$

This is just an optimization of the Fiat-Shamir heuristic of Schnorr-like proofs.

## 5   Conclusion

With this construction, we are able to propose a new kind of scheme that let us derive testable, privacy-preserving, fingerprints from arbitrary messages. This allows us to propose a solution to the initial motivation of organ donation, where the requirement of encrypting low-entropy messages in such a way that they could be publicly tested against each other seemed to imply highly-interactive protocols. In contrast, our construction allows plaintext-equality tests between fingerprints to be performed fully offline, while only their generation requires an interactive process, to guarantee some level of confidentiality despite the low min-entropy.

We hope that this solution will prove useful in practical applications and allow cryptography to be used in more numerous situations. It might also be feasible to design systems which requires fewer interactions, or rely on more mainstream assumptions.

**Acknowledgments.** This work was supported in part by the European Research Council under the European Community's Seventh Framework Programme (FP7/2007-2013 Grant Agreement no. 339563 – CryptoCloud).

## A   Proof of Theorem 1

*Proof.* We prove $q$-DMSDH-1 in the generic bilinear group model. The generic group model (not bilinear) was used by Victor Shoup in [Sho97] to assess more tightly the difficulty of computing the discrete logarithm and related problems. A vastly clarified introduction to this technique can be found in [Jag12]. The generic bilinear group model is presented in appendix A of [BBG05]. It is essentially a formal way to enumerate the values that an adversary can compute from a restricted number of inputs, using only the group laws.

We use the classical approach of simulating group operations by an oracle $\mathcal{G}$, which operates on arbitrary representations $(\xi_{i,1})_i$, $(\xi_{i,2})_i$, $(\xi_{T,i})_i$ of the elements of $\mathbb{G}_1$, $\mathbb{G}_2$ and $\mathbb{G}_3$ (respectively). The oracle is built such that all interactions are done without relation to the secret values, hence reducing the attack to a guess.

For instance, $\mathcal{G}(\times, \xi_{i,1}, \xi_{1,j})$ returns a representation of the product of the underlying values in $\mathbb{G}_1$. The oracle $\mathcal{G}$ similarly allows the adversary $\mathcal{A}$ to compute products in $\mathbb{G}_2$ and $\mathbb{G}_T$, evaluate the pairing $e$, and test two representations for the equality of the underlying values.

To simulate the operations, the oracle $\mathcal{G}$ stores the values known to the adversary $\mathcal{A}$ (at beginning, and following a request) into lists $L_1$, $L_2$ and $L_T$ (for each group). To track how the adversary $\mathcal{A}$ obtained these values, we save with each representation $\xi_{\square,i}$ a polynomial $p_{\square,i}$ corresponding to the operations used to compute the value. The representations used are not important, and the reader must simply remember that a new random representation is generated for each new computed value; testing whether the value is fresh or not is done by searching the polynomial in the relevant list $L_1$, $L_2$ or $L_T$.

The values initially provided to the adversary $\mathcal{A}$ are:

- in $\mathbb{G}_1$: $(g^{x^i})_{0 \le i \le q}$, $g^a$, $g^{a \cdot x}$, $h^{\frac{1}{x+w}}$, $h^{\frac{a}{P(x)}}$
- in $\mathbb{G}_2$: $(\tilde{g}^{x^i})_{0 \le i \le q}$, $\tilde{g}^a$

To simulate operations over these elements, we set $r$ such that $h = g^r$ and introduce the indeterminate values $\bar{x}$, $\bar{a}$, $\bar{r}$. Then, we initialize $L_1 = \{\bar{x}^i\}_i \cup \{\bar{a}, \bar{a}\bar{x}, \frac{\bar{r}}{\bar{x}+w}, \frac{\bar{a} \cdot \bar{r}}{P(\bar{x})}\}$, $L_2 = \{\bar{x}^i\}_i \cup \{\bar{a}\}$ and $L_T = \varnothing$ (along with arbitrary representations), and set:

- $\mathcal{G}(\times, \xi_{\square,i}, \xi_{\square,j})$: append $p_{\square,i} + p_{\square,j}$ to $L_\square$
- $\mathcal{G}(=, \xi_{\square,i}, \xi_{\square,j})$: return whether $p_{\square,i} = p_{\square,j}$
- $\mathcal{G}(e, \xi_{1,i}, \xi_{2,j})$: append $p_{1,i} \times p_{2,j}$ to $L_T$

*Remark 4.* Comparing the representations directly is equivalent to calling the group oracle for testing, because the representations are generated so as to be equal when the corresponding polynomials are equal

We now have to show two things: the simulation does not allow the adversary to distinguish between $(h^{\frac{1}{x+w}}, h^{\frac{a}{P(x)}})$ and a pair of random elements from $\mathbb{G}_1$; the simulation is indistinguishable from the initial game.

**Indistinguishability in Simulation.** Since representations are opaque, the adversary can only obtain information from testing two values for equality (either of representations or through the group oracle $\mathcal{G}$).

*Comparing elements of $\mathbb{G}_1$.* Consider a comparison of $\xi_{1,i}$ to $\xi_{1,j}$; the difference of their polynomials, $p_{1,i} - p_{1,j}$, is of the form:

$$\sum_i \left( C_x^{(i)} \bar{x}^i + C_a \bar{a} + C_{ax} \bar{a}\bar{x} + C_1 \frac{\bar{r}}{\bar{x} + w} + C_2 \frac{\bar{a} \cdot \bar{r}}{P(\bar{x})} \right)$$

as a polynomial in $\bar{r}$, the linear term implies that, if this polynomial were equal to zero, then:

$$C_1 P(\bar{x}) + C_2 \bar{a}(\bar{x} + w) = 0$$

as a polynomial in $\bar{a}$, this implies $C_1 = C_2 = 0$. Thus, the polynomial does not depend on the challenge pair.

*Comparing elements of* $\mathbb{G}_2$. Elements in $\mathbb{G}_2$ do not depend on the challenge pair.

*Comparing elements of* $\mathbb{G}_T$. Since $L_T$ starts out empty, a comparison of $\xi_{T,i}$ to $\xi T, j$ will correspond to polynomials whose difference $p_{T,i} - p_{T,j}$ is the sum of products of one element from $\mathbb{G}_1$ and one element from $G_2$, thus of the form:

$$\sum_i \left( Q(\bar{x}) + C_{i,a}\bar{a} + C_{i,ax}\bar{a}\bar{x} + C_{i,1}\frac{\bar{r}}{\bar{x}+w} + C_{i,2}\frac{\bar{a}\cdot\bar{r}}{P(\bar{x})} \right) \times \left( R(\bar{x}) + \tilde{C}_{i,a}\bar{a} \right)$$

where $Q$ and $R$ are polynomials of degrees at most $q$. As a polynomial in $\bar{r}$, if this were the zero polynomial, then the linear term would imply that:

$$\sum_i \left( C_{i,1}P(\bar{x}) + C_{i,2}\bar{a}(\bar{x}+w) \right) \times \left( R(\bar{x}) + \tilde{C}_{i,a}\bar{a} \right) = 0$$

as a polynomial in $\bar{a}$, then the linear term would imply that:

$$\sum_i \left( C_{i,1}P(\bar{x})\tilde{C}_{i,a} + C_{i,2}(\bar{x}+w)R(\bar{x}) \right) = 0$$

that is, $CP(\bar{x}) + S(\bar{x})(\bar{x}+w) = 0$ for $C$ a constant and $S$ a polynomial. Since $P(\bar{x})$ and $(\bar{x}+w)$ are relatively prime, this means that $C = 0$ and $S = 0$ and thus that the original equation does not depend on the challenge pair.

**Undistinguishability of Simulation.** Let $q_{\mathcal{G}}$ be the number of queries to the group oracle $\mathcal{G}$. The simulation is undistinguishable from the original game unless the adversary assembles two distinct polynomials $(p, q)$ with $(p - q)(x, a, r) = 0$.

The adversary can adaptively test whether $(x, a, r)$ is a root of one of the at most $q' = (5 + 2q + q_{\mathcal{G}})^2/2$ differences of polynomials of degrees at most $d = 2q$. Per the Schwartz-Zippel lemma, which states that a multivariate polynomial of degree $d$ has at most $d$ roots, this is equivalent to testing whether $(x, a, r)$ pertains to one of $q'$ subsets of $\mathbb{Z}_p^3$ of sizes at most $d$. Finally, the probability of adaptively finding such subsets is bounded above by $\frac{q'\cdot d}{p^3}$, which is negligible.

# References

[BBG05]  Boneh, D., Boyen, X., Goh, E.-J.: Hierarchical identity based encryption with constant size ciphertext. Cryptology ePrint Archive, Report 2005/015 (2005). http://eprint.iacr.org/2005/015

[BBO06]  Bellare, M., Boldyreva, A., O'Neill, A.: Deterministic and efficiently searchable encryption. Cryptology ePrint Archive, Report 2006/186 (2006). http://eprint.iacr.org/2006/186

[BDOP04] Boneh, D., Di Crescenzo, G., Ostrovsky, R., Persiano, G.: Public key encryption with keyword search. In: Cachin, C., Camenisch, J.L. (eds.) EUROCRYPT 2004. LNCS, vol. 3027, pp. 506–522. Springer, Heidelberg (2004). https://doi.org/10.1007/978-3-540-24676-3_30

[CFGL12] Canard, S., Fuchsbauer, G., Gouget, A., Laguillaumie, F.: Plaintext-checkable encryption. In: Dunkelman, O. (ed.) CT-RSA 2012. LNCS, vol. 7178, pp. 332–348. Springer, Heidelberg (2012). https://doi.org/10.1007/978-3-642-27954-6_21

[Cha82] Chaum, D.: Blind signatures for untraceable payments. In: Chaum, D., Rivest, R.L., Sherman, A.T. (eds.) CRYPTO 1982, pp. 199–203. Plenum Press, New York (1982)

[FNP04] Freedman, M.J., Nissim, K., Pinkas, B.: Efficient private matching and set intersection. In: Cachin, C., Camenisch, J.L. (eds.) EUROCRYPT 2004. LNCS, vol. 3027, pp. 1–19. Springer, Heidelberg (2004). https://doi.org/10.1007/978-3-540-24676-3_1

[GM84] Goldwasser, S., Micali, S.: Probabilistic encryption. J. Comput. Syst. Sci. **28**(2), 270–299 (1984)

[Jag12] Jager, T.: Black-Box Models of Computation. Vieweg+Teubner Verlag, Wiesbaden (2012)

[LZL13] Lu, Y., Zhang, R., Lin, D.: Stronger security model for public-key encryption with equality test. In: Abdalla, M., Lange, T. (eds.) Pairing 2012. LNCS, vol. 7708, pp. 65–82. Springer, Heidelberg (2013). https://doi.org/10.1007/978-3-642-36334-4_5

[Ped92] Pedersen, T.P.: Non-interactive and information-theoretic secure verifiable secret sharing. In: Feigenbaum, J. (ed.) CRYPTO 1991. LNCS, vol. 576, pp. 129–140. Springer, Heidelberg (1992). https://doi.org/10.1007/3-540-46766-1_9

[PS16] Pointcheval, D., Sanders, O.: Short randomizable signatures. In: Sako, K. (ed.) CT-RSA 2016. LNCS, vol. 9610, pp. 111–126. Springer, Cham (2016). https://doi.org/10.1007/978-3-319-29485-8_7

[PS18] Pointcheval, D., Sanders, O.: Reassessing security of randomizable signatures. In: Smart, N.P. (ed.) CT-RSA 2018. LNCS, vol. 10808, pp. 319–338. Springer, Cham (2018). https://doi.org/10.1007/978-3-319-76953-0_17

[Sha79] Shamir, A.: How to share a secret. Commun. Assoc. Comput. Mach. **22**(11), 612–613 (1979)

[Sho97] Shoup, V.: Lower bounds for discrete logarithms and related problems. In: Fumy, W. (ed.) EUROCRYPT 1997. LNCS, vol. 1233, pp. 256–266. Springer, Heidelberg (1997). https://doi.org/10.1007/3-540-69053-0_18

[SWP00] Song, D.X., Wagner, D., Perrig, A.: Practical techniques for searches on encrypted data. In: 2000 IEEE Symposium on Security and Privacy, pp. 44–55. IEEE Computer Society Press, May 2000

[YTHW10] Yang, G., Tan, C.H., Huang, Q., Wong, D.S.: Probabilistic public key encryption with equality test. In: Pieprzyk, J. (ed.) CT-RSA 2010. LNCS, vol. 5985, pp. 119–131. Springer, Heidelberg (2010). https://doi.org/10.1007/978-3-642-11925-5_9

# Nothing Refreshes Like a RePSI: Reactive Private Set Intersection

Andrea Cerulli[1], Emiliano De Cristofaro[1(✉)], and Claudio Soriente[2]

[1] University College London, London, UK
e.decristofaro@ucl.ac.uk
[2] NEC Laboratories Europe, Heidelberg, Germany

**Abstract.** Private Set Intersection (PSI) is a popular cryptographic primitive that allows two parties, a client and a server, to compute the intersection of their private sets, so that the client only receives the output of the computation, while the server learns nothing besides the size of the client's set. A common limitation of PSI is that a dishonest client can progressively learn the server's set by enumerating it over different executions. Although these "oracle attacks" do not formally violate security according to traditional secure computation definitions, in practice, they often hamper real-life deployment of PSI instantiations, especially if the server's set does not change much over multiple interactions.

In a first step to address this problem, this paper presents and studies the concept of Reactive PSI (RePSI). We model PSI as a reactive functionality, whereby the output depends on previous instances, and use it to limit the effectiveness of oracle attacks. We introduce a general security model for RePSI in the (augmented) semi-honest model and a construction which enables the server to control how many inputs have been used by the client across several executions. In the process, we also present the first practical construction of a Size-Hiding PSI (SHI-PSI) protocol in the standard model, which may be of independent interest.

## 1 Introduction

Private Set Intersection (PSI) lets two parties compute the intersection of their private sets, drawn from a common universe, without disclosing items outside the intersection. In its most common formulation, only one party, usually referred to as the *client*, obtains the intersection, while the other, aka *server*, only learns the size of the client's set. Over the past few years, PSI has been used in numerous privacy-friendly applications, including ridesharing [HOS17], collaborative threat mitigation [FDCB15], genomic testing [BBD+11], and online advertising [IKN+17].

Nonetheless, there are some challenging issues limiting the adoption of PSI in practice. In particular, if two parties run the protocol several times, the server

The research leading to these results has received funding from the European Research Council under the European Union's Seventh Framework Programme (FP/2007-2013)/ERC Grant Agreement no. 307937.

© Springer International Publishing AG, part of Springer Nature 2018
B. Preneel and F. Vercauteren (Eds.): ACNS 2018, LNCS 10892, pp. 280–300, 2018.
https://doi.org/10.1007/978-3-319-93387-0_15

is vulnerable to *oracle attacks*. In such an attack, a dishonest client progressively learns the server's set by enumerating it over different executions. Although this does not formally violate security definitions of two-party computation [Gol04], it may hamper real-life deployment of PSI, especially if the server's set is mostly static. Moreover, in the *Size-Hiding* variant of PSI [ADT11], where the server does not learn the size of client's set, the problem is further compounded as the server cannot limit the size of client's input.

Aiming to mitigate oracle attacks in PSI protocols, we start reasoning about the security of this cryptographic primitive across multiple runs. To this end, we introduce the notion of Reactive PSI (RePSI), along with a general security model in the augmented semi-honest model [Gol04], and set to propose provably secure instantiations.

Let us first consider a naïve solution. In the non size-hiding setting, using certain PSI protocols, e.g., [DT10], one could in theory let the client re-use the randomness for the elements in its input set that do not change across runs. This way, the server learns how many of the client's elements are "fresh" in the current run and imposes an upper-bound. However, this approach at the very least makes two protocol executions linkable as it reveals the patterns of the client's inputs. Moreover, if the distribution of client's elements is somewhat predictable, this might actually reveal too much information. By contrast, our goal is to provide stronger definitions whereby the client does not reveal its input patterns, but only proves that number of unique elements input from the first run up to the current one is below a given threshold.

## 1.1   Roadmap

In this paper, we tackle the issue of oracle attacks in Private Set Intersection (PSI) by extending security definitions to account for reactive functionalities, whereby the output of the current execution can depend on previous executions.

First, we introduce the notion of Reactive PSI (RePSI), along with a general security model in the augmented semi-honest model [Gol04]. In this model, the adversary is assumed to follow the specifications of the protocol (as in the standard semi-honest model) but it is allowed to adaptively modify the inputs used by the controlled party at each protocol run. We argue that the augmented semi-honest model can effectively model oracle attacks in PSI, whereas, the standard semi-honest model cannot, since it prevents the adversary to change the input of the corrupted party between protocol executions. That is, the adversary can only leverage honestly generated transcripts. Also, although we do not yet provide security in the fully malicious setting, we believe that ours is an important first step towards the development of efficient protocols. In fact, there exist general transformations [GMW87, Gol04] allowing to compile a semi-honest secure protocol into one secure against malicious adversaries, and efficient PSI-like protocols are also traditionally in semi-honest settings (see Sect. 1.2). Moreover, our definitions are general enough to capture various types of reactive functionalities and they cover the sequential composition of standard (i.e., stateless) PSI protocols.

Then, we provide two constructions, one static and one reactive. We focus on the size-hiding setting since, as mentioned above, the fact that the server cannot even check and limit the number of client's inputs in a single execution, makes oracle attacks significantly worse. Our static construction, named **Bounded-Input PSI** limits the size of the client's input set at every protocol run. We achieve this by adapting the Bounded Size-Hiding PSI recently presented by Bradley et al. [BFT16], which provided security in the Random Oracle Model (ROM). As an additional contribution, we instantiate Bounded Size-Hiding PSI in the standard model, thus also presenting the first practical Size-Hiding PSI protocol not in ROM. Our reactive construction, called **Input Controlling RePSI**, enables the server to control how many inputs have been used by the other party across several executions. Specifically, it limits the size of the unions set stemming from the union of client's input sets across all protocol runs. Input Controlling RePSI, therefore, addresses oracle attacks in practical scenarios where a client and a server engage in multiple PSI executions.

By modeling PSI as a reactive functionality, we require that client and server keep *state* across protocol executions. Nevertheless, the amount of state information kept by the two parties in our constructions is small and independent of the number of runs.

## 1.2   Related Work

To the best of our knowledge, the problem of Reactive PSI has not been studied in literature. Standard security definitions for semi-honest and malicious two-party and multiparty computation can be extended to model security of generic protocols computing reactive functionalities. The augmented semi-honest model was introduced by Goldreich [Gol04] to bridge the semi-honest model and the malicious model and used it as an intermediate step in the compilation of secure protocols from the semi-honest to the malicious settings. Hazay and Lindell [HL10a] observed that security in the malicious settings sometime does not imply security in the semi-honest settings, while this anomaly does not happen in the augmented semi-honest model.

Overall, prior work on PSI can be grouped in protocols using special-purpose constructions [FNP04, DT10], oblivious transfer and its extensions [PSZ14, PSSZ15], and/or generic garbled circuits [PSSZ15]. Most protocols are secure against semi-honest adversaries [FNP04, DT10, PSZ14, PSSZ15], with fewer, less efficient ones, against malicious ones [DKT10, JL10, RR17]. Also, protocols by Hazay and Lindell [HL08] operate in the covert model (i.e., a malicious adversary may be able to cheat but it can get caught with at least a certain probability).

There are also a few variants to the standard PSI functionality. Besides the size-hiding one discussed above [ADT11, BFT16], Authorized PSI [CZ09, DT10] partially mitigates malicious behavior by introducing a trusted party that authorizes (i.e., signs) the elements that a client can use as input. However, finding a common trusted party may be hard in most practical use cases.

More closely related to our work are the protocols proposed in [BFT16] and [DMV13]. Bradley et al. [BFT16] introduce the concept of Bounded Size-Hiding PSI, which allows the client to hide the size of its input, and the server to impose an upper-bound on the size of the client's set *for the current run*. We start from the protocol of [BFT16] and cast it within the framework of RePSI to counter oracle attacks *across multiple runs*. Furthermore, while [BFT16] works in the random oracle model, we instantiate it in the standard model. Dagdelen et al. [DMV13] introduce the concept of rate-limited Secure Function Evaluation (SFE), whereby protocol participants can monitor and limit the number of distinct inputs (i.e., rate) used by their counterparts in multiple executions of an SFE. They present compilers by which any SFE scheme can be turned into a rate-limited one. In particular, the "rate-hiding" compiler [DMV13] may be applied to a PSI protocol to achieve the same provisions of our Input Controlling RePSI. We take a less general approach and focus on PSI, by incorporating reactiveness in the functionality and achieving a more efficient construction (see Sect. 5.3). A theoretical construction based on fully-homomorphic encryption for size-hiding PSI in the standard model was recently presented in [COV15].

### 1.3   Paper Organization

Next section introduces some preliminaries, then, Sect. 3 provides security definitions for the Reactive PSI primitive in the augmented semi-honest model. Next, in Sects. 4 and 5, we present our constructions of Bounded Input RePSI and Input Controlling RePSI, respectively. Finally, the paper concludes in Sect. 6.

## 2   Preliminaries

In this section, we introduce notation, cryptographic assumptions and building blocks used later on in the paper.

We write $y \leftarrow \mathcal{A}(x)$ for a probabilistic algorithm returning output $y$ given as input $x$. In case we want to specify the randomness $r$ used, we write $y = \mathcal{A}(x; r)$. We implicitly assume all the algorithms considered in this paper to receive as input the security parameter $\lambda$. For functions $f, g : \mathbb{N} \rightarrow [0, 1]$ we write $f(\lambda) \approx g(\lambda)$ if $|f(\lambda) - g(\lambda)| = \lambda^{\omega(1)}$. We say a function $f$ is *overwhelming* if $f(\lambda) \approx 1$ and *negligible* if $f(\lambda) \approx 0$.

### 2.1   Bilinear Groups

A bilinear group is a tuple $(p, \mathbb{G}, \mathbb{G}_T, e, g)$ s.t. $\mathbb{G}$ and $\mathbb{G}_T$ are groups of prime order $p$ and $g \in \mathbb{G}$ generates the group $\mathbb{G}$. The function $e$ is an efficiently computable bilinear map $e : \mathbb{G} \times \mathbb{G} \rightarrow \mathbb{G}_T$ such that $e(g, g)$ is a generator of $\mathbb{G}_T$. We assume there are probabilistic polynomial time generators $\mathcal{G}$ and $\mathcal{BG}$ that, given as input the security parameter, return the description of a group $(p, \mathbb{G}, g) \leftarrow \mathcal{G}(\lambda)$ and bilinear group $(p, \mathbb{G}, \mathbb{G}_T, e, g) \leftarrow \mathcal{BG}(\lambda)$, respectively. In the constructions of Sects. 4 and 5, we rely on the exponent Strong Diffie-Hellman (Exponent $q$-SDH) and the Decisional Bilinear Diffie-Hellmann Inversion problem ($q$-DBDHI).

## 2.2   Bilinear Accumulators

A cryptographic accumulator is a primitive that allows to give a compact representation of a set and that enables to efficiently prove membership of an element into the accumulated set. Accumulators were firstly introduced by Benaloh and de Mare [BDM94] and were later extended and provided with additional properties [BP97, CL02, Ngu05, DHS15, GOP+16, CKS09].

A (static) accumulator consists of four algorithms (KeyGen, Eval, WitGen, Verify). The key generation algorithm KeyGen takes as input the security parameter and generates a secret and an evaluation key pair $(sk, ek)$ for the accumulator. The evaluation algorithm Eval gets as input the evaluation key $ek$ and a set $A$ of values and returns an accumulator $\mathrm{acc}_A$. The WitGen and Verify are deterministic algorithms for, respectively, producing and verifying a witness wit for the membership of an element $a \in A$ in a given accumulator $\mathrm{acc}_A$. We follow [DHS15] on modelling Eval and WitGen to optionally get as input the secret key $sk$, since this makes the algorithms more efficient. We denote the optional input by writing $\boxed{sk}$.

The main security properties required from accumulators are: *correctness*, i.e. honestly generated witnesses should verify; *collision-freeness*, i.e. that it is unfeasible to compute a witness for elements not included in the accumulated set; and *indistinguishability*, i.e. the accumulator does not reveal any information on the accumulated set.

In our constructions of PSI we will later use the accumulator introduced by Nguyen in [Ngu05] based on bilinear pairings. Since we will not require the possibility of removing elements from an accumulator, we restrict Nguyen's construction [Ngu05] to a static accumulator, description of which can be found in Fig. 1.

---

KeyGen$(\lambda) \to (sk, ek)$:
- $(p, \mathbb{G}, \mathbb{G}_T, e, g) \leftarrow \mathcal{BG}(\lambda)$
- $x \leftarrow \mathbb{Z}_p^*$
- $sk := x$
- $ek := (g, g^x, g^{x^2}, \ldots, g^{x^q})$

Eval$(\boxed{sk}, ek, A) \to \mathrm{acc}_A$:
- Parse $A = (a_1, \ldots, a_n)$ for $a_i \in \mathbb{Z}_p$
- $\mathrm{Ch}_A(X) = \sum_{i=0}^n c_i X^i$
- $r \leftarrow \mathbb{Z}_p^*$
- $\mathrm{acc}_A := g^{r\mathrm{Ch}_A(x)} = \left(\prod_{i=0}^n (g^{x^i})^{c_i}\right)^r$

WitGen$(\boxed{sk}, ek, \mathrm{acc}_A, r, A, a) \to \mathrm{wit}$:
- Parse $A = (a_1, \ldots, a_n)$ for $a_i \in \mathbb{Z}_p$
- $\mathrm{Ch}_{A \setminus \{a\}}(X) = \sum_{i=0}^n d_i X^i$
- $\mathrm{wit} := \mathrm{acc}_A^{\frac{1}{a+x}} = g^{r\mathrm{Ch}_{A \setminus \{a\}}(x)} = \left(\prod_{i=0}^n (g^{x^i})^{d_i}\right)^r$

Verify$(ek, \mathrm{acc}_A, a, \mathrm{wit}) \to 0/1$:
- If $e(\mathrm{acc}_A, g) = e(\mathrm{wit}, g^x \cdot g^a)$ : Return 1
- Else: Return 0

**Fig. 1.** Bilinear accumulators.

---

Let $A = \{a_1, \ldots a_n\}$ be a set of elements $a_i \in \mathbb{Z}_p$ that we wish to include into an accumulator. We first start by computing the *characteristic polynomial* representation of set $A$. This is the monic polynomial $\mathsf{Ch}_A(X) \in \mathbb{Z}_p[X]$ which has roots in the elements contained in the set $A$, namely $\mathsf{Ch}_A(X) = \prod_{i=1}^{n}(X + a_i)$. In order to efficiently evaluate the accumulator, it will be convenient to express such polynomial using its coefficient representation, i.e. computing $c_j$ such that $\mathsf{Ch}_A(X) = \prod_{i=1}^{n}(X + a_i) = \sum_{j=0}^{n} c_j X^j$. We stress that given $A$ it is always possible to efficiently compute the coefficient $c_j$ of $\mathsf{Ch}_A(X)$.

The evaluation key of [Ngu05] bilinear accumulator consists of $ek = (g, g^x, g^{x^2}, \ldots, g^{x^q}) \in \mathbb{G}^{q+1}$, where $g$ is a generator of the group $\mathbb{G}$ and $x \in \mathbb{Z}_p$ is a secret value.

Given the evaluation key and polynomial $\mathsf{Ch}_A(X)$ of degree at most $q$, it is possible to compute $g^{\mathsf{Ch}_A(x)}$. This is done by first expanding $\mathsf{Ch}_A(X)$ into its coefficient representation, i.e $\mathsf{Ch}_A(X) = \sum_{i=0}^{q} c_i X^i$, and then computing $g^{\mathsf{Ch}_A(x)} = \prod_{i=0}^{q}(g^{x^i})^{c_i}$. An accumulator $\mathsf{acc}_A$ to a set $A$ is computed by picking a random $r \leftarrow \mathbb{Z}_p$ and setting $\mathsf{acc}_A = (g^{\mathsf{Ch}_A(x)})^r$.

We recall the following result from [Ngu05, DHS15].

**Lemma 1.** *Under the $q$-SDH assumption, the accumulator described in Fig. 1 is collision-free and indistinguishable.*

**Subset Queries.** The $\mathsf{WitGen}$ algorithm described in Fig. 1 is used to compute witnesses for the membership of single elements in $\mathsf{acc}_A$. We now extend it to compute witnesses for multiple elements, namely to show that a set $B \subseteq A$ is included in $\mathsf{acc}_A$. We write $\mathsf{WitGen}^*(\boxed{sk}, ek, A, \mathsf{acc}_A, r, B)$ for the computation of the witness $\mathsf{wit} = \mathsf{acc}_A^{\frac{1}{\mathsf{Ch}_B(x)}} = g^{r\mathsf{Ch}_{A \setminus B}(x)}$. Similarly, we let $\mathsf{Verify}^*(ek, \mathsf{acc}_A, B, \mathsf{wit})$ to return 1 in case $e(\mathsf{acc}_A, g) = e(\mathsf{wit}, g^{\mathsf{Ch}_B(x)})$ holds, and 0 otherwise.

Furthermore, we can extend $\mathsf{WitGen}$ to compute witnesses for an accumulator $\mathsf{acc}_B$ to accumulate a subset of the set accumulated into $\mathsf{acc}_A$. Let $r$ and $r'$ be the randomness used to generate $\mathsf{acc}_A$ and $\mathsf{acc}_B$, respectively. We define the following

- $\mathsf{WitGen}^*(\boxed{sk}, ek, (\mathsf{acc}_A, r, A), (r', B))$ : it computes the witness $\mathsf{wit}^* = \mathsf{acc}_A^{\frac{1}{r' \mathsf{Ch}_B(x)}} = g^{\frac{r}{r'} \mathsf{Ch}_{A \setminus B}(x)}$
- $\mathsf{Verify}^*(ek, \mathsf{acc}_A, \mathsf{acc}_B, \mathsf{wit}^*)$ : it returns 1 if $e(\mathsf{acc}_A, g) = e(\mathsf{acc}_B, \mathsf{wit}^*)$ holds, and 0 otherwise.

### 2.3   Hard Relations

Let $p$ be a polynomial and $\mathcal{R}_{\mathsf{pp}} \subseteq \{0,1\}^{p(\lambda)} \times \{0,1\}^{p(\lambda)}$ be a binary relation indexed by some public parameters $\mathsf{pp}$. We call $(u, w) \in \mathcal{R}$ *instance* and *witness*, respectively. We assume the public parameters $\mathsf{pp} \leftarrow \mathcal{G}(\lambda)$ to be efficiently computable given as input the security parameter. Also, let $L_{\mathsf{pp}} := \{u : \exists w \text{ s.t. } (u, w) \in \mathcal{R}\}$ to be the NP language corresponding to $\mathcal{R}_{\mathsf{pp}}$. We require the language $L$ to be efficiently sampleable and denote with $u \leftarrow \mathcal{D}(L)$ the process of picking a random element from $L$. A relation $(\mathcal{G}, \mathcal{R}, \mathcal{D})$ is said to be *hard* if for any probabilistic polynomial time adversary $\mathcal{A}$ the following probability is negligible

$$\Pr\left[\mathsf{pp} \leftarrow \mathcal{G}(\lambda); u \leftarrow \mathcal{D}(L_{\mathsf{pp}}); w \leftarrow \mathcal{A}(\mathsf{pp}, u) : (u, w) \in \mathcal{R}_{\mathsf{pp}}\right] \approx 0$$

More concretely, we are interested in relations corresponding to hard search problems associated with cryptographic accumulators. For example the relation corresponding to the following language

$$L_{ek}(a) := \{(\mathsf{acc}_A, a) \in \mathbb{G} \times \mathbb{Z}_p : \exists \, \mathsf{wit} \in \mathbb{G} \text{ s.t. } \mathsf{Verify}(ek, \mathsf{acc}_A, a, \mathsf{wit}) = 1\}$$

The above language consists of all accumulators $\mathsf{acc}_A$ for which there exists a witness for the accumulation of $a \in \mathbb{Z}_p$. We note that the above language is efficiently sampleable by letting $\mathsf{acc}_A \leftarrow \mathsf{Eval}(ek, a)$. We now state the following straightforward Lemma and refer to the full version of the paper [CDS18] for the proof.

**Lemma 2.** *Assuming the accumulator is collision-free and indistinguishable, then the above the binary relation corresponding to $L_{ek}(a)$ is hard for any $a \in \mathbb{Z}_p$.*

### 2.4 Smooth Projective Hash Function

Smooth Projective Hash Functions (SPHF) were introduced by Cramer and Shoup [CS02] (with the name of hash proof system) as a kind of designated-verifier proof systems for certain classes of algebraic languages. These found great applications towards the development of several primitives such as CCA2 secure public key encryption [CS02] and password authenticated key exchange [GL03,KV09]. Here we define a simpler hash proof system for the language of elements accumulated using the above bilinear accumulator.

An SPHF consists of three algorithms $(\mathsf{HGen}, \mathsf{Hash}, \mathsf{PHash})$. The key generation algorithm $\mathsf{HGen}$ takes as input the security parameter and returns a relation[1], and a pair of secret and public keys $(hsk, hpk)$; we sometimes refer to $hpk$ as the projection key. The keys specify an hash function from the relation $\mathcal{R}$ to an abelian group $\mathbb{G}$. The hash function can be privately evaluated using $hsk$ on any instance in $L_{\mathcal{R}}$, namely $\mathsf{Hash}_{hsk} : L_{\mathcal{R}} \to \mathbb{G}$. The hash function allows also for public evaluation given $hpk$ but only on instances for which a witness is known, namely $\mathsf{PHash}_{hpk} : \mathcal{R} \to \mathbb{G}$. An SPHF satisfies two main properties: correctness and smoothness.

– Correctness: for any $(u, w) \in R$, the private and public evaluation algorithms $\mathsf{Hash}, \mathsf{PHash}$ of the SPHF return the same result, i.e.

$$\mathsf{Hash}_{hsk}(u) = \mathsf{PHash}_{hpk}(u, w)$$

---

[1] The original definition of SPHF was introduced for languages related with hard subset membership problems, while here we define SPHF for languages related with a hard search problem.

– (Computational) Smoothness: for any instance for which a witness is not known, the evaluation of the hash function is (computationally) indistinguishable from random. Namely, we say that an SPHF on a relation $(\mathcal{G}, \mathcal{R}, \mathcal{D})$ is smooth if for any probabilistic polynomial time adversary $\mathcal{A}$, the following advantage is negligible

$$\left| \Pr \left[ \begin{array}{c} (L_{\mathsf{pp}}, hsk, hpk) \leftarrow \mathsf{HGen}(\lambda); \\ u \leftarrow \mathcal{D}(L_{\mathsf{pp}}); \\ H \leftarrow \mathsf{Hash}_{hsk}(u); \end{array} : \mathcal{A}(hpk, u, H) = 1 \right] - \Pr \left[ \begin{array}{c} (L_{\mathsf{pp}}, hsk, hpk) \leftarrow \mathsf{HGen}(L_{\mathsf{pp}}); \\ u \leftarrow \mathcal{D}(L_{\mathsf{pp}}); \\ H \leftarrow \mathbb{G}; \end{array} : \mathcal{A}(hpk, u, H) = 1 \right] \right| \approx 0$$

We now show the construction for an SPHF defined on the relation specified by $L_{ek}(a)$, for any $a \in \mathbb{Z}_p$, to the target group $\mathbb{G}_T$ of a bilinear group. The construction of the SPHF is described in Fig. 2 and is a simple combination of the bilinear accumulators of [Ngu05] and the verifiable random function (VRF) constructed by Dodis and Yampolskiy [DY05]. A VRF is a pseudorandom function which admits proofs of correct evaluation that can be publicly verified. In our SPHF we apply the VRF to an accumulator and an element accumulated in it. The proof of evaluation for the function corresponds to the accumulation witness, and the secret key of the SPHF is the secret key of the accumulator. Since the secret key of the accumulator allows to compute witnesses for every element in $\mathbb{Z}_p$ it also allows to evaluate the SPHF in every pair $(\mathsf{acc}, a) \in \mathbb{G} \times \mathbb{Z}_p$.

| $\mathsf{HGen}(\lambda) \to (L_{ek}, hsk, hpk):$ | $\mathsf{Hash}_{hsk}(\mathsf{acc}, a) \to H:$ |
|---|---|
| $\cdot\ (sk, ek) \leftarrow \mathsf{KeyGen}(\lambda)$ | $\cdot\ H := e(\mathsf{acc}, g^z)^{\frac{1}{sk+a}}$ |
| $\cdot\ L_{ek} := \cup_{a \in \mathbb{Z}_p} L_{ek}(a)$ | $\mathsf{PHash}_{hpk}((\mathsf{acc}, a), \mathsf{wit}) \to H:$ |
| $\cdot\ z \leftarrow \mathbb{Z}_p^*$ | $\cdot\ \mathrm{If}\ ((\mathsf{acc}, a), \mathsf{wit}) \in \mathcal{R}_{L_{ek}}:$ |
| $\cdot\ hsk := (sk, z)$ | $\cdot\ H := e(\mathsf{wit}, g^z)$ |
| $\cdot\ hpk := (ek, g^z)$ | $\cdot\ \mathrm{Else:\ Return}\ H := \perp.$ |

Fig. 2. SPHF for accumulators.

The security of the SPHF constructed in Fig. 2 follows from the security of the verifiable random function of [DY05], based on the $q$-DHDBI assumption. We refer to the full version of the paper [CDS18] for a proof of the following Lemma.

**Lemma 3.** *Under the $q$-DBDHI assumption over a bilinear group $(p, \mathbb{G}, \mathbb{G}_T, e, g)$, the construction in Fig. 2 is a smooth projective hash function.*

## 3   Reactive PSI in the Augmented Semi-honest Model

Aiming to prevent oracle attacks in scenarios where two parties engage in several PSI executions, we consider stateful PSI protocols computing reactive functionalities, whereby their outputs can depend on previous instances of the protocol.

We set our security definitions in the augmented semi-honest model of [Gol04]. In this model, the adversary is restricted to follow the specifications of the protocol as in the standard semi-honest settings. In addition, the adversary is allowed to adaptively modify the inputs used by the controlled party before each instance of the protocol. Apart from being more natural [HL10b] to give semi-honest adversaries this capability, we argue that the augmented model is more appropriate than the standard one to study composition of protocols.

Let $t = t(\lambda)$ be a polynomial. We define the *reactive functionality* ReF $=$ $(F_1, F_2, \ldots, F_t)$ as a sequence of stateful functionalities[2] $F_i$ each taking as input a client set $C_i$ and a server set $S_i$ and returning a pair $\text{ReF}_i(C_i, S_i) = (I_i, b_i)$. These correspond to the outputs of the client and server should have at the at the end of each execution, respectively.

Next, we state our security definitions in terms of a generic reactive functionality and refer to the end of the section for specific instantiations of ReF for private set intersection protocols.

**Definition 1 (RePSI).** *A private set intersection protocol is a tuple* $(Setup, \Pi)$ *s.t.*

- $Setup(\lambda) \rightarrow (\text{param}_C; \text{param}_S)$: *it takes as input the security parameter and returns a pair of initial parameters for the client and the server. These can include public parameters and secret keys for the client and the server. If a specific protocol does not require a setup algorithm, this can be simply regarded as copying the security parameter into the initial parameters.*
- $\Pi \langle \mathcal{C}(C; St_C); \mathcal{S}(S; St_S) \rangle \rightarrow ((\text{out}_C; St_C); (\text{out}_S; St_S))$: *this is a stateful probabilistic polynomial time interactive protocol between a client $\mathcal{C}$ and a server $\mathcal{S}$. Each party takes as input a set and a state information (initialised to $St_C := \text{param}_C, St_S := \text{param}_S$ in the first instance of the protocol) and returns an output and an updated the state.*

*We say that private set intersection protocol $(Setup, \Pi)$ is a RePSI if it securely realizes a reactive functionality ReF in the augmented semi-honest model, i.e. if it satisfies* correctness, server privacy *and* client privacy *as defined below.*

Correctness is defined by the security game $\mathbf{Exp}_{\mathcal{A}}^{\text{Corr}}(\lambda)$ described in Fig. 3. Informally, a protocol is correct if at the end of each instance both parties return their prescribed outputs.

**Definition 2 (Correctness).** *Let $t = t(\lambda)$ a polynomial in the security parameter $\lambda$, and ReF defined as above. A protocol $(Setup, \Pi)$ is correct if for any probabilistic polynomial time adversary $\mathcal{A}$*

$$\Pr\left[\mathbf{Exp}_{\mathcal{A}}^{Corr}(\lambda) = 1\right] \approx 1$$

---

[2] In this paper we restrict our attention to the case of deterministic functionalities.

---

$\mathbf{Exp}_{\mathcal{A}}^{\mathrm{Corr}}(\lambda)$:

- $(\mathsf{param}_{\mathcal{C}}; \mathsf{param}_{\mathcal{S}}) \leftarrow Setup(\lambda)$
- $(\mathsf{C}_1, \mathsf{S}_1, \ldots, \mathsf{C}_t, \mathsf{S}_t) \leftarrow \mathcal{A}(\mathsf{param}_{\mathcal{C}}; \mathsf{param}_{\mathcal{S}})$
- $St_{\mathcal{C}} := \mathsf{param}_{\mathcal{C}}, St_{\mathcal{S}} := \mathsf{param}_{\mathcal{S}}$
- For $i = 1$ to $t$:
    - $((\mathsf{out}_{\mathcal{C},i}; St_{\mathcal{C}}); (\mathsf{out}_{\mathcal{S},i}; St_{\mathcal{S}})) \leftarrow \Pi\langle\mathcal{C}(\mathsf{C}_i; St_{\mathcal{C}}); \mathcal{S}(\mathsf{S}_i; St_{\mathcal{S}})\rangle$
    - $(I_i, b_i) = \mathsf{ReF}_i(\mathsf{C}_i, \mathsf{S}_i)$
- If $(\mathsf{out}_{\mathcal{C},i}, \mathsf{out}_{\mathcal{S},i}) = (I_i, b_i)$ for all $i \in [1, \ldots, t]$: Return 1
- Else: Return 0

**Fig. 3.** Correctness game

---

$O_\Pi(\mathsf{S}^*, St_{\mathcal{S}}^*)$:

- If $i = 0$: $St_{\mathcal{C}} := \mathsf{param}_{\mathcal{C}}$
- $i = i + 1$
- $((\mathsf{out}_{\mathcal{C},i}; St_{\mathcal{C}}); (\mathsf{out}_{\mathcal{S},i}; St_{\mathcal{S}})) \leftarrow \Pi\langle\mathcal{C}(\mathsf{C}_i; St_{\mathcal{C}}); \mathcal{S}(\mathsf{S}^*; St_{\mathcal{S}}^*)\rangle$
- Return $\mathsf{view}_{i,\mathcal{S}}((\mathsf{C}_i; St_{\mathcal{C}}); (\mathsf{S}^*; St_{\mathcal{S}}^*))$

$O_{Sim}(\mathsf{S}^*, St_{\mathcal{S}}^*)$:

- $i = i + 1$
- $(I_i; b_i) = \mathsf{ReF}_i(\mathsf{C}_i, \mathsf{S}^*)$
- $\mathsf{view}_{i,\mathcal{S},Sim} \leftarrow Sim((\mathsf{S}^*, St_{\mathcal{S}}^*), b_i, \mathsf{param}_{\mathcal{S}}, |\mathsf{C}_i|)$
- Return $\mathsf{view}_{i,\mathcal{S},Sim}$

**Fig. 4.** Oracles used in the client privacy game.

Client privacy is specified by two oracles $O_\Pi, O_{Sim}$ described in Fig. 4. The oracle $O_\Pi$ allows the adversary to run the next interaction between client and server on server's inputs of her choice. The oracle then returns the server's view in the protocol $\mathsf{view}_{i,\mathcal{S}}((\mathsf{C}_i; St_{\mathcal{C}}); (\mathsf{S}^*; St_{\mathcal{S}}^*))$, which contains the server's input, random coins and messages received from the client in the execution of the protocol. Oracle $O_{Sim}$ returns instead a simulated view, based only on the input and output of the server. Informally, we say that the protocol achieves client privacy if an adversary is not able to distinguish which oracle she is interacting with.

**Definition 3 (Client Privacy).** *Let $t = t(\lambda)$ and $\mathsf{ReF}$ defined as above. A protocol $(Setup, \Pi)$ has client privacy if for any probabilistic polynomial time adversary $\mathcal{A}$ there exists a probabilistic polynomial time simulator $Sim$, such that for every sequence $\mathsf{S}_1, \ldots, \mathsf{S}_t$ the following advantage is negligible*

$$Adv_{\mathcal{A}}^{\mathrm{CPriv}}(\lambda) = \Big| \Pr\Big[(\mathsf{param}_{\mathcal{C}}; \mathsf{param}_{\mathcal{S}}) \leftarrow Setup(\lambda) : \mathcal{A}^{O_\Pi}(\mathsf{param}_{\mathcal{S}}) = 1\Big]$$
$$- \Pr\Big[(\mathsf{param}_{\mathcal{C}}; \mathsf{param}_{\mathcal{S}}) \leftarrow Setup(\lambda) : \mathcal{A}^{O_{Sim}}(\mathsf{param}_{\mathcal{S}}) = 1\Big]\Big|$$

$O_\Pi(\mathsf{C}^*, St_{\mathcal{C}}^*)$:
. If $i = 0$: $St_{\mathcal{S}} := \mathsf{param}_{\mathcal{S}}$
. $i = i + 1$
. $((\mathsf{out}_{\mathcal{C},i}; St_{\mathcal{C}}); (\mathsf{out}_{\mathcal{S},i}; St_{\mathcal{S}})) \leftarrow \Pi\langle\mathcal{C}(\mathsf{C}^*; St_{\mathcal{C}}^*); \mathcal{S}(\mathsf{S}_i; St_{\mathcal{S}})\rangle$
. Return $\mathsf{view}_{i,\mathcal{C}}((\mathsf{C}^*; St_{\mathcal{C}}^*); (\mathsf{S}_i; St_{\mathcal{S}}))$

$O_{Sim}(\mathsf{C}^*, St_{\mathcal{C}}^*)$:
. $i = i + 1$
. $(I_i; b_i) = \mathsf{ReF}_i(\mathsf{C}^*, \mathsf{S}_i)$
. $\mathsf{view}_{i,\mathcal{C},Sim} \leftarrow Sim((\mathsf{C}^*, St_{\mathcal{C}}^*), I_i, \mathsf{param}_{\mathcal{C}}, |\mathsf{S}_i|)$
. Return $\mathsf{view}_{i,\mathcal{C},Sim}$

**Fig. 5.** Details of the oracles used in the server privacy game.

Server privacy is also specified in terms of two oracles $O_\Pi$, $O_{Sim}$ described in Fig. 5. The oracle $O_\Pi$ allows the adversary to run the next interaction between client and server on client's inputs of her choice. The oracle then returns the client's view $\mathsf{view}_{i,\mathcal{C}}$ in the protocol. Oracle $O_{Sim}$ returns instead a simulated view, based only on the input and output of the client. Informally, we say that the protocol achieves server privacy if an adversary is not able to distinguish which oracle she is interacting with.

**Definition 4 (Server Privacy).** *Let $t = t(\lambda)$ and $\mathsf{ReF}$ defined as above. A protocol $(Setup, \Pi)$ has server privacy if for any probabilistic polynomial time adversary $\mathcal{A}$ there exists a probabilistic polynomial time simulator $Sim$, such that for every sequence $\mathsf{C}_1, \ldots, \mathsf{C}_t$ the following advantage is negligible*

$$Adv_{\mathcal{A}}^{\mathrm{SPriv}}(\lambda) = \Big| \Pr\Big[(\mathsf{param}_{\mathcal{C}}; \mathsf{param}_{\mathcal{S}}) \leftarrow Setup(\lambda) : \mathcal{A}^{O_\Pi}(\mathsf{param}_{\mathcal{C}}) = 1\Big]$$
$$- \Pr\Big[(\mathsf{param}_{\mathcal{C}}; \mathsf{param}_{\mathcal{S}}) \leftarrow Setup(\lambda) : \mathcal{A}^{O_{Sim}}(\mathsf{param}_{\mathcal{C}}) = 1\Big]\Big|$$

**Size-Hiding.** In the previous definitions of client and server privacy we gave the simulator the size of the honest party's input set. This captures the security of most protocols in which participants learn information about the size of the other party's input. However, in certain cases the size of the inputs represents confidential information which should not be leaked in a protocol execution. Protocols achieving this stronger property are usually referred as *size-hiding* [ADT11]. To formalise size-hiding variants of client and server privacy it is sufficient to remove the size of the honest party's input from the input of the simulator. Looking ahead to the next sections, our protocols achieve size-hiding only in the case of client privacy.

The above definitions are general enough to capture various types of reactive functionalities $\mathsf{ReF}$. Moreover, they can also be used to formalise security for the sequential composition of standard PSI stateless protocols. In this case it is sufficient to replace $\mathsf{ReF}$ with $t$ copies of the same functionality $\mathsf{F}$ and replace protocol $\Pi$ with a stateless protocol that does not update the states $(St_{\mathcal{C}}, St_{\mathcal{S}})$, which are initialised as $(\mathsf{param}_{\mathcal{C}}, \mathsf{param}_{\mathcal{S}})$.

Next, we specify two functionalities, one static ($\mathsf{PSI}$) and one reactive ($\mathsf{RePSI}$), which we call *Bounded Input* PSI and *Input Controlling* RePSI, respectively.

**Bounded Input PSI.** A Bounded Input PSI limits the maximum size of the set the client can use in each instance of the protocol. More precisely, let $R$ be a polynomial in the security parameter $\lambda$, a Bounded Input $\mathsf{PSI} = (\mathsf{PSI}_1, \mathsf{PSI}_2, \ldots, \mathsf{PSI}_t)$ is defined as

$$\mathsf{PSI}_i(\mathsf{C}_i, \mathsf{S}_i) = \begin{cases} (\mathsf{C}_i \cap \mathsf{S}_i; \bot) & \text{If } |\mathsf{C}_i| \leq R \\ (\bot; \bot) & \text{Otherwise} \end{cases}$$

**Input Controlling RePSI.** An Input Controlling RePSI limits the number of maximum distinct elements a client can includes in its sets across all the executions. In this case the server's outputs is a predicate on whether the client has exceeded the allowed bound. More precisely, let $R$ be a polynomial in the security parameter $\lambda$, an Input Controlling $\mathsf{RePSI} = (\mathsf{RePSI}_1, \mathsf{RePSI}_2, \ldots, \mathsf{RePSI}_t)$ is defined as

$$\mathsf{RePSI}_i(\mathsf{C}_i, \mathsf{S}_i) = \begin{cases} (\mathsf{C}_i \cap \mathsf{S}_i; 1) & \text{If } |\cup_{j \leq i} \mathsf{C}_i| \leq R \\ (\bot; 0) & \text{Otherwise} \end{cases}$$

# 4    Bounded Input PSI

In this section we introduce our construction for a Bounded Input PSI. Bounded Input PSI allows client and server to compute the intersection of their private sets while imposing a bound $R$ on the size of the client set at each execution of the protocol. Bounded Input PSI is not a reactive RePSI but we will us it as a stepping stone for constructing our Input Controlling RePSI in the next section.

We notice that in several PSI protocols the size of the client set is naturally revealed during the interaction. Hence, a Bounded Input PSI variant can be easily achieved with simple modifications. The server can check the number of inputs used by the client and abort in case it exceeds the bound. This strategy is not viable in size-hiding PSI protocols [ADT11] where the use of cryptographic accumulators hides the size of the client set. We also leverage cryptographic accumulators, thus the server cannot directly check the number of inputs used by the client as just explained. Moreover, we will start from the Bounded Input PSI introduced in this section to construct our Input Controlling RePSI. In the latter, apart from hiding the size of the client set and reducing the communication, the use of accumulators will enable to use compact states for the server whose size does not depend on the number of protocol executions.

Our Bounded Input protocol is a modification of the bounded size-hiding protocol of Bradley et al. [BFT16], whose security is based on the $q$-SDH assumption in the random oracle model. The idea behind the protocol of Bradley et al. [BFT16] is to have the client to accumulate its input set using a cryptographic

$$\begin{array}{|l|}
\hline
Setup(\lambda) \rightarrow (\mathsf{param}_C; \mathsf{param}_S): \\
\hline
\cdot\ (p, \mathbb{G}, \mathbb{G}_T, e, g) \leftarrow \mathcal{BG}(\lambda) \\
\cdot\ \text{Set } R := R(\lambda) \\
\cdot\ x \leftarrow \mathbb{Z}_p^* \\
\cdot\ sk := x \\
\cdot\ ek := (g, g^x, g^{x^2}, \ldots, g^{x^R}) \\
\cdot\ \mathsf{param}_C := ((p, \mathbb{G}, \mathbb{G}_T, e, g), ek) \\
\cdot\ \mathsf{param}_S := ((p, \mathbb{G}, \mathbb{G}_T, e, g), sk, ek) \\
\hline
\end{array}$$

**Fig. 6.** Setup algorithm for bounded input PSI.

accumulator and send it to the server. The server would then use the accumulator secret key to *remove* her elements from the accumulator. This amounts to compute witnesses for elements in the server set. Then, the server hashes the witnesses using a random oracle and sends back the hash values to the client. The client is able to compute witnesses for each accumulated element and then hash them on the random oracle. The intersection can be then retrieved by checking matches between the two sets of hash values.

The protocol of [BFT16], as well as ours, relies on the boundedness of the underlying accumulator to limit the size of the sets that can be accumulated.

Informally, the protocol of [BFT16] fulfils server privacy because the random oracle hides all the information about the witnesses computed by the server, apart from the ones the client can compute on its own. We modify the protocol and remove the need of random oracles. The idea is to replace it with a function that can be efficiently computed by the client given a witness, but for which the evaluation looks random if a witness is not known. This is exactly the smoothness property of the SPHF we introduced in Sect. 2.4. Thus, we are able to remove the random oracle assumption and reduce the security to the $q$-DBDHI assumption, on which the SPHF relies on. We note that our Bounded Input PSI is, to the best of our knowledge, the first instantiation of size-hiding PSI in the standard model.

## 4.1   Bounded Input PSI Without Random Oracles

The setup of the protocol of the bounded-size PSI consists of generating a pair of secret key and evaluation key for a bilinear accumulator, as shown in Fig. 1. The length of the evaluation key $ek$ of the accumulator matches the input bound $R$ allowed to the client input size. The setup algorithm then sets the initial parameters for the client to be the evaluation key of the accumulator, and the initial parameters for the server to include both the secret key and evaluation key. The complete description of the *Setup* algorithm of our Bounded Input PSI is described in Fig. 6. Note that since we are in semi-honest settings, we can allow the server to run the setup and send the initial parameters to the client in a preliminary interaction with the client.

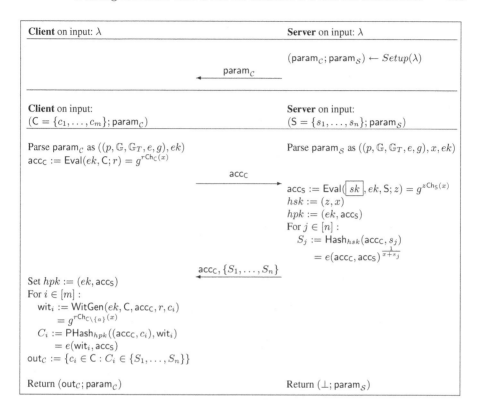

**Fig. 7.** Bounded input PSI without random oracles.

In the first move of the protocol, the client starts by computing an accumulator $\mathsf{acc_C}$ of its input set $\mathsf{C}$ and send it to the server. The evaluation of the accumulator can be done efficiently by first computing the characteristic polynomial of the set $\mathsf{C}$, expanding its coefficients, and then performing a multi-exponentiation of the evaluation key $ek$, using the coefficients of $\mathsf{Ch_C}(X)$ as exponents.

In the second move of the protocol, the server then picks a pair of keys $(hsk, hpk)$ for a SPHF associated with the witness relation of the accumulator. The secret key for the SPHF consists of the secret key $x$ of the accumulator and a random element $z \leftarrow \mathbb{Z}_p^*$. The projective key of the hash function corresponds to the accumulator $\mathsf{acc_S}$ of the server set, using randomness $z$. Then for every $s_i$ contained in its input set $\mathsf{S}$, the server evaluates the SPHF on instances $(\mathsf{acc_C}, s_i)$ using the secret key $x$. The server ends its move by forwarding the projective key $\mathsf{acc_S}$ to the client together with the set of SPHF evaluations. Without loss of generality we assume the server to sort the set of evaluations in lexicographic order before sending it to the client. Note that the server is not strictly required to know the secret key of the accumulator. However this can be used to speed up computation. For example, the server can avoid to accumulate its own set and simply set $acc_S = g^z$.

In the last move of the protocol, the client computes a witnesses $wit_i$ for the accumulation of his input elements $c_i \in C$ in the accumulator $acc_C$. Then, the client evaluates the SPHF using the projective key $acc_S$ on each witness $wit_i$ for $(acc_C, c_i)$. The clients then compares the set of its evaluations of the SPHF with the evaluations received from the server, looking for matches. Finally, the client outputs the subset of elements in $C$, for which the evaluation of the SPHF gave a match.

The full description of our Bounded Input PSI protocol is given in Fig. 7. We discuss its security in the following Theorem and refer to the full version of the paper [CDS18] for the proof.

**Theorem 1.** *Under the R-SDH and n-DBDHI assumptions, the protocol (Setup, $\Pi$) as described in Figs. 6 and 7 is a secure instantiation of a Bounded Input PSI in the augmented semi-honest model.*

## 5    Input Controlling RePSI

We now introduce our Input Controlling RePSI protocol. The starting point is the Bounded Input protocol introduced in the previous section. The idea is to turn the previous protocol into a stateful one where both parties keep track of previous executions.

### 5.1    Description of the Protocol

The *Setup* phase of the protocol is the same as the one described in Fig. 6 for the Bounded Input protocol. We stress that in this case the bound $R$ is not (only) the bound on the size of the client input of a single execution, but also a bound on the maximum number of elements the client can use across multiple executions. Again, since the client initial parameters only include public information we can allow the (semi-honest) server to run the *Setup* and forward the client the initial parameters $param_C$.

The first instance of Input Controlling RePSI is similar to an execution of a Bounded Input RePSI described in Fig. 7. The only difference here is that at the end of the first instance the client and the server update their output state. The client returns state $St_C = (param_C, C, r)$, which includes the initial parameter $param_C$, its current input set $C$ and the randomness used to create the accumulator $acc_C$. The server returns state $St_S = (param_S, acc_C)$, which includes the initial parameters $param_S$ as well as the accumulator $acc_C$ received from the client. In the rest of the description we implicitly assume that initial parameters $param_C$ and $param_S$ are always part of the states $St_C$ and $St_S$, respectively, and omit them from the notation to improve readability.

All the instances following the first one proceed as described in Fig. 8. In the first move of the protocol, the client retrieves the set $C'$ stored in state $St_C$

| **Client** on input: | **Server** on input: |
|---|---|
| $(C = \{c_1, \ldots, c_m\}; St_C)$ | $(S = \{s_1, \ldots, s_n\}; St_S)$ |

Parse $St_C$ as $(param_C, C', r')$                                Parse $St_S$ as $(param_S, acc_{C'})$

Pick $r, s \leftarrow \mathbb{Z}_p^*$

Set $U := C \cup C'$

$acc_C := \mathsf{Eval}(ek, C; r)$

$acc_U := \mathsf{Eval}(ek, U; s)$

$wit_C := \mathsf{WitGen}^*(ek, (acc_U, s, U), (r, C))$

$wit_{C'} := \mathsf{WitGen}^*(ek, (acc_U, s, U), (r', C'))$

$$\xrightarrow{\quad acc_C, acc_U, wit_C, wit_{C'} \quad}$$

If $\Big( \mathsf{Verify}^*(ek, acc_U, acc_C, wit_C) = 0 \; \vee$

$\quad \mathsf{Verify}^*(ek, acc_U, acc_C', wit_{C'}) = 0 \Big):$

     ▪ Return $(0; St_S)$

Else: Set $St_S := (param_S, acc_U)$

$acc_S := \mathsf{Eval}(\boxed{sk}, ek, S; z) = g^{z\mathsf{Chs}(x)}$

$hsk := (z, x)$

$hpk := (ek, acc_S)$

For $j \in [n]$ :

    $S_j := \mathsf{Hash}_{hsk}(acc_C, s_j)$

$$\xleftarrow{\quad acc_S, \{S_1, \ldots, S_n\} \quad} \qquad\qquad = e(acc_C, acc_S)^{\frac{1}{x+s_j}}$$

Set $hpk := (ek, acc_S)$

For $i \in [m]$ :

    $wit_i := \mathsf{WitGen}(ek, C, acc_C, r, c_i)$

       $= g^{r\mathsf{Ch}_{C \setminus \{a\}}(x)}$

    $C_i := \mathsf{PHash}_{hpk}((acc_C, c_i), wit_i)$

       $= e(wit_i, acc_S)$

$out_C := \{c_i \in C : C_i \in \{S_1, \ldots, S_n\}\}$

$St_C := (param_C, U, s)$

Return $(out_C; St_C)$                                       Return $(1; St_S)$

**Fig. 8.** Input controlling RePSI.

which contains all the elements used in previous executions of the protocol and computes the union with its current input set, i.e. $U = C \cup C'$. Then, the client computes fresh accumulators for both the current input set $C$ and the union set $U$. The client computes also witnesses for the accumulation in $acc_U$ of subsets accumulated into $acc_C$ and $acc_{C'}$. Here $acc_{C'}$ corresponds to the accumulator of the union of all previous client input set, which was generated in the last execution. The client ends its move by sending the accumulators $acc_C, acc_U$ and witnesses $wit_C, wit_{C'}$ to the server.

In the second move of the protocol, the server retrieves the accumulator $acc_{C'}$ from its state, which contains the union of the sets of all previous client sets. Then, the server verifies the witnesses $wit_C, wit_{C'}$ for the accumulation of $C$ and $C'$ in $U$. If any of these checks fails, then the server terminates the execution of the protocol with output $(0; St_S)$. Note that in this case both client and server do not update their states and might later enter a new instance of the protocol with different inputs. In case both checks pass, the server continues the execution as in the Bounded Input protocol: he sets a public and private key for the SPHF

**Table 1.** Efficiency. Computation is expressed in number of pairings $\mathbb{P}$ and group exponentiations $\mathbb{E}$, communication in terms of the number of group elements $\mathbb{G}$, target group elements $\mathbb{G}_T$ and field elements $\mathbb{Z}_p$. The size of the client and server sets are $m$ and $n$, respectively. While the total size of the inputs used by the client up to the current iteration is denoted with $M$. The client's state does not include the total number of elements used by the client, i.e. $M$.

|  | Bounded input | Input controlling |
|---|---|---|
| Client computation | $m\mathbb{P} + O(\frac{m^2}{\log m})\mathbb{E}$ | $m\mathbb{P} + O(\frac{m^2}{\log m} + \frac{M}{\log M})\mathbb{E}$ |
| Server computation | $n\mathbb{P} + (n+1)\mathbb{E}$ | $(n+4)\mathbb{P} + (n+1)\mathbb{E}$ |
| Communication | $n\mathbb{G}_T + 2\mathbb{G}$ | $n\mathbb{G}_T + 5\mathbb{G}$ |
| Client's state | n.a | $1\mathbb{Z}_p$ |
| Server's state | n.a | $1\mathbb{G}$ |

and evaluates it on instances $(\mathsf{acc}_C, s_i)$ for elements $s_i \in S$. The server ends its move by sending the public key for the SPHF and the set of evaluations to the client, updates its state with the accumulator $\mathsf{acc}_U$ and terminates its execution by outputting $(1, St_S)$.

In the last move of the protocol the client continues the execution as in the case of the Bounded Input RePSI. It computes witnesses for the accumulation of elements in $C$ into $\mathsf{acc}_C$ and computes evaluations of the SPHF on these. Then it looks for matches between the sets of evaluations and includes the corresponding elements in $C$ in the intersection $\mathsf{out}_C$. The client updates its state with $(U, s)$, where $s$ is the randomness used in the generation of the accumulator $\mathsf{acc}_U$, and terminates the instance execution with output $(\mathsf{out}_C; St_C)$.

### 5.2   Security of Input Controlling RePSI

**Theorem 2.** *Under the R-SDH and n-DBDHI assumptions, the protocol $(Setup, \Pi)$ as described in Figs. 6 and 8 is a secure instantiation of an Input Controlling RePSI in the augmented semi-honest model.*

*Proof.* Correctness as for the case of the Bounded Input RePSI follows from the correctness of accumulators and of SPHF.

Client privacy follows again from indistinguishability property of the accumulator. In the first instance of the protocol the only message the server receives from the client is the accumulator $\mathsf{acc}_C$. In this case the simulator $Sim$ picks $r \leftarrow \mathbb{Z}_p$ and sets $\mathsf{acc}_C = g^r$. As in the case of Bounded Input RePSI the simulated view is distributed identically to the real view. In the following calls of $O_{Sim}$ the simulator picks $s, t \leftarrow \mathbb{Z}_p$ and sets $\mathsf{acc}_U = g^s$ and $\mathsf{acc}_C = g^t$ and retrieves $\mathsf{acc}_{C'} = g^r$ from the previous instance. The simulator then sets the witnesses to be $\mathsf{wit}_C = g^{\frac{s}{t}}$ and $\mathsf{wit}_{C'} = g^{\frac{s}{r}}$. The distribution of the simulated $\mathsf{acc}_C, \mathsf{acc}_U, \mathsf{wit}_C, \mathsf{wit}_{C'}$ is uniformly random, conditioned on satisfying the two witness verification equations, as in a real distribution. Again, the simulator does not need the size of the client' set and thus client privacy is achieved with respect to the Size-Hiding variant.

The proof of server privacy unfolds as in the case of the Bounded Input RePSI (see [CDS18]) since the messages sent from the server to the client are the same.

### 5.3 Efficiency

We summarize the efficiency of both our Bounded Input PSI and Input Controlling RePSI in Table 1. The dominant computational cost for the client in the Bounded Input PSI is $O(m)$ pairings and multi-exponentiations of length at most $m$, where $m$ is the size of the client's set. With respect to the Bounded Input PSI, the overhead incurred by the client in our Input Controlling RePSI is only of a single multi-exponentiation of length $M$, the total number of elements used so far in the protocol.

For both the Bounded Input PSI and the Input Controlling RePSI. the computational cost for the server is $O(n)$ pairings and exponentiations, where $n$ is the size of the server set in that run. The overall communication is linear in the size of the server set in that particular instance for both protocols. The communication overhead of the Input Controlling RePSI is of only 3 group elements more than the Bounded Input PSI.

The table also shows that both server and client keep constant state in case of Input Controlling RePSI. When computing the state size for the client, we *do not* consider the elements input thus far by the client. We argue that any instantiation of Input Controlling RePSI requires the client to include in its state the inputs thus far. This is because the client will have to tell whether the next input is "fresh" or not. This is also true for the instantiation of the protocol via a trusted third party. In this case, the trusted party will have to remember all inputs up to the current run, in order to tell whether the next input violates the bound. If we do not consider the inputs thus far as part of the client's state, our instantiation of Input Controlling RePSI is optimal from the point of view of storage overhead since it only requires constant state at both the client and the server. In particular the state for each of them is independent of the number of runs.

**Comparison with [DMV13].** To the best of our knowledge, the only possible alternative to instantiate an Input Controlling RePSI would be to use the "rate-hiding" compiler of [DMV13] with a PSI protocol such as [HN10]. Since [DMV13] only hints at how to build a rate-hiding PSI,[3] we cannot compare its communication/computation complexity with the one of our Input Controlling RePSI. However, note that the rate-hiding compiler of [DMV13] requires the client to commit to the inputs of the current run and both parties to keep the commitments to the client's inputs across all runs. (The client must prove that the

---

[3] In [DMV13], the authors only show that the PSI protocol of [HN10] fulfills a property called "commit-first" and that it can be used in the rate-hiding compiler. However, the compiled protocol is not available.

number of unique inputs hidden by the commitments does not exceed the rate.). As such, even if we exclude the client's input from its state, both the client and the server keep a state that is linear in the number of elements used by the client across all executions. Whereas, our protocol features constant state at both parties and communication complexity that is independent on the size of the client's set.

## 6    Conclusions

Although a large number of Private Set Intersection (PSI) protocols have been proposed in recent years, their adoption in real-life applications is still hindered by a few challenges. In this paper, we focused on oracle attacks, whereby the client learns the server's private set by enumerating it across several executions. To address this problem, we set out to model PSI as a reactive functionality, namely, Reactive PSI (RePSI), and provided a construction that allow the server to set an upper bound to the number of elements the client has input up to the current protocol run. Essentially, we made PSI a stateful protocol but provided a construction where the state kept by the two parties is small and independent of the number of runs thus far and, for the server only, independent on the number of elements in either input set.

To the best of our knowledge, our work is the first to formalize and instantiate Reactive PSI. In the process, we also presented the first size-hiding PSI protocol in the standard model, which may be of independent interest.

## References

[ADT11]  Ateniese, G., De Cristofaro, E., Tsudik, G.: (If) Size matters: size-hiding private set intersection. In: Catalano, D., Fazio, N., Gennaro, R., Nicolosi, A. (eds.) PKC 2011. LNCS, vol. 6571, pp. 156–173. Springer, Heidelberg (2011). https://doi.org/10.1007/978-3-642-19379-8_10

[BBD+11]  Baldi, P., Baronio, R., De Cristofaro, E., Gasti, P., Tsudik, G.: Countering GATTACA: efficient and secure testing of fully-sequenced human genomes. In: ACM CCS, pp. 691–702 (2011)

[BDM94]  Benaloh, J., de Mare, M.: One-way accumulators: a decentralized alternative to digital signatures. In: Helleseth, T. (ed.) EUROCRYPT 1993. LNCS, vol. 765, pp. 274–285. Springer, Heidelberg (1994). https://doi.org/10.1007/3-540-48285-7_24

[BFT16]  Bradley, T., Faber, S., Tsudik, G.: Bounded size-hiding private set intersection. In: Zikas, V., De Prisco, R. (eds.) SCN 2016. LNCS, vol. 9841, pp. 449–467. Springer, Cham (2016). https://doi.org/10.1007/978-3-319-44618-9_24

[BP97]  Barić, N., Pfitzmann, B.: Collision-free accumulators and fail-stop signature schemes without trees. In: Fumy, W. (ed.) EUROCRYPT 1997. LNCS, vol. 1233, pp. 480–494. Springer, Heidelberg (1997). https://doi.org/10.1007/3-540-69053-0_33

[CDS18]  Cerulli, A., De Cristofaro, E., Soriente, C.: Nothing Refreshes Like a RePSI: Reactive Private Set Intersection (Full Version). eprint.iacr.org (2018)

[CKS09] Camenisch, J., Kohlweiss, M., Soriente, C.: An accumulator based on bilinear maps and efficient revocation for anonymous credentials. In: Jarecki, S., Tsudik, G. (eds.) PKC 2009. LNCS, vol. 5443, pp. 481–500. Springer, Heidelberg (2009). https://doi.org/10.1007/978-3-642-00468-1_27

[CL02] Camenisch, J., Lysyanskaya, A.: Dynamic accumulators and application to efficient revocation of anonymous credentials. In: Yung, M. (ed.) CRYPTO 2002. LNCS, vol. 2442, pp. 61–76. Springer, Heidelberg (2002). https://doi.org/10.1007/3-540-45708-9_5

[COV15] Chase, M., Ostrovsky, R., Visconti, I.: Executable proofs, input-size hiding secure computation and a new ideal world. In: Oswald, E., Fischlin, M. (eds.) EUROCRYPT 2015. LNCS, vol. 9057, pp. 532–560. Springer, Heidelberg (2015). https://doi.org/10.1007/978-3-662-46803-6_18

[CS02] Cramer, R., Shoup, V.: Universal hash proofs and a paradigm for adaptive chosen ciphertext secure public-key encryption. In: Knudsen, L.R. (ed.) EUROCRYPT 2002. LNCS, vol. 2332, pp. 45–64. Springer, Heidelberg (2002). https://doi.org/10.1007/3-540-46035-7_4

[CZ09] Camenisch, J., Zaverucha, G.M.: Private intersection of certified sets. In: Dingledine, R., Golle, P. (eds.) FC 2009. LNCS, vol. 5628, pp. 108–127. Springer, Heidelberg (2009). https://doi.org/10.1007/978-3-642-03549-4_7

[DHS15] Derler, D., Hanser, C., Slamanig, D.: Revisiting cryptographic accumulators, additional properties and relations to other primitives. In: Nyberg, K. (ed.) CT-RSA 2015. LNCS, vol. 9048, pp. 127–144. Springer, Cham (2015). https://doi.org/10.1007/978-3-319-16715-2_7

[DKT10] De Cristofaro, E., Kim, J., Tsudik, G.: Linear-complexity private set intersection protocols secure in malicious model. In: Abe, M. (ed.) ASIACRYPT 2010. LNCS, vol. 6477, pp. 213–231. Springer, Heidelberg (2010). https://doi.org/10.1007/978-3-642-17373-8_13

[DMV13] Dagdelen, Ö., Mohassel, P., Venturi, D.: Rate-limited secure function evaluation: definitions and constructions. In: Kurosawa, K., Hanaoka, G. (eds.) PKC 2013. LNCS, vol. 7778, pp. 461–478. Springer, Heidelberg (2013). https://doi.org/10.1007/978-3-642-36362-7_28

[DT10] De Cristofaro, E., Tsudik, G.: Practical private set intersection protocols with linear complexity. In: Sion, R. (ed.) FC 2010. LNCS, vol. 6052, pp. 143–159. Springer, Heidelberg (2010). https://doi.org/10.1007/978-3-642-14577-3_13

[DY05] Dodis, Y., Yampolskiy, A.: A verifiable random function with short proofs and keys. In: Vaudenay, S. (ed.) PKC 2005. LNCS, vol. 3386, pp. 416–431. Springer, Heidelberg (2005). https://doi.org/10.1007/978-3-540-30580-4_28

[FDCB15] Freudiger, J., De Cristofaro, E., Brito, A.E.: Controlled data sharing for collaborative predictive blacklisting. In: Almgren, M., Gulisano, V., Maggi, F. (eds.) DIMVA 2015. LNCS, vol. 9148, pp. 327–349. Springer, Cham (2015). https://doi.org/10.1007/978-3-319-20550-2_17

[FNP04] Freedman, M.J., Nissim, K., Pinkas, B.: Efficient private matching and set intersection. In: Cachin, C., Camenisch, J.L. (eds.) EUROCRYPT 2004. LNCS, vol. 3027, pp. 1–19. Springer, Heidelberg (2004). https://doi.org/10.1007/978-3-540-24676-3_1

[GL03] Gennaro, R., Lindell, Y.: A framework for password-based authenticated key exchange. In: Biham, E. (ed.) EUROCRYPT 2003. LNCS, vol. 2656, pp. 524–543. Springer, Heidelberg (2003). https://doi.org/10.1007/3-540-39200-9_33

[GMW87] Goldreich, O., Micali, S., Wigderson, A.: How to play any mental game or a completeness theorem for protocols with honest majority. In: Proceedings of the 19th Annual ACM Symposium on Theory of Computing, pp. 218–229 (1987)

[Gol04] Goldreich, O.: The Foundations of Cryptography - Volume 2, Basic Applications. Cambridge University Press, Cambridge (2004)

[GOP+16] Ghosh, E., Ohrimenko, O., Papadopoulos, D., Tamassia, R., Triandopoulos, N.: Zero-knowledge accumulators and set algebra. In: Cheon, J.H., Takagi, T. (eds.) ASIACRYPT 2016. LNCS, vol. 10032, pp. 67–100. Springer, Heidelberg (2016). https://doi.org/10.1007/978-3-662-53890-6_3

[HL08] Hazay, C., Lindell, Y.: Efficient protocols for set intersection and pattern matching with security against malicious and covert adversaries. In: Canetti, R. (ed.) TCC 2008. LNCS, vol. 4948, pp. 155–175. Springer, Heidelberg (2008). https://doi.org/10.1007/978-3-540-78524-8_10

[HL10a] Hazay, C., Lindell, Y.: Efficient Secure Two-Party Protocols - Techniques and Constructions. Information Security and Cryptography. Springer, Heidelberg (2010). https://doi.org/10.1007/978-3-642-14303-8

[HL10b] Hazay, C., Lindell, Y.: A note on the relation between the definitions of security for semi-honest and malicious adversaries. ePrint (2010)

[HN10] Hazay, C., Nissim, K.: Efficient set operations in the presence of malicious adversaries. In: Nguyen, P.Q., Pointcheval, D. (eds.) PKC 2010. LNCS, vol. 6056, pp. 312–331. Springer, Heidelberg (2010). https://doi.org/10.1007/978-3-642-13013-7_19

[HOS17] Hallgren, P., Orlandi, C., Sabelfeld, A.: PrivatePool: privacy-preserving ridesharing. In: CSF, pp. 276–291 (2017)

[IKN+17] Ion, M., Kreuter, B., Nergiz, E., Patel, S., Saxena, S., Seth, K., Shanahan, D., Yung, M.: Private intersection-sum protocol with applications to attributing aggregate ad conversions. ePrint 2017/738 (2017)

[JL10] Jarecki, S., Liu, X.: Fast secure computation of set intersection. In: Garay, J.A., De Prisco, R. (eds.) SCN 2010. LNCS, vol. 6280, pp. 418–435. Springer, Heidelberg (2010). https://doi.org/10.1007/978-3-642-15317-4_26

[KV09] Katz, J., Vaikuntanathan, V.: Smooth projective hashing and password-based authenticated key exchange from lattices. In: Matsui, M. (ed.) ASIACRYPT 2009. LNCS, vol. 5912, pp. 636–652. Springer, Heidelberg (2009). https://doi.org/10.1007/978-3-642-10366-7_37

[Ngu05] Nguyen, L.: Accumulators from bilinear pairings and applications. In: Menezes, A. (ed.) CT-RSA 2005. LNCS, vol. 3376, pp. 275–292. Springer, Heidelberg (2005). https://doi.org/10.1007/978-3-540-30574-3_19

[PSSZ15] Pinkas, B., Schneider, T., Segev, G., Zohner, M.: Phasing: private set intersection using permutation-based hashing. In: USENIX Security Symposium (2015)

[PSZ14] Pinkas, B., Schneider, T., Zohner, M.: Faster private set intersection based on OT extension. In: USENIX Security Symposium, pp. 797–812 (2014)

[RR17] Rindal, P., Rosulek, M.: Improved private set intersection against malicious adversaries. In: Coron, J.-S., Nielsen, J.B. (eds.) EUROCRYPT 2017. LNCS, vol. 10210, pp. 235–259. Springer, Cham (2017). https://doi.org/10.1007/978-3-319-56620-7_9

# Multi-party Computation

# New Protocols for Secure Equality Test and Comparison

Geoffroy Couteau$^{(\boxtimes)}$

Karsruhe Institute of Technology, Karlsruhe, Germany
geoffroy.couteau@kit.edu

**Abstract.** Protocols for securely comparing private values are among the most fundamental building blocks of multiparty computation. introduced by Yao under the name millionaire's problem, they have found numerous applications in a variety of privacy-preserving protocols; however, due to their inherent non-arithmetic structure, existing construction often remain an important bottleneck in large-scale secure protocols.

In this work, we introduce new protocols for securely computing the greater-than and the equality predicate between two parties. Our protocols rely solely on the existence of oblivious transfer, and are UC-secure against passive adversaries. Furthermore, our protocols are well suited for use in large-scale secure computation protocols, where secure comparisons (SC) and equality tests (ET) are commonly used as basic routines: they perform particularly well in an amortized setting, and can be preprocessed efficiently (they enjoy an extremely efficient, information-theoretic online phase). We perform a detailed comparison of our protocols to the state of the art, showing that they improve over the most practical existing solutions regarding both communication and computation, while matching the asymptotic efficiency of the best theoretical constructions.

**Keywords:** Two-party computation · Equality test
Secure comparison · Oblivious transfer

## 1 Introduction

Multiparty Computation (MPC) addresses the challenge of performing computation over sensitive data without compromising its privacy. In the past decades, several general-purpose solutions to this problem have been designed, starting with the seminal works of Yao [53] and Goldreich et al. [27]. Among the large variety of problems related to MPC that have been considered, the *secure comparison* problem, in which the players wish to find out whether $x \geq y$ for given $x, y$ without disclosing them, is probably the one that received the most attention. Indeed, in addition to being the first MPC problem ever considered (introduced

---

Part of this work was made while the author was at École Normale Supérieure de Paris, France.

B. Preneel and F. Vercauteren (Eds.): ACNS 2018, LNCS 10892, pp. 303–320, 2018.
https://doi.org/10.1007/978-3-319-93387-0_16

in [53] under the name of millionaire's problem), it has proven to be a fundamental primitive in a considerable number of important applications of multiparty computation. Examples include auctions, signal processing, database queries, machine learning and statistical analysis, biometric authentication, combinatorial problems, or computation on rational numbers. Secure comparison is at the heart of any task involving sorting data, finding a minimum value, solving any optimization problem, or even in tasks as basic as evaluating the predicate of a while loop, among countless other examples. The related task of *secure equality test*, known as the socialist millionaires' problem, in which the players wish to find out whether $x = y$ for given $x, y$ without disclosing them, enjoys comparably many applications.

Two-party and multiparty computation seem now at the edge of becoming practical, with increasing evidence that they are no more beyond the reach of the computational power of today's computers. However, secure equality tests and comparisons appear to be a major bottleneck in secure algorithms that use them as a basic routines. Various implementations of secure algorithms unanimously lead to the conclusion that secure comparison is the most computationally involved primitive, being up to two orders of magnitude slower than, e.g., secure multiplication. Hence, we believe that designing improved protocols for these tasks is an important road toward making multiparty computation truly practical.

In this work, we consider secure equality test and comparison on inputs secretely shared between the parties, with output shared between the parties as well. This is the natural setting of large-scale computation, where inputs and outputs cannot always be disclosed to the parties. Our new two-party protocols compare very favorably to state-of-the-art solutions. In particular, our protocols are well suited for large scale secure computation protocols using secure comparison as a basic routine. Our protocols are secure in the universal composability framework of Canetti [11], which ensures that security is preserved under general composition. As this is the model used in most practical applications, we focus on the passive adversarial model, in which players are assumed to follow the specifications of the protocol. We leave as open the interesting question of extending our protocols to handle malicious adversaries, while preserving (as much as possible) their efficiency.

## 1.1 State of the Art for Secure Equality Test and Comparison

To avoid unnecessary details in the presentation, we assume some basic knowledge on classical cryptographic primitives, such as garbled circuits, oblivious transfers and cryptosystems. Preliminaries on oblivious transfers are given in the full version of this work [15]. In the following, we let $\ell$ denote an input length, and $\kappa$ denote a security parameter. As secure protocols for equality tests and comparisons were commonly built together in the literature, the state of the art for both remains essentially the same, hence we unify the presentation.

- *From Garbled Circuits.* The first category regroups protocols following the garbled circuit approach of Yao [53]. The protocols of [37], which were later improved in [36,55], are amongst the most communication-efficient protocols for secure equality test or comparison. The protocols of [36] proceed by letting the first player garble a circuit containing $\ell$ comparison gates (resp. $\ell - 1$ equality test gates), which amounts to $\ell$ AND gates with the free-xor trick (resp. $\ell - 1$ AND gates). In a setting where several instances of the protocols will be invoked, oblivious transfer extensions [33] can be used for an arbitrary number of executions, using a constant number of public key operations and only cheap symmetric operations for each invocation of the secure protocol, making them very efficient.

– *From Homomorphic Encryption.* Solutions to the millionaire problem from homomorphic-encryption originated in [7]. The most efficient method in this category, to our knowledge, is [20], which uses an ad hoc cryptosystem. This protocol was corrected in [21], and improved in [51]. The protocol communicates $4\ell$ ciphertexts (in the version that outputs shares of the result) and is often regarded as one of the most computationally efficient. The more recent construction of [25] relies on the flexibility of lattice based cryptosystems to design a secure comparison protocol. Using a degree-8 somewhat homomorphic encryption scheme and ciphertext packing techniques, the (amortized) bit complexity of their protocol is $\tilde{O}(\ell + \kappa)$. Although asymptotically efficient, this method is expected to remain less efficient than alternative methods using simpler primitives for any realistic parameters.

– *From the Arithmetic Black Box Model.* The third category consists of protocols built on top of an arithmetic black box [17] (ABB), which is an ideal reactive functionality for performing securely basic operations (such as additions and multiplications) over secret values loaded in the ABB. The ABB itself can be implemented from various primitives, such as oblivious transfer [23,45] or additively homomorphic encryption (most articles advocate the Paillier scheme [44]). Protocols in this category vary greatly in structure. Most protocols [12,19,43] involve $\tilde{O}(\ell)$ private multiplications, each typically requiring $O(1)$ operations over a field of size $O(\ell + \kappa)$, resulting in an overall $\tilde{O}(\ell(\ell + \kappa))$ bit complexity. The protocols of Toft [50], and Toft and Lipmaa [40], use only a sublinear (in $\ell$) number of invocations to the cryptographic primitive; however, the total bit complexity remains superlinear in $\ell$. For large values of $\ell$ ($\kappa^2/\ell = o(1)$) the protocol of [54] enjoys an optimal $O(\ell)$ communication complexity; however, the constants involved are quite large: it reduces to $84\lambda + 96$ bit oblivious transfer and 6 $\ell$-bit secure multiplications for a $1/2^\lambda$ error probability, and becomes competitive with e.g. [36] only for inputs of at least 500 bits (assuming a $1/2^{40}$ error probability).

– *From Generic Two-Party Computation.* Generic two-party computation (2PC) techniques can be used to securely compute functions represented as boolean circuits. An elegant logarithmic-depth boolean circuit, computing simultaneously the greater-than and the equality predicates, was suggested in [24]. It uses a natural recursive formula, and has $3\ell - \log \ell - 2$ AND gates. This circuit can be evaluated using $6\ell - 2 \log \ell - 4$ oblivious transfers on bits, which can be precomputed and amortized using oblivious transfer extensions. In the amortized setting, we found this approach to be (by far) the most efficient in terms of communication and computation; however, it is more interactive than the garbled circuit approach, which still enjoy efficient communication and computation.

In this paper, we will compare our protocols to the two most efficient alternatives in the amortized setting, namely, the garbled circuit approach, and the generic 2PC approach (which is more interactive, but has lower communication and computation). For fairness of the comparison, we will apply all optimizations that we apply to our protocols to these alternatives, when it is relevant.

## 1.2  Our Contribution

In this work, we construct new protocols for secure equality tests and comparisons which improve over the best state-of-the-art protocols. Our protocols are secure in the universal composability framework, assuming only an oblivious transfer. Using oblivious transfer extensions allows to confine all public-key operations to a one-time setup phase. The online phase of our protocols enjoys information theoretic security, and is optimal regarding both communication and computation: $O(\ell)$ bits are communicated, and $O(\ell)$ binary operations are performed, with small constants. Regarding overall complexity, our protocols match the best existing constructions in terms of asymptotic efficiency (and have in particular an optimal $O(\ell)$ complexity for large values of $\ell$, see Table 1), and outperform the most efficient constructions for practical parameters, by 70% to 80% for equality test, and by 20% to 40% for secure comparison. Our protocols have non-constant round complexity: $O(\log^* \kappa)$ rounds for equality test (2 to 4 online rounds in practice), and $O(\log \log \ell)$ rounds for comparison (2 to 10 online rounds). Our secure comparison protocol relies on a new technique to (non-interactively) reduce comparison of values shared between the players to comparison of values held by each players, which might be of independent interest. Due to space restriction, we only focus on our new protocols for equality tests here; our protocols for secure comparison are described in the full version of this work [15].

**Further Contributions of the Full Version.** In addition to detailed security proofs, the full version of our work [15] contains further contributions, including a new simple method which reduces by 25% the communication of the Naor-Pinkas oblivious transfer protocol [41] when the size of the transmitted strings is lower than $\kappa/2$, and a variant of our equality test protocol in a batch settings (where many equality tests are performed "by blocks"), which uses additively homomorphic encryption to further improve the communication of our equality test protocol by up to 50%.

## 1.3  Our Method

The high level intuition of our approach is an observation that was already made in previous works [40,50]: to compare two strings, it suffices to divide them in equal length blocks, and compare the first block on which they differ. Therefore, a protocol for (obliviously) finding this block can be used to reduce the secure comparison problem on large strings to the secure comparison problem on smaller strings. One can then recursively apply this size-reduction protocol, until the strings to be compared are small enough, and compute the final result using a second protocol tailored to secure comparison on small strings. However, this intuition was typically implemented in previous work using heavy public-key primitives, such as homomorphic encryption. In this work, we show how this strategy can be implemented using exclusively oblivious transfers on small strings.

To implement the size-reduction protocol, we rely on a protocol to obliviously determine whether two strings are equal. Therefore, a first step toward realizing a secure comparison protocol is to design a protocol for testing equality between two strings, which outputs shares (modulo 2) of a bit which is 1 if and only if the strings are equal. Keeping this approach in mind, we start by designing an equality test protocol which is based solely on oblivious transfer. Recall that in an oblivious transfer protocol, one party (the sender) inputs a pair $(s_0, s_1)$, while the other party (the receiver) inputs a bit $b$; the receiver receives $s_b$ as output and learns nothing about $s_{1-b}$, while the sender learns nothing about $b$. Our protocol relies on a classical observation: two strings are equal if and only if their Hamming distance is zero. More specifically, our protocols proceed as follows:

**Equality Test.** Consider two inputs $(x, y)$, of length $\ell$. We denote $(x_i, y_i)_{i \le \ell}$ their bits. The parties execute $\ell$ parallel oblivious transfers over $\mathbb{Z}_{\ell+1}$, where the first player input pairs $(a_i + x_i \bmod \ell + 1, a_i + 1 - x_i \bmod \ell + 1)$ ($a_i$ is a random mask over $\mathbb{Z}_{\ell+1}$), and the second party input his secret bits $y_i$; let $b_i$ be his output ($b_i = a_i + x_i \oplus y_i \bmod \ell + 1$, where $\oplus$ is the exclusive or). Observe that $x' \leftarrow \sum_i a_i \bmod \ell + 1$ and $y' \leftarrow \sum_i b_i \bmod \ell + 1$ are equal if and only if the Hamming distance between $x$ and $y$ is 0, if and only if $x = y$. Note that $(x', y')$ are of length $\log(\ell + 1)$.

The players repeatedly invoke the above method, starting from $(x', y')$, to shrink the input size while preserving equality, until they end up with string of length at most (say) 3 bits (it takes about $O(\log^* \ell)$ invocations of the protocol, where the first invocation dominates the communication cost). The players then perform a straightforward equality test on these small strings, using oblivious transfers to evaluate an explicit exponential-size formula for equality checking on the small entries.

The core feature of this compression method is that it can be almost entirely preprocessed: by executing the compression protocol on random inputs $(r, s)$ in a preprocessing phase (and storing the masks generated), the players can reconstruct the output of the protocol on input $(x, y)$ simply by exchanging $x \oplus r$ and $s \oplus y$ in the online phase. Therefore, the communication of the entire equality test protocol can be made as low as a few dozens to a few hundreds of bits in the online phase. Furthermore, in the preprocessing phase, the protocol involves only oblivious transfers on very small entries (each entry has size at most $\log \ell$ bits), for which particularly efficient constructions exist [35].

**Secure Comparison.** We now describe our solution to the secure comparison problem. This protocol has a structure somewhat comparable to the previous one, but is more involved. The parties break their inputs $(x, y)$ in $\sqrt{\ell}$ blocks of length $\sqrt{\ell}$ each. In the first part of the protocol, the parties will construct $\sqrt{\ell}$ shares of bits, which are all equal to 0 except for the $i$th bit, where $i$ is the index of the first block on which $x$ differs from $y$. This step relies on parallel invocations to the equality test functionality, and on oblivious transfers. Then, using these bit-shares and oblivious transfers, the players compute shares of the first block on which $x$ differs from $y$.

At this point, we cannot directly repeat the above method recursively, as this method takes inputs *known to the parties*, while the output values are only shared between the parties. However, under a condition on the size of the group on which the shares are computed, we prove a lemma which shows that the parties can *non-interactively* reduce the problem of securely comparing shared value to the problem of securely comparing known values, using only local computations on their shares. From that point, the parties can apply the compression protocol again (for $O(\log \log \ell)$ rounds), until they obtain very small values, and use (similarly as before) a straightforward protocol based on an explicit exponential-size formula for comparison. Alternatively, to reduce the interactivity, the compression protocol can be executed a fixed (constant) number of times, before applying, e.g., a garbled-circuit-based protocol or a generic 2PC protocol on the reduced-size inputs.

This protocol involves $O(\sqrt{\ell})$ equality tests and oblivious transfers on small strings, both of which can be efficiently preprocessed. This leads to a secure comparison protocol that communicates about a thousand bits in the online phase, for 64-bit inputs.

### 1.4   Comparison with Existing Works

**For Secure Comparisons.** We provide Table 1 a detailed comparison between the state of the art, our logarithmic-round protocol $\mathsf{SC}_1$, and its constant-round variants $\mathsf{SC}_2$ and $\mathsf{SC}_3$. We evaluate efficiency in an amortized setting and ignore one-time setup costs. We considered two methods based on garbled circuit, the protocol of [36] and the same protocol enhanced with the method of [3] to optimize the online communication. We also considered the solution based on the DGK cryptosystem [20,21,51], the protocol of [40], the probabilistically correct protocol of [54], and generic 2PC applied to the protocol of [24]. Note that [40,54] are described with respect to an arithmetic black box, hence their cost depends on how the ABB is implemented. For [40], which requires an ABB over large order fields, we considered a Paillier based instantiation, as advocated by the authors. For [54], which involves (mainly) an ABB over $\mathbb{F}_2$, we considered the same optimizations than in our protocols, implementing the ABB with oblivious transfers on bits.

As illustrated in Table 1, our protocols improve over existing protocols (asymptotically) regarding both communication and computation. This comes at the cost of a non-constant $O(\log \log \ell)$ interactivity (or $O(c \cdot \log^* \kappa)$ in the constant-round setting). In particular, for large values of $\ell$ (and for any value of $\ell$ in the online phase), our protocols enjoy an optimal $O(\ell)$ communication and computation complexity. The hidden constants are small, making our protocols more efficient than the state of the art for any practical parameter. For values of $\ell$ between 4 and 128, the protocols of [24,36] (which enjoy tiny constants) outperforms all other existing protocols regarding communication and computation. We therefore focus on these protocols as a basis for comparison with our protocols in our concrete efficiency estimations.

**Equality Tests.** The state of the art given Table 1 remains essentially the same for equality tests. Indeed, all the papers listed in the table (at the exception of [20], but including the present paper) do also construct equality tests protocols, with the same (asymptotic) complexity and from the same assumptions. The only difference in asymptotic complexity between our equality test protocol and the protocol $SC_1$ is with respect to the round complexity: while $SC_1$ has $O(\log \log \ell)$ rounds, our equality test protocol has an almost-constant number of rounds $O(\log^* \kappa)$. Note that we consider only equality tests whose output is shared between the players (as this is necessary for our secure comparison protocol); if the players get to learn the output in the clear (this is known as the socialist millionaires problem), more efficient solutions exist, but there is no simple way of designing equality tests with shared outputs from these solutions.

### 1.5   Applications

Equality test protocols enjoy many applications as building blocks in various multiparty computation protocols. Examples include, but are not limited to, protocols for switching between encryption schemes [16], secure linear algebra [18], secure pattern matching [31], and secure evaluation of linear programs [49]. Secure comparisons have found a tremendous number of applications in cryptography; we provide thereafter a non-exhaustive list of applications for which our protocols lead to increased efficiency. We note that in applications for which implementations have been described, the communication of secure comparisons was generally pointed out as the main efficiency bottleneck.

- *Obliviously sorting data* [28,29] has proven useful in contexts such as private auctions [42], oblivious RAM [26], or private set intersection [32], but it remains to date quite slow (in [30], sorting over a million 32-bit words takes between 5 and 20 min). All existing methods crucially rely on secure comparisons and require at least $O(m \log m)$ secure comparisons in $O(\log m)$ rounds to sort lists of size $m$.
- *Biometric authentication*, while solving issues related to the use of passwords, raises concerns regarding the privacy of individuals, and received a lot of attention from the cryptographic community. Protocols for tasks such as

**Table 1.** Amortized costs of state of the art secure comparison

| Protocol | [36] | [20,21,51][a] | [40][a] | [36]+[3][a] | [54] |
|---|---|---|---|---|---|
| *Preprocessing phase* | | | | | |
| Communication | $O(\kappa\ell)$ | – | $O(n\kappa \log \ell)$ | $O(n\ell)$ | $O(\frac{\kappa^2}{\log \kappa} + \ell)$ |
| Computation | $O(\kappa\ell)$ | $O(\ell(\kappa+\ell)\cdot C_n)$ | $O(n\kappa \log \ell \cdot C_n)$ | $O(n\ell \cdot C_n)$ | $O(\frac{\kappa^2}{\log^2 \kappa} + \ell)$ |
| Rounds | 1 | – | $O(1)$ | 1 | $O(1)$ |
| Assumption | OT | – | ABB | RSA | ABB |
| *Online phase* | | | | | |
| Communication | $O(\kappa\ell)$ | $O(n\ell)$ | $O(n \log \ell)$ | $O(\ell + n)$ | $O(\kappa + \ell)$ |
| Computation | $O(\kappa\ell)$ | $O(\ell \log \ell \cdot C_n)$ | $O(n \log \ell \cdot C_n)$ | $O(\kappa\ell + n \cdot C_n)$ | $O(\kappa + \ell)$ |
| Rounds | 2 | 2 | $O(\log \ell)$ | 2 | $O(\log \kappa)$ |
| Assumption | OWF | DGK | ABB | RSA | None |

| Protocol | [24] | $SC_1$ | $SC_2, SC_3$ ($c$ is some fixed constant) |
|---|---|---|---|
| *Preprocessing phase* | | | |
| Communication | $O(\frac{\kappa\ell}{\log \kappa})$ | $O(\frac{\kappa\ell}{\log \kappa})$ if $\ell = o(\kappa^2)$<br>$O(\ell)$ else | $O(\frac{\kappa\ell}{\log \kappa})$ if $\ell^{1-1/c} = o(\kappa^2)$<br>$O(\ell)$ else |
| Computation | $O(\frac{\kappa\ell}{\log \kappa})$ | $O(\frac{\kappa\ell}{\log \kappa})$ if $\ell = o(\kappa^2)$<br>$O(\ell)$ else | $O(\frac{\kappa\ell}{\log \kappa})$ if $\ell^{1-1/c} = o(\kappa^2)$<br>$O(\ell)$ else |
| Rounds | $O(\log \ell)$ | $O(\log \log \ell)$ | $O(c \log^* \kappa)$ |
| Assumption | OT | OT | OT |
| *Online phase* | | | |
| Communication | $O(\ell)$ | $O(\ell)$ | $O(\ell)$ |
| Computation | $O(\ell)$ | $O(\ell)$ | $O(\ell)$ |
| Rounds | $O(\log \ell)$ | $O(\log \log \ell)$ | $O(c \log^* \kappa)$ |
| Assumption | None | None | OWF ($SC_2$) or none ($SC_3$) |

[a]$n > \ell + \kappa$ is the length of an RSA modulus. $C_n$ denotes the cost of a modular multiplication modulo $n$. Note that [3] can also be instantiated from the DDH or the LWE assumption.

secure face recognition [47] require finding the minimum value in a database, which reduces to $O(m)$ secure comparisons in $O(\log m)$ rounds.

- Secure protocols for *machine learning* employ secure comparisons as a basic routine for tasks such as classification [10], generating private recommendations [22], spam classification [52], multimedia analysis [14], clinical decisions [46], evaluation of disease risk [5], or image feature extraction [39].
- Secure algorithms for *combinatorial problems*, such as finding the flow of maximum capacity in a weighted graph, or searching for the shortest path between two nodes, have been investigated in several works, e.g. [38], and have applications in protocols such as private fingerprint matching [8], privacy-preserving GPS guidance, or privacy-preserving determination of topological features in social networks [2]. They typically involve a very large number of secure comparisons (e.g. $n^2$ comparisons for Dijkstra's shortest path algorithm on an $n$-node graph [2]).
- Other applications that heavily rely on comparisons include computing on non integer values [1], various types of secure auctions [20], range queries over encrypted databases [48], or algorithms for optimization problems [13,49].

## 1.6   Organization

In Sect. 2, we recall definitions and classical results on oblivious transfers, as well as on oblivious transfer extensions. Section 3 introduces our new equality test protocol, and constitutes the main body of our work. Due to space constraints, we postpone our protocols for secure comparisons, as well as our detailed security proofs, to the full version [15]; we note that most of the security proofs are quite standard.

## 1.7   Notations

Given a finite set $S$, the notation $x \leftarrow_R S$ means that $x$ is picked uniformly at random from $S$. For an integer $n$, $\mathbb{Z}_n$ denotes the set of integers modulo $n$. Throughout this paper, $+$ will always denote addition over the integers, and not modular additions. We use bold letters to denote vectors. For a vector $\boldsymbol{x}$, we denote by $\boldsymbol{x}[i]$ its $i$'th coordinate; we identify $k$-bit-strings to vectors of $\mathbb{Z}_2^k$ (but do not use bold notations for them). We denote by $\boldsymbol{x} * \boldsymbol{y}$ the Hadamard product $(\boldsymbol{x}[i] \cdot \boldsymbol{y}[i])_i$ between $\boldsymbol{x}$ and $\boldsymbol{y}$. Let $\oplus$ denote the xor operation (when applied on bit-strings, it denotes the bitwise xor). For integers $(x, y)$, $[x = y]$, $[x < y]$, and $[x \leq y]$ denote a bit which is 1 if the equality/inequality holds, and 0 otherwise. The notation $(x \bmod k)$, between parenthesis, indicates that $x \bmod t$ is seen as an integer between 0 and $t - 1$, not as an element of $\mathbb{Z}_t$. For an integer $k$, let $\langle \cdot \rangle_k$ denote the randomized function that, on input $x$, returns two uniformly random shares of $x$ over $\mathbb{Z}_k$ (i.e., a random pair $(a, b) \in \mathbb{Z}_k$ such that $a + b = x \bmod k$). We extend this notation to vectors in a natural way: for an integer vector $\boldsymbol{x}$, $(\boldsymbol{a}, \boldsymbol{b}) \leftarrow_R \langle \boldsymbol{x} \rangle_k$ denote the two vectors obtained by applying $\langle \cdot \rangle_k$ to the coordinates of $\boldsymbol{x}$. Finally, for an integer $x$, we denote by $|x|$ the bit-size of $x$.

## 2   Oblivious Transfer

Oblivious transfers (OT) were introduced in [45]. An oblivious transfer is a two-party protocol between a sender and a receiver, where the sender obliviously transfers one of two string to the receiver, according to the selection bit of the latter. The ideal functionality for $k$ oblivious transfers on $l$-bit strings is specified as follows:

$$\mathscr{F}_{\mathsf{OT}}^{k,l} : ((\boldsymbol{s}_0, \boldsymbol{s}_1), x) \mapsto \left( \bot, \left( \boldsymbol{s}_{x[i]}[i] \right)_{i \leq k} \right)$$

where $(\boldsymbol{s}_0, \boldsymbol{s}_1) \in (\mathbb{F}_2^l)^k \times (\mathbb{F}_2^l)^k$ is the input of the sender, and $x \in \mathbb{F}_2^k$ is the input of the receiver. In a *random oblivious transfer* (ROT), the input of the sender is picked at random:

$$\mathscr{F}_{\mathsf{ROT}}^{k,l} : (\bot, x) \mapsto \left( (\boldsymbol{s}_0, \boldsymbol{s}_1), \left( \boldsymbol{s}_{x[i]}[i] \right)_{i \leq k} \right)$$

The primitive can be extended naturally to $k$-out-of-$n$ oblivious transfers; we let $\binom{n}{k}$-$\mathsf{OT}_\ell^t$ denote $t$ invocations of a $k$-out-of-$n$ OT on strings of length $\ell$. Oblivious transfer is a fundamental primitive in MPC as it implies general multiparty computation [34] and can be made very efficient.

## 2.1   Oblivious Transfer Extension

Although oblivious transfer requires public-key cryptographic primitives, which can be expensive, *oblivious transfer extension* allows to execute an arbitrary number of oblivious transfers, using only cheap, symmetric operations, and a small number of base OTs. OT extensions were introduced in [6]. The first truly practical OT extension protocol was introduced in [33], assuming the random oracle model.[1] We briefly recall the intuition of the OT extension protocol of [33]. A $\binom{2}{1}$-OT$_t^\kappa$ can be directly obtained from a $\binom{2}{1}$-OT$_\kappa^\kappa$: the sender associates two $\kappa$-bit keys to each pair of messages and obliviously transfer one key of each pair to the receiver. Then, the receiver stretches two $t$-bit strings from the two keys of each pair, using a pseudo-random generator, and sends the xor of each of these strings and the corresponding message to the receiver. The $\binom{2}{1}$-OT$_\ell^t$ itself can be implemented with a single call to a $\binom{2}{1}$-OT$_t^\kappa$ functionality, in which the receiver plays the role of the sender (and reciprocally). The total communication of the reduction from $\binom{2}{1}$-OT$_\ell^t$ to $\binom{2}{1}$-OT$_\kappa^\kappa$ is $2t\ell + 2t\kappa$ bits. Regarding the computational complexity, once the base OTs have been performed, each OT essentially consists in three evaluations of a hash function. An optimization to the protocol of [33] was proposed in [4] (and discovered independently in [35]). It reduces the communication of the OT extension protocol from $2t\ell + 2t\kappa$ bits to $2t\ell + t\kappa$ bits, and allows to perform the base OTs without an a-priori bound on the number of OTs to be performed later (the OTs can be continuously extended).

**Oblivious Transfer of Short Strings.** An optimized OT extension protocol for short strings was introduced in [35], where the authors describe a reduction of $\binom{2}{1}$-OT$_\ell^t$ to $\binom{2}{1}$-OT$_\kappa^\kappa$ with $t(2\kappa/\log n + n \cdot \ell)$ bits of communication, $n$ being a parameter that can be chosen arbitrarily so as to minimize this cost. Intuitively, this is done by reducing $\log n$ invocations of $\binom{2}{1}$-OT to one invocation of $\binom{n}{1}$-OT; the result is then obtained by combining this reduction with a new $\binom{n}{1}$-OT extension protocol introduced in [35]. In our concrete efficiency estimations, we will heavily rely on this result as our equality test protocol involves only OTs on very short strings.

**Correlated and Random Oblivious Transfers.** The authors of [4] described several OT extension protocols, tailored to OTs on inputs satisfying some particular conditions. In particular, the communication of the OT extension protocol can be reduced from $2t\ell + t\kappa$ bits to $t\ell + t\kappa$ bits when the inputs to each OT are *correlated*, i.e. when each input pair is of the form $(r, f(r))$ for a uniformly random $r$ and a function $f$ known by the sender (which can be different for each OT). For random oblivious transfer extension, the bit-communication can be further reduced to $t\kappa$. We note that the optimizations of [4,35] can be combined: $\log n$ correlated $\binom{2}{1}$-OT can be reduced to one correlated $\binom{n}{1}$-OT (defined

---

[1] The random oracle model can be avoided by assuming that the hash function is a correlation-robust function, see [35], Appendix A.2.

by input pairs of the form $(r, f_1(r), \cdots f_{n-1}(r))$ for a random $r$ and functions $f_1 \cdots f_{n-1}$ known by the sender). This gives a correlated short-string oblivious transfer extension protocol which transmits $t(2\kappa/\log n + (n-1) \cdot \ell)$ bits.

## 3    Equality Test

In this section, we design an equality-test (ET) protocol to securely compute shares over $\mathbb{Z}_2$ of the equality predicate.

**Ideal Functionalities.** The ideal functionality for our ET protocol is represented on Fig. 1. Following the common standard for multiparty computation, we design our protocol in the preprocessing model, where the players have access to a preprocessing functionality $\mathscr{F}_{ET\text{-}prep}$. The preprocessing functionality is used in an initialization phase to generate material for the protocol; it does not require the inputs of the players. Our ideal preprocessing functionality is also represented on Fig. 1.

---

**Functionality $\mathscr{F}_{ET}$**

The functionality runs with two parties, Alice and Bob. Upon receiving $(ET, x)$ from Alice and $(ET, y)$ from Bob, set $\beta \leftarrow 1$ if $x = y$, and $\beta \leftarrow 0$ else. Set $(a, b) \leftarrow_R \langle \beta \rangle_2$. Return $a$ to Alice and $b$ to Bob.

---

**Functionality $\mathscr{F}_{ET\text{-}prep}$**

The functionality runs with two parties, Alice and Bob.

**Size Reduction:** Upon receiving $(SR, j)$ from both players, the functionality picks $(x, y) \leftarrow_R (\mathbb{Z}_2^j)^2$ and sets $(a, b) \leftarrow_R \langle x \oplus y \rangle_{j+1}$. $\mathscr{F}_{ET\text{-}prep}$ outputs $(x, a)$ to Alice and $(y, b)$ to Bob.

**Product Sharing:** Upon receiving $(PS, n)$ from both players, the functionality picks $(x, y) \leftarrow_R (\mathbb{Z}_2^{2^n-2})^2$ and sets $(a, b) \leftarrow_R \langle x * y \rangle_2$. $\mathscr{F}_{ET\text{-}prep}$ outputs $(x, a)$ to Alice and $(y, b)$ to Bob.

---

**Fig. 1.** Ideal functionalities for equality test and preprocessing

**Protocol.** We now describe our implementation of $\mathscr{F}_{ET}$ in the $\mathscr{F}_{ET\text{-}prep}$-hybrid model, with respect to passive corruption. The protocol runs with two players, Alice and Bob. It is parametrized by two integers $(\ell, n)$, where $n$ is called the *threshold* of the protocol. The players recursively perform size reduction steps using the material produced by the size reduction procedure of $\mathscr{F}_{ET\text{-}prep}$. Each step reduces inputs of size $\ell$ to inputs of size $|\ell + 1|$ while preserving the equality predicate. The players stop the reduction when the bitsize of their inputs becomes smaller than the threshold $n$ (taken equal to 3 or 4 in our concrete estimations). The equality predicate is computed on the small inputs with the material produced by the product sharing procedure of $\mathscr{F}_{ET\text{-}prep}$. The protocol is represented on Fig. 2.

---

### Protocol $\Pi_{\mathsf{ET}}$

---

**Initialize:** Let $i \leftarrow 1$ and $j \leftarrow \ell$. The players perform the following operations:
- (size reduction) While $j > n$, both players call $\mathscr{F}_{\mathsf{ET\text{-}prep}}$ on input $(\mathsf{SR}, j)$ to get outputs $(r_i, \boldsymbol{a}_i)$ and $(s_i, \boldsymbol{b}_i)$. The players set $i \leftarrow i + 1$ and $j \leftarrow \lfloor j + 1 \rfloor$.
- (product sharing) Both players call $\mathscr{F}_{\mathsf{ET\text{-}prep}}$ on input $(\mathsf{PS}, n)$ to get outputs $(r, a)$ and $(s, b)$.

**Equality Test:** On input two $\ell$-bit integers, $x$ from Alice and $y$ from Bob, let $x_1 \leftarrow x$ and $y_1 \leftarrow y$. Let $i \leftarrow 1$ and $j \leftarrow \ell$. The players perform the following operations:

1. While $j > n$, Alice sends $x_i' \leftarrow r_i \oplus x_i$ to Bob, and Bob sends $y_i' \leftarrow s_i \oplus y_i$ to Alice. Let $z_i \leftarrow x_i' \oplus y_i'$. Alice sets $x_{i+1} \leftarrow -\sum_{l=1}^{j}(-1)^{z_i[l]}\boldsymbol{a}_i[l] \bmod j + 1$, and Bob sets $y_{i+1} \leftarrow \sum_{l=1}^{j}(-1)^{z_i[l]}\boldsymbol{b}_i[l] + z_i[l] \bmod j + 1$. The players set $i \leftarrow i + 1$ and $j \leftarrow \lfloor j + 1 \rfloor$. Note that $(x_i, y_i) \in \mathbb{Z}_j^2$.

2. Once $j \leq n$, let $(I_k)_{1 \leq k \leq 2^n - 2}$ denote the list of non-empty strict subsets of $\{1, \cdots, n\}$ (in any arbitrary fixed order). For $k = 1$ to $2^n - 2$, Alice, sets $X_k \leftarrow \prod_{l \in I_k}(1 \oplus x_i[l])$ and $\alpha_k \leftarrow r[k] \oplus X_k$. Then, Bob sets $Y_k \leftarrow \prod_{l \notin I_k} y_i[l]$, and $\beta_k \leftarrow s[k] \oplus Y_k$. Alice picks $\alpha \leftarrow_R \{0, 1\}$ and sends $(\alpha, (\alpha_k)_{k \leq 2^n - 2})$, and Bob picks $\beta \leftarrow_R \{0, 1\}$ and sends $(\beta, (\beta_k)_{k \leq 2^n - 2})$.

3. Alice outputs
$$\bigoplus_{k \leq 2^n - 2} (a[k] \oplus \beta_k X_k) \oplus \prod_{l \leq n}(1 \oplus x_i[l]) \oplus \alpha \oplus \beta$$

   Bob outputs
$$\bigoplus_{k \leq 2^n - 2} (b[k] \oplus \alpha_k s[k]) \oplus \prod_{l \leq n} y_i[l] \oplus \alpha \oplus \beta$$

---

**Fig. 2.** Protocol for equality test

**Theorem 1.** *The protocol $\Pi_{\mathsf{ET}}$ securely implements $\mathscr{F}_{\mathsf{ET}}$ in the $\mathscr{F}_{\mathsf{ET\text{-}prep}}$-hybrid model, with respect to passive corruption.*

Due to space constraints, the proof of Theorem 1 is postponed to the full version.

### 3.1   Implementing the Preprocessing Functionality

We now describe the implementation of the functionality $\mathscr{F}_{\mathsf{ET\text{-}prep}}$, in the $\mathscr{F}_{\mathsf{OT}}$-hybrid model. The protocol is represented on Fig. 3.

**Theorem 2.** *The protocol $\Pi_{\mathsf{ET}}$ securely implements $\mathscr{F}_{\mathsf{ET}}$ when calls to $\mathscr{F}_{\mathsf{ET\text{-}prep}}$ in $\Pi_{\mathsf{ET}}$ are replaced by executions of $\Pi_{\mathsf{ET\text{-}prep}}$ in the $\mathscr{F}_{\mathsf{OT}}$-hybrid model, with respect to passive corruption.*

Due to lack of space, we postpone the proof to the full version. While the proof is rather straightforward, observe that we do not claim that $\Pi_{\mathsf{ET\text{-}prep}}$ UC-securely implements $\mathscr{F}_{\mathsf{ET\text{-}prep}}$ with respect to passive corruption, but rather that the entire protocol remain secure when calls to $\mathscr{F}_{\mathsf{ET\text{-}prep}}$ are replaced by executions of $\Pi_{\mathsf{ET\text{-}prep}}$. The reason for this distinction is that $\Pi_{\mathsf{ET\text{-}prep}}$ does in fact

---

**Protocol $\Pi_{\mathsf{ET\text{-}prep}}$**

---

**Size-Reduction($\ell$):** Alice picks $(x, a) \leftarrow_R \mathbb{Z}_2^{\ell} \times \mathbb{Z}_{\ell+1}^{\ell}$, and Bob picks $y \leftarrow_R \mathbb{Z}_2^{\ell}$. The players call $\mathcal{F}_{\mathsf{OT}}^{\ell, |\ell+1|}$, on input $(x[i] - a[i] \bmod \ell + 1, 1 - a[i] - x[i] \bmod \ell + 1)_{i \leq \ell}$ for Alice and $y$ for Bob. Let $b$ denote Bob's output. Alice outputs $(x, a)$ and Bob outputs $(y, b)$.

**Product-Sharing($n$):** Alice picks $(x, a) \leftarrow_R (\mathbb{Z}_2^{2^n-2})^2$, and Bob picks $y \leftarrow_R \mathbb{Z}_2^{2^n-2}$. The players call $\mathcal{F}_{\mathsf{OT}}^{2^n-2, 2}$ on input $(a[i], a[i] \oplus x[i])_{i \leq 2^n-2}$ for Alice and $y$ for Bob. Let $b$ denote Bob's output. Alice outputs $(x, a)$ and Bob outputs $(y, b)$.

---

**Fig. 3.** Preprocessing protocol for equality test

not UC-securely implement $\mathcal{F}_{\mathsf{ET\text{-}prep}}$. Intuitively, this comes from the fact that in $\Pi_{\mathsf{ET\text{-}prep}}$, the parties choose (part of) their outputs themselves; hence, no simulator can possibly force the parties to set their outputs to being equal to the outputs of $\mathcal{F}_{\mathsf{ET\text{-}prep}}$. While this can be solved by adding a resharing step at the end of the protocol, this would add some unnecessary interaction and communication to the protocol. Instead, we rely on an approach of [9], which was developed exactly for this purpose: we prove that the protocol is *input-private* (meaning that there is a simulator producing a view indistinguishable from an execution of the protocol for any environment that ignores the output of the protocol), which, as shown in [9], suffices to argue the security of the composed protocol as soon as some rules on ordered composition are respected.

## 3.2 Communication Complexity

By a classical observation (see e.g. [40]), we can always assume that the inputs of the players are less than $\kappa$-bit long: if this is not the case, each party can hash its input first, preserving the correctness of the protocol with overwhelming probability. Therefore, as the largest strings obliviously transferred during the protocol $\Pi_{\mathsf{ET}}$ are $|\ell+1| \leq |\kappa+1|$ bit long (for $\kappa = 128$, this corresponds to 8-bit strings), we can benefit from the short-string oblivious transfer extension protocol of [35]. Ignoring the computation of the base $\mathsf{OTs}$, which is performed a single time for an arbitrary number of equality tests, $k$ size reduction procedures on $\ell$-bit inputs transmit $O(k\ell(\kappa/\log x + x \cdot |\ell|))$ bits, where $x$ is a parameter that can be arbitrarily set so as to minimize this cost. This minimizes to $O(k\ell\kappa/\log\kappa)$, up to some $\log\log$ term. As a consequence, when performing many equality tests, the (amortized) cost of a single equality test is $O(\kappa\ell/\log\kappa)$ bits in the preprocessing phase (and still $O(\ell)$ bits in the online phase). For inputs of size $\ell > \kappa$, where the players can hash their input first, the complexity becomes $O(\kappa^2/\log\kappa)$ in the preprocessing phase, and $O(\kappa)$ in the online phase.

## 3.3 Concrete Efficiency

We now analyze the efficiency of our protocol for various input-lengths. In all our numerical applications, we set the security parameter $\kappa$ to 128. We estimate the efficiency in an amortized setting, where we can use oblivious transfer extension.

**Comparison with Equality Test from Garbled Circuit and from 2PC.**
We compare our protocol to the garbled-circuit-based protocol of [36], and to the solution based on generic 2PC, using the optimized circuit of [24]. We apply all possible optimizations to these two alternative approaches, using random OTs in the offline phase to precompute the online OTs, as well as oblivious transfer extensions. We use optimized OT extensions of short strings for [24], but not for [36], as it involves OT on large keys.

**Amortized Setting.** We now provide a concrete efficiency analysis of the protocol in an amortized setting, using oblivious transfer extensions. We do not take into account the cost of the base oblivious transfers for the OT extension scheme, as this is a constant independent of the number of equality tests performed, which is the same for both our protocol and the protocol of [36]. Adapting the construction of [35] to the case of correlated short inputs, the exact cost of reducing $m$ oblivious transfers of $t$-bit strings to $\kappa$ oblivious transfers of $\kappa$-bit strings is $m(2\kappa/\log x + (x-1)t)$ (this takes into account an optimization described in

**Table 2.** Communication of $\ell$-bit ETs

| $\ell$ | Our ET | | [36] | | [24] | |
|---|---|---|---|---|---|---|
| | Comm.[b] | Rounds | Comm. | Rounds | Comm. | Rounds |
| *Preprocessing phase* | | | | | | |
| 4 | 1106 | 2 | 1288 | 1 | 1264 | 3 |
| 8 | 2018 | 3 | 2832 | 1 | 3002 | 4 |
| 16 | 2945 | 4 | 5920 | 1 | 6636 | 5 |
| 32 | 5212 | 4 | 12096 | 1 | 14062 | 6 |
| 64 | 9863 | 4 | 24448 | 1 | 29072 | 7 |
| 128 | 20194 | 4 | 49152 | 1 | 59250 | 8 |
| *Online phase* | | | | | | |
| 4 | 28 | 1 | 1540 | 2 | 96 | 3 |
| 8 | 44 | 2 | 3080 | 2 | 228 | 4 |
| 16 | 54 | 3 | 6160 | 2 | 504 | 5 |
| 32 | 88 | 3 | 12320 | 2 | 1068 | 6 |
| 64 | 154 | 3 | 24640 | 2 | 2208 | 7 |
| 128 | 300 | 3 | 49280 | 2 | 4500 | 8 |

[a]The one-time cost of the base OTs is ignored in the amortized setting.
[b]Comm. denotes the number of bits exchanged during a protocol run.

[35, Appendix A] and the optimization for correlated inputs of [4]).Therefore, the amortized cost of a size reduction protocol on input $k$ is $k(2\kappa/\log x + (x-1)k)$, where $x$ can be chosen so as to minimize this cost. Table 2 sums up the amortized costs of our equality test protocol for various values of $\ell$; oblivious transfers for the garbled circuit approach of [36] are performed using the OT extension protocol of [4] on $\kappa$-bit inputs, which transmits $3\kappa$ bits per OT. As shown in Table 2, our protocol improves over the communication of [36] by up to 80% overall. During the online phase, our protocol is extremely efficient, two orders of magnitude faster than [36]. Our protocol also improves over [24] by about 70% overall, and by 95% in the online phase. Furthermore, it is considerably less interactive, although it remains more interactive than the garbled-circuit-based approach.

**Amortized Computational Complexity.** The computational complexity of [24,36] and our protocol are directly proportional to their communication in the amortized setting (and it is dominated by the evaluation of hash functions in both, which are required for (extended) OTs and garbled gates), hence our constructions improve upo these protocols regarding computation by factors similar to those listed in Table 2.

**Acknowledgements.** We thank David Pointcheval for insightful discussions and comments, and Thomas Schneider for pointing out inaccuracies in our cost estimations for the garbled circuit-based constructions of equality tests and secure comparison. The author was supported by ERC grant 339563 (project CryptoCloud) and ERC grant 724307 (project PREP-CRYPTO).

# References

1. Aliasgari, M., Blanton, M., Zhang, Y., Steele, A.: Secure computation on floating point numbers. In: NDSS 2013, February 2013
2. Aly, A., Cuvelier, E., Mawet, S., Pereira, O., Van Vyve, M.: Securely solving simple combinatorial graph problems. In: Sadeghi, A.-R. (ed.) FC 2013. LNCS, vol. 7859, pp. 239–257. Springer, Heidelberg (2013). https://doi.org/10.1007/978-3-642-39884-1_21
3. Applebaum, B., Ishai, Y., Kushilevitz, E., Waters, B.: Encoding functions with constant online rate or how to compress garbled circuits keys. In: Canetti, R., Garay, J.A. (eds.) CRYPTO 2013. LNCS, vol. 8043, pp. 166–184. Springer, Heidelberg (2013). https://doi.org/10.1007/978-3-642-40084-1_10
4. Asharov, G., Lindell, Y., Schneider, T., Zohner, M.: More efficient oblivious transfer and extensions for faster secure computation. In: Sadeghi, A.R., Gligor, V.D., Yung, M. (eds.) ACM CCS 2013, pp. 535–548. ACM Press, November 2013
5. Ayday, E., Raisaro, J.L., Laren, M., Jack, P., Fellay, J., Hubaux, J.P.: Privacy-preserving computation of disease risk by using genomic, clinical, and environmental data. In: Proceedings of USENIX Security Workshop on Health Information Technologies (HealthTech 2013), No. EPFL-CONF-187118 (2013)
6. Beaver, D.: Correlated pseudorandomness and the complexity of private computations. In: 28th ACM STOC, pp. 479–488. ACM Press, May 1996

7. Blake, I.F., Kolesnikov, V.: Strong conditional oblivious transfer and computing on intervals. In: Lee, P.J. (ed.) ASIACRYPT 2004. LNCS, vol. 3329, pp. 515–529. Springer, Heidelberg (2004). https://doi.org/10.1007/978-3-540-30539-2_36

8. Blanton, M., Saraph, S.: Oblivious maximum bipartite matching size algorithm with applications to secure fingerprint identification. In: Pernul, G., Ryan, P.Y.A., Weippl, E. (eds.) ESORICS 2015. LNCS, vol. 9326, pp. 384–406. Springer, Cham (2015). https://doi.org/10.1007/978-3-319-24174-6_20

9. Bogdanov, D., Laud, P., Laur, S., Pullonen, P.: From input private to universally composable secure multiparty computation primitives. Cryptology ePrint Archive, Report 2014/201 (2014). http://eprint.iacr.org/2014/201

10. Bost, R., Popa, R.A., Tu, S., Goldwasser, S.: Machine learning classification over encrypted data. Cryptology ePrint Archive, Report 2014/331 (2014). http://eprint.iacr.org/2014/331

11. Canetti, R.: Universally composable security: a new paradigm for cryptographic protocols. In: 42nd FOCS, pp. 136–145. IEEE Computer Society Press, October 2001

12. Catrina, O., de Hoogh, S.: Improved primitives for secure multiparty integer computation. In: Garay, J.A., De Prisco, R. (eds.) SCN 2010. LNCS, vol. 6280, pp. 182–199. Springer, Heidelberg (2010). https://doi.org/10.1007/978-3-642-15317-4_13

13. Catrina, O., de Hoogh, S.: Secure multiparty linear programming using fixed-point arithmetic. In: Gritzalis, D., Preneel, B., Theoharidou, M. (eds.) ESORICS 2010. LNCS, vol. 6345, pp. 134–150. Springer, Heidelberg (2010). https://doi.org/10.1007/978-3-642-15497-3_9

14. Chu, W.T., Chang, F.C.: A privacy-preserving bipartite graph matching framework for multimedia analysis and retrieval. In: Proceedings of the 5th ACM on International Conference on Multimedia Retrieval, pp. 243–250. ACM (2015)

15. Couteau, G.: New protocols for secure equality test and comparison. Cryptology ePrint Archive, Report 2016/544 (2016). http://eprint.iacr.org/2016/544

16. Couteau, G., Peters, T., Pointcheval, D.: Encryption switching protocols. In: Robshaw, M., Katz, J. (eds.) CRYPTO 2016. LNCS, vol. 9814, pp. 308–338. Springer, Heidelberg (2016). https://doi.org/10.1007/978-3-662-53018-4_12. http://eprint.iacr.org/2015/990

17. Cramer, R., Damgård, I., Nielsen, J.B.: Multiparty computation from threshold homomorphic encryption. In: Pfitzmann, B. (ed.) EUROCRYPT 2001. LNCS, vol. 2045, pp. 280–300. Springer, Heidelberg (2001). https://doi.org/10.1007/3-540-44987-6_18

18. Cramer, R., Kiltz, E., Padró, C.: A note on secure computation of the moore-penrose pseudoinverse and its application to secure linear algebra. In: Menezes, A. (ed.) CRYPTO 2007. LNCS, vol. 4622, pp. 613–630. Springer, Heidelberg (2007). https://doi.org/10.1007/978-3-540-74143-5_34

19. Damgård, I., Fitzi, M., Kiltz, E., Nielsen, J.B., Toft, T.: Unconditionally secure constant-rounds multi-party computation for equality, comparison, bits and exponentiation. In: Halevi, S., Rabin, T. (eds.) TCC 2006. LNCS, vol. 3876, pp. 285–304. Springer, Heidelberg (2006). https://doi.org/10.1007/11681878_15

20. Damgård, I., Geisler, M., Krøigaard, M.: Efficient and secure comparison for on-line auctions. In: Pieprzyk, J., Ghodosi, H., Dawson, E. (eds.) ACISP 2007. LNCS, vol. 4586, pp. 416–430. Springer, Heidelberg (2007). https://doi.org/10.1007/978-3-540-73458-1_30

21. Damgard, I., Geisler, M., Kroigard, M.: A correction to 'efficient and secure comparison for on-line auctions'. Int. J. Appl. Crypt. 1(4), 323–324 (2009)

22. Erkin, Z., Veugen, T., Toft, T., Lagendijk, R.L.: Generating private recommendations efficiently using homomorphic encryption and data packing. IEEE Trans. Inf. Forensics Secur. **7**(3), 1053–1066 (2012)
23. Even, S., Goldreich, O., Lempel, A.: A randomized protocol for signing contracts. In: Chaum, D., Rivest, R.L., Sherman, A.T. (eds.) CRYPTO 1982, pp. 205–210. Plenum Press, New York (1982)
24. Garay, J., Schoenmakers, B., Villegas, J.: Practical and secure solutions for integer comparison. In: Okamoto, T., Wang, X. (eds.) PKC 2007. LNCS, vol. 4450, pp. 330–342. Springer, Heidelberg (2007). https://doi.org/10.1007/978-3-540-71677-8_22
25. Gentry, C., Halevi, S., Jutla, C., Raykova, M.: Private database access with HE-over-ORAM architecture. In: Malkin, T., Kolesnikov, V., Lewko, A.B., Polychronakis, M. (eds.) ACNS 2015. LNCS, vol. 9092, pp. 172–191. Springer, Cham (2015). https://doi.org/10.1007/978-3-319-28166-7_9
26. Goldreich, O.: Towards a theory of software protection and simulation by oblivious RAMs. In: Aho, A. (ed.) 19th ACM STOC, pp. 182–194. ACM Press, May 1987
27. Goldreich, O., Micali, S., Wigderson, A.: How to prove all NP statements in zero-knowledge and a methodology of cryptographic protocol design (extended abstract). In: Odlyzko, A.M. (ed.) CRYPTO 1986. LNCS, vol. 263, pp. 171–185. Springer, Heidelberg (1987). https://doi.org/10.1007/3-540-47721-7_11
28. Goodrich, M.T.: Randomized shellsort: a simple oblivious sorting algorithm. In: Charika, M. (ed.) 21st SODA, pp. 1262–1277. ACM-SIAM, January 2010
29. Goodrich, M.T.: Zig-zag sort: a simple deterministic data-oblivious sorting algorithm running in $O(n \log n)$ time. In: 46th ACM STOC, pp. 684–693. ACM Press (2014)
30. Hamada, K., Ikarashi, D., Chida, K., Takahashi, K.: Oblivious radix sort: an efficient sorting algorithm for practical secure multi-party computation. Cryptology ePrint Archive, Report 2014/121 (2014). http://eprint.iacr.org/2014/121
31. Hazay, C., Toft, T.: Computationally secure pattern matching in the presence of malicious adversaries. J. Cryptol. **27**(2), 358–395 (2014)
32. Huang, Y., Evans, D., Katz, J.: Private set intersection: are garbled circuits better than custom protocols? In: NDSS 2012, February 2012
33. Ishai, Y., Kilian, J., Nissim, K., Petrank, E.: Extending oblivious transfers efficiently. In: Boneh, D. (ed.) CRYPTO 2003. LNCS, vol. 2729, pp. 145–161. Springer, Heidelberg (2003). https://doi.org/10.1007/978-3-540-45146-4_9
34. Kilian, J.: Founding cryptography on oblivious transfer. In: 20th ACM STOC, pp. 20–31. ACM Press, May 1988
35. Kolesnikov, V., Kumaresan, R.: Improved OT extension for transferring short secrets. In: Canetti, R., Garay, J.A. (eds.) CRYPTO 2013. LNCS, vol. 8043, pp. 54–70. Springer, Heidelberg (2013). https://doi.org/10.1007/978-3-642-40084-1_4
36. Kolesnikov, V., Sadeghi, A.-R., Schneider, T.: Improved garbled circuit building blocks and applications to auctions and computing minima. In: Garay, J.A., Miyaji, A., Otsuka, A. (eds.) CANS 2009. LNCS, vol. 5888, pp. 1–20. Springer, Heidelberg (2009). https://doi.org/10.1007/978-3-642-10433-6_1
37. Kolesnikov, V., Schneider, T.: Improved garbled circuit: free XOR gates and applications. In: Aceto, L., Damgård, I., Goldberg, L.A., Halldórsson, M.M., Ingólfsdóttir, A., Walukiewicz, I. (eds.) ICALP 2008. LNCS, vol. 5126, pp. 486–498. Springer, Heidelberg (2008). https://doi.org/10.1007/978-3-540-70583-3_40
38. Laud, P.: A private lookup protocol with low online complexity for secure multi-party computation. In: Hui, L.C.K., Qing, S.H., Shi, E., Yiu, S.M. (eds.) ICICS 2014. LNCS, vol. 8958, pp. 143–157. Springer, Cham (2015). https://doi.org/10.1007/978-3-319-21966-0_11

39. Li, P., Li, T., Yao, Z.A., Tang, C.M., Li, J.: Privacy-preserving outsourcing of image feature extraction in cloud computing. Soft Comput. **21**, 1–11 (2016)
40. Lipmaa, H., Toft, T.: Secure equality and greater-than tests with sublinear online complexity. In: Fomin, F.V., Freivalds, R., Kwiatkowska, M., Peleg, D. (eds.) ICALP 2013. LNCS, vol. 7966, pp. 645–656. Springer, Heidelberg (2013). https://doi.org/10.1007/978-3-642-39212-2_56
41. Naor, M., Pinkas, B.: Efficient oblivious transfer protocols. In: Kosaraju, S.R. (ed.) 12th SODA, pp. 448–457. ACM-SIAM, January 2001
42. Nishide, T., Iwamoto, M., Iwasaki, A., Ohta, K.: Secure $(M + 1)$ st-price auction with automatic tie-break. In: Yung, M., Zhu, L., Yang, Y. (eds.) INTRUST 2014. LNCS, vol. 9473, pp. 422–437. Springer, Cham (2015). https://doi.org/10.1007/978-3-319-27998-5_27
43. Nishide, T., Ohta, K.: Multiparty computation for interval, equality, and comparison without bit-decomposition protocol. In: Okamoto, T., Wang, X. (eds.) PKC 2007. LNCS, vol. 4450, pp. 343–360. Springer, Heidelberg (2007). https://doi.org/10.1007/978-3-540-71677-8_23
44. Paillier, P.: Public-key cryptosystems based on composite degree residuosity classes. In: Stern, J. (ed.) EUROCRYPT 1999. LNCS, vol. 1592, pp. 223–238. Springer, Heidelberg (1999). https://doi.org/10.1007/3-540-48910-X_16
45. Rabin, M.: How to exchange secrets by oblivious transfer. Technical report TR-81, Harvard University (1981)
46. Rahulamathavan, Y., Phan, R.C.W., Veluru, S., Cumanan, K., Rajarajan, M.: Privacy-preserving multi-class support vector machine for outsourcing the data classification in cloud. IEEE Trans. Dependable Secure Comput. **11**(5), 467–479 (2014)
47. Sadeghi, A.-R., Schneider, T., Wehrenberg, I.: Efficient privacy-preserving face recognition. In: Lee, D., Hong, S. (eds.) ICISC 2009. LNCS, vol. 5984, pp. 229–244. Springer, Heidelberg (2010). https://doi.org/10.1007/978-3-642-14423-3_16
48. Samanthula, B.K., Jiang, W., Bertino, E.: Lightweight and secure two-party range queries over outsourced encrypted databases. arXiv:1401.3768 (2014)
49. Toft, T.: Solving linear programs using multiparty computation. In: Dingledine, R., Golle, P. (eds.) FC 2009. LNCS, vol. 5628, pp. 90–107. Springer, Heidelberg (2009). https://doi.org/10.1007/978-3-642-03549-4_6
50. Toft, T.: Sub-linear, secure comparison with two non-colluding parties. In: Catalano, D., Fazio, N., Gennaro, R., Nicolosi, A. (eds.) PKC 2011. LNCS, vol. 6571, pp. 174–191. Springer, Heidelberg (2011). https://doi.org/10.1007/978-3-642-19379-8_11
51. Veugen, T.: Improving the DGK comparison protocol. In: 2012 IEEE International Workshop on Information Forensics and Security (WIFS), pp. 49–54. IEEE (2012)
52. Wu, D.J., Feng, T., Naehrig, M., Lauter, K.: Privately evaluating decision trees and random forests. Cryptology ePrint Archive, Report 2015/386 (2015). http://eprint.iacr.org/2015/386
53. Yao, A.C.C.: How to generate and exchange secrets (extended abstract). In: 27th FOCS, pp. 162–167. IEEE Computer Society Press, October 1986
54. Yu, C.-H., Yang, B.-Y.: Probabilistically correct secure arithmetic computation for modular conversion, zero test, comparison, MOD and exponentiation. In: Visconti, I., De Prisco, R. (eds.) SCN 2012. LNCS, vol. 7485, pp. 426–444. Springer, Heidelberg (2012). https://doi.org/10.1007/978-3-642-32928-9_24
55. Zahur, S., Rosulek, M., Evans, D.: Two halves make a whole - reducing data transfer in garbled circuits using half gates. In: Oswald, E., Fischlin, M. (eds.) EUROCRYPT 2015. LNCS, vol. 9057, pp. 220–250. Springer, Heidelberg (2015). https://doi.org/10.1007/978-3-662-46803-6_8

# Minimising Communication in Honest-Majority MPC by Batchwise Multiplication Verification

Peter Sebastian Nordholt[1] and Meilof Veeningen[2]([⊠])

[1] Alexandra Institute, Copenhagen, Denmark
peter.s.nordholt@alexandra.dk
[2] Philips Research, Eindhoven, The Netherlands
meilof@gmail.com

**Abstract.** In this paper, we present two new and very communication-efficient protocols for maliciously secure multi-party computation over fields in the honest-majority setting with abort. Our first protocol improves a recent protocol by Lindell and Nof. Using the so far over-looked tool of batchwise multiplication verification, we speed up their technique for checking correctness of multiplications (with some other improvements), reducing communication by 2× to 7×. In particular, in the 3PC setting, each party sends only two field elements per multiplication. We also show how to achieve fairness, which Lindell and Nof left as an open problem. Our second protocol again applies batchwise multiplication verification, this time to perform 3PC by letting two parties perform the SPDZ protocol using triples generated by a third party and verified batchwise. In this protocol, each party sends only $\frac{4}{3}$ field elements during the online phase and $\frac{5}{3}$ field elements during the preprocessing phase.

## 1 Introduction

Multi-party computation (MPC) allows a number of parties to compute a function on their respective sensitive inputs without leaking anything but the computation result. Recently, there has been a lot of interest in concretely efficient actively secure MPC in the honest-majority setting with abort, in which fewer than $n/2$ out of $n$ parties may be corrupted. In this setting, very efficient solutions are known and it is also possible to achieve *fairness*, i.e., either all parties learn the result or none do, which is not possible without a honest majority.

A number of recent works have achieved particularly striking performance numbers. Binary circuits can be evaluated at a cost of sending 10 bits per AND gate for three parties due to [11], and arithmetic circuits can be evaluated at a cost of sending 4 (for $n = 3$), $5(n - 1)$, or 42 field elements per multiplication due to [16]. However, this still leaves at least a factor four communication increase compared to passive security. Moreover, these best known protocols unfortunately do not satisfy fairness (unlike other honest-majority protocols).

© Springer International Publishing AG, part of Springer Nature 2018
B. Preneel and F. Vercauteren (Eds.): ACNS 2018, LNCS 10892, pp. 321–339, 2018.
https://doi.org/10.1007/978-3-319-93387-0_17

In this work, we improve on the state-of-the-art of concretely efficient honest-majority MPC by further decreasing communication complexity, while also supporting fairness. Concerning communication complexity, we decrease communication in the three main variants of the protocol of Lindel and Nof by factors of approximately 2, 5, and 7, respectively. In all cases, the gap between passive and active security becomes only a factor 2. Moreover, in the three-party setting, the best protocol now requires sending just two messages per party per multiplication. Some of this improvement comes from better use of PRNGs; a more significant improvement comes from applying the tool of batchwise multiplication verification [2], a technique that allows to check that many multiplications have been performed correctly by essentially checking a single multiplication.

We additional provide a novel three-party protocol, based on the SPDZ protocol [8], that reduces *online* communication from 2 in our protocol described above to $\frac{4}{3}$ messages per party per multiplication. This comes at the expense of requiring a *preprocessing* phase with $\frac{5}{3}$ messages per party per multiplication. Our SPDZ-based protocol also makes heavy use of PRNGs and batchwise multiplication verification, but additionally incorporates the idea of taking a two-party protocol in the preprocessing model, and replacing the distributed preprocessing protocol by in-the-plain preprocessing by a third party. This idea was known before but, as far as we know, has never been applied; we extend this idea by allowing the preprocessing to be spread evenly between the three parties. By way of comparison, in the two-party dishonest majority setting, a recent SPDZ variant by Keller *et al.* [14] requires the equivalent of around 130 field elements to be sent per party, highlighting the communication gap between the honest- and dishonest-majority settings.

In both our Lindell-Nof and our SPDZ based protocol, the decrease in communication implies an increase in computation, but we show that in many practical settings, communication is still the bottleneck.

Finally, we show how to add fairness both of our constructions. We employ general principles to achieve fairness such as using signature-based broadcast for agreement and MACs or signatures to prevent output manipulation. Our solutions are especially crafted to ensure that they add as little practical overhead as possible; in particular, they do not affect the above communication complexity results. This means that communication-efficient, actively secure MPC is possible in practice without having to sacrifice fairness.

## 1.1  Outline

We discuss preliminaries in Sect. 2, before presenting our Lindell-Nof-based and SPDZ-based constructions in Sects. 3 and 4, respectively. We give a brief performance analysis in Sect. 5.

## 1.2  Related Work

Several recent works are closely related to this paper. Concerning efficient honest-majority MPC, the most relevant work is the framework for communication-efficient MPC from [16] that forms the basis of our first protocol. It is also the closest competitor in terms of overall communication complexity that we are aware of. Another recent honest-majority MPC framework is due to [7]. Although their construction is quite a bit less communication-efficient than ours, it does work for arbitrary rings as opposed to just fields. They also provide a (less efficient) construction for fairness largely based on the same principles as ours.

Concerning the technique of batchwise multiplication verification, the groundwork was laid out in several earlier works. Ben-Sasson *et al.* [2] first proposed batchwise multiplication verification. As discussed below, there it was used to get an asymptotic result; we are not aware of works using it to improve practical performance. Works such as the Pinocchio verifiable computation system [19] and the Trinocchio protocol that combines it with MPC [20] were a main inspiration to start seeing batchwise multiplication verification also as a tool that may deliver practical efficiency. Corrigan-Gibbs and Boneh [4] first proposed to use batchwise multiplication verification where one party provides data and a number of other parties verify it, as in our SPDZ-based protocol; but there it is not for performing the MPC but for checking its inputs.

## 2 Preliminaries

In this section, we present our notation and the security model for honest-majority MPC with abort, and the main technique we will use to minimise its communication: batchwise multiplication verification.

### 2.1 Notation and Security Model

The protocols in this paper are for $n$ parties $\mathcal{P} = \{\mathcal{P}_1, \mathcal{P}_2, \ldots, \mathcal{P}_n\}$, where an adversary may statically corrupt a minority of up to $t$ parties, i.e., $2t < n$. We generally work in the field $\mathbb{Z}_p$ for some prime $p > 2^\sigma$, where $\sigma$ is a statistical security parameter. We use $[x]$ to denote a Shamir secret sharing of $x$; $[\![x]\!]$ to denote an additive sharing; and $\langle x \rangle = ([\![x]\!], [\![\alpha x]\!])$ to denote a SPDZ sharing consisting of an additive sharing of the value and its MAC. $[x]_i$, $[\![x]\!]_i$, $\langle x \rangle_i$ refer to shares held by party $\mathcal{P}_i$. We heavily use pseudorandom number generators (PRNGs) to sample random data. For a pseudorandom number generator prng we use the notation $r \leftarrow$ prng to indicate sampling $r$ uniformly at random (from the relevant domain). $[a, b]$ denotes the interval $[a, a+1, \ldots, b]$.

We define security in the traditional standalone security model from [3] as adapted in [16]. Security in this model is captured by demanding indistinguishability of the real-world protocol execution to an ideal-world execution with a trusted third party. In the real-world model, the protocol is run between honest parties in the presence of a non-uniform probabilistic polynomial time adversary $\mathcal{A}$ that acts on behalf of the corrupted parties. We assume a synchronous network with pairwise private channels and a rushing adversary (that receives its messages in each round before it sends them). A party may *abort*, meaning it sends a special abort message to all parties, who abort in the next round.

An execution of a protocol $\pi$ in this model with inputs $x_1, \ldots, x_n$, adversarial auxiliary input $z$ and security parameter $\kappa$ is denoted $\mathrm{Real}_{\pi, \mathcal{A}(z), \mathcal{C}}(x_1, \ldots, x_n, \kappa)$. This is a tuple containing the outputs of the honest parties and an arbitrary output chosen by the adversary.

The ideal-world model defines how an idealised protocol execution looks like in which the computation is performed by an incorruptible trusted party executing a certain *functionality*. The functionality defines the exact security guarantees; we will define variants with and without fairness. In the ideal-world model, the trusted party executes the functionality in the presence of the honest parties and a non-uniform probabilistic polynomial time adversary $\mathcal{S}$.

The functionalities for fair and non-fair MPC both start with each party $\mathcal{P}_i$ sending its input $x_i$ to the trusted party. The adversary may choose an arbitrary input for corrupted parties and may also provide $\perp$ to indicate an abort. The trusted party computes output $y$ as specified by $f$, or sets $y = \perp$ if the adversary supplied $\perp$. In the *fair variant*, the trusted party sends the outputs to all of the parties. In the *non-fair variant*, the trusted party sends $y$ to the adversary who returns $c \in \{\top, \perp\}^n$. For each party $\mathcal{P}_i$, if $c_i = \top$ the trusted party sends $y$ to $\mathcal{P}_i$, otherwise it sends $\perp$. Ideal-world executions with these functionalities are denoted $\mathrm{Ideal}_{f, \mathcal{S}(z), \mathcal{C}}(x_1, \ldots, x_n, \kappa)$ or $\mathrm{Ideal}_{f, \ldots}^{\mathrm{fair}}(\ldots)$: a tuple containing the outputs of the honest parties and an arbitrary output chosen by the adversary.

Security is defined as indistinguishability between real-world and ideal-world executions. Precisely, we say that a protocol $\pi$ *securely computes $f$ with statistical security parameter $\sigma$ for honest majority* if, for every adversary $\mathcal{A}$, there exists a simulator $\mathcal{S}$ such that, for all $x_i, z, \mathcal{C}$ with $|\mathcal{C}| \leq t$, the distinguishing probability between $\mathrm{Ideal}_{f, \mathcal{S}(z), \mathcal{C}}(x_1, \ldots, x_n, \kappa)$ and $\mathrm{Real}_{\pi, \mathcal{A}(z), \mathcal{C}}(x_1, \ldots, x_n, \kappa)$ is at most $2^{-\sigma} + \mu(\kappa)$ for some $\mu$ negligible in $\kappa$. Protocol $\pi$ *fairly computes $f$ with statistical security parameter $\sigma$ for honest majority* if the same holds with respect to $\mathrm{Ideal}_{f, \ldots}^{\mathrm{fair}}(\ldots)$. Security can also be defined more generally for any functionality $\mathcal{F}$. As is well-known, we can design protocols containing calls to an ideal functionality $\mathcal{F}$ (in the so-called $\mathcal{F}$-*hybrid model*) and then replace the ideal functionality by a secure protocol implementing it [3].

The above model describes standalone executions with synchronous communication, but we believe that neither limitation is inherent to our protocol. In asynchronous models, unlike above, there is no global round clock. In general, synchronous protocols can be made asynchronous by having each party confirm to all other parties that it has received all messages for round $t$, and only proceeding to send messages for round $t+1$ after receiving all confirmations [15], but this is of course costly. We expect that such confirmations are only necessary at a few points in our protocol. In composable models, unlike the standalone model above, protocols are proven secure also in the presence of simultaneous other protocols and protocol instances. Here, we note that we use only black-box non-rewinding simulators, so adding "start synchronisation" should be enough to achieve composability [15]. We leave details for future work.

## 2.2  Batchwise Multiplication Verification

Batchwise multiplication verification was introduced in [2] to improve the asymptotic complexity of verifying preprocessed multiplication triples over small fields. Standard multiplications checks, e.g. based on sacrificing, scale with the security parameter (which is larger than the field size), but using batchwise multiplication verification, these costs can be spread over a batch.

In particular, given secret-shared values $[a_1], \ldots, [a_N], [b_1], \ldots, [b_N], [c_1], \ldots, [c_N]$, the goal is to verify that $c_i = a_i \cdot b_i$ for all $i$. This is done by translating these $N$ equalities of field elements into a single equality of polynomials, and verifying this equality based on the Schwartz-Zippel lemma [21,22]. Fix nonzero $\omega_1, \ldots, \omega_{2N-1}$, and let $A(x), B(x)$ be of degree $\leq N - 1$ such that for $i \in [1, N]$, $A(\omega_i) = a_i$ and $B(\omega_i) = b_i$. If we let $C(x) = A(x)B(x)$, then obviously $C(\omega_i) = c_i$ for $i \in [1, N]$, but the converse is also true: if there exists a polynomial $C(x)$ of degree $\leq 2N - 1$ such that $C(x) = A(x)B(x)$ and $C(\omega_i) = c_i$ for $i \in [1, N]$, this implies $c_i = a_i \cdot b_i$.

In batchwise multiplication verification, first, $C(x)$ is constructed by computing $C(\omega_j) = A(\omega_j) \cdot B(\omega_j)$, $j \in [N + 1, 2N - 1]$ using passively secure MPC and deriving its coefficients by interpolation. Then, $A$, $B$, and $C$ are evaluated in a random point $s \notin \{\omega_1, \ldots, \omega_{2N-1}\}$. This can be done with local linear operations given shares of the $a_i$, $b_i$, $c_i$, and $C(\omega_j)$. Finally, a multiplication check protocol is run to check that $A(s) \cdot B(s) = C(s)$. The Schwartz-Zippel lemma, states that for a non-zero degree $d$ polynomial, $P$, over field $\mathcal{F}$ of and a random $r \in S$ for a finite $S \subseteq \mathcal{F}$ the probability that $P(r) = 0$ is at most $d/|S|$. Thus if $A(s) \cdot B(s) = C(s)$ then with high probability, $A(x) \cdot B(x) = C(x)$ as polynomials and hence $a_i \cdot b_i = c_i$. Note that for each triple, an additional passively secure multiplication is needed, but the multiplication check is performed only once per batch, giving the asymptotic advantage.

In [4], the above idea is used in a different setting: some party provides inputs to MPC, and we want to verify that inputs satisfy a certain property. This property is phrased in terms of a number of multiplications of linear combinations of inputs, and the multiplications are checked similarly to above. In this case, the inputter determines and provides the "witness" values $C(\omega_j)$ proving that the multiplications are correct, and the computing parties again use a simple protocol to check that $A(s) \cdot B(s) = C(s)$. It is also shown there that the various polynomial computations can be performed efficiently using FFTs.

## 3  Lindell-Nof with Fewer Messages and More Fairness

In this section, we show how to reduce the communication complexity of the Lindell-Nof protocol for honest-majority MPC [16] and how to add fairness. We outline their construction (Sect. 3.1); plug in batchwise multiplication verification (Sect. 3.2); analyse and further reduce communication complexity (Sect. 3.3); finally, we show how to achieve fairness and discuss two other improvements (Sect. 3.4).

### 3.1 The Lindell-Nof Construction

Lindell and Nof present a framework for efficient actively secure MPC with a honest majority [16]. The basic observation underlying this framework is that many passively secure MPC protocols are "actively secret", essentially meaning that an active attack can break correctness of the computation, but not privacy. Hence, to perform a computation in an actively secure way, one can simply perform the computation using a passively secure protocol and, prior to opening the result, retrospectively check that all multiplications, as these are the only operations that require interaction, have been performed correctly.

In slightly more detail, the Lindell-Nof construction uses of $t$-out-of-$n$ secret sharing, such as Shamir secret sharing or replicated secret sharing. The protocol starts with all parties secret-sharing their inputs, and checking whether they are "correct", in the sense that the shares of all honest parties reconstruct to a unique value. Next, a passively secure MPC is executed, with linear operations performed locally on shares and multiplication using known protocols for Shamir by Gennaro et al. [12], Damgård and Nielsen [6] and for replicated secret sharing by Araki et al. [1]. We will refer to these three multiplication methods as GRR, DN and AFL+ respectively. Finally, the correctness of the performed multiplications is checked using one of two possible methods, and if this check passes, the secret shares of the output are reconstructed to obtain the output. Overall, this gives active security without fairness with relatively little communication.

### 3.2 Plugging in Batchwise Multiplication Verification

We now show how batchwise multiplication verification can be used to efficiently implement the multiplication check in the Lindell-Nof protocol. As discussed above, the multiplication check is called at the end of the protocol to check correctness of a number of passively secure multiplications performed before.

Our protocol performing this multiplication check is shown in Fig. 1. The protocol uses functionalities $\mathcal{F}_{\text{RAND}}$ for generating share $r$ for random $r \in \mathbb{Z}_p$ and $\mathcal{F}_{\text{COIN}}$ for generating a public field element $r \in \mathbb{Z}_p \backslash \{0\}$ known to all parties as described in [16]. Moreover, it uses a passively secure multiplication protocol that, as described by Lindell and Nof [16], needs to be "secure up to additive attacks", meaning that the adversary can manipulate its result only by adding an additive offset to its result. The GRR, DN and AFL+ protocols mentioned above all meet this requirement.

Our multiplication protocol follows the basic idea of [2], but avoids its actively secure $A(s) \cdot B(s) = C(s)$ check. We add a random multiplication triple $(a_N, b_N, c_N)$ to the batch of triples and choose $s$ uniformly at random from $\mathbb{Z}_p$. Then, the values of $A(s), B(s), C(s)$ are uniformly random and can be opened so that the check $A(s) \cdot B(s) = C(s)$ can be performed in the plain. (Note that this option was not available to the authors of [2] since they need $s$ from an extension field so $A(s), B(s), C(s)$ are not uniform).

We now prove correctness of our multiplication check. In Lindell-Nof, correctness of their multiplication check is shown in [16, Lemma 3.9]. We prove

---

**Protocol: Batchwise multiplication check for Lindell-Nof (batch size $N$):**

**Inputs:** The parties hold a list of triples $([a_i], [b_i], [c_i])_{i=1}^{N-1}$ they want to verify.

1. Generate random $[a_N], [b_N]$ with $\mathcal{F}_{\text{RAND}}$ and together compute $[c_N] \leftarrow [a_N] \cdot [b_N]$
2. Let $A(x), B(x)$ be of degree $\leq N - 1$ such that $A(\omega_i) = a_i$; $B(\omega_i) = b_i$ for $i \in [1, N]$. Using $[a_i]$ and $[b_i]$, locally compute $[a_j] = [A(\omega_j)]$, $[b_j] = [B(\omega_j)]$ for $j \in [N + 1, 2N - 1]$
3. Together compute $[c_j] \leftarrow [a_j] \cdot [b_j]$ for $j \in [N + 1, 2N - 1]$
4. Generate random $s$ with $\mathcal{F}_{\text{COIN}}$. Repeat until $s \notin \{0, \omega_1, \ldots, \omega_{2N-1}\}$.
5. Let $C(x)$ be of degree $\leq 2N - 2$ such that $C(\omega_i) = c_i$ for $i \in [1, 2N - 1]$. Locally compute $[A(s)]$, $[B(s)]$ and $[C(s)]$ as linear combinations of $([a_i])_{i=1}^{N}$, $([b_i])_{i=1}^{N}$ and $([c_i])_{i=1}^{2N-1}$ respectively
6. Exchange secret shares $[A(s)]$, $[B(s)]$ and $[C(s)]$ between all parties. Output accept if the shares are correct and $A(s)B(s) = C(s)$.

---

Fig. 1. Batchwise multiplication check for Lindell-Nof

that the same result holds for our multiplication check, implying that it can be used as a drop-in replacement in their protocol. Actually, our result is slightly more complete since we do not just prove correctness but also privacy of the multiplication check. In the full version, we use this result for a self-contained proof of an optimised version of the Lindell-Nof protocol.

**Proposition 1.** *Suppose shares $([a_i], [b_i])_{i=1}^{N-1}$ are correct and $([c_i])_{i=1}^{N-1}$ are valid, and that $[\cdot] \leftarrow [\cdot] \cdot [\cdot]$ is a multiplication protocol secure up to additive attack. There exists a simulator that, on input $\Delta_i := c_i - (a_i \cdot b_i)$ and the shares held by the corrupted parties, simulates an execution of the protocol from Fig. 1 with respect to an active adversary corrupting a minority of parties with statistical distance at most negligibly greater than $(2N-2)/(|\mathbb{Z}_p| - 2N)$. In particular, if any $\Delta_k \neq 0$, then the honest parties output accept with at most this probability; if all $\Delta_k = 0$ then honest parties fail or succeed at the will of the adversary.*

*Proof.* The simulator proceeds as follows. The simulator first simulates the generation of random $[a_N]$ and $[b_N]$ and the computation of $[c_N], [a_{N+1}], \ldots, [a_{2N-1}]$, $[b_{N+1}], \ldots, [b_{2N-1}], [c_{N+1}], \ldots, [c_{2N-1}]$, learning the errors $\Delta_N, \ldots, \Delta_{2N-1}$ to the $c_i$ introduced by the adversary (which is possible since the protocol is secure up to additive attack). Simulate the generation of $s$ and the computation of $[A(s)]$, $[B(s)]$, and $[C(s)]$. Let $D(x)$ be of degree $\leq 2N - 2$ such that $D(\omega_1) = \Delta_1, \ldots, D(\omega_{2N-1}) = \Delta_{2N-1}$. If $(\Delta_1, \ldots, \Delta_{2N-1}) \neq \mathbf{0}$ but $D(s) = 0$, abort. Generates random $A(s)$ and $B(s)$, and let $C'(s) = A(s) \cdot B(s)$ and $C(s) = C'(s) + D(s)$. Simulate the opening of $[A(s)]$ to $A(s)$, $[B(s)]$ to $B(s)$, and $[C(s)]$ to $C(s)$. Let the honest parties output success if $D(s) = 0$ and the adversary provides the correct shares of $[A(s)], [B(s)], [C(s)]$ and fail otherwise.

We argue that this simulation is indeed indistinguishable. For this, we need to check that the view of the adversary and the outputs of the honest parties in the simulation are indistinguishable from a real execution. Concerning the view of the adversary, note that the values $A(s)$ and $B(s)$ that are opened are uniformly random because of the inclusion of the random $[a_N]$, $[b_N]$. Given these values $A(s)$ and $B(s)$, $C'(s) = A(s) \cdot B(s)$ is the value that is opened for $[C(s)]$ if all multiplications are correct. By linearity of the computation of $C(s)$, given $A(s)$ and $B(s)$ the value the adversary expects for $[C(s)]$ is $C'(s) + D(s)$. Hence, the simulation of the multiplication check is indistinguishable to the adversary and its success implies $(\Delta_1, \ldots, \Delta_{c_1}) = \mathbf{0}$, unless $(\Delta_1, \ldots, \Delta_{2N-1}) \neq \mathbf{0}$ and $D(s) = 0$. But $D(s)$ is the evaluation of a polynomial of degree at most $2N - 2$ in a random point from $\mathbb{Z}_p \setminus \{0, \omega_1, \ldots \omega_{2N-1}\}$, so by the Schwartz-Zippel lemma, if $(\Delta_1, \ldots, \Delta_{c_1}) \neq \mathbf{0}$ then $D(s) = 0$ with probability $(2N-2)/(|\mathbb{Z}_p|-2N)$. Hence, except with this probability, the adversary cannot make wrong multiplications pass the check, so also the honest parties' outputs are indistinguishable.     □

**Corollary 1 (Informal).** *The protocol for computing an arithmetic circuit over a finite field from [16] with the batchwise multiplication check from Fig. 1 computes any n-party functionality f with computational security in the presence of a malicious adversary controlling up to $t < n/2$ corrupted parties.*

In the full version of this paper, we present an optimised and slightly simplified version of the Lindell-Nof protocol and prove its security in detail.

### 3.3   Performance Analysis and Optimisation with PRNGs

Table 1 shows how the amount of communication in the Lindell-Nof protocol is reduced by batchwise multiplication verification, and how it can be further reduced with PRNGs. As mentioned above Lindel and Nof give three concrete instantiations of their protocol based on the GRR, DN and AFL+ multiplication protocols respectively [1,6,12]. (The exact variants of the protocols used for this comparison are given in the full version of this paper.) They instantiate three core operations, multiplying, opening shared values and generating a random shared value, and use them in two multiplication checks. The first check uses 2 multiplications, 2 random values and 3 openings; the second check uses 6 multiplications and 3 random values. In GRR, the first check is used; in DN, the second check is used; and in AFL+, a slight optimisation of the first check is used, leading to the given performance in Table 1.

As shown, using batchwise multiplication verification, checking a multiplication requires essentially one additional multiplication. As a result, using it instead of either of the Lindell-Nof multiplication checks reduces communication by a factor 2 to 3.5. The constant cost of the check (hidden behind the $\gtrsim$ symbol in the table) is spread over the triples in a batch but pretty small: e.g., for $\leq 10$ parties the batch size needed to make the overhead less than one is always less than 50 and to make it less than 0.1 it is less than 500. As shown in Sect. 5, this is possible without affecting computational complexity too much.

Using PRNGs, we can reduce communication in the GRR and DN constructions even further. For instance, consider the re-sharing of values that takes place

**Table 1.** Field elements sent per party for the Lindell-Nof protocol instantiated with GRR, DN (both with or without PRNG optimizations) and AFL+ (with PRNG optimization). The number of parties and the threshold is denoted by $n$ and $t$ respectively (generally $n \approx 2t$). Grey areas are our results

| Operation | GRR | GRR-PRNG | DN | DN-PRNG | AFL+ |
|---|---|---|---|---|---|
| Random value | 0 | 0 | $\lesssim 2$ | $\lesssim 1$ | 0 |
| Opening | $n-1$ | $n-1$ | $n-1$ | $n-1$ | 1 |
| Passive mult. | $n-1$ | $n-t-1$ | $\lesssim 6$ | $\lesssim 3$ | 1 |
| LN mul + check | $5(n-1)$ | $6(n-t-1)$ | $\lesssim 42$ | $\lesssim 18$ | 4 |
| Batch mul + check | $\gtrsim 2(n-1)$ | $\gtrsim 2(n-t-1)$ | $\gtrsim 12$ | $\gtrsim 6$ | $\gtrsim 2$ |

in GRR multiplication: instead of sending shares to each party, the dealing party can simply set the shares of $t$ parties by pairwise PRNGs between him and the recipients so that he only needs to send $n - t - 1$ shares, halving communication if $n = 2t + 1$. This idea is of course not new, but it is still important for us since applying it reduces communication in the Shamir constructions by an additional factor of at least two. In particular, using PRNGs, the Shamir-based construction with GRR becomes as communication-efficient as the PRNG-based construction. Details appear in the full version of this paper.

### 3.4 Further Improvements

**Adding Fairness.** To achieve fairness, we first let the parties reach agreement on whether to produce an output. Once there is agreement, we let the parties derive the output in such a way that the adversary cannot force a failure anymore.

To reach agreement, we use detectable broadcast [10]. Detectable broadcast lets a party send a message to all parties so that either all parties receive the same message, or all parties agree that the broadcast has failed. In our case, the adversary may cause this failure after seeing the value to be broadcast. Unlike full broadcast, it can be achieved over private channels without set-up assumptions. Essentially, [10] achieves detectable broadcast by letting each party once pick and distribute a public key, and performing a pairwise check if all parties consistently sent out their keys. After this setup, broadcasts are performed with the standard Dolev-Strong protocol [9]. In our protocol, parties detectably broadcast their shares of $A(s)$, $B(s)$, and $C(s)$ in the last round of the multiplication check; the parties decide to produce an output only if all parties have successfully broadcast a value; all shares consistently reconstruct to some values $A(s)$, $B(s)$, and $C(s)$; and $A(s) \cdot B(s) = C(s)$.

To derive the output, we need to ensure that honest parties can detect wrong values sent by corrupted parties. If there are only few parties, each party $\mathcal{P}_i$ can input a random information-theoretic MAC key $\alpha_i, \beta_i$ into the MPC (with PRSS, this requires no communication) and the parties compute MAC $\alpha_i \cdot x + \beta_i$ on output $x$. After the multiplication check, all parties send their shares of $x$ and $\alpha_i x + \beta_i$ to $\mathcal{P}_i$, who selects whichever reconstructed $x$ has a correct MAC. For many parties, this technique is not secure since it costs $\log((t+1)\binom{n-1}{t}) \approx n$ bits security; for that case see the full version of this paper.

**Efficient Inner Products.** One particularly appealing property of MPC based on secret sharing schemes like Shamir and replicated secret sharing, is that they allow inner products $[c] = \sum_{i=1}^{l}[a_i] \cdot [b_i]$ to be computed at the cost of a single multiplication. Such multiplication protocols first locally perform the multiplication (turning $t$-out-of-$n$ shared inputs into a $2t$-out-of-$n$ sharing of the product) and then re-share the result (turning the product from a $2t$-out-of-$n$ sharing back into a $t$-out-of-$n$ sharing). To compute an inner product, several local multiplications are first summed up and then the result is re-shared.

We can make such inner product computations actively secure by generalising batchwise multiplication verification to verify many inner products of the same length. Instead of generating two random values and computing their product, we generate $2l$ random values and compute their inner product. We then define polynomials $(A_i(x))_{i=1}^{l}, (B_i(x))_{i=1}^{l}, C(x)$ in the natural way; exchange shares of $(A_i(s))_{i=1}^{l}, (B_i(s))_{i=1}^{l}, C(s)$; and check whether $\sum_{i=1}^{l} A_i(s)B_i(s) = C(s)$. This gives the same security guarantees as batchwise multiplication verification.

**Smaller Fields.** Because of the false positive rate of the Schwartz-Zippel lemma, our construction requires a field of size at least $2N \cdot 2^{\sigma}$, where $\sigma$ is the statistical security parameter. When working over a smaller field, the multiplication check can be performed repeatedly. This way, statistical security can be boosted arbitrarily: repeating the check $k$ times increases statistical security from $\log((|\mathbb{Z}_p|-2N)/(2N-2))$ to $\log(\binom{|\mathbb{Z}_p|-2N}{k}/\binom{2N-2}{k})$ bits. Note that repeated checking can be done more efficiently than by just repeating the full check as follows. Instead of adding one random triple to a batch of multiplications, we add $k$ of them; and instead of generating one random challenge $s$, we generate $k$ challenges $s_i$ and evaluate $A(s_i), B(s_i),$ and $C(s_i)$ for $i = 1, \ldots, k$. (These can be opened because of the inclusion of the $k$ random triples).

## 4    SPDZ with an Untrusted Dealer

In this section, we present a protocol for honest-majority 3PC. The main contribution is a communication efficient protocol implementing the preprocessing phase for the 2PC SPDZ protocol using batchwise multiplication verification to check the correctness of Beaver triples generated locally by a third party dealer $\mathcal{P}_3$. In the online phase two parties $\mathcal{P}_1, \mathcal{P}_2$ use the preprocessed values in the regular two party SPDZ[1] to compute the desired function. Using a small addition to the online SPDZ protocol, based on ideas from [13], we can allow the

---

[1] The version by Damgård *et al.* refered to as SPDZ-2 [5].

dealer to provide input to and receive output from the 2PC protocol, thus giving an actively secure 3PC protocol in the honest-majority setting. We leave these modifications as an exercise.

We note that, the resulting 3PC protocol is highly asymmetric; in the preprocessing phase the $\mathcal{P}_3$ is doing most of the work while in the online phase $\mathcal{P}_1, \mathcal{P}_2$ do all the work. To better utilise resources across all three parties, we also develop a load balanced version of the protocol. This works by letting each of party play the role of the dealer in separate runs of the preprocessing phase. In the online phase, we then partition the multiplications to be performed into three sets to be evaluated by each pair of parties in a 2PC fashion. The overall communication per multiplication required in both versions is 5 field elements for the preprocessing phase and 4 field elements in the online phase (as per the regular 2PC SPDZ protocol). Thus using the load balanced version of the protocol we get $4/3$ and $5/3$ fields elements an average per party in the preprocessing and online phases respectively. We defer the load balancing version of the protocol to the full version of the paper. In this section we focus on our protocol for the SPDZ preprocessing phase.

We note that, compared to our Lindell-Nof based protocol, the protocol presented in this section does communicate three additional field elements per multiplication. However, the *online* phase communicates two field elements less than the Lindell-Nof based protocol. Thus the setting were preprocessing is available our SPDZ-based protocol is preferable.

### 4.1   Data Needed for the Online Phase

Before we describe our protocol for the preprocessing phase we here first summarise the data that should be generated: We use $\langle a \rangle = (\llbracket a \rrbracket, \llbracket \alpha a \rrbracket)$ to denote a *SPDZ sharing* of $a \in \mathbb{Z}_p$, where the sharing is between the parties $\mathcal{P}_1, \mathcal{P}_2$. Here $\alpha \in \mathbb{Z}_p$ is a random *MAC key* fixed at initialisation and unknown to both $\mathcal{P}_1, \mathcal{P}_2$, but which they share additively. The shared value $\alpha a$ of is an *information theoretic MAC* on $a$, which is used in the online phase to ensure active security.

The online phase of SPDZ needs preprocessed *multiplication triples* and *input masks*. A multiplication triple is SPDZ sharings $(\langle a \rangle, \langle b \rangle, \langle c \rangle)$ where $a, b \in \mathbb{Z}_p$ are random values and $c = ab$. In the online phase each multiplication will consume one triple. An input mask is a pair $(r, \langle r \rangle)$ for a random value $r \in \mathbb{Z}_p$ known to, say, $\mathcal{P}_1$. In the online phase each input provided by $\mathcal{P}_1$ consumes one such mask. For security in the online phase we require that the preprocessed data should be *correct* in the sense that the shared values and their MACs should obey the correlations described above. Furthermore, the shared values should be unknown and random in the view of any corrupt party participating in the online phase (i.e., either $\mathcal{P}_1$ or $\mathcal{P}_2$). We describe the ideal functionality more formally in the full version of the paper.

## 4.2   Preprocessing Phase

The basic idea of our protocol is to let $P_3$ generate the all the preprocessed data locally, and send the appropriate shares to $P_1, P_2$. Batchwise multiplication verification is then used to check that $P_3$ generated the multiplication triples correctly, and a separate check is used to check that the MACs are correct. To save communication our protocol heavily relies on joint PRNGs $\mathsf{prng}_{i,j}$ between each pair of parties $P_i, P_j$ in order to non-interactively share values.

Our protocol $\Pi_{\mathrm{DEAL}}$ implementing the preprocessing phase is described in detail in Figs. 2 and 3. In Fig. 2 we show how the protocol is initialised by using the joint PRNGs to sample a random MAC key $\alpha$ in such a way that $\alpha$ is unknown to all parties but is additively secret shared between each pair of parties $P_i, P_j$, denoted $[\![\alpha]\!]_i^{i,j}, [\![\alpha]\!]_j^{i,j}$. Additionally, $P_1$ and $P_2$ use $\mathsf{prng}_{1,2}$ to sample a challenge $s_{1,2}$ used for multiplication checks.

In Fig. 2 we also describe two subprotocols which will be used through out the $\Pi_{\mathrm{DEAL}}$ protocol. These protocols use the PRNGs to non-interactively generate a random additive sharing $[\![r]\!]$ between $P_1, P_2$, where $r$ is known to $P_3$ (4a of Fig. 2), and given any such shared $r$ an additive sharing of $[\![\alpha r]\!]$ between *all* the parties (4b of Fig. 2). Note, that this means that by sending $P_3$'s share $[\![\alpha r]\!]_3$ of $\alpha r$ to, say, $P_1$ we can trivially compute a SPDZ sharing $\langle r \rangle$ by adding $[\![\alpha r]\!]_3$ to $[\![\alpha r]\!]_1$. The protocol we slightly abuse notation in this case by saying that $P_1$ *updates* her share $[\![\alpha r]\!]_1 = [\![\alpha r]\!]_1 + [\![\alpha r]\!]_3$. Note that this requires $P_3$ so send exactly one field element per SPDZ sharing.

In Fig. 3 we describe how to generate and verify the actually preprocessed data to be used in the online phase. Multiplication triples are generated by first using the 4a and 4b subprotocols to generate $\langle a \rangle$ and $\langle b \rangle$ as described above. $P_3$ then computes $c = ab$ and additively shares it among the parties, using 4b on $c$ we get its MAC. This requires $P_3$ to send four field elements.

For a batch of triples $(\langle a_i \rangle, \langle b_i \rangle, \langle c_i \rangle)_{i=1}^{N-1}$ the multiplicative property $a_i b_i = c_i$ is verified using batch multiplication verification similar to the Lindell-Nof case above. In this case we let the dealer $P_3$ compute and additively share (without MACs) the values $c_{N+1} = C(\omega_{N+1}), \ldots, c_{2N-1} = C(\omega_{2N-1})$, as in [4]. $P_1, P_2$ verify the multiplications by checking the polynomials evaluated in the challenge point $s$ generated at initialisation. Again we can open $A(s), B(s), C(s)$ by sacrificing one triple. The check requires a single field element sent per triple and an additional element per batch of $N - 1$ triples. Overall, a total of 5 field elements are sent to generate each multiplication triples and verify the multiplicative property plus one additional field element per batch.

Input masks are simply generated by first using the 4a and 4b subprotocols to generate $\langle r \rangle$, and then letting $P_3$ send the value $r$ to the party using the input mask. This requires sending two field elements for each input mask.

Finally, $P_1, P_2$ must check that all the MACs resulting from invocations of the 4b subprotocol are correct. We do this using protocol similar to the MAC check subprotocol of the regular SPDZ protocol. Essentially, the parties take a pseudorandom linear combination of all the shared values generated, and check that the MACs a consistent with the result. This takes constant communication.

The intuition for security of the protocol goes as follows. Consider first a corrupt $\mathcal{P}_i$ for $i \in \{1, 2\}$, i.e., one of the parties that will run the online phase. In this case, the dealer $\mathcal{P}_3$ is honest, and only deals correct random additive shares, which does not reveal information on the shared values. Furthermore, since $\mathcal{P}_i$ only sends messages in the protocols checking correctness of the dealt shares, $\mathcal{P}_i$ can only influence the protocol by making it abort (which we allow anyway), but cannot influence the values of any of the shared values. Thus the preprocessed data will be correct and $\mathcal{P}_i$ will not get information on the shared values. Consider then a corrupt dealer $\mathcal{P}_3$. By the security of the multiplication verification and MAC check, if the protocol does not abort, then with overwhelming probability the preprocessed data will be correct. $\mathcal{P}_3$ will learn all values shared in the preprocessing phase, but since these are independent of the parties' input to the online phase and since $\mathcal{P}_3$ does not directly participate in the online phase of the protocol, this does not leak any private information.

In the full version we prove security more formally, giving this result:

**Corollary 2 (Informal).** *Combining the $\Pi_{\mathrm{DEAL}}$ with the 2PC online phase of SPDZ and the outsourced MPC additions of [13] leads to an over all protocol that computes any 3-party functionality f with computational security in the presence of a malicious adversary controlling at most one corrupted party.*

### 4.3    Variants and Extensions

*Fairness.* Fairness is easily achieved in the load-balanced variant of the protocol described in the fullversion, similarly to the Lindell-Nof case. Essentially, each party $\mathcal{P}_i$ inputs MAC key $\alpha_i, \beta_i$ and mask $\delta_i$ (for which we can use input masks). Then, $\alpha_i x + \beta_i$ and $x + \delta_i$ are opened to the other two parties. These values are checked with the SPDZ MAC check and then provided to $\mathcal{P}_i$. The SPDZ MAC check needs to be performed such that everybody agrees on its result, which essentially means that we need to compute a sum $\sum [\![\sigma]\!]_1 + [\![\sigma]\!]_2 + [\![\sigma]\!]_3$ in a fair way. This can be done by letting each party secret-share its summand in a digitally signed way and the other parties forwarding these secret shares, similarly to Dolev-Strong broadcast. We omit the details because of space.

*Preprocessing Other Material.* Apart from multiplication triples, other random data can be preprocessed in order to speed up specific computations in the SPDZ online phase. For example, Damgård *et al.* [5] show how to preprocess random square pairs $\langle a \rangle, \langle a^2 \rangle$ for random $a$. In the online phase $\langle z \rangle = \langle x^2 \rangle$ can be computed from $\langle x \rangle$ by revealing $\varepsilon = x - a$ and setting $\langle z \rangle = 2\varepsilon \langle x \rangle + \langle a^2 \rangle - \varepsilon^2$, which requires only half the communication of regular online multiplications. Our dealer based protocol allows such material to be generated very efficiently.

To preprocess $N - 1$ pairs of squares $(\langle a_i \rangle, \langle a_i^2 \rangle)_{i=1}^{N-1}$, we run the protocol for generating multiplication triples as above, except the dealer sets all $b_i = a_i$ (including $b_N$ in the triple to be sacrificed). Note that in this case $B(s) = A(s)$ does not need to be computed or exchanged separately.

---

Protocol $\Pi_{\text{DEAL}}$

**Inputs:** The amount of multiplication triples $M$, random input masks $I_1, I_2$ and a batch size $N$.

1. *(PRNG setup)* Each pair of parties $\mathcal{P}_i, \mathcal{P}_j$ sets up joint PRNG $\mathsf{prng}_{i,j}$ (one party generates it and sends it to the other)
2. *(MAC key generation)* The parties generate a random secret MAC key $\alpha$, additively shared between each pair of parties:
   (a) Let $\alpha_1, \alpha_2 \leftarrow \mathsf{prng}_{1,3}$; $\alpha_3, \alpha_4 \leftarrow \mathsf{prng}_{1,2}$; $\alpha_5, \alpha_6 \leftarrow \mathsf{prng}_{2,3}$
   (b) Parties $\mathcal{P}_1, \mathcal{P}_2$ set $[\![\alpha]\!]_1^{1,2} = \alpha_1 + \alpha_2 + \alpha_3$, $[\![\alpha]\!]_2^{1,2} = \alpha_4 + \alpha_5 + \alpha_6$
   (c) Parties $\mathcal{P}_1, \mathcal{P}_3$ set $[\![\alpha]\!]_1^{1,3} = \alpha_3 + \alpha_4 + \alpha_1$, $[\![\alpha]\!]_3^{1,3} = \alpha_5 + \alpha_6 + \alpha_2$
   (d) Parties $\mathcal{P}_2, \mathcal{P}_3$ set $[\![\alpha]\!]_2^{2,3} = \alpha_3 + \alpha_4 + \alpha_5$, $[\![\alpha]\!]_3^{2,3} = \alpha_1 + \alpha_2 + \alpha_6$
3. *(Sample Challenge)* $\mathcal{P}_1, \mathcal{P}_2$ sample $s_{1,2} \in \mathbb{Z}_p \setminus \{0, \omega_1, \ldots, \omega_{2N-1}\}$ using $\mathsf{prng}_{1,2}$
4. *(Subprotocols)* Throughout the parties use two subprotocols to non-interactively generate random value $r$ known by $\mathcal{P}_3$ and secret-shared between $\mathcal{P}_1, \mathcal{P}_2$ and a corresponding MAC secret shared among all three parties:
   (a) *(Random)* Let $[\![r]\!]_1 \leftarrow \mathsf{prng}_{1,3}$; $[\![r]\!]_2 \leftarrow \mathsf{prng}_{2,3}$. $\mathcal{P}_3$ sets $r = [\![r]\!]_1 + [\![r]\!]_2$.
   (b) *(Additive MAC shares)* Let $\delta_{1,3} \leftarrow \mathsf{prng}_{1,3}$; $\delta_{2,3} \leftarrow \mathsf{prng}_{2,3}$; $\delta_{1,2} \leftarrow \mathsf{prng}_{1,2}$.
   For an additively shared $[\![r]\!]$ as above
   $\mathcal{P}_1$ sets $[\![\alpha r]\!]_1 = [\![\alpha]\!]_1^{1,3} \cdot [\![r]\!]_1 + \delta_{1,2} - \delta_{1,3}$.
   $\mathcal{P}_2$ sets $[\![\alpha r]\!]_2 = [\![\alpha]\!]_2^{2,3} \cdot [\![r]\!]_2 + \delta_{2,3} - \delta_{1,2}$.
   $\mathcal{P}_3$ sets $[\![\alpha r]\!]_3 = [\![\alpha]\!]_3^{1,3} \cdot [\![r]\!]_1 + [\![\alpha]\!]_3^{2,3} \cdot [\![r]\!]_2 + \delta_{1,3} - \delta_{2,3}$.

*(continued in Fig. 3)*

---

**Fig. 2.** Protocol $\Pi_{\text{DEAL}}$

Damgård *et al.* also preprocess random bits, i.e., values $\langle x \rangle$ so that $x \in \{0, 1\}$. Such preprocessed values are useful to speed up the online computation of e.g. comparisons [17]. To preprocessed random bits $\langle x_1 \rangle, \ldots, \langle x_{N-1} \rangle$, we run the protocol for generating multiplication triples as above, except the dealer sets all $a_i = x_i$ and $b_i = 1 - x_i$ (implying $c_i = 0$). If we use $(\langle a_N \rangle, (1 - \langle a_N \rangle), \langle a_N \rangle (1 - \langle a_N \rangle))$ for random $a_N$ as the extra multiplication triple to be sacrificed, we have $B(x) = 1 - A(x)$ so $B(s)$ does not need to be computed or exchanged. Thus the preprocessing of both a square pair and a bit requires communicating one less field element than a multiplication.

Similarly, we can compute other useful preprocessed material by having the dealer prove the appropriate multiplicative relations using the batchwise multiplication check. For example, random values with their negative powers $\langle r \rangle, \langle r^{-1} \rangle, \ldots, \langle r^{-k} \rangle$ are useful to compute $\langle x^2 \rangle, \ldots, \langle x^k \rangle$ from $\langle x \rangle$ by opening $(rx)$ and taking $\langle x^i \rangle = (rx)^i \langle r^{-i} \rangle$ (e.g., for secure equality [17]). Correctness is verified from triples $\langle a_1 \rangle = \langle r \rangle, \langle b_1 \rangle = r^{-1}, \langle c_1 \rangle = 1, \langle a_i \rangle = \langle r^{-1} \rangle$, $\langle b_i \rangle = \langle r^{-i+1} \rangle, \langle c_i \rangle = \langle r^{-i} \rangle$, $i = 2, \ldots, k$.

Secret-shared random matrix products can be used to efficiently compute matrix products [18]: given random matrices $\langle \mathbf{U} \rangle, \langle \mathbf{V} \rangle$, and $\langle \mathbf{W} \rangle = \langle \mathbf{U} \cdot \mathbf{V} \rangle$ of

Protocol $\Pi_{\text{DEAL}}$ *(continued from Fig. 2)*

5. *(Triple generation)* Generate $M$ multiplication triples in $M/(N-1)$ batches $(\langle a_i \rangle, \langle b_i \rangle, \langle c_i \rangle)_{i=1}^{N-1}$ of size $N-1$:

   (a) Generate $N$ multiplication triples by doing the following for each $i \in [1, \ldots, N]$:

       i. *(Shares of $a_i, b_i$)* Repeat 4a twice to get $[\![a_i]\!]$, $[\![b_i]\!]$.

       ii. *(Shares of $c_i$)* Let $\delta_{2,3} \leftarrow \mathsf{prng}_{2,3}$, $\delta_{1,2} \leftarrow \mathsf{prng}_{1,2}$. $\mathcal{P}_3$ sets $c_i \leftarrow a_i \cdot b_i$, and sends $c_i - \delta_{2,3}$ to $\mathcal{P}_1$. $\mathcal{P}_1, \mathcal{P}_2$ set $[\![c_i]\!]_1 = (c_i - \delta_{2,3}) + \delta_{1,2}$, $[\![c_i]\!]_2 = \delta_{2,3} - \delta_{1,2}$ respectively.

       iii. *(MAC shares)* Repeat 4b to get $[\![\alpha a_i]\!], [\![\alpha b_i]\!], [\![\alpha c_i]\!]$ shared between the three parties. $\mathcal{P}_3$ sends $[\![\alpha a_i]\!]_3$ to $\mathcal{P}_1$, who updates his MAC share $[\![\alpha a_i]\!]_1 = [\![\alpha a_i]\!]_1 + [\![\alpha a_i]\!]_3$; and similarly for $[\![\alpha b_i]\!]_k$, $[\![\alpha c_i]\!]_k$ sent to $\mathcal{P}_2$.

   (b) Check correctness of $(\langle a_i \rangle, \langle b_i \rangle, \langle c_i \rangle)_{i=1}^{N-1}$ by sacrificing $(\langle a_N \rangle, \langle b_N \rangle, \langle c_N \rangle)$:

       i. $\mathcal{P}_3$ computes $c_j = C(\omega_j)$ for $j \in [N+1, 2N-1]$ where $C(x) = A(x)B(x)$; $A(x), B(x)$ of degree $\leq N-1$ s.t. $A(\omega_i) = a_i$, $B(\omega_i) = b_i$

       ii. $\mathcal{P}_3$ secret-shares $(c_j)_{j=N+1}^{2N-1}$ by sampling $[\![c_j]\!]_2 \leftarrow \mathsf{prng}_{2,3}$ and sending $[\![c_j]\!]_1 = c_j - [\![c_j]\!]_2$ to $\mathcal{P}_1$

       iii. $\mathcal{P}_1, \mathcal{P}_2$ compute $[\![A(s_{1,2})]\!]$, $[\![B(s_{1,2})]\!]$, $[\![C(s_{1,2})]\!]$ linearly from $([\![a_i]\!], [\![b_i]\!], [\![c_i]\!])_{i=1}^N$ and $([\![c_i]\!])_{i=N+1}^{2N-1}$

       iv. $\mathcal{P}_1$ sends $[\![A(s_{1,2})]\!]_1$, $[\![B(s_{1,2})]\!]_1$, $[\![C(s_{1,2})]\!]_1$ to $\mathcal{P}_2$. $\mathcal{P}_2$ reconstructs $A(s_{1,2})$, $B(s_{1,2})$, and $C(s_{1,2})$, and aborts if $A(s_{1,2}) \cdot B(s_{1,2}) \neq C(s_{1,2})$

6. *(Input generation)* To generate an input mask $(r, \langle r \rangle)$ for party $\mathcal{P}_i$ the parties run 4a and 4b. Without loss of generality assume $i = 1$. $\mathcal{P}_3$ sends $r$ and $[\![\alpha r]\!]_3$ to $\mathcal{P}_1$ who updates his MAC share $[\![\alpha r]\!]_1 = [\![\alpha r]\!]_1 + [\![\alpha r]\!]_3$.

7. *(MAC check)* The parties check all the MACs on all the generated sharings (input masks and triples). Denote these $([\![a_i]\!])_{i=1}^L$ for $L = I_1 + I_2 + 3M$:

   (a) Repeat 4a,4b to get random $\langle a_{L+1} \rangle$ known by $\mathcal{P}_3$ and shared between $\mathcal{P}_1, \mathcal{P}_2$. $\mathcal{P}_3$ sends $[\![\alpha a_{L+1}]\!]_3$ to $\mathcal{P}_1$, who updates his MAC share $[\![\alpha a_{L+1}]\!]_1 = [\![\alpha a_{L+1}]\!]_1 + [\![\alpha a_{L+1}]\!]_3$

   (b) $\mathcal{P}_1, \mathcal{P}_2$ sample PRNG seed $s \leftarrow \mathsf{prng}_{1,2}$. Both send $s$ to $\mathcal{P}_3$, who aborts if inconsistent. All three generate $r_1, \ldots, r_{L+1}$ from the PRNG with seed $s$.

   (c) $\mathcal{P}_3$ computes $S = \sum_{i=1}^{L+1} r_i a_i$ and sends $S$ to $\mathcal{P}_1$

   (d) $\mathcal{P}_1$ computes $[\![\sigma]\!]_1 \leftarrow (\sum_{i=1}^{L+1} r_i [\![\alpha a_i]\!]_1) - S \cdot [\![\alpha]\!]_1^{1,2}$ and sends $S, [\![\sigma]\!]_1$ to $\mathcal{P}_2$

   (e) $\mathcal{P}_2$ computes $[\![\sigma]\!]_2 \leftarrow (\sum_{i=1}^{L+1} r_i [\![\alpha a_i]\!]_2) - S \cdot [\![\alpha]\!]_2^{1,2}$, aborts if $[\![\sigma]\!]_1 + [\![\sigma]\!]_2 \neq 0$

8. Finally, each party returns its preprocessed MAC key, masks, and triples.

**Fig. 3.** Protocol $\Pi_{\text{DEAL}}$ (cont'd)

the correct size, matrix product $\langle \mathbf{Z} \rangle = \langle \mathbf{X} \cdot \mathbf{Y} \rangle$ is computed by opening $\langle \mathbf{X} - \mathbf{U} \rangle$ and $\langle \mathbf{Y} - \mathbf{V} \rangle$ and letting

$$\langle \mathbf{Z} \rangle = (\mathbf{X} - \mathbf{U}) \cdot (\mathbf{Y} - \mathbf{V}) + (\mathbf{X} - \mathbf{U}) \cdot \langle \mathbf{V} \rangle + (\mathbf{Y} - \mathbf{V}) \cdot \langle \mathbf{U} \rangle + \langle \mathbf{W} \rangle.$$

To preprocess a random matrix product, the dealer provides secret shares of all $U_{i,j}$, $V_{j,k}$ and products $U_{i,j} \cdot V_{j,k}$, and proves their correctness. The elements of $W$ are computed as linear combinations of these products. Preprocessing in this

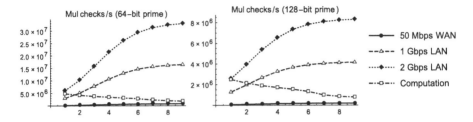

**Fig. 4.** Number of Lindell-Nof multiplications that can be checked for correctness per second based on the given network capacity or computation effort, with batches of size $2^1, \ldots, 2^9$ for a 64-bit prime (left) or 128-bit prime (right)

case reduces *overall* communication, e.g., by a factor 1.5 for $2 \times 2$ matrices or a factor 2.5 for $10 \times 10$ matrices. Similarly, in the common case of multiplying value (i.e., 1-by-1 matrix) $\langle x \rangle$ with each element in vector (i.e., 1-by-$n$ matrix) $\langle y \rangle$, online communication halves and overall communication decreases by 33%.

*Smaller Fields.* As in the Lindell-Nof case, we need a field of size at least $2N \cdot 2^\sigma$, but as there, we can enhance the statistical security of $\Pi_{\mathrm{DEAL}}$ by repeating the multiplication check. Of course, for an overall secure protocol for fields smaller than $2^\sigma$, also modifications to the SPDZ online phase are needed, cf. [8].

## 5   Performance Evaluation

In this section we present performance estimates suggesting that, despite the computations in our protocols, communication is often still the main bottleneck.

### 5.1   Implementation Details

To estimate the computation effort of our protocol, we have implemented batch-wise multiplication verification both in the Lindell-Nof and the SPDZ setting. In both cases, we implemented only computation (including PRNG evaluation, secret sharing, reconstruction, and the MAC check) and not communication. For the PRNG, we used the SPDZ-2 implementation based on AES-NI[2].

We implemented the batch check in batch sizes of $2^k$ using fields $\mathbb{Z}_p$ that allow efficient modular arithmetic and efficient FFTs for those batch sizes (batches do not need to be completely filled up). Batch verification relies heavily on performing FFTs of the size of the batch for performing interpolation; with batch size $2^k$, we can use the efficient Cooley-Tukey FFT algorithm. This requires a $(2^k)$th root of unity in $\mathbb{Z}_p$, or equivalently, $2^k | p - 1$. To have fast modular arithmetic, we use pseudo-Mersenne primes $p = 2^s - 2^l + 1$; note that if $k \leq l$ then $2^k | 2^l | p - 1$. (We cannot use regular Mersenne primes $2^s - 1$ since $2^k \nmid 2^s - 1$.) In particular, we use our own modular arithmetic/FFT implementation for primes $2^{64} - 2^{10} + 1$ and $2^{128} - 2^{54} + 1$, allowing batches up to $2^9$, and $2^{53}$, respectively.

---

[2] https://github.com/bristolcrypto/SPDZ-2/.

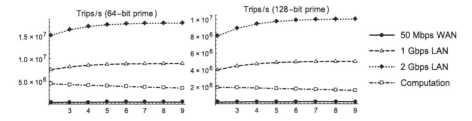

**Fig. 5.** Number of SPDZ multiplication triples that can be preprocessed per second based on the given network capacity or computation effort (excluding online phase), with batches of size $2^2, \ldots, 2^9$ for a 64-bit prime (left) or 128-bit prime (right).

To estimate communication complexity, we compute the number of bits that each party needs to send to check correctness of one multiplication. For Lindell-Nof, this is the same for each party; for SPDZ, we use load-balancing so that communication is also evenly spread. The number of multiplications per second is computed as the bandwidth divided by that amount of bits.

## 5.2 Evaluation Results

Figure 4, estimates the number of multiplications that can be checked in the Lindell-Nof protocol using Shamir secret sharing, GRR multiplication, and our batchwise check. (Note that this does not include the multiplication to be checked itself.) We show, for different batch sizes $2^k$, how many checks are allowed by the bandwidth of a 50 Mbps WAN, a 1 Gbps LAN, and a 2 Gbps LAN. We also show, on a single core of a Amazon M4.large machine (a 2.3/2.4 GHz Intel Xeon E5), how many checks can be handled by the processor. As expected, larger batches are good for communication complexity but bad for computation complexity. With a 1 Gbps LAN and a single core, computation quickly becomes the bottleneck, but still it is possible to process check around 5 million multiplications per second for 64-bit primes and 2 million for 128-bit primes. Note that batchwise verification is trivially parallelizable by checking each batch on a different core, so the number of checks per second can easily be increased by increasing the number of cores. With less than 1 Gbps available, communication quickly becomes the bottleneck rather than computation. We did not run experiments for more than three parties, but in general, the amount of computation should stay roughly the same (since it is dominated by the FFTs) whereas the amount of communication increases as shown in Table 1.

Figure 5 similarly estimates the number of multiplication triples per second of our SPDZ preprocessing, load-balanced between the three parties. As above, for different batch sizes $2^k$, we plot the number of triples that can be generated on a 50 Mbps WAN, a 1 Gbps LAN, and a 2 Gbps LAN; and a single Amazon M4.large core. Note that SPDZ has less communication than Lindell-Nof for small batch sizes; this is because the constant overhead of the SPDZ batch check is very small (just a few field elements). However, for larger batches, Lindell-Nof has less communication (each party sends one field element per check vs. the dealer sends five field elements for one third of the checks). In SPDZ, on a 1Gbps network with a single core, computation is the bottleneck, and around 5 million triples per second are possible for a 64-bit primes or around 2 million triples for a 128-bit prime; with two to four cores, it is possible to reach around 10 million triples for a 64-bit prime or 5 million triples for a 128-bit prime.

**Acknowledgements.** We thank the anonymous reviewers for their useful suggestions. This work has received funding from the European Union's Horizon 2020 research and innovation programme under grant agreement #731583 (SODA).

# References

1. Araki, T., Furukawa, J., Lindell, Y., Nof, A., Ohara, K.: High-throughput semi-honest secure three-party computation with an honest majority. In: Proceedings of CCS 2016. ACM (2016)
2. Ben-Sasson, E., Fehr, S., Ostrovsky, R.: Near-linear unconditionally-secure multiparty computation with a dishonest minority. In: Safavi-Naini, R., Canetti, R. (eds.) CRYPTO 2012. LNCS, vol. 7417, pp. 663–680. Springer, Heidelberg (2012). https://doi.org/10.1007/978-3-642-32009-5_39
3. Canetti, R.: Security and composition of multi-party cryptographic protocols. J. Cryptol. **13**(1), 143–202 (2000)
4. Corrigan-Gibbs, H., Boneh, D.: Prio: private, robust, and scalable computation of aggregate statistics. In: Proceedings of NSDI (2017)
5. Damgård, I., Keller, M., Larraia, E., Pastro, V., Scholl, P., Smart, N.P.: Practical covertly secure MPC for dishonest majority – or: breaking the SPDZ limits. In: Crampton, J., Jajodia, S., Mayes, K. (eds.) ESORICS 2013. LNCS, vol. 8134, pp. 1–18. Springer, Heidelberg (2013). https://doi.org/10.1007/978-3-642-40203-6_1
6. Damgård, I., Nielsen, J.B.: Scalable and unconditionally secure multiparty computation. In: Menezes, A. (ed.) CRYPTO 2007. LNCS, vol. 4622, pp. 572–590. Springer, Heidelberg (2007). https://doi.org/10.1007/978-3-540-74143-5_32
7. Damgård, I., Orlandi, C., Simkin, M.: Yet another compiler for active security or: efficient MPC over arbitrary rings. Cryptology ePrint Archive, Report 2017/908 (2017). http://eprint.iacr.org/2017/908
8. Damgård, I., Pastro, V., Smart, N., Zakarias, S.: Multiparty computation from somewhat homomorphic encryption. In: Safavi-Naini, R., Canetti, R. (eds.) CRYPTO 2012. LNCS, vol. 7417, pp. 643–662. Springer, Heidelberg (2012). https://doi.org/10.1007/978-3-642-32009-5_38
9. Dolev, D., Strong, H.R.: Authenticated algorithms for Byzantine agreement. SIAM J. Comput. **12**(4), 656–666 (1983)
10. Fitzi, M., Gisin, N., Maurer, U., von Rotz, O.: Unconditional Byzantine agreement and multi-party computation secure against dishonest minorities from scratch. In: Knudsen, L.R. (ed.) EUROCRYPT 2002. LNCS, vol. 2332, pp. 482–501. Springer, Heidelberg (2002). https://doi.org/10.1007/3-540-46035-7_32
11. Furukawa, J., Lindell, Y., Nof, A., Weinstein, O.: High-throughput secure three-party computation for malicious adversaries and an honest majority. In: Coron, J.-S., Nielsen, J.B. (eds.) EUROCRYPT 2017. LNCS, vol. 10211, pp. 225–255. Springer, Cham (2017). https://doi.org/10.1007/978-3-319-56614-6_8

12. Gennaro, R., Rabin, M.O., Rabin, T.: Simplified VSS and fact-track multiparty computations with applications to threshold cryptography. In: Proceedings of PODC (1998)
13. Jakobsen, T.P., Nielsen, J.B., Orlandi, C.: A framework for outsourcing of secure computation. In: Proceedings of CCSW 2014 (2014)
14. Keller, M., Pastro, V., Rotaru, D.: Overdrive: making SPDZ great again. Cryptology ePrint Archive, Report 2017/1230 (2017). https://eprint.iacr.org/2017/1230
15. Kushilevitz, E., Lindell, Y., Rabin, T.: Information-theoretically secure protocols and security under composition. In: Proceedings of STOC 2006 (2006)
16. Lindell, Y., Nof, A.: A framework for constructing fast MPC over arithmetic circuits with malicious adversaries and an honest-majority. In: Proceedings of CCS 2017. ACM (2017)
17. Lipmaa, H., Toft, T.: Secure equality and greater-than tests with sublinear online complexity. In: Fomin, F.V., Freivalds, R., Kwiatkowska, M., Peleg, D. (eds.) ICALP 2013. LNCS, vol. 7966, pp. 645–656. Springer, Heidelberg (2013). https://doi.org/10.1007/978-3-642-39212-2_56
18. Mohassel, P., Zhang, Y.: SecureML: a system for scalable privacy-preserving machine learning. In: Proceedings of S&P (2017)
19. Parno, B., Howell, J., Gentry, C., Raykova, M.: Pinocchio: nearly practical verifiable computation. In: Proceedings of S&P (2013)
20. Schoenmakers, B., Veeningen, M., de Vreede, N.: Trinocchio: privacy-preserving outsourcing by distributed verifiable computation. In: Manulis, M., Sadeghi, A.-R., Schneider, S. (eds.) ACNS 2016. LNCS, vol. 9696, pp. 346–366. Springer, Cham (2016). https://doi.org/10.1007/978-3-319-39555-5_19
21. Schwartz, J.T.: Fast probabilistic algorithms for verification of polynomial identities. J. ACM $27(4)$, 701–717 (1980)
22. Zippel, R.: Probabilistic algorithms for sparse polynomials. In: Ng, E.W. (ed.) Symbolic and Algebraic Computation. LNCS, vol. 72, pp. 216–226. Springer, Heidelberg (1979). https://doi.org/10.1007/3-540-09519-5_73

# Best of Both Worlds in Secure Computation, with Low Communication Overhead

Daniel Genkin[1,3], S. Dov Gordon[2(✉)], and Samuel Ranellucci[2,3]

[1] University of Pennsylvania, Philadelphia, USA
danielg3@cis.upenn.edu
[2] George Mason University, Arlington, USA
gordon@gmu.edu
[3] University of Maryland, College Park, USA
samuel@umd.edu

**Abstract.** When performing a secure multiparty computation with a few hundred parties, using the best protocols known today, bandwidth constraints are the primary bottleneck. A long line of work demonstrates that $n$ parties can compute a circuit $C$ of depth $d$ while communicating $O(|C| \log |C| + \mathsf{poly}(d, n))$ field elements per party, as long as a majority of parties are honest. However, in the malicious majority setting, a lot less is known. The work of Nielsen and Ranellucci is the first to provide constant-overhead in the communication complexity when a majority of parties are malicious; their result demonstrates feasibility, but is quite complex and impractical.

In this work, we construct a new MPC protocol in the pre-processing model. We introduce a new middle-ground: our protocol has low communication and provides robustness when a majority of parties are honest, and gives security with abort (possibly with higher communication cost) when a majority of players are malicious. Robustness is impossible when a majority of parties are malicious; viewing the increased communication complexity as a form of denial of service, similar to an abort, we view our result as providing the "best of both worlds".

## 1 Introduction

After a decade of improvements in the computational cost of secure multiparty computation, we have reached a point where the primary performance bottleneck is the communication complexity, even when computing with only a moderate number of parties Most constructions require that $n$ participants communicate a total of $O(Cn^2)$ field elements to compute a circuit of size $C$. The $n^2$ term stems from point-to-point communication at every multiplication gate, which, at first glance, seems hard to avoid. Amazingly, when a majority of parties are honest, there are several constructions that require communicating only $O(C)$ field elements.[1] Very broadly, these constructions make use of two ideas to

---

[1] Additionally, they have an additive term that is polynomial in $n$.

B. Preneel and F. Vercauteren (Eds.): ACNS 2018, LNCS 10892, pp. 340–359, 2018.
https://doi.org/10.1007/978-3-319-93387-0_18

lower communication cost. First, by using a randomly chosen dealer, they can reduce the communication channels from $O(n^2)$ to $O(n)$. This requires care, to ensure that a malicious dealer cannot corrupt the computation. Second, by using "packed secret sharing", the participants can communicate just one field element to compute $O(n)$ multiplication gates. In a bit more detail, multiple wire values are simultaneously encoded using a single threshold secret sharing scheme: to encode $\ell$ wire values, $w_1, \cdots, w_\ell$, a random polynomial $p$ is chosen such that $p(-j) = w_j$. As usual, $p(1), \cdots, p(n)$ define the secret shares of the $n$ parties, and, for a degree $t + \ell$ polynomial, all $\ell$ secrets remain perfectly hidden against $t$ colluding parties. Since $t + \ell < n$, this provides a tradeoff between security and efficiency; as more values are packed into the secret sharing, the number of corruptions that can be tolerated decreases. With a small blowup in the circuit description, these polynomials can be used to compute $\ell$ multiplication gates at a time, cutting the communication cost by a factor of $\ell = O(n)$ [9].

In the malicious majority setting, a lot less is known about reducing the communication complexity. The recent work of Nielsen and Ranellucci is the first and only protocol with constant communication cost per circuit gate [16]. The result of their work is exciting, as it demonstrates feasibility for the first time. However, as the authors state, their protocol "is solely of theoretical interest"; it has constants that are large and difficult to compute, and, conceptually, it requires parsing a complex composition of player emulations and subprotocols.

In this work, we propose an optimistic approach to communication complexity. Our protocol has constant *expected* communication complexity if a majority of players are *honest*. However, unlike prior work in the honest majority setting, we stress that our protocol also remains secure when a majority of players are malicious, albeit with higher communication complexity. At a high level, the variation in communication complexity stems from the following feature of our approach. We choose a random dealer and hope that they are honest. If the dealer happens to be malicious, he can force a re-start of the protocol, and if $O(n)$ consecutive dealers are malicious, then they can force the communication complexity to blow up. Taking the view that this increased communication cost is simply a form of denial of service, we view our result as providing "the best of both worlds" with respect to denial of service; when a majority of parties are malicious, it is impossible to prevent a denial of service attack, as the adversary can always force an abort. While Nielsen and Ranellucci show that, technically, it is possible to achieve low communication when a majority of players are malicious, the benefit of our relaxation is that it allows us to construct a much simpler protocol, both in concept and in concrete complexity.

The phrase "best of both worlds" has been used before in the MPC literature, referring to the more common notion of denial of service: guaranteed output delivery [8,13,15]. With only a few exceptions, protocols for secure multiparty computation are usually designed with a particular corruption threshold in mind. They either provide security with guaranteed output delivery when a majority of parties are honest, but provide no security at all when a majority are malicious, or they provide security with abort when a majority of parties are corrupt, but allow a denial of service even if only a single party is corrupt. Our protocol provides the best of both worlds in this sense as well, giving security with guaranteed output delivery when the adversary fails to corrupt a majority of parties, and security with abort when a majority are corrupt.

Our construction relies on offline (data independent) preprocessing that, currently, we do not know how to compute with constant overhead (short of using Nielsen and Ranellucci). While we hope this reliance can be removed in future work, we note that there are settings where it might be very reasonable to use such preprocessing. The obvious case is where the parties can afford to send a lot of data prior to the arrival of their inputs, but another setting in which preprocessing is available is where the parties have access to some trusted setup.

**Formal Description of Our Result.** For privacy threshold $t_p$, and packing parameter $\ell$, our protocol enables $n$ players to compute any arithmetic circuit $C$, guaranteeing security with abort when fewer than $t < t_p$ players are corrupt. It achieves guaranteed output delivery (aka: robustness, full security) when $t < t_r$, where $t_r = (n - t_p - 2 \cdot \ell)/2$. In addition, if $t < t_r$ and $\ell \in \Omega(n)$, then for a circuit $C$ of size $|C|$ and depth $d$, our protocol has expected communication complexity of $O(|C| \log |C| + \mathsf{poly}(n, d))$.

**Related Work.** Our work follows from two lines of work. The first line focuses on achieving low overhead computation in the majority setting, this includes the work of [2,14]. The paper of [3] achieved a sublinear overhead in the number of players, but only in the computational setting and with overhead in the security parameter that is not sublinear. The paper of [2] showed how by selecting $\ell \in \Omega(n)$, it was possible to construct a protocol for $n$ parties with communication overhead of $O(|C| \log |C| + \mathsf{poly}(n, d))$ for a circuit $C$ of size $|C|$ and depth $d$.

The second line of work, [8,13,15] focuses on finding MPC protocols with tradeoffs between how many corruptions can be tolerated before privacy is compromised $(t_p)$, and how many corruptions can be tolerated before the robustness guarantee is lost $(t_r)$. Ishai et al. demonstrated that this is possible when there is some slack in the parameters: there exist $n$-party protocols where, for $t_p + t_r < n$, the protocol maintains security with guaranteed output delivery against $t_r$ malicious players and security with abort against $t_p$ malicious parties [13]. In the same work, they demonstrated that this slackness is inherent, by giving an example of a function that cannot be securely computed with these same guarantees if $t + s = n$.

In parallel to our work, the work of [12] used the assumption that a certain number of parties are honest to improve the efficiency of semi-honest GMW and BMR-style MPC protocols. Other approaches that use preprocessing (such as [4, 6,7]) require each player to communicate one field element per multiplication since they do not use packing.

## 1.1   Technical Overview

In this section we present a high level overview of our protocol. We begin by describing a semi-honest version of our protocol, in order to provide insight into how we achieve low communication complexity. (Note that we never give a formal description of this semi-honest version, and it is meant purely for intuition.) Borrowing techniques from [2,3,5], we use a $t_p$-private packed Shamir secret sharing scheme with packing parameter $\ell$. These polynomials have degree $t_p + \ell$, and we will maintain this degree as we compute the circuit.

To compute multiplication gates, our protocol uses a special designated party (called the dealer), and Beaver triples $[a], [b], [c]$, which are secret sharings of values $a, b, c \in \mathbb{F}^\ell$, where $a, b$ are randomly sampled and $c = a \cdot b$ (introduced in [1]). These triples are shared using a $t_p$-private Shamir packed secret sharing scheme with packing parameter $\ell$. The packing parameter $\ell$ allows players to compute pointwise multiplication on vectors of field elements by having each player compute and send a constant number of field elements to the dealer.

Our protocol evaluates an arithmetic circuit $C$ in topological order from the input to the output gates. Since packed Shamir secret sharing is linear, the players can locally compute on their shares in order to evaluate the addition gates of $C$. To compute the product $[z] = [x] \cdot [y]$, the players execute the following steps, using a Beaver triple $[a], [b], [c]$. First, the players locally compute shares of $x - a$ and $y - b$ and send them to the dealer. The dealer reshares $x - a$, $y - b$ and $(x - a) \cdot (y - b)$ using degree $\ell$ polynomials. By resharing and packing those values instead of sending them in the clear, we cut down the communication cost by a factor $\ell$; the secret sharing in this step has nothing to do with privacy. The players then compute shares of $w \leftarrow y \cdot (x - a) + x \cdot (y - b) + r$, where the random mask $r$ is sampled and secret shared during preprocessing, using a degree $t_p + \ell$ polynomial. Since $x$ and $y$ are of degree $t_p + \ell$, and $(y - b)$ and $(x - a)$ are of degree $\ell$, it follows that $w$ is of degree $t_p + 2\ell$. The players send their shares of $w$ to the dealer. The dealer re-shares $w$ using a degree $\ell$ polynomial, and the players compute $z = w - r$. Since $r$ is shared using a degree $t_p + \ell$ polynomial, this results in shares of a degree $t_p + \ell$ polynomial, maintaining the invariant.

The use of a dealer allows each user to send secret shares to one party, instead of $n$ parties, cutting the cost per gate from $O(n^2)$ to $O(n)$. Packed secret sharing further reduces the complexity from $O(n)$ to $O(n/\ell)$. However, this also forces us to increase the degree of the polynomial to $t_p + \ell$, which creates a tradeoff between privacy and efficiency: the closer $t_p$ is to $n$, the smaller $\ell$ must be.

**Attacks by Malicious Adversaries.** The protocol above is only secure against a semi-honest adversary. At a high level, an active adversary, which instructs the players or the dealer to deviate from the protocol specification, can mount two types of attacks.

**Additive Attacks.** The first class of attacks occur either when a corrupt dealer re-shares the wrong value, or when malicious players send invalid shares to an honest dealer, thereby causing the dealer to reconstruct and re-share the wrong value. As we describe in our proof sketch in Sect. 4, these attacks are actually instances of additive attacks, in which an adversary can tamper with the evaluation of circuits by adding or subtracting values on individual wires, but cannot impact the computation in any other way. See the full version of this paper for more detail. By running the protocol on an additively secure circuit, obtained from the compiler of Genkin et al. [10], we are able to construct a protocol for MPC that renders such an attack ineffective. At a high level, the compiler of Genkin et al. takes any circuit and transforms it into a new circuit that will output $\perp$ if the adversary applies an additive attack (i.e. tampers with the value of any wire). By showing that any attack on our protocol is equivalent to an additive attack, we can apply the protocol of [10] to make it secure. We note that [10] has a constant overhead.

**Divide and Conquer Attacks.** The second class of attacks can only be performed by a malicious dealer. At a high level, during the evaluation of multiplication gates, instead of re-sharing values using a degree-$\ell$ polynomial, the dealer can create two sets of shares, each consistent with a different degree-$\ell$ polynomial.

More formally, consider the following situation: let $n$ be the number of parties, let $M$ be a set of corrupted parties, and let $S_1, S_2$ be distinct sets of honest parties (not necessarily disjoint). The adversarial dealer sends shares to $S_1$ such that the secret recovered from those shares is $x - a$. He sends shares to $S_2$ such that the secret recovered from those shares is $x - a + 1$. Then, when the players try to compute shares of $(x - a) \cdot y + r$, where $r$ is a random mask, note that both $S_1 \cup M$ and $S_2 \cup M$ give the dealer enough shares to reconstruct the blinded secret: from $S_1 \cup M$, the dealer can recover $(x - a) \cdot y + r$ and from the shares of $S_2 \cup M$, the dealer can recover $(x - a + 1) \cdot y + r$. By subtracting $(x - a + 1) \cdot y + r$ from $(x - a) \cdot y + r$ the malicious dealer can recover $y$, even though the value of $(x - a) \cdot y$ is supposedly hidden by a random mask.

**The Degree-Test Protocol.** Dealing with this second type of attack is one of our main technical contributions. In Sect. 3 we present a novel *degree-test* protocol that takes secret shares from the dealer and transmits them to the players if only if the shares of the honest players are consistent with a polynomial of degree-$d$. This degree test is also efficient, requiring each player to exchange only a constant number of field of element with the dealer. The main idea behind this protocol is as follows. During preprocessing, all parties learn a portion of a secret that is encoded in a degree $n - 1$ polynomial, $w$. Additionally, they receive shares of a degree $n - d - 1$ polynomial, $v$, such that $v(0) = 0$. To prove that he shared a degree $d$ polynomial, the dealer collects $n$ shares of $z$, defined as $z \leftarrow p \cdot v + w$. If $p$ is of appropriate degree, this suffices to learn $w(0)$, revealing the secret value, while if the degree of $p$ is too high, $w(0)$ remains hidden and the dealer fails to prove that he acted honestly.

## 2   Best of Both Worlds Security

We prove our protocols secure under the ideal-world, real-world paradigm. We define $f_C$ as the ideal functionality that takes an input $x$ from the players and outputs $C(x)$. The functionality $f_C^A$ takes an input $x$ from the players, and a vector $A$ from the adversary. It also evaluates $C$ on $x$, but it allows an adversary to tamper with the evaluation by adding values on individual wires; the variable $A$ specifies the values that are added to each wire.

**Definition 1.** *Let $t_p \leq n$ be positive integers, let* SD *denote the statistical distance, and let $0 \leq \epsilon \leq 1$. We say that an n-party protocol $\pi$ $(t_p, \epsilon)$-securely realizes a functionality $\mathcal{F}$ if for every PPT real-world adversary $A$ which corrupts at most $t_p$ players, there exists a simulator $S$ such that*

$$\mathsf{SD}(Real_{\pi,A}, Ideal_{\mathcal{F},S}) \leq \epsilon.$$

*We naturally extend this definition to protocol in the g-hybrid model by replacing $Real_{\pi,A}$ above with $Real_{\pi,A,g}$. In this case we say that $\pi$ $(t_p, \epsilon)$-securely realizes $\mathcal{F}$ in the g-hybrid model.*

**Definition 2.** *Let $n \geq t_p \geq t_r$ be positive integers and let $0 \leq \epsilon \leq 1$. We say that an n-party protocol $\pi$ $(t_r, t_p, \epsilon)$-robustly realizes $(f_C, f_C^A)$ if it meets the following two conditions.*

1. ***Security.** If $t_p > t \geq t_r$ then $\pi$ $(t_p, \epsilon)$-securely realizes $f_C^A$ as per Definition 1. This property does not guarantee that players receive outputs, because the adversary can cause the protocol to abort in the real world.*
2. ***Robustness.** If $t_r > t$ then $\pi$ $(t_p, \epsilon)$-securely realizes $f_C$, and it is guaranteed that the protocol will successfully terminate, with each honest player receiving output. More formally, if less than $t_r$ players are corrupt, the output generated in the real world is the same that is produced by the functionality $f_C$ in the ideal world where (i) each honest player $P_i$ provides input $x_i$ to the functionality, and (ii) the ideal functionality selects a default input for each corrupted player that does not provide an input $x_i$.*

## 3   Degree Test

Our degree test protocol is an interactive proof between a single prover (dealer) and multiple verifiers (players). The dealer sends a field element to each player, and proves that these elements are consistent with a polynomial $p$ of degree at most $d$. We construct a proof where the prover can only convince a given verifier with probability $2^{(-4s/n-t_p-\ell)}$. The aim is that at least $n - t_p - \ell$ verifiers will not be convinced by a cheating prover. The protocol proceeds as follows. The preprocessing functionality randomly samples a binary string of size $\frac{4s}{n-t_p-\ell}$, encodes it as $\mathsf{secret} \in \mathbb{F}$, and sends a portion of $\mathsf{secret}$ to each player. After sharing the polynomial $p$, the players will interact with the dealer in a manner that allows the dealer to learn this secret if and only if $p$ is of degree $d$ or less. The dealer then proves that he learned secret by sending to each player the portion of the binary string that they received during the preprocessing. If some player does not receive the correct part of the secret that was given to him during preprocessing, the player complains about the dealer.

In more detail, the preprocessing phase will generate a random degree-$(n - d - 1)$ polynomial $v$ such that $v(0) = 0$. Additionally, the preprocessing phase generates a random string, encodes it in $\mathbb{F}$, and shares secret $\in \mathbb{F}$ using a random degree-$(n - 1)$ polynomial $w$ (that is, $w(0) =$ secret). Finally, the individual bits of the binary string are distributed among the $n$ participating players (we assume a large enough field $\mathbb{F}$ to facilitate this). Upon receiving $p(i)$ from the dealer in the online phase, the player $P_i$ computes $z(i) \leftarrow p(i) \cdot v(i) + w(i)$ and sends it to the dealer. In case $(p(1), \cdots, p(n))$ are not consistent with any degree-$d$ polynomial, the dealer cannot reconstruct the value secret since the degree of $z$ is larger than $n - 1$. As a result, the dealer would only be able to break soundness with a small number of players. The remaining players will complain, and conclude that the dealer is a cheater. On the other hand, if the dealer shared a low degree polynomial, the dealer can reconstruct secret by interpolating $z(1), \cdots, z(n)$, and can then use secret as a proof that indeed $(p(1), \cdots, p(n))$ define a degree-$d$ polynomial. This can be done by sending each $P_i$ its portion of the binary string encoded as secret.

**Attack on Shares by Corrupt Players.** Even if the dealer gives shares $p(1), \cdots, p(n)$ consistent with a low degree polynomial, it may be that corrupt players would send back bad shares to prevent the dealer from reconstructing the correct secret, or by refusing to send shares altogether. To solve this problem, we allow the dealer to verify shares and eliminate players that send bad shares.

We allow the dealer to verify that $P_i$ sent a share that equals $p(i) \cdot v(i) + w(i)$ by (1) having the preprocessing phase authenticate the shares $v(i), w(i)$ that it sends to each player $P_i$, (2) using the linearly homomorphic MAC from SPDZ, and (3) by giving the verification keys to the dealer. When a dealer complains about a player, the player will be eliminated and will no longer take part in any future degree tests with that dealer.[2] We use $E$ to denote the set of eliminated players.

**Properties About the Set of Eliminated Players.** We need certain guarantees about the set of eliminated players. First, if the dealer is honestly sharing a low degree polynomial, then no honest player will complain about the dealer. Second, if the dealer is malicious and does not share a low degree polynomial, then a large number of honest players will eliminate themselves. Third, we must ensure that every player has a consistent view of the set of eliminated players. We satisfy this last property using a secure broadcast anytime a player is eliminated. If a large number of players are eliminated, then the dealer is replaced

---

[2] If the protocol re-starts because the dealer is thrown out, the party will rejoin the computation.

and protocol restarts with a new dealer. We can safely remove the dealer in this case, because, either the dealer is corrupt, or there are enough corrupt players that we can give up on robustness.

**Recovering from Eliminated Players.** The fact that the dealer can eliminate players creates a new problem: how does the dealer reconstruct secret when a few players have been eliminated? Recall that secret is shared using a degree-$n-1$ polynomial, and that eliminated players no longer provide shares to the dealer. In order to replace the eliminated players, we have the non-eliminated players send additional information that will allow the dealer to recover the missing shares of $z$. A natural approach for this is to have each remaining player send the dealer a share (generated during the preprocessing phase) of the eliminated player's share. While this solution works, it is too costly, as it introduces a quadratic overhead in the number of players. This overhead stems from two facts: first, a linear number of players could be eliminated, and second, for each execution of the degree test, for each eliminated player, each non-eliminated player would have to send one share to the dealer.

**Reducing Recovery Overhead.** We employ a couple of strategies to reduce the communication required of the honest players when they help the dealer to reconstruct the shares of eliminated players. First, we will reuse the same $v$ for each execution of the degree test. Now, when a player $P_i$ is eliminated by the dealer, each player will only need to send a share of $v_i$ to the dealer once, ensuring that the dealer learns $v_i$ for all further executions of the degree test protocol. Next, we notice that the dealer recovers secret from the shares of $z$ by performing Lagrange interpolation, which is a linear operation. That is, the dealer computes secret $= \sum_{i=1}^{n} \alpha_i z_i = \sum_{i=1}^{n} \alpha_i(p(i) \cdot v_i + w_i)$ where $\alpha_1, \cdots, \alpha_n$ are the Lagrange interpolation coefficients. Rewriting the above equation,

$$\texttt{secret} = \sum_{i=1}^{n} \alpha_i z_i = \sum_{P_i \notin E} \alpha_i z_i + \sum_{P_i \in E} \alpha_i z_i = \sum_{P_i \notin E} \alpha_i z_i + \sum_{P_i \in E} \alpha_i(p(i) \cdot v_i + w_i)$$

$$= \sum_{P_i \notin E} \alpha_i z_i + \sum_{P_i \in E} \alpha_i p(i) \cdot v_i + \sum_{P_i \in E} \alpha_i w_i.$$

Since the dealer knows $p(i)$ for all players, knows $v_i$ for all eliminated players, and has the shares $z_i$ for all non-eliminated players, he only needs to learn $\bar{c} = \sum_{i \in E} \alpha_i w_i$. Thus, each non-eliminated player can locally compute a single share of $\bar{c}$, using a share of $w_i$ for each $P_i \in E$. Sending just this single share to the dealer, instead of one share for every eliminated player, allows us to avoid the linear overhead that arose in the naive approach previously suggested.

### 3.1   Formal Description of the Degree Test Protocol

In this section we formally present and analyze our degree test protocol. Let $H$ be the set of honest players and let $E$ denote a global, shared variable, indicating the set of eliminated players. We denote the inputs to the degree test protocol by $p(1), \cdots, p(n)$. For some honest player, $P_i$, we let $\eta$ denote the probability that a malicious dealer wrongly convinces $P_i$ that $p$ is of degree less than or equal to $d$. Finally, we denote the set of parties complaining about the dealer by $C$. The ideal functionality, $\mathcal{F}_{\mathrm{dt}}$, is formally described in Fig. 1, and the degree test protocol realizing this functionality is described in Fig. 2. Consider the following theorem.

---

We denote $E$ to be a global variable which denotes the set of eliminated players.

**Input**

1. Dealer: $\{p(i)\}_{P_i \notin E}$. In case the dealer is honest we require that $(p(1), \cdots, p(n))_{P_i \notin E}$ is the evaluation of a polynomial of degree at most $d$.

**Compute**

1. Initialize a set of complaining players $C \leftarrow \emptyset$.
2. Let $p$ be the polynomial that results from interpolating the shares $\{p(i)\}_{P_i \in H}$
3. On receipt of (bad_share_complaint, $i$) from the adversary set $C \leftarrow C \cup \{P_i\}$, unless both the dealer and $P_i$ are honest.
4. If $C \neq \emptyset$ , set $E \leftarrow E \cup C$ and terminate.
5. If $\mathsf{degree}(p) > d$, each honest party is added to $C$ with probability $1 - \eta$.
6. On receipt of (bad_proof_complaint, $i$) from the adversary set $C \leftarrow C \cup \{P_i\}$ unless both the dealer and $P_i$ are honest.
7. If $C \neq \emptyset$, set $E \leftarrow E \cup C$ and terminate.

**Output**

1. Party $P_i$ receives $p(i)$

**Fig. 1.** Degree test functionality $\mathcal{F}_{\mathrm{dt}}$

**Theorem 1.** $\pi_{dt}$ *securely realizes* $\mathcal{F}_{dt}$ *in the preprocessing-hybrid model.*

In order to prove Theorem 1, we provide two simulators, one simulator for the case when the dealer is honest, and a second simulator for the case when the dealer is corrupt. In each case the simulator simply follows the description of the protocol, determines if players or the dealer needs to complain, and adds players to the set of eliminated players $E$ that would be eliminated. We recall that $H$ denotes the set of honest players. $E$ denotes the set of eliminated parties. The point $v_i \in \mathbb{F}$ is a share of a degree $n - t_p - \ell$ polynomial that evaluates to zero at zero. The point $w_i \in \mathbb{F}$ is a share of a polynomial that evaluates to a random value $\mathsf{secret}$. The share $v_{i,j}$ is a resharing of $v_i$ that will help the dealer to reconstruct $v_i$ if $P_i$ is eliminated.

**Degree Test Simulation Honest Case.** The simulator queries the ideal functionality and receives $p(i)$ for each $P_i \in \bar{H}$.

1. The simulator simulates the preprocessing by following its description.
2. The simulator sends $p(i)$ to each non-eliminated corrupt player $P_i \in \bar{E} \cup \bar{H}$

The degree test protocol is parameterized by security parameter $s$, $n$ players, threshold $t$, degree $d$, and field $\mathbb{F}$ where $|\mathbb{F}| \geq \frac{2ns}{n-t}$. Each player gets a point $p(i) \in \mathbb{F}$ from the dealer. The global variable $E$ stores the set of eliminated players and may be updated. If $E$ is updated, all parties will halt and discard their shares. Players in $E$ do not send shares to dealer. Otherwise, they know that $\{p(i)\}_{P_i \in H}$ lies on a polynomial of degree at most $d$. We define $\alpha_1, \cdots, \alpha_n$ as the lagrange coefficients. We use a homomorphic mac scheme (setup, keygen, mac, verify)

**One-time preprocessing**
1. $(v_1, \cdots, v_n) \leftarrow \mathsf{share}_{n-d}(0)$
2. Send $\gamma \leftarrow \mathsf{setup}(1^s, \mathbb{F})$ to the dealer.　　　　(global key for mac scheme).
3. Send $k_i \leftarrow \mathsf{keygen}(1^s, \mathbb{F})$ to the dealer. (key used to authenticate $p(i) \cdot v_i$)
4. Send $v_i, t_i \leftarrow \mathsf{mac}(\gamma, k_i, v_i)$ to $P_i$
5. Generate shares to reconstruct values in case players are eliminated.
   　$v_{i,j} \leftarrow \mathsf{share}_t(v_i)$ and send $v_{1,j}, \cdots, v_{n,j}$ to $P_j$

**Preprocessing (per instance)**
1. Set $m = \frac{2ns}{n-t-\ell}$ and sample a random $\mathsf{secret} \in \{0,1\}^m$.
2. $(w_1, \cdots, w_n) \leftarrow \mathsf{share}_n(\mathsf{secret})$　　　　(Hides the secret.)
3. Send $\delta_i \leftarrow \mathsf{keygen}(1^s, \mathbb{F})$ to the dealer.
4. $\tau_i \leftarrow \mathsf{mac}(\gamma, \delta_i, w_i)$　　　($\tau_i + p(i) \cdot t_i$ produces a mac tag for $p(i) \cdot v_i + w_i$)
5. Send $(w_i, \tau_i)$ and $\mathsf{secret}_{m/n \cdot (i-1)+1, \cdots, m/n \cdot i}$ to $P_i$.
6. Generate shares to recover in case players are eliminated.
   　$w_{i,1}, \cdots, w_{i,n} \leftarrow \mathsf{share}_{t_p}(w_i)$ and send $w_{1,j}, \cdots, w_{n,j}$ to $P_j$.

**Protocol online phase**
1. **dealer**
   　　Send $p(i)$ to $P_i$ for each $P_i \notin E$.
2. **players**
   　i. $z_i \leftarrow p(i) \cdot v_i + w_i$　　　($z_i$ is a share of $z$ such that $z(0) = \mathsf{secret}$)
   　ii. Send $z_i, \sigma_i \leftarrow p(i) \cdot t_i + \tau_i$ to the dealer.
   　iii. Generate shares when players are eliminated.
   　　　Send $a_i \leftarrow \sum_{P_j \in E} \alpha_j \cdot w_{j,i}$ to the dealer. (local shares of $\sum_{P_j \in E} \alpha_j w_j$)
3. **dealer**
   　i. Dealer complains about each non-eliminated player $P_i$ who either: did not send a $z_i$ with a tag $\sigma_i$ such that $\mathsf{verify}(\gamma, p(i) \cdot k_i + \delta_i, z_i, \sigma_i) = \mathsf{accept}$; or did not send an $a_i$ when players have been eliminated. If the dealer complained, $E$ is updated to include all the players that he complained about, and the dealer skips to 5.i.
   　ii. Generate shares when players are eliminated.
   　　　$- \bar{c} \leftarrow \mathsf{recover}([\, a_i \mid P_i \notin E \,])$　　　($\bar{c} = \sum_{P_j \in E} \alpha_j \cdot w_j$)
   　　　$- \bar{c} \leftarrow \bar{c} + \sum_{P_i \in E} \alpha_i (v_i \cdot p(i))$
   　iii. $\mathsf{secret} \leftarrow \left( \sum_{P_i \notin E} \alpha_i \cdot z_i \right) + \bar{c}$ and send $\mathsf{secret}_{m \cdot (i-1)+1, \cdots, m \cdot i}$ to $P_i$
4. **players**
   　i. If dealer did not complain, and $P_i$ received a different value for $\mathsf{secret}$ from the dealer then what he got in the preprocessing, then he complains. $P_i$ is added to $E$. Each player $P_i$ who received a complaint from the dealer (resp. $P_j$) about $P_j$ (resp. Dealer) sends $(i, j, v_{j,i})$ to the dealer.
5. **dealer**
   　i. The dealer reconstructs $v_j$ from the $v_{j,i}$ he receives using Reed-Solomon decoding. If the dealer cannot reconstruct $v_j$, the dealer broadcasts failure, and then $E$ is set to be the set of all players.

**Fig. 2.** Degree test $\pi_{\mathrm{dt}}$

3. The simulator await that corrupted non-eliminated player $P_i \in \bar{E} \cup \bar{H}$ sends $(z_i, \mathsf{m}(z_i))$ and $a_i$ to the dealer.
4. The simulator computes $\mathsf{k}(z_i) \leftarrow p(i) \cdot \mathsf{k}(v_i) + \mathsf{k}(w_i)$, assigns to $S$ the subset of corrupted non-eliminated players $P_i$ who either did not send a $z_i$ with a valid mac tag or who did not send an $a_i$. All players in $S$ are added to $E$. If any players were added to $E$, he runs the player elimination simulation (below).
5. Send $\mathsf{secret}_{m \cdot (i-1)+1, \cdots, m \cdot i}$ to each non-eliminated corrupt player $P_i$
6. For each player $P_i$ who complains about the dealer, the simulator sends (bad_proof_complaint, $i$) to the functionality and then add $P_i$ to $E$. The simulator then runs the Player elimination simulation (below).

**Honest Dealer Elimination Simulation.** Whenever a player is eliminated, we require that the simulator do the following. After a set $S$ of players are added to $E$, the simulator awaits $(i, j, v'_{j,i})$ from each non-eliminated corrupt player for each $P_j \in S$. The, for each $P_j \in S$, the simulator tries to reconstruct $v_j$ from the $v'_{j,i}$ that come from non-eliminated corrupt players, and the $v_{j,i}$ that were generated in the preprocessing for the honest players. If the simulator does not reconstruct a valid share $v_j$, the dealer broadcasts failure, and the full set of players is added $E$. The simulation then halts.

**Description of the Simulator When Dealer Is Corrupt**

1. The simulator simulates the preprocessing by following its description.
2. The simulator await that the dealer send $p(i)$ to each non-eliminated honest player $P_i$.
3. The simulator computes $z_i \leftarrow p(i) \cdot v_i + w_i$, $a_i \leftarrow \sum_{P_j \in E} \alpha_j \cdot w_{j,i}$ (local shares of $\sum_{P_j \in E} \alpha_j w_j$), $\mathsf{m}(z_i) \leftarrow p(i) \cdot \mathsf{m}(v_i) + \mathsf{m}(w_i)$ and sends $(z_i, \mathsf{m}(z_i))$ and $a_i$ to the dealer.
4. For each non-eliminated player $P_i$ that the dealer complains about, the simulator send (bad_proof_complaint, $i$) to the functionality. The simulator executes the player elimination simulation.
5. The simulator await $\mathsf{secret}_{m \cdot (i-1)+1, \cdots, m \cdot i}$ from the dealer for each honest non-eliminated player $P_i$.
6. For each non-eliminated honest player $P_i \in \bar{E} \cup H$, if the dealer did not send the same value of $\mathsf{secret}$ that would have been to $P_i$, the simulator sends (bad_proof_complaint, $i$) to the functionality. The simulator executes the player elimination simulation.

**Corrupt Dealer Elimination Simulation.** Whenever a player is eliminated players we require that the simulator do the following. After a set $S$ of players are added to $E$, the simulator sends $(i, j, v'_{j,i})$ for each eliminated player $P_j \in S$ and non-eliminated honest player $P_i$. If the corrupt dealer broadcasts failure, then $E$ is set to be the set of all players. The simulation then halts.

## 3.2   Properties of the Degree-Test Protocol

We already know that the degree test protocol securely realizes the degree test functionality. Within the context of our main protocol, we want to show that our degree test protocol has more features than what is directly provided by the functionality. The first is that the online cost of the degree test is low, namely that if we use the protocol many times, the overhead of the degree test per player will be small. The second condition that we want is that if the dealer is honest, and less than some threshold of players are dishonest, then in each execution of the degree test, either it succeeds, or some malicious party is eliminated.

The third condition that we are interested in is that if a corrupt dealer cheats by sharing a high degree polynomial, and does not complain about the shares and tags given to him by honest players, then less than half of the honest player's will accept the secret. (Recall, if he does complain about some of the shares and tags that he was given, then all parties are eliminated and the protocol re-starts with a new dealer.)

**Lemma 1.** *The total communication cost of running $m$ executions of the degree test with the same dealer is $O(s \cdot n \cdot m + \mathsf{poly}(n))$ bits.*

*Proof.* We enumerate over each item that is communicated and compute its associated communication overhead. A player will broadcast a complaint about the dealer at most once $(O(n^2))$. The dealer will broadcast a complaint about a player at most once. $(O(n^2))$. Each player will send a constant number of field elements to the dealer per execution of the degree test $(O(s \cdot n \cdot m))$. The dealer will send a constant number of field elements to each player per execution of the degree test $(O(s \cdot n \cdot m))$.

The communication complexity of all these items is $O(s \cdot n \cdot m + \mathsf{poly}(n))$. This completes the proof of this lemma.

**Lemma 2.** *If the dealer is honest, and less than $\frac{(n - t_p - 2\ell)}{2}$ players are corrupt, then both of the following conditions will be met (except with negligible probability).*

1. *No honest player will be eliminated.*
2. *The degree test will succeed, or at least one corrupt player will be eliminated.*

*Proof.* First, we show that an honest player will not be eliminated by an honest dealer except with negligible probability. Since honest players always send correct shares, the dealer would only eliminate an honest player if he reconstructs an incorrect value for the secret in step 3.iii. This can only occur if the adversary is able to successfully forge a mac tag in step 2.ii. Otherwise, the dealer would complain about a corrupt player and the degree test would terminate. Since forging a mac tag only succeeds with negligible probability, this completes the first part of the proof.

Next we proceed to show that either the degree test will succeed, or at least one corrupt player will be eliminated. If the dealer reconstructs the correct secret, the dealer will send the correct part of the secret to each honest player in step

3.iii, and each honest player will accept the secret in step 4.i. This leaves only two strategies for the adversary to prevent the degree test from succeeding: he can either send bad shares, or not send shares at all. In either case, the dealer will complain about corrupt players in step 3.i and the dealer will eliminate corrupt players. This completes the second part of the proof.

**Lemma 3.** *If less than $t_p$ players are corrupt and the following conditions all hold, then more than $\frac{n-t_p-2\ell}{2}$ honest players will be eliminated.*

1. *The dealer is malicious and does not complain about a player in step 3.i.*
2. *The degree of the polynomial $p$ is greater than $\ell$.*

*Proof.* First, we show that if all the above conditions hold then the dealer cannot learn any information about the secret. Since by condition 2, the dealer shares a polynomial $p$ of degree higher than $d$, then the degree $p \cdot v$ is greater than $n$. Since $w$ was selected at random, and less than $t_p$ players are corrupt, then the dealer cannot recover the secret from $(p \cdot v + w)(0)$.

By the first condition of the lemma, the dealer did not complain in step 3.i. This means that the dealer, to convince an honest player that he is honest must correctly guess the part of the secret given to that player. Since the probability of correctly guessing the secret for a given player is $2^{-\frac{4s}{n-t_p-\ell}}$, we can finally show that more than half the honest players will abort.

By combining the following two statements with the lemma below, we have what we want: (1) the probability of correctly guessing a player's secret is $p = 1 - 2^{-4s/(n-t_p-\ell)}$ and (2) the random variables associated to the dealer successfully guessing players' part of the secret are independent.

**Lemma 4.** *Given $s, m \in \mathbb{N}$, let $X_1, \ldots, X_m$ be independant Bernoulli variables with success probability $p = 1 - 2^{-4s/m}$ and let $X = \sum_{i=1}^{m} X_i$ then*

$$\Pr\left[X < \tfrac{m}{2}\right] \le 2^{-\theta(s)}$$

*Proof.* If $m \ge s$, we can directly apply Chernoff's bound to get this result. We have that $\mu = m \cdot (1 - 2^{-4s/m})$ and let $\delta = \frac{1}{2(1-2^{-4s/m})}$. We note that $\delta \ge \frac{1}{2}$ and that $\mu \cdot \delta = \frac{m}{2}$ and thus we have that

$$\Pr\left[X \le \tfrac{m}{2}\right] = \Pr\left[X < (1-\delta) \cdot \mu\right] \le e^{\frac{-\delta^2 \mu}{3}} \le e^{-\frac{m}{12}} \in 2^{-\theta(s)}$$

This leaves only the case where $m < s$ and we show that this also holds by using the following combinatorial argument.

$$\Pr\left[X < \tfrac{m}{2}\right] = \sum_{i=0}^{m/2} \binom{m}{i} \left(1 - 2^{-4s/m}\right)^i \left(2^{-4s/m}\right)^{m-i} \le \sum_{i=0}^{m/2} \binom{m}{i} \left(2^{-4s/m}\right)^{m-i}$$

$$\le \sum_{i=0}^{m/2} 2^m \left(2^{-4s/m}\right)^{m/2} \le 2^{-2s+m+\log m} \in 2^{-\theta(s)}$$

# 4   Additively-Secure Protocol

We now construct a protocol which is secure in the preprocessing-hybrid model, aside from allowing additive attacks. (Recall, these are then handled using the compiler of Genkin et al. [10].) The players will randomly elect (without repetition) a dealer that will be used to run the computation. If at some point too many players claim the dealer is cheating, the protocol will be restarted with a new dealer. During the evaluation phases (routing, multiplication and addition), the players will add, multiply and subtract shares locally, and they will also send and receive shares to and from the dealer. The dealer will be responsible for receiving, reconstructing values and resharing them. In particular, the dealer will be responsible for reconstructing values when less than $t_r$ shares are corrupted. This will be done by having the dealer apply Reed-Solomon decoding to the shares he receives. If at any point, the dealer fails to reconstruct the secret, the dealer will eliminate himself and the protocol will be restarted with a new dealer. The protocol employs the degree testing protocol to ensure that when the dealer reshares values, he cannot use a polynomial of degree greater than $\ell$. Since degree testing involves eliminating players, the protocol will need to keep track of who has been eliminated.

At the beginning, the players will randomly elect a dealer. While that dealer is active, each party will keep track of a set of eliminated players denoted by the variable $E$. Players can eliminate themselves if they detect malicious behavior, or they can be eliminated, either by an honest dealer for acting maliciously, or by a malicious dealer, arbitrarily. If the set of eliminated players grows too big, all parties kick out the dealer and rejoin the protocol with a new dealer (chosen without replacement). To simplify exposition, we assume that the set $E$ is a global variable, and that all honest parties agree on its members. In practice, this can be achieved using a broadcast channel, without impacting the claimed communication cost. Our main protocol consists of four phases: the preprocessing phase, the input phase, the evaluation phase, and the output phase. The input, evaluation, and output phase will all rely on values generated by the preprocessing. We will not describe the preprocessing phase in its entirety but rather describe which values each of the other phases need from the preprocessing.

Throughout the computation, parties hold shares of wire values, encoded using polynomials of degree $t = t_p + \ell$. This ensures that $t_p$ parties cannot learn anything about these values. Because we need to multiply these polynomials by degree $\ell$ polynomials that encode masked wire values, the degree of the polynomials becomes $t_p + 2\ell$ during the evaluation. This allows us to error-correct in the presence of less than $\frac{n-t_p-2\ell}{2}$ corruptions, maintaining robustness as claimed in our theorem. When we do not specify the degree of a sharing, we mean that the polynomial has degree $t_p + \ell$ (Figs. 3 and 4).

**Input Phase.** In the input phase, a sender provides his input $x$, and the other parties receive shares of that input, which can then be used in the evaluation phase. The preprocessing functionality randomly samples $r \in \mathbb{F}^\ell$, gives the value

Below, we let $t = t_p + \ell$.

**Input**
1. Randomly sample $r \in \mathbb{F}^\ell$ and send it to the sender.
2. Send $[\,y\,] \leftarrow \mathsf{share}_t(r)$ to players

**$\rho$-gate**
1. Randomly sample $u,\ v \in \mathbb{F}^\ell$ such that $\rho(u) = v$.
2. Send $[\,c\,] \leftarrow \mathsf{share}_t(u),\ [\,z\,] \leftarrow \mathsf{share}_t(v)$ to players.

**Multiplication**
1. Randomly sample $\alpha, \beta, \gamma, \upsilon \in \mathbb{F}^\ell$ such that $\alpha \cdot \beta = \gamma$.
2. $[\,a\,] \leftarrow \mathsf{share}_t(\alpha),\ [\,b\,] \leftarrow \mathsf{share}_t(\beta),\ [\,c\,] \leftarrow \mathsf{share}_t(\gamma),$
   $[\,u\,] \leftarrow \mathsf{share}_t(\upsilon)$
3. Send $[\,a\,], [\,b\,], [\,c\,], [\,u\,]$ to players.

**Output**
1. $r \in_R \mathbb{F}^\ell.\ [\,r\,] \leftarrow \mathsf{share}_t(r)$
2. Send $[\,r\,], [\![\,r\,]\!]$ to players. ($[\![\,r\,]\!]$ is a VSS sharing of $r$.)

**Fig. 3.** Preprocessing

to the sender, and provides $[r]$ to the other players. The sender broadcasts $y = x - r$. The players then compute $[x] = [r] + y$. Due to a lack of space, we provide the full description in the full version of the paper.

**Output Phase.** In the output phase, parties take shares $[x]$ of the output and reconstruct $x$. We have to limit the adversary to an additive attack on the revealed output, ensuring that the adversary cannot arbitrarily choose the output. The preprocessing functionality creates two shares of a value $r \in \mathbb{F}^\ell$, once using packed Shamir secret sharing resulting, in $[r]$, and once using a VSS, resulting in $[\![r]\!]$. The players will use $[r]$ and $[\![r]\!]$ to mask and then unmask $x$. That is, they locally, homomorphically add $r$ to the output by adding their shares of $[x]$ and $[r]$, and then reveal $r$ by opening the VSS sharing. Because VSS is binding, the adversary can only modify the value before it is unmasked. As such, the only attack that can be done is an additive attack. Due to a lack of space, we provide the full description in the full version of our paper.

**Multiplication.** The multiplication is the most complex operation, the goal is to take shares $[x], [y]$ and produce shares of $[x \cdot y]$. To do so, we will use beaver triple $[a], [b], [a \cdot b]$, and a sharing of a random $r \in \mathbb{F}^\ell$, $[r]$. First the players will send $[x - a], [y - b]$. The dealer will reconstructs values $x - a, y - b, (x-a)(y-b)$, and re-shares them using degree $\ell$ polynomials. The players verify that the shares given to them by the dealer are of degree $\ell$, using the degree test protocol. The players will then compute $[u] = [x - a]_\ell \cdot [y] + [y - b]_\ell \cdot [x] + [r]$ and send the shares to the dealer. The dealer re-shares $u$ using a degree $\ell$ polynomial, and the players again test that the degree is no more than $\ell$. Finally, the players will compute $[x \cdot y] = [u] - [a \cdot b] - [r]$.

The players want to evaluate a SIMD circuit $C$ with $m$ input gates $g_1, \cdots, g_m$ with output gates $g_{|C|-O+1}$ to $g_{|C|}$. We denote $g_{m+1}, \cdots, g_{|C|-O}$ as evaluation gates. For each input gate $g$, we denote $p_g$ as the player who provides input $x_g$ and we will use the variable $[\, i_g \,]$ to store the shares generated by $\mathcal{F}_{\mathrm{pre}}$ for the gate $g$.

For each multiplication gate $g$, we will use the variable $[\, a_g \,], [\, b_g \,], [\, c_g \,]$ and $[\, u_g \,]$ to store the shares generated by $\mathcal{F}_{\mathrm{pre}}$ for the gate $g$. For each $\rho$-gate, we will use the variable $[\, v_g \,], [\, w_g \,]$ to store the shares generated by $\mathcal{F}_{\mathrm{pre}}$ for gate $g$. We use $t_g$ to denote the shares generated by evaluating the gate $g$. For each output gate, We will use the variable $[\, \Upsilon_g \,]$ to store the shares generated by packed secret sharing for the output phase and define $[\, \Phi_g \,]$ to denote the shares generated using the VSS.

We use $E$ to denote the set of eliminated players; it is a global variable which is sometimes updated in the sub-protocols. Each round will have a fresh dealer. We denote $\mathcal{D}$ as the set of eliminated dealers.

## Preprocessing

1. For each input gate $g$
   The players execute $\mathcal{F}_{\mathrm{pre}}(\mathsf{input})$ where $p_g$ taking the role of the sender. The sender stores the value he receives as $r_g$ and the shares received by players are assigned to $[\, i_g \,]$.
2. For each $\rho$-gate $g$, $[\, v_g \,], [\, w_g \,] \leftarrow \mathcal{F}_{\mathrm{pre}}(\rho)$
3. For each multiplication gate $g$, $[\, a_g \,], [\, b_g \,], [\, c_g \,], [\, u_g \,] \leftarrow \mathcal{F}_{\mathrm{pre}}(\mathsf{multiplication})$
4. For each output gate $g$,
   (a) $[\, y_g \,], [[\, r_g \,]] \leftarrow \mathcal{F}_{\mathrm{pre}}(\mathsf{output})$
   (b) $[\, \Upsilon_g \,] \leftarrow [\, y_g \,] \qquad [\, \Phi_g \,] \leftarrow [[\, r_g \,]]$

## Dealer replacement rule.

If at any point $|E_i| \geq \frac{n-t_p}{2} - \ell$, the player sets $\mathcal{D} \leftarrow \mathcal{D} \cup \{ D \}$ and return to step 3 of the evaluation.

## Evaluation

1. For each input gate $g$, $[\, t_g \,] \leftarrow \mathsf{Input}(x_g, r_g, [\, i_g \,])$ where $x_g$ and $r_g$ are the inputs of sender $p_g$.
2. $\mathcal{D} \leftarrow \emptyset, E \leftarrow \emptyset$.
3. Sample a random dealer not in $\mathcal{D}$.
4. For each evaluation layer $L$ and for each gate $g \in L$.
   (a) If $L$ is an addition layer then $[\, t_g \,] \leftarrow [\, x \,] + [\, y \,]$
   (b) Otherwise
      − If $L$ is a routing layer then
         $[\, x \,] \leftarrow [\, t_{\mathsf{input}(g)} \,]$
         $[\, t_g \,] \leftarrow \mathsf{routing}([\, x \,], [\, v_g \,], [\, w_g \,])$
      − If $L$ is a multiplication layer then
         $[\, x \,] \leftarrow t_{\mathsf{left}(g)}, \; [\, y \,] \leftarrow t_{\mathsf{right}(g)}$
         $[\, t_g \,] \leftarrow \mathsf{multiplication}([\, x \,], [\, y \,], [\, a_g \,], [\, b_g \,], [\, c_g \,], [\, u_g \,])$
      − If $|E| \geq \frac{n-t_p}{2} - \ell$, $\mathcal{D} \leftarrow \mathcal{D} \cup \{ D \}$ and return to step 3 of the evaluation.
      − If $[\, t_g \,] = \bot$, return to step 4.b (This occurs when a player is eliminated during a degree test.)
5. For each output gate $g$
   (a) $[\, x \,] \leftarrow [\, t_{\mathsf{input}(g)} \,]$
   (b) $v \leftarrow \mathsf{output}([\, x \,])$
   (c) Output $v$

**Fig. 4.** Main protocol

**Routing.** The input is $[x]$ and the output should be $[\rho(x)]$. The preprocessing functionality generates shares $[r], [r']$ such that $\rho(r) = r'$. Then when provided $[x]$, the players will send $[x + r]$ to the dealer who will reshare $[\rho(x + r)]$. The players will then verify that the dealer reshared $x + r$ using a low degree polynomial via the degree test. The players will then compute $[x] = [\rho(x + r)] - [r']$. Due to a lack of space, we provide the full description in the full version of our paper.

Formally, we prove that our protocol realizes two things. First, we show that the protocol securely realizes $f_C$ *with low expected communication overhead* if less than $t_r$ players are corrupt. Second, we prove that our protocol securely realizes $f_C^A$ (the functionality that allows the adversary to tamper with each wire individually) if less than $t_p$ players are corrupt. Then, by running our protocol on a circuit secure against tampering on individual wires, our protocol securely realizes $f_C$. The compilers of [10,11] allow us to compile any circuit into an equivalent circuit that is secure against individual tampering with only a constant blowup in circuit size. As a result, it is easy to see that by employing our protocol with the results of [10,11], we achieve the desired security properties as well as the desired level of efficiency (Fig. 5).

**Theorem 2.** *For any number of players $n$, privacy threshold $n \geq t_p \geq \frac{n}{2}$, packing parameter $\ell < \frac{n-t_p}{2}$, $\pi_{mpc}$ $(t_p, O(1/|\mathbb{F}|))$-securely realizes $f_C^A$ with abort in the $\mathcal{F}_{pre}$-hybrid model.*

**Theorem 3.** *For any number of players $n$, privacy threshold $n \geq t_p \geq \frac{n}{2}$, robustness threshold $t_r \leq \frac{n-t_p-2\ell}{2}$, $\ell < \frac{n-t_p}{2}$. $\pi_{mpc}$ $(t_p, t_r, O(1/|\mathbb{F}|))$-securely realizes $(f_C, f_C^A)$ for arithmetic circuit $C$ with depth $d$ in the $\mathcal{F}_{pre}$-hybrid model, with full security, and expected communication overhead*

$$O\big(|C|\log(|C|) \cdot \frac{n}{\ell} + d^2 \cdot n + \mathsf{poly}(n, s)\big).$$

Due to space constraint, we only provide a short summary of how we prove our main protocol secure. A more complete argument appears in the full version of the paper.

**Security Under Honest Dealer.** Since our protocol is in a hybrid-model, the simulator can simulate a run of the preprocessing functionality and store the generated values. This allows the simulator to extract the adversary's inputs. The simulator runs the honest parties with dummy inputs and determines whether the adversary causes the honest dealer to abort, or causes an additive attack. We show that if the adversary sends bad shares to the dealer, then the simulator can determine, based solely on these shares, which of these three things happen: (1) the dealer aborts because he failed to reconstruct a secret, (2) the bad shares can be ignored (which is the case if enough players are honest), or (3) the attack by the adversary can be mapped to an additive attack. We prove the previous statement by using the fact that Shamir secret sharing is a linear error correcting code, and from the following fact about such codes.

The players input sharings $[\,x\,], [\,y\,]$, a triple of shares $[\,a\,], [\,b\,]$ and $[\,c\,]$ such that $c = a \cdot b$, and sharing $[\,r\,]$ of a random value $r \in \mathbb{F}^{\ell}$. All of these values are shared using polynomials of degree $t_p + \ell$. The shares $[\,r\,]$ are used to hide values from the dealer. The global variable $E$, which stores the set of eliminated players, may be updated. If it is updated, all players terminate, discard their shares, and output $\perp$. Otherwise, the players produce shares $[\,z\,]$ such that $z = x \cdot y$.

**Evaluation**
1. **players**
    i. $[\,d\,] \leftarrow [\,y\,] - [\,b\,]$
    ii. $[\,e\,] \leftarrow [\,x\,] - [\,a\,]$
    iii. Send $[\,d\,], [\,e\,]$ to dealer.
2. **dealer**
    i. $v \leftarrow \mathsf{recover}([\,d\,]) \cdot \mathsf{recover}([\,e\,])$
    ii. $[\,\alpha\,]_{\ell} \leftarrow \mathsf{share}_{\ell}(v)$
    iii. $[\,\epsilon\,]_{\ell} \leftarrow \mathsf{reshare}_{\ell}([\,e\,])$
    iv. $[\,\delta\,]_{\ell} \leftarrow \mathsf{reshare}_{\ell}([\,d\,])$
3. **Degree Test**
    i. Execute degree-testing with dealer input $[\,\alpha\,]_{\ell}$.
    ii. Execute degree-testing with dealer input $[\,\delta\,]_{\ell}$.
    iii. Execute degree-testing with dealer input $[\,\epsilon\,]_{\ell}$.
    iv. If the degree test outputs $\perp$ in any of these executions, then all players terminate and output $\perp$.
4. **players**
    i. $[\,g_1\,] \leftarrow [\,\delta\,]_{\ell} \cdot [\,x\,] + [\,\epsilon\,]_{\ell} \cdot [\,y\,]$
    ii. $[\,g\,] \leftarrow [\,g_1\,] - [\,\alpha\,]_{\ell} + [\,r\,]$
    iii. Send $[\,g\,]$ to dealer.
5. **dealer**
    i. $[\,h\,]_{\ell} \leftarrow \mathsf{reshare}_{\ell}([\,g\,])$
6. **Degree Test**
    i. Execute degree-testing with dealer input $[\,h\,]_{\ell}$.
    ii. If the degree test outputs $\perp$, then all players terminate and output $\perp$.
7. **players**
    i. Set $O \leftarrow [\,h\,]_{\ell} + [\,c\,] - [\,r\,]$
    ii. Output $O$

**Recovery failure subroutine**
1. If $\mathsf{recover}(\cdot)$ ever fails to output a polynomial of degree $t_p + \ell$ that agrees with $\frac{n+t_p}{2} + \ell$ shares, then the dealer broadcasts "failure", sets $E \leftarrow P$, and all players terminate with output $\perp$. The parameters in this subroutine are chosen so that it is guaranteed that either the Berklaml-welch algorithm reconstruct a correct value for the secret or that the $\mathsf{recover}$ operation will output $\perp$.

**Fig. 5.** Multiplication

Let (encode, decode) be a linear error-correcting, let $c = \mathsf{encode}(m)$ be an encoding of $m$, and let be $\mu$ be an error vector. By linearity of the error-correcting code, we have that $\mathsf{decode}(\mathsf{encode}(m) + \mu) = \mathsf{decode}(\mathsf{encode}(m)) + \mathsf{decode}(\mu)$. In particular, this implies that $\mathsf{decode}(\mathsf{encode}(m) + \mu) = \perp$ if and only if

$\mathsf{decode}(\mu) = \perp$. The error vector $\mu$ in this case represents the difference between the shares the adversary should have sent, versus the shares it actually sent.

**Security Under Malicious Dealer.** At a high level, the simulation of a malicious dealer is similar to that of an honest dealer. The main difference is that this simulator must ensure that the dealer does not share a polynomial of too high a degree. This is easily detected by inspecting the shares sent to the degree-test functionality, and the dealer can then be replaced. If the dealer's polynomial is of the appropriate degree, the simulator can compute the value of an additive attack by reconstructing the shared secret and comparing it with the secret that the dealer should have sent.

**Acknowledgments.** This material is based upon work supported by the National Science Foundation under Grants No. #1564088, #1111599, #1514261, #1652259 and #1563722. Daniel Genkin was also supported by financial assistance award 70NANB15H328 from the U.S. Department of Commerce, NIST, the 2017–2018 Rothschild Postdoctoral Fellowship, and DARPA Contract #FA8650-16-C-7622.

# References

1. Beaver, D.: Efficient multiparty protocols using circuit randomization. In: Feigenbaum, J. (ed.) CRYPTO 1991. LNCS, vol. 576, pp. 420–432. Springer, Heidelberg (1992). https://doi.org/10.1007/3-540-46766-1_34

2. Damgård, I., Ishai, Y., Krøigaard, M.: Perfectly secure multiparty computation and the computational overhead of cryptography. In: Gilbert, H. (ed.) EUROCRYPT 2010. LNCS, vol. 6110, pp. 445–465. Springer, Heidelberg (2010). https://doi.org/10.1007/978-3-642-13190-5_23

3. Damgård, I., Ishai, Y., Krøigaard, M., Nielsen, J.B., Smith, A.: Scalable multiparty computation with nearly optimal work and resilience. In: Wagner, D. (ed.) CRYPTO 2008. LNCS, vol. 5157, pp. 241–261. Springer, Heidelberg (2008). https://doi.org/10.1007/978-3-540-85174-5_14

4. Damgård, I., Keller, M., Larraia, E., Pastro, V., Scholl, P., Smart, N.P.: Practical covertly secure MPC for dishonest majority – or: breaking the SPDZ limits. In: Crampton, J., Jajodia, S., Mayes, K. (eds.) ESORICS 2013. LNCS, vol. 8134, pp. 1–18. Springer, Heidelberg (2013). https://doi.org/10.1007/978-3-642-40203-6_1

5. Damgård, I., Nielsen, J.B.: Scalable and unconditionally secure multiparty computation. In: Menezes, A. (ed.) CRYPTO 2007. LNCS, vol. 4622, pp. 572–590. Springer, Heidelberg (2007). https://doi.org/10.1007/978-3-540-74143-5_32

6. Damgård, I., Pastro, V., Smart, N., Zakarias, S.: Multiparty computation from somewhat homomorphic encryption. In: Safavi-Naini, R., Canetti, R. (eds.) CRYPTO 2012. LNCS, vol. 7417, pp. 643–662. Springer, Heidelberg (2012). https://doi.org/10.1007/978-3-642-32009-5_38

7. Damgård, I., Zakarias, S.: Constant-overhead secure computation of Boolean circuits using preprocessing. In: Sahai, A. (ed.) TCC 2013. LNCS, vol. 7785, pp. 621–641. Springer, Heidelberg (2013). https://doi.org/10.1007/978-3-642-36594-2_35

8. Dowsley, R., Müller-Quade, J., Otsuka, A., Hanaoka, G., Imai, H., Nascimento, A.C.A.: Universally composable and statistically secure verifiable secret sharing scheme based on pre-distributed data. IEICE Trans. $94\text{-}\mathbf{A}(2)$, 725–734 (2011)

9. Franklin, M.K., Yung, M.: Communication complexity of secure computation (extended abstract). In: Proceedings of the 24th Annual ACM Symposium on Theory of Computing, pp. 699–710 (1992)

10. Genkin, D., Ishai, Y., Polychroniadou, A.: Efficient multi-party computation: from passive to active security via secure SIMD circuits. In: Gennaro, R., Robshaw, M. (eds.) CRYPTO 2015. LNCS, vol. 9216, pp. 721–741. Springer, Heidelberg (2015). https://doi.org/10.1007/978-3-662-48000-7_35

11. Genkin, D., Ishai, Y., Prabhakaran, M., Sahai, A., Tromer, E.: Circuits resilient to additive attacks with applications to secure computation. In: Symposium on Theory of Computing, STOC 2014, pp. 495–504 (2014)

12. Hazay, C., Orsini, E., Scholl, P., Soria-Vazquez, E.: Efficient MPC from syndrome decoding (or: Honey, I shrunk the keys). IACR Cryptology ePrint Archive 2018:208 (2018)

13. Ishai, Y., Katz, J., Kushilevitz, E., Lindell, Y., Petrank, E.: On achieving the "best of both worlds" in secure multiparty computation. SIAM J. Comput. $\mathbf{40}(1)$, 122–141 (2011)

14. Ishai, Y., Kushilevitz, E., Prabhakaran, M., Sahai, A., Yu, C.-H.: Secure protocol transformations. In: Robshaw, M., Katz, J. (eds.) CRYPTO 2016. LNCS, vol. 9815, pp. 430–458. Springer, Heidelberg (2016). https://doi.org/10.1007/978-3-662-53008-5_15

15. Katz, J.: On achieving the "best of both worlds" in secure multiparty computation. In: Proceedings of the 39th Annual ACM Symposium on Theory of Computing, pp. 11–20 (2007)

16. Nielsen, J.B., Ranellucci, S.: On the computational overhead of MPC with dishonest majority. In: Fehr, S. (ed.) PKC 2017. LNCS, vol. 10175, pp. 369–395. Springer, Heidelberg (2017). https://doi.org/10.1007/978-3-662-54388-7_13

# 3PC ORAM with Low Latency,
# Low Bandwidth, and Fast Batch Retrieval

Stanislaw Jarecki$^{(\boxtimes)}$ and Boyang Wei

University of California, Irvine, USA
{sjarecki,boyanw1}@uci.edu

**Abstract.** Multi-Party Computation of Oblivious RAM (MPC ORAM) implements secret-shared random access memory in a way that protects access pattern privacy against a threshold of corruptions. MPC ORAM enables secure computation of any RAM program on large data held by different entities, e.g. MPC processing of database queries on a secret-shared database. MPC ORAM can be constructed by any (client-server) ORAM, but there is an efficiency gap between known MPC ORAM's and ORAM's. Current asymptotically best MPC ORAM is implied by an "MPC friendly" variant of *Path-ORAM* [26] called *Circuit-ORAM*, due to Wang et al [27]. However, using garbled circuit for Circuit-ORAM's client implies MPC ORAM which matches Path-ORAM in rounds but increases *bandwidth* by $\Omega(\kappa)$ factor, while using GMW or BGW protocols implies MPC ORAM which matches Path-ORAM in bandwidth, but increases *round complexity* by $\Omega(\log n \log \log n)$ factor, where $\kappa$ is a security parameter and $n$ is memory size.

In this paper we bridge the gap between MPC ORAM and client-server ORAM by showing a specialized 3PC ORAM protocol, i.e. MPC ORAM for 3 parties tolerating 1 fault, which uses only symmetric ciphers and asymptotically matches client-server Path-ORAM in round complexity and for large records also in bandwidth.

Our 3PC ORAM also allows for fast pipelined processing: With postponed clean-up it processes $b = O(\log n)$ accesses in $O(b + \log n)$ rounds with $O(D + \mathsf{poly}(\log n))$ bandwidth per item, where $D$ is record size.

## 1 Introduction

**MPC ORAM.** Multi-Party Computation Oblivious Random Access Memory (MPC ORAM), or Secure-Computation ORAM (SC ORAM), is a protocol which lets $m$ parties implement access to a secret-shared memory in such a way that both memory records and the accessed locations remain hidden, and this security guarantee holds as long as no more than $t$ out of $m$ parties are corrupted. Applications of MPC ORAM stem from the fact that it can implement random memory access subprocedure within secure computation of any RAM program. Classic approaches to secure computation [3,8,17,29] express computation as

---

The full version of this paper appears in Cryptology ePrint Archive [21].

© Springer International Publishing AG, part of Springer Nature 2018
B. Preneel and F. Vercauteren (Eds.): ACNS 2018, LNCS 10892, pp. 360–378, 2018.
https://doi.org/10.1007/978-3-319-93387-0_19

a Boolean or arithmetic circuit, thus their size, and consequently efficiency, is inherently lower-bounded by the size of their inputs. In practice this eliminates the possibility of secure computation involving large data, including such fundamental computing functionality as search and information retrieval. MPC ORAM makes such computation feasible because it generalizes secure computation from circuits to RAM programs: All RAM program instruction can be implemented using circuit-based MPC, since they involves only local variables, while access to (large) memory can be implemented with MPC ORAM.

As an application of MPC of RAM program, and hence of MPC ORAM, consider an MPC Database, i.e. an MPC implementation of processing of database queries over a secret-shared database. A typical database implementation would hash a searched keyword to determine an address of a hash table page whose content is then matched against the queried keyword. Standard MPC techniques can implement the hashing step, but the retrieval of the hash page is a random access to a large memory. Implementing this RAM access via garbled circuits requires $\Omega(nD\kappa)$ bandwidth, where $n$ is the number of records, $D$ is the record size, and $\kappa$ is the cryptographic security parameter, which makes such computation unrealistic even for 1MB databases. By contrast, using MPC ORAM can cost $O(\mathsf{poly}(\log n)D\kappa)$ and hence, in principle, can scale to large data.

**Inefficiency Gap in MPC ORAM Constructions.** The general applicability of MPC ORAM to MPC of any RAM program motivates searching for efficient MPC ORAM realizations. As pointed out in [10,23], any ORAM with its client implemented with an MPC protocol yields MPC ORAM. This motivates searching for an ORAM with an MPC-friendly client, i.e. a client which can be efficiently computed using MPC techniques [16,19,22,27,28]. Indeed, the recent *Circuit-ORAM* proposal of Wang et al. [27] exhibits a variant of *Path-ORAM* of Stefanov et al. [26] whose client has a Boolean circuit of an asymptotically optimal size, i.e. a constant factor of the data which Path-ORAM client retrieves from the server, and which forms an input to its computation.

Still, in spite of the circuit-size optimality of Circuit-ORAM,[1] applying generic honest-but-curious MPC protocols to it yields MPC ORAM solutions which are two orders of magnitude more expensive than Path-ORAM.[2] Using Yao's garbled circuit [29] on Circuit-ORAM yields a 2PC ORAM of [27] which has (asymptotically) the same round complexity as Path-ORAM, but its bandwidth, both online and in offline precomputation, is larger by $\Omega(\kappa)$ factor. Alternatively, applying GMW [17] or BGW [3] to the Boolean circuit for Circuit-ORAM yields 2PC or MPC ORAM which asymptotic preserves Path-ORAM bandwidth, but its round complexity is larger by $\Omega(\log n \log \log n)$ factor (compare footnote 3).

---

[1] In this paper we call the client-server ORAM implicit in [27] "Circuit-ORAM", and its garbled-circuit 2PC implementation, also shown in [27], "2PC Circuit-ORAM".

[2] We use Path-ORAM as a client-server baseline for these comparisons because Path-ORAM has the most "MPC-friendly" client, hence most MPC ORAM's emulate securely either Path-ORAM or its predecessor, *Binary-Tree ORAM* [25]. (The recent 2PC ORAM of [12] is an exception, discussed below.).

**Our Contribution: 3PC ORAM with Low Latency *and* Bandwidth**
We show that the gap between MPC ORAM and client-server ORAM can be bridged by exhibiting a 3PC ORAM, i.e. MPC for $m = 3$ servers with $t = 1$ fault, which uses *customized*, i.e. non-generic, 3PC protocols and *asymptotically matches Path-ORAM* in rounds, and, for records size $D = \Omega(\kappa \log^2 n)$, bandwidth. Specifically, our 3PC ORAM securely emulates the Circuit-ORAM client in 3PC setting, using $O(\log n)$ rounds and $O(\kappa \log^3 n + D \log n)$ bandwidth (see Fig. 1). We note that the 3PC setting of $(t, m) = (1, 3)$ gives weaker security than 2PC setting of $(t, m) = (1, 2)$, but it was shown to enable lower-cost solutions to many secure computation problems compared to both 2PC or general $(t, m)$-MPC (e.g. [1,5]) and for that reason it's often chosen in secure computation implementations (e.g. [4,6]). Here we show that 3PC benefits extend to MPC ORAM.

| | rounds | bandwidth |
|---|---|---|
| Path-ORAM ($^{\text{client-server}}_{\text{baseline}}$) [26] | $O(\log n)$ | $O(\log^3 n + D \log n)$ |
| 2PC Circuit-ORAM [27]+[29] | $O(\log n)$ | $O(\kappa \log^3 n + \kappa D \log n)$ |
| 2PC SQRT-ORAM [30] | $O(\log n)$ | $O(\kappa D \sqrt{n} \log^3 n)$ |
| 2PC FLORAM [12] | $O(\log n)$ | $O(\sqrt{\kappa D n} \log n)$ |
| generic 3PC Circ.-ORAM [27]+[1] | $O(\log^2 n \log \log n)$ | $O(\log^3 n + D \log n)$ |
| 3PC ORAM of [14] | $O(\log n)$ | $O(\kappa \lambda \log^3 n + \lambda D \log n)$ |
| *Our 3PC Circuit-ORAM* | $O(\log n)$ | $O(\kappa \log^3 n + D \log n)$ |

**Fig. 1.** Round and bandwidth comparisons, for $n$: array size, $D$: record size, $\kappa$: cryptographic security parameter, $\lambda$: statistical security parameter.

We show the benefits of our 3PC ORAM contrasted with previous 2PC and 3PC ORAM approaches in Fig. 1. In the 3PC setting we include a *generic 3PC Circuit-ORAM*, which results from implementing Circuit-ORAM with the generic 3PC protocol of Araki et al. [1], which is the most efficient 3PC instantiation we know of either the BGW or the GMW framework.[3] The second 3PC ORAM we compare to is Faber et al. [14], which uses non-generic 3PC techniques, like we do, but it emulates in 3PC with a less efficient Binary-Tree ORAM variant than Circuit-ORAM, yielding 3PC ORAM with bandwidth worse than ours by $\Omega(\lambda)$ factor. Regarding 2PC ORAM, several 2PC ORAM's based on Binary-Tree ORAM variants were given prior to Circuit-ORAM [16,19,22,28], but we omit them from Fig. 1 because Circuit-ORAM outperforms them [27]. We include two recent alternative approaches, 2PC ORAM of [30] based on Square-Root ORAM of [18], and 2PC FLORAM of [12] based on the Distributed Point Function (DPF) of [20]. However, both of these 2PC ORAM's use $O(\sqrt{n})$

---

[3] Using the BGW-style MPC over an *arithmetic* circuit for Circuit-ORAM, as was done by Keller and Scholl for another Path-ORAM variant [22], should also yield a bandwidth-competitive 3PC ORAM, but with round complexity at least $\Omega(\log^2 n)$.

bandwidth, and [12] also uses $O(n)$ local computation, which makes them not scale well for large $n$'s.[4] Restricting the comparison to poly($\log n$) MPC ORAM, our 3PC ORAM offers the following trade-offs:

(1) Compared to the *generic* 3PC Circuit-ORAM [1] applied to Circuit-ORAM, we increase bandwidth from $O(\log^3 n + D\log n)$ to $O(\kappa\log^3 n + D\log n)$ but reduce round complexity from $O(\log^2 n \log\log n)$ to $O(\log n)$;
(2) Compared to the *generic* garbled circuit 2PC [29] applied to Circuit-ORAM, we weaken the security model, from $(t, m) = (1, 2)$ to $(t, m) = (1, 3)$, but reduce bandwidth from $O(\kappa\log^3 n + \kappa D\log n)$ to $O(\kappa\log^3 n + D\log n)$.

Thus for medium-sized records, $D = \Omega(\kappa\log^2 n)$, our 3PC ORAM asymptotically matches client-server Path-ORAM in all aspects, and beats 2PC Circuit-ORAM by $\Omega(\kappa)$ factor in bandwidth, without dramatic increase in round complexity incurred using generic 3PC techniques. In concrete terms, our round complexity is 50x lower than the generic 3PC Circuit-ORAM,[5] and, for $D > 1\,\text{KB}$, our bandwidth is also >50x lower than 2PC Circuit-ORAM. Our protocol is also competitive for small record sizes, e.g. $D = 4B$: First, our bandwidth is only about 2x larger than the generic 3PC Circuit-ORAM; Second, our bandwidth is lower than the 2PC Circuit-ORAM by a factor between 10x and 20x for $20 \leq \log n \leq 30$.

**Fast System Response and Batch Retrieval.** Another benefit of our 3PC ORAM is a fast system response, i.e. the time we call a *Retrieval Phase*, from an access request to the retrieval of the record. In fact, our protocol supports fast retrieval of a *batch* of requests, because the expensive post-processing of each access (i.e. the Circuit-ORAM eviction procedure) can be postponed for a batch of requests, allowing all of them to be processed at a smaller cost. Low-bandwidth batch retrieval with postponed eviction was recently shown for client-server Path-ORAM variants [11,24] (see also [15]), and our protocol allows MPC ORAM to match this property in the 3PC setting.

Specifically, our protocol processes $b = O(\log n)$ requests in $3b + 3h$ rounds, using $3D + O(\log^2 n \log\log n)$ bandwidth per record, and to the best of our knowledge no other MPC ORAM allows batch-processing with such costs. After retrieving $b$ requests the protocol must perform all evictions, using $6b$ rounds and $O(b(\kappa\log^3 n + D\log n))$ total bandwidth, but this can be postponed for any batch size that benefits the higher-level MPC application. Concretely, for $\log n \leq 30$, the per-record bandwidth for $b \leq 4\log n$ is only $\leq 3D + 10\,\text{KB}$.

**Brief Overview of our 3PC ORAM.** We sketch the main ideas behind our 3PC protocol that emulates Circuit-ORAM ORAM. Observe that

---

[4] 2PC ORAM cost of [12] has stash linear scan $O(T\kappa\log n)$ and amortized re-init $O(nD/T)$. Picking $T = O(\sqrt{nD/\kappa\log n})$ we get $O(\sqrt{\kappa Dn\log n})$. In [12] this is rendered as $O(\sqrt{n})$ *overhead*, assuming $D = \Omega(\log n)$ and omitting $\kappa$. [12] also show $O(1)$-round 2PC ORAM, but at the price of increased bandwidth and computation.
[5] We estimate that the circuit depth of the Circuit-ORAM client, and hence the round complexity of the generic 3PC Circuit-ORAM, is > 1000 even for $n = 2^{20}$, compared to $\approx 15$ rounds in our 3PC ORAM and $\approx 8$ in the client-server Path-ORAM.

Circuit-ORAM client, like a client in any Binary-Tree ORAM variant, performs the following steps: (1) locate the searched record in the retrieved tree path, (2) post-process that record (free-up its current location, update its labels, and add the modified record to the path root), (3) determine the *eviction map*, i.e. the permutation on positions in the retrieved path according to which the records will be moved in eviction, and (4) move the records on the path according to the eviction map. The main design principle in our 3PC emulation of Circuit-ORAM is to implement steps (1), (2), and (4) using *customized* asymptotically bandwidth-optimal *and* constant-round protocols (we explain some of the challenges involved in Sect. 2), and leave the eviction map computation step as in 2PC Circuit-ORAM, implemented with *generic* constant-round secure computation, namely garbled circuits. Circuit-ORAM computes the eviction map via data-dependent scans, which we do not know how to implement in constant rounds without the garbled circuit overhead. However, computation of the eviction map involves only on metadata, and is independent of record payloads. Hence even though using garbled circuits in this step takes $O(\kappa)$ bandwidth per input bit, this is upper-bounded by the cost of bandwidth-optimal realization of the data movement step (4) already for $D \approx 140B$.

Secondly, we utilize the 3PC setting in the retrieval phase, to keep its bandwidth especially low, namely $O(D + \log^2 n \log \log n)$. The key ingredient is a 3-party *Secret-Shared* PIR (SS-PIR) gadget, which computes a secret-sharing of record M[N] given a secret-sharing of array M and of address N. We construct SS-PIR from any 2-server PIR [13] whose servers' responses form an xor-sharing of the retrieved record, which is the case for many 2-PIR schemes [2,9,20]. Another component is a one-round bandwidth-optimal compiler from 3PC SS-PIR to 3PC *Keyword* SS-PIR, which retrieves shared value given a sharing of keyword and of (keyword,value) list. With a careful design we use *only three rounds* for the retrieval and post-processing steps, which allows pipelined processing of a batch of accesses using *only three rounds* per tree.

**Roadmap.** We overview the technical challenges of our construction in Sect. 2. We present our 3PC ORAM protocol in Sect. 3, argue its security in Sect. 4, and discuss our prototype performance in Sect. 5. For lack of space, all specialized sub-protocols our protocol requires are deferred to [21], Appendix A. The full security argument, the specification of garbled circuits we use, and further prototype performance data, are all included in [21], Appendices B-E.

## 2    Technical Overview

**Overview of Path ORAM [26].** Our 3PC Circuit-ORAM is a 3PC secure computation of Circuit-ORAM of [27] (see footnote 1), which is a variant of Path-ORAM of Shi et al. [26]. We thus start by recalling Path-ORAM of [26], casting it in terms which are convenient in our context. Let M be an array of $n$ records of size $D$ each. Server S keeps a binary tree of depth $\log n$, denoted tree, shown in Fig. 2, where each node is a bucket of a small constant size $w$, except

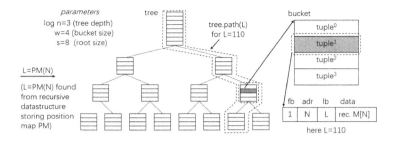

**Fig. 2.** Path ORAM (*final*) tree

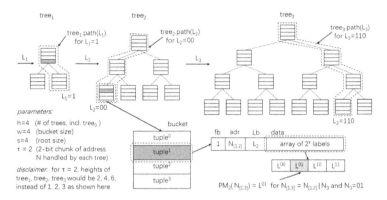

**Fig. 3.** Path ORAM recursive access

the root bucket (a.k.a. a *stash*) which has size $s = O(\log n)$. Each tree bucket is a list of *tuples*, which are records with four fields, fb, lb, adr, and data. For each address $N \in \{0,1\}^{\log n}$, record M[N] is stored in a unique tuple T in tree s.t. T.(fb, lb, adr, data) $= (1, L, N, M[N])$ where fb is a full/empty tuple status bit and L is a *label* which defines a tree leaf assigned at random to address N.

Data-structure tree satisfies an invariant that a tuple with label L lies in a bucket on the path from the root to leaf L, denoted tree.path(L). To access address N, client C uses a (recursive) *position map* PM : N → L (see below) to find leaf L corresponding to N, sends L to S to retrieve path = tree.path(L), searches path for T $= (1, L, N, M[N])$ with fields (fb, adr) matching $(1, N)$, assigns new random leaf L′ to N, adds a modified tuple T′ $= (1, L′, N, M[N])$ to the root bucket in path (In case of *write* access C also replaces M[N] in T′ with a new entry), and erase old T from path by flipping T.fb to 0. Finally, to avoid overflow, C evicts tuples in path as far down as possible without breaking the invariant or overflowing any bucket.

Position map PM : N → L is stored using the same data-structure, with each tuple storing labels corresponding to a batch of $2^\tau$ consecutive addresses, for some constant $\tau$. Since such position map has only $2^{\log n}/2^\tau = 2^{\log n - \tau}$ entries, this recursion results in $h = (\log n/\tau) + 1$ trees $tree_0, , .., tree_{h-1}$ which work as follows (see Fig. 3): Divide N into $\tau$-bit blocks $N_1, ..., N_{h-1}$. The top-level tree, $tree_{h-1}$ contains the records of M as described above, shown in Fig. 2, while for

$i < h-1$, $\mathsf{tree}_i$ is a binary tree of depth $d_i = i\tau$ which implements position map $\mathsf{PM}_i$ that matches address prefix $\mathsf{N}_{[1,...,i+1]} = \mathsf{N}_1|...|\mathsf{N}_{i+1}$ to leaf $\mathsf{L}_{i+1}$ assigned to this prefix in $\mathsf{tree}_{i+1}$. Access algorithm ORAM.Access traverses this data-structure by sequentially retrieving the labels assigned to each prefix of the searched-for address, using an algorithm we denote ORAM.ML For $i$ from 0 to $h-1$, algorithm ORAM.ML retrieves $\mathsf{L}_{i+1} = \mathsf{PM}_i(\mathsf{N}_1|...|\mathsf{N}_{i+1})$ from $\mathsf{tree}_i$ using the following steps: (1) it identifies path $\mathsf{path} = \mathsf{tree}_i.\mathsf{path}(\mathsf{L}_i)$ in $\mathsf{tree}_i$ using label $\mathsf{L}_i$, (2) it identifies tuple $\mathsf{T}$ in $\mathsf{path}$ s.t. $\mathsf{T}.\mathsf{adr} = \mathsf{N}_1|...|\mathsf{N}_i$, and (3) it returns $\mathsf{L}_{i+1} = \mathsf{T}.\mathsf{data}[\mathsf{N}_{i+1}]$.

**Circuit-ORAM vs. Path-ORAM.** Circuit-ORAM (see footnote 1) follows the same algorithm as Path-ORAM except (1) the eviction procedure is *restricted* in that it moves only selected tuples down the path in $\mathsf{path}$, as we discuss further below; and (2) it performs the eviction on two paths in each tree per access. Our 3PC emulation of Circuit-ORAM also runs twice per each tree per access, but since the second execution is limited to eviction, for simplicity of presentation we omit it in all discussion below, except when we report performance data.

**Top-Level Design of 3PC Circuit-ORAM.** The client algorithm in all variants of Binary-Tree ORAM, which includes Path-ORAM and Circuit-ORAM, consists of the following phases:

1. *Retrieval*, which given $\mathsf{path} = \mathsf{tree}.\mathsf{path}(\mathsf{L})$ and address prefix N, locates tuple $\mathsf{T} = (1, \mathsf{L}, \mathsf{N}, \mathsf{data})$ in $\mathsf{path}$ and retrieves next-level label (or record) in $\mathsf{data}$;
2. *Post-Process*, which removes $\mathsf{T}$ from $\mathsf{path}$, injects new labels into $\mathsf{T}$, and re-inserts it in the root (=stash);
3. *Eviction*, which can be divided into two sub-steps:
   (a) *Eviction Logic*: An eviction map EM is computed, by function denoted Route, on input label L and the *metadata* fields $(\mathsf{fb}, \mathsf{lb})$ of tuples in $\mathsf{path}$,
   (b) *Data Movement*: Permute tuples in $\mathsf{path}$ according to map EM.

Our 3PC ORAM is a secure emulation of the above procedure, with the Eviction Logic function Route instantiated as in Circuit-ORAM, and it performs all the above steps on the *sharings* of inputs $\mathsf{tree}$ and N, given label L as a public input known to all parties. With the exception of the next-level label recovered in Retrieval, all other variables remain secret-shared. Our implementation of the above steps resembles the 3PC ORAM emulation of Binary-Tree ORAM by [14] in that we use garbled circuit for Eviction Logic, and specialized 3PC protocols for Retrieval, Post-Process, and Data Movement. However, our implementations are different from [14]: First, to enable low-bandwidth batch processing of retrieval we use different sharings and protocols in Retrieval and Post-Process. Second, to securely "glue" Eviction Logic and Data Movement we need to mask mapping EM computed by Eviction Logic and implement Data Movement given this masked mapping. We explain both points in more detail below.

**Low-Bandwidth 3PC Retrieval.** The Retrieval phase realizes a *Keyword Secret-Shared PIR* (Kw-SS-PIR) functionality: The parties hold a *sharing* of an array of (keyword, value) pairs, and a *sharing* of a searched-for keyword, and the protocol must output a *sharing* of the value in the (keyword, value) pair that contains the matching keyword. In our case the address prefix $N_{[1,i]}$ is the searched-for keyword and path is the array of the (keyword, value) pairs where keywords are address fields adr and values are payload fields data.

The 3PC implementation of Retrieval in [14] has $O(\ell D)$ bandwidth where $\ell = O(\log n)$ is the number of tuples in path, and here we reduce it to $3D + O(\ell \log \ell)$ as follows: First, we re-use the *Keyword Search* protocol KSearch of [14] to create a secret-sharing of index $j$ of a location of the keyword-matching tuple in path. This subprotocol reduces the problem to finding an index where a secret-shared array of length $\ell$ contains an all-zero string, which has $\Theta(\ell \log \ell)$ communication complexity. Our KSearch implementation has $2\ell(c + \log \ell)$ bandwidth where $2^{-c}$ is the probability of having to re-run KSearch because of collisions in $\ell$ pairs of $(c + \log \ell)$-bit hash values. The overall bandwidth is optimal for $c \approx \log \log \ell$, but we report performance numbers for $c = 20$.

Secondly, we use a *Secret-Shared PIR* (SS-PIR) protocol, which creates a fresh sharing of the $j$-th record given the shared array and the shared index $j$. We implement SS-PIR in two rounds from any 2-server PIR [13] whose servers' PIR responses form an xor-sharing of the retrieved record. Many 2-PIR's have this property, e.g. [2,9,20], but we exemplify this generic construction with the simplest form of 2-server PIR of Chor et al. [9] which has $3\ell + 3D$ bandwidth. This is not optimal in $\ell$, but in our case $\ell \leq 150 + b$ where $b$ is the number of accesses with postponed eviction, the optimized version of SS-PIR sends only $\approx \ell + 3D$ bits *on-line*, and KSearch already sends $O(\ell \log \ell)$ bits. Our generic 2-PIR to 3PC-SS-PIR compiler is simple (a variant of it appeared in [20]) but the 3-round 3PC Kw-SS-PIR protocol is to the best of our knowledge novel.

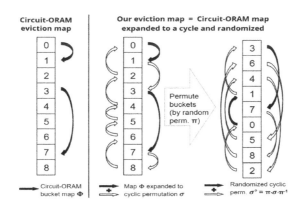

**Fig. 4.** Randomization of circuit ORAM's bucket map

**Efficient 3PC Circuit-ORAM Eviction.** In Eviction we use a simple Data Movement protocol, with 2 round and $\approx 2|path|$ bandwidth. With three parties denoted as $(C, D, E)$, our protocol creates a two-party $(C, E)$-sharing of path$' = $ EM(path) from a $(C, E)$-sharing of path *if* party D holds eviction map EM in the clear. Naively outputting $\mathsf{EM} = \mathsf{Route}(\mathsf{path})$ to party $\mathsf{D}$ is insecure, as eviction map is correlated with the ORAM access pattern, so the question is whether $\mathsf{EM}$ can be *masked* by some randomizing permutation known by $\mathsf{C}$ and $\mathsf{E}$. [14] had an easy solution for its binary tree ORAM variant because its algorithm Route outputs a *regular* $\mathsf{EM}$, that buckets on every except the last level of the retrieved path always move two tuples down to the next level, so all [14] needed to do is to randomly permute tuples on each bucket level of path, and the resulting new $\mathsf{EM}'$ on the permuted path leaks no information on $\mathsf{EM}$. By contrast, Circuit-ORAM eviction map is *non-regular* (see Fig. 4): Its bucket level map $\varPhi$ of $\mathsf{EM}$ can move a tuple by variable distance and can leave some buckets untouched, both of which are correlated with the density of tuples in path, and thus with ORAM access pattern.

Thus our goal is to transform the underlying Circuit-ORAM eviction map $\mathsf{EM} = (\varPhi, \mathsf{t})$ into a map whose distribution does not depend on the data ($\varPhi$ describes the bucket-level movement, while $\mathsf{t}$ is an array containing one tuple index from each bucket that will be moved). We do so in two steps. First, we add an extra empty tuple to each bucket and we modify Circuit-ORAM algorithm Route to *expand* function $\varPhi : \mathsf{Z}_d \rightarrow \mathsf{Z}_d \cup \{\bot\}$ into a cyclic permutation $\sigma$ on $\mathsf{Z}_d$ ($d$ is the depth of path, $\mathsf{Z}_d$ is the set $\{0, ..., d-1\}$), by adding spurious edges to $\varPhi$ in the deterministic way illustrated in Fig. 4. Second, we apply two types of masks to the resulting output $(\sigma, \mathsf{t})$ of Route, namely a random permutation $\pi$ on $\mathsf{Z}_d$ and two arrays $(\delta, \rho)$, each of which contains a random tuple index in each bucket. Our Eviction Logic protocol will use $(\pi, \delta, \rho)$ to mask $(\sigma, \mathsf{t})$ by computing $(\sigma^\circ, \mathsf{t}^\circ)$ s.t. $\sigma^\circ = \pi \cdot \sigma \cdot \pi^{-1}$ (permutation composition) and $\mathsf{t}^\circ = \rho \oplus \pi(\mathsf{t} \oplus \delta)$. And now we have a masked eviction map $\mathsf{EM}_{\sigma^\circ, \mathsf{t}^\circ}$ that can be revealed to party $\mathsf{D}$ but does not leak information on $\mathsf{EM}_{\sigma, \mathsf{t}}$ or $\mathsf{EM}_{\varPhi, \mathsf{t}}$.

# 3    Our Protocol: 3PC Emulation of Circuit-ORAM

**Protocol Parties.** We use $\mathsf{C}, \mathsf{D}, \mathsf{E}$ to denote the three parties participating in 3PC-ORAM. We use $x^\mathsf{P}$ to denote that variable $x$ is known only to party $\mathsf{P} \in \{\mathsf{C}, \mathsf{D}, \mathsf{E}\}$, $x^{\mathsf{P}_1 \mathsf{P}_2}$ if $x$ is known to $\mathsf{P}_1$ and $\mathsf{P}_2$, and $x$ if known to all parties.

**Shared Variables, Bitstrings, Secret-Sharing.** Each pair of parties $\mathsf{P}_1, \mathsf{P}_2$ in our protocol is initialized with a shared seed to a Pseudorandom Generator (PRG), which allows them to generate any number of shared (pseudo)random objects. We write $x^{\mathsf{P}_1 \mathsf{P}_2} \xleftarrow{\$} \mathsf{S}$ if $\mathsf{P}_1$ and $\mathsf{P}_2$ both sample $x$ uniformly from set $\mathsf{S}$ using the PRG on a jointly held seed. We use several forms of secret-sharing, and here introduce four of them which are used in our high level protocols 3PC-ORAM.Access and 3PC-ORAM.ML (Algorithms 1 and 2):

$$\langle x \rangle = (x_1^{\mathsf{DE}}, x_2^{\mathsf{CE}}, x_3^{\mathsf{CD}}) \text{ for } x_1, x_2, x_3 \xleftarrow{\$} \{0,1\}^{|x|} \text{ where } x_1 \oplus x_2 \oplus x_3 = x$$

$$\langle x \rangle_{\mathsf{xor}}^{\mathsf{P}_1 - \mathsf{P}_2} = (x_1^{\mathsf{P}_1}, x_2^{\mathsf{P}_2}) \text{ for } x_1, x_2 \xleftarrow{\$} \{0,1\}^{|x|} \text{ where } x_1 \oplus x_2 = x$$

$$\langle x \rangle_{\mathsf{shift}}^{\mathsf{P}_1 \mathsf{P}_2 - \mathsf{P}_3} = (x_{12}^{\mathsf{P}_1 \mathsf{P}_2}, x_3^{\mathsf{P}_3}) \text{ for } x \in \mathsf{Z}_m, x_{12}, x_3 \xleftarrow{\$} \mathsf{Z}_m \text{ s.t. } x_{12} + x_3 = x \bmod m$$

$$\langle x \rangle_{\mathsf{shift}} = (\langle x \rangle_{\mathsf{shift}}^{\mathsf{CD} - \mathsf{E}}, \langle x \rangle_{\mathsf{shift}}^{\mathsf{CE} - \mathsf{D}}, \langle x \rangle_{\mathsf{shift}}^{\mathsf{DE} - \mathsf{C}})$$

**Integer Ranges, Permutations.** We define $Z_n$ as set $\{0, ..., n-1\}$, and $\mathsf{perm}_n$ as the set of permutations on $Z_n$. If $\pi, \sigma \in \mathsf{perm}_n$ then $\pi^{-1}$ is an inverse permutation of $\pi$, and $\pi \cdot \sigma$ is a composition of $\sigma$ and $\pi$, i.e. $(\pi \cdot \sigma)(i) = \pi(\sigma(i))$.

**Arrays.** We use $\mathsf{array}^m[\ell]$ to denote arrays of $\ell$ bitstrings of size $m$, and we write $\mathsf{array}[\ell]$ if $m$ is implicit. We use $x[i]$ to denote the $i$-th item in array $x$. Note that $x \in \mathsf{array}^m[\ell]$ can also be viewed as a bitstring in $\{0,1\}^{\ell m}$.

**Permutations, Arrays, Array Operations.** Permutation $\sigma \in \mathsf{perm}_\ell$ can be viewed as an array $x \in \mathsf{array}^{\log \ell}[\ell]$, i.e. $x = [\sigma(0), ..., \sigma(\ell-1)]$. For $\pi \in \mathsf{perm}_\ell$ and $y \in \mathsf{array}[\ell]$ we use $\pi(y)$ to denote an array containing elements of $y$ permuted according to $\pi$, i.e. $\pi(y) = [y_{\pi^{-1}(0)}, ..., y_{\pi^{-1}(\ell-1)}]$.

**Garbled Circuit Wire Keys.** If variable $x \in \{0,1\}^m$ is an input/output in circuit $C$, and $\mathsf{wk} \in \mathsf{array}^\kappa[m, 2]$ is the set of wire key pairs corresponding to this variable in the garbled version of $C$, then $\{\mathsf{wk} : x\} \in \mathsf{array}^\kappa[m]$ denotes the wire-key representation of value $x$ on these wires, i.e. $\{\mathsf{wk} : x\} = \{\mathsf{wk}[x[i]]\}_{i=1}^m$. If the set of keys is implicit we will denote $\{\mathsf{wk} : x\}$ as $\overline{x}$.

---

**Algorithm 1.** 3PC-ORAM.Access: 3PC Circuit-ORAM

---

**Params:** Address size $\log n$, address chunk size $\tau$, number of trees $h = \frac{\log n}{\tau} + 1$

**Input:** $\langle \mathsf{OM}, \mathsf{N}, \mathsf{rec}' \rangle$, for $\mathsf{OM} = (\mathsf{tree}_0, ..., \mathsf{tree}_{h-1})$, $\mathsf{N} = (\mathsf{N}_1, ..., \mathsf{N}_{h-1})$

**Output:** $\langle \mathsf{rec} \rangle$: record stored in $\mathsf{OM}$ at address $\mathsf{N}$

1: $\{\langle L'_i \rangle \xleftarrow{\$} \{0,1\}^{i \cdot \tau}\}_{i=1}^{h-1}$ ;   $\langle \mathsf{N}_0, \mathsf{N}_h, L'_0, L'_h \rangle := \bot$ ;   $L_0 := \bot$

2: **for** $i = 0$ **to** $h-1$ **do**

$\quad$ 3PC-ORAM.ML: $L_i, \langle \mathsf{tree}_i, (\mathsf{N}_0|...|\mathsf{N}_i), \mathsf{N}_{i+1}, L'_i, L'_{i+1}, {}^* \mathsf{rec}' \rangle$

$\qquad\qquad \longrightarrow \quad L_{i+1}$ (* $\langle \mathsf{rec} \rangle$ instead of $L_{i+1}$), $\langle \mathsf{tree}_i \rangle$

---

\*: On top-level ORAM tree, i.e. $i = h - 1$

**3PC ORAM Protocol.** Our 3PC ORAM protocol, 3PC-ORAM.Access, Algorithm 1, performs the same recursive scan through data-structure $\mathsf{tree}_0, ..., \mathsf{tree}_{h-1}$ as the client-server Path-ORAM (and Circuit-ORAM) described in Sect. 2, except it runs on inputs in $\langle \cdot \rangle$ secret-sharing format. The main loop of 3PC-ORAM.Access, i.e. protocol 3PC-ORAM.ML, Algorithm 2, also follows the corresponding client-server algorithm ORAM.ML, except that apart of the current-level leaf label L which is known to all parties, all its other inputs are secret-shared as well.

$\quad$ Protocol 3PC-ORAM.ML calls subprotocols whose round/bandwidth specifications are stated in Fig. 5. (We omit computation costs because they are all comparable to link-encryption of communicated data). The low costs of these subprotocols are enabled by different forms of secret-sharings, e.g. xor versus additive, or 2-party versus 3-party, and by low-cost (or no cost) conversions between them. For implementations of these protocols we refer to [21] Appendix A.

---

**Algorithm 2.** 3PC-ORAM.ML: Main Loop of 3PC Circuit-ORAM

---

**Param:** Tree level index $i$. path depth $d$ (number of buckets). Bucket size $w$.

**Input:** $L_i$, $\langle \text{tree}, N, \Delta N, L'_i, L'_{i+1} \rangle$ ($*\langle \text{rec}' \rangle$)

**Output:** (1) $L_{i+1} = \text{T.data}[\Delta N]$ for tuple $T$ on $\text{tree.path}(L_i)$ s.t.
$\quad\quad$ T.(fb|adr) = 1|N ($*\langle \text{rec} \rangle := \langle \text{T.data} \rangle$)
$\quad\quad$ (2) $\langle \text{tree.path}(L) \rangle$ modified by eviction, with $\text{T.lb} := L'_i$ and
$\quad\quad$ $\text{T.data}[\Delta N] := L'_{i+1}$ ($*$ T.data := rec')

**Offline:** pick $(\pi, \delta, \rho)^{CE}$, for $\pi \xleftarrow{\$} \text{perm}_d$, $\delta, \rho \xleftarrow{\$} \text{array}^{\log(w+1)}[d]$

## Retrieval of Next Label/Record ##

$\quad \langle \text{path} \rangle := \langle \text{tree.path}(L_i) \rangle$

1: KSearch: $\langle \text{path.(fb|adr)}, 1|N \rangle \rightarrow \langle j \rangle_{\text{shift}}$ $\quad\quad\quad \triangleright$ path[$j$].(fb|adr) = 1|N

2: 3ShiftPIR: $\langle \text{path.data} \rangle, \langle j \rangle_{\text{shift}} \rightarrow \langle X \rangle$ ($*\langle \text{rec} \rangle := \langle X \rangle$) $\quad \triangleright X = \text{path}[j].\text{data}$

3: 3ShiftXorPIR: $\langle \text{path.data}, \Delta N \rangle, \langle j \rangle_{\text{shift}} \rightarrow L_{i+1}(*\text{skip}) \triangleright L_{i+1} = \text{path}[j].\text{data}[\Delta N]$

## Post-Process of Found Tuple ##

4: ULiT: $\langle X, N, \Delta N, L'_i, L'_{i+1} (* \text{rec}') \rangle, L_{i+1} \rightarrow \langle T \rangle$

$\quad\quad\quad\quad\quad\quad\quad\quad \triangleright X[\Delta N] := L'_{i+1}$ ($* X := \text{rec}'$), $T = (1, N, L'_i, X)$

5: FlipFlag: $\langle \text{path.fb} \rangle, \langle j \rangle_{\text{shift}} \rightarrow \langle \text{path.fb} \rangle$ $\quad\quad\quad\quad \triangleright$ path[$j$].fb := 0

$\quad \langle \text{path} \rangle := \langle \text{path.append-to-root}(T) \rangle$

## Eviction ##

6: GC(Route): $L_i, \delta^{CE}, \langle \text{path.(fb, lb)} \rangle \rightarrow (\overline{\sigma}, t')^D$, $\text{wk}^E$

$\quad \triangleright \overline{\sigma} = \{\text{wk} : \sigma\}$ and $t' = t \oplus \delta$ for expanded Circ-ORAM eviction map $(\sigma, t)$

7: PermBuckets: $\overline{\sigma}^D, \pi^{CE}, \text{wk}^E \rightarrow \sigma^{\circ D}$ $\quad\quad\quad\quad\quad\quad \triangleright \sigma^{\circ} = \pi \cdot \sigma \cdot \pi^{-1}$

8: PermTuples: $t'^D, (\pi, \rho)^{CE} \rightarrow t^{\circ D}$ $\quad\quad\quad\quad\quad\quad\quad \triangleright t^{\circ} = \rho \oplus \pi(t')$

9: XOT: $\langle \text{path} \rangle, (\pi, \delta, \rho)^{CE}, (\sigma^{\circ}, t^{\circ})^D \rightarrow \langle \text{path}' \rangle$ $\quad\quad \triangleright$ path' = $\text{EM}_{\sigma,t}(\text{path})$

$\quad \langle \text{tree.path}(L_i) \rangle := \langle \text{path}' \rangle$

---

$*$: On top-level ORAM tree, i.e. $i = h - 1$.  $\quad \triangleright$: Comments.

**Three Phases of 3PC-ORAM.ML:** Protocol 3PC-ORAM.ML computes on sharing $\langle \text{path} \rangle$ for path = tree.path(L) and it contains the same three phases as the client-server Path-ORAM, but implemented with specialized 3PC protocols:

**(1) Retrieval** runs protocol KSearch to compute "shift" (i.e. additive) sharing $\langle j \rangle_{\text{shift}}$ of index for tuple $T = \text{path}[j]$ in path s.t. path[$j$].adr = N and path[$j$].fb = 1, i.e. it is the unique (and non-empty) tuple pertaining to address prefix N; Then it runs protocol 3ShiftPIR to extract sharing $\langle X \rangle$ of the payload $X = \text{path}[j].\text{data}$ of this tuple, given sharings $\langle \text{path} \rangle$ and $\langle j \rangle_{\text{shift}}$; In parallel to 3ShiftPIR it also runs protocol 3ShiftXorPIR to publicly reconstruct the next-level label stored at position $\Delta N$ in this tuple's payload, i.e. $L_{i+1} = (\text{path}[j].\text{data})[\Delta N]$, given sharing

| | rounds | bandwidth |
|---|---|---|
| KSearch | 2 | $\approx 2\ell(c + \log \ell)$ |
| 3ShiftPIR | 2 | $3\ell + 3\lvert \text{data}\rvert$ for $\lvert \text{data}\rvert = 2^\tau \lvert \text{L}\rvert$ |
| 3ShiftXorPIR | 2 | $3 \cdot 2^\tau \ell + 6\lvert \text{L}\rvert$ |
| ULiT | 2 | $\approx 4\lvert \text{data}\rvert$ $(+4\lvert \text{data}\rvert$ offline$)$ |
| FlipFlag | 2 | $4\ell$ |
| GC(Route) | 1 | $2\lvert x\rvert \kappa$ $(+4\lvert \text{circ}\rvert + 2\lvert x\rvert)\kappa$ offline$)$ |
| PermBuckets | 2 | $3d \log d$ $(+d^2(\kappa + 2\log d) + 3d\log d$ offline$)$ |
| PermTuples | 2 | $2d(w+1)$ $(+d(w+1)$ offline$)$ |
| XOT | 3 | $4\lvert \text{path}\rvert + 2\ell \log(\ell)$ $(+2\lvert \text{path}\rvert$ offline$)$ |

**Fig. 5.** Round and bandwidth for subprotocols of Algorithm 2, for $\ell$ the number of tuples on path and $x$ the circuit input size $(\approx \ell(d + \log n) + d\log(w + 1))$

$\langle \text{path} \rangle$ and $\langle \Delta \text{N} \rangle$. This construction of the Retrieval emulation allows for presenting protocols 3ShiftPIR and 3ShiftXorPIR (see resp. Algorithm 9 and 11 in [21], Appendix A) as *generic* SS-PIR constructions from a class of 2-Server PIR protocols. However, a small modification of this design achieves better round *and* on-line bandwidth parameters, see an *Optimizations and Efficiency Discussion* paragraph below.

**(2) Post-process** runs the Update-Label-in-Tuple protocol ULiT to form sharing $\langle \text{T} \rangle$ of a new tuple using sharing $\langle X \rangle$ of the retrieved tuple's payload, sharings $\langle \text{N} \rangle$ and $\langle \Delta \text{N} \rangle$ of the address prefix and the next address chunk, and sharings $\langle \text{L}'_i \rangle, \langle \text{L}'_{i+1} \rangle$ of new labels; In parallel to ULiT it also runs protocol FlipFlag to flip the full/empty flag to 0 in the old version of this tuple in path, which executes on inputs the sharings $\langle \text{path.fb} \rangle$ of field fb of tuples in path and on the "shift" sharing $\langle j \rangle_{\text{shift}}$; Once ULiT terminates the parties can insert $\langle \text{T} \rangle$ into sharing of the root bucket in path. At this point the root bucket has size $s+1$ (or $s+b$ if we postpone eviction for a batch of $b$ accesses).

**(3) Eviction** emulates Circuit-ORAM eviction on sharing $\langle \text{path} \rangle$ involved in retrieval (or another path because 3PC-ORAM.Access, just like client-server Circuit-ORAM, performs eviction on two paths per access). It uses the generic garbled circuit protocol GC(Route) to compute the Circuit-ORAM eviction map (appropriately masked), and then runs protocols PermBuckets, PermTuples, and XOT to apply this (masked) eviction map to the secret-shared $\langle \text{path} \rangle$. We discuss the eviction steps in more details below.

**Eviction Procedure.** As we explain in Sect. 2, we split Eviction into Eviction Logic, which uses garbled circuit subprotocol to compute the eviction map EM, and Eviction Movement, which uses special-purpose protocols to apply EM to the shared path, which in protocol 3PC-ORAM.ML will be $\langle \text{path} \rangle$. However, recall that revealing the eviction map to any party would leak information about path density, and consequently the access pattern. We avoid this leakage in two steps: First, we modify the Circuit-ORAM eviction logic computation Route, so that when it computes bucket-level map $\Phi$ and the tuple pointers array t, which define an eviction map $\mathsf{EM}_{\Phi,\mathsf{t}}$, the algorithm scans through the buckets once more to *expand* the partial map $\Phi$ into a complete cycle $\sigma$ over the $d$ buckets (see Fig. 4). (We include the modified Circuit-ORAM algorithm Route in [21], Appendix D.) Second, the garbled circuit computation $\mathsf{GC}(\mathsf{Route})$, see Step 6, Algorithm 2, does not output $(\sigma,\mathsf{t})$ to $\mathsf{D}$ in the clear: Instead, it outputs $\mathsf{t}'=\mathsf{t}\oplus\delta$ where $\delta$ is a random array, used here as a one-time pad, and the *garbled wire encoding* of the bits of $\sigma=[\sigma(1),...,\sigma(d)]$, i.e. the output wire keys $\{\mathsf{wk}:\sigma\}=\mathsf{wk}[i][\sigma[i]]\}_{i=1}^{d\log d}$.

Recall that we want $\mathsf{D}$ to compute $(\sigma^\circ,\mathsf{t}^\circ)$, a masked version of $(\sigma,\mathsf{t})$, where $\sigma^\circ=\pi\cdot\sigma\cdot\pi^{-1}$ and $\mathsf{t}^\circ=\rho\oplus\pi(\mathsf{t}\oplus\delta)$, for $\pi$ a random permutation on $\mathsf{Z}_d$ and $\delta,\rho$ random arrays, all picked by $\mathsf{C}$ and $\mathsf{E}$. This is done by protocol PermBuckets, which takes 2 on-line rounds to let $\mathsf{D}$ translate $\{\mathsf{wk}:\sigma\}$ into $\sigma^\circ=\pi\cdot\sigma\cdot\pi^{-1}$ given $\mathsf{wk}$ held by $\mathsf{E}$ and $\pi$ held by $\mathsf{C},\mathsf{E}$, and (in parallel) PermTuples, which takes 2 rounds to let $\mathsf{D}$ translate $\mathsf{t}'=\mathsf{t}\oplus\delta$ into $\mathsf{t}^\circ=\rho\oplus\pi(\mathsf{t}')$ given $\pi,\rho$ held by $\mathsf{C},\mathsf{E}$. Then $\mathsf{C},\mathsf{E}$ permute $\langle\mathsf{path}\rangle_{\mathsf{xor}}^{\mathsf{C-E}}$ (implied by $\langle\mathsf{path}\rangle$, because $\langle x\rangle = (x_1^{\mathsf{DE}},x_2^{\mathsf{CE}},x_3^{\mathsf{CD}}) \rightarrow (x_1^{\mathsf{E}},x_2^{\mathsf{E}},x_3^{\mathsf{C}}) = \langle x\rangle_{\mathsf{xor}}^{\mathsf{C-E}})$ by $\Pi = \tilde\rho\cdot\ddot\pi\cdot\tilde\delta$ where $\ddot\pi$, $\tilde\delta$, and $\tilde\rho$ are permutations on $\ell = d\cdot(w+1)$ tuples in the path induced by $\pi,\delta,\rho$:

- $\pi \in \mathsf{perm}_d$ defines $\ddot\pi \in \mathsf{perm}_\ell$ s.t. $\ddot\pi(j,t) = (\pi(j),t)$, i.e. $\ddot\pi$ moves position $t$ in bucket $j$ to position $t$ in bucket $\pi(j)$;
- $\delta \in \mathsf{array}^{\log(w+1)}[d]$ defines $\tilde\delta \in \mathsf{perm}_\ell$ s.t. $\tilde\delta(j,t) = (j,t\oplus\delta)$, i.e. $\tilde\delta$ moves position $t$ in bucket $j$ to position $t\oplus\delta[j]$ in bucket $j$; same for $\rho$ and $\tilde\rho$;

Now use protocol XOT in 2 round and $\approx 2|\mathsf{path}|$ bandwidth to apply map $\mathsf{EM}_{\sigma^\circ,\mathsf{t}^\circ}$ held by $\mathsf{D}$ to $\langle\Pi(\mathsf{path})\rangle_{\mathsf{xor}}^{\mathsf{C-E}}$. The result is $\langle\mathsf{path}^\circ\rangle_{\mathsf{xor}}^{\mathsf{C-E}}$ for $\mathsf{path}^\circ = (\mathsf{EM}_{\sigma^\circ,\mathsf{t}^\circ} \cdot \Pi)(\mathsf{path})$, and when $\mathsf{C},\mathsf{E}$ apply $\Pi^{-1}$ to it they get $\langle\mathsf{path}'\rangle_{\mathsf{xor}}^{\mathsf{C-E}}$ for $\mathsf{path}' = (\Pi^{-1}\cdot \mathsf{EM}_{\sigma^\circ,\mathsf{t}^\circ}\cdot\Pi)(\mathsf{path})$. Finally $\langle\mathsf{path}'\rangle$ can be reconstructed from $\langle\mathsf{path}'\rangle_{\mathsf{xor}}^{\mathsf{C-E}}$ in 1 round and $2|\mathsf{path}|$ bandwidth (see [21], Appendix A for secret-sharing conversions and reasoning), and can then be injected into $\langle\mathsf{tree}\rangle$.

**Eviction Correctness.** We claim that the eviction protocol described above implements mapping $\mathsf{EM}_{\sigma,\mathsf{t}}$ applied to $\mathsf{path}$, i.e. that (note that $(\tilde x)^{-1} = \tilde x$):

$$\mathsf{EM}_{\sigma,\mathsf{t}} = \Pi^{-1}\cdot \mathsf{EM}_{\sigma^\circ,\mathsf{t}^\circ}\cdot\Pi = (\tilde\delta\cdot\ddot\pi^{-1}\cdot\tilde\rho)\cdot(\mathsf{EM}_{\pi\sigma\pi^{-1},\rho\oplus\pi(\mathsf{t}\oplus\delta)})\cdot(\tilde\rho\cdot\ddot\pi\cdot\tilde\delta) \quad (1)$$

Consider the set of points $S = \{(j,\mathsf{t}[j]) \mid j \in \mathsf{Z}_d\}$ which are moved by the left hand side (LHS) permutation $\mathsf{EM}_{\sigma,\mathsf{t}}$. To argue that Eq. (1) holds we first show that the RHS permutation maps any point $(j,\mathsf{t}[j])$ of $S$ in the same way as the LHS permutation:

$$(j,\mathsf{t}[j]) \xrightarrow{(\tilde\rho\cdot\ddot\pi\cdot\tilde\delta)} (\pi(j),\rho[\pi(j)]\oplus\mathsf{t}[j]\oplus\delta[j]) = (\pi(j),\mathsf{t}^\circ[\pi(j)])$$

$$\xrightarrow{\mathsf{EM}_{\pi\sigma\pi^{-1},\mathsf{t}^\circ}} (\pi\sigma\pi^{-1}(\pi(j)),\mathsf{t}^\circ[\pi\sigma\pi^{-1}(\pi(j))]) = (\pi\sigma(j),\mathsf{t}^\circ[\pi\sigma(j)])$$

$$= (\pi\sigma(j),\rho[\pi\sigma(j)]\oplus\mathsf{t}[\sigma(j)]\oplus\delta[\sigma(j)])$$

$$\xrightarrow{\tilde\rho} (\pi\sigma(j),\mathsf{t}[\sigma(j)]\oplus\delta[\sigma(j)]) \xrightarrow{\ddot\pi^{-1}} (\sigma(j),\mathsf{t}[\sigma(j)]\oplus\delta[\sigma(j)])$$

$$\xrightarrow{\tilde\delta} (\sigma(j),\mathsf{t}[\sigma(j)])$$

It remains to argue that RHS is an identity on points not in $S$, just like LHS. Observe that set $S'$ of tuples moved by $\mathsf{EM}_{\sigma^\circ, \mathsf{t}^\circ}$ consists of the following tuples:

$$(k, \mathsf{t}^\circ[k]) = (k, \rho[k] \oplus \mathsf{t}[\pi^{-1}(k)] \oplus \delta[\pi^{-1}(k)]) = (\pi(j), \rho[\pi(j)] \oplus \mathsf{t}[j] \oplus \delta[j])$$

Also note that:

$$(\tilde{\rho} \cdot \tilde{\pi} \cdot \tilde{\delta})(j, \mathsf{t}[j]) = (\tilde{\rho} \cdot \tilde{\pi})(j, \mathsf{t}[j] \oplus \delta[j]) = \tilde{\rho}(\pi(j), \mathsf{t}[j] \oplus \delta[j]) = (\pi(j), \rho[\pi(j)] \oplus \mathsf{t}[j] \oplus \delta[j])$$

which means that $S' = \Pi(S)$, so if $(j, t) \notin S$ then $\Pi(j, t) \notin S'$, hence $(\mathsf{EM}_{\sigma^\circ, \mathsf{t}^\circ} \cdot \Pi)(j, t) = \Pi(j, t)$, and hence $\Pi^{-1} \cdot \mathsf{EM}_{\sigma^\circ, \mathsf{t}^\circ} \cdot \Pi$ and $\mathsf{EM}_{\sigma, \mathsf{t}}$ are equal on $(j, t) \notin S$.

**Optimizations and Efficiency.** As mentioned above, we can improve on both bandwidth and rounds in the Retrieval phase of 3PC-ORAM.ML shown in Algorithm 2. The optimization comes from an observation that our protocol KSearch (see Algorithm 6, Appendix A) takes just one round to compute shift-sharing $\langle j \rangle_{\mathsf{shift}}^{\mathsf{DE-C}}$ of index $j$, and its second round is a resharing which transforms $\langle j \rangle_{\mathsf{shift}}^{\mathsf{DE-C}}$ into $\langle j \rangle_{\mathsf{shift}}$. This round of resharing can be saved, and we can re-arrange protocols 3ShiftPIR and 3ShiftXorPIR so they use only $\langle j \rangle_{\mathsf{shift}}^{\mathsf{DE-C}}$ as input and effectively piggyback creating the rest of $\langle j \rangle_{\mathsf{shift}}$ in such a way that the modified protocols, denoted resp. 3ShiftPIR-Mod and 3ShiftXorPIR-Mod take 2 rounds, which makes the whole Retrieval take only 3 rounds, hence access protocol 3PC-ORAM.Access takes $3h$ rounds in Retrieval, and, surprisingly, the same is true for Retrieval *with Post-Processing*. For further explanations we refer to [21].

## 4    Security

Protocol 3PC-ORAM of Sect. 3 is a three-party secure computation of an Oblivious RAM functionality, i.e. it can implement RAM for any 3PC protocol in the RAM model. To state this formally we define a Universally Composable (UC) Oblivious RAM functionality $\mathsf{F}_{\mathsf{ORAM}}$ for 3-party computation (3PC) in the framework of Canetti [7], and we argue that our 3PC ORAM realizes $\mathsf{F}_{\mathsf{ORAM}}$ in the setting of $m = 3$ parties with *honest majority*, i.e. only $t = 1$ party is (statically) corrupted, assuming *honest-but-curious* (HbC) adversary, i.e. corrupted party follows the protocol. We assume secure pairwise links between the three parties. Since we have static-corruptions, HbC adversary, and non-rewinding simulators, security holds even if communication is asynchronous.

**3PC ORAM Functionality.** Functionality $\mathsf{F}_{\mathsf{ORAM}}$ is parametrized by address and record sizes, resp. $\log n$ and $D$, and it takes command Init, which initializes an empty array $\mathsf{M} \in \mathsf{array}^D[n]$, and Access(instr, $\langle \mathsf{N}, \mathsf{rec}' \rangle$) for (instr, $\mathsf{N}, \mathsf{rec}') \in \{\mathsf{read}, \mathsf{write}\} \times \{0,1\}^{\log n} \times \{0,1\}^D$, which returns a *fresh* secret-sharing $\langle \mathsf{rec} \rangle$ of record $\mathsf{rec} = \mathsf{M}[\mathsf{N}]$, and if instr $=$ write it also assigns $\mathsf{M}[\mathsf{N}] := \mathsf{rec}'$. Technically, $\mathsf{F}_{\mathsf{ORAM}}$ needs each of the three participating parties to make the call, where each party provides their part of the sharing, and $\mathsf{F}_{\mathsf{ORAM}}$'s output $\langle \mathsf{rec} \rangle$ is also delivered in the form of a corresponding share to each party. However, in the HbC setting all parties are assumed to follow the instructions provided by an *environ-ment* algorithm Z, which models higher-level protocol which utilizes $F_{ORAM}$ to implement oblivious memory access. Hence we can simply assume that Z sends Init and Access(instr, $\langle N, rec' \rangle$) to $F_{ORAM}$ and receives $\langle M[N] \rangle$ in return.

**Security of our 3PC ORAM.** Since our protocol is a three-party secure *emulation* of Circuit-ORAM, we prove that it securely realizes $F_{ORAM}$ in the $(t, m) = (1, 3)$ setting *if* Circuit-ORAM defines a secure Client-Server ORAM, which implies security of 3PC-ORAM by the argument for Circuit-ORAM security given in [27]. We note that protocol 3PC-ORAM.Access of Sect. 3 implements only procedure Access. Procedure Init can be implemented by running 3PC-ORAM.Access with instr = write in a loop for N from 0 to $n-1$ (and arbitrary rec''s), but this requires some adjustments in 3PC-ORAM.Access and 3PC-ORAM.ML to deal with initialization of random label assignments and their linkage. We leave the specification of these (straightforward) adjustments to the full version, and our main security claim, stated as Corollary 1 below, assumes that Init is executed by a trusted-party.

For lack of space we defer the proof of Corollary 1 to [21], Appendix C. Very briefly, the proof uses UC framework, arguing that each protocol securely realizes its intended input/output functionality *if* each subprotocol it invokes realizes its idealized input/output functionality. All subprotocols executed by protocol 3PC-ORAM.ML of Sect. 3 are accompanied with brief security arguments which argue precisely this statement. As for 3PC-ORAM.ML, its security proof, given in [21], Appendix C, is centered around two facts argued in Sect. 3, namely that our way of implementing Circuit-ORAM eviction map, with D holding $\sigma^\circ = \pi \cdot \sigma \cdot \pi^{-1}$ and $t^\circ = \rho \oplus \pi(t \oplus \delta)$ and E, C holding $\pi, \rho, \delta$ is (1) correct, because $\Pi^{-1} \cdot EM_{\sigma^\circ, t^\circ} \cdot \Pi = EM_{\sigma, t}$ for $\Pi = \tilde\rho \cdot \tilde\pi \cdot \tilde\delta$, and (2) it leaks no information to either party, because random $\pi, \rho, \delta$ induce random $\sigma^\circ, t^\circ$ in D's view.

**Corollary 1** *(from [21], Appendix C). Assuming secure initialization,* 3PC-ORAM.Access *is a UC-secure realization of 3PC ORAM functionality* $F_{ORAM}$.

## 5    Performance Evaluation

We tested a Java prototype of our 3PC Circuit-ORAM, with garbled circuits implemented using the ObliVM library by Wang [27], on three AWS EC2 c4.2xlarge servers, with communication links encrypted using AES-128. Each c4.2xlarge instance is equipped with eight Intel Xeon E5-2666 v3 CPU's (2.9 GHz), 15 GB memory, and has 1 Gbps bandwidth. (However, our tested prototype utilizes multi-threading only in parallel Eviction, see below.)

In the discussion below we use the following acronyms:
- cust-3PC: our 3PC Circuit-ORAM protocol;
- gen-3PC: generic 3PC Circuit-ORAM using 3PC of Araki et al. [1];
- 2PC: 2PC Circuit-ORAM [27];
- C/S: the client-server Path-ORAM [26].

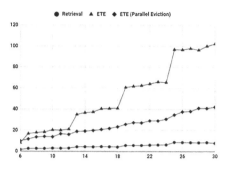

**Fig. 6.** Our 3PC-ORAM online wall-clock time (ms) vs $\log n$ for $D = 4B$

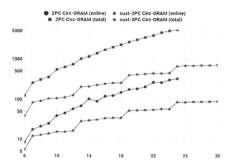

**Fig. 7.** CPU time (ms) vs $\log n$, for $D = 4B$

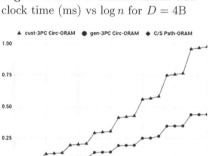

**Fig. 8.** Online bndw.(MB) vs $\log n$ for $D = 4B$

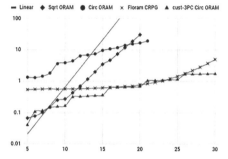

**Fig. 9.** Comparison with 2PC-ORAM's in online+offline bndw.(MB) vs $\log n$ for $D = 4B$

**Wall Clock Time.** Figure 6 shows online timing of cust-3PC for small record sizes ($D = 4B$) as a function of address size $\log n$. It includes Retrieval wall clock time (WC), End-to-End (Retrieval+PostProcess+Eviction) WC, and End-to-End WC with *parallel* Eviction for all trees, which shows 60% reduction in WC due to better CPU utilization. Note that Retrieval takes about 8 milliseconds for $\log n = 30$ (i.e. $2^{30}$ records), and that Eviction takes only about 4–5 times longer. Recall that Retrieval phase has $3h$ rounds while Eviction has 6, which accounts for much smaller CPU utilization in Retrieval.

**CPU Time.** We compare total and online CPU time of cust-3PC and 2PC in Fig. 7 with respect to memory size $n$, for $D = 4B$.[6] Since 2PC implementation [27] does not provide online/offline separation, we approximate 2PC online CPU time by its garbled circuit evaluation time, because 2PC costs due to OT's can be

---

[6] We include CPU comparisons only with 2PC Circuit-ORAM, and not SQRT-ORAM [30] and DPF-ORAM [12], because the former uses the same Java ObliVM GC library while the latter two use the C library Obliv-C. Still, note that for $n = 30$, the on-line computation due to FSS evaluation and linear memory scans contributes over 1 sec to wall-clock in [12], while our on-line wall-clock comes to 40 msec.

pushed to precomputation. As Fig. 7 shows, the cust-3PC CPU costs are between 6x and 10x lower than in 2PC, resp. online and total, already for $\log n = 25$, and the gap widens for higher $n$. In [21], Appendix E.2 we include CPU time comparison with respect to $D$, which shows CPU ratio of 2PC over cust-3PC grows to $\approx 25$ for $D \geq 10\,\mathrm{KB}$.

**Bandwidth Comparison with Generic 3PC.** Timing results depend on many factors (language, network, CPU, and more), and bandwidth is a more reliable predictor of performance for protocols using only light symmetric crypto. In Fig. 8 we compare online bandwidth of cust-3PC, gen-3PC, and C/S, as a function of the address size $\log n$, for $D = 4\mathrm{B}$. We see for small records our cust-3PC is only a factor of 2x worse than the optimal-bandwidth gen-3PC (which, recall, has completely impractical round complexity). In [21], Appendix E.2 we show that as $D$ grows, cust-3PC beats gen-3PC in bandwidth for $D \geq 1\,\mathrm{KB}$.

**Bandwidth Comparison with 2PC ORAMs.** In Fig. 9 we compare total bandwidth of cust-3PC and several 2PC ORAM schemes, including 2PC, the DPF-based FLORAM scheme of [12], the 2PC SQRT-ORAM of [30], and a trivial linear-scan scheme. Our cust-3PC bandwidth is competitive to FLORAM for all $n$'s, but for $n \geq 24$ the $O(\sqrt{n})$ asymptotics of FLORAM takes over. Note also that FLORAM uses $O(n)$ local computation vs. our $O(\log^3 n)$, so in the FLORAM case bandwidth comparison does not suffice. Indeed, for $n = 2^{30}$ and $D = 4\mathrm{B}$, [12] report $> 1\,\mathrm{s}$ overall processing time on LAN vs. 40 msec for us.

For further discussions of bandwidth and CPU time with respect to record size $D$, and cust-3PC CPU time component, refer to [21], Appendix E.2.

# References

1. Araki, T., Furukawa, J., Lindell, Y., Nof, A., Ohara, K.: High-throughput semi-honest secure three-party computation with an honest majority. In: Proceedings of the 2016 ACM SIGSAC Conference on Computer and Communications Security, Vienna, Austria, 24–28 October 2016, pp. 805–817 (2016)
2. Beimel, A., Ishai, Y., Malkin, T.: Reducing the servers computation in private information retrieval: PIR with preprocessing. J. Cryptol. **17**, 125–151 (2004)
3. Ben-Or, M., Goldwasser, S., Wigderson, A.: Completeness theorems for non-cryptographic fault-tolerant distributed computation. In: Proceedings of the Twentieth Annual ACM Symposium on Theory of Computing, STOC 1988, pp. 1–10. ACM, New York (1988)
4. Bogdanov, D., Kamm, L., Kubo, B.: Students and taxes: a privacy-preserving study using secure computation. In: Proceedings on Privacy Enhancing Technologies (PET), pp. 117–135 (2016)
5. Bogdanov, D., Laur, S., Willemson, J.: Sharemind: a framework for fast privacy-preserving computations. In: Jajodia, S., Lopez, J. (eds.) ESORICS 2008. LNCS, vol. 5283, pp. 192–206. Springer, Heidelberg (2008). https://doi.org/10.1007/978-3-540-88313-5_13

6. Bogetoft, P., et al.: Secure multiparty computation goes live. In: Dingledine, R., Golle, P. (eds.) FC 2009. LNCS, vol. 5628, pp. 325–343. Springer, Heidelberg (2009). https://doi.org/10.1007/978-3-642-03549-4_20

7. Canetti, R.: Universally composable security: a new paradigm for cryptographic protocols. In: Proceedings of the 42nd IEEE Symposium on Foundations of Computer Science, FOCS 2001. IEEE Computer Society, Washington, DC (2001)

8. Chaum, D., Crépeau, C., Damgård, I.: Multiparty unconditionally secure protocols (extended abstract). In: Proceedings of the 20th Annual ACM Symposium on Theory of Computing, 2–4 May 1988, Chicago, Illinois, USA, pp. 11–19 (1988)

9. Chor, B., Kushilevitz, E., Goldreich, O., Sudan, M.: Private information retrieval. J. ACM **45**(6), 965–981 (1998)

10. Damgård, I., Meldgaard, S., Nielsen, J.B.: Perfectly secure oblivious RAM without random oracles. In: Ishai, Y. (ed.) TCC 2011. LNCS, vol. 6597, pp. 144–163. Springer, Heidelberg (2011). https://doi.org/10.1007/978-3-642-19571-6_10

11. Devadas, S., van Dijk, M., Fletcher, C.W., Ren, L., Shi, E., Wichs, D.: Onion ORAM: a constant bandwidth blowup oblivious RAM. In: Kushilevitz, E., Malkin, T. (eds.) TCC 2016. LNCS, vol. 9563, pp. 145–174. Springer, Heidelberg (2016). https://doi.org/10.1007/978-3-662-49099-0_6

12. Doerner, J., Shelat, A.: Scaling ORAM for secure computation. In: Proceedings of the 2017 ACM SIGSAC Conference on Computer and Communications Security, CCS 2017, pp. 523–535. ACM, New York (2017)

13. Dvir, Z., Gopi, S.: 2 server PIR with subpolynomial communication. J. ACM **63**(4), 391–3915 (2016)

14. Faber, S., Jarecki, S., Kentros, S., Wei, B.: Three-party ORAM for secure computation. In: Iwata, T., Cheon, J.H. (eds.) ASIACRYPT 2015. LNCS, vol. 9452, pp. 360–385. Springer, Heidelberg (2015). https://doi.org/10.1007/978-3-662-48797-6_16

15. Fletcher, C.W., Naveed, M., Ren, L., Shi, E., Stefanov, E.: Bucket ORAM: single online roundtrip, constant bandwidth oblivious RAM. IACR Cryptology ePrint Archive, 2015:1065 (2015)

16. Gentry, C., Goldman, K.A., Halevi, S., Julta, C., Raykova, M., Wichs, D.: Optimizing ORAM and using it efficiently for secure computation. In: De Cristofaro, E., Wright, M. (eds.) PETS 2013. LNCS, vol. 7981, pp. 1–18. Springer, Heidelberg (2013). https://doi.org/10.1007/978-3-642-39077-7_1

17. Goldreich, O., Micali, S., Wigderson, A.: How to play any mental game. In: Proceedings of the Nineteenth Annual ACM Symposium on Theory of Computing, STOC 1987, pp. 218–229. ACM, New York (1987)

18. Goldreich, O., Ostrovsky, R.: Software protection and simulation on oblivious RAMs. J. ACM **43**(3), 431–473 (1996)

19. Gordon, S.D., Katz, J., Kolesnikov, V., Krell, F., Malkin, T., Raykova, M., Vahlis, Y.: Secure two-party computation in sublinear (amortized) time. In: Computer and Communications Security (CCS), CCS 2012, pp. 513–524 (2012)

20. Ishai, Y., Kushilevitz, E., Lu, S., Ostrovsky, R.: Private large-scale databases with distributed searchable symmetric encryption. In: Sako, K. (ed.) CT-RSA 2016. LNCS, vol. 9610, pp. 90–107. Springer, Cham (2016). https://doi.org/10.1007/978-3-319-29485-8_6

21. Jarecki, S., Wei, B.: 3PC ORAM with low latency, low bandwidth, and fast batch retrieval. IACR Cryptology ePrint Archive, 2018:347 (2018)

22. Keller, M., Scholl, P.: Efficient, oblivious data structures for MPC. In: Sarkar, P., Iwata, T. (eds.) ASIACRYPT 2014. LNCS, vol. 8874, pp. 506–525. Springer, Heidelberg (2014). https://doi.org/10.1007/978-3-662-45608-8_27

23. Ostrovsky, R., Shoup, V.: Private information storage (extended abstract). In: Proceedings of the Twenty-Ninth Annual ACM Symposium on the Theory of Computing, El Paso, Texas, USA, 4–6 May 1997, pp. 294–303 (1997)
24. Ren, L., Fletcher, C., Kwon, A., Stefanov, E., Shi, E., Van Dijk, M., Devadas, S.: Constants count: practical improvements to oblivious RAM. In: Proceedings of the 24th USENIX Conference on Security Symposium, SEC 2015, pp. 415–430. USENIX Association, Berkeley (2015)
25. Shi, E., Chan, T.-H.H., Stefanov, E., Li, M.: Oblivious RAM with $O((\log N)^3)$ worst-case cost. In: Lee, D.H., Wang, X. (eds.) ASIACRYPT 2011. LNCS, vol. 7073, pp. 197–214. Springer, Heidelberg (2011). https://doi.org/10.1007/978-3-642-25385-0_11
26. Stefanov, E., van Dijk, M., Shi, E., Fletcher, C., Ren, L., Yu, X., Devadas, S.: Path ORAM: an extremely simple oblivious ram protocol. In: Proceedings of the 2013 ACM SIGSAC Conference on Computer Communications Security, CCS 2013, pp. 299–310. ACM, New York (2013)
27. Wang, X., Chan, H., Shi, E.: Circuit ORAM: on tightness of the goldreich-ostrovsky lower bound. In: Proceedings of the 22nd ACM SIGSAC Conference on Computer and Communications Security, CCS 2015, pp. 850–861 (2015). ACM, New York
28. Wang, X.S., Huang, Y., Chan, T.-H.H., Shelat, A., Shi, E.: SCORAM: oblivious ram for secure computation. In Proceedings of the 2014 ACM SIGSAC Conference on Computer and Communications Security, CCS 2014, pp. 191–202. ACM, New York (2014)
29. Yao, A.C.-C.: Protocols for secure computations (extended abstract). In: Proceedings of the 23rd Annual Symposium on Foundations of Computer Science, FOCS 1982, pp. 160–164 (1982)
30. Zahur, S., Wang, X., Raykova, M., Gascón, A., Doerner, J., Evans, D., Katz, J.: Revisiting square-root ORAM efficient random access in multi-party computation. In: Proceedings of the 37th IEEE Symposium on Security and Privacy ("Oakland"). IEEE 2016 (2016)

# Symmetric Key Primitives

# MergeMAC: A MAC for Authentication with Strict Time Constraints and Limited Bandwidth

Ralph Ankele[1(✉)], Florian Böhl[2], and Simon Friedberger[2]

[1] Royal Holloway University of London, Egham, UK
`ralph.ankele.2015@rhul.ac.uk`
[2] NXP Semiconductors, Leuven, Belgium
`{florian.boehl,simon.friedberger}@nxp.com`

**Abstract.** This paper presents MergeMAC, a MAC that is particularly suitable for environments with strict time requirements and extremely limited bandwidth. MergeMAC computes the MAC by splitting the message into two parts. We use a pseudorandom function (PRF) to map messages to random bit strings and then merge them with a very efficient keyless function. The advantage of this approach is that the outputs of the PRF can be cached for frequently needed message parts. We demonstrate the merits of MergeMAC for authenticating messages on the CAN bus where bandwidth is extremely limited and caching can be used to recover parts of the message counter instead of transmitting it. We recommend an instantiation of the merging function Merge and analyze the security of our construction. Requirements for a merging function are formally defined and the resulting EUF-CMA security of MergeMAC is proven.

**Keywords:** Symmetric-key cryptography
Message Authentication Code · Lightweight · Efficient · Automotive
CAN bus

## 1 Introduction

In constrained environments, such as embedded devices, wireless sensor networks, control systems and automated devices, the Internet of Things (IoT) in general, and more particularly to save bandwidth in highly time constrained scenarios it is important to reduce the latency while still ensure that the throughput of a communication channel does not fall below a critical threshold. A common practice is to omit parts with low entropy in the communication of transmitted messages when the communication overhead is more expensive than simply

---

R. Ankele and S. Friedberger—This research was partially supported by the European Union's Horizon 2020 research and innovation programme under grant agreement No. H2020-MSCA-ITN-2014-643161 ECRYPT-NET.

© Springer International Publishing AG, part of Springer Nature 2018
B. Preneel and F. Vercauteren (Eds.): ACNS 2018, LNCS 10892, pp. 381–399, 2018.
https://doi.org/10.1007/978-3-319-93387-0_20

reconstructing the message by brute-force guessing the missing parts. As attacks on IoT devices become more and more of a threat [Lan11, RSWO17], it is important to ensure the authenticity of an entity and the integrity of transmitted messages. Message Authentication Codes (MAC) allow an receiver of a message to verify the integrity of a received message and ensure that the sender has to be an authenticated entity.

MERGEMAC is a MAC function optimized exactly for the requirements of communicating in extremely constrained environments and still ensuring strict time requirements even with limited bandwidth. In our proposal, we omit parts of the transmitted message with very little information content. The missing information can then be reconstructed by the receiver by brute-forcing all possibilities as only the correct solution will be verified as the received MAC. Even though the missing parts are not transmitted they are included in the MAC computation. Our proposed construction achieves the strict timing constraints, while still recalculating parts of the MAC, by splitting the MAC computation into several parts, and further allowing fast recombination of intermediate values into MACs. We will now introduce the scenario which prompted the development of our solution.

**Security Under Extreme Conditions.** Modern cars rely on the Controller Area Network (CAN) bus for car-internal communication between different components, usually referred to in this context as electronic control units (ECUs). The CAN bus connects everything - from critical systems like breaks or airbags to convenience features like built-in navigation or entertainment systems. When the bus was developed in the 1980's, the connected world of today was still merely science fiction. Security was not a concern. This started to change when hackers first used the CAN bus as an entry point to steal a car, accessing it by taking off a side mirror [KCR+10, CMK+11]. Nowadays, more and more components with an interface to the CAN bus are also connected to the Internet. This allows hackers to mount a powerful attack, by attacking the car from an online attack surface. A remote attack on the complete fleet is the nightmare of every CTO in the automotive industry. Consequentially, the call for more security grew louder quickly. However, adding security to legacy systems is a complicated and error prone process. The ramifications specifically for the CAN bus are summarized as:

- **High costs:** The cost pressure is high. Many ECUs are simple microcontrollers and a security solution that adds significant costs is unlikely to be adopted.
- **Time constraints:** Several components, such as breaks or airbags, are running under strict time constraints. This confines the latency a security solution may introduce to the system.
- **Limited bandwidth:** The bandwidth on the CAN bus is limited. Hence a security solution should need as little additional bandwidth as possible.

In this paper we describe an approach how to establish authenticated communication between ECUs on the CAN bus under these extreme conditions. Our construction allows for very efficient hardware implementations as we demonstrate with the specific instantiation based on MergeMAC and Present or Prince. It addresses bandwidth constraints by not transmitting low-entropy parts of messages and recovering them at the receiver in an efficient way.

**Message Authentication Codes.** Message Authentication Codes (MACs) are a popular standard technique to authenticate messages using a shared secret key [ISO11,Dwo16]. Using a shared key and a message as input, a user can compute a MAC tag and attach it to the message. The recipient can then verify the authenticity of the message using the secret key. The most striking advantage of MACs is their efficiency. MACs can be constructed directly from symmetric block ciphers or from cryptographic hash functions and are hence much more efficient than digital signatures, their asymmetric relatives. This also makes them the tool of choice on constrained devices, like microcontrollers and lightweight IoT devices. Therefore, they are the correct building blocks for our scenario.

**Authentication.** The CAN bus itself does not provide any message authentication mechanism. Every connected ECU can send arbitrary frames including a forged sender identity. Our goal is to define an authentication mechanism that is tailored towards the most common scenario: A sender (e.g. a sensor) addressing one or more receivers. The sender includes a counter into each message to prevent replay attacks and adds a MAC tag to each message sent. Receivers keep track of the counter value. They will reject incoming messages with a counter value not higher than the current one. Skipping messages is acceptable, i.e. the counter value will always be updated to the last one received with a valid MAC tag. The authentication mechanism we propose significantly reduces the attack surface if it is used for all ECUs on the CAN bus. Moreover, the attack surface is drastically reduced, as an attacker from the outside (e.g. by accessing the CAN bus from the side mirrors) will not be able to impersonate an internal device. Furthermore, an attacker from the inside (e.g. through a corrupted ECU) is confined to the receivers that trust this ECU.

**A Bandwidth Saving Technique.** Bandwidth can be saved by only including the $n$ least significant bits of the counter in the messages, i.e. the counter is divided into $n$ low bits, called $l$ and the remaining high bits called $h$. The sender computes the MAC tag on the message as usual based on the complete counter value. The receiver recovers the complete counter as follows: He takes the high bits $h$ from his local storage and combines them with the transmitted low bits $l$. If the MAC verification is successful and the combined counter is greater than the locally stored counter value, the message is accepted. Otherwise, the message may still be valid if a wrap of the lower bits $l$ has occurred on the sender side leading to an incremented $h$. Consequentially, the receiver will try again with $h+1, h+2, \ldots$ up to $h+w_{max}$ for a parameter $w_{max}$ of the maximum number of wraps that are allowed to occur. We apply this idea to the counter only, but it can be used more broadly to recover predictable information to save bandwidth. With 8 bytes, payload sizes on the standard CAN bus are relatively short and we will see that saving a few bytes on the counter saves us a complete additional frame in many cases. While this mechanism allows us to save bandwidth, it has an impact on security. If the counter is transferred fully, the probability of the adversary to guess a MAC tag correctly is $1/2^\ell$ where $\ell$ is the length of the tag, this increases to $w_{max}/2^\ell$. For $w_{max}$ we recommend a value below 4 bits. An attacker with the ability to suppress more than $w_{max}$ messages can permanently desynchronize the sender and receiver. Since such an attacker could just suppress all messages achieving the same effect we consider it an implementation detail to mitigate this attack.

**Worst Case Run Times.** While the technique just described allows us to omit transferring parts of the message counter and reconstruct them with the MAC, this comes at the cost of additional MAC computations. To be specific, $w_{max}$ in the worst case. Here, time constraints become a concern: There is an upper bound on the time the processing of a message may take, i.e. $w_{max}$ MAC calculations to recover the counter must not take longer than $t_{max}$ ms. Of course, with a sufficiently powerful receiver, a standard MAC construction could be used and either the receiver would have a sufficiently strong CPU or MAC computation could be parallelized. However, the high cost pressure in the automobile sector makes powerful receivers impossible.

**Pre-compute and Merge.** In this paper we present MERGEMAC, a dedicated MAC constructions for these constrained environments. One of the main features of MERGEMAC is that it is particularly well suited for the recovery of predictable information, e.g., such as the most significant bits of the counter as described above. The idea is, basically, to split the messages in two parts, the predictable information that is not transferred and the payload part that actually is. Then a pre-MAC is computed for both parts independently (see Fig. 1). For the predictable information, these pre-MACs can be pre-computed and cached - e.g. this would be the pre-MACs for the current and the $w_{max} - 1$ counter values. Two pre-MACs can then be merged into the final MAC. As the pre-MACs are already PRF outputs, we can significantly relax the security requirements for the merging function. This allows to speed this step up significantly, e.g. by roughly 70% in contrast to using a lightweight cipher for merging the PRF outputs. Our merging function MERGE is a round-reduced variant of CHASKEY [MMVH+14]. MERGEMAC has the following features:

– Our merge function MERGE is derived from CHASKEY and hence inherits its features: First and foremost, it is a dedicated design for microcontrollers and easy to implement in hardware.
– We define a construction for the merge function based on lightweight ciphers. Other constructions based on more secures primitives are possible but we focus on the lightweight scenario. On top, MERGE is keyless allowing for very efficient hardware implementation. We further detail this in Sect. 2.

**Contributions. Efficient Merging Function.** We introduce the concept of a merging function and present an efficient candidate based on CHASKEY. We conduct a thorough cryptanalysis for this candidate and provide a performance analysis using the SUPERCOP framework [Ber16].

**Practical Application.** We use our merging function to define the MAC scheme MergeMAC. We analyze and compare different recommendations to instantiate MAC with a 128-bit and a 64-bit version of our merging function. Overall, we demonstrate the benefits of this construction for a practical proposal to secure communication on the CAN bus.

**A Security Definition for Merging Functions.** We formally define security requirements for merging functions. We show how our security definition can be applied by proving the MergeMAC to be EUF-CMA secure based on the assumption that Merge is a secure merging function and we have two secure PRFs. Consequentially, we show generically that every secure merging function can be used to instantiate MergeMAC.

**Information Recovery with MACs.** To the best of our knowledge this paper is the first to introduce recovery of low-entropy information through a MAC to save bandwidth.

**Related Work.** The most popular MAC schemes today are HMAC [BCK96, Tur08] and CMAC [IK03, Dwo16]. Both cannot be parallelized and do not allow for merging messages in the way outlined above. Bellare et al. [BGR95] first discussed the possibility of parallelizing MAC calculations for increased efficiency when introducing XMAC. Later Black and Rogaway [BR02] introduced PMAC with the express goal of providing a parallelizable MAC construction. Both approaches allow reusing partial results in a way that also allows merging of pre-computed MACs for message parts. However, merging requires an additional keyed block cipher operation which is what we avoid with our lightweight key-less merging function (see also the discussion in Sect. 5). In XMACR the block cipher operation is needed as the randomness is fed to the block cipher. In PMAC the final block cipher call always has to be performed, no matter if parts of the message have been reused or not. In XMACC the counter has to be fed to the block cipher. Considering that we will have several possible values for the high bits of the counter and that the low bits will be included in the message this also depends on sender input. One way to view our construction in relation to these proposals is as a specific kind of merging function which can be made more efficient than a generic constructions because the attacker has little control over the inputs.

**Outline.** In Sect. 2 we present the construction for MergeMAC and introduce the merging function Merge. In Sect. 3 we define the security requirements for a merging function and prove that any merging function satisfying these requirements can be used to instantiate MergeMAC. Section 4 presents the results of the cryptanalysis we conducted for our candidate of the merging function from Sect. 2. In Sect. 5 we discuss the performance of our construction before we conclude in Sect. 6.

## 2    The MERGEMAC Construction

In this Section, we define the MERGEMAC construction in detail and give concrete parameters. MERGEMAC uses two independent keys $K_1, K_2$ of $k$-bit each, to process a message msg of arbitrary size into a tag tag of $n$ bits. These keys are used to instantiate the variable input length PRFs $\mathcal{P}_1, \mathcal{P}_2$ using any MAC scheme that is a secure PRF as outlined in Sect. 3, for example AES-CMAC or CHASKEY. The message msg is split into two parts, the size of both parts is flexible since we use variable input length PRFs. These parts are then combined into the MAC using a function MERGE which has relaxed security requirements because it only operates on random and secret inputs. We suggest three rounds of the permutation $\pi$ as defined in Sect. 2.3 and combine the PRF outputs by XORing them together as input to the permutation $\pi$. Furthermore, we also XOR the outputs of the PRF to the output of the permutation $\pi$. Calling the input parts $\rho, \tilde{\rho}$ this is a Davies-Meyer construction for $\rho \oplus \tilde{\rho}$. MERGEMAC is illustrated in Fig. 1.

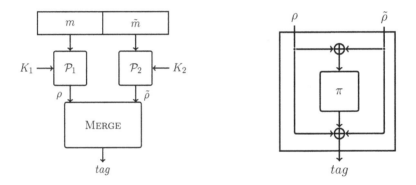

**Fig. 1.** (Left): MERGEMAC construction, (Right): MERGE function.

### 2.1    Variations

Our construction allows for several design choices. It is possible to define variations of MERGEMAC with different PRF instantiations or a different merging function. Since we are targeting constrained environments we suggest using lightweight functions, specifically PRESENT or PRINCE in CMAC mode and a slightly adapted CHASKEY round function, which will be described in more detail in Sect. 2.3. If further optimizations are needed for applications with higher security requirements different PRFs and merging function can be chosen. The only constraints are that any used MACs have good PRF properties and that the merging function MERGE provides enough confusion to prevent an attacker from combining previous results into MACs for unknown messages. We discuss sufficient requirements for the proof in Sect. 3.

## 2.2   Caching

The main design goal when constructing MERGEMAC was to provide a way to re-use calculations performed for similar messages to speed up MAC verification. This was achieved and MERGEMAC allows caching the outputs of both PRFs. If a message $\mathsf{msg}' = m'||\tilde{m}$ is received the evaluation of $\tilde{\rho} = \mathcal{P}_2(m)$ can be omitted by using a cached version of $\tilde{\rho}$. This is particularly beneficial for message parts which are constant or have low entropy for example a recipient ID. Compared to other constructions we can combine cached intermediate results without a full evaluation of any PRF. Common cache-able constructions require that at least one computationally intensive part must be repeated, usually a call to a block cipher or compression function. We improve on this by making use of the fact that the intermediate results are outputs of a PRF and a simpler computation is therefore sufficient.

## 2.3   The Merging Function $F$

Efficiently combining the outputs of the two PRFs in a secure manner is a challenging task. The natural building block for this situation would be a hash function. An ideal hash function would completely hide the PRF outputs from any adversary making them inaccessible from the top by the property of the PRFs and inaccessible from the bottom by the property of the hash function. It would also perfectly mix the two input parts preventing any attacks based on recombining individual parts of previous messages. Unfortunately hash functions or even just compression functions usually require several repetitions of a round function and are not efficient enough.

Our proposal MERGE for such a function tackles the problem with a construction similar to the Lai-Massey construction [LM91] which has been used in block ciphers like IDEA [LMM91]. The purpose of our MERGE-function is to provide enough mixing of the inputs of our MERGE-function so that it is computationally infeasible to find a pre-image of MERGE or to combine outputs for different PRFs into new MACs.

We use a modified version of the $\pi$ function of CHASKEY, with a reduced word size of 16 bits to match the 64-bit block size of PRESENT or PRINCE used for the PRF. The permutation $\pi$ is based on modular additions, rotations and XOR functions (ARX). The advantages of ARX-based designs are high performance, compact implementations and the possibility of constant-time implementations, preventing timing side channel attacks. The rotation constants in our permutation are chosen to be optimal for microcontrollers which often only allows efficient rotations/shifts by one or two bits, and byte-permutations by 8-bits.

# 3   Proof of Security

In this Section, we show that given the function MERGE satisfies easily achieved requirements and secure PRFs, our scheme is a provably secure MAC. According

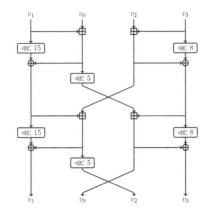

**Fig. 2.** One round of the permutation $\pi$ that is used within our merging function MERGE.

to Daemen and Rijmen [DR05] a MAC is considered secure if it is impossible to recover the key faster than exhaustive enumeration and impossible to forge a MAC with higher success probability than random guessing. We are not especially concerned about key recovery since it implies forgery and we want the chances of forgery to be sufficiently small to make the difference irrelevant.

We use the following experiment to define a forgery, according to Bellare et al. [BGR95]:

**Definition 1** (EUF-CMA). *The existential unforgability under chosen message experiment* EUF-CMA *consists of three algorithms*

- *The* Setup() *algorithm randomly generates a key k. It must be called first.*
- *The* MAC(msg) *algorithm will return a valid MAC for any message* msg *from the message space* $\{0,1\}^*$.
- *The verification algorithm,* Verify(msg, tag), *will return* Valid *if* tag *is valid for* msg *and* Invalid *otherwise.*

*The result of the experiment is* Broken, *and the adversary wins, if a pair* (msg, tag) *verifies correctly and* MAC(msg) *has not been called, otherwise the result is* Unbroken. *An adversary which makes* $q_m$ *distinct calls to* MAC, $q_v$ *distinct calls to* Verify, *runs in time t and wins the game with probability at least* $\epsilon$ *is called a* $(t, q_m, q_v, \epsilon)$,*-adversary.*

**Definition 2.** *A MAC is considered* $(t, q_m, q_v, \epsilon)$*-secure if there is no* $(t, q_m, q_v, \epsilon)$*-adversary.*

### 3.1 Random Input Indistinguishability

We define a property, called Random Input Indistinguishability, which is easy to achieve in practice and which allows us to prove that our construction is a secure

MAC. For simple analysis we use an unkeyed primitive similar to a hash function for the MERGE function. The usual security definitions for hash functions are collision resistance, second preimage resistance and preimage resistance. They are extensively discussed by Rogaway and Shrimpton [RS04]. Random Input Indistinguishability is even weaker than preimage resistance. Intuitively the definition is based on the following reasoning: Assuming that the PRFs are secure the only way for an adversary to learn anything about the intermediate values which are inputs to MERGE is by inverting MERGE. However finding any preimage to MERGE$(x, y)$ is not sufficient, instead an adversary would have to find the original $x$ and $y$. Finding any other preimage is not useful since the adversary cannot find a suitable message to generate those values as long as the PRFs are secure. The only other way to mount an attack would be to find an operation that can be performed on known outputs to transform them into some other output, effectively calculating MERGE$(\mathcal{P}_1(m), \mathcal{P}_2(\tilde{m}))$ for known $m$ and $\tilde{m}$ but in a new combination. We formalize our requirements for MERGE using the following Random Input Indistinguishability experiment RII$_F$:

**Definition 3** (RII$_F$). *The experiment consists of the following five algorithms*

- *The* Setup() *algorithm picks five uniformly random values: a bit $b$ and $X, Y, U, V \in \{0,1\}^N$ where $N$ is the bit length of our output which is the same as for the used PRFs. It must be called first.*
- *The* Query1$(a)$ *algorithm, given any input $a \in \{0,1\}^N$ returns* MERGE$(a, Y)$.
- *The* Query2$(a)$ *algorithm, given any input $a \in \{0,1\}^N$ returns* MERGE$(X, a)$.
- *The adversary can request the challenge at any time during the game. For $b = 0$* Challenge() *will return* MERGE$(X, Y)$ *for $b = 1$ it will return* MERGE$(U, V)$.
- *Eventually the adversary outputs a bit $b'$ by calling* Guess$(b')$.

*The adversary wins the game if $b' = b$.*

We parameterize an adversary $\mathcal{A}$ by the total amount of queries he makes $q$, its running time $t$ and its probability to win $\epsilon$. Our adversary therefore becomes a $(t, q, \epsilon)$-adversary. MERGE is $(t, q, \epsilon)$-secure if $(t, q, \epsilon)$-adversaries do not exist.

## 3.2   Reduction

In this Section, we prove the security of our scheme using two assumptions. First, the used PRFs are $(t, q, \epsilon_P)$-secure, i.e. an adversary making $q$ queries to the PRF and taking at most time $t$ cannot distinguish the PRF from a random function with probability at least $\epsilon$. Second, the function MERGE is $(t, q, \epsilon)$-secure which we will use to bound any adversary in the EUF-CMA experiment.

Our first game is $\mathcal{G}_0 = $ EUF-CMA, $\mathcal{G}_1$ is the same construction but whenever $\mathcal{P}_1$ is used we replace the output with a random value. We use the notation Rnd$(\cdot)$ to denominate such random oracle values and define $r_i = $ Rnd$(m_i)$ and $\tilde{r}_i = $ Rnd$(\tilde{m}_i)$ for brevity. Let $\mathcal{A}$ be a $(t, q_m, q_v, \epsilon_0)$-adversary for $\mathcal{G}_0$ and assuming that $\mathcal{P}_1$ is $(t, q_v + q_m, \epsilon_P)$-secure it follows that there must be a $(t, q_m, q_v, \epsilon_1)$-adversary for $\mathcal{G}_1$ where

$$\epsilon_0 < \epsilon_1 + \epsilon_P.$$

Game $\mathcal{G}_2$ proceeds similarly for $\mathcal{P}_2$ giving us a $(t, q_m, q_v, \epsilon_2)$-adversary such that

$$\epsilon_0 < \epsilon_2 + 2\epsilon_P.$$

We now continue with a hybrid game, successively replacing $\text{MERGE}(r_i, \tilde{r}_i)$ with $\text{MERGE}$ evaluated on new random values. Eventually all the adversary gets is $\text{MERGE}$ evaluated on independent random values and security follows. We show an example of the initial game $\mathcal{G}_2$ in Fig. 3 and give the general definition of the game $\mathcal{G}_{l+2}(l \in \mathbb{N}_{>0})$ next.

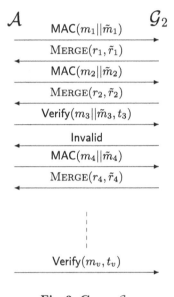

**Fig. 3.** Game $\mathcal{G}_2$

**Definition 4 (Game $\mathcal{G}_{l+2}$).** *The game $\mathcal{G}_{l+2}$ consists of three algorithms*

- *The Setup() algorithm randomly picks a key $k$. It must be called first.*
- *The result of the MAC algorithm call MAC($m_i \| \tilde{m}_i$), for a message* msg $= m_i \| \tilde{m}_i$, *depends on $i$:*
  - *For $i \leq l$ it will return $\text{MERGE}(\text{Rnd}(m_i \| \tilde{m}_i))$. Here we slightly abuse notation and let Rnd return two values.*
  - *For $i > l$ it will return $\text{MERGE}(r_i, \tilde{r}_i)$ just like $\mathcal{G}_2$.*
- *The verification algorithm, Verify(msg, tag), will compute the MAC like MAC does and compare the result to tag.*

Going from game $\mathcal{G}_{l+1}$ to $\mathcal{G}_{l+2}$ we remove all occurrences of $\text{MERGE}(r_l, \tilde{r}_l)$ and replace them with $\text{MERGE}$ evaluated at new random inputs $\text{MERGE}(\text{Rnd}(m_l \| \tilde{m}_l))$. We now define a simulator for these two games and show that a distinguisher for $\mathcal{G}_{l+2}$ and $\mathcal{G}_{l+3}$ wins the Random Input Indistinguishability game against MERGE. To simplify, we assume that the messages in queries $l$ and $l+1$ are different. Since queries are deterministic, if a msg is repeated we simply give the same answer as the for the first query.

**Definition 5 (Simulator).** *The simulator for games $\mathcal{G}_{l+1}$ and $\mathcal{G}_{l+2}$ consists of three algorithms*

- *The Setup() algorithm simply calls Setup() for the Random Input Indistinguishability game.*
- *The result of the MAC algorithm MAC(msg), depends on $i$:*
  - *For $i < l$ it returns $\mathrm{MERGE}(\mathrm{Rnd}(m_i || \tilde{m}_i))$.*
  - *For $i = l$ it returns the result of a call to Challenge() for the Random Input Indistinguishability game.*
  - *For $i > l$ the result depends on the input message $\mathsf{msg}_i = m_i || \tilde{m}_i$:*
    * *If $m_i = m_l, \tilde{m}_i \neq \tilde{m}_l$ it returns the result of a call to Query1($\tilde{m}_l$) for the Random Input Indistinguishability game.*
    * *If $m_i \neq m_l, \tilde{m}_i = \tilde{m}_l$ it returns the result of a call to Query2($m_l$) for the Random Input Indistinguishability game.*
    * *If $m_i \neq m_l, \tilde{m}_i \neq \tilde{m}_l$ it returns $\mathrm{MERGE}(r_i, \tilde{r}_i)$ just like $\mathcal{G}_2$.*
    * *If $m_i = m_l, \tilde{m}_i = \tilde{m}_l$ this value has been queried before and the same result is used again.*
- *The verification algorithm, Verify(msg, tag), will compute the MAC like MAC does and compare the result to tag.*

This implicitly maps $X = r_l, Y = \tilde{r}_l$ in the Random Input Indistinguishability game. For $i < l$ the simulator behaves like both $\mathcal{G}_{l+1}$ and $\mathcal{G}_{l+2}$. For $i = l$ it returns Challenge() from the Random Input Indistinguishability game. If $b = 0$ this will be $\mathrm{MERGE}(X, Y)$ which implicitly maps to $\mathrm{MERGE}(r_l, \tilde{r}_l)$. For $b = 1$ it will be $\mathrm{MERGE}(U, V)$ which is just MERGE evaluated at new random values just like $\mathrm{MERGE}(\mathrm{Rnd}(m_i || \tilde{m}_i))$ in $\mathcal{G}_{l+2}$. For $i > l$ the simulator uses the query algorithms for the Random Input Indistinguishability game to uphold the implicit mapping and return $\mathrm{MERGE}(X, \tilde{r}_i)$ if $r_i$ is reused or $\mathrm{MERGE}(r_i, Y)$ if $\tilde{r}_i$ is reused. Given a completely different input message it will behave just like $\mathcal{G}_2$ and also like both games by returning $\mathrm{MERGE}(r_i, \tilde{r}_i)$. If game $\mathcal{G}_{l+1}$ requires $q_m, q_v$ queries to the simulator then at most $q_m + q_v$ queries to MERGE are made. Assuming that we have a $(t, q_m, q_v, \epsilon_{l+1})$-adversary for $\mathcal{G}_{l+1}$ and that MERGE is $(t, q_m + q_v, \epsilon_{\mathrm{MERGE}})$-secure, we have a $(t, q_m, q_v, \epsilon_{l+2})$-adversary for $\mathcal{G}_{l+2}$ with

$$\epsilon_{l+1} < \epsilon_{l+2} + \epsilon_{\mathrm{MERGE}}.$$

If the initial game contained $q_m$ MAC queries and $q_v$ verify queries all the answers will have been replaced after $q_m + q_v$ steps. So for $\mathcal{G}_{q_m + q_v + 2}$ the adversary receives no useful information anymore.

At this point the probability of an adversary to create a valid message-tag-pair amounts to guessing the tag. We have

$$\epsilon_{q_m + q_v + 2} < 2^{-N}(q_m + q_v).$$

It follows that

$$\epsilon_0 < 2^{-N}(q_m + q_v) + \epsilon_{\text{MERGE}}(q_m + q_v) + 2\epsilon_P.$$

This bounds all adversaries against $\mathcal{G}_0$ since we started with an arbitrary one.

# 4   Cryptanalysis

In this Section, we give an overview of the security related cryptographic properties of our construction. First, we discuss the security of the two initial PRFs in MERGEMAC. Second, we discuss relevant attacks for the recommended merging function MERGE in detail. The goal of the second analysis is to methodogically provide evidence that MERGE satisfies Random Input Indistinguishability.

Table 1. Security claims according to the underlying primitives

| Underlying BC | Block size | Key size | Existential forgery resistance |
|---|---|---|---|
| PRESENT | 64 | 80 | $2^{-64}$ |
| PRESENT | 64 | 128 | $2^{-64}$ |
| PRINCE | 64 | 128 | $2^{-64}$ |

## 4.1   Security of the PRFs

The security of the two initial PRFs in MERGEMAC depends on the underlying block ciphers used in CMAC mode. Table 1 gives an overview of the security claims related to the recommended MAC functions and their underlying primitives.

**Birthday Attacks.** While standard block ciphers, like AES have a block size of 128-bits, a majority of lightweight block ciphers have a block size of 64-bits. Bhargavan and Leurent [BL16] showed in their Sweet32 attack, that many lightweight block ciphers with 64-bit block size can be practically attacked when used in a mode like CBC. Consequently, the amount of data blocks that are processed by the initial PRFs of our construction must be limited appropriately.

**Forgeries by Reordering of Messages.** An adversary is capable of creating a simple forgery attack, as the first operation in the merging function MERGE is an XOR of its two inputs. The adversary just has to reorder the output tags of the PRFs as the XOR operation is commutative. Such a simple forgery attack can be prevented by using independent keys for both PRFs.

## 4.2  Security of the MERGE Function

We chose a round-reduced and slightly adapted version of the permutation $\pi$ from CHASKEY with initial and final XORs for our MERGE function. We now provide a detailed security analysis of relevant attacks on this function.

**Meet-in-the-Middle Attacks.** Meet-in-the-middle attacks (MITM) were introduced by Diffie and Hellman [DH77] in 1977 and showed that the security of double DES with two independent 56-bit keys is not as expected 112-bits, but still 56-bits. In their simplest form, MITM attacks can be described as follows: The goal is to attack a cipher $E$ which is composed of two subciphers $E = E'_{K_1} \circ E''_{K_2}$ with keys $K_1, K_2$ and decryption function $D = D''_{K_2} \circ D'_{K_1}$. The adversary uses a plaintext/ciphertext pair $(P, C)$ and computes $E''_{K_2}(P)$ under the set of all possible key values for $K_2$ and stores the results in a table. For the corresponding ciphertexts, the adversary computes $v = D'_{K_1}(C)$ for each value of $K_1$. If $v$ is in the table, the adversary has a key candidate $(K_1, K_2)$ which can be verified with further plaintext/ciphertext pairs.

This has a time complexity of $2^{\#K_1} + 2^{\#K_2}$ and a memory complexity of $2^{min\{\#K_1, \#K_2\}}$ compared to exhaustive key search with a time complexity of $2^{\#K_1 + \#K_2}$ and constant memory complexity.

Applying a meet-in-the-middle attack to our construction, would require an adversary to find a pre-image of the tag by inverting the MERGE function. We show that finding a pre-image of MERGE is as hard as exhaustively guessing the internal state after the initial PRFs in Sect. 4.2. Moreover, as MERGEMAC does not implement an inverse function for the merging function MERGE, we also limit more advanced meet-in-the-middle attacks such as partial matching/sieve-in-the-middle attacks [BR11], splice and cut attacks [AS09] and biclique attacks [KRS12].

**State Recovery Attacks.** The goal of state recovery attacks is to recover internal state of a cipher or parts thereof. Those attacks are especially powerful against stream ciphers [MK08], as they may allow an adversary to predict the remaining key stream. Recovering the internal state in a MAC scheme could potentially lead to forgery attacks.

In MERGEMAC, recovering the internal state before the merging function MERGE would require guessing one of the PRF outputs, while keeping the other one constant. An adversary can also try to exploit the two XOR operations in the beginning and end of MERGE. However, the $\pi$ function provides full diffusion after 3 rounds canceling any correlation between the input and output of $\pi$.

**Differential Attacks.** Differential Cryptanalysis [BS91] is one of the most powerful cryptanalytic techniques. Leurent [Leu16] applied a partitioning technique on CHASKEY, breaking 7 out of 8 rounds. We searched for differential trails of our $\pi$-function using the automated tool CryptoSMT [Ste15]. The tool is based

**Table 2.** Differential trails for 3 of the $\pi$ function.

| # Rounds | $\Delta_{in}(v_0, v_1, v_2, v_3) \rightarrow \Delta_{out}(v_0, v_1, v_2, v_3)$ | Probability |
|---|---|---|
| 1 | (0000, 0000, 8000, 0000) | 1 |
|   | (8000, 0080, 0080, 8001) | |
| 2 | (1040, 1000, 2000, 2000) | $2^{-5}$ |
|   | (8001, 0080, 0080, 8002) | |
| 3 | (4010, 0010, 0020, 0020) | $2^{-14}$ |
|   | (0201, 0A22, 0800, 0302) | |

on the constraint solver STP and the SAT solver CryptoMiniSat. Table 2 shows the results for three rounds of the $\pi$ functions.

However, one can deduce that the reduced-round $\pi$-functions are not differential secure. Nevertheless, to successfully mount a differential attack on MergeMAC an adversary needs access to differential pairs at the input and output of Merge. Since the outputs of the PRFs are unknown an adversary does not have access to such pairs.

**Internal Collisions.** An internal collision is defined as any input difference $\Delta_{in}$ that maps to a zero output difference $\Delta_{out} = 0$. An adversary could use the information from internal collisions to set up a forgery attack by constructing message pairs that fulfill the input difference $\Delta_{in}$ that when colliding lead to the same tag. We experimentally verified that there are no internal collision in the merging function Merge with our differential search tool CryptoSMT. Hence, we defined a zero difference after a selected number of rounds and checked if we can find any possible input differences that would lead to this all zero difference. We tested our $\pi$-function for up to five rounds and concluded that there are no internal collisions in our Merge-function.

**Rotational Cryptanalysis.** Rotational cryptanalysis [KN10] is a generic cryptanalytic attack against ARX ciphers. Let us consider a pair $(x, x \lll r)$, consisting of plaintext $x$ and a rotated plaintext $x$ by $r$ positions. Then, the pair $(x, x \lll r)$ forms a rotational pair. Rotational cryptanalysis exploits that a rotational pair remains steady through binary operations like XOR and rotation. In MergeMAC the inputs for merging function Merge are uniformly random and unknown thereby preventing rotational attacks.

**Slide Attacks.** Slide attacks were introduced by Biryukov and Wagner [BW99] in 1999 and later extended to advanced slide attacks [BW00]. Both can be used against ciphers with identical round functions. Accordingly, the number of rounds for a cipher is irrelevant against slide attacks. In our construction, each round of the permutation $\pi$ in our merging function Merge is identical and therefore vulnerable to slide attacks. However, as we XOR the inputs of the merging function MERGE before and after the permutation $\pi$, an adversary will not be able to exploit a slide attack as she would still be required to invert the XOR operation. Therefore, slide attacks do not pose a threat to our construction.

**Rebound Attacks.** Rebound attacks were introduced by Mendel et al. [MRST09] and are an important technique for differential cryptanalysis of hash functions. While standard rebound attacks are only applicable to AES-like compression functions Khovratovich et al. [KNR10] applied rotational cryptanalysis with rebound attacks to the SHA-3 finalist SKEIN with its THREEFISH compression function. The general idea behind the attack is to split the compression function in three parts $E = E_{fw} \circ E_{in} \circ E_{bw}$. In the inbound phase, $E_{in}$ parts of a differential characteristic that are difficult to satisfy probabilistically are covered with a match-in-the-middle approach. In the outbound phases, the solutions from the inbound phases are propagated outwards in both directions, while it is checked if the characteristic holds. Rebound attacks are no threat to MERGE, as the adversary needs to be able to verify the differentials which is impossible because the input values are unknown. Moreover, even if an adversary uses an outbound phase over the initial PRFs, the selection of our MAC function precludes the existence of any high probability differential trails that an adversary could use to succeed.

**Fixed Points.** The permutation in CHASKEY, which is structurally the same as our permutation $\pi$, has one fixed point. Since it only contains modular additions XOR and bit wise rotations the all zero input leads to $\pi(\mathbf{0}) = \mathbf{0}$. Fixed points can be used in a differentiability attack as shown by Maurer et al. [MRH04].

For our construction, this would mean that if an adversary can construct a message leading to an internal all zero state $\mathbf{0}$ before the application of MERGE, then the tag would also be $\mathbf{0}$. However, constructing an all zero-state as input to MERGE, means constructing matching PRF outputs. Since each output occurs uniformly at random an adversary will not be able to find such a plaintext with a complexity better than $2^{64}$.

**Algebraic Attacks.** Higher-order cryptanalysis and zero-sum distinguisher were introduced by Lai in 1994 [Lai94] and first applied to block ciphers by Knudsen in 1995 [Knu95]. In 2009, Dinur and Shamir introduced Cube attacks [DS09]. All of those algebraic attacks exploit a low algebraic degree of a block cipher to attack it. In our merging function MERGE, the only non-linear operation is a modular addition. This modular addition ensures that the algebraic degree grows sufficiently for each output bit. Furthermore, as each input to the merging function MERGE is first processed by the underlying block cipher of the PRFs, we can ensure that the degree of the input bits are already sufficiently large (i.e. the degree is n − 1, where n is the block size of the block cipher of the PRFs).

## 5  Performance

We benchmarked both CHASKEY and our function MERGE using SUPER-COP [Ber16] on an Intel i7-4600U CPU running at 2.10 GHz. While this is not a platform requiring lightweight cryptography we are only interested in comparing relative timings for which it is sufficient. We give the median of required cycles for CHASKEY for several input sizes in Table 3. As is to be expected, our simplified version is faster than CHASKEY on even the shortest messages since we only apply the round function three times. The median of the required cycles for MERGE was 38 which, compared to the second row of Table 3, is close to 3 out of 8 rounds. The difference becomes more pronounced for longer messages. To consider the overhead of our construction let $t_1, t_2$ be the time required for $\mathcal{P}_1$ and $\mathcal{P}_2$ and let $t_{\text{MERGE}}$ be the time required by the merging function. So in the least favorable comparison, when the entire message would fit into one block, our construction requires time $t_1 + t_2 + t_{\text{MERGE}}$ where simply using $\mathcal{P}_1$ as a MAC would only require $t_1$. Using our performance values for CHASKEY this would be an overhead of 132%. However, since $\mathcal{P}_1$ and $\mathcal{P}_2$ can execute in parallel this immediately comes down to only 32%. For a message size of over 16 bytes, so at least two blocks, and leveraging parallel execution our construction is already as fast as the simple MAC. In the ideal case when both message parts are known and the PRF outputs are cached our construction is three times faster. Note that in the case of CHASKEY the overhead required by our merging function is less than the overhead required for creating the padding for messages as shown in the first line of Table 3.

**Table 3.** Required cycles for hashing with CHASKEY

| Input size | Median cycles |
|:----------:|:-------------:|
| 0          | 153           |
| 16         | 111           |
| 32         | 147           |
| 64         | 216           |
| 128        | 354           |
| 256        | 639           |
| 512        | 1182          |
| 1024       | 2259          |
| 2048       | 4461          |
| 4096       | 8835          |

For the CAN bus application this means that in the case of a correct counter our construction will at most have an overhead of 32%. In case of an incorrect counter trying additional values only costs one third of a normal MAC evaluation. In the worst case, if the counter has wrapped many times, our construction would require only one third of the time.

# 6  Conclusions

We presented MERGEMAC, a MAC construction specifically tailored to accomplish authenticated communication in very constrained environments with limited bandwidth and the need to satisfy strict time constraints. The construction is based on a merging function for which we conducted a thorough cryptanalysis and provided performance figures. We demonstrated the applicability of MERGEMAC for authenticating messages on the CAN bus. In case of different security requirements it is perfectly possible to instantiate this MAC construction with different PRFs like AES-CMAC and a suitable merging function.

One of the questions left for future work is whether there are more efficient merging functions that still meet the security requirements as defined in Sect. 3. The merging function MERGE we defined merges two pre-MACs into the final MAC. For other use cases it is possible to canonically increase the number of pre-MACs.

# References

[AS09] Aoki, K., Sasaki, Y.: Preimage attacks on one-block MD4, 63-step MD5 and more. In: Avanzi, R.M., Keliher, L., Sica, F. (eds.) SAC 2008. LNCS, vol. 5381, pp. 103–119. Springer, Heidelberg (2009). https://doi.org/10.1007/978-3-642-04159-4_7

[BCK96] Bellare, M., Canetti, R., Krawczyk, H.: Keying hash functions for message authentication. In: Koblitz, N. (ed.) CRYPTO 1996. LNCS, vol. 1109, pp. 1–15. Springer, Heidelberg (1996). https://doi.org/10.1007/3-540-68697-5_1

[Ber16] Bernstein, D.J.: Supercop (2016). https://bench.cr.yp.to/supercop.html

[BGR95] Bellare, M., Guérin, R., Rogaway, P.: XOR MACs: new methods for message authentication using finite pseudorandom functions. In: Coppersmith, D. (ed.) CRYPTO 1995. LNCS, vol. 963, pp. 15–28. Springer, Heidelberg (1995). https://doi.org/10.1007/3-540-44750-4_2

[BL16] Bhargavan, K., Leurent, G.: On the practical (in-)security of 64-bit block ciphers: collision attacks on HTTP over TLS and OpenVPN. In: Proceedings of the 2016 ACM SIGSAC Conference on Computer and Communications Security, CCS 2016, pp. 456–467. ACM, New York (2016)

[BR02] Black, J., Rogaway, P.: A block-cipher mode of operation for parallelizable message authentication. In: Knudsen, L.R. (ed.) EUROCRYPT 2002. LNCS, vol. 2332, pp. 384–397. Springer, Heidelberg (2002). https://doi.org/10.1007/3-540-46035-7_25

[BR11] Bogdanov, A., Rechberger, C.: A 3-subset meet-in-the-middle attack: cryptanalysis of the lightweight block cipher KTANTAN. In: Biryukov, A., Gong, G., Stinson, D.R. (eds.) SAC 2010. LNCS, vol. 6544, pp. 229–240. Springer, Heidelberg (2011). https://doi.org/10.1007/978-3-642-19574-7_16

[BS91] Biham, E., Shamir, A.: Differential cryptanalysis of DES-like cryptosystems. In: Menezes, A.J., Vanstone, S.A. (eds.) CRYPTO 1990. LNCS, vol. 537, pp. 2–21. Springer, Heidelberg (1991). https://doi.org/10.1007/3-540-38424-3_1

[BW99]  Biryukov, A., Wagner, D.: Slide attacks. In: Knudsen, L. (ed.) FSE 1999. LNCS, vol. 1636, pp. 245–259. Springer, Heidelberg (1999). https://doi. org/10.1007/3-540-48519-8_18

[BW00]  Biryukov, A., Wagner, D.: Advanced slide attacks. In: Preneel, B. (ed.) EUROCRYPT 2000. LNCS, vol. 1807, pp. 589–606. Springer, Heidelberg (2000). https://doi.org/10.1007/3-540-45539-6_41

[CMK+11] Checkoway, S., McCoy, D., Kantor, B., Anderson, D., Shacham, H., Savage, S., Koscher, K., Czeskis, A., Roesner, F., Kohno, T., et al.: Comprehensive experimental analyses of automotive attack surfaces. In: USENIX Security Symposium, San Francisco (2011)

[DH77]  Diffie, W., Hellman, M.E.: Special feature exhaustive cryptanalysis of the NBS data encryption standard. Computer $10$(6), 74–84 (1977)

[DR05]  Daemen, J., Rijmen, V.: A new MAC construction ALRED and a specific instance ALPHA-MAC. In: Gilbert, H., Handschuh, H. (eds.) FSE 2005. LNCS, vol. 3557, pp. 1–17. Springer, Heidelberg (2005). https://doi.org/10.1007/11502760_1

[DS09]  Dinur, I., Shamir, A.: Cube attacks on tweakable black box polynomials. In: Joux, A. (ed.) EUROCRYPT 2009. LNCS, vol. 5479, pp. 278–299. Springer, Heidelberg (2009). https://doi.org/10.1007/978-3-642-01001-9_16

[Dwo16] Dworkin, M.J.: Recommendation for block cipher modes of operation: the CMAC mode for authentication. Special Publication (NIST SP)-800-38B (2016)

[IK03]  Iwata, T., Kurosawa, K.: OMAC: one-key CBC MAC. In: Johansson, T. (ed.) FSE 2003. LNCS, vol. 2887, pp. 129–153. Springer, Heidelberg (2003). https://doi.org/10.1007/978-3-540-39887-5_11

[ISO11] Message Authentication Codes (MACs) - Part 1: Mechanisms Using a Block Cipher. Standard, International Organization for Standardization, Geneva, CH, March 2011

[KCR+10] Koscher, K., Czeskis, A., Roesner, F., Patel, S., Kohno, T., Checkoway, S., McCoy, D., Kantor, B., Anderson, D., Shacham, H., et al.: Experimental security analysis of a modern automobile. In: 2010 IEEE Symposium on Security and Privacy (SP), pp. 447–462. IEEE (2010)

[KN10]  Khovratovich, D., Nikolić, I.: Rotational cryptanalysis of ARX. In: Hong, S., Iwata, T. (eds.) FSE 2010. LNCS, vol. 6147, pp. 333–346. Springer, Heidelberg (2010). https://doi.org/10.1007/978-3-642-13858-4_19

[KNR10] Khovratovich, D., Nikolić, I., Rechberger, C.: Rotational rebound attacks on reduced skein. In: Abe, M. (ed.) ASIACRYPT 2010. LNCS, vol. 6477, pp. 1–19. Springer, Heidelberg (2010). https://doi.org/10.1007/978-3-642-17373-8_1

[Knu95] Knudsen, L.R.: Truncated and higher order differentials. In: Preneel, B. (ed.) FSE 1994. LNCS, vol. 1008, pp. 196–211. Springer, Heidelberg (1995). https://doi.org/10.1007/3-540-60590-8_16

[KRS12] Khovratovich, D., Rechberger, C., Savelieva, A.: Bicliques for preimages: attacks on Skein-512 and the SHA-2 family. In: Canteaut, A. (ed.) FSE 2012. LNCS, vol. 7549, pp. 244–263. Springer, Heidelberg (2012). https://doi.org/10.1007/978-3-642-34047-5_15

[Lai94] Lai, X.: Higher order derivatives and differential cryptanalysis. In: Blahut, R.E., Costello, D.J., Maurer, U., Mittelholzer, T. (eds.) Communications and Cryptography, pp. 227–233. Springer, Boston (1994). https://doi.org/10.1007/978-1-4615-2694-0_23

[Lan11] Langner, R.: Stuxnet: dissecting a cyberwarfare weapon. IEEE Secur. Priv. **9**(3), 49–51 (2011)

[Leu16] Leurent, G.: Improved differential-linear cryptanalysis of 7-round Chaskey with partitioning. In: Fischlin, M., Coron, J.-S. (eds.) EUROCRYPT 2016. LNCS, vol. 9665, pp. 344–371. Springer, Heidelberg (2016). https://doi. org/10.1007/978-3-662-49890-3_14

[LM91] Lai, X., Massey, J.L.: A proposal for a new block encryption standard. In: Damgård, I.B. (ed.) EUROCRYPT 1990. LNCS, vol. 473, pp. 389–404. Springer, Heidelberg (1991). https://doi.org/10.1007/3-540-46877-3_35

[LMM91] Lai, X., Massey, J.L., Murphy, S.: Markov ciphers and differential cryptanalysis. In: Davies, D.W. (ed.) EUROCRYPT 1991. LNCS, vol. 547, pp. 17–38. Springer, Heidelberg (1991). https://doi.org/10.1007/3-540-46416-6_2

[MK08] Maximov, A., Khovratovich, D.: New state recovery attack on RC4. In: Wagner, D. (ed.) CRYPTO 2008. LNCS, vol. 5157, pp. 297–316. Springer, Heidelberg (2008). https://doi.org/10.1007/978-3-540-85174-5_17

[MMVH+14] Mouha, N., Mennink, B., Van Herrewege, A., Watanabe, D., Preneel, B., Verbauwhede, I.: Chaskey: an efficient MAC algorithm for 32-bit microcontrollers. In: Joux, A., Youssef, A. (eds.) SAC 2014. LNCS, vol. 8781, pp. 306–323. Springer, Cham (2014). https://doi.org/10.1007/978-3-319-13051-4_19

[MRH04] Maurer, U., Renner, R., Holenstein, C.: Indifferentiability, impossibility results on reductions, and applications to the random oracle methodology. In: Naor, M. (ed.) TCC 2004. LNCS, vol. 2951, pp. 21–39. Springer, Heidelberg (2004). https://doi.org/10.1007/978-3-540-24638-1_2

[MRST09] Mendel, F., Rechberger, C., Schläffer, M., Thomsen, S.S.: The rebound attack: cryptanalysis of reduced whirlpool and Grøstl. In: Dunkelman, O. (ed.) FSE 2009. LNCS, vol. 5665, pp. 260–276. Springer, Heidelberg (2009). https://doi.org/10.1007/978-3-642-03317-9_16

[RS04] Rogaway, P., Shrimpton, T.: Cryptographic hash-function basics: definitions, implications, and separations for preimage resistance, second-preimage resistance, and collision resistance. In: Roy, B., Meier, W. (eds.) FSE 2004. LNCS, vol. 3017, pp. 371–388. Springer, Heidelberg (2004). https://doi.org/10.1007/978-3-540-25937-4_24

[RSWO17] Ronen, E., Shamir, A., Weingarten, A.O., O'Flynn, C.: IoT goes nuclear: creating a ZigBee chain reaction. In: 2017 IEEE Symposium on Security and Privacy (SP), pp. 195–212, May 2017

[Ste15] Kölbl, S.: CryptoSMT: an easy to use tool for cryptanalysis of symmetric primitives (2015). https://github.com/kste/cryptosmt

[Tur08] Turner, J.M.: The keyed-hash message authentication code (HMAC). Federal Information Processing Standards Publication (2008)

# KangarooTwelve: Fast Hashing Based on Keccak-$p$

Guido Bertoni[3], Joan Daemen[1,2], Michaël Peeters[1], Gilles Van Assche[1(✉)],
Ronny Van Keer[1], and Benoît Viguier[2]

[1] STMicroelectronics, Diegem, Belgium
gilles.vanassche@st.com
[2] Radboud University, Nijmegen, The Netherlands
[3] Security Pattern, Brescia, Italy

**Abstract.** We present KangarooTwelve, a fast and secure arbitrary output-length hash function aiming at a higher speed than the FIPS 202's SHA-3 and SHAKE functions. While sharing many features with SHAKE128, like the cryptographic primitive, the sponge construction, the eXtendable Output Function (XOF) and the 128-bit security strength, KangarooTwelve offers two major improvements over its standard counterpart. First it has a built-in parallel mode that efficiently exploits multi-core or SIMD instruction parallelism for long messages, without impacting the performance for short messages. Second, relying on the cryptanalysis results on Keccak over the past ten years, we tuned its permutation to require twice less computation effort while still offering a comfortable safety margin. By combining these two changes KangarooTwelve consumes less than 0.55 cycles/byte for long messages on the latest Intel®'s SkylakeX architectures. The generic security of KangarooTwelve is guaranteed by the use of Sakura encoding for the tree hashing and of the sponge construction for the compression function.

**Keywords:** Symmetric cryptography · Hash function · Tree hashing
Keccak · Software performance

## 1 Introduction

Most cryptography involves careful trade-offs between performance and security. The performance of a cryptographic function can be objectively measured, although it can yield a wide spectrum of figures depending on the variety of hardware and software platforms that the users may be interested in. Out of these, performance on widespread processors is easily measurable and naturally becomes the most visible feature. Security on the other hand cannot be measured. The best one can do is to obtain security assurance by relying on public scrutiny by skilled cryptanalysts. This is a scarce resource and the gaining of

© Springer International Publishing AG, part of Springer Nature 2018
B. Preneel and F. Vercauteren (Eds.): ACNS 2018, LNCS 10892, pp. 400–418, 2018.
https://doi.org/10.1007/978-3-319-93387-0_21

insight requires time and reflection. With the growing emphasis on provable security reduction of modes, the fact that the security of the underlying primitives is still based on public scrutiny should not be overlooked.

In this paper we present the hash function KANGAROOTWELVE, or more exactly an *eXtendable Output Function* (XOF). KANGAROOTWELVE makes use of a tree hash mode with SAKURA encoding [9,30] and the sponge construction [7], both proven secure. Its underlying permutation is a member of the KECCAK-$p[1600, n_r]$ family, differing from that of KECCAK only in the number of rounds. Since its publication in 2008, the round function of KECCAK was never tweaked [6]. Moreover, as for most symmetric cryptographic primitives, third-party cryptanalysis has been applied to reduced-round versions of KECCAK. Hence KANGAROOTWELVE's security assurance directly benefits from nearly ten years of public scrutiny, including all cryptanalysis during and after the SHA-3 competition [13].

KANGAROOTWELVE gets its low computational workload per bit from using the KECCAK-$f[1600]$ permutation reduced to 12 rounds. Clearly, 12 rounds provide less safety margin than the full 24 rounds in SHA-3 and SHAKE functions. Still, the safety margin provided by 12 rounds is comfortable as, e.g., the best published collision attacks at time of writing break KECCAK only up to 6 rounds [15,16,36,37].

The other design choice that gives KANGAROOTWELVE great speed for long messages is the use of a tree hash mode. This mode is transparent for the user in the sense that the message length fully determines the tree topology. Basically, the mode calls an underlying sponge-based compression function for each 8192-byte chunk of message and finally hashes the concatenation of the resulting digests. We call this the *final node growing* approach. Clearly, the chunks can be hashed in parallel.

The main advantage of the final node growing approach is that implementers can decide on the degree of parallelism their programs support. A simple implementation could compute everything serially, while another would process two, four or more branches in parallel using multiple cores, or more simply, a SIMD instruction set such as the Intel® AVX2™. Future processors can even contain an increasing number of cores, or wider SIMD registers as exemplified by the recent AVX-512™ instruction set, and KANGAROOTWELVE will be readily able to exploit them. The fixed length of the chunks and the fact that the tree topology is fully determined by the message length improves interoperability: The hash result is independent of the amount of parallelism exploited in the implementation.

KANGAROOTWELVE is not the only KECCAK-based parallel hash mode. In late 2016, NIST published the SP 800-185 standard, including a parallelized hash mode called ParallelHash [31]. Compared to ParallelHash, KANGAROOTWELVE improves on the speed for short messages. ParallelHash compresses message chunks to digests in a first stage and compresses the concatenation of the digests in a second stage. This two-stage hashing introduces an overhead that is costly for short messages. In KANGAROOTWELVE we apply a technique called *kangaroo hopping*: It merges the hashing of the first chunk of the message and that of the chaining values of the remaining chunks [9]. As a result, the two stages reduce to one if the input fits in one chunk with no overhead whatsoever.

Finally, KANGAROOTWELVE is a concrete application of the SAKURA encoding, which yields secure tree hash modes by construction [9].

After setting up some notation conventions in Sect. 2, we specify KANGA-ROOTWELVE in Sect. 3. Section 4 gives a rationale and Sect. 5 introduces a closely related variant called MARSUPILAMIFOURTEEN. In Sect. 6, we discuss implementation aspects and display benchmarks for recent processors.

## 2    Notation

A bit is an element of $\mathbb{Z}_2$. A string of bits is denoted using single quotes, e.g., '0' or '111'. The concatenation of two strings $a$ and $b$ is denoted $a\|b$. The truncation of a string $s$ to its first $n$ bits is denoted $\lfloor s \rfloor_n$. The $n$ times repetition of a bit 's' is denoted 's$^n$', e.g. '110$^4$' = '110000'. The empty string is denoted as $*$.

A byte is a string of 8 bits. The byte $b_0, b_1, \ldots, b_7$ can also be represented by the integer value $\sum_i 2^i b_i$ written in hexadecimal. E.g., the bit string 11110010 can be equivalently written as 0x4F as depicted in Fig. 1. The function $\mathrm{enc}_8(x)$ encodes the integer $x$, with $0 \leq x \leq 255$, as a byte with value $x$.

The length in of a byte string $s$ is denoted $\|s\|$. (0x00)$^n$ denotes the $n$ times repetition of the byte 0x00.

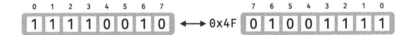

**Fig. 1.** Example of byte representation

## 3    Specifications of KANGAROOTWELVE

KANGAROOTWELVE is an eXtendable Output Function (XOF). It takes as input a message $M$ and an optional customization string $C$, both byte strings of variable length.

KANGAROOTWELVE produces unrelated outputs on different couples $(M, C)$. The customization string $C$ is meant to provide *domain separation*, namely, for two different customization strings $C_1 \neq C_2$, KANGAROOTWELVE gives two independent functions of $M$. In practice, $C$ is typically a short string, such as a name, an address or an identifier (e.g., URI, OID). KANGAROOTWELVE naturally maps to a XOF with a single input string $M$ by setting the customization string input $C$ to the empty string. This allows implementing it with a classical hash function API.

As a XOF, the output of KANGAROOTWELVE is unlimited, and the user can request as many output bits as desired. It can be used for traditional hashing simply by generating outputs of the desired digest size.

We provide a reference implementation and test vectors in [11].

## 3.1    The Inner Compression Function $F$

The core of KANGAROOTWELVE is the KECCAK-$p[1600, n_r = 12]$ permutation, i.e., a version of the permutation used in SHAKE and SHA-3 instances reduced to $n_r = 12$ rounds [30]. We build a sponge function $F$ on top of this permutation with capacity set to $c = 256$ bits and therefore with rate $r = 1600 - c = 1344$. It makes use of multi-rate padding, indicated by pad10*1. Following [30], this is expressed formally as:

$$F = \text{SPONGE}[\text{KECCAK-}p[1600, n_r = 12], \text{pad}10^*1, r = 1344].$$

On top of the sponge function $F$, KANGAROOTWELVE uses a SAKURA-compatible tree hash mode, which we describe shortly.

## 3.2    The Merged Input String $S$

First, we merge $M$ and $C$ to a single input string $S$ in a reversible way by concatenating:

– the input message $M$;
– the customization string $C$;
– the length in bytes of $C$ encoded using length_encode$(\|C\|)$ as in Algorithm 1.

---

**Algorithm 1.** The function length_encode$(x)$

---

**Input:** an integer $x$ in the range $0 \le x \le 256^{255} - 1$
**Output:** a byte string

Let $l$ be the smallest integer in the range $0 \le l \le 255$ such that $x < 256^l$
Let $x = \sum_{i=0}^{l-1} x_i 256^i$ with $0 \le x_i \le 255$ for all $i$
**return** $\text{enc}_8(x_{l-1})\| \ldots \|\text{enc}_8(x_1)\|\text{enc}_8(x_0)\|\text{enc}_8(l)$

**Examples:**
  length_encode$(0)$ returns 0x00
  length_encode$(12)$ returns 0x0C||0x01
  length_encode$(65538)$ returns 0x01||0x00||0x02||0x03

---

Then, the input string $S$ is cut into chunks of $B = 8192$ bytes, i.e.,

$$S = S_0\|S_1\| \ldots \|S_{n-1},$$

with $n = \left\lceil \frac{\|S\|}{B} \right\rceil$ and where all chunks except the last one must have exactly $B$ bytes. Note that there is always one block as $S$ consists of at least one byte.

### 3.3 The Tree Hash Mode

When $\|S\| > B$, we have $n > 1$ and KANGAROOTWELVE builds a tree with the following final node $\texttt{Node}_*$ and inner nodes $\texttt{Node}_i$ with $1 \leq i \leq n - 1$:

$$\texttt{Node}_i = S_i\|\text{'110'}$$
$$\text{CV}_i = \lfloor F(\texttt{Node}_i) \rfloor_{256}$$
$$\texttt{Node}_* = S_0\|\text{'110}^{62}\text{'}\|\text{CV}_1\|\dots\|\text{CV}_{n-1}\|\texttt{length\_encode}(n - 1)$$
$$\|\texttt{0xFF}\|\texttt{0xFF}\|\text{'01'}$$
$$\text{KANGAROOTWELVE}(M, C) = F(\texttt{Node}_*).$$

The chaining values $\text{CV}_i$ have length $c = 256$ bits. This is illustrated in Fig. 2.

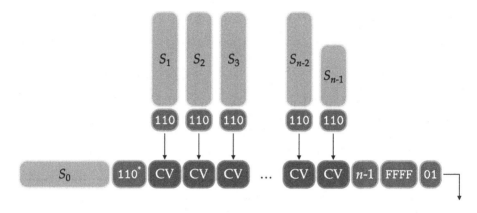

**Fig. 2.** Schematic of KANGAROOTWELVE for $\|S\| > B$, with arrows denoting calls to $F$.

When $\|S\| \leq B$, we have $n = 1$ and the tree reduces to its single final node $\texttt{Node}_*$ and KANGAROOTWELVE becomes:

$$\texttt{Node}_* = S\|\text{'11'}$$
$$\text{KANGAROOTWELVE}(M, C) = F(\texttt{Node}_*).$$

### 3.4 Security Claim

We make a flat sponge claim [8] with 255 bits of claimed capacity in Claim 1. Informally, it means that KANGAROOTWELVE shall offer the same security strength as a random oracle whenever that offers a strength below 128 bits and a strength of 128 bits in all other cases. We discuss the implications of the claim more in depth in Sect. 4.1.

**Claim 1 (Flat Sponge Claim [8]).** *The success probability of any attack on* KANGAROOTWELVE *shall not be higher than the sum of that for a random oracle and*

$$1 - e^{-\frac{N^2}{2^{256}}},$$

*with $N$ the attack complexity in calls to* KECCAK-$p[1600, n_r = 12]$ *or its inverse. We exclude from the claim weaknesses due to the mere fact that the function can be described compactly and can be efficiently executed, e.g., the so-called random oracle implementation impossibility [24], as well as properties that cannot be modeled as a single-stage game [33].*

Note that $1 - e^{-\frac{N^2}{2^{256}}} < \frac{N^2}{2^{256}}$.

## 4 Rationale

In this section, we provide some more in-depth explanations on the design choices in KANGAROOTWELVE.

### 4.1 Implications of the Security Claim

The flat sponge claim covers all attacks up to a given *security strength* of 128 bits. Informally, saying that a cryptographic function has a security strength of $s$ bits means that no attacks exist with complexity $N$ and success probability $p$ such that $N/p < 2^s$ [26].

The claim covers quasi all practically revelant security of KANGAROOTWELVE including that of traditional hashing: collision, preimage and second preimage resistance. To achieve 128-bit security strength, the output $n$ must be chosen long enough so that there are no generic attacks (i.e., also applicable to a random oracle) that violate 128-bit security. So for 128-bit (second) preimage security the output should be at least 128 bits, and for 128-bit collision security the output should be at least 256 bits.

For many primitives the security strength that can be claimed degrades under multi-target attacks by $\log_2 M$ bits with $M$ the number of targets. This is not the case for the flat sponge claim. As an example, let us take the case of a multi-target preimage attack versus a single-target preimage attack.

– In a (single-target) preimage attack, the adversary is given a $n$-bit challenge $y$ and has to find an input $x$ such that $\lfloor f(x) \rfloor_n = y$. A random oracle offers $n$ bits of security strength: After $N$ attempts, the total success probability is $p$ with $p \approx N2^{-n}$. So we have that $N/p \approx 2^n$ for $N < 2^n$ and the security strength for a random oracle is $n$. For KANGAROOTWELVE we claim security strength $\min(n, 128)$ bits in this case.

– In an $M$-target preimage attack, the adversary is given $M$ challenges, $y_1$ to $y_M$, and she succeeds if she find an input $x$ such that $\lfloor f(x) \rfloor_n = y_i$ for any of the challenges. A random oracle with $N$ attempts has success probability $p$ with of $p \approx MN2^{-n}$, and hence $N/p \approx 2^n/M$. So the security strength for the random oracle reduces to $n - \log M$ bits. For KANGAROOTWELVE we claim security strength $\min(n - \log M, 128)$ bits in this case.

Clearly, the reduction in security due to $M$ targets is generic and independent of the security strength. It can be compensated for by increasing the output length $n$ by $\log M$ bits.

### 4.2  Security of the Mode

The security of the mode, or the generic security, relies on both the sponge construction and on the tree hash mode. The latter is SAKURA-compatible so that it automatically satisfies the conditions of soundness and guarantees security against generic attacks, see [9, Theorem 1] and [10, Theorem 1]. In both cases, the bottleneck is the ability to generate collisions in the chaining values, or equivalently, collisions of the inner hash function.

The probability of inner collisions in the sponge construction is $N^2/2^{c+1}$, with $N$ the number of blocks [7]. Regarding the collisions in the chaining values of the tree hash mode, the probability is at most $q^2/2^{c+1}$ [10, Theorem 1] with $q$ the number of queries to $F$. Since each query to $F$ implies at least one block to be processed by the sponge construction, we have $q \leq N$ and we can bound the sum of the two probabilities as $N^2/2^{c+1} + q^2/2^{c+1} \leq N^2/2^{(c-1)+1}$. This expression is equivalent as if $c$ was one bit less than with a single source of collisions, and Claim 1 takes this into account by setting the claimed capacity to $c - 1 = 255$ bits.

We formalize the security of KANGAROOTWELVE's mode of operation in the following theorem. We can see the combination of the tree hash mode and the sponge construction as applied in KANGAROOTWELVE as a mode of operation of a permutation and call it $\mathcal{K}$.

**Theorem 1.** *The advantage of differentiating $\mathcal{K}$, where the underlying permutation is uniformly chosen among all the possible 1600-bit permutations, is upper bounded by*

$$\frac{2N^2 + N}{2^{c+1}},$$

*with $N$ the number of calls to the underlying permutation.*

*Proof.* By the triangle inequality, the advantage in distinguishing $\mathcal{K}$ calling a random permutation from a random oracle is upper bounded by the sum of two advantages:

– that of distinguishing the tree hash mode calling as inner function a random function $\mathcal{F}$ from a random oracle;
– that of distinguishing the sponge construction calling a random permutation from a random function.

The former advantage is upper bounded by $q^2/2^{c+1}$, where $q$ is the number of calls to $\mathcal{F}$. This follows from Theorem 1 of [10] for any sound tree hash mode, and from Theorem 1 of [9] that says that any SAKURA-compatible tree hash mode is sound. We show that the tree hash mode is indeed SAKURA-compatible in Sect. 4.3.

Following Theorem 2 of [7], the latter advantage is upper bounded by $(N^2 + N)/2^{c+1}$. Adding the two bounds and using $q \leq N$ proves our theorem.  □

### 4.3   SAKURA Compatibility

To show SAKURA-compatibility, we use the following terminology. The inputs to the underlying hash function are called *nodes*. Each node consists of one or more *hops*, and a hop is either a chunk of the message or a sequence of chaining values.

The encoding of the nodes follows [9, Sect. 3.1]:

– When $n = 1$, the tree reduces to a single node. This is the final node, and it contains a single message hop consisting of the input string $S$ followed by the frame bits "message hop" '1' and "final node" '1'.
– When $n > 1$, there are inner nodes and the final node.
  • Each inner node contains a message hop consisting of a chunk $S_i$ followed by the frame bit "message hop" '1'; a simple padding bit '1' and "inner node" '0'.
  • The final node contains two hops: a message hop followed by a chaining hop. The message hop is the first chunk of the input string $S_0$ followed by the frame bit "message hop" '1' and a padding string '1'||'$0^{62}$' to align the chaining hop to 64-bit boundaries. The chaining hop consists of the concatenation of the chaining values, the coded number of chaining values (`length_encode`$(n-1)$), the indication that there was no interleaving ($I = \infty$, coded with the bytes `0xFF`||`0xFF`) and the frame bits "chaining hop" '0' and "final node" '1'.

### 4.4   Choice of $B$

We fix the size of the message chunks to make KANGAROOTWELVE a function without parameters. This frees the user from the burden of this technical choice and facilitates interoperability.

In particular, we chose $B = 8192$. First, we chose a power of two as this can help fetching bulk data in time-critical applications. For instance, when hashing a large file, we expect the implementation to be faster and easier if the chunks contain a whole number of disk sectors.

As for the order of magnitude of $B$, we took into account following considerations. For each $B$-byte block there is a 32-byte chaining value in the final node, giving rise to a relative processing overhead of about $32/B$. Choosing $B = 2^{13}$, this is only $2^{-8} \approx 0.4\%$.

Another concern is the number of *unused bytes* in the last $r$-bit block of the input to $F$. We have $r = 1344$ bits or $R = r/8 = 168$ bytes. When cutting the chunk $S_i$ into blocks of $R$ bytes, it leaves $W = -(B+1) \bmod R$ unused bytes in the last block. It turns out that $W$ reaches a minimum for $B = 2^{7+6n}$ with $n \geq 0$ an integer. Its relative impact, $\frac{W}{B}$, decreases as $B$ increases. For small values, e.g., $B \in \{128, 256, 512\}$, this is about 30%, while for $B = 8192$ it drops below 0.5%.

There is a tension between a larger $B$ and the exploitable parallelism. Increasing $B$ would further reduce these two overhead factors, but it would also delay the benefits of parallelism to longer messages.

Finally, the choice of $B$ bounds the degree of parallelism that an implementation can fully exploit. An implementation can in principle compute the final node and leaves in parallel, but if more than $B/32$ leaves are processed at once, the final node grows faster than $B$ bytes at a time. The chosen value of $B$ allows a parallelism up to degree $B/32 = 256$.

### 4.5   Choice of the Number of Rounds

Opting for the KECCAK-$p[1600, n_r = 12]$ permutation is a drastic reduction in the number of rounds compared to the nominal KECCAK and to the SHA-3 standard. Still, there is ample evidence from third-party cryptanalysis that the switch to KECCAK-$p[1600, n_r = 12]$ leaves a safety margin similar to the one in the SHA-2 functions.

Currently, the best collision attack applicable to KANGAROOTWELVE or any SHA-3 instance works only when the permutation is reduced to 5 rounds [36]. The attack extends to 6 rounds if more degrees of freedom are available and requires a reduction of the capacity from 256 to 160 bits. Preimage attacks reach an even smaller number of rounds [21]. Hence our proposal has a safety margin of 7 out of 12 rounds w.r.t. collision and (second) preimage resistance.

Structural distinguishers is the term used for properties of a specific function that are very unlikely to be present in a random function. Zero-sum distinguishers were applied to the KECCAK-$p[1600, n_r]$ family of permutations in a number of publications [3,14,21]. They allow producing a set of input and of output values that both sum to zero, and this in about half the time it would be needed on a random permutation with only black-box access. These structural distinguishers are of nice theoretical interest, but they do not pose a threat as they do not extend to distinguishers on sponge functions that use KECCAK-$p[1600, n_r]$, see, e.g., [35].

The structural distinguisher on the KECCAK sponge function that does reach the highest number of rounds is the keystream prediction by Dinur et al. [17]. It works when the permutation is reduced to 9 rounds, with a time and data complexity of $2^{256}$, and allows to predict one block of output. This is above the security claim of KANGAROOTWELVE, but the same authors propose a variant that works on 8 rounds with a time and data complexity of $2^{128}$, leaving a safety margin of 4 rounds or 33% for KANGAROOTWELVE against this rather academic attack. Examples of structural distinguishers for the KECCAK sponge function with practical complexity and reaching the highest number of rounds are reported by Huang et al. and work up to 7 rounds [22].

In comparison, SHA-256 has a collision attack on 31 (out of 64) steps and its compression function on 52 steps [23,25]. SHA-512's compression function admits collision attacks with practical complexities for more than half of its steps [18].

## 5   MARSUPILAMIFOURTEEN

While KANGAROOTWELVE claims a strong notion of 128-bit security strength, and we believe any security beyond it is purely of theoretical interest, some users may wish to use a XOF or hash function with higher security strength. In particular, when defining a cipher suite or protocol aiming for 256-bit security strength, all cryptographic functions shall have at least 256-bit security. Coming forward to such requests, in this section we present a variant of KANGAROOTWELVE with 511-bit claimed capacity.

Addressing a claimed capacity of 511 bits requires an increase of both the capacity in $F$ and length of chaining values in the tree hash mode to at least 512 bits. Taking exactly $c = 512$ bits is sufficient for resisting generic attacks below the claim. As for KECCAK-$p$-specific attacks, the increase of the claimed capacity to 511 bits increases the available budget of attackers and hence reduces the safety margin. In many types of attack, adding a round in the primitive (permutation or block cipher) increases the attack complexity by a large factor. Or the other way round, if one wishes to keep the same safety margin, an increase of the attack complexity must be compensated by adding rounds.

We did the exercise and the result is MARSUPILAMIFOURTEEN. It has the same specifications as KANGAROOTWELVE, with the following exceptions:

- The capacity and chaining values are 64-byte long instead of 32 bytes. This reduces the sponge rate in $F$ to 136 bytes.
- The number of rounds of KECCAK-$p[1600, n_r]$ is 14 instead of 12.
- The claimed capacity in the flat sponge claim is 511 bits instead of 255.

The computational workload per bit is roughly 45% higher than that of KANGAROOTWELVE.

Naturally, even thicker safety margins are achieved with the standard FIPS 202 instances or ParallelHash [30,31].

## 6   Implementation

We implemented KANGAROOTWELVE in C and made it available in the KECCAK code package (KCP) [12]. We now review different aspects of this implementation and its performance.

### 6.1   Byte Representation

KANGAROOTWELVE assumes that its inputs $M$ and $C$ are byte strings. SAKURA encoding works at the bit level and adds padding and suffixes so that the input to the function $F$ is a string of bits whose length is in general not a multiple of 8.

It is common practice in implementations of KECCAK to represent the last few bits of a string as a *delimited suffix* [12]. The delimited suffix is a byte that contains the last $|X| \bmod 8$ bits of a string $X$, with $|X|$ the length of $X$ in bits, followed by the delimiter bit '1', and ending with the necessary number of bits '0' to reach a length of 8 bits. When absorbing the last block in the sponge function $F$, the delimiter bit coincides with the first bit '1' of the pad10*1 padding rule. An implementation can therefore process the first $\lfloor|X|/8\rfloor$ bytes of the string $S$ and, in the last block, simply add the delimited suffix and the second bit of the pad10*1 padding rule at the last position of the outer part of the state (i.e., at position $r-1$, with $r$ the rate).

Following the convention in Sect. 2, the delimited suffix of a string with last bits $(s_0, \ldots, s_{n-1})$ can be represented by the value $2^n + \sum_{i=0}^{n-1} s_i 2^i$ in hexadecimal. For KANGAROOTWELVE, this concretely means that the final node with $\|S\| \le B$ has suffix '11' and delimited suffix 0x07. With $\|S\| > B$ the intermediate nodes with trailing bits '110' use 0x0B (as depicted in Fig. 3), and the final node ending with '01' will have 0x06 as delimited suffix.

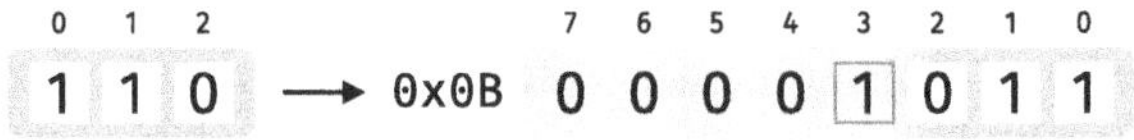

**Fig. 3.** Example of delimited suffix

On a similar note, the 64-bit string '$110^{62}$' in the final node is represented by the bytes 0x03||(0x00)$^7$, still following the convention in Sect. 2.

This approach is taken by the Internet Research Task Force RFC draft describing KANGAROOTWELVE [38] and in the reference source code in [11].

## 6.2  Structuring the Implementation

The implementation has an interface that accepts the input message $M$ in pieces of arbitrary sizes. This is useful if a file, larger than the memory size, must be processed. The customization string $C$ can be given at the end.

We have integrated the KANGAROOTWELVE code in KCP as illustrated on Fig. 4. In particular, we instantiate the sponge construction on top of KECCAK-$p[1600, n_r = 12]$ to implement the function $F$, at least to compute the final node. The function $F$ on the leaves is computed as much in parallel as possible, i.e., if at least $8B$ input bytes are given by the caller, it uses a function that computes 8 times KECCAK-$p[1600, n_r = 12]$ in parallel; if it is not available and if at least $4B$ bytes are given, it computes $4 \times$ KECCAK-$p[1600, n_r = 12]$ in parallel; and so on. If no parallel implementation exists for the given platform, or if not enough bytes are given by the caller, it falls back on a serial implementation like for the final node.

The KCP foresees that the serial and parallel implementations of the KECCAK-$p$ permutation can be optimized for a given platform. In contrast, the code for the tree hash mode and the sponge construction is generic C, without optimizations for specific platforms, and it accesses the optimized permutation-level functions through an interface called $SnP$ (for a single permutation) or $PlSnP$ (for permutations computed in parallel) [12].

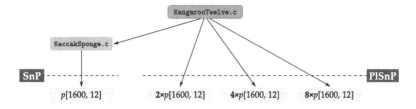

**Fig. 4.** The structure of the code implementing KANGAROOTWELVE in the KCP.

To input large messages $M$, the state to maintain between two calls internally uses two queues: one for the final node and one for the current leaf. To save memory, the input bytes are absorbed directly into the state of $F$ as they arrive. Hence, the state reduces to two times the state of $F$. Of course, if a message is known to be smaller than or equal to $B$ bytes, one could further save one queue.

### 6.3  256-bit SIMD

Current mainstream PC processors, in the Intel® Haswell and Skylake families, support a 256-bit SIMD instruction set called AVX2™. We can exploit it to compute $4 \times$ KECCAK-$p[1600, n_r = 12]$ efficiently, even on a single core.

On an Intel® Core™ i5-6500 (Skylake), we measured that one evaluation of KECCAK-$p[1600, n_r = 12]$ takes about 450 cycles, while 2 in parallel about 730 cycles and $4 \times$ KECCAK-$p[1600, n_r = 12]$ about 770 cycles. This does not include the time needed to add the input bytes to the state. Yet, this clearly points out that the time per byte decreases with the degree of parallelism.

Figure 5 displays the number of cycles for input messages up to 150,000 bytes. Microscopically, the computation time steps up for every additional $R = 168$ bytes, but this is not visible on the figure. The time needed to hash messages of length smaller than 168 bytes thus represents the smallest granularity and is reported in Table 1. Note that if many very short messages have to be processed, they can be batched so as to use a parallel implementation. This case is also reported in Table 1.

Macroscopically, when $\|S\| < B$, the time is a straight line with a slope of about 2.89 cycles/byte, i.e., the speed for $F$ implemented serially. At $\|S\| = B = 8192$, there is a slight bump (a) as the tree gets a leaf, which causes an extra evaluation of KECCAK-$p[1600, n_r = 12]$. When $\|S\| = 3B = 24,576$, two leaves can be computed in parallel and the number of cycles drops. When $\|S\| = 5B = 40,960$, four leaves can be computed in parallel and we see another drop. From then on, the same pattern repeats and one can easily identify the slopes of serial, $\times 2$ and $\times 4$ parallel implementations of KECCAK-$p[1600, n_r = 12]$.

In our implementation, the final node is always processed with a serial implementation. In principle, a more advanced implementation could process the final node in parallel with the leaves. In more details, it would process the first chunk $S_0$ in parallel with the first few leaves, and it would buffer about $B$ bytes of chaining values and so as to process them in parallel with leaves. However, at

**Table 1.** The overall speed for very short messages ($\|S\| < 168$) in cycles, very short messages when batched in cycles/message, for short messages ($\|S\| \leq 8192$) and for long ($\|S\| \gg 8192$) messages in cycles/byte. The figures assume a single core in each case.

| Intel®Core™ | Very short m. | Batched v.s.m. | Short m. | Long m. |
|---|---|---|---|---|
| Intel®Core™ i5-4570 (Haswell) | 618 c | 242 c/m | 3.68 c/b | 1.44 c/b |
| Intel®Core™ i5-6500 (Skylake) | 486 c | 205 c/m | 2.89 c/b | 1.22 c/b |
| Intel®Core™ i7-7800X (SkylakeX) | 395 c | 92 c/m | 2.35 c/b | 0.55 c/b |

this point, we preferred code simplicity over speed optimization. Similarly, one could in principle remove the peaks of Fig. 5 and make it monotonous. It could be achieved by using, e.g., the fast $4 \times$ KECCAK-$p[1600, n_\mathrm{r} = 12]$ implementation even if there are less than $4B$ bytes available, with some dummy input bytes.

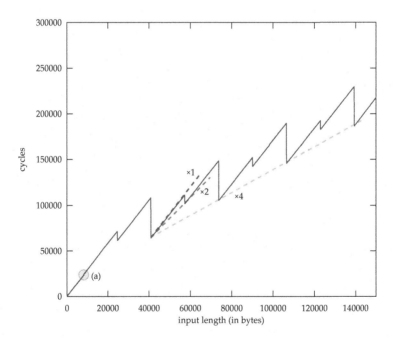

**Fig. 5.** The number of cycles of KANGAROOTWELVE on an Intel®Core$^{TM}$ i5-6500 (Skylake) as a function of the input message size.

Figure 6 shows the implementation cost in cycles per bytes. To determine the speed in cycles per byte for long messages in our implementation, we need to take into account both the time to process $4B$ input bytes in 4 leaves (or a multiple thereof) and 4 chaining values in the final node. Regarding the latter, 21 chaining values fit in exactly 4 blocks of $R = 168$ bytes. Hence, we measure

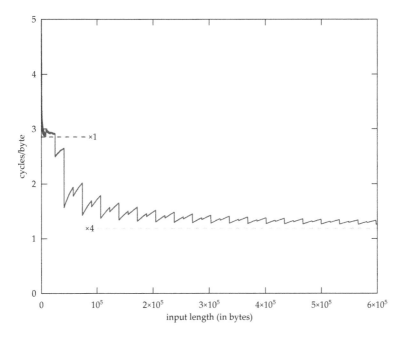

**Fig. 6.** The number of cycles per byte of KANGAROOTWELVE on an Intel®Core™ i5-6500 (Skylake) as a function of the input message size.

the time taken to process an extra $84B = \text{lcm}(4B, 21B)$ bytes. These results are reported in Table 1, together with measurements on short messages.

### 6.4 512-bit SIMD

Recently, Intel® started shipping processors with the AVX-512™ instruction set. It supports 512-bit SIMD instructions, enabling efficient implementations of $8 \times$ KECCAK-$p[1600, n_{\mathrm{r}} = 12]$. In addition to a higher degree of parallelism, some new features of AVX-512™ benefit to the implementation of KANGA-ROOTWELVE, of ParallelHash and of KECCAK in general.

- *Rotation instructions.* With the exception of AMD's XOP™, earlier SIMD instruction sets did not include a rotation instruction. This means that the cyclic shifts in $\theta$ and $\rho$ had to be implemented with a sequence of three instructions (shift left, shift right, XOR). With a rotation instruction, cyclic shifts are thus reduced from three to one instruction.
- *Three-input binary functions.* AVX-512™ offers an instruction that produces an arbitrary bitwise function of three binary inputs. In $\theta$, computing the parity takes four XORs, which can be reduced to two applications of this new instruction. Similarly, the non-linear function $\chi$ can benefit from it to directly compute $a_x + (a_{x+1} + 1)a_{x+2}$.

**Table 2.** Speed comparison. All figures are in cycles per byte for long messages, unless otherwise specified.

| Function | SkylakeX | Skylake | Haswell |
|---|---|---|---|
| KANGAROOTWELVE | 0.55 | 1.22 | 1.44 |
| KANGAROOTWELVE ($\leq$8KiB) | 2.35 | 2.89 | 3.68 |
| ParallelHash128 | 0.96 | 2.31 | 2.73 |
| Blake2bp | 1.39 | 1.34 | 1.37 |
| Blake2sp | 1.22 | 1.29 | 1.39 |
| SHAKE128 | 4.28 | 5.56 | 7.09 |
| MD5 | 4.33 | 4.54 | 4.93 |
| SHA-1 | 3.05 | 3.07 | 4.15 |
| SHA-256 | 6.65 | 6.91 | 9.27 |
| SHA-512 | 4.44 | 4.64 | 6.54 |
| Blake2b | 2.98 | 3.04 | 3.08 |
| Blake2s | 4.26 | 4.85 | 5.34 |
| Blake-256 | 5.95 | 6.76 | 7.52 |
| Blake-512 | 4.48 | 5.19 | 5.68 |
| Grøstl-256 | 7.24 | 8.13 | 9.35 |
| Grøstl-512 | 9.95 | 11.31 | 13.51 |
| JH | 13.04 | 15.14 | 15.09 |
| Skein | 4.48 | 5.18 | 5.34 |

– *32 registers.* Compared to AVX2$^{\text{TM}}$, the new processors increase the number of registers from 16 to 32. As KECCAK-$p$ has 25 lanes, this significantly decreases the need to move data between memory and registers.

We report in Table 1 the speed of our current implementation on a machine equipped with a processor in the Intel® SkylakeX family, supporting this instruction set [12].

## 6.5   Comparison with Other Functions

To put the speed of KANGAROOTWELVE in perspective, we compare it to typical hash functions, including the traditional standards MD5, SHA-1 and SHA-2 [28,29,34], the SHA-3 finalists [2,19,20,39], the popular Blake2 functions [4] and some SHA-3 instances [30,31]. For consistency, wherever possible we performed benchmarks on three machines in our possession. Moreover, we cross-checked with the publicly available eBASH results [5] and in case of discrepancy, we selected the fastest. For the traditional hash functions, the fastest implementation often came from OpenSSL [32]. For Blake2, we included some specific AVX2$^{\text{TM}}$ code by Samuel Neves [27]. Note that the comparison on SkylakeX must be taken with care, as not all implementations available at the time of this benchmarking are fully optimized for the AVX-512$^{\text{TM}}$ instruction set.

Table 2 shows the results. We first list hash functions that explicitly exploit SIMD instructions with a built-in tree hash mode, such as ParallelHash and Blake2{b, s}p, and compare them to KANGAROOTWELVE for long messages (or when it is used for hashing multiple messages in parallel).

It is interesting to compare the other hash functions to KANGAROOTWELVE when it is restricted to serial processing (as for short messages), to see its speed gain already before the parallelism kicks in. Of course, such a restriction does not exist when hashing a large file, and in practice the comparison should also be made with KANGAROOTWELVE for long messages.

## 7  Conclusion

KANGAROOTWELVE can be seen as a new member of the KECCAK family. It inherits all the properties of the family such as suitability in hardware and resistance against side-channel attacks, but grew up with a strong focus on software performance and interoperability. We tuned the mode and the primitive to offer a tremendous computational speedup in many applications while keeping a comfortable security margin. The latter is confirmed by the cryptanalysis results on KECCAK accumulated over the last ten years, which are directly applicable to the new sibling. Also, all existing KECCAK implementations can be reused with minimal effort thanks to the layered approach in the design. For instance, KANGAROOTWELVE benefits immediately from the new SHA-3 hardware support recently introduced in the ARMv8.2 instruction set [1].

The speedup benefits to both low-end and high-end processors. For the low end, one immediately benefits from the reduction in the number of rounds, and care was taken not to add overhead in the case of short messages.

At the high end, we observed that KANGAROOTWELVE gets significant performance improvements in recent processors, which go beyond the mere gain due to parallelism. Part of these improvements come from the choice of low-latency Boolean operations in the primitive that superscalar architectures can implement efficiently, as demonstrated in the latest Intel®'s SkylakeX processors with the introduction of three-input binary functions.

On such a processor, KANGAROOTWELVE processes long messages at 0.55 cycles/byte. At this speed, it would require only one of its cores to process, in real-time, the output of 10 high-speed solid-state drives (SSD), i.e., accumulated bandwidth of more than 7 GB/s per core (assuming a clock frequency of 4 GHz). This simply illustrates that with KANGAROOTWELVE the speed of hashing is no longer a bottleneck in software applications.

**Acknowledgements.** Our implementation for the serial processing is based on the AVX2$^{\text{TM}}$ code written by Andy Polyakov for OpenSSL. We would also like to thank the anonymous reviewers for their constructive comments.

# References

1. ARM corporation: ARM architecture reference manual ARMv8, for ARMv8-A architecture profile, document ARM DDI 0487C.a (ID121917). http://www.arm.com/

2. Aumasson, J.-P., Henzen, L., Meier, W., Phan, R. C.-W., SHA-3 proposal BLAKE. Submission to NIST (2008)

3. Aumasson, J.-P., Meier, W.: Zero-sum distinguishers for reduced Keccak-f and for the core functions of Luffa and Hamsi (2009). http://131002.net/data/papers/AM09.pdf

4. Aumasson, J.-P., Neves, S., Wilcox-O'Hearn, Z., Winnerlein, C.: BLAKE2: simpler, smaller, fast as MD5. In: Jacobson, M., Locasto, M., Mohassel, P., Safavi-Naini, R. (eds.) ACNS 2013. LNCS, vol. 7954, pp. 119–135. Springer, Heidelberg (2013). https://doi.org/10.1007/978-3-642-38980-1_8

5. Bernstein, D.J., Lange, T., (eds.) eBACS: ECRYPT benchmarking of cryptographic systems. http://bench.cr.yp.to

6. Bertoni, G., Daemen, J., Peeters, M., Van Assche, G.: KECCAK specifications. NIST SHA-3 Submission, October 2008

7. Bertoni, G., Daemen, J., Peeters, M., Van Assche, G.: On the indifferentiability of the sponge construction. In: Smart, N. (ed.) EUROCRYPT 2008. LNCS, vol. 4965, pp. 181–197. Springer, Heidelberg (2008). https://doi.org/10.1007/978-3-540-78967-3_11

8. Bertoni, G., Daemen, J., Peeters, M., Van Assche, G.: Cryptographic sponge functions, January 2011. https://keccak.team/files/SpongeFunctions.pdf

9. Bertoni, G., Daemen, J., Peeters, M., Van Assche, G.: Sakura: a flexible coding for tree hashing. In: Boureanu, I., Owesarski, P., Vaudenay, S. (eds.) ACNS 2014. LNCS, vol. 8479, pp. 217–234. Springer, Cham (2014). https://doi.org/10.1007/978-3-319-07536-5_14

10. Bertoni, G., Daemen, J., Peeters, M., Van Assche, G.: Sufficient conditions for sound tree and sequential hashing modes. Int. J. Inf. Secur. **13**, 335–353 (2014). https://doi.org/10.1007/s10207-013-0220-y

11. Bertoni, G., Daemen, J., Peeters, M., Van Assche, G., Van Keer, R.: KangarooTwelve: fast hashing based on KECCAK-*p*. Cryptology ePrint Archive, Report 2016/770 (2016). http://eprint.iacr.org/2016/770

12. Bertoni, G., Daemen, J., Peeters, M., Van Assche, G., Van Keer, R.: KECCAK code package, June 2016. https://github.com/gvanas/KeccakCodePackage

13. Bertoni, G., Daemen, J., Peeters, M., Van Assche, G., Van Keer, R.: KECCAK third-party cryptanalysis (2017). https://keccak.team/third_party.html

14. Boura, C., Canteaut, A., De Cannière, C.: Higher-order differential properties of KECCAK and *Luffa*. In: Joux, A. (ed.) FSE 2011. LNCS, vol. 6733, pp. 252–269. Springer, Heidelberg (2011). https://doi.org/10.1007/978-3-642-21702-9_15

15. Dinur, I., Dunkelman, O., Shamir, A.: Collision attacks on up to 5 rounds of SHA-3 using generalized internal differentials. In: Moriai, S. (ed.) FSE 2013. LNCS, vol. 8424, pp. 219–240. Springer, Heidelberg (2014). https://doi.org/10.1007/978-3-662-43933-3_12

16. Dinur, I., Dunkelman, O., Shamir, A.: Improved practical attacks on round-reduced Keccak. J. Cryptol. **27**(2), 183–209 (2014)

17. Dinur, I., Morawiecki, P., Pieprzyk, J., Srebrny, M., Straus, M.: Cube attacks and cube-attack-like cryptanalysis on the round-reduced Keccak sponge function. In: Oswald, E., Fischlin, M. (eds.) EUROCRYPT 2015. LNCS, vol. 9056, pp. 733–761. Springer, Heidelberg (2015). https://doi.org/10.1007/978-3-662-46800-5_28

18. Dobraunig, C., Eichlseder, M., Mendel, F.: Analysis of SHA-512/224 and SHA-512/256. In: Iwata, T., Cheon, J.H. (eds.) ASIACRYPT 2015. LNCS, vol. 9453, pp. 612–630. Springer, Heidelberg (2015). https://doi.org/10.1007/978-3-662-48800-3_25

19. Ferguson, N., Lucks, S., Schneier, B., Whiting, D., Bellare, M., Kohno, T., Callas, J., Walker, J.: The skein hash function family. Submission to NIST (Round 2) (2009)

20. Gauravaram, P., Knudsen, L.R., Matusiewicz, K., Mendel, F., Rechberger, C., Schläffer, M., Thomsen, S.S.: Grøstl - a SHA-3 candidate. Submission to NIST (Round 3) (2011)

21. Guo, J., Liu, M., Song, L.: Linear structures: applications to cryptanalysis of round-reduced KECCAK. In: Cheon, J.H., Takagi, T. (eds.) ASIACRYPT 2016. LNCS, vol. 10031, pp. 249–274. Springer, Heidelberg (2016). https://doi.org/10.1007/978-3-662-53887-6_9

22. Huang, S., Wang, X., Xu, G., Wang, M., Zhao, J.: Conditional cube attack on reduced-round Keccak sponge function. In: Coron, J.-S., Nielsen, J.B. (eds.) EUROCRYPT 2017. LNCS, vol. 10211, pp. 259–288. Springer, Cham (2017). https://doi.org/10.1007/978-3-319-56614-6_9

23. Li, J., Isobe, T., Shibutani, K.: Converting meet-in-the-middle preimage attack into pseudo collision attack: application to SHA-2. In: Canteaut, A. (ed.) FSE 2012. LNCS, vol. 7549, pp. 264–286. Springer, Heidelberg (2012). https://doi.org/10.1007/978-3-642-34047-5_16

24. Maurer, U., Renner, R., Holenstein, C.: Indifferentiability, impossibility results on reductions, and applications to the random oracle methodology. In: Naor, M. (ed.) TCC 2004. LNCS, vol. 2951, pp. 21–39. Springer, Heidelberg (2004). https://doi.org/10.1007/978-3-540-24638-1_2

25. Mendel, F., Nad, T., Schläffer, M.: Improving local collisions: new attacks on reduced SHA-256. In: Johansson, T., Nguyen, P.Q. (eds.) EUROCRYPT 2013. LNCS, vol. 7881, pp. 262–278. Springer, Heidelberg (2013). https://doi.org/10.1007/978-3-642-38348-9_16

26. Micciancio, D., Walter, M.: On the bit security of cryptographic primitives. Eurocrypt (2018, to appear)

27. Neves, S.: BLAKE2 AVX2 implementations. https://github.com/sneves/blake2-avx2

28. NIST: Federal information processing standard 180–1, secure hash standard, April 1995

29. NIST: Federal information processing standard 180–2, secure hash standard, August 2002

30. NIST: Federal information processing standard 202, SHA-3 standard: Permutation-based hash and extendable-output functions, August 2015. http://dx.doi.org/10.6028/NIST.FIPS.202

31. NIST: NIST special publication 800–185, SHA-3 derived functions: cSHAKE, KMAC, TupleHash and ParallelHash, December 2016. https://doi.org/10.6028/NIST.SP.800-185

32. OpenSSL community: OpenSSL - cryptography and SSL/TLS toolkit. https://github.com/openssl/openssl

33. Ristenpart, T., Shacham, H., Shrimpton, T.: Careful with composition: limitations of the indifferentiability framework. In: Paterson, K.G. (ed.) EUROCRYPT 2011. LNCS, vol. 6632, pp. 487–506. Springer, Heidelberg (2011). https://doi.org/10.1007/978-3-642-20465-4_27

34. Rivest, R.: The MD5 message-digest algorithm. Internet Request for Comments, RFC 1321, April 1992
35. Saha, D., Kuila, S., Chowdhury, D.R.: Symsum: symmetric-sum distinguishers against round reduced SHA3. IACR Trans. Symmetric Cryptol. **2017**(1), 240–258 (2017)
36. Song, L., Liao, G., Guo, J.: Non-full sbox linearization: applications to collision attacks on round-reduced KECCAK. In: Katz, J., Shacham, H. (eds.) CRYPTO 2017. LNCS, vol. 10402, pp. 428–451. Springer, Cham (2017). https://doi.org/10. 1007/978-3-319-63715-0_15
37. Song, L., Liao, G., Guo, J.: Solution to the 6-round collision challenge (2017). https://keccak.team/crunchy_contest.html
38. Viguier, B.: KangarooTwelve. Internet Research Task Force draft, March 2018. https://datatracker.ietf.org/doc/draft-viguier-kangarootwelve/
39. Wu, H.: The hash function JH. Submission to NIST (Round 3) (2011)

# Symmetric Key Cryptanalysis

# Related-Key Boomerang Attacks on Full ANU Lightweight Block Cipher

Yu Sasaki[✉]

NTT Secure Platform Laboratories,
3-9-11, Midori-cho, Musashino-shi, Tokyo 180-8585, Japan
sasaki.yu@lab.ntt.co.jp

**Abstract.** This paper presents related-key attacks against lightweight block cipher ANU that requires only 1015 gate equivalents for a 128-bit key, which is less than all existing lightweight ciphers. The design of ANU appears to be a mixture of other decent lightweight ciphers such as SIMON, PRESENT, Piccolo, TWINE etc., however, the security arguments especially against related-key attacks are not theoretically supported. In this paper, we observe that the mixture of a SIMON-like round function and a PRESENT-like key schedule function causes a very sparse differential trail that avoids non-linear update in the key schedule function. By exploiting it, a distinguishing attack against full-round ANU works only with $2^{19}$ queries in the related-key setting, in which the attack is verified by our machine experiment. This also leads to a key recovery attack for a 128-bit key with $2^{112}$ computations.

**Keywords:** Cryptanalysis · Symmetric-key · Block cipher
Lightweight · IoT · Boomerang attacks · Related-key
Dependent S-boxes

## 1 Introduction

Lightweight cryptography, which is one of the most actively discussed topics in the current symmetric-key community, studies cryptographic technologies that are particularly useful for extremely resource-constraint environments, e.g. sensor networks and radio frequency identifier (RFID) systems. Those technologies are important for the coming age of Internet-of-Things, in which a lot of sensitive data is measured by sensors that are not equipped with a powerful CPU and the data is communicated through the public space.

Block ciphers are one of the most fundamental primitives for symmetric-key cryptographic schemes. Since the proposal of the pioneering design of ultra-lightweight block ciphers PRESENT [11], a huge number of lightweight block ciphers have been designed especially during the last decade. Readers may refer to [1] for a list of existing lightweight block-cipher designs, in which the list is well-managed by researchers at University of Luxembourg.

© Springer International Publishing AG, part of Springer Nature 2018
B. Preneel and F. Vercauteren (Eds.): ACNS 2018, LNCS 10892, pp. 421–439, 2018.
https://doi.org/10.1007/978-3-319-93387-0_22

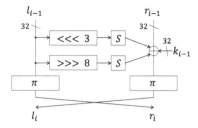

**Fig. 1.** ANU round function. '$\mathcal{S}$', '$\pi$', '$\ggg x$', and '$\lll x$' are an S-box layer, a bit-permutation, $x$-bit right cyclic shift and $x$-bit left cyclic shift, respectively.

Given a lot of lightweight block ciphers, it is now necessary for the community to choose good designs. Indeed, lightweight block ciphers have recently been discussed extensively not only in academia but also by standardization bodies such as ISO, NIST and CRYPTREC. The primary evaluation criteria should be security in the standard usage and implementation efficiency, whereas additional security features, e.g. related-key security, multi-key security, post-quantum security, misimplementation security, are also important. In particular, the recent standardization activity for lightweight cryptography by NIST [15] explicitly mentions that additional security features are taken into account during the standardization process.

In this paper, we investigate the security of a lightweight block cipher ANU that was designed by Bansod et al. in 2016 [3,4]. ANU adopts a balanced Feistel-based network, supports 64-bit block size and 128- or 80-bit key size, and consists of 25 rounds. According to the designers, it requires only 1015 gate equivalents for a 128-bit key, which is less than all existing lightweight ciphers. The computation structure of ANU appears to be a mixture of other lightweight ciphers SIMON [5], PRESENT [11], Piccolo [17], TWINE [19] or LBlock [22].

Although the formal description will only be explained later, we show the schematic diagram of the ANU round function in Fig. 1. As the designs of SIMON [5] and Simeck [23], the round function of ANU makes two rotated copies of the left half of the state. Then, instead of applying bitwise-AND of those two states like SIMON and Simeck, ANU applies the S-box layer for both of two states and XORs the outputs. Such a design, to the best of our knowledge, has never been adopted in other primitives. Hence its security evaluation is of interest.

The key schedule function of ANU is a minor modification of the PRESENT key schedule function. In short, it maintains a $|K|$-bit key state, and for each round, a round key is extracted and then the key state is updated partially non-linearly. The designers briefly mention the security against related-key attacks [3]. The designers did not provide any specific analysis, i.e. how the difference in the master key diffuses to the round keys or the lower bound of the number of active S-boxes. The security arguments simply rely on the fact that no successful related-key attack exists against PRESENT. This seems a risky design choice because the round function and even parameters of the key schedule function are modified from the original.

Table 1. Summary of attacks against ANU with 128-bit key.

| Rounds | Setting | Goal | Time | Data | Memory | #keys |
|--------|---------|------|------|------|--------|-------|
| 25 (full) | Related-key | Distinguisher | $2^{17}$ | $2^{17}$ | negl. | 2 |
| 25 (full) | Related-key | Key recovery | $2^{111}$ | $2^{30}$ | negl. | 2 |

**Our Contributions.** In this paper, we present related-key boomerang attacks [9,20] against full (25) rounds of ANU using a 128-bit key. The ANU cipher can be distinguished from an ideal cipher with $2^{17}$ queries. Owing to its low complexity, the attack is implemented and the correctness is verified. By extending the distinguisher, a 128-bit key can be recovered with $2^{112}$ computations. (Note that the complexity of the generic attack using 2 related keys is $2^{127}$.) The results are summarized in Table 1.

The core observation is that minor modifications of the PRESENT key schedule function made by the designers allow very sparse differential propagation in the key state. For example, the sizes of round keys in PRESENT and ANU are 64- and 32-bits respectively. Hence the PRESENT key schedule function extracts 64 bits from a 128-bit key state per round whereas ANU key schedule function only extracts 32 bits from a 128-bit key state. This allows the attacker to have only 6 active round keys in 25 round. Moreover, the differential trail in the key schedule function skips all non-linear operations.

From a technical point of view, we provide the precise probability evaluation of the differential propagation through the round function. Suppose that there is a single active-bit in the left-half of the state $l_{i-1}$ in Fig. 1. This activates two S-boxes in the round function: one for $\mathcal{S}(l_{i-1} \lll 3)$ and one for $\mathcal{S}(l_{i-1} \ggg 8)$. The designers evaluated the probability of those two active S-boxes *under the independent assumption*. That is, because the maximum differential probability of each S-box is $2^{-2}$, the lower bound of the probability of the differential trail is $2^{-4}$. However, two S-boxes are clearly dependent. We observe that the analysis by Canteaut et al. [12] can be applied to ANU. After the detailed analysis, we exploit the trails such that two active S-boxes are satisfied with probability $2^{-3}$ by avoiding the cases that dependency leads to disadvantages to the attacker, i.e. two active S-boxes are satisfied with probability 0.

Another interesting feature of our attacks is that our attacks only require 2 related-key oracles, whereas typical related-key boomerang attacks require 4 related-key oracles. This can be achieved by using the same master-key difference for two sub-ciphers and only chooses the state differences independently, whereas typical related-key boomerang attacks choose both of state- and key-differences independently for two sub-ciphers.

The results presented in this paper do not have any impact in the single-key security of ANU. However, we believe that our results provide meaningful intuition about the security of ANU as follows.

- The key-relation in our attacks is minimal, i.e. 2 keys with 1-bit difference. Owing to its minimal difference, a careless key-management may face our attacks.

- When users have two choices of ciphers, one is vulnerable in the relate-key setting and the other is not, there is no reason to choose the vulnerable one. Indeed, many of other competitive designs such as SIMON, TWINE, Piccolo, RECTANGLE [24], SKINNY [6], GIFT [2] etc. do not allow related-key attacks.
- In general, simply mixing a part of designs from various ciphers may cause undesired properties. Our attacks well-demonstrate the risk of such designs.

**Paper Outline.** The remaining of this paper is organized as follows. Section 2 describes the specification of ANU and briefly recalls the framework of related-key boomerang attacks. Section 3 shows the analysis of the PRESENT-like key schedule function in ANU. Section 4 presents the full-round distinguisher and extension to the key recovery. We conclude this paper in Sect. 5.

## 2    Related Work

The specification of ANU is briefly described in Sect. 2.1. The framework of the related-key boomerang attacks is introduced in Sect. 2.2. We note that throughout this paper we use the notation "$\Delta$" to denote the difference. We also use typefont to denote hexadecimal numbers.

### 2.1    Specification of Block Cipher ANU

ANU [3,4] is a block cipher supporting 64-bit block size and 128- or 80-bit key size. Overall, a 64-bit plaintext $P$ is first loaded to the state $s_0$. Then the state is updated by iteratively applying a round function $RF : \{0,1\}^{64} \times \{0,1\}^{32} \mapsto \{0,1\}^{64}$ 25 times as $s_i \leftarrow RF(s_{i-1}, k_{i-1})$ for $i = 1, 2, \cdots, 25$, where $k_i$ are 25 round keys generated from a 128- or 80-bit master key $K$ by a key scheduling function $KSF : \{0,1\}^{|K|} \mapsto (\{0,1\}^{32})^{25}$ as $(k_0, k_1, \cdots, k_{24}) \leftarrow KSF(K)$. We call the computation for $i$ "*round $i$*." The last state, $s_{25}$, is output as the ciphertext.

**Round Function    (RF).** The round function of ANU adopts the 2-branch balanced Feistel network along with the block-shuffle mechanism [18] that was adopted in the design of TWINE [19]. The state $s_i$ is represented by a concatenation of two 32-bit words $l_i$ and $r_i$, namely $s_i = l_i \| r_i$. The round function consists of the three operations: $F$-function, round-key addition, and block-shuffle.

*$F$-function:* A function $F : \{0,1\}^{32} \mapsto \{0,1\}^{32}$ is applied to the left word $l_{i-1}$ and $F(l_{i-1})$ is XORed to the right word $r_{i-1}$. Inside $F$, two rotated copies of $l_{i-1}$ are generated by $l_{i-1} \lll 3$ and $l_{i-1} \ggg 8$, where "$\lll 3$" and "$\ggg 8$" are the left cycle shift by 3 bits and right cycle shifts by 8 bits, respectively. Then an S-box layer $\mathcal{S}$ is applied to both words, which applies the 4-bit to 4-bit S-box $S$ shown in Table 2 to 8 nibbles of each word in parallel. Finally,

**Table 2.** 4-bit S-box of ANU.

| $x$ | 0 1 2 3 4 5 6 7 8 9 a b c d e f |
|---|---|
| $S(x)$ | 2 9 7 e 1 c a 0 4 3 8 d f 6 5 b |

**Table 3.** Bit-permutation of ANU.

| $x$ | 0 | 1 | 2 | 3 | 4 | 5 | 6 | 7 | 8 | 9 | 10 | 11 | 12 | 13 | 14 | 15 |
|---|---|---|---|---|---|---|---|---|---|---|---|---|---|---|---|---|
| $\pi(x)$ | 20 | 16 | 28 | 24 | 17 | 21 | 25 | 29 | 22 | 18 | 30 | 26 | 19 | 23 | 27 | 31 |
| $x$ | 16 | 17 | 18 | 19 | 20 | 21 | 22 | 23 | 24 | 25 | 26 | 27 | 28 | 29 | 30 | 31 |
| $\pi(x)$ | 11 | 15 | 3 | 7 | 14 | 10 | 6 | 2 | 9 | 13 | 1 | 5 | 12 | 8 | 4 | 0 |

the results of two S-layers are XORed to the right half of the branch $r_{i-1}$. In summary, the $F$-function part can be described as

$$F(l_{i-1}) = \mathcal{S}(l_{i-1} \lll 3) \oplus \mathcal{S}(l_{i-1} \ggg 8),$$
$$r_{i-1} \leftarrow r_{i-1} \oplus F(l_{i-1}).$$

**Round-key addition:** A round key $k_{i-1}$ is not used inside the $F$ function but is XORed to $r_{i-1}$ directly as done in SIMON [5] or Piccolo [17].

**Block-shuffle:** A bit-permutation $\pi$ specified in Table 3 is applied to both of the left and right words. After that the left and the right branches are swapped as the ordinary 2-branch Feistel network.

**Key Schedule Function  *(KSF)*.** The $KSF$ in ANU is a minor modification of the $KSF$ in PRESENT [11]. Because the target in this paper is ANU with 128-bit keys, we mainly explain the $KSF$ for 128-bit keys.

A 128-bit master key $K$ is loaded to a 128-bit key state denoted by $w = w_{127}, w_{126}, \cdots, w_0$. The KSF, for each round, performs four operations: round-key extract, key-state rotate, S-box update, and round-number XOR.

**Round-key extract:** In round $i$, set the round key $k_{i-1}$ as the least significant 32 bits of the current key state $w$, namely $k_{i-1} \leftarrow w_{31}, w_{30}, \cdots, w_0$.

**Key-state rotate:** Apply the left cyclic shift by 13 bits to the key state $w$.

**S-box update:** Apply the 4-bit S-box $S$ to the least significant 2 nibbles. Namely, $w_3 w_2 w_1 w_0 \leftarrow S(w_3 w_2 w_1 w_0)$ and $w_7 w_6 w_5 w_4 \leftarrow S(w_7 w_6 w_5 w_4)$.

**Round-number XOR:** In round $i$, XOR the 5-bit binary representation of $i$ to the 5 bits of the key state $w$ in bit-position 59–63. Namely, $w_{63} w_{62} w_{61} w_{60} w_{59} \leftarrow w_{63} w_{62} w_{61} w_{60} w_{59} \oplus (i)_2$.

*Remarks on KSF for 80-Bit Keys.* The $KSF$ for 80-bit keys is almost the same as one for 128-bit keys. The size of the key state is 80 bits. The rotation number and the positions of XORing the round number are identical.

**Security.** The designers mention the security against related-key attacks [3, Sect. 3.7] as follows.

> *Related-key attack and Slide attack are two important attacks that show weakness related to the key scheduling algorithms*
>
> $\cdots$
>
> *There is no successful key-related attack that has been found on the key scheduling algorithm of PRESENT, so a similar style of key scheduling to the PRESENT block cipher was adopted. For designing of the key scheduling algorithm, two approaches were considered which are given as follows: (1) Use of nonlinear component, that is, S-box in the design. (2) XOR operation of 5-bits from the key register with round constant RCi.*

The designers did not provide any specific analysis, i.e. how the difference in the master key diffuses to the round keys. Their security arguments simply rely on the fact that no successful related-key attack exists against PRESENT. This seems a risky design choice because the round function and even detailed parameters of *KSF* are modified from the original.

**Differences from *KSF* in PRESENT.** In PRESENT, the round key size is 64 bits that is double of ANU. Hence, in each round, 64-bits are extracted from the 128-bit key state. Moreover, the key state is rotated by 61 bits in each round. Those differences make the number of active round keys significantly smaller and the speed of involving non-linear operations in *KSF* significantly slower in ANU than in PRESENT. Our attacks later exploit those features.

### 2.2 Boomerang Attacks

Boomerang attacks [20] and their variants combine two short differential trails with high probability. Here we briefly introduce the framework.

Boomerang attacks regard the target cipher as a composition of two sub-ciphers $E_0$ and $E_1$. The first sub-cipher is supposed to have a differential $\alpha \rightarrow \beta$, and the second one to have a differential $\gamma \rightarrow \delta$, with probabilities $p$ and $q$, respectively. The basic boomerang attacks require an adaptive chosen plaintext/ciphertext scenario, and plaintext pairs result in a right quartet with probability $p^2 q^2$. The amplified boomerang attacks (also called the rectangle attacks) work in a chosen-plaintext scenario and a right quartet is obtained with probability $p^2 q^2 2^{-n}$ [13]. Further, it was pointed out in [7,8] that any value of $\beta$ and $\gamma$ is allowed as long as $\beta \neq \gamma$. As a result, the probability of the right quartet increases to $2^{-n} \hat{p}^2 \hat{q}^2$, where

$$\hat{p} = \sqrt{\sum_i \Pr^2(\alpha \rightarrow \beta_i)} \text{ and } \hat{q} = \sqrt{\sum_j \Pr^2(\gamma_j \rightarrow \delta)}.$$

---

**Algorithm 1.** Basic Procedure of Related-Key Boomerang Distinguishers.

---

**Input:** $\alpha, \delta, K_1, K_2, K_3, K_4, \hat{p}\hat{q}$
**Output:** $b \in \{0,1\}$
1: **for** $i \leftarrow 1, 2, \ldots, (\hat{p}\hat{q})^{-2}$ **do**
2:     Choose distinct input $P_1$. Set $P_2 \leftarrow P_1 \oplus \alpha$.
3:     Obtain $C_1 = E_{K_1}(P_1)$ and $C_2 = E_{K_2}(P_2)$ by making encryption queries.
4:     Set $C_3 \leftarrow C_1 \oplus \delta$ and $C_4 \leftarrow C_2 \oplus \delta$.
5:     Obtain $P_3 = D_{K_3}(C_3)$ and $P_4 = D_{K_4}(C_4)$ by making decryption queries.
6:     **if** $P_3 \oplus P_4 = \alpha$ **then**
7:         **return** 1
8:     **end if**
9: **end for**
10: **return** 0

---

Boomerang and rectangle attacks under related-key setting were formulated in [9]. Let $\Delta K$ and $\nabla K$ be the key differences for the first and second sub-ciphers, respectively. The attack generally requires access to four related-key oracles with $K_1 \in \{0,1\}^{|K|}$, $K_2 = K_1 \oplus \Delta K$, $K_3 = K_1 \oplus \nabla K$ and $K_4 = K_1 \oplus \Delta K \oplus \nabla K$. In the related-key boomerang attack, paired plaintexts $P_1, P_2$ such that $P_1 \oplus P_2 = \alpha$ are queried to $K_1$ encryption oracle and $K_2$ encryption oracle, and the attacker receives ciphertexts $C_1$ and $C_2$. Then $C_3$ and $C_4$ are calculated by $C_3 = C_1 \oplus \delta$ and $C_4 = C_2 \oplus \delta$, and then queried to $K_3$ decryption oracle and $K_4$ decryption oracle. The resulting plaintext difference $P_3 \oplus P_4$ equals to $\alpha$ with probability $\hat{p}^2\hat{q}^2$. The distinguishing game can be described more formally in an algorithmic form as Algorithm 1. The game returns a distinguishing bit $b \in \{0,1\}$ that is set to 1 if the oracle is a target algorithm and 0 if the oracle is an ideal permutation. Algorithm 1 is $(\hat{p}\hat{q})^{-2}$ many iterations of 2 chosen-plaintext and 2 adaptively chosen-ciphertext queries. Hence the attack complexity is $(time, data, memory) = (4 \cdot (\hat{p}\hat{q})^{-2}, 4 \cdot (\hat{p}\hat{q})^{-2}, negligible)$.

**Related-Key Boomerang Attacks Against Non-linear Key Schedule.** If the key schedule function adopts non-linear operations, related-key boomerang attacks cannot be applied in a straightforward manner. This is because the differential for $E_1$ (including round-key differences for $E_1$) is usually chosen independently of $E_0$, but the key relation must be specified as the difference between two master keys. For a linear key schedule function, any round key difference for $E_1$ suggests the corresponding master-key difference deterministically, whereas for a non-linear key schedule function, the master-key difference may probabilistically be obtained. Hence, attacks only work for a portion of keys, and are regarded as weak-key attacks.

One possible trick to avoid this issue is changing the way to define key relations. For example, the related-key boomerang attacks on full AES-192 and AES-256 [10] allow the attacker to access to related-key oracles such that two keys have a pre-specified XOR difference in a single round-key of the attacker's choice. With this direction, the attacks are still theoretically interesting, but practical implication becomes smaller.

However, for ANU, we will show in the next section that the attacker can construct the differential trail for $E_1$ so that non-linear operations are skipped thus the master-key difference can be deterministically obtained. Moreover, the attack requires only 2 related keys by setting $\Delta K = \nabla K$.

## 3    Analysis of Key Schedule Function of ANU

We observe that to borrow the $KSF$ of PRESENT in the design of ANU causes significantly sparse round-key differences, which will lead to full-round distinguishers in a practical complexity. In specific, we determine the key difference according to the following two observations.

– Given that the state size is 128 bits, the round key size is 32 bits, and the key state is rotated only 13 bits per round, the attacker can control the key state difference so that round key differences are zero for up to $\lfloor 96/13 \rfloor + 1 = 8$ rounds.
– Moreover, given that non-linear operations are applied only 8 bits of the key state per round, the attacker can inject 1-bit difference in the key state so that the active bit position will skip those 8 bits several times.

As a result, we identified a 128-bit master-key difference that avoids making active bits updated by the non-linear operations for the subsequent 39 rounds. Non-zero round-key differences appear only in 8 rounds during those 39 rounds. The identified differences in the key state and round keys are shown in Table 4.

ANU has 25 rounds. Considering the optimization of differential trails, we determined to set $E_0$ and $E_1$ in rounds 8 to 20 and 21 to 32, respectively. Hence the key relation $\Delta K$ in our attack is as follows.

$$\Delta K = 00004000\ 00000000\ 00000000\ 00000000$$

**Number of Oracles.** In boomerang attacks, round-key differences for $E_0$ and $E_1$ can generally be chosen independently as specified in Algorithm 1, thus we do not have to locate them to be consecutive 25 rounds. In contrast, if the attack works in such a setting, two key relations $K_1 \oplus K_2 = \Delta K$ and $K_1 \oplus K_3 = \nabla K$ become identical, thus the attack works only with 2 related-key oracles instead of 4 related-key oracles in the ordinary related-key boomerang attacks. Indeed, $K_1, K_2, K_3, K_4$ are defined as

$$K_1 = K, \qquad\qquad K_2 = K \oplus \Delta K,$$
$$K_3 = K \oplus \Delta K = K_2, \qquad K_4 = K \oplus \Delta K \oplus \Delta K = K_1.$$

**Table 4.** Sparse linear differential propagation in $KSF$ and attack configuration.

| Round $i$ | Difference in the Key State | $\Delta k_{i-1}$ |
|---|---|---|
| 0 | 00000000 00000000 00000000 00000040 | 00000040 |
| 1 | 00000000 00000000 00000000 00080000 | 00080000 |
| 2 | 00000000 00000000 00000001 00000000 | 00000000 |
| 3 | 00000000 00000000 00002000 00000000 | 00000000 |
| 4 | 00000000 00000000 04000000 00000000 | 00000000 |
| 5 | 00000000 00000080 00000000 00000000 | 00000000 |
| 6 | 00000000 00100000 00000000 00000000 | 00000000 |
| 7 | 00000002 00000000 00000000 00000000 | 00000000 |
| 8 | 00004000 00000000 00000000 00000000 | 00000000 |
| 9 | 08000000 00000000 00000000 00000000 | 00000000 |
| 10 | 00000000 00000000 00000000 00000100 | 00000100 |
| 11 | 00000000 00000000 00000000 00200000 | 00200000 |
| 12 | 00000000 00000000 00000004 00000000 | 00000000 |
| 13 | 00000000 00000000 00008000 00000000 | 00000000 |
| 14 | 00000000 00000000 10000000 00000000 | 00000000 |
| 15 | 00000000 00000200 00000000 00000000 | 00000000 |
| 16 | 00000000 00400000 00000000 00000000 | 00000000 |
| 17 | 00000008 00000000 00000000 00000000 | 00000000 |
| 18 | 00010000 00000000 00000000 00000000 | 00000000 |
| 19 | 20000000 00000000 00000000 00000000 | 00000000 |
| 20 | 00000000 00000000 00000000 00000400 | 00000400 |
| 21 | 00000000 00000000 00000000 00800000 | 00800000 |
| 22 | 00000000 00000000 00000010 00000000 | 00000000 |
| 23 | 00000000 00000000 00020000 00000000 | 00000000 |
| 24 | 00000000 00000000 40000000 00000000 | 00000000 |
| 25 | 00000000 00000800 00000000 00000000 | 00000000 |
| 26 | 00000000 01000000 00000000 00000000 | 00000000 |
| 27 | 00000020 00000000 00000000 00000000 | 00000000 |
| 28 | 00040000 00000000 00000000 00000000 | 00000000 |
| 29 | 80000000 00000000 00000000 00000000 | 00000000 |
| 30 | 00000000 00000000 00000000 00001000 | 00001000 |
| 31 | 00000000 00000000 00000000 02000000 | 02000000 |
| 32 | 00000000 00000000 00000040 00000000 | 00000000 |
| 33 | 00000000 00000000 00080000 00000000 | 00000000 |
| 34 | 00000000 00000001 00000000 00000000 | 00000000 |
| 35 | 00000000 00002000 00000000 00000000 | 00000000 |
| 36 | 00000000 04000000 00000000 00000000 | 00000000 |
| 37 | 00000080 00000000 00000000 00000000 | 00000000 |
| 38 | 00100000 00000000 00000000 00000000 | 00000000 |
| 39 | 00000000 00000000 00000000 0000000* | 0000000* |

Boomerang distinguishers

| Round | Prob | | |
|---|---|---|---|
| | End | Dec | |
| 1 | 1 | 1 | |
| 2 | $2^{-8}$ | 1 | |
| 3 | $2^{-3}$ | 1 | |
| 4 | 1 | 1 | |
| 5 | 1 | 1 | |
| 6 | 1 | 1 | |
| 7 | 1 | 1 | $E_0$ |
| 8 | 1 | 1 | |
| 9 | 1 | 1 | |
| 10 | 1 | 1 | |
| 11 | 1 | 1 | |
| 12 | 1 | 1 | |
| 13 | 1 | 1 | |
| 14 | 1 | 1 | |
| 15 | 1 | 1 | |
| 16 | 1 | 1 | |
| 17 | 1 | 1 | |
| 18 | 1 | 1 | |
| 19 | 1 | 1 | $E_1$ |
| 20 | 1 | 1 | |
| 21 | 1 | 1 | |
| 22 | 1 | 1 | |
| 23 | 1 | 1 | |
| 24 | $2^{-3}$ | $2^{-3}$ | |
| 25 | 1 | 1 | |

# 4    Related-Key Boomerang Attacks on Full ANU

In this section, we present our related-key distinguishers on full ANU that is composed of a 20-round deterministic differential trail (Sect. 4.1), 3-round probabilistic extension (Sect. 4.2), and 2-round deterministic extension that is common to ciphers with a SIMON-like round function (Sect. 4.3). Further, we explain extension to a key-recovery attack in Sect. 4.4.

## 4.1    20-Round Deterministic Properties

First, we describe a simple deterministic boomerang distinguisher with 20 rounds. The attack target here is from rounds 4 to 23 (rounds 11 to 30 in Table 4). Readers may refer to differential trails illustrated in Fig. 6 in Appendix A.

$E_0$ covers from rounds 4 to 13. The round key difference only exists in the very beginning ($\Delta k_3$) and the very last ($\Delta k_{12}$). By setting the plaintext difference $\Delta l_3 \| \Delta r_3 \leftarrow 0 \| \Delta k_3$, the state difference becomes 0 after the round-key addition and the zero-difference state continues until round 12. Another difference $\Delta k_{12}$ is injected in round 13 and this will make $\Delta l_{13} = \pi(\Delta k_{12})$ with probability 1.

The very similar occurs in $E_1$ that covers from rounds 14 to 23. The input difference $\Delta l_{13} \| \Delta r_{13} = 0 \| \Delta k_{13}$ makes the state difference 0, and $\Delta k_{22}$ in round 23 makes the ciphertext difference $\Delta l_{23} \| \Delta r_{23} = \pi(\Delta k_{22}) \| 0$ with probability 1.

Those will form the deterministic related-key boomerang distinguisher for 20 rounds. We implemented the attack according to the framework of Algorithm 1 to check whether or not incompatibility pointed out by [16] occurs. We verified that the right quartet is generated with probability 1.

## 4.2    23-Round Distinguishers with Two Dependent S-Layers

We then extend the 20-round trail in Sect. 4.1 by three rounds; by appending 2 rounds at the beginning and 1 round at the end. We begin with the last extended round depicted in Fig. 2. In this round, we have one active S-box for $\mathcal{S}(l_{23} \lll 3)$ with input difference 4 and one active S-box for $\mathcal{S}(l_{23} \ggg 8)$ with input

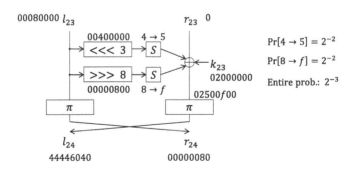

**Fig. 2.** The last round extension in the 23-round distinguisher.

difference 8. According to the differential distribution table (DDT) of the ANU S-box shown in Table 5 in Appendix B, the following differential propagations can be satisfied with probability $2^{-2}$.

$$\Pr[4 \xrightarrow{S} 5] = 2^{-2}, \qquad\qquad \Pr[8 \xrightarrow{S} a] = 2^{-2},$$
$$\Pr[4 \xrightarrow{S} d] = 2^{-2}, \qquad\qquad \Pr[8 \xrightarrow{S} f] = 2^{-2}.$$

Hence, there are $2 \times 2 = 4$ choices of differential trails with probability $2^{-4}$ under the assumption that they can be independently evaluated.

However, in reality, none of the above four choices is satisfied with probability $2^{-4}$. Two are satisfied with probability $2^{-3}$ and the other two are never satisfied (probability 0). The issue here is that the two S-box layers, $S(l_{23} \lll 3)$ and $S(l_{23} \ggg 8)$, are not independent. Therefore, the analysis under independent assumption by the designers [3,4] cannot be applied. Instead, we can apply the similar approach by Canteaut et al. [12] against unkeyed construction.

By following the notation by Canteaut et al. [12], let $\mathcal{X}_S(\Delta_i, \Delta_o)$ denote a set of values that map the input difference $\Delta_i$ to the output difference $\Delta_o$ through the ANU S-box $S$. Namely,

$$\mathcal{X}_S(\Delta_i, \Delta_o) \triangleq \{i \in \{0,1\}^4 : S(i) \oplus S(i \oplus \Delta_i) = \Delta_o\}.$$

We then have

$$\mathcal{X}_S(4,5) = \{1,5,9,d\} = \{0001, 0101, 1001, 1101\}, \tag{1}$$
$$\mathcal{X}_S(4,d) = \{2,6,a,e\} = \{0010, 0110, 1010, 1110\}, \tag{2}$$
$$\mathcal{X}_S(8,a) = \{1,5,9,d\} = \{0001, 0101, 1001, 1101\}, \tag{3}$$
$$\mathcal{X}_S(8,f) = \{2,6,a,e\} = \{0010, 0110, 1010, 1110\}. \tag{4}$$

The four input bits to the active S-box in $S(l_{23} \lll 3)$ are $l_{23}[20,19,18,17]$, where $a[b_1, b_2, \cdots]$ denote the bit positions $b_1, b_2, \cdots$ of a variable $a$. The four input bits to the active S-box in $S(l_{23} \ggg 8)$ are $l_{23}[19,18,17,16]$. Hence, three bits involved in both propagations cause dependence. In the following, we evaluate the exact probability for each case.

**Case $4 \to 5$ and $8 \to a$:** From Eq. (1), the necessary condition to satisfy the differential propagation of $4 \to 5$ is $l_{23}[18] = 0$ and $l_{23}[17] = 1$. In contrast, from Eq. (3), the necessary condition for $8 \to a$ is $l_{23}[17] = 0$ and $l_{23}[16] = 1$. Two conditions on $l_{23}[17]$ contradict each other. Hence, the probability to satisfy those two propagations simultaneously is 0.

**Case $4 \to 5$ and $8 \to f$** (Fig. 2): The condition for $4 \to 5$ is mentioned above, and for $8 \to f$ is $l_{23}[17] = 1$ and $l_{23}[16] = 0$. Two conditions on $l_{23}[17]$ match. In the end, if the propagation $4 \to 5$ is satisfied with $2^{-2}$ and the condition $l_{23}[16] = 0$ is satisfied with $2^{-1}$, the propagation $8 \to a$ is satisfied. The probability of simultaneously satisfying the two propagations is $2^{-3}$.

**Other two cases:** The other two cases can be analyzed similarly. To avoid redundancy we omit the details. $4 \to d$ and $8 \to a$ simultaneously occur with probability $2^{-3}$, while $4 \to d$ and $8 \to f$ never occur simultaneously.

The choice of $(4 \to 5, 8 \to f)$ and $(4 \to d, 8 \to a)$ does not impact to the 25-round attack. If one wants to attack more than 25 rounds, $(4 \to d, 8 \to a)$ seems better with respect to the smaller Hamming weight, which brings advantage for further extension. In this paper, we pick $(4 \to 5, 8 \to f)$.

**Extension in the First Two Rounds.** The first two extended rounds are depicted in Fig. 3. The analysis in round 3 is very similar to the one in round 24 in Fig. 2. First, we chose output differences 9 and c because they are only choices that can be satisfied with $2^{-2}$ under the independent assumption according to DDT. Thus, it is unlikely to improve the entire trail by changing those choices.

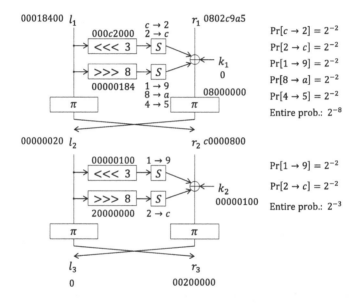

**Fig. 3.** The first two-round extension in the 23-round distinguisher.

There exists only 1 active bit in $l_2$ and this activates one S-box in each of $\mathcal{S}(l_2 \lll 3)$ and $\mathcal{S}(l_2 \ggg 8)$ that are dependent each other. From $\mathcal{X}_S(1, 9) = \{2, 3, c, d\}$ and $\mathcal{X}_S(2, c) = \{5, 7, 8, a\}$, we obtain that two active S-boxes in round 3 for our trail can be satisfied with probability $2^{-3}$.

Extension for another round is rather complicated. There are five active S-boxes. The 4 input bits for each active S-box is $l_1[19, 18, 17, 16], l_1[16, 15, 14, 13], l_1[15, 14, 13, 12], l_1[12, 11, 10, 9], l_1[11, 10, 9, 8]$. Owing to the complicated dependence, we determined to run an experiment to identify output differences that can be satisfied with high probability. Indeed, only 12 bits are involved in these five active S-boxes and the input differences are fully fixed. Hence, the experiment is feasible, namely for all $2^{12}$ input values, we compute the corresponding output differences and count the number of occurrences for each output difference. As a result, we identified 32 output differences that can be satisfied with probability $2^{-8}$, rather than $2^{-10}$ under the independent assumption. We chose one of the 32 output differences as depicted in Fig. 3.

In the end, $p = 2^{-11}$ and $q = 2^{-3}$. According to the basic framework in Algorithm 1, the complexity of the simple 23-round attack is $4 \cdot (pq)^{-2} = 2^{30}$.

**Optimization for Distinguishers.** The distinguishing attack complexity (may not be suitable to be used in the key-recovery attack) can be further reduced by relaxing the differential propagation for the second pair through decryption queries. Namely in Fig. 3, we change to accept any output difference from the active S-boxes in round 3 and from the $F$-function in round 2. This will make the differences for the second pair in those two rounds as

$$(\Delta l_1, \Delta r_1) = \left(\pi^{-1}(\texttt{X0000X00}), \texttt{XXXXXXXX}\right),$$
$$(\Delta l_2, \Delta r_2) = (\texttt{00000020}, \texttt{X0000X00}),$$

where $X$ can be any 4-bit difference. In Step 6 of the basic attack in Algorithm 1, the attacker checks the difference for all 64-bits of the state. However, checking only a part of the state is sufficient as long as the filtering effect is strong enough to discard all wrong quartets. In the end, the probability of the boomerang trail becomes $2^{-17}$ ($p$ for the second pair becomes 1) and the attacker can check if the 24 bits of $l_1$ is zero or not. By multiplying the factor of 4, the attack complexity is $(time, data, memory) = (2^{19}, 2^{19}, negl.)$.

### 4.3   Full-Round Distinguishers

It is well-known that for the SIMON-like structure that XORs round keys outside the $F$-function, differential-based distinguishers can be extended by 1 round at the beginning and the end, e.g. exploited in [14,21]. This is because the first and the last round keys are not used in the non-linear layer of those rounds.

The differential trail for round 1 is depicted in Fig. 4. To obtain a pair of plaintexts that has the desired difference after round 1, the attacker first chooses any value of $r_1$ and computes $l_0 \leftarrow \pi^{-1}(r_1)$ and $l'_0 \leftarrow \pi^{-1}(r_1 \oplus \texttt{0802c9a5})$. Then the attacker computes $F(l_0) \oplus F(l'_0)$ and chooses any value for $r_0$ and computes $r'_0 \leftarrow r_0 \oplus F(l_0) \oplus F(l'_0) \oplus \texttt{00220002}$. This ensures the desired difference at the input of round 2.

The procedure for the last round can be defined similarly. Due to the lack of the round key, the attacker can fully control the difference before the last round.

To fit it to the boomerang attack, the attacker generates plaintext pairs according to the above procedures to ensure the difference after the first round. For each ciphertext received, the attacker computes the ciphertext pair so that the desired difference at the output of round 24 is obtained. Finally, they are

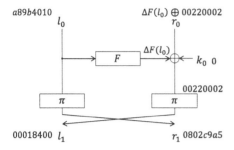

**Fig. 4.** Full-round attack (round 1).

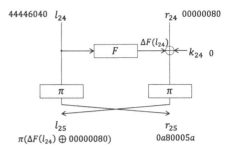

**Fig. 5.** Full-round attack (round 25).

passed to decryption oracles, and the attacker computes the corresponding difference after the first round to check if a right quartet is generated or not.

The same arguments are applied to the last round (Fig. 5). In the end, the 23-round distinguisher can be extended to 25 rounds with free of cost. The attack complexity for the full rounds is the same as for 23 rounds, namely $(time, data, memory) = (2^{17}, 2^{17}, negl.)$.

**Experimental Verification.** To demonstrate the correctness and practicalness of our attack, we implemented the related-key boomerang distinguisher against full ANU. The key difference is $\Delta K = 00004000\|00000000\| 00000000\|00000000$. The plaintext difference is $\texttt{a89b4010}\|\Delta F(l_0) \oplus 00220002$ and the ciphertext differences is $\pi(\Delta F(l_{24}) \oplus 00000080)\|\texttt{0a80005a}$. The probability to be a right quartet is $2^{-11} \cdot 1 \cdot (2^{-3})^2 = 2^{-17}$. We randomly choose $K_1$ and set $K_2 \leftarrow K_1 \oplus \Delta K$, $K_3 \leftarrow K_2$, and $K_4 \leftarrow K_1$.

We randomly picked $2^{23}$ random plaintexts and ran Algorithm 1 but checking only 24 bits of the state at Step 6. Moreover, we iterated the experiments by changing the value of $K_1$ several times. As a result, 66 right quartets are generated on average thus the probability to be a right quartet is $66/2^{23} = 2^{-17.0}$ that matches the theoretical evaluation well. We provide an example of a right quartet in Table 6 in Appendix C.

### 4.4 Key Recovery on Full ANU

The full-round distinguisher allows to recover a part of 128-bit master-key, which makes the exhaustive search on the remaining bits faster than $2^{128}$.

For the key-recovery, we used the differential trail with probability $2^{-30}$ rather than the one with $2^{-17}$. This is because the amount of the efficiently recovered key bits increases when more key bits are involved in the non-linear operations. Recall that the non-linear operations in round 2 involve 12 bits of $l_1$ (bit-position 8 to 19) and the trail is satisfied with probability $2^{-8}$. Hence, after the attacker obtains a right quartet on the full ANU with $2^{30}$ queries, the value of 12 bits of $l_1$ can be reduced to $2^4$ possibilities. From each possibility, the attacker can reduce the corresponding 12 bits (the bit-positions after $\pi^{-1}$ is applied, namely bit-positions $29, 28, 25, 24, 21, 20, 17, 16, 12, 9, 4, 1$) of the first round key $k_0$ by computing

$$k_0 \bullet \Gamma = (F(l_0) \oplus r_0) \bullet \Gamma \oplus \pi^{-1}(l_1) \bullet \Gamma,$$

where $\Gamma$ is $33331212$ that is a mask to represent the target 12 bit-positions and '$\bullet$' is a masking operation, i.e. $V \bullet \Gamma$ extracts the target 12 bits of $V$. In the end, the space of 12 bits of $k_0 \bullet \Gamma$ is reduced by $2^{-8}$ per pair. Because there are 2 pairs in the right quartet, those 12 key bits are uniquely identified.

Similarly, recall that the non-linear operations in round 24 involve 5 bits of $l_{23}$ (bit-position 16 to 20) and the trail is satisfied with probability $2^{-3}$. With the same argument, this reduces the space of 5 bits of $k_{24}$ to 1 after analyzing 2 pairs in the right quartet. Note that $k_{24}$ is completely independent of $k_0$ due the $KSF$, thus there is no overlap between the recovered key bits.

Overall, $12 + 5 = 17$ key bits out of 128 bits are identified, which reduces the cost of the exhaustive search to $2^{111}$.

**Remarks.** We believe that a few more bits can be recovered cleverly by modifying the differential trail in the boomerang distinguisher. For example, by exhaustive guessing the first round-key, constructing other boomerang trail for 24 rounds may lead to more knowledge of the master-key bits. Because our main target is a very efficient distinguisher with rigorous analysis of dependent S-layers, we leave the very detailed optimization work open.

## 5   Concluding Remarks

In this paper, we showed related-key boomerang attacks against full ANU. Our attack exploits the property that simply using a PRESENT-like key schedule function for shorter round keys (32 bits for ANU instead of 64 bits for PRESENT) leads to a sparse differential trail in the key schedule function. The SIMON-like key insertion that XORs round keys outside the $F$-function further allows the attacker to extend the attack efficiently.

Moreover, we show that applying the independent assumption for multiple active S-boxes in the ANU round function is inappropriate. We showed how to precisely evaluate the probability of differential propagations thorough dependent S-layers of ANU. Indeed, the differential trail in our attack has higher probability than the one evaluated under the independent assumption.

Our attack reveals the risk of mixing a part of other designs, even though each of them is well-known to be good. We believe that our attacks give some insight for future designers about the importance of applying extensive security evaluation under the designers' responsibility.

## A     Differential Trails for 20-Round Distinguishers

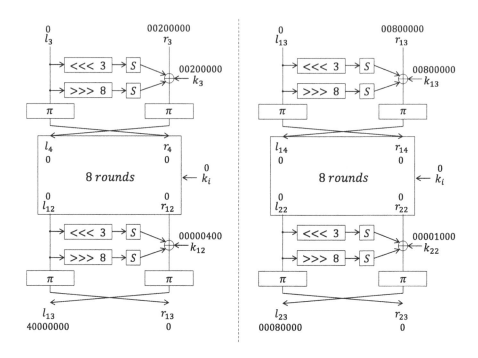

**Fig. 6.** 10-round differential trails for $E_0$ (left) and $E_1$ (right).

## B     Differential Distribution Table of ANU S-Box

**Table 5.** Difference distribution table (DDT) of the ANU S-box.

$\Delta_o$

|  $\Delta_i$ | 0 | 1 | 2 | 3 | 4 | 5 | 6 | 7 | 8 | 9 | a | b | c | d | e | f |
|---|---|---|---|---|---|---|---|---|---|---|---|---|---|---|---|---|
| 0 | 16 | 0 | 0 | 0 | 0 | 0 | 0 | 0 | 0 | 0 | 0 | 0 | 0 | 0 | 0 | 0 |
| 1 | 0 | 0 | 0 | 0 | 0 | 2 | 0 | 2 | 0 | 4 | 2 | 2 | 0 | 2 | 2 | 0 |
| 2 | 0 | 0 | 0 | 0 | 0 | 2 | 0 | 2 | 0 | 0 | 2 | 2 | 4 | 2 | 2 | 0 |
| 3 | 0 | 2 | 0 | 2 | 2 | 0 | 2 | 0 | 0 | 2 | 0 | 2 | 2 | 0 | 2 | 0 |
| 4 | 0 | 0 | 0 | 2 | 0 | 4 | 2 | 0 | 0 | 0 | 0 | 2 | 0 | 4 | 2 | 0 |
| 5 | 0 | 0 | 2 | 2 | 2 | 0 | 0 | 2 | 4 | 0 | 0 | 0 | 2 | 0 | 2 | 0 |
| 6 | 0 | 2 | 2 | 0 | 0 | 0 | 2 | 2 | 4 | 2 | 0 | 2 | 0 | 0 | 0 | 0 |
| 7 | 0 | 0 | 4 | 2 | 0 | 0 | 2 | 0 | 0 | 0 | 0 | 2 | 0 | 0 | 2 | 4 |
| 8 | 0 | 0 | 0 | 2 | 0 | 0 | 2 | 0 | 0 | 0 | 4 | 2 | 0 | 0 | 2 | 4 |
| 9 | 0 | 4 | 0 | 2 | 0 | 2 | 2 | 2 | 2 | 0 | 0 | 2 | 0 | 0 | 2 | 0 |
| a | 0 | 0 | 0 | 2 | 4 | 2 | 2 | 2 | 2 | 0 | 0 | 2 | 0 | 0 | 2 | 0 |
| b | 0 | 2 | 0 | 0 | 2 | 0 | 0 | 0 | 0 | 2 | 4 | 0 | 2 | 0 | 0 | 4 |
| c | 0 | 0 | 4 | 0 | 0 | 4 | 0 | 0 | 0 | 0 | 0 | 0 | 0 | 4 | 0 | 4 |
| d | 0 | 0 | 2 | 0 | 2 | 0 | 2 | 2 | 4 | 0 | 0 | 2 | 2 | 0 | 0 | 0 |
| e | 0 | 2 | 2 | 2 | 0 | 0 | 2 | 2 | 4 | 2 | 0 | 0 | 0 | 0 | 2 | 0 |
| f | 0 | 4 | 0 | 0 | 4 | 0 | 0 | 0 | 0 | 4 | 0 | 0 | 4 | 0 | 0 | 0 |

# C    An Example of Related-Key Boomerang Quartet

**Table 6.** An example of related-key boomerang quartet for full ANU. $P_2' \oplus P_3'$ is an XOR of $\pi(\pi(F(l_0) \oplus r_0))$ for $P_2$ and for $P_3$ that is used for the 24-bit filter.

| | | | | |
|---|---|---|---|---|
| $K_0$ | 5fdcdba5 | 841fe8eb | 7c45f3e1 | 2bb46b59 |
| $K_1$ | 5fdc9ba5 | 841fe8eb | 7c45f3e1 | 2bb46b59 |
| $\Delta K$ | 00004000 | 00000000 | 00000000 | 00000000 |
| $P_0$ | f353ed75 | ef2bc597 | | |
| $P_1$ | 5bc8ad65 | 125dffb6 | | |
| $P_2$ | 9db0b2a6 | fee4fc4e | | |
| $P_3$ | 3656b0e4 | a48a98f1 | | |
| $P_0 \oplus P_1$ | a89b4010 | fd763a21 | | |
| $P_2' \oplus P_3'$ | c0000c00 | | | |
| $C_0$ | 683433eb | 07a93b5c | | |
| $C_2$ | f34d9ef5 | d93d2b3d | | |
| $C_1$ | d8894ec7 | 0d293b06 | | |
| $C_3$ | 62f3a6d9 | d3bd2b67 | | |
| $C_0 \oplus C_2$ | b0bd7d2c | 0a80005a | | |
| $C_1 \oplus C_3$ | 91be382c | 0a80005a | | |

# References

1. Biryukov, A., Großschädl, J., Le Corre, Y.: CryptoLUX, Lightweight Cryptography (2015). https://www.cryptolux.org/index.php/Lightweight_Cryptography
2. Banik, S., Pandey, S.K., Peyrin, T., Sasaki, Y., Sim, S.M., Todo, Y.: GIFT: a small present. In: Fischer, W., Homma, N. (eds.) CHES 2017. LNCS, vol. 10529, pp. 321–345. Springer, Cham (2017). https://doi.org/10.1007/978-3-319-66787-4_16
3. Bansod, G., Patil, A., Sutar, S., Pisharoty, N.: ANU: an ultra lightweight cipher design for security in IoT. Secur. Commun. Netw. **9**(18), 5238–5251 (2016)
4. Bansod, G., Patil, A., Sutar, S., Pisharoty, N.: An ultra lightweight encryption design for security in pervasive computing. In: Conference article for 2016 IEEE 2nd International Conference on Big Data Security on Cloud, IEEE International Conference on High Performance and Smart Computing, IEEE International Conference on Intelligent Data and Security, pp. 79–84, April 2016. http://ieeexplore.ieee.org/document/7502268/
5. Beaulieu, R., Shors, D., Smith, J., Treatman-Clark, S., Weeks, B., Wingers, L.: The SIMON and SPECK families of lightweight block ciphers. Cryptology ePrint Archive, Report 2013/404 (2013)
6. Beierle, C., Jean, J., Kölbl, S., Leander, G., Moradi, A., Peyrin, T., Sasaki, Y., Sasdrich, P., Sim, S.M.: The SKINNY family of block ciphers and its low-latency variant MANTIS. In: Robshaw, M., Katz, J. (eds.) CRYPTO 2016. LNCS, vol. 9815, pp. 123–153. Springer, Heidelberg (2016). https://doi.org/10.1007/978-3-662-53008-5_5

7. Biham, E., Dunkelman, O., Keller, N.: The rectangle attack—rectangling the serpent. In: Pfitzmann, B. (ed.) EUROCRYPT 2001. LNCS, vol. 2045, pp. 340–357. Springer, Heidelberg (2001). https://doi.org/10.1007/3-540-44987-6_21

8. Biham, E., Dunkelman, O., Keller, N.: New results on boomerang and rectangle attacks. In: Daemen, J., Rijmen, V. (eds.) FSE 2002. LNCS, vol. 2365, pp. 1–16. Springer, Heidelberg (2002). https://doi.org/10.1007/3-540-45661-9_1

9. Biham, E., Dunkelman, O., Keller, N.: Related-key boomerang and rectangle attacks. In: Cramer, R. (ed.) EUROCRYPT 2005. LNCS, vol. 3494, pp. 507–525. Springer, Heidelberg (2005). https://doi.org/10.1007/11426639_30

10. Biryukov, A., Khovratovich, D.: Related-key cryptanalysis of the full AES-192 and AES-256. In: Matsui, M. (ed.) ASIACRYPT 2009. LNCS, vol. 5912, pp. 1–18. Springer, Heidelberg (2009). https://doi.org/10.1007/978-3-642-10366-7_1

11. Bogdanov, A., Knudsen, L.R., Leander, G., Paar, C., Poschmann, A., Robshaw, M.J.B., Seurin, Y., Vikkelsoe, C.: PRESENT: an ultra-lightweight block cipher. In: Paillier, P., Verbauwhede, I. (eds.) CHES 2007. LNCS, vol. 4727, pp. 450–466. Springer, Heidelberg (2007). https://doi.org/10.1007/978-3-540-74735-2_31

12. Canteaut, A., Lambooij, E., Neves, S., Rasoolzadeh, S., Sasaki, Y., Stevens, M.: Refined probability of differential characteristics including dependency between multiple rounds. IACR Trans. Symmetric Cryptol. **2017**(2), 203–227 (2017)

13. Kelsey, J., Kohno, T., Schneier, B.: Amplified boomerang attacks against reduced-round MARS and serpent. In: Goos, G., Hartmanis, J., van Leeuwen, J., Schneier, B. (eds.) FSE 2000. LNCS, vol. 1978, pp. 75–93. Springer, Heidelberg (2001). https://doi.org/10.1007/3-540-44706-7_6

14. Kondo, K., Sasaki, Y., Todo, Y., Iwata, T.: Analyzing key schedule of SIMON: iterative key differences and application to related-key impossible differentials. In: Obana, S., Chida, K. (eds.) IWSEC 2017. LNCS, vol. 10418, pp. 141–158. Springer, Cham (2017). https://doi.org/10.1007/978-3-319-64200-0_9

15. McKay, K.A., Bassham, L., Turan, M.S., Mouha, N.: NISTIR 8114 report on lightweight cryptography. Technical report, U.S. Department of Commerce, National Institute of Standards and Technology (2017). https://doi.org/10.6028/NIST.IR.8114

16. Murphy, S.: The return of the cryptographic boomerang. IEEE Trans. Inf. Theory **57**(4), 2517–2521 (2011)

17. Shibutani, K., Isobe, T., Hiwatari, H., Mitsuda, A., Akishita, T., Shirai, T.: *Piccolo*: an ultra-lightweight blockcipher. In: Preneel, B., Takagi, T. (eds.) CHES 2011. LNCS, vol. 6917, pp. 342–357. Springer, Heidelberg (2011). https://doi.org/10.1007/978-3-642-23951-9_23

18. Suzaki, T., Minematsu, K.: Improving the generalized Feistel. In: Hong, S., Iwata, T. (eds.) FSE 2010. LNCS, vol. 6147, pp. 19–39. Springer, Heidelberg (2010). https://doi.org/10.1007/978-3-642-13858-4_2

19. Suzaki, T., Minematsu, K., Morioka, S., Kobayashi, E.: TWINE: a lightweight block cipher for multiple platforms. In: Knudsen, L.R., Wu, H. (eds.) SAC 2012. LNCS, vol. 7707, pp. 339–354. Springer, Heidelberg (2013). https://doi.org/10.1007/978-3-642-35999-6_22

20. Wagner, D.: The boomerang attack. In: Knudsen, L. (ed.) FSE 1999. LNCS, vol. 1636, pp. 156–170. Springer, Heidelberg (1999). https://doi.org/10.1007/3-540-48519-8_12

21. Wang, Q., Liu, Z., Varıcı, K., Sasaki, Y., Rijmen, V., Todo, Y.: Cryptanalysis of reduced-round SIMON32 and SIMON48. In: Meier, W., Mukhopadhyay, D. (eds.) INDOCRYPT 2014. LNCS, vol. 8885, pp. 143–160. Springer, Cham (2014). https://doi.org/10.1007/978-3-319-13039-2_9

22. Wu, W., Zhang, L.: LBlock: a lightweight block cipher. In: Lopez, J., Tsudik, G. (eds.) ACNS 2011. LNCS, vol. 6715, pp. 327–344. Springer, Heidelberg (2011). https://doi.org/10.1007/978-3-642-21554-4_19
23. Yang, G., Zhu, B., Suder, V., Aagaard, M.D., Gong, G.: The Simeck family of lightweight block ciphers. In: Güneysu, T., Handschuh, H. (eds.) CHES 2015. LNCS, vol. 9293, pp. 307–329. Springer, Heidelberg (2015). https://doi.org/10.1007/978-3-662-48324-4_16
24. Zhang, W., Bao, Z., Lin, D., Rijmen, V., Yang, B., Verbauwhede, I.: RECTANGLE: a bit-slice lightweight block cipher suitable for multiple platforms. Sci. China Inf. Sci. **58**(12), 1–15 (2015)

# Generic Round-Function-Recovery Attacks for Feistel Networks over Small Domains

F. Betül Durak[(✉)] and Serge Vaudenay

Ecole Polytechnique Fédérale de Lausanne (EPFL), 1015 Lausanne, Switzerland
betul.durak@epfl.ch

**Abstract.** Feistel Networks (FN) are now being used massively to encrypt credit card numbers through format-preserving encryption. In our work, we focus on FN with two branches, entirely unknown round functions, modular additions (or other group operations), and when the domain size of a branch (called N) is small. We investigate round-function-recovery attacks.

The best known attack so far is an improvement of Meet-In-The-Middle (MITM) attack by Isobe and Shibutani from ASIACRYPT 2013 with optimal data complexity $q = r\frac{N}{2}$ and time complexity $N^{\frac{r-4}{2}N+o(N)}$, where $r$ is the round number in FN. We construct an algorithm with a surprisingly better complexity when $r$ is too low, based on partial exhaustive search. When the data complexity varies from the optimal to the one of a codebook attack $q = N^2$, our time complexity can reach $N^{O\left(N^{1-\frac{1}{r-2}}\right)}$. It crosses the complexity of the improved MITM for $q \sim N\frac{e^3}{r}2^{r-3}$.

We also estimate the lowest secure number of rounds depending on N and the security goal. We show that the format-preserving-encryption schemes FF1 and FF3 standardized by NIST and ANSI cannot offer 128-bit security (as they are supposed to) for $N \leqslant 11$ and $N \leqslant 17$, respectively (the NIST standard only requires $N \geqslant 10$), and we improve the results by Durak and Vaudenay from CRYPTO 2017.

## 1 Introduction

Feistel Networks (FN) have been used in constructing many block ciphers such as DES [1]. In the classical FN, we construct a permutation from $2n$ bits to $2n$ bits with round functions from $n$ bits to $n$ bits. We call it as balanced Feistel network. Figure 1 represents a 4-round FN with modular addition (modulo the size of the domain for a branch). Other well known types of Feistel networks are unbalanced FN, alternating between contracting and expanding round functions.

Although block ciphers only encrypt blocks of a fixed format (typically: a binary string of length 128), there are many applications requiring to encrypt data of another format (such as a decimal string of a given length) and to have encrypted data in the same format. For example, Credit Card Numbers (CCN)

© Springer International Publishing AG, part of Springer Nature 2018
B. Preneel and F. Vercauteren (Eds.): ACNS 2018, LNCS 10892, pp. 440–458, 2018.
https://doi.org/10.1007/978-3-319-93387-0_23

consist of 16 decimal numbers, whose 6 digits must be kept confidential. For this reason, these 6 digits are typically encrypted in digital transactions using a Format-Preserving Encryption (FPE). Recently, FPE based on FN [5,6,9] have been standardized [2,3]. As an example, the FPE solution of the terminal manufacturer company Verifone encrypts about 30M credit card transactions per day in the United States alone.

In this work, we are specifically interested in FN with two branches (not necessarily balanced) with secret round functions and modular addition operation. Moreover, we are interested in small domain size over larger key space. We investigate the security when the round function is entirely unknown instead of a publicly known round function that mixes the input with a secret key (i.e. round function is $F_i = f_i(k_i, .)$, where $k_i$ is the round key in $i^{th}$ round). We do not assume that round functions are bijective. This applies to FF1 [6] by Bellare et al. and FF3 [9] by Brier et al. which have been standardized by The National Institute of Standards an Technology (NIST) published in March, 2016 [2]. This standard aims at a 128-bit security for any $N \geqslant 10$. FF3 was broken and repaired by Durak and Vaudenay [15]. Herein, we denote by FF3* the repaired scheme.

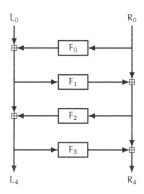

**Fig. 1.** 4-round Feistel network

Since their invention, Feistel networks and their security analysis have been studied. Many cryptanalysis studies have been done to give key-recovery, message-recovery, round-function-recovery, and differential attacks on different types of Feistel networks [7,12,16,18,21,24]. We summarize the best function recovery attacks in Table 1.[1] The complexities are given in terms of number of encryptions. In Appendix, we present a brief survey of existing attacks. So far, the best generic attack was a variant of Meet-In-The-Middle (MITM) attack.

The most famous security result dates back to late 80's given by Luby-Rackoff [20]. In their seminal paper, Luby and Rackoff first showed that a three round Feistel construction is a secure pseudorandom permutation from $2n$ bits

---

[1] Table 1 only reports function recovery attacks. It does not include attacks applying with round functions in a small space of $N$ (instead of $N^N$). It does not include distinguishers such as the ones from Patarin [22] either.

to $2n$ bits. Moreover, they showed that for more than three rounds FN, all generic chosen-plaintext attacks on Feistel schemes require $q = \Omega(2^{\frac{n}{2}})$ queries where $n$ is the input/output size to the round function. Information theoretically, the number $q$ of queries provides $2qn$ bits of information. For $r$-round FN, we need $rn2^n$ bits of information to recover the round functions (each round function can be represented with a string of size $n2^n$). Therefore, $q = \frac{r}{2}2^n$ is enough to reconstruct the round function, in theory. Patarin [23] further showed that for $q \ll 2^n$, four rounds are secure against known-plaintext attacks (the advantage would be bounded by $\frac{4q}{2^n} + \frac{q^2}{2 \cdot 2^n}$ for $q \leqslant \frac{2^n}{67n}$), five rounds are secure against chosen-plaintext attacks (the advantage would be bounded by $\frac{5q}{2^n} + \frac{q^2}{2 \cdot 2^n}$ for $q \leqslant \frac{2^n}{67n}$) and six rounds are secure against chosen-plaintext and ciphertext attacks (the advantage would be bounded by $\frac{8q}{2^n} + \frac{q^2}{2 \cdot 2^n}$ for $q \leqslant \frac{2^n}{128n}$).

As we will not necessarily assume messages in binary, we use the notation $N_l, N_r$ as the domain size of the round functions. We introduce some known attacks on Feistel networks with our focused properties: two branches with domain size $N_l$ and $N_r$, with modular addition modulo $N_l$ and $N_r$, secret random round functions which are balanced ($N = N_l = N_r$) or unbalanced but with $N_l \approx N_r$.

**Table 1.** Round-function-recovery attacks against generic balanced 2-branch $r$-round FN with domain branch size $N$. (All $\beta$ are different constants such that $\beta < 1$.)

| Roundsc | Method | Type | Requirement | Time complexity T | Data q | Ref |
|---|---|---|---|---|---|---|
| 3 | Yo-yo | Known pt | | $O(N \ln N)$ | $N \ln N$ | [15] |
| 4 | Cycle finding | Known pt | | $O(N^3)$ | $N^{\frac{3}{2}}$ | [15] |
| 4 | Guess and determine | Chosen pt | | $O\left(N^{\frac{3}{2}}\right)$ | $N^{\frac{3}{2}}$ | [7] |
| 5 | Cycle finding | Chosen pt | | $O\left(N^{\sqrt{N}+3}\right)$ | $N^{\frac{3}{2}}$ | [15] |
| 5 | Integral attack | Chosen pt | $F_1$ or $F_3$ invertible | $O\left(N^{2.81}\right)$ | $N^2$ | [7] |
| 5 | Yo-yo | Codebook | $\oplus$-Feistel | $O\left(N^2\right)$ | $N^2$ | [7] |
| 5 | Guess and determine | Codebook | | $O\left(N N^{\frac{3}{4}}\right)$ | $N^2$ | [7] |
| 5 | SAT solver | Codebook | | Not specified | $N^2$ | [8] |
| 6 | Yo-yo | Codebook | $\oplus$-Feistel | $O\left(N^{\frac{1}{2}N}\right)$ | $N^2$ | [7] |
| 7 | Yo-yo | Codebook | $\oplus$-Feistel | $O\left(N^N\right)$ | $N^2$ | [7] |
| $r$ | Cycle finding | Chosen pt | | $O\left(N^{(r-5)N+\sqrt{N}+3}\right)$ | $N^{\frac{3}{2}}$ | [15] |
| $r$ | MITM | Known pt | | $O\left(N^{\lceil \frac{r}{2} \rceil N}\right)$ | $r\frac{N}{2}$ | Eq. (1) |
| $r$ | MITM* | Chosen pt | | $N^{\frac{r-4}{2}N}(1+o(1))$ | $r\frac{N}{2}$ | Eq. (2) |
| $r$ | Iterated partial exhst search | Known pt | | $N^{\frac{(r-2)^2}{r-1}N}\left(\frac{N}{q}\right)^{\frac{1}{r-2}}(\beta+o(1))$ | $q \leqslant N^2$ | Eq. (5) |
| $r$ | Iterated partial exhst search | Chosen pt | | $N^{(r-3)N^{1-\frac{1}{r-2}}}(\beta+o(1))$ | $\beta N^{2-\frac{1}{r-2}}$ | Eq. (8) |
| $r$ | Iterated partial exhst search | Chosen pt | | $N^{\frac{q}{N}-1+\frac{(r-3)^2}{r-2}N}\left(\frac{N}{q}\right)^{\frac{1}{r-3}}(\beta+o(1))$ | $q \leqslant N^2$ | Eq. (7) |

*Our Contributions.* In this work, we propose the best known generic exhaustive search attack on Feistel networks with two branches and random functions with arbitrary number $r$ of rounds. We compare it with MITM. It is better for some parameters. When the data complexity varies in between the optimal (based on information theory) and the one of the codebook attack, our best time complexity goes from $N^{\frac{r-2}{2}N+o(N)}$ (MITM-based, see Eq. (2) for $r$ even) to $N^{O(N^{1-\frac{1}{r-2}})}$ (based on partial exhaustive search, see Eq. (8)), where $N$ is the domain size of the branch. More precisely, the optimal data complexity is $q = r\frac{N}{2}$. MITM works with the optimal data complexity and with time complexity $T^{MITM^*} = N^{\frac{r-2}{2}N+o(N)}$ (see Eq. (2)). Our partial exhaustive search attack can use any data complexity from the optimal to the one of a codebook $q = N^2$, but it is better than MITM for $q > \frac{N \times e^3}{r} 2^{r-3}$. It reaches the time complexity (called $T^{Iter^*}$) $N^{(r-3)N^{1-\frac{1}{r-2}}(\beta+o(1))}$ for some constant $\beta < 1$ (see Eq. (8)) using $q = \beta N^{2-\frac{1}{r-2}}$ chosen plaintexts.

We plot in Fig. 2 the $(r, N)$ parameters for which we have $T^{Iter^*} = T^{MITM^*}$. As we can see, for any constant $N$ and a low $r$ (including $r = 8$ and $r = 10$ as the NIST standards suggest), $Iter^*$ is the best attack. The same figure includes two curves that correspond to the 128-bit and 256-bit security parameters $(r, N)$. The curves are computed with the minimum between $T_{Iter^*}$ and $T^{MITM^*}$. It can be read that an intended 128-bit security level in FF3* with $r = 8$, $N \leqslant 17$ and in FF1 with $r = 10$, $N \leqslant 11$ has not been satisfied.[2] E.g., for 6-bit messages and 2-digit messages.[3]

Another application could be to reverse engineer an S-box based on FN [8].

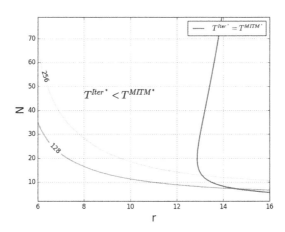

**Fig. 2.** Parameters $(r, N)$ for $T^{Iter^*} = T^{MITM^*}$ and parameters to meet a 128-bit and a 256-bit security level.

---

[2] It was shown by Durak and Vaudenay [15] that 128-bit security was not reached by FF3* and FF1 for $7 \leqslant N \leqslant 10$ and $N = 7$, respectively.

[3] Note that the NIST standard [2] requires $N \geqslant 10$.

*Structure of Our Paper.* In Sect. 2, we review the symmetries in the set of tuples of round functions which define the same FN and we describe the MITM attacks. Our algorithm is described and analyzed in Sect. 3. Section 4 applies our results to format preserving encryption standards. Finally, we conclude.[4]

# 2    Preliminaries

In this section, we present known techniques to recover the $r$-tuple of round functions in FN. Note that we actually recover an *equivalent tuple of round functions*. Indeed, we can see that round functions differing by constants can define the actual same cipher [13,15]. Concretely, let $(F_0, \ldots, F_{r-1})$ be a tuple defining a cipher C. For every $a_0, \ldots, a_{r-1}, b_0, \ldots b_{r-1}$ such that $a_i = b_{i-1} + b_{i-3} + b_{i-5} + \cdots$ and $b_0 + b_2 + b_4 + \cdots = b_1 + b_3 + b_5 + \cdots = 0$, we can define $(F'_0, \ldots, F'_{r-1})$ by $F'_i(x) = F_i(x - a_i) + b_i$. We obtain a tuple defining the same cipher C. Therefore, we can fix arbitrarily one point of $F_0, \ldots, F_{r-3}$ and we are ensured to find an equivalent tuple of functions including those points.

## 2.1    Meet-In-The-Middle (MITM) Attack

The MITM attack was introduced by Diffie and Hellman [10]. It is a generic known-plaintext attack. Briefly, consider an $r$ round encryption $E_0, E_1, \ldots, E_{r-1}$ and corresponding $D_0, D_1, \ldots, D_{r-1}$ decryption algorithms. We assume each algorithm uses a $k$-bit key and we denote the keys by $K_0, K_1, \ldots, K_{r-1}$. Let $M_1, M_2, \ldots, M_q$ be the plaintexts and $C_1, C_2, \ldots, C_q$ be the corresponding ciphertexts. Let the intermediate values entering to round $i$ be $M_1^{(i)}, M_2^{(i)}, \ldots, M_q^{(i)}$ for $1 \leqslant i < r$. The adversary enumerates each possible combination of the keys $K_0, K_1, \ldots, K_{u-1}$ for the first $u = \lfloor \frac{r}{2} \rfloor$ rounds and it computes the intermediate values for each plaintexts as $M_1^{(u)}, M_2^{(u)}, \ldots, M_q^{(u)}$ until round $u$. Then, these values along with their possible keys are stored in a table (The memory complexity is $2^{uk}$ messages). Then, the adversary partially decrypts the ciphertext $C_1, C_2, \ldots, C_q$ for each value of the keys $K_{r-1}, K_{r-2}, \ldots, K_u$ backward. Finally, the adversary looks for a match between the partially decrypted values and the rows of the stored table. Each match suggests keys for $K_0, K_1, \ldots K_{r-1}$ and the adversary recovers all the keys. The time complexity of the MITM attack is $2^{(r-u)k}$ and memory complexity is $2^{uk}$.[5]

We can apply the MITM attack to the Feistel networks with $r$ rounds and $q$ known plaintext/ciphertext pairs. In our setting, $N$ is quite small, thus we can focus on a generic FN with functions specified by tables. This is equivalent to

---

[4] The full version of our paper [14] includes appendices with: a description of the message recovery attacks from Bellare et al. [4], the generic round-function-recovery attack from Durak and Vaudenay [13,15], an attack exploiting the bias in the modulo-N reduction inspired by Bleichenbacher (as described by Vaudenay [25]), and the generic round-function-recovery attacks by Biryukov et al. [7].

[5] In order to improve the memory complexity of MITM attack, a new technique called dissection attack has been introduced by Dinur et al. in [11].

using a key of $k = N \log_2 N$ bits. Therefore, the standard MITM attack has a time complexity of $N^{(r-u)N}$ with same memory complexity. We label the time complexity as follows:

$$T^{MITM} = O\left(N^{\lceil \frac{r}{2} \rceil N}\right) \tag{1}$$

with $q = \frac{rN}{2}$ **known plaintexts**. The pseudocode is given in Algorithm 1.

---

**Algorithm 1.** Meet-In-The-Middle Attack (MITM)

---

1  Collect $q$ plaintext-ciphertext pairs $(M_i, C_i)$, $i = 1, \ldots, q$.
2  **foreach** $K_0, \ldots, K_{u-1}$ **do**
3  |    Compute $M_1^{(u)}, \ldots, M_q^{(u)}$ forward from $M_1, \ldots, M_q$.
4  |    Store $(K_0, \ldots, K_{u-1})$ in $h(M_1^{(u)}, \ldots, M_q^{(u)})$.
5  **end**
6  **foreach** $K_u, \ldots, K_{r-1}$ **do**
7  |    Compute $M_1^{(u)}, \ldots, M_q^{(u)}$ backward from $C_1, \ldots, C_q$.
8  |    **foreach** $K_0, \ldots, K_{u-1}$ *in* $h(M_1^u, \ldots, M_q^u)$ **do**
9  |    |    Output $K_0, \ldots, K_{r-1}$.
10 |    **end**
11 **end**

---

## 2.2  Improved MITM

In this section, we elaborate and extend the attack mentioned briefly in [11,12] on $r$-round FN. The same attack appears in [17,18] with $k = \log_2 N$. We are only adapting the algorithm to our settings. We take $u = \lceil \frac{r}{2} \rceil - 1$ and $v = \lfloor \frac{r}{2} \rfloor - 1$ so that $r = u + v + 2$ and $u \approx v$. Consider the FN in Fig. 3 for $r$ even (When $r$ is odd, we can set $u = \lfloor \frac{r}{2} \rfloor - 1$ so that $r - u - 2 = \lceil \frac{r}{2} \rceil - 1$). We can split the $(2u+2)$- round FN in 4 parts: starting with a single round $F_0$; a $u$-round Feistel Network called $G$, the $(u+2)^{\text{th}}$ round with function $F_{u+1}$, and finally another $v$-round Feistel Network called $H$.

An intuitive attack works as follows. Fix a value $M_R^{(0)} = a$ and consider all possible $M_L^{(0)}$ so that we obtain $N$ plaintexts. We do it $\frac{q}{N}$ times to obtain $q$ plaintexts. Hence, we have $\frac{q}{N}$ values for $a$. We set the output of $F_0$ for one value of $a$ arbitrarily. For all the plaintexts, we query $(M_L^{(0)} \| M_R^{(0)})$ and obtain $q$ $(C_L \| C_R)$ values. We enumerate all the functions of $H$, and compute $(M_L^{(u+2)} \| M_R^{(u+2)})$ from $(C_L \| C_R)$ by decrypting. We set $Z = M_L^{(u+2)} = M_L^{(u+1)}$ if $u$ is even and set $Z = M_R^{(u+2)} = M_R^{(u+1)}$ if $u$ is odd. We store each $Z$ in a hash table. We then enumerate all the functions of $G$, and compute $(M_L^{(u+1)} \| M_R^{(u+1)})$ from $(M_L^{(0)} \| M_R^{(0)})$. For each computed values of $M_L^{(u+1)}$ (for $u$ even) or $M_R^{(u+1)}$ (for $u$ odd), we look for a match in the hash table storing $Z$ values (since they have to be equal). The time complexity of this approach consists of enumerating many values and functions with memory complexity $vN \log_2(N)$ to store the hash table.

Enumerating $F_0, (F_1, \ldots, F_u)$ and $F_{u+2}, \ldots, F_{r-1}$ gives $N^{\frac{q}{N}-1+(u+v)(N-1)}$ tuples which are filtered by $N^{-q}$. We obtain $N^{\frac{q}{N}-1+(u+v)(N-1)-q}$ tuples. Thus, for each filtered tuple, we can deduce input/output values for $F_{u+1}$ and rule out inconsistent tables to isolate the solutions $(F_0, \ldots, F_{r-1})$. This post-filtering has a complexity $N^{\frac{q}{N}-1+(u+v)(N-1)}$. We will see that it is lower than the complexity of the rest of the algorithm. Thus, it disappears in the big-O. The pseudocode is given in Algorithm 2.

---

**Algorithm 2.** Improved Meet-In-The-Middle Attack (MITM*)

---

1  Take $a_1, \ldots, a_{\frac{q}{N}}$ pairwise different half blocks.
2  Take $M_1, \ldots, M_q$ pairwise different such that $(M_i)_R \in \{a_1, \ldots, a_{\frac{q}{N}}\}$.
3  Collect the encryption $C_1, \ldots, C_q$ of $M_1, \ldots, M_q$.
4  **foreach** $v$-*round Feistel Network* H **do**
5      Compute $M_1^{(u+2)}, \ldots, M_q^{(u+2)}$ backward from $C_1, \ldots, C_q$.
6      Set $Z_i = M_L^{(u+2)}$ if $u$ is even and $Z_i = M_R^{(u+2)}$ if $u$ is odd, $i = 1, \ldots, q$.
7      Store H in $h(Z_1, \ldots, Z_q)$.
8  **end**
9  Set $b_1$ arbitrarily.
10  **foreach** $b_2, \ldots, b_{\frac{q}{N}}$ **do**
11      Set $F_0(a_i) = b_1$, $i = 1, \ldots, \frac{q}{N}$.
12      **foreach** $u$-*round Feistel Network* G **do**
13          Compute $M_1^{(u+1)}, \ldots, M_q^{(u+1)}$ forward from $M_1, \ldots, M_q$.
14          Set $Z_i = M_L^{(u+1)}$ if $u$ is even and $Z_i = M_R^{(u+1)}$ if $u$ is odd, $i = 1, \ldots, q$.
15          **foreach** H *stored in* $h(Z_1, \ldots, Z_q)$ **do**
16              Deduce input/output values for $F_{u+1}$.
17              **if** *consistent* **then**
18                  Output $(F_0, G, H)$.
19              **end**
20          **end**
21      **end**
22  **end**

---

In this attack, we have to guess $N^{\frac{q}{N}-1}$ values for $F_0$, $N^{u(N-1)}$ values (we have $N-1$ instead of $N$ because one value per round is free to select) for enumerating $F_1, F_2, \ldots, F_u$ (we guess $N^{\frac{q}{N}-1+u(N-1)}$ values in total). And, we guess $N^{v(N-1)}$ values for enumerating $F_{u+2}, F_{u+3}, \ldots, F_{r-1}$ (we guess $N^{v(N-1)}$ in total). Therefore, the complexity is $O\left(N^{\frac{q}{N}-1+(\frac{r}{2}-1)(N-1)}\right)$ for $r$ is even and $O\left(N^{\frac{q}{N}-1+(\frac{r-1}{2})(N-1)}\right)$ for $r$ is odd. We label the time complexity for described attack as:

$$T^{MITM^*} = O\left(N^{(\frac{r}{2}-1)N}\right), \quad \text{for } r \text{ even} \tag{2}$$

$$T^{MITM^*} = O\left(N^{\frac{r-1}{2}N-\frac{1}{2}}\right), \quad \text{for } r \text{ odd}$$

with $q = \frac{rN}{2}$ **chosen plaintexts.**

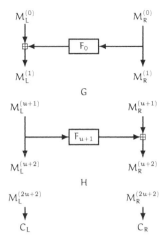

**Fig. 3.** $(2u+2)$-round Feistel network (with $u$ even on the picture)

## 3   Round-Function-Recovery by Partial Exhaustive Search

We consider exhaustive search algorithms dealing with partial functions. Normally, a function $F_j$ is defined by its set of all possible $(z, F_j(z))$ pairs. We call a table as *partial table* if it is a subset of its table. It is a set of pairs such that

$$\forall x, y, z \quad (x, y) \in F_i \text{ and } (x, z) \in F_i \Longrightarrow y = z.$$

If $(x, y) \in F_i$, we say that $F_i(x)$ is defined and we denote $F_i(x) = y$. The *density* of a partial table is the ratio $\theta$ of its cardinality by $N$. For example, $\theta = \frac{1}{N}$ corresponds to a partial table defined on a single point $z$ and $\theta = 1$ corresponds to the full table. Our aim is to enumerate possible partial tables of increasing density by exhaustive search. So, we will "extend" partial functions. A partial table is an *extension* of another partial table if the former is a superset of the latter.

We deal with partial tables for each round function. We define $r$-tuples $T$ of partial tables in which $T_j$ denotes the partial table of $F_j$ in $T$.[6] We say that $T$ is homogeneous with density $\theta$ if for all $j$, $T_j$ has density $\theta$. Similarly, a tuple $T'$ is an extension of $T$ if for each $j$, $T_j'$ is an extension of $T_j$. An *elementary tuple* is a homogeneous tuple of density $\frac{1}{N}$. This means that each of its partial functions are defined on a single point.

---

[6] We denote an $r$-tuple with capital letter $T$. Each tuple $T$ consists of $r$ tables, i.e. $T = \{T_0, \dots T_{r-1}\}$. When we have multiple $r$-tuples, we denote different tuples indexed with a superscript $T^1, T^2, \dots$.

Again, our aim is to start with an elementary tuple and to list all extensions, as long as they are compatible (as defined below) with the collected pairs of plaintexts and ciphertexts $(M, C)$. We say that a tuple $T$ *encrypts* a plaintext $M_i$ into a ciphertext $C_i$ (or *decrypts* $C_i$ into $M_i$ or even that $T$ encrypts the pair $(M_i, C_i)$) if we can evaluate the FN on $M_i$ with the partial information we have about the round functions and if it gives $C_i$. We say that a pair $(M_i, C_i)$ is *computable except for $r'$ rounds* for a tuple $T$ if there exists a round number $j$ such that the partial functions are enough to encrypt $M_i$ for up to $j$ rounds and to decrypt $C_i$ for up to $r - j - r'$ rounds.

We want to define what it means for a tuple to be compatible with $(M, C)$. Roughly, it is compatible if for each $i$, there exists an extension encrypting $M_i$ into $C_i$. (However, it does not mean there exists an extension encrypting each $M_i$ to $C_i$.) More precisely, we say that a tuple $T$ of partial tables is *compatible* with $(M, C)$ if for each $i$, at least one of the following conditions is satisfied:

(i)  $T$ encrypts $M_i$ into $C_i$
     (in this case, there is no need to extend $T$);
(ii) $(M_i, C_i)$ is computable except for two rounds or more
     (indeed, if two rounds are undetermined, we know that we can extend $T$ to encrypt $M_i$ to $C_i$);
(iii) $(M_i, C_i)$ is computable except for one round (numbered $s$ below) and their is a match in the value skipping the missing round: more precisely, their exists $s \in \{0, \ldots, r-1\}$ and one $(x, y)$ pair such that if $T'_s = T_s \cup \{(x, y)\}$, the tuple $T' = (T_0, \ldots, T_{s-1}, T'_s, T_{s+1}, \ldots, T_{r-1})$ encrypts $M_i$ to $C_i$
     (indeed, we know we can extend the missing round with $T_s(x) = y$).

Clearly, if no condition is satisfied for $i$, then no extension of $T$ can encrypt $M_i$ into $C_i$, so we can prune an exhaustive search.

## 3.1   Iter: Iterative Partial Exhaustive Search

Assume that $q$ plaintext/ciphertext pairs $(M_i, C_i)$ are known to the adversary. Due to the symmetries in the set of tuples which are compatible with the codebook, we can focus on the tuples which are extensions of an arbitrarily fixed elementary tuple $T^1$ which encrypts the pair $(M_1, C_1)$. So, we define $\mathsf{Pool}_i$ as the set of all extensions $T$ of $T^1$ encrypting the pairs $(M_1, C_1), \ldots, (M_i, C_i)$, which are compatible with all other pairs, and which are *minimal* (in the sense that removing any entry in the partial tables of $T$ makes at least one $(M_j, C_j)$ pair not computable, for $1 \leqslant j \leqslant i$).

We iteratively construct $\mathsf{Pool}_i$. For that, we take all possible minimal extensions of tuples from $\mathsf{Pool}_{i-1}$ which encrypt the $i^{\text{th}}$ pair and remain compatible with all others. We proceed as defined by Algorithm 3.

With an appropriate data structure, we can avoid to retry to encrypt $M_j$ or decrypt $C_j$ and directly go to the next computable round (if any) in every pair. For each tuple $T$ in $\mathsf{Pool}_i$, we maintain a hash table $h$ in which $h(u, x)$ is a list of pairs of the form $(j, +)$ or $(j, -)$ with $j > i$. If $(j, +)$ is in $h(u, x)$, this means that

---

**Algorithm 3.** Iterative partial exhaustive search round-function-recovery attack

---

1  Collect $q$ plaintext-ciphertext pairs $(M_i, C_i)$, $i = 1, \ldots, q$.
2  Get an arbitrary elementary tuple $T^1$ which encrypts $M_1$ to $C_1$.
3  Initialize $\text{Pool}_1 = \{T^1\}$.
4  **foreach** $i = 2, \ldots, q$ **do**
5    |  Initialize $\text{Pool}_i$ to empty.
6    |  **foreach** $T \in \text{Pool}_{i-1}$ **do**
7    |  |  **foreach** *minimal extension* $T'$ *of* $T$ *encrypting* $M_i$ *to* $C_i$ **do**
8    |  |  |  **if** *all* $(M_{i+1}, C_{i+1}), \ldots, (M_q, C_q)$ *are compatible with* $T'$ **then**
9    |  |  |  |  Add $T'$ in $\text{Pool}_i$.
10   |  |  |  **end**
11   |  |  **end**
12   |  **end**
13 **end**
14 Output $\text{Pool}_q$.

---

$T$ encrypts $M_j$ up to round $u-1$ and that the input to $F_u$ (the output of which is unknown) is $x$. If $(j, -)$ is in $h(u, x)$, this means that $T$ decrypts $M_j$ up to round $u+1$ and that the input to $F_u$ is $x$. Concretely, this means that $h(u, x)$ lists the indices of $(M_j, C_j)$ pairs who need the value of $F_u(x)$ to encrypt/decrypt one more round. With this type algorithmic trick, we save the inner loop and the complexity is expected to be close to the total size of the pools: $\sum_{i=1}^{q} |\text{Pool}_i|$.

### 3.2  A Heuristic Complexity Analysis of Iter

We heuristically estimate $|\text{Pool}_i|$. First, we recall that $\text{Pool}_i$ is the subset of all minimal extensions of the elementary tuple $T^1$ which encrypt the first $i$ plaintext/ciphertext pairs, restricted to the ones which are compatible with all others.

We approximate $|\text{Pool}_i|$ by $N^{X-Y}$ where $X$ is the number of entries in the partial tables (i.e. the number of defined points throughout all rounds) and $Y$ is the number of independent equations modulo $N$ which a tuple must satisfy to be compatible. So, $N^{-Y}$ is the probability for a tuple to satisfy the conditions in $\text{Pool}_i$. In other words, the $N^X$ possible tuples are decimated by a factor $N^Y$. To treat the fact that we start with only $T^1$ in $\text{Pool}_1$, we decrease $X$ by $r$ (it means that entries defined in $T^1$ do not have to be enumerated as they are fixed) and we decrease $Y$ by 2 (i.e., we consider that the $(M_1, C_1)$ pair never decimates tuples as it is always compatible by the choice of $T^1$).

Although it would be inefficient to proceed this way, we could see $\text{Pool}_i$ as follows. For all sets $(T^2, \ldots, T^i)$ of elementary tuples in which $T^j$ encrypts the $j^{th}$ pair, we check if $\{T^1, T^2, \ldots, T^i\}$ are non-conflicting, and check if merging them defines partial tables which are compatible with the $q-i$ other pairs. We consider that picking an elementary tuple $T^j$ encrypting the $j$th plaintext (irrespective of the ciphertext) corresponds to picking one random input in each of the $r$ round functions. We call this a trial. An input to one round function corresponds to a ball with a number from 0 to $N - 1$. A round function is a bag of $N$ balls. So, we have $r$ bags of balls and a trial consists of picking one ball in each bag. Balls are replaced in their respective bags after picking them. Each $T^j$ makes one trial. Consequently, we have $i$ trials. The balls which are picked during these $i$ trials are called *good balls*. Then, checking compatibility with the remaining $q - i$ pairs corresponds to making $q - i$ additional trials. In those additional trials, we simply look at the number of good balls to see how many rounds can be processed for encryption/decryption.

We estimate the random variable $X$ as the total number of good balls (to which we subtract the $r$ balls corresponding to the trial of $T^1$). Conditioned to a density of good balls of $\theta_{i,j}$ in round $j$, we have $E(X|\theta_{i,.}) = \sum_{j=1}^{r} \theta_{i,j} N - r$. All $\theta_{i,j}$ are random, independent, and with expected value $\theta_i$. So, $E(X) = r\theta_i N - r$.

The random variable $Y$ is set to $Y = Y_1 + Y_2 + Y_3$. The variable $Y_1$ counts the number of modulo $N$ equations so that the encryption of the first $i$ plaintexts match the corresponding ciphertext. So, $Y_1 = 2(i - 1)$ (the first pair $(M_1, C_1)$ is satisfied by default, and each of the $i - 1$ other ones define two equations due to the two halves of the ciphertexts). The variable $Y_2$ counts the number of equations coming from pairs encrypted for all but one round. So, $Y_2$ counts the number of trials (out of the last $q-i$ ones) picking exactly $r-1$ good balls, as they encrypt for all but one round so they define a single equation. The variable $Y_3$ counts the number of equations coming from pairs in $(M_{i+1}, C_{i+1}), \ldots, (M_q, C_q)$ which are fully encrypted. So, $Y_3$ is twice the number of trials (out of the last $q - i$ ones) with $r$ good balls, as they fully encrypt their corresponding pair and thus define two equations each. Conditioned to a density of good balls of $\theta_{i,j}$ in round $j$, we have

$$E(Y|\theta_{i,.}) = \underbrace{2(i - 1)}_{Y_1} + \underbrace{(q - i) \sum_{j=1}^{r} (1 - \theta_{i,j}) \prod_{j' \neq j} \theta_{i,j}}_{Y_2} + \underbrace{2(q - i) \prod_{j} \theta_{i,j}}_{Y_3}.$$

All $\theta_{i,j}$ are random and independent, with expected value $\theta_i$. Thus,

$$E(Y) = 2(i - 1) + r\theta_i^{r-1}(1 - \theta_i)(q - i) + 2\theta_i^r(q - i).$$

We obtain $|Pool_i| \approx cns \times N^{E(X-Y)}$ where $cns$ is adjusted such that $|Pool_1| = 1$. Hence,

$$|Pool_i| \approx cns \times N^{r\theta_i N - r - 2(i-1) - r\theta_i^{r-1}(1-\theta_i)(q-i) - 2\theta_i^r(q-i)} \qquad (3)$$

with $cns \approx 1$ such that $|Pool_1| = 1$.

To estimate $\theta_i$, we look at how it grows compared to $\theta_{i-1}$. During the $i^{th}$ trial, with probability $\theta_{i-1}$ a picked ball is already good (so the density remains the same), and with probability $1 - \theta_{i-1}$, picking a ball defines an additional good one (so the density increases by $\frac{1}{N}$).[7] Therefore, on average we have

---

[7] It would increase with a probability a bit larger than $1 - \theta_{i-1}$, namely $\frac{N^2(1-\theta_{i-1})}{N^2 - (i-1)}$ if the messages are not independent but conditioned to being pairwise different.

$$\theta_i = \theta_{i-1} + \frac{1}{N} \times (1 - \theta_{i-1}).$$

As $\theta_1 = \frac{1}{N}$, we deduce $\theta_i = 1 - \left(1 - \frac{1}{N}\right)^i$.

Assuming that the above model fits well with $\mathsf{Iter}$, the expected value of $\log|\mathsf{Pool}_i|$ should match Eq. (3). However, Eq. (3) cannot represent well the expected value of $|\mathsf{Pool}_i|$ as exponential with bigger exponents will have a huge impact on the average. This motivates an abort strategy when the pool becomes too big. The abort strategy has known and influenced many works [19]. The way we use this strategy will be discussed in Sect. 3.5.

Finally, the heuristic complexity is computed by

$$T^{\mathsf{Iter}} = \sum_{i=1}^{N} N^{r\theta_i N - 2i - r\theta_i^{r-1}(1-\theta_i)(q-i) - 2\theta_i^r(q-i) - r + 2}. \tag{4}$$

### 3.3 Approximation of the Complexity

For $i \ll N$, we can write $\theta_i = \frac{i}{N}$. By neglecting $\theta_i^r$ against $\theta_i^{r-1}$, the complexity is approximated by the maximum of $N^{r\theta N - 2N\theta - r\theta^{r-1}q - r + 2}$. We can easily show that the maximum is reached by $\theta = \theta_c$ with

$$\theta_c = \left(\frac{r-2}{r(r-1)}\right)^{\frac{1}{r-2}} \left(\frac{N}{q}\right)^{\frac{1}{r-2}}.$$

We obtain the complexity

$$T^{\mathsf{Iter}} \approx N^{\frac{(r-2)^2}{r-1}} \left(\frac{r-2}{r(r-1)}\right)^{\frac{1}{r-2}} N\left(\frac{N}{q}\right)^{\frac{1}{r-2} - r + 2} \tag{5}$$

with $q$ **known plaintexts**. We will see later that (5) approximates well (4).

The best complexity is reached with **the full codebook** $q = N^2$ with

$$T^{\mathsf{Iter}} \approx N^{\frac{(r-2)^2}{r-1}} \left(\frac{r-2}{r(r-1)}\right)^{\frac{1}{r-2}} N^{1 - \frac{1}{r-2} - r + 2} \tag{6}$$

which is $T^{\mathsf{Iter}} = N^{\frac{(r-2)^2}{r-1}} (\beta + o(1)) N^{1 - \frac{1}{r-2}}$ for some $\beta < 1$.

### 3.4 Iter*: A Chosen Plaintext Extension to Iter

Finally, if $q$ is not too close to $N^2$, a chosen plaintext attack variant consists of fixing the right half of the plaintext as much as possible, then guessing $F_0$ on these points and run the known-plaintext attack on $r - 1$ rounds to obtain

$$T^{\mathsf{Iter}^*} = N^{\frac{q}{N} - 1} T_{r-1}^{\mathsf{Iter}} \approx N^{\frac{q}{N} - 1 + \frac{(r-3)^2}{r-2}} \left(\frac{r-3}{(r-1)(r-2)}\right)^{\frac{1}{r-3}} N\left(\frac{N}{q}\right)^{\frac{1}{r-3} - r + 3} \tag{7}$$

with $q$ **chosen plaintexts** such that $q \leqslant N^2$.

*Discussion.* For $N^2 > q > N^{\frac{r-3}{(r-1)(r-2)}} \left( 2 \frac{(r-3)^2}{(r-2)(r-4)} \right)^{r-3} \sim \frac{Ne^3}{r} 2^{r-3}$, we have $T^{Iter^*} < N^{\frac{d}{N}-r+2+\frac{r-4}{N}}$ and that means $T^{Iter^*} < T^{MITM^*}$. Therefore, **our Iter*** **algorithm becomes better than** MITM*. Also, for $N \geqslant \frac{(r-3)^{r-2}}{r-1}$, we have $T^{Iter^*} < N^{N-r+2}$ so Iter* **is faster than exhaustive search on a single round function.**

*Optimization with Larger* q. We easily obtain that $T^{Iter^*}$ in (7) is optimal with

$$T^{Iter^*} = N^{\frac{d}{N}-1}T_{r-1}^{Iter} \approx N^{(r-3)N^{1-\frac{1}{r-2}} \left( \frac{1}{r-1} \right)^{\frac{1}{r-2}} -r+2} \tag{8}$$

for

$$q = \frac{r-3}{r-2}N^{2-\frac{1}{r-2}} \left( \frac{1}{r-1} \right)^{\frac{1}{r-2}}.$$

**chosen plaintexts.**

### 3.5  Variants of Iter and Iter*

*Optimized Algorithm.* We can speed up the algorithm by adding more points in the tuples as soon as we can compute them. Concretely, if one plaintext/ciphertext pair can be "computed" except in one or two rounds, we can deduce the values in the missing rounds and define them in the tuple. Adding $x$ points reduce the number of iterations to define the next pool by $N^x$.

*Abort Strategy.* Our complexity is not an average complexity but its logarithm is an average logarithmic complexity. To avoid having a too high average complexity, we may change the algorithm to make it abort if the pool exceeds a threshold to be defined. For instance, if our theoretical formula predicts a complexity $Th$, to make sure that the worst case complexity does not exceed $Th \times N^x$, we set this to the threshold value. This will affect the success probability, which is 100% without the abort strategy, but may be lower for any real number $x$.

*Other Improvements.* We believe that we could improve our algorithms in many ways. For instance, we could take the $(M_i, C_i)$ pairs in an optimized order so that we do not have too many new values appearing in the first and last round functions. This would decrease the number of tuples to consider.

### 3.6  Experimental Results

We implemented Algorithm 3 with known plaintext, $r = 5$, $N = 8$, $q = 40$. Our algorithm always ended with a pool limited to a correct set of full tables.

With these parameters, Eq. (3) estimates $Pool_3$ to be the largest, and estimates $|Pool_3| = N^{2.49}$. We checked over 100 executions, that $\log_N |Pool_3|$ has an average of 4.37 and a standard deviation of 0.60. This is a bad news as it is quite larger than what is predicted. More precisely, each partial function in $Pool_3$ has on average 2.9 defined entries, which is slightly more than the $N\theta_3 \approx 2.64$ which is predicted.[8] But adjusting $\theta_3$ to $\frac{2.9}{N}$ in Eq. (3) gives $N^{3.04}$, which is not enough to explain the high $|\mathsf{Pool}_3|$ which is observed. So, our model for the random variable $X$ may be correct but $Y$ may be overestimated: $\mathsf{Iter}$ decimates less than expected. Although we thought $\mathsf{Pool}_3$ would be the largest from our theory, the largest observed pool during our experiment were $\mathsf{Pool}_4$ with logarithmic size with average 5.28. This indicates that our model for $\mathsf{Iter}$ is not accurate.

All these problems find several explanations. First of all, our parameter $N$ is so small that a tiny variation of number of defined entries (supposed to be $\theta_i N$) in each round has a dramatic impact on the number of tuples. Second, our approach takes the $\theta_i$ as uniform in all rounds and runs although there are variations. Some rounds have more than $\theta_i N$ entries and some others have less. The function we analyze is not linear in $\theta_i$. It is exponential. So, any round with more than $\theta_i N$ defined entries increase the complexity quite a lot.

The good news is that using our optimized variant reduced the gap substantially. The largest $\mathsf{Pool}$ becomes $\max_i \log_N(|\mathsf{Pool}_i|) = 3.46$. Using the abort strategy with $x = 1$ gives a success rate of 42% and $\max_i \log_N(|\mathsf{Pool}_i|) = 3.08$. So, we believe that **our anticipated complexities are achievable with a good success probability**. However, finding a good model for decimation and for the improved algorithm remains an open question.

We summarize our experiments in the Table 2. For the $\max|\mathsf{Pool}|$ column is the average (logarithmically) of the largest observed pool. The logarithm is the maximum over each iteration of the average over the runs of the logarithm of the pool size. The computed average only includes successful runs, as unsuccessful ones are all on the abort threshold.

## 4    Applications

In the standards, the supported domain size of messages in FF1 and FF3* is greater than 100 (i.e. $N^2 \geqslant 100$). For FF1 and FF3*, the best attack is roughly $\mathsf{Iter}^*$ for very low $N$, then $\mathsf{MITM}^*$ for larger $N$. More precisely, we achieve the results shown in Table 3.[9]

For a better precision, we did the computation without approximations, i.e. by using Eq. (4) instead of Eq. (5) in Eq. (7). In any case, we have checked that the figures with approximation do not differ much. They are reported in the Table 4.

As an example, for FF3* with $N = 2^3$ (i.e., messages have 6 bits), $\mathsf{MITM}^*$ uses $q = 2^5$ pairs (half of the codebook) and search on three points for $F_0$, the entire (but one point) $F_1$ and $F_2$, one bit of $F_3$ in the encryption direction, and the entire (but one point) $F_7$ and $F_6$ and one bit of $F_5$ in the decryption direction. This is $N^{3+2(N-1)} \times 2^{N-1} = 2^{58}$. With $\mathsf{Iter}^*$, we also use $q = 2^5$ and the pool reaches its critical density for $\theta_c \approx \frac{4.4}{N}$. The complexity is $T^{\mathsf{Iter}^*} = 2^{42}$.

---

[8] This is partially explained by the fact that plaintexts are pairwise different.
[9] Note that the standard requires $N \geqslant 10$. Hence, the first three rows are not relevant in practice.

**Table 2.** Experimental results with parameters $r = 5$, $N = 8$, and $q = 40$ and with parameters $r = 5$, $N = 10$, and $q = 40$. The max$|$Pool$|$ column reports $\max_i E_{runs}(\log_N |Pool_i|)$: the average (logarithmically) of the largest observed pool. It is compared with Th which is derived as the largest theoretical pool size by our theory. The column opt shows whether we used the optimization trick. The abort column indicates when we used the abort strategy, and with which bound.

| $r = 5$, $N = 8$, $q = 40$ | | | | |
|---|---|---|---|---|
| #runs | success | max$|$Pool$|$ | opt | abort |
| 100 | 100% | Th $\times$ $N^{2.79}$ | no | no |
| 10 000 | 0% | | no | Th |
| 1 000 | 0% | | no | Th $\times$ N |
| 1 000 | 3% | Th $\times$ $N^{1.76}$ | no | Th $\times$ $N^2$ |
| 100 | 100% | Th $\times$ $N^{0.93}$ | yes | no |
| 10 000 | 1% | Th $\times$ $N^{-0.29}$ | yes | Th |
| 100 | 42% | Th $\times$ $N^{0.59}$ | yes | Th $\times$ N |
| 100 | 99% | Th $\times$ $N^{0.90}$ | yes | Th $\times$ $N^2$ |

| $r = 5$, $N = 10$, $q = 40$ | | | | |
|---|---|---|---|---|
| #runs | success | max$|$Pool$|$ | opt | abort |
| 10 000 | 0% | | no | Th |
| 1 000 | 0% | | no | Th $\times$ N |
| 100 | 0% | | no | Th $\times$ $N^2$ |
| 14 | 100% | Th $\times$ $N^{1.40}$ | yes | no |
| 10 000 | 1% | Th $\times$ $N^{-0.31}$ | yes | Th |
| 100 | 19% | Th $\times$ $N^{0.60}$ | yes | Th $\times$ N |
| 19 | 68% | Th $\times$ $N^{1.25}$ | yes | Th $\times$ $N^2$ |

**Table 3.** Time complexity of the chosen-plaintext attacks MITM$^*$ ($T^{MITM^*}$) and Iter$^*$ ($T^{Iter^*}$) with query complexity $q$ for various values of $N$ and $r = 8$ or $r = 10$. Computations for $T^{Iter^*}$ were done without using approximations.

| $r = 8$ (FF3$^*$) | | | $r = 10$ (FF1) | | |
|---|---|---|---|---|---|
| N | $T^{MITM^*}[q]$ (2) | $T^{Iter^*}[q]$ (8) | N | $T^{MITM^*}[q]$ (2) | $T^{Iter^*}[q]$ (8) |
| $2^1$ | $2^6[\ 2^{2.0}\ ]$ | $2^2[2^{2.0}]$ | $2^1$ | $2^8[\ 2^{2.0}\ ]$ | $2^3[\ 2^{2.0}\ ]$ |
| $2^2$ | $2^{24}[\ 2^{4.0}\ ]$ | $2^{13}[2^{4.0}]$ | $2^2$ | $2^{32}[\ 2^{4.0}\ ]$ | $2^{21}[\ 2^{4.0}\ ]$ |
| $2^3$ | $2^{72}[\ 2^{5.0}\ ]$ | $2^{42}[2^{5.0}]$ | $2^3$ | $2^{96}[\ 2^{5.3}\ ]$ | $2^{72}[\ 2^{5.3}\ ]$ |
| $2^4$ | $2^{192}[\ 2^{6.0}\ ]$ | $2^{116}[2^{6.6}]$ | $2^4$ | $2^{256}[\ 2^{6.3}\ ]$ | $2^{199}[\ 2^{6.8}\ ]$ |
| $2^5$ | $2^{480}[\ 2^{7.0}\ ]$ | $2^{279}[2^{8.3}]$ | $2^5$ | $2^{640}[\ 2^{7.3}\ ]$ | $2^{487}[\ 2^{8.6}\ ]$ |
| $2^6$ | $2^{1152}[\ 2^{8.0}\ ]$ | $2^{627}[2^{10.1}]$ | $2^6$ | $2^{1536}[\ 2^{8.3}\ ]$ | $2^{1115}[\ 2^{10.5}\ ]$ |
| $2^7$ | $2^{2688}[\ 2^{9.0}\ ]$ | $2^{1343}[2^{12.0}]$ | $2^7$ | $2^{3584}[\ 2^{9.3}\ ]$ | $2^{2445}[\ 2^{12.4}\ ]$ |
| $2^8$ | $2^{6144}[\ 2^{10.0}\ ]$ | $2^{2788}[2^{13.8}]$ | $2^8$ | $2^{8192}[\ 2^{10.3}\ ]$ | $2^{5202}[\ 2^{14.3}\ ]$ |

We may wonder for which $N$ the ciphers offer a 128-bit security. Durak and Vaudenay [15] showed that this is not the case for FF3$^*$ with $N \leqslant 10$ and FF1 with $N \leqslant 7$. By doing computations for Iter$^*$, we extend this to show that **FF3$^*$**

**Table 4.** Time complexity of the chosen-plaintext attacks MITM* ($T^{MITM*}$) and Iter* ($T^{Iter*}$) with query complexity q for various values of N and $r = 8$ or $r = 10$. Computations for $T^{Iter*}$ were done using approximations.

| $r = 8$ (FF3*) | | | $r = 10$ (FF1) | | |
|---|---|---|---|---|---|
| N | $T^{MITM*}$[q] (2) | $T^{Iter*}$[q] (8) | N | $T^{MITM*}$[q] (2) | $T^{Iter*}$[q] (8) |
| $2^1$ | $2^6$[ $2^{2.0}$ ] | $2^1$[$2^{2.0}$] | $2^1$ | $2^8$[ $2^{2.0}$ ] | $2^2$[ $2^{2.0}$ ] |
| $2^2$ | $2^{24}$[ $2^{4.0}$ ] | $2^{13}$[$2^{4.0}$] | $2^2$ | $2^{32}$[ $2^{4.0}$ ] | $2^{21}$[ $2^{4.0}$ ] |
| $2^3$ | $2^{72}$[ $2^{5.0}$ ] | $2^{44}$[$2^{5.0}$] | $2^3$ | $2^{96}$[ $2^{5.3}$ ] | $2^{75}$[ $2^{5.3}$ ] |
| $2^4$ | $2^{192}$[ $2^{6.0}$ ] | $2^{122}$[$2^{6.6}$] | $2^4$ | $2^{256}$[ $2^{6.3}$ ] | $2^{209}$[ $2^{6.9}$ ] |
| $2^5$ | $2^{480}$[ $2^{7.0}$ ] | $2^{295}$[$2^{8.4}$] | $2^5$ | $2^{640}$[ $2^{7.3}$ ] | $2^{512}$[ $2^{8.8}$ ] |
| $2^6$ | $2^{1152}$[ $2^{8.0}$ ] | $2^{658}$[$2^{10.3}$] | $2^6$ | $2^{1536}$[ $2^{8.3}$ ] | $2^{1166}$[ $2^{10.7}$ ] |
| $2^7$ | $2^{2688}$[ $2^{9.0}$ ] | $2^{1401}$[$2^{12.1}$] | $2^7$ | $2^{3584}$[ $2^{9.3}$ ] | $2^{2543}$[ $2^{12.5}$ ] |
| $2^8$ | $2^{6144}$[ $2^{10.0}$ ] | $2^{2890}$[$2^{13.9}$] | $2^8$ | $2^{8192}$[ $2^{10.3}$ ] | $2^{5383}$[ $2^{14.4}$ ] |

does not offer a 128-bit security for $N \leqslant 17$, and **FF1 does not offer a 128-bit security for $N \leqslant 11$.**

Genuinely, we can compute in Table 5 the minimum $r_{opt} \geqslant 4$ of the number of rounds for which $\min(T^{MITM*}, T^{Iter*}) \geqslant 2^s$ depending on s and N. Again, we computed without using our approximations. For $s = 128$ and $s = 256$, we fetch the following table.[10]

**Table 5.** Minimal number $r_{opt}$ of rounds for various N in order to have complexities at least $2^{128}$ or $2^{256}$. Computations for $T^{Iter*}$ were done without using approximations.

| $s = 128$ | | | | $s = 256$ | | | |
|---|---|---|---|---|---|---|---|
| N | $r_{opt}$ | $T^{MITM*}$ | $T^{Iter*}$ | N | $r_{opt}$ | $T^{MITM*}$ | $T^{Iter*}$ |
| $2^1$ | 260 | $2^{258.0}$ | $2^{128.5}$ | $2^1$ | 516 | $2^{514.0}$ | $2^{256.5}$ |
| $2^2$ | 40 | $2^{152.0}$ | $2^{129.3}$ | $2^2$ | 77 | $2^{228.0}$ | $2^{257.6}$ |
| $2^3$ | 14 | $2^{144.0}$ | $2^{136.5}$ | $2^3$ | 24 | $2^{264.0}$ | $2^{272.2}$ |
| $2^4$ | 9 | $2^{240.0}$ | $2^{155.8}$ | $2^4$ | 12 | $2^{320.0}$ | $2^{289.1}$ |
| $2^5$ | 7 | $2^{465.0}$ | $2^{187.9}$ | $2^5$ | 8 | $2^{480.0}$ | $2^{279.3}$ |
| $2^6$ | 6 | $2^{768.0}$ | $2^{236.2}$ | $2^6$ | 7 | $2^{1134.0}$ | $2^{415.8}$ |
| $2^7$ | 5 | $2^{1778.0}$ | $2^{195.4}$ | $2^7$ | 6 | $2^{1792.0}$ | $2^{485.0}$ |
| $2^8$ | 5 | $2^{4080.0}$ | $2^{370.4}$ | $2^8$ | 5 | $2^{4080.0}$ | $2^{370.4}$ |

Even by adding a safety margin, this shows that we do not need many rounds to safely encrypt a byte (that is, $N = 2^4$) with respect to our best attacks. However, with low r, we should care about other attacks as in Table 1. Indeed, for $\oplus$-FN, we recommend never to take $r \leqslant 7$ due to the yo-yo attack [7]. For other FN, we recommend never to take $r \leqslant 5$.

---

[10] In this table, we computed the value of q suggested by our formulas but rounded in the $\left[\frac{rN}{2}, N^2\right]$ interval.

In Fig. 4, we plot complexities for $r = 8$ or $r = 10$ and various ranges of $N$. The regions for $T^{Iter^*}$ we plot have a minimum for the optimal $q$ and a maximum for $r = \frac{rN}{2}$. The region corresponds to all complexities for $q \in [\frac{rN}{2}, N^2]$.

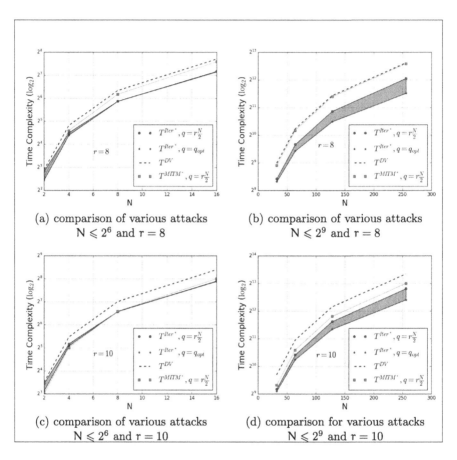

(a) comparison of various attacks $N \leqslant 2^6$ and $r = 8$

(b) comparison of various attacks $N \leqslant 2^9$ and $r = 8$

(c) comparison of various attacks $N \leqslant 2^6$ and $r = 10$

(d) comparison for various attacks $N \leqslant 2^9$ and $r = 10$

**Fig. 4.** Time complexity of attacks against generic 8-round and 10-round FN for Iter* with $q$ minimal or $q$ making the complexity optimal, for DV [15], and MITM*.

## 5    Conclusion

Standard Feistel Networks and its variations have created an active research area since their invention and have been used in constructions of many cryptographic systems to a wide extent. The security of FN has been studied for many decades resulting in many interesting results for cryptanalysis purpose. In this work, we analyze the security of a very specific type of FN with two branches, secure random round functions, and modular addition to analyze its security. Additionally, we consider small domains. The best attack was believed to be MITM. However, we show that partial exhaustive search can be better. Concretely, we show that the number of rounds recommended by NIST is insufficient in FF1 and FF3* for very small N.

This specific FN with the described properties has been used to build Format-Preserving Encryption and perhaps will inspire many other constructions. However, the security of FN with various properties is not clear (regardless of the significant security analyses mentioned in the introduction) and has to be investigated more. Our work shows only that a caution should be taken in order to meet the desired security level in the systems.

We proposed a new algorithm based on partial exhaustive search. We observed a gap between our heuristic complexity and experiments and suggested possible explanations. However, the problem to reduce this gap is left as an open problem.

# References

1. Data Encryption Standard, National Bureau of Standards, NBS FIPS PUB 46, January 1977. National Bureau of Standards. U.S, Department of Commerce (1977)
2. Recommendation for Block Cipher Modes of Operation: Methods for Format Preserving Encryption, NIST Special Publication (SP) 800-38G, 29 March 2016. National Institute of Standards and Technology
3. Retail Financial Services - Requirements for Protection of Sensitive Payment Card Data - Part 1: Using Encryption Method. American National Standards Institute (2016)
4. Bellare, M., Hoang, V.T., Tessaro, S.: Message-recovery attacks on Feistel-based format-preserving encryption. In: Proceedings of the 2016 ACM SIGSAC Conference on Computer and Communications Security, CCS 2016, pp. 444–455. ACM, New York (2016)
5. Bellare, M., Ristenpart, T., Rogaway, P., Stegers, T.: Format-preserving encryption. In: Jacobson, M.J., Rijmen, V., Safavi-Naini, R. (eds.) SAC 2009. LNCS, vol. 5867, pp. 295–312. Springer, Heidelberg (2009). https://doi.org/10.1007/978-3-642-05445-7_19
6. Bellare, M., Rogaway, P., Spies, T.: The FFX Mode of Operation for Format-Preserving Encryption. draft 1.1. Submission to NIST, February 2010. http://csrc.nist.gov/groups/ST/toolkit/BCM/documents/proposedmodes/ffx/ffx-spec.pdf
7. Biryukov, A., Leurent, G., Perrin, L.: Cryptanalysis of feistel networks with secret round functions. In: Dunkelman, O., Keliher, L. (eds.) SAC 2015. LNCS, vol. 9566, pp. 102–121. Springer, Cham (2016). https://doi.org/10.1007/978-3-319-31301-6_6
8. Biryukov, A., Perrin, L.: On reverse-engineering S-boxes with hidden design criteria or structure. In: Gennaro, R., Robshaw, M. (eds.) CRYPTO 2015. LNCS, vol. 9215, pp. 116–140. Springer, Heidelberg (2015). https://doi.org/10.1007/978-3-662-47989-6_6
9. Brier, E., Peyrin, T., Stern, J.: BPS: A Format-Preserving Encryption Proposal. http://csrc.nist.gov/groups/ST/toolkit/BCM/documents/proposedmodes/bps/bps-spec.pdf
10. Diffie, W., Hellman, M.E.: Special feature exhaustive cryptanalysis of the NBS data encryption standard. Computer **10**(6), 74–84 (1977)

11. Dinur, I., Dunkelman, O., Keller, N., Shamir, A.: Efficient dissection of composite problems, with applications to cryptanalysis, knapsacks, and combinatorial search problems. In: Safavi-Naini, R., Canetti, R. (eds.) CRYPTO 2012. LNCS, vol. 7417, pp. 719–740. Springer, Heidelberg (2012). https://doi.org/10.1007/978-3-642-32009-5_42

12. Dinur, I., Dunkelman, O., Keller, N., Shamir, A.: New attacks on feistel structures with improved memory complexities. In: Gennaro, R., Robshaw, M. (eds.) CRYPTO 2015. LNCS, vol. 9215, pp. 433–454. Springer, Heidelberg (2015). https://doi.org/10.1007/978-3-662-47989-6_21

13. Durak, F.B., Vaudenay, S.: Breaking the FF3 format-preserving encryption. In: Proceedings of ESC 2017. https://www.cryptolux.org/mediawiki-esc2017/images/8/83/Proceedings_esc2017.pdf

14. Durak, F.B., Vaudenay, S.: Generic Round-Function-Recovery attacks for Feistel Networks over Small Domains. https://eprint.iacr.org/2018/108.pdf

15. Durak, F.B., Vaudenay, S.: Breaking the FF3 format-preserving encryption standard over small domains. In: Katz, J., Shacham, H. (eds.) CRYPTO 2017. LNCS, vol. 10402, pp. 679–707. Springer, Cham (2017). https://doi.org/10.1007/978-3-319-63715-0_23

16. Hoang, V.T., Rogaway, P.: On generalized Feistel networks. In: Rabin, T. (ed.) CRYPTO 2010. LNCS, vol. 6223, pp. 613–630. Springer, Heidelberg (2010). https://doi.org/10.1007/978-3-642-14623-7_33

17. Isobe, T., Shibutani, K.: All subkeys recovery attack on block ciphers: extending meet-in-the-middle approach. In: Knudsen, L.R., Wu, H. (eds.) SAC 2012. LNCS, vol. 7707, pp. 202–221. Springer, Heidelberg (2013). https://doi.org/10.1007/978-3-642-35999-6_14

18. Isobe, T., Shibutani, K.: Generic key recovery attack on Feistel scheme. In: Sako, K., Sarkar, P. (eds.) ASIACRYPT 2013. LNCS, vol. 8269, pp. 464–485. Springer, Heidelberg (2013). https://doi.org/10.1007/978-3-642-42033-7_24

19. Lu, J., Kim, J., Keller, N., Dunkelman, O.: Improving the efficiency of impossible differential cryptanalysis of reduced Camellia and MISTY1. In: Malkin, T. (ed.) CT-RSA 2008. LNCS, vol. 4964, pp. 370–386. Springer, Heidelberg (2008). https://doi.org/10.1007/978-3-540-79263-5_24

20. Luby, M., Rackoff, C.: How to construct pseudorandom permutations from pseudorandom functions. SIAM J. Comput. **17**(2), 373–386 (1988)

21. Nachef, V., Volte, E., Patarin, J.: Differential attacks on generalized Feistel schemes. In: Abdalla, M., Nita-Rotaru, C., Dahab, R. (eds.) CANS 2013. LNCS, vol. 8257, pp. 1–19. Springer, Cham (2013). https://doi.org/10.1007/978-3-319-02937-5_1

22. Patarin, J.: Generic attacks on Feistel schemes (2008). http://eprint.iacr.org/2008/036

23. Patarin, J.: Security of Balanced and Unbalanced Feistel Schemes with Non-linear Equalities (2010). http://eprint.iacr.org/2010/293

24. Patarin, J., Nachef, V., Berbain, C.: Generic attacks on unbalanced Feistel schemes with contracting functions. In: Lai, X., Chen, K. (eds.) ASIACRYPT 2006. LNCS, vol. 4284, pp. 396–411. Springer, Heidelberg (2006). https://doi.org/10.1007/11935230_26

25. Vaudenay, S.: The security of DSA and ECDSA. In: Desmedt, Y.G. (ed.) PKC 2003. LNCS, vol. 2567, pp. 309–323. Springer, Heidelberg (2003). https://doi.org/10.1007/3-540-36288-6_23

# Differential Cryptanalysis
# of Round-Reduced Sparx-64/128

Ralph Ankele[1]([✉]) and Eik List[2]

[1] Royal Holloway University of London, Egham, UK
ralph.ankele.2015@rhul.ac.uk
[2] Bauhaus-Universität Weimar, Weimar, Germany
eik.list@uni-weimar.de

**Abstract.** SPARX is a family of ARX-based block ciphers designed according to the *long-trail strategy* (LTS) that were both introduced by Dinu et al. at ASIACRYPT'16. Similar to the wide-trail strategy, the LTS allows provable upper bounds on the length of differential characteristics and linear paths. Thus, the cipher is a highly interesting target for third-party cryptanalysis. However, the only third-party cryptanalysis on SPARX-64/128 to date was given by Abdelkhalek et al. at AFRICACRYPT'17 who proposed impossible-differential attacks on 15 and 16 (out of 24) rounds.

In this paper, we present chosen-ciphertext differential attacks on 16 rounds of SPARX-64/128. First, we show a truncated-differential analysis that requires $2^{32}$ chosen ciphertexts and approximately $2^{93}$ encryptions. Second, we illustrate the effectiveness of boomerangs on SPARX by a rectangle attack that requires approximately $2^{59.6}$ chosen ciphertexts and about $2^{122.2}$ encryption equivalents. Finally, we also considered a yoyo attack on 16 rounds that, however, requires the full codebook and approximately $2^{126}$ encryption equivalents.

**Keywords:** Symmetric-key cryptography · Cryptanalysis
Boomerang · Truncated differential · Yoyo · ARX

## 1 Introduction

ARX CIPHERS. The design and cryptanalysis of block ciphers is a heuristic competition between designers and analysts. With the introduction of the wide- trail design strategy in Rijndael, designers could finally provide provable bounds for the expected probabilities and therefore for the maximal length of differential characteristics and linear trails of block ciphers. Rijndael and similar designs are substitution-permutation networks (SPNs), which left the earlier path of using

R. Ankele—This research was partially supported by the European Union's Horizon 2020 research and innovation programme under grant agreement No. H2020-MSCA-ITN-2014-643161 ECRYPT-NET.

only the omnipresent modular addition, XOR, rotation, and shift operations that most processors support out-of-the-box. Thus, SPNs demand an expertised tailoring of their implementations to the operating platform to be comparably efficient as bit-based designs. However, in resource-constrained environments, the most efficient software implementations are still ciphers that employ only logical operations and/or addition, e.g., ciphers based on modular additions, rotations, and XOR (ARX). Hence, until recently, there has been a gap between the provable bounds of wide-trail designs, and the efficiency of ARX-based constructions.

SPARX. At ASIACRYPT'16, Dinu et al. introduced SPARX [7], the first ARX-based family of block ciphers that provides provable bounds on the maximal length of differential characteristics and linear trails. Alongside SPARX, the authors developed the long-trail design strategy, a general approach for ARX-based symmetric-key primitives to obtain provable bounds. Both the long-trail strategy in general, and SPARX in particular, are interesting targets of cryptanalysis as they try to bridge the gap between efficiency and providing security bounds. The question arises if it is also secure against (truncated) differential and boomerang attacks that can exploit clustering effects of many differential characteristics.

RESEARCH GAP AND RELATED WORK. In the specification of SPARX, the designers reported on their results of a first automated analysis that no differential characteristic with probability higher than $2^{-n}$ nor any linear characteristic with bias higher than $2^{-n/2}$ exists over five or more steps. Moreover, they described integral attacks on up to five out of eight steps of SPARX-64/128, and six out of ten steps of SPARX-128. Though, those initial attacks are naturally limited due to time constraints when designing a new cipher, and therefore demand a deeper analysis by the cryptographic community. At AFRICACRYPT'17, Abdelkhalek et al. [1] proposed 12- and 13-round impossible-differential distinguishers on SPARX-64/128, using the four-step distinguisher for balanced Type-1 Feistel networks. They extended their attacks by three rounds, respectively, where they exploited dependencies between the key words from the key-schedule. Recently, Tolba et. al. proposed multi-dimensional zero-correlation linear attacks on up to 26 rounds of SPARX-128/128, and on up to 29 rounds of SPARX-128/256 [13].

CONTRIBUTION AND OUTLINE. This work adds two chosen-ciphertext attacks on SPARX-64/128 in the single-key model: (1) a truncated-differential attack on 16 rounds and (2) a rectangle attack on 16 rounds; moreover, we further considered yoyo attacks on the same number of rounds, which, however, requires the full codebook. Due to space constraints, that attacks will be available in a full version alongside this work [2]. Table 1 compares their parameters with the previous attacks on SPARX-64/128 from the literature. In the remainder, we briefly revisit the necessary notions as well as the details of SPARX-64 in Sect. 2. We describe our truncated-differential attack in Sect. 5. We continue with an informal introduction to boomerang and rectangle attacks in Sect. 3. In Sect. 4, we describe our search of differential trails before we detail our rectangle attack on SPARX-64/128 in Sect. 6. Finally, Sect. 7 concludes this work.

**Table 1.** Previous and proposed attacks on SPARX-64/128. KP/CP/CC = known plaintext/chosen plaintext/chosen ciphertext. ID = Impossible differential, TD = Truncated differentials.

| Rounds | Attack type | Time | Data | | Memory | Ref. |
|--------|-------------|------|------|---|--------|------|
| 15/24 | Integral | $2^{101.0}$ | $2^{37.0}$ | CP | $2^{64.0}$ | [7] |
| 15/24 | ID | $2^{94.1}$ | $2^{51.0}$ | CP | $2^{43.5}$ | [1] |
| 16/24 | ID | $2^{94.0}$ | $2^{61.5}$ | KP | $2^{61.5}$ | [1] |
| 16/24 | TD | $2^{93.0}$ | $2^{32.0}$ | CC | $2^{61.0}$ | Sect. 5 |
| 16/24 | Rectangle | $2^{122.2}$ | $2^{59.6}$ | CC | $2^{61.6}$ | Sect. 6 |
| 16/24 | Yoyo | $2^{126.0}$ | $2^{64.0}$ | CP | $2^{64.0}$ | Full version [2] |

## 2  Preliminaries

GENERAL NOTATIONS. We denote by $\mathbb{F}_2$ the finite field of two elements $x \in \{0,1\}$. For positive integer $n$, we denote by $\mathbb{F}_2^n$ the space of $n$-element vectors from $\mathbb{F}_2$. We represent functions by upper case letters and indices by lowercase letters. $\{0,1\}^n$ is the set of all $n$-bit strings and $\{0,1\}^*$ the set of bit strings of arbitrary length. Let $x, y \in \{0,1\}^n$ for some positive integer $n$ in the following. Then, we denote by $x \parallel y$ the concatenation of $x$ and $y$, by $x \oplus y$ their bitwise XOR, by $x \lll r$ a rotation by $r$ bit to the left and by $x \ggg r$ rotation by $r$ bit to the right; moreover, we denote by $x \boxplus y = (x + y) \bmod 2^n$ modular addition, and by $x \boxminus y = (x - y) \bmod 2^n$ modular subtraction. For all bit strings $x \in \{0,1\}^n$, we index the bits $x = (x_{n-1} \ldots x_1 x_0)$ where $x_{n-1}$ is the most significant and $x_0$ the least significant bit of $x$. Given a bit string $x = (x^1 \parallel \ldots \parallel x^m) \in (\{0,1\}^{mn})$ consisting of $m$ words of $n$ bit each, we denote by

$$x \lll_n r \stackrel{\text{def}}{=} (x^1 \lll r) \parallel \ldots \parallel (x^m \lll r)$$

the word-wise independent rotated value. We overload the notation for tuples of bit strings $x \in (\{0,1\}^n)^m$: $x = (x^1, \ldots, x^m)$, to still mean wordwise independent rotation $x \lll_n r \stackrel{\text{def}}{=} (x^1 \lll r), \ldots, (x^m \lll r)$. We use typewriter font to represent hexadecimal values, e.g., $\texttt{0110} = 272$. We use the same font but with annotation to represent bit strings, e.g., $(\texttt{0110})_2 = 6$; moreover, we will use the symbol $*$ at the position of that certain bits to indicate that they can take arbitrary values, e.g., $(0*10)_2 \in \{2,6\}$. As a shorthand notation for probabilities $p$, we often write $h_w = -\log_2(p)$ when the meaning of $p$ is clear from the context.

### 2.1  The Sparx Family of Ciphers

The SPARX-$n/k$ family comprises three versions, SPARX-64/128, SPARX-128/128, and SPARX-128/256, where $n$ indicates the block size, and $k$ the key length $k$. The cipher is based on a Feistel network with two state words for SPARX-64 and four state words for SPARX-128, consisting of $n_s$ Feistel steps. Each step

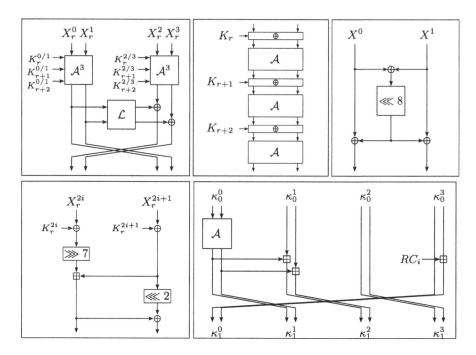

**Fig. 1.** High-level view of SPARX-64. **Top left:** The step function. **Top center:** The $\mathcal{A}^3$ layer in SPARX-64. **Top right:** The linear layer $\mathcal{L}$. **Bottom left:** The $\mathcal{A}$ function SPECKEY. **Bottom right:** One iteration of the key schedule of SPARX-64/128.

consists of $r_a$ rounds of an ARX-based round function; plain- and ciphertexts consist of $w = n/32$ words $X^0, \ldots, X^{w-1}$ of 32 bit each; the key is divided into 32-bit words $(\kappa^0, \ldots, \kappa^{v-1})$. The values for the individual versions of SPARX are summarized in Table 2, the components of the cipher are also depicted in Fig. 1.

SPARX-64/128. The structure of SPARX-64 is reminiscent of a Feistel network of eight steps. Each step consists of $r_a = 3$ rounds of the ARX-box $\mathcal{A}$, (i.e. three rounds of SPECKEY) on each branch. The Feistel function $\mathcal{L}$ is a linear involutive permutation $\mathcal{L} : \mathbb{F}_2^{32} \rightarrow \mathbb{F}_2^{32}$ inspired by [8]. Given the left 32-bit state word $x \parallel y$, the input is split into 16-bit parts $x, y$, and is mapped to

$$\mathcal{L}(x \parallel y) \stackrel{\text{def}}{=} (x \oplus ((x \oplus y) \lll 8)) \parallel (y \oplus ((x \oplus y) \lll 8)).$$

We denote the 64-bit state after Round $r$ interchangeably as $(L_r, R_r) = (X_r^0 \parallel X_r^1, X_r^2 \parallel X_r^3) = (X_r^L \parallel Y_r^L, X_r^R \parallel Y_r^R)$, and the round key used in Round $r$ interchangeably as $(K_r^L, K_r^R) = (K_r^0 \parallel K_r^1, K_r^2 \parallel K_r^3)$.

THE KEY SCHEDULE OF SPARX-64. The 128-bit secret key of SPARX-64/128 is divided into four initial 32-bit words $(\kappa_0^0, \kappa_0^1, \kappa_0^2, \kappa_0^3)$. In each step, the key schedule transforms the leftmost 32-bit word $\kappa_s^0$ in one iteration of the ARX-box $\mathcal{A}$, adds the output to the right neighboring word $\kappa_s^1$, adds a round constant $RC_i$

**Table 2.** Parameters of the individual versions of SPARX.

| Cipher | #state-words $w$ | #key-words $v$ | #rounds/step $r_a$ | #steps $n_s$ |
|---|---|---|---|---|
| SPARX-64/128 | 2 | 2 | 3 | 8 |
| SPARX-128/128 | 4 | 4 | 4 | 8 |
| SPARX-128/256 | 4 | 8 | 4 | 10 |

to the rightmost 16-bit half of $\kappa_{2s}^3$ to prevent slide attacks, and finally rotates the four words by one position to the right. The $r_a = 3$ leftmost words $\kappa_{2s}^0$, $\kappa_{2s}^1$, $\kappa_{2s}^2$ are used as round keys for the first, second, and third round of the left branch of Step $s + 1$; the $r_a = 3$ left-most words $\kappa_{2s+1}^0$, $\kappa_{2s+1}^1$, $\kappa_{2s+1}^2$ are used for the first, second, and third round of the right branch of Step $s + 1$. For example, $(\kappa_0^0, \kappa_0^1, \kappa_0^2)$ are used as round keys for the left branch in the first step, and $(\kappa_1^0, \kappa_1^1, \kappa_1^2)$ are used as round keys for the right branch in the first step.

### 2.2 Properties

As observed by Abdelkhalek et al. [1], one can obtain the rounds keys for 2.5 consecutive rounds by guessing only 64 bit of key material. More precisely, one obtains the round keys for Round $3r + 1$ and the round key for the right 32-bit branch in Round $3r + 2$ by guessing the 64 bit of the key material of Round $3r$:

*Property 1.* Given $\kappa_{s+1}^2$ and $\kappa_{s+1}^3$, one can directly derive the key words $\kappa_s^2 = \kappa_{s+1}^3$, $\kappa_{s+2}^0 = \kappa_{s+1}^3$, $\kappa_{2s+3}^1 = \mathcal{A}(\kappa_{s+2}^0)$, and $\kappa_{s+3}^0 = \kappa_{s+1}^2$.

We learnt Property 2 from Leurent [10].

*Property 2.* Assume, $\Delta \in \mathbb{F}_2^n$ is a fixed difference, and $x^0, \ldots, x^m \in \mathbb{F}_2^n$ represent $m$ values for which the goal is to find pairs $(x^i, x^j)$ that result in $x^i \oplus x^j = \Delta$. Then, one can define a linear function $F : \mathbb{F}_2^n \to \mathbb{F}_2^n$ with rank $n - 1$, s.t. $F(\Delta) = 0^n$; thus, all pairs $(x^i, x^j)$ with $x^i \oplus x^j = \Delta$ will collide in $F(x^i) = F(x^j)$.

It finds pairs with some difference without studying all combinations of pairs but by comparing their outputs from $F$. One can reduce the rank of $F$ to $n - d$ so that outputs of $F$ collide if and only if their inputs have one of $2^d$ differences.

## 3  Boomerang and Rectangle Attacks

Boomerang attacks, as proposed by Wagner [15], allow an attacker to concatenate two short differentials with high probability when long differentials with sufficient probability are absent or hard to find. In the basic setting, an adversary splits an encryption function $E : \{0,1\}^k \times \{0,1\}^n \to \{0,1\}^n$ into two subciphers $E = E_2 \circ E_1$, s.t. $E(P) \stackrel{\text{def}}{=} E_2(E_1(P))$. Then, it considers a first differential $\alpha \to \beta$ with probability $p$ over $E_1$ and a second differential $\gamma \to \delta$ with probability $q$ over $E_2$. These are often called upper and lower differentials or trails, respectively. They can then be combined in a chosen-plaintext and adaptive chosen-ciphertext attack to construct a boomerang distinguisher consisting of the following steps:

1. Choose a plaintext pair $(P, P')$ with difference $\alpha = P \oplus P'$ and encrypt it through $E$ to obtain its ciphertext pair $(C, C')$ with difference $\beta$.
2. Derive $D = C \oplus \delta$ and $D' = C' \oplus \delta$ (the $\delta$-shift) and decrypt $D$ and $D'$ through $E^{-1}$ to obtain the corresponding plaintext pair $(Q, Q')$.
3. If the plaintext pair $(Q, Q')$ has difference $\alpha = Q \oplus Q'$, then $(P, P', Q, Q')$ form a correct quartet.

**Proposition 1.** For a quartet $(P, P', Q, Q')$, there exists a differential with an input difference $\alpha$ for $P' = P \oplus \alpha$, $Q' = Q \oplus \alpha$, and a corresponding output difference $\beta$ for $U' = U \oplus \beta$, $V' = V \oplus \beta$ with probability $p$. If we consider a differential $\delta \rightarrow \gamma$ with input difference $D = C \oplus \delta$, $D' = C' \oplus \delta$ and a corresponding output difference $\gamma$ for $V = U \oplus \gamma$, it holds with probability $q$ that $V' = U' \oplus \gamma$. Then, we can connect both differentials if we consider $V = U \oplus \gamma$, it follows that $V' = V \oplus \beta = (U \oplus \gamma) \oplus \beta = (U \oplus \beta) \oplus \gamma = U' \oplus \gamma$.

Calculating the probabilities for a correct quartet requires to consider both plaintext pairs $(P, P')$ and $(Q, Q')$ and results in a probability of $(pq)^2$. For the differentials to exist, the resulting probability has to satisfy $(pq)^2 \geq 2^{-n/2}$.

The probability of a correct quartet can be increased if one fixes input differences $\alpha$ and $\delta$ but allows all possible differences for $\beta$ and $\gamma$, requiring only that $\beta \neq \gamma$. A boomerang distinguisher would then consider all trails of the form $\alpha \rightarrow \beta'$ for the upper trail and $\delta \rightarrow \gamma'$ for the lower trail. This increases the probability to $(\widehat{p}\widehat{q})^2$ where $\widehat{p} = \sqrt{\sum_{\beta'} \text{Pr}^2 [\alpha \rightarrow \beta']}$ and $\widehat{q} = \sqrt{\sum_{\gamma'} \text{Pr}^2 [\delta \rightarrow \gamma']}$ where $\widehat{p}$ is evaluated over $E_1$ and $\widehat{q}$ over $E_2^{-1}$, respectively.

THE RECTANGLE ATTACK. In boomerang attacks, the adversary needs to query its oracles with chosen plaintexts and adaptively chosen ciphertexts. Since our boomerang attack will have to guess a considerable amount of key bits, which would require an oracle query for every obtained text and key guess, we will employ a *rectangle* attack instead. *Rectangle* attacks [3] have been derived from the *amplified boomerang* [9], both of which transform the boomerang into a purely chosen-plaintext attack (or chosen-ciphertext if the adversary starts from the opposite direction). The core idea is to encrypt many pairs $(P, P')$ with difference $P' \oplus P = \alpha$ in the hope that some of those will form a quartet with the desired differences in the middle with probability $2^{-n}$. Given $N$ plaintext pairs, the number of correct quartets is reduced to $N^2 \cdot 2^{-n} \cdot (\widehat{p}\widehat{q})^2$. Note that two pairs $(U, U')$ and $(V, V')$ can be combined in two distinct ways to a quartet in the middle: $U \oplus V = U' \oplus V' = \beta$ or $U \oplus U' = V \oplus V' = \beta$. [4] presented further improvements to the technique. The disadvantages of rectangle compared to boomerang attacks are the increased data complexity and the large number of potential quartets that have to be filtered to find correct quartets.

LADDER SWITCH. There exist a few approaches for increasing the transitional probability of boomerang trails in the middle. Two well-known approaches are

**Table 3.** An optimal six-round differential trail.

| Rd. | $\Delta L_i$ | $\Delta R_i$ | $h_w$ | |
|---|---|---|---|---|
| 0 | 00000000 | 02110a04 | – | – |
| 1 | 00000000 | 28000010 | 0 | 4 |
| 2 | 00000000 | 00400000 | 0 | 2 |
| 3 | 00000000 | 80008000 | 0 | 0 |
| $\mathcal{L}$ | 80008000 | 00000000 | 0 | 0 |
| 4 | 81008102 | 00000000 | 1 | 0 |
| 5 | 8000840a | 00000000 | 2 | 0 |
| 6 | 850a9520 | 00000000 | 4 | 0 |
| $\mathcal{L}$ | af1abf30 | 850a9520 | 0 | 0 |

**Table 4.** Optimal differentials through up to ten rounds of Sparx-64; $t$ is the run time of each search.

| #Rds. | $\Delta_{in}$ | $\Delta_{out}$ | $h_w$ | $t$ |
|---|---|---|---|---|
| 1 | (00408000, 00000000) | (00000002, 00000000) | 0.00 | 0.02 s |
| 2 | (00102000, 00000000) | (80008002, 00000000) | 1.00 | 0.10 s |
| 3 | (28000010, 00000000) | (83008302, 81008102) | 3.00 | 0.46 s |
| 4 | (00000000, 28000010) | (8000840a, 00000000) | 4.99 | 2.40 s |
| 5 | (00000000, 02110a04) | (8000840a, 00000000) | 8.99 | 25.07 s |
| 6 | (00000000, 02110a04) | (af1abf30, 850a9520) | 12.99 | 0.06 h |
| 7 | (00000000, 14881008) | (82048e0e, 8000840a) | 23.95 | 47.80 h |
| 8 | (00000000, 540a0120) | (8000840a, 8000840a) | 28.53 | 15.20 d |
| 9 | (28000010, 28000010) | (d2609263, d1209123) | 32.87 | 22.30 d |
| 10 | (28000010, 28000010) | (80818283, 80008002) | 38.12 | 32.50 d |

the Feistel switch and the ladder switch; recently, Sasaki et al. [6] observed a number of more ways. Here, we concentrate on the ladder switch by [5]. It exploits that start and end of upper and lower trails can be located at different locations for each part of the state. For Sparx, it is intuitive to consider full steps: e.g., assume that the top trail has a nonzero difference in the left branch through the step in the middle. If the right branch has a zero difference in the left branch, one can put the switch for the left branch before the step and consider it to be part of the bottom trail, which has probability one. Clearly, this approach can be generalized further to probabilities smaller than one. For Sparx, an optimal switch has one active (e.g., the left) and one inactive (e.g., the right) branch in the top trail, and mirrored in the bottom trail (e.g., right active and left inactive), which allows to pass the step in the middle with probability one.

## 4 Differential Trails and Boomerang Distinguishers

We employed a two-step approach: first, we searched for optimal differential characteristics for up to ten rounds of Sparx-64. Those formed the base of the wrapping rounds before and after the boomerang switches. Thereupon, we considered three interesting types of boomerangs over five steps.

### 4.1 Searching Optimal Differential Trails

We implemented variants of Sparx in CryptoSMT [12], an open- source tool based on the SAT/SMT solvers CryptoMiniSat [11] and STP [14] to search for optimal differential characteristics[1]. In this case, the problem to find optimal differential characteristics is modeled as a Boolean satisfiability problem, and can then be solved by a SAT solver. As the differential model of a cipher can be rather complex, we modeled the problem as a more general SMT (Satisfiability Modular Theories) problem. The difference to SAT problems is that SMT problems can express richer languages where, e.g., sets of variables can be expressed

---

[1] The differential models for Sparx are available at: https://github.com/TheBan anaMan/sparx-differential-attacks.

**Table 5. Top** (left to right): best trails found for our differentials of Type 1a, Type 1b, Type 1c, and Type 1d. **Middle**: best trails found for our differentials of Type 2a, Type 2b, Type 2d, and Type 2e. **Bottom**: Type 2c, Type 3a, Type 3b, and Type 3c. $\Sigma$ denotes the sum of $h_w$ over all rounds.

**Top** (Type 1a, Type 1b, Type 1c, Type 1d):

| Rd. | $\Delta L_i$ | $\Delta R_i$ | $h_w$ | Rd. | $\Delta L_i$ | $\Delta R_i$ | $h_w$ | Rd. | $\Delta L_i$ | $\Delta R_i$ | $h_w$ | Rd. | $\Delta L_i$ | $\Delta R_i$ | $h_w$ |
|---|---|---|---|---|---|---|---|---|---|---|---|---|---|---|---|
| 0 | 00000000 | 28000010 | - - | 0 | 28000010 | 28000010 | - - | 0 | 40404000 | 00400000 | - - | 0 | 80008000 | 80008000 | - - |
| 1 | 00000000 | 00400000 | 0 2 | 1 | 00400000 | 00400000 | 2 2 | 1 | 40804081 | 80008000 | 2 0 | 1 | 81008102 | 81008102 | 1 1 |
| 2 | 00000000 | 80008000 | 0 0 | 2 | 80008000 | 80008000 | 0 0 | 2 | 40004205 | 81008102 | 3 1 | 2 | 8004840e | 8004840e | 3 3 |
| 3 | 00000000 | 81008102 | 0 1 | 3 | 81008102 | 83008302 | 1 2 | 3 | 42854a90 | 8000840a | 5 2 | 3 | bd1aad20 | 870a9730 | 7 8 |
| $\mathcal{L}$ | 81008102 | 00000000 | 0 0 | $\mathcal{L}$ | 00000000 | 81008102 | 0 0 | $\mathcal{L}$ | d78ddb92 | 42854a90 | 0 0 | $\mathcal{L}$ | 00000000 | bd1aad20 | 0 0 |
| $\Sigma$ | | | 3 | $\Sigma$ | | | 7 | $\Sigma$ | | | 13 | $\Sigma$ | | | 23 |

**Middle** (Type 2a, Type 2b, Type 2d, Type 2e):

| Rd. | $\Delta L_i$ | $\Delta R_i$ | $h_w$ | Rd. | $\Delta L_i$ | $\Delta R_i$ | $h_w$ | Rd. | $\Delta L_i$ | $\Delta R_i$ | $h_w$ | Rd. | $\Delta L_i$ | $\Delta R_i$ | $h_w$ |
|---|---|---|---|---|---|---|---|---|---|---|---|---|---|---|---|
| 0 | 02110a04 | 02110a04 | - - | 0 | 02110a04 | 00000000 | - - | | | | | | | | |
| 1 | 28000010 | 28000010 | 4 4 | 1 | 28000010 | 00000000 | 4 0 | 0 | 28000010 | | - | 0 | 28000010 | | - |
| 2 | 00400000 | 00400000 | 2 2 | 2 | 00400000 | 00000000 | 2 0 | 1 | 00400000 | 00400000 | 2 - | 1 | 00400000 | 00000000 | 2 - |
| 3 | 80008000 | 80008000 | 0 0 | 3 | 80008000 | 80008000 | 0 0 | 2 | 80008000 | 80008000 | 0 0 | 2 | 80008000 | 00000000 | 0 0 |
| $\mathcal{L}$ | 00000000 | 80008000 | 0 0 | $\mathcal{L}$ | 00000000 | 80008000 | 0 0 | $\mathcal{L}$ | 00000000 | 80008000 | 0 0 | $\mathcal{L}$ | 00000000 | 80008000 | 0 0 |
| 4 | 00000000 | 81008102 | 0 1 | 3 | 81008102 | 81008102 | 1 1 | 3 | 00000000 | 81008102 | 0 1 | 3 | 81008102 | 81008102 | 1 1 |
| 5 | 00000000 | 8000840a | 0 2 | 4 | 8000840a | 8000840a | 2 2 | 4 | 00000000 | 8000840a | 0 2 | 4 | 8000840a | 8000840a | 2 2 |
| 6 | 00000000 | 850a9520 | 0 4 | 5 | 850a9520 | 2a102a10 | 4 4 | 5 | 00000000 | 850a9520 | 0 4 | 5 | 850a9520 | 850a9520 | 4 4 |
| $\mathcal{L}$ | 850a9520 | 00000000 | 0 0 | $\mathcal{L}$ | 2a102a10 | 850a9520 | 0 0 | $\mathcal{L}$ | 850a9520 | 00000000 | 0 0 | $\mathcal{L}$ | 2a102a10 | 850a9520 | 0 0 |
| $\Sigma$ | | | 19 | $\Sigma$ | | | 20 | $\Sigma$ | | | 9 | $\Sigma$ | | | 16 |

**Bottom** (Type 2c, Type 3a, Type 3b, Type 3c):

| Rd. | $\Delta L_i$ | $\Delta R_i$ | $h_w$ | Rd. | $\Delta L_i$ | $\Delta R_i$ | $h_w$ | Rd. | $\Delta L_i$ | $\Delta R_i$ | $h_w$ | Rd. | $\Delta L_i$ | $\Delta R_i$ | $h_w$ |
|---|---|---|---|---|---|---|---|---|---|---|---|---|---|---|---|
| 0 | 00000000 | 02110a04 | - - | 0 | 28000010 | 28000010 | - - | 0 | 00000000 | 00508402 | - - | | | | |
| 1 | 00000000 | 28000010 | 0 4 | 1 | 00400000 | 00400000 | 2 2 | 1 | 00000000 | 24023408 | 0 4 | 0 | 00000000 | | - |
| 2 | 00000000 | 00400000 | 0 2 | 2 | 80008000 | 80008000 | 0 0 | 2 | 00000000 | 50c080e0 | 0 7 | 1 | 00000000 | 0a204205 | 0 - |
| 3 | 00000000 | 80008000 | 0 0 | 3 | 83008302 | 81008102 | 2 1 | 3 | 00000000 | 01810203 | 0 5 | 2 | 00000000 | 02110a04 | 0 5 |
| $\mathcal{L}$ | 80008000 | 00000000 | 0 0 | $\mathcal{L}$ | 00000000 | 83008302 | 0 0 | $\mathcal{L}$ | 01810203 | 00000000 | 0 0 | $\mathcal{L}$ | 02110a04 | 00000000 | 0 0 |
| 4 | 81008102 | 00000000 | 1 0 | 4 | 00000000 | 80088c02 | 0 5 | 4 | 000c0800 | 00000000 | 5 0 | 3 | 28000010 | 00000000 | 4 0 |
| 5 | 8000840a | 00000000 | 2 0 | 5 | 00000000 | 8502b508 | 0 5 | 5 | 20000000 | 00000000 | 3 0 | 4 | 00400000 | 00000000 | 2 0 |
| 6 | 850a9520 | 00000000 | 4 0 | 6 | 00000000 | d0020420 | 0 7 | 6 | 00400040 | 00000000 | 1 0 | 5 | 80008000 | 80008000 | 0 0 |
| $\mathcal{L}$ | af1abf30 | 850a9520 | 0 0 | $\mathcal{L}$ | d0020420 | 00000000 | 0 0 | $\mathcal{L}$ | 00400040 | 00400040 | 0 0 | $\mathcal{L}$ | 00000000 | 80008000 | 0 0 |
| | | | | 7 | 00801000 | 00000000 | 4 0 | 7 | 80408140 | 80408140 | 2 2 | 6 | 81008102 | 81008102 | 1 1 |
| | | | | 8 | 10015001 | 00000000 | 2 0 | 8 | 00400542 | 00400542 | 3 3 | 7 | 8000840a | 8000840a | 2 2 |
| | | | | 9 | 52211224 | 00000000 | 5 0 | 9 | 8542904a | 8542904a | 4 4 | 8 | 850a9520 | 850a9520 | 4 4 |
| | | | | $\mathcal{L}$ | 57611764 | 52211224 | 0 0 | $\mathcal{L}$ | 08150815 | 8542904a | 0 0 | $\mathcal{L}$ | 2a102a10 | 850a9520 | 0 0 |
| $\Sigma$ | | | 13 | $\Sigma$ | | | 35 | $\Sigma$ | | | 37 | $\Sigma$ | | | 25 |

as predicates or the problem can be modeled on word level. We describe the differential behavior of SPARX using the CVC language. This allows us to define specific constraints that can be used to limit the search space for the SAT solver. The solver then tries to find all possible valid differential characteristics for the given parameters with increasing probability.

Table 3 shows an optimal six-round differential trail. Note that $h_w$ denotes $h_w = -\log_2(p)$, for the differential probability $p$ through a round. One can observe that optimal differential characteristics for SPARX-64 possess an hour-glass structure, i.e., the number of active bits is minimal in the middle and increases outwards. Using the probability of the best characteristic is often assumed to be an adequate approximation of the probability of the best differential. However, this approximation is not always sufficiently accurate for

ARX-based ciphers. Therefore, we tried to evaluate the probability of differentials where feasible. For the best differentials for SPARX-64, we provide an overview in Table 4.

TYPES OF DIFFERENTIAL CHARACTERISTICS. After searching differentials incrementality for a given interval of rounds, we searched for optimal characteristics among the following types. The first category consists of single-step characteristics:

- **Type 1a.** Arbitrary single-step characteristics.
- **Type 1b.** Single-step characteristics with two active branches that have a single active branch after the step.
- **Type 1c.** Single-step characteristics with two active branches that have a single active branch before the step.
- **Type 1d.** Single-step characteristics with two active branches that have a single active branch before and afterwards.

The best characteristic for single-steps is a Type 1a characteristic with the left branch all zeros. Type 1d is especially interesting for our truncated-differential attack. The second category consists of two-step characteristics, that are also used in our boomerang/rectangle distinguishers:

- **Type 2a.** Two-step top characteristics which collide after the XOR in the right branch after the first step.
- **Type 2b.** Two-step bottom characteristics with only the left branch active at the first step.
- **Type 2c.** Two-step characteristics where only the left branch is active in the first, and therefore only the right branch is active in the second step.
- **Type 2d.** 4.5-round versions of Type 2a, but only two rounds before the collision for the left and one round before for the right branch.
- **Type 2e.** We further investigated the versions of Type 2a where the first step covers only one round.

We use the two-step characteristic of Type 2c for the top trail and Type 2b for the bottom trail of our rectangle distinguisher. We further considered three-step characteristics for boomerang/rectangle attacks in our third category:

- **Type 3a.** Three-step characteristics where both branches are active in the first step, and only one branch is active in the subsequent steps, as is used in both top and bottom trail of the single- sided bottom type of boomerang.
- **Type 3b.** Three-step characteristics where the first two steps are of Type 3a, and both branches are active in the third step.
- **Type 3c.** 7.5-round versions of Type 3b, where only one round is considered for the first step.

Our results for the best characteristics found are summarized in Table 5.

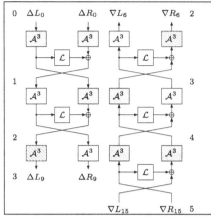

(a) Free-middle boomerang

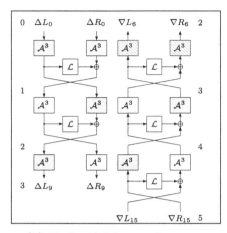

(b) Single-sided-bottom boomerang

**Fig. 2.** Types of five-step boomerangs. White $\mathcal{A}^3$ boxes are inactive (zero difference); gray $\mathcal{A}^3$-boxes are active (non-zero difference). Hatched $\mathcal{A}^3$ boxes indicate active branches that do not have to be taken into account at the switch.

### 4.2 Boomerangs

From the combination of the best identified characteristics, we continued to form boomerangs. We considered three types of boomerangs over five steps.

- **Free middle.** This type exploits that we can obtain the middle step for free if we choose our top and bottom trails such that one of them possesses a zero difference in the left branch, and the other one has a zero difference in the right branch, which is a direct application of the Ladder switch. We can obtain a five-step boomerang in this way, but have active differences in both branches in the first and in the fifth step of the wrapping rounds.
- **Single-sided bottom.** This type has both branches active at the start of the top trail, but only one active branch at the end of the bottom trail.
- **Single-sided top.** This type has both branches active at the end of the bottom trail, but only one active branch at the beginning of the top trail.

As examples, the former two types are visualized in Fig. 2.

From our experiments, it became clear soon that free-middle boomerangs possessed higher probabilities. Table 6 summarizes the best boomerang that consist of a single characteristic that we could find for one up to five steps. Through a single step, there exist various boomerangs with probability one:

$$\Pr\left[(\Delta L_0, \Delta R_0) \xrightarrow{\text{1 step}} (\Delta L_3, \Delta R_3)\right] = 1,$$

for all characteristics with $\Delta L_0 = 0$ and $\Delta L_3 = \mathcal{L}(\Delta R_3)$; alternatively, it also holds for all characteristics with $\Delta R_0 = \Delta R_3 = 0$.

Over two steps, there exist two-step boomerangs with

$$\Pr\left[(\Delta L_0, \Delta R_0) \xrightarrow{\text{2 steps}} (\Delta L_6, \Delta R_6)\right] \geq 2^{-6},$$

namely for characteristics of the form

- $\Delta L_0 = 0$ and $\Delta R_0 \in \{28000010, 00400000\}$ and $\Delta L_6 = \mathcal{L}(\Delta R_6)$, or
- $\Delta R_0 = 0$ and $\Delta R_6 \in \{81008102, 8000840a\}$ and $\Delta L_6 = \mathcal{L}(\Delta R_6)$.

For three steps, the best boomerangs have probability $2^{-12}$, using the single-step characteristic with the highest probability of Type 1a for the top trail, and a similar characteristic mirrored vertically and starting from the bottom difference $(\Delta L_9, \Delta R_9) = (83008302, 81008102)$. Similarly, we obtain from the combination of the characteristics of Type 2a (as the top trail) and Type 1a (horizontally mirrored, as the bottom trail; this is a free-middle boomerang) boomerangs with probability of $2^{-44}$ over four steps. Over five steps, the highest theoretical probability of a boomerang with fixed characteristics results from combining a characteristic of Type 2a with the highest probability at the top with a characteristic of Type 2b with the highest probability at the bottom.

NEAR-OPTIMAL DIFFERENTIAL TRAILS. Boomerangs that employ a single characteristic are of limited expressiveness in practice as we noticed strong differential clustering effects in SPARX. For boomerangs, they are particularly strong in the switching rounds. Our purpose was to find good boomerangs of five steps, where we focused on the free-middle approach. We used the best characteristics of Type 1b and Type 2a as top and Type 1a and Type 2b as bottom trails as a base to study their probability empirically over a feasible subset of the three steps in the middle. Moreover, our automated search for optimal differential characteristics yielded many near-optimal differentials with probability slightly smaller than that of the optimal ones; as one could anticipate, this small change in the probability stemmed from the fact that bits adjacent to the active bits in the optimal differentials were also active in the near-optimal ones, mainly in the first or the last round. Hence, we also considered those near-optimal trails in our investigation of potential start and end differences for boomerangs. The subset of our results is given in Table 7. We used a variant of them for our rectangle attack in Sect. 6.

## 5   Truncated-Differential Attack on Sparx-64/128

HIGH-LEVEL VIEW. This section describes a truncated-differential attack on 16-round SPARX-64/128. On a high level, the Feistel-like structure allows generic trails that pass through almost two steps so that only one branch is active. The core observation of our attack is the existence of differentials of Type 1d, i.e., trails that have an inactive branch before and after a step with probability $\gg 2^{-32}$. One such trail is illustrated in Table 8. The trail is truncated after Round 9; thereupon, its precise differences are irrelevant as long as it will cancel

**Table 6.** Best found boomerangs on step-reduced SPARX-64/128; for up to three steps, we verified them experimentally with 100 random keys and $2^{20}$ random pairs each. Values in parentheses are products of the empirical probabilities over the three steps in the middle from Table 7 with the theoretical probabilities over the remaining step(s).

| #Steps | Input difference | | Output difference | | $h_w$ | |
|---|---|---|---|---|---|---|
| | $\Delta L_0$ | $\Delta R_0$ | $\Delta L_{3s}$ | $\Delta R_{3s}$ | Theor. | Empiric. |
| 1 | 00000000 | 00400000 | 83008302 | 81008102 | 0 | 0 |
| 2 | 00000000 | 28000010 | 8000840a | 00000000 | 6 | 5.11 |
| 2 | 00000000 | 28000010 | 81008102 | 00000000 | 6 | 5.16 |
| 2 | 00000000 | 28000010 | 850a9520 | 00000000 | 6 | 5.31 |
| 3 | 00000000 | 28000010 | 83008302 | 81008102 | 12 | 10.55 |
| 3 | 00000000 | 28000010 | 8a048e0e | 8000840a | 12 | 11.43 |
| 4 | 28000010 | 28000010 | 83008302 | 81008102 | 42 | (36.78) |
| 5 | 28000010 | 28000010 | 2a102a10 | 850a9520 | 78 | (68.54) |
| 5 | 02110a04 | 02110a04 | 2a102a10 | 850a9520 | 76 | (72.18) |

**Table 7.** Relevant experimental probabilities of free-middle boomerangs over three steps. Values represent $-\log_2(p)$, where $p$ is the average probability of correct quartets from 100 test runs of random independent keys with $2^{30}$ random text pairs each.

| $(\Delta L_9, \Delta R_9)$ | $(\Delta L_0, \Delta R_0)$ | |
|---|---|---|
| | $(00000000, 80008000)$ | $(00000000, 81008102)$ |
| $(80008000, 80008000)$ | 20.18 | 26.54 |
| $(83008302, 81008102)$ | 16.32 | 22.78 |

in the right branch after the linear layer, and the zero-difference branch can propagate through two further steps (i.e. Rounds $13-18$ in Table 8). Thus, an adversary can observe that only a single branch will be active after five steps; the final linear layer can then be easily inverted. On the downside, the probability of truncated trails must exceed $2^{-32}$ for a useful distinguisher.

To ensure a sufficient probability of the differential, we employ Property 1 at the plaintext side to reduce the number of steps to trace through. So, we obtain the round keys of Round 3, 4, and that for the right branch of Round 5 from guessing only 64 bits of key material. At the ciphertext side, we choose structures of $2^{32}$ texts, such that all texts in a structure have a constant value in the right branch, and iterate over all values on the left branch through Rounds $16-18$. In the following, we mount a chosen-ciphertext attack on 16-round SPARX-64/128 covering Rounds 3 through 18; the used differential trail is given in Table 8.

STRUCTURES AND SETS. We choose $2^m$ structures of $2^{32}$ ciphertexts each from a base text $S_{18}^0 = (L_{18}, R_{18})$, and $2^{32} - 1$ derived texts $S_{18}^i = (L_{18}^i, R_{18})$ from iterating over all $2^{32}$ values $L_{18}$, and derive the $2^{32}$ ciphertexts $C^i \leftarrow \mathcal{L}(S^i)$ that form the structure. Since we employ all $2^{32}$ possible values for the right branch

**Table 8.** The truncated differential trail through 16 rounds. A ∗ symbol marks a truncated difference which can take any possible value.

| Rd. $i$ | $\Delta L_i$ | $\Delta R_i$ | $h_w$ | Rd. $i$ | $\Delta L_i$ | $\Delta R_i$ | $h_w$ | Rd. $i$ | $\Delta L_i$ | $\Delta R_i$ | $h_w$ |
|---|---|---|---|---|---|---|---|---|---|---|---|
| | | | | 7 | 28000010 | 00000000 | 4 0 | 13 | 00000000 | ******** | 0 ? |
| 2 | ******** ******** | | – – | 8 | 00400000 | 00000000 | 2 0 | 14 | 00000000 | ******** | 0 ? |
| 3 | ******** ******** | | – – | 9 | 80008000 | 00000000 | 0 0 | 15 | 00000000 | ******** | 0 ? |
| $\mathcal{L}$ | 00000000 | ******** | – – | $\mathcal{L}$ | 80008000 | 80008000 | 0 0 | $\mathcal{L}$ | ******** | 00000000 | 0 0 |
| 4 | 00000000 | ******** | – – | 10 | ******** ******** | | ? ? | 16 | ******** | 00000000 | ? 0 |
| 5 | 00000000 | 0a204205 | 0 – | 11 | ******** ******** | | ? ? | 17 | ******** | 00000000 | ? 0 |
| 6 | 00000000 | 02110a04 | 0 5 | 12 | ******** ******** | | ? ? | 18 | ******** | 00000000 | ? 0 |
| $\mathcal{L}$ | 02110a04 | 00000000 | 0 0 | $\mathcal{L}$ | 00000000 | ******** | 0 0 | $\mathcal{L}$ | ******** ******** | | 0 0 |

of Rounds 16 to 18, their $2^{63}$ pairs will form all possible differences in this branch about $2^{31}$ times at any point until the end of Round 12, i.e., $\Delta_{12}$. From experiments, we observed that the truncated differential (80008000, 80008000) leads to (00000000, ********) with probability $2^{-17.36}$. Hence, there is a subset of *good* differences $\Delta_{12}$ that can lead to (80008000, 80008000) with this accumulated probability. Since we have $2^{31}$ pairs for each such $\Delta_{12}$, we expect that there are about $2^{31-17.36} \approx 2^{13.64}$ pairs with $\Delta_9 = (80008000, 80008000)$, and $2^{13.64-6-5} = 2^{2.64}$ pairs that follow our trail up to $\Delta_5$. We have approximately $2^{63}$ pairs in a structure that have our desired difference with probability $2^{-64}$, so we expect $2^{-1}$ false positive pairs from the structure.

EXPERIMENTAL VERIFICATION. We verified a variant of our distinguisher experimentally using 100 random keys and $2^{32}$ random pairs. For practicality, we considered it in encryption direction, i.e., we chose random pairs with start difference $(\Delta L_5, \Delta R_5) = (00000000, 0a204205)$, encrypted them to the states after Round 18 and inverted the final linear layer. On average, we obtained $2^{3.75}$ pairs with zero difference in the right branch, which corresponds to a probability of $2^{3.75-32} = 2^{-28.25}$, which is close to the expected $2^{-28.36}$.

ATTACK STEPS. Using Property 2, we define a linear function $F : \mathbb{F}_2^{32} \times \mathbb{F}_2^{32} \to \mathbb{F}_2^{64}$ with rank $n - 1 = 63$, so that $F(\Delta) = 0^{64}$ for $\Delta = (00000000, 0a204205)$. The attack consists of the following steps:

1. Construct $2^m$ structures as described above. For each structure, request the corresponding $2^{32}$ plaintexts $P^i$ from a 16-round decryption oracle.
2. Initialize a list $\mathcal{K}$ of $2^{64}$ key counters.
3. For each of the $2^{64}$ guesses of $K_2^0, K_2^1, K_2^2, K_2^3$, i.e., the key of Round 2:
   3.1 Re-encrypt all plaintexts over one round until the state after the linear layer of Round 3 and store them in a list $\mathcal{H}$ according to the values of their left branches. Only consider pairs that collide in $L_3$ after the application of the linear layer $\mathcal{L}$, and store those in a distinct list $\mathcal{H}'$.

3.2 For all texts, compute $(L_3, R_5)$, apply $F(R_r)$, and store the updated states in $\mathcal{H}$. Discard all pairs that do not collide. For each colliding pair, increment the counter for the current key candidate in $\mathcal{K}$.

4. Output the keys in descending order of their corresponding counters.

COMPLEXITY. The computational complexity results from:

- **Step 1** requires $2^{m+32}$ 16-round decryptions. We assume that the computational costs for decryption and encryption are equal.
- **Step 3.1** requires $2^{64} \cdot 2^{m+32} \cdot 1/16 \cdot 2 \approx 2^{m+92}$ encryption equivalents since we consider one out of 16 rounds. From the $\binom{2^{32}}{2} \approx 2^{63}$ pairs of one structure, we expect $2^{63-32} = 2^{31}$ false positive pairs for each structure at this step.
- We approximate the costs for a call to $F$ by those of a call to two SPECKEY rounds since both branches are used. The complexity of **Step 3.2** is therefore given by $2^{64} \cdot 2^{31+m} \cdot 4/32 \approx 2^{m+92}$ encryption equivalents on average. We expect about $2^{63-64} = 2^{-1}$ false-positive pairs per structure and key candidate, whereas we have $2^{31-28.36} \approx 2^{2.64}$ correct pairs for the correct key candidate, again per structure.

The computational complexity sums to

$$2^{m+32} + 2^{m+92} + 2^{m+92} \approx 2^{m+93} \text{ Encryptions.}$$

The memory complexity stems from storing a byte counter for the current key candidate, i.e., $2^{64} \cdot 8/64 = 2^{61}$ states, plus $2^{32}$ texts. The data complexity is given by $2^{m+32}$. A single structure, i.e., $m = 1$, suffices to obtain at least two correct pairs for the correct round-key candidate.

## 6  Rectangle Attack on 16-Round Sparx-64/128

HIGH-LEVEL VIEW. This section describes a rectangle attack on 16-round SPARX-64/128. Our attack starts after the second round of the cipher, i.e., it starts with Round 3. Again, we guess 64 key bits to get through Rounds 3 and 4 and the right branch of Round 5. The attack covers then Rounds 3 through 18.

DIFFERENTIAL TRAILS. Table 9 illustrates the employed differential trails. The top trail covers Rounds 3 through 9 and the right part of Rounds 10 to 12 since the right part contains a zero difference which propagates for free through the $\mathcal{A}^3$ box of Rounds 10 to 12. The bottom trail covers Rounds 13 through 18, and the left part of Rounds 10 through 12 in decryption direction. Again, the bottom trail has a zero difference in that part, which propagates for free through the $\mathcal{A}^3$ box backwards through Rounds 12 through Round 10.

Again, we experimentally verified the boomerang switch in the middle. From 100 experiments with random keys and $2^{26}$ independently at random chosen pairs $(P, P')$ with difference $\alpha = (80008000, 80008000)$, encrypted through three steps to $(C, C')$, applied the $\delta$-shift (80008000, 80008000) to obtain $(D, D')$, decrypted

**Table 9.** Our used differential characteristic through the top (left) and bottom (right) trail for our 16-round rectangle attack on SPARX-64/128.

| Rd. $i$ | $\Delta L_i$ | $\Delta R_i$ | $h_w$ | Rd. $i$ | $\Delta L_i$ | $\Delta R_i$ | $h_w$ |
|---|---|---|---|---|---|---|---|
| 4 | 28000010 | | – – | 10 | 00000000 | ******** | 0 – |
| 5 | 00400000 | 00400000 | 2 – | 11 | 00000000 | ******** | 0 – |
| 6 | 80008000 | 80008000 | 0 0 | 12 | 00000000 | ******** | 0 – |
| $\mathcal{L}$ | 00000000 | 80008000 | 0 0 | $\mathcal{L}$ | 02110a04 | 00000000 | 0 0 |
| 7 | 00000000 | ******** | 0 – | 13 | ******** | 00000000 | – 0 |
| 8 | 00000000 | ******** | 0 – | 14 | ******** | 00000000 | – 0 |
| 9 | 00000000 | ******** | 0 – | 15 | ******** | 00000000 | – 0 |
| $\mathcal{L}$ | ******** | 00000000 | 0 – | $\mathcal{L}$ | 80008000 | 80008000 | 0 0 |
| 10 | ******** | 00000000 | – 0 | 16 | 81008102 | 81008102 | 1 1 |
| 11 | ******** | 00000000 | – 0 | 17 | 8000840a | 8000840a | 2 2 |
| 12 | ******** | 00000000 | – 0 | 18 | 850a9520 | 850a9520 | 4 4 |
| $\mathcal{L}$ | ******** | ******** | – 0 | $\mathcal{L}$ | 2a102a10 | 850a9520 | 0 0 |

those back to $(Q, Q')$, and counted the number of times that $Q \oplus Q' = \alpha$. We observed an average probability of approximately $2^{-20.18}$. So, for the correct key, we obtain a probability of approximately $(\widehat{pq})^2 \approx (2^{-2})^2 \cdot 2^{-20.18} \cdot (2^{-14})^2 \approx 2^{-52.18}$ for a valid quartet.

ATTACK PROCEDURE. Choose a linear function $F : \mathbb{F}_2^{64} \to \mathbb{F}_2^{64}$ of rank 63 s.t. $F(\Delta L_4 \| \Delta R_5) = 0^{64}$. The attack consists of the following steps:

1. Initialize a list of key counters $\mathcal{L}$ to zero, for all $2^{64}$ possible values for the round keys of Round 2.
2. Initialize two empty hash maps $\mathcal{P}$ and $\mathcal{Q}$. Choose $2^m$ ciphertext pairs $(C, D)$ with difference (2a102a10, 850a9520), and ask for their corresponding plaintexts $(P, Q)$. Store the pairs into $\mathcal{P}$ indexed by $P$.
3. For each of the $2^{64}$ guesses of $(K_2^0, K_2^1, K_2^2, K_2^3)$:
   3.1 Partially re-encrypt all plaintext pairs $(P, Q)$ to their corresponding states $(L_4^P, R_5^P)$ and $(L_4^Q, R_5^Q)$.
   3.2 Apply $F((L_4, R_5))$ to all states and store the corresponding outputs $(\widehat{L}_4^P, \widehat{R}_5^P)$ and $(\widehat{L}_4^Q, \widehat{R}_5^Q)$ into a hash table $\mathcal{Q}$. Only consider pairs of pairs $p = (\widehat{L}_4^P, \widehat{R}_5^P)$, $q = (\widehat{L}_4^Q, \widehat{R}_5^Q)$, $p' = (\widehat{L}_4^{P'}, \widehat{R}_5^{P'})$, $q' = (\widehat{L}_4^{Q'}, \widehat{R}_5^{Q'})$ that collide in either $(p, q) = (p', q')$ or $(p, q) = (q', p')$ and discard all further quartets. We expect $2^{2m} \cdot 2^{2 \cdot -64} \approx 2^{2m-128}$ quartets on average.
   3.3 If a quartet survives, increment the counter for the current key guess. Choose a plaintext pair with our desired difference – w.l.o.g., $(p, p')$ – from the current quartet, and check for all remaining key bits if it follows our path until Round 6. If yes, encrypt it further roundwise until Round 9. If all roundwise checks pass, check for $p$ if it encrypts to ciphertext $C$. If yes, test again for $(q, q')$ and output the key candidate if it also matches.
4. If no key candidate has been returned, return $\bot$.

For $m = 58.6$ pairs, we can expect $(2^m \widehat{pq})^2 / 2^n \approx 2^{117.2} \cdot 2^{-52.18} / 2^{64} \approx 2$ valid quartets for the correct key guess. In contrast, we can expect $2^{117.2 - 2 \cdot 64} = 2^{-10.8}$ quartets for a wrong key guess.

COMPLEXITY. The computational complexity results from:

- **Step 2** requires $2 \cdot 2^{58.6} \approx 2^{59.6}$ 16-round decryptions. We assume that the computational costs for a decryption and encryption are equal.
- **Steps 3.1 and 3.2** require $2^{64} \cdot 2 \cdot 2^m \cdot 6/32 \approx 2^{122.2}$ encryption equivalents since we consider five out of 32 SPECKEY rounds in the 16-round cipher for re-encryption and approximate the costs for computing $F$ by the costs of a SPECKEY round.
- **Step 3.2** will require $2^{64} \cdot 2 \cdot 2^m = 2^{m+65}$ memory accesses (MAs) and comparisons.
- **Step 3.3** will require at most $2^{64} \cdot 2^{2m-128} \cdot 2^{64} \approx 2^{117.2}$ encryption equivalents to identify the correct key.

Hence, the computations are upper bounded by approximately

$$2^{59.6} + 2^{122.2} \approx 2^{122.2} \text{ encryptions} \quad \text{and} \quad 2^{59.6} + 2^{123.6} \approx 2^{123.6} \text{ MAs.}$$

The data complexity is upper bounded by $2^{59.6}$ chosen ciphertexts. The memory complexity is upper bounded by storing at most $4 \cdot 2^{59.6}$ states at a time, which is equivalent to storing approximately $2^{61.6}$ states.

# 7    Conclusion

This work presents two standard differential attacks using truncated differentials and rectangle attacks on 16-round SPARX-64/128. The former attack builds upon a nine-round (three-step) differential trail that is extended by a six-round (two-step) truncated trail. Adopting the observation by Abdelkhalek et al. [1], we can turn the distinguishers into a 16-round chosen-ciphertext attack and recover the round keys by just guessing 64-bit of the key material. Our truncated- differential attack requires approximately $2^{32}$ chosen ciphertexts, about $2^{32}$ states, and approximately $2^{93}$ encryption equivalents. Our proposed rectangle attack exploits the Feistel structure of SPARX using differential trails with inactive branches over their middle step; similarly, the yoyo attack in the full version of this paper [2] profits from the structure over the end. It may be interesting for further studies to investigate yoyo cycles of more iterations of en- and decryption.

We stress that our attacks do not threaten the security of SPARX-64/128, but provide deeper insights in its security against attacks in the single-key setting. We can observe a strong clustering effect of many differential characteristics in our studies and exploit them in our attacks; it remains subject to further studies to employ them for further rounds. For public verification and future works, our trails, tests, and implementations of SPARX-64/128 will be published into the public domain[2].

---

[2] https://github.com/TheBananaMan/sparx-differential-attacks.

# References

1. Abdelkhalek, A., Tolba, M., Youssef, A.M.: Impossible differential attack on reduced round SPARX-64/128. In: Joye, M., Nitaj, A. (eds.) AFRICACRYPT 2017. LNCS, vol. 10239, pp. 135–146. Springer, Cham (2017). https://doi.org/10.1007/978-3-319-57339-7_8

2. Ankele, R., List, E.: Differential cryptanalysis of round-reduced Sparx-64/128. Cryptology ePrint Archive, Report 2018/332 (2018). https://eprint.iacr.org/2018/332

3. Biham, E., Dunkelman, O., Keller, N.: The rectangle attack — rectangling the serpent. In: Pfitzmann, B. (ed.) EUROCRYPT 2001. LNCS, vol. 2045, pp. 340–357. Springer, Heidelberg (2001). https://doi.org/10.1007/3-540-44987-6_21

4. Biham, E., Dunkelman, O., Keller, N.: New results on boomerang and rectangle attacks. In: Daemen, J., Rijmen, V. (eds.) FSE 2002. LNCS, vol. 2365, pp. 1–16. Springer, Heidelberg (2002). https://doi.org/10.1007/3-540-45661-9_1

5. Biryukov, A., Khovratovich, D.: Related-key cryptanalysis of the full AES-192 and AES-256. In: Matsui, M. (ed.) ASIACRYPT 2009. LNCS, vol. 5912, pp. 1–18. Springer, Heidelberg (2009). https://doi.org/10.1007/978-3-642-10366-7_1

6. Cid, C., Huang, T., Peyrin, T., Sasaki, Y., Song, L.: Boomerang connectivity table (BCT) for Boomerang attack. In: EUROCRYPT. LNCS (2018, to appear)

7. Dinu, D., Perrin, L., Udovenko, A., Velichkov, V., Großschädl, J., Biryukov, A.: Design strategies for ARX with provable bounds: SPARX and LAX. In: Cheon, J.H., Takagi, T. (eds.) ASIACRYPT 2016. LNCS, vol. 10031, pp. 484–513. Springer, Heidelberg (2016). https://doi.org/10.1007/978-3-662-53887-6_18

8. Daemen, J., Peeters, M., Van Assche, G., Rijmen, V.: Nessie Proposal: NOEKEON (2000). http://gro.noekeon.org/Noekeon-spec.pdf

9. Kelsey, J., Kohno, T., Schneier, B.: Amplified boomerang attacks against reduced-round MARS and serpent. In: Goos, G., Hartmanis, J., van Leeuwen, J., Schneier, B. (eds.) FSE 2000. LNCS, vol. 1978, pp. 75–93. Springer, Heidelberg (2001). https://doi.org/10.1007/3-540-44706-7_6

10. Leurent, G.: Improved differential-linear cryptanalysis of 7-round chaskey with partitioning. In: Fischlin, M., Coron, J.-S. (eds.) EUROCRYPT 2016. LNCS, vol. 9665, pp. 344–371. Springer, Heidelberg (2016). https://doi.org/10.1007/978-3-662-49890-3_14

11. Soos, M.: CryptoMiniSat SAT solver (2009). https://github.com/msoos/cryptominisat/

12. Kölbl, S.: CryptoSMT: an easy to use tool for cryptanalysis of symmetric primitives (2015). https://github.com/kste/cryptosmt

13. Tolba, M., Abdelkhalek, A., Youssef, A.M.: Multidimensional zero-correlation linear cryptanalysis of reduced round SPARX-128. In: Adams, C., Camenisch, J. (eds.) SAC 2017. LNCS, vol. 10719, pp. 423–441. Springer, Cham (2018). https://doi.org/10.1007/978-3-319-72565-9_22

14. Ganesh, V., Hansen, T., Soos, M., Liew, D., Govostes, R.: STP constraint solver (2017). https://github.com/stp/stp

15. Wagner, D.: The boomerang attack. In: Knudsen, L. (ed.) FSE 1999. LNCS, vol. 1636, pp. 156–170. Springer, Heidelberg (1999). https://doi.org/10.1007/3-540-48519-8_12

# Can Caesar Beat Galois?
## Robustness of CAESAR Candidates Against Nonce Reusing and High Data Complexity Attacks

Serge Vaudenay and Damian Vizár[(⊠)]

EPFL, Lausanne, Switzerland
damian.vizar@epfl.ch

**Abstract.** The Competition for Authenticated Encryption: Security, Applicability and Robustness (CAESAR) has as its official goal to "identify a portfolio of authenticated ciphers that offer advantages over [the Galois-Counter Mode with AES]" and are suitable for widespread adoption." Each of the 15 candidate schemes competing in the currently ongoing $3^{\mathrm{rd}}$ round of CAESAR must clearly declare its security claims, i.e. whether it can tolerate nonce misuse, and what is the maximal data complexity for which security is guaranteed. These claims appear to be valid for all 15 candidates. Interpreting "Robustness" in CAESAR as the ability to mitigate damage when security guarantees are void, we describe attacks with 64-bit complexity or above, and/or with nonce reuse for each of the 15 candidates. We then classify the candidates depending on how powerful does an attacker need to be to mount (semi-)universal forgeries, decryption attacks, or key recoveries. Rather than invalidating the security claims of any of the candidates, our results provide an additional criterion for evaluating the security that candidates deliver, which can be useful for e.g. breaking ties in the final CAESAR discussions.

**Keywords:** Authenticated encryption · CAESAR competition
Forgery · Decryption attack · Key recovery · Birthday bound
Nonce misuse

## 1 Introduction

Authenticated encryption (AE) is a symmetric key primitive that simultaneously ensures confidentiality, integrity and authenticity of encrypted messages [4,29] and typically also allows to authenticate a public string, the associated data, along with the message [37]. During the two decades of its existence, AE has been not just a frequent research object but also a frequently used tool (e.g. in IEEE 802.11i, IPsec ESP and IKEv2, NIST SP 800-38D, ANSI C12.22, and ISO/IEC 19772:2009), especially because most practical applications of symmetric key cryptography require both confidentiality and integrity at the same time.

In 2013, the Competition for Authenticated Encryption: Security, Applicability and Robustness (CAESAR) was announced. The reason for its launch was,

© Springer International Publishing AG, part of Springer Nature 2018
B. Preneel and F. Vercauteren (Eds.): ACNS 2018, LNCS 10892, pp. 476–494, 2018.
https://doi.org/10.1007/978-3-319-93387-0_25

in part, a startling amount of recently discovered issues with the applications of symmetric cryptography, and with the most popular AE schemes CCM [27,43] and GCM (Galois Counter Mode) [32]. The security misses in the applications constituted practically exploitable vulnerabilities [7] and for CCM and GCM, concerns were expressed about their applicability [39], the security proofs [25] or their susceptibility to serious attacks when not used correctly [16,28].

Thus CAESAR's main goal was set to "identify a portfolio of authenticated ciphers that offer advantages over AES-GCM and are suitable for widespread adoption" [6]. GCM instantiated with the AES blockcipher has been used as a reference that ought to be surpassed by the CAESAR candidates, while the name of the competition spells out the properties the candidates are expected to guarantee: security, applicability and robustness. Out of 57 submissions to the first round of CAESAR, 15 candidates still compete in the $3^{\mathrm{rd}}$ round [5]. The security claims of each of them are supported by solid cryptanalysis and/or security proofs, and are generally believed to be sound.

**Table 1.** An overview of $3^{\mathrm{rd}}$ round CAESAR candidates based on their *claimed* security guarantees w.r.t the nonce misuse and quantitative security; 64-bit-bound refers to about $2^{64}$ processed bits. For security in presence of nonce misuse, we consider MRAE [38], OAE [17] or RAE [21]. For each candidate, we consider an instance with 128-bit secret key. Deoxys II is listed twice due to its graceful degradation of security.

|  | Up to 64-bit-bound | Beyond 64-bit-bound |
|---|---|---|
| Unique nonces | OCB, NORX, Jambu, CLOC& SILC | Tiaoxin, Morus, Keyak, Ketje, Deoxys I& II, Ascon, AEGIS, ACORN |
| Nonce misuse | Deoxys II, COLM, AEZ | - |

**64-bit Bound and Nonce-Misuse.** All of CAESAR candidates must accept a nonce, a secret key, AD and a message as an input. The nonce is akin to an initialization vector, and it can be assumed to have a unique value for every encryption query. The candidates are allowed to request that the nonce must not repeat in order for their security guarantees to apply. This is the case for 12 $3^{\mathrm{rd}}$ round CAESAR candidates. AEZ and Deoxys guarantee no degradation of authenticity, and the minimal (and unavoidable [38]) degradation of confidentiality[1] even if the nonces are misused, i.e. repeated. COLM guarantees a weaker version of confidentiality protection in presence of nonce misuse, so called online-misuse resistance [17]. Each candidate must also specify how much data can be securely processed with a single secret key. Most CAESAR candidates guarantee security up to the so called birthday-bound; for AES-based AE schemes, this means processing no more than about $2^{64}$ blocks of data per key and making no

---

[1] As the encryption is required to be a deterministic algorithm, repeating all inputs unavoidably means repeating the ciphertexts as well.

more than $2^{64}$ encryption queries. In this paper, we use the 64-bit data/query complexity as a reference threshold for comparison of candidates, denoted by 64-bit-bound.

In Table 1, we categorize the $3^{rd}$ round candidates, as well as CCM and GCM, based on their security claims w.r.t. the nonce misuse and quantitative security. We consider a scheme to claim security against nonce reuse if it targets MRAE [38], OAE [17] or RAE [21] security. For each candidate, we consider an instance with a 128-bit secret key.

**Robustness: (In)security Beyond Guarantees.** All CAESAR candidates clearly state what security properties do they guarantee as long as the conditions on the nonces or data limits are respected. However, they give little or no information on the actual impact of attacks that violate these usage conditions.

This is what we aim to determine in this work. We take the liberty to interpret robustness of AE schemes as the ability to resist powerful attacks, possibly beyond the limitations guaranteed by the designers, and analyze the security of all 15 third round CAESAR candidates against attacks with very high data complexity, and against nonce-misuse attacks. In order to make the result comparable, we consider instances using secret keys of 128 bits, and use the 64-bit-bound (i.e. the "birthday bound" of AES-GCM) as a point of reference.

**An Overview.** For each candidate we describe one or more attacks, unless relevant attacks already exist. We sort the CAESAR candidates into six categories based on the adversarial powers necessary to break them: **(A)** Those for which we have a nonce-respecting universal forgery *and* a decryption attack at the 64-bit-bound. **(B)** Others for which we have a nonce-respecting universal forgery *and* a decryption attack above the 64-bit-bound, but below exhaustive search. **(C)** Those for which we have a reusable forgery *and* a reusable decryption attack with small complexity, possibly with nonce-misuse. **(D)** Others for which we have a forgery *or* a decryption attack with small complexity, possibly with nonce-misuse. **(E)** Others for which we have a forgery *or* a decryption attack at the 64-bit-bound, possibly with nonce-misuse. **(F)** Remaining ones. Our results are summarized in Table 2. For each candidate, we indicate the type of attack, the query complexity[2], whether the attack needs nonce misuse, and whether it is reusable. All attacks presented in Table 2 succeed with high probability.

The categories can be ordered by a decreasing level of resilience as follows: $(\mathbf{F}) \geq (\mathbf{E}) \geq (\mathbf{D}) \geq (\mathbf{C})$ and $(\mathbf{F}) \geq (\mathbf{E}) \geq (\mathbf{B}) \geq (\mathbf{A})$. The categories $(\mathbf{A})$ and $(\mathbf{C})$ are incomparable (same for $(\mathbf{B})$ and $(\mathbf{D})$), as the impacted schemes succumb to different kinds of misuse. However, the attacks in category $(\mathbf{C})$ may be seen as a more serious threat than those in $(\mathbf{A})$, as they are much more likely in practice.

**Our Contribution.** Table 2 sheds more light on the actual impact of nonce-reuse/high-data attacks, and arguably provides much more information than the guarantees provided by the authors (summarized in Table 1). This can be very useful to break ties at the end of $3^{rd}$ round of CAESAR competition. Some of

---

[2] The time and memory complexities of the attacks mentioned in the Table 2 are small multiples/small powers of the query complexity.

**Table 2.** A summary of attacks on $3^{\text{rd}}$ round CAESAR candidates and their clustering based on the type of attack. The categories (**A**), (**B**), (**C**), (**D**), (**E**) and (**F**) are listed from top to bottom. The column "source" lists the sections and/or bibliography references that describe the relevant attacks. The comments "$(N, A)$", "$(N)$" and "$(A)$" in the reusability column (see Sect. 2) mean that the reusability is limited to fixed values of the listed parameters. The values in the column "nonce-reuse" indicate maximal number of times any nonce is used (so 1 means nonce respecting), $q$ denotes the number of independent forgeries made in a single attack, and $m$ is used as a parameter. #The attack applies only if $|N| > 128$.

| | Algorithm | Source(s) | Type of attack | Nonce-reuse | # Queries | Reusable |
|---|---|---|---|---|---|---|
| **A** | **AES-GCM** [32]# | 4 | Univ. forgery | 1 | $3 \cdot 2^{64}$ | Yes |
| | AEZ [22] | 5, [12] | Key recovery | 1 | $3 \cdot 2^{64}$ | |
| | OCB [30] | 6, [15] | Univ. forgery & CCA decryp. | 1 | 2 (one w/ $2^{64}$ blocks) | Yes |
| | AES-OTR [34] | 3, 7 | Univ. forgery & CPA decryp. | 1 | 2 (one w/ $2^{64}$ blocks) | Yes |
| **B** | CLOC [24] | 8 | Univ. forgery & CPA decryp. | 1 | $2^{80}$ | Yes |
| **C** | **AES-GCM** [32] | 3, 4, [28] | Univ. forgery & CPA decryp. | 2 | 2 | Yes |
| | Deoxys-I [26] | 3 | Univ. forgery & CCA decryp. | 3 | 3 | Yes $(A)$ |
| | OCB [30] | 3 | Univ. forgery & CCA decryp. | 2 | 2 | Yes $(A)$ |
| | Tiaoxin [35] | 10 | Key recovery | 30 | 30 | |
| | AEGIS-128 [47] | 11 | Univ. forgery & CPA decryp. | 15 | 15 | Yes $(N, A)$ |
| | ACORN-128 [44] | 12 | Univ. forgery & CPA decryp. | 586 | 586 | Yes $(N, A)$ |
| | Ketje Sr [9] | 13 | Key recovery | 50 | 50 | |
| | MORUS 640 [45] | 14 | Univ. forgery & CPA decryp. | 8 | 8 | Yes $(N)$ |
| **D** | **AES-CCM** [43] | 3 | CPA decryp. | 2 | 1 | |
| | CLOC & SILC [24] | 3 | CPA decryp | 2 | 1 | No |
| | JAMBU [46] | 3 | CPA decryp. | $1 + |C|/64$ | $|C|/64$ | No |
| | NORX32-4-1 [2] | 3 | CPA decryp. | $1 + |C|/384$ | $|C|/384$ | No |
| | Ascon-128 [14] | 3 | CPA decryp. | $1 + |C|/64$ | $|C|/64$ | No |
| | Lake Keyak [10] | 3 | CPA decryp. | $1 + |C|/1344$ | $|C|/1344$ | No |
| **E** | COLM [1] | 3 | Semi-univ. forgery | $1 + q$ | $2^{64}$ | Yes $(N, A)$ |
| **F** | Deoxys-II [26] | 9 | Semi-univ. forgery & CCA decryp. | $2^m$ | $2^{128-m}$ | Yes $(A)$ |

these attacks can also be viewed as disturbingly powerful (e.g. low-complexity key recoveries). Taking into consideration the circumstances that led to the start of CAESAR competition, we do not think that schemes that succumb to such attacks should be recommended as CAESAR finalists (in this sense, not every candidate for CAESAR can beat Galois).

The attacks we present also shed more light on the weaknesses and strengths of different constructions. For example, many designs in cat. (C) use aggressively optimized state update functions which give up the key (or secret state) with the slightest nonce reuse, which we find worrisome. The collection of generic attacks in Sect. 3 is especially helpful to identify common security phenomena related to certain construction principles, such as the decryption attacks for streamciphers, or easy nonce-reusing forgeries on ciphertext-translation based schemes.

We found it interesting that the state recovery on AEGIS and Tiaoxin works thanks to the differential properties of the AES Sbox. The "$E_K$ oracle" attack on CLOC is nonce respecting because CLOC processes the nonce in a place that is usual for the last associated data block. COLM, in turn, resists to nonce-respecting collision attacks thanks to having the nonce restricted to 64 bits. Finally, we have not seen the trade-off between the degree of nonce-reuse and the attack complexity used for Deoxys-II in the literature before.

**Disclaimer and Open Problems.** We understand that **none** of the attacks we present violates the security claims of any of the CAESAR candidates. That is not the goal of our work. Our goal is to determine to what degree will the security of respective candidates deteriorate *after* the guarantees become void.

We leave the investigation of security of CAESAR candidates within other adversarial models (such as related-key security, release of unverified plaintext or multi-user security) as open problems.

**Related Work.** The (in)security of GCM mode was treated by a number of works [20,25,36,40], in particular Joux authored the "forbidden" nonce misusing attack [28]. Collision attack similar to ours, or inspiring ours, were described for previous versions of AEZ by Fuhr et al. [19], and Chaigneau and Gilbert [12]. Collision attack on OCB were given by Ferguson [15] and Sun et al. [41]. Reusable forgery attacks on OCB, OTR and COLM were described by Forler et al. [18]. Collision-based attacks on COPA and ELmD (the predecessors of COPA) were described by Bay et al. [3] and Lu [31]. Bost and Sanders found a flaw in the masking scheme of an earlier version of OTR [11], Huang and Wu described a collision based forgery [23]. Mileva et al. describe a nonce misusing distinguisher attack for MORUS [33]. The collision-based forgeries on NORX, Ascon and Keyak are matching Lemma 2 of the work on provable generic security of full-state keyed duplex by Daemen et al. [13].

**Organization of the Paper.** In Sect. 2 we introduce notations, AE syntax and the attack model. In Sect. 3 we give generic attacks that apply to several schemes that share a particular structure. Then in Sects. 4 to 14, we address attacks specific to GCM and several CAESAR candidates, each in a separate section. For descriptions of CCM, GCM, and the CAESAR candidates in, we refer the reader either to the full version of this paper [42], or to the respective submission documents [5].

## 2    Preliminaries

When presenting the CAESAR candidates, we try to respect the original notations but deviate a bit to unify the notation of the common input/output values.
Hence, the secret key is denoted by $K$, the nonce (or IV) is denoted by $N$, the
associated data (AD) is denoted by $A$, the plaintext is denoted by $M$, the ciphertext is denoted by $C$, and the tag (if any) is denoted by $T$. We further use $\tau$ to
denote the ciphertext expansion/stretch, which is in most cases the same as the
tag length.

**Notations.**    All strings are binary strings. We let $\varepsilon$ denote the empty string
and $|X|$ the length of a string $X$ in bits. For two strings $X, Y$ with $|X| =
|Y|$, we let $X\&Y$ denote the bitwise AND of $X$ and $Y$ and $X \oplus Y$ the bitwise
xor. We let $\{0,1\}^n$ denote the set of all strings of $n$ bits, and let $\{0,1\}^* =
\bigcup_{n \in \{0,1,2,\dots\}} \{0,1\}^n$. Each of the candidates internally partitions the inputs into
blocks of constant size. We use several symbols to denote the length of the
blocks, e.g. $n, r$ or $\nu$, in order to respect the notation of each candidate as much
as possible. We use subscript to index blocks in a query and superscript to index
queries, e.g. $M_i^j$ is the $i^{\text{th}}$ message block in $j^{\text{th}}$ query. We let $M_1, \dots, M_\ell \xleftarrow{n} M$
denote the partitioning of a string $M$ into blocks of $n$ bits, except for $1 \leq
|M_\ell| \leq n$, such that $\ell = \lceil |M|/n \rceil$. We let $|M|_n = \lceil |M|/n \rceil$. With a slight abuse
of notation, we let $X0^*1$ denote extending a string $X$ with the smallest number
of zero bits followed by a "1" that will yield a string whose length is a multiple
of a block size, when a block size is implicit from the context. We let $\mathsf{msb}_a(X)$
denote the $a$ most significant bits of a string $X$, and similar applies to $\mathsf{lsb}_a$. We
let $\mathsf{enc}_n(a)$ denote the $n$-bit canonical encoding of an integer $0 \leq a \leq 255$. For
blockcipher-based schemes, we let $E$ denote the underlying blockcipher.

**Syntax.**    A scheme for authenticated encryption (AE) $\Pi$ consists of a key space
$\mathcal{K} \subset \{0,1\}^*$ (for most candidates $\mathcal{K} = \{0,1\}^k$ for a positive $k$), and two deterministic algorithms $\mathcal{E}$ and $\mathcal{D}$. The encryption algorithm maps a key, a nonce, associated data (AD) and a message $(K, N, A, M)$ to a ciphertext $C = \mathcal{E}(K, N, A, M)$,
such that $|C| = |M| + \tau$ where the stretch is either a constant parameter, or user-
selectable (only for candidate AEZ). For most candidates, the ciphertext con-
sists of a core ciphertext and a tag, i.e. $\mathcal{E}(K, N, A, M) = C\|T$ with $|T| = \tau$. The
decryption algorithm $\mathcal{D}$ that maps $(K, N, A, C)$ (or $(K, N, A, C\|T)$) to a mes-
sage $M$ or to an error symbol $\perp$, if the authentication fails. It is required that for
every valid input tuple $(K, N, A, M)$, we have $M = \mathcal{D}(K, N, A, \mathcal{E}(K, N, A, M))$.
We denote the sets of nonces, AD and messages valid for $\Pi$ by $\mathcal{N}$, $\mathcal{A}$ and $\mathcal{M}$
respectively.

**Attack Model.**    We focus on three types of attacks: decryption attacks, (semi)
universal forgeries and key recovery attacks. To make the results comparable, for
each candidate we attack an instance that uses 128-bit keys (i.e. $\mathcal{K} = \{0,1\}^{128}$),
and we define our attacks models to correspond to the 128-bit security level.

In each type of attack on a scheme $\Pi$, an attacker $\mathscr{A}$ has blackbox oracle
access to an instance of the encryption and the decryption algorithms $\mathcal{E}_K, \mathcal{D}_K$

of $\Pi$ that use a secret key $K$ unknown to $\mathscr{A}$. We call $\mathscr{A}$ *nonce respecting* if each encryption query it makes uses a distinct nonce. We say that $\mathscr{A}$ mounts a *chosen plaintext attack* (CPA) if it never makes a decryption query, otherwise we say $\mathscr{A}$ mounts a *chosen ciphertext attack* (CCA).[3] $\mathscr{A}$ is free to make any queries beyond the explicit restrictions.

For each attack, we keep track of the data complexity (in blocks of some constant size) and/or the query complexity, the maximal number (over the values of the nonce) of encryption queries made with the same nonce. We call a forgery (resp. decryption) attack *reusable* if, after having forged (resp. decrypted) for the first time, the query and computational complexity of the consequent forgeries (resp. decryptions) are significantly lower than the complexity of the initial forgery (resp. decryption).

**(Semi)-universal Forgery.** $\mathscr{A}^{\mathcal{E}_K, \mathcal{D}_K}(N, A, M)$ receives an a nonce, AD and a message and tries to produce a decryption query $(N, A, C)$ that will correctly decrypt to $M$, such that $C$ was not an output of a previous encryption query made with $N, A$. We call the forgery *semi-universal* if $\mathscr{A}$ only gets target AD and message (i.e. $\mathscr{A}^{\mathcal{E}_K, \mathcal{D}_K}(A, M)$) or target message only (i.e. $\mathscr{A}^{\mathcal{E}_K, \mathcal{D}_K}(M)$) and is allowed to use arbitrary values for the remaining inputs.

**Decryption Attack.** $\mathscr{A}^{\mathcal{E}_K, \mathcal{D}_K}(N, A, C)$ receives a nonce, AD and ciphertext-tuple that is an encryption of a secret random message $M$ of fixed length $\mu \geq 128$, and tries to produce $M$.

**Key Recovery.** $\mathscr{A}^{\mathcal{E}_K, \mathcal{D}_K}()$ tries to compute $K$.

## 3    Generic Attacks

In this section, we list attacks that trivially apply to certain construction principles, rather than being construction-specific. Nevertheless, these attacks are relevant for the comparison of "robustness" of CAESAR candidates.

**CPA Decryption: Streamciphers (Nonce Reuse, Constant Complexity).** AE schemes that produce a core ciphertext $C$ and a tag $T$ such that $C = M \oplus f(K, N, |M|)$ (or $C = M \oplus f(K, N, A, |M|)$), i.e. the message is xored with a sequence of masking bits derived as a function of the nonce and the secret key (or the nonce, secret key and AD) will necessarily succumb to this attack. To decrypt $(N, A, C\|T)$, we make a single encryption query $f(K, N, A, |M|)\|T' = \mathcal{E}_K(N, A, 0^{|C|})$ that reveals the key stream and compute $M = C \oplus f(K, N, A, |M|)$. This attack applies to **CCM, GCM**.

**CPA Decryption: Self-synchronizing Streamciphers (Nonce Reuse, Tiny Complexity).** The previous attack can be adapted to AE schemes that produce the core ciphertext $C$ block by block, by xoring the current message block with masking bits dependent on the key, the nonce, AD and the previous message blocks. I.e. $M_1, \ldots, M_\ell \xleftarrow{n}$ and then $C_i =$

---

[3] Note that a forgery is always a CCA, due to the final decryption query.

$M_i \oplus f(K, N, A, M_1 \| \ldots M_{i-1}, |M_i|)$, where the value of $n$ depends on the scheme. To decrypt $(N, A, C\|T)$, we make $|C|_n = \lceil |C|/n \rceil$ encryption queries as follows:

1: Compute $C_1, \ldots, C_\ell \xleftarrow{n} C$.
2: **for** $i \leftarrow 1$ **to** $\ell$ **do**
3:     Query $C'\|T' \leftarrow \mathcal{E}_K(N, A, M_1 \| \ldots \| M_{i-1} \| 0^{|C_i|})$.
4:     Compute $C'_1, \ldots, C'_i \xleftarrow{n} C'$ and then $M_i \leftarrow C'_i \oplus C_i$.
5: **end for**

This attack applies to **CLOC, SILC, AEGIS, ACORN, MORUS, Ketje, NORX, Ascon, Keyak** and **JAMBU**.

**Semi-universal Forgery: AD Preprocessing (Nonce-Reuse, Varying Complexity).** Several candidates internally process an encryption query $(K, N, A, M)$ by first computing a value $V = f(K, N, A)$ dependent on the key, nonce and the AD, and then compute the (tagged) ciphertext as a function of the secret key, the message and the value $V$ as $C = g(K, V, M)$, such that $|V| = v$ for constant $v$. If $|\mathcal{N}| \geq 2^{v/2}$, then it is possible to find a pair $(N_1, A_1), (N_2, A_2)$ such that $f(K, N_1, A_1) = f(K, N_2, A_2)$ in a nonce-respecting birthday attack, and then use it to forge for $M$ (hence semi-universal forgery):

1: Initialize empty table $\mathsf{T}$, pick arbitrary $\hat{M} \in \{0,1\}^v$.
2: **for** $i \leftarrow 1$ **to** $2^{v/2}$ **do**
3:     Pick $(N', A')$ with a fresh $N'$ randomly.
4:     Query $C' \leftarrow \mathcal{E}_K(N', A', \hat{M})$, then insert $(C', (N', A'))$ to $\mathsf{T}$.
5: **end for**
6: Find entries $(C', (N_1, A_1))$, $(C', (N_2, A_2))$ (with collision on $C'$) in $\mathsf{T}$.
7: Query $C \leftarrow \mathcal{E}_K(N_1, A_1, M)$ and forge with $(N_2, A_2, C)$.

The attack succeeds with a probability close to $1/2$, in particular choosing $\hat{M} \in \{0,1\}^{2v}$ ensures that a $C'$ collision implies a $V$ collision with overwhelming probability (thanks to the ciphertext expansion). It is reusable with the same $(N_1, A_1), (N_2, A_2)$, and uses every nonce no more than $1 + q$ times, with $q$ the number of desired forgeries.

    The attack applies with **64-bit-bound** complexity (as $v = 128$) to, **AEZ, CLOC, SILC, COLM** and with some care to **CCM**.[4] This attack applies with complexity above **64-bit-bound** (as $v = 192$) to **JAMBU**.

**Semi-universal Forgery: Sponges (Nonce Reuse, Varying Complexity).** In sponge-based modes, the processing can again be expressed with two functions $f$ and $g$ but nonce reuse allows the attacker to force arbitrary values to the outer $r$ bits of the sponge state after processing the first message block. Using this, the previous attack can be adapted to work with complexity $2^{c/2}$ (where $c$ is the capacity of the sponge-based scheme) to forge for arbitrary $(A, M)$:

1: Initialize empty tables $\mathsf{T}$, pick arbitrary $\hat{M} \in \{0,1\}^c$.
2: **for** $i \leftarrow 1$ **to** $2^{c/2}$ **do**
3:     Pick a fresh $N'$ randomly.

---

[4] With $\tau = 128$, we must use $A'$ of 240 bits to make sure that the encoding of the nonce and AD for the CBC MAC is block-aligned.

4:    Query $C'\|T' \leftarrow \mathcal{E}_K(N', A, 0^r)$, then query $C''\|T'' \leftarrow \mathcal{E}_{(}N', A, C'\|\hat{M})$.

5:    Compute $C_1'', \ldots, C_\ell'' \xleftarrow{r} C''$, then insert $(C_2''\|\ldots\|C_\ell''\|T'', N')$ to T.

6:  **end for**

7:  Find entries $(C''\|T'', N_1)$, $(C''\|T'', N_2)$ (with collision on $C''\|T''$) in T.

8:  Query $C\|T \leftarrow \mathcal{E}_K(N_1, A, M)$ and forge with $(N_2, A, C\|T)$.

The success probability is close to $1/2$. The second query in the attacks forces the internal state of the sponge to become $0^r\|S$ for some $S \in \{0,1\}^c$, hence the birthday complexity in $c$. The attack is reusable with the same $(N_1, A), (N_2, A),$[5] and uses every nonce no more than $2+q$ times, with $q$ the number of desired forgeries. The attack applies with 64-bit-bound complexity (as $c = 128$) to **NORX** and with above-64-bit-bound complexity (as $c = 256$) to **Keyak** and **Ascon**. We note that for Keyak and Ascon, the exhaustive key search has the same time complexity as this attack, but needs only a single query.

**Universal Forgery and CCA Decryption: Ciphertext Translation (Nonce Misuse, Tiny Complexity).** Some candidates use so called *ciphertext translation* [37] to incorporate the authentication of AD with a message-only encryption core $\bar{\mathcal{E}}$. These schemes compute the tagged ciphertext as $\mathcal{E}_K(N, A, M) = \bar{\mathcal{E}}_K(N, M) \oplus 0^{|M|}\|H_K(A)$ where $\bar{\mathcal{E}}_K(N, M)$ returns a core-ciphertext and a $\tau$-bit tag and $H$ is an AXU hash with $\tau$-bit output. To forge for $(N, A, M)$, we pick arbitrary $\hat{N} \neq N$, $\hat{M} \neq M$ and $A' \neq A$ and we do:

1:  Query $C^1\|T^1 \leftarrow \mathcal{E}_K(\hat{N}, A, \hat{M})$ and $C^2\|T^2 \leftarrow \mathcal{E}_K(\hat{N}, A', \hat{M})$.

2:  Compute $\Delta \leftarrow T^1 \oplus T^2$.

3:  Query $C'\|T' \leftarrow \mathcal{E}_K(N, A', M)$ and forge with $(N, A, C'\|(T' \oplus \Delta))$.

It is easily verified that the forgery is correct. This attack can be modified to decrypt a ciphertext $N, A, C\|T$; knowing $\Delta$, we query $N, A', C\|(T \oplus \Delta)$ and learn the message $M$. This attack applies to **OCB**, **AES-OTR** and **Deoxys-I**.

# 4    AES-GCM

**Universal Forgery (Nonce Misuse, Tiny Complexity).** This attack has been first described by Joux as the "forbidden attack" [28]. The main idea is that recovering the derived key $L$ makes forging very easy. We assume that $\tau = 128$. To forge for $N, A, M$, we pick random $\hat{N}$ and $M^1 \neq M^2 \in \{0,1\}^{128}$ and do:

1:  Query $C^1\|T^1 \leftarrow \mathcal{E}_K(N, \varepsilon, M^1)$ and $C^2\|T^2 \leftarrow \mathcal{E}_K(N, \varepsilon, M^2)$.

2:  Compute $L$ as root of $P(\Lambda) = (C_1^1 \oplus C_1^2) \cdot \Lambda^2 \oplus (T^1 \oplus T^2)$ over $GF(2^{128})$.

3:  Query $C'\|T' \leftarrow \mathcal{E}_K(N, A', M)$ with arbitrary $A'$ and $M'$ s.t. $|M'| = |M|$.

4:  Forge with $(N, A, (C' \oplus M' \oplus M)\|(T' \oplus GHASH_L(A', C') \oplus GHASH_L(A, C)))$.

We note that $L$ will be the only root of $P(\Lambda)$ as squaring yields a bijection over $GF(2^{128})$. Once $L$ is computed, forgeries become easy.

**Universal Forgery (Nonce Respecting, 64-bit-Bound, $|N| > 128$).** If nonces longer than 128 bits are allowed, it is possible to recover $L$ in a nonce-respecting birthday attack. We note, however, that the use of nonce length other

---

[5] For Keyak, the attack attack can be reused with arbitrary AD, because AD and message are being processed simultaneously.

than 96 bits is uncommon and discouraged [25]. Assuming that $\tau = 128$, for each $i$ we use distinct $N^i$ of 256 bits and $M^i = B \| M_2^i$ for a fixed $B \in \{0,1\}^{128}$ and distinct $M_2^i \in \{0,1\}^{128}$, and do:

1: **for** $i \leftarrow 1$ **to** $2^{64}$ **do** query $C^i \| T^i \leftarrow \mathcal{E}_K(N^i, \varepsilon, M^i)$.
2: For $i \neq j$ s.t. $C_1^i = C_1^j$ find $L$ as root of $P(\Lambda) = (C_2^i \oplus C_2^j) \cdot \Lambda^2 \oplus (T^1 \oplus T^2)$.
3: Forge using $L$.

Note that the collision in line 2 must imply $\text{GHASH}_L(\varepsilon, N^i) = \text{GHASH}_L(\varepsilon, N^{i'})$, so if it occurs, the attack succeeds. We note that a forgery allows to mount a CCA decryption attack (by changing AD).

## 5   AEZ v5

We present three nonce-respecting attacks that respectively recover the subkeys $I$, $J$ and $L$, each at the 64-bit-bound complexity.

**$J$-Recovery Attack.** The Chaigneau-Gilbert attack [12] on AEZ v4.1 can be applied to AEZ v5 to extract $J$ by a nonce-respecting chosen message attack at the birthday bound. When $N$ and $A$ are single blocks, then based on the AEZ v5 specification [22] $H$ becomes

$$h_k(\tau, N, A) = \qquad\qquad E_K^{3,1}(\tau) \oplus E_K^{4,1}(N) \oplus E_K^{5,1}(A)$$
$$= E_K^{3,1}(\tau) \oplus \mathsf{AES4}_k(N \oplus 4J \oplus 2I \oplus L) \oplus \mathsf{AES4}_k(A \oplus 5J \oplus 2I \oplus L).$$

If we limit ourselves to queries with $A = N \oplus c$ for a fixed block $c$ and variable nonces, a ciphertext collision with the pair $(N, N')$ will mean that $N' = N \oplus c \oplus J$. The attack runs as follows:

1: Initialize an empty table $\mathsf{T}$.
2: Pick an arbitrary block $c \in \{0,1\}^{128}$ and message $M \in \{0,1\}^{2 \cdot 128}$.
3: **for** $i \leftarrow 1$ **to** $2^{64}$ **do**
4:     Pick a fresh $N$ randomly, set $A \leftarrow N \oplus c$.
5:     Query $C \leftarrow \mathcal{E}_K(N, A, \tau, M)$, store $(C, N)$ in $\mathsf{T}$.
6: **end for**
7: Find $(C, N), (C', N')$ in $\mathsf{T}$ with $C = C'$, compute $J = N \oplus N' \oplus c$.

The Chaigneau-Gilbert attack requires a little effort to be adapted to AEZ v5 but it can recover $I$ and $L$ with nonce-misuse. A nonce respecting recovery of $I$ and $L$ is possible if we can use nonces of several blocks (a feature of AEZ [22]), to have a similar attack as the one above.

**$L$-Recovery Attack.** If $|N|_{128} = 2$ and $A = \varepsilon$, then following the AEZ v5 specifications $H$ becomes

$$h_k(\tau, (N_1, N_2)) = E_K^{3,1}(\tau) \oplus E_K^{4,1}(N_1) \oplus E_K^{4,2}(N_2)$$
$$= E_K^{3,1}(\tau) \oplus \mathsf{AES4}_k(N_1 \oplus 4J \oplus 2I \oplus L) \oplus \mathsf{AES4}_k(N_2 \oplus 4J \oplus 2I \oplus 2L).$$

We modify the $J$-recovery attack to use 2-block nonces with $N_2 = N_1 \oplus c$ for a fixed block $c$. A ciphertext collision with $N$ and $N'$ will then

**I-Recovery Attack.** Next, we see that when $|N|_{128} = 9$, the hash function $H$ becomes

$$
\begin{aligned}
h_k(\tau, (N_1, \dots, N_9)) &= E_K^{3,1}(\tau) \oplus E_K^{4,1}(N_1) \oplus \cdots \oplus E_K^{4,9}(N_9) \\
&= E_K^{3,1}(\tau) \oplus \mathsf{AES4}_k(N_1 \oplus 4J \oplus 2I \oplus L) \oplus \cdots \oplus \\
&\quad \mathsf{AES4}_k(N_7 \oplus 4J \oplus 2I \oplus 7L) \oplus \mathsf{AES4}_k(N_8 \oplus 4J \oplus 2I) \oplus \\
&\quad \mathsf{AES4}_k(N_9 \oplus 4J \oplus 4I \oplus L).
\end{aligned}
$$

We again modify the $J$-recovery attack to use 9-block nonces with $N_2, \dots, N_8$ constant and $N_9 = N_1 \oplus c$ for a fixed block $c$. A ciphertext collision with $N$ and $N'$ yields $6I = N_1 \oplus N_1' \oplus c$. So, we recover $I, J, L$ with a nonce-respecting chosen message attack 64-bit-bound.

# 6 OCB3 (OCB v1.1)

**L-Recovery Attack.** An attack by Ferguson [15] allows to recover the derived key $L$ at 64-bit-bound using a single huge query. In the nonce-misuse setting, we can make many queries with empty message and two-block AD:

1: **for** $i \leftarrow 1$ **to** $2^{64}$ **do** query $T^i \leftarrow \mathcal{E}_K(N, A^i \| A^i, \varepsilon)$ with fresh $A^i \in \{0, 1\}^{128}$.
2: Find $i \neq j$ with $T^i = T^j$, compute $L = (A^i \oplus A_j) \cdot (\gamma_1 \oplus \gamma_2)^{-1}$.

If tag collision occurs, we must have $A_1^i = A_1^j \oplus (\gamma_1 \oplus \gamma_2) \cdot L$. We need to reuse the nonce $2^{64}$ times.

**Universal Forgery (Tiny Complexity, Using $L$).** Using $L$, we can make a universal forgery for $(N, A, M')$. If $|M'|_{128} = \ell > 1$, we do:

1: Define a permutation $\pi : \{1, \dots, \ell\} \to \{1, \dots, \ell\}$ as $\pi(i) = (i + 1 \bmod \ell) + 1$.
2: **for** $i \leftarrow 1$ **to** $\ell$ **do** $M_i \leftarrow M'_{\pi(i)} \oplus \gamma_i \cdot L \oplus \gamma_{\pi(i)} \cdot L$.
3: Query $C \| T \leftarrow \mathcal{E}_K(N, A, M)$.
4: **for** $i \leftarrow 1$ **to** $\ell$ **do** $C'_i = C_{\pi^{-1}(i)} \oplus (\gamma_i \oplus \gamma_{\pi^{-1}(i)}) \cdot L$.
5: Forge with $(N, A, C' \| T)$.

If $|M'|_{128} = 1$, we construct $M = M' \| (\gamma_1 \oplus \gamma_2) \cdot L$, make a query with $(N, A, M)$ to get $C \| T$, and take $C' = C_1$, which again gives a valid encryption $C' \| T$ of $(N, A, M')$.

**$E_K$ Oracle (Tiny Complexity, Using $L$).** We can also implement an $E_K$ oracle. To compute $y_i = E_K(x_i)$ for arbitrary $x_1, \dots, x_s \in \{0, 1\}^{128}$ set $\ell = 2^{14}$, and do:

1: Pick $M \in \{0, 1\}^{\ell \cdot 128}$ with $\bigoplus_{i > 1} M_i = (2^{-1} \oplus \gamma_1 \oplus \gamma_\ell) \cdot L$ randomly.
2: Query $C \| T \leftarrow \mathcal{E}_K(N, \varepsilon, M)$, compute $R \leftarrow C_1 \oplus T \oplus \gamma_1 \cdot L$.
3: Find $i$ s.t. $M_i \oplus R \oplus \gamma_i \cdot L = 0^7 \| 1 \| N'' \| 0^6$ for $N' \in \{0, 1\}^{114}$.
4: Set $N' \leftarrow N'' \| 0^6$, compute $R' = C_i \oplus R \oplus \gamma_i \cdot L$.
5: **for** $i \leftarrow 1$ **to** $s$ **do** set $M'_i \leftarrow x_i \oplus R' \oplus \gamma_i \cdot L$.
6: Query $C' \| T' \leftarrow \mathcal{E}_K(N', \varepsilon, M')$.
7: **for** $i \leftarrow 1$ **to** $s$ **do** compute $y_i \leftarrow C'_i \oplus R' \oplus \gamma_i \cdot L$.

The $R$ computed on line 2 is correct as $T = E_K(M_1 \oplus R \oplus \gamma_1 \cdot L) = C_1 \oplus R \oplus \gamma_1 \cdot L$. We can also add an unused nonce to the list of $x_i$-s to avoid making the $2^{14} \cdot$

128bit$= 256$ KB query more than once. Then the attack uses a single encryption query per list of blocks $x_1, \ldots, x_s$, of size $s + 1$ blocks.

**CCA Decryption Attack For Messages Of Odd Length (Tiny Complexity, Using $L$).** Assume that we want to decrypt $(N, A, C, T)$ (let $M$ be its decryption). We can first compute $R$ associated with $N$ with the above $E_K$ oracle, as well as some fresh $N'$ and its associated $R'$ with tiny complexity. The message $M'$ defined by $M'_i = M_i \oplus R \oplus R'$ encrypts into $(C', T')$ such that $C'_i = C_i \oplus R \oplus R'$ and $T' = T$ when $\ell$ is odd. So, a CCA decryption query with $(N', A, C', T)$ gives $M'$ from which we deduce $M$.

# 7 AES-OTR v3.1

**$L$-Recovery Attack.** If we use the same nonce $N$ $2^{64}$ times, we can recover $L$:

1: **for** $i \leftarrow 1$ **to** $2^{64}$ **do** query $C \| T \leftarrow \mathcal{E}_K(N, \varepsilon, M^i)$ with fresh $M^i \in \{0, 1\}^{4 \cdot 128}$.
2: Find $i \neq j$ s.t. $C_1^i \oplus M_2^i = C_3^j \oplus M_4^j$, compute $L = (M_1^i \oplus M_3^j) \cdot (1 \oplus 2)^{-1}$.

In a nonce respecting attack, we can encrypt a huge random message (with $|M|_{128} \approx 2^{64}$) with a nonce $N$ and look for an internal collision with $i \neq j$

$$C_{2i} \oplus M_{2i-1} = C_{2j} \oplus M_{2j-1} \text{ implying } C_{2i-1} \oplus 2^{i-1} \cdot 2 \cdot L = C_{2j-1} \oplus 2^{j-1} \cdot 2 \cdot L,$$

revealing $L$ for this $N$. We further expect to find many values of $1 \leq i \leq |M|_{128}/2$ for which $2^{i-1} \cdot L \oplus M_{2i-1}$ (or $2^{i-1} \cdot 3 \cdot L \oplus C_{2i-1}$) will be a string of the form $\epsilon(\tau) \| 1 \| N'$. For any such $N'$ we can use $L' = C_{2i-1}$ (or $L' = C_{2i}$) to bootstrap the following attack.

**$E_K$ Oracle (Using $(N, L)$ Pair).** Assuming that we know an $(N, L)$ pair $E_K(x_1), \ldots, E_K(x_r)$ for a list $x_1, \ldots, x_r$ as follows:

1: **for** $i \leftarrow 1$ **to** $r$ **do** set $M_{2i-1} \leftarrow x_i \oplus 2^{2i-1} \cdot L$ and pick $M_i$ arbitrarily.
2: Query $C \| T \leftarrow \mathcal{E}_K(N, \varepsilon, M)$.
3: **for** $i \leftarrow 1$ **to** $r$ **do** compute $E_K(x_i) = M_{2i} \oplus C_{2i-1}$.

In each execution of this attack, we can add one block to the list of $x_i$-s to prepare a fresh pair $N', L'$ for the next execution of the attack, allowing for its nonce respecting repetition.

# 8 CLOC

**$E_K$ Oracle in CLOC (Nonce-Respecting, Above 64-bit-Bound).** In CLOC, the processing of AD and nonce has the form $V = f_1(f_2(K, A) \oplus \mathsf{ozp}(\mathsf{param} \| N))$ where the function $f_1$ is easy to invert. To compute $E_K(x)$ for an $x \in \{0, 1\}^{128}$, we pick fixed AD $A$ and do:

1: **for** $i \leftarrow 1$ **to** $2^{64}$ **do** query $C^i \| T^i \leftarrow \mathcal{E}_K(N^i, A, M^i)$ with random $M^i \in \{0, 1\}^{2 \cdot 128}$.
2: Find $i \neq j$ s.t. $M_1^i \oplus C_1^i = M_2^j \oplus C_2^j$, compute $W \leftarrow f_1^{-1}(\mathsf{fix1}(C_1^j)) \oplus \mathsf{ozp}(\mathsf{param} \| N^i)$.
3: **if** $f_1^{-1}(x) \oplus W$ of the form $\mathsf{ozp}(\mathsf{param} \| \bar{N})$ query $E_K(x) \| T \leftarrow \mathcal{E}_K(\bar{N}, A, 0^{128})$.
4: **else** abort.

The attack works as the collision on line 2 implies that $V^i = \text{fix1}(C_1^j)$ so we deduce the $V^i$ value for a random nonce $N^i$ with $A$. This allows us to recover $W = f_2(K, A)$. If $x$ is not of the correct form, it is bad luck. When using nonces of 112 bits, which is the maximum, the probability to have the correct form is $2^{-16}$. But we can run this attack $2^{16}$ times to get many $W^i = f_2(K, A^i)$ with complexity $2^{80}$. Then at least one is $W^i$ will be such that $f_1^{-1}(x) \oplus W_i$ is of the correct format for any $x$.

This attack does not work on SILC, in which $W$ depends on both $N$ and $A$.

**Universal Forgery and CPA Decryption Attack in CLOC (Nonce-Respecting, Above 64-bit-Bound).** With the previous $\mathcal{E}_K$ oracle, we can simulate the encryption or the decryption process and thus mount universal forgeries and CPA decryption.

## 9    Deoxys v1.41

**Semi-universal Forgery, CCA Decryption Attack: Deoxys-II (Reusable, Nonce-Misuse).** The encryption algorithm of Deoxys-II can be expressed as $\mathcal{E}_K(N, A, M) = \bar{\mathcal{E}}(K, N, f_2(f_1(K, A), M), M)$ where $\bar{\mathcal{E}}$ produces a (stretched) ciphertext and $f_1$ and $f_2$ are keyed functions with constant-size output. The attacks are based on finding a collision on $f_1$. Assuming each nonce can be used up to $2^m$ times, to forge for $(N, M)$ we use $N^1, \ldots, N^{2^{128-2m}} \neq N$ all distinct and $M' \neq M$ of 2 blocks, and do:

1: **for** $i \leftarrow 1$ **to** $2^{128-2m}$ **do**
2:      **for** $j \leftarrow 1$ **to** $2^m$ **do** query $C^{i,j} \| T^{i,j} \leftarrow \mathcal{E}_K(N^i, A^{i,j}, M')$ with random $A^{i,j}$.
3: **end for**
4: Find $i, j \neq j'$ s.t. $A^{i,j} \neq A^{i,j'}$ and $T^{i,j} = T^{i,j'}$.
5: Query $C \| T \leftarrow \mathcal{E}_K(N, A^{i,j}, M)$ and forge with $(N, A^{i,j'}, C \| T)$.

We can modify this attack to decrypt $(N, A^{i,j}, C \| T)$ by making a CCA decryption query on $(N, A^{i,j'}, C, T)$. This can only decrypt messages using $A^{i,j}$ as associated data. The total complexity of the attack is $2^{128-m}$ queries. Note that if $m = 64$, the complexity becomes birthday bounded.

## 10    Tiaoxin-346

**Nonce-Misuse Key Recovery.** [6] We pick $M, \bar{M}, \tilde{M} \in \{0, 1\}^{4 \cdot 128}$ such that $M_i \oplus \bar{M}_i = \Delta$ and $M_i \oplus \tilde{M}_i = \tilde{\Delta}$ for $i = 0, 1, 2, 3$ and $\Delta \neq \tilde{\Delta}$. We pick arbitrary $N$ and $A$ and recover two 128 bit words $T'[4]_0$ and $T'[3]_0$ of the internal state right after processing of $N$, $A$ and the first two blocks of $M$ by:

1: Query $C \| T \leftarrow \mathcal{E}_K(N, A, M)$, $\bar{C} \| \bar{T} \leftarrow \mathcal{E}_K(N, A, \bar{M})$ and $\tilde{C} \| \tilde{T} \leftarrow \mathcal{E}_K(N, A, \tilde{M})$.
2: **for** $i \leftarrow 2, 3$ **do** set $\gamma_i \leftarrow \text{ShiftRows}^{-1}(\text{MixColumns}^{-1}(\bar{C}_i \oplus C_i))$.
3: **for** $i \leftarrow 2, 3$ **do** set $\tilde{\gamma}_i \leftarrow \text{ShiftRows}^{-1}(\text{MixColumns}^{-1}(\tilde{C}_i \oplus C_i))$.

---

[6] Note that we change the meaning of subscript and square brackets compared to the original Tiaoxin description [35].

4: **for** byte index $j \leftarrow 0$ to 15 **do**

5:     **for** $i \leftarrow 2, 3$ **do** Find $X_{i,j} = \{\gamma_{i,j} \mid \gamma_{i,j} = \mathsf{SubBytes}(x) \oplus \mathsf{SubBytes}(x \oplus \Delta)\}$.

6:     **for** $i \leftarrow 2, 3$ **do** Find $\tilde{X}_{i,j} = \{\tilde{\gamma}_{i,j} \mid \tilde{\gamma}_{i,j} = \mathsf{SubBytes}(x) \oplus \mathsf{SubBytes}(x \oplus \tilde{\Delta})\}$.

7:     Set $T'[4]_{0,j} \leftarrow X_{2,j} \cap \tilde{X}_{2,j}$ and $T'[3]_{0,j} \leftarrow X_{3,j} \cap \tilde{X}_{3,j}$.

8: **end for**

The above works, as we can verify that in the encryption of $M$ we have

1. $T'[3] = R(T[3], M_0)$,
2. $T'[4] = R(T[4], M_1)$,
3. $T'[6] = R(T[6], M_0 \oplus M_1)$,
4. $C_0 = T'[3]_0 \oplus T'[3]_2 \oplus T'[4]_1$ $\oplus (T'[6]_3 \& T'[4]_3)$,
5. $C_1 = T'[6]_0 \oplus T'[4]_2 \oplus T'[3]_1$ $\oplus (T'[6]_5 \& T'[3]_2)$,

6. $T''[3] = R(T'[3], M_2)$,
7. $T''[4] = R(T'[4], M_3)$,
8. $T''[6] = R(T'[6], M_2 \oplus M_3)$,
9. $C_2 = T''[3]_0 \oplus T''[3]_2 \oplus T''[4]_1$ $\oplus (T''[6]_3 \& T''[4]_3)$,
10. $C_3 = T''[6]_0 \oplus T''[4]_2 \oplus T''[3]_1$ $\oplus (T''[6]_5 \& T''[3]_2)$.

In the encryption of $\bar{M}$ we have the following (and similar for $\tilde{M}$ and $\tilde{\Delta}$)

1. $\bar{T}'[3] = R(T[3], M_0 \oplus \Delta)$,
2. $\bar{T}'[4] = R(T[4], M_1 \oplus \Delta)$,
3. $T'[6] = R(T[6], M_0 \oplus M_1)$,
4. $\bar{C}_0 = \bar{T}'[3]_0 \oplus \bar{T}'[3]_2 \oplus \bar{T}'[4]_1$ $\oplus (T'[6]_3 \& \bar{T}'[4]_3)$,
5. $\bar{C}_1 = T'[6]_0 \oplus \bar{T}'[4]_2 \oplus \bar{T}'[3]_{10}$ $\oplus (T'[6]_5 \& \bar{T}'[3]_2)$,

6. $\bar{T}''[3] = R(\bar{T}'[3], M_2 \oplus \Delta)$,
7. $\bar{T}''[4] = R(\bar{T}'[4], M_3 \oplus \Delta)$,
8. $T''[6] = R(T'[6], M_2 \oplus M_3)$,
9. $\bar{C}_2 = \bar{T}''[3]_0 \oplus \bar{T}''[3]_2 \oplus \bar{T}''[4]_1$ $\oplus (T''[6]_3 \& \bar{T}''[4]_3)$,
10. $\bar{C}_3 = T''[6]_0 \oplus \bar{T}''[4]_2 \oplus \bar{T}''[3]_1$ $\oplus (T''[6]_5 \& \bar{T}''[3]_2)$.

We can easily see that

$$\bar{T}'[3] \oplus T'[3] = (\Delta, 0, 0) \text{ and } \bar{T}''[3] \oplus T''[3] = (0, A(T'[3]_0) \oplus A(T'[3]_0 \oplus \Delta), 0),$$

$$\bar{T}'[4] \oplus T'[4] = (\Delta, 0, 0, 0) \text{ and } \bar{T}''[4] \oplus T''[4] = (0, A(T'[4]_0) \oplus A(T'[4]_0 \oplus \Delta), 0, 0).$$

It follows that the differences of ciphertext blocks used in the lines 5 and 6 are a result of a differential equation for a single round of AES. This can be reduced to a collection of 16 differential equations for AES Sbox, allowing to recover the parts of the secret state as intersections of solutions found in the said lines (we can check that we always have $|S_{i,j} \cap \tilde{S}_{i,j}| = 1$).

We can then repeat this process with longer messages to obtain $T[3]$ and $T[4]$ and we recover $T'[4]$ and $T'[3]$ with 12 queries (3 queries per 128-bit word of $T[4]$). The state $T[6]$ follows in a similar method using 18 queries. Once the state $(T[3], T[4], T[6])$ is recovered, we invert the initialization and obtain $K$.

## 11 AEGIS v1.1

**Universal Forgery, Decryption Attack (Tiny Complexity, Nonce-Misuse).** To forge for $(N, A, M)$ or to decrypt $(N, A, C, T)$, we only need to recover the secret state $S$ after processing $A$ with nonce $N$, the rest of encryption/decryption can then be reconstructed.

We pick three messages $M', \bar{M}, \tilde{M} \in \{0,1\}^{3 \cdot 128}$ with the same criteria as for Tiaoxin (with $\Delta \neq \tilde{\Delta}$). To recover a part $S_0'$ of the state $A'$ right after processing $M_1'$ with $N$ and $A$, we:

1: Query $C' \| T' \leftarrow \mathcal{E}_K(N, A, M')$, $\bar{C} \| \bar{T} \leftarrow \mathcal{E}_K(N, A, \bar{M})$ and $\tilde{C} \| \tilde{T} \leftarrow \mathcal{E}_K(N, A, \tilde{M})$.
2: Set $\gamma \leftarrow \mathsf{ShiftRows}^{-1}(\mathsf{MixColumns}^{-1}(\bar{C}_3 \oplus \bar{M}_3 \oplus C_3' \oplus M_3'))$.
3: Set $\tilde{\gamma} \leftarrow \mathsf{ShiftRows}^{-1}(\mathsf{MixColumns}^{-1}(\tilde{C}_3 \oplus \tilde{M}_3 \oplus C_3' \oplus M_3'))$.
4: Recover bytes of $S_0'$ using $\gamma, \tilde{\gamma}, \Delta, \tilde{\Delta}$ in differential equations as with Tiaoxin.

The attack works because the difference $(C_3' \oplus M_3') \oplus (\bar{C}_3 \oplus \bar{M}_3)$ (associated to $M_1' \neq \bar{M}_1$) is equal to the difference $R(R(S_4) \oplus S_0 \oplus M_1') \oplus R(R(S_4) \oplus S_0 \oplus \bar{M}_1)$ (where $R(S_4) \oplus S_0 = S_0'$), with $R$ just a single AES round. We can repeat this strategy to recover the remaining four 128-bit words of $S_1', \ldots, S_4'$ with 3 queries each. Then we can recover $S$, having done 15 nonce reusing queries. The possibility of a low-complexity nonce reusing attack is mentioned in the AEGIS v1.1 specifications [47].

## 12   ACORN v3

**Universal Forgery, Decryption Attack (Tiny Complexity, Nonce-Misuse).** To forge the encryption of $(N, A, M)$ or to decrypt $(N, A, C, T)$, we only need to recover the internal state $S_o$ after processing $N, A$, which allows to finish the rest of encryption/decryption. We sketch the main idea of the attack.

We make two encryption queries $C^1 \| T^1 \leftarrow \mathcal{E}_K(N, A, 0 \| B)$ and $C^2 \| T^2 \leftarrow \mathcal{E}_K(N, A, 1 \| B)$ for any $B \in \{0,1\}^{58}$. We can see that $\mathsf{ks}_{i+o}^j$ is constant for $j = 1, 2$ and $i = 0, \ldots, 57$ and that $\mathsf{ks}_{58+o}^1 \oplus \mathsf{ks}_{58+o}^2 = S_{58+o,61} \oplus S_{58+o,193}$, which is a linear equation in the bits of $S_o$. We recover 292 more equations by making 292 pairs of (longer) queries that differ only in a single bit, and solve the system for $S_o$. The knowledge of $S_o$ allows arbitrary forgeries and decryptions with $N, A$.

## 13   Ketje

**Key Recovery (Tiny Complexity, Nonce-Misusing).** The authors of Ketje themselves point at the possibility of this attack. Because Ketje uses only a single round of the Keccak$-f$ function [9], the diffusion between two consecutive sponge states is low. In addition, the algebraic degree of a single round of Keccak$-f$ is only 2. We use this to recover the internal state $S$ after processing of $N$ and $A$, and then the secret key $K$ by inverting the processing of $N, A$. We sketch the main idea of the attack.

We make queries $C^i \| T^i \leftarrow \mathcal{E}_K(N, A, M^i)$ with some fixed $(N, A)$ and $M^i \in \{0,1\}^{2 \cdot (r-4)}$ s.t. $M_2^i = 0^r$ for $i = 1, \ldots, \theta$. For each $i$ we can use $M_1^i$ and $C_2^i$ to derive degree-2 polynomial equations with the bits in the inner (capacity) part of $S$ as unknowns. Each bit in $C_2^i$ depends on 31 bits of the previous state on average [8], so we expect an overwhelming majority of the bits of the attacked state to be covered by the derived equations. We need the number of nonce misusing queries $\theta$ to be a small multiple of $\frac{b-r+4}{r-4} = 11,5$ in order to fully determine the system. Moreover, no more than a single unique monomial of degree 2 per every bit of the state appears in the system, so with $\theta = 60$, we should be able to linearize the system and solve it for $S$.

## 14   Morus

**Nonce-Misuse Universal Forgery and CPA Decryption.** If we recover the state $S$ right after the initialization with $N$, we can forge ciphertexts with this $N$ and decrypt any ciphertext using this $N$. We sketch the $S$ recovery attack.

We first recover $S_2$ and $S_3$ by querying $C^i \| T^i \leftarrow \mathcal{E}_K(N, \varepsilon, M^i)$ with $M^i \in \{0,1\}^{256}$ for $i = 1, \ldots, 4$. Letting $\delta_i = M_0^1 \oplus M_0^i$ with $i \neq 1$, we have that

$$
\begin{aligned}
(C^1 \oplus M^1) \oplus (C^i \oplus M^i) =& (\mathsf{Rotl}(\delta_i, b_1) \lll (w_3 + 96)) \oplus S_2 \& \mathsf{Rotl}(\delta_i \oplus \mathsf{Rotl}(\delta_i, b_1), b_3) \\
& \oplus S_3 \& (\mathsf{Rotl}(\delta_i, b_2) \lll w_4) \\
& \oplus (\mathsf{Rotl}(\delta_i, b_2) \lll w_4) \& \mathsf{Rotl}(\delta_i \oplus \mathsf{Rotl}(\delta_i, b_1), b_3),
\end{aligned}
$$

where $\mathsf{Rotl}$ is a linear function, $\lll$ denotes a circular rotation, and all $b_r$-s and $w_t$-s are constants. Each $\delta_i$ provides 128 linear equations in 256 binary unknowns, so with $\delta_1, \delta_2, \delta_3$, we are able to recover the values of $S_2$ and $S_3$ with high probability. Once $S_2$ and $S_3$ are known, $C_1^1 \oplus M_1^1$ can be expressed as a linear function of $S_0$ and $S_1$ and we learn their xor-difference.

We still need to recover $S_0, S_1, S_4$, i.e. 384 bits, and have 128 linear equations (so 256 unknown bits). We query $\bar{C}^j \| \bar{T}^j \leftarrow \mathcal{E}_K(N, \varepsilon, \bar{M}^j)$ with $\bar{M}^j = M_0^1 \| \bar{M}_1^j \| 0^{128}$ and $\bar{M}_1^j \in \{0,1\}^{128}$ for $j = 1, \ldots, \theta$. Each $\bar{C}_2^j$ will supply 128 polynomial equations in $S_0, S_1, S_4$ of degree at most 3. By examining the StateUpdate and the keystream generation functions of Morus, we verify that there will be no more than $19 \cdot 128$ unique monomials of degree higher than 1 present in all equations in the worst case and only $9.25 \cdot 128$ on average. Thus by taking $\theta = 16$, we should be able to linearise the system and recover $S_0, S_1$ and $S_4$ with high probability, using 20 queries for the entire attack.

**Acknowledgements.** We would like to thank all CAESAR designers who provided us with their feedback. We would like to thank the Ascon team for pointing out that generic attacks with the same time but much lower data complexity than our forgery exist, and the Deoxys team for suggesting a better way to measure adversarial resources for nonce misuse. We would also like to thank the attendants of the Dagstuhl seminar 2018, and the anonymous reviewers for constructive comments.

## References

1. Andreeva, E., Bogdanov, A., Datta, N., Luykx, A., Mennink, B., Nandi, M., Tischhauser, E., Yasuda, K.: COLM v1 (2016). https://competitions.cr.yp.to/round3/colmv1.pdf
2. Aumasson, J., Jovanovic, P., Neves, S.: NORX v3.0 (2016). https://competitions.cr.yp.to/round3/norxv30.pdf

3. Bay, A., Ersoy, O., Karakoç, F.: Universal forgery and key recovery attacks on ELmD authenticated encryption algorithm. In: Cheon, J.H., Takagi, T. (eds.) ASIACRYPT 2016. LNCS, vol. 10031, pp. 354–368. Springer, Heidelberg (2016). https://doi.org/10.1007/978-3-662-53887-6_13

4. Bellare, M., Rogaway, P.: Encode-then-encipher encryption: how to exploit nonces or redundancy in plaintexts for efficient cryptography. In: Okamoto, T. (ed.) ASIACRYPT 2000. LNCS, vol. 1976, pp. 317–330. Springer, Heidelberg (2000). https://doi.org/10.1007/3-540-44448-3_24

5. Bernstein, D.J.: Cryptographic competitions: CAESAR submissions. http://competitions.cr.yp.to/caesar-submissions.html

6. Bernstein, D.J.: Cryptographic competitions: CAESAR (2014). https://competitions.cr.yp.to/caesar-call.html

7. Bernstein, D.J.: Cryptographic competitions: disasters (2014)

8. Bertoni, G., Daemen, J., Peeters, M., Van Assche, G.: Keccak sponge function family main document. Submission NIST (Round 2) **3**(30) (2009)

9. Bertoni, G., Daemen, J., Peeters, M., Van Assche, G., Keer, R.V.: CAESAR submission: Ketje v2 (2016). https://competitions.cr.yp.to/round3/ketjev2.pdf

10. Bertoni, G., Daemen, J., Peeters, M., Van Assche, G., Keer, R.V.: CAESAR submission: Keyak v2 (2016). https://competitions.cr.yp.to/round3/keyakv22.pdf

11. Bost, R., Sanders, O.: Trick or tweak: on the (in)security of OTR's tweaks. In: Cheon, J.H., Takagi, T. (eds.) ASIACRYPT 2016. LNCS, vol. 10031, pp. 333–353. Springer, Heidelberg (2016). https://doi.org/10.1007/978-3-662-53887-6_12

12. Chaigneau, C., Gilbert, H.: Is AEZ v4.1 sufficiently resilient against key-recovery attacks? IACR Trans. Symmetric Cryptol. **2016**(1), 114–133 (2016). https://doi.org/10.13154/tosc.v2016.i1.114-133

13. Daemen, J., Mennink, B., Van Assche, G.: Full-state keyed duplex with built-in multi-user support. IACR Cryptology ePrint Archive 2017/498 (2017). http://eprint.iacr.org/2017/498

14. Dobraunig, C., Eichlseder, M., Mendel, F., Schläffer, M.: Ascon v1.2 (2016). https://competitions.cr.yp.to/round3/asconv12.pdf

15. Ferguson, N.: Collision attacks on OCB. NIST CSRC website (2002)

16. Ferguson, N.: Authentication weaknesses in GCM (2005)

17. Fleischmann, E., Forler, C., Lucks, S.: McOE: a family of almost foolproof online authenticated encryption schemes. In: Canteaut, A. (ed.) FSE 2012. LNCS, vol. 7549, pp. 196–215. Springer, Heidelberg (2012). https://doi.org/10.1007/978-3-642-34047-5_12

18. Forler, C., List, E., Lucks, S., Wenzel, J.: Reforgeability of authenticated encryption schemes. In: Pieprzyk, J., Suriadi, S. (eds.) ACISP 2017. LNCS, vol. 10343, pp. 19–37. Springer, Cham (2017). https://doi.org/10.1007/978-3-319-59870-3_2

19. Fuhr, T., Leurent, G., Suder, V.: Collision attacks against CAESAR candidates. In: Iwata, T., Cheon, J.H. (eds.) ASIACRYPT 2015. LNCS, vol. 9453, pp. 510–532. Springer, Heidelberg (2015). https://doi.org/10.1007/978-3-662-48800-3_21

20. Handschuh, H., Preneel, B.: Key-recovery attacks on universal hash function based MAC algorithms. In: Wagner, D. (ed.) CRYPTO 2008. LNCS, vol. 5157, pp. 144–161. Springer, Heidelberg (2008). https://doi.org/10.1007/978-3-540-85174-5_9

21. Hoang, V.T., Krovetz, T., Rogaway, P.: Robust authenticated-encryption AEZ and the problem that it solves. In: Oswald, E., Fischlin, M. (eds.) EUROCRYPT 2015. LNCS, vol. 9056, pp. 15–44. Springer, Heidelberg (2015). https://doi.org/10.1007/978-3-662-46800-5_2

22. Hoang, V.T., Krovetz, T., Rogaway, P.: AEZ v5: authenticated encryption by enciphering (2017). https://competitions.cr.yp.to/round3/aezv5.pdf

23. Huang, T., Wu, H.: Attack on AES-OTR. https://groups.google.com/forum/#!topic/crypto-competitions/upaRX2jdVCQ

24. Iwata, T., Minematsu, K., Guo, J., Morioka, S., Kobayashi, E.: CLOC and SILC (2016). https://competitions.cr.yp.to/round3/clocsilcv3.pdf

25. Iwata, T., Ohashi, K., Minematsu, K.: Breaking and repairing GCM security proofs. In: Safavi-Naini, R., Canetti, R. (eds.) CRYPTO 2012. LNCS, vol. 7417, pp. 31–49. Springer, Heidelberg (2012). https://doi.org/10.1007/978-3-642-32009-5_3

26. Jean, J., Nikolić, I., Peyrin, T.: Deoxys v1.41 (2016). https://competitions.cr.yp.to/round3/deoxysv141.pdf

27. Jonsson, J.: On the security of CTR + CBC-MAC. In: Nyberg, K., Heys, H. (eds.) SAC 2002. LNCS, vol. 2595, pp. 76–93. Springer, Heidelberg (2003). https://doi.org/10.1007/3-540-36492-7_7

28. Joux, A.: Authentication failures in NIST version of GCM (2006)

29. Katz, J., Yung, M.: Unforgeable encryption and chosen ciphertext secure modes of operation. In: Goos, G., Hartmanis, J., van Leeuwen, J., Schneier, B. (eds.) FSE 2000. LNCS, vol. 1978, pp. 284–299. Springer, Heidelberg (2001). https://doi.org/10.1007/3-540-44706-7_20

30. Krovetz, T., Rogaway, P.: OCB (v1.1) (2016). https://competitions.cr.yp.to/round3/ocbv11.pdf

31. Lu, J.: Almost universal forgery attacks on the COPA and marble authenticated encryption algorithms. In: Proceedings of the 2017 ACM on Asia Conference on Computer and Communications Security, pp. 789–799. ACM (2017)

32. McGrew, D.A., Viega, J.: The security and performance of the galois/counter mode (GCM) of operation. In: Canteaut, A., Viswanathan, K. (eds.) INDOCRYPT 2004. LNCS, vol. 3348, pp. 343–355. Springer, Heidelberg (2004). https://doi.org/10.1007/978-3-540-30556-9_27

33. Mileva, A., Dimitrova, V., Velichkov, V.: Analysis of the authenticated cipher MORUS (v1). In: Pasalic, E., Knudsen, L.R. (eds.) BalkanCryptSec 2015. LNCS, vol. 9540, pp. 45–59. Springer, Cham (2016). https://doi.org/10.1007/978-3-319-29172-7_4

34. Minematsu, K.: AES-OTR v3.1 (2016). https://competitions.cr.yp.to/round3/aesotrv31.pdf

35. Nikolić, I.: Tiaoxin - 346 (2016). https://competitions.cr.yp.to/round3/tiaoxinv21.pdf

36. Procter, G., Cid, C.: On weak keys and forgery attacks against polynomial-based MAC schemes. J. Cryptology 28(4), 769–795 (2015). https://doi.org/10.1007/s00145-014-9178-9

37. Rogaway, P.: Authenticated-encryption with associated-data. In: Proceedings of the 9th ACM Conference on Computer and Communications Security, CCS 2002, Washington, DC, USA, 18–22 November 2002, pp. 98–107 (2002)

38. Rogaway, P., Shrimpton, T.: A provable-security treatment of the key-wrap problem. In: Vaudenay, S. (ed.) EUROCRYPT 2006. LNCS, vol. 4004, pp. 373–390. Springer, Heidelberg (2006). https://doi.org/10.1007/11761679_23

39. Rogaway, P., Wagner, D.A.: A critique of CCM. IACR Cryptology ePrint Archive 2003/70 (2003)

40. Saarinen, M.-J.O.: Cycling attacks on GCM, GHASH and other polynomial MACs and hashes. In: Canteaut, A. (ed.) FSE 2012. LNCS, vol. 7549, pp. 216–225. Springer, Heidelberg (2012). https://doi.org/10.1007/978-3-642-34047-5_13

41. Sun, Z., Wang, P., Zhang, L.: Collision attacks on variant of OCB mode and its series. In: Kutyłowski, M., Yung, M. (eds.) Inscrypt 2012. LNCS, vol. 7763, pp. 216–224. Springer, Heidelberg (2013). https://doi.org/10.1007/978-3-642-38519-3_14

42. Vaudenay, S., Vizár, D.: Under pressure: security of caesar candidates beyond their guarantees. Cryptology ePrint Archive, Report 2017/1147 (2017). https://eprint.iacr.org/2017/1147

43. Whiting, D., Ferguson, N., Housley, R.: Counter with CBC-MAC (CCM) (2003)

44. Wu, H.: ACORN: A lightweight authenticated cipher (v3) (2016). https://competitions.cr.yp.to/round2/acornv2.pdf

45. Wu, H., Huang, T.: The authenticated cipher MORUS (v2) (2016). https://competitions.cr.yp.to/round3/morusv2.pdf

46. Wu, H., Huang, T.: The JAMBU lightweight authentication encryption mode (v2.1) (2016). https://competitions.cr.yp.to/round3/jambuv21.pdf

47. Wu, H., Preneel, B.: AEGIS: a fast authenticated encryption algorithm (v1.1) (2016). https://competitions.cr.yp.to/round3/aegisv11.pdf

# Public Key Encryption

# Improved Anonymous Broadcast Encryptions
## Tight Security and Shorter Ciphertext

Jiangtao Li[1] and Junqing Gong[2(✉)]

[1] East China Normal University, Shanghai, China
`lijiangtao@stu.ecnu.edu.cn`
[2] ENS de Lyon, Laboratoire LIP (U. Lyon, CNRS, ENSL, INRIA, UCBL),
Lyon, France
`junqing.gong@ens-lyon.fr`

**Abstract.** We investigate anonymous broadcast encryptions (ANOBE) in which a ciphertext hides not only the message but also the target recipients associated with it. Following Libert *et al.*'s generic construction [PKC, 2012], we propose two concrete ANOBE schemes with tight reduction and better space efficiency.

- The IND-CCA security and anonymity of our two ANOBE schemes can be tightly reduced to standard $k$-Linear assumption (and the existence of other primitives). For a broadcast system with $n$ users, Libert *et al.*'s security analysis suffers from $O(n^3)$ loss while our security loss is constant.
- Our first ANOBE supports fast decryption and has a shorter ciphertext than the fast-decryption version of Libert *et al.*'s concrete ANOBE. Our second ANOBE is adapted from the first one. We sacrifice the fast decryption feature and achieve shorter ciphertexts than Libert *et al.*'s concrete ANOBE with the help of bilinear groups.

Technically, we start from an instantiation of Libert *et al.*'s generic ANOBE [PKC, 2012], but we work out all our proofs from scratch instead of relying on their generic security result. This intuitively allows our optimizations in the concrete setting.

**Keywords:** Broadcast encryption · Full anonymity
Chosen-ciphertext security · Tight reduction · Short ciphertext

## 1 Introduction

**Broadcast Encryption.** *Broadcast encryption* [Ber91,FN94] (BE) is a public-key cryptosystem designed for securely sending information to multiple users via

J. Li—Shanghai Key Laboratory of Trustworthy Computing, School of Computer Science and Software Engineering. Supported by the National Key R&D program of China (No. 2017YFB0802000) and NSF of China (Nos. 61572198, 61632012, 61672239). Part of this work was done while the author was visiting ENS de Lyon.
J. Gong—Supported by the French ANR ALAMBIC project (ANR-16-CE39-0006).

© Springer International Publishing AG, part of Springer Nature 2018
B. Preneel and F. Vercauteren (Eds.): ACNS 2018, LNCS 10892, pp. 497–515, 2018.
https://doi.org/10.1007/978-3-319-93387-0_26

a public channel. In a BE system, we may index each user by integers $1, \ldots, n$ and name set $U := \{1, \ldots, n\}$ the *universe*. It would be convenient to describe BE in the framework of *Functional Encryption* [BSW11]. An authority publishes a set of public parameters generated by the Setup algorithm. Each user's secret key is then created by the KeyGen algorithm from the master secret key which is the output of Setup. By invoking the encryption algorithm Enc, a sender can create a ciphertext for users specified by a target set $S \subseteq U$. Any user with an index $i \in S$ is able to decrypt the ciphertext using the Dec algorithm.

The basic security requirement is *collusion-resistance* which ensures that a ciphertext leaks no information about the message even when multiple users outside the target set $S$ decide to cooperate. More formally, it is required that

$$\{\mathsf{ct} \leftarrow_{\mathrm{R}} \mathsf{Enc}(\mathsf{mpk}, S, m_0)\} \approx_c \{\mathsf{ct} \leftarrow_{\mathrm{R}} \mathsf{Enc}(\mathsf{mpk}, S, m_1)\}$$

where mpk is the public parameters, $(S \subseteq U, m_0, m_1)$ are chosen by the adversary; and we allow the adversary to adaptively learn secret keys for all $i \notin S$.

With more powerful functional encryptions such as attribute-based encryptions [SW05, GPSW06, OT10, LOS+10, CGW15], we can securely broadcast information in a structural way which is more efficient and much easier to manage. However the classical BE still serves as the most general tool for broadcasting information in the systems where users are not well-organized, e.g., a country-wide pay-TV system.

**Anonymity.** Since been introduced, a series of BE schemes have been published [FN94, NNL01, YFDL04, BGW05, DPP07, GW09, Wee16], but they only ensure the confidentiality of the message while the target set $S$ is entirely exposed to the public. In fact, the description of $S$ will be directly transmitted through the insecure channel for decryption. However in many applications, the confidentiality of the target set is also crucial. For instance, in the pay-TV setting, everyone has access to the full list of subscribers, which is not acceptable. Therefore, it is desirable and non-trivial to build a BE system taking both the message and the target set into account in terms of confidentiality. In this paper, we call the latter feature *anonymity* and name such a BE as *anonymous broadcast encryption* [LPQ12] (ANOBE). More formally, it is required that

$$\{\mathsf{ct} \leftarrow_{\mathrm{R}} \mathsf{Enc}(\mathsf{mpk}, S_0, m_0)\} \approx_c \{\mathsf{ct} \leftarrow_{\mathrm{R}} \mathsf{Enc}(\mathsf{mpk}, S_1, m_1)\}$$

where $(m_0, m_1, S_0, S_1)$ are chosen by the adversary and secret keys for all $i \notin (S_0 \setminus S_1) \cup (S_1 \setminus S_0)$ can be revealed. The subtlety is that any secret key for $i \in S_0 \cap S_1$ will give an adversary the power to correctly decrypt both ciphertexts above. In this case, $m_0 \neq m_1$ is disallowed in order to avoid the trivial attack.

**State of the Art.** Although anonymity is crucial for BE, it has not received much attentions to construct ANOBE with the proper security guarantee.

In 2006, Barth *et al.* [BBW06] first identified the *anonymity* (i.e., *recipient privacy* in their work) in the context of encrypted file system. They introduced the notion of ANOBE in the name of *private broadcast encryption*. In their work, two constructions were described. The first one is a generic construction from an IND-CCA secure PKE with key-privacy and a strongly unforgeable signature scheme. They claimed that it achieves IND-CCA security and anonymity but in the *selective* (or static) model which means that the adversary must commit the challenge target sets $(S_0, S_1)$ in advance. Basically, a BE ciphertext there is a set of PKE ciphertexts intended for every recipient in $S$ bound together via a signature. One drawback of this construction is that the decryption time is proportional to $|S|$ since each receiver has to try to decrypt each PKE ciphertext one by one. In their second construction, they introduced a method helping a receiver to find the right PKE ciphertext and reduced the decryption cost to constant. However, it unfortunately relies on the random oracle model.

At PKC 2012, Libert *et al.* [LPQ12] formally revisited Barth *et al.*'s results. They described the *adaptive* security for ANOBE where the adversary can choose the challenge target sets $(S_0, S_1)$ at any time (i.e., the security notion we have reviewed), and showed that it can be achieved from IND-CCA secure PKE (plus strongly secure signatures). Note that this result is quite strong in that the underlying PKE is not necessarily key-private. Moreover, the receiver can decrypt in a constant time. However, the size of ciphertext depends on $n$, the size of universe. They then demonstrated that Barth *et al.*'s first BE is actually IND-CCA secure and anonymous in an *adaptive* sense and provided an alternative construction from IBE [Sha84, CHK04]. This ANOBE has shorter ciphertext (of size $O(|S|)$) but requires the underlying PKE to be weakly robust [ABN10, Moh10] and key-private, and the decryption cost increases to $O(|S|)$. They also formalized the method helping to reduce the decryption cost in Barth *et al.*'s second construction [BBW06] as *anonymous hint system*, which can be viewed as a variant of extractable hash proof systems [Wee10]. The classical randomness-reuse technique [Kur02, BBS03] was then formally studied to reduce the ciphertext size. Finally, a concrete ANOBE based on the Kurosawa-Desmedt PKE [KD04] was proposed. Having their generic ANOBE, they showed that the Kurosawa-Desmedt PKE can be adapted to be key-private and robust, and also support randomness-reuse technique.

Also at PKC 2012, Fazio and Perera [FP12] proposed an ANOBE scheme with sublinear-size ciphertexts but with a much weaker *outsider-anonymity* where users identified by $S_0 \cap S_1$ are not considered to be malicious. More formally, the adversary is forbidden to get any secret key for $i \in S_0 \cap S_1$. However Barth *et al.*'s early work [BBW06] has actually recognized such an inside attacker as a hazard and illustrated how serious the issue is under a chosen-ciphertext attack. In the end, we want to note that Libert *et al.*'s results [LPQ12] are still the best in the sense that they achieve (1) IND-CCA security, (2) *fully* anonymity and (3) random-oracle-freeness. To our best knowledge, there is no follow-up result with all these features simultaneously even when taking the *identity-based* variant into account (see recent work [HWL+16] for more details).

## 1.1   Contributions

In this paper, we propose two concrete ANOBE schemes. Both of them are obtained by optimizing an instantiation of Libert *et al.*'s generic construction [LPQ12] with *Cramer-Shoup PKE* [CS98, CS02]. We prove, *from scratch*, that they are secure in the sense of [LPQ12] from the standard $k$-Linear ($k$-Lin) assumption and the existence of several other cryptographic primitives (such as strongly unforgeable signature and collision-resistant hash function).

Although our proposals do not deviate from Libert *et al.*'s generic framework [LPQ12], our new start point and customized security proof allow us to gain shorter ciphertexts and tighter reduction than the concrete instantiation in [LPQ12]. (Recall that it is based on Kurosawa-Desmedt PKE [KD04] and the security result follows the generic construction directly.) A comparison between them is shown in Table 1 where we consider instantiations of our two ANOBE under DDH = 1-Lin (or SXDH = 1-Lin) assumption[1]. We note that these two instantiations are the most efficient ones.

**Table 1.** Comparison of our two proposals and the concrete ANOBE from [LPQ12] in terms of ciphertext size and reduction tightness. Table (a) is for the schemes supporting fast decryption while we tolerate linear decryption cost in Table (b). In our comparison, the system has $n$ users and $\ell$ is the size of target set $S$. We let $\mathbb{G}$ be a finite group where DDH holds while $\mathbb{G}_1$ denotes the first source group of a bilinear group where SXDH holds. The column "Reduction" shows the security loss.

(a) Comparing our first ANOBE with [LPQ12] plus anonymous hint system.

(b) Comparing our second ANOBE with [LPQ12] *without* anonymous hint system.

| Scheme | \|ct\| | Reduction | Scheme | \|ct\| | Reduction |
|--------|--------|-----------|--------|--------|-----------|
| [LPQ12] | $(4\ell + 5)\|\mathbb{G}\| + 2\|\mathbb{Z}_p\|$ | $O(n^3)$ | [LPQ12] | $(2\ell + 5)\|\mathbb{G}\| + 2\|\mathbb{Z}_p\|$ | $O(n^3)$ |
| Sect. 3 | $(2\ell + 5)\|\mathbb{G}\| + 2\|\mathbb{Z}_p\|$ | $O(1)$ | Sect. 4 | $(\ell + 6)\|\mathbb{G}_1\|$ | $O(1)$ |

**Shorter Ciphertext.** Our first ANOBE scheme supports fast decryption. Compared with the concrete ANOBE in [LPQ12] equipped with their DDH-based anonymous hint system[2], our ANOBE can save roughly 50% bandwidth. Our second ANOBE is derived from the first one. We sacrifice fast decryption and peruse shorter ciphertext. Compared with concrete ANOBE in [LPQ12], our second ANOBE works with bilinear groups and roughly saves 50% bandwidth[3]. We highlight that this construction almost touches the lower bound of ciphertext size in an anonymous broadcast encryption [KS12]. It is quite surprising that we start from a less efficient basic PKE scheme but finally achieves better space efficiency. We note that the Cramer-Shoup PKE [CS98, CS02] is indeed

---

[1] We assume that (1) the verification key and signature for strongly unforgeable one-time signatures consist of 3 group elements and 2 integers, respectively [Gro06] (see Sect. 4, [CCS09]); (2) the authenticated encryption with key-binding property has a ciphertext of roughly 2 group elements (see Sect. 6, [LPQ12]).

[2] The resulting ANOBE will also support fast decryption, here we share the randomness between ANOBE and anonymous hint system.

[3] Here we implement the concrete ANOBE from [LPQ12] using elliptic curve.

less efficient than Kurosawa-Desmedt PKE [KD04], but it permits us to use some customized method to optimize the system.

**Tighter Reduction.** In [LPQ12], their security reduction suffers from $O(n^3)$ loss where $n$ is the size of the universe. This makes it infeasible for large-scale systems such as aforementioned pay-TV application. In particular, we need to use a larger group to compensate the loss, which of course increases the bandwidth and computation costs. In our work, we prove the security of two ANOBE from basic assumption and only suffer constant security loss, which is of both theoretical and practical interest. We argue that the result is non-trivial: A potential solution is to employ an IND-CCA secure PKE with tight reduction for multiple users (like [GHKW16,Hof17]) in Libert *et al.*'s generic construction [LPQ12]. However, the simulator still needs to guess which public keys will be associated with target set which is chosen adversarially and causes significant security loss.

## 1.2  Technical Overview

Our starting point is an instantiation of Libert *et al.*'s generic construction with Cramer-Shoup PKE [CS98, CS02]. In this overview, we first give this instantiation and describe how to derive our two ANOBE schemes from it.

**Starting Point.** Assume a *prime-order group* $(p, \mathbb{G}, g)$. We let $[a] := g^a \in \mathbb{G}$ for all $a \in \mathbb{Z}_p$ and extend it to matrix over $\mathbb{Z}_p$. Assume $S := \{i_1, \ldots, i_\ell\}$. We can instantiate Libert *et al.*'s construction using Cramer-Shoup PKE under $k$-Lin assumption as below:

$$\mathsf{mpk} : \{\ [\mathbf{A}]\ , [\mathbf{A}^\top \mathbf{k}_i], [\mathbf{A}^\top \mathbf{x}_i], [\mathbf{A}^\top \mathbf{y}_i]\ \}_{i \in [n]}, (\mathsf{Gen}_{\mathsf{ots}}, \mathsf{Sig}, \mathsf{Ver}), \mathsf{h}$$

$$\mathsf{sk}_i : \mathbf{k}_i, \mathbf{x}_i, \mathbf{y}_i$$

$$\mathsf{ct}_S : \{\ [\mathbf{r}^\top \mathbf{A}^\top]\ , [\mathbf{r}^\top \mathbf{A}^\top \mathbf{k}_{i_j}] \cdot m, [\mathbf{r}^\top \mathbf{A}^\top (\mathbf{x}_{i_j} + \alpha \cdot \mathbf{y}_{i_j})]\ \}_{j \in [\ell]}, \mathsf{pk}_{\mathsf{ots}}, \sigma$$

where $\mathbf{A} \leftarrow_{\mathrm{R}} \mathbb{Z}_p^{(k+1) \times k}$, $\mathbf{k}_i, \mathbf{x}_i, \mathbf{y}_i \leftarrow_{\mathrm{R}} \mathbb{Z}_p^{k+1}$ for $i \in [n]$ and $\mathbf{r} \leftarrow_{\mathrm{R}} \mathbb{Z}_p^k$. The public parameter $\mathsf{mpk}$ is basically $n$ public keys of Cramer-Shoup PKE[4] sharing $[\mathbf{A}]$ which is a common technique in the multi-user setting. The ciphertext for $S$ contains $\ell$ ciphertexts of Cramer-Shoup PKE with randomness $[\mathbf{r}^\top \mathbf{A}^\top]$ reused as [LPQ12]. Following Libert *et al.*'s suggestion, they are then bound together via a strongly unforgeable signature $\sigma$ under fresh verification key $\mathsf{pk}_{\mathsf{ots}}$ instead of encrypting $m \| \mathsf{pk}_{\mathsf{ots}}$.

The above BE is IND-CCA secure and anonymous according to Libert *et al.*'s generic result. However, we can do better by showing a tighter reduction for this concrete ANOBE. The security loss of Libert *et al.*'s reduction (which is $O(n^3)$) is mainly caused by black-box-reduction to the underlying PKE where the simulation need to guess some information about challenge target set. We prove our security result *from scratch*. In particular, we employ the proof technique for

---

[4] Here we use a direct generalization of Cramer-Shoup PKE under the $k$-Lin assumption. The original Cramer-Shoup PKE corresponds to the case $k = 1$.

IND-CCA PKE in the multi-user setting [GHKW16, Hof17] but adapt it to our broadcast encryption case. We found that we can now avoid guessing adversary's behavior and also corresponding reduction loss.

**Our First ANOBE: Shorter Ciphertext for Fast Decryption.** The above instantiation has not been equipped with anonymous hint system [LPQ12], so the decryption cost should be $O(\ell)$. (Recall that, intuitively, an anonymous hint system can help the decryptor to find the right ciphertext component intended for him and avoid $O(\ell)$ factor.) However we observe that $\{[\mathbf{r}^\top \mathbf{A}^\top (\mathbf{x}_{i_j} + \alpha \cdot \mathbf{y}_{i_j})]\}_{j \in [\ell]}$ can serve as the hints for fast decryption. This benefits from the fact that tag $\alpha$ is shared by all users in $S$. In the decryption procedure, a user with secret key $\mathbf{k}_i, \mathbf{x}_i, \mathbf{y}_i$ can recover $v = [\mathbf{r}^\top \mathbf{A}^\top (\mathbf{x}_i + \alpha \cdot \mathbf{y}_i)]$ and try to find the index $j^*$ such that $v = [\mathbf{r}^\top \mathbf{A}^\top (\mathbf{x}_{i_{j^*}} + \alpha \cdot \mathbf{y}_{i_{j^*}})]$, which indicates the right ciphertext.

This already saves the bandwidth since we need the DDH-based anonymous hint system in [LPQ12] to upgrade Libert *et al.*'s concrete ANOBE in order to achieve fast decryption. Even with randomness reuse technique, this will introduce $2 \cdot |S|$ additional group elements to the ciphertext. The perspective here is that $\{[\mathbf{r}^\top \mathbf{A}^\top (\mathbf{x}_{i_j} + \alpha \cdot \mathbf{y}_{i_j})]\}_{j \in [\ell]}$ act as crucial components for achieving IND-CCA security and hints for fast decryption at the same time while they are realized separately in Libert *et al.*'s concrete ANOBE.

**Our Second ANOBE: Compressing Ciphertext Again.** We now ask:

*Can we reduce the ciphertext size if we can tolerate slower decryption?*

Observe that we have $\ell$ group elements (i.e., $\{[\mathbf{r}^\top \mathbf{A}^\top (\mathbf{x}_{i_j} + \alpha \cdot \mathbf{y}_{i_j})]\}_{j \in [\ell]}$) for consistency check (which is necessary for IND-CCA security) in our first ANOBE. If we assume that each recipient can correctly guess which part is intended for him/her, we can see that only one of these $\ell$ elements will be used in the decryption procedure. Therefore a promising idea is to ask all recipients to share the consistency check process. A direct way to do so is to

$$\text{replace} \quad \{[\mathbf{r}^\top \mathbf{A}^\top (\mathbf{x}_{i_j} + \alpha \cdot \mathbf{y}_{i_j})]\}_{j \in [\ell]} \quad \text{with} \quad [\mathbf{r}^\top \mathbf{A}^\top (\mathbf{x} + \alpha \cdot \mathbf{y})]$$

and publish $[\mathbf{A}^\top \mathbf{x}]$ and $[\mathbf{A}^\top \mathbf{y}]$ in mpk. Unfortunately, there is a fatal issue. To do the consistency check, we should give each user $\mathbf{x}$ and $\mathbf{y}$ directly and they will be leaked to an adversary through any corrupted user. This totally breaks the IND-CCA security. We circumvent the difficulty by making the consistency check public using the technique by Kiltz and Wee [KW15]. In particular, we adapt our first ANOBE to $\mathbb{G}_1$ of a pairing group $(p, \mathbb{G}_1, \mathbb{G}_2, \mathbb{G}_T, e)$ and

$$\text{replace} \quad [\mathbf{r}^\top \mathbf{A}^\top (\mathbf{x} + \alpha \cdot \mathbf{y})]_1 \quad \text{with} \quad [\mathbf{r}^\top \mathbf{A}^\top (\mathbf{X} + \alpha \cdot \mathbf{Y})]_1$$

where $\mathbf{X}, \mathbf{Y} \leftarrow_{\mathrm{R}} \mathbb{Z}_p^{(k+1) \times (k+1)}$. In the public parameter mpk, we publish

$$([\mathbf{A}^\top \mathbf{X}]_1, [\mathbf{A}^\top \mathbf{Y}]_1) \quad \text{and} \quad ([\mathbf{B}]_2, [\mathbf{X}\mathbf{B}]_2, [\mathbf{Y}\mathbf{B}]_2)$$

where $\mathbf{B} \leftarrow_{\mathrm{R}} \mathbb{Z}_p^{(k+1) \times k}$ and the right-hand side part allow *anyone* to *publicly* check the ciphertext consistency.

We have successfully compressed the ciphertext but lose the correctness of decryption since we do not have hint system now. It is easy to fix using *key-binding* symmetric encryption scheme $(\mathsf{E}, \mathsf{D})$. That is we pick session key $K$ from the key space of $(\mathsf{E}, \mathsf{D})$ and

$$\text{replace} \quad [\mathbf{r}^\top \mathbf{A}^\top \mathbf{k}_{i_j}]_1 \cdot m \quad \text{with} \quad [\mathbf{r}^\top \mathbf{A}^\top \mathbf{k}_{i_j}]_1 \cdot K, \mathsf{E}_K(m).$$

We note that we are not pursuing fast decryption now. We can further get rid of $\sigma$ by defining $\alpha$ as in Cramer-Shoup PKE [CS98, CS02]. We sketch our second ANOBE as follows:

$\mathsf{mpk} : (\mathsf{E}, \mathsf{D}), \mathsf{h}; \; \{\, [\mathbf{A}^\top]_1 \,, [\mathbf{A}^\top \mathbf{k}_i]_1, \; [\mathbf{A}^\top \mathbf{X}]_1, [\mathbf{A}^\top \mathbf{Y}]_1 \,\}_{i \in [n]}; \; [\mathbf{B}]_2, [\mathbf{XB}]_2, [\mathbf{YB}]_2$

$\mathsf{sk}_i : \mathbf{k}_i$

$\mathsf{ct}_S : \{\, [\mathbf{r}^\top \mathbf{A}^\top]_1 \,, [\mathbf{r}^\top \mathbf{A}^\top \mathbf{k}_{i_j}]_1 \cdot K, \; \mathsf{E}_K(m) \,, \; [\mathbf{r}^\top \mathbf{A}^\top (\mathbf{X} + \alpha \cdot \mathbf{Y})]_1 \,\}_{j \in [\ell]}$

where all terms in gray box are shared by all users/receivers. As our first ANOBE, the reduction loss is constant.

Compared with Libert *et al.*'s concrete ANOBE [LPQ12], our second ANOBE is based on weaker assumptions — we don't require the existence of strongly one-time signature and $(\mathsf{E}, \mathsf{D})$ is not necessarily authenticated encryption. Furthermore, in the ciphertext, we share as many components as possible among receivers in the target set, the remaining $\ell$ group elements seem to be inevitable by the lower bound [KS12].

**Organization.** Our paper is organized as follows. We review some basic notions in Sect. 2. Our two ANOBE constructions along with security analysis will be presented in Sects. 3 and 4, respectively. We finally conclude the paper in Sect. 5.

## 2   Preliminaries

**Notations.** For $n \in \mathbb{N}$, we define $[n] := \{1, 2, \ldots, n\}$. We use $a \leftarrow_{\mathrm{R}} A$ to denote the process of uniformly sampling an element from set $A$ and assigning it to variable $a$. For two sets $S_0, S_1$, define $S_0 \triangle S_1 := (S_0 \setminus S_1) \cup (S_1 \setminus S_0)$. "p.p.t." stands for probabilistic polynomial time.

### 2.1   Anonymous Broadcast Encryption

**Algorithms.** Let $U := [n]$ be the universe. A *broadcast encryption* (BE) scheme consists of four algorithms $(\mathsf{Setup}, \mathsf{KeyGen}, \mathsf{Enc}, \mathsf{Dec})$: Algorithm $\mathsf{Setup}$ takes security parameter $1^\lambda$ and $n$ as input and outputs a master public key $\mathsf{mpk}$ and a master secret key $\mathsf{msk}$; Algorithm $\mathsf{KeyGen}$ takes $\mathsf{mpk}, \mathsf{msk}$ and an index $i \in U$ as input and outputs a secret key $\mathsf{sk}_i$; Algorithm $\mathsf{Enc}$ takes $\mathsf{mpk}$, a message $m$ and a subset $S \subseteq U$ as input and outputs a ciphertext $\mathsf{ct}_S$; Algorithm $\mathsf{Dec}$ takes $\mathsf{mpk}, \mathsf{ct}_S$ and $\mathsf{sk}_i$ as input and outputs $m$ or a failure symbol $\bot$.

**Correctness.** For all $\lambda$, all $(\mathsf{mpk}, \mathsf{msk}) \leftarrow_{\mathrm{R}} \mathsf{Setup}(1^\lambda, n)$, all $m$, all $S \subseteq U$, and all $i \in S$, it is required that $\mathsf{Dec}(\mathsf{mpk}, \mathsf{Enc}(\mathsf{mpk}, m, S), \mathsf{KeyGen}(\mathsf{mpk}, \mathsf{msk}, i)) = m$.

**Chosen-Ciphertext Security and Anonymity.** For any adversary $\mathcal{A}$, define

$$\mathsf{Adv}_{\mathcal{A}}^{\mathsf{BE}}(1^\lambda) := \left| \Pr \left[ b = b' \left| \begin{array}{c} (\mathsf{mpk}, \mathsf{msk}) \leftarrow_{\mathrm{R}} \mathsf{Setup}(1^\lambda, n), \; b \leftarrow_{\mathrm{R}} \{0, 1\} \\ (m_0, m_1, S_0, S_1) \leftarrow_{\mathrm{R}} \mathcal{A}^{\mathsf{KeyO}(\cdot), \mathsf{DecO}(\cdot, \cdot)}(1^\lambda, \mathsf{mpk}) \\ \mathsf{ct}^* \leftarrow_{\mathrm{R}} \mathsf{Enc}(\mathsf{mpk}, m_b, S_b) \\ b' \leftarrow_{\mathrm{R}} \mathcal{A}^{\mathsf{KeyO}(\cdot), \mathsf{DecO}(\cdot, \cdot)}(1^\lambda, \mathsf{mpk}, \mathsf{ct}^*) \end{array} \right. \right] - \frac{1}{2} \right|$$

where oracles work as follows:

– KeyO: on input $i$, *key extraction oracle* KeyO outputs $\mathsf{sk}_i \leftarrow_{\mathrm{R}}$ $\mathsf{KeyGen}(\mathsf{msk}, \mathsf{mpk}, i)$ and sets $Q_{\mathsf{sk}} := Q_{\mathsf{sk}} \cup \{i\}$ which is initialized to be $\emptyset$ at the beginning.
– DecO: on input $(\mathsf{ct}, i)$, *decryption oracle* DecO outputs $\mathsf{Dec}(\mathsf{mpk}, \mathsf{ct}, \mathsf{sk}_i)$ when $\mathsf{ct}^*$ (a.k.a. *challenge ciphertext*) has not been defined or $\mathsf{ct} \neq \mathsf{ct}^*$.

A broadcast encryption scheme achieves chosen-ciphertext security and anonymity (ANO-IND-CCA) if, for all p.p.t. adversary $\mathcal{A}$, $\mathsf{Adv}_{\mathcal{A}}^{\mathsf{BE}}(\lambda)$ is negligible in $\lambda$ under the restrictions that (1) $|m_0| = |m_1|$ and $|S_0| = |S_1|$; (2) $Q_{\mathsf{sk}} \cap (S_0 \triangle S_1) = \emptyset$; (3) if $Q_{\mathsf{sk}} \cap (S_0 \cap S_1) \neq \emptyset$, then $m_0 = m_1$.

## 2.2 Prime-Order (Bilinear) Groups

**Prime-Order Group.** A group generator GGen is a p.p.t. algorithm which takes $1^\lambda$ as input and outputs a description $\mathcal{G} := (p, \mathbb{G}, g)$. Here $\mathbb{G}$ is a finite cyclic group of prime order $p$ and $g$ is a random generator of $\mathbb{G}$. Throughout the paper, we will use *implicit representation* [EHK+13]. We let $[a] := g^a \in \mathbb{G}$ for all $a \in \mathbb{Z}_p$. For a matrix $\mathbf{A} = (a_{ij}) \in \mathbb{Z}_p^{m \times n}$, we let $[\mathbf{A}] = (g^{a_{ij}}) \in \mathbb{G}^{m \times n}$.

**Prime-Order Bilinear Group.** A group generator PGGen is a p.p.t. algorithm which takes $1^\lambda$ as input and outputs a description $\mathcal{PG} := (p, \mathbb{G}_1, \mathbb{G}_2, \mathbb{G}_T, e, g_1, g_2)$ of (asymmetric) bilinear group. Here $\mathbb{G}_1, \mathbb{G}_2, \mathbb{G}_T$ are finite cyclic groups of prime order $p$ and $e$ is an admissible bilinear map. $g_1 \in \mathbb{G}_1$ and $g_2 \in \mathbb{G}_2$ are random generators of $\mathbb{G}_1$ and $\mathbb{G}_2$, and $g_T := e(g_1, g_2)$ will be a generator of group $\mathbb{G}_T$. The implicit representation is also be applied to prime-order *bilinear* groups: We let $[a]_s := g_s^a \in \mathbb{G}_s$ for all $a \in \mathbb{Z}_p$ and $s \in \{1, 2, T\}$. The notation can be easily extended to matrices analogously and we let $e([\mathbf{A}]_1, [\mathbf{B}]_2) := [\mathbf{AB}]_T$ for matrices $\mathbf{A}$ and $\mathbf{B}$ when the multiplication is well-defined.

**Cryptographic Assumption.** For any $k \in \mathbb{N}$, we call $\mathcal{D}_k$ a *matrix distribution* if it outputs full-rank matrices in $\mathbb{Z}_p^{(k+1) \times k}$ in polynomial time. We may assume that for all $\mathbf{A} \leftarrow_{\mathrm{R}} \mathcal{D}_k$, the first $k$ rows of $\mathbf{A}$ form an invertible matrix.

We will use the $\mathcal{D}_k$-Matrix Diffie-Hellman ($\mathcal{D}_k$-MDDH) assumption in $\mathbb{G}$ described as follows. The $\mathcal{D}_k$-MDDH assumption in $\mathbb{G}_1$ and $\mathbb{G}_2$ are analogous.

**Assumption 1 ($\mathcal{D}_k$-MDDH).** *We say that the $\mathcal{D}_k$-Matrix Diffie-Hellman assumption holds relative to* GGen, *if for any p.p.t. adversary $\mathcal{A}$, the following advantage function is negligible in $\lambda$.*

$$\mathsf{Adv}^{\mathsf{mddh}}_{\mathcal{A},\mathbb{G}}(\lambda) := |\Pr[\mathcal{A}(\mathcal{G},[\mathbf{A}],[\mathbf{As}]) = 1] - \Pr[\mathcal{A}(\mathcal{G},[\mathbf{A}],[\mathbf{u}]) = 1]|$$

*where $\mathcal{G} \leftarrow_R \mathsf{GGen}(1^\lambda)$, $\mathbf{A} \leftarrow_R \mathcal{D}_k$, $\mathbf{s} \leftarrow_R \mathbb{Z}_p^k$, and $\mathbf{u} \leftarrow_R \mathbb{Z}_p^{k+1}$.*

The famous $k$-Linear ($k$-Lin) assumption is an instantiation of the $\mathcal{D}_k$-MDDH assumption. The classical *decisional Diffie-Hellman* (DDH) assumption (a.k.a *symmetric external Diffie-Hellman* (SXDH) assumption in *asymmetric* bilinear groups) is just the $k$-Lin assumption with $k = 1$. See [EHK+13] for more details.

For bilinear groups, we also use the $\mathcal{D}_k$-Matrix Kernel Diffie-Hellman ($\mathcal{D}_k$-KerMDH) Assumption [MRV16], which is implied by the $\mathcal{D}_k$-MDDH assumption.

**Assumption 2 ($\mathcal{D}_k$-KerMDH).** *Let $s \in \{1,2\}$. We say that the $\mathcal{D}_k$-Kernel Matrix Diffie-Hellman Assumption holds relative to* PGGen, *if for any p.p.t. adversary $\mathcal{A}$, the following advantage function is negligible in $\lambda$.*

$$\mathsf{Adv}^{\mathsf{kmdh}}_{\mathcal{A},\mathbb{G}_s}(\lambda) := \Pr[\mathbf{A}^\top \mathbf{a}^\perp = \mathbf{0} \wedge \mathbf{a}^\perp \neq \mathbf{0} \mid [\mathbf{a}^\perp]_{3-s} \leftarrow_R \mathcal{A}(\mathcal{PG},[\mathbf{A}]_s)]$$

*where $\mathcal{PG} \leftarrow_R \mathsf{PGGen}(1^\lambda)$, $\mathbf{A} \leftarrow_R \mathcal{D}_k$.*

## 2.3 Cryptographic Primitives

Our constructions will use the following cryptographic primitives:

- A semantically secure and key-binding symmetric encryption scheme $(\mathsf{E},\mathsf{D})$ with key space $\mathcal{K}$. Let $\mathsf{E}_K(\cdot)$ and $\mathsf{D}_K(\cdot)$ denote the encryption and decryption procedures under secret key $K \in \mathcal{K}$. By *key-binding* [Fis99], we mean that, for any message $m$ and any secret key $K \in \mathcal{K}$, there exists no $K' \in \mathcal{K}$ such that $K \neq K'$ and $\mathsf{D}_{K'}(\mathsf{E}_K(m)) \neq \perp$ (Here $\perp$ indicates a decryption failure).
- A family of collision-resistant hash function $\mathcal{H}$. It ensures that, given $\mathsf{h} \leftarrow_R \mathcal{H}$, it is hard to find $x \neq y$ such that $\mathsf{h}(x) = \mathsf{h}(y)$ (i.e., a collision).
- A strongly unforgeable one-time signature scheme $(\mathsf{Gen}_{\mathsf{ots}}, \mathsf{Sign}, \mathsf{Ver})$. Let $(\mathsf{pk}_{\mathsf{ots}}, \mathsf{sk}_{\mathsf{ots}}) \leftarrow_R \mathsf{Gen}_{\mathsf{ots}}(1^\lambda)$ be a verification key and a signing key. It is guaranteed that, given $\mathsf{pk}_{\mathsf{ots}}$ and a signature $\sigma \leftarrow_R \mathsf{Sign}(\mathsf{sk}_{\mathsf{ots}}, m)$ for some adversarially chosen message $m$, it is infeasible to output another message-signature pair $(m^*, \sigma^*) \neq (m, \sigma)$ satisfying $\mathsf{Ver}(\mathsf{pk}_{\mathsf{ots}}, m^*, \sigma^*) = 1$.

We will use $\mathsf{Adv}^{\mathsf{se}}_{\mathcal{A}}(\lambda)$, $\mathsf{Adv}^{\mathsf{hash}}_{\mathcal{A}}(\lambda)$ and $\mathsf{Adv}^{\mathsf{ots}}_{\mathcal{A}}(\lambda)$ to denote the advantage of adversary $\mathcal{A}$ in violating the security of above primitives under security parameter $\lambda$. Formal definitions can be found in the full version of the paper.

## 2.4    Core Lemma

We review the core lemma in [KW15].

**Lemma 1 (Core lemma, [KW15]).** *Let $k \in \mathbb{N}$. For any $\mathbf{A}, \mathbf{B} \in \mathbb{Z}_p^{(k+1) \times k}$ and any (possibly unbounded) adversary $\mathcal{A}$, we have*

$$
\Pr\left[
\begin{array}{c}
\mathbf{u} \notin \mathrm{span}(\mathbf{A}) \wedge \alpha \neq \alpha^* \\
\wedge \ \boldsymbol{\pi}^\top = \mathbf{u}^\top(\mathbf{X} + \alpha \cdot \mathbf{Y})
\end{array}
\left|
\begin{array}{c}
\mathbf{X}, \mathbf{Y} \leftarrow_{\mathrm{R}} \mathbb{Z}_p^{(k+1) \times (k+1)} \\
(\mathbf{u}, \alpha, \boldsymbol{\pi}) \leftarrow_{\mathrm{R}} \mathcal{A}^{\mathcal{O}(\cdot)}(\mathbf{A}^\top\mathbf{X}, \mathbf{A}^\top\mathbf{Y}, \mathbf{XB}, \mathbf{YB})
\end{array}
\right.
\right] \leq \frac{1}{p}
$$

*where $\mathcal{O}(\alpha^*) \to \mathbf{X} + \alpha^* \cdot \mathbf{Y}$ may only be called one time.*

# 3    Tightly Secure ANOBE with Fast Decryption

## 3.1    Construction

Our first broadcast encryption scheme is described as follows.

- Setup($1^\lambda, n$): Run $\mathcal{G} := (p, \mathbb{G}, g) \leftarrow_{\mathrm{R}} \mathsf{GGen}(1^\lambda)$. Sample

$$
\mathbf{A} \leftarrow_{\mathrm{R}} \mathcal{D}_k \quad \text{and} \quad \mathbf{k}_i, \mathbf{x}_i, \mathbf{y}_i \leftarrow_{\mathrm{R}} \mathbb{Z}_p^{k+1} \quad \text{for} \ \ i \in [n].
$$

Select a strongly unforgeable one-time signature scheme $(\mathsf{Gen}_{\mathsf{ots}}, \mathsf{Sig}, \mathsf{Ver})$ and a hash function $\mathsf{h} : \{0,1\}^* \to \mathbb{Z}_p$ from $\mathcal{H}$. The master public key is

$$
\mathsf{mpk} := (\mathcal{G}, \mathsf{h}, (\mathsf{Gen}_{\mathsf{ots}}, \mathsf{Sig}, \mathsf{Ver}), [\mathbf{A}], \{[\mathbf{A}^\top\mathbf{k}_i], [\mathbf{A}^\top\mathbf{x}_i], [\mathbf{A}^\top\mathbf{y}_i]\}_{i=1}^n)
$$

and the master secret key is $\mathsf{msk} := (\{\mathbf{k}_i, \mathbf{x}_i, \mathbf{y}_i\}_{i=1}^n)$.
- KeyGen($\mathsf{msk}, \mathsf{mpk}, i$): Output the secret key $\mathsf{sk}_i = (\mathbf{k}_i, \mathbf{x}_i, \mathbf{y}_i)$.
- Enc($\mathsf{mpk}, m, S$): Let $\ell := |S|$ and $S = \{i_1, \ldots, i_\ell\} \subseteq U = [n]$. Sample $\mathbf{r} \leftarrow_{\mathrm{R}} \mathbb{Z}_p^k$ and compute $[\mathbf{u}^\top] := [\mathbf{r}^\top \mathbf{A}^\top]$. Generate $(\mathsf{sk}_{\mathsf{ots}}, \mathsf{pk}_{\mathsf{ots}}) \leftarrow_{\mathrm{R}} \mathsf{Gen}_{\mathsf{ots}}(1^\lambda)$, compute $\alpha := \mathsf{h}(\mathsf{pk}_{\mathsf{ots}})$ and $c_1 := [\mathbf{r}^\top \mathbf{A}^\top \mathbf{k}_{i_1}] \cdot m, v_1 := [\mathbf{r}^\top \mathbf{A}^\top (\mathbf{x}_{i_1} + \alpha \cdot \mathbf{y}_{i_1})], \ldots, c_\ell := [\mathbf{r}^\top \mathbf{A}^\top \mathbf{k}_{i_\ell}] \cdot m, v_\ell := [\mathbf{r}^\top \mathbf{A}^\top (\mathbf{x}_{i_\ell} + \alpha \cdot \mathbf{y}_{i_\ell})]$. Choose a random permutation $\tau$ over $[\ell]$ and compute $\sigma := \mathsf{Sig}(\mathsf{sk}_{\mathsf{ots}}, ([\mathbf{u}^\top], c_{\tau(1)}, v_{\tau(1)}, \ldots, c_{\tau(\ell)}, v_{\tau(\ell)}))$. The ciphertext is

$$
\mathsf{ct} := ([\mathbf{u}^\top], c_{\tau(1)}, v_{\tau(1)}, \ldots, c_{\tau(\ell)}, v_{\tau(\ell)}, \mathsf{pk}_{\mathsf{ots}}, \sigma).
$$

- Dec($\mathsf{mpk}, \mathsf{ct}, \mathsf{sk}_i$): Parse the ciphertext $\mathsf{ct}$ as $([\mathbf{u}^\top], \bar{c}_1, \bar{v}_1, \ldots, \bar{c}_\ell, \bar{v}_\ell, \mathsf{pk}_{\mathsf{ots}}, \sigma)$ and the secret key $\mathsf{sk}_i$ as $(\mathbf{k}_i, \mathbf{x}_i, \mathbf{y}_i)$. Return $\bot$ if

$$
\mathsf{Ver}(\mathsf{pk}_{\mathsf{ots}}, ([\mathbf{u}^\top], \bar{c}_1, \bar{v}_1, \ldots, \bar{c}_\ell, \bar{v}_\ell), \sigma) = 0,
$$

otherwise, compute
$$
v := [\mathbf{u}^\top(\mathbf{x}_i + \alpha \cdot \mathbf{y}_i)],
$$

where $\alpha = \mathsf{h}(\mathsf{pk}_{\mathsf{ots}})$. If there exists $j \in [\ell]$ such that $v = \bar{v}_j$, return $m' := \bar{c}_j / [\mathbf{u}^\top \mathbf{k}_i]$; otherwise, return $\bot$.

It is direct to check the correctness.

## 3.2    Security Result and Proof Overview

We prove the following theorem.

**Theorem 1.** *Our broadcast encryption scheme in Sect. 3.1 is adaptively ANO-IND-CCA secure assuming that: (1) $\mathcal{H}$ is collision-resistant; (2) the $\mathcal{D}_k$-MDDH assumption holds in $\mathbb{G}$; (3) signature scheme* $(\mathsf{Gen}_{ots}, \mathsf{Sig}, \mathsf{Ver})$ *is strongly unforgeable under one-time chosen message attack. Concretely, for any adversary $\mathcal{A}$, there exist algorithms $\mathcal{B}_1, \mathcal{B}_2, \mathcal{B}_3$ such that*

$$\mathsf{Adv}_{\mathcal{A}}^{\mathsf{BE}}(\lambda) \le \mathsf{Adv}_{\mathbb{G},\mathcal{B}_1}^{\mathsf{mddh}}(\lambda) + \mathsf{Adv}_{\mathcal{B}_2}^{\mathsf{ots}}(\lambda) + \mathsf{Adv}_{\mathcal{B}_3}^{\mathsf{hash}}(\lambda) + O(1/p)$$

*and* $\mathsf{Time}(\mathcal{B}_1), \mathsf{Time}(\mathcal{B}_2), \mathsf{Time}(\mathcal{B}_3) \approx \mathsf{Time}(\mathcal{A})$.

We prove the theorem via the following game sequence. A proof sketch for each step will be given and more details can be found in the full paper.

$\mathsf{Game}_0$. This game is identical to the real game described in Sect. 2.1. The challenge ciphertext for $(m_0, m_1, S_0, S_1)$ where $S_0 = \{i_{1,0}, \ldots, i_{\ell,0}\}$ and $S_1 = \{i_{1,1}, \ldots, i_{\ell,1}\}$ is of form

$$\mathsf{ct}^* := (\, \mathsf{ct}_1^* := ([\mathbf{u}^{*\top}], c_1^*, v_1^*, \ldots, c_\ell^*, v_\ell^*), \mathsf{pk}_{ots}^*, \sigma^* := \mathsf{Sig}(\mathsf{sk}_{ots}^*, \mathsf{ct}_1^*)\,)$$

where $\mathbf{u}^* \leftarrow_{\mathrm{R}} \mathrm{span}(\mathbf{A})$, $(\mathsf{sk}_{ots}^*, \mathsf{pk}_{ots}^*) \leftarrow_{\mathrm{R}} \mathsf{Gen}_{ots}(1^\lambda)$, and we compute

$$c_j^* = [\mathbf{u}^{*\top} \mathbf{k}_{i_{\tau(j),b}}] \cdot m_b \quad \text{and} \quad v_j^* = [\mathbf{u}^{*\top}(\mathbf{x}_{i_{\tau(j),b}} + \alpha^* \cdot \mathbf{y}_{i_{\tau(j),b}})], \quad \forall j \in [\ell]$$

with $b \leftarrow_{\mathrm{R}} \{0, 1\}$, $\alpha^* = \mathsf{h}(\mathsf{pk}_{ots}^*)$ and a random permutation $\tau$ over $[\ell]$. On input $(\mathsf{ct}, i)$, DecO parses

$$\mathsf{ct} = (\mathsf{ct}_1 = ([\mathbf{u}^\top], c_1, v_1, \ldots, c_\ell, v_\ell), \mathsf{pk}_{ots}, \sigma),$$

and rejects the query if

$$(a) \quad \mathsf{ct} = \mathsf{ct}^* \quad \text{or} \quad (b) \quad \mathsf{Ver}(\mathsf{pk}_{ots}, \mathsf{ct}_1, \sigma) = 0.$$

Then compute $v = [\mathbf{u}^\top(\mathbf{x}_i + \alpha \cdot \mathbf{y}_i)]$ with $\alpha = \mathsf{h}(\mathsf{pk}_{ots})$. If there exists $j \in [\ell]$ such that $v = v_j$, return $m' := c_j/[\mathbf{u}^\top \mathbf{k}_i]$; otherwise, return $\perp$. Let $\mathsf{Win}_i$ denote the event that $\mathcal{A}$ in $\mathsf{Game}_i$ guesses $b$ correctly. Since $\mathsf{Game}_0$ perfectly simulates the real game, we have $\mathsf{Adv}_{\mathcal{A}}^{\mathsf{BE}}(1^\lambda) = |\Pr[\mathsf{Win}_0] - 1/2|$.

$\mathsf{Game}_1$. This game is identical to $\mathsf{Game}_0$ except that we sample $\mathbf{u}^* \leftarrow_{\mathrm{R}} \mathbb{Z}_p^{k+1}$ when generating the challenge ciphertext $\mathsf{ct}^*$. It is easy to see that this game is indistinguishable from $\mathsf{Game}_0$ under the $\mathcal{D}_k$-MDDH assumption. Formally, we have the following lemma.

**Lemma 2 ($\mathsf{Game}_1 \approx_c \mathsf{Game}_0$).** *There exists an adversary $\mathcal{B}_1$ such that*

$$|\Pr[\mathsf{Win}_1] - \Pr[\mathsf{Win}_0]| \le \mathsf{Adv}_{\mathbb{G},\mathcal{B}_1}^{\mathsf{mddh}}(\lambda).$$

$\mathsf{Game}_2$. This game is identical to $\mathsf{Game}_1$ except that $\mathsf{DecO}$, on input $(\mathsf{ct}, i)$, rejects the query if $(a)$ or $(b)$ or

$$(c) \quad \mathsf{pk}_{\mathsf{ots}} = \mathsf{pk}^*_{\mathsf{ots}}.$$

This game is identical to $\mathsf{Game}_1$ until $\mathcal{A}$ submits a query with $\mathsf{pk}_{\mathsf{ots}} = \mathsf{pk}^*_{\mathsf{ots}}$ which survives under condition $(a)$ and $(b)$. However $\sigma$ in such a query will violate the strong unforgeability of $(\mathsf{Gen}_{\mathsf{ots}}, \mathsf{Sig}, \mathsf{Ver})$, and this game is indistinguishable from $\mathsf{Game}_1$. Formally, we have the following lemma.

**Lemma 3 ($\mathsf{Game}_2 \approx_c \mathsf{Game}_1$).** *There exists an adversary $\mathcal{B}_2$ such that*

$$|\Pr[\mathsf{Win}_2] - \Pr[\mathsf{Win}_1]| \leq \mathsf{Adv}^{\mathsf{ots}}_{\mathcal{B}_2}(\lambda).$$

$\mathsf{Game}_3$. This game is identical to $\mathsf{Game}_2$ except the following substitution:

$$(c) \quad \mathsf{pk}_{\mathsf{ots}} = \mathsf{pk}^*_{\mathsf{ots}} \quad \longmapsto \quad (c') \quad \alpha = \alpha^*$$

This game is identical to $\mathsf{Game}_2$ until $\mathcal{A}$ submits a query with $\mathsf{pk}_{\mathsf{ots}} \neq \mathsf{pk}^*_{\mathsf{ots}}$ but $\alpha = \alpha^*$. This immediately violates the collision-resistance of $\mathcal{H}$, and this game is indistinguishable from $\mathsf{Game}_2$. Formally, we have the following lemma.

**Lemma 4 ($\mathsf{Game}_3 \approx_c \mathsf{Game}_2$).** *There exists an algorithm $\mathcal{B}_3$ such that*

$$|\Pr[\mathsf{Win}_3] - \Pr[\mathsf{Win}_2]| \leq \mathsf{Adv}^{\mathsf{hash}}_{\mathcal{B}_3}(\lambda).$$

$\mathsf{Game}_4$. This game is identical to $\mathsf{Game}_3$ except that except that $\mathsf{DecO}$, on input $(\mathsf{ct}, i)$, rejects the query if $(a)$ or $(b)$ or $(c')$ or

$$(d) \quad \mathbf{u} \notin \mathsf{span}(\mathbf{A})$$

We have the following lemma stating that this game is statistically indistinguishable with $\mathsf{Game}_3$.

**Lemma 5 ($\mathsf{Game}_4 \approx_s \mathsf{Game}_3$).** $|\mathsf{Win}_4 - \mathsf{Win}_3| \leq O(1/p)$.
Let $q_D$ be the number of decryption queries. The lemma can be proved in $q_D$ steps. In the $j$-th step, assuming that the first $j - 1$ decryption queries have been processed with condition $(d)$, we demonstrate that the $j$-th query will finally be rejected if it survives under condition $(a), (b), (c')$ with $\mathbf{u} \notin \mathsf{span}(\mathbf{A})$. In other words, we can introduce condition $(d)$ here without changing adversary's view. The proof (for the $j$-th step) relies on the observation that we leak no more information than $\{\mathbf{A}^\top \mathbf{x}_\eta, \mathbf{A}^\top \mathbf{y}_\eta\}_{\eta \in [n]}$ when answering the first $j - 1$ queries to $\mathsf{DecO}$. With the help of condition $(c')$, which ensures that $\alpha \neq \alpha^*$, we can claim that $\mathbf{u}^\top (\mathbf{x}_i + \alpha \cdot \mathbf{y}_i)$ is independently and uniformly distributed and thus hard to guess.

Finally, we have the following lemma which proves Theorem 1 when combining with all previous lemmas and claims.

**Lemma 6.** $\Pr[\mathsf{Win}_4] = 1/2$.

This follows from the fact that $(\mathbf{u}^* \mathbf{k}_i, \mathbf{u}^* (\mathbf{x}_i + \alpha \cdot \mathbf{y}_i))$ are uniformly distributed over $\mathbb{G}^2$, especially unrelated to $b$, for all $i \in S_b$ (resp. $i \in S_b / S_{1-b}$) when $Q_{\mathsf{sk}} \cap (S_0 \cap S_1) = \emptyset$ (resp. $Q_{\mathsf{sk}} \cap (S_0 \cap S_1) \neq \emptyset$), conditioned on $\mathsf{mpk}, \mathsf{KeyO}$ and $\mathsf{DecO}$. The analysis is similar to that for Lemma 5.

**Perspective.** Lemmas 5 and 6 are at the core of our proof. Although our proofs still rely on the proof technique of underlying Cramer-Shoup PKE, we get rid of large reduction loss by carrying out the argument in the broadcast setting *directly*. In particular, we employ the technique beneath the core lemma from Kiltz and Wee [KW15] (see Lemma 1), which allows us to take *all* users into account in a *non-adaptive* way first and then upgrade to the adaptive setting for free. This avoids guessing adversary's behaviour in the simulation which caused large security loss in Libert *et al.*'s work [LPQ12]. Furthermore, we note that our proof indeed involves *robustness* [ABN10, Moh10, LPQ12] but in an *implicit* manner since we are not working with generic PKE anymore.

## 4 Tightly Secure ANOBE with Shorter Ciphertext

### 4.1 Construction

– Setup $(1^\lambda, n)$: Run $\mathcal{PG} := (p, \mathbb{G}_1, \mathbb{G}_2, \mathbb{G}_T, e, g_1, g_2) \leftarrow_{\mathrm{R}} \mathsf{PGGen}(1^\lambda)$. Sample

$$\mathbf{A}, \mathbf{B} \leftarrow_{\mathrm{R}} \mathcal{D}_k, \ \mathbf{X}, \mathbf{Y} \leftarrow_{\mathrm{R}} \mathbb{Z}_p^{(k+1) \times (k+1)}, \ \mathbf{k}_i \leftarrow_{\mathrm{R}} \mathbb{Z}_p^{k+1} \ \text{for } i \in [n].$$

Select a key-binding secure symmetric encryption scheme $(\mathsf{E}, \mathsf{D})$ with the key space $\mathcal{K} := \mathbb{G}_1$ and a collision-resilient hash function $\mathsf{h} \leftarrow_{\mathrm{R}} \mathcal{H}$ mapping from $\{0,1\}^*$ to $\mathbb{Z}_p$. The master public key is

$$\mathsf{mpk} := \left( \mathcal{PG}, (\mathsf{E}, \mathsf{D}), \mathsf{h}; \ \begin{array}{l} [\mathbf{A}^\top]_1, \{[\mathbf{A}^\top \mathbf{k}_i]_1\}_{i=1}^n, [\mathbf{A}^\top \mathbf{X}]_1, [\mathbf{A}^\top \mathbf{Y}]_1 \\ [\mathbf{B}]_2, \qquad\qquad\qquad [\mathbf{X}\mathbf{B}]_2, \ [\mathbf{Y}\mathbf{B}]_2 \end{array} \right)$$

and the master secret key is $\mathsf{msk} := \{\mathbf{k}_i\}_{i=1}^n$.
– KeyGen $(\mathsf{msk}, \mathsf{mpk}, i)$: Output the secret key $\mathsf{sk}_i := \mathbf{k}_i$.
– Enc $(\mathsf{mpk}, m, S)$: Let $\ell := |S|$ and $S = \{i_1, \dots, i_\ell\} \subseteq U$. Sample $\mathbf{r} \leftarrow_{\mathrm{R}} \mathbb{Z}_p^k$ and compute $[\mathbf{u}^\top]_1 := [\mathbf{r}^\top \mathbf{A}^\top]_1$. Select session key $K \leftarrow_{\mathrm{R}} \mathbb{G}_1$ and compute

$$c_0 := \mathsf{E}_K(m), \ c_1 := [\mathbf{r}^\top \mathbf{A}^\top \mathbf{k}_{i_1}]_1 \cdot K, \ \dots, \ c_\ell := [\mathbf{r}^\top \mathbf{A}^\top \mathbf{k}_{i_\ell}]_1 \cdot K$$

Choose a random permutation $\tau$ over $[\ell]$ and compute

$$[\boldsymbol{\pi}]_1 := [\mathbf{r}^\top \mathbf{A}^\top (\mathbf{X} + \alpha \cdot \mathbf{Y})]_1$$

where $\alpha := \mathsf{h}([\mathbf{u}^\top]_1, c_0, c_{\tau(1)}, \dots, c_{\tau(\ell)})$. The ciphertext is

$$\mathsf{ct} := ( \ [\mathbf{u}^\top]_1, \ c_0, \ c_{\tau(1)}, \ \dots, \ c_{\tau(\ell)},, \ [\boldsymbol{\pi}]_1 \ ).$$

– Dec$(\mathsf{mpk}, \mathsf{ct}, \mathsf{sk}_i)$: Parse $\mathsf{ct}$ as $([\mathbf{u}^\top]_1, c_0, \bar{c}_1, \dots, \bar{c}_\ell, [\boldsymbol{\pi}]_1)$ and $\mathsf{sk}_i$ as $\mathbf{k}_i$. Compute $\alpha = \mathsf{h}([\mathbf{u}^\top]_1, c_0, \bar{c}_1, \dots, \bar{c}_\ell)$ and check

$$e([\boldsymbol{\pi}]_1, [\mathbf{B}]_2) \overset{?}{=} e([\mathbf{u}^\top]_1, [(\mathbf{X} + \alpha \cdot \mathbf{Y})\mathbf{B}]_2). \tag{1}$$

If Eq. (1) does not hold, return $\perp$; otherwise, do the following two steps from $j := 1$.
1. Compute $K' := \bar{c}_j / [\mathbf{u}^\top \mathbf{k}_i]_1$ and $m' := \mathsf{D}_{K'}(c_0)$. If $m' \neq \perp$, return $m'$ and halt; otherwise, go to the second step.
2. If $j = \ell$, return $\perp$ and halt; otherwise, do the first step with $j := j + 1$.

**Correctness.** For any ciphertext $\mathsf{ct} := ([\mathbf{u}^\top]_1, c_0, \bar{c}_1, \dots, \bar{c}_\ell, [\boldsymbol{\pi}]_1)$ for set $S \subseteq U$ produced by Enc, we have

$$e([\boldsymbol{\pi}]_1, [\mathbf{B}]_2) = e([\mathbf{r}^\top \mathbf{A}^\top (\mathbf{X} + \alpha \cdot \mathbf{Y})]_1, [\mathbf{B}]_2) = e([\mathbf{u}^\top]_1, [(\mathbf{X} + \alpha \cdot \mathbf{Y})\mathbf{B}]_2)$$

where $\alpha = \mathsf{h}([\mathbf{u}^\top]_1, c_0, \bar{c}_1, \dots, \bar{c}_\ell)$. That is, the ciphertext always satisfies Eq. (1). Given a secret key $\mathsf{sk}_i = \mathbf{k}_i$ for $i \in S$, we know that there exists $i' \in [\ell]$ such that $c_{i'} = [\mathbf{r}^\top \mathbf{A}^\top \mathbf{k}_i]_1 \cdot K$. The correctness of our ANOBE then follows from the following two observations:

1. For each $j < i'$, we know that $c_j = [\mathbf{r}^\top \mathbf{A}^\top \mathbf{k}_{j'}]_1 \cdot K$ for some $j' \in S \setminus \{i\}$, and thus we have

$$c_j / [\mathbf{u}^\top \mathbf{k}_i]_1 \neq K$$

   with overwhelming probability. From the key-binding feature of $(\mathsf{E}, \mathsf{D})$, the decryption algorithm Dec will return nothing before the $i'$-th iteration.
2. It is easy to see that

$$c_{i'} / [\mathbf{u}^\top \mathbf{k}_i]_1 = K.$$

   By the correctness of $(\mathsf{E}, \mathsf{D})$, the decryption algorithm Dec will return $m$ in the $i'$-th iteration.

### 4.2    Security Result and Proof Overview

We prove the following theorem.

**Theorem 2.** *Our broadcast encryption described in Sect. 4.1 is ANO-IND-CCA secure assuming that: (1) $\mathcal{H}$ is collision-resistant; (2) the $\mathcal{D}_k$-MDDH assumption holds in $\mathbb{G}_1$; (3) the $\mathcal{D}_k$-KerMDH assumptions holds in $\mathbb{G}_2$; (4) $(\mathsf{E}, \mathsf{D})$ is semantically secure. Concretely, for any adversary $\mathcal{A}$, there exist algorithms $\mathcal{B}_1, \mathcal{B}_2, \mathcal{B}_3, \mathcal{B}_4$, such that*

$$\mathsf{Adv}_{\mathcal{A}}^{\mathsf{BE}}(\lambda) \leq \mathsf{Adv}_{\mathcal{B}_1, \mathbb{G}_1}^{\mathsf{mddh}}(\lambda) + \mathsf{Adv}_{\mathcal{B}_2}^{\mathsf{hash}}(\lambda) + \mathsf{Adv}_{\mathcal{B}_3, \mathbb{G}_2}^{\mathsf{kmdh}}(\lambda) + 2 \cdot \mathsf{Adv}_{\mathcal{B}_4}^{\mathsf{se}}(\lambda) + O(1/p)$$

*and* $\mathsf{Time}(\mathcal{B}_1), \mathsf{Time}(\mathcal{B}_2), \mathsf{Time}(\mathcal{B}_3), \mathsf{Time}(\mathcal{B}_4) \approx \mathsf{Time}(\mathcal{A})$.

We prove the theorem via the following game sequence. A proof sketch for each step will be given and more details can be found in the full paper.

$\mathsf{Game}_0$. This game is identical to the real game described in Sect. 2.1. The challenge ciphertext for $(m_0, m_1, S_0, S_1)$ where $S_0 = \{i_{1,0}, \dots, i_{\ell,0}\}$ and $S_1 = \{i_{1,1}, \dots, i_{\ell,1}\}$ is of form

$$\mathsf{ct}^* := (\ \mathsf{ct}_1^* := ([\mathbf{u}^{*\top}]_1, c_0^*, c_1^*, \dots, c_\ell^*),\ [\boldsymbol{\pi}^*]_1 := [\mathbf{u}^{*\top}(\mathbf{X} + \alpha^* \cdot \mathbf{Y})]_1\ )$$

where $\mathbf{u}^* \leftarrow_R \mathsf{span}(\mathbf{A})$, $\alpha^* = \mathsf{h}(\mathsf{ct}_1^*)$ and we compute

$$c_0^* = \mathsf{E}_{K^*}(m_b) \quad \text{and} \quad c_j^* = [\mathbf{u}^{*\top} \mathbf{k}_{i_{\tau(j),b}}]_1 \cdot K^*, \quad \forall j \in [\ell]$$

with $K^* \leftarrow_R \mathbb{G}_1$ and random permutation $\tau$ over $[\ell]$. On input $(\mathsf{ct}, i)$, parse

$$\mathsf{ct} = (\mathsf{ct}_1 = ([\mathbf{u}^\top]_1, c_0, c_1, \ldots, c_\ell), [\boldsymbol{\pi}]_1),$$

compute $\alpha = \mathsf{h}(\mathsf{ct}_1)$ and reject the query if

$$(a) \quad \mathsf{ct} = \mathsf{ct}^* \quad \text{or} \quad (b) \quad e([\boldsymbol{\pi}]_1, [\mathbf{B}]_2) \neq e([\mathbf{u}^\top]_1, [(\mathbf{X} + \alpha \cdot \mathbf{Y})\mathbf{B}]_2).$$

Then recover $m$ using $\mathbf{k}_i$ as Dec and return $m$. We let $\mathsf{Win}_i$ denote the event that $\mathcal{A}$ guesses $b$ correctly in $\mathsf{Game}_i$. Since $\mathsf{Game}_0$ perfectly simulates the real game, we have $\mathsf{Adv}_{\mathcal{A}}^{\mathsf{BE}}(1^\lambda) = |\Pr[\mathsf{Win}_0] - 1/2|$.

$\mathsf{Game}_1$. This game is identical to $\mathsf{Game}_0$ except that we sample $\mathbf{u}^* \leftarrow_R \mathbb{Z}_p^{k+1}$ when generating the challenge ciphertext $\mathsf{ct}^*$. This game is indistinguishable from $\mathsf{Game}_0$ under the $\mathcal{D}_k$-MDDH assumption. Formally, we have the following lemma and the proof is analgous to that for Lemma 2.

**Lemma 7 ($\mathsf{Game}_1 \approx_c \mathsf{Game}_0$).** *There exists an adversary $\mathcal{B}_1$ such that*

$$|\Pr[\mathsf{Win}_1] - \Pr[\mathsf{Win}_0]| \leq \mathsf{Adv}_{\mathcal{B}_1, \mathbb{G}_1}^{\mathsf{mddh}}(\lambda)$$

$\mathsf{Game}_2$. This game is identical to $\mathsf{Game}_1$ except that $\mathsf{DecO}$, on input $(\mathsf{ct}, i)$, returns $\bot$ if $(a)$ or $(b)$ or

$$(c) \quad \mathsf{ct}_1 \neq \mathsf{ct}_1^* \text{ but } \alpha = \alpha^*.$$

By the collision-resilience of $\mathcal{H}$, this game is indistinguishable from $\mathsf{Game}_1$. Formally, we have the following lemma and the proof is similar to that for Lemma 4.

**Lemma 8 ($\mathsf{Game}_2 \approx_c \mathsf{Game}_1$).** *There exists an algorithm $\mathcal{B}_2$ such that*

$$|\Pr[\mathsf{Win}_2] - \Pr[\mathsf{Win}_1]| \leq \mathsf{Adv}_{\mathcal{B}_2}^{\mathsf{hash}}(\lambda)$$

$\mathsf{Game}_3$. This game is identical to $\mathsf{Game}_2$ except the following substitution:

$$(b)\ e([\boldsymbol{\pi}]_1, [\mathbf{B}]_2) \neq e([\mathbf{u}^\top]_1, [(\mathbf{X} + \alpha \cdot \mathbf{Y})\mathbf{B}]_2) \longmapsto (b')\ [\boldsymbol{\pi}]_1 \neq [\mathbf{u}^\top(\mathbf{X} + \alpha \cdot \mathbf{Y})]_1.$$

This game is the same as $\mathsf{Game}_2$ until $\mathcal{A}$ sends $\mathsf{DecO}$ a query which is rejected by condition $(b')$ but survives under condition $(b)$. One can see that such a query immediately gives a solution to the $\mathcal{D}_k$-KerMDH problem w.r.t $[\mathbf{B}]_2$. Formally, we have the following lemma.

**Lemma 9 ($\mathsf{Game}_3 \approx_c \mathsf{Game}_2$).** *There exists an algorithm $\mathcal{B}_3$ such that*

$$|\Pr[\mathsf{Win}_3] - \Pr[\mathsf{Win}_2]| \leq \mathsf{Adv}_{\mathcal{B}_3, \mathbb{G}_2}^{\mathsf{kmdh}}(\lambda)$$

$\mathsf{Game}_4$. This game is identical to $\mathsf{Game}_3$ except the following substitution

$$(b')\ [\boldsymbol{\pi}]_1 \neq [\mathbf{u}^\top(\mathbf{X} + \alpha \cdot \mathbf{Y})]_1 \longmapsto (b'')\ \mathbf{u} \notin \mathsf{span}(\mathbf{A}) \parallel [\boldsymbol{\pi}]_1 \neq [\mathbf{u}^\top(\mathbf{X} + \alpha \cdot \mathbf{Y})]_1.$$

Here "$\parallel$" denotes the OR operation which neglects the second operand if the first one is satisfied. We have the following lemma stating that this game is statistically close to $\mathsf{Game}_3$.

**Lemma 10** (Game$_4 \approx_s$ Game$_3$). $|\Pr[\mathsf{Win}_4] - \Pr[\mathsf{Win}_3]| \leq O(1/p)$.
Let $q_D$ be the number of decryption queries. The lemma will be proved in $q_D$ steps. In the $j$-th step, assuming that the first $j-1$ decryption queries have been processed with condition $(b'')$, we demonstrate that the $j$-th query with $\mathbf{u} \notin \mathsf{span}(\mathbf{A})$ can be rejected by condition $(a), (b'), (c)$ with high probability. This simply follows from Lemma 1 (the core lemma).

To complete the proof of Theorem 2, we show the following lemma.

**Lemma 11. (Bounding** $\Pr[\mathsf{Win}_4]$**).** *There exists an algorithm* $\mathcal{B}_4$ *such that*

$$\Pr[\mathsf{Win}_4] \leq 1/2 + 2 \cdot \mathsf{Adv}^{\mathsf{se}}_{\mathcal{B}_4}(\lambda)$$

To prove the lemma, we consider two cases: (1) when $Q_{\mathsf{sk}} \cap (S_0 \cap S_1) = \emptyset$, we can prove that $[\mathbf{u}^{*\top}\mathbf{k}_i]_1$ for $i \in S_b$ are independently and uniformly distributed over $\mathbb{G}_1$, which hide both $S_b$ and $K^*$. The proof is similar to the proof of Lemma 6. Then the semantic security of $(\mathsf{E}, \mathsf{D})$ allows us to hide $m_b$; (2) when $Q_{\mathsf{sk}} \cap (S_0 \cap S_1) \neq \emptyset$, we can only prove that $[\mathbf{u}^{*\top}\mathbf{k}_i]_1$ for $i \in S_b \setminus S_{1-b}$ are randomly distributed, but it is sufficient for proving the lemma since $m_0 = m_1$.

# 5    Conclusion

In this paper, we described two concrete ANOBE schemes. The first one is an instantiation of Libert *et al.*'s generic ANOBE. However, by working out the proof directly, we achieved a constantly tight reduction to standard assumptions. Furthermore, we pointed out that this scheme supports fast decryption for free and thus enjoys shorter ciphertexts. By the second scheme, we showed how to shorten the ciphertext again while preserving the tightness at the cost of slower decryption.

**Acknowledgment.** We greatly thank Benoît Libert for his encouragement and support. We also thank all anonymous reviewers for their constructive comments.

# References

[ABN10]  Abdalla, M., Bellare, M., Neven, G.: Robust encryption. In: Micciancio, D. (ed.) TCC 2010. LNCS, vol. 5978, pp. 480–497. Springer, Heidelberg (2010). https://doi.org/10.1007/978-3-642-11799-2_28

[BBS03]  Bellare, M., Boldyreva, A., Staddon, J.: Randomness re-use in multi-recipient encryption schemeas. In: Desmedt, Y.G. (ed.) PKC 2003. LNCS, vol. 2567, pp. 85–99. Springer, Heidelberg (2003). https://doi.org/10.1007/3-540-36288-6_7

[BBW06]  Barth, A., Boneh, D., Waters, B.: Privacy in encrypted content distribution using private broadcast encryption. In: Di Crescenzo, G., Rubin, A. (eds.) FC 2006. LNCS, vol. 4107, pp. 52–64. Springer, Heidelberg (2006). https://doi.org/10.1007/11889663_4

[Ber91]   Berkovits, S.: How to broadcast a secret. In: Davies, D.W. (ed.) EURO-
          CRYPT 1991. LNCS, vol. 547, pp. 535–541. Springer, Heidelberg (1991).
          https://doi.org/10.1007/3-540-46416-6_50

[BGW05]   Boneh, D., Gentry, C., Waters, B.: Collusion resistant broadcast encryp-
          tion with short ciphertexts and private keys. In: Shoup, V. (ed.) CRYPTO
          2005. LNCS, vol. 3621, pp. 258–275. Springer, Heidelberg (2005). https://
          doi.org/10.1007/11535218_16

[BSW11]   Boneh, D., Sahai, A., Waters, B.: Functional encryption: definitions
          and challenges. In: Ishai, Y. (ed.) TCC 2011. LNCS, vol. 6597, pp.
          253–273. Springer, Heidelberg (2011). https://doi.org/10.1007/978-3-642-
          19571-6_16

[CCS09]   Camenisch, J., Chandran, N., Shoup, V.: A public key encryption scheme
          secure against key dependent chosen plaintext and adaptive chosen cipher-
          text attacks. In: Joux, A. (ed.) EUROCRYPT 2009. LNCS, vol. 5479, pp.
          351–368. Springer, Heidelberg (2009). https://doi.org/10.1007/978-3-642-
          01001-9_20

[CGW15]   Chen, J., Gay, R., Wee, H.: Improved dual system ABE in prime-order
          groups via predicate encodings. In: Oswald, E., Fischlin, M. (eds.) EURO-
          CRYPT 2015. LNCS, vol. 9057, pp. 595–624. Springer, Heidelberg (2015).
          https://doi.org/10.1007/978-3-662-46803-6_20

[CHK04]   Canetti, R., Halevi, S., Katz, J.: Chosen-ciphertext security from identity-
          based encryption. In: Cachin, C., Camenisch, J.L. (eds.) EUROCRYPT
          2004. LNCS, vol. 3027, pp. 207–222. Springer, Heidelberg (2004). https://
          doi.org/10.1007/978-3-540-24676-3_13

[CS98]    Cramer, R., Shoup, V.: A practical public key cryptosystem provably
          secure against adaptive chosen ciphertext attack. In: Krawczyk, H. (ed.)
          CRYPTO 1998. LNCS, vol. 1462, pp. 13–25. Springer, Heidelberg (1998).
          https://doi.org/10.1007/BFb0055717

[CS02]    Cramer, R., Shoup, V.: Universal hash proofs and a paradigm for adaptive
          chosen ciphertext secure public-key encryption. In: Knudsen, L.R. (ed.)
          EUROCRYPT 2002. LNCS, vol. 2332, pp. 45–64. Springer, Heidelberg
          (2002). https://doi.org/10.1007/3-540-46035-7_4

[DPP07]   Delerablée, C., Paillier, P., Pointcheval, D.: Fully collusion secure dynamic
          broadcast encryption with constant-size ciphertexts or decryption keys. In:
          Takagi, T., Okamoto, T., Okamoto, E., Okamoto, T. (eds.) Pairing 2007.
          LNCS, vol. 4575, pp. 39–59. Springer, Heidelberg (2007). https://doi.org/
          10.1007/978-3-540-73489-5_4

[EHK+13]  Escala, A., Herold, G., Kiltz, E., Ràfols, C., Villar, J.: An algebraic
          framework for Diffie-Hellman assumptions. In: Canetti, R., Garay, J.A.
          (eds.) CRYPTO 2013. LNCS, vol. 8043, pp. 129–147. Springer, Heidelberg
          (2013). https://doi.org/10.1007/978-3-642-40084-1_8

[Fis99]   Fischlin, M.: Pseudorandom function tribe ensembles based on one-way
          permutations: improvements and applications. In: Stern, J. (ed.) EURO-
          CRYPT 1999. LNCS, vol. 1592, pp. 432–445. Springer, Heidelberg (1999).
          https://doi.org/10.1007/3-540-48910-X_30

[FN94]    Fiat, A., Naor, M.: Broadcast encryption. In: Stinson, D.R. (ed.) CRYPTO
          1993. LNCS, vol. 773, pp. 480–491. Springer, Heidelberg (1994). https://
          doi.org/10.1007/3-540-48329-2_40

[FP12]  Fazio, N., Perera, I.M.: Outsider-anonymous broadcast encryption with sublinear ciphertexts. In: Fischlin, M., Buchmann, J., Manulis, M. (eds.) PKC 2012. LNCS, vol. 7293, pp. 225–242. Springer, Heidelberg (2012). https://doi.org/10.1007/978-3-642-30057-8_14

[GHKW16]  Gay, R., Hofheinz, D., Kiltz, E., Wee, H.: Tightly CCA-secure encryption without pairings. In: Fischlin, M., Coron, J.-S. (eds.) EUROCRYPT 2016. LNCS, vol. 9665, pp. 1–27. Springer, Heidelberg (2016). https://doi.org/10.1007/978-3-662-49890-3_1

[GPSW06]  Goyal, V., Pandey, O., Sahai, A., Waters, B.: Attribute-based encryption for fine-grained access control of encrypted data. In: ACM CCS 2006, pp. 89–98. ACM Press (2006)

[Gro06]  Groth, J.: Simulation-sound NIZK proofs for a practical language and constant size group signatures. In: Lai, X., Chen, K. (eds.) ASIACRYPT 2006. LNCS, vol. 4284, pp. 444–459. Springer, Heidelberg (2006). https://doi.org/10.1007/11935230_29

[GW09]  Gentry, C., Waters, B.: Adaptive security in broadcast encryption systems (with short ciphertexts). In: Joux, A. (ed.) EUROCRYPT 2009. LNCS, vol. 5479, pp. 171–188. Springer, Heidelberg (2009). https://doi.org/10.1007/978-3-642-01001-9_10

[Hof17]  Hofheinz, D.: Adaptive partitioning. In: Coron, J.-S., Nielsen, J.B. (eds.) EUROCRYPT 2017. LNCS, vol. 10212, pp. 489–518. Springer, Cham (2017). https://doi.org/10.1007/978-3-319-56617-7_17

[HWL+16]  He, K., Weng, J., Liu, J., Liu, J.K., Liu, W., Deng, R.H.: Anonymous identity-based broadcast encryption with chosen-ciphertext security. In: ASIACCS 2016, pp. 247–255. ACM Press (2016)

[KD04]  Kurosawa, K., Desmedt, Y.: A new paradigm of hybrid encryption scheme. In: Franklin, M. (ed.) CRYPTO 2004. LNCS, vol. 3152, pp. 426–442. Springer, Heidelberg (2004). https://doi.org/10.1007/978-3-540-28628-8_26

[KS12]  Kiayias, A., Samari, K.: Lower bounds for private broadcast encryption. In: Kirchner, M., Ghosal, D. (eds.) IH 2012. LNCS, vol. 7692, pp. 176–190. Springer, Heidelberg (2013). https://doi.org/10.1007/978-3-642-36373-3_12

[Kur02]  Kurosawa, K.: Multi-recipient public-key encryption with shortened ciphertext. In: Naccache, D., Paillier, P. (eds.) PKC 2002. LNCS, vol. 2274, pp. 48–63. Springer, Heidelberg (2002). https://doi.org/10.1007/3-540-45664-3_4

[KW15]  Kiltz, E., Wee, H.: Quasi-adaptive NIZK for linear subspaces revisited. In: Oswald, E., Fischlin, M. (eds.) EUROCRYPT 2015. LNCS, vol. 9057, pp. 101–128. Springer, Heidelberg (2015). https://doi.org/10.1007/978-3-662-46803-6_4

[LOS+10]  Lewko, A., Okamoto, T., Sahai, A., Takashima, K., Waters, B.: Fully secure functional encryption: attribute-based encryption and (hierarchical) inner product encryption. In: Gilbert, H. (ed.) EUROCRYPT 2010. LNCS, vol. 6110, pp. 62–91. Springer, Heidelberg (2010). https://doi.org/10.1007/978-3-642-13190-5_4

[LPQ12]  Libert, B., Paterson, K.G., Quaglia, E.A.: Anonymous broadcast encryption: adaptive security and efficient constructions in the standard model. In: Fischlin, M., Buchmann, J., Manulis, M. (eds.) PKC 2012. LNCS, vol. 7293, pp. 206–224. Springer, Heidelberg (2012). https://doi.org/10.1007/978-3-642-30057-8_13

[Moh10]  Mohassel, P.: A closer look at anonymity and robustness in encryption schemes. In: Abe, M. (ed.) ASIACRYPT 2010. LNCS, vol. 6477, pp. 501–518. Springer, Heidelberg (2010). https://doi.org/10.1007/978-3-642-17373-8_29

[MRV16]  Morillo, P., Ràfols, C., Villar, J.L.: The kernel matrix Diffie-Hellman assumption. In: Cheon, J.H., Takagi, T. (eds.) ASIACRYPT 2016. LNCS, vol. 10031, pp. 729–758. Springer, Heidelberg (2016). https://doi.org/10.1007/978-3-662-53887-6_27

[NNL01]  Naor, D., Naor, M., Lotspiech, J.: Revocation and tracing schemes for stateless receivers. In: Kilian, J. (ed.) CRYPTO 2001. LNCS, vol. 2139, pp. 41–62. Springer, Heidelberg (2001). https://doi.org/10.1007/3-540-44647-8_3

[OT10]  Okamoto, T., Takashima, K.: Fully secure functional encryption with general relations from the decisional linear assumption. In: Rabin, T. (ed.) CRYPTO 2010. LNCS, vol. 6223, pp. 191–208. Springer, Heidelberg (2010). https://doi.org/10.1007/978-3-642-14623-7_11

[Sha84]  Shamir, A.: Identity-based cryptosystems and signature schemes. In: Blakley, G.R., Chaum, D. (eds.) CRYPTO 1984. LNCS, vol. 196, pp. 47–53. Springer, Heidelberg (1985). https://doi.org/10.1007/3-540-39568-7_5

[SW05]  Sahai, A., Waters, B.: Fuzzy identity-based encryption. In: Cramer, R. (ed.) EUROCRYPT 2005. LNCS, vol. 3494, pp. 457–473. Springer, Heidelberg (2005). https://doi.org/10.1007/11426639_27

[Wee10]  Wee, H.: Efficient chosen-ciphertext security via extractable hash proofs. In: Rabin, T. (ed.) CRYPTO 2010. LNCS, vol. 6223, pp. 314–332. Springer, Heidelberg (2010). https://doi.org/10.1007/978-3-642-14623-7_17

[Wee16]  Wee, H.: Déjà Q: encore! Un petit IBE. In: Kushilevitz, E., Malkin, T. (eds.) TCC 2016. LNCS, vol. 9563, pp. 237–258. Springer, Heidelberg (2016). https://doi.org/10.1007/978-3-662-49099-0_9

[YFDL04]  Yao, D., Fazio, N., Dodis, Y., Lysyanskaya, A.: ID-based encryption for complex hierarchies with applications to forward security and broadcast encryption. In: ACM CCS 2004, pp. 354–363. ACM Press (2004)

# Time-Based Direct Revocable Ciphertext-Policy Attribute-Based Encryption with Short Revocation List

Joseph K. Liu[1(✉)], Tsz Hon Yuen[2], Peng Zhang[3], and Kaitai Liang[4]

[1] Faculty of Information Technology, Monash University, Melbourne, Australia
joseph.liu@monash.edu
[2] Huawei, Singapore, Singapore
[3] Shenzhen University, Shenzhen, China
[4] University of Surrey, Guildford, UK

**Abstract.** In this paper, we propose an efficient revocable Ciphertext-Policy Attribute-Based Encryption (CP-ABE) scheme. We base on the direct revocation approach, by embedding the revocation list into ciphertext. However, since the revocation list will grow longer as time goes by, we further leverage this by proposing a secret key time validation technique so that users will have their keys expired on a date and the revocation list only needs to include those user keys revoked before their intended expired date (e.g. those user keys which have been stolen before expiry). These keys can be removed from the revocation list after their expiry date in order to keep the revocation list short, as these keys can no longer be used to decrypt ciphertext generated after their expiry time. This technique is derived from Hierarchical Identity-based Encryption (HIBE) mechanism and thus time periods are in hierarchical structure: year, month, day. Users with validity of the whole year can decrypt any ciphertext associated with time period of any month or any day within the year. By using this technique, the size of public parameters and user secret key can be greatly reduced. A bonus advantage of this technique is the support of discontinuity of user validity (e.g. taking no-paid leave).

## 1 Introduction

Attribute-Based Encryption (ABE) is a generalization of Identity-Based Encryption (IBE) [5,6,11–13,48]. It provides flexibility of data sharing for system users in the sense that a data encryptor is allowed to specify some descriptive values $x$ for an encryption and thus, the encryption can be decrypted successfully by a secret key associated with some descriptive values $y$ matching $x$. ABE has many network applications, such as cloud computing [23,35], cloud storage systems [20,21,34,50] and medical e-healthcare systems [7,17,22,38] etc. ABE can be classified into two different types: one is Key-Policy ABE (KP-ABE), and the other is Ciphertext-Policy ABE (CP-ABE). In a KP-ABE system, ciphertexts are associated with attribute sets and secret keys are associated with access

© Springer International Publishing AG, part of Springer Nature 2018
B. Preneel and F. Vercauteren (Eds.): ACNS 2018, LNCS 10892, pp. 516–534, 2018.
https://doi.org/10.1007/978-3-319-93387-0_27

policies. On the opposite side, in a CP-ABE scheme ciphertexts are related to access policies, and attribute sets are tagged with secret keys.

Before deploying ABE into any practical scenarios, one has to solve for the user revocation problem. No organization will be happy to see that any of its revoked users can still be able to decrypt the document designated for its users.

When we talk about revocability in ABE, there are different levels of revocation:

1. **Attribute Revocation.** In this case, the user has changed his/her attributes. For example, the original attributes for Alice are {Physics, Student, University A}. Now she has changed to {Chemistry, Student, University A}. Therefore, the original Physics attribute should be revoked (but not Student or University A).
2. **User Revocation.** In this case, the user has left the organization. That is, all attributes have to be revoked. In the previous example of Attribute Revocation, Alice has left University A and therefore the user Alice should be revoked.
3. **Key Revocation.** In this case, the secret key of the user is revoked. This is the most generalized level of revocation. This can be happened in different scenarios. For example, the user has left the organization (case (2)). Or if the user has lost his secret key (and got a replacement key), the old one has to be revoked. It can also cover case (1): If Alice changes her attribute from Physics to Chemistry, her old key is revoked while she has been issued with a new key associated with her new attribute.

   Usually in this case the key is also associated with an identity or a serial number, which is used in the revocation process by the authority. The encryptor does not need to know this identity or number. In the rest of this paper, we refer to *revocation* as this case (key revocation).

## 1.1 Different Approaches for Revocable ABE

There are several approaches to tackle the problem of revocability in ABE:

1. **Key Update for Non-revoked Users.** This is also called the *Indirect Approach*. In this approach, every user has a secret key with a state. The authority will execute a key update algorithm for every non-revoked users. The keys for revoked users will not be updated. Upon the update, a new state will be issued to the secret key. Ciphertext is generated according to the current state. Therefore those revoked users who only have the secret keys of previous state(s) cannot decrypt the ciphertext which is associated with the new state.

   If the ciphertext is stored on cloud, those revoked users however are still able to decrypt the old ciphertext (generated with previous states). In order to hinder this vulnerability, a ciphertext update algorithm can be executed so that all old ciphertexts will be modified to associate with the current state. In this way, revoked users (whose secret keys are associated with an old state) can no longer decrypt any old ciphertext from the cloud as it has been updated to the current state which is only decryptable by a secret key with the new state.

Nevertheless we only regard the ciphertext update as an optional feature, as we have no way to prevent a revoked user from downloading the ciphertext (and thus decrypting the ciphertext) before he has been revoked.

*The main issue of the key update approach is the inability of instant user revocation.* Suppose Alice is revoked now and the next key update algorithm is scheduled at the 1st of coming month. Alice is still able to decrypt any newly generated ciphertext from now to the end of this month. (Even if the cloud is equipped with ciphertext update, Alice cannot decrypt only those old ciphertext but still can decrypt those newly generated one.) One may try to argue that the authority may execute the key update algorithm once there is any revoked user. In the point of view of security, this action can block the loophole of inability instant user revocation. Nevertheless, it is definitely not practical especially if there are a large number of non-revoked users. In a large organization, there may be a new revoked user in every hour or even every minute. It is impossible to ask every non-revoked user to update their key every minute! If we schedule a longer key update period, the instant user revocation problem will be worse then.

2. **Embedding Revocation List into Ciphertext.** This is also called the *Direct Approach.* In this approach, there is a public revocation list. The encryptor embeds the latest revocation list into the ciphertext so that only those users not in the revocation list and satisfying the predicate (attributes-policy matching) can decrypt the ciphertext. This approach can provide instant user revocation (and thus solve the problem from the indirect approach). No key update is required in this approach.

*However, there is another practical problem with this approach.* The revocation list will grow longer as time goes by. If the organization is large, the revocation list will become an efficiency bottleneck for the encryption and decryption as it will continue to grow all the time. There is no way to reduce or delete the revocation list, unless the revoked user re-joins the organization in the future. This is not likely to happen in most of the scenarios though.

3. **Cloud-Assisted.** Another approach is to make use of the cloud assistance. In this approach, the decryption ability is split into two halves. The first half is owned by the user while another half is owned by the cloud. The cloud needs to partially decrypt the ciphertext into an intermediate data first, which is then sent to the user for the second level decryption. If the user is revoked, the cloud refuses to execute the first level decryption. Then the revoked user cannot decrypt the ciphertext without the assistance from the cloud.

This is the simplest way to achieve user revocation for ABE. *In spite of that, the cloud will be very busy if the number of users is large*, as the decryption of every user requires the assistance from the cloud.

More examples on each approach will be given in Sect. 2.

## 1.2   A Naïve Approach

One may immediately think of a naïve approach by combining the indirect and direct approaches together in order to possess the merits from both sides. Intuitively the simple combination is to use a key update ABE (the indirect revocable ABE) to encrypt the plaintext first into the first-level ciphertext. Then the resulting ciphertext is further encrypted using another ABE with revocation list embedded into the ciphertext (the direct revocable ABE) as the second-level. If a user is revoked before the next key update period, since his identity has been put into the revocation list embedded into the second-level ciphertext (generated by the direct revocable ABE), he cannot decrypt it. On the other side, if the revoked user's key has been expired (that is, not being updated as it has been revoked), his identity is not needed to be put into the revocation list by the direct revocable ABE as the revoked key cannot be used to decrypt the first-level ciphertext (generated by the indirect revocable ABE) even though it can still decrypt the second level ciphertext. In this way, the revocation list can be kept short while instant revocation can be achieved and thus no frequent key update is required.

This naïve approach seems working fine, if we do not consider collusion attack. Simply speaking, collusion attack in ABE refers to two different users who both cannot decrypt the ciphertext individually but they can succeed to do so if they are colluding with each other. Suppose Alice is revoked just right now (before the next key update period) and therefore her identity Alice is in the revocation list embedded into the second-level ciphertext. Bob is another revoked user who was revoked in the previous time period. Thus his key has not been updated in the current time period and his identity Bob is not in the revocation list embedded into the second-level ciphertext. It is obviously that both Alice and Bob cannot decrypt the combined ciphertext individually. However, if they are working together, they can successfully decrypt it: Bob can use his secret key to decrypt the second-level ciphertext (as his identity is not in the revocation list) and he can pass the resulting intermediate data (which has become the first-level ciphertext) to Alice. Alice can use her secret key to decrypt this first-level ciphertext as her key is the most updated one. As a result, Alice and Bob can get the final plaintext if they are working together.

We definitely have to avoid this kind of collusion attack in any circumstance.

## 1.3   Our Contribution

In this paper, we propose an efficient and practical revocable CP-ABE scheme. Our scheme is motivated from the (non-revocable) CP-ABE given in [36] and incorporates the merit from all existing approaches for revocation, yet we do not have the emerged trade-off and we are immune to the collusion attack mentioned above in the naive approach. Namely,

- We have a revocation list, which is used by the encryptor to be embedded into the ciphertext. On the other side, we also have a key update process for non-revoked users at a *reasonable* interval (e.g. once every two years). The revocation list only contains those revoked users whose keys are not expired yet. If their keys are expired (they are not allowed to update their keys as they are revoked), they should not be able to decrypt any ciphertext generated after their expiry date even though they are not included in the revocation list. In other words, they can be removed from the revocation list after the expiry date of their keys and thus *the revocation list can be kept short.*

- Although we still require a key update process for all non-revoked users, we do not need to execute it frequently in order to provide instant key revocation. We argue that most organizations will require their users to renew their contracts at a reasonable time interval (e.g. once every two years). It is practical to renew their secret keys at the time they are renewing their contracts. This time does not need to be synchronized. Every user may have his own time for expiry and renewal.
- We do not need the cloud in our basic system (a cloud-free system). Extension can be made to provide ciphertext update in the cloud (e.g. using the ciphertext update technique in [31,47]) so that revoked users are no longer able to decrypt any ciphertext generated in the past.
- We are immune to the collusion attack mentioned in the naïve approach. Suppose there is a set of users. Anyone in this set cannot decrypt the ciphertext individually. They cannot succeed to do so even if they are working together, or by someone who has the secret keys for all users in this set.
- We use Hierarchical Identity-based Encryption (HIBE) technique to further shorten the size of user secret key. Our time period is *hierarchical.* That is, we have *year*, *month* and *day*. A user with secret key valid for the whole year can derive the key with validity for the underlying months of that year. A user with secret key valid for the whole month can derive the key with validity for the underlying days of that month. With this technique, we can further support discontinuity of user validity, which is believed as a common scenario in the practical world (e.g. no-paid leave).

We provide a concrete construction for our proposed scheme. The size of the ciphertext only depends on the embedded policy (access structure) but NOT the revocation list, though the size of the secret key is linear with the maximum length of the revocation list and the number of attributes of the user. In the decryption, the number of pairing operations only depends on the access structure but NOT the number of users in the revocation list or the total number of users in the system. The performance of our construction enjoys a significant improvement over other similar schemes.

Table 1 gives a functional comparison between other approaches and our proposed approach.

**Table 1.** Features comparison

| Approach | Examples | Features | | | | |
|---|---|---|---|---|---|---|
| | | Instant revoke | No freq. key update | Cloud free | Ciphertext update | Short revo. it. |
| Key update | [9], [1], [47], [31], [39], [40], [26], [29], [27] | × | × | ✓ | Optional | ✓ |
| Embedding revocation list | [2], [1], [4], [33], [28], [8], [49], [15], [25], [16] | ✓ | ✓ | ✓ | Optional | × |
| Cloud-assisted | [30], [19], [43], [32], [44], [14], [45] | ✓ | ✓ | × | ✓ | × |
| Our approach | | ✓ | ✓ | ✓ | Optional | ✓ |

## 2    Related Works

There are several schemes in the literature addressing the problem of revocation in ABE. We briefly describe them using the classification in Sect. 1.[1]

1. **Key Update for Non-revoked Users (Indirect) Approach**. The first revocable ABE was proposed by Boldyreva et al. [9]. It is a KP-ABE. Revocation list is stored in the authority which executes key update algorithm with each non-revoked users (those users not in the revocation list) during a regular time interval. Revoked users (without having their keys updated) cannot decrypt any newly generated ciphertext. Yu et al. [47] proposed another revocable ABE in the context of CP-ABE using key update approach. In addition, they provide a mechanism to update ciphertext so that revoked users cannot decrypt the updated ciphertext in the cloud. Nevertheless, they support policies with logical AND only. A more promising construction was given by Sahai et al. [31]. They provided constructions for both KP-ABE and CP-ABE. There are key update and ciphertext update algorithms. Ciphertext is decryptable only if the encryption time $t < t'$ where $t'$ is the key expiry time. If the user is revoked, ciphertext will be updated so that the newly revoked users cannot decrypt those old ciphertext (those ciphertext generated before the user is revoked). All other users will then run the key update algorithm except the revoked user.

   Later on, Xie et al. [39] (the full version of [40]), proposed a revocable CP-ABE. In their construction, each user has two keys. There is an individual key and also a group key. A group is defined as a set of users with the

---

[1] We exclude the discussion for [46] as it is not an ABE scheme. They require every user to have a private key and public key. Public key is generated by the authority and private key is generated by the encryptor! The encryptor needs to use the private key to encrypt the message. This is not a formal ABE that we are considering and thus it is excluded in our discussion. We also exclude [41,42] as they are pointed out as insecure in [18].

same attributes. Decryption requires to have the group key and the individual user secret key. Revocation is done by updating the keys of non-revoked users. Ciphertext update is also allowed as in [47]. Naruse et al. [26] proposed another CP-ABE with attribute update by the cloud server. The cloud re-encrypts the ciphertext and re-generates new secret key for users, who have updated their attributes. Similar approach has also been suggested in [27,29].

2. **Embedding Revocation List into Ciphertext (Direct) Approach.** Another approach is called direct approach, which requires the encryptor to incorporate the revocation list in the ciphertext. In this way, users in the revocation list cannot decrypt the ciphertext even though their attributes/policy satisfy the policy/attributes associated with the ciphertext. No key update is required using this approach. Attrapadung and Imai [2] proposed a revocable ABE by incorporating the revocation information into the ciphertext. Their approach is to use broadcast encryption. That is, the encryptor needs to know the identities of those *unrevoked* users. They provide a KP-ABE constructions. Later, Attrapadung et al. [4] proposed another revocable KP-ABE. Different from the previous one, this construction only requires the encryptor to know the identities of revoked users (instead of unrevoked users). Wang et al. [33] proposed another revocable KP-ABE using broadcast encryption which requires the encryptor to know the list of unrevoked users. Nieto et al. [28] generalize the revocability technique to Predicate Encryption. They require the encryptor to embed the revocation list into the ciphertext. They use dual pairing vector space as the primitive and thus the number of pairing operations in the decryption is very large (linear with the number of users in the system). Balu and Kuppusamy [8] proposed a revocable CP-ABE by incorporating the revocation list. Encryptor only needs to know the identities of revoked users. However, their model is very weak. They only allow the adversary to query secret key that does not satisfy the challenge access structure AND not in the revocation list. In other words, it does not allow adversary to query a secret key that satisfies the access structure but in the revocation list. (This models the case for revoked users.) Zhang [49] proposed another revocable CP-ABE scheme using similar approach. In addition, the scheme also supports leakage resilient. But the construction only supports attribute-level revocation (the basic level of revocation). Datta et al. [15] proposed a KP-ABE construction using similar approach using multilinear maps. Liu and Wong [25] proposed a CP-ABE construction. Again they deploy similar approach but using matrix representation for users. Thus the size of ciphertext is of size $O(\sqrt{N})$, where $N$ is the total number of users in the system. Recently, Datta et al. [16] proposed another KP-ABE that supports revocability with this approach. This time they use subset difference technique to achieve the purpose.

There is also a construction using either direct and indirect approach. Attrapadung and Imai [1] proposed a KP-ABE which allows the encryptor to use whether direct or indirect mode (but not both).

3. **Cloud-Assisted Approach.** With the assistance of cloud, revocation becomes easier without letting the encryptor to get the revocation list, or

executing any key update for non-revoked users. Earlier stage cloud-assisted scheme [30] only provides ciphertext-update so that revoked users cannot decryp the ciphertext in the cloud. Later on, other cloud-assisted schemes require all decryption must go through the cloud as a partial process. The cloud has the control to refuse the assistance of decryption for revoked users. Without the help from the cloud, no one can decrypt the ciphertext. Hur and Noh [19] proposed a revocable CP-ABE scheme. The data owner first out-sourced the data into the cloud. The cloud then re-encrypts (using a double-encryption technique) according the set of authenticated (valid) membership. The revocation is easy. The cloud just deletes the revoked user from the mem-bership (which is a binary tree). Decryption requires the cloud to process first. It then sends the partially decrypt data to the user. Yang et al. [43] and Shi et al. [32] proposed another cloud-assisted scheme independently. In their schemes, the decryption is split into two halves. The cloud stores the first half and the user stores another half. A complete decryption requires both parts. Yang et al. [44] use similar approach. They further reduce the trust on cloud by increasing the risk of collusion with users. Recently, Cui et al. [14] reduced the trust to the cloud server by letting the cloud server to use a kind of proxy re-encryption key only.

## 3    Definition

### 3.1    Time Period

A time period can be a day, a month or a year.[2] For example, we use "2016-Jun-15" to represent a day; "2016-Dec" to represent a month etc. Our scheme can also support some special case for non-continuity. For example, if the user is going to take no-paid leave from 01 August 2016 to 29 November 2016, then we can just assign the valid period from 15 June 2016 to 31 July 2016 and from 30 November 2016 to 31 December 2016. (Assume today is 15 June 2016 and the user expiries at the end of 2016.)

A decryptable time period is a time period set by the encryptor such that only users with validity completely covered the period can decrypt. (A specific setting is to let the encrypting time to be the decryptable time period.) For example, suppose the decryptable time period is December 2016 and the validity of user secret key is only limited to 31 December 2016. This is not a complete cover and thus this secret key is not able to decrypt. On the opposite, if the decryptable time period is 01 December 2016 and the validity of user secret key is December 2016, then it is able to decrypt as it has a complete cover for the decryptable time period (provided that other conditions are also satisfied).

---

[2] Our scheme can further support more levels of time period, e.g. hours, minutes etc. Yet for simplicity, we limit the description to the *day* level only.

## 3.2    Definition of Revocable Ciphertext-Policy Attribute-Based Encryption

A revocable ciphertext-policy attribute based encryption scheme consists of four algorithms: Setup, KeyGen, Encrypt, Decrypt.

- Setup($1^\kappa, U, R, \mathsf{T}$). Take as input the security parameter $\kappa$, the number of attributes in the system $U$, the maximum number of revoked users in the revocation list $R$ and the depth of the time tree $\mathsf{T}$. It outputs the public parameters $PK$ and a master key $MK$. We omit the description of $\kappa$ in the rest of this paper.
- KeyGen($MK, ID, S, \mathsf{T}$). Take as input the master key $MK$, a user's identity $ID^3$, a set of attributes $S$ and a range of validity time periods $\mathsf{T}$. It outputs a private key $SK_{(ID,S,\mathsf{T})}$.
- Encrypt($PK, m, \mathsf{T}_c, \mathcal{R}, \mathbb{A}$). Take as input the public parameters $PK$, a message $m$, a decryptable time period $\mathsf{T}_c$, a revoked set $\mathcal{R}$ and an access structure $\mathbb{A}$ over the universe of attributes. It outputs a ciphertext $CT$.
- Decrypt($PK, CT, \mathcal{R}, \mathbb{A}, \mathsf{T}_c, SK_{(ID,S,\mathsf{T})}$). Take as input the public parameters $PK$, a ciphertext $CT$, along with a description of a revoked set $\mathcal{R}$, an access policy $\mathbb{A}$ and a decryptable time period $\mathsf{T}_c$, and a private key $SK_{(ID,S,\mathsf{T})}$, which is a private key for the user's identity $ID$, attributes set $S$ and the range of validity time periods $\mathsf{T}$. If the user's identity $ID$ is not in the revoked set $\mathcal{R}$, the set $S$ of attributes satisfies the access structure $\mathbb{A}$ and the range of validity time periods $\mathsf{T}$ completely covers the decryptable time period $\mathsf{T}_c$, then the algorithm will decrypt the ciphertext and return a message $m$. Otherwise it outputs $\perp$.

Note that we do not explicitlly define the key update algorithm as its function can be implicitly covered by the KeyGen algorithm with the new validity time period.

## 3.3    Security Model

We now describe a selective security model for the revocable ciphertext-policy ABE scheme. The security model is described by the following game between a challenger $\mathcal{C}$ and an adversary $\mathcal{A}$. In the game, $\mathcal{A}$ needs to submit an access structure $\mathbb{A}^*$, a revocation list $\mathcal{R}^*$ and a decryptable time period $\mathsf{T}_c^*$ to $\mathcal{C}$ before seeing the public parameter $PK$. At any time $\mathcal{A}$ can query for any private keys that cannot be used to decrypt the challenge ciphertext.

- **Init.** $\mathcal{A}$ needs to submit the challenge access structure $\mathbb{A}^*$, the challenge revocation list $\mathcal{R}^*$ and the challenge decryptable time period $\mathsf{T}_c^*$ to the Challenger $\mathcal{C}$.
- **Setup.** $\mathcal{C}$ runs the Setup algorithm and gives the public parameters $PK$ to the adversary.

---

[3] In practice, this can also be the serial number of a user key in order to achieve key-level revocation.

- **Phase 1.** Adversary $\mathcal{A}$ makes repeated private key queries corresponding to the identity ID, the attribute set $S$ and the range of validity time periods T such that for any single returned secret key $SK_{(ID,S,T)}$, at least one of the following conditions must be fulfilled:
  - $S$ does not satisfy the access structure $\mathbb{A}^*$.
  - $ID \in \mathcal{R}^*$.
  - $T_c^*$ is not completely covered in T.
- **Challenge.** Adversary $\mathcal{A}$ submits two equal length messages $m_0$ and $m_1$. Challenger $\mathcal{C}$ flips a random coin $\beta \in \{0,1\}$ and encrypts $m_\beta$ under the access structure $\mathbb{A}^*$, the revoked set $\mathcal{R}^*$ and the time $T_c^*$. The ciphertext $CT^*$ is given to adversary $\mathcal{A}$.
- **Phase 2.** It is the same as in Phase 1.
- **Guess.** The adversary outputs a guess $\beta'$ for $\beta$.

The advantage of adversary $\mathcal{A}$ in the above game is defined as $Adv_{\mathcal{A}} = Pr[\beta' = \beta] - 1/2$.

**Definition 3.1.** *A revocable ciphertext-policy attribute-based encryption scheme is secure if all polynomial time adversaries have at most a negligible advantage in the above game.*

Other mathematical background is provided in the full version [24].

## 4   Our Scheme

### 4.1   Overview

Our scheme is motivated by the (non-revocable) CP-ABE scheme in [36]. We first add a revocation list in the ciphertext so that users in the revocation list cannot decrypt. We then add time validity to user secret key and a decryptable time period in the ciphertext. Users without having a complete cover of validity for the decryptable time period cannot decrypt. (Readers may refer to Sect. 3.1 for more details.)

Observe that the valid time always have the "AND" relation with the user attributes. Therefore, we have to attach the *time validity* tightly to the secret key in order to avoid the collusion attack. A naïve approach is to treat each time period as an attribute. In the policy, we just need to add the "AND" relation with all valid time periods (that is, time-attributes) together with the original policy. It works fine, if the number of valid time periods in the system is small. Otherwise, the size of public parameters and user secret key will be very large as they grow linear with the number of attributes (that is, number of time periods in this naïve approach). For example, if the system supports up to 10 years and the smallest unit of time period is *day*, then there will be more than 3000 time-attributes in the system!

If the user is revoked before the normal expiry time, the user ID will be put into the revocation list until his expiry time has passed. Anyone whose ID is in the revocation list will not be able to decrypt any ciphertext, regardless of his attributes. The idea of the revocation approach is motived from [3,4].

Also note that we have the same restriction as the scheme in [36] using the decisional BDHE assumption (the first scheme). That is, an attribute can only be used in at most one row in the ciphertext access matrix $M$ (the function $\rho(\cdot)$ is injective). This can be thought of as an attribute appearing in at most one node in a formula. However, this limitation can be easily mitigated by assigning a different string for each time an attribute is associated with a row in an access structure.

## 4.2   Technical Construction

We borrow the idea from the Boneh-Boyen-Goh Hierarchical Identity-based Encryption (HIBE) scheme [10] to apply in our time validity control. We take advantage of the fact that the validity period of a user's key or ciphertext is usually represented as some time interval (e.g. from January to December), instead of some discrete time segments (e.g. January and March and July and December). Therefore, we use a tree-based approach to further improve the efficiency for continuous time interval. The advantage is two-fold. Firstly, the size of the user secret key is reduced. Secondly, if the encryptor wants to encrypt the message for some time interval, then only the user with keys valid in the complete time interval can decrypt. At the same time, the size of the ciphertext is still independent of the length of the time interval.

We use the set-cover approach to select the minimum number of nodes that can represent all the valid time periods. A node (except the root node) in the tree represents a time period. By using HIBE, the user obtains the keys corresponding to these nodes only. Consider the following example:

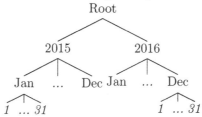

The first level represents the *year*. The second level represents the *month*. The third level represents the *day*.

Suppose an employee joins the company on 29 November 2015 and his contract ends on 31 December 2016. He should obtain keys for the nodes of "2015-Nov-29", "2015-Nov-30", "2015-Dec" and "2016". For the encryptor, he can choose to encrypt a message for a specific day, for a whole month or whole year. The employee who is authorized for the whole month can decrypt the ciphertext for the whole month. On the other hand, if the ciphertext is specified for a single day only, the employee can derive the decryption key from the corresponding month or year key using the HIBE approach.

In order to simplify the description, suppose the time tree has depth $T$ and each node have $z$ children. A time period (e.g. a day, a month, a year) can be represented by a $z$-ary element $(\tau_1, \tau_2, \ldots, \tau_k)$ for some $k < \mathsf{T}$. Our construction is as follows.

1. $\mathsf{Setup}(U, R, \mathsf{T})$: $U$ is the number of attributes in the system. Time is represented as a $z$-ary string $\{1, z\}^{\mathsf{T}-1}$. The maximum number of revoked users is $R - 1$. Choose a bilinear group $\mathbb{G}$ of prime order $p$ with a random generator $g$ and $U$ random elements $h_1, \ldots, h_U, \in \mathbb{G}$. Randomly choose $\alpha, \alpha_0 \in \mathbb{Z}_p$ and $\boldsymbol{\alpha} = (\alpha_1, \ldots, \alpha_R)^\top \in_R \mathbb{Z}_p^R$, $V_0, V_1, \ldots, V_\mathsf{T} \in_R \mathbb{G}$, set

$$\mathbf{F} = g^{\boldsymbol{\alpha}} = (g^{\alpha_1}, \cdots, g^{\alpha_R})^\top = (f_1, \ldots, f_R)^\top.$$

Output $PK = \left\{ g, g^{\alpha_0}, e(g, g)^\alpha, h_1, \ldots, h_U, V_0, V_1, \ldots, V_\mathsf{T}, \mathbf{F} \right\}$ and $MK = \alpha$.

2. $\mathsf{KeyGen}(MK, ID, S, \mathsf{T})$: $S$ is the set of attributes of a user with identity $ID$. $\mathsf{T}$ is the range of validity time periods for the user $ID$. Denote $\mathbb{T}$ as the set-cover representing $\mathsf{T}$ which consists of some time elements $\tau = (\tau_1, \tau_2, \ldots, \tau_{k_\tau}) \in \{1, z\}^{k_\tau}$ where $k_\tau < \mathsf{T}$ for any $\tau \in \mathbb{T}$.[4] Randomly choose $u, t, v_\tau \in_R \mathbb{Z}_p$ for all $\tau \in \mathbb{T}$ and compute

$$D_0 = g^t, \qquad D_0' = g^u, \qquad \left\{ D_{0,\tau}'' = g^{v_\tau} \right\}_{\tau \in \mathbb{T}},$$

$$\left\{ D_{1,\tau} = g^\alpha g^{\alpha_0 t} g^{\alpha_1 u} (V_0 \prod_{j=1}^{k_\tau} V_j^{\tau_j})^{v_\tau} \right\}_{\tau \in \mathbb{T}}, \qquad \{ L_{j,\tau} = V_j^{v_\tau} \}_{j=k_\tau+1, \ldots, \mathsf{T}, \tau \in \mathbb{T}},$$

$$\{ K_x = h_x^t \}_{x \in S}, \qquad \left\{ F_i = (f_1^{-ID^{i-1}} \cdot f_i)^u \right\}_{i=2, \cdots, R}.$$

Output

$$SK_{(ID, S, \mathsf{T})} = \left\{ D_0, D_0', \{ D_{0,\tau}'', D_{1,\tau}, L_{k_\tau+1,\tau}, \ldots, L_{\mathsf{T},\tau} \}_{\tau \in \mathbb{T}}, \{ K_x \}_{x \in S}, \{ F_i \}_{i=2, \cdots, R} \right\}$$

as the user secret key for the user with identity $ID$, attribute set $S$ and time validity period $\mathsf{T}$.

3. $\mathsf{Encrypt}(PK, m, \mathsf{T}_c, \mathcal{R}, \mathbb{A} = (M, \rho))$: $\mathcal{R} = (ID_1, \ldots, ID_r)$ is the revocation list with $r$ revoked users and $r < R$. $m \in \mathbb{G}_T$ is the plaintext message and $\mathsf{T}_c$ is the decryptable time period of this ciphertext. Let $\tau_c = (\tau_1, \ldots, \tau_k) \in \{1, z\}^k$ be the $z$-ary representation of $\mathsf{T}_c$, where $k < \mathsf{T}$.[5] Take as input an LSSS access structure $\mathbb{A} = (M, \rho)$. The function $\rho$ associates rows of $M$ to attributes. Let $M$ be an $\ell \times n$ matrix. The algorithm first chooses a random vector $\mathbf{v} = (s, y_2, \ldots, y_n) \in \mathbb{Z}_p^n$. These values will be used to share the encryption

---

[4] For example, if the user is valid from 2015-Nov-29 to 2016-Dec-31, $\mathbb{T} = \{(2015, Nov, 29), (2015, Nov, 30), (2015, Dec), (2016)\}$.

[5] Note that if $k < \mathsf{T}$, it means that only the users valid throughout a period of time $(\tau_1, \ldots, \tau_k, 1, 1, \ldots, 1)$ and $(\tau_1, \ldots, \tau_k, z, z, \ldots, z)$ can decrypt. For example, if the decryptable time period of this ciphertext is "2015-Dec" (and thus $\tau = (2015, Dec)$), only user with secret key valid for the whole December can decrypt this ciphertext.

exponent $s$. For $i = 1$ to $\ell$, it calculates $\lambda_i = \langle \mathbf{v}, M_i \rangle$, where $M_i$ is the vector corresponding to the $i$th row of $M$. Also let

$$\mathcal{F}_{\mathcal{R}}(Z) = (Z - ID_1) \cdots (Z - ID_r) = y_1 + y_2 Z + \cdots + y_r Z^{r-1} + y_{r+1} Z^r. \quad (1)$$

If $r + 1 < R$, the coefficients $y_{r+2}, \cdots, y_R$ are set to 0. Compute

$$C_0 = m \cdot e(g, g)^{\alpha s}, \quad C_0' = g^s, \quad C_0'' = (f_1^{y_1} \cdots f_R^{y_R})^s, \quad C_0''' = (V_0 \prod_{j=1}^{k} V_j^{\tau_j})^s,$$

$$C_1 = g^{\alpha_0 \lambda_1} h_{\rho(1)}^{-s}, \quad \ldots, \quad C_\ell = g^{\alpha_0 \lambda_\ell} h_{\rho(\ell)}^{-s}.$$

Output a ciphertext $CT = \{C_0, C_0', C_0'', C_0''', C_1, \ldots, C_\ell\}$ along with a description of $\mathsf{T}_c, (M, \rho)$ and the revoked set $\mathcal{R}$.

4. Decrypt($CT, \mathcal{R}, SK_{(ID,S,\mathsf{T})}$): First define $\mathbf{X} = (1, ID, \cdots, ID^{R-1})$ from the identity $ID$ and $\mathbf{Y} = (y_1, \cdots, y_R)$ from the revoked set $\mathcal{R}$ (where $y_i$, $i = 1, \ldots, R$ are defined as in equation (1)). Note that

$$\langle \mathbf{X}, \mathbf{Y} \rangle = y_1 + y_2 ID + \ldots + y_r ID^{r-1} + y_{r+1} ID^r = \mathcal{F}_{\mathcal{R}}(ID),$$

and if $r + 1 < R$, the coefficients $y_{r+2}, \cdots, y_R$ are 0. If any one of the following conditions occurs, output $\perp$:

- $S$ does not satisfy the access structure $(M, \rho)$.
- $ID \in \mathcal{R}$. That is, $\langle \mathbf{X}, \mathbf{Y} \rangle = \mathcal{F}_{\mathcal{R}}(ID) = 0$.
- $\mathsf{T}_c$ is not completely covered in $\mathsf{T}$. That is, $\tau_c$ and all its prefixes are not in $\mathbb{T}$, where $\tau_c$ is the $z$-ary representation for $\mathsf{T}_c$ and $\mathbb{T}$ is the set-cover for $\mathsf{T}$.

Otherwise, now we have $ID \notin \mathcal{R}$ (that is, $\langle \mathbf{X}, \mathbf{Y} \rangle \neq 0$). First compute

$$F = \prod_{i=2}^{R} F_i^{y_i} = \left( f_1^{-\langle \mathbf{X}, \mathbf{Y} \rangle} \cdot \prod_{i=1}^{R} f_i^{y_i} \right)^u \text{ and } \varsigma_1 = \left( \frac{e(F, C_0')}{e(D_0', C_0'')} \right)^{\frac{-1}{\langle \mathbf{X}, \mathbf{Y} \rangle}} = e(g, g)^{\alpha_1 s u}.$$

Further let $I \subset \{1, 2, \ldots, \ell\}$ be defined as $I = \{i : \rho(i) \in S\}$. Then, let $\{\omega_i \in \mathbb{Z}_p\}_{i \in I}$ be a set of constants such that if $\{\lambda_i\}$ are valid shares of any secret $s$ according to $M$, then $\sum_{i \in I} \omega_i \lambda_i = s$. Compute

$$\varsigma_2 = \prod_{i \in I} (e(C_i, D_0) \cdot e(C_0', K_{\rho(i)}))^{\omega_i} = e(g, g)^{\alpha_0 s t}.$$

If $\tau_c = (\tau_1, \ldots, \tau_k) \in \mathbb{T}$, $D_{1,\tau_c}$ should be one of the components in the secret key. Otherwise, let its prefix $\tau_c' = (\tau_1, \ldots, \tau_{k'})$, where $k' < k$, such that $\tau_c' \in \mathbb{T}$. Then derive the key from the secret key with respect to $\tau_c'$ as follows: $D_{1,\tau_c} = D_{1,\tau_c'} \prod_{j=k'+1}^{k} L_{j,\tau_c'}^{\tau_j}$, and set $\tau_c = \tau_c'$. Finally, compute

$$m = \frac{C_0 \cdot \varsigma_1 \cdot \varsigma_2 \cdot e(D_{0,\tau_c}'', C_0''')}{e(D_{1,\tau_c}, C_0')}.$$

We provide the correctness and security analysis in the full version [24].

### 4.3   Future Enhancements

There are some future enhancements that we can further improve upon the current construction:

- To lift the restriction for repeated attributes while keeping simple or standard assumption. We note that [37] provided a construction for non-revocable CP-ABE that has removed this restriction. Yet they use a non-standard assumption (decisional parallel BDHE assumption). Theoretically speaking, we can build up a system based on this scheme. However, the resulting system will also rely on the decisional parallel BDHE assumption.
- To add ciphertext update for revoked users (so that they cannot decrypt those ciphertext generated in the past). We can use the technique of proxy re-encryption to achieve this. But we believe this is not the most essential feature of a revocable ABE since revoked users can anyway decrypt the past ciphertext before they are revoked. If they have done so, it has no use to re-encrypt the ciphertext unless the system is fully cloud-based (e.g. cloud-assisted approach).

## 5   Performance Analysis

We first compare the efficiency of our scheme with other revocable ABE schemes. We present our comparison in Table 2. We use the following symbols in our comparison table:

**Table 2.** Efficiency comparison

| Scheme | PK size | SK size | Ciphertext size | Decryption Time (# of pairing) | KP/CP-ABE | Selective / Adaptive |
|---|---|---|---|---|---|---|
| [1] | $(\log R + U)G + G_T$ | $((\ell + 1) \log N)G$ | $(1 + S + \log r)G + G_T$ | $2\ell$ | KP-ABE | Selective |
| [4] | $(R + U + 1)G + G_T$ | $((R + 1) \cdot \ell)G$ | $3G + G_T$ | $2I$ | KP-ABE | Selective |
| [33] | $(3 + 2U + R)G$ | $4\ell G$ | $(2 + 2S)G + G_T$ | $2I$ | KP-ABE | Selective |
| [15] | $(\log N + L + 3)G$ | $(1 + L + Q)G$ | $(2 + S)G + G_T$ | $2L + 3Q + 3$ (multilinear) | KP-ABE | Selective |
| [16] | $11G + G_T$ | $(5 + 16\ell + 16(\log^2 N + \log N)G$ | $(16S + 64R - 27)G + G_T$ | $16S + 37$ | KP-ABE | Adaptive |
| [28] | $32NG$ | $8NG$ | $4NG + G_T$ | $(2 + r)N$ | CP-ABE | Adaptive |
| [25] | $(5 + 8\sqrt{N})G + \sqrt{N}G_T$ | $(2 + 2S + \sqrt{N})G$ | $(16\sqrt{N} + 3\ell)G + G_T$ | $9 + 3I$ | CP-ABE | Selective |
| Our | $(U + R + T + 3)G + G_T$ | $(S + Z + R + 1)G$ best case: $Z = 2$ worst case: $Z = \frac{T(T+3)}{2}$ | $(3 + \ell)G + G_T$ | $4 + 2I$ | CP-ABE | Selective |

- $R$: max number of revoked users; $U$: max number of attributes in the system
- $T$: number of time period level (depth of time tree)
- $N$: max number of users in the system; $S$: number of attributes of the user
- $r$: number of revoked users in the revocation list
- $\ell$: number of rows of the access structure matrix
- $I$: number of attributes used in the decryption
- $L$: max number of length of input wires (exclusive for [15] only)
- $Q$: max number of gates (exclusive for [15] only)
- $G_T$: number $G_T$ elements; $G$: number $G$ elements

Note that we exclude the following for the comparison as they are of different features or security level with our scheme:

- Using indirect approach and cloud-assisted approach (such as those listed in Sect. 2), as they cannot support instant revocation or require a cloud server to assist decryption.
- Using broadcast encryption technique (such as [2,33]) as they require the encryptor to know the identity of all possible decryptors, which is not exactly an ABE but more or less similar to a broadcast encryption in nature.
- Weak security model [8]. Their model is very week. They only allow the adversary to query secret key that does not satisfy the challenge access structure AND not in the revocation list. Under this model, the collusion attack we mentioned in Sect. 1.2 is NOT considered as a valid attack. That means their model cannot capture such a low-level attack.
- Attribute-level revocation only [49]. They only support attribute-level revocation, instead of the more generalized user-level or key-level revocation.

From the comparison, we can see that our scheme is the most efficient CP-ABE using direct approach for revocation. In practice, T can be very small. For example, if we only consider *year*, *month* and *day*, T = 3. Our space and computation complexity do not depend on $N$, the total number of users in the system, which is supposed to be a very large number.

## 6    Conclusion

In this paper, we proposed a revocable CP-ABE scheme based on the direct revoke approach. That is, the revocation list is embedded into the ciphertext so that instant revocation can be achieved. In order to shorten the revocation list, we further propose a time validity technique so that expired users cannot decrypt ciphertext associated with a decryptable time period not completely covered under their validity period. We deploy a tree-based structure and HIBE technique to construct the time validity part. The efficiency analysis also shows that our scheme is practical enough to be deployed.

**Acknowledgement.** This work was supported by Australian Research Council (ARC) Grant DP180102199, the National Natural Science Foundation of China (61702342), the Science and Technology Innovation Projects of Shenzhen (JCYJ20160 307150216309, JCYJ20170302151321095) and Tencent "Rhinoceros Birds" -Scientific Research Foundation for Young Teachers of Shenzhen University.

## References

1. Attrapadung, N., Imai, H.: Attribute-based encryption supporting direct/indirect revocation modes. In: Parker, M.G. (ed.) IMACC 2009. LNCS, vol. 5921, pp. 278–300. Springer, Heidelberg (2009). https://doi.org/10.1007/978-3-642-10868-6_17

2. Attrapadung, N., Imai, H.: Conjunctive broadcast and attribute-based encryption. In: Shacham, H., Waters, B. (eds.) Pairing 2009. LNCS, vol. 5671, pp. 248–265. Springer, Heidelberg (2009). https://doi.org/10.1007/978-3-642-03298-1_16

3. Attrapadung, N., Libert, B.: Functional encryption for inner product: achieving constant-size ciphertexts with adaptive security or support for negation. In: Nguyen, P.Q., Pointcheval, D. (eds.) PKC 2010. LNCS, vol. 6056, pp. 384–402. Springer, Heidelberg (2010). https://doi.org/10.1007/978-3-642-13013-7_23

4. Attrapadung, N., Libert, B., de Panafieu, E.: Expressive key-policy attribute-based encryption with constant-size ciphertexts. In: Catalano, D., Fazio, N., Gennaro, R., Nicolosi, A. (eds.) PKC 2011. LNCS, vol. 6571, pp. 90–108. Springer, Heidelberg (2011). https://doi.org/10.1007/978-3-642-19379-8_6

5. Au, M.H., Huang, Q., Liu, J.K., Susilo, W., Wong, D.S., Yang, G.: Traceable and retrievable identity-based encryption. In: Bellovin, S.M., Gennaro, R., Keromytis, A., Yung, M. (eds.) ACNS 2008. LNCS, vol. 5037, pp. 94–110. Springer, Heidelberg (2008). https://doi.org/10.1007/978-3-540-68914-0_6

6. Au, M.H., Liu, J.K., Yuen, T.H., Wong, D.S.: Practical hierarchical identity based encryption and signature schemes without random oracles. IACR Cryptology ePrint Archive 2006/368 (2006)

7. Au, M.H., Yuen, T.H., Liu, J.K., Susilo, W., Huang, X., Xiang, Y., Jiang, Z.L.: A general framework for secure sharing of personal health records in cloud system. J. Comput. Syst. Sci. **90**, 46–62 (2017)

8. Balu, A., Kuppusamy, K.: Ciphertext-policy attribute-based encryption with user revocation support. In: Singh, K., Awasthi, A.K. (eds.) QShine 2013. LNICST, vol. 115, pp. 696–705. Springer, Heidelberg (2013). https://doi.org/10.1007/978-3-642-37949-9_61

9. Boldyreva, A., Goyal, V., Kumar, V.: Identity-based encryption with efficient revocation. In: CCS, pp. 417–426. ACM (2008)

10. Boneh, D., Boyen, X., Goh, E.-J.: Hierarchical identity based encryption with constant size ciphertext. In: Cramer, R. (ed.) EUROCRYPT 2005. LNCS, vol. 3494, pp. 440–456. Springer, Heidelberg (2005). https://doi.org/10.1007/11426639_26

11. Boneh, D., Franklin, M.: Identity-based encryption from the Weil pairing. In: Kilian, J. (ed.) CRYPTO 2001. LNCS, vol. 2139, pp. 213–229. Springer, Heidelberg (2001). https://doi.org/10.1007/3-540-44647-8_13

12. Chow, S.S.M., Liu, J.K., Zhou, J.: Identity-based online/offline key encapsulation and encryption. In: ASIACCS, pp. 52–60. ACM (2011)

13. Chu, C., Liu, J.K., Zhou, J., Bao, F., Deng, R.H.: Practical id-based encryption for wireless sensor network. In: ASIACCS, pp. 337–340. ACM (2010)

14. Cui, H., Deng, R.H., Li, Y., Qin, B.: Server-aided revocable attribute-based encryption. In: Askoxylakis, I., Ioannidis, S., Katsikas, S., Meadows, C. (eds.) ESORICS 2016. LNCS, vol. 9879, pp. 570–587. Springer, Cham (2016). https://doi.org/10.1007/978-3-319-45741-3_29

15. Datta, P., Dutta, R., Mukhopadhyay, S.: General circuit realizing compact revocable attribute-based encryption from multilinear maps. In: Lopez, J., Mitchell, C.J. (eds.) ISC 2015. LNCS, vol. 9290, pp. 336–354. Springer, Cham (2015). https://doi.org/10.1007/978-3-319-23318-5_19

16. Datta, P., Dutta, R., Mukhopadhyay, S.: Adaptively secure unrestricted attribute-based encryption with subset difference revocation in bilinear groups of prime order. In: Pointcheval, D., Nitaj, A., Rachidi, T. (eds.) AFRICACRYPT 2016. LNCS, vol. 9646, pp. 325–345. Springer, Cham (2016). https://doi.org/10.1007/978-3-319-31517-1_17

17. He, K., Weng, J., Liu, J.K., Zhou, W., Liu, J.-N.: Efficient fine-grained access control for secure personal health records in cloud computing. In: Chen, J., Piuri, V., Su, C., Yung, M. (eds.) NSS 2016. LNCS, vol. 9955, pp. 65–79. Springer, Cham (2016). https://doi.org/10.1007/978-3-319-46298-1_5

18. Hong, J., Xue, K., Li, W.: Comments on "DAC-MACS: effective data access control for multiauthority cloud storage systems"/security analysis of attribute revocation in multiauthority data access control for cloud storage systems. IEEE Trans. Inf. Forensics Secur. **10**(6), 1315–1317 (2015)

19. Hur, J., Noh, D.K.: Attribute-based access control with efficient revocation in data outsourcing systems. IEEE Trans. Parallel Distrib. Syst. **22**(7), 1214–1221 (2011)

20. Liang, K., Au, M.H., Liu, J.K., Susilo, W., Wong, D.S., Yang, G., Phuong, T.V.X., Xie, Q.: A dfa-based functional proxy re-encryption scheme for secure public cloud data sharing. IEEE Trans. Inf. Forensics Secur. **9**(10), 1667–1680 (2014)

21. Liang, K., Au, M.H., Liu, J.K., Susilo, W., Wong, D.S., Yang, G., Yu, Y., Yang, A.: A secure and efficient ciphertext-policy attribute-based proxy re-encryption for cloud data sharing. Future Gener. Comput. Syst. **52**, 95–108 (2015)

22. Liu, J., Huang, X., Liu, J.K.: Secure sharing of personal health records in cloud computing: ciphertext-policy attribute-based signcryption. Future Gener. Comput. Syst. **52**, 67–76 (2015)

23. Liu, J.K., Au, M.H., Huang, X., Lu, R., Li, J.: Fine-grained two-factor access control for web-based cloud computing services. IEEE Trans. Inf. Forensics Secur. **11**(3), 484–497 (2016)

24. Liu, J.K., Yuen, T.H., Zhang, P., Liang, K.: Time-based direct revocable ciphertext-policy attribute-based encryption with short revocation list. IACR Cryptology ePrint Archive (2018)

25. Liu, Z., Wong, D.S.: Practical ciphertext-policy attribute-based encryption: traitor tracing, revocation, and large universe. In: Malkin, T., Kolesnikov, V., Lewko, A.B., Polychronakis, M. (eds.) ACNS 2015. LNCS, vol. 9092, pp. 127–146. Springer, Cham (2015). https://doi.org/10.1007/978-3-319-28166-7_7

26. Naruse, T., Mohri, M., Shiraishi, Y.: Attribute-based encryption with attribute revocation and grant function using proxy re-encryption and attribute key for updating. In: Park, J., Stojmenovic, I., Choi, M., Xhafa, F. (eds.) Future Information Technology. LNEE, vol. 276, pp. 119–125. Springer, Heidelberg (2014). https://doi.org/10.1007/978-3-642-40861-8_18

27. Naruse, T., Mohri, M., Shiraishi, Y.: Provably secure attribute-based encryption with attribute revocation and grant function using proxy re-encryption and attribute key for updating. Hum.-Centric Comput. Inf. Sci. **5**(1), 1–13 (2015)

28. González-Nieto, J.M., Manulis, M., Sun, D.: Fully private revocable predicate encryption. In: Susilo, W., Mu, Y., Seberry, J. (eds.) ACISP 2012. LNCS, vol. 7372, pp. 350–363. Springer, Heidelberg (2012). https://doi.org/10.1007/978-3-642-31448-3_26

29. Qian, H., Li, J., Zhang, Y., Han, J.: Privacy-preserving personal health record using multi-authority attribute-based encryption with revocation. Int. J. Inf. Sec. **14**(6), 487–497 (2015)

30. Ruj, S., Nayak, A., Stojmenovic, I.: DACC: distributed access control in clouds. In: TrustCom 2011, pp. 91–98. IEEE Computer Society (2011)

31. Sahai, A., Seyalioglu, H., Waters, B.: Dynamic credentials and ciphertext delegation for attribute-based encryption. In: Safavi-Naini, R., Canetti, R. (eds.) CRYPTO 2012. LNCS, vol. 7417, pp. 199–217. Springer, Heidelberg (2012). https://doi.org/10.1007/978-3-642-32009-5_13

32. Shi, J., Huang, C., Wang, J., He, K., Wang, J.: An access control scheme with direct cloud-aided attribute revocation using version key. In: Sun, X., Qu, W., Stojmenovic, I., Zhou, W., Li, Z., Guo, H., Min, G., Yang, T., Wu, Y., Liu, L. (eds.) ICA3PP 2014. LNCS, vol. 8630, pp. 429–442. Springer, Cham (2014). https://doi.org/10.1007/978-3-319-11197-1_33

33. Wang, P., Feng, D., Zhang, L.: Towards attribute revocation in key-policy attribute based encryption. In: Lin, D., Tsudik, G., Wang, X. (eds.) CANS 2011. LNCS, vol. 7092, pp. 272–291. Springer, Heidelberg (2011). https://doi.org/10.1007/978-3-642-25513-7_19

34. Wang, S., Liang, K., Liu, J.K., Chen, J., Yu, J., Xie, W.: Attribute-based data sharing scheme revisited in cloud computing. IEEE Trans. Inf. Forensics Secur. **11**(8), 1661–1673 (2016)

35. Wang, S., Zhou, J., Liu, J.K., Yu, J., Chen, J., Xie, W.: An efficient file hierarchy attribute-based encryption scheme in cloud computing. IEEE Trans. Inf. Forensics Secur. **11**(6), 1265–1277 (2016)

36. Waters, B.: Ciphertext-policy attribute-based encryption: an expressive, efficient, and provably secure realization. Cryptology ePrint Archive, Report 2008/290 (2008). http://eprint.iacr.org/

37. Waters, B.: Ciphertext-policy attribute-based encryption: an expressive, efficient, and provably secure realization. In: Catalano, D., Fazio, N., Gennaro, R., Nicolosi, A. (eds.) PKC 2011. LNCS, vol. 6571, pp. 53–70. Springer, Heidelberg (2011). https://doi.org/10.1007/978-3-642-19379-8_4

38. Xhafa, F., Wang, J., Chen, X., Liu, J.K., Li, J., Krause, P.: An efficient PHR service system supporting fuzzy keyword search and fine-grained access control. Soft Comput. **18**(9), 1795–1802 (2014)

39. Xie, X., Ma, H., Li, J., Chen, X.: An efficient ciphertext-policy attribute-based access control towards revocation in cloud computing. J. UCS **19**(16), 2349–2367 (2013)

40. Xie, X., Ma, H., Li, J., Chen, X.: New ciphertext-policy attribute-based access control with efficient revocation. In: Mustofa, K., Neuhold, E.J., Tjoa, A.M., Weippl, E., You, I. (eds.) ICT-EurAsia 2013. LNCS, vol. 7804, pp. 373–382. Springer, Heidelberg (2013). https://doi.org/10.1007/978-3-642-36818-9_41

41. Yang, K., Jia, X., Ren, K., Zhang, B.: DAC-MACS: effective data access control for multi-authority cloud storage systems. In: INFOCOM, pp. 2895–2903. IEEE (2013)

42. Yang, K., Jia, X., Ren, K., Zhang, B., Xie, R.: DAC-MACS: effective data access control for multiauthority cloud storage systems. IEEE Trans. Inf. Forensics Secur. **8**(11), 1790–1801 (2013)

43. Yang, Y., Ding, X., Lu, H., Wan, Z., Zhou, J.: Achieving revocable fine-grained cryptographic access control over cloud data. In: Desmedt, Y. (ed.) ISC 2013. LNCS, vol. 7807, pp. 293–308. Springer, Cham (2015). https://doi.org/10.1007/978-3-319-27659-5_21

44. Yang, Y., Liu, J.K., Liang, K., Choo, K.-K.R., Zhou, J.: Extended proxy-assisted approach: achieving revocable fine-grained encryption of cloud data. In: Pernul, G., Ryan, P.Y.A., Weippl, E. (eds.) ESORICS 2015. LNCS, vol. 9327, pp. 146–166. Springer, Cham (2015). https://doi.org/10.1007/978-3-319-24177-7_8

45. Yang, Y., Liu, J., Wei, Z., Huang, X.: Towards revocable fine-grained encryption of cloud data: reducing trust upon cloud. In: Pieprzyk, J., Suriadi, S. (eds.) ACISP 2017. LNCS, vol. 10342, pp. 127–144. Springer, Cham (2017). https://doi.org/10.1007/978-3-319-60055-0_7

46. Ye, J., Zhang, W., Wu, S., Gao, Y., Qiu, J.: Attribute-based fine-grained access control with user revocation. In: Linawati, L., Mahendra, M.S., Neuhold, E.J., Tjoa, A.M., You, I. (eds.) ICT-EurAsia 2014. LNCS, vol. 8407, pp. 586–595. Springer, Heidelberg (2014). https://doi.org/10.1007/978-3-642-55032-4_60
47. Yu, S., Wang, C., Ren, K., Lou, W.: Attribute based data sharing with attribute revocation. In: ASIACCS, pp. 261–270. ACM (2010)
48. Yuen, T.H., Zhang, Y., Yiu, S.M., Liu, J.K.: Identity-based encryption with post-challenge auxiliary inputs for secure cloud applications and sensor networks. In: Kutyłowski, M., Vaidya, J. (eds.) ESORICS 2014. LNCS, vol. 8712, pp. 130–147. Springer, Cham (2014). https://doi.org/10.1007/978-3-319-11203-9_8
49. Zhang, M.: New model and construction of ABE: achieving key resilient-leakage and attribute direct-revocation. In: Susilo, W., Mu, Y. (eds.) ACISP 2014. LNCS, vol. 8544, pp. 192–208. Springer, Cham (2014). https://doi.org/10.1007/978-3-319-08344-5_13
50. Zuo, C., Shao, J., Liu, J.K., Wei, G., Ling, Y.: Fine-grained two-factor protection mechanism for data sharing in cloud storage. IEEE Trans. Inf. Forensics Secur. **13**(1), 186–196 (2018)

# Almost Tight Multi-Instance Multi-Ciphertext Identity-Based Encryption on Lattices

Xavier Boyen and Qinyi Li$^{(\boxtimes)}$

Queensland University of Technology, Brisbane, Australia
qinyi.li@hdr.qut.eud.au

**Abstract.** Boyen and Li [AsiaCrypt, 2016] proposed the first almost tightly secure lattice identity-based encryption scheme in the standard model. The security of such scheme is proved under learning with errors assumption in the single-instance, single-challenge setting. In this work, we show how to extend the Boyen-Li scheme to obtain an almost tight security reduction in the multi-instance, multi-ciphertext setting, in which the security loss incurred is $\mathsf{poly}(\kappa)$ in the security parameter $\kappa$ and independent of the number of adversarial queries.

## 1 Introduction

To prove that the security of a cryptosystem is based on some computational problem, we provide a reductionist proof (in a properly defined security model) that states: If there exists an efficient adversary with runtime $t$ that breaks the cryptosystem with non-negligible probability $\epsilon$, then an efficient algorithm can be constructed to solve the computational problem with non-negligible probability $\epsilon' = \epsilon/L$ in time $t' \approx t$, which contradicts the assumed hardness of such computational problem. The parameter $L \geq 1$ measures the tightness of such a reduction proof. $L$ usually can be affected by several factors, including the reductionist proof itself, the security parameter, the number of deployed instance of a cryptosystem, the number of adversarial queries and so on. We say a reductionist proof is tight if $L$ is a small constant, and almost tight if $L$ is a polynomial of the security parameter and independent of other factors. An (almost) tight reduction usually has smaller and fixed $L$, which allows us to implement the cryptosystem with shorter parameters in a more accurate way. In contrast, the parameter $L$ in loose reductions is often large and depends on some uncontrollable quantities, e.g., the number of adversarial queries and the number of system instances. These quantities are difficult to determine accurately when the cryptosystem is deployed. Once these quantities are increased by adversaries, $L$ could go beyond

---

X. Boyen—Research supported in part by ARC Discovery Project grant number DP140103885 and ARC Future Fellowship FT140101145 from the Australian Research Council.

B. Preneel and F. Vercauteren (Eds.): ACNS 2018, LNCS 10892, pp. 535–553, 2018.
https://doi.org/10.1007/978-3-319-93387-0_28

some bound fixed by the implementation, obscuring the cryptosystem's security. Therefore, (almost) tight reduction is a desirable feature for cryptosystems.

In [11] the authors propose an almost tightly secure identity-based encryption (IBE) scheme from lattice. Its security is based on the hardness of learning-with-errors (LWE) problem and the security of an instantiated pseudorandom function (PRF). The reduction is *tight* in the sense that the security loss during the reduction is independent of the number of key generation queries, say $Q_{\mathsf{key}}$, made by the adversary. To make the whole reduction tight, a PRF with tight reduction is required. However, the security reduction given by Boyen and Li [11] is within the "single instance, single challenge" (SISC) setting where the adversary is only given one instance of the IBE scheme and one challenge ciphertext to attack. In a more realistic scenario, many instances of an IBE scheme would be deployed and there would be many ciphertexts targeted by an adversary. To model this "multi-instance, multi-ciphertext" setting, the adversary is allowed to see any polynomial number of scheme instances, say $N$, adaptively make any polynomial number of identity key generation queries, say $Q_{\mathsf{key}}$, and receive any polynomial number of challenge ciphertexts, say $Q_{\mathsf{enc}}$. Generically, via a hybrid argument, if an IBE scheme $\Pi$ is $\epsilon$ secure (meaning that adversary breaks $\Pi$ with probability $\epsilon$ in a defined model) in the SISC setting, then $\Pi$ is $\epsilon' = \epsilon \cdot N \cdot Q_{\mathsf{enc}}$ secure in the MIMC setting. This security loss (i.e., $N \cdot Q_{\mathsf{enc}}$) could be significant since $N$ and $Q_{\mathsf{enc}}$ are controlled by the adversary and, therefore, could be large. So it is preferable to have IBE schemes whose security does not depend on $Q_{\mathsf{key}}$, $Q_{\mathsf{enc}}$ and $N$ in the MIMC setting.

The first construction of IBE schemes from bilinear pairings with tight reductions in the MIMC setting was given by Hofheinz et al. [24]. Several subsequent works, e.g., [4,17,19,20], show various improvements in weakening underlying assumptions, computational efficiency and size of parameters. On the other hand, there is no tightly secure IBE scheme in the MIMC setting from lattices.

In this work, we propose the first lattice-based IBE scheme that has almost tight security reduction in the MIMC setting. We start from the almost tightly secure lattice IBE scheme by Boyen and Li [11] (the only known such scheme, albeit in the SISC setting), and extend it to have a tight security reduction in the MIMC setting under the LWE assumption.

## 1.1   Our Techniques

We first briefly review the proof idea of Boyen-Li IBE scheme. Let $C_{\mathsf{PRF}}$ be a Boolean circuit of a secure one-bit output pseudorandom function $\mathsf{PRF}$. In the security reduction, given any identity, a simulator devises two publicly computable matrices $\mathbf{F}_b = [\mathbf{A}|\mathbf{A}\mathbf{R}_{\mathsf{id}}]$ and $\mathbf{F}_{1-b} = [\mathbf{A}|\mathbf{A}\tilde{\mathbf{R}}_{\mathsf{id}} + (1 - 2C_{\mathsf{PRF}}(\mathbf{k}, \mathsf{id}))\,\mathbf{G}]$ in which $b = \mathsf{PRF}(\mathbf{k}, \mathsf{id}) \in \{0, 1\}$, $\mathbf{G}$ is the gadget matrix, and the low-norm matrices $\mathbf{R}_{\mathsf{id}}, \tilde{\mathbf{R}}_{\mathsf{id}}$ are only known to the simulator. For a key generation query on identity id, the simulator uses the $\mathbf{G}$ trapdoor of the matrix $\mathbf{F}_{1-b}$ to sample a decryption key. For the encryption (challenge) query, using its LWE samples, the simulator constructs a challenge ciphertext $\mathbf{c}_b^\top = \mathbf{s}^\top[\mathbf{A}|\mathbf{A}\mathbf{R}_{\mathsf{id}}] + \mathbf{e}^\top$ where $\mathbf{e}$ is correlated with the secret matrix $\mathbf{R}_{\mathsf{id}}$. Since $b$ is pseudorandom (if PRF is secure), the adversary would attack $\mathbf{c}_b^\top$ with probability $\approx 1/2$, providing non-trivial information for solving the LWE problem.

While this idea works well in the single instance and single ciphertext setting, it runs into issues in the MIMC setting, particularly when we aim for an (almost) tight reduction. Firstly, for, say, $N$ instances of such IBE scheme, we will have to provide $N$ instances of PRF (specified by the key $\mathbf{k}_i$). In order to make the reduction independent of $N$, we need to, at some point, switch all instances of PRF to random function in a single step (or with $\mathsf{poly}(\kappa)$ steps that only depends on the security parameter $\kappa$). It is not known how to achieve this with existing normal PRFs (a straightforward hybrid argument introduces a factor $N$ in the security loss). Secondly, in the Boyen-Li IBE scheme, the noise $\mathbf{e}$ of the challenge ciphertext is setup by using $\mathbf{R}_{\mathsf{id}}$. By adding a small "smoothing" noise to $\mathbf{e}$, Boyen and Li showed that $\mathbf{R}_{\mathsf{id}}$ remains hidden under polynomial LWE modulus (assuming the PRF circuit is in $\mathsf{NC}^1$). If adversary is able to make multiple challenge queries with the same identity or correlated identities, such an information-theoretic argument would not work any more. Because the adversary can gradually learn the information about $\mathbf{R}_{\mathsf{id}}$ from multiple challenge ciphertexts on identities that are the same as/correlated to $\mathsf{id}$, and fail the reduction.

We deal with the two issues as follows. Firstly, recall one-bit output PRFs are sufficient for Boyen-Li IBE scheme. We notice that the single-instance security of a PRF with certain key-homomorphism could be tightly extend to the security in multi-instance setting, as long as different PRF instances do not evaluate the same input. A PRF $\mathsf{PRF} : \mathcal{K} \times \mathcal{X} \to \mathcal{Y}$ is key homomorphic if $(\mathcal{K}, \boxplus)$ and $(\mathcal{Y}, +)$ are groups, and given $\mathsf{PRF}(\mathbf{k}, \mathbf{x}), \mathsf{PRF}(\mathbf{k}', \mathbf{x})$, then $\mathsf{PRF}(\mathbf{k} \boxplus \mathbf{k}', \mathbf{x}) = \mathsf{PRF}(\mathbf{k}, \mathbf{x}) + \mathsf{PRF}(\mathbf{k}', \mathbf{x})$. Given an oracle access to $\mathsf{PRF}(\mathbf{k}^*, \cdot)$ one can simulate a PRF with a uniformly random key $\mathbf{k}_i$ by freshly choosing a key $\tilde{\mathbf{k}}_i$ and setting its output as $\mathsf{PRF}(\mathbf{k}^*, \cdot) + \mathsf{PRF}(\tilde{\mathbf{k}}_i, \cdot)$. On the other hand, given an oracle access to a random function $F(\cdot)$, one can simulate a random function as $F'(\cdot) = F(\cdot) + \mathsf{PRF}(\tilde{\mathbf{k}}_i, \cdot)$ if all queries are different. However, only approximate key-homomorphic PRFs from lattices are known which satisfy $\mathsf{PRF}(\mathbf{k} \boxplus \mathbf{k}') = \mathsf{PRF}(\mathbf{k}, \mathbf{x}) + \mathsf{PRF}(\mathbf{k}', \mathbf{x}) + \varepsilon$ for a small error term $\varepsilon$. We can set parameters such that $\varepsilon$ barely affects the most significant bits of outputs: with overwhelming probability, $\mathsf{MSB}\,(\mathsf{PRF}(\mathbf{k} \boxplus \mathbf{k}')) = \mathsf{MSB}\,(\mathsf{PRF}(\mathbf{k}, \mathbf{x}) + \mathsf{PRF}(\mathbf{k}', \mathbf{x}))$. This idea was used in a very different context, i.e., building distributed PRFs from approximate key-homomorphic PRFs [10].

For the issue of constructing multiple challenge ciphertexts (or answering multiple encryption queries), we use the lossy mode of LWE: embedding an instance of LWE problem into the matrix $\mathbf{A}$ make $\mathbf{s}^\top [\mathbf{A}|\mathbf{A}\mathbf{R}_{\mathsf{id}}] + \mathbf{e}^\top$ statistically lose the information of $\mathbf{s}$. While $\mathbf{s}$ and $\mathbf{e}$ now are independent of the LWE problem that we embedded, we can pick fresh $\mathbf{s}, \mathbf{e}$ for each challenge ciphertext and, thus, eliminate the problem that we have in Boyen-Li IBE scheme. Moreover, while one instance of LWE problem is embedded (trough multiple samples) to all scheme instances (i.e., different matrix $\mathbf{A}$), we can switch half of the challenge ciphertexts (the ones indexed by the bit $b_{\mathsf{id}}^{(j)} = \mathsf{PRF}(\mathbf{k}^{(j)}, \mathsf{id})$ for the scheme instance $j$.) to random in a single step. Such an idea stems from the notion of lossy trapdoor function [6,27] and has recently been used in [12,25].

## 2 Preliminaries

We use PPT to denote "probabilistic polynomial-time". We denote by $x\|y$ the concatenation of bit $x$ and $y$. For a positive integer $n$, we denote by $[n]$ the set of positive integers no greater than $n$. We use bold lowercase letters (e.g. $\mathbf{a}$) to denote vectors and bold capital letters (e.g. $\mathbf{A}$) to denote matrices. For a positive integer $q \geq 2$, let $\mathbb{Z}_q$ be the ring of integers modulo $q$. We denote the group of $n \times m$ matrices in $\mathbb{Z}_q$ by $\mathbb{Z}_q^{n \times m}$. Vectors are treated as column vectors. The transpose of a vector $\mathbf{a}$ (resp. a matrix $\mathbf{A}$) is denoted by $\mathbf{a}^\top$ (resp. $\mathbf{A}^\top$). For $\mathbf{A} \in \mathbb{Z}_q^{n \times m}$ and $\mathbf{B} \in \mathbb{Z}_q^{n \times m'}$, let $[\mathbf{A}|\mathbf{B}] \in \mathbb{Z}_q^{n \times (m+m')}$ be the concatenation of $\mathbf{A}$ and $\mathbf{B}$. We write $\|\mathbf{x}\|_\infty$ for the infinity norm of a vector $\mathbf{x}$. The Euclidean norm of a matrix $\mathbf{R} = \{\mathbf{r}_1, \ldots, \mathbf{r}_m\}$ is denoted by $\|\mathbf{R}\| = \max_i \|\mathbf{r}_i\|$. We denote $\|\mathbf{R}\|_{\mathsf{GS}}$ by the Euclidean norm of the Gram-Schmidt orthogonalization of the column vector of $\mathbf{R}$. The spectral norm of $\mathbf{R}$ is denoted by $s_1(\mathbf{R}) = \sup_{\mathbf{x} \in \mathbb{R}^{m+1}} \|\mathbf{R} \cdot \mathbf{x}\|$. For a security parameter $\kappa$, a function $\mathsf{negl}(\kappa)$ is negligible in $\kappa$ if it is smaller than all polynomial fractions for a sufficiently large $\kappa$.

### 2.1 Randomness Extractor

Let $X$ and $Y$ be two random variables over some finite set $S$. The statistical distance between $X$ and $Y$, denoted as $\Delta(X, Y)$, is defined as $\Delta(X, Y) = \frac{1}{2} \sum_{s \in S} |\Pr[X = s] - \Pr[Y = s]|$. Let $X_\lambda$ and $Y_\lambda$ be ensembles of random variables indexed by the security parameter $\lambda$. $X$ and $Y$ are statistically close if $\Delta(X_\lambda, Y_\lambda) = \mathsf{negl}(\lambda)$. The min-entropy of a random variable $X$ over a set $S$ is defined as $H_\infty(X) = -\log(\max_{s \in S} \Pr[X = s])$. A random variable $X$ has $\varepsilon$-smooth min-entropy at least $k$, denoted by $H_\infty^\varepsilon(X) \geq k$, if there exists some variable $X'$ such that $\Delta(X, X') \leq \varepsilon$ and $H_\infty(X') \geq k$. We write $H_\infty^{\mathsf{smooth}}(\cdot)$ for some (unspecified) negligible $\varepsilon$.

**Definition 1 (Universal Hash Functions).** *$\mathcal{H} = \{H : \mathcal{X} \to \mathcal{Y}\}$ is called a family of universal hash functions if for all $x, x' \in \mathcal{X}$, with $x \neq x'$, we have $\Pr[H(x) = H(x')] \leq \frac{1}{|\mathcal{Y}|}$ over the random choice of $H \leftarrow \mathcal{H}$.*

**Lemma 1 ([27], Lemma 2.2).** *Let $X, Y$ be random variables such that $X \in \{0,1\}^n$ and $\tilde{H}_\infty(X|Y) \geq k$. Let $\mathcal{H} : \{0,1\}^n \to \{0,1\}^\ell$ be a family of universal hash functions where $k \geq \ell + 2\lambda$. It holds that for $H \xleftarrow{\$} \mathcal{H}$ and $r \xleftarrow{\$} \{0,1\}^\ell$, $\Delta((H, H(X), Y), (H, r, Y)) \leq 2^{-\lambda}$.*

**Lemma 2 ([1], Lemma 4).** *Suppose that $m > (n+1) \log q + \omega(\log n)$ and that $q > 2$ is prime. Let $\mathbf{R}$ be an $m \times k$ matrix chosen uniformly in $\{1, -1\}^{m \times k} \mod q$ where $k = k(n)$ is polynomial in $n$. Let $\mathbf{A}$ and $\mathbf{B}$ be matrices chosen uniformly in $\mathbb{Z}_q^{n \times m}$ and $\mathbb{Z}_q^{n \times k}$ respectively. Then, for all vectors $\mathbf{w} \in \mathbb{Z}_q^m$, the distribution $(\mathbf{A}, \mathbf{A}\mathbf{R}, \mathbf{R}^\top \mathbf{w})$ is statistically close to the distribution $(\mathbf{A}, \mathbf{B}, \mathbf{R}^\top \mathbf{w})$.*

## 2.2  Lattice Background

**Definition 2.** *Let a basis* $\mathbf{B} = [\mathbf{b}_1 \mid \ldots \mid \mathbf{b}_m] \in (\mathbb{R}^m)^m$ *of linearly indepen-dent vectors. The lattice generated by* $\mathbf{B}$ *is defined as* $\Lambda = \{\mathbf{y} \in \mathbb{R}^m : \exists s_i \in \mathbb{Z},\ \mathbf{y} = \sum_{i=1}^m s_i \mathbf{b}_i\}$. *For* $q$ *prime,* $\mathbf{A} \in \mathbb{Z}_q^{n \times m}$, *we define the* $m$-*dimensional (full-rank) random integer lattice* $\Lambda_q^\perp(\mathbf{A}) = \{\mathbf{e} \in \mathbb{Z}^m : \mathbf{Ae} = \mathbf{0} \pmod{q}\}$.

We denote the discrete Gaussian distribution over a lattice $\Lambda$ with Gaussian parameter $s > 0$, center $\mathbf{0}$ by $D_{\Lambda,s}$. We refer to [18] for the definition of discrete Gaussian distribution. We recall the following facts of "gadget matrix" [26].

**Lemma 3 ([26], Theorem 1).** *Let* $q$ *be a prime, and* $n$, $m$ *be integers with* $m = n \log q$. *There is a fixed full-rank matrix* $\mathbf{G} \in \mathbb{Z}_q^{n \times m}$ *such that the lattice* $\Lambda_q^\perp(\mathbf{G})$ *has a publicly known trapdoor matrix* $\mathbf{T_G} \in \mathbb{Z}^{n \times m}$ *with* $\|\mathbf{T_G}\|_{GS} \leq \sqrt{5}$.

**Lemma 4 ([9], Lemma 2.1).** *There is a deterministic algorithm, denoted* $\mathbf{G}^{-1}(\cdot) : \mathbb{Z}_q^{n \times m} \to \mathbb{Z}^{m \times m}$, *that takes any matrix* $\mathbf{A} \in \mathbb{Z}_q^{n \times m}$ *as input, and outputs the preimage* $\mathbf{G}^{-1}(\mathbf{A})$ *of* $\mathbf{A}$ *such that* $\mathbf{G} \cdot \mathbf{G}^{-1}(\mathbf{A}) = \mathbf{A} \pmod{q}$ *and* $\|\mathbf{G}^{-1}(\mathbf{A})\| \leq \sqrt{m}$.

*Lattice Trapdoors.* It is shown in [2] how to sample a "nearly" uniform random matrix $\mathbf{A} \in \mathbb{Z}^{n \times m}$ along with a trapdoor matrix $\mathbf{T_A} \in \mathbb{Z}^{m \times m}$ which is a short or low-norm basis of the induced lattice $\Lambda_q^\perp(\mathbf{A})$.

**Lemma 5.** *There is a PPT algorithm* TrapGen *that takes as input integers* $n \geq 1$, $q \geq 2$ *and a sufficiently large* $m = O(n \log q)$, *outputs a matrix* $\mathbf{A} \in \mathbb{Z}_q^{n \times m}$ *and a trapdoor matrix* $\mathbf{T_A} \in \mathbb{Z}^{m \times m}$, *such that* $\mathbf{A} \cdot \mathbf{T_A} = 0 \pmod{q}$, *the distribution of* $\mathbf{A}$ *is statistically close to the uniform distribution over* $\mathbb{Z}_q^{n \times m}$ *and* $\|\mathbf{T_A}\|_{GS} = O(\sqrt{n \log q})$.

**Lemma 6.** *Let* $n, q, m$ *be integers with* $m = O(n \log q)$. *Let* $\mathbf{s} \in \mathbb{Z}_q^n$, $\mathbf{A} \in \mathbb{Z}_q^{n \times m}$, $\mathbf{e} \in \mathbb{Z}^m$. *Given* $\mathbf{y}^\top = \mathbf{s}^\top \mathbf{A} + \mathbf{e}^\top \bmod q$ *and a basis* $\mathbf{T}$ *of* $\Lambda_q^\perp(\mathbf{A})$ *such that* $\left\|\mathbf{e}^\top \mathbf{T}\right\|_\infty \leq q/4$, *there is an algorithm* Invert$(\mathbf{y}, \mathbf{A}, \mathbf{T})$ *that outputs* $\mathbf{s}$ *with over-whelming probability.*

We use the following lattice basis sampling algorithms due to [1,16,26].

**Lemma 7.** *There is an efficient algorithm* SampleLeft *which takes as input a full-rank matrix* $\mathbf{A} \in \mathbb{Z}_q^{n \times m}$, *a matrix* $\mathbf{B} \in \mathbb{Z}_q^{n \times m}$, *a short basis* $\mathbf{T_A} \in \mathbb{Z}^{m \times m}$, *a Gaussian parameter* $s$ *where* $s > \|\mathbf{T_A}\|_{GS} \cdot \omega(\sqrt{\log 2m})$, *and for* $\mathbf{F} = [\mathbf{A}|\mathbf{B}]$, *outputs a full-rank basis* $\mathbf{T_F}$ *of* $\Lambda_q^\perp(\mathbf{F})$ *where the distribution of* $\mathbf{T_F}$ *is statistically close to* $D_{\Lambda_q^\perp(\mathbf{F}),s}$ *and* $\|\mathbf{T_F}\|_\infty \leq s\sqrt{2m}$.

**Lemma 8.** *There is an efficient algorithm* SampleRight *which takes as input* $\mathbf{A} \in \mathbb{Z}_q^{n \times m}$, *low-norm matrix* $\mathbf{R} \in \mathbb{Z}^{m \times m}$, *non-zero scalar* $h \in \mathbb{Z}_q$, *gadget matrix* $\mathbf{G} \in \mathbb{Z}_q^{n \times m}$, *a Gaussian parameter* $s$ *where* $s > \sqrt{5} \cdot s_1(\mathbf{R}) \cdot \omega(\sqrt{\log m})$, *and for* $\mathbf{F} = [\mathbf{A}|\mathbf{AR} + h\mathbf{G}]$, *outputs a full-rank basis* $\mathbf{T_F}$ *of* $\Lambda_q^\perp(\mathbf{F})$ *where the distribution of* $\mathbf{T_F}$ *is statistically close to* $D_{\Lambda_q^\perp(\mathbf{F}),s}$ *and* $\|\mathbf{T_F}\|_\infty \leq s\sqrt{2m}$.

*Homomorphic Evaluation Algorithm.* We adopt the following lemma.

**Lemma 9 ([11]).** *Let $C : \{0,1\}^\ell \to \{0,1\}$ be a NAND Boolean circuit. Let $\{\mathbf{A}_i = \mathbf{AR}_i + x_i\mathbf{G} \in \mathbb{Z}_q^{n \times m}\}_{i \in [\ell]}$ be $\ell$ different matrices correspond to each input wire of $C$ where $\mathbf{A} \xleftarrow{\$} \mathbb{Z}_q^{n \times m}$, $\mathbf{R}_i \xleftarrow{\$} \{1, -1\}^{m \times m}$, $x_i \in \{0,1\}$ and $\mathbf{G} \in \mathbb{Z}_q^{n \times m}$ is the gadget matrix. There is an efficient deterministic algorithm $\mathsf{Eval_{BV}}$ that takes as input $C$ and $\{\mathbf{A}_i\}_{i \in [\ell]}$ and outputs a matrix $\mathbf{A}_C = \mathbf{AR}_C + C(x_1, \ldots, x_\ell)\mathbf{G} = \mathsf{Eval_{BV}}(C, \mathbf{A}_1, \ldots, \mathbf{A}_\ell)$ where $\mathbf{R}_C \in \mathbb{Z}^{m \times m}$ and $C(x_1, \ldots, x_\ell)$ is the output of $C$ on the arguments $x_1, \ldots, x_\ell$, $s_1(\mathbf{R}_C) \leq O(4^d \cdot m^{3/2})$. $\mathsf{Eval_{BV}}$ runs in time $\mathrm{poly}(4^d, \ell, n, \log q)$. Particularly, if $C$ has depth $d = c \log \ell$ for some constant $c$, i.e. $C$ is in $\mathsf{NC}^1$, we have $s_1(\mathbf{R}_C) \leq O(\ell^{2c} \cdot m^{3/2})$.*

*Computational Assumptions.* We recall the following variant of decision learning with errors assumption.

**Definition 3 (Decision LWE).** *Let $n$ and $q$ be positive integers. Let $\chi$ be a distribution over $\mathbb{Z}_q$. Let $\mathbf{s} \xleftarrow{\$} \mathbb{Z}_q^n$ be a secret vector. Define oracles :*

- *$\mathcal{O}_\mathbf{s}$: samples $\mathbf{a} \xleftarrow{\$} \mathbb{Z}_q^n$, column vector $\mathbf{e} \leftarrow \chi$; returns $(\mathbf{a}, \mathbf{s}^\top \mathbf{a} + e \bmod q)$.*
- *$\mathcal{O}_\$$: samples $\mathbf{a} \xleftarrow{\$} \mathbb{Z}_q^n$, $b \xleftarrow{\$} \mathbb{Z}_q$; returns $(\mathbf{a}, b)$.*

*The decision LWE problem, denote $\mathsf{LWE}_{n,q,\chi}$, asks to distinguish between $\mathcal{O}_\mathbf{s}$ and $\mathcal{O}_\$$. The (decision) LWE assumption says that for an efficient algorithm $\mathcal{A}$, there is a negligible functuon $\mathsf{negl}(\kappa)$ such that*

$$\mathsf{Adv}_{\mathcal{A}}^{\mathsf{LWE}_{n,q,\chi}}(\kappa) = \left|\Pr[\mathcal{A}^{\mathcal{O}_\mathbf{s}}(1^\kappa) = 1] - \Pr[\mathcal{A}^{\mathcal{O}_\$}(1^\kappa) = 1]\right| \leq \mathsf{negl}(\kappa)$$

Notice that the decision LWE problem does not restrict the number of oracle calls (or the number of samples available to $\mathcal{A}$). In the security proof of our IBE scheme, we use this fact to obtain enough samples from a single instance of LWE problem to simulate multiple challenge ciphertexts. Usually, the noise distribution $\chi$ is a discrete Gaussian distribution $D_{\mathbb{Z},\alpha q}$ where $\alpha \in (0,1)$ and $\alpha q > 3\sqrt{n}$. For fix dimension $n$, the modulus-to-noise ratio $q/\alpha$ measures the hardness of LWE problem. The larger the ratio, the easier the LWE problem.

   In our construction, we use a variant of LWE problem where the secret is a random matrix $\mathbf{S} \in \mathbb{Z}_q^{n \times h}$ (we choose the noise as vectors where coordinates are independently sampled according to $\chi$). Via a hybrid argument, such a variant is polynomially equivalent to the LWE problem we define above up to a factor of $h$ in the reduction.

### 2.3   Lossy Mode for LWE

A series of works [3,6,25] show that LWE/LWR problem (with a-priori polynomially bounded number of samples) has a lossy mode in which the samples only reveal partial information of its secret. More precisely, given $m$ LWE samples $\mathbf{y}^\top = \mathbf{s}^\top \mathbf{A} + \mathbf{e}^\top \pmod{q}$ where $\mathbf{A} \in \mathbb{Z}_q^{n \times m}$, if $\mathbf{A}$ is generated in the lossy mode, then $\mathbf{s}$ still has some entropy given $\mathbf{y}, \mathbf{A}$. The following lemma states this fact.

**Lemma 10 ([3], Lemma B.4).** *Let $\kappa$ be a security parameter. Let $n$, $n'$, $m^*$, $q$, $\beta^*$, $\gamma$, $\sigma$ and $\lambda$ be integers and $\chi$ be the LWE error distribution over $\mathbb{Z}_q$ where $\mathrm{Pr}_{x \leftarrow \chi}[|x| \geq \beta^*] \leq \mathsf{negl}(\kappa)$ and $\sigma \geq \beta^* \gamma nm^*$. For random variables $\mathbf{s} \in [-\gamma, \gamma]^n$, $\mathbf{e} \xleftarrow{\$} [\sigma, \sigma]^{m^*}$ and $\mathbf{A} = \mathbf{CB} + \mathbf{F} \pmod{q}$ where $\mathbf{C} \xleftarrow{\$} \mathbb{Z}_q^{n \times n'}$, $\mathbf{B} \xleftarrow{\$} \mathbb{Z}_q^{n' \times m^*}$ and $\mathbf{F} \leftarrow \chi^{n \times m^*}$, we have*

$$H_\infty^{smooth}(\mathbf{s}|\mathbf{A}, \mathbf{s}^\top \mathbf{A} + \mathbf{e}^\top) \geq H_\infty(\mathbf{s}) - (n' + 2\kappa)\log q$$

The following theorem, which is a direct consequence of Lemma 10, is essential for the security proof of our IBE scheme.

**Theorem 1.** *Let $\kappa$ be a security parameter. Let $n, n', m, q, \gamma, \sigma, \lambda$ be integers, $q$ prime, $\beta$ real, such that $n \geq \kappa$, $m \geq O(n \log q)$. Let $\chi$ be the LWE error distribution over $\mathbb{Z}_q$ where $\mathrm{Pr}_{x \leftarrow \chi}[|x| \geq \beta] \leq \mathsf{negl}(\kappa)$. Let $\mathbf{R} \in \mathbb{Z}^{m \times m}$ be a low-norm matrix with $\|\mathbf{R}\|_\infty \leq B$. Assume $n \geq (n' + 2\kappa + \frac{\lambda}{\log q})\frac{\log q}{\log 2\gamma} + \frac{2\kappa}{\log q}$ and $\sigma \geq 2B\beta\gamma nm$. For random variables $\mathbf{s} \in [-\gamma, \gamma]^n$, $\mathbf{e} \xleftarrow{\$} [\sigma, \sigma]^{2m}$ and $\mathbf{A} = \mathbf{CB} + \mathbf{F} \pmod{q}$ where $\mathbf{C} \xleftarrow{\$} \mathbb{Z}_q^{n \times n'}$, $\mathbf{B} \xleftarrow{\$} \mathbb{Z}_q^{n' \times m}$ and $\mathbf{F} \leftarrow \chi^{n \times m}$ such that given $\mathbf{FR}$, $\mathbf{BR}$ is statistically close to the uniform distribution over $\mathbb{Z}_q^{n' \times m}$, we have*

$$H_\infty^{smooth}(\mathbf{s}|\mathbf{A}, \mathbf{s}^\top[\mathbf{A}|\mathbf{AR}] + \mathbf{e}^\top) \geq H_\infty(\mathbf{s}) - (n' + 2\kappa)\log q$$
$$\geq 2\kappa + \lambda$$

*Proof.* The proof follows from the proof of Theorem 7.3, [3]. We can write $[\mathbf{A}|\mathbf{AR}] = \mathbf{CB}^* + \mathbf{F}^*$ where $\mathbf{B}^* = [\mathbf{B}|\mathbf{BR}]$ and $\mathbf{F}^* = [\mathbf{F}|\mathbf{FR}]$. First of all, the statistical distance between the distribution of $\mathbf{B}^*$ and the uniform distribution over $\mathbb{Z}_q^{n' \times 2m}$ is $\mathsf{negl}(\kappa)$. Secondly, we can bound each entry of $\mathbf{F}^*$ by $mB\beta$. Therefore, invoking Lemma 10 with $m^* = 2m$, $\beta^* = B\beta$, $n \geq (n' + 2\kappa + \frac{\lambda}{\log q})\frac{\log q}{\log 2\gamma} + \frac{2\kappa}{\log q}$, $\sigma \geq 2B\beta\gamma nm^2$ and concealing $\mathsf{negl}(\kappa)$ by the term smooth, we have

$$H_\infty^{smooth}(\mathbf{s}|\mathbf{A}, \mathbf{s}^\top[\mathbf{A}|\mathbf{AR}] + \mathbf{e}^\top) \geq H_\infty(\mathbf{s}) - (n' + 2\kappa)\log q$$
$$\geq n\log(2\gamma) - (n' + 2\kappa)\log q$$
$$\geq 2\kappa + \lambda$$

## 2.4 Identity-Based Encryption

An identity-based encryption (IBE) scheme with identity space $\mathcal{ID}$ and message space $\mathcal{M}$ consists of the following five PPT algorithms:

- $\mathsf{Para}(1^\kappa) \to \mathsf{pub}$. The public parameter generation algorithm $\mathsf{Para}$ takes as input a security parameter $\kappa$, and outputs a set of global parameters $\mathsf{pub}$.
- $\mathsf{Setup}(\mathsf{pub}) \to (\mathsf{mpk}, \mathsf{msk})$. The setup algorithm $\mathsf{Setup}$ takes as input $\mathsf{pub}$, and outputs a master public key $\mathsf{mpk}$ and a master secret key $\mathsf{msk}$.
- $\mathsf{KeyGen}(\mathsf{mpk}, \mathsf{msk}, \mathsf{id}) \to \mathsf{ct}_{\mathsf{id}}$. The key generation algorithm $\mathsf{KeyGen}$ takes as input the master public key $\mathsf{mpk}$, the master private key $\mathsf{msk}$, and an identity $\mathsf{id}$, and outputs a user private key $\mathsf{sk}_{\mathsf{id}}$.

- Encrypt(mpk, id, m) → $ct_{id}$. The encryption algorithm Encrypt takes as input the master public key mpk, an identity id, and a message m, outputs a ciphertext $ct_{id}$.
- Decrypt(mpk, $sk_{id}$, $ct_{id}$) → m or ⊥. The decryption algorithm Decrypt takes as input the master public key mpk, a private key $sk_{id}$ and a ciphertext $ct_{id}$, outputs message m or ⊥.

For correctness, we require that for all $\kappa$, all pub ← Para($1^\kappa$), all (mpk, msk) ← Setup(pub), all id ∈ $\mathcal{ID}$, all $ct_{id}$ ← KeyGen(mpk, msk, id), all m ∈ $\mathcal{M}$ and for all $ct_{id}$ ← Encrypt(mpk, id, m), Decrypt(mpk, $sk_{id}$, $ct_{id}$) outputs m except negligible probability.

*Security Definition.* The multi-instance, multi-ciphertext security for an IBE scheme $\Pi$ = (Para, Setup, KeyGen, Encrypt, Decrypt) is defined through the following security game between a challenger $\mathcal{B}$ and an adversary $\mathcal{A}$.

**Initial.** $\mathcal{B}$ runs pub ← Para($1^\kappa$) and randomly picks coin ← {0, 1}, and gives pub to $\mathcal{A}$. $\mathcal{A}$ selects $N$ = poly($\kappa$). Then $\mathcal{B}$ runs ($mpk^{(j)}$, $msk^{(j)}$) ← Setup(pub) for $j \in [N]$, and gives $\{mpk^{(j)}\}_{j \in [N]}$ to $\mathcal{A}$.

**Query.** $\mathcal{A}$ adaptively issues the following two types of queries:
- Key Generation Query. The adversary $\mathcal{A}$ submits ($j \in [N]$, id ∈ $\mathcal{ID}$) to the challenger $\mathcal{B}$. $\mathcal{B}$ runs $sk_{id}^{(j)}$ ← KeyGen($mpk^{(j)}$, $msk^{(j)}$, id) and gives $sk_{id}^{(j)}$ to $\mathcal{A}$.
- Encryption Query. The adversary submits the $k$-th encryption query ($k \in [Q_{enc}]$, $j \in [N]$, id ∈ $\mathcal{ID}$, $m_0, m_1 \in \mathcal{M}$) to $\mathcal{B}$. $\mathcal{B}$ runs $ct_{id,k}^{(j)}$ ← Encrypt($mpk^{(j)}$, id, $m_{coin}$) and returns $ct_{id,k}^{(j)}$ to $\mathcal{A}$. In addition, $\mathcal{A}$ is allowed to submit two encryption queries with same instance index $j$ (but the index $k$ will be different)[1].

**Guess.** $\mathcal{A}$ outputs coin′ ∈ {0, 1} and it wins if coin′ = coin.

The advantage of $\mathcal{A}$ in wining the game is defined as $\mathsf{Adv}_{\mathcal{A}, \Pi, (N, Q_{key}, Q_{enc})}^{\mathsf{IND\text{-}ID\text{-}CPA}}(\kappa)$ = | Pr[coin′ = coin] − 1/2|, where $Q_{key}$ and $Q_{enc}$ are the number of key generation queries and encryption queries, respectively. We say that an IBE scheme $\Pi$ is secure if for all PPT adversary $\mathcal{A}$, there is a negligible function negl($\kappa$) such that $\mathsf{Adv}_{\mathcal{A}, \Pi, (N, Q_{key}, Q_{enc})}^{\mathsf{IND\text{-}ID\text{-}CPA}}(\kappa) \leq$ negl($\kappa$).

### 2.5   Almost Key-Homomorphic Pseudorandom Functions

**Definition 4 (Pseudorandom Functions).** *Let $\kappa$ be the security parameter. A pseudorandom function PRF : $\mathcal{K} \times \mathcal{X} \rightarrow \mathcal{Y}$ is an efficiently computable, deterministic function. Let $\Omega$ be the set of all functions from $\mathcal{X}$ to $\mathcal{Y}$. We define the advantage of an adversary $\mathcal{A}$ in attacking the PRF as*

$$\mathsf{Adv}_{PRF, \mathcal{A}}(\kappa) = \left| \Pr[\mathcal{A}^{PRF(K, \cdot)}(1^\kappa) = 1] - \Pr[\mathcal{A}^{F(\cdot)}(1^\kappa) = 1] \right|$$

---

[1] This refers to the strong/full adaptive MIMC security [17,24].

*where the probability is taken over a uniform choice of key $K \xleftarrow{\$} \mathcal{K}$ and $F \xleftarrow{\$} \Omega$, and the randomness of $\mathcal{A}$. We say that $\mathsf{PRF}$ is secure if for all PPT adversaries $\mathcal{A}$, $\mathsf{Adv}_{\mathsf{PRF},\mathcal{A}}(\kappa) \leq \mathsf{negl}(\kappa)$ for some negligible function $\mathsf{negl}(\kappa)$.*

**Definition 5.** *A PRF $\mathsf{PRF} : \mathcal{K} \times \mathcal{X} \to \mathbb{Z}_q$ is $\varepsilon$-almost key-homomorphic if $(\mathcal{K}, \boxplus)$ is a group, and for $\mathbf{k}_1, \mathbf{k}_2 \in \mathcal{K}$, $\mathbf{x} \in \mathcal{X}$, we have*

$$\mathsf{PRF}(\mathbf{k}_1 \boxplus \mathbf{k}_2, \mathbf{x}) = \mathsf{PRF}(\mathbf{k}_1, \mathbf{x}) + \mathsf{PRF}(\mathbf{k}_2, \mathbf{x}) + e$$

*where $e \in [0, \varepsilon]$.*

Let $\mathsf{Prefix} \colon \mathbb{Z}_p \to \{0,1\}^\ell$ where $\ell \leq \log p$ be a deterministic function that takes as input an element in $\mathbb{Z}_q$ and outputs its binary prefix of length $\ell$.

**Definition 6.** *We say a $\varepsilon$-almost key-homomorphic PRF has prefix correction with respect to the function $\mathsf{Prefix}$ if*

$$\mathsf{Prefix}\left(\mathsf{PRF}(\mathbf{k}_1 \boxplus \mathbf{k}_2, \mathbf{x})\right) = \mathsf{Prefix}\left(\mathsf{PRF}(\mathbf{k}_1, \mathbf{x}) + \mathsf{PRF}(\mathbf{k}_2, \mathbf{x})\right)$$

*holds with overwhelming probability. Particularly, we say $\varepsilon$-almost key-homomorphic PRF $\mathsf{PRF}$ has most-significant-bit correction:*

$$\mathsf{MSB}\left(\mathsf{PRF}(\mathbf{k}_1 \boxplus \mathbf{k}_2, \mathbf{x})\right) = \mathsf{MSB}\left(\mathsf{PRF}(\mathbf{k}_1, \mathbf{x}) + \mathsf{PRF}(\mathbf{k}_2, \mathbf{x})\right)$$

*with all but negligible probability where $\mathsf{MSB} : \mathbb{Z}_p \to \{0,1\}$ be a deterministic function that takes as input an $\mathbb{Z}_p$-element and outputs its most significant bit.*

To base our IBE scheme on lattice assumptions with a (almost) tight reduction, we can instantiate the PRF in our construction with the lattice-based almost key-homomorphic PRF by Boneh et al. [10] (BLMR-PRF). Here we recall the construction of BLMR-PRF. Let $n, m, p, q$ be integers where $m = n\lfloor \log q \rfloor$ and $p|q$. Let $\mathbb{Z}_q$-invertible matrices $\mathbf{B}_0, \mathbf{B}_1 \in \{0,1\}^{m \times m}$ be public parameter. For an input $\mathbf{x} = \mathbf{x}[1]\mathbf{x}[2]...\mathbf{x}[\ell] \in \{0,1\}^\ell$, a secret key $\mathbf{k} \leftarrow \mathbb{Z}_q^m$, the BLMR-PRF $\mathsf{PRF}_{\mathsf{BLMR}} : \mathbb{Z}_q^m \times \{0,1\}^\ell \to \mathbb{Z}_p^m$ is defined as

$$\mathsf{PRF}_{\mathsf{BLMR}}(\mathbf{k}, \mathbf{x}) = \left\lfloor \prod_{i=1}^\ell \mathbf{B}_{\mathbf{x}[i]} \cdot \mathbf{k} \right\rfloor_p \tag{1}$$

where for any $x \in \mathbb{Z}_q$, the function $\lfloor x \rfloor_p = \lfloor (p/q) \cdot x \rfloor \mod p$, and it naturally extends to vectors by applying the function to each coordinate of the vector individually. While the output space (of the original description) of BLMR-PRF is $\mathbb{Z}_p^m$, we can always output the first $\mathbb{Z}_p$ coordinate as an input to the function $\mathsf{Prefix}$ (and MSB). Assume $2|p$, for $x \in \mathbb{Z}_p$, we define

$$\mathsf{MSB}(x) = \lfloor x \rfloor_2 = \lfloor (2/p) \cdot x \rfloor \mod 2$$

The 1-almost key-homomorphism of BLMR-PRF was proved in [10] (Theorem 5.5). To make the BMLR-PRF have the most-significant-bit correction property, we can set the parameter $p$ slightly super-polynomial, e.g., $p = n^{\omega(1)}$

(and set up $q$ accordingly), to make sure the noise always properly being rounded off. This fact has already been mentioned in [10] in applying almost key-homomorphic PRFs to obtain distributed PRFs.

Very recently, Libert et al. ([25], Theorem 7) showed that BLMR-PRF has a (almost) tight reduction from non-uniform LWE (NLWE) problem (in the sense that the security loss during the security reduction is independent of the number of PRF queries being made) which in turn has a tight security reduction to LWE problem with certain parameters ([10], Theorem 4.3). These results together demonstrate that for input length $\ell$, BLMR-PRF is (almost) tightly secure under the LWE assumption where the modulus-to-noise ratio is $n^{\Omega(\ell)}$.

Similar to the Boyen-Li IBE scheme, using shallow depth almost key-homomorphic PRFs (e.g., the ones can be implemented by $\mathsf{NC}^1$ circuits) will allow us to use polynomial modulus for the IBE scheme (not the PRF itself). BLMR-PRF satisfies this requirement. As it is mentioned in [25], the computation of BLMR-PRF can be divided into two phases, a matrices product followed by rounding an inner-product. The matrices product $\prod_{i=1}^{\ell} \mathbf{B}_{\mathbf{x}[i]}$ can be computed publicly without knowing the secret key. So the actual circuit needed to be evaluated is the "inner-product-then-rounding" circuit which is in $\mathsf{NC}^1$.

## 3   The Scheme

In our scheme, we require that the same identity is never used for requesting private identity keys from different scheme instances. Such a requirement is natural and essential for the security proof. It is done by appending a unique instance identifier to users' actual identities. A user with identity $\mathsf{id}'$ uses the actual identity $\mathsf{id} = \mathsf{ID}\|\mathsf{id}'$ for the scheme instance whose identifier is $\mathsf{ID}$.

$\mathsf{Para}(1^\kappa)$. The public parameter generation algorithm does the following.

1. Choose a LWE hardness parameter $n'$, integer $n \geq n'$, integer $m = 2n \log q + \omega(\log n)$, LWE modulo $q$ and integers $\gamma, \sigma$. Set message space $\mathcal{M} = \{0,1\}^\lambda$ for some integer $\lambda$.
2. Select an almost key-homomorphic PRF $\mathsf{PRF} : \{0,1\}^t \times \{0,1\}^\ell \to \{0,1\}^r$, where $r = \omega(\log \kappa)$, which has the most-significant-bit correction (as per Definition 6). Set a depth $d$, NAND Boolean circuit $C_{\mathsf{PRF}}\{0,1\}^t \times \{0,1\}^\ell \to \{0,1\}$ which outputs the most significant bits of the output stings of $\mathsf{PRF}$. That is $C_{\mathsf{PRF}}$ computes $\mathsf{MSB}(\mathsf{PRF}(\cdot,\cdot))$.
3. Let $B = O(4^d \cdot m^{3/2})$ (as the bound given in Lemma 9), we choose $s \geq \sqrt{5} \cdot B \cdot \omega(\sqrt{\log 2m})$.
4. Randomly sample a universal hash function $\mathsf{H} : [-\gamma, \gamma]^n \to \{0,1\}^\lambda$ from a family of universal hash functions $\mathcal{H}$.
5. Output the global public parameters

$$\mathsf{pub} = (n, m, q, \gamma, \delta, \lambda, \mathsf{PRF}, C_{\mathsf{PRF}}, \mathsf{H}, s)$$

$\mathsf{Setup}(\mathsf{pub})$. On input $\mathsf{pub}$, the setup algorithm does the following.

1. Select a random key $\mathbf{k} \leftarrow \{0,1\}^t$ for PRF.
2. Run $\mathsf{TrapGen}(n, m, q)$ to generate a matrix $\mathbf{A} \in \mathbb{Z}_q^{n \times m}$ along with a trapdoor $\mathbf{T_A} \in \mathbb{Z}^{m \times m}$.
3. Choose random matrices $\mathbf{A}_0, \mathbf{A}_1, \mathbf{C}_1, ..., \mathbf{C}_t \leftarrow \mathbb{Z}_q^{n \times m}$.
4. Choose a unique system identifier $\mathsf{ID}$, and output the master public key

$$\mathsf{mpk} = \left(\mathsf{ID}, \mathbf{A}, \mathbf{A}_0, \mathbf{A}_1, \{\mathbf{C}_i\}_{i \in [t]}\right)$$

and master secret key $\mathsf{msk} = (\mathbf{T_A}, \mathbf{k})$.

$\mathsf{Encrypt}(\mathsf{mpk}, \mathsf{id}, \mathsf{m})$. Let $\mathsf{ID}\|\mathsf{id} = \mathsf{id}[1]...\mathsf{id}[\ell] \in \{0,1\}^\ell$, the algorithm encrypts $\mathsf{m} \in \{0,1\}^\lambda$ as follows.

1. Compute $\mathbf{A}_{C_{\mathsf{PRF}},\mathsf{id}} = \mathsf{Eval}(C_{\mathsf{PRF}}, \{\mathbf{C}_i\}_{i \in [t]}, \mathsf{id}[1]\mathbf{G}, ..., \mathsf{id}[\ell]\mathbf{G}) \in \mathbb{Z}_q^{n \times m}$.
2. Set $\mathbf{F}_{\mathsf{id},\mu} = [\mathbf{A}|\mathbf{A}_\mu - \mathbf{A}_{C_{\mathsf{PRF}},\mathsf{id}}]$ for $\mu = 0, 1$.
3. Select $\mathbf{x}_0, \mathbf{x}_1 \leftarrow [-\gamma, \gamma]^n, \mathbf{e}_0, \mathbf{e}_1 \leftarrow [-\sigma, \sigma]^{2m}$. Output the ciphertext $\mathsf{ct}_{\mathsf{id}} = (\mathbf{c}_0, \mathbf{c}'_0, \mathbf{c}_1, \mathbf{c}'_1)$ where

$$\begin{cases} \mathbf{c}_0 = \mathsf{m} \oplus \mathsf{H}(\mathbf{x}_0) \\ \mathbf{c}'_0{}^\top = \mathbf{x}_0^\top \cdot \mathbf{F}_{\mathsf{id},0} + \mathbf{e}_0^\top \bmod q \end{cases} \quad ; \quad \begin{cases} \mathbf{c}_1 = \mathsf{m} \oplus \mathsf{H}(\mathbf{x}_1) \\ \mathbf{c}'_1{}^\top = \mathbf{x}_1^\top \cdot \mathbf{F}_{\mathsf{id},1} + \mathbf{e}_1^\top \bmod q \end{cases}$$

$\mathsf{KeyGen}(\mathsf{mpk}, \mathsf{msk}, \mathsf{id})$. On input $\mathsf{mpk}, \mathsf{msk}$ and an identity $\mathsf{id}$, the algorithm does the following to generate a private key.

1. Compute $\mu = \mathsf{MSB}(\mathsf{PRF}(\mathbf{k}, \mathsf{ID}\|\mathsf{id})) \in \{0,1\}$.
2. Compute $\mathbf{A}_{C_{\mathsf{PRF}},\mathsf{id}} = \mathsf{Eval}(C_{\mathsf{PRF}}, \{\mathbf{C}_i\}_{i \in [t]}, \mathsf{id}[1]\mathbf{G}, ..., \mathsf{id}[\ell]\mathbf{G}) \in \mathbb{Z}_q^{n \times m}$.
3. Set $\mathbf{F}_{\mathsf{id},1-\mu} = [\mathbf{A}|\mathbf{A}_{1-\mu} - \mathbf{A}_{C_{\mathsf{PRF}},\mathsf{id}}] \in \mathbb{Z}_q^{n \times 2m}$.
4. Run $\mathsf{SampleLeft}([\mathbf{A}|\mathbf{A}_{1-\mu} - \mathbf{A}_{C_{\mathsf{PRF}},\mathsf{id}}], \mathbf{T_A}, s)$ to get trapdoor $\mathbf{T}_{\mathsf{id}} \in \mathbb{Z}^{2m \times 2m}$ for $\mathbf{F}_{\mathsf{id},1-\mu}$.
5. Return $\mathsf{sk}_{\mathsf{id}} = (1 - \mu, \mathbf{T}_{\mathsf{id}})$.

$\mathsf{Decrypt}(\mathsf{mpk}, \mathsf{sk}_{\mathsf{id}}, \mathsf{ct}_{\mathsf{id}})$. On input ciphertext $(\mathbf{c}_0, \mathbf{c}'_0), (\mathbf{c}_1, \mathbf{c}'_1)$, and private key $(1 - \mu, \mathbf{T}_{\mathsf{id}})$, the decryption algorithm does:

1. Compute $\mathbf{F}_{\mathsf{id},1-\mu} = [\mathbf{A}|\mathbf{A}_{1-\mu} - \mathbf{A}_{C_{\mathsf{PRF}},\mathsf{id}}]$.
2. Compute $\mathsf{m} = \mathbf{c}_{1-\mu} \oplus \mathsf{H}\left(\mathsf{Invert}(\mathbf{F}_{\mathsf{id},1-\mu}, \mathbf{T}_{\mathsf{id}}, \mathbf{c}'_{1-\mu})\right)$.

*Parameters.* With $s \geq \sqrt{5} \cdot B \cdot \omega(\sqrt{\log 2m})$, we ensure that the algorithm $\mathsf{SampleLeft}$ can be simulated by $\mathsf{SampleRight}$ in the security proof. We set $n \geq (n' + 2\kappa + \frac{\lambda}{\log q})\frac{\log q}{\log 2\gamma} + \frac{2\kappa}{\log q}$, $\sigma \geq 2B\beta\gamma nm$ for invoking Theorem 1. For decryption correctness, we need $\left\|\mathbf{e}_{1-\mu}^\top \cdot \mathbf{T}_{\mathsf{id}}\right\|_\infty \leq q/4$. So we set $q$ large enough such that $s\sigma m \leq q/4$.

If the we instantiate PRF by BMLR-PRF (Eq. 1), we can set the circuit $C_{\mathsf{PRF}}$ compute the function $\mathsf{MSB}(\lfloor \cdot, \cdot \rceil)$ where the first argument of the function is, say, the first row of the identity-dependent matrix $\prod_{i=1}^\ell \mathbf{B}_{\mathsf{id}[i]}$ and the second argument is the secret key $\mathbf{k}$. By doing that, the PRF computation is separated into a publicly computable "heavy" part (matrix product) and a "light" part (inner-product-then-rounding). With this change, for an identity $\mathsf{id}$, $\mathsf{KeyGen}$ and

Encrypt will first compute the bit string of the first row of $\prod_{i=1}^{\ell} \mathbf{B}_{\mathsf{id}[i]}$, and run Eval according to such string[2]. This makes $C_{\mathsf{PRF}}$ in $\mathsf{NC}^1$ and we can set $d = c \log(t + \ell)$, for some constant $c > 0$, such that $q = \mathsf{poly}(\kappa)$.

## 4  Security

**Theorem 2.** *For any PPT adversary $\mathcal{A}$ against the IND-ID-CPA security of above scheme $\Pi$ with advantage $\mathsf{Adv}^{\mathsf{IND\text{-}ID\text{-}CPA}}_{\mathcal{A},\Pi,(N,Q_{key},Q_{enc})}(\kappa)$, there exists PPT adversaries $\mathcal{A}_1, \mathcal{A}_2$ such that*

$$\mathsf{Adv}^{\mathsf{IND\text{-}ID\text{-}CPA}}_{\Pi,\mathcal{A},(N,Q_{key},Q_{enc})}(\kappa) \leq 3n \cdot \mathsf{Adv}^{\mathsf{LWE}_{n',q,\chi}}_{\mathcal{A}_1}(\kappa) + 2 \cdot \mathsf{Adv}^{\mathsf{PRF}}_{\mathcal{A}_2}(\kappa) + \mathsf{negl}(\kappa) \qquad (2)$$

*for some negligible error $\mathsf{negl}(\kappa)$.*

We prove the above theorem through game-sequence technique. Let $S_i$ denote the event that the IBE adversary $\mathcal{A}$ outputs $\mathsf{coin}' = \mathsf{coin}$ in $\mathbf{Game}_i$. We first define two simulation algorithms Sim.Setup and Sim.KeyGen. which are used only for security proof. Without loss of generality, assume the adversary asks for $N$ instances of the IBE scheme.

Sim.Setup($\mathsf{pub}, j$). For generating parameters for $j$-th instance, the algorithm does the following.

1. Choose a unique system identifier $\mathsf{ID}^{(j)}$.
2. Select $\mathbf{k}^{(j)} = \mathbf{k}^{(j)}[1]...\mathbf{k}^{(j)}[t] \leftarrow \{0,1\}^t$ for PRF.
3. Select a random matrix $\mathbf{A}^{(j)} \in \mathbb{Z}_q^{n \times m}$.
4. Select $\mathbf{R}^{(j)}_{\mathbf{A}_0}, \mathbf{R}^{(j)}_{\mathbf{A}_1}, \mathbf{R}^{(j)}_{\mathbf{C}_1}, ..., \mathbf{R}^{(j)}_{\mathbf{C}_t} \leftarrow \{-1,1\}^{m \times m}$.
5. Set $\mathbf{A}^{(j)}_0 = \mathbf{A}^{(j)}\mathbf{R}^{(j)}_{\mathbf{A}_0}$, $\mathbf{A}^{(j)}_1 = \mathbf{A}^{(j)}\mathbf{R}^{(j)}_{\mathbf{A}_1} + \mathbf{G}$, and $\mathbf{C}^{(j)}_i = \mathbf{A}^{(j)}\mathbf{R}^{(j)}_{\mathbf{C}_i} + \mathbf{k}^{(j)}[i]\mathbf{G}$ for $i \in [t]$.
6. Output $\mathsf{mpk}^{(j)} = \left(\mathsf{ID}^{(j)}, \mathbf{A}^{(j)}, \mathbf{A}^{(j)}_0, \mathbf{A}^{(j)}_1, \{\mathbf{C}^{(j)}_i\}_{i \in [t]}\right)$ and $\mathsf{msk}^{(j)} = \left(\mathbf{R}^{(j)}_{\mathbf{A}_0}, \mathbf{R}^{(j)}_{\mathbf{A}_1}, \{\mathbf{R}^{(j)}_{\mathbf{C}_i}\}_{i \in [t]}\right)$.

Sim.KeyGen($\mathsf{mpk}^{(j)}, \mathsf{msk}^{(j)}, \mathsf{id}$) On input $\mathsf{id} \in \{0,1\}^\ell$, the algorithm does:

1. For $\mathsf{ID}^{(j)} \| \mathsf{id} = \mathsf{id}[1], ..., \mathsf{id}[\ell]$, compute the $\mathbb{Z}_q^{n \times m}$-matrix

$$\begin{aligned}\mathbf{A}^{(j)}_{C_{\mathsf{PRF}},\mathsf{id}} &= \mathsf{Eval}(C_{\mathsf{PRF}}, \{\mathbf{C}^{(j)}_i\}_{i \in [t]}, \mathsf{id}[1]\mathbf{G}, ..., \mathsf{id}[\ell]\mathbf{G}) \\ &= \mathbf{A}^{(j)}\mathbf{R}^{(j)}_{C_{\mathsf{PRF}},\mathsf{id}} + \mathsf{MSB}(\mathsf{PRF}(\mathbf{k}^{(j)}, \mathsf{id}))\mathbf{G} \\ &= \mathbf{A}^{(j)}\mathbf{R}^{(j)}_{C_{\mathsf{PRF}},\mathsf{id}} + \mu\mathbf{G}\end{aligned}$$

---

[2] In this case we need to set parameter $t$ to be the length of such string.

2. Set the $\mathbb{Z}_q^{n \times 2m}$-matrix

$$
\begin{aligned}
\mathbf{F}_{\text{id},1-\mu}^{(j)} &= \left[ \mathbf{A}^{(j)} | \mathbf{A}_{1-\mu}^{(j)} - \mathbf{A}_{C_{\text{PRF}},\text{id}}^{(j)} \right] \\
&= \left[ \mathbf{A}^{(j)} | \mathbf{A}^{(j)}(\mathbf{R}_{\mathbf{A}_{1-\mu}}^{(j)} - \mathbf{R}_{C_{\text{PRF}},\text{id}}^{(j)}) + (1 - 2\mu)\mathbf{G}) \right] \\
&= \left[ \mathbf{A}^{(j)} | \mathbf{A}^{(j)}\mathbf{R}_{1-\mu}^{(j)} + (1 - 2\mu)\mathbf{G} \right]
\end{aligned}
$$

3. Run $\mathsf{SampleRight}(\mathbf{A}^{(j)}, \mathbf{R}_{1-\mu}^{(j)}, 1 - 2\mu, \mathbf{G}, s)$ to get a trapdoor $\mathbf{T}_{\text{id}}^{(j)}$ for $\mathbf{F}_{\text{id},1-\mu}^{(j)}$.
4. Return $\mathsf{sk}_{\text{id}}^{(j)} = (1 - \mu, \mathbf{T}_{\text{id}})$.

The first game **Game** 0 is the same as the real IND-ID-CPA security game. **Game** 1 is the same as **Game** 1 except it runs Sim.Setup and Sim.KeyGen instead of Setup and KeyGen.

**Lemma 11. Game** *0 and* **Game** *1 are statistically indistinguishable, i.e., there exist a negligible function* $\mathsf{negl}(\lambda)$ *such that* $|\Pr[S_0] - \Pr[S_1]| \le \mathsf{negl}(\lambda)$.

*Proof.* For $j$-th instance, the differences between **Game** 0 and **Game** 1 are:

1. In **Game** 0, $\mathbf{A}^{(j)}$ is generated by TrapGen. By Lemma 5 it has a distribution that is statistically close to uniform distribution on $\mathbb{Z}_q^{n \times m}$. On the other hand, $\mathbf{A}^{(j)}$ is sampled uniformly at random in **Game** 1.
2. By Lemma 2, matrices $\mathbf{A}_0, \mathbf{A}_0, \{\mathbf{C}_i\}_{i \in [t]}$ in **Game** 1 are statistically close to uniform distribution on $\mathbb{Z}_q^{n \times m}$. In **Game** 0 those matrices are sampled uniformly from $\mathbb{Z}_q^{n \times m}$.
3. In **Game** 0, the decryption key $\mathbf{T}_{\text{id}}^{(j)}$ is sampled by SampleLeft with the trapdoor of $\mathbf{A}^{(j)}$. In **Game** 1, $\mathbf{T}_{\text{id}}^{(j)}$ is sampled by SampleRight with the gadget matrix $\mathbf{G}$ and knowledge of the low-norm matrix $\mathbf{R}_{1-\mu}^{(j)}$. By Lemmas 7 and 8, for sufficiently large $s$ (e.g., $s \ge \sqrt{5}s_1(\mathbf{R}_{1-\mu}^{(j)}) \cdot \omega(\sqrt{\log 2m})$), $\mathbf{T}_{\text{id}}^{(j)}$ generated in **Game** 0 and **Game** 1 are statistically close.

We therefore conclude that **Game** 0 and **Game** 1 are statistically close up to some error $\mathsf{negl}(\lambda)$.

**Game** 2 is the same as **Game** 1 except that the public matrices $\{\mathbf{A}^{(j)}\}_{j \in [N]}$ for $N$ scheme instances are generated as LWE samples. More specifically, one firstly samples $\mathbf{C} \leftarrow \mathbb{Z}_q^{n' \times n}$. For constructing $\mathbf{A}^{(j)}$, it samples $\mathbf{B}^{(j)} \leftarrow \mathbb{Z}_q^{n' \times m}$, and $\mathbf{F}^{(j)} \leftarrow \chi^{m \times n}$ and sets $\mathbf{A}^{(j)} = \mathbf{C} \cdot \mathbf{B}^{(j)} + \mathbf{F}^{(j)} \bmod q$. Here $\mathbf{C}$ serves as the secret of LWE instances for all $\mathbf{A}^{(j)}$. It is easy to see that under the LWE assumption, **Game** 2 and **Game** 3 are computationally indistinguishable. So we have the following lemma in which the factor $n$ accounts for a $n$-step hybrid argument for reducing the LWE problem with matrix secret $\mathbf{C}$ to the LWE problem with single vector secret defined in Definition 3[3].

---

[3] Recall that the LWE problem is hard for arbitrary number of samples.

**Lemma 12.** $|\Pr[S_2] - \Pr[S_1]| \leq n \cdot \mathbf{Adv}_{\mathcal{A}_1}^{LWE_{n',q,\chi}}(\lambda)$ *for some adversary $\mathcal{A}_1$.*

**Game** 3 is the same as **Game** 2 except that it answers the encryption query in a slightly different way. Concretely, for encryption query $(k, j, \mathrm{id}, \mathsf{m}_0, \mathsf{m}_1)$ where $k \in [Q_{\mathsf{enc}}]$, $j \in [N]$, $\mathrm{id} \in \mathcal{ID}$ and $\mathsf{m}_0, \mathsf{m}_1 \in \mathcal{M}$, encryption (of message $\mathsf{m}_{\mathsf{coin}}$) is done by normal encryption algorithm except the ciphertext component $c_\mu^{(j)}$ is chosen uniformly at random from $\{0,1\}^\lambda$, where $\mu = \mathsf{MSB}(\mathsf{PRF}(\mathbf{k}^{(j)}, \mathsf{ID}^{(j)}||\mathrm{id}))$. We have the following lemma.

**Lemma 13. Game** *2 and* **Game** *3 are statistically indistinguishable, i.e., there exists a negligible error* $\mathsf{negl}(\kappa)$ *such that* $|\Pr[S_3] - \Pr[S_2]| \leq \mathsf{negl}(\kappa)$.

*Proof.* First of all, we have $\mu = \mathsf{MSB}(\mathsf{PRF}(\mathbf{k}^{(j)}, \mathsf{ID}^{(j)}||\mathrm{id})) \in \{0,1\}$. By the construction of encryption algorithm, we have

$$
\begin{aligned}
\mathbf{F}_{\mathrm{id},\mu}^{(j)} &= [\mathbf{A}^{(j)} | \mathbf{A}_\mu^{(j)} - \mathbf{A}_{C_{\mathsf{PRF}},\mathrm{id}}^{(j)}] \\
&= [\mathbf{A}^{(j)} | (\mathbf{A}^{(j)} \mathbf{R}_{\mathbf{A}_\mu}^{(j)} + \mu \mathbf{G}) - (\mathbf{A}^{(j)} \mathbf{R}_{C_{\mathsf{PRF}},\mathrm{id}}^{(j)} + \mathsf{MSB}(\mathsf{PRF}(\mathbf{k}^{(j)}, \mathsf{ID}^{(j)}||\mathrm{id})) \mathbf{G})] \\
&= [\mathbf{A}^{(j)} | \mathbf{A}^{(j)} (\mathbf{R}_{\mathbf{A}_\mu}^{(j)} - \mathbf{R}_{C_{\mathsf{PRF}},\mathrm{id}}^{(j)})] \\
&= [\mathbf{A}^{(j)} | \mathbf{A}^{(j)} \mathbf{R}_\mu{}^{(j)}]
\end{aligned}
$$

So for the ciphertext components $(\mathbf{c}_\mu'^{(j)}, \mathbf{c}_\mu{}^{(j)})$, we have

$$
\mathbf{c}_{\mu,k}'^{(j)}{}^\top = \mathbf{x}_{\mu,k}^{(j)}{}^\top \cdot \mathbf{F}_{\mathrm{id},\mu}^{(j)} + \mathbf{e}_{\mu,k}^{(j)}{}^\top \quad ; \quad c_{\mu,k}^{(j)} = \mathsf{m}_{\mathsf{coin}} \oplus \mathsf{H}(\mathbf{x}_{\mu,k}^{(j)})
$$

where $\mathbf{x}_{\mu,k}^{(j)}, e_{\mu,k}^{(j)}$ are chosen randomly and freshly for each ciphertext query with index $k$.[4] Recall $\mathbf{A}^{(j)} = \mathbf{C} \cdot \mathbf{B}^{(j)} + \mathbf{F}^{(j)}$ where $\mathbf{B}^{(j)} \in \mathbb{Z}_q^{n' \times m}$ is randomly chosen and $m = 2n \log q + \omega(\log q)$. By Lemma 2, $\mathbf{B}^{(j)} \mathbf{R}_\mu^{(j)}$ is statistically close to uniform (given $\mathbf{F}^{(j)} \mathbf{R}_\mu^{(j)}$) by itself, as required by Theorem 1. Since here we consider the left entropy of randomly and independently chosen $\mathbf{x}_{\mu,k}^{(j)}$, we can still apply Theorem 1 even though $\mathbf{B}^{(j)} \mathbf{R}_\mu^{(j)}$ is not statistically uniform given $\mathbf{F}_{\mathrm{id}',\mu}^{(j)}$ from another encryption query with $\mathrm{id}' \neq \mathrm{id}$. By Theorem 1 we get

$$
\begin{aligned}
H_\infty\left(\mathbf{x}_{\mu,k}{}^{(j)} | \mathbf{c}_{\mu,k}'^{(j)}\right) &\geq H_\infty\left(\mathbf{x}_{\mu,k}^{(j)}\right) - (n' + 2\kappa) \log q \\
&\geq n \log(2\gamma) - (n' + 2\kappa) \log q \\
&\geq \lambda + 2\kappa
\end{aligned}
$$

By Lemma 1, we have

$$
\Delta\left((\mathsf{H}, \mathsf{H}(\mathbf{x}_{\mu,k}^{(j)})), (\mathsf{H}, \rho_k^{(j)})\right) \leq 2^{-\kappa} = \mathsf{negl}(\kappa)
$$

for uniformly random string $\rho_k^{(j)} \leftarrow \{0,1\}^\lambda$. This makes $\mathbf{c}_{\mu,k}^{(j)}$ uniformly random and independent of $\mathsf{m}_{\mathsf{coin}}$.

---

[4] This is why our scheme achieves strong/full adaptive MIMC security.

**Game** 4 is the same as **Game** 3 except that it uses Sim.Setup to generate the public parameters. In particular, $\mathbf{A}^{(j)}$ is sampled uniform at random. Looking ahead, this step allows us to run Setup (instead of Sim.Setup) in the next game where we are able to have trapdoor for the matrix $\mathbf{A}^{(j)}$. A straightforward reduction gives us the following lemma.

**Lemma 14.** $|\Pr[S_4] - \Pr[S_3]| \leq n \cdot \mathsf{Adv}_{\mathcal{A}_1}^{LWE_{n',q,\chi}}(\kappa)$ *for some adversary* $\mathcal{A}_1$.

**Game** 5 is the same as **Game** 4 except that it runs algorithms Setup and KeyGen instead of the simulation algorithms. Similar to Lemma 11, we have

**Lemma 15. Game** *4 and* **Game** *5 are statistically indistinguishable, i.e.* $|\Pr[S_5] - \Pr[S_4]| \leq \mathsf{negl}(\kappa)$ *for some negligible function* $\mathsf{negl}(\kappa)$.

**Game** 6 is the same as **Game** 5 except that the simulator samples the bit value $\mu$ uniformly instead of computing it by PRF as in **Game** 5. The simulator also keeps the record of tuples $(j, \mathsf{id}, \mu)$. For a private key generation query or encryption query on instance $j$ and identity id that has been made before, the simulator simply finds the recorded $\mu$ and uses it for further operations. We prove the following lemma.

**Lemma 16.** $|\Pr[S_6] - \Pr[S_5]| \leq \mathsf{Adv}_{\mathcal{A}_2}^{PRF}(\kappa)$ *for some adversary* $\mathcal{A}_2$ *against* PRF.

*Proof.* We build a simulator $\mathcal{A}_2$ who uses a PRF challenger to simulate **Game** 5 or **Game** 6. $\mathcal{A}_2$ flips a fair coin $\mathsf{coin} \in \{0,1\}$ and follows $\mathsf{Para}(1^\kappa)$ to generate all the parameters of pub except the almost key-homomorphic PRF PRF. Instead, $\mathcal{A}_2$ receives PRF from its challenger.

$\mathcal{A}_2$ chooses $N$ random PRF keys $\{\tilde{\mathbf{k}}^{(j)}\}_{j \in [N]}$. Then it runs Setup to generate $\{\mathsf{mpk}^{(j)}, \mathsf{msk}^{(j)}\}_{j \in [N]}$ except the PRF keys. Notice that $\mathsf{mpk}^{(j)}$ has exactly the same distribution as in the real scheme. $\mathcal{A}_2$ answers the following two types of query.

1. For a key generation query $(j, \mathsf{id})$, $\mathcal{A}_2$ first sends $\mathsf{ID}^{(j)} \| \mathsf{id}$ to its challenger and receives back $y$. It sets $\mu = \mathsf{MSB}\left(y + \mathsf{PRF}(\tilde{\mathbf{k}}^{(j)}, \mathsf{ID}^{(j)} \| \mathsf{id})\right)$ and runs steps 2 to step 5 of KeyGen to generates the private identity key.
2. For an encryption query $(k, j, \mathsf{id}, \mathsf{m}_0, \mathsf{m}_1)$, $\mathcal{A}_2$ first sends $\mathsf{ID}^{(j)} \| \mathsf{id}$ to its challenger, receives back $y$, and sets $\mu = \mathsf{MSB}(y + \mathsf{PRF}(\tilde{\mathbf{k}}^{(j)}, \mathsf{ID}^{(j)} \| \mathsf{id}))$. It then runs Encrypt to generate ciphertext on message $\mathsf{m}_{\mathsf{coin}}$ based on the bit value $\mu$, except it samples the component $c_{\mu,k}^{(j)}$ randomly.

If $y = \mathsf{PRF}(\mathbf{k}^*, \mathsf{ID}^{(j)} \| \mathsf{id})$ for some key $\mathbf{k}^*$, i.e., $\mathcal{A}_2$ interacts with PRF, we have

$$\mu = \mathsf{MSB}(y + \mathsf{PRF}(\tilde{\mathbf{k}}^{(j)}, \mathsf{ID}^{(j)} \| \mathsf{id}))$$
$$= \mathsf{MSB}(\mathsf{PRF}(\mathbf{k}^*, \mathsf{ID}^{(j)} \| \mathsf{id}) + \mathsf{PRF}(\tilde{\mathbf{k}}^{(j)}, \mathsf{ID}^{(j)} \| \mathsf{id}))$$
$$= \mathsf{MSB}(\mathsf{PRF}(\mathbf{k}^* \boxplus \tilde{\mathbf{k}}^{(j)}, \mathsf{ID}^{(j)} \| \mathsf{id}))$$

This shows that $\mathcal{A}_2$ simulates **Game** 5 with random PRF key $\mathbf{k}^{(j)} = \mathbf{k}^* + \tilde{\mathbf{k}}^{(j)}$. On the other hand, if $y = F(\mathsf{ID}^{(j)}\|\mathsf{id})$ for some random function $F : \{0,1\}^\ell \to \{0,1\}^r$, as $F(\cdot)$ is never takes the same input, $\mu$ is uniformly random from the adversary's view. In this case, $\mathcal{A}_2$ simulates **Game** 6. Therefore we have $\Pr[S_6] - \Pr[S_5] \le \mathsf{Adv}_{\mathcal{A}_2}^{\mathsf{PRF}}(\kappa)$.

Let $(\mathbf{c}_{0,k}^{(j)}, \mathbf{c}_{0,k}'^{(j)}, \mathbf{c}_{1,k}^{(j)}, \mathbf{c}_{1,k}'^{(j)})$ be the challenge ciphertext generated for answering the $k$-th encryption query $(k, j, \mathsf{id}, \mathsf{m}_0, \mathsf{m}_1)$. Recall that in **Game** 6, depending on the bit value $\mu = \mathsf{MSB}(\mathsf{PRF}(\mathbf{k}^{(j)}, \mathsf{id}))$, $\mathbf{c}_\mu^{(j)}$ is chosen randomly. **Game** 7 is the same as **Game** 6 except that it chooses $\mathbf{c}_{1-\mu,k}^{(j)}$ randomly and computes other components honestly. Since $\mu$ is random, we have the following lemma.

**Lemma 17. Game** 6 *and* **Game** 7 *are identical, i.e.,* $\Pr[S_6] = \Pr[S_7]$.

**Game** 8 is the same as **Game** 7 except that for encryption and key generation queries on $j$-th instance and identity $\mathsf{id}$, the bit value $\mu$ is computed as $\mu = \mathsf{MSB}(\mathsf{PRF}(\mathbf{k}^{(j)}, \mathsf{ID}^{(j)}\|\mathsf{id}))$. Similar to Lemma 16, we have the following lemma for which we omit the proof as it is identical to the proof of Lemma 16.

**Lemma 18.** $|\Pr[S_7] - \Pr[S_8]| \le \mathsf{Adv}_{\mathcal{A}_2}^{\mathsf{PRF}}(\kappa)$ *for some adversary* $\mathcal{A}_2$ *against* **PRF**.

**Game** 9 is the same as **Game** 8 except that the simulation algorithms Sim,Setup and Sim.KeyGen are invoked instead of Setup and KeyGen. Notice that this difference is exactly the difference between **Game** 0 and **Game** 1. So we have the following lemma which can be proved using the proof of Lemma 11.

**Lemma 19. Game** 8 *and* **Game** 9 *are statistically indistinguishable, i.e., there exist a negligible function* $\mathsf{negl}(\kappa)$ *such that* $|\Pr[S_9] - \Pr[S_8]| \le \mathsf{negl}(\kappa)$.

In the next game **Game** 10, instead of sampling the public matrices $\{\mathbf{A}^{(j)}\}_{j\in[N]}$ for $N$ instances randomly, we again generate them by LWE samples as in **Game** 2, i.e., $\mathbf{A}^{(j)} = \mathbf{C} \cdot \mathbf{B}^{(j)} + \mathbf{F}^{(j)} \bmod q$. This change is not noticeable for efficient adversary under LWE assumption which can be stated by the lemma below.

**Lemma 20.** $|\Pr[S_{10}] - \Pr[S_9]| \le n \cdot \mathsf{Adv}_{\mathcal{A}_1}^{\mathsf{LWE}_{n',q,\chi}}(\kappa)$ *for some adversary* $\mathcal{A}_1$.

**Game** 11 is the same as **Game** 10 except that for any encryption query $(k, j, \mathsf{id}, \mathsf{m}_0, \mathsf{m}_1)$, the ciphertext component $\mathbf{c}_{\mu,k}^{(j)}$ are chosen randomly, where $\mu = \mathsf{PRF}(\mathbf{k}^{(j)}, \mathsf{ID}^{(j)}\|\mathsf{id})$. Notice that we have already switched the ciphertext component $\mathbf{c}_{1-\mu,k}^{(j)}$ to random since **Game** 7. So in **Game** 11, both $\mathbf{c}_{0,k}^{(j)}$ and $\mathbf{c}_{1,k}^{(j)}$ (which were used to mask the message $\mathsf{m}_{\mathsf{coin}}$) are random, meaning that the challenge ciphertexts replied to encryption queries are random and independent of the messages chosen by the adversary. So the adversary has no advantage in wining **Game** 11. The proof of the following lemma is omitted as it is the same as the proof of Lemma 13.

**Lemma 21. Game** *10 is statistically close to* **Game** *11, and in* **Game** *11, no adversary has any advantage in guessing the bit* **coin***, i.e.,* $|\Pr[S_{11}] - \Pr[S_{10}]| \leq$ negl$(\kappa)$ *for some statistically error* negl$(\kappa)$ *and* $\Pr[S_{11}] = 1/2$.

To sum up, we have:

$$\mathsf{Adv}^{\mathsf{IND\text{-}ID\text{-}CPA}}_{\Pi,\mathcal{A},(N,Q_{\mathsf{key}},Q_{\mathsf{enc}})}(\kappa) = |\Pr[S_1] - 1/2|$$

$$= |\Pr[S_1] - \Pr[S_{11}]|$$

$$\leq \sum_{i=0}^{10} |\Pr[S_i] - \Pr[S_{i+1}]|$$

$$= 3n \cdot \mathsf{Adv}^{\mathsf{LWE}_{n',q,\chi}}_{\mathcal{A}_1} + 2 \cdot \mathsf{Adv}^{\mathsf{PRF}}_{\mathcal{A}_2}(\kappa) + \mathsf{negl}(\kappa)$$

for some function negl$(\kappa)$ which stands for the negligible statistical error in the reduction. The security loss is independent of the number of instances $N$, the number of encryption queries $Q_{\mathsf{enc}}$ and the number of key generation queries $Q_{\mathsf{key}}$.

# 5   Discussion and Conclusion

For generality, we reduce the security of the IBE scheme to the LWE problem $\mathsf{LWE}_{n',q,\chi}$ and the security of the PRF as shown by Theorem 2. To make the whole IBE scheme (almost) tightly secure, we need (almost) tightly secure PRFs. The instantiation of PRF also affects the LWE problem $\mathsf{LWE}_{n',q,\chi}$ quantitatively by the depth $d$ of the circuit $C_{\mathsf{PRF}}$. For example, employing an almost tightly secure (based on the LWE problem) BLMR-PRF [10] allows us to use a polynomial modulo $q$. Meanwhile, the computational assumption we make for the PRF affects the final assumption that we need to make for the IBE scheme. The (almost) tight security proof of the BLMR-PRF requires an LWE assumption with modulus-to-noise ratio $n^{\Omega(\ell)}$ ($\ell$ is the PRF input length) which is quantitatively stronger than the LWE problem $\mathsf{LWE}_{n',q,\chi}$ we use for the LWE lossy mode. This means the IBE scheme needs a strong LWE assumption on which the BLMR-PRF is based. However any future improvement in (lattice-based) key-homomorphic PRFs will directly improve the efficiency and security of our scheme without weakening the underlying assumption.

Under a suitable BLMR-PRF instantiation, our IBE scheme, based on a strong LWE assumption (sub-exponential modulus-to-noise ratio), achieves almost tight security in the strong MIMC setting. Under the same assumption, the Boyen-Li IBE scheme from [11] (using almost tightly secure PRFs from [5,10]) only had an almost tight security reduction in the SISC setting. The (strong) LWE assumption that we use is believed to be hard and has been widely used in other contexts, including fully-homomorphic encryption [14], attribute-based/predicate encryption [9,21,22] and lattice-based constrained PRFs [13,15]. How to obtain an (almost) tightly secure IBE scheme in the MIMC setting was not known before, even with such a strong LWE assumption. By applying the standard BCHK transformation [8] with tightly secure one-time signature schemes (e.g., [7]), our IBE scheme leads to the first almost tightly CCA2 secure public-key encryption scheme from lattices in the multi-instance and multi-ciphertext setting [23].

Our work motivates two future directions: to improve efficiency and key sizes; and to design tightly secure key-homomorphic PRFs from weaker assumptions.

# References

1. Agrawal, S., Boneh, D., Boyen, X.: Efficient lattice (H)IBE in the standard model. In: Gilbert, H. (ed.) EUROCRYPT 2010. LNCS, vol. 6110, pp. 553–572. Springer, Heidelberg (2010). https://doi.org/10.1007/978-3-642-13190-5_28

2. Ajtai, M.: Generating hard instances of lattice problems (extended abstract). In: STOC, pp. 99–108 (1996)

3. Alwen, J., Krenn, S., Pietrzak, K., Wichs, D.: Learning with rounding, revisited. In: Canetti, R., Garay, J.A. (eds.) CRYPTO 2013. LNCS, vol. 8042, pp. 57–74. Springer, Heidelberg (2013). https://doi.org/10.1007/978-3-642-40041-4_4

4. Attrapadung, N., Hanaoka, G., Yamada, S.: A framework for identity-based encryption with almost tight security. In: Iwata, T., Cheon, J.H. (eds.) ASIACRYPT 2015. LNCS, vol. 9452, pp. 521–549. Springer, Heidelberg (2015). https://doi.org/10.1007/978-3-662-48797-6_22

5. Banerjee, A., Peikert, C., Rosen, A.: Pseudorandom functions and lattices. In: Pointcheval, D., Johansson, T. (eds.) EUROCRYPT 2012. LNCS, vol. 7237, pp. 719–737. Springer, Heidelberg (2012). https://doi.org/10.1007/978-3-642-29011-4_42

6. Bellare, M., Kiltz, E., Peikert, C., Waters, B.: Identity-based (lossy) trapdoor functions and applications. In: Pointcheval, D., Johansson, T. (eds.) EUROCRYPT 2012. LNCS, vol. 7237, pp. 228–245. Springer, Heidelberg (2012). https://doi.org/10.1007/978-3-642-29011-4_15

7. Blazy, O., Kakvi, S.A., Kiltz, E., Pan, J.: Tightly-secure signatures from chameleon hash functions. In: Katz, J. (ed.) PKC 2015. LNCS, vol. 9020, pp. 256–279. Springer, Heidelberg (2015). https://doi.org/10.1007/978-3-662-46447-2_12

8. Boneh, D., Canetti, R., Halevi, S., Katz, J.: Chosen-ciphertext security from identity-based encryption. SIAM J. Comput. $\mathbf{36}(5)$, 1301–1328 (2006)

9. Boneh, D., Gentry, C., Gorbunov, S., Halevi, S., Nikolaenko, V., Segev, G., Vaikuntanathan, V., Vinayagamurthy, D.: Fully key-homomorphic encryption, arithmetic circuit ABE and compact garbled circuits. In: Nguyen, P.Q., Oswald, E. (eds.) EUROCRYPT 2014. LNCS, vol. 8441, pp. 533–556. Springer, Heidelberg (2014). https://doi.org/10.1007/978-3-642-55220-5_30

10. Boneh, D., Lewi, K., Montgomery, H., Raghunathan, A.: Key homomorphic PRFs and their applications. In: Canetti, R., Garay, J.A. (eds.) CRYPTO 2013. LNCS, vol. 8042, pp. 410–428. Springer, Heidelberg (2013). https://doi.org/10.1007/978-3-642-40041-4_23

11. Boyen, X., Li, Q.: Towards tightly secure lattice short signature and id-based encryption. In: Cheon, J.H., Takagi, T. (eds.) ASIACRYPT 2016. LNCS, vol. 10032, pp. 404–434. Springer, Heidelberg (2016). https://doi.org/10.1007/978-3-662-53890-6_14

12. Boyen, X., Li, Q.: All-but-many lossy trapdoor functions from lattices and applications. In: Katz, J., Shacham, H. (eds.) CRYPTO 2017. LNCS, vol. 10403, pp. 298–331. Springer, Cham (2017). https://doi.org/10.1007/978-3-319-63697-9_11

13. Brakerski, Z., Tsabary, R., Vaikuntanathan, V., Wee, H.: Private constrained PRFs (and more) from LWE. In: Kalai, Y., Reyzin, L. (eds.) TCC 2017. LNCS, vol. 10677, pp. 264–302. Springer, Cham (2017). https://doi.org/10.1007/978-3-319-70500-2_10

14. Brakerski, Z., Vaikuntanathan, V.: Efficient fully homomorphic encryption from (standard) LWE. In: FOCS, pp. 97–106 (2011)

15. Brakerski, Z., Vaikuntanathan, V.: Constrained key-homomorphic PRFs from standard lattice assumptions. In: Dodis, Y., Nielsen, J.B. (eds.) TCC 2015. LNCS, vol. 9015, pp. 1–30. Springer, Heidelberg (2015). https://doi.org/10.1007/978-3-662-46497-7_1

16. Cash, D., Hofheinz, D., Kiltz, E., Peikert, C.: Bonsai trees, or how to delegate a lattice basis. J. Cryptol. **25**(4), 601–639 (2012)

17. Chen, J., Gong, J., Weng, J.: Tightly secure IBE under constant-size master public key. In: Fehr, S. (ed.) PKC 2017. LNCS, vol. 10174, pp. 207–231. Springer, Heidelberg (2017). https://doi.org/10.1007/978-3-662-54365-8_9

18. Gentry, C., Peikert, C., Vaikuntanathan, V.: Trapdoors for hard lattices and new cryptographic constructions. In: STOC, pp. 197–206 (2008)

19. Gong, J., Chen, J., Dong, X., Cao, Z., Tang, S.: Extended nested dual system groups, revisited. In: Cheng, C.-M., Chung, K.-M., Persiano, G., Yang, B.-Y. (eds.) PKC 2016. LNCS, vol. 9614, pp. 133–163. Springer, Heidelberg (2016). https://doi.org/10.1007/978-3-662-49384-7_6

20. Gong, J., Dong, X., Chen, J., Cao, Z.: Efficient IBE with tight reduction to standard assumption in the multi-challenge setting. In: Cheon, J.H., Takagi, T. (eds.) ASIACRYPT 2016. LNCS, vol. 10032, pp. 624–654. Springer, Heidelberg (2016). https://doi.org/10.1007/978-3-662-53890-6_21

21. Gorbunov, S., Vaikuntanathan, V., Wee, H.: Attribute-based encryption for circuits. In: STOC, pp. 545–554 (2013)

22. Gorbunov, S., Vaikuntanathan, V., Wee, H.: Predicate encryption for circuits from LWE. In: Gennaro, R., Robshaw, M. (eds.) CRYPTO 2015. LNCS, vol. 9216, pp. 503–523. Springer, Heidelberg (2015). https://doi.org/10.1007/978-3-662-48000-7_25

23. Hofheinz, D., Jager, T.: Tightly secure signatures and public-key encryption. In: Safavi-Naini, R., Canetti, R. (eds.) CRYPTO 2012. LNCS, vol. 7417, pp. 590–607. Springer, Heidelberg (2012). https://doi.org/10.1007/978-3-642-32009-5_35

24. Hofheinz, D., Koch, J., Striecks, C.: Identity-based encryption with (almost) tight security in the multi-instance, multi-ciphertext setting. In: Katz, J. (ed.) PKC 2015. LNCS, vol. 9020, pp. 799–822. Springer, Heidelberg (2015). https://doi.org/10.1007/978-3-662-46447-2_36

25. Libert, B., Sakzad, A., Stehlé, D., Steinfeld, R.: All-but-many lossy trapdoor functions and selective opening chosen-ciphertext security from LWE. In: Katz, J., Shacham, H. (eds.) CRYPTO 2017. LNCS, vol. 10403, pp. 332–364. Springer, Cham (2017). https://doi.org/10.1007/978-3-319-63697-9_12

26. Micciancio, D., Peikert, C.: Trapdoors for lattices: simpler, tighter, faster, smaller. In: Pointcheval, D., Johansson, T. (eds.) EUROCRYPT 2012. LNCS, vol. 7237, pp. 700–718. Springer, Heidelberg (2012). https://doi.org/10.1007/978-3-642-29011-4_41

27. Peikert, C., Waters, B.: Lossy trapdoor functions and their applications. SIAM J. Comput. **40**(6), 1803–1844 (2011)

28. Regev, O.: On lattices, learning with errors, random linear codes, and cryptography. In: STOC, pp. 84–93 (2005)

# Authentication and Biometrics

# In-Region Authentication

Mamunur Rashid Akand$^{(\boxtimes)}$ and Reihaneh Safavi-Naini

University of Calgary, Calgary, AB, Canada
{mdmamunurrashid.akan,rei}@ucalgary.ca

**Abstract.** Location information has wide applications in customization and personalization of services, as well as secure authentication and access control. We introduce *in-Region Authentication (inRA)*, a novel type of authentication, that allows a prover to prove to a set of cooperating verifiers that they are in possession of the correct secret key, and are inside a specified (policy) region of arbitrary shape. These requirements naturally arise when a privileged service is offered to registered users within an area. Locating a prover without assuming GPS (Global Positioning System) signal however, incurs error. We discuss the challenge of designing secure protocols that have quantifiable error in this setting, define and formalize correctness and security properties of the protocols, and propose a systematic approach to designing a family of protocols with provable security where error can be flexibly defined and efficiently minimized. We give an instance of this family that requires only two verifiers, prove its security and evaluate its performance in four typical policy regions. Our results show that in all cases false acceptance and false rejection of below 6% can be achieved. We compare our results with related works, and propose directions for future research.

**Keywords:** In-region · Distance bounding · Authentication

## 1 Introduction

Location-based services (LBS) have provided exciting opportunities to use position related information such as location, proximity or distance in improving system security, control access, and personalized service delivery [14,16,29]. One of the earliest applications of user location is for securing authentication systems [9] against man-in-the-middle (MiM) attack. Secure authentication protocols are challenge-response protocols between a *prover* and a *verifier*. In an MiM attack against these protocols, an attacker runs two simultaneous sessions of the protocol, one with an honest prover and one with the (honest) verifier, and by passing the responses of the prover to the verifier, succeeds in making the protocol accept their claim. Desmedt *et al.* [9] showed that protection against this attack, that does not any cryptographic solution, can be provided if the verifier uses an estimate of the location of the prover (e.g. distance to the verifier) as a second factor in authentication. Distance (Upper) Bounding (DUB)

© Springer International Publishing AG, part of Springer Nature 2018
B. Preneel and F. Vercauteren (Eds.): ACNS 2018, LNCS 10892, pp. 557–578, 2018.
https://doi.org/10.1007/978-3-319-93387-0_29

protocols [5] are challenge-response authentication protocols that provide cryptographic authentication security with the extra guarantee that the user is within a distance bound to the verifier. These protocols have been widely studied, their security has been formalized, and protocols with provable properties have been proposed [4,5,10,22]. Successful authentication allows the user to perform privileged actions, e.g., open the car door [12], or access a special system resource.

In this paper we consider the problem of controlling access with respect to a region $\mathcal{R}$, that is called *policy region*. The user has to "prove" to the verifier(s) that, (i) they have the secret key $k_u$, and (ii) they are within the region $\mathcal{R}$. This setting naturally arises when a privileged service is offered in a region $\mathcal{R}$. For example a project team in a software development company can access proprietary project information when they are within their work area. In this setting authentication protocol must prove the conjunction,

$$User \text{ has the shared secret } k_u \wedge (User \text{ is in } \mathcal{R}). \tag{1}$$

We propose a new authentication system that is called *in-Region Authentication (inRA)*, that proves that the above conjunction holds.

A simplistic solution to prove the conjunction (1) is to use a secure cryptographic authentication to allow the user to prove that they know the secret $k_u$, and then use a secure location verification protocol to prove their location. This solution however will be insecure because, firstly, proving the two clauses separately allows new attacks, for example the prover changing the location in between the two steps, and secondly, secure location verification protocols [8,19] start with the prover claiming a location, which needs them to access GPS signal. This not only limits the application of the protocol to locations where GPS signal is available, but also opens the possibility of GPS spoofing attacks [24].

One can combine the two steps when $\mathcal{R}$ is a circular region by employing a secure DUB protocol: the verifier of the DUB protocol will be placed at the center of the region and the distance bound will be chosen as the radius of $\mathcal{R}$ (Fig. 1a). The approach works perfectly because $\mathcal{R}$ is perfectly covered with the circle associated with the boundary of the DUB protocol. For arbitrary $\mathcal{R}$, one can use an *approximate cover* by using one or more verifiers (See Fig. 1b and c): the prover must prove its distance to the corresponding verifier of each part of the region. This is the approach in [17] to solve the closely related problem of *in-region location verification* where the goal is to verify that the prover is within the region, *without requiring secured authentication of the user* or quantifying error.

Using multiple verifiers to cover $\mathcal{R}$ requires one to determine the *verifier configuration*, which is specified by (i) the number of verifiers, (ii) their locations, and (iii) their associated distance bounds. Note that the error associated to a configuration does not have an algebraic form and one cannot use traditional optimization methods to find the optimal configuration, and this is true even if the number and location of verifiers are known.

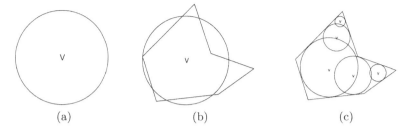

**Fig. 1.** Location verification for (a) circular region $\mathcal{R}$ that is perfectly covered by a single verifier placed at the center of $\mathcal{R}$, (b) arbitrary shaped region $\mathcal{R}$, a single verifier does not give perfect coverage, and (c) arbitrary shaped region $\mathcal{R}$, multiple verifiers are placed inside $\mathcal{R}$ ([17]'s approach), also does not give perfect coverage.

## Our Work

*Model.* Our goal is to design provably secure authentication protocols that allow the prover to prove the conjunction (1), while minimizing protocol error. In Sect. 3 we formally define an inRA system for a set of registered (provers) and a set of unregistered users, a set of collaborating verifiers, and an inRA protocol whose correctness is defined using FA (False acceptance) and FR (False rejection) with respect to the policy region $\mathcal{R}$. Our security definition formalizes attacks that involve a malicious prover outside $\mathcal{R}$, an unregistered user inside $\mathcal{R}$, and a collusion of a malicious prover and a helper who is inside $\mathcal{R}$. A significant challenge in modelling and achieving security is the possibility of the prover moving between their interactions with different verifiers. Our security model uses ITMs (Interactive Turing Machines) to model the prover and verifiers and does not formalize time (movement of the prover). We assume prover movement will be detected through other mechanisms, and our protocol introduces a mechanism that does that, allowing us to use our security model.

*Construction.* Armed with this model and definition, we propose a systematic approach to designing inRA protocols for the proof of the conjunction (1) and with *quantifiable correctness error*, and give an efficient algorithm to minimizing the error (see below). The approach in its basic form uses two verifiers $V_0$ and $V_1$, and covers the region $\mathcal{R}$ with a *pseudo-rectangle (P-rect)* $R'(V_0, V_1)$ that is formed by two rings centered at the two verifiers (See Fig. 2 and Sect. 3). A ring is formed by a verifier running a DUB protocol followed by a *Distance Lower Bounding (DLB)* protocol [28] (that guarantees a lower bound on the distance of the prover to the verifier- See Sect. 2), with the prover. The two verifiers work in tandem, with the second immediately following the first. Verifiers use omnidirectional antennas during the protocol initialization, and use *directional antennas* for the challenge-response phase.

This basic inRA protocol approximates $\mathcal{R}$ with a P-rect and results in FA and FR. We define the total error as the sum of FA and FR errors and aim at minimizing it. Our approach however can be easily extended to the case that the two types of errors have different significance – see Sect. 6.

*Minimizing Error.* For fixed locations of $V_0$ and $V_1$, the total error is a function of the distance bounds of the two verifiers. To minimize error one can use brute force method and for every possible values of distance bounds, find the error and select the minimal value. This is an infeasible task in practice. We give an innovative approach that uses *maximum subarray problem* [13] algorithm to solve the optimization problem of finding a P-rect that is proved to minimize the total error in approximate coverage of $\mathcal{R}$ with a P-rect. The algorithm has complexity $O(n^3)$ where $n$ is the size of $\mathcal{R}$ represented as a point set. This basic algorithm can be employed multiple times using more verifiers, to increase accuracy. In Sect. 6 we show that using two P-rects to cover the region reduces the total error by up to 15%. We leave the problem of optimizing the number and the locations of the verifiers as an interesting direction for future work.

*Security Proof.* In our basic protocol (Sect. 4) we will use a novel approach to detecting movement of the prover during protocol execution, by using each verifier to play the role of an observer for the other verifier's interaction with the prover. We will then use our security model to prove security against attacks. We discuss how protection against a new attack called *key splitting attack* that is the result of using a pair of DUB and DLB protocols with two verifiers, can be avoided by using keys shared with $V_0$ and $V_1$ both, to generate the fast phase responses to each verifier.

*Implementation and Experimental Results.* We implemented the optimization algorithm for two verifiers and applied it to four policy regions corresponding to buildings in our University (Sect. 6). We started with a $640 \times 640$ Google Map image of the policy region, and converted it into a binary image for point-set representation of the policy regions. To achieve higher accuracy, we used two P-rects to cover the policy region. Table 1 summarizes our results. The highest accuracy is obtained for the most regularly shaped rectangular region. In all cases FA and FR range between 0.81% to 5.16%, and 3.89% to 5.58%, respectively.

We compared our approach with the scheme in Sastry et al. [17]. This is the only system with comparable security goals and assumptions. Comparison (Sect. 6) clearly shows superior performance of our approach: [17] uses 5 verifiers to achieve 93% accuracy and uses informal security analysis, while we use 2 verifiers, achieve 96.4% accuracy, and provide formal security proof.

*Extensions.* One can define weights for each type of FA and FR error depending on the application, and use optimization approach on the weighted error function. The approach raises numerous interesting open questions such as optimizing the total error when there are more than two verifiers, and one needs to select their locations and distance bounds. We leave these for future work.

*Organization.* Section 2 is preliminaries. Section 3 describes our inRA model. Section 4 details the inRA protocol $\Pi_{rect}$, and the security analysis. Section 5 provides our approach to minimize error. Section 6 includes our experimental results. Section 7 presents related works and Sect. 8 concludes the paper.

## 2 Preliminaries

**Distance Bounding.** Secure *distance bounding protocols* have three phases: (i) initialization phase, (ii) Challenge-response phase, and (iii) Verification phase. The round-trip time of a challenge and response is used to estimate distance. The goal of a distance Upper bounding (DUB) protocol is to ensure that a prover $P$ located at distance $d_{PV}$ satisfies $d_{PV} \leq \mathcal{B}_U$ where $\mathcal{B}_U$ is a fixed upperbound.

The main attacks on distance bounding protocols are, (i) Distance fraud attack: a far away dishonest prover tries to claim a shorter $d_{PV}$ and be accepted by $V$; (ii) Mafia fraud attack: an external attacker uses the communication of an honest prover to get accepted by the verifier, and (iii) Terrorist attack (also known as collusion attack): a dishonest prover gets help from a helper that is close to the verifier, to get accepted by the verifier. A number of formal security models that capture above attacks, and protocols with provable security have been proposed [10, 22]. Secure DUB protocols are vulnerable to distance enlargement attack but not to distance reduction attack [6].

The goal of distance lower bounding (DLB) protocols [28] is the converse: a prover wants to prove that their distance to the verifier is larger than a given bound. Zheng *et al.* [28] showed that one cannot simply use DUB protocols to guarantee a lower bound on the distance of the prover. They proposed a security model for DLB that is inline with the DUB security model, and constructed a DLB protocol with provable security in their model. Our construction of inRA protocol $\Pi_{Prect}$ uses DLB protocol together with a DUB protocol.

**Maximum Subarray Problem.** Optimizing P-rect uses *maximum subarray problem (MSP)*, first proposed in [13]. The problem is to select a contiguous segment of an array that has the largest sum over all possible array segments. Efficient algorithms for MSP problem have applications in computer vision, data mining and genomic sequence analysis [11, 21, 25]. For a 2D array $a[1...m][1...n]$, the maximum sub-array $M$ is given by [3],

$$M = \max \sum_{x=i,y=g}^{j,h} a[x][y] | 1 \leq i \leq j \leq m, 1 \leq g \leq h \leq n \tag{2}$$

Solutions have complexity cubic or sub-cubic [20]. To find the P-rect with the lowest total error, or equivalently maximum accuracy, we will use *FindOptimalBounds* algorithm (Sect. 4) that uses the extended Kadane's algorithm [3].

## 3 In-Region Authentication Systems

Consider a two-dimensional planar connected (path connected) geographic area represented by an array of points, each point representing a geolocation[1]. Let $\mathcal{U}$

---

[1] A point set corresponding to a geographic area can be constructed using a bitmap image of the area, at the required resolution level. Thus each point corresponds to a geographic square of size $u$ where $u$ is determined by the resolution of the mapping.

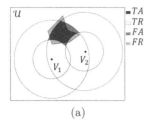 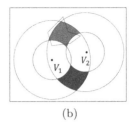

(a)                                        (b)

**Fig. 2.** (a) The policy region $\mathcal{R}$ is the yellow arbitrary shaped region. The blue (almost) rectangular area is P-rect $\mathcal{R}_\Pi$ for the inRA protocol in Sect. 4. The dark blue area of $\mathcal{R}$ is correctly covered. The remaining yellow and blue areas are $FR_{\Pi,\mathcal{R}}$ and $FA_{\Pi,\mathcal{R}}$, respectively. (b) The upper intersection forms $R_{rect}$ to cover $\mathcal{R}$ (blue). The lower intersection forms $R'_{rect}$ (red), an ambiguous region. (Color figure online)

denote the universe of all points of interest, and $\mathcal{R} \subset \mathcal{U}$, be the *policy region*. There are multiple parties, each represented by a polynomially bounded Interactive Turing Machine (ITM), and associated with a location *loc*.

A *protocol instance* between two honest parties $P$ and $V$ is modelled by a probabilistic *experiment* where each party uses its algorithm on its input and random coin. This is shown by $P(x; r_P) \leftrightarrow V(y; r_V)$, $x$ and $y$ are the inputs, $r_P$ and $r_V$ are the random coins of the two participants, respectively. We can "enlarge" the experiment to include an adversary's algorithm, shown as: $P(x; r_P) \leftrightarrow A(r_A) \leftrightarrow V(y; r_V)$. This means that an adversary $A$ is interfering with the communication between the honest participants.

**inRA Protocols.** Let $\mathcal{R}$ be a connected policy region (Fig. 2). The *verifying system* consists of a set of verifiers $\mathcal{V} = \{V_0 \cdots V_{m-1}\}$, with publicly known locations. Verifiers are trusted to follow the protocol and can communicate among themselves through secure channels to exchange information and coordinate their actions. Verifiers are equipped with *directional antennas* whose signals can be received in a conic region of space that covers $\mathcal{R}$. A prover $P$ with location $loc_P$, has shared keys with the verifier set $\mathcal{V}$. The prover is not trusted.

An *in-region authentication protocol* is a protocol $\Pi$ between $P$ and $\mathcal{V}$, at the end of which $\mathcal{V}$ outputs $Out_\mathcal{V} = 0$ or 1, denoting reject and accept of the prover's claim, respectively. Prover does not have an output and so $Out_\mathcal{V}$ is the protocol output. The prover's claim is stated as the conjunction in (1).

DUB protocols can be seen as inRA protocols where the second proposition is, *P is within a distance bound from the verifier.*

**Error and Accuracy in inRa Protocols.** Consider an instance of a protocol $\Pi$ between an honest prover $P$ and the verifier set, in the absence of an adversary. Let $\mathcal{R}_\Pi \subset \mathcal{U}$ denote the set of points $u \in \mathcal{U}$ that $\Pi$ will have $Out_\mathcal{V} = 1$. We define two types of errors for the protocol $\Pi$ with respect to the region $\mathcal{R}$: $FA_{\Pi,\mathcal{R}}$ and $FR_{\Pi,\mathcal{R}}$, denoting false acceptance and false rejection of the protocol $\Pi$, respectively, where, (i) $FA_{\Pi,\mathcal{R}}$ is the *set of locations* that are in $R_\Pi \setminus \mathcal{R}$,[2]

---

[2] $A \setminus B$ denotes the set of points that are in $A$ and not in $B$.

and $FR_{\Pi,\mathcal{R}}$ is the *set of locations* that are in $\mathcal{R} \setminus \mathcal{R}_{\Pi}$. *Accuracy ratio* can be defined as follows [15]:

$$Accuracy\ ratio = \frac{TA_{\Pi,\mathcal{R}} + TR_{\Pi,\mathcal{R}}}{TA_{\Pi,\mathcal{R}} + TR_{\Pi,\mathcal{R}} + FA_{\Pi,\mathcal{R}} + FR_{\Pi,\mathcal{R}}} \tag{3}$$

where $TA_{\Pi,\mathcal{R}}$ and $TR_{\Pi,\mathcal{R}}$ denote the true acceptance and true rejection sets, $TA_{\Pi,\mathcal{R}}$ is the set of points in $\mathcal{R} \cap \mathcal{R}_{\Pi}$ and are accepted by the algorithm, and $TR_{\Pi,\mathcal{R}}$ is the set of points in $\mathcal{U} \setminus \{\mathcal{R} \cup \mathcal{R}_{\Pi}\}$ and are rejected by the algorithm. Now, *Error ratio* = 1 − *Accuracy ratio*, and can be expressed as,

$$Error\ ratio = \frac{FA_{\Pi,\mathcal{R}} + FR_{\Pi,\mathcal{R}}}{TA_{\Pi,\mathcal{R}} + TR_{\Pi,\mathcal{R}} + FA_{\Pi,\mathcal{R}} + FR_{\Pi,\mathcal{R}}} \tag{4}$$

Since $\mathcal{U} = (TA_{\Pi,\mathcal{R}} + TR_{\Pi,\mathcal{R}} + FA_{\Pi,\mathcal{R}} + FR_{\Pi,\mathcal{R}})$ is constant, to minimize error one needs to minimize $(FA_{\Pi,\mathcal{R}} + FR_{\Pi,\mathcal{R}})$. In our work we use *error* $E_{\Pi,\mathcal{R}}$ given by,

$$\text{Error:} \qquad E_{\Pi,\mathcal{R}} = FA_{\Pi,\mathcal{R}} + FR_{\Pi,\mathcal{R}} \tag{5}$$

Note that one can attach weights to points in $FA_{\Pi,\mathcal{R}}$ or $FR_{\Pi,\mathcal{R}}$ to reflect their importance in a particular application. In this paper we assume the same significance for the two types of errors. For $\mathcal{R} = TA_{\Pi,\mathcal{R}} + FR_{\Pi,\mathcal{R}}$, we can write,

$$FA_{\Pi,\mathcal{R}} + FR_{\Pi,\mathcal{R}} = FA_{\Pi,\mathcal{R}} + (\mathcal{R} - TA_{\Pi,\mathcal{R}})$$
$$= \mathcal{R} - (TA_{\Pi,\mathcal{R}} - FA_{\Pi,\mathcal{R}}).$$

$\mathcal{R}$ is fixed and so *minimizing* $(FA_{\Pi,\mathcal{R}} + FR_{\Pi,\mathcal{R}})$ *is equivalent to maximizing* $(TA_{\Pi,\mathcal{R}} - FA_{\Pi,\mathcal{R}})$. We say that in our $\mathcal{R}$ coverage problem, error is minimized by minimizing $(FA_{\Pi,\mathcal{R}} + FR_{\Pi,\mathcal{R}})$, or equivalently, accuracy is maximized by maximizing $(TA_{\Pi,\mathcal{R}} - FA_{\Pi,\mathcal{R}})$. Therefore, we define Accuracy $A_{\Pi,\mathcal{R}}$ as:

$$\text{Accuracy:} \qquad A_{\Pi,\mathcal{R}} = TA_{\Pi,\mathcal{R}} - FA_{\Pi,\mathcal{R}} \tag{6}$$

**Definition 1 (in-Region Authentication).** *An in-region authentication (inRA) protocol $\Pi$ is a tuple $\Pi = (Gen, P, \mathcal{V} = \{V_0 \cdots V_{m-1}\}, \mathcal{R})$ where:*

1. $\mathcal{X} \leftarrow Gen(1^s, r_k)$ *is a randomized key generation algorithm that generates a vector $\mathcal{X} = \{x_0, \ldots, x_{m-1}\}$ of $n$ secret keys, where $x_i$ is the prover's shared secret key with $V_i$, and $r_k$ denoting the random coins of Gen. $s$ is the security parameter.*
2. $P(\mathcal{X}; r_P)$, *is a ppt. (probabilistic polynomial time) ITM (Interactive Turing Machine) running the prover algorithm with random input $r_P$ and the secret key vector $\mathcal{X} = \{x_0, \ldots, x_m - 1\}$.*
3. $\mathcal{V} = (V_0, \ldots, V_{m-1})$ *is a set of verifiers, each verifier $V_i(x_i; r_{V_i}) \in \mathcal{V}$ is a ppt. ITM running algorithm with random input $r_{V_i}$ and shared secret $x_i$. We write $\mathcal{V}(\mathcal{X}, r_{\mathcal{V}})$ to denote the set of the verifiers' algorithms.*
4. $\mathcal{R}$ *is a set of points corresponding to a contiguous region. This is the* policy region.

*The protocol satisfies the following properties:*

- **Termination:** $(\forall s)$ $(\forall \mathcal{Z})$ $(\forall (r_k, r_V))$ $(\forall loc_V)$ if $\mathcal{X} \leftarrow Gen(1^s, r_k)$ and $(\mathcal{Z} \longleftrightarrow V(\mathcal{X}; r_V))$ *is the execution where $\mathcal{Z}$ is any set of prover algorithms, then $V$ halts in polynomial number of computational steps (Poly(s));*
- **p-Completeness:** $(\forall s)$ $(\forall (loc_V, loc_P))$ *such that $loc_P \in \mathcal{R}$ we have*

$$\Pr_{r_k, r_P, r_V} \left[ Out_V = 1 : \begin{array}{c} \mathcal{X} \leftarrow Gen(1^s, r_k) \\ P(\mathcal{X}; r_P) \leftrightarrow V(\mathcal{X}; r_V) \end{array} \right] \geq p. \tag{7}$$

Similar definition of termination and completeness is used for DB prortocols [1,22,28].

## 3.1   inRA Security

We consider a prover, possibly malicious, who may receive help from a helper who is in $\mathcal{R}$ but does not have a secret key.

The adversary attempts to prove that their location is inside $\mathcal{R}$ (while they are actually outside) and their success chance must be negligible even if they know the shared key. We use a game-based approach in defining security, and define security in terms of the success chance of an adversary in the following security games against a challenger. Each game starts with a setup phase where the challenger sets the keys and locations of participants. This is followed by the adversary corrupting some of the participants (depending on the game), engaging them in a learning phase and finally the attack phase. We omit the details because of space and outline the steps of each game in the definition of each attack. In the following, a dishonest prover is denoted by $P^*$.

**in-Region Fraud (inF).** In this attack, a corrupted prover $P^*$ who has the secret key and is in $\mathcal{U} \setminus \mathcal{R}$ wants to prove that they are inside $\mathcal{R}$.

**Definition 2 (inF-resistance).** *An inRA protocol $\Pi$ is $\alpha$-resistant to in-region fraud if $(\forall s)(\forall P^*)(\forall loc_V)$ such that $loc_P \notin \{\mathcal{R} \cup FA_{\Pi, \mathcal{R}}\}$, and $(\forall r_k)$ we have,*

$$\Pr_{r_V} \left[ Out_V = 1 : \begin{array}{c} \mathcal{X} \leftarrow Gen(1^s, r_k) \\ P^*(\mathcal{X}) \leftrightarrow V(\mathcal{X}; r_V) \end{array} \right] \leq \alpha. \tag{8}$$

The above definition also captures a special type of attack - *in-region hijacking* (follows from a similar type of attack in DB protocols - *distance hijacking*). A dishonest prover $P^*$ located outside $\mathcal{R}$ uses the inRA communications of unaware honest provers (inside $\mathcal{R}$) to get authenticated as an honest prover.

**in-Region Man-in-the-Middle (inMiM).** A corrupted participant who does not have a key but is inside $\mathcal{R}$, interacts with multiple provers $P$'s and the verifier set $V$, and uses transcripts of these protocols to succeed in the inRA protocol.

**Definition 3 (inMiM-resistance).** *An inRA protocol $\Pi$ is $\beta$-resistant to inMiM attack if, $(\forall s)(\forall m, l, z)$ that are polynomially bounded, $(\forall \mathcal{A}_1, \mathcal{A}_2)$ that are polynomially bounded, for all locations s.t. $loc_{P_j} \notin \{\mathcal{R} \cup FA_{\Pi,\mathcal{R}}\}$, where $j \in \{q+1, \ldots, t\}$, we have*

$$Pr \left[ Out_{\mathcal{V}} = 1 : \begin{array}{l} \mathcal{X} \longleftarrow Gen(1^s, r_k) \\ P_1(\mathcal{X}), \ldots, P_q(\mathcal{X}) \longleftrightarrow \mathcal{A}_1 \longleftrightarrow \mathcal{V}_1(\mathcal{X}), \ldots, \mathcal{V}_z(\mathcal{X}) \\ P_{q+1}(\mathcal{X}), \ldots, P_t(\mathcal{X}) \longleftrightarrow \mathcal{A}_2(View_{\mathcal{A}_1}) \longleftrightarrow \mathcal{V}(\mathcal{X}) \end{array} \right] \leq \beta. \quad (9)$$

The attacker is a pair of algorithms $(\mathcal{A}_1, \mathcal{A}_2)$, where $\mathcal{A}_1$ denotes the learning phase during which the attacker interacts with the protocol-runs of $q$ provers that can be anywhere, and provides this view to $\mathcal{A}_2$ in the second stage of the attack. Definition 3 is general and captures other attack settings that are traditionally referred to as mafia fraud and impersonation attack, in DB protocols. Mafia fraud is an MiM attack as defined above but without a learning phase. In impersonation attack the attacker uses multiple possibly concurrent interactions with the verifiers to make the verifier output 1.

**in-Region Collusion Fraud (inCF).** Arguably the strongest attack and involves the collusion of a corrupted prover who is in $\mathcal{U} \setminus \mathcal{R}$, and a helper who is inside $\mathcal{R}$. In collusion fraud the assumption is that the corrupted prover does not want their long-term secret key to be learnt by the helper as otherwise the helper would have a better chance to succeed in other attacks individually. The prover however attempts to use the helper's location to succeed in the attack. In the following definition of rCF-resistance, success of the attacker in inCF implies that - the attacker in a MiM attacker as defined above (and realized by the helper), will also succeed. $P^{(*)}(\mathcal{X})$ denotes honest or dishonest prover.

**Definition 4 (inCF-resistance).** *An inRA protocol $\Pi$ is $(\gamma, \eta)$-resistant to collusion fraud if $(\forall s)$ $(\forall P^*)$ $(\forall loc_{\mathcal{V}_0}$ s.t. $loc_{P^*} \notin \{\mathcal{R} \cup FA_{\Pi,\mathcal{R}}\}$ $(\forall \mathcal{A}^{CF} ppt.)$ s.t.*

$$Pr \left[ Out_{\mathcal{V}_0} = 1 : \begin{array}{l} \mathcal{X} \longleftarrow Gen(1^s) \\ P^{(*)}(x) \longleftrightarrow \mathcal{A}^{CF} \longleftrightarrow \mathcal{V}_0(\mathcal{X}) \end{array} \right] \geq \gamma, \quad (10)$$

*over all random coins, there is a two stage attacker $(\mathcal{A}_1, \mathcal{A}_2)$ as defined in MiM with the additional relaxation that in the learning phase, the attacker can interact with the malicious prover also, such that,*

$$Pr \left[ Out_{\mathcal{V}} = 1 : \begin{array}{l} \mathcal{X} \leftarrow Gen(1^s) \\ P_1^{(*)}(\mathcal{X}), \ldots, P_q^{(*)}(\mathcal{X}) \longleftrightarrow \mathcal{A}_1 \longleftrightarrow \mathcal{V}_1(\mathcal{X}), \ldots, \mathcal{V}_z(\mathcal{X}) \\ P_{q+1}(\mathcal{X}), \ldots, P_r(\mathcal{X}) \longleftrightarrow \mathcal{A}_2(View_{\mathcal{A}_1}) \longleftrightarrow \mathcal{V}(\mathcal{X}) \end{array} \right] \geq \eta.$$
$$(11)$$

The above definition of inCF captures a widely used attack model for DB protocols, which we call *in-Region Terrorist fraud (inTF)* in which $P^*$, with

$loc_{P^*} \notin \{\mathcal{R} \cup FA_{\Pi,\mathcal{R}}\}$, uses a helper who does not have the secret key, to succeed in an instance of the protocol.

We do not consider jamming attacks blocking all communication. A *secure inRA protocol* provides security against inF, inMiM and inCF.

# 4    Pseudo-rectangle (P-rect) Cover Approach to inRA

We assume the setting of Sect. 3 and describe our approach using *basic inRA protocol* that uses two verifiers $V_0, V_1$ with (publicly known) location $loc_{V_0}$ and $loc_{V_1}$. The prover $P$ shares the secret keys $x_0$ and $x_1$ with $V_0, V_1$, respectively.

## 4.1    Basic (Two-Verifier) P-rect Approach

**Protocol Communication.** We assume radio signal travel at the speed of light and the round trip time of a challenge and response can provide a reliable estimate of distance. There are two collaborating verifiers who interact with the prover using, *slow communication* that is used for time-insensitive messages over reliable channels, and *fast communication* that are time sensitive messages that are used for estimating distance and are sent over the physical channel that is noisy. For simplicity, we do not consider noise. Our results however can be easily extended to noisy channels by modifying the protocol parameters (thresholds). Verifiers are equipped with omnidirectional and directional antennas, although in each run of the protocol we require only one of them to use their directional antenna for communication with the prover. Communication between the verifiers takes place over a secure and reliable channel and is not time sensitive.

**P-rectangle.** For a fixed pair of verifiers, $V_0$ and $V_1$, with lower and upper bound pairs, $\{\ell_{V_0}, u_{V_0}\}, \{\ell_{V_1}, u_{V_1}\}$, respectively, a P-rect is defined as the set of points $x \in \mathcal{U}$ that satisfy the following inequalities:

$$d(x, loc_{V_0}) \leq u_{V_0}, \; d(x, loc_{V_0}) \geq \ell_{V_0}, \; d(x, loc_{V_1}) \leq u_{V_1}, \; d(x, loc_{V_1}) \geq \ell_{V_1}$$

where $d(.,.)$ is the Euclidean distance. Consider the two pairs of concentric circles, centered at $loc_{V_0}$ with radii $\{\ell_{V_0}, u_{V_0}\}$ and at $loc_{V_1}$ with radii $\{\ell_{V_1}, u_{V_1}\}$, respectively. The intersection of the four circles defines two P-rects (Fig. 2b).

We denote the two mirrored rectangles by $R_{rect}(loc_{V_0}, loc_{V_1}, \ell_{V_0}, u_{V_0}, \ell_{V_1}, u_{V_1})$ and $R'_{rect}(loc_{V_0}, loc_{V_1}, \ell_{V_0}, u_{V_0}, \ell_{V_1}, u_{V_1})$. We use $R_{rect}$ and $R'_{rect}$ when parameters are known from the context. These P-rects are formed when $V_0$ and $V_1$ each executes a pair of DUB and DLB protocols with corresponding upper and lower bounds. To distinguish between the two, one of the verifiers can use a directional challenge towards the target region $\mathcal{R}$. The inRA protocol $\Pi_{rect}$ below uses a P-rect to cover $\mathcal{R}$. We quantify the error and prove security of this protocol.

**Protocol $\Pi_{rect}$.** For given values of $loc_{V_0}, loc_{V_1}, \ell_{V_0}, u_{V_0}, \ell_{V_1}, u_{V_1}$, the protocol bounds the prover within- $R_{rect}(loc_{V_0}, loc_{V_1}, \ell_{V_0}, u_{V_0}, \ell_{V_1}, u_{V_1})$ (see Fig. 3).

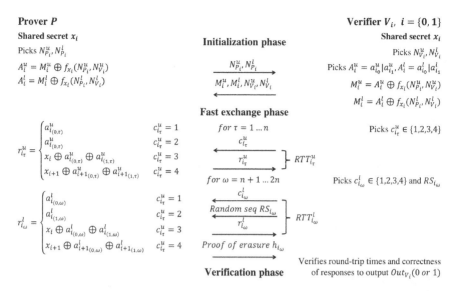

**Fig. 3.** inRA protocol $\Pi_{rect}$ between a prover and 2 verifiers. In initialization phase prover and verifiers generate and exchange nonces $N_{v_i}^l, N_{v_i}^u$. Fast Exchange phase is $2n$ rounds of challenge $(c_{i_\tau}^u, c_{i_\omega}^l)$ and responses $(r_{i_\tau}^u, r_{i_\omega}^l)$ for DUB and DLB. The responses are calculated using a pseudo-random function with special properties. In verification phase, verifiers check round-trip time and correctness of responses.

*Initialization Phase.* Prover $P$ and verifiers $V_0, V_1$ have shared secret $x_i, i = 0, 1$ and security parameter $k$ at the start of the protocol. Prover picks four independently generated nonces $N_{p_i}^l, N_{p_i}^u, i = \{0, 1\}$, each of length $k$, and sends a pair of nonces to each verifier $V_i, i = \{0, 1\}$. Each verifier $V_i$ picks two independently generated nonces of the same length, $N_{v_i}^l, N_{v_i}^u$, and two random strings $A_i^u, A_i^l$, each of length $2n$ ($2n$ corresponds to number of rounds in fast-exchange phase) and calculates, $M_i^u = A_i^u \oplus f_x(N_{p_i}^l, N_{v_i}^l)$ and $M_i^l = A_i^l \oplus f_x(N_{p_i}^u, N_{v_i}^u)$. $f$ is a Pseudo Random Function (PRF). $N_{p_i}^u, N_{v_i}^u, M_i^u, M_i^l$ are sent to the prover who decrypts and stores $A_i^u, A_i^l$. These are the response tables of the distance upper and lower bound challenges for the respective verifiers, in the fast-exchange phase. All communications between the prover and the verifiers use omnidirectional antenna in the initialization phase.

*Fast-Exchange (FE) Phase.* WLOG assume $V_0$ starts the FE phase and notifies $V_1$ to start its FE phase right after sending its last challenge[3].

$V_0$ will use an omnidirectional antenna to send its challenges, while $V_1$ will use a directional antenna with the direction and the angle of the beam chosen to cover only one of the two mirrored P-rects $R_{rect}$ and $R'_{rect}$ (See Fig. 2b). This means that only the points in $R_{rect}$ will receive the challenge from $V_1$.

---

[3] We assume verifiers have agreed on the order.

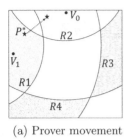
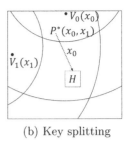

| (a) Prover movement | (b) Key splitting |

**Fig. 4.** (a) Prover movement attack: Prover responds to DUB and DLB challenges of verifier $V_0$ while in *Region 1* (R1), and DUB and DLB challenges of verifier $V_1$ while in *Region 2* (R2). (b) Key splitting attack: Prover responds to DUB and DLB challenges of $V_1$, and also DUB challenges of $V_0$ while asking the helper to respond to the DLB challenges of $V_0$.

The FE phase of each verifier consists of $2n$ consecutive rounds of challenge-response ($n \in \Omega(k)$), where the first $n$ rounds are used for distance upper bounding, and the last $n$ rounds for distance lower bounding. In each distance upper bounding round $\tau, \tau = \{1, \dots, n\}$, verifier $V_i$ picks a challenge value $c_{i_\tau}^u \in \{1, 2, 3, 4\}$, and sends it to the prover, who must respond immediately with $r_{i_\tau}^u$, as shown in Fig. 3.

Note that the prover's response, when the challenge value is in the set $\{1, 2\}$, depends on the nonces of the verifier that has sent the challenge, but when the challenge value is in the set $\{3, 4\}$, their response value depends on both verifiers' nonces. This is to prevent *key-splitting attack* in which a malicious prover who is located in specific parts of the plane (outside $\mathcal{R}$), can combine parts of the secret keys of the two verifiers to succeed in their attack (more in Sect. 4.2). Verifiers will verify the responses at the end of the protocol and after sharing their nonces. To estimate the distance, each verifier measures the round-trip-time $RTT_{i_\tau}^u$, from sending $c_{i_\tau}^u$ to receiving $r_{i_\tau}^u$, of a round.

Rounds $\omega, \omega = \{n+1, \dots, 2n\}$, are for DLB protocol. In each such round the verifier $V_i$ picks a random challenge $c_{i_\omega}^l \in \{1, 2, 3, 4\}$, together with an erasure sequence $RS_{i_\omega}$ of length $z_{i_\omega}$ [4], that is used to prevent prover from delaying the response and claiming a farther distance. Prover has to send a response as shown in Fig. 3, as well as the proof of receiving the erasure sequence. Verifier also measures and stores the round-trip-time $RTT_{i_\omega}^l$, from sending $c_{i_\omega}^l$ to receiving $r_{i_\omega}^l$, in each round.

*Verification Phase.* Firstly, verifiers check correctness of the responses $(r_{i_\tau}^u, r_{i_\omega}^l)$, as well as the proof of erasures, $h_{i_\omega}$. Then each verifier checks if the round-trip-time of the FE challenge-responses in each of the first $n$ rounds satisfies:

---

[4] An erasure sequence is a pseudo-random sequence of defined length that is used in secure DLB protocols to prevent the prover from storing malicious codes in device memory to delay their responses. We follow the construction of erasure sequence of [28], which is also explained in the full version of this paper [2].

$\frac{RTT_{i_x}^u}{2} \leq u_{V_i}$, and each of the last $n$ rounds satisfies $\frac{RTT_{i_\omega}^l}{2} \geq \ell_{V_i} + T(z_{i_\omega} - 1)$. $T(z_{i_\omega} - 1)$ is the maximum processing time required by the prover to store the erasure and compute the proof of erasure. If the above checks succeed, then verifier $V_i$ outputs $Out_{V_i} = 1$. If both verifiers output 1, then $P$ is accepted, otherwise $P$ is rejected.

## 4.2   Security Analysis

$\Pi_{rect}$ uses a pair of DUB and DLB protocols with two verifiers. To prove security of the protocol we first eliminate attacks that are because of the ability of the prover to change its location between its interaction with the two verifiers, or leaking part of its key to the helper such that it succeeds in lying about its location without enabling the helper to succeed in its individual attack.

**Prover Movement.** Location verification protocols that consider prover's communication with multiple verifiers are vulnerable to attacks that involve movement of the prover. Figure 4a shows such a scenario. A malicious prover located outside the P-rect attempts to get accepted by moving from one place to another. Consider two regions: *Region 1* (*R1*) contains all the points that are within the ring centered at $V_0$ and inside the lower bound of $V_1$, and *Region 2* (*R2*) contains all the points that are within the ring centered at $V_1$ and inside the lower bound of $V_0$. Now the prover changes its location, and can succeed by responding to DUB and DLB challenges of verifier $V_0$ while in *Region 1*, and DUB and DLB challenges of verifier $V_1$ while in *Region 2*. Similar attack can take place by the prover moving between *Region 2,3*, or *Region 3,4*, or *Region 4,1*.

Chiang *et al.* proposed a solution to prover movement [8] that uses simultaneous challenge from the verifiers. However, this requires the prover to claim a location first and this needs GPS signal (or other location determination infrastructure) and so not directly applicable to indoor area. We propose a novel approach to detecting the prover movement in which each verifier acts as an observer for the other verifier. More details below.

Let $V_0$ be an observer who passively records the timing of the signals for the communication between the prover and verifier $V_1$, and $V_1$ play a similar role for $V_0$. Let us revisit the prover movement scenario in Fig. 4a. First, we consider the prover movement between *Region 1,2*. In this case, we only consider the communication in the fast exchange phase of the DLB protocols. Notice that $P^*$ must be in *Region 1* (*R1*) while responding to the DLB challenge from $V_0$, and in *Region 2* (*R2*) while responding to the DLB challenge from $V_1$. Consider the following time-stamps (all challenges are DLB challenges): $t_0$: $V_0$ sends challenge to $P^*$ in *Region 1*; $t_1$: $V_1$ sends challenge to $P^*$ in *Region 2*; $T_0$: $V_0$ receives response from $P^*$ sent from *Region 1*; $T_1$: $V_1$ receives response from $P^*$ sent from *Region 2*; $T_0'$: $V_0$ listens to the response of $P^*$ sent from *Region 2*; $T_1'$: $V_1$ listens to the response of $P^*$ sent from *Region 1*.

We assume the prover's processing time is known and is public. $V_0$, from DLB communication, will compute the distance between itself and $P^*$ using their challenge and response round trip time as: $d_{V_0 P^*} = \frac{(T_0 - t_0) \times C}{2}$, where $C$ is the speed of radio wave. Similarly, $V_1$ will compute its distance to $P^*$ as: $d_{V_1P^*} = \frac{(T_1-t_1)\times C}{2}$. By listening to the other DLB communication, $V_0$ will compute the distance between itself and $P^*$ based on the response times of $P^*$ as: $d'_{V_0P^*} = \left(T'_0 - \frac{T_1-t_1}{2}\right) \times C$. This is because the response from $P^*$ at *Region 2* leaves $P^*$ at time $(T_1 - t_1)/2$, and reaches $V_0$ at time $T'_0$. Similarly, $V_1$ will compute the distance between itself and $P^*$ at *Region 1*, using its listening time of the response of $P^*$, as: $d'_{V_1P^*} = \left(T'_1 - \frac{T_0-t_0}{2}\right) \times C$. This is because the response from $P^*$ at *Region 1* leaves $P^*$ at time $(T_0 - t_0)/2$, and reaches $V_1$ at time $T'_1$. The system detects movement of the prover if any of the following checks do not hold:

$$d_{V_0P^*} = d'_{V_0P^*}, d_{V_1P^*} = d'_{V_1P^*}. \tag{12}$$

The protocol immediately rejects and aborts when multiple provers are detected.

A similar approach for each type of communication, e.g., DLB or DUB, can detect the prover movement between *Region 2,3*, or *Region 3,4*, or *Region 4,1*.

**Key Splitting Attack.** This attack is a result of using a pair of DUB and DLB protocols with two verifiers. In a key splitting attack, the prover leaks part of their key information to a helper to allow them to succeed in its attack, without allowing the helper to have a better chance to succeed on its own. Figure 4b shows a scenario for such an attack. Here, a malicious prover $P^*$ is located within the ring centered at $V_1$ and inside the lower bound of verifier $V_0$. $P^*$ shares key $x_0, x_1$ with $V_0, V_1$ respectively. A helper $H$ is located inside the P-rect. $P^*$ gives $x_0$ to $H$. Now the prover will succeed by correctly responding to DUB and DLB challenges of $V_1$, and also DUB challenges of $V_0$ while asking the helper to respond to the DLB challenges of $V_0$. Note that the attack is successful because this key leakage will not directly result in a successful inMiM ($H$ requires both keys $(x_0, x_1)$ to succeed in inMiM) and so according to inCF Definition (Definition 4), the protocol is not secure.

We thwart this attack by including both keys $(x_0, x_1)$ in generating the response to the challenges of each verifier. As shown in Fig. 3, upon receiving a challenge $c^u_{i_\tau} = 3$ from verifier $V_i$ ($i = \{0,1\}$), generating the response $r^u_{i_\tau}$ requires key and response table shared with verifier $V_i$. If $c^u_{i_\tau} = 4$, it requires key and response table shared with verifier $V_{i+1}$.

Revisiting the above key splitting scenario, to get accepted in $\Pi_{rect}$, $P^*$ must share both keys $x_0, x_1$ with the helper, otherwise helper would not be able to generate the responses to the DLB challenges $c^l_i = 4$ from $V_0$. This will lead to a successful inMiM by $H$ - which guarantees security (Definition 4) of our protocol.

**Security Against inF, inMiM and inCF.** By removing the threats described above, we are ready to analyze the security of $\Pi_{rect}$ against the three attacks defined in Sect. 3.1: inF, inMiM and inCF.

Let, $\Pi^{DUB}_{rect}$ and $\Pi^{DLB}_{rect}$ denote DUB and DLB protocols used in $\Pi_{rect}$. The detailed inRA protocol is presented in Fig. 3. We use the constructions of [22] and [28] for DUB and DLB protocols, respectively. These protocols are provably secure against the main three attacks (distance fraud, man-in-the-middle and collusion fraud) of distance bounding protocols that have been defined consistent with the corresponding attacks of inRA in Sect. 3. Security of these component protocols does not directly lead to the security of inRA with respect to the P-rect formed by these protocols,i.e., we need to consider attack scenarios that yield from a single verifier running two different protocols (DUB and DLB).

For each verifier $V_i \in \mathcal{V}$, the response table $a_u$ of the DUB protocol $\Pi_{rect}^{DUB}$ and $a_l$ of the DLB protocol $\Pi_{rect}^{DLB}$ are independently generated from each other and for each verifier. This holds because verifiers are honest and a response tables is constructed using the randomness of the prover and corresponding verifier.

Because of space limitation, we put security models for $\Pi_{rect}^{DUB}$ and $\Pi_{rect}^{DLB}$ (including Definitions 5–10) as well as the proof of following theorem in the full version of this paper [2].

**Theorem 1.** *For a region* $\mathcal{R}$*, the protocol* $\Pi_{rect}$ *satisfies the following:*

1. *If* $\Pi_{rect}^{DUB}$ *and* $\Pi_{rect}^{DLB}$ *are secure against distance fraud attack with probability* $\alpha_u, \alpha_\ell$ *in Definition 5 and Definition 8, respectively, then* $\Pi_{rect}$ *is secure against in-region fraud attack with probability* $\alpha \geq \max(\alpha_u, \alpha_\ell)$ *in Definition 2.*
2. *If* $\Pi_{rect}^{DUB}$ *and* $\Pi_{rect}^{DLB}$ *are secure against man-in-the-middle attack with probability* $\beta_u, \beta_\ell$ *in Definition 6 and Definition 9 respectively, then* $\Pi_{rect}$ *is secure against in-region man-in-the-middle with probability* $\beta \geq \max(\beta_u, \beta_\ell)$ *in Definition 3.*
3. *If* $\Pi_{rect}^{DUB}$ *and* $\Pi_{rect}^{DLB}$ *are secure against collusion fraud with probability* $(\gamma_u, \eta_u)$ *in Definition 7 and* $(\gamma_\ell, \eta_\ell)$ *in 10 respectively, then* $\Pi_{rect}$ *is secure against in-region collusion fraud with probability* $(\gamma, \eta)$ *where* $\gamma \geq \max(\gamma_u, \gamma_\ell)$ *and* $\eta \geq \max(\eta_u, \eta_\ell)$ *in Definition 4.*

## 5   Optimizing Error

The basic $\Pi_{rect}$ protocol covers $\mathcal{R}$ with a P-rect. For given locations of verifiers $loc_{V_0}, loc_{V_1}$, and and distance bounds $\{\ell_{V_0}, u_{V_0}\}, \{\ell_{V_1}, u_{V_1}\})$, the error in the coverage can be computed. In this paper we consider the total error which is $FA + FR$. To minimize this error, one can use a two step algorithm: (i) for fixed $loc_{V_0}, loc_{V_1}$, find $\{\ell_{V_0}, u_{V_0}\}, \{\ell_{V_1}, u_{V_1}\})$ that minimizes the error, Denote it by $E_{min}(loc_{V_0}, loc_{V_1})$. (ii) find $loc_{V_0}, loc_{V_1}$ that minimizes $E_{min}(loc_{V_0}, loc_{V_1})$. Both these minimizations can be solved by exhaustive search, which for an $n \times n$ size universe $\mathcal{U}$ will have the cost of $O(n^4)$ each.

In the following we provide an efficient algorithm *FindOptimalBounds*, or $FOB$ for short (Algorithm 1) to solve (i). Let the *size of a P-rectangle* be the number of points in the rectangle. The algorithm works as follows.

(i) Selects an initial $R_{rect}$ (Line 1). This rectangle $\mathcal{R} \subset R_{rect}$ is constructed by choosing the radii to touch the region $\mathcal{R}$;

**Algorithm 1.** *FindOptimalBounds* algorithm to find P-rectangle with maximum accuracy for $\Delta$

---

**Input:**
    Policy region $\mathcal{R}$, Verifiers' location $loc_{V_1}, loc_{V_2}$, P-square size $\Delta$
**Output:**
    P-rect with maximum *accuracy* for $\Delta$

1:  $R_{rect} \leftarrow initR_{rect}(R, loc_{V_0}, loc_{V_1})$     ▷ Initial P-rectangle, covering $\mathcal{R}$ completely
2:  $R_{rect}^{\Delta} \leftarrow makeGrid(R_{rect}, \Delta)$     ▷ $R_{rect}$ is subdivided into P-squares of size $\Delta$
3:  **for** each P-square $ps \in R_{rect}^{\Delta}$ **do**
4:     $ps.TA \leftarrow 0; \quad ps.FA \leftarrow 0$
5:     **for** each point $p \in ps$ **do** ▷ Each point contributes to either TA or FA value of
    the P-square
6:         **if** $p \in \mathcal{R}$ **then**
7:             $ps.TA = ps.TA + 1$
8:         **else**
9:             $ps.FA = ps.FA + 1$
10:       **end if**
11:     **end for**
12:     $ps.accuracy = ps.TA - ps.FA$     ▷ See Expression 6 for accuracy.
13: **end for**
14: $OptR_{rect} \leftarrow MaxSubArray(R_{rect}^{\Delta})$     ▷ $R_{rect}^{\Delta}$, which is a 2D
    array with each element representing a *ps.accuracy* value, is input to a Maximum
    Subarray Algorithm.
15: **return** $OptR_{rect}$

---

(ii)  $R_{rect}$ is subdivided into P-squares (equal size sides) of size $\Delta$ (Line 2). P-squares are used as measuring units, and is used to quantify the *accuracy* (given by expression 6 in Sect. 3) of $R_{rect}$ in covering $\mathcal{R}$;

(iii) The P-rect that maximizes the *accuracy* (therefore minimizes total *error* - see Sect. 3) for this $\Delta$, is found by formulating the *accuracy* as the objective function of a maximum sum sub-array problem and using an algorithm (presented in Algorithm 7, page 18 of [3]) to efficiently solve the problem (Lines 3–14).

The output of *FOB* is $OptR_{rect}$, a contiguous 2D sub-array (P-rect) with maximum sum (Line 15), that is the *optimal P-rect* for P-squares of size $\Delta$.

**Lemma 1.** *For fixed values of $loc_{V_0}, loc_{V_1}$, the initial P-rect in FindOptimal-Bounds algorithm achieves higher accuracy compared to any larger P-rect.*

*Proof.* Let, the initial P-rectangle be denoted by $initR_{rect}$. This rectangle is chosen to be the smallest P-rectangle that contains all points in $\mathcal{R}$. That is, $initR_{rect}$ has maximum $TA$. Let the false acceptance associated with this P-rectangle be $FA_{initR_{rect}}$. The accuracy of $initR_{rect}$ is given by, $A_{initR_{rect}} = TA_{max} - FA_{initR_{rect}}$. Let $R_{rect}$ be a P-rectangle that is larger than $initR_{rect}$ and fully covers $\mathcal{R}$. The accuracy of $R_{rect}$ is expressed as - $A_{R_{rect}} = TA_{R_{rect}} -$

$FA_{R_{rect}}$. Because $initR_{rect}$ is the "smallest" P-rectangle that covers $\mathcal{R}$, $R_{rect}$ must have larger false acceptance. That is, $FA_{R_{rect}} > FA_{initR_{rect}}$.

Because $TA_{max} \geq TA_{R_{rect}}$, we conclude that, $A_{initR_{rect}} > A_{R_{rect}}$.

**Theorem 2 (Optimality).** *Let the maximum sub-array algorithm return a contiguous 2D sub-array with the largest sum. Then the FindOptimalBounds algorithm returns the P-rectangle with maximum accuracy, for $loc_{V_0}, loc_{V_1}$ and P-square size $\Delta$.*

*Proof.* A P-rectangle can be expressed as a 2D array with each point being an element of that array. $FOB$ algorithm is initialized with a 2D array $initR_{rect}$ of size $m \times n$ (unit $\Delta$). For maximum accuracy, using Lemma 1 we need not consider larger P-rectangles that contain $\mathcal{R}$. The accuracy is given by the size of the set $A_{initR_{rect}} = TA_{max} - FA_{initR_{rect}} = \mathcal{R} \cap initR_{rect} - initR_{rect} \setminus \mathcal{R}$. Thus the contribution of a point $initR_{rect}[x][y]$ to the accuracy is 1, if it is in $\mathcal{R} \cap initR_{rect}$ and $-1$, if it is in $initR_{rect} \setminus \mathcal{R}$.[5]

Let $OptR_{rect}$ denote the 2D sub-array with maximum sum that is returned by $MaxSubArray()$. Using Expression 2 for maximum sum sub-array (see Sect. 2), the 2D array $OptR_{rect}$ can be written as:

$$OptR_{rect} = \max \left\{ \sum_{x=i,y=g}^{j,h} R_{rect}[x][y] | 1 \leq i \leq j \leq m, 1 \leq g \leq h \leq n \right\}$$

$$= \max \left\{ \sum_{x=i,y=g}^{j,h} \left( TA_{R_{rect}[x][y]} - FA_{R_{rect}[x][y]} \right) \right\}$$

The right hand side of this equation is the 2D sub-array of maximum accuracy, and this concludes the proof.

**Location of the Verifiers.** The Algorithm 1 assumes that the verifiers' location are outside $\mathcal{R}$, and satisfy the following restriction: the initial rings centered at the verifiers $V_0$ and $V_1$ must intersect pairwise. This is to ensure a well-formed P-rectangle is constructed. The restriction discards many candidate locations for the verifiers. We leave the problem of efficiently finding the location of the verifiers that results in the smallest error for future work. One can remove the restriction on the location of verifiers, including being outside region $\mathcal{R}$, by subdividing the region into smaller regions. See Sect. 6.

**Higher Accuracy.** One can increase the accuracy of the algorithm by subdividing $\mathcal{R}$ into sub-regions, and for each, choose verifiers' location and find upper and lower bounds (using $FOB$). We show this in Sect. 6.

---

[5] Here we consider equal weights for $FA, FR$. Section 6 shows a flexible way to define these errors.

# 6    Experimental Evaluation

The error in covering $\mathcal{R}$ with a P-rect depends on the shape of $\mathcal{R}$, the number of subregions and the distance bounds. We consider the following cases for four policy regions shown in Fig. 5.

- *Direct approach:* $\mathcal{R}$ is completely covered by the P-rect formed by rings centered at $V_0$ and $V_1$ and being the narrowest rings that contain all locations of $\mathcal{R}$. The resulting P-rect is the smallest P-rectangle covering $\mathcal{R}$ completely (Fig. 6a).
- *Basic FindOptimalBounds algorithm (FOB):* Fig. 6b shows the implementation of basic error optimization algorithm presented in Sect. 5.
- *FindOptimalBounds with adjusted verifiers' location ($FOB_{loc}$):* We have adjusted the verifiers' locations heuristically to observe the impact on accuracy.
- *FindOptimalBounds algorithm with partitioned regions ($FOB_{part}$):* We partitioned each policy region into two smaller regions, and applied *FindOptimalBounds* algorithm on each independently. Figure 6c, d show this settings.

**Experimental Setup.** We take images from Google Map for point-set representation of the policy region, where the pixels represent points. We use "road-map" images with zoom level of 17, and of dimension $640 \times 640$ containing the policy region $\mathcal{R}$. Each pixel represents $0.7503$ m, which is obtained using the formula for "ground resolution" [18]. Ground resolution is the distance on the ground that can be represented by a single pixel in the map. We convert it into binary image containing only the policy region and store values for all the pixels in a binary matrix. Measurements, including locations, distance, area and errors are all in pixels.

|     |     |     |     |
| :-: | :-: | :-: | :-: |
| (a) | (b) | (c) | (d) |

**Fig. 5.** Policy regions (from left to right): Building B1, B2, B3, B4 in binary image. We considered both regular shaped (B1) and relatively irregularly shaped regions (B2, B3, B4) to provide diversity to the experiment

**Error and Coverage Comparison.** Table 1 compares four approaches when applied to B1, B2, B3, B4. Notice that comparatively "regular" shaped policy regions (e.g., B1 in Fig. 5a,) can be covered more accurately than other regions; if we compare the best found errors, B1 has (FA, FR) error only $(0.81, 3.89)\%$ against $(4.16, 5.58)\%$ (B2), $(3.34, 4.53)\%$ (B3) and $(5.16, 4.4)\%$ (B4). $FOB_{part}$ algorithm reduces this irregularity to some extent reduces the total error of $FOB$

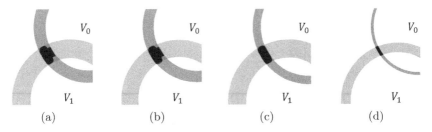

**Fig. 6.** (a) B4 is covered using direct approach, each ring touches two sides of the region (b) FOB approach: to reduce total error, a small amount of false rejection area is introduced (c, d) partitioning B4 into two separate regions and applying FOB on each.

by 7.82 ($B2$), 15.48 ($B3$) and 12.78% ($B4$). Our algorithm trades much better than naively covering a region (the direct approach), $FOB$ reduces total error from direct approaches by 10.84 ($B1$), 12.68 ($B2$), 10.78 ($B3$) and 4.31%($B4$).

**Comparison to Existing Approaches.** Computing optimal bounds for verifiers so that the two types of errors are optimized - is only attempted once in existing literature on in-region verification and localization methods, by Sastry *et al.* [17]. They have placed 5 verifiers inside a 100 m by 100 m room. They were able to achieve a coverage (True Acceptance) of 93% with 7% total error. We compare by considering a policy region of $100 \times 100$ resolution in the universe of $640 \times 640$ pixels. Each pixel represents 1 m, so we replicate the scenario of covering a 100 m by 100 m room. Using two verifiers, we achieved a 96.4% coverage (TA) and 4.1% total error. An illustration of the two approaches is given in the full version of this paper [2].

**FA, FR Weight Analysis.** In some applications $FA$ is more tolerable, while in others $FR$. A notable advantage of our error formulation (Eq. 5) is that it can be adjusted to capture requirements of different applications. We give the concept of weighted error metric: $E_{\Pi,\mathcal{R}}{}^w = W_{FA} \times FA_{\Pi,\mathcal{R}} + W_{FR} \times FR_{\Pi,\mathcal{R}}$. The increased weight for FA reduces FA error. For this analysis, we considered policy region $B2$ (Fig. 5b) and $FOB_{Loc}$ approach, and found that for FA weights $\{1, 2, 3, 4, 5\}$, the resulting FA errors are $\{7.09, 3.14, 1.43, 0.95, 0.75\}$% (Fig. 7).

## 7 Related Work

There are hundreds of papers on location aware security and services. Because of space we only consider those that are directly relevant and consider location verification with respect to a region. As noted earlier, our goal, that is to provide provably secure authentication for users inside $\mathcal{R}$ together with quantifiable error, for arbitrary region, is novel and not shared by any existing work. The system in [23] provides location verification for a region without using a secret key and without requiring user authentication.

**Table 1.** Four coverage approaches are applied to B1, B2, B3, B4. E = FA + FR is total error. Best found FA, FR and E range from 0.81 to 5.16%, 3.89 to 5.58% and 4.71 to 9.74%. Best found total coverage ranges from 94.41 to 96.1%

| | | Direct | $FOB$ | $FOB_{Loc}$ | $FOB_{part}$ |
|---|---|---|---|---|---|
| B1 | TA | 100 | 94.2 | 94.1 | 96.1 |
| | FA | 20.94 | 4.31 | 2.32 | 0.81 |
| | FR | 0 | 5.79 | 5.89 | 3.89 |
| | E | 20.94 | 10.1 | 8.22 | 4.71 |
| B2 | TA | 100 | 90.77 | 95.3 | 94.41 |
| | FA | 30.24 | 8.33 | 7.09 | 4.16 |
| | FR | 0 | 9.22 | 4.69 | 5.58 |
| | E | 30.24 | 17.56 | 11.78 | 9.74 |
| B3 | TA | 100 | 77.63 | 90.61 | 95.47 |
| | FA | 34.13 | 9.5 | 9.69 | 3.34 |
| | FR | 0 | 13.84 | 9.38 | 4.53 |
| | E | 34.13 | 23.35 | 19.08 | 7.87 |
| B4 | TA | 100 | 93.35 | 94.7 | 95.6 |
| | FA | 26.65 | 15.7 | 12.21 | 5.16 |
| | FR | 0 | 6.64 | 5.3 | 4.4 |
| | E | 26.65 | 22.34 | 21.07 | 9.56 |

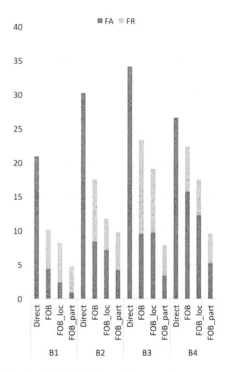

**Fig. 7.** FA, FR Error Comparison among different approaches when applied to B1, B2, B3, B4. The regularly shaped region B1 has the lowest FA and FR errors compared to other relatively irregular shaped regions, in all four approaches.

Secure positioning in multiple verifier settings is considered in [7], who proved that security against multiple adversaries (adversaries at multiple locations) is only achievable in the bounded retrieval model. [27] use bounded retrieval model, and like us, they also take advantage of directional antennas to provide in-region security. However, they cannot provide security against adversaries that reside inside the region.

[26] proposed an in-region location verification that uses the inconsistencies between claimed location of the sensor (prover) and observations of their neighbor sensors to detect a false location claim. However, their security is dependent on other sensors' trust, which is often not desirable.

Numerous distance upper bounding protocols have been proposed to date [4,5,10,22]. However the only distance lower bounding protocol with provable security against three main kind of attacks is [28]. inRA uses the formal model and protocol constructions of [22] and [28] for its DUB and DLB components.

# 8    Concluding Remarks

We motivated and defined the problem of in-region authentication, and defined correctness and security of inRA protocols for a region $\mathcal{R}$. We proposed an approach to constructing secure inRA protocols that uses distance bounding protocols to cover $\mathcal{R}$ with a P-rect, and gave an efficient algorithm to optimize the P-rect by minimizing the total error. We also proposed a basic two-verifier protocol with provable properties. Our approach provides flexibility to define error functions that are suitable for particular applications, and increase accuracy by choosing more verifiers.

We showed error performance of our optimization algorithm on different shaped policy region and verified improved accuracy when the region is subdivided into two. Optimizing error under real life constraints on the location of verifiers, the number of verifiers, particular error function, and optimization in three dimensional spaces are challenging directions for future research.

# References

1. Ahmadi, A., Safavi-Naini, R.: Distance-bounding identifiaction. In: 3rd International Conference on Information Systems Security and Privacy (2017)
2. Akand, M.R., Safavi-Naini, R.: In-region authentication. Cryptology ePrint Archive, Report 2018/345 (2018). https://eprint.iacr.org/2018/345
3. Bae, S.E.: Sequential and parallel algorithms for the generalized maximum subarray problem. Ph.D. thesis, University of Canterbury (2007)
4. Boureanu, I., Mitrokotsa, A., Vaudenay, S.: Secure and lightweight distance-bounding. In: Avoine, G., Kara, O. (eds.) LightSec 2013. LNCS, vol. 8162, pp. 97–113. Springer, Heidelberg (2013). https://doi.org/10.1007/978-3-642-40392-7_8
5. Brands, S., Chaum, D.: Distance-bounding protocols. In: Helleseth, T. (ed.) EUROCRYPT 1993. LNCS, vol. 765, pp. 344–359. Springer, Heidelberg (1994). https://doi.org/10.1007/3-540-48285-7_30
6. Čapkun, S., Hubaux, J.P.: Secure positioning of wireless devices with application to sensor networks. In: Proceedings of the 24th Annual Joint Conference of the IEEE Computer and Communications Societies, vol. 3, pp. 1917–1928. IEEE (2005)
7. Chandran, N., Goyal, V., Moriarty, R., Ostrovsky, R.: Position based cryptography. In: Halevi, S. (ed.) CRYPTO 2009. LNCS, vol. 5677, pp. 391–407. Springer, Heidelberg (2009). https://doi.org/10.1007/978-3-642-03356-8_23
8. Chiang, J.T., Haas, J.J., Hu, Y.: Secure and precise location verification using distance bounding and simultaneous multilateration. In: Proceedings of the 2nd ACM Conference on Wireless Network Security (WiSec 2009). pp. 181–192. ACM, New York (2009)
9. Desmedt, Y.: Major security problems with the 'unforgeable'(Feige)-Fiat-Shamir proofs of identity and how to overcome them. In: Proceedings of SECURICOM, vol. 88, pp. 15–17 (1988)
10. Dürholz, U., Fischlin, M., Kasper, M., Onete, C.: A formal approach to distance-bounding RFID protocols. In: Lai, X., Zhou, J., Li, H. (eds.) ISC 2011. LNCS, vol. 7001, pp. 47–62. Springer, Heidelberg (2011). https://doi.org/10.1007/978-3-642-24861-0_4

11. Fan, T.-H., Lee, S., Lu, H.-I., Tsou, T.-S., Wang, T.-C., Yao, A.: An optimal algorithm for maximum-sum segment and its application in bioinformatics. In: Ibarra, O.H., Dang, Z. (eds.) CIAA 2003. LNCS, vol. 2759, pp. 251–257. Springer, Heidelberg (2003). https://doi.org/10.1007/3-540-45089-0_23

12. Francillon, A., Danev, B., Čapkun, S.: Relay attacks on passive keyless entry and start systems in modern cars. In: NDSS (2011)

13. Grenander, U.: Pattern Analysis. Applied Mathematical Sciences, vol. 24. Springer, New York (1978). https://doi.org/10.1007/978-1-4684-9354-2

14. Hammad, A., Faith, P.: Location based authentication, US Patent 9,721,250, 1 August 2017

15. Metz, C.E.: Basic principles of ROC analysis. In: Seminars in Nuclear Medicine, vol. 8, pp. 283–298. Elsevier (1978)

16. Rasmussen, K.B., Castelluccia, C., Heydt-Benjamin, T.S., Čapkun, S.: Proximity-based access control for implantable medical devices. In: Proceedings of the 16th ACM Conference on Computer and Communications Security (CCS 2009), Chicago, Illinois, USA, pp. 410–419, November 2009

17. Sastry, N., Shankar, U., Wagner, D.: Secure verification of location claims. In: Proceedings of the 2nd ACM Workshop on Wireless Security, pp. 1–10. ACM, New York (2003)

18. Schwartz, J.: Bing maps tile system. https://msdn.microsoft.com/en-us/library/bb259689.aspx. Accessed 13 Apr 2016

19. Singelee, D., Preneel, B.: Location verification using secure distance bounding protocols. In: IEEE International Conference on Mobile Adhoc and Sensor Systems Conference, pp. 7-pp. IEEE (2005)

20. Takaoka, T.: Efficient algorithms for the maximum subarray problem by distance matrix multiplication. Electron. Notes Theor. Comput. Sci. **61**, 191–200 (2002)

21. Takaoka, T., Pope, N.K., Voges, K.E.: Algorithms for data mining. In: Business Applications and Computational Intelligence, pp. 291–315. IGI Global (2006)

22. Boureanu, I., Mitrokotsa, A., Vaudenay, S.: Practical and provably secure distance-bounding. In: Desmedt, Y. (ed.) ISC 2013. LNCS, vol. 7807, pp. 248–258. Springer, Cham (2015). https://doi.org/10.1007/978-3-319-27659-5_18

23. Vora, A., Nesterenko, M.: Secure location verification using radio broadcast. IEEE Trans. Dependable Secur. Comput. **3**(4), 377–385 (2006)

24. Warner, J.S., Johnston, R.G.: A simple demonstration that the global positioning system (GPS) is vulnerable to spoofing. J. Secur. Adm. **25**(2), 19–27 (2002)

25. Weddell, S., Langford, B.: Hardware implementation of the maximum subarray algorithm for centroid estimation. In: Proceedings of the Twenty-First Image and Vision Computing Conference New Zealand (IVCNZ 2006), pp. 511–515 (2006)

26. Wei, Y., Guan, Y.: Lightweight location verification algorithms for wireless sensor networks. IEEE Trans. Parallel Distrib. Syst. **24**(5), 938–950 (2013)

27. Yang, R., Xu, Q., Au, M.H., Yu, Z., Wang, H., Zhou, L.: Position based cryptography with location privacy: a step for Fog computing. Future Gener. Comput. Syst. **78**, 799–806 (2017)

28. Zheng, X., Safavi-Naini, R., Ahmadi, H.: Distance lower bounding. In: Hui, L.C.K., Qing, S.H., Shi, E., Yiu, S.M. (eds.) ICICS 2014. LNCS, vol. 8958, pp. 89–104. Springer, Cham (2015). https://doi.org/10.1007/978-3-319-21966-0_7

29. Zickuhr, K.: Location-Based Services, pp. 679–695. Pew Research (2013)

# Formal Analysis of Distance Bounding with Secure Hardware

Handan Kılınç$^{(\boxtimes)}$ and Serge Vaudenay

EPFL, Lausanne, Switzerland
handan.kilinc@epfl.ch

**Abstract.** A distance bounding (DB) protocol is a two-party authentication protocol between a prover and a verifier which is based on the distance between the prover and the verifier. It aims to defeat threats by malicious provers who try to convince that they are closer to the verifier or adversaries which seek to impersonate a far-away prover. All these threats are covered in several security definitions and it is not possible to have a single definition covering all. In this paper, we describe a new DB model with three parties where the new party is named hardware. In this model, called secure hardware model (SHM), the hardware is held by the prover without being able to tamper with. We define an all-in-one security model which covers all the threats of DB and an appropriate privacy notion for SHM. In the end, we construct the most efficient (in terms of computation by the prover-hardware and number of rounds) and secure DB protocols achieving the optimal security bounds as well as privacy.

**Keywords:** Distance bounding · RFID · NFC · Relay attack
Tamper resistance · Terrorist fraud

## 1 Introduction

Distance bounding (DB) protocols are two-party (a prover and a verifier) authentication protocols. A prover authenticates itself and proves that the distance between its location and the verifier's location is less than a predetermined bound. The verifier estimates the distance of the prover by computing the round trip time of sending a challenge to the prover and receiving a response from the prover. Brands and Chaum [6] first defined this notion as a solution to relay attacks. However, it may also provide a solution for the following threats:

*Mafia Fraud (MiM)* [12]: A man-in-the-middle (MiM) adversary between a verifier and a far-away honest prover makes the verifier accept the access of the prover. Malicious and far-away provers who want to convince that they are close to a verifier appear in the followings:

*Distance Fraud (DF)*: A malicious far-away prover tries to prove that he is close enough to the verifier to make the verifier accept.

© Springer International Publishing AG, part of Springer Nature 2018
B. Preneel and F. Vercauteren (Eds.): ACNS 2018, LNCS 10892, pp. 579–597, 2018.
https://doi.org/10.1007/978-3-319-93387-0_30

*Distance Hijacking (DH)* [11]: A far-away malicious prover takes advantage of some honest and active provers who are close to the verifier to make the verifier grant privileges to the far-away prover.

*Terrorist Fraud (TF)* [12]: A far-away malicious prover, with the help of an adversary, tries to make the verifier accept the access of the prover.

Clearly, the strongest security notion is the resistance to TF. So, if we can construct a DB protocol that is secure against TF, then the DB protocol will be secure against MiM, DF and DH. However, it is not possible to achieve the TF-security because of a trivial attack: the malicious prover gives his secret (key) to a close adversary, and the adversary authenticates on behalf of the malicious prover by running the protocol. To achieve the TF-security, the trivial attack is artificially excluded from the TF model in the literature by assuming that malicious provers would never share their keys (in this paper, we call this weaker version "TF'-security"). However, we cannot adapt TF'-security as an all-in-one security notion because no connection between TF'-security and MiM, DF or DH security can be established. Because of this disconnection, all DB protocols require separate security analysis for each of them. The only public-key DB protocols that are secure against all of them (MiM, DF, DH, TF') are ProProx [27], its variant eProProx [25] and TREAD [2]. Some important distance bounding protocols [6,8,10,15,19,21,23] are all vulnerable to TF'. The protocol by Bultel et al. [7] is TF'-secure thanks to a 'cheat option' (as explained below) but it is not DH-secure since it aims for anonymity against verifier.

Moreover, the formal definition of TF'-security is controversial. The TF'-security definition of Dürholz et al. [13] allows treatment of the partial disclosure of the secret key. Essentially, the TF' security in this definition implies that any information forwarded to a close-by adversary would allow another adversary to later pass, without a help of the prover, with the same probability, but through a "cheat option" in the protocol. Fischlin and Onete [14] adapted the Swiss-Knife protocol [20] to have this definition. However, it was proven that this technique weakens Swiss-Knife for MiM-security [24]. Clearly, it is not reasonable to weaken the most relevant security to protect it against the least relevant one. There are also extractor based TF'-security definitions [5,24,27] stronger than the definition of Dürholz et al. model [13]. However, all TF'-security definitions are constructed with the assumption that the malicious prover do not reveal any secret key related information. This assumption is considered **weak and not realistic** [1]. In short, none of the models in the literature fully covers TF.

Apparently, there is no way of achieving TF-security without hiding the secret key from the prover. This intuitive idea has been noticed [9,22], but never formally defined. A natural question to ask here is whether this idea really prevents TF. The answer is "yes and no" because hiding the key is necessary but not sufficient.

In a nutshell, state of the art DB results says that TF-security is not possible in the existing models of DB and it could be possible by hiding the key but this is not enough. However, it is still not formally noted how it can be achievable.

Therefore, in this paper, we define a new formal model where constructing TF-secure protocols are possible.

Our formal model for DB, which we call secure hardware model (SHM), provides a solution to all DB related problems that we mention. We denote the two-algorithm (Prover and Verifier) DB corresponding to the classical DB in the literature as "plain model" (PM) [4–6,13,26]. In the SHM, we have another entity called "Hardware" that is always honest and only communicate with their holder (the prover). Mainly, this hardware runs some part of the prover algorithm honestly and neither a malicious prover nor an adversary can corrupt it. In the real world, we can realize our new entity as e.g. tamper-resistant modules in smart-cards. In more detail, *our contribution* in this paper is the following:

- We define a new type of DB with three algorithms $(V, P, H)$: verifier, prover, hardware. Then, we design a communication and adversarial model for three-algorithm DB which we call secure hardware model (SHM). In SHM, it is possible to have TF-secure DB protocols without excluding trivial attacks. We give a new security definition in SHM for a three-algorithm DB. In this security definition, achieving TF-security means achieving MiM, DF and DH-security. So, we obtain an all-in-one definition.
- We obtain a convincing model for TF based on SHM. We show that the TF-security of $(V, P, H)$ in SHM is equivalent to the MiM-security of $(V, H)$ in PM where $H$ in PM corresponds to the prover algorithm. This result implies that **$P$ plays no role in security but only in the correctness of the protocol to have TF-security**.
- We establish security relations between PM and SHM. We show that the MiM-security in SHM and the MiM-security in PM are equivalent where the prover algorithm in PM is the union $P^H$ of the prover $P$ and the hardware $H$ in SHM. Additionally, we show that a MiM-secure DB protocol in PM can be converted into a fully-secure DB protocol in SHM. This result shows that if we have only a MiM-secure DB protocol in PM, **we can easily construct an efficient DB protocol secure against all threats in SHM**.
- We define a strong privacy notion of DB in SHM. Strong privacy in DB requires that the adversary cannot identify a prover even after getting his secret (e.g. by a corruption).
- We construct a symmetric DB protocol **MiM-symDB which is the most efficient optimally secure MiM-secure protocol in PM (in terms of computation and number of rounds) among the protocols with binary challenges and responses.** Then, we convert it into a DB protocol in SHM (Full-symDB$^H$) and obtain the most efficient symmetric DB protocol secure against all threats and achieving optimal security bounds.
- We also consider a secure and private public-key DB protocol in SHM. Instead of designing a new one we take advantage from existing public-key DB's Eff-pkDB and Simp-pkDB [19] to convert them into SHM. We slightly modify Eff-pkDB to increase its efficiency in SHM, and we modify Simp-pkDB such that its new version in SHM is secure and private.

We underline that the **only assumption on the secure hardware is that it is honest** which means that it runs the specified algorithm only. By doing so, we give a model here where the TF-security is achievable.

One may argue that our assumption on secure hardware is too strong for the real world applications. For example, in the real world, if the secure hardware is implemented using a tamper-resistant hardware, it is always possible that a side-channel attack will break our assumption. However, we believe that relying on our assumption is more reasonable than relying on some adversarial intention (e.g., that the adversary never shares his secret). We can never prevent a TF-adversary to share his secret-key, but we can construct a strong tamper-resistant hardware which requires very expensive devices to be tampered. Besides, MiM-security would be preserved even if the tamper resistance assumption is broken.

## 2    Definitions and Security in SHM

We first give the formal definitions of SHM and security in this model. Then, we provide some security relations related to PM and SHM.

### 2.1    Definitions

Parties of a DB protocol are a prover and a verifier [6]. However, we define a new version of it called three-algorithm (symmetric or public-key) DB where the algorithms are prover, verifier, and hardware.

**Definition 1 (Three-Algorithm Symmetric DB).** *Three-algorithm symmetric DB is a probabilistic polynomial-time (PPT) protocol. It consists of a tuple $(\mathcal{K}, V, P, B, H)$ where $\mathcal{K}$ is the key generation algorithm, $P$ is the proving algorithm, $H$ is the hardware algorithm, $V$ is the verifying algorithm and $B$ is the distance bound. The input of $V$ and $H$ is $K$ generated by $\mathcal{K}$. $P$ interacts with $H(K)$ and $V(K)$. At the end of the protocol, $V(K)$ outputs a final message $\mathsf{Out}_V \in \{0,1\}$. If $\mathsf{Out}_V = 1$, then $V$ accepts. If $\mathsf{Out}_V = 0$, then $V$ rejects.*

In symmetric DB, $V$ knows that it needs to use $K$ (possibly resulting from a prior identification protocol).

**Definition 2 (Three-Algorithm Public Key DB).** *Three-algorithm public key distance bounding is a PPT protocol. It consists of a tuple $(\mathcal{K}_P, \mathcal{K}_V, V, P, B, H)$ where $(\mathcal{K}_P, \mathcal{K}_V)$ are the key generation algorithms of $P$ and $V$, respectively. The output of $\mathcal{K}_P$ is a secret/public key pair $(\mathsf{sk}_P, \mathsf{pk}_P)$ and the output of $\mathcal{K}_V$ is a secret/public key pair $(\mathsf{sk}_V, \mathsf{pk}_V)$. $V$ is the verifying algorithm with the input $(\mathsf{sk}_V, \mathsf{pk}_V)$, $P$ is the proving algorithm with the input $(\mathsf{pk}_P, \mathsf{pk}_V)$ and $H$ is the hardware algorithm with the input $(\mathsf{sk}_P, \mathsf{pk}_P)$. $B$ is the distance bound. $P$ interacts with $H(\mathsf{sk}_P, \mathsf{pk}_P)$ and $V(\mathsf{sk}_V, \mathsf{pk}_V)$. At the end of the protocol, $V(\mathsf{sk}_V, \mathsf{pk}_V)$ outputs a final message $\mathsf{Out}_V \in \{0,1\}$ and has $\mathsf{pk}_P$ as a private output. If $\mathsf{Out}_V = 1$, then $V$ accepts. If $\mathsf{Out}_V = 0$, then $V$ rejects.*

This definition assumes a priori identification of $\mathsf{pk}_V$ for $P$.

**Definition 3 (Correctness of DB).** *A public-key (resp. symmetric) DB protocol is correct if and only if under an honest execution, whenever the distance between $P$ and $V$ is at most $B$, $V$ always outputs $\mathsf{Out}_V = 1$ and $\mathsf{pk}_P$ (resp. $\emptyset$).*

In all definitions below, verifiers, provers, and hardware are parties running $V$, $P$ and $H$, respectively. The parties can move and run their algorithms multiple times. Each new execution of a party's algorithm is an **instance** of this party.

Classical DB in the literature is very similar to three-algorithm DB with the following differences: no $H$ algorithm exists and the input of $P$ in public-key and symmetric DB is $(\mathsf{sk}_P, \mathsf{pk}_P, \mathsf{pk}_V)$ and $K$, respectively. The plain model is the model corresponding to the classical DB.

*Plain Model (PM):* Parties of PM are provers, verifiers and other actors.

- Honest parties run their assigned algorithms only.
- Verifiers are always honest. Provers are either malicious or honest.
- Each instance of a party has a location.
- A malicious party may run its instances concurrently, while an honest party runs its instances only sequentially.
- Communication between instances has a latency proportional to the distance (e.g., it travels at the speed of light).

The secure hardware model is the model corresponding to three-algorithm DB: $P$, $V$ and $H$.

*Secure Hardware Model (SHM):* Parties of SHM are provers, hardware, verifiers and other actors. SHM includes all the characteristics of PM and the additional ones:

- Secure hardware are honest parties.
- Each prover possesses its own secure hardware.
- The secure hardware of an honest prover can only communicate with its prover and they are both at the same location.

In the rest of the paper, whenever we say "a distance bounding protocol in SHM", it refers to the three-algorithm DB.

Remark that since secure hardware are honest parties, they always run their assigned algorithms even if malicious provers hold them. They should be taken as a subroutine of a prover algorithm running on a secure enclave where the prover can never change or interfere it.

SHM and PM follow the communication model from [5,18]: instances can only communicate by sending messages which are delivered with a delay proportional to the distance, and malicious instances can prevent delivery or change the destination of messages [27].

Now, we give our security definition for a DB protocol in SHM. The definition covers distance fraud, mafia fraud (MiM), distance hijacking and terrorist fraud which are the threat models in PM.

**Definition 4 (Security in SHM).** *Consider a public-key DB. The game consists of a verifier and provers $P_1, P_2, \ldots, P_t$ with their corresponding hardware $H_1, H_2, \ldots, H_t$. It begins by running the key setup algorithm $\mathcal{K}_V$ outputting $(\mathsf{sk}_V, \mathsf{pk}_V)$ for $V$ and $\mathcal{K}_P$ outputting $(\mathsf{sk}_{P_i}, \mathsf{pk}_{P_i})$ for $H_i$. The game consists of instances of the verifier, provers, hardware and actors. $V$ is a distinguished instance of the verifier. One prover (let's denote $P$) is the target prover. The winning condition of the game is $V$ outputs $\mathsf{Out}_V = 1$ and privately $\mathsf{pk}_P$ (public key of $P$) if no close instance of $P$'s hardware exists during the execution of $V$.*

- *The DB protocol is MiM-secure if the winning probability is always negligible whenever $P$ is honest[1].*
- *The DB protocol is DF-secure if the winning probability is always negligible whenever there is no instance of any party close to $V$.*
- *The DB protocol is DH-secure if the winning probability is always negligible whenever all close instances are honest provers other than $P$ and their hardware.*
- *The DB protocol is TF-secure if the winning probability is always negligible.*

*The same security definition holds for a symmetric DB where we replace $\mathcal{K}_V$ and $\mathcal{K}_P$ with $\mathcal{K}$ and $\mathsf{sk}_{P_i}/\mathsf{pk}_{P_i}$ with $K_i$.*

Without loss of generality, we can consider all other actors as adversaries.

It is clear that TF-security implies DF-security, MiM-security, and DH-security. So, we have an all-in-one security notion in SHM. Hence, we say **"secure" instead of "TF-secure"** in SHM.

*Security in PM:* The security in PM is almost the same as Definition 4 except that in PM, we do not have hardware. In PM, there is always a trivial TF-attack in which a malicious prover can give his secret key to another malicious party so that the party authenticates the prover while it is far-away. So, TF-security is not possible in PM. Clearly, this trivial attack is preventable in SHM if we can assure that $H$ never leaks $K$.

Note that we do not consider the weaker version of TF-security [13,20,24] (TF'-security) which artificially excludes trivial attack. So, when we refer to TF-security in PM, we indeed refer to an impossible-to-achieve notion.

### Notations

$\boldsymbol{P_{dum}}$ is a dummy prover algorithm in SHM which only relays the messages between the outside world and $H$ without even using any of its input. Remark that if the prover who should run $P_{dum}$ is malicious, then it can still play with its hardware or other parties maliciously.

$\boldsymbol{P^H}$ is the algorithm which is constructed from joining $P$ and $H$ in SHM. More precisely, $P^H$ runs $P$ and instead of interacting with $H$, it executes the same computation that $H$ would do if $P$ had interacted. Therefore, $\boldsymbol{P^H_{dum}}$ is the hardware algorithm $H$.

---

[1] Recall that it implies that $H$ communicates with only $P$ and that they are at the same location.

"Challenge phase" is informally defined as the phase where $V$ comprehends the proximity of $P$. In the challenge phase, $V$ sends challenges and receives responses from $P$. If all the responses are correct and arrive on time, then $V$ decides that the distance between $V$ and $P$ is less than the bound $B$.

## 2.2   Security Results

We give some security relations between a DB protocol in PM and SHM.

**Theorem 1 (MiM in SHM $\Rightarrow$ MiM in PM).** *Let $DB = (\mathcal{K}, V, P, B, H)$ be a symmetric-key DB protocol in SHM. We define a DB protocol $DB' = (\mathcal{K}, V, P^H, B)$ in PM. If DB is MiM-secure then $DB'$ is MiM-secure.*
   *The same holds with public-key DB.*

The proof is trivial by adding a hardware to every honest prover at the same location: A MiM-game against $DB'$ becomes a MiM-game against $DB$.

**Theorem 2 (MiM-security in PM with $P_{dum}^H \Leftrightarrow$ Security in SHM).** *Let $DB = (\mathcal{K}, V, P, B, H)$ be a symmetric DB in SHM and $DB' = (\mathcal{K}, V, P_{dum}^H, B)$ be a symmetric-key DB in PM where $H$ in $DB'$ corresponds $H$ of DB. $DB'$ is MiM secure in PM if and only if DB is TF-secure in SHM.*

Here, the prover algorithm of $DB'$ is just $H$ because $P_{dum}^H \equiv H$.
   Note that $DB'$ in Theorem 2 is not a correct DB protocol in general if $P \neq P_{dum}$ as the algorithm $P$ disappeared. However, we can still consider MiM-security for $DB'$ without correctness.

*Proof.* ($\Rightarrow$) Consider a TF-game in SHM. We run this game in PM by simulating the secure hardware $H$ of $DB$ with the prover $P_{dum}^H$ of $DB'$ and simulating the prover $P$ in SHM with an actor in PM (it is possible because $P$ in SHM does not have any secret key as an input). Then, we obtain MiM-game of $DB'$.
   ($\Leftarrow$) If $\mathcal{A}$ wins the MiM-game of $DB'$, then a TF adversary runs $\mathcal{A}$ and wins the TF-game for $DB$.                                         □

Remark that it is not possible to prove "MiM-security of $DB' = (\mathcal{K}, V, P^H, B) \Leftrightarrow$ security of $DB = (\mathcal{K}, V, P, B, H)$" where $P$ in $DB'$ is not necessarily $P_{dum}$ because we could not simulate $H$ and $P$ in "$\Rightarrow$" case of the proof in Theorem 2.
   Theorem 2 clearly shows that hiding the key is necessary to have security in $DB$. Because if $H$ in $DB$ does not hide the key, then the prover algorithm of $DB'$ which is $H$ does not hide as well. So, $DB'$ would not be MiM-secure. However, hiding may not be enough as explained below:
   We consider the algorithm $P$ of $DB$ which does the computations $\mathcal{C} = \{C_1, C_2, \ldots, C_k\}$ and where $P$ does learn any key related information. So, all computations in $\mathcal{C}$ are executed independently from the key. Assume that the success probability of an adversary to break the TF-security of $DB$ is at most $p$. Then, thanks to Theorem 2, the success probability of a MiM-adversary $\mathcal{A}$ in

$DB'$ is at most $p$. In addition, assume that there exists $C_i \in \mathcal{C}$ and the success probability of a TF-adversary in $DB$ is $p' > p$ without $C_i$. If such $C_i$ exists, we can have another MiM-adversary $\mathcal{A}'$ which runs $P$ without $C_i^2$ and wins MiM-game with $p' > p$. So, this contradicts with our assumption which says that the success probability of a MiM-adversary can be at most $p$. As a result, Theorem 2 actually shows that the TF-security is not possible in SHM if the computations of $P$ has an effect on $p$.

We agree that having a secure hardware running whole algorithm without its prover's effect on the security is a trivial solution to have TF-security. However, here, we show that **the other way around is not possible.** We underline that it does not mean that prover cannot do any computation to have TF-security. For example, in our TF-secure protocols in Sect. 4, the prover algorithm in SHM still executes some part of the algorithm $P^H$ in PM but it does not have any effect on the security of the protocol (as it can be seen in their security proofs Theorems 8 and 10).

Some more results of Theorem 2:

- We can conclude if $DB' = (\mathcal{K}, V, P_{dum}^H, B)$ is **MiM-secure** and correct DB protocol, then we can construct a **secure** DB protocol $DB = (\mathcal{K}, V, P, B, H)$ in SHM for any algorithm $P$. $DB$ is further correct when $P = P_{dum}$.
- In order to prove security of $DB = (\mathcal{K}, V, P, B, H)$ in SHM, it is enough to prove MiM-security of $DB' = (\mathcal{K}, V, P_{dum}^H, B)$ in PM.
- **MiM security and security of a DB protocol $DB = (\mathcal{K}, V, P, B, H)$ in SHM are equivalent if $P = P_{dum}$** due to Theorems 1 and 2. Note that this result may not hold without $P_{dum}$.

In Fig. 1, we give the security (non)-implications in SHM and PM. The proof of these (non)-implications are in the full version of the paper. In Fig. 2, we give the same for SHM when the prover is $P_{dum}$. In this case, **the full security is equivalent to MiM-security.** The rest of the (non)-implications in Fig. 2 can be proven the same as in the non-implications in Fig. 1.

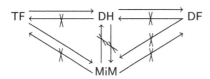

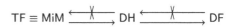

**Fig. 1.** Security implications of DB protocols in PM and SHM. TF-security implies all of them, DH-security implies DF security and no relation exists between MiM and DH (also DF).

**Fig. 2.** Security implications in SHM with the prover $P_{dum}$. TF-security and MiM security are equivalent in SHM with $P_{dum}$. The relations between DF, DH and MiM are the same as in Fig. 1.

---

[2] Remark that any adversary can compute the computations in $\mathcal{C}$ because they do not require any secret.

## 2.3   Privacy

In strong-privacy definition of PM, the adversary can corrupt the provers and learn the secrets. However, the hardware in SHM is honest by nature. So, it cannot be corrupted. Hence, we define semi-strong privacy with no such corruption. Achieving semi-strong privacy in a DB protocol is good enough assuming that the hardware is tamper-resistant. Nevertheless, we also allow corruption of hardware in order to define the strong privacy notion.

**Definition 5 (Privacy in SHM).** *The privacy game consists of a verifier, provers* $P_1, P_2, \ldots, P_t$ *and their corresponding hardware* $\{H_1, H_2, \ldots, H_t\}$. *We generate the secret/public key pairs of them with* $\mathcal{K}_V$ *and* $\mathcal{K}_P$ *for the verifier and the hardware of provers. We pick* $b \in \{0, 1\}$ *and start the game:*
*The adversary can create instances of the verifier and any prover. It can send/receive messages to/from instances of the verifier. It can corrupt any prover and hardware which let it learn the current state of their memory. At some moment, it picks two provers* $P_i, P_j$ *as a challenge of the game. If* $b = 0$, *we create a virtual prover of* $P_i$ *with its hardware and if* $b = 1$, *we create a virtual prover of* $P_j$ *with its hardware. The adversary can communicate with the virtual prover and its virtual hardware. It can also release a virtual prover, if it exists. In this case, we remove the virtual prover from the game, anonymously. The game has to have at most one virtual prover. In the end, the adversary outputs* $b'$. *If* $b' = b$, *the adversary wins. Otherwise, it loses.*
*We say a DB protocol in SHM is* **strong private** *if the advantage of the adversary in this game is bounded by a negligible probability. We say a DB protocol in SHM is* **semi-strong private** *if the advantage of the adversary in a version of this game, where the corruption only lets the adversary communicate with the hardware non-anonymously, is bounded by a negligible probability.*

In semi-strong privacy, even though we do not allow corruption of hardware, we let semi-strong corruption occur by allowing interaction with the secure hardware. In SHM, we stress that when $P$ interacts with its secure hardware, this interaction remains private.

Hermans et al. [16] defined a similar game for the **strong privacy** of DB in PM. In that game, no hardware exists, so the definition of semi-strong privacy is not considered. Instead, the **weak privacy** notion exists where no corruption on provers are allowed.

Note that we obtain a notion of strong privacy of $DB = (K, V, P, B, H)$ in SHM which is equivalent to the strong privacy of $DB' = (K, V, P^H, B)$ in PM.

# 3   Optimal Symmetric DB Protocol in SHM

In this section, we show our new protocol MiM-symDB in PM which is only MiM-secure (not DF, DH or TF-secure). We construct a DB at this level of security because having MiM-security in PM is enough to achieve (full) security in SHM as a result of Theorem 2. The security bounds of MiM-symDB is very close to optimal security bounds [5][3]. Its conversion into SHM reaches the same bound as well. It is proved [5] that an optimal security bound in PM for a MiM-adversary is $(\frac{1}{2})^n$ given that challenges and responses are bits and the challenge phase consists of $n$ rounds. The same bound applies in SHM as well.

We note that using other optimally MiM-secure DB protocols such as DB1, DB2, DB3 [5] is reasonable as well to have fully secure DB protocols in SHM. However, these protocols are also secure against DF or TF' in PM which is an overkill since we need only MiM-security. By constructing an optimal MiM-only secure DB in PM, we can save some computations and rounds.

***Notation:*** When we use $H$ as a superscript in the name of a protocol, it shows that it is in SHM.

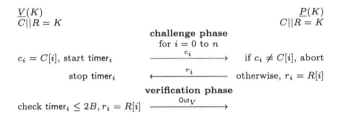

**Fig. 3.** MiM-OTDB

**MiM-OTDB:** First, we describe our MiM-OTDB protocol which is MiM-secure when it is executed *only once*. The prover $P$ and the verifier $V$ share a secret key $K = C\|R$. Here, the bits of $C$ correspond to the challenges and the bits of $R$ correspond to the responses. In the challenge phase, in each round $i$, $V$ sends the challenge $c_i = C[i]$ to $P$ and $P$ sends the response $r_i = R[i]$ to $V$. If $P$ receives a challenge which is different from $C[i]$, then $P$ does not continue the protocol. In the verification phase, $V$ checks if the responses are correct and on time. (See Fig. 3.)

**MiM-symDB:** The prover $P$ and the verifier $V$ share a secret key $K$. They use a pseudo random function (PRF) $f$ returning strings of $2n$ bits. $P$ and $V$ exchange the nonces $N_P, N_V \in \{0,1\}^s$, respectively, where $s$ is a security parameter. Then, $P$ and $V$ compute $f(K, N_P, N_V)$ which outputs $C\|R$. Finally, $V$ and $P$ run MiM-OTDB with using $C\|R$ as a key. (See Fig. 4.)

We prove the following theorem by using a lemma in [18]. The lemma shows that any message $m$ sent by a party is independent from the messages seen by another party at the time which is less than arrival time of $m$. This lemma is correct in SHM as well.

---

[3] A security bound of a DB means an upper bound of the success probability of an adversary.

$$\underline{V}(K) \hspace{6cm} \underline{P}(K)$$

pick $N_V \in \{0,1\}^s$ $\quad \xleftarrow{\hspace{1cm} N_P \hspace{1cm}} \quad$ pick $N_P \in \{0,1\}^s$

$C\|R = f(K, N_P, N_V) \quad \xrightarrow{\hspace{1cm} N_V \hspace{1cm}} \quad C\|R = f(K, N_P, N_V)$

$$\xleftarrow{\hspace{0.8cm} \text{MiM-OTDB}(C\|R) \hspace{0.8cm}}$$

**Fig. 4.** MiM-symDB

**Theorem 3 (MiM-security of MiM-symDB).** *If $f$ is a secure PRF, then the winning probability of a probabilistic polynomial time (PPT) adversary in a MiM-game of MiM-symDB in PM is at most $\frac{3}{2^{n+1}} + \frac{q^2}{2^{s+1}} + \frac{q'^2}{2^{s+1}} + \mathsf{Adv}_{PRF}(q + q', t)$. For a PPT game, this is negligible.*

*Here, $q$ is the number of prover instances, $q'$ is the number of verifier instances, $t$ is the total complexity of the game and $\mathsf{Adv}_{PRF}$ is the advantage for distinguishing the output of $f$ from the output of a random function with $q + q'$ queries and complexity $t$.*

*Proof.* $\Gamma_0$: It is a MiM-game where $P$'s instances and $V$'s instances with the distinguished instance $\mathcal{V}$ play in PM. The winning probability in $\Gamma_0$ is $p$.

$\Gamma_1$: We reduce $\Gamma_0$ to $\Gamma_1$ where the nonces of the prover instances and the nonces of the verifier instances do not repeat. The probability that a prover (resp. verifier) instance selects the same nonce with the one of the other prover (resp. verifier) instances is bounded by $\frac{q^2}{2}\frac{1}{2^s}$ (resp. $\frac{q'^2}{2}\frac{1}{2^s}$). So, the winning probability of $\Gamma_1$ is at least $p - \frac{q^2}{2^{s+1}} - \frac{q'^2}{2^{s+1}}$.

$\Gamma_2$: We reduce $\Gamma_1$ to $\Gamma_2$ where $\mathcal{V}$ and the prover's instances replace $f(K,.,.)$ by a random function. Clearly, the winning probability in $\Gamma_2$ is at least $p - \frac{q^2}{2^{s+1}} - \frac{q'^2}{2^{s+1}} - \mathsf{Adv}_{PRF}(q + q', t)$.

In $\Gamma_2$, we have a game where at most one prover instance P seeing $(N_P, N_V)$ pair with $\mathcal{V}$ and $C\|R$ is completely random meaning that it is independent from $N_P$ and $N_V$. If P exists, it has to be far from $\mathcal{V}$ because of the winning condition of MiM-game. Assuming that $\mathcal{V}$ and P see the same $(N_P, N_V)$, we look each round $i$ for the case where $r_i$ arrived on time. If $r_i$ arrived on time, thanks to the lemma in [18], the response sent by P is independent from $r_i$ or the challenge that P received is independent from $c_i$ sent by $\mathcal{V}$. In any case, the adversary's probability to pass each round is $\frac{1}{2}$ because the response $r_i$ has to be correct and on time: the adversary guesses either $r_i$ or $c_i$ (post-ask or pre-ask attack). There may also be one round where the pre-ask strategy is done for a constant number of rounds until it makes P abort. After abort, there is an additional opportunity (in the last of these rounds) for the adversary to pass the round by guessing the response. Therefore,

$$p = \frac{3}{2^{n+1}} + \frac{q^2}{2^{s+1}} + \frac{q'^2}{2^{s+1}} + \mathsf{Adv}_{PRF}(q + q', t).$$

$\square$

Assuming that $\frac{q^2}{2^{s+1}} + \frac{q'^2}{2^{s+1}} + \mathsf{Adv}_{PRF}(q+q',t)$ is negligible, the success probability of a MiM-adversary is $\frac{3}{2^n+1}$ very close to the optimal security $\frac{1}{2^n}$.

**MiM-symDB is More Efficient than the Existing Optimally MiM-secure Protocols DB1, DB2, DB3** [5]. $P$ in DB1, DB2, DB3 compute a PRF function two times and some other mappings too. So, with parameter $n_c = n_r = 2$ in common structure, for a given target security, we construct a nearly optimal protocol, both in terms of number of round and computation complexity.

**Theorem 4 (OT-MiM security of MiM-OTDB).** *Any MiM-game against MiM-OTDB with **only one instance** of $V(K)$ and one instance of $P(K)$ has a winning probability bounded by $\frac{3}{2^n+1}$. In short, MiM-OTDB is OT-MiM-secure (one time MiM-secure)* [26].

*Proof.* Using the last game in the proof of Theorem 3, we can show that MiM-OTDB is OT-MiM-secure.                                                                                    □

MiM-OTDB is the most efficient one-time MiM-secure protocol [26] since it does not need any computation.

**Adaptation of MiM-symDB to SHM (Full-symDB$^H$).** We define Full-symDB$^H$ with the tuple $(\mathcal{K}, V, P_{dum}, B, H)$ where $B, V$ and $\mathcal{K}$ are as in MiM-symDB, $H$ is the same with $P$ in MiM-symDB.

**Theorem 5 (Security of Full-symDB$^H$).** *If $f$ is a secure PRF, Full-symDB$^H$ is secure in SHM.*

*Proof.* The conversion of Full-symDB$^H$ in PM is $(\mathcal{K}, V, P_{dum}^H, B)$ which is equal to MiM-symDB. We know that MiM-symDB is MiM-secure since $f$ is a secure PRF. Hence, Full-symDB$^H$ with $(\mathcal{K}, V, P_{dum}, B.H)$ is secure thanks to Theorem 2. The security bound of Full-symDB$^H$ is the same as MiM-symDB's.                                                                                    □

Full-symDB$^H$ is the first protocol that reaches the optimal secure bounds for MiM, DH, DF and TF secure.

# 4    Optimal Public-Key DB Protocols in SHM

In this section, we give two public key DB protocols in SHM: Full-pkDB1$^H$ and Full-pkDB2$^{H\,4}$ which is correct, private and secure. The first one is derived from Simp-pkDB [19] in PM. We modify Simp-pkDB to make it private in SHM because Simp-pkDB is not private in PM. The second one is derived from Eff-pkDB$^p$ [19] in PM which is a variant of Eff-pkDB [19] with privacy protection. We slightly modify Eff-pkDB$^p$ as well as Eff-pkDB to increase its efficiency. We use these protocols because of their efficiency in PM.

---

[4] Full refers full security (MiM, DF, DH, TF) and privacy.

**Full-pkDB1$^H$:** This protocol is derived from Simp-pkDB [19]. However, Simp-pkDB is not private. Therefore, we add an extra encryption process on the prover side to achieve privacy. The details of Full-pkDB1$^H$ is as follows:

The input of the verifier $V$ is its secret/public key pair $(\mathsf{sk}_V, \mathsf{pk}_V)$ which is generated from the key generation algorithm of an encryption scheme $(\mathsf{Enc'}, \mathsf{Dec'})$. The input of $H$ is the prover's secret/public key pair $(\mathsf{sk}_P, \mathsf{pk}_P)$ which is generated by the key generation algorithm of the encryption scheme $(\mathsf{Enc}, \mathsf{Dec})$. The input of $P$ is $(\mathsf{pk}_P, \mathsf{pk}_V)$. $H$ picks a nonce $N$ from $\{0,1\}^s$ and sends it to $P$ along with $\mathsf{pk}_P$. Then, $P$ encrypts $\mathsf{pk}_P, N$ with $\mathsf{pk}_V$ and sends the encryption $e_P$ to $V$. $V$ learns $\mathsf{pk}_P$ and $N$ by decrypting $e_P$ with $\mathsf{sk}_V$. Then, it picks $C||R$ from $\{0,1\}^{2n}$ and encrypts $C||R||N$ with $\mathsf{pk}_P$. Next, it sends the encryption $e_V$ to $P$ and $P$ relays it to $H$. $H$ decrypts $e_V$ and learns $C||R||N$. If $N$ is the same nonce that it picked, it runs MiM-OTDB$(C||R)$ with $V$. The protocol is depicted in Fig. 5.

The conversion of Full-pkDB1$^H$ into PM is called as "Simp-pkDB$^p$". Its prover algorithm is $P^{H(\mathsf{sk}_P, \mathsf{pk}_P)}$ where $P$ and $H$ is from Full-pkDB1$^H$. Simp-pkDB$^p$ is the same as Simp-pkDB except that the prover encrypts its public key and the nonce, and the verifier learns the public key and the nonce via decryption. Clearly, Simp-pkDB$^p$ is MiM secure since Simp-pkDB is MiM-secure [19].

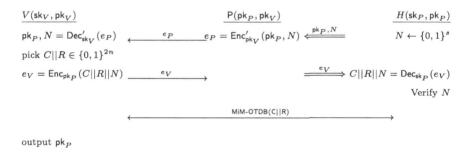

**Fig. 5.** Full-pkDB1$^H$. The double arrow shows the communication between $P$ and $H$

**Theorem 6 (Security of Full-pkDB1$^H$).** *If the encryption scheme* $(\mathsf{Enc}, \mathsf{Dec})$ *is IND-CCA secure and MiM-OTDB is OT-MiM-secure, Full-pkDB1$^H$ is secure in SHM.*

*Proof.* Consider $DB = (\mathcal{K}_V, \mathcal{K}_P, V, P^H_{dum}, B)$ with $V$ and $H$ from Full-pkDB1$^H$. Actually, $DB =$ Simp-pkDB. Using Theorem 2, Full-pkDB1$^H$ is secure because $DB =$ Simp-pkDB is MiM-secure [19] assuming that $(\mathsf{Enc}, \mathsf{Dec})$ is IND-CCA secure and MiM-OTDB is OT-MiM-secure. □

Full-pkDB1$^H$ achieves almost optimal security bounds because MiM-security of Simp-pkDB is reduced to MiM-security of MiM-OTDB [19].

We see that Full-pkDB1$^H$ is secure without encryption. Actually, the encryption is only used for achieving privacy. So, if privacy is not a concern, we can use

Full-pkDB1$^H$ without the encryption and decryption. In this case, the verifier has no secret/public key pair. This can be useful in practical applications.

We first prove that Simp-pkDB$^p$ achieves weak privacy. This helps us to prove Full-pkDB1$^H$ is semi-strong private in SHM.

**Theorem 7 (Weak privacy of Simp-pkDB$^p$).** *Assuming the encryption scheme with* (Enc′, Dec′) *is IND-CCA secure and the encryption scheme with* (Enc, Dec) *is IND-CCA and IK-CPA [3] secure, then Simp-pkDB$^p$ is weak private in PM.*

*Proof.* $\Gamma_i$ is a game where $p_i$ is the probability that the adversary in $\Gamma_i$ succeeds.

$\Gamma_0$: The adversary $\mathcal{A}$ plays the weak-privacy game in PM. The success probability of $\mathcal{A}$ is $p_0$.

$\Gamma_1$: We reduce $\Gamma_0$ to $\Gamma_1$ where the verifiers do not decrypt (with Dec′) any encryptions sent by the provers and the provers do not decrypt (with Dec) the encryptions generated by the verifiers. Instead, they directly use the values inside the encryption. Because of the correctness of both encryption schemes $p_1 = p_0$.

$\Gamma_2$: We reduce $\Gamma_1$ to $\Gamma_2$ where all provers encrypt (with Enc′) a random value instead of $\mathsf{pk}_P, N$ and all verifiers encrypt (with Enc) a random value instead of $(C||R||N)$. Note that the change on $e_V$ is indistinguishable by an adversary since it does not know $\mathsf{sk}_P$ because we prove here weak privacy. Thanks to the IND-CCA security of the encryption schemes $p_1 - p_2$ is negligible.

$\Gamma_3$: We reduce $\Gamma_2$ to $\Gamma_3$ where the prover does not decrypt (with Dec) the encryptions $e_V$ generated by the adversaries and it aborts. Since $N$ has never been used, the probability that $\mathcal{A}$ sends a valid encryption of $N$ is negligible. Therefore, $p_3 - p_2$ is negligible. Remark that in $\Gamma_3$, $\mathsf{Dec}_{\mathsf{sk}_P}$ has never used.

$\Gamma_4$: We reduce $\Gamma_3$ to $\Gamma_4$ where the prover replaces $\mathsf{pk}_P$ by a freshly generated public-key (that $\mathcal{V}$ uses if $e_P$ is correctly forwarded). The only visible change from $\Gamma_3$ is that now $e_V$ is encrypted using a new key. Because of IK-CPA security of the encryption scheme (with Enc, Dec), $p_4 - p_3$ is negligible.

Now, in $\Gamma_4$, no identity is used by the verifiers and the provers, so adversary succeeds $\Gamma_4$ with $\frac{1}{2}$ probability. Therefore, $p_0 - \frac{1}{2}$ is negligible.     □

Simp-pkDB$^p$ is not strong private due to the following attack: Assume that an adversary corrupts a prover $P$ and learns $\mathsf{sk}_P$. Later, he can decrypt all $e_V$ sent by the verifier with $\mathsf{sk}_P$. If $e_V$ is sent to $P$, then it means the adversary learns the challenges and responses. When these challenges and responses become known during MiM-OTDB, the adversary can identify $P$.

**Theorem 8 (Semi-strong privacy of Full-pkDB1$^H$).** *Assuming that the encryption scheme with* (Enc′, Dec′) *is IND-CCA secure and the encryption scheme with* (Enc, Dec) *is IND-CCA and IK-CCA [3] secure, then Full-pkDB1$^H$ is semi-strong private in SHM.*

*Proof.* The proof works like in Theorem 7. We only let non-anonymous hardware decrypt $e_V$ from the adversary with the right key through a CCA query in the IK-CCA game.     □

**Full-pkDB2$^H$:** Eff-pkDB$^p$ [19] is the most efficient public-key DB protocol which is secure against MiM, DF, DH and strong private. Briefly, in Eff-pkDB$^p$, after the prover transmits its public key via encryption, $V$ and $P$ run a key agreement protocol with the algorithms ($\mathsf{Gen}_V, \mathsf{Gen}_P, A_{N_V}, B_{N_V}, D$). In the end, with the agreed key, they run a symmetric DB protocol.

One of the assumptions in MiM-security of Eff-pkDB$^p$ is that the symmetric DB is "one-time multi-verifier MiM-secure"[5] [19]. It is not possible to use MiM-OTDB on current Eff-pkDB$^p$ as a symmetric DB because MiM-OTDB does not fulfill the assumption. Hence, we modify Eff-pkDB$^p$ so that one time MiM-security is enough. In this way, we are able to use MiM-OTDB as a symmetric DB which does not require any computation.

$V(\mathsf{sk}_V, \mathsf{pk}_V)$          $P(\mathsf{pk}_P, \mathsf{pk}_V)$          $H(\mathsf{sk}_P, \mathsf{pk}_P)$

$N_V \leftarrow \{0,1\}^s$     $\xrightarrow{N_V}$     $\xrightarrow{N_V, \mathsf{pk}_V}$     $N_P \leftarrow D(1^s)$,

$\mathsf{pk}_P, N_P = \mathsf{Dec}_{\mathsf{sk}_{V_1}}(e)$,     $\xleftarrow{e}$     $e = \mathsf{Enc}_{\mathsf{pk}_{V_1}}(\mathsf{pk}_P, N_P) \xleftarrow{N_P, \mathsf{pk}_P}$

$C||R =$                                                $C||R =$

$A_{N_V}(\mathsf{sk}_{V_2}, \mathsf{pk}_{V_2}, \mathsf{pk}_P, N_P)$                $B_{N_V}(\mathsf{sk}_P, \mathsf{pk}_P, \mathsf{pk}_{V_2}, N_P)$

$\xleftrightarrow{\text{MiM-OTDB}(C||R)}$

output $\mathsf{pk}_P$

**Fig. 6.** Full-pkDB2$^H$. Double arrow shows the communication with $H$.

We slightly change the verifier algorithm of Eff-pkDB$^p$ and convert Eff-pkDB$^p$ into SHM. We call this new version in SHM as Full-pkDB2$^H$ (in Fig. 6). The description of Full-pkDB2$^H$ is as follows: The verifier $V$ has the secret/public key pair $(\mathsf{sk}_V, \mathsf{pk}_V) = ((\mathsf{sk}_{V_1}, \mathsf{sk}_{V_2}), (\mathsf{pk}_{V_1}, \mathsf{pk}_{V_2}))$ which has two parts where the first part is generated from the key generation algorithm of an encryption scheme and the second part is generated by $\mathsf{Gen}_V$. $H$ has the input $(\mathsf{sk}_P, \mathsf{pk}_P)$ generated by $\mathsf{Gen}_P$. The input of $P$ is $(\mathsf{pk}_P, \mathsf{pk}_V)$. First, $V$ picks a nonce $N_V$ from $\{0,1\}^s$ and sends it to $P$. Then, $P$ relays it to $H$. Similarly, $H$ picks $N_P$ from the distribution $D(1^s)$ and gives it $P$. $P$ encrypts $N_P$ and $\mathsf{pk}_P$ with $\mathsf{pk}_{V_1}$. Then, $P$ sends the encryption $e$ to $V$. $V$ decrypts it with $\mathsf{sk}_V$ and learns $N_P, \mathsf{pk}_P$. $H$ and $V$ run the algorithms $B_{N_V}(\mathsf{sk}_P, \mathsf{pk}_P, \mathsf{pk}_{V_2}, N_P)$ and $A_{N_V}(\mathsf{sk}_{V_2}, \mathsf{pk}_{V_2}, \mathsf{pk}_P, N_P)$ which output $C||R$, respectively. In the end, they run MiM-OTDB using $C||R$ as a secret key.

The conversion of Full-pkDB2$^H$ into PM is called as "our variant of Eff-pkDB$^p$". In this variant, the prover algorithm is $P^{H(\mathsf{sk}_P, \mathsf{pk}_P)}$ where $P$ and $H$ are from Full-pkDB2$^H$. The difference between the verifier algorithms of Eff-pkDB$^p$ [19] and our variant of Eff-pkDB$^p$ is the following: In Eff-pkDB$^p$, $V$ does not select any nonce (equivalently, we can say that $N_V$ is a constant) and the

---

[5] It is equivalent to MiM-security with one prover instance and multiple verifier's instances.

algorithms $A_{N_V}$ and $B_{N_V}$ generate a one-time secret key to run a symmetric DB protocol. Remember that we do this change in the verifier algorithm of Eff-pkDB$^p$ to increase its efficiency in SHM since we can use MiM-OTDB with this version.

**Theorem 9 (Security of Full-pkDB2$^H$).** *If the key agreement protocol* $(\mathsf{Gen}_V, \mathsf{Gen}_P, A_{N_V}, B_{N_V}, D)$ *is D-AKA secure* [19] *for all fixed* $N_V \in \{0,1\}^s$ *and MiM-OTDB is* **one time MiM-secure** *then Full-pkDB2$^H$ is secure in SHM.*

*Proof.* We prove it by using Theorem 2. Consider that $DB = (\mathcal{K}_V, \mathcal{K}_P, V, P_{dum}^H, B)$ with $V$ and $H$ from Full-pkDB2$^H$ is MiM-secure in PM. Actually, $DB$ is our variant of Eff-pkDB. Using Theorem 2, Full-pkDB2$^H$ is secure because our variant of EffpkDB is MiM-secure assuming that the key agreement proto-col $(\mathsf{Gen}_V, \mathsf{Gen}_P, A_{N_V}, B_{N_V}, D)$ is D-AKA secure for all fixed $N_V \in \{0,1\}^s$ and MiM-OTDB is **one time MiM-secure**. The MiM security proof of our variant of Eff-pkDB is in the full version of the paper. □

Full-pkDB2$^H$ achieves almost optimal security bounds because MiM-security of our variant of Eff-pkDB is reduced to MiM-security of MiM-OTDB.

We see that Full-pkDB2$^H$ is secure without encryption. Actually, the encryp-tion is used for achieving privacy. So, if privacy is not a concern, we can use Full-pkDB2$^H$ without the encryption and decryption.

**Theorem 10 (Strong privacy of Full-pkDB2$^H$).** *Assuming that the key-agreement protocol* $(\mathsf{Gen}_V, \mathsf{Gen}_P, A_{N_V}, B_{N_V}, D)$ *is D-AKA$^p$ secure* [19] *for all fixed* $N_V \in \{0,1\}^n$ *and the crypto system is IND-CCA secure, Full-pkDB2$^H$ is strong private in SHM.*

*Proof.* We first show that our variant of Eff-pkDB$^p$ is strong private in PM. Actually, the strong privacy proof of our variant of Eff-pkDB$^p$ is the same with the proof of Eff-pkDB$^p$ (Theorem 7 of [19]) where first it reduces the privacy game to the game where all the encryptions are random (the reduction showed by using IND-CCA security) and then reduces to the game where the provers use a random secret and public key pair with $B_{N_V}$ (the reduction showed by using D-AKA$^p$). Because of the equivalence of strong privacy of a DB in SHM and its conversion in PM, we can conclude that Full-pkDB2$^H$ is strong private. □

The prover algorithms of Full-pkDB1$^H$ and Full-pkDB2$^H$ are not $P_{dum}$, but it can be easily seen from the proofs of Theorems 6 and 9 that the computations in these algorithms do not have any effect on the security (i.e., the security of Full-pkDB1$^H$ and Full-pkDB1$^H$ do not need any security assumptions on the encryption scheme with $(\mathsf{Enc}', \mathsf{Dec}')$ which is used by $P$.)

## 5    Conclusion

In this paper, we defined a new DB with three algorithms and designed its adversarial and communication model of SHM. According to our new model, we define a new security definition. We showed that the trivial attack of TF is preventable in our definition. By showing implications between different threat models, we deduced that if a DB protocol achieves TF-security in SHM, then it is secure against all other security notions. This result cannot be applied in PM because TF-security is not possible. We also gave some security relations between PM and SHM. One of the relations shows that we can construct a DB protocol that is secure against all the threat models including TF in SHM, if its conversion into PM is MiM-secure. This result is significant because it shows that many MiM-secure DB protocols in the literature [4–6,17,19,24,26] can be used to achieve higher security level in our model.

We constructed a new only MiM-secure symmetric key DB in PM called MiM-symDB. It achieves optimal security bounds and it is the most efficient DB achieving this. We did not need to achieve other security models with MiM-symDB because MiM-security is enough to have a secure DB protocol in SHM by using $P_{dum}$. In addition, we constructed another symmetric DB protocol MiM-OTDB. It is MiM-secure when it is run at most one time. It does not require any computation, so it is the most efficient one.

We also considered public key DB protocols in SHM. For this, we derived protocols Full-pkDB1$^H$ and Full-pkDB2$^H$ from Eff-pkDB$^p$ and Simp-pkDB [19], respectively. Full-pkDB1$^H$ was constructed through some modifications on Eff-pkDB$^p$ to be able to use computation free sub-protocol MiM-OTDB. We formally proved that Full-pkDB1$^H$ is strong private and secure in SHM. By adding one extra encryption, we added privacy to Simp-pkDB and constructed Full-pkDB2$^H$ from its private version. We proved Full-pkDB2$^H$ is semi-strong private and secure in SHM.

Compared to the previous models [1,5,13] which do not have any practical and secure solution against all the threats, SHM lets us construct more efficient protocols while achieving the **highest security**.

# References

1. Avoine, G., Bingöl, M.A., Kardaş, S., Lauradoux, C., Martin, B.: A framework for analyzing RFID distance bounding protocols. J. Comput. Secur. Spec. Issue RFID Syst. Secur. **19**, 289–317 (2010)
2. Avoine, G., Bultel, X., Gambs, S., Gérault, D., Lafourcade, P., Onete, C., Robert, J.-M.: A terrorist-fraud resistant and extractor-free anonymous distance-bounding protocol. In: Proceedings of the 2017 ACM on Asia Conference on Computer and Communications Security, pp. 800–814. ACM (2017)
3. Bellare, M., Boldyreva, A., Desai, A., Pointcheval, D.: Key-privacy in public-key encryption. In: Boyd, C. (ed.) ASIACRYPT 2001. LNCS, vol. 2248, pp. 566–582. Springer, Heidelberg (2001). https://doi.org/10.1007/3-540-45682-1_33
4. Boureanu, I., Mitrokotsa, A., Vaudenay, S.: Secure and lightweight distance-bounding. In: Avoine, G., Kara, O. (eds.) LightSec 2013. LNCS, vol. 8162, pp. 97–113. Springer, Heidelberg (2013). https://doi.org/10.1007/978-3-642-40392-7_8

5. Boureanu, I., Vaudenay, S.: Optimal proximity proofs. In: Lin, D., Yung, M., Zhou, J. (eds.) Inscrypt 2014. LNCS, vol. 8957, pp. 170–190. Springer, Cham (2015). https://doi.org/10.1007/978-3-319-16745-9_10

6. Brands, S., Chaum, D.: Distance-bounding protocols. In: Helleseth, T. (ed.) EURO-CRYPT 1993. LNCS, vol. 765, pp. 344–359. Springer, Heidelberg (1994). https://doi.org/10.1007/3-540-48285-7_30

7. Bultel, X., Gambs, S., Gérault, D., Lafourcade, P., Onete, C., Robert, J.-M.: A prover-anonymous and terrorist-fraud resistant distance-bounding protocol. In: Proceedings of the 9th ACM Conference on Security & Privacy in Wireless and Mobile Networks, pp. 121–133. ACM (2016)

8. Bussard, L., Bagga, W.: Distance-bounding proof of knowledge to avoid real-time attacks. In: Sasaki, R., Qing, S., Okamoto, E., Yoshiura, H. (eds.) SEC 2005. IAICT, vol. 181, pp. 223–238. Springer, Boston, MA (2005). https://doi.org/10.1007/0-387-25660-1_15

9. Bussard, L., Roudier, Y.: Embedding distance-bounding protocols within intuitive interactions. In: Hutter, D., Müller, G., Stephan, W., Ullmann, M. (eds.) Security in Pervasive Computing. LNCS, vol. 2802, pp. 143–156. Springer, Heidelberg (2004). https://doi.org/10.1007/978-3-540-39881-3_14

10. Capkun, S., Buttyan, L., Hubaux, J.-P.: SECTOR: secure tracking of node encounters in multi-hop wireless networks. In: ACM Workshop on Security of Ad Hoc and Sensor Networks (SASN), pp. 21–32 (2003)

11. Cremers, C., Rasmussen, K.B., Schmidt, B., Capkun, S.: Distance hijacking attacks on distance bounding protocols. In: 2012 IEEE Symposium on Security and Privacy (SP), pp. 113–127. IEEE (2012)

12. Desmedt, Y.: Major security problems with the "unforgeable" (Feige-) Fiat-Shamir proofs of identity and how to overcome them. In: Congress on Computer and Communication Security and Protection, SECURICOM, pp. 147–159. SEDEP, Paris (1988)

13. Dürholz, U., Fischlin, M., Kasper, M., Onete, C.: A Formal Approach to Distance-Bounding RFID Protocols. In: Lai, X., Zhou, J., Li, H. (eds.) ISC 2011. LNCS, vol. 7001, pp. 47–62. Springer, Heidelberg (2011). https://doi.org/10.1007/978-3-642-24861-0_4

14. Fischlin, M., Onete, C.: Terrorism in distance bounding: modeling terrorist-fraud resistance. In: Jacobson, M., Locasto, M., Mohassel, P., Safavi-Naini, R. (eds.) ACNS 2013. LNCS, vol. 7954, pp. 414–431. Springer, Heidelberg (2013). https://doi.org/10.1007/978-3-642-38980-1_26

15. Hancke, G.P.: A practical relay attack on ISO 14443 proximity cards. Technical report, University of Cambridge Computer Laboratory, vol. 59, pp. 382–385 (2005)

16. Hermans, J., Pashalidis, A., Vercauteren, F., Preneel, B.: A new RFID privacy model. In: Atluri, V., Diaz, C. (eds.) ESORICS 2011. LNCS, vol. 6879, pp. 568–587. Springer, Heidelberg (2011). https://doi.org/10.1007/978-3-642-23822-2_31

17. Hermans, J., Peeters, R., Onete, C.: Efficient, secure, private distance bounding without key updates. In: WiSec Proceedings of the Sixth ACM Conference on Security and Privacy in Wireless and Mobile Networks, pp. 207–218 (2013)

18. Kılınç, H., Vaudenay, S.: Optimal proximity proofs revisited. In: Malkin, T., Kolesnikov, V., Lewko, A.B., Polychronakis, M. (eds.) ACNS 2015. LNCS, vol. 9092, pp. 478–494. Springer, Cham (2015). https://doi.org/10.1007/978-3-319-28166-7_23

19. Kılınç, H., Vaudenay, S.: Efficient public-key distance bounding protocol. In: Cheon, J.H., Takagi, T. (eds.) ASIACRYPT 2016. LNCS, vol. 10032, pp. 873–901. Springer, Heidelberg (2016). https://doi.org/10.1007/978-3-662-53890-6_29

20. Kim, C.H., Avoine, G., Koeune, F., Standaert, F.-X., Pereira, O.: The swiss-knife RFID distance bounding protocol. In: Lee, P.J., Cheon, J.H. (eds.) ICISC 2008. LNCS, vol. 5461, pp. 98–115. Springer, Heidelberg (2009). https://doi.org/10.1007/978-3-642-00730-9_7

21. Reid, J., Nieto, J.M.G., Tang, T., Senadji, B.: Detecting relay attacks with timing-based protocols. In: Proceedings of the 2nd ACM Symposium on Information, Computer and Communications Security, pp. 204–213. ACM (2007)

22. Singelee, D., Preneel, B.: Location verification using secure distance bounding protocols. In: 2005 IEEE International Conference on Mobile Adhoc and Sensor Systems Conference, 7 p. IEEE (2005)

23. Singelée, D., Preneel, B.: Distance bounding in noisy environments. In: Stajano, F., Meadows, C., Capkun, S., Moore, T. (eds.) ESAS 2007. LNCS, vol. 4572, pp. 101–115. Springer, Heidelberg (2007). https://doi.org/10.1007/978-3-540-73275-4_8

24. Vaudenay, S.: On modeling terrorist frauds. In: Susilo, W., Reyhanitabar, R. (eds.) ProvSec 2013. LNCS, vol. 8209, pp. 1–20. Springer, Heidelberg (2013). https://doi.org/10.1007/978-3-642-41227-1_1

25. Vaudenay, S.: On privacy for RFID. In: Au, M.-H., Miyaji, A. (eds.) ProvSec 2015. LNCS, vol. 9451, pp. 3–20. Springer, Cham (2015). https://doi.org/10.1007/978-3-319-26059-4_1

26. Vaudenay, S.: Private and secure public-key distance bounding. In: Böhme, R., Okamoto, T. (eds.) FC 2015. LNCS, vol. 8975, pp. 207–216. Springer, Heidelberg (2015). https://doi.org/10.1007/978-3-662-47854-7_12

27. Vaudenay, S.: Sound proof of proximity of knowledge. In: Au, M.-H., Miyaji, A. (eds.) ProvSec 2015. LNCS, vol. 9451, pp. 105–126. Springer, Cham (2015). https://doi.org/10.1007/978-3-319-26059-4_6

# KRB-CCN: Lightweight Authentication and Access Control for Private Content-Centric Networks

Ivan O. Nunes[✉] and Gene Tsudik

University of California Irvine, Irvine, USA
{ivanoliv,g.tsudik}@uci.edu

**Abstract.** Content-Centric Networking (CCN) is an internetworking paradigm that offers an alternative to today's IP-based Internet Architecture. Instead of focusing on hosts and their locations, CCN emphasizes addressable named content. By decoupling content from its location, CCN allows opportunistic in-network content caching, thus enabling better network utilization, at least for scalable content distribution. However, in order to be considered seriously, CCN must support basic security services, including content authenticity, integrity, confidentiality, authorization and access control. Current approaches rely on content producers to perform authorization and access control, which is typically attained via public key encryption. This general approach has several disadvantages. First, consumer privacy vis-a-vis producers is not preserved. Second, identity management and access control impose high computational overhead on producers. Also, unnecessary repeated authentication and access control decisions must be made for each content request. (This burden is particularly relevant for resource-limited producers, e.g., anemic IoT devices.)

These issues motivate our design of KRB-CCN – a complete authorization and access control system for private CCN networks. Inspired by Kerberos in IP-based networks, KRB-CCN involves distinct authentication and authorization authorities. By doing so, KRB-CCN obviates the need for producers to make consumer authentication and access control decisions. KRB-CCN preserves consumer privacy since producers are unaware of consumer identities. Producers are also not required to keep any hard state and only need to perform two symmetric key operations to guarantee that sensitive content is confidentially delivered only to authenticated and authorized consumers. Furthermore, KRB-CCN works transparently on the consumer side. Most importantly, unlike prior designs, KRB-CCN leaves the network (i.e., CCN routers) out of any authorization, access control or confidentiality issues. We describe KRB-CCN design and implementation, analyze its security, and report on its performance.

## 1 Introduction

Content-Centric Networking (CCN) is an emerging internetworking paradigm that emphasizes transfer of named data (aka content) instead of host-to-host

B. Preneel and F. Vercauteren (Eds.): ACNS 2018, LNCS 10892, pp. 598–615, 2018.
https://doi.org/10.1007/978-3-319-93387-0_31

communication [1, 2]. All CCN content is uniquely named. Content *producers* are entities that publish content under namespaces. Entities that wish to obtain content, called *consumers*, do so by issuing an *interest* message specifying desired content by its unique name. The network is responsible for forwarding the interest, based on the content name, to the nearest copy of requested content. Interests do not carry source or destination addresses. Each interest leaves state in every router it traverses. This state is later used to forward, along the reverse path, requested *content* back to the consumers. As content is forwarded to the consumer, each router can choose to cache it. If a popular content is cached, subsequent interests for it can be satisfied by the caching router and not forwarded further. This can lead to lower delays, better throughput and improved network utilization.

Due to CCN's unique characteristics, security focus shifts from securing host-to-host tunnels to securing the content itself. CCN mandates that each content must be signed by its producer. This is the extent of CCN network-layer security. In particular, CCN does not make any provisions for confidentiality, authorization or access control, leaving these issues to individual applications. We believe that this approach makes sense, since involving the network (i.e., routers) in such issues is generally problematic for both performance and security reasons.

Access control (AC) in CCN has been explored in recent years. Most approaches [3–9][1] rely on using public key encryption. Specifically, producers encrypt content with a public key of an authorized consumer or a group thereof. The latter use their corresponding private keys to decrypt. Although it seems to work, this approach exhibits several problems:

- First, producers are responsible for handling consumer authentication and content AC on their own. Thus, they must deal with (1) consumer identity management and authentication, (2) AC policy representation and storage, (3) updates of access rights, and (4) content encryption. In some cases, producers might not want (or be able) to deal with this burden, e.g., resource-constrained IoT devices. On the consumer side, this means keeping track of producer-specific authentication contexts and keys.
- Second, AC enforced by producers implies sacrificing consumer privacy, which is an important and appealing CCN feature. Since CCN interests do not carry source addresses, a content producer (or a router) normally does not learn the identity of the consumer. However, if the producer enforces AC, it needs to learn consumers identities.
- Third, if multiple producers are in the same administrative domain and each enforces its AC policy, it is difficult to react to policy changes, e.g., access revocation for a given consumer or a consumer's credential. Implementing such changes requires notifying each producer individually.
- Finally, since public keys are associated with identities, if AC is based on public keys, authentication of consumers is attained via consumer-owned private keys. However, if a consumer is authenticated by other means, e.g., passwords

---

[1] We overview them in Sect. 6.

and biometrics, each producer would have to store and manage potentially sensitive state information (password files or biometric templates) for each consumer.

Since mid-1980s, Kerberos [10] has been successfully and widely used to address these exact issues in private IP-based networks or so-called stub Autonomous Systems. Kerberos de-couples authentication and authorization services via short-term *tickets*. It also allows services (e.g., storage, compute or web servers) to be accessed by clients over a secure ephemeral session. By checking a client's ticket for freshness of authentication information, a service limits the period of vulnerability due to revocation.

In this paper, we present KRB-CCN, a system inspired by Kerberos for authentication and access control (AC) enforcement in CCN, that aims at addressing the aforementioned issues[2]. KRB-CCN treats consumer authentication and authorization as separate services. It uses tickets to allow consumers to convey authorization permissions to servers, e.g., content producers or repositories. Servers use tickets to determine whether requested content should be provided. KRB-CCN also introduces a novel namespace based AC policy, which allows a consumer to securely retrieve content without revealing its identity to the content producer, thus preserving consumer privacy. In addition, KRB-CCN is transparent to the users; they need not be aware of KRB-CCN or perform any additional tasks. It is also completely invisible to the network, i.e., CCN routers are unaware of KRB-CCN.

**Organization:** Section 2 overviews CCN and Sect. 3 overviews Kerberos. Next, Sect. 4 introduces KRB-CCN, including its system architecture, namespace based AC scheme, and the protocol for authentication, authorization, and secure content retrieval. Then, performance of KRB-CCN is evaluated in Sect. 5. Finally, Sect. 6 discusses related work and Sect. 7 concludes this paper. Security analysis of KRB-CCN is available in the extended version of this paper[3].

## 2   CCN Overview

We now overview key features of CCN. Given basic familiarity with CCN, this section can be skipped with no loss of continuity.

In contrast to today's IP-based Internet architecture which focuses on endpoints of communication (i.e., interfaces/hosts and their addresses) CCN [1,11] centers on content by making it named, addressable, and routable within the network. Moreover, a content must be signed by its producer. A content name is a URI-like string composed of one or more variable-length name segments, separated by the '/' character. To obtain content, a user (consumer) issues an explicit request message, called an *interest* containing the name of desired content. This

---

[2] KRB-CCN source-code is available at: https://github.com/ivanolive/krb-ccn.
[3] See: http://arxiv.org/abs/1804.03820.

interest can be *satisfied* by either: (1) a router cache, or (2) the content producer. A *content object* message is returned to the consumer upon satisfaction of the interest. Name matching is exact, e.g., an interest for /edu/uni-X/ics/cs/fileA can only be satisfied by a content object named /edu/uni-X/ics/cs/fileA.

In addition to a payload, a content object includes several other fields. In this paper, we are only interested in the following three: Name, Validation, and ExpiryTime. Validation is a composite of validation algorithm information (e.g., the signature algorithm, its parameters, and the name of the public verification key), and validation payload, i.e., the content signature. We use the term "signature" to refer to the entire Validation field. ExpiryTime is an optional, producer-recommended duration for caching a content object. Interest messages carry a name, optional payload, and other fields that restrict the content object response. We refer to [11] for a complete description of all CCN message types, fields and their semantics.

Packets are moved within the network by routers. Each CCN router has two mandatory (and one optional) components:

- *Forwarding Interest Base* (FIB) – a table of name prefixes and corresponding outgoing interfaces. The FIB is used to route interests based on longest-prefix-matching (LPM) of their names.
- *Pending Interest Table* (PIT) – a table of outstanding (pending) interests and a set of corresponding incoming interfaces.
- An optional *Content Store* (CS) used for content caching. The timeout for cached content is specified in the ExpiryTime field of the content header. From here on, we use the terms *CS* and *cache* interchangeably.

A router uses its FIB to forward interests toward the producer of requested content. Whereas, a router uses its PIT to forward content along the reverse path towards consumers. Specifically, upon receiving an interest, a router $R$ first checks its cache (if present) to see if it can satisfy this interest locally. In case of a cache miss, $R$ checks its PIT for an outstanding version of the same interest. If there is a PIT match, the new interest's incoming interface is added to the PIT entry. Otherwise, $R$ creates a new PIT entry and forwards the interest to the next hop according to its FIB (if possible). For each forwarded interest, $R$ stores some state information in the PIT entry, including the name in the interest and the interface from which it arrived, such that content may be returned to the consumer. When content is returned, $R$ forwards it to all interfaces listed in the matching PIT entry and then removes the entry. A content that does not match any PIT entry is discarded.

## 3   Kerberos Overview

We now summarize Kerberos. We refer to [12] for a more extensive description. Kerberos includes four types of entities: clients, services, an Authentication Server (AS), and a Ticket-Granting Server (TGS). The AS/TGS pair (which are often collocated within the same host) is also known as a Key Distribution Center (KDC). Should a new client/user or a new service be added to the network, it must first be properly registered into KDC's (AS and TGS) databases.

In Kerberos' terminology, a *realm* corresponds to a single administrative domain, e.g., a private network or a stub Autonomous System. Each realm has one KDC and any authorization or AC decision by a KDC is only valid within its realm. Thus, identities, tickets, and encryption keys (see below) are also realm-specific.

*Principal* is the term used to refer to names of entries in the KDC database. Each user/client and service has an associated principal. User principals are generally their usernames in the system. Service principals are used to specify various applications. A service principal has the format: `service/hostname@realm`. A service specification is needed in addition to a hostname, since a single host often runs multiple services. With Kerberos operation in IP Networks, principals are resolved to host IP addresses via DNS look-ups [13]. As can be expected, CCN obviates the need for DNS look-ups, since all content objects are uniquely named by design. Moreover, routing is done based on content names. As discussed below, `KRB-CCN` enforces AC based on content namespaces, instead of service principals.

Each client/user principal (i.e., username) stored in the AS database is associated with a key, which can be either a public-key or a symmetric key derived from the user's password. Also, the same client/user principal also exists in the TGS database. However, it is associated with a list principals for services that such user has permission to access.

Before attempting to access any content, a client must first authenticate to its local AS. This is done by either typing a password, or proving possession of a secret key associated with the client's identity in the AS database. If the client proves its identity, AS issues a *Ticket-Granting Ticket (TGT)* – a temporary proof of identity required for the authorization. This TGT might be cached and used multiple times until its expires.

The client uses a valid TGT to request, from TGS, authorization for a service. The TGS is responsible for access control decisions – verifying whether the requested service is within the set of permitted services for the identity ascertained in the provided TGT. If the result is positive, TGS issues a *Service Ticket (ST)* to be used for requesting the actual service.

## 4   `KRB-CCN` Design

There are three fundamental requirements for any authentication and authorization system. First, AC policies must effectively bind identities to their access rights. Second, once AC policies are established, there must be a way to enforce them, thus preventing unauthorized access. Third, authentication mechanisms must ensure that identities can not be spoofed; this includes both producers and consumers. The system must also not involve the network elements (i.e., routers) where authentication and authorization burden is both misplaced and simply unnecessary.

In the rest of this section, we describe how KRB-CCN achieves each of these requirements. We start by introducing KRB-CCN system architecture and its namespace-based AC policy, which takes advantage of CCN hierarchical content name structure to provide AC based on content prefixes. Next, we describe KRB-CCN communication protocol, which enforces AC policies while providing a single sign-on mechanism for user authentication. Though KRB-CCN is inspired by Kerberos for IP-based networks, it also takes advantage of unique CCN features to effectively satisfy basic authentication and authorization requirements. Throughout the protocol description we discuss the intuition behind the security of KRB-CCN.

As it is the case for IP-based Kerberos, KRB-CCN targets private (content-centric) networks, such as intra-corporation/intra-Autonomous Systems settings.

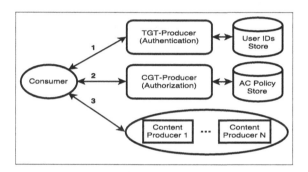

**Fig. 1.** KRB-CCN system architecture

## 4.1   System Architecture

Recall that Kerberos has 4 types of entities: AS, TGS, client, and server. A Kerberos realm (domain) typically has one AS/TGS pair, usually collocated in the same host, as well as multiple clients and servers. KRB-CCN also includes four types of entities that map to Kerberos entities as follows:

- Consumer: corresponds to Kerberos client. It issues interests for content and services according to KRB-CCN protocol. Each consumer has an identity and a set of associated permissions registered in the system.
- Producer: subsumes one or more Kerberos servers. A producer is required to register its namespace(s) in the system, by registering with a TGS (see below). A single namespace, i.e., a name prefix, can correspond to a single Kerberos server. Alternatively, a group of namespaces of the same producer can be treated as a single server. A producer does not perform any direct consumer authentication or authorization. A producer only checks whether a content-requesting consumer possesses a valid TGS-issued ticket.
- As in Kerberos, authentication and authorization are handled by two logically separated entities which can be collocated:

*Authentication Server (AS) (aka TGT-Prod):* treated as a special type of producer that generates so-called Ticket-Granting Tickets (TGT-s) for consumers once their identities are verified. These tickets can then be used as temporary proofs of identity. We refer to the AS as *TGT-Prod*.

*Ticket − Granting Server (TGS) (aka CGT-Prod):* performs authorization and is also treated as a special type of producer. Based on a valid consumer TGT and a request to access to a given namespace (server), TGS checks whether this consumer is allowed access to the requested namespace. If so, TGS issues a Content-Granting Ticket (CGT), which proves to the producer that this consumer is granted access to any content under the requested namespace. We refer to TGS as *CGT-Prod*.

Figure 1 illustrates KRB-CCN system architecture. As part of the log-in procedure (aka single sign-on or SSO), a consumer authenticates to TGT-Prod (round 1) and obtains a TGT, which it caches. Whenever a consumer wants to initially access content from a particular producer, it requests authorization from CGT-Prod using its cached TGT (round 2) and obtains a CGT, which it also caches. A CGT authorizes access to one or more namespaces belonging to the same producer. Finally, a consumer requests content from the producer using the corresponding CGT (round 3). TGT and CGT-s remain valid and re-usable until their expiration time runs out. Note that each round (1, 2 and 3) is realized as a single interest-content exchange.

Subsequent requests from the namespace(s) specified in the CGT require no involvement of either *TGT-Prod* or *CGT-Prod*. A consumer retrieves another content by directly issuing an interest containing the cached CGT. To access content under a different namespace, a consumer uses its cached TGT to contact CGT-Prod and request a new CGT.

For authentication and authorization, KRB-CCN must ensure that TGT-s and CGT-s issued to a specific consumer $C_r$ are unforgeable, and not usable by clients other than $C_r$. Moreover, it must make sure that content authorized for $C_r$ can only be decrypted by $C_r$. In the rest of this section we go into the details of how KRB-CCN achieves these requirements and functionalities.

### 4.2   Namespace-Based AC Policies

Instead of traditional service principals in Kerberos, KRB-CCN AC policies refer to namespaces, i.e, prefixes of content names that correspond to a producer. Recall that a content name is a URI-like string composed of arbitrary number of elastic name segments, separated by a '/' character. For example, consider a content named:

> /edu/uni-X/ics/cs/students/alice/images/img1.png

The leftmost part, /edu/uni-X/ics/cs, defines this content's original producer's location. Subsequent name segments get increasingly specific, defining, e.g., location of the content in a directory structure on the producer.

KRB-CCN leverages this hierarchical name structure to implement AC policies based on content prefixes. For example, to grant Alice permission to retrieve contents under the prefix /edu/uni-X/ics/cs/students/alice, namespace /edu/uni-X/ics/cs/students/alice/* must be included under Alice's ID in the AC Policy Store, as shown in Fig. 1. This entry would allow Alice to retrieve /edu/uni-X/ics/cs/students/alice/images/img1.png, as well as any content with that same prefix.

Suppose that Bob is a faculty member of the faculty in the same institution and has privileges to retrieve contents under own (Bob's) private directory and any content of students' directories. Bob's entry in the AC Policy store would include two namespaces:

> /edu/uni-X/ics/cs/faculty/bob/* and /edu/uni-X/ics/cs/students/*

The former allows Bob to access its own private directory under the faculty directory, but no other faculty's private directories. The latter allows Bob to access contents of any student directory under /edu/uni-X/ics/cs/students/*. Finally, suppose that Carl is a system administrator. As such, he has access to all content. Carl's entry in the AC Policy Store would be the namespace /edu/uni-X/ics/*, allowing access to any content with a name starting with this prefix; this includes all faculty and students' content.

If Alice (who is not yet "logged in", i.e., has no current TGT) wants to issue an interest for /edu/uni-X/ics/cs/students/alice/images/img1.png she first authenticates to TGT-Prod to get a TGT. Alice then uses the TGT to request a CGT from CGT-Prod for namespace /edu/uni-X/ics/cs/students/alice/*. Notice that Alice does not need to specify the actual content name – only the namespace. Therefore, CGT-Prod does not learn which content Alice wants to retrieve, only the producer's name. Since CGT is associated with /edu/uni-X/ics/cs/students/alice/*, it can be used for future interests within the same namespace, e.g., /edu/uni-X/ics/cs/students/alice/docs/paper.pdf.

### 4.3   Protocol

To retrieve protected content, $C_r$ must go through all of KRB-CCN's three phases, in sequence: authentication, authorization, and content retrieval. As discuss below, transition between phases is automated on the consumer side, i.e., it requires no extra actions. Table 1 summarizes our notation.

**Authentication**

The first phase on KRB-CCN verifies consumer identity via authentication. The authentication protocol in Fig. 2 is executed between $C_r$ and TGT-Prod. If it succeeds, $C_r$ receives a TGT, used in the authorization phase, as proof that $C_r$'s identity has been recently verified.

$C_r$ starts by issuing an interest with TGT suffix in the content name (e.g., /uni-X/ics/TGT). This interest carries as payload consumer's UID, i.e, $C_r$'s username. Hence, the actual interest name also contains a hash of the payload as its suffix[4]. The interest is routed by CCN towards TGT-Prod. Upon the interest,

---

[4] In CCN design, an interest carrying a payload must have the hash of the payload appended to its name.

**Table 1.** Notation summary

| Notation | Description |
|---|---|
| $N$ | A namespace prefix (e.g., edu/uni-X/ics/alice/) |
| $C_r$ | Consumer |
| $TGT\_Name$ | Ticket-granting ticket name (e.g., edu/uni-X/ics/TGT) that will be routed towards TGT-Prod |
| $CGT\_Name$ | Content-granting ticket name (e.g., edu/uni-X/ics/CGT) that will be routed towards CGT-Prod |
| $sk_C$ | Consumer secret key |
| $pk_C$ | Consumer public key, including public UID and certificate |
| $k_A$ | Long-term symmetric key shared between TGT-Prod and CGT-Prod |
| $k_P$ | Long-term symmetric key shared between CGT-Prod and a given content producer |
| $s \leftarrow_\$ \{0,1\}^\lambda$ | Random $\lambda$-bits number generation |
| $ct \leftarrow Enc_k(pt)$ | Authenticated encryption of $pt$ using symmetric key $k$ |
| $pt \leftarrow Dec_k(ct)$ | Decryption of $ct$ using symmetric key $k$ |
| $ct \leftarrow Enc_{pk}(pt)$ | Authenticated encryption of $pt$ using public key $pk$ |
| $pt \leftarrow Dec_{sk}(ct)$ | Decryption of $ct$ using secret key $sk$ |

TGT-Prod looks up $UID$ in its user database and retrieves the corresponding public key. The protocol assumes that, when a user enrolls in the system, a public/private key-pair is generated. Alternatively, a password can be used for the same purpose, as discussed later. Once TGT-Prod successfully locates the user and retrieves the public-key, it proceeds with TGT generation. Otherwise, it replies with a special error content message indicating unknown user.

TGT is an encrypted structure with three fields: $UID$, $k_{CGT}$, and expiration date $t_1$. It is encrypted using $k_A$ – a long-term symmetric key shared between TGT-Prod and CGT-Prod. Only CGT-Prod can decrypt and access cleartext fields of a TGT. Since $C_r$ needs to present the TGT to CGT-Prod during the authorization phase, $UID$ binds the TGT to $C_r$. This same $UID$ is used later for namespace access rights verification. CGT-Prod uses $t_1$ to verify whether a TGT is still valid. TGT expiration time is a realm-specific (and usually realm-wide) parameter reflecting the duration of a typical user authenticated session, e.g., 8 h. After TGT expires, $C_r$ needs to repeat the authentication protocol with TGT-Prod. A TGT also contains a short-term symmetric key $k_{CGT}$, encrypted separately for CGT-Prod and $C_r$. The purpose of $k_{CGT}$ is to allow $C_r$ and CGT-Prod to communicate securely in the subsequent authorization protocol phase. In addition to the TGT, TGT-Prod generates $token_{CGT}^C$, which contains the same $t_1$ and $k_{CGT}$ encrypted with the $pk_C$ associated with $UID$.

To transmit the TGT to $C_r$, TGT-Prod responds with a content message containing the TGT and $token_{CGT}^C$, which is routed by CCN back to $C_r$. $C_r$

**Consumer** | `TGT-Prod`

I.name = TGT_Name

$\xrightarrow{payload=UID}$

$pk_C \leftarrow fetch(UID)$
$t_1 \leftarrow \mathsf{setTGTExpiration}()$
$k_{CGT} \leftarrow_{\$} \{0,1\}^{\lambda}$
$\mathsf{token}^{C}_{CGT} \leftarrow \mathsf{Enc}_{pk_C}(k_{CGT}||t_1)$
$\mathsf{TGT} \leftarrow \mathsf{Enc}_{k_A}(\mathsf{UID}||t_1||k_{CGT})$

$\xleftarrow{payload=\mathsf{TGT},\mathsf{token}^{C}_{CGT}}$

$k_{CGT}||t_1 \leftarrow \mathsf{Dec}_{sk_C}(\mathsf{token}^{C}_{CGT})$
$\mathsf{store}(\mathsf{TGT}, \mathsf{t_1}, \mathsf{k_{CGT}})$

**Fig. 2.** Consumer authentication protocol

**Consumer** | `CGT-Prod`

I.name = CGT_Name

$\xrightarrow{payload=N,\mathsf{TGT}}$

$\mathsf{UID}||t_1||k_{CGT} \leftarrow \mathsf{Dec}_{k_A}(TGT)$
Verify: $t_1$ not expired
$k_P \leftarrow \mathsf{verifyPolicyAndFetchKey}(N, \mathsf{UID})$
$k_N \leftarrow_{\$} \{0,1\}^{\lambda}$
$t_2 \leftarrow \mathsf{setCGTExpiration}()$
$\mathsf{CGT} \leftarrow \mathsf{Enc}_{k_P}(N||k_N||t_2)$
$\mathsf{token}^{C}_{N} \leftarrow \mathsf{Enc}_{k_{CGT}}(k_N||t_2)$

$\xleftarrow{payload=\mathsf{CGT},\mathsf{token}^{C}_{N}}$

$k_N||t_2 \leftarrow \mathsf{Dec}_{k_{CGT}}(\mathsf{token}^{C}_{N})$
$\mathsf{store}(\mathsf{N}, \mathsf{CGT}, \mathsf{t_2}, \mathsf{k_N})$

**Fig. 3.** Consumer-data authorization protocol

cannot decrypt, access, or modify the TGT due to the use of authenticated encryption. $C_r$ decrypts $token^{C}_{CGT}$ and caches the TGT for the duration of $t_1$, along with $k_{CGT}$. The TGT is presented to `CGT-Prod` every time $C_r$ needs to request authorization for a new namespace.

**Authorization**

The authorization phase (Fig. 3) is executed between $C_r$ and `CGT-Prod`. It requires $C_r$ to have a valid TGT, acquired from the authentication phase described above. Upon successful completion of the authorization protocol, $C_r$ obtains a namespace-specific CGT, which demonstrates $C_r$'s authorization to access a particular restricted content namespace. However, the CGT does not reveal $C_r$'s identity to the content producer; $C_r$'s authorization is ascertained based on possession of a correct session key.

$C_r$ starts the protocol by sending an interest with name set to *CGT_Name*. The payload includes the namespace prefix $N$ (e.g., `/edu/uni-X/ics/cs/students/alice/*`) for which authorization is being requested and a non-expired TGT. Optionally, if confidentiality for namespace

$N$ is an issue, $C_r$ can compute $Enc_{k_{CGT}}(N)$. instead of sending $N$ in clear. When CGT-Prod receives this interest, it uses $k_A$ (long-term symmetric key shared by TGT-Prod and CGT-Prod) to decrypt the TGT and obtains $UID$, $t_1$ and $k_{CGT}$. Next, CGT-Prod checks TGT for expiration. It then optionally (if encryption was used in the interest) computes $N \leftarrow Dec_{k_{CGT}}(Enc_{k_{CGT}}(N))$.

If the TGT is successfully verified, CGT-Prod invokes *verifyPolicyAnd-FetchKey* procedure, which (1) fetches AC rules for user $UID$; (2) verifies if $N$ is an authorized prefix for $UID$; and (3) returns $k_P$ – symmetric key associated with the producer for $N$. $k_P$ is later used to encrypt the CGT such that only the appropriate producer can decrypt it.

Similar to a TGT, a CGT carries an expiration $t_2$ and a fresh key $k_N$. The latter is used between $C_r$ and the content producer for confidentiality and mutual authentication, as discussed later. However, instead of $UID$, a CGT includes $N$, i.e., a CGT proves to the content producer that whoever possesses $k_N$ is authorized to access content under $N$. Also, a $token_N^C \leftarrow Enc_{k_{CGT}}(k_N \| t_2)$ is sent to $C_r$, such that $C_r$ can obtain $k_N$ and $t_2$.

In response to a CGT interest, $C_r$ receives a content packet containing the CGT and $token_N^C$. $C_r$ decrypts $token_N^C$ using $K_{CGT}$ and creates a cache entry containing: $N$, the CGT, $k_N$, and $t_2$. This cached information is used (until time $t_2$) in all future requests for content under $N$.

**Authorized Content Request**

On the consumer (client) side, a KRB-CCN content request is similar to a regular CCN interest, except that $C_r$ needs to include a valid CGT in the payload. An authorized interest name has the format: $N \| suffix$ (e.g., /edu/uni-X/ics/cs/students/alice/images/img1.png), where $N$ is authorized by the CGT, and $suffix$ specifies which content is being requested under namespace $N$. Note that, as long as $C_r$ has proper access rights, a single CGT allows accessing any content with prefix $N$.

The secure content retrieval phase is in Fig. 4. When the producer receives an interest for a restricted content, it first decrypts the CGT and verifies its expiration. Note that $k_P$ used to decrypt the CGT is shared between the producer and CGT-Prod. Thus, successful decryption (recall that we use authenticated encryption) implies that CGT was indeed generated by CGT-Prod and has not been modified. The producer obtains $k_N$, which is also known to $C_r$. The producer encrypts requested content using $k_N$, i.e., $D' \leftarrow Enc_{k_N}(D)$. $D'$ is returned to $C_r$, which decrypts it to obtain $D$.

Note that, by replaying the interest issued by $C_r$, anyone can retrieve $D'$. This might not appear problematic since only the authorized consumer (who has $k_N$) can decrypt $D'$. However, in some application scenarios this might be troublesome, e.g.:

- Production of content requires a lot of computation, e.g., expensive encryption. In this case, an adversary can replay legitimate interests previously issued by authorized consumers. The adversary's goal might be to mount a DoS attack on the producer.

– The producer might be a peripheral device, e.g., a printer. In this setting, the interest might be a request to print a (perhaps very large) document and returned content $D$ might be a mere confirmation of it having been printed. In this case, the replay attack allows the adversary to print the same document multiple times, resulting in DoS.

This issue occurs since the producer does not authenticate $C_r$ for each interest. A modified version of the protocol, shown in Fig. 5, addresses the problem. It uses a challenge-response protocol that allows the producer to confirm that $C_r$ possesses $k_N$ before producing the content or providing service. As a down-side, this incurs an additional round of communication for the challenge-response protocol.

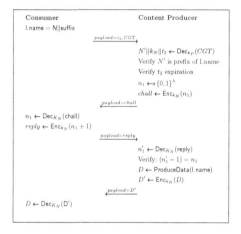

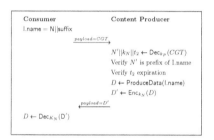

**Fig. 4.** Content retrieval *without* optional challenge-response based consumer authentication

**Fig. 5.** Content retrieval **including** optional challenge-response based consumer authentication

## Transparent Execution and Ticket Caching

Recall that $C_r$ must issue three types of interests, for: authentication, authorization, and the actual content request. This process is transparent to the user since KRB-CCN consumer-/client-side code handles these steps by following the work-flow in Fig. 6.

Whenever $C_r$ issues an interest, KRB-CCN client intervenes and checks whether the name is part of any restricted namespace. If so, it looks up the local cache of CGT-s to find a CGT for prefix $N$. If a valid CGT is found, it is added to the interest payload and the interest is issued. A cached and valid CGT can be used to skip the first two phases, allowing authenticated and authorized content retrieval in one round.

If no valid cached CGT is found, KRB-CCN client looks up a cached TGT. If a valid TGT is found, the authentication phase is skipped. The client requests a CGT and uses it to request the actual content. This process takes two rounds.

In the worst case all three phases are executed, which results in three rounds of communication. Since consumers only request TGT and/or CGT-s when these tickets expire, ticket caching also reduces the number of requests (and overall traffic volume) flowing to TGT-Prod and CGT-Prod. In practice, we expect CGT-s and TGT-s to be long-lived, i.e., on the order of hours or days, similar to current single sign-on systems. This means that the bulk of authorized content retrieval can be performed in one round. If mutual authentication (per protocol in Fig. 5) is demanded by the producer, one extra round is required.

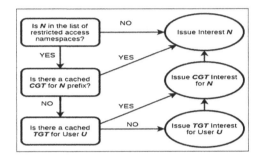

**Fig. 6.** KRB-CCN work-flow for transparent execution on consumers

## 5   Implementation and Performance Evaluation

This section discusses our KRB-CCN prototype implementation and its performance.

### 5.1   Methodology

KRB-CCN is implemented as an application service running as specific purpose producers that produce tickets. Also, consumer-side code is modified to implement the work-flow for authenticated and authorized content request in Fig. 6. Our implementation uses the CCNx software stack [14] and the cryptographic library Sodium [15]. Both publicly available and written in C. For authenticated PKE operations, we use Sodium Sealed-Boxes [16], implemented over X25519 elliptic curves. AES256-GCM [17] is used to encrypt-then-MAC, i.e., for authenticated symmetric-key encryption.

Experiments presented in this section were ran on an Intel Core i7-3770 octa-core CPU @3.40 GHz, with 16 GB of RAM, running Linux (Ubuntu 14.04LTS). Content payload sizes for interests were set to 10 kilobytes. Payload sizes of TGT and CGT contents are 228 bytes and 165 bytes, respectively. Each carries the respective ticket/token pair, as described in Sect. 4. In every experiment, each participating entity's process was assigned as a high priority, and each ran in a single processor core. Unless stated otherwise, results are an average of 10 executions, presented with 95% confidence intervals.

Figure 7 presents our network testbed. The goal is to evaluate KRB-CCN's overhead. To avoid topology-specific delays, we used a minimal setup containing a single producer $P$, TGT-Prod, and CGT-Prod. These entities are interconnected by an unmodified CCNx Athena router.

### 5.2   Experiments

We start by measuring per-request processing times at each producer: TGT-Prod, CGT-Prod, and $P$. Each of these processes was executed 1,000 times. Figure 8 presents the distribution, as box-plots, of processing time for verifying an incoming interest and replying with the content (either ticket, or authorized encrypted content) at each producer type. Figure 8 shows that the most computationally expensive part is TGT issuance (about 500 μs per request). Higher computational overhead for TGT issuance makes sense because the authentication token ($token^C_{CGT}$ in Fig. 2) is encrypted with $C_r$'s public key. In case of password-based authentication, public key encryption is replaced by much faster symmetric key encryption using a password-derived key. This incurs much lower computational overhead on TGT-Prod.

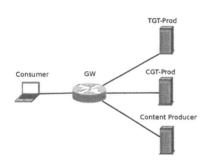

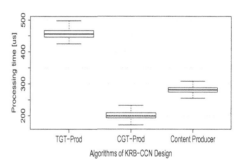

**Fig. 7.** Experimental testbed

**Fig. 8.** Statistical distribution of the per-interest processing time (in μs) at each of KRB-CCN producers

Times for CGT issuance and content production are around 200 μs and 300 μs, respectively. Time is naturally higher for the latter, since encrypted data is larger. In case of content production, the whole content (10 kB) is encrypted. In a CGT request, only the CGT and the token need to be encrypted, resulting in a faster processing time.

To investigate how KRB-CCN entities cope under increasing congestion, we flood them with a massive number of simultaneous interests: from 300 to 3000. We then measure average Round-Trip Time (RTT) per type of issued interest.

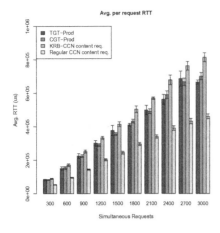

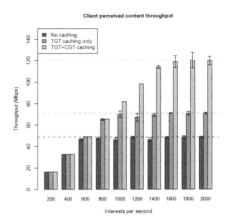

**Fig. 9.** Average RTT/request with massive simultaneous requests to same producer

**Fig. 10.** Consumer perceived throughput under different ticket caching policies

Figure 9 shows the RTTs for each response type. We also include the RTT for regular CCN content retrieval. Since it incurs no extra processing overhead, the regular content RTT is the lower bound for RTTs in CCNx implementation.

The average RTT for interests for TGT, CGT, and authorized encrypted content are similar. The latter is slightly higher as more data (10 kB per interest) must traverse the reverse path back to the consumer. KRB-CCN requests incur in average ~60% higher RTT than unmodified content retrieval. In the largest scale test case, with 3000 simultaneous interests issued for each producer, content replies are received in less than 800 ms.

Finally, we also measure the overall throughput perceived by the consumer in three possible scenarios:

- **Cached TGT and CGT:** in this case the consumer requests contents under the same namespace. Therefore, the same (non-expired) cached CGT can be used for authorized content retrieval, allowing the client to skip the authentication and authorization phases.
- **Cached TGT only:** this is the case in which no AC ticket caching happens. It happens when the consumer always requests contents under different namespaces or because the realm owner demands consumers to request a fresh CGT for each content. In this case only the authentication part of the protocol is skipped at each request.
- **No caching:** This is the case in which the realm owner does not allow single sign-on through TGT caching nor authorization reuse through CGT caching. Three requests (authentication, authorization, and content retrieval) are required for each content packet.

Recall that issuance of appropriate interests in each of the cases is automatically handled by KRB-CCN client software running on the consumer.

For each of the above cases, we gradually increase the rate of interests requested per second until throughput reaches its asymptotic limit. By analyzing throughput results, presented in Fig. 10, we can observe the benefit of ticket caching. When both TGT and CGT caching are enabled, the client perceived throughput is higher than in the other cases, as actual content can be retrieved with a single interest. Conversely, caching only TGT-s is still better than not caching any type of ticket, because in this case the authentication phase can be skipped.

## 6   Related Work

Previous related efforts provide other types of security services currently available in IP-based networks. ANDaNA [18] is an anonymity service analogous to Tor [19] that uses CCN application-layer onion routing. Mosko et al. [20] proposed a TLS-like key exchange protocol for building secure sessions for ephemeral end-to-end security in CCN. Similar to IPSec-based VPNs [21], CCVPN [22] is a network-layer approach for providing content confidentiality and interest name privacy via secure tunnels between physically separated private networks.

There are several CCN-based techniques that implement so-called Content-Based Access Control (CBAC). They tend to rely on content encryption under appropriate consumer keys to enforce AC. A group-based AC scheme for early versions of CCN was proposed in [3]. Policies tie groups of consumers to content, ensuring that only consumers belonging to authorized groups can decrypt restricted content. Similarly, Misra et al. [4] proposed an AC scheme based on broadcast encryption [23,24]. Wood and Uzun [5] proposed several AC schemes based on proxy re-encryption [25,26] to enable consumer personalized content caching. An attribute-based AC system, using attribute-based cryptography [27,28] was proposed in [6]. CCN-AC [7] is a framework that unifies CBAC-type methods by providing a flexible encryption-based AC framework. It relies on manifest-based content retrieval specification (defined in CCNx 1.0 [29]) to enable flexible and extensible AC policy specification and enforcement. A similar approach is proposed in NDN-NBAC [8] framework. In these frameworks, data owners generate and distribute private keys to consumers via out-of-band channels. Producers receive corresponding public keys also via out-of-band channels. These public keys are used to encrypt one-time (per-content) symmetric keys.

In a different vein, Ghali et al. [9] proposed an Interest-Based Access Control (IBAC) scheme, wherein access to protected content is enforced by making names secret and unpredictable – based on encryption with keys known only to authorized consumers. Compared with CBAC, IBAC has the advantage of preserving interest name privacy and allowing content caching. However, IBAC must be used in conjunction with CBAC to preclude unauthorized content retrieval via replay of previously issued obfuscated interest names.

In all schemes discussed above, authentication, authorization/AC, and confidentiality are often convoluted. In particular, producers are assumed to be implicitly responsible for authentication and authorization. This implies dealing with identity management and thus violating consumer privacy. Moreover, authentication and AC are enforced on a per-content basis which is unscalable and expensive. To the best of our knowledge KRB-CCN is the first comprehensive approach to address these issues by (1) separating authentication, authorization and content production among distinct entities; and (2) issuing re-usable authentication and authorization tickets for restricted namespaces.

## 7   Conclusions

We presented KRB-CCN – a comprehensive design for handling authentication, authorization, and access control in private CCN networks, while preserving consumer privacy. KRB-CCN is transparent to consumers and incurs fairly low overhead. We analyzed KRB-CCN security and assessed its performance based on a prototype implementation. Experimental results show that KRB-CCN is a practical and efficient means of providing multiple security services in private (stub AS) CCNs.

**Acknowledgments.** The authors would like to thank Christopher Wood for fruitful discussions and feedback. This work was supported by CISCO University Research Award (2017).

## References

1. Jacobson, V., Smetters, D.K., Thornton, J.D., Plass, M.F., Briggs, N.H., Braynard, R.L.: Networking named content. In: Proceedings of the 5th International Conference on Emerging Networking Experiments and Technologies, pp. 1–12. ACM (2009)
2. Zhang, L., Estrin, D., Burke, J., Jacobson, V., Thornton, J.D., Smetters, D.K., Zhang, B., Tsudik, G., Massey, D., Papadopoulos, C., et al.: Named data networking (NDN) project. Relatório Técnico NDN-0001, Xerox Palo Alto Research Center-PARC (2010)
3. Smetters, D.K., Golle, P., Thornton, J.: CCNx access control specifications. Technical report, PARC (2010)
4. Misra, S., Tourani, R., Majd, N.E.: Secure content delivery in information-centric networks: design, implementation, and analyses. In: Proceedings of the 3rd ACM SIGCOMM Workshop on Information-Centric Networking, pp. 73–78. ACM (2013)
5. Wood, C.A., Uzun, E.: Flexible end-to-end content security in CCN. In: 2014 IEEE 11th Consumer Communications and Networking Conference (CCNC), pp. 858–865. IEEE (2014)
6. Ion, M., Zhang, J., Schooler, E.M.: Toward content-centric privacy in ICN: attribute-based encryption and routing. In: Proceedings of the 3rd ACM SIGCOMM Workshop on Information-Centric Networking, pp. 39–40. ACM (2013)
7. Kuriharay, J., Uzun, E., Wood, C.A.: An encryption-based access control framework for content-centric networking. In: 2015 IFIP Networking Conference (IFIP Networking), pp. 1–9. IEEE (2015)
8. Yu, Y., Afanasyev, A., Zhang, L.: Name-based access control, Named Data Networking Project, Technical Report NDN-0034 (2015)

9. Ghali, C., Schlosberg, M.A., Tsudik, G., Wood, C.A.: Interest-based access control for content centric networks. In: Proceedings of the 2nd International Conference on Information-Centric Networking, pp. 147–156. ACM (2015)
10. Neuman, B.C., Ts'o, T.: Kerberos: an authentication service for computer networks. IEEE Commun. Mag. **32**(9), 33–38 (1994)
11. Mosko, M., Solis, I., Wood, C.: CCNx semantics, IRTF Draft, Palo Alto Research Center, Inc. (2016)
12. Ricciardi, F.: Kerberos protocol tutorial. The National Institute of Nuclear Physics Computing and Network Services, LECCE, Italy (2007)
13. Mockapetris, P.V.: Domain names-concepts and facilities (1987)
14. PARC: CCNx distillery (2016). https://github.com/parc/CCNx_Distillery
15. Sodium: The sodium crypto library (libsodium) (2017). https://github.com/jedisct1/libsodium
16. Bernstein, D.J.: Curve25519: new Diffie-Hellman speed records. In: Yung, M., Dodis, Y., Kiayias, A., Malkin, T. (eds.) PKC 2006. LNCS, vol. 3958, pp. 207–228. Springer, Heidelberg (2006). https://doi.org/10.1007/11745853_14
17. Dworkin, M.: Recommendation for block cipher modes of operation: Galois/Counter Mode (GCM) and GMAC. US Department of Commerce, National Institute of Standards and Technology (2007)
18. DiBenedetto, S., Gasti, P., Tsudik, G., Uzun, E.: ANDaNA: anonymous named data networking application, arXiv preprint arXiv:1112.2205 (2011)
19. Dingledine, R., Mathewson, N., Syverson, P.: Tor: The second-generation onion router. Technical report, Naval Research Lab Washington DC (2004)
20. Mosko, M., Uzun, E., Wood, C.A.: Mobile sessions in content-centric networks. In: IFIP Networking (2017)
21. Doraswamy, N., Harkins, D.: IPSec: The New Security Standard for the Internet, Intranets, and Virtual Private Networks. Prentice Hall Professional, Upper Saddle River (2003)
22. Nunes, I.O., Tsudik, G., Wood, C.A.: Namespace tunnels in content-centric networks. In: 2017 IEEE 42nd Conference on Local Computer Networks (LCN), pp. 35–42. IEEE (2017)
23. Fiat, A., Naor, M.: Broadcast encryption. In: Stinson, D.R. (ed.) CRYPTO 1993. LNCS, vol. 773, pp. 480–491. Springer, Heidelberg (1994). https://doi.org/10.1007/3-540-48329-2_40
24. Boneh, D., Gentry, C., Waters, B.: Collusion resistant broadcast encryption with short ciphertexts and private keys. In: Shoup, V. (ed.) CRYPTO 2005. LNCS, vol. 3621, pp. 258–275. Springer, Heidelberg (2005). https://doi.org/10.1007/11535218_16
25. Ateniese, G., Fu, K., Green, M., Hohenberger, S.: Improved proxy re-encryption schemes with applications to secure distributed storage. ACM Trans. Inf. Syst. Secur. (TISSEC) **9**(1), 1–30 (2006)
26. Canetti, R., Hohenberger, S.: Chosen-ciphertext secure proxy re-encryption. In: Proceedings of the 14th ACM Conference on Computer and Communications Security, pp. 185–194. ACM (2007)
27. Goyal, V., Pandey, O., Sahai, A., Waters, B.: Attribute-based encryption for fine-grained access control of encrypted data. In: Proceedings of the 13th ACM Conference on Computer and Communications Security, pp. 89–98. ACM (2006)
28. Bethencourt, J., Sahai, A., Waters, B.: Ciphertext-policy attribute-based encryption. In: 2007 IEEE Symposium on Security and Privacy, SP 2007, pp. 321–334. IEEE (2007)
29. Solis, I., Scott, G.: CCN 1.0 (tutorial). In: ACM ICN (2014)

# Assentication: User De-authentication and Lunchtime Attack Mitigation with Seated Posture Biometric

Tyler Kaczmarek$^{(\boxtimes)}$, Ercan Ozturk, and Gene Tsudik

UC Irvine, Irvine, USA
{tkaczmar,ercano,gtsudik}@uci.edu

**Abstract.** Biometric techniques are often used as an extra security factor in authenticating human users. Numerous biometrics have been proposed and evaluated, each with its own set of benefits and pitfalls. Static biometrics (such as fingerprints) are geared for discrete operation, to identify users, which typically involves some user burden. Meanwhile, behavioral biometrics (such as keystroke dynamics) are well-suited for continuous and more unobtrusive operation. One important application domain for biometrics is *de-authentication*: a means of quickly detecting absence of a previously-authenticated user and immediately terminating that user's secure sessions. De-authentication is crucial for mitigating so-called *Lunchtime Attacks*, whereby an insider adversary takes over an authenticated state of a careless user who leaves her computer.

Motivated primarily by the need for an unobtrusive and continuous biometric to support effective de-authentication, we introduce Assentication – a new hybrid biometric based on a human user's seated posture pattern. Assentication captures a unique combination of physiological and behavioral traits. We describe a low-cost fully functioning prototype that involves an office chair instrumented with 16 tiny pressure sensors. We also explore (via user experiments) how Assentication can be used in a typical workplace to provide continuous authentication (and de-authentication) of users. We experimentally assess viability of Assentication in terms of uniqueness by collecting and evaluating posture patterns of a cohort of 30 users. Results show that Assentication yields very low false accept and false reject rates. In particular, users can be identified with 94.2% and 91.2% accuracy using 16 and 10 sensors, respectively.

## 1 Introduction and Motivation

Secure, correct and efficient user authentication is an integral component of any meaningful security system. Authentication schemes implemented in a typical modern workplace typically include two factors: (1) a user demonstrates knowledge of a secret password or PIN, and (2) a user proves possession of a secure device or token. However, it is becoming more popular to augment this approach with a third factor – biometrics that reflect inherent human traits or behaviors. Biometric techniques are considered as the best means of evaluating

© Springer International Publishing AG, part of Springer Nature 2018
B. Preneel and F. Vercauteren (Eds.): ACNS 2018, LNCS 10892, pp. 616–633, 2018.
https://doi.org/10.1007/978-3-319-93387-0_32

human inherence and they range widely: from a very simple (e.g., fingerprints) to rather complex, such as iris scans.

After initial authentication, users often spend long stretches of time continuously using computing devices and services. During that time, continuous presence of the originally authenticated user must be periodically re-affirmed, especially, in a shared workplace setting. Failure to do so can result in so-called *Lunchtime Attacks*. Such an attack occurs when a previously authenticated user walks away from her workplace, thus allowing the adversary to take over her login session and engage in potentially nefarious activity. This prompts the need for periodic re-authentication and/or continuous authentication. Unfortunately, the former can be quite annoying, as is the case with too-short inactivity time-outs requiring frequent password re-entry.

Meanwhile, continuous authentication (or presence verification) is challenging in its own right. For example, camera-based methods that use face recognition [1] or gaze tracking [2] might be viewed as intrusive in terms of personal privacy, since cameras can be abused (e.g., by malware) to surreptitiously record users. Furthermore, face recognition is prone to attacks, while gaze tracking requires the user to maintain line-of-sight with the camera, which can result in unnecessary de-authentication when the user turns away while remaining at the workplace. Whereas, keyboard or mouse activity profiling and monitoring, though effective in some settings, are poorly suited for cases when a user temporarily halts input activity, e.g., in order to chat with co-workers or answer the phone. Other techniques continuously measure physical distance between the user and her workplace, by requiring each user to wear an extra device, e.g., a wristband or smart badge. Such methods are: (1) potentially burdensome due to imposing an extra device, and (2) ultimately authenticate only the presence of the device and not of its owner.

Based on the above discussion, we believe that the "design space" for continuous authentication (or, equivalently, de-authentication) techniques needs to be explored further. From the outset, we acknowledge that a perfect continuous authentication method is unlikely to materialize; in fact, one might not even exist. In other words, since each previous method has a distinct set of advantages and limitations/flaws, the same will certainly hold for our current efforts.

In this paper, we propose and evaluate a new biometric called Assentication. It is based on a user's seated posture patterns in an average office chair over the course of a typical workday. We examine the applicability of Assentication for continuous user authentication, i.e., ensuring that – after the initial successful login – the person currently using a particular computer is the same as the one who initially logged in. One of Assentication's key advantages over many other de-authentication methods is its ability to operate in an unobtrusive manner, with no effort on the part of the user.[1] To evaluate its viability and effectiveness, we built a low-cost Assentication prototype by instrumenting a commodity office

---

[1] This is in contrast with, for example, fingerprint-based continuous authentication, which would prompt the user to periodically swipe her finger(s) on the fingerprint reader; which is obtrusive and disrupts the typical workflow.

chair with ultra-thin flexible sensors that gather user posture data. Its purpose was to assess whether users are correctly authenticated, based on their own training data. The same platform was used to test the uniqueness of Assentication within a sample population of measured users. Our results demonstrate that the prototype unobtrusively captures the necessary data for continuous authentication and identification while the user engages in a typical use of a desktop or laptop computer.

The rest of this paper is organized as follows: Sect. 2 overviews related work. Next, Sect. 3 provides the background on continuous authentication and de-authentication. Section 4 describes the Assentication biometric. Then, Sect. 5 outlines the adversarial model. Section 6 describes the Assentication prototype and methodology used for data collection, followed by results in Sect. 7, a detailed discussion of Assentication is provided in Sect. 8. The paper concludes with directions for future work in Sect. 9 and a summary in Sect. 10.

## 2    Related Work

Biometric traits have been extensively explored in the context of authentication. Jain et al. [3] provides an authoritative overview of many well-known techniques, including: fingerprint, face, iris, palm-print and keystroke dynamics. However, since our focus is on biometric-based continuous authentication which can be used to achieve effective de-authentication, we do not discuss methods that are not amenable for the intended application.

Eberz et al. [4] provide an overview of the state of the art of the evaluation of biometric techniques for authentication. Additionally they provide recommendations for the evaluation of future methods. Our evaluation strategy is informed by this framework.

Rasmussen et al. [5] use human body's response to electric signals as a biometric. In the proposed system, a weak pulse signal is applied to the palm of one hand and measured on the palm of the other hand. Pulse-response biometric can be used as a second or third factor in user authentication and/or as a continuous authentication mechanism. The system achieves 100% accuracy over a static set, and 88% accuracy on permanence tests performed over several weeks.

Eberz et al. [2] investigate eye movement patterns as a biometric. Based on gazing data gathered from 30 participants, pupil, temporal and spatial features are defined. Reported equal error rate is 3.98% in a single session and 92.2% of attacks are detected within 40 s. Measurements done two weeks apart show that this biometric is stable over time.

Mare et al. [6] propose wearing a bracelet that has a gyroscope and an accelerometer for continuous authentication. When the user interacts with the computer (e.g., typing or scrolling), the bracelet transfers collected sensor data to the computer, which evaluates whether user actions match the sensor data. The proposed system, ZEBRA, achieves continuous authentication with 85% accuracy and detects attacks within 11 s. However, a recent study by Huhta et al. [7] presents a set of credible attacks on ZEBRA.

Keystroke dynamics are another means of continuous authentication. Ahmed and Traore use $1,500$ digraphs from each user as a base profile and applies neural networks to guess missing digraphs [8]. In a 53-user experiment, a false reject rate of $0.0152\%$, a false accept rate of $4.82\%$ and an equal error rate of $2.46\%$ are achieved.

Finally, Conti et al. [9] describe FADEWICH, a continuous authentication system that uses attenuation of wireless signals when a human body is on the signal's path. FADEWICH is **not** based on any biometrics. It tracks the user by placing 9 sensors in a 6m-by-3m office environment. Once detected as having left the environment, the user is logged out. FADEWICH successfully de-authenticates users with $90\%$ accuracy within 4s, and $100\%$ accuracy within 6s.

There have been prior attempts to use posture and seated pressure for both identification and continuous authentication. Gia et al. [10] use data gathered from: (1) four pressure sensors placed on the seat bottom, (2) an accelerometer, and (3) light sensors placed on the seat-back, to identify the user. Pressure sensors are used to differentiate among users, while weight and accelerometer readings determine chair movements when someone sits down. Light sensors help determine how much space is covered by the sitting user. In an experiment involving only 10 people, a rather low accuracy of $72\%$ is achieved.

Furthermore, Yamada et al. [11] describe a hip-print authentication method which uses pressure data from 32 sensors placed along the seat bottom. However, in experiments that use only first 1.5s of measurement, quite low accuracies of $74.3\%$ and $59.9\%$ are reported for 10 and 25 subjects, respectively.

Among prior work, the one closest to this paper is [12]. It proposes a continuous driver identification system for automobiles that uses pressure data from two mats, each containing $32 \times 32$ sensors, placed on the seat cushion and backrest of the driver seat. Features used for classification are based on one's pelvic bone signature, mid- to high-pressure distribution and weight. In a study involving 34 participants, a fairly low uniqueness rate is reported. The authors assert that this is because a car setting is not appropriate for detecting pressure distribution changes. Most drivers adopt a single, constant posture adjusted to their preferred driving position.

Finally, Mutlu et al. [13] investigate how to use fewer sensors to detect posture. To determine optimal sensor placement, a classifier is constructed that learns the probabilistic model between the chosen subset of sensor values and feature vectors used for posture classification. With 19 sensors, classification accuracy of $87\%$ is reported. As discussed later, this study guides our sensor placement strategy.

# 3    Background

This section sets the stage for the rest of the paper by overviewing user authentication, de-authentication, attack scenarios and continuous authentication requirements.

## 3.1   User Authentication

User authentication can involve one or more of the following factors:

F1:  What one knows, or what one recognizes.
    The former corresponds to knowledge of: passwords, PINs, drawing pat-
    terns and free-text answers to security questions. The latter corresponds
    to recognition of: correct answers to multiple-choice questions, faces or
    other types of images.

F2:  What one has in their possession.
    This generally means some form of a personal (even passive) device, such
    as a badge, bracelet, key-fob, token or smartphone.

F3:  What one is, or how one behaves.
    The former type is referred to as a *static* and includes biometrics based on:
    fingerprints, irises, palms, wrists, faces, ears and pulse-response. The latter
    type is called *behavioral* and includes biometrics based on: gait, keystroke
    dynamics, head movements, hand gestures and gaze tracking.

Though widely used, F1-type authentication alone is widely considered to be
insufficient, mainly due to the low entropy of secrets involved. By itself, F2 is also
inadequate, since a personal device is not guaranteed to always be in possession
of its intended owner. Finally, F3 can be subverted, at least for some static
methods, e.g., via cloned fingerprint moulds [14], fake irises using contact lenses
[15], and face masks[2]. It also usually requires a non-trivial training or enrollment
phase. Meanwhile, some behavioral biometrics are unstable or fragile, e.g., gait,
breathing patterns, blinking and head movements. Consequently, multi-factor
user authentication is usually recommended in order to achieve better security.

## 3.2   De-authentication and Lunchtime Attacks

As part of everyday office or workplace activity, an average user might engage
in one or more of the following activities (not an exhaustive list):

[A1]: Work by continuously utilizing one or more traditional input devices, such
    as a keyboard, touchscreen or mouse.
[A2]: Take a quick seated nap or meditation break.
[A3]: Read some printed matter, e.g., a paper or book.
[A4]: Use another personal device, e.g., a smartphone.
[A5]: Turn away from one's desk to talk to other people directly, or on the phone.
[A6]: Watch videos and/or listen to music without using any input devices.
[A7]: Take part in an audio or video conference.
[A8]: Get up momentarily to fetch something from the immediate vicinity (or
    simply to stretch) and return.

---

[2] "Biometric Update", "spoofing iris recognition technology with pictures", http://
www.biometricupdate.com/201503/spoofing-iris-recognition-technology-with-
pictures, 2015, accessed: 2017-05-19.

[A9]: Walk away from the workplace for a short (e.g., bathroom), longer (e.g., lunch), or long (e.g., done for the day) time, before returning.

In a security-conscious setting, these activities might require periodic reassurance that the same user (who initially authenticated and/or logged in) is still present. Ideally, when the original user remains present [A1–A7], no reassurance should be needed. However, [A9] results in leaving the workplace unattended, while [A8] might. (Also, [A2] could be viewed as the user not really being there.) An important challenge is to distinguish among these types of activities. The term *de-authentication* denotes the process of deciding whether the original user is no longer present and, if so, terminating active secure sessions.

In a perfect world, each user would always log out or otherwise terminate all active sessions before stepping away. Unfortunately, this is far from reality, which triggers the threat of *Lunchtime Attacks*. As the name suggests, attack of this type occurs when the adversary takes over the secure session(s) of a legitimate user who has left, even for a short time. Such attacks are quite common, as noted in the recent work of Marques et al. [16].

### 3.3   Default Approach: Inactivity Timeouts

The most common current means of dealing with Lunchtime Attacks and reassuring original user presence is inactivity timeouts. Most users of personal and workplace computing devices are familiar with them: whenever keyboard and/or mouse inactivity exceeds a certain threshold, de-authentication takes place, i.e., log-in and other (previously authenticated) sessions are terminated. Various operating systems, apps and websites set their own timeout rules and policies. In some cases (e.g., macOS or Windows) users can select their own timeouts. At a typical workplace, mandatory timeouts are often imposed.

Inactivity timeouts are almost universally disliked. As noted in [6], most users find too-short timeouts annoying, while too-long timeouts are insecure, since they defeat the purpose of Lunchtime Attack mitigation (by extending the attack time window). Even more importantly, timeouts achieve their desired effect only in case [A1] and fail in several other ways:

- They operate under the assumption that keyboard/mouse inactivity (i.e., "NOT [A1]") indicates user absence. This is often not true, e.g., in cases [A2]–[A5] and [A8]. De-authenticating the user in these cases is both unnecessary and annoying.
- Conversely, timeouts naïvely suppose that resumption of activity (within the timeout threshold) indicates presence of *the same* user. This is clearly wrong in situations where the original walks away [A9] and the adversary quickly starts typing.
- In case [A6], if timeouts are activated, the user is also unnecessarily burdened. Otherwise, if timeouts are automatically disabled while music and/or videos are playing, the user can walk away for a potentially long time, thus leaving the computing device(s) open to Lunchtime Attacks.

- The same holds for case [A7], except that user's voice and/or camera movements might be used to infer continuous presence. However, this would require additional voice or visual authentication.
- In case [A9], timeouts only work correctly (by de-authenticating the original user) if no attack occurs. Knowing the timeout threshold, which is usually not secret, allows the adversary to easily succeed in a Lunchtime Attack.

### 3.4    Continuous Authentication

Given the inadequacy of inactivity timeouts, one appealing alternative is continuous authentication. Methods of this variety are generally unobtrusive, i.e., require none or very little user burden. As discussed in Sect. 2, these include: keystroke dynamics [8], wrist movement [6], pulse response [5], gaze tracking [2], and wireless signal monitoring [9]. (Note that only the first four are biometric-based methods, while the last is purely a de-authentication technique.)

### 3.5    Design Goals

Since our main goal is the design of a biometric-based de-authentication method, we first consider general design goals for biometrics. A popular survey of biometric techniques by Jain et al. [3] provides a comprehensive overview of many popular methods, and discusses design criteria, which include the following:

*Universality:* The biometric must be (ideally) universally applicable. For example, an iris scanner is not useful for users who are missing an eye or have cataracts, while fingerprint readers are similarly useless for people with severe eczema.

*Uniqueness:* The biometric must be unique within the target population. It must be possible to distinguish users using the biometric.

*Unobtrusiveness:* The biometric should be maximally transparent. Ideally, it should be used in a passive manner, without any extra requirements or interference with users' normal behavior.

*Circumvention Difficulty:* To be meaningful in any security context, the biometric must be difficult to circumvent. That is, false accept (fraud) rate (FAR) should be minimal, i.e., it should be hard to impersonate a genuine user.

*Low Error Rate:* The biometric must have a low false reject (insult) rate (FRR), i.e., should very rarely fail to recognize an enrolled user.

*Collectability:* The biometric should be measurable in a fast, easy and meaningful quantitative way.

*Cost Effectiveness:* The biometric's distinguishing power as related to the cost of deployment and maintenance. In our design, this is a key goal.

*Easy enrollment:* The biometric's initial (training) phase should be as short and burden-free as possible.

*Acceptability:* The ideal biometric is one which (most) users are comfortable to use.

We now present design goals for an ideal de-authentication method, not necessarily based on biometrics.[3]

- Minimal extra components (particularly, physical or hardware) and monetary cost
- Quick and correct detection of activities requiring de-authentication, i.e., [A9] or a circumvention attempt, e.g., another user sits down
- Minimal False Reject Rate (FRR), i.e., probability of mistaking [A1]-[A8] for [A9]
- Minimal False Accept Rate (FAR), i.e., probability of mistaking [A9] for [A1]-[A8]
- Maximal user transparency, i.e., unobtrusiveness

We recognize that the last goal might be ethically dubious. De-authentication methods with user transparency can be abused, e.g., by unscrupulous employers, to surreptitiously spy on unsuspecting users. We acknowledge that it is very difficult to reconcile positive and negative connotations.

# 4   Assentication Biometric

Assentication works by monitoring, over time, changing pressure patterns exerted by a person seated in a typical office chair. This pattern is influenced by both behavioral and physical characteristics. The former stem from one's seating preferences. For example, some people cross their legs, which leads to an asymmetric pressure distribution, while others keep both feet firmly on the ground which results in nearly symmetric pressure distribution. Other contributing factors include height, hip width and weight.

## 4.1   Strengths and Weaknesses

Since exact distribution of seated pressure depends on the user's physical dimensions as well as on adopted postures, Assentication is a hybrid biometric blending physiological and behavioral factors. This allows it to benefit from some strengths of both. In particular, one's posture pattern can be captured in a strictly passive manner. Even though this property is shared by other biometrics, such as facial recognition or pulse response, posture pattern is not easily circumventable (unlike, e.g., facial recognition), and does not alter normal user behavior, unlike, e.g., pulse-response. We believe that this combination of unobtrusiveness, difficulty of circumvention, and behavior agnosticism make Assentication an attractive biometric.

Additionally, Assentication requires very little in terms of specialized hardware to capture the physiological biometric it uses. As discussed later in Sect. 6, we constructed a Assentication prototype of an instrumented office chair.

---

[3] We do this while keeping in mind that all of them are unlikely to be achievable.

## 4.2  Liveness and Replay

In any biometric system used for continuous authentication, liveness detection is a serious concern. For example, a face recognition system needs to detect blinking, breathing, and/or some other artifact of a user being alive and present. Otherwise, as has been demonstrated in the past, it can be subverted by a photo or a mask (face-cast). Traditionally, liveness is attained via some form of a challenge by the system that requires the user to act. In case of facial recognition, the system might prompt the user to turn her head or look in a particular direction. While this helps achieve liveness and protect against subversion, it also sacrifices transparency and increases user burden.

Some modern de-authentication systems, such as gaze tracking or keystroke patterns, can passively check for liveness by relying on dynamic user behavior instead of constant physical characteristics. However, they require the user to act in a particular (not necessarily free or natural) manner. For example, gaze tracking requires the user to face in the general direction of the gaze tracking apparatus, which may not always be in the user's typical workflow. Furthermore, gaze tracking requires the user's eyes to be open. In the same vein, keystroke analysis requires the user to type on the keyboard. For its part, the pulse-response biometric needs the user to complete an electrical circuit by touching conductive implements with both hands. With all these systems, if the user fails to behave in the required manner, the likely outcome is a false accept.

In contrast, Assentication is more forgiving in such cases. It does not rely on specific user actions. Instead, Assentication is based merely on user's physical presence. It monitors seated pressure distribution regardless of whether the user faces the workstation, touches the keyboard with both hands, is currently typing, or keeps their eyes open. The only requirement for collection of posture pattern data is that the user must be seated in the chair. We believe that this makes our system a good candidate for both continuous authentication and de-authentication.

## 5  Adversarial Model and Attacks

The Assentication biometric focuses on protecting against insider threats. We are particularly concerned with aforementioned Lunchtime Attacks whereby the adversary steps in to access a co-worker's computer after the latter walks away. Insider threats are not limited to such attacks, and might include scenarios ranging from a disgruntled employee staying after hours to sabotage a colleague, to the trivial case of a user deliberately giving access to a co-worker. In all scenarios, the adversary "wins" by gaining access to secure log-in or application sessions.

We assume that the original user provides authentic log-in credentials at session initiation time. However, the same user neglects to log-out before physically leaving the workplace. Once the original user leaves, the adversary approaches the computer, accesses secure log-in sessions and performs some actions, e.g., copy or erase sensitive files, read or send private email. Such attacks are particularly dangerous since they originate from valid and logged-in user accounts. Also, it might be very difficult for the victim to repudiate the adversary's actions.

Insider attacks are unfortunately quite commonplace. In fact, they account for about 28% of all electronic crimes in industry [17]. This includes some high-publicity attacks, such as the infamous 2014 Sony hack [18].

We consider two types of insider adversaries: *casual* and *determined*. In both cases, the adversary is aware of Assentication's use and presence. The adversary is considered successful if it manages to circumvent the system, either by physically imitating the victim's pressure patterns, or by constructing an accurate model (replica) that does the same. We assume that the adversary cannot disable the system, or interfere with its correct operation through physical sabotage, since such manipulation would leave traces.

The *casual* adversary aims to subvert Assentication through behavioral imitation of the victim's posture patterns. We assume that this adversary is familiar with the habits and schedule of the victim, and has physical access to the victim's workplace. Success of the *casual* adversary relies on the discriminating power of the system. In our prototype design (discussed later), posture pattern data is aggregated and evaluated against the previously constructed profile every 10 s. Even in the unrealistically ideal scenario where the *casual* adversary instantly appears in the victim's chair immediately after the victim walks away, only 10 s would remain to perform any attack. However, in our experimental office setting, this attack time window is substantially shorter, ≈2-to-4 s, since it takes 3–4 s for the victim to leave and about as long for the adversary to enter and sit down. After that, posture data is flagged as incorrect, the victim is de-authenticated and all active secure sessions are terminated.

The *determined* adversary seeks to defeat the system by fabricating a physical model of the victim user. We assume that this adversary has access to the exact sensor data of the victim, as well as precise measurements of the victim's posterior and lower back. This data might be obtained if the adversary manages to previously trick the victim to sit (for a sufficiently long period) in a staged chair instrumented the same way as the victim's.

A perfect mold or cast of the victim with the correct pressure distribution would circumvent Assentication. However, creation and deployment of such a mold is not trivial. The determined adversary would have to create a bulky and heavy object that accurately replicates the victim's posterior as well as lower back and weighs enough to exert the necessary pressure upon the instrumented chair, in the right places. Physically and logistically, deploying the mold onto the victim's chair is burdensome and likely to be detected by extraneous means.

However, we recognize that a mold is not the only way to subvert Assentication. We conjecture that a more effective and discrete approach is to use a set of strategically placed hydraulic or pneumatic contraptions, each calibrated to exert an accurate amount of pressure on each sensor on the victim's chair. This kind of precision is difficult to achieve and, unlike a monolithic mold, placing the entire set of contraptions onto the chair at the same time is also quite hard.

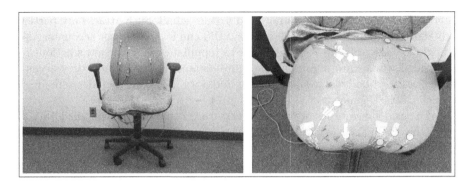

**Fig. 1.** Assentication prototype chair: (a) as seen by the user, and (b) uncovered seat-bottom sensor placements.

All in all, we consider this attack to be quite improbable and close to the realm of "Mission: Impossible".

# 6    Methodology

This section describes our Assentication prototype design, experimental setup, procedures, subject parameters as well as classifiers used for data analysis.

## 6.1    Prototype Design

To demonstrate viability and facilitate ease of experimentation, we built the Assentication prototype by modifying a standard inexpensive office chair with commodity (off-the-shelf) sensor components. Figure 1(a) shows the prototype chair, and Fig. 1(b) focuses on the placement of sensors across the seat and back of the chair. Our sensor placement was guided by the experience in Mutlu et al. [13].

The prototype consists of three components:

1. One 2003/2004 Hon Mid-Back Task Chair.[4]
2. Sixteen (16) Tekscan Flexiforce A401 Large Force Sensing Resistors.
3. Two Arduino 101 modules[5], one of which is connected to 6 A401 resistors. The other module is connected to the remaining 10 sensors in a similar configuration, augmented with an analog multiplexer in its 6-th analog port, in order to support the use of 10 sensor inputs.

Acquired measurements are sent from the Arduino to a commodity desktop PC for collection and evaluation. Arduinos are connected to the desktop via USB cables. Obviously, in a real office setting, having wires running between the chair

---

[4] See https://www.hon.com.
[5] See https://www.arduino.cc/en/Main/ArduinoBoard101.

and the computer would be highly undesirable. We expect that either Bluetooth or WiFi would be used instead.

Total instrumentation cost of \$275 was incurred for the initial single-chair prototype, for feasibility and testing purposes. For a medium-size office with 50 chairs, the per-chair cost can be cut significantly, to approximately \$150 due to volume pricing of Tekscan A401.

## 6.2  Data Collection Procedure

To collect data in a realistic setting, rather than bringing subjects to an unfamiliar office and encountering complications cited by Yamada et al. [11] in collecting posture data in a lab setting, we brought the prototype instrumented chair to the subjects' workplace. Each subject was briefed on the nature of the experiment, and was asked to sit naturally. Subjects allowed us to swap out their office chair with the prototype, and continued their normal work activities while sitting on the latter. We collected posture data in rounds of 10 min per subject. 17 subjects participated in two collection sessions over the course of several days and 13 subjects participated in a single session only. We sampled subjects in order to accommodate typical day-to-day fluctuations in mood and posture, e.g., one session in the morning, and the other – shortly after lunch, on a different day.

A total of 30 subjects were recruited primarily from the student population of a large public university. Because of this, overwhelming majority (27 out of 30) were between the ages of 22 and 30, while the remaining 3 were somewhat older faculty and staff. The gender break-down was: 10 female and 20 male.

Finally, despite its somewhat ungainly appearance (as shown in Fig. 1), the prototype chair is rather comfortable for sitting and none of the subjects expressed any unease or discomfort during the data collection phase.

## 6.3  Features

We collected data in the form of 1, 200 sample time-series reflecting the force exerted on each of the 16 pressure sensors captured each 0.5 s over a 10-min session, for a total of 19, 200 samples per subject, per session.

For continuous authentication, we treat the first 5 min of each session as a training phase, and evaluate the subject on the next 3 frames of sensor data, representing 1.5 s of measurement. If this data is consistent with the training set, it is accepted as valid and included in the training set for future evaluations. If the data is deemed inconsistent with the training set, it is marked as adversarial and de-authentication takes place.

## 6.4  Feature Selection and Quality

Riener and Ferscha [12] use the highest pressure points on a car seat instrumented with a uniform array of 1, 024 pressure sensors to determine a subject's gender. Based on these results, we constructed a Random Forest (RF) classifier

**Table 1.** RF-based gender classification results.

| Gender | TPR | FPR |
|--------|------|------|
| Female | 96.5% | 1.4% |
| Male | 98.6% | 3.5% |

**Table 2.** Pressure sensors ranked according to information gain.

| Sensor | Inf. gain | Sensor | Inf. gain |
|--------|-----------|--------|-----------|
| 15 | 2.4054 | 1 | 1.3519 |
| 4 | 1.9285 | 5 | 1.2846 |
| 12 | 1.8822 | 0 | 1.063 |
| 3 | 1.7893 | 8 | 1.034 |
| 13 | 1.7332 | 14 | 1.021 |
| 2 | 1.6246 | 6 | 0.5634 |
| 7 | 1.4498 | 10 | 0.3578 |
| 11 | 1.4407 | 9 | 0.0128 |

to identify subjects' gender in order to assess the quality of gender information of our features. We obtained a 97.9% True Positive Rate (TPR), and a 2.7% False Positive Rate (FPR), as shown in Table 1. This demonstrates that our strategy of utilizing 16 well-placed sensors preserves gender information reflected by pressure data. However, preliminary stratification of subjects by gender before classification did not yield a higher true acceptance rate, and we do not utilize such an approach.

Table 2 shows the ranking of our extracted features based on their information gain for all 16 sensors. The Information gain is measured with respect to the class as follows:

$$InformationGain(Class, Feature) = H(Class) - H(Class|Feature)$$

where $H$ is entropy function and $H(A|B)$ is entropy of $B$ conditioned on $A$.

### 6.5 Classification Algorithm

Since we are dealing with a fairly commonplace time series clustering problem, there are many well-known candidate techniques. We compared three popular classification algorithms to determine the one that yields the best results.

*Random Forest (RF):* we found that it consistently yields the best results. It produces precise, accurate results, closely clustered for all subjects. Both FNR and FPR are acceptably low in cross-validation of user data, as discussed in more detail below.

*K-Nearest Neighbors (KNN):* we tested the KNN classifier for $k = 1$, 3 and 5 using Euclidean Distance. KNN is a simple lazy classifier that is quite effective in many settings. However, for our classification needs, it did not perform as well as RF.

*Support Vector Machine (SVM):* For each subject, we trained a single binary classifier in a one-against-one case. The final prediction was determined by voting. While SVM provided extremely consistent and highly accurate results for

some users, it did not perform as well as RF, on average. It also had a few outliers with unacceptably high FPRs. We tried different kernel functions, degrees,
cost and $\gamma$ values.

## 7 Results

We present results for two classifiers: one for identification and the other – for
continuous authentication. The former is based on RF and provides verification
of a one-to-$n$ match of a sample of a known user against every sample in a
database. The continuous authentication classifier is based on anomaly detection
in training data's inter-quartile range and provides verification of a one-to-one
match of a sample of unknown origin against that of a single known user.

### 7.1 Identification

Identification is a classification problem across many classes. Our RF-based classifier is ideal for this – it achieves, on average, 94.2% TAR, as shown in Fig. 2.
We also achieve an average FAR of 0.2%, as shown in Fig. 3 using 16 sensors.
Moreover, Assentication with only 10 sensors achieves a TAR of 91.2% and FAR
of 0.3%, as shown in Figs. 4 and 5, respectively.

The low FAR indicates that the *casual adversary* (as described in Sect. 5)
can not successfully impersonate another enrolled user in a Lunchtime Attack
with a reasonably high probability. Furthermore, the insult rate of 0.2% suggests
that users experience minimal annoyance through mis-identification.

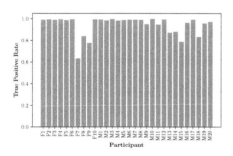

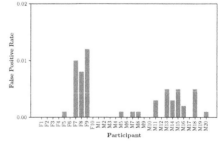

**Fig. 2.** Identification classifier (16 sensors)

**Fig. 3.** FPR for RF cross-validation on all
subject data (16 sensors).

### 7.2 Continuous Authentication

Our classifier for continuous authentication is focused on identifying outliers and
extreme values in fresh incoming data. After a 5-min training window, subject
training data is compared to the next 3 data slices collected by the sensors.

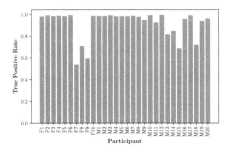
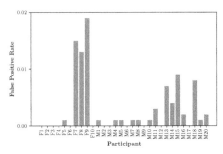

**Fig. 4.** RF identification TPR by subject (10 sensors).

**Fig. 5.** RF identification FPRs by subject (10 sensors).

Each data slice is then classified as an "extreme" value (i.e. an outlier) or not. If all three measurement sets are "extreme", data is considered invalid, and de-authentication results. Otherwise, data slices are added to the training set. This comparison occurs every 1.5 s as new data is collected.

This approach results in no (0% rate) false de-authentications. Hence, a valid user who sits down on an instrumented chair will not – with very high probability – be erroneously de-authenticated while remaining seated. Additionally we find that 91% of imposters are de-authenticated in the first measurement frame (after 1.5 s) and all imposters are de-authenticated by the end of the first 45 s (30 measurement cycles). This demonstrates further resistance to *casual* adversary attacks in the continuous authentication case.

## 8  Discussion

We now assess Assentication in the context of design goals for an ideal de-authentication system outlined in Sect. 3.

Assentication was designed with the emphasis on *minimal extra components and monetary cost*. The use of an instrumented chair does require specialized hardware. However, it does not impose any behavioral requirements on the user. Furthermore, the per-unit cost of $150 (at scale of about 50) is reasonable in the context of other posture-based techniques, which can easily cost thousands of dollars, as noted by Mutlu et al. [13].

We claim that *maximal user transparency* is achieved by Assentication because of the ubiquitous nature of sitting in office or workplace settings. In fact, over 70% of the workforce in a traditional office setting spend upwards of 6 hours a day seated [19]. Enrollment, authentication and de-authentication phases of Assentication all occur transparently while the user is seated and engaged in normal workflow activities. Because of this, there are no behavioral modifications required from the user to participate in Assentication and no need for modifying everyday activities.

*Quick detection of activities requiring de-authentication* is trivial in Assentication. A user who engages in any activity covered by [A9] is de-authenticated as soon as a single collection window passes. Though in the initial prototype implementation this window was set to 1.5 s, it can be adjusted up or down.

As evidenced by the average 94.2% accuracy of user identification and 100% accuracy for continuous authentication, false rejections would only occur in exceptional circumstances, which satisfies the *minimal insult rate* design goal. This holds during most typical office activities [A1–A7] that are typically performed while the users is seated. However, if a user leaves the chair to grab something nearby [A8] and spends over 10 s away, potentially erroneous de-authentication can occur.

### 8.1 Deployment Scenario

The physical and behavioral features measured as part of Assentication are somewhat ephemeral in nature. An individual's weight can fluctuate over a kilogram (2.2 pounds) day-to-day [20]. Also, one's posture is influenced by the emotive state [21]. This makes permanence of user posture rather doubtful. Therefore, we believe that an Assentication-like de-authentication system should be operated as follows:

- At the start of a session, a user sits down in an instrumented chair, and authenticates to the system normally, e.g., via username and password.
- Upon successful authentication, Assentication system collects posture data and forms a temporary profile.
- After enrollment period of 10 min, the system evaluates new posture data against the profile throughout the day.
- Once the user leaves at the end of the session (e.g., for the day), the profile is deleted.

This provides several benefits. First, no additional configuration is needed to deploy Assentication in an enviroment where several users are authorized to use the same physical terminal or workstation under different authorized accounts. Second, unlike more permanent biometrics, there is no costly institution-wide enrollment or re-enrollment required to initialize the system. Finally, the use of temporary profiles avoids the need for permanent secure storage of sensitive biometric data, which is currently an open problem for long-lived biometrics.

### 8.2 Ethical Considerations

All experiments described in this paper were duly authorized by the Institutional Review Board (IRB) of the authors' employer, well ahead of the commencement of the study. The level of review was: Exempt, Category II. No sensitive data was collected during the experiments and minimal identifying information was retained. In particular, no subject names, phone numbers or other personally identifying information (PII) was collected. All data was stored pseudonymously.

## 9    Future Work

There are several directions for future work:

First, we plan to conduct a larger-scale, longer-term (longitudinal) study, obtaining multiple measurement sessions from each subject over the course of several weeks. This would lead to a better understanding of the posture pattern biometric as a whole.

Second, we intend to evaluate accuracy of Assentication in its typical deployment scenario, as described in Sect. 8.1. For this, we intend to have the subjects replace their office chair with our prototype for an entire workday. We would use this data to obtain the rate of both false rejects and accepts, throughout the day, as well as measure associated user burden.

Next, we plan to evaluate attack vectors outlined in Sect. 5, starting with a *casual* adversary. This will entail recruiting pairs of subjects with similar physical characteristics, and training them to impersonate each other's posture patterns. Finally, we explore the attacks by a *determined* adversary. For this, we need to construct a contraption that imitates the victim's posture pattern.

## 10    Conclusions

In summary, this paper proposed and described a new Assentication biometric based on seated posture patterns. We built and experimented with a prototype implementation of Assentication. Furthermore, experimental results show that posture pattern biometric captures a unique combination of physiological and behavioral traits. We found that users can be identified with, on average, 94.2% accuracy from a population of 30. We also believe that it is infeasible for a *casual* adversary to circumvent Assentication by impersonation of the victim's posture patterns. We also argue that physical and logistical burdens of fabricating and deploying an accurate mold (replica) of the victim's relevant body parts make circumvention very challenging even for the *determined* adversary. Finally, we provided a thorough comparison of several prominent modern biometric-based techniques for continuous authentication.

## References

1. Chang, K., Bowyer, K.W., Sarkar, S., Victor, B.: Comparison and combination of ear and face images in appearance-based biometrics. IEEE Trans. Pattern Anal. Mach. Intell. **25**(9), 1160–1165 (2003)
2. Eberz, S., Rasmussen, K.B., Lenders, V., Martinovic, I.: Preventing lunchtime attacks: fighting insider threats with eye movement biometrics. In: NDSS (2015)
3. Jain, A.K., Ross, A., Pankanti, S.: Biometrics: a tool for information security. IEEE Trans. Inf. Forensics Secur. **1**(2), 125–143 (2006)
4. Eberz, S., Rasmussen, K.B., Lenders, V., Martinovic, I.: Evaluating behavioral biometrics for continuous authentication: challenges and metrics. In: Proceedings of the 2017 ACM on Asia Conference on Computer and Communications Security, pp. 386–399. ACM (2017)

5. Rasmussen, K.B., Roeschlin, M., Martinovic, I., Tsudik, G.: Authentication using pulse-response biometrics. In: NDSS (2014)
6. Mare, S., Markham, A.M., Cornelius, C., Peterson, R., Kotz, D.: Zebra: zero-effort bilateral recurring authentication. In: 2014 IEEE Symposium on Security and Privacy (SP), pp. 705–720. IEEE (2014)
7. Huhta, O., Shrestha, P., Udar, S., Juuti, M., Saxena, N., Asokan, N.: Pitfalls in designing zero-effort deauthentication: opportunistic human observation attacks. arXiv preprint arXiv:1505.05779 (2015)
8. Ahmed, A.A., Traore, I.: Biometric recognition based onfree-text keystroke dynamics. IEEE Trans. Cybern. **44**(4), 458–472 (2014)
9. Conti, M., Lovisotto, G., Martinovic, I., Tsudik, G.: Fadewich: fast deauthentication over the wireless channel. In: 2017 IEEE 37th International Conference on Distributed Computing Systems (ICDCS), pp. 2294–2301. IEEE (2017)
10. Gia, N., Takimoto, T., Giang, N.D.M., Nakazawa, J., Takashio, K., Tokuda, H.: People identification based on sitting patterns. In: Workshop on Ubiquitous Data Mining, p. 33 (2012)
11. Yamada, M., Kamiya, K., Kudo, M., Nonaka, H., Toyama, J.: Soft authentication and behavior analysis using a chair with sensors attached: hipprint authentication. Pattern Anal. Appl. **12**(3), 251–260 (2009)
12. Riener, A., Ferscha, A.: Supporting implicit human-to-vehicle interaction: driver identification from sitting postures. In: The First Annual International Symposium on Vehicular Computing Systems (ISVCS 2008), p. 10 (2008)
13. Mutlu, B., Krause, A., Forlizzi, J., Guestrin, C., Hodgins, J.: Robust, low-cost, non-intrusive sensing and recognition of seated postures. In: Proceedings of the 20th Annual ACM Symposium on User Interface Software and Technology, pp. 149–158. ACM (2007)
14. Uludag, U., Jain, A.K.: Attacks on biometric systems: a case study in fingerprints. Proc. SPIE **5306**, 622–633 (2004)
15. Bowyer, K.W., Doyle, J.S.: Cosmetic contact lenses and iris recognition spoofing. Computer **47**(5), 96–98 (2014)
16. Marques, D., Muslukhov, I., Guerreiro, T.J., Carriço, L., Beznosov, K.: Snooping on mobile phones: prevalence and trends. In: Twelfth Symposium on Usable Privacy and Security, SOUPS 2016, Denver, CO, USA, 22–24 June 2016, pp. 159–174. USENIX (2016)
17. Mickelberg, K., Pollard, N., Schive, L.: US cybercrime: rising risks, reduced readiness key findings from the 2014 US state of cybercrime survey. US Secret Service. National Threat Assessment Center, Pricewaterhousecoopers (2014)
18. Robb, D.: Sony hack: a timeline (2014). http://deadline.com/2014/12/sony-hack-timeline-any-pascal-the-interview-north-korea-1201325501/
19. Ryan, C.G., Dall, P.M., Granat, M.H., Grant, P.M.: Sitting patterns at work: objective measurement of adherence to current recommendations. Ergonomics **54**(6), 531–538 (2011)
20. Jéquier, E., Tappy, L.: Regulation of body weight in humans. Physiol. Rev. **79**(2), 451–480 (1999)
21. Jaimes, A.: Sit straight (and tell me what i did today): a human posture alarm and activity summarization system. In: Proceedings of the 2nd ACM Workshop on Continuous Archival and Retrieval of Personal Experiences, pp. 23–34. ACM (2005)

# Cloud and Peer-to-Peer Security

# Stateful Multi-client Verifiable Computation

Christian Cachin[1], Esha Ghosh[2], Dimitrios Papadopoulos[3], and Björn Tackmann[1(✉)]

[1] IBM Research – Zurich, Rüschlikon, Switzerland
{cca,bta}@zurich.ibm.com
[2] Microsoft Research, Redmond, USA
esha.ghosh@microsoft.com
[3] Hong Kong University of Science and Technology, Kowloon, Hong Kong
dipapado@cse.ust.hk

**Abstract.** This paper develops an asynchronous cryptographic protocol for outsourcing arbitrary stateful computation among multiple clients to an untrusted server, while guaranteeing integrity of the data. The clients communicate only with the server and merely store a short authenticator to ensure that the server does not cheat. Our contribution is two-fold. First, we extend the recent hash&prove scheme of Fiore et al. (CCS 2016) to *stateful* computations that support arbitrary updates by the untrusted server, in a way that can be verified by the clients. We use this scheme to *generically* instantiate authenticated data types. Second, we describe a protocol for multi-client verifiable computation based on an authenticated data type, and prove that it achieves a computational version of *fork linearizability*. This is the strongest guarantee that can be achieved in the setting where clients do not communicate directly; it ensures correctness and consistency of outputs seen by the clients individually.

**Keywords:** Cloud computing · Authenticated data types
Verifiable computation · Byzantine emulation · Fork linearizability

## 1  Introduction

Cloud services are nowadays widely used for outsourcing data and computation because of their competitive pricing and immediate availability. They also allow for online collaboration by having multiple clients operate on the same data; such online services exist for, e.g., shared file storage, standard office applications, or software solutions for specific domains. For authenticity, confidentiality, and integrity of the data, however, the clients have to fully trust the cloud providers, which can access and modify the raw data without the clients' consent or notice.

The scenario we are concerned with in this paper involves multiple clients that mutually trust each other and collaborate through an untrusted server. A

© Springer International Publishing AG, part of Springer Nature 2018
B. Preneel and F. Vercauteren (Eds.): ACNS 2018, LNCS 10892, pp. 637–656, 2018.
https://doi.org/10.1007/978-3-319-93387-0_33

practical example is a group of co-workers using a shared calendar or editing a text document hosted on a cloud server. The protocol emulates multi-client access to an abstract data type $F$. Given an operation $o$ and a current state $s$, the protocol computes $(s', r) \leftarrow F(s, o)$ to generate an updated state $s'$ and an output $r$. The role of a client $C_v$ is to invoke operation $o$ and obtain response $r$; the purpose of the server is to store the state of $F$ and to perform the computation. As an example, let $F$ be defined for a set of elements where $o$ can be adding or deleting an element to the set. The state of the functionality will consist of the entire set. The protocol requires that all clients have public keys for digital signatures. Clients communicate only with the server; no direct communication between the clients occurs. Our protocol guarantees the integrity of responses and ensures fork linearizability, in the scenario where the server is untrusted and may be acting maliciously.

*Related Work.* The described problem has received considerable attention from the viewpoint of distributed systems, starting with protocols for securing *untrusted storage* [33]. Without communication among clients, the server may always perform a *forking attack* and omit the effects of operations by some clients in the communication with other clients. Clients cannot detect this attack unless they exchange information about the protocol progress or rely on synchronized clocks; the best achievable consistency guarantee has been called *fork lineariz-ability* by Mazières and Shasha [33] and has been investigated before [11,13,30] and applied to actual systems [8,12,13,28,44]. Early works [13,28] focused on simple read/write accesses to a storage service. More recent protocols such as BST [44] and COP [12] allow for emulating arbitrary data types, but require that the entire state be stored and the operations be computed on the client. ACOP [12] and VICOS [8] describe at a high level how to outsource both the state and the computation in a generic way, but neither work provides a cryptographic security proof.

The purpose of an *authenticated data type* (ADT; often also referred to as authenticated data structure) is to outsource storage of data, and the computation on it, to a server, while guaranteeing the integrity of the data. In a nutshell, while the server stores the data, the client holds a small *authenticator* (sometimes called *digest*) that relates to it. Operations on the data are performed by the server, and for each operation the server computes an integrity proof relative to the authenticator. ADTs originated as a generalization of Merkle trees [34], but instantiations of ADTs for various data types have been developed. There exist schemes for such diverse types as sets [14,40], dictionaries [2,24,36], range trees [31], graphs [25], skip lists [23,24], B-trees [35], or hash tables [39].

Non-interactive verifiable computation has been introduced as a concept to outsource computational tasks to untrusted workers [20]; schemes that achieve this for arbitrary functionalities exist [16,20,21,41] and are closely related to SNARKs (e.g., [6]). These works have the disadvantage, however, that the client verifying the proof needs to process the complete input to the computation as well. This can be avoided by having the client first hash its input and then outsource it storing only the hash locally. The subsequent verifiable computation protocol must then ensure not only the correctness of the computation but also that the input used matches the pre-image of the stored hash (which increases the concrete overhead), an approach that has been adopted in several works [9, 16, 17, 43]. In this work, we build on the latest in this line of works, the hash&prove scheme of Fiore et al. [17], by a mechanism that allows for stateful computation in which an *untrusted* party can update the state in a verifiable manner, and that can handle multiple clients. An alternative approach for verifiable computation focuses on specific computation tasks (restricted in generality, but often more efficient), such as polynomial evaluation [4, 7], database queries [37, 45], or matrix multiplication [18].

All these works target a setting where a *single* client interacts with the server, they do not support *multiple* clients collaborating on outsourced data. The only existing approaches that capture multi-client verifiable computation are by Choi et al. [15] and Gordon et al. [26]; yet, they only support stateless computations where all clients send their inputs to the server once, the latter evaluates a function on the joint data and returns the output. Another recent related work provides multi-key homomorphic authenticators for circuits of (bounded) polynomial depth [19]. Our work differs in that it allows stateful computation on data that is permanently outsourced to the server and updated through computations initiated by the clients. López-Alt et al. [29] address a complementary goal: they achieve privacy, but do not target consistency in terms of linearizability of a stateful multi-client computation. Also, their protocol requires a round of direct communication between the clients, which we rule out.

*Contributions.* Our first contribution is a new and general definition of a two-party ADT, where the server manages the state of the computation, performs updates and queries; the client invokes operations and receives results from the server. This significantly deviates from standard three-party ADTs (e.g. [40, 42]) that differentiate between a data owner, the untrusted server, and client(s). The owner needs to store the entire data to perform updates and publish the new authenticator in a *trusted* manner, while the client(s) may only issue read-only queries to the server. Our definition allows the untrusted server to perform updates such that the resulting authenticator can be verified for its correctness, eliminating the need to have a trusted party store the entire data. The definition also generalizes existing two-party ADTs [22, 38], as we discuss in Sect. 3.

We then provide a *general-purpose* instantiation of an ADT, based on verifiable computation from the work of Fiore et al. [17]. Our instantiation captures *arbitrary* stateful deterministic computation, and the client stores only a short authenticator which consists of two elements in a bilinear group.

We also devise *computational* security definitions that model the distributed-systems concepts of *linearizability* and *fork linearizability* [33] via cryptographic games. This allows us to prove the security of our protocol in a computational model by reducing from the security of digital signatures and ADTs—all previous work on fork linearizability idealized the cryptographic schemes.

Finally, we describe a "lock-step" protocol to satisfy the computational fork linearizability notion, adapted from previous work [13, 33]. The protocol guarantees fork-linearizable multi-client access to a data type. It is based on our definition of ADTs; if instantiated with our ADT construction, it is an asynchronous protocol for outsourcing any stateful (deterministic) computation with shared access in a multi-client setting.

## 2   Preliminaries

We use the standard notation for the sets of natural numbers $\mathbb{N}$, integers $\mathbb{Z}$, and integers $\mathbb{Z}_p$ modulo a number $p \in \mathbb{N}$. We let $\epsilon$ denote the empty string. If $Z$ is a string then $|Z|$ denotes its length, and $\circ$ is an operation to concatenate two strings. We consider lists of items, where $[\ ]$ denotes the empty list, $L[i]$ means accessing the $i$-th element of the list $L$, and $L \leftarrow L \circ x$ means storing a new element $x$ in $L$ by appending it to the end of the list. If $\mathcal{X}$ is a finite set, we let $x \leftarrow_\$ \mathcal{X}$ denote picking an element of $\mathcal{X}$ uniformly at random and assigning it to $x$. Algorithms may be randomized unless otherwise indicated. If $A$ is an algorithm, we let $y \leftarrow A(x_1, \ldots; r)$ denote running $A$ with uniform random coins $r$ on inputs $x_1, \ldots$ and assigning the output to $y$. We use $y \leftarrow_\$ A(x_1, \ldots)$ as shorthand for $y \leftarrow A(x_1, \ldots; r)$. For an algorithm that returns pairs of values, $(y, \_) \leftarrow A(x)$ means that the second parameter of the output is ignored; this generalizes to arbitrary-length tuples. The security parameter of cryptographic schemes is denoted by $\lambda$.

We formalize cryptographic security properties via games, following in particular the syntax of Bellare and Rogaway [5]. By $\Pr[\mathbf{G}]$ we denote the probability that the execution of game $\mathbf{G}$ returns TRUE. We target concrete-security definitions, specifying the security of a primitive or protocol directly in terms of the adversary advantage of winning a game. Asymptotic security follows immediately from our statements. In games, integer variables, set, list and string variables, and boolean variables are assumed initialized, respectively, to $0, \emptyset, [\,]$ and $\epsilon$, and FALSE.

*System Model.* The security definition for our protocol is based on well-established notions from the distributed-systems literature. In order to make *cryptographic* security statements and not resort to modeling all cryptography as ideal, we provide a computational definition that captures the same intuition.

Recall that our goal is to enable multiple clients $C_1, \ldots, C_u$, with $u \in \mathbb{N}$, to evaluate an abstract deterministic *data type* $F : (s, o) \mapsto (s', r)$, where $s, s' \in S$ describe the global state of $F$, $o \in O$ is an *input* of a client, and $r \in A$ is the corresponding *output* or *response*. Each client may exchange messages with a server over an asynchronous network channel. The clients can provide inputs to $F$ in an arbitrary order. Each execution defines a *history* $\sigma$, which is a sequence of input events $(C_v, o)$ and output events $(C_v, r)$; for simplicity, we assume $O \cap A = \emptyset$. An operation directly corresponds to an input/output event pair and vice versa, and an operation is *complete* in a history $\sigma$ if $\sigma$ contains an output event matching the input event.

In a *sequential* history, the output event of each operation directly follows the corresponding input event. Moreover, an operation $o$ *precedes* an operation

$o'$ in a history $\sigma$ if the *output* event of $o$ occurs before the *input* event of $o'$ in $\sigma$. Another history $\sigma'$ *preserves* the (real-time) order of $\sigma$ if all operations of $\sigma'$ occur in $\sigma$ as well and their precedence relation in $\sigma$ is also satisfied in $\sigma'$. The goal of a protocol is to *emulate* $F$. The clients only observe their own input and output events. The security of a protocol is defined in terms of how close the histories it produces are to histories produced through invocations of an ideal shared $F$.

*Linearizability.* A history $\sigma$ is *linearizable with respect to a type $F$* [27] if and only if there exists a sequential permutation $\pi(\sigma)$ of $\sigma$ such that

- $\pi(\sigma)$ preserves the (real-time) order of $\sigma$; and
- the operations of $\pi(\sigma)$ satisfy the sequential specification of $F$.

Satisfying the sequential specification of $F$ means that if $F$ starts in a specified initial state $s_0$, and all operations are performed sequentially as determined by $\pi(\sigma) = o_1, o_2, \ldots$, then with $(s_j, r_j) \leftarrow F(s_{j-1}, o_j)$, the output event corresponding to $o_j$ contains output $r_j$.

Linearizability is a strong guarantee as it specifies that the history $\sigma$ could have been observed by interacting with the ideal $F$, by only (possibly) exchanging the order of operations which were active concurrently. Unfortunately, as described in the introduction, linearizability cannot be achieved in the setting we are interested in.

*Fork Linearizability.* A history $\sigma$ is called *fork-linearizable with respect to a type $F$* [13,33] if and only if, for each client $C_v$, there exists a subsequence $\sigma_v$ of $\sigma$ consisting only of complete operations and a sequential permutation $\pi_v(\sigma_v)$ of $\sigma_v$ such that:

- All complete operations in $\sigma$ occurring at client $C_v$ are in $\sigma_v$, and
- $\pi_v(\sigma_v)$ preserves the real-time order of $\sigma_v$, and
- the operations of $\pi_v(\sigma_v)$ satisfy the sequential specification of $F$, and
- for every $o \in \pi_v(\sigma_v) \cap \pi_{v'}(\sigma_{v'})$, the sequence of events preceding $o$ in $\pi_v(\sigma_v)$ is the same as the sequence of events that precede $o$ in $\pi_{v'}(\sigma_{v'})$.

Fork linearizability is weaker than linearizability in that it requires consistency with $F$ only with respect to permutations of sub-sequences of the history. This models the weaker guarantee that is achieved relative to a dishonest server that partitions the set of clients and creates independent *forks* of the computation in each partition. Intuitively, fork linearizability formalizes that this partitioning attack is the only possible attack; the partitions will remain split forever, and the executions within the partitions are linearizable. Fork linearizability is the strongest achievable guarantee in the setting we consider [33].

*Abortable Services.* When operations of $F$ cannot be served immediately, a protocol may decide to either block or abort. Aborting and giving the client a chance to retry the operation at his own rate often has advantages compared to blocking, which might delay an application in unexpected ways. As in previous work that permitted aborts [1,8,12,30], we allow operations to abort and augment $F$ to an *abortable* type $F'$ accordingly. $F'$ is defined over the same set of states $S$ and operations $O$ as $F$, but returns a tuple defined over $S$ and $A \cup \{\text{BUSY}\}$. $F'$ may return the same output as $F$, but $F'$ may also return BUSY and leave the state unchanged, denoting that a client is not able to execute $F$. Hence, $F'$ is a non-deterministic relation and satisfies $F'(s, o) = \{(s, \text{BUSY}), F(s, o)\}$ .

*Verifiable Computation.* A *verifiable computation scheme* VC specifies the following. A key-generation algorithm VC.KEYGEN that takes as input security parameter $\lambda$ and relation $R \subset U \times W$ and produces a pair $(ek, vk) \leftarrow_\$ \text{VC.KEYGEN}(\lambda, R)$ of evaluation key $ek$ and verification key $vk$. An algorithm VC.PROVE that takes as input evaluation key $ek, u \in U$, and witness $w \in W$ such that $(u, w) \in R$, and returns a proof $\xi \leftarrow_\$ \text{VC.PROVE}(ek, u, w)$. As a concrete example, in the case of a circuit-based SNARK [16,41] the witness $w$ consists of the assignments of the internal wires of the circuit. An algorithm VC.VERIFY that takes as input the verification key $vk$, input $u$, and proof $\xi$, and returns a Boolean TRUE/FALSE $\leftarrow \text{VC.VERIFY}(vk, u, \xi)$ that signifies whether $\xi$ is valid.

The correctness error of VC is the probability that the verification of an honestly computed proof for a correct statement returns FALSE. The soundness error is the advantage of a malicious prover to produce an accepting proof of a false statement. Both quantities must be small for a scheme to be useful.

The verifiable computation schemes we use in this work have a special property referred to as *offline-online verification*, and which is defined when the set $U$ can be written as $U = X \times V$. In particular, for those schemes there exist algorithms VC.OFFLINE and VC.ONLINE such that

$$\text{VC.VERIFY}(vk, (x, v), \xi) = \text{VC.ONLINE}(vk, \text{VC.OFFLINE}(vk, x), v, \xi).$$

*Hash&prove Schemes.* We again consider the relation $R \subseteq U \times W$. A hash&prove scheme HP then allows to prove statements of the type $\exists w \in W : R(u, w)$ for a given $u \in U$; one crucial property of hash&prove schemes is that one can produce a short proof of the statement (using the witness $w$), such that the verification does not require the element $u \in U$ but only a short representation of it.

In more detail, a multi-relation hash&prove scheme as defined by Fiore et al. [17] consists of five algorithms:

- HP.SETUP takes as input security parameter $\lambda$ and produces public parameters $pp \leftarrow_\$ \text{HP.SETUP}(\lambda)$.
- HP.HASH takes as input public parameters $pp$ and a value $x \in X$ and produces a hash $h_x \leftarrow \text{HP.HASH}(pp, x)$.
- HP.KEYGEN takes as input public parameters $pp$ and a relation $R$ and outputs a key pair $(ek_R, vk_R) \leftarrow_\$ \text{HP.KEYGEN}(pp, R)$ of evaluation key and verification key.
- HP.PROVE takes as input evaluation key $ek_R$, values $(x, v) \in X \times V$ and witness $w \in W$ such that $((x, v), w) \in R$, and produces a proof $\pi \leftarrow_\$ \text{HP.PROVE}(ek_R, (x, v), w)$.

– Finally, HP.VERIFY takes as input verification key $vk_R$, hash $h_x$, value $v$, and proof $\pi$ and outputs a Boolean denoting whether it accepts the proof, written TRUE/FALSE ← HP.VERIFY($vk_R, h_x, v, \pi$).

An *extractable* hash&prove scheme has an additional (deterministic) algorithm HP.CHECK that takes as input $pp$ and a hash $h$ and outputs TRUE/FALSE ← HP.CHECK($pp, h$), a Boolean that signifies whether the hash is well-formed (i.e., there is a pre-image).

Correctness of HP is defined by requiring that the honest evaluation of the above algorithms leads to HP.VERIFY accepting. A hash&prove scheme has two soundness properties, *soundness* and *hash-soundness*. At a high level, both soundness games require an adversary to produce a proof for a false statement that will be accepted by HP.VERIFY. Adversary $\mathcal{A}$ is given public parameters $pp$, evaluation key $ek$, and verification key $vk$. To break soundness, $\mathcal{A}$ has to produce a proof for a statement $(x, v)$ that is wrong according to relation $R$, but the proof is accepted by HP.VERIFY for $h_x$ ← HP.HASH($pp, x$) computed honestly.

The purpose of hash soundness is to capture the scenario where HP supports arguments on untrusted, opaque hashes provided by the adversary. For this, the HP.HASH algorithm must be extractable. The hash-soundness game operates almost as the soundness game, but instead of $x$, the adversary provides a hash $h$. The adversary wins if the hash $h$ cannot be opened consistently (by the extractor $\mathcal{E}$) to satisfy the relation; for further explanation, we point the readers to [17, Appendix A.1], but we stress that the extraction is needed in our context.

Finally, we define the collision advantage of adversary $\mathcal{A}$ as

$$\text{Adv}_{\text{HP}}^{\text{CR}}(\mathcal{A}) := \Pr \left[ \begin{array}{l} pp \leftarrow_{\$} \text{HP.SETUP}; (x, y) \leftarrow_{\$} \mathcal{A}(pp); \\ \text{HP.HASH}(pp, x) \stackrel{?}{=} \text{HP.HASH}(pp, y) \end{array} \right]$$

*Hash&Prove for Multi-exponentiation.* We recall the hash&prove scheme for multi-exponentiation introduced as $\text{XP}_{\mathcal{E}}$ in [17], but keep the details light since we do not use properties other than those already used there. The scheme, which we call MXP here, uses asymmetric bilinear prime-order groups $\mathcal{G}_\lambda = (e, \mathbb{G}_1, \mathbb{G}_2, \mathbb{G}_T, p, g_1, g_2)$, with an admissible bilinear map $e : \mathbb{G}_1 \times \mathbb{G}_2 \to \mathbb{G}_T$, generators $g_1 \in \mathbb{G}1$ and $g_2 \in \mathbb{G}_2$, and group order $p$. The main aspect we need to know about MXP is that, it works for inputs of the form $x = (x_1, \ldots, x_n) \in \mathbb{Z}_p^n$ and admissible relations of MXP are described by a vector $(G_1, \ldots, G_n) \in \mathbb{G}_1^n$. The proved relation is the following: $\prod_{i=1}^n G_i^{x_i} = c_x$ for a given $c_x$. MXP uses a hash of the input $x = (x_1, \ldots, x_n) \in \mathbb{Z}_p^n$ to prove correctness across different admissible relations. The hash function is described by a vector $(H_1, \ldots, H_n) \in \mathbb{G}_1^n$. For an input $x = (x_1, \ldots, x_n) \in \mathbb{Z}_p^n$, the hash is computed as $h_x = \prod_{i=1}^n H_i^{x_i}$. In a nutshell, this will be used for proving that $h_x$ and $c_x$ encode the same vector $x$, with respect to a different basis.

Fiore et al. [17] prove MXP adaptively hash-sound under the Strong External DDH and the Bilinear $n$-Knowledge of Exponent assumptions. They then combine MXP with schemes for online-offline verifiable computation that use an encoding of the form $\prod_{i=1}^{n} G_i^{x_i} = c_x$ as its intermediate representation, to obtain a hash&prove scheme that works for arbitrary (stateless) computations. We describe their construction in more detail in Sect. 4, before explaining our scheme that follows the same idea but extends to *stateful* computations.

# 3    Authenticated Data Types

Authenticated data types, which originated as an abstraction and generalization of Merkle trees [34], associate with a (potentially large) state of the data type a short *authenticator* (or *digest*) that is useful for verification of the integrity of operations on the state. In more detail, an abstract data type is described by a state space $S$ with a function $F : S \times O \to S \times A$ as before. $F$ takes as input a state $s \in S$ of the data type and an operation $o \in O$ and returns a new state $s'$ and the response $r \in A$. The data type also specifies the initial state $s_0 \in S$.

Here, we present a definition for what is known in the literature as a "two-party" *authenticated data type (ADT)* [38]. The interaction is between a *client*, i.e., a party that owns $F$ and wants to outsource it, and an untrusted *server* that undertakes storing the state of this outsourced data type and responding to subsequent operations issued. The client, having access only to a succinct *authenticator* and the secret key of the scheme, wishes to be able to efficiently test that requested operations have been performed honestly by the server (see [38] for a more detailed comparison of variants of ADT modes of operation). An authenticated data type ADT for $F$ consists of the following algorithms:

$(sk, ad, a) \leftarrow_\$ \text{ADT.INIT}(\lambda)$: This algorithm sets up the secret key and the public key for the ADT scheme, for security parameter $\lambda$. It also outputs an initial amended state $ad$ and a succinct authenticator $a$. We implicitly assume from now on that the public key $pk$ is part of the secret key $sk$ as well as the server state $ad$. We also assume that the actual initial state $s_0$ and authenticator $a$ are part of $ad$.

$\pi \leftarrow_\$ \text{ADT.EXEC}(ad, o)$: This algorithm takes an operation $o$, applies it on the current version of $ad$, and provides a correctness proof $\pi$, from which a response $r$ can be extracted.

$(\text{TRUE/FALSE}, r, a', t) \leftarrow_\$ \text{ADT.VERIFY}(sk, a, o, \pi)$: The algorithm takes the current authenticator $a$, an operation $o$, and a proof $\pi$, verifies the proof with respect to the authenticator and the operation, outputting local output $r$, the updated authenticator $a'$, and an additional authentication token $t$.

$ad' \leftarrow_\$ \text{ADT.REFRESH}(ad, o, t)$: The algorithm updates the amended state from $ad$ to $ad'$, using operation $o$ and authentication token $t$ provided by the client.

An ADT has to satisfy two conditions, correctness and soundness. Correctness formalizes that if the ADT is used faithfully, then the outputs received by the client are according to the abstract data type $F$.

**Definition 1 (Correctness).** *Let $s_0$ be the initial state of data type $F$ and $o_1, \ldots, o_m$ be a sequence of operations. The ADT scheme ADT is correct if in the following computation, the assertions are always satisfied.*

$(sk, ad, a) \leftarrow\!\!\text{\$ } \text{ADT.INIT}(\lambda) \; ; \; s \leftarrow s_0$
*For* $j = 1, \ldots, m$ *do*
$\quad \pi \leftarrow\!\!\text{\$ } \text{ADT.EXEC}(ad, o_j)$
$\quad (b, r, a', t) \leftarrow \text{ADT.VERIFY}(sk, a, o_j, \pi)$
$\quad (s', r') \leftarrow F(s, o_j)$
$\quad$ **assert** $b$ *and* $r = r'$
$\quad ad' \leftarrow\!\!\text{\$ } \text{ADT.REFRESH}(ad, o_j, t)$
$\quad (ad, a, s) \leftarrow (ad', a', s')$

The second requirement for the ADT, soundness, states that a dishonest server cannot cheat. The game $\mathbf{G}^{\text{sound}}_{\text{ADT}}$ described in Fig. 1 formalizes that it must be infeasible for the adversary (a misbehaving server) to produce a proof that makes a client accept a wrong response of an operation. The variable *forged* tracks whether the adversary has been successful. The list $L[\ ]$ is used to store valid pairs of state and authenticator of the ADT, and is consequently initialized with $(s_0, a)$ of a newly initialized ADT in position 0. The adversary $\mathcal{A}$ is initialized with $(ad, a)$ and can repeatedly query the VERIFY oracle in the game by specifying an operation $o$, the index $pos \in \mathbb{N}$ of a state on which $o$ shall be executed, and a proof $\pi$. The challenger obtains state $s$ and authenticator $a$ of the $pos$-th state from the list $L[\ ]$. The challenger (a) checks whether ADT.VERIFY accepts the proof $\pi$, and (b) computes the new state $s'$ and the output $r'$ using the correct $F$ and state $s$, and sets *forged* if the proof verified but the output $r$ generated by ADT.VERIFY does not match the "ideal" output $r'$.

This game formulation ensures the outputs provided to the clients are always correct according to $F$ and the sequence of operations performed, but also allows the adversary to "fork" and compute different operations based on the same state. This is necessary for proving the security of the protocol described in Sect. 6. Unlike for the output $r$, the game does not formalize an explicit correctness condition for $ad'$ to properly represent the state $s'$ of $F$ as updated by $o'$; this is only modeled through the outputs generated during subsequent operations. Indeed, in the two-party model, the internal state of the server cannot be observed, and only the correctness of the responses provided to clients matters.

**Definition 2 (Soundness).** *Let $F$ be an abstract data type and* ADT *an ADT for $F$. Let $\mathcal{A}$ be an adversary. The* soundness *advantage of $\mathcal{A}$ against* ADT *is defined as* $\text{Adv}^{\text{SOUND}}_{\text{ADT}}(\mathcal{A}) := \Pr\left[\mathbf{G}^{\text{sound}}_{\text{ADT}}\right].$

To exclude trivial schemes in which the server always sends the complete state to the clients, we explicitly require that the authenticator of the clients must be *succinct*. More concretely, we require that the size of the authenticator is independent of the size of the state.

**Definition 3 (Succinctness).** *Let $F$ be an abstract data type and* ADT *an ADT with security parameter $\lambda$ for $F$. Then* ADT *is* succinct *if the bit-length of the authenticator $a$ is always in $\mathcal{O}(\lambda)$.*

Very few existing works seek to define a two-party authenticated data structure [22,38], since most of the literature focuses on a three-party model where

| Game $\mathbf{G}_{\mathrm{ADT}}^{\mathrm{sound}}(\mathcal{A})$ | VERIFY$(o, pos, \pi)$ |
|---|---|
| *forged* ← FALSE | If $pos > \lvert L \rvert$ then return $\perp$ |
| $(sk, ad, a) \leftarrow_{\$} \mathrm{ADT.INIT}(\lambda)$ | $(s, a) \leftarrow L[pos]$ |
| $L[0] \leftarrow (s_0, a)$ | $(b, r, a', t) \leftarrow_{\$} \mathrm{ADT.VERIFY}(sk, a, o, \pi)$ |
| $\mathcal{A}^{\mathrm{VERIFY}}(ad, a)$ | If $b$ then |
| Return *forged* | $\quad (s', r') \leftarrow F(s, o)$ |
| | $\quad$ If $r' \neq r$ then *forged* ← TRUE |
| | $\quad L \leftarrow L \circ (s', a')$ |
| | $\quad$ Return (TRUE, $a', t, r$) |
| | Else return (FALSE, $\perp, \perp, \perp$) |

**Fig. 1.** The security game formalizing soundness of an ADT.

the third party is a trusted data manager that permanently stores the data and is the sole entity capable of issuing updates.

The definition of [38] differs from ours as it only supports a limited class of functionalities. It requires the update issuer to appropriately modify *ad* himself and provide the new version to the server and, as such, this definition can only work for structures where the part of the *ad* that is modified after an update is "small" (e.g., for a binary hash tree, only a logarithmic number of nodes are modified). The definition of [22] supports general functionalities however, unlike ours, it cannot naturally support randomized ADT schemes as it requires the client to be able to check the validity of the new authenticator $a'$ after an update; in case a scheme is randomized, it is not clear whether this check can be performed. In our soundness game from Fig. 1, the adversary can only win by providing a bad local output $r$ (which, by default, is empty in the case of updates) and not with a bad authenticator, which makes it possible to handle randomized constructions. We note that our construction from Sect. 4 does not exploit this, as it is deterministic.

## 4   A General-Purpose Instantiation of ADT

This section contains one main technical contribution of this work, namely a general-purpose instantiation of ADTs defined in Sect. 3. Our scheme builds on the work of Fiore et al. [17], which defined hash&prove schemes in which a server proves the correctness of a computation (relative to a state) to a client that only knows a hash value of the state. The main aspect missing from [17] is the capability for an untrusted server to *update* the state and produce a new (verifiable) hash. The hash of an updated state *can* be computed incrementally as described in [17, Sect. 4.4].

Before we start describing our scheme, we recall some details of the hash&prove scheme of Fiore et al. [17]. Their scheme allows to verifiably compute a function $f : Z \rightarrow V$ on an untrusted server, where the verification by the client does not require $z \in Z$ but only a hash $h_z$ of it. In accordance with the verifiable computation schemes for proving correctness of the computation, they set $U = Z \times V$ and consider a relation $R_f \subseteq U \times W$ such that for a pair $(z, v) \in U$ there is a witness $w \in W$ with $((z, v), w) \in R_f$ if and only if $f(z) = v$. In other words, proving $\exists w : ((z, v), w) \in R_f$ implies that $f(z) = v$. The format of the witness $w$ depends on the specific verifiable computation scheme in use, e.g., it may be the assignments to the wires of the circuit computing $f(z)$.

Fiore et al. proceed via an offline-online verifiable computation scheme VC and a hash-extractable hash&prove scheme for multi-exponentiations MXP. Recall that MXP uses a hash function that is described by a vector $pp = (H_1, \ldots, H_n) \in \mathbb{G}_1^n$ and computed as $h_z \leftarrow \text{MXP.HASH}(pp, z) = \prod_{i=1}^{n} H_i^{z_i}$ for $z = (z_1, \ldots, z_n) \in \mathbb{Z}_p^n$. The hash $h_z$, which is known to the client, is computed via $\text{MXP.HASH}(pp, \cdot)$. The offline-online property of the scheme VC states that

$$\text{VC.VERIFY}(vk, (z, v), \xi) = \text{VC.ONLINE}(vk, \text{VC.OFFLINE}(vk, z), v, \xi).$$

Fiore et al. further assume that VC uses an intermediate representation of the form $\text{VC.OFFLINE}(vk, z) = c_z = \prod_{i=1}^{n} G_i^{z_i}$, where the group elements $G_1, \ldots, G_n$ are included in the verification key $vk$. This means, in a nutshell, that MXP can be used to prove that, for a given $z$, the hashes $c_z$ and $h_z$ encode the same $z$.

In the complete scheme, the server computes $\xi \leftarrow_\$ \text{VC.PROVE}(ek, z, w)$, using the scheme-dependent witness $w$ referred to above, and the evaluation key $ek$ for the function $f$. It also computes $c_z = \text{VC.OFFLINE}(vk, z)$ and sends $\xi$ and $c_z$ to the client. The server proves to the client via MXP that $c_z$ contains the same value $z$ as the hash $h_z$ known to the client. The client concludes by verifying the proof via VC.ONLINE with input $c_z$.

*Building the New Hash&Prove Scheme.* Our goal is to model stateful computations of the type $F(s, o) = (s', r)$, using the syntax of the hash&prove scheme. Recall that the syntax of [17] does not handle stateful computations with state updates explicitly. On a high-level, our approach can be seen as computing a stateful $F$ verifiably by first computing $(s', \_) \leftarrow F(s, o)$ *without verification* (where $\_$ means that the second component of the output is ignored) and then *verifiably* computing $\tilde{F}((s, s'), o) \mapsto (d, r)$ defined via $(\bar{s}, r) \leftarrow F(s, o); d \leftarrow \bar{s} \stackrel{?}{=} s'$. In this approach, the client has to check the proof of the verifiable computation *and* that $d = \text{TRUE}$. Putting the output state $s'$ into the input of the verifiable computation of $\tilde{F}$ has the advantage that we already know how to handle hashes there: via a hash&proof scheme similar to the one of [17]. In the following, we describe our scheme more technically. It can be seen as a variant of [17] with two hashed inputs $x$ and $y$.

In [17], the output of $\text{VC.OFFLINE}(vk, z)$ is a single value $c_z$ that is then related to the hash $h_z$ known to the client via MXP. As we have two individual hashes $h_x$ and $h_y$ for the components $x$ and $y$, respectively, we modify the construction of [17]. For $z \in X \times Y$ with $X = Y = \mathbb{Z}_p^n$, we modify $\text{VC.OFFLINE}(vk, z)$ to compute $c_x \leftarrow \prod_{i=1}^{n} G_i^{x_i}$ and $c_y \leftarrow \prod_{i=1}^{n} G_{n+i}^{y_i}$ for elements $G_1, \ldots, G_{2n}$ that are specified in $vk$, and prove consistency of $c_x$ with $h_x$ and of $c_y$ with $h_y$, again

$\text{SHP.SETUP}(\lambda)$

$pp \leftarrow_\$ \text{MXP.SETUP}(\lambda)$
Return $pp$

$\text{SHP.HASH}(pp, (x, y))$

$h_x \leftarrow \text{MXP.HASH}(pp, x)$ ; $h_y \leftarrow \text{MXP.HASH}(pp, y)$
Return $(h_x, h_y)$

$\text{SHP.KEYGEN}(pp, R)$

$(ek, vk) \leftarrow_\$ \text{VC.KEYGEN}(\lambda, R)$
Let $G_1, \ldots, G_{2n}$ be the "offline" elements in $vk$, see discussion in text.
$(ek_i, vk_i) \leftarrow_\$ \text{MXP.KEYGEN}(pp, (G_1, \ldots, G_n))$
$(ek_o, vk_o) \leftarrow_\$ \text{MXP.KEYGEN}(pp, (G_{n+1}, \ldots, G_{2n}))$
Return $(ek_R, vk_R) = ((ek, vk, ek_i, ek_o), (vk, vk_i, vk_o))$

$\text{SHP.PROVE}(ek_R, (x, y), v, w)$

$(c_x, c_y) \leftarrow \text{VC.OFFLINE}(vk, (x, y))$
$\xi \leftarrow_\$ \text{VC.PROVE}(ek, ((x, y), v), w)$
$\pi_x \leftarrow_\$ \text{MXP.PROVE}(ek_i, x, c_x)$ ; $\pi_y \leftarrow_\$ \text{MXP.PROVE}(ek_o, y, c_y)$
Return $\pi_R = (c_x, c_y, \xi, \pi_x, \pi_y)$

$\text{SHP.CHECK}(pp, (h_x, h_y))$

Return $\text{MXP.CHECK}(pp, h_x) \wedge \text{MXP.CHECK}(pp, h_y)$

$\text{SHP.VERIFY}(vk_R, (h_x, h_y), v, \pi_R)$

Return $\text{VC.ONLINE}(vk, (c_x, c_y), v, \xi) \wedge \text{SHP.CHECK}(pp, (h_x, h_y))$
$\wedge \text{MXP.VERIFY}(vk_i, h_x, c_x, \pi_x) \wedge \text{MXP.VERIFY}(vk_o, h_y, c_y, \pi_y)$

**Fig. 2.** The hash&prove scheme SHP for updates by untrusted servers.

using MXP. (Note that this is $c_z = c_x c_y$.) As argued by [17], many existing VC/SNARK constructions can be written in this way.

Summarizing the above, the main modifications over [17] are (i) that we transform a stateful $F$ into a stateless $\tilde{F}$, (ii) that VC.ONLINE obtains two elements $c_x$ and $c_y$ from VC.OFFLINE, and (iii) that the output bit $d$ has to be checked. Our stateful hash&prove system SHP for $\tilde{F}$ is specified formally in Fig. 2. We formally prove that SHP is hash sound (analogously to [17, Corollary 4.1]) in the full version [10].

*Building a General-Purpose ADT Using Our HP.* The scheme SHP constructed above lends itself well to building a general-purpose ADT. Note that verifiable computation schemes explicitly construct the witness $w$ required for the correctness proof; in fact, the computation of $F$ can also be used to produce a witness $w$ for the correctness according to $\tilde{F}$, which is immediate for VC schemes that actually model $F$ as a circuit [21,41].

The general-purpose ADT GA, which is more formally described in Fig. 3, works as follows. Algorithm GA.INIT generates public parameters $pp$ and a

| $\text{GA.INIT}_F(\lambda)$ | $\text{GA.VERIFY}(sk, a, o, \pi)$ |
|---|---|
| $pp \leftarrow_\$ \text{SHP.SETUP}(\lambda)$ | $(\xi, a', r') \leftarrow \pi \; ; \; (d, r) \leftarrow r'$ |
| $(ek, vk) \leftarrow_\$ \text{SHP.KEYGEN}(pp, R_{\tilde{F}})$ | $b \leftarrow d \wedge \text{SHP.VERIFY}(sk, (a, a'), (o, r'), \xi)$ |
| $(a, \_) \leftarrow \text{SHP.HASH}(pp, (s_0, \epsilon))$ | Return $(b, r, a', \epsilon)$ |
| Return $(vk, (s_0, a, ek, vk), a)$ | |
| | $\text{GA.REFRESH}_F(ad, o, t)$ |
| $\text{GA.EXEC}_F(ad, o)$ | $(s, a, ek, vk) \leftarrow ad$ |
| $(s, a, ek, vk) \leftarrow ad$ | $(s', r) \leftarrow F(s, o)$ |
| $(s', r) \leftarrow F(s, o)$    ▷ Get witness $w$ | $(a', \_) \leftarrow \text{SHP.HASH}(pp, (s', \epsilon))$ |
| $\xi \leftarrow_\$ \text{SHP.PROVE}(ek, (s, s'), (o, r), w)$ | Return $(s', a', ek, vk)$ |
| $(a', \_) \leftarrow \text{SHP.HASH}(pp, (s', \epsilon))$ | |
| Return $\pi = (\xi, a', r)$ | |

**Fig. 3.** The general-purpose ADT scheme GA that can be instantiated for any data type $F$. While GA.REFRESH does not use the value $t$, it is included in the definition of ADT as it could be useful in other schemes.

key pair $(ek, vk)$ for SHP, and then computes the authenticator $(a, \_) \leftarrow \text{SHP.HASH}(pp, (s_0, \epsilon))$ for the initial state $s_0$ of $F$. Algorithm GA.EXEC computes the new state $s'$ via $F$ and authenticator $(a', \_) \leftarrow \text{SHP.HASH}(pp, (s', \epsilon))$, and generates a correctness proof $\xi$ for the computation of $\tilde{F}$ via SHP.PROVE. We note that we explicitly write out the empty string $\epsilon$, and ignore the second output component, in algorithm $(a, \_) \leftarrow \text{SHP.HASH}(pp, (s_0, \epsilon))$ to be consistent with the hash&prove scheme syntax. We can safely ignore this argument at the implementation level. Algorithm GA.VERIFY checks the proof $\xi$ via SHP.VERIFY and also checks the bit $d$ output by $\tilde{F}$ to ensure that the authenticator $a'$ is correct. Algorithm GA.REFRESH simply updates the server state—recomputing $s'$ and $a'$ can be spared by caching the values from GA.EXEC. Instantiating GA with the schemes of [17] leads to a succinct ADT. We defer the soundness proof to the full version [10].

## 5    Computational Fork-Linearizable Byzantine Emulation

The application we target in this paper is verifiable multiple-client computation of an ADT $F$ with an untrusted server for coordination. As the clients may not be online simultaneously, we do not assume any direct communication among them. The goal of the protocol is to emulate an abstract data type $F : (s, o) \mapsto (s', r)$. As the server may be malicious, this setting is referred to as *Byzantine emulation* in the literature [13].

A Byzantine emulation protocol BEP specifies the following: A setup algorithm BEP.SETUP takes as parameter the number $u \in \mathbb{N}$ of clients and outputs, for each client $v \in \mathbb{N}$, key information $clk_v$, server key information $svk$, and public key information $pks$. (The variable $pks$ models information that is considered public, such as the clients' public keys.) A client algorithm BEP.INVOKE takes as input an operation $o \in \{0,1\}^*$, secret information $clk \in \{0,1\}^*$, public keys $pks \in \{0,1\}^*$ and state $S \in \{0,1\}^*$, and outputs a message $m \in \{0,1\}^*$ and a new state $S' \in \{0,1\}^*$. A client algorithm BEP.RECEIVE takes as input a message $m \in \{0,1\}^*$, and $clk, pks$, and $S$ as above, and outputs a value $r \in \{0,1\}^* \cup \{\text{ABORT}, \text{BUSY}\}$, a message $m' \in \{0,1\}^* \cup \{\bot\}$, and a new state $S' \in \{0,1\}^*$. The return value ABORT means that the operation has been aborted because of an error or inconsistency of the system, whereas BUSY means that the server is busy executing a different operation and the client shall repeat the invocation later. A server algorithm BEP.PROCESS takes as input a message $m \in \{0,1\}^*$, purported sender $v \in \mathbb{N}$, secret information $svk \in \{0,1\}^*$, public keys $pks \in \{0,1\}^*$ and state $S_s \in \{0,1\}^*$, and outputs a message $m' \in \{0,1\}^*$, intended receiver $v' \in \mathbb{N}$, and updated state $S'_s \in \{0,1\}^*$.

We then define the security game $\mathbf{G}^{\text{emu}}_{\text{BEP},u,\text{P}}$ described in Fig. 4. Initially, the game calls BEP.SETUP to generate the necessary keys; the setup phase modeled here allows the clients to generate and distribute keys among them. This allows for modeling, for instance, a public-key infrastructure, or just a MAC key that is shared among all clients. (Note that we consider all clients as honest.) The adversary $\mathcal{A}$, which models the network as well as the malicious server, is executed with input $pks$—the public keys of the scheme—and has access to four oracles. Oracle INVOKE$(v, o)$ models the invocation of operation $o$ at client $C_v$, updates the state $S_v$, and appends the input event $(C_v, o)$ to the history $\sigma$. The oracle returns a message $m$ directed at the server. Oracle RECEIVE$(v, m)$ delivers the message $m$ to $C_v$, updates the state $S_v$, and outputs a response $r$ and a message $m'$. If $r \neq \bot$, the most recently invoked operation of $C_v$ completes and the output event $(C_v, r)$ is appended to $\sigma$. If $m' \neq \bot$, then $m'$ is a further message directed at the server. Oracle CORRUPT returns the server state $S_s$, and oracle PROCESS$(v, m)$ corresponds to delivering message $m$ to the server as being sent by $C_v$. This updates the server state $S_s$, and may return a message $m'$ to be given to $C_v$. The game returns the result of predicate P on the history $\sigma$, which is initially empty and extended through calls of the types INVOKE$(v, o)$ and RECEIVE$(v, m)$. We define two classes of adversaries: *full* and *benign*, that we use in the security definition.

*Full Adversaries:* A *full* adversary $\mathcal{A}_{\text{FULL}}$ invokes oracles in an arbitrary order. The only restriction is that, for each $v \in [1, u]$, after $\mathcal{A}_{\text{FULL}}$ has invoked an operation of $C_v$ (with INVOKE$(v, \cdot)$), then $\mathcal{A}_{\text{FULL}}$ must not invoke another operation of $C_v$ until after the operation completes (when RECEIVE$(v, \cdot)$ returns $r \neq \bot$). This condition means that a single client does not run concurrent operations and is often called *well-formedness*.

*Benign Adversaries:* A *benign* adversary $\mathcal{A}_{\text{BEN}}$ is restricted like $\mathcal{A}_{\text{FULL}}$. Additionally, it makes no query to the CORRUPT oracle and delivers exactly the messages generated by the protocol; the order of messages belonging to different client operations can be modified as long as the server is allowed to finish each operation before starting the next one.

The protocol must satisfy two conditions, which are made formal in Definition 4. The first condition models the security against malicious servers, and uses

| Game $\mathbf{G}^{\mathrm{emu}}_{\mathrm{BEP},u,\mathrm{P}}(\mathcal{A})$ | RECEIVE$(v, m)$ |
|---|---|
| $(clk_1, \ldots, clk_u, svk, pks)$ | $(r, m', S_v) \leftarrow\!\!\text{\$}\, \text{BEP.RECEIVE}(m, clk_v, pks, S_v)$ |
| $\quad \leftarrow\!\!\text{\$}\, \text{BEP.SETUP}(u)$ | $\sigma \leftarrow \sigma \circ (C_v, r)$ |
| $\mathcal{A}^{\text{INVOKE,RECEIVE,PROCESS,CORRUPT}}(pks)$ | Return $(r, m')$ |
| Return $\neg\mathrm{P}(\sigma)$ | |
| | CORRUPT |
| INVOKE$(v, o)$ | Return $S_{\mathsf{s}}$ |
| $(m, S_v) \leftarrow\!\!\text{\$}\, \text{BEP.INVOKE}(o, clk_v, pks, S_v)$ | |
| $\sigma \leftarrow \sigma \circ (C_v, o)$ | PROCESS$(v, m)$ |
| Return $m$ | $(m', v', S_{\mathsf{s}})$ |
| | $\quad \leftarrow\!\!\text{\$}\, \text{BEP.PROCESS}(m, v, svk, pks, S_{\mathsf{s}})$ |
| | Return $(v', m')$ |

**Fig. 4.** The emulation game parametrized by a predicate P.

the concept of fork linearizability as defined in Sect. 2. In more detail, we use a predicate $\mathrm{fork}_{F'}$ that determines whether the history $\sigma$ is fork linearizable with respect to the abortable type $F'$, and the advantage of adversary $\mathcal{A}_{\mathrm{FULL}}$ is defined as the probability of producing a history that is not fork-linearizable. The second condition formalizes linearizability with respect to benign adversaries $\mathcal{A}_{\mathrm{BEN}}$ and is defined using a predicate $\mathrm{lin}_{F'} \wedge \mathrm{live}_{F'}$ that formalizes both linearizability and liveness.

**Definition 4.** *Let* BEP *be a protocol and* $F$ *an abstract data type. The FLBE-advantage of* $\mathcal{A}_{\mathrm{FULL}}$ *w.r.t.* BEP *and* $F$ *is defined as the probability of winning the game* $\mathbf{G}^{\mathrm{emu}}_{\mathrm{BEP},u,\mathrm{fork}_{F'}}$, *where* $\mathrm{fork}_{F'}$ *denotes the predicate that formalizes fork linearizability with respect to* $F'$. *The* linearizability advantage *of* $\mathcal{A}_{\mathrm{BEN}}$ *is defined as the probability of winning the game* $\mathbf{G}^{\mathrm{emu}}_{\mathrm{BEP},u,\mathrm{lin}_F \wedge \mathrm{live}_F}$, *using the predicate* $\mathrm{lin}_F$ *that formalizes linearizability with respect to* $F$, *and* $\mathrm{live}_F$ *that formalizes that no operations abort.*

The predicates $\mathrm{fork}_{F'}$ and $\mathrm{lin}_F$ are easily made formal following the descriptions in Sect. 2. The predicate $\mathrm{live}_F$ simply formalizes that for every operation $o \in \sigma$ there is a corresponding output event.

## 6   A Lock-Step Protocol for Emulating Shared Data Types

We describe a *lock-step* protocol that uses an ADT to give multiple clients access to a data type $F$, and achieves fork linearizability via vector clocks [13,32,33] in a setting where the server may be malicious. By *lock-step* we mean that while the server processes the request of one client, all other clients will be blocked. We prove the security of the scheme based on the unforgeability of the underlying signature scheme and the soundness of the underlying ADT.

The lock-step protocol LS, which is specified formally in Fig. 5, has a setup phase in which the keys of the ADT and one signature key pair per client are

$\underline{\text{LS.SETUP}(u, \lambda)}$

$(sk, ad, a) \leftarrow_\$ \text{ADT.INIT}(\lambda)$
For $v = 1$ to $u$ do $(ssk_v, spk_v) \leftarrow_\$ \text{DS.KEYGEN}(\lambda)$
Return $((ssk_1, sk, 1), \dots, (ssk_u, sk, u), ad, (spk_1, \dots, spk_u, a))$

$\underline{\text{LS.INVOKE}(o_v, clk_v, pks, T)}$

If $s = \epsilon$ then $T \leftarrow (0, \dots, 0)$          ▷ Obtain number of users from $pks$
Return $(\langle \text{SUBMIT}, o_v \rangle, T)$

$\underline{\text{LS.RECEIVE}(m, (ssk_v, sk, v), (spk_1, \dots, spk_u, a_0), T)}$

If $m = \langle \text{BUSY} \rangle$ then return $(\text{BUSY}, \perp, T)$
$\langle \text{REPLY}, V, \ell, a, \varphi', \xi \rangle \leftarrow m$ (or abort if not possible)
$(b, r, a', t) \leftarrow \text{ADT.VERIFY}(sk, a, o_v, \xi)$
$b \leftarrow b \wedge ((V = (0, \dots, 0) \wedge a = a_0) \vee \text{DS.VERIFY}(spk_\ell, \varphi', \text{COMMIT} \circ a \circ V))$
If $\neg ((T \leq V) \wedge (T[v] = V[v]) \wedge b)$ then return $(\text{ABORT}, \perp, T)$
$T \leftarrow V + 1_v$
$\varphi \leftarrow \text{DS.SIGN}(ssk_v, \text{COMMIT} \circ a' \circ T)$
Return $(r, \langle \text{COMMIT}, T, a', \varphi, t \rangle, T)$

$\underline{\text{LS.PROCESS}(m, v, ad_0, pks, s)}$

If $s = \epsilon$ then $s \leftarrow (ad, a, 0, \epsilon, (0, \dots, 0), 0)$          ▷ Initialize server state
$(ad, a, \ell, \omega, V, i) \leftarrow s$
If $i = 0$ and $m = \langle \text{SUBMIT}, o \rangle$ then          ▷ Expect a submit message
    $\pi \leftarrow \text{ADT.EXEC}(ad, o)$
    Return $(v, \langle \text{REPLY}, V, \ell, a, \omega, \pi \rangle, (ad, a, \ell, \omega, V, v))$
Else if $i = v$ and $m = \langle \text{COMMIT}, T, a', \varphi, t \rangle$ then          ▷ Expected commit
    $ad' \leftarrow \text{ADT.REFRESH}(ad, a, o, t)$
    Return $(0, \perp, (ad', a', i, \varphi, T, 0))$
Else return $(v, \langle \text{BUSY} \rangle, s)$

**Fig. 5.** The lock-step protocol LS.

generated and distributed. Each client has access to the verification keys of all other clients; this is in practice achieved by means of a PKI. The processing then works as follows. A client $C_v$ initiates an operation $o$ by calling LS.INVOKE, which generates a SUBMIT message with $o$ for the server. When this message is delivered to the server, then it generates a REPLY message for the client. The client performs local computation, generates a COMMIT message for the server, finally completes the operation by returning the output $r$.

*Authenticated data types* ensure the validity of each individual operation invoked by a client. After the client submits operation $o$, the server executes $o$ via ADT.EXEC and returns the proof $\pi$ together with the previous authenticator in REPLY. The client verifies the server's computation against the previous authenticator, computes the output and the new authenticator via ADT.VERIFY, and sends them to the server in COMMIT. Finally, the new authenticator and the authentication token of the ADT are sent to the server, which updates the state via ADT.REFRESH.

*Digital signatures* are used to authenticate the information that synchronizes the protocol state among the clients. After computing a new authenticator $a'$ via ADT.VERIFY, a client signs $a'$ and sends it back to the server in COMMIT. When the next client initiates an operation $o$, the REPLY message from the server contains the authenticator $a'$ together with the signature. Checking the validity of this signature ensures that all operations are performed on a valid (though possibly outdated) state.

*Vector clocks* represent causal dependencies among events occurring in different parts of a network [3]. For clients $C_1, \ldots, C_u$, a logical clock is described by a vector $V \in \mathbb{N}^u$, where the $v$-th component $V[v]$ contains the logical time of $C_v$. In our protocol, clients increase their local logical with each operation they perform; the vector clock therefore ensures a partial order on the operations. Each client ensures that all operations it observes are totally ordered by updating its vector clock accordingly, and signing and communicating it together with the authenticator. Together with the above mechanism, this ensures that the only attack that is feasible for a server is partitioning the client set and *forking* the execution.

We prove in the full version [10] that the protocol achieves fork linearizability if the signature scheme and the ADT are secure. On a high level, we first perform game hops in which we idealize the guarantees of the signature scheme and the ADT used by protocol LS. We then show that the history $\sigma$ produced with idealized cryptography is fork-linearizable.

**Theorem 1.** *The protocol described above emulates the abortable type $F'$ on a Byzantine server with fork linearizability. Furthermore, if the server is correct, then all histories of the protocol are linearizable w.r.t. $F$.*

**Acknowledgments.** This work has been supported in part by the European Commission through the Horizon 2020 Framework Programme (H2020-ICT-2014-1) under grant agreements 644371 WITDOM and 644579 ESCUDO-CLOUD and in part by the Swiss State Secretariat for Education, Research and Innovation (SERI) under contracts 15.0098 and 15.0087. The work by Esha Ghosh was supported in part by NSF grant CNS-1525044.

# References

1. Aguilera, M.K., Frölund, S., Hadzilacos, V., Horn, S.L., Toueg, S.: Abortable and query-abortable objects and their efficient implementation. In: ACM PODC, pp. 23–32 (2007)
2. Anagnostopoulos, A., Goodrich, M.T., Tamassia, R.: Persistent authenticated dictionaries and their applications. In: Davida, G.I., Frankel, Y. (eds.) ISC 2001. LNCS, vol. 2200, pp. 379–393. Springer, Heidelberg (2001). https://doi.org/10.1007/3-540-45439-X_26
3. Attiya, H., Welch, J.: Distributed Computing: Fundamentals, Simulations and Advanced Topics, 2nd edn. Wiley, Hoboken (2004)

4. Backes, M., Fiore, D., Reischuk, R.M.: Verifiable delegation of computation on outsourced data. In: ACM CCS, pp. 863–874 (2013)
5. Bellare, M., Rogaway, P.: The security of triple encryption and a framework for code-based game-playing proofs. In: Vaudenay, S. (ed.) EUROCRYPT 2006. LNCS, vol. 4004, pp. 409–426. Springer, Heidelberg (2006). https://doi.org/10.1007/11761679_25
6. Ben-Sasson, E., Chiesa, A., Genkin, D., Tromer, E., Virza, M.: SNARKs for C: verifying program executions succinctly and in zero knowledge. In: Canetti, R., Garay, J.A. (eds.) CRYPTO 2013. LNCS, vol. 8043, pp. 90–108. Springer, Heidelberg (2013). https://doi.org/10.1007/978-3-642-40084-1_6
7. Benabbas, S., Gennaro, R., Vahlis, Y.: Verifiable delegation of computation over large datasets. In: Rogaway, P. (ed.) CRYPTO 2011. LNCS, vol. 6841, pp. 111–131. Springer, Heidelberg (2011). https://doi.org/10.1007/978-3-642-22792-9_7
8. Brandenburger, M., Cachin, C., Knežević, N.: Don't trust the cloud, verify: integrity and consistency for cloud object stores. ACM TOPS **20**(3), 8:1–8:30 (2017)
9. Braun, B., Feldman, A.J., Ren, Z., Setty, S.T.V., Blumberg, A.J., Walfish, M.: Verifying computations with state. In: SOSP, pp. 341–357. ACM (2013)
10. Cachin, C., Ghosh, E., Papadopoulos, D., Tackmann, B.: Stateful multi-client verifiable computation. Cryptology ePrint Archive, Report 2017/901 (2017)
11. Cachin, C., Keidar, I., Shraer, A.: Fork sequential consistency is blocking. Inf. Process. Lett. **109**(7), 360–364 (2009)
12. Cachin, C., Ohrimenko, O.: Verifying the consistency of remote untrusted services with commutative operations. In: Aguilera, M.K., Querzoni, L., Shapiro, M. (eds.) OPODIS 2014. LNCS, vol. 8878, pp. 1–16. Springer, Cham (2014). https://doi.org/10.1007/978-3-319-14472-6_1
13. Cachin, C., Shelat, A., Shraer, A.: Efficient fork-linearizable access to untrusted shared memory. In: ACM PODC, pp. 129–138. ACM (2007)
14. Canetti, R., Paneth, O., Papadopoulos, D., Triandopoulos, N.: Verifiable set operations over outsourced databases. In: Krawczyk, H. (ed.) PKC 2014. LNCS, vol. 8383, pp. 113–130. Springer, Heidelberg (2014). https://doi.org/10.1007/978-3-642-54631-0_7
15. Choi, S.G., Katz, J., Kumaresan, R., Cid, C.: Multi-client non-interactive verifiable computation. In: Sahai, A. (ed.) TCC 2013. LNCS, vol. 7785, pp. 499–518. Springer, Heidelberg (2013). https://doi.org/10.1007/978-3-642-36594-2_28
16. Costello, C., Fournet, C., Howell, J., Kohlweiss, M., Kreuter, B., Naehrig, M., Parno, B., Zahur, S.: Geppetto: versatile verifiable computation. In: IEEE S&P. IEEE (2015)
17. Fiore, D., Fournet, C., Ghosh, E., Kohlweiss, M., Ohrimenko, O., Parno, B.: Hash first, argue later: adaptive verifiable computations on outsourced data. In: ACM CCS, pp. 1304–1316. ACM (2016)
18. Fiore, D., Gennaro, R.: Publicly verifiable delegation of large polynomials and matrix computations, with applications. In: ACM CCS, pp. 501–512 (2012)
19. Fiore, D., Mitrokotsa, A., Nizzardo, L., Pagnin, E.: Multi-key homomorphic authenticators. In: Cheon, J.H., Takagi, T. (eds.) ASIACRYPT 2016. LNCS, vol. 10032, pp. 499–530. Springer, Heidelberg (2016). https://doi.org/10.1007/978-3-662-53890-6_17
20. Gennaro, R., Gentry, C., Parno, B.: Non-interactive verifiable computing: outsourcing computation to untrusted workers. In: Rabin, T. (ed.) CRYPTO 2010. LNCS, vol. 6223, pp. 465–482. Springer, Heidelberg (2010). https://doi.org/10.1007/978-3-642-14623-7_25

21. Gennaro, R., Gentry, C., Parno, B., Raykova, M.: Quadratic span programs and succinct NIZKs without PCPs. In: Johansson, T., Nguyen, P.Q. (eds.) EUROCRYPT 2013. LNCS, vol. 7881, pp. 626–645. Springer, Heidelberg (2013). https://doi.org/10.1007/978-3-642-38348-9_37

22. Ghosh, E., Goodrich, M.T., Ohrimenko, O., Tamassia, R.: Verifiable zero-knowledge order queries and updates for fully dynamic lists and trees. In: Zikas, V., De Prisco, R. (eds.) SCN 2016. LNCS, vol. 9841, pp. 216–236. Springer, Cham (2016). https://doi.org/10.1007/978-3-319-44618-9_12

23. Goodrich, M.T., Papamanthou, C., Tamassia, R.: On the cost of persistence and authentication in skip lists. In: Demetrescu, C. (ed.) WEA 2007. LNCS, vol. 4525, pp. 94–107. Springer, Heidelberg (2007). https://doi.org/10.1007/978-3-540-72845-0_8

24. Goodrich, M.T., Tamassia, R., Schwerin, A.: Implementation of an authenticated dictionary with skip lists and commutative hashing. In: DISCEX (2001)

25. Goodrich, M.T., Tamassia, R., Triandopoulos, N.: Efficient authenticated data structures for graph connectivity and geometric search problems. Algorithmica 60(3), 505–552 (2011)

26. Gordon, S.D., Katz, J., Liu, F.-H., Shi, E., Zhou, H.-S.: Multi-client verifiable computation with stronger security guarantees. In: Dodis, Y., Nielsen, J.B. (eds.) TCC 2015. LNCS, vol. 9015, pp. 144–168. Springer, Heidelberg (2015). https://doi.org/10.1007/978-3-662-46497-7_6

27. Herlihy, M.P., Wing, J.M.: Linearizability: a correctness condition for concurrent objects. ACM Trans. Program. Lang. Syst. 12(3), 463–492 (1990)

28. Li, J., Krohn, M., Mazières, D., Shasha, D.: Secure untrusted data repository (SUNDR). In: USENIX, p. 9. USENIX Association (2004)

29. López-Alt, A., Tromer, E., Vaikuntanathan, V.: On-the-fly multiparty computation on the cloud via multikey fully homomorphic encryption. In: STOC (2012)

30. Majuntke, M., Dobre, D., Serafini, M., Suri, N.: Abortable fork-linearizable storage. In: Abdelzaher, T., Raynal, M., Santoro, N. (eds.) OPODIS 2009. LNCS, vol. 5923, pp. 255–269. Springer, Heidelberg (2009). https://doi.org/10.1007/978-3-642-10877-8_21

31. Martel, C., Nuckolls, G., Devanbu, P., Gertz, M., Kwong, A., Stubblebine, S.G.: A general model for authenticated data structures. Algorithmica 39, 21–41 (2004)

32. Mattern, F.: Virtual time and global states of distributed systems. In: Cosnard, M. (ed.) Proceedings of the Workshop on Parallel and Distributed Algorithms, pp. 215–226 (1988)

33. Mazières, D., Shasha, D.: Building secure file systems out of Byzantine storage. In: ACM PODC, pp. 108–117. ACM (2002)

34. Merkle, R.C.: A certified digital signature. In: Brassard, G. (ed.) CRYPTO 1989. LNCS, vol. 435, pp. 218–238. Springer, New York (1990). https://doi.org/10.1007/0-387-34805-0_21

35. Mykletun, E., Narasimha, M., Tsudik, G.: Authentication and integrity in out-sourced databases. TOS 2(2), 107–138 (2006)

36. Naor, M., Nissim, K.: Certificate revocation and certificate update. IEEE J. Sel. Areas Commun. 18(4), 561–570 (2000)

37. Papadopoulos, D., Papadopoulos, S., Triandopoulos, N.: Taking authenticated range queries to arbitrary dimensions. In: ACM CCS, pp. 819–830 (2014)

38. Papamanthou, C.: Cryptography for efficiency: new directions in authenticated data structures. Ph.D. thesis, Brown University (2011)

39. Papamanthou, C., Tamassia, R., Triandopoulos, N.: Authenticated hash tables. In: ACM CCS. pp. 437–448. ACM (2008)

40. Papamanthou, C., Tamassia, R., Triandopoulos, N.: Optimal verification of operations on dynamic sets. In: Rogaway, P. (ed.) CRYPTO 2011. LNCS, vol. 6841, pp. 91–110. Springer, Heidelberg (2011). https://doi.org/10.1007/978-3-642-22792-9_6
41. Parno, B., Howell, J., Gentry, C., Raykova, M.: Pinocchio: nearly practical verifiable computation. In: 2013 IEEE Symposium on Security and Privacy (SP) (2013)
42. Tamassia, R.: Authenticated data structures. In: Di Battista, G., Zwick, U. (eds.) ESA 2003. LNCS, vol. 2832, pp. 2–5. Springer, Heidelberg (2003). https://doi.org/10.1007/978-3-540-39658-1_2
43. Wahby, R.S., Setty, S.T.V., Ren, Z., Blumberg, A.J., Walfish, M.: Efficient RAM and control flow in verifiable outsourced computation. In: NDSS (2015)
44. Williams, P., Sion, R., Shasha, D.: The blind stone tablet: outsourcing durability to untrusted parties. In: NDSS (2009)
45. Zhang, Y., Katz, J., Papamanthou, C.: IntegriDB: verifiable SQL for outsourced databases. In: ACM CCS, pp. 1480–1491 (2015)

# VeriCount: Verifiable Resource Accounting Using Hardware and Software Isolation

Shruti Tople[1(✉)], Soyeon Park[2], Min Suk Kang[1], and Prateek Saxena[1]

[1] National University of Singapore, Singapore, Singapore
{shruti90,kangms,prateeks}@comp.nus.edu.sg
[2] Georgia Tech, Atlanta, Georgia
spark720@gatech.edu

**Abstract.** In cloud computing, where clients are billed based on the consumed resources for outsourced tasks, both the cloud providers and the clients have the incentive to manipulate claims about resource usage. Both desire an accurate and verifiable resource accounting system, which is neutral and can be trusted to refute any disputes. In this work, we present VeriCount—a verifiable resource accounting system coupled with refutable billing support for Linux container-based applications. To protect VeriCount logic, we propose a novel approach called *self-accounting* that combines hardware-based isolation guarantees from trusted computing mechanisms and software fault isolation techniques. The self-accounting engine in VeriCount leverages security features present in trusted computing solutions, such as Intel SGX, to measure user CPU time, memory, I/O bytes and network bandwidth while simultaneously detecting resource usage inflation attacks. We claim three main results. First, VeriCount incurs an average performance overhead of 3.62% and 16.03% over non-accounting but SGX-compatible applications in hardware and simulation mode respectively. Next, it contributes only an additional 542 lines of code to the trusted computing base. Lastly, it generates highly accurate, fine-grained resource accounting, with no discernible difference to the resource measuring tool available with the OS.

## 1 Introduction

*Verifiable resource accounting* is a security primitive that checks whether the measured resource accounting (e.g., CPU cycles, memory, network bandwidth, or I/O resources) of cloud computing infrastructure is accurate for an outsourced computing task. In today's "pay-as-you-use" model of cloud computing, where clients are billed based on the usage of the computing resources, verifiable resource accounting is increasingly desirable [12]. As the accounting result determines the final bill, both a cloud provider and a client have strong motivation to manipulate the results in favor of their economic interests; e.g., cloud providers

---

S. Park—Research done when visiting National University of Singapore.

B. Preneel and F. Vercauteren (Eds.): ACNS 2018, LNCS 10892, pp. 657–677, 2018.
https://doi.org/10.1007/978-3-319-93387-0_34

overcharge clients or clients try to be undercharged. This demands for a *refutable* billing system where denying charges is possible based on a decision from a neutral backdrop. In the last decade, serious concerns have been raised about the billing problem in an untrusted cloud model [12,15,26,34]. Several attacks such as mis-attribution of resources, false accounting, tampering execution to increase resource utilization have been demonstrated in presence of a malicious operating system (OS) [22,31,32,38]. This is particularly hazardous for widely accepted container-based virtualization techniques, such as Docker [3] where resources are shared at finer granularity than virtual machines and thus accurate accounting is more challenging. Worse yet, even cloud providers seem to be struggling to implement accurate fine grained accounting and safe billing systems. Research has shown bugs in EC2 that lead to free CPU time and over-charging for storage in Rackspace [18]. Given the indisputable necessity of fairness in billing, we ask *whether it is to build a refutable billing system for cloud computing that allows significant security assurance?*

Currently, many OSes offer resource accounting features (e.g., `cgroups`); yet, such OS-based resource accounting mechanisms in commercial clouds (e.g., Amazon EC2 [2]) are not ideal due to their large TCB and attack surface. We discuss a class of attacks called *resource usage inflation* that a malicious OS can perpetrate to overcharge clients in Sect. 3.1. Research has demonstrated isolating resource accounting from the untrusted OS [13,28]. In particular, Alibi [13] utilizes nested virtualization and Trusted Platform Modules (TPMs) to implement an observer placed at the hypervisor layer. However, Alibi includes a huge TCB (entire Linux kernel and KVM) for accounting. In this paper, we present VERICOUNT, a verifiable resource accounting system that accounts for four major computing resources used for executing outsourced computing tasks within secure containers (e.g., [10,17,30]). These containers ensure secure execution of applications assuming trusted computing solutions. VERICOUNT guarantees untampered resource accounting operations while allowing the clients and the cloud providers to explicitly establish a pre-agreed policy (e.g., maximum recoveries from crashes) for the execution and reports any violation of the policy. This eventually enables a *refutable billing* model which is a desirable feature in today's cloud computing.

At its core, VERICOUNT aims to implement strong isolation of the resource accounting logic from *both* the underlying OS and the client-submitted applications. However, it is challenging because the accounting logic is easily dependent either on the OS or the client applications based on where it is placed in the system. In VERICOUNT, we address this system dependency problem by combining both *hardware and software isolation* techniques. We isolate the OS and other privilege code using hardware isolation supported by trusted computing mechanisms (such as Intel SGX [1]), and implement sandboxing mechanisms for untrusted client applications. First, we show that a novel system architecture, which we call *self-accounting*, coupled with an execution policy enforcement provides strong independence of VERICOUNT's accounting logic from the underlying OS. Self-accounting lets the client application perform its own resource accounting efficiently *within* the same isolated memory region during its execution and thereby identify false accounting. Second, to ensure that the accounting logic is independent of untrusted client applications, VERICOUNT sandboxes the client-code using software fault isolation [14,19,24,33]. A second challenge is to design an efficient yet accurate self-accounting approach. Basic approach of generating huge execution logs at runtime and verifying them later are expensive in terms of performance and verification effort [16]. To address this, we investigate an alternate way to effectively detect attacks that manipulate resource usage. We explore several trusted features that recent SGX-enabled CPUs support and leverage them to design accurate resource accounting system. Our solution exhibits desirable properties such as low performance overhead, low verification effort and a small trusted computing base (TCB).

**System and Results.** We build a proof-of-concept implementation for our design and evaluate it on SPEC CPUINT 2006 Benchmarks and H2O web server. Our prototype adds 542 source lines of code (SLoC) to the TCB and is simple enough to be formally verified later. We observe that VERICOUNT-enabled applications incur an average performance overhead of **3.62%** and **16.03%** as compared to non-accounting SGX applications in hardware and simulation mode respectively.

**Contributions.** We outline our main contribution below:

– *Self-Accounting* - Our novel approach of self-accounting lets each application account for its own resources, while employing hardware and software isolation.
– VERICOUNT *System* - VERICOUNT system consists of a compiler, a static verifier and a post-execution analyzer to guarantee verifiable accounting and refutable billing.
– *Evaluation* - We evaluate our prototype of VERICOUNT for performance overhead and accuracy of SPEC CPUINT 2006 Benchmarks and H2O web-server.

## 2    Problem Definition

Hosting containerized (docker-based) applications on the cloud is gaining popularity. Securing such applications is shown to be possible using trusted computing mechanism [10]. In this work, we support an additional primitive of verifiable resource accounting.

### 2.1    Threat Model

Our is the first work to consider two different adversary models simultaneously: a malicious cloud provider and a malicious client. Both adversaries have strong motivation to manipulate the resource accounting information in favor of their economic interests. A malicious provider receives a task of executing an application $A$ from a client and aims to manipulate the resource usage summary $R_A$, to *increase* the final bill $\mathcal{B}_A$ of the task; i.e., overcharging the client. We consider that the malicious provider has full control over the operating system (OS), which allows the attacker to access any system resource that the OS controls and break any security mechanism that rely on it (e.g., process isolation, access control in reference monitor, shown in Sect. 3.1). At the same time, a malicious client aims to manipulate the resource usage summary $R_A$ to *decrease* the bill $\mathcal{B}_A$; i.e., being undercharged. We consider that the malicious client has full control over the application code that are submitted for the outsourced computation. Both the provider and the client must trust VERICOUNT components and SGX.

**Scope.** We consider that the two adversaries would not collude, as they have contradictory goals. Moreover, the execution of $A$ is strictly constrained to the input provided by the client. This restriction is necessary for verifiable accounting since it is in general impossible to define the notion of correct resource accounting between a client and a provider when applications expect to run with arbitrary inputs due to the undecidable problem. We do not consider denial-of-service attacks caused by arbitrary inputs to the application $A$; i.e., VERICOUNT does not detect resource usage manipulation if the cloud provider can generate valid inputs to the application.

### 2.2    Problem Statement

Verifiable resource accounting has three protocol steps between a client and a provider. First, a client and a provider agree on an *execution policy* $\phi = (\mathsf{p}, \mathsf{c}, \mathsf{t})$, where $\phi$ is a tuple of three parameters: a per-resource pricing scheme ($\mathsf{p}$), a crash recovery limit ($\mathsf{c}$), and the maximum OS response time ($\mathsf{t}$). The per-resource pricing scheme $\mathsf{p}$ includes the unit price for CPU, memory, I/O operations and network bandwidth usage. The crash recovery limit $\mathsf{c}$ is an integer number that permits the cloud provider to recover a crashed instance without informing the client. The maximum OS response time $\mathsf{t}$ is the time that an OS requires to respond to a service request from the application. Second, the client sends an application $A$ along with an authenticated input $I$ for the execution.

After the provider executes $A$, the accounting logic generates the resource usage summary $R_A$ and the final bill $\mathcal{B}_A$ and sends them to the client for verification. $\mathcal{B}_A$ is calculated with the knowledge of $R_A$ and $\phi$. We seek the following security properties.

(a) **Isolation from compromised OS.** A compromised OS cannot interfere with the resource accounting operation for any client-submitted application.
(b) **Isolation from malicious client application.** A maliciously generated client application cannot tamper with the resource accounting information.
(c) **Verifiable execution policy.** At the end of outsourced computation, a client and a provider can efficiently check any violation of the pre-agreed execution policy; i.e., confirm whether $\mathcal{B}_A \leftarrow (\phi, R_A)$.

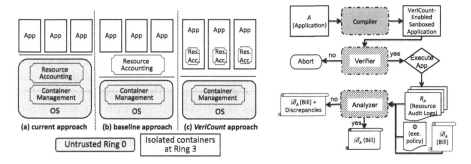

**Fig. 1.** Three isolation approaches: (a) current approach, (b) baseline approach, and (c) VERICOUNT approach. The shaded region is untrusted components and non-shaded is isolated container.

**Fig. 2.** Workflow of VERICOUNT system. The verifier and the analyzer (hatched) are trusted whereas the compiler (shaded) is untrusted.

Moreover, our verifiable resource accounting offers three desirable properties:

(1) *Low performance overhead.* A VERICOUNT-enabled application should incur low performance overhead. The advantage of verifiable resource utilization should not unacceptably slow down as compared to the original application.

(2) *Low verification overhead.* Verifying resource utilization should not require a client or a cloud provider to spend large resources for either repeating the outsourced execution or accessing huge logs of execution process [16]. This is critical for clients who outsource their computations to a remote cloud due to their insufficient local resources.

(3) *Small TCB.* The solution should have small trusted software base, beyond that is implied by use of SGX, to avoid bugs that are present in large software.

**Assumptions.** We assume cloud providers support SGX-enabled CPUs and SGX guarantees are preserved throughout the execution lifetime. We assume that all hardware chip-sets are not malicious and do not contain backdoor that would violate the isolation properties of our verifiable resource accounting [37]. We assume no side-channels in the hardware architecture of the cloud provider. Attacks exploiting side-channels are outside the scope of the present work [20, 27, 29, 35].

## 3   Baseline Approaches and Attacks

Previous solutions have proposed using an external observer for resource accounting [13]. We discuss a baseline with a similar approach and discuss attacks on it.

**Baseline Solution.** A straightforward approach for verifiable resource accounting is to isolate the resource accounting engine from the underlying OS. Figure 1(b) shows the design of such a baseline approach. One can use any trusted computing mechanism such as TPM or Intel SGX and port the resource accounting engine to a secure container using an existing system [10,30]. Compared to the existing resource accounting architecture in Fig. 1(a), where the accounting engine resides in the underlying OS, the accounting engine in Fig. 1(b) is isolated and acts as an external observer and accounts the resource utilization for each secure containerized application. Compromising the OS and gaining privilege access does not enable the attacker to directly tamper with the accounting information. This baseline solution ensures accurate attribution of resource utilization as it eliminates any direct method of attacking the accounting system. However, we show that there still exists indirect dependency, which we call the execution dependency, on the underlying OS. The adversary can easily influence the execution operations to inflate the resource consumption.

### 3.1 Resource Usage Inflation Attacks

Although the baseline places the accounting engine within a secure container, the adversary can increase the resource usage of containers in the absence of support for refuting spurious charges. We discuss these resource usage inflation (RUI) attacks below.

**Invoking Multiple Container Instances.** The underlying OS is responsible for launching the container with the application on request from a client. Although the client requests to launch a single instance of the application, the OS can execute multiple instances of the same container. This results in inflated resource consumption corresponding to client's container. The accounting system incorrectly attributes the resources utilized by the unrequested instances to the client. In the absence of verifiable accounting, the client and the cloud provider have no way to refute disputed claims.

**Replaying Inputs.** The OS can replay the given input and increase the utilization of resources for the particular container. Note that the adversary cannot generate new set of valid inputs and hence is limited to replaying existing inputs arbitrary number of times. This inflates the resource consumption causing overcharging.

**Arbitrary Halts.** The application may experience unexpected crashes during its execution and the client is supposed to be informed about it so that she can request for starting a new execution. The malicious OS can exploit this property to silently crash an instance and restart it arbitrary number of times. The OS can forcefully halt the execution of the container before completion. The accounting engine being unaware of the malicious OS intention accounts the resources utilized for all the crashed instances and bills the client for the inflated resource usage.

**Slowing Down OS Service.** The application depends on the OS for several services like system calls, interrupts and others. If the user is charged based on the total time that the container is up and running then the OS may maliciously delay to execute the requested service. Thus, increasing the amount of time utilized by the particular container [22].

## 3.2    Towards Self-accounting

All these RUI attacks demonstrate that the malicious OS has several ways to increase resource consumption even when the accounting engine is isolated as shown in Fig. 1(b). Note that the baseline approach places the accounting engine outside every application and thus cannot detect such malicious execution strategies by the OS. One can consider establishing inter-container communication channels between applications and the isolated accounting engine to address the RUI attacks; e.g., every I/O operation, user-kernel context switch or network usage is performed via the isolated resource accounting engine. Such an approach would incur prohibitively large overhead due to continuous IPC involved. Thus, we propose a novel *self-accounting* approach where each accounting engine runs alongside the client application within the container as shown in Fig. 1(c). That is, the accounting engine is tied with the atomic execution unit, which is the application itself, removing the execution dependency on the OS. The operation of the accounting engine is always executed with its application and thus the malicious execution strategies presented above cannot be effective. Thus, shifting the accounting engine from Ring $O$ to Ring 3 removes the execution dependency from the OS and provides protection against an adversary perpetrating RUI attacks.

**Client-Code Dependency Attacks.** The self accounting design choice, however, creates another system dependency, which we call the client-code dependency. It makes the trusted accounting logic susceptible to attacks from a malicious client trying to undercharge itself. First, the client may not use the prescribed procedure for enabling verifiable resource accounting and hence result in undercharging. Second, the client can embed subtle vulnerabilities to exploit during runtime and tamper the accounting engine data. Since the accounting engine and client-code share the same memory space (see Fig. 1(c)), the malicious application can tamper the accounting data to decrease its resource consumption. This demands isolating the accounting engine from client's application as well. To protect against dynamic attacks during runtime, we sandbox the untrusted application (explained in detail in Sect. 5.2). To address the compile-time threat, we statically verify the correctness of the client application.

## 3.3    Basic Self-accounting Approach

One way to realize the self-accounting approach is to let the accounting engine log sufficient information related to each run of the application. First, to prevent execution replays or invocation of multiple instances, the accounting engine calculates and records a measurement or hash of the executing application before initiating its execution. Note that same application generates same measurement every time. Thus observing the frequency with which the same measurement appears in the resource consumption logs lets us detect execution replays. Next, to detect spurious executions due to input replay, the accounting engine records the hash of all the inputs of the application. Observing all the records of hashed inputs along with the application measurement helps in detecting executions with replayed inputs. Further, to detect arbitrary crashes, the logs are generated on the fly throughout the execution. Any arbitrary crash results in partial records of the hashed inputs. Presence of such partial records in resource logs lets us detect whether the same application is halted more than the pre-agreed crash recovery limit. A simple post-execution analyzer running in trusted environment either at the client or cloud provider side can perform analysis of these logs and detect the occurrence of RUI attacks [16]. The post-execution analyzer can further generate valid bill based on legitimate resource utilization and pre-agreed policy.

**Inefficiency.** Although the above basic solution detects RUI attacks, it demands continuous hashing and logging operations, thus making it highly inefficient. The accounting engine computes a hash of every input and invokes a system call to write it to the resource consumption logs. The accounting engine easily becomes a bottleneck for the executing application and incurs a non-negligible performance overhead. Our experimental evaluation confirm that performance overhead of an application is directly proportional to the number of system calls performed during its execution (see Sect. 6.1). Moreover, it generates huge logs that need to be processed at either the client or the cloud provider. This violates our desirable property of low verification overhead. In this work, we investigate the problem of designing a significantly more efficient verifiable accounting system than the basic approach. To this end, we advocate the novel use of SGX features to design an efficient solution thwarting RUI attacks.

## 4   Our Design

VERICOUNT comprises of three components: a compiler, a static verifier, and a post-execution analyzer. Figure 2 shows the workflow of our VERICOUNT system. The hatched components (verifier and analyzer) run in an untampered environment.

### 4.1   Overview

**Compiler.** VERICOUNT provides its own compiler that transforms client's application to support resource accounting based on our accounting library that executes with the application. The compiler inserts APIs in the application to invoke the accounting engine. This VERICOUNT-enabled application generates encrypted and integrity-protected resource consumption logs at the end of the execution. To eliminate client-code dependency and isolate the accounting engine from the client's application, VERICOUNT compiler sandboxes the application and protects the accounting engine data. Further, to remove trust from the underlying OS, the transformed application executes in a trusted execution environment in the cloud. Note that the compiler itself is executed in a potentially-malicious (thus *untrusted*) client platform.

**Static Verifier.** Clients may not use prescribed compiler with the intention to reduce charges. To detect against such static compile-time misbehavior, the verifier runs in a trusted environment and lets the cloud provider validate the correctness of the client-submitted, transformed application. On successful verification, the provider launches the application; otherwise, the execution is aborted. It verifies these properties:

(a) *Correctness* - The VERICOUNT-enabled application has all the API calls to the accounting engine at appropriate interfaces in the application.
(b) *Safety* - The application code does not access the memory region of the accounting engine; i.e., it verifies the sandboxing of the application code.
(c) *Integrity* - It verifies the accounting engine integrity embedded in the application.

**Post-Execution Analyzer.** The trusted post-execution analyzer takes the resource consumption logs, pre-agreed execution policy $\phi = (\mathsf{p}, \mathsf{c}, \mathsf{t})$, and the cloud provider generated bill $\mathcal{B}_A$ as inputs and verifies whether the bill $\mathcal{B}_A$ adheres to the execution policy $\phi$. The analyzer outputs a *yes* if the bill correctly reflects the resource consumption as per $\phi$. Otherwise, it outputs *no* along with a discrepancy report in the bill.

## 4.2   Background on SGX

Intel SGX supports creating hardware isolated execution environment called enclaves that execute at Ring 3. Such execution is termed as *enclaved-execution*. Enclave code and data pages reside in a hardware protected memory region during execution called Enclaved Page Cache (EPC). The hardware protects a compromised OS or any other process from tampering pages in EPC. For more details, readers can refer to Intel SGX Manual [1]. SGX introduces OCALLs to call functions that reside outside the enclave from within an enclave and ECALLs for vice versa. Hence, to invoke OS services, existing system perform OCALLs to access filesystem, network and I/O services [30]. We describe the important primitives supported in the SGX platform.

(1) *Remote attestation* - SGX allows to attest enclave code such that any remote entity can verify the integrity of the code and authenticity of the executing hardware.
(2) *True random number* - In SGX, the use of rand and srand functions in the C/C++ library within an enclave is disabled as these are susceptible to bias. Instead, SGX supports sgx_read_rand API that generates a true random number using the RDRAND instruction directly from the hardware and returns it to the enclave.
(3) *Monotonic counter* - SGX supports creating a limited number of monotonic counters (MC) for each enclave. Monotonic counters are shared among enclaves that have the same code. On creating a MC, it gets written to the non-volatile memory in the platform. The sgx_create_monotonic_counter returns a UUID and a value.
(4) *Trusted elapsed time* - The function call to sgx_get_trusted_time returns the current time from a reference point. The difference between the returned time of two calls gives the trusted elapsed time between two events from the same reference point.

### 4.3    Protection Against Malicious Provider

**Self-Accounting.** VERICOUNT places the resource accounting engine along-side a secure enclaved application that guarantees tamper-resistant accounting of resources used within the enclave against a compromised OS. Self-accounting enables fine-grained accounting of resources utilized during the application execution. Moreover, it offers transparent method to report to clients about exact operations and executions invoked by the underlying OS. Along with enclaved execution, remote attestation allows client to verify correct execution of their application on the cloud provider's platform. Enclaved execution combined with remote-attestation enables VERICOUNT to move the accounting engine from Ring 0 to Ring 3.

**Preventing Replay Attacks.** After remote attestation of enclaved application, the client establishes a secure channel with the enclave to provision encrypted and integrity protected inputs [1,10]. To prevent replays, instead of hashing and logging every input to the application, we utilize the support for creating monotonic counters and true random number in SGX. In VERICOUNT system, the accounting engine registers a UUID corresponding to a monotonic counter using `sgx_create_monotonic_counter` API for the application. This UUID is sent to the client over the secure channel and acts as a hardware identity of the enclave. If the client legitimately wants to create multiple instances of the same enclaved application, she requests for multiple UUIDs. VERICOUNT appends these UUIDs and there value in the final bill, thereby allowing the client to validate the resource consumption details. Since the UUID is accessible only from within the enclave and is securely transferred to the client, an adversary cannot learn this value. Moreover, since all enclaves with the same measurement share common set of monotonic counters on same machine, different instances of the same application cannot have the same UUID. Therefore, invocation of an unrequested application instance results in a new UUID which is unknown to the client. Thus, the client can match the registered UUID of its application enclave with the UUID present in the final bill to detect execution replay attacks. As monotonic counters are written to non-volatile memory, they provide rollback protection from platform reboots as well. VERICOUNT can benefit from any additional security from recent solutions (e.g., ROTE [23]), however, we do not encapsulate them in our current design. Along with the UUID, the enclaved container uses the trusted randomness primitive to generate a random nonce corresponding to this enclave. This random nonce is sent to the client along with the UUID. To ensure the freshness of data, the client is enforced to append this random nonce to every authenticated-and-encrypted input data. To legitimately send multiple copies of the same input, the client increments the random nonce each time and appends with the input. Since this random value is generated from hardware and kept secret, the adversary cannot learn it. This prevents the attacker from generating copies of the input to inflate resource usage.

**Preventing Arbitrary-Halt Attacks.** Every time the enclave halts or exits, the accounting engine seals the monotonic counter UUID and value using sgx_seal_data [1]. On invoking the enclave instance again, it unseals the monotonic counter UUID and value using sgx_unseal_data and verifies the value using sgx_read_monotonic_counter. On successful verification, it increments the value using sgx_increment_monotonic_counter. Thus, if the adversary tries to arbitrarily halt and restart the execution to inflate resource usage, the counter corresponding to the UUID value increases and the final value is reported in the bill. Based on the monotonic counter value, the client can detect whether the application is invoked for more than the requested number of executions. The c value in $\phi$ specifies an upper bound for recovery of crashed instances allowed to the provider. This also applies to crashes that occur due to bugs in client's application and are required to be restarted legitimately. The policy agreement between the client and cloud provider captures both these cases. Thus, the use of monotonic counters helps in designing a simple solution and brings transparency with respect to the enclave invocations. Note that a forced system shutdown that does not allow a clean enclave exit results in an incomplete resource log. Such incomplete logs allows us to detect if an enclave process is killed arbitrarily.

**Detecting Slow-OS Attacks.** A malicious OS can slowdown the kernel mode of operation to overcharge clients. VERICOUNT enables fine grained accounting by measuring the CPU time spent in an enclave and outside the enclave separately. The sgx_get_trusted_time API is invoked just before switching from enclave to non-enclave mode and when it switches back. Hence, we support specifying an upper bound for time spent outside the enclave necessary for replying to any system level request from the user. If the OS exceeds this time, then it indicates that the adversary intentionally delays the response to increase the total time and thereby overcharging client. In VERICOUNT, we use t value in $\phi$ as the upper bound for delay in OS response for all system calls. Ideally, the billing model should charge the container for only CPU time within an enclave and provide a fixed charge for OS services. VERICOUNT supports both these models and can be decided in the execution policy between a client and a cloud provider.

### 4.4    Protection Against Malicious Client

Self-accounting allows a client-submitted application to run in the same enclave and thus the client application may overwrite the accounting engine's data at runtime. To remove this client-code runtime dependency, VERICOUNT compiler sandboxes the application from the trusted accounting engine. Worse yet, a client may not use the prescribed protection mechanism or modify the compiler to ignore the sandboxing and API insertion logic entirely. The client's code may exclude executing APIs which invoke the resource accounting engine. There are three possible approaches to address this: (1) To enforce the clients to submit their source codes and compile them in a trusted environment; (2) To assume all the clients are equipped with a hardware-based trusted execution environment (e.g., SGX) to compile their applications in their local machine; and (3) To statically verify the client-compiled, sandboxed applications in a trusted environment at the cloud provider. Although all these approaches are technically feasible, we choose the third approach as the former two approaches impose too strong requirements for the clients in practice. VERICOUNT's trusted static verifier checks that the client-application satisfies a set of rules correctly to perform accurate resource accounting. The static verifier is responsible for ensuring correct sandboxing of unsafe instructions, appropriate API insertion and integrity of accounting engine. The cloud provider rejects the execution of the application if the verifier fails.

### 4.5   Measuring Resources

**CPU Elapsed Time.** The billing metric for CPU differ for every cloud provider. While Amazon EC2 charges in hours, Google Compute Engine is moving towards a more granular accounting and charges per minute. VERICOUNT measures the time at the fine granularity of per second [2,4]. To perform fine-grained accounting at Ring 3, we use the trusted elapsed time feature of SGX hardware that supports calculating time with a precision of seconds. The accounting engine invokes sgx_get_trusted_time function on a switch from enclave mode to non-enclave mode and vice versa. Finally, before exiting the enclave, the engine records final value at the end of the execution. As per VERICOUNT design, the *user time* corresponds to the time spent for execution within the enclaved region. The execution time spend in untrusted region outside enclave at the user level and in the OS are accounted towards *service time*. We consider this as a valid design since a compromised OS can always tamper the execution of non-isolated application code executing outside the enclaved environment to delay the execution.

**Memory.** For SGX CPUs, BIOS allocates a certain region called processor reserved memory (PRM) of sizes of 32, 64 or 128 MB [1]. The underlying CPU reserves a part of this PRM as EPC memory. Enclave pages are loaded in EPC which is a hardware protected memory region. Thus, the billing of memory resource is restricted to the allowed physical memory region by SGX. VERICOUNT currently does not calculate the allocated memory from within the enclave. However, SGX2 instructions support reporting page faults to the enclave [25]. VERICOUNT can utilize this feature to correctly report the number of page faults during the execution of an application.

**Network Bandwidth.** Cloud providers charge bandwidth usage based on the amount of bytes transferred over the network. To calculate network bandwidth, VERICOUNT records the inputs and outputs from the enclave via network system calls. All the data that is sent over the network is accounted towards the bandwidth utilization for the application. As the accounting is performed within the enclave, it ensures that the bandwidth accounting is correctly attributed to the application and avoids mis-accounting.

**I/O Resources.** VERICOUNT records the I/O bytes that are read/written using system calls. Due to the restriction of SGX on direct invocation of system calls, applications use OCALLs to request I/O service from the underlying OS. A VERICOUNT-enabled application invokes the accounting engine to account the I/O bytes after every such OCALL. The engine considers only the actual data passed as arguments to these system calls. Hence, if the OS responds with fewer or more bytes than requested, VERICOUNT fairly charges for the actual I/O bytes read / written. This design guarantees that only the I/O operations made from within the enclave are accounted to the particular enclave.

# 5   Implementation

VERICOUNT consists of library, a compiler, a static verifier and a post-execution analyzer. It relies on existing proposals to port legacy applications to enclaves [10,30].

## 5.1   VERICOUNT Library

VERICOUNT library contains functions to compute resources utilized during application execution. It accounts for user and service time, I/O bytes, total I/O calls and network bandwidth. We implement the VERICOUNT accounting engine as a statically linkable C library libvericount.a. The application, accounting library and SGX libraries are linked together to create the trusted enclave file. The accounting library invokes the sgx_create_pse_session function to start the trusted platform service at the start of enclave execution. Once a session is started, the library invokes appropriate calls to the trusted runtime functions to get elapsed time and monotonic counter.

**API Insertion.** We implement our VERICOUNT compiler as a pass in LLVM v3.8.1. The compiler inserts APIs to invoke resource accounting logic in VERICOUNT library. At the entry of an Ecall function inside an enclave, it inserts vericount_init_user_time() which starts the counter for accounting user time. The compiler inserts vericount_init_service_time() before every Ocall from within the enclave which essentially stops the user time counter and starts the counter for service time. After return of every Ocall, vericount_end_service_time() API is inserted which stops the service time counter and starts the user time counter again. Finally, before end of every Ecall function in the enclaved application, the compiler inserts vericount_end_user_time() which calculates the final user time. All these APIs invoke the trusted time function to account for elapsed time and add them to corresponding counter value. For accounting I/O bytes and network bandwidth, the VERICOUNT compiler inserts vericount_io_bytes() and vericount_net_bytes() APIs after the return of every Ocall to libc function related to I/O such as fread, fwrite, fgets, fputs, and others and network, such as send, recv. The library accounts the total usage based on their arguments and return values.

**Output Logs.** A simple way to log resource consumption is to ensure every API invocation logs the usage to the output. However, this incurs overhead since a write operation requires an `Ocall` that performs context switch from trusted to untrusted region. Thus, in our implementation, we choose to begin accounting on enclave entry and write resource consumption logs only before the enclave executes the `EEXIT` instruction. The `vericount_init_user_time()` API logs the enclave UUID to the output file and marks the start of the accounting procedure and the `vericount_end_user_time()` API logs the accounted usage to the output. The total enclave memory required to hold the accounting information is as small as storing 4 counters (user_time, service_time, io_bytes and net_bytes). We enable a provision for cloud provider's to send a user signal to fetch the resource consumption logs on demand or at a timer expiration.

## 5.2 Sandboxing Within Enclaves

While sandboxing is not a new idea, implementing it in enclaves involves a number of non-trivial challenges. For e.g., enclaved applications have specific limitations about execution, such as no system calls making use of existing sandboxing tools impossible for enclaved applications [36]. Hence, we implement our sandbox logic compatible with Linux SGX SDK based on standard SFI techniques [19,33].

**Fault Domain Isolation.** We divide the enclave virtual address space into two regions: application memory and VERICOUNT memory. The VERICOUNT memory is the region that contains the code and data of the accounting library and SDK trusted libraries. The application memory is a shadow memory or SFI section that is created to confine the application's code and data. We use portable SFI techniques to implement the application memory [19]. We add our own `malloc` function alongside the `malloc` function in SDK to create a separate heap in SFI section for application variables. The VERICOUNT compiler instruments all `malloc` calls in the application to invoke our added `malloc` function. The library code continues to use the SDK `malloc` that allocates memory in the default section. We add sandboxing instructions to all unsafe instructions in the application memory as per standard SFI sandboxing rules [33].

**Static Verifier.** The VERICOUNTstatic verifier checks a set of rules in a disassembled executable of a VERICOUNT-enabled application to ensure its correctness, safety, and integrity before executing it. We include all standard SFI checks to ensure instruction safety, control flow and trusted memory protection against attacks that exploit indirect jumps, code-reuse attacks and others [14,24]. In addition, all call instructions to `sgx_ocall` are immediately followed by VERICOUNT APIs and there are no jump instructions between them. This ensures that the client-code cannot bypass the accounting logic when invoking an `Ocall`. Moreover, the call to `vericount_init_user_time()` and `vericount_init_end_time()` are the first and last instructions of every `Ecall` function in the enclave.

**Post-Execution Analyzer.** The post-execution analyzer executes within an enclave and takes the execution policy $\phi$, resource consumption logs, and the bill from the cloud provider. The post-execution analyzer first checks that every

UUID entry and its value is followed by resource consumption details in the output log. Next, the analyzer computes charges based on resource consumed and $\phi = (\mathbf{p}, \mathbf{c}, \mathbf{t})$ and compares it with the cloud provider's bill. The analyzer outputs the difference, if any, between VERICOUNT computed and cloud provider's bill. The enclaved post-execution analyzer cryptographically signs this final bill to be verified by the client. The client can refute provider's charges based on the output of VERICOUNT.

**TCB Size.** We measure the size of our TCB that includes the accounting engine, the verifier, the analyzer and trusted libraries from Intel SGX SDK using `CLOC` tool. The application code along with glibc libraries are not a part of our TCB. Our VERICOUNT compiler consists of 872 SLoC, which is outside of our TCB well. The accounting engine library consists of 230 lines of `C` code. The verifier and the analyzer contribute 180 and 132 SLoC respectively. Thus, VERICOUNT contributes only **542** SLoC to the total TCB beyond the trusted SDK libraries of 80 K SLoC. The total TCB is orders of magnitude smaller than any privileged software which consists of millions of LoC.

# 6    Evaluation

We evaluate our system on a Lenovo Thinkpad T460s with Ubuntu Desktop-14.04-LTS 64bits and Intel Core i7-6600U CPU running at 2.60 GHz × 4 with 4 MB cache and 12 GB of RAM. We use open source version of Intel SGX SDKv1.8 available for Linux systems [6]. We perform our evaluation with two goals (a) To evaluate the performance overhead of VERICOUNT application as compared to non-accounting secure (enclaved) applications (b) To evaluate the accuracy of VERICOUNT accounting engine.

**Selection of Benchmark.** To evaluate the effectiveness of VERICOUNT, we select standard SPEC CPUINT 2006 v1.2 benchmarks [9] and H2O web server which is an optimized HTTP server [5]. We do *not* claim contribution in porting our benchmarks to execute on SGX CPUs, which by itself is a hard problem [10,11,30]. At present, support for creating secure enclaved containers and the corresponding libraries is not available for public use. Hence, we use a recently proposed and open source Panoply system that supports executing legacy applications on SGX-enabled CPUs [8]. Yet, VERICOUNT system is general and compatible with any other enclaved execution system.

**Evaluation Methodology.** VERICOUNT system extends the guarantees of enclaved applications to support verifiable accounting. We use enclaved application executed using Panoply libraries as our base for comparison throughout our evaluation. We calculate the overall execution time of our benchmarks using `time` command in Linux. Each measurement is averaged over 5 runs. All benchmarks are compiled using Clang v3.8.1. We do not include time for compiling and verifying our applications as these are offline operations and do not incur any overhead. We divide our experiments into three sets.

**Table 1.** Table reporting OS and VERICOUNT accounted user and service time, VERI-COUNT accounted I/O bytes, no. of I/O `Ocalls` and total no. of `Ocalls` for our benchmarks.

| Benchmarks | User time (s) | | Service time (s) | | VeriCount I/O operations | | VeriCount total Ocalls |
|---|---|---|---|---|---|---|---|
| | OS | VeriCount | OS | VeriCount | I/O Bytes | I/O Ocalls | |
| mcf | 20.05 | 20 | 1.01 | 0 | 2360827 | 192458 | 192462 |
| bzip2 | 31.83 | 31 | 1.00 | 0 | 653190 | 32 | 34 |
| astar | 77.99 | 78 | 0.99 | 0 | 3146654 | 68 | 92 |
| hmmer | 127.31 | 127 | 1.02 | 0 | 16633 | 766 | 1265 |
| h264ref | 11.96 | 11 | 1.02 | 1 | 969975 | 360 | 1646052 |
| libquantum | 5.15 | 5 | 1.03 | 0 | 261 | 7 | 8 |
| sjeng | 229.40 | 229 | 1.00 | 0 | 17211 | 1601 | 4587 |
| gobmk | 0.91 | 0 | 1.10 | 0 | 11876 | 10024 | 10412 |
| gcc | 18.21 | 17 | 1.04 | 1 | 1744658 | 827474 | 827494 |
| H2O (10000 req.) file size = 10 KB | 16.12 | 5 | 0.81 | 13 | 102400000 | 10000 | 122073 |

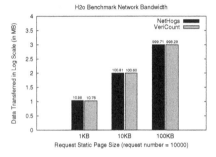

**Fig. 3.** Comparison of data bytes transferred using VERICOUNT and NetHogs. VERICOUNT accounting differs by 0.66% as compared to NetHogs.

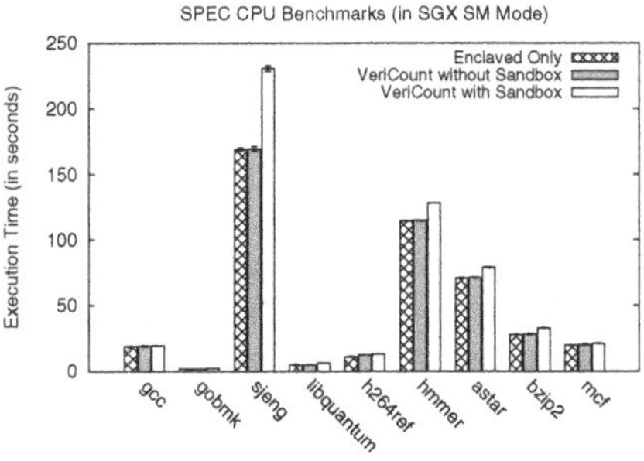

**Fig. 4.** Execution time of (a) Enclaved only (b) VERICOUNT without sandbox and (c) VERICOUNT with sandbox in simulation mode.

**(1) Simulation Mode.** We first evaluate all benchmarks in simulation mode to observe the performance overhead due to VERICOUNT design and implementation. To understand the overhead breakdown, we measure the overall execution time for enclaved only, VERICOUNT without sandbox, and VERICOUNT with sandbox applications.

**(2) Hardware Mode.** Further, to understand the overhead of using SGX, we perform experiments in hardware mode. We compare the execution time of VERICOUNT and non-VERICOUNT enclaved applications in hardware mode.

**(3) Resource Measurements.** To evaluate the accuracy of our accounting engine, we measure the user time, service time, I/O bytes, and network bandwidth using VERICOUNT and compare them to resource accounting tools from the OS.

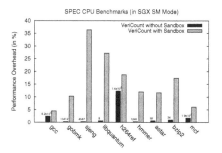

**Fig. 5.** Performance overhead of VERI-COUNT with and without sandbox application over enclaved only applications in simulation mode.

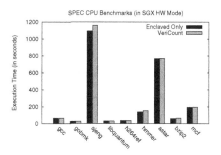

**Fig. 6.** Execution time of VERICOUNT applications and enclaved only applications in hardware mode.

### 6.1 Performance Overhead

**Simulation Mode Overhead.** Figure 4 shows the execution time of VERI-COUNT without and with sandbox for our benchmarks as compared to enclaved benchmarks in simulation mode. We observe that VERICOUNT without sandbox benchmarks incur an average overhead of only **2.28%** as compared to non-accountable enclaved applications. Thus, the accounting engine contributes a small overhead to perform resource accounting. This relatively small overhead of VERICOUNT's resource accounting engine (without sandbox) suggests that a trusted application (which does not tamper with the accounting engine) can exclude the sandbox logic and enjoy the low performance overhead. The maximum overhead in VERICOUNT applications without sandbox is for applications with large number of `Ocalls`, thereby causing higher number of invocations to accounting engine. Figure 5 shows the performance overhead where `h264ref` benchmark invokes $1.6 \times 10^5$ `Ocalls` and hence incurs maximum overhead of 12.3%. We observe that VERICOUNT with sandbox benchmarks incur an average overhead of **16.03%**. This shows that the sandboxing logic in VERICOUNT contributes to major portion of the overall overhead. The overhead is directly proportional to the number of sandboxing instructions added to the application. Applications with higher number of sandboxing instructions (e.g., `sjeng`) show a higher overhead.

**Hardware Mode Overhead.** To get the estimate of VERICOUNT overhead in hardware mode, we compare the execution time of VERICOUNT and enclaved only applications (shown in Fig. 6). VERICOUNT-enabled applications incur an average overhead of **3.62%** as compared to enclaved only applications in hardware mode. 3.62% approximately captures the overall overhead (i.e., sandboxing and accounting engine) of VERICOUNT design in hardware mode. Thus, we observe that the performance overhead due to VERICOUNT is less in hardware mode than in simulation mode. Figures 4 and 6 show that porting enclaved applications from simulation to hardware mode increases the execution time by a large margin which essentially hides the overhead due to VERICOUNT. Since enclaved application in HW mode take longer to finish than in simulation mode (the denominator increases), it reduces the overall overhead.

## 6.2   Resource Utilization Measurement

**User-Service Time.** The `time` command provides user and kernel time along with the overall execution time. We compare the user time measured by VERI-COUNT with that of the OS service. Column 2 in Table 1 shows that the VERI-COUNT calculated user time differs from the OS user time within a fraction of second for the SPEC CPUINT 2006 benchmarks. One exception is the H2O web server, where the VERICOUNT user time does not match the OS time. This is because the web server spends most of its time waiting for requests in the untrusted library outside the enclave while VERICOUNT guarantees are scoped only within the enclaved applications. Column 3 in Table 1 shows the difference between VERICOUNT service time and OS accounted kernel time. VERICOUNT's service time includes the kernel time and waiting time of untrusted library residing outside the enclave. This results in a difference between OS kernel time and VERICOUNT's service time. Arguably, service time should not be considered when accounting the user resources. Or, if client and cloud provider agree, they can decide an upper bound of $t$ in policy $\phi$ or use fixed pricing for service time.

**I/O Operations.** VERICOUNT calculates the I/O bytes, I/O calls and total number of `Ocalls` invoked by the application (shown in Column 4, 5, and 6 in Table 1). As there is no precise OS supported tool to measure I/O operations executed within the enclave, we confirm the correctness of our accounting engine using the `strace` and `ltrace` commands. We use `ltrace` command to verify the number of I/O `Ocalls` and total number of `Ocalls` which invoke the glibc library functions in the untrusted region. We use the `strace` command to calculate total bytes read & written after `open(app.signed.so)` call i.e., once the control switches to the enclave. We observe that VERICOUNT accurately accounts the I/O bytes for all our benchmarks. For eg., the I/O bytes and `Ocalls` for H2O web server is exactly 102400000 Bytes and 10000 for 10000 requests of 10 KB file size. As all the values match, we do not report the OS generated values in Table 1.

**Network Bandwidth.** We calculate the data transferred over the network by VERICOUNT-enabled H2O web server and compare it to `NetHogs` tool available in most Linux distributions [7]. We observe that VERICOUNT accounted network bytes differ from NetHogs results on an average by 0.66% (shown in Fig. 3). We were unable to determine the cause for the extra data traffic accounted by NetHogs but speculate it to be due to TLS handshakes before the actual response is sent over the network. We use `h2load` performance measurement tool to generate workload of 10000 requests for static web pages of size of 1 KB, 10 KB and 100 KB.

# 7    Related Work

**Issues in Cloud Accounting and Billing.** Previous work like Bouchenak et al. [12], Fernandes et al. [15], Xiao and Xiao [34] have discussed the importance of verifying resource consumption, accountability and billing. The key message is that users benefit from the ability to reason about the operations at the server. VERICOUNT realizes this idea and provides a refutable billing model for both users and cloud providers. Jellinek et al. [18] perform a study of billing systems in current cloud systems such as Amazon EC2, Google Compute Engine, Rackspace and others. Their results show that cloud billing systems have bugs that cause over-charging or free CPU time for users. VERICOUNT solve this issue with a verifiable accounting engine and a refutable billing primitive.

**Solutions for Verifiable Resource Accounting.** Sekar and Maniatis proposed the first practical design for resource accounting based on nested virtualization and TPMs [28]. They propose the idea of an observer placed at the hypervisor layer which accounts for the resources utilized by guest virtual machines. Alibi is a system based on this solution extending Turtles nested virtualization framework [13]. In contrast to this, VERICOUNT uses a self-accounting approach ensuring effective protection from resource usage inflation attacks. Moreover, their implementation based on Linux kernel and KVM incurs a huge TCB which we avoid in our solution. A second line of research uses execution logs but suffers from similar inefficiency problems as in our baseline approach. Haerberlen et. al propose accountable virtual machines that generate logs during execution that are sent to user [16]. A user can replay a "good" known execution and identify discrepancies in the server logs to detect maliciousness. This solution is hard to use where resource-constrained clients do not have enough bandwidth to download huge logs.

**Combining Trusted Computing and Sandboxing.** Previous work has proposed the idea of two-way protection using trusted computing and sandboxing approaches for different reasons. MiniBox [21] provides the first sandbox mechanism for native code in platform-as-a-service cloud computing. Though MiniBox uses TrustVisor and NaCl, the core idea applies to SGX as well. Ryoan uses a similar idea to create distributed sandbox for computing on secret data [17]. In VERICOUNT we use this idea to protect the execution of accounting engine from both the client-code and the underlying OS.

# 8    Conclusion

VERICOUNT achieves a verifiable resource accounting with a refutable billing mechanism for Linux containerized applications with Intel SGX support with low overhead.

**Acknowledgements.** We thank the anonymous reviewers of this paper for their helpful feedback. We also thank Zhenkai Liang, Shweta Shinde, and Loi Luu for useful feedback on an early version of the paper. This research was partially supported by a grant from Singapore Ministry of Education Academic Research Fund Tier 1 (R-252-000-624-133), and the National Research Foundation, Prime Ministers Office, Singapore under its National Cybersecurity R&D Program (TSUNAMi project, No. NRF2014NCR-NCR001-21) and administered by the National Cybersecurity R&D Directorate.

# References

1. Software Guard Extensions Programming Reference, September 2013. https://software.intel.com/sites/default/files/329298-001.pdf
2. Amazon EC2 container service (2017). https://aws.amazon.com/ecs/
3. Docker (2017). https://www.docker.com/
4. Google container engine (GKE) (2017). https://cloud.google.com/
5. H2O web server (2017). https://github.com/h2o/h2o
6. Intel SGX linux SDK (2017). https://github.com/01org/linux-sgx
7. NetHogs (2017). https://github.com/raboof/nethogs
8. Panoply source code (2017). https://shwetasshinde24.github.io/Panoply/
9. SPEC CPU2006 benchmarks (2017). https://www.spec.org/cpu2006/
10. Arnautov, S., Trach, B., Gregor, F., Knauth, T., Martin, A., Priebe, C., Lind, J., Muthukumaran, D., OKeeffe, D., Stillwell, M.L., et al.: Scone: secure Linux containers with intel SGX. In: 12th USENIX Symposium Operating Systems Design and Implementation (2016)
11. Baumann, A., Peinado, M., Hunt, G.: Shielding applications from an untrusted cloud with haven. ACM Trans. Comput. Syst. (TOCS) **33**(3), 8 (2015)
12. Bouchenak, S., Chockler, G., Chockler, H., Gheorghe, G., Santos, N., Shraer, A.: Verifying cloud services: present and future. ACM SIGOPS Oper. Syst. Rev. **47**, 6–19 (2013)
13. Chen, C., Maniatis, P., Perrig, A., Vasudevan, A., Sekar, V.: Towards verifiable resource accounting for outsourced computation. In: VEE (2013)
14. Erlingsson, Ú., Abadi, M., Vrable, M., Budiu, M., Necula, G.C.: XFI: software guards for system address spaces. In: OSDI (2006)
15. Fernandes, D.A., Soares, L.F., Gomes, J.V., Freire, M.M., Inácio, P.R.: Security issues in cloud environments: a survey. International J. Inf. Secur. **13**, 113–170 (2014)
16. Haeberlen, A., Aditya, P., Rodrigues, R., Druschel, P.: Accountable virtual machines. In: OSDI, pp. 119–134 (2010)
17. Hunt, T., Zhu, Z., Xu, Y., Peter, S., Witchel, E.: Ryoan: a distributed sandbox for untrusted computation on secret data. In: OSDI (2016)
18. Jellinek, R., Zhai, Y., Ristenpart, T., Swift, M.: A day late and a dollar short: the case for research on cloud billing systems. In: HotCloud (2014)
19. Kroll, J.A., Stewart, G., Appel, A.W.: Portable software fault isolation. In: 27th 2014 IEEE Computer Security Foundations Symposium (CSF), pp. 18–32. IEEE (2014)
20. Lee, S., Shih, M.W., Gera, P., Kim, T., Kim, H., Peinado, M.: Inferring fine-grained control flow inside SGX enclaves with branch shadowing. arXiv preprint arXiv:1611.06952 (2016)

21. Li, Y., McCune, J.M., Newsome, J., Perrig, A., Baker, B., Drewry, W.: Minibox: A two-way sandbox for x86 native code. In: USENIX Annual Technical Conference (2014)
22. Liu, M., Ding, X.: On trustworthiness of CPU usage metering and accounting. In: IEEE 30th International Conference on Distributed Computing Systems Workshops (2010)
23. Matetic, S., Kostiainen, K., Dhar, A., Sommer, D., Ahmed, M., Gervais, A., Juels, A., Capkun, S.: ROTE: rollback protection for trusted execution. In: Usenix Security (2017)
24. McCamant, S., Morrisett, G.: Evaluating SFI for a CISC architecture. In: Usenix Security (2006)
25. McKeen, F., Alexandrovich, I., Anati, I., Caspi, D., Johnson, S., Leslie-Hurd, R., Rozas, C.: Intel® software guard extensions (Intel® SGX) support for dynamic memory management inside an enclave. In: HASP 2016
26. Mihoob, A., Molina-Jimenez, C., Shrivastava, S.: A case for consumer-centric resource accounting models. In: IEEE 3rd International Conference on Cloud Computing (2010)
27. Shih, M.-W., Lee, S., Kim, T., Peinado, M.: T-SGX: eradicating controlled-channel attacks against enclave programs. In: NDSS (2017)
28. Sekar, V., Maniatis, P.: Verifiable resource accounting for cloud computing services. In: ACM Workshop on Cloud Computing Security Workshop (2011)
29. Shinde, S., Chua, Z.L., Narayanan, V., Saxena, P.: Preventing page faults from telling your secrets. In: ASIACCS (2016)
30. Shinde, S., Le Tien, D., Tople, S., Saxena, P.: Panoply: low-TCB Linux applications with SGX enclaves. In: NDSS (2017)
31. Tsafrir, D., Etsion, Y., Feitelson, D.G.: Secretly monopolizing the CPU without superuser privileges. In: USENIX Security, vol. 7, pp. 1–18 (2007)
32. Varadarajan, V., Kooburat, T., Farley, B., Ristenpart, T., Swift, M.M.: Resource-freeing attacks: improve your cloud performance (at your neighbor's expense). In: CCS (2012)
33. Wahbe, R., Lucco, S., Anderson, T.E., Graham, S.L.: Efficient software-based fault isolation. In: ACM SIGOPS Operating Systems Review, pp. 203–216. ACM (1994)
34. Xiao, Z., Xiao, Y.: Security and privacy in cloud computing. IEEE Commun. Surv. Tutor. **15**(2), 843–859 (2013)
35. Xu, Y., Cui, W., Peinado, M.: Controlled-channel attacks: deterministic side channels for untrusted operating systems. In: IEEE Symposium on Security and Privacy (SP) (2015)
36. Yee, B., Sehr, D., Dardyk, G., Chen, J.B., Muth, R., Ormandy, T., Okasaka, S., Narula, N., Fullagar, N.: Native client: a sandbox for portable, untrusted x86 native code. In: 2009 30th IEEE Symposium on Security and Privacy, pp. 79–93. IEEE (2009)
37. Zhang, F., Zhang, H.: SoK: a study of using hardware-assisted isolated execution environments for security. In: Proceedings of the Hardware and Architectural Support for Security and Privacy 2016, HASP 2016 (2016)
38. Zhou, F., Goel, M., Desnoyers, P., Sundaram, R.: Scheduler vulnerabilities and coordinated attacks in cloud computing. J. Comput. Secur. **21**(4), 533–559 (2013)

# Message-Locked Encryption with File Update

Suyash Kandele$^{(\boxtimes)}$ and Souradyuti Paul

Indian Institute of Technology Bhilai, Raipur, Chhattisgarh, India
{suyashk,souradyuti}@iitbhilai.ac.in

**Abstract.** *Message-locked encryption (MLE)* (formalized by Bellare et al. [5]) is an important cryptographic primitive that supports deduplication in the *cloud*. *Updatable block-level message-locked encryption (UMLE)* (formalized by Zhao and Chow [13]) adds the *update* functionality to the *MLE*. In this paper, we formalize and extensively study a new cryptographic primitive *file-updatable message-locked encryption (FMLE)*. *FMLE* can be viewed as a generalization of the *UMLE*, in the sense that unlike the latter, the former does not require the existence of *BL-MLE (block-level message-locked encryption)*. *FMLE* allows more flexibility and efficient methods for updating the ciphertext and tag.

Our second contribution is the design of two efficient *FMLE* constructions, namely, RevD-1 and RevD-2, whose design principles are inspired from the very unique *reverse decryption* functionality of the *FP* hash function (designed by Paul et al. [11]) and the *APE* authenticated encryption (designed by Andreeva et al. [2]). With respect to *UMLE* – which provides so far the most efficient update function – RevD-1 and RevD-2 reduce the total update time by at least 50%, on average. Additionally, our constructions are storage efficient. We also give extensive comparison between our and the existing constructions.

## 1 Introduction

MLE. *Message-locked encryption (MLE)* is a special type of encryption, where the decryption key is derived from the message itself. The main application of *MLE* is in the secure deduplication of data in the *cloud*, where *MLE* removes the need for storing multiple copies of identical data, without compromising their privacy and, thereby, helps to reduce the storage costs. Given the cloud services being on the rise, this primitive is gaining importance.

The first attempt to solve the problem of deduplication was made in 2002 by Douceur *et al.* [8], who came up with the idea of *Convergent Encryption (CE)*. Bellare et al. [5] studied this subject in a formal way and named it *message-locked encryption (MLE)*. They also gave efficient constructions of *MLE*.

UMLE. As seen before, *MLE* does not inherently support the *file-update* and the *proof of ownership* functionalities in its definition. *UMLE* solves this issue by adding three functionalities – file-update, PoW algorithms for prover and verifier

B. Preneel and F. Vercauteren (Eds.): ACNS 2018, LNCS 10892, pp. 678–695, 2018.
https://doi.org/10.1007/978-3-319-93387-0_35

– to the existing definition of *MLE*. The main drawback of *UMLE* is that the functionalities are constructed from another cryptographic primitive, namely, *BL-MLE*, which is nothing but *MLE* executed on a fixed-sized block. Such a *BL-MLE*-based *UMLE* entails degradation of performance for encryption and decryption [13]. Another drawback of *UMLE* is that the update of file-tag is an expensive operation.

MOTIVATION FOR STUDYING FMLE. From the high level, both *UMLE* and *FMLE* have identical functionalities; the main difference, however, is that the former is necessarily based on *BL-MLE*, but the latter may or may not be. Therefore, the definition of *FMLE* can be viewed as a generalisation of *UMLE*, where we remove the constraint of using *BL-MLE*. The motivation for studying *FMLE* is clear from the drawbacks of *UMLE* mentioned above. These motivations are:

*Does there exist an* FMLE *scheme which is not based on* BL-MLE*? If such a construction exists, is it more efficient than* UMLE*?*

Studying *FMLE* is a futile exercise, if both the answers are in the negative. A moment's reflection suggests that the answer to the first question is actually 'Yes'. A trivial *FMLE* construction – not based on *BL-MLE* – always exists, where the file-update function is designed the following way: apply decryption to the ciphertext to recover the original plaintext; edit/modify the original message; and finally encrypt the updated message. Note that this trivial file-update function does not need any *BL-MLE*, therefore, it is an *FMLE*, but certainly not a *UMLE* scheme. The main drawback of this *FMLE* scheme is that this is several orders of magnitude slower than a *UMLE* scheme. Therefore, the main challenge is:

*Does there exists an* FMLE *scheme more efficient than* UMLE*?*

Searching for such a construction is the main motivation of this paper.

OUR CONTRIBUTION. Our first contribution is formalizing the new cryptographic notion *file-updatable message-locked encryption (FMLE)*. We also propose two efficient *FMLE* constructions RevD-1 and RevD-2: their update functions are at least 50% faster (on average).[1] Also, our constructions are more space efficient than the so-far best *MLE* variants; in particular, the *ciphertext expansion* and *tag storage* in RevD-1 and RevD-2 are constant, while they are logarithmic and linear (or may be worse) for other similar time-efficient cases. In order to obtain this improvement in the performance, our constructions critically exploit a very unique feature – what we call *reverse decryption* – of the hash function *FP* and the authenticated encryption *APE*. We also present proofs of security of our constructions. Extensive comparison of our constructions with the others – in terms of time complexity, storage requirements and security properties – have also been provided (see Table 1). Being randomized, our constructions

---

[1] The term RevD is a shorthand for ***Rev**erse **D**ecryption*.

are secure against the *dictionary attacks*, however, they lack STC security, like all other randomized *MLE*s.

RELATED WORK. We now describe various pieces of work done by several researchers that are related to *FMLE*. Douceur *et al.* are the first to come up with the idea of *Convergent Encryption (CE)* in 2002, where the key was calculated as a hash of the message, and then this key was used for encryption [8]. Bellare, Keelveedhi and Ristenpart formalized *CE* in the form of *message-locked encryption (MLE)* [5]. They also provided a systematic discussion of various *MLE* schemes. In a separate paper, these authors also designed a new system DupLESS that supports deduplication even if the message entropy is low [4].

Beelare and Keelveedhi extended *message-locked encryption* to *interactive message-locked encryption*, and have addressed the cases when the messages are correlated as well as dependent on the public parameters, leading to weakened privacy [3]. Abadi *et al.* gave two new constructions for the *i-MLE*; these fully randomized schemes also supported equality-testing algorithm for finding ciphertexts derived from identical messages [1]. Jiang *et al.* gave an efficient logarithmic-time deduplication scheme that substantially reduces the equality-testing in the *i-MLE* schemes [10].

Canard, Laguillaumie and Paindavoine introduced *deduplication consistency* – a new security property – that prevents the clients from bypassing the deduplication protocol. This is accomplished by introducing a new feature named *verifiability (of the well-formation) of ciphertext at the server* [6]. They also proposed a new ElGamal-based construction satisfying this property. Wang *et al.* proposed a stronger security notion PRV-CDA3 and showed that their new construction *ME* is secure in this model [12].

Chen *et al.* proposed the *block-level message-locked encryption (BL-MLE)*, which is nothing but breaking a big message into smaller chunks – called *blocks* – and then applying *MLE* on the individual *blocks* [7]. Huang, Zhang and Wang showed how to integrate the functionality *proof of storage (PoS)* with *MLE* by using a new data structure *Quadruple Tags* [9]. Zhao and Chow proposed the use of *BL-MLE* to design *Efficiently Updatable Block-Level Message-Locked Encryption (UMLE)* scheme which has an additional functionality of updating the ciphertext that costs sub-linear time [13].

ORGANIZATION OF THE PAPER. In Sect. 2, we discuss the preliminaries including the notation and basic definitions. Section 3 describes the deduplication protocol. In Sect. 4, we give the formal definition of *FMLE*. In Sect. 5, we construct the *FMLE* schemes by tweaking the existing *MLE* and *UMLE* schemes. In Sect. 6, we describe the two new efficient *FMLE* schemes and we compare them with the various *FMLE* schemes and conclude our paper in Sect. 7.

## 2    Preliminaries

### 2.1    Notation

The expression $M := x$ denotes that the value of $x$ is assigned to $M$, and $M := \mathcal{D}(x)$ denotes that the value returned by function $\mathcal{D}(\cdot)$, on input $x$, is assigned to $M$. $M = x$ denotes the equality comparison of the two variables $M$ and $x$, and $M = \mathcal{D}(x)$ denotes the equality comparison of the variable $M$ with the output of $\mathcal{D}(\cdot)$, on input $x$. The XOR or $\oplus$ denotes the bit-by-bit *exclusive-or* operation on two binary strings of same length. The concatenation operation of $p \geq 1$ strings $s_1, s_2, \cdots, s_p$ and assignment to the variable $s$ is denoted by $s := s_1 || s_2 || \cdots || s_p$. The parsing of string $s$ into $p \geq 1$ strings $s_1, s_2, \cdots, s_p$ is denoted by $s_1 || s_2 || \cdots || s_p := s$. The length of string $M$ is denoted by $|M|$. The set of all binary strings of length $\ell$ is denoted by $\{0,1\}^\ell$. The set of all binary strings of any length is denoted by $\{0,1\}^*$. A vector of strings is denoted by $\boldsymbol{M}$ and $i$-th string in $\boldsymbol{M}$ is denoted by $\boldsymbol{M}^{(i)}$. The number of strings in $\boldsymbol{M}$ is denoted by $\|\boldsymbol{M}\|$. The infinite set of all binary strings of any length is denoted by $\{0,1\}^{**}$. The set of all Natural numbers is denoted by $\mathbb{N}$. We denote that $M$ is assigned a binary string of length $k$ chosen randomly and uniformly by $M \xleftarrow{\$} \{0,1\}^k$. To mark any invalid string (may be input string or output string), the symbol $\perp$ is used. $(\boldsymbol{M}, Z) \xleftarrow{\$} \mathcal{S}(1^\lambda)$ denotes the assignment of outputs given randomly and uniformly by $\mathcal{S}$ to $\boldsymbol{M}$ and $Z$.

## 2.2 Dictionary Attack

A *dictionary attack* is defined to be a *brute-force attack*, where the adversary first builds a dictionary off-line, and then processes every element of the dictionary to determine the correct solution against an online challenge. For example, suppose that the hash of a message is given as a challenge to the adversary for her to determine the correct message. If the entropy of the message is low, then the adversary generates the dictionary of all possible messages and their corresponding hash values off-line; and given the online challenge, she selects the message whose hash value matches the challenge. *Any deterministic MLE with low message entropy is broken by dictionary attack.*

## 2.3 Proof of Ownership

Proof-of-ownership (PoW) is an interactive protocol where the owner of file proves the ownership of a file to the cloud storage. This protocol assumes that the adversary does not have access to the entire ciphertext which was uploaded onto the cloud by some previous (or first) owner, but he may know the tag, which is a small fraction of the entire information. In this protocol, the cloud storage provider generates a challenge $Q$ and sends it to the client, along with some other information. The client computes the proof $P$ corresponding to the given challenge $Q$ and sends it back to the cloud. The cloud verifies it and if the verification is successful, then the client is granted access, otherwise the access is denied.

## 2.4 Ideal Permutation

Let $\pi / \pi^{-1} \colon \{0,1\}^n \mapsto \{0,1\}^n$ be a pair of oracles. The pair $\pi / \pi^{-1}$ is called an *ideal permutation* if the following three properties are satisfied.

1. $\pi^{-1}(\pi(x)) = x$ and $\pi(\pi^{-1}(x)) = x$, for all $x \in \{0,1\}^n$.
2. Suppose, $x_k$ is the $k$-th query $(k \geq 1)$, submitted to the oracle $\pi$, and $y \in \{0,1\}^n$. Then, for the current query $x_i$:

$$\Pr\left[\pi(x_i) = y \,\middle|\, \pi(x_1) = y_1, \pi(x_2) = y_2, \cdots, \pi(x_{i-1}) = y_{i-1}\right]$$

$$= \begin{cases} 1, & \text{if } x_i = x_j, y = y_j, j < i. \\ 0, & \text{if } x_i = x_j, y \neq y_j, j < i, \\ 0, & \text{if } x_i \neq x_j, y = y_j, j < i, \\ \frac{1}{2^n - i + 1}, & \text{if } x_i \neq x_j, y \neq y_j, j < i. \end{cases}$$

3. Suppose, $y_k$ is the $k$-th query $(k \geq 1)$, submitted to the oracle $\pi^{-1}$, and $x \in \{0,1\}^n$. Then, for the current query $y_i$:

$$\Pr\left[\pi^{-1}(y_i) = x \,\middle|\, \pi^{-1}(y_1) = x_1, \pi^{-1}(y_2) = x_2, \cdots, \pi^{-1}(y_{i-1}) = x_{i-1}\right]$$

$$= \begin{cases} 1, & \text{if } y_i = y_j, x = x_j, j < i. \\ 0, & \text{if } y_i = y_j, x \neq x_j, j < i, \\ 0, & \text{if } y_i \neq y_j, x = x_j, j < i, \\ \frac{1}{2^n - i + 1}, & \text{if } y_i \neq y_j, x \neq x_j, j < i. \end{cases}$$

### 2.5   Other Definitions

Due to space constraints, the definitions of *unpredictable sources*, *message-locked encryption (MLE)*, *updatable block-level message-locked encryption (UMLE)*, *hash function* and *one-time symmetric encryption* will appear in the full version of the paper.

## 3   Deduplication: An Application of *FMLE*

Deduplication is a mechanism by which a protocol removes the requirement for storing multiple copies of an identical file in memory. This is highly beneficial for the better utilization of space in the *cloud*, where multiple users often store identical files. Loosely speaking, it does so, by identifying the identical files, removing all the copies except one, and then attaching a special file called the *list of owners* to it. In Fig. 1, we give the details of the deduplication protocol supporting *file-update* and *proof of ownership (PoW)* functionalities. Although, intuitively clear, we would like to point out that the *authentication of users* is not a part of this protocol; the system, otherwise, takes care of that through various well-known means such as password-based/bio-metric authentications, etc.

The deduplication protocol with file-update and PoW functionalities, has three functions: client uploading data to the server, as shown in Fig. 1(a); client downloading data from the server, as shown in Fig. 1(b); and client updating data to the server, as shown in Fig. 1(c). Due to space constraints, the textual description has been omitted and will appear in the full version of the paper.

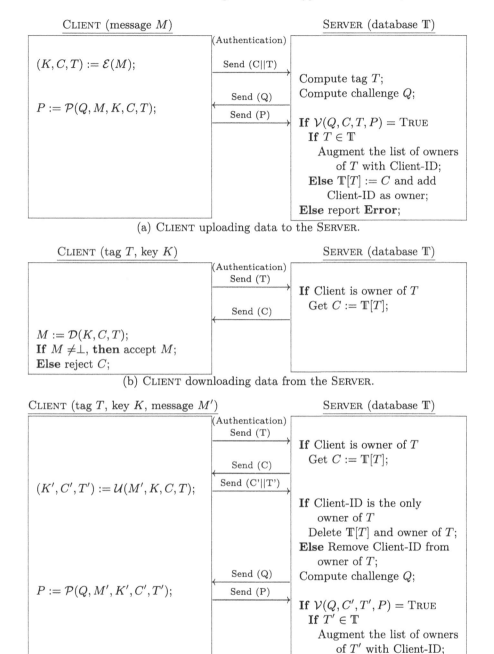

(a) CLIENT uploading data to the SERVER.

(b) CLIENT downloading data from the SERVER.

(c) CLIENT updating data to the SERVER.

**Fig. 1.** Upload, download and update protocols in the deduplication protocol.

# 4   *FMLE*: A New Cryptographic Primitive

The *File updatable Message-Locked Encryption (FMLE)* is a generalisation of *Efficiently Updatable Block-Level Message-Locked Encryption (UMLE)* as given by Zhao and Chow [13]. The difference between the definitions of *UMLE* and *FMLE* is that the former requires the existence of a *BL-MLE* scheme, while the latter does not.[2] Therefore, any *UMLE* scheme can be viewed as an *FMLE* scheme too, not the other way round.

Below we elaborately discuss the syntax, correctness and security definition of the new notion *FMLE*.

## 4.1   Syntax

Suppose $\lambda \in \mathbb{N}$ is the security parameter. An *FMLE* scheme $\Pi = (\Pi.\mathcal{E}, \Pi.\mathcal{D}, \Pi.\mathcal{U}, \Pi.\mathcal{P}, \Pi.\mathcal{V})$ is five-tuple of algorithms over a PPT setup $\Pi.\mathsf{Setup}$. $\Pi$ satisfies the following conditions.

1. The PPT setup algorithm $\Pi.\mathsf{Setup}(1^\lambda)$ outputs the parameter *params* and the sets $\mathcal{K}$, $\mathcal{M}$, $\mathcal{C}$ and $\mathcal{T}$, denoting the *key, message, ciphertext* and *tag spaces* respectively.
2. The PPT encryption algorithm $\Pi.\mathcal{E}$ takes as inputs *params* and $M \in \mathcal{M}$, and returns a 3-tuple $(K, C, T) := \Pi.\mathcal{E}(params, M)$, where $K \in \mathcal{K}$, $C \in \mathcal{C}$ and $T \in \mathcal{T}$.
3. The decryption algorithm $\Pi.\mathcal{D}$ is a deterministic algorithm that takes as inputs *params*, $K \in \mathcal{K}$, $C \in \mathcal{C}$ and $T \in \mathcal{T}$, and returns $\Pi.\mathcal{D}(params, K, C, T) \in \mathcal{M} \cup \{\bot\}$. The decryption algorithm $\mathcal{D}$ returns $\bot$ if the key $K$, ciphertext $C$ and tag $T$ are not generated from a valid message.
4. The PPT update algorithm $\Pi.\mathcal{U}$ takes as inputs *params*, the index of starting and ending bits $i_{st}$ and $i_{end}$, new message bits $M_{new} \in \mathcal{M}$, the decryption key $K \in \mathcal{K}$, the ciphertext to be updated $C \in \mathcal{C}$, the tag to be updated $T \in \mathcal{T}$ and the bit $app \in \{0,1\}$ indicating change in length of new message, and returns a 3-tuple $(K', C', T') := \Pi.\mathcal{U}(params, i_{st}, i_{end}, M_{new}, K, C, T, app)$, where $K' \in \mathcal{K}$, $C' \in \mathcal{C}$ and $T' \in \mathcal{T}$.
5. The PPT proof-of-ownership (PoW) algorithm for prover $\Pi.\mathcal{P}$ takes as inputs parameter *params*, challenge $Q$, a file $M \in \mathcal{M}$, the decryption key $K \in \mathcal{K}$, the ciphertext $C \in \mathcal{C}$, the tag $T \in \mathcal{T}$, and returns the proof $P := \Pi.\mathcal{P}(params, Q, M, K, C, T)$.
6. The PPT proof-of-ownership (PoW) algorithm for verifier $\Pi.\mathcal{V}$ takes as inputs parameter *params*, challenge $Q$, ciphertext $C \in \mathcal{C}$, tag $T \in \mathcal{T}$ and proof $P$, and returns the value $val := \Pi.\mathcal{V}(params, Q, C, T, P)$, where $val \in \{\mathsf{TRUE}, \mathsf{FALSE}\}$.
7. We restrict $|C|$ to be a linear function of $|M|$.

---

[2] A *block-level message-locked encryption (BL-MLE)* is an *MLE* that works on the fixed-sized messages, called *blocks*.

## 4.2   Correctness

KEY CORRECTNESS. Suppose $(K, C, T) := \Pi.\mathcal{E}(params, M)$, and $(K', C', T')$ $:= \Pi.\mathcal{E}(params, M')$. Then *key correctness* of $\Pi$ requires that if $M = M'$, then $K = K'$, for all $\lambda \in \mathbb{N}$ and all $M, M' \in \mathcal{M}$.

DECRYPTION CORRECTNESS. Suppose $(K, C, T) := \Pi.\mathcal{E}(params, M)$. Then *decryption correctness* of $\Pi$ requires that $\Pi.\mathcal{D}(params, K, C, T) = M$, for all $\lambda \in \mathbb{N}$ and all $M \in \mathcal{M}$.

TAG CORRECTNESS. Suppose $(K, C, T) := \Pi.\mathcal{E}(params, M)$, and $(K', C', T')$ $:= \Pi.\mathcal{E}(params, M')$. Then *tag correctness* of $\Pi$ requires that if $M = M'$, then $T = T'$, for all $\lambda \in \mathbb{N}$ and all $M, M' \in \mathcal{M}$.

UPDATE CORRECTNESS. Suppose $\ell = |M|$, $(K, C, T) := \Pi.\mathcal{E}(params, M)$, and $(K', C', T') := \Pi.\mathcal{U}(params, i_{st}, i_{end}, M_{new}, K, C, T, app)$. Then *update correctness* of $\Pi$ requires that, for all $\lambda \in \mathbb{N}$, all $M \in \mathcal{M}$, $1 \leq i_{st} \leq \ell$ and $i_{st} < i_{end}$:

- for $app = 1$, $\Pi.\mathcal{D}(params, K', C', T') = M[1] \,||\, M[2] \,||\cdots||\, M[i_{st}-1] \,||\, M_{new}$, and
- for $app = 0$, $\Pi.\mathcal{D}(params, K', C', T') = M[1] \,||\, M[2] \,||\cdots||\, M[i_{st}-1] \,||\, M_{new}$ $||\, M[i_{end}+1] || M[i_{end}+2] ||\cdots|| M[\ell]$.

PoW CORRECTNESS. Suppose $(K, C, T) := \Pi.\mathcal{E}(params, M)$, $Q$ is any challenge and $P := \Pi.\mathcal{P}(params, Q, M, K, C, T)$. Then *PoW correctness* of $\Pi$ requires that $\Pr[\Pi.\mathcal{V}(params, Q, C, T, P) = \mathsf{TRUE}] = 1$, for all $\lambda \in \mathbb{N}$ and all $M \in \mathcal{M}$.

## 4.3   Security Definitions

Security definitions of *FMLE* are naturally adapted from those of *UMLE*. For the sake of completeness, we describe them below in full detail. As usual, all the games are written in the form of challenger-adversary framework.

PRIVACY. Let $\Pi = (\Pi.\mathcal{E}, \Pi.\mathcal{D}, \Pi.\mathcal{U}, \Pi.\mathcal{P}, \Pi.\mathcal{V})$ be an *FMLE* scheme. Since, no *MLE* scheme can provide security for predictable messages, we are modelling the security based on the unpredictable message source $\mathcal{S}(\cdot)$. According to the PRV\$-CDA game, as in Fig. 2, the challenger gets a vector of messages, $\boldsymbol{M}$ and the auxiliary information $Z$, from the source $\mathcal{S}(\cdot)$. The challenger does the following operations: computes the decryption key $\boldsymbol{K}_1^{(i)}$, ciphertext $\boldsymbol{C}_1^{(i)}$ and tag $\boldsymbol{T}_1^{(i)}$ for each message string $\boldsymbol{M}^{(i)}$ using $\Pi.\mathcal{E}$, where $i \in \{1, 2, \cdots, m(1^\lambda)\}$; computes the random strings $\boldsymbol{K}_0^{(i)}, \boldsymbol{C}_0^{(i)}$ and $\boldsymbol{T}_0^{(i)}$ of length $|\boldsymbol{K}_1^{(i)}|, |\boldsymbol{C}_1^{(i)}|$ and $|\boldsymbol{T}_1^{(i)}|$ respectively; and returns $(\boldsymbol{C}_b, \boldsymbol{T}_b, Z)$ to the adversary. The adversary has to return a bit $b'$ indicating whether the ciphertext $\boldsymbol{C}_b$ and tag $\boldsymbol{T}_b$ corresponds to message $\boldsymbol{M}$ or is it a collection of random strings. If the values of $b$ and $b'$ coincide, then the adversary wins the game.

| Game PRV\$-CDA$_{\Pi}^{S,A}(1^\lambda, b)$ | Game CXH$_{\Pi}^{A}(1^\lambda, \sigma, b)$ |
|---|---|
| $(M, Z) \xleftarrow{\$} S(1^\lambda);$ <br> **for** $(i := 1, 2, \cdots, m(1^\lambda))$ <br> $\quad (K_1^{(i)}, C_1^{(i)}, T_1^{(i)}) := \Pi.\mathcal{E}(params, M^{(i)});$ <br> $\quad K_0^{(i)} \xleftarrow{\$} \{0,1\}^{\lvert K_1^{(i)} \rvert};$ <br> $\quad C_0^{(i)} \xleftarrow{\$} \{0,1\}^{\lvert C_1^{(i)} \rvert};$ <br> $\quad T_0^{(i)} \xleftarrow{\$} \{0,1\}^{\lvert T_1^{(i)} \rvert};$ <br> $b' := A(1^\lambda, C_b, T_b, Z);$ <br> **return** $b';$ | $(M_0, M_1) := A_1(1^\lambda, \sigma);$ <br> Determine bit-positions $i_1, i_2, \cdots, i_\rho$ <br> $\quad$ where $M_0$ and $M_1$ differ; <br> **If** $\rho > \sigma$, **then** return 0; <br> $(K_0, C_0, T_0) := \Pi.\mathcal{E}(params, M_0);$ <br> $(K_1, C_1, T_1) := \Pi.\mathcal{E}(params, M_1);$ <br> $(K_1', C_1', T_1') := \Pi.\mathcal{U}(params, i_1, i_\rho,$ <br> $\quad M_0[i_1, i_1 + 1, \cdots, i_\rho], K_1, C_1, T_1, 0);$ <br> **If** $b = 0$, **then** $C^* := C_0;$ <br> **Else** $C^* := C_1';$ <br> $b' := A_2(1^\lambda, C^*);$ <br> **return** $b';$ |
| Game STC$_{\Pi}^{A}(1^\lambda)$ $\boxed{\text{TC}_{\Pi}^{A}(1^\lambda)}$ | Game UNC-CDA$_{\Pi}^{A}(1^\lambda)$ |
| $(M, C', T') := A(1^\lambda);$ <br> **If** $(M =\perp) \vee (C' =\perp)$, **then return** 0; <br> $(K, C, T) := \Pi.\mathcal{E}(params, M);$ <br> $M' := \Pi.\mathcal{D}(params, K, C', T');$ <br> **If** $(T = T') \wedge (M \neq M')$ $\boxed{\wedge (M' \neq \perp)}$ <br> $\quad$ **return** 1; <br> **Else return** 0; | $S := A_1(1^\lambda), (M, Z) \xleftarrow{\$} S(1^\lambda);$ <br> $(K, C, T) := \Pi.\mathcal{E}(params, M)$ <br> $P^* := A_2(1^\lambda, Q, Z);$ <br> $P := \Pi.\mathcal{P}(params, Q, M, K, C, T);$ <br> **If** $(\Pi.\mathcal{V}(params, Q, C, T, P^*) = \text{TRUE})$ <br> $\quad \wedge (P^* \neq P)$ <br> $\quad$ **return** 1; <br> **Else return** 0; |

**Fig. 2.** Games defining PRV\$-CDA, STC, TC, CXH and UNC-CDA security of *FMLE* scheme $\Pi = (\Pi.\mathcal{E}, \Pi.\mathcal{D}, \Pi.\mathcal{U}, \Pi.\mathcal{P}, \Pi.\mathcal{V})$. In CXH and UNC-CDA games, adversary $A = (A_1, A_2)$

We define the advantage of an PRV\$-CDA adversary $A$ against $\Pi$ for the message source $S(\cdot)$ as:

$$Adv_{\Pi,S,A}^{\text{PRV\$-CDA}}(1^\lambda) \stackrel{def}{=} \Big| \Pr[\text{PRV\$-CDA}_{\Pi,S}^{A}(1^\lambda, b = 1) = 1]$$
$$- \Pr[\text{PRV\$-CDA}_{\Pi,S}^{A}(1^\lambda, b = 0) = 1] \Big|.$$

An *FMLE* scheme $\Pi$ is said to be PRV\$-CDA secure over a set of valid PT sources for *FMLE* scheme $\Pi$, $\overline{S} = \{S_1, S_2, \cdots\}$, for all PT adversaries $A$ and for all $S_i \in \overline{S}$, if $Adv_{\Pi,S_i,A}^{\text{PRV\$-CDA}}(\cdot)$ is negligible. An *FMLE* scheme $\Pi$ is said to be PRV\$-CDA secure, for all PT adversaries $A$, if $Adv_{\Pi,S,A}^{\text{PRV\$-CDA}}(\cdot)$ is negligible, for all valid PT source $S$ for $\Pi$.

TAG CONSISTENCY. Let $\Pi = (\Pi.\mathcal{E}, \Pi.\mathcal{D}, \Pi.\mathcal{U}, \Pi.\mathcal{P}, \Pi.\mathcal{V})$ be an *FMLE* scheme. For an *FMLE* scheme, we have designed the STC and TC security games in Fig. 2, which aim to provide security against duplicate faking attacks. In addition, STC provides safeguards against erasure attack. In a duplicate faking attack, two unidentical messages – one fake message produced by an adversary and a legitimate one produced by an honest client – produce the same tag, thereby cause loss of message and hamper the integrity. In an erasure attack, the adversary replaces the ciphertext with a fake message that decrypts successfully.

The adversary returns a message $M$, a ciphertext $C'$ and a tag $T'$. If the message or ciphertext is invalid, the adversary loses the game. Otherwise, the challenger computes decryption key $K_D$, ciphertext $C$ and tag $T$ corresponding to message $M$, and computes the message $M'$ corresponding to ciphertext $C'$ and tag $T'$ using key $K_D$. If the two tags are equal, i.e. $T = T'$, the message $M'$ is valid, i.e. $M' \neq \perp$, and the two messages are unequal, i.e. $M \neq M'$, then the adversary wins.

Now, we define the advantage of a TC adversary $\mathcal{A}$ against $\Pi$ as:

$$Adv^{\mathsf{TC}}_{\Pi,\mathcal{A}}(1^\lambda) \stackrel{def}{=} \Pr[\mathsf{TC}^{\mathcal{A}}_{\Pi}(1^\lambda) = 1].$$

Now, we define the advantage of an STC adversary $\mathcal{A}$ against $\Pi$ as:

$$Adv^{\mathsf{STC}}_{\Pi,\mathcal{A}}(1^\lambda) \stackrel{def}{=} \Pr[\mathsf{STC}^{\mathcal{A}}_{\Pi}(1^\lambda) = 1].$$

An *FMLE* scheme $\Pi$ is said to be TC (or STC) secure, for all PT adversaries $\mathcal{A}$, if $Adv^{\mathsf{TC}}_{\Pi,\mathcal{A}}(\cdot)$ (or $Adv^{\mathsf{STC}}_{\Pi,\mathcal{A}}(\cdot)$) is negligible.

CONTEXT HIDING. Let $\Pi = (\Pi.\mathcal{E}, \Pi.\mathcal{D}, \Pi.\mathcal{U}, \Pi.\mathcal{P}, \Pi.\mathcal{V})$ be an *FMLE* scheme. For an *FMLE*, we have designed the CXH game in Fig. 2, which aims to provide security against distinguishing between an updated ciphertext and a ciphertext encrypted from scratch, to ensure that the level of privacy is not compromised during update process.

According to the CXH game, as in Fig. 2, the adversary returns two messages $M_0$ and $M_1$ such that $M_0$ and $M_1$ are identical for all bits except $\sigma$ bits. The challenger calculates the bit-positions $i_1, i_2, \cdots, i_\rho$ where $M_0$ and $M_1$ differ, and the adversary loses if $\rho > \sigma$. The challenger encrypts the two messages $M_0$ and $M_1$ to generate $(K_0, C_0, T_0)$ and $(K_1, C_1, T_1)$ and updates the $C_1$ with $M_0[i_1, i_1 + 1, \cdots, i_\rho]$ to obtain $(K'_1, C'_1, T'_1)$. The challenger then sends either $C_0$ or $C'_1$, depending on the value of $b$, to the adversary. The adversary has to return a bit $b'$ indicating whether the ciphertext is built from scratch or is an updated ciphertext. If the values of $b$ and $b'$ are equal, then the adversary wins the game.

Now, we define the advantage of a CXH adversary $\mathcal{A}$ for $\sigma$-bit update in message, against $\Pi$ as:

$$Adv^{\mathsf{CXH}}_{\Pi,\mathcal{A}}(1^\lambda, \sigma) \stackrel{def}{=} \left| \Pr[\mathsf{CXH}^{\mathcal{A}}_{\Pi}(1^\lambda, \sigma, b = 1) = 1] - \Pr[\mathsf{CXH}^{\mathcal{A}}_{\Pi}(1^\lambda, \sigma, b = 0) = 1] \right|.$$

An *FMLE* scheme $\Pi$ is said to be CXH secure, for $\sigma$-bit update in message, for all PT adversaries $\mathcal{A}$, if $Adv^{\mathsf{CXH}}_{\Pi,\mathcal{A}}(\cdot, \cdot)$ is negligible.

PROOF OF OWNERSHIP. Let $\Pi = (\Pi.\mathcal{E}, \Pi.\mathcal{D}, \Pi.\mathcal{U}, \Pi.\mathcal{P}, \Pi.\mathcal{V})$ be an *FMLE* scheme. For an *FMLE*, we have designed the UNC-CDA game in Fig. 2, which aims to provide security against the adversary in proving that they possess the entire file when they actually have only a partial information about the file. This is to block the unauthorised ownership of the file.

According to the UNC-CDA game, as in Fig. 2, the adversary returns an unpredictable message source $\mathcal{S}(\cdot)$. The challenger gets a message $M$ and the auxiliary information $Z$, from this source. The challenger then send the challenge $Q$ and the auxiliary information $Z$ to the adversary and the adversary returns a proof $P^*$. The challenger generates the proof $P$ for the same challenge. If $P^*$ is successfully verified by the PoW verifier algorithm $\Pi.\mathcal{V}$ and $P$ is different from $P^*$, then the adversary wins the game.

Now, we define the advantage of a UNC-CDA adversary $\mathcal{A}$ against an uncheatable chosen distribution attack against $\Pi$ for a message source source $\mathcal{S}(\cdot)$ as:

$$Adv_{\Pi,\mathcal{A}}^{\mathsf{UNC\text{-}CDA}}(1^\lambda) \overset{def}{=} \Pr[\mathsf{UNC\text{-}CDA}_{\Pi}^{\mathcal{A}}(1^\lambda) = 1].$$

An *FMLE* scheme $\Pi$ is said to be UNC-CDA secure, for all PT adversaries $\mathcal{A}$, if $Adv_{\Pi,\mathcal{A}}^{\mathsf{UNC\text{-}CDA}}(\cdot)$ is negligible.

# 5    Practical *FMLE* Constructions from Existing *MLE* and *UMLE* Schemes

The description and security properties of F-CE, F-HCE2 & F-RCE and F-UMLE schemes will appear in the full version of the paper.

# 6    New Efficient *FMLE* Schemes

In this section we present the two new efficient constructions for *FMLE* – namely RevD-1 and RevD-2 – which are based on a $2\lambda$-bit easy-to-invert permutation $\pi$. We assume that the length of message is a multiple of $\lambda$; $\lambda$ is the security parameter.

## 6.1    The RevD-1 Scheme

We describe our first *FMLE* scheme, namely, RevD-1. This construction is motivated by the design of the hash function mode of operation *FP* [11].

**Description of RevD-1.** The pictorial and algorithmic descriptions are given in Figs. 3 and 4; all wires are $\lambda$-bit long. Let $M$ denote the message to be encrypted, $M[i]$ denote the $i$-th block of message, and $M[i][j]$ denote the $j$-th bit of $i$-th block of message. It is worth noting that the decryption is executed in the reverse direction of encryption. The detailed textual description of the 5-tuple of algorithms will appear in the full version of the paper.

**Security of RevD-1.** The details of the proofs for the PRV\$-CDA, TC, CXH and UNC-CDA security of RevD-1 will appear in the full version.

## 6.2    The RevD-2 Scheme

We describe our second *FMLE* scheme, namely, RevD-2. This construction is motivated by the design of the authenticated encryption *APE* [2].

**Description of RevD-2.** The pictorial and algorithmic descriptions are given in Figs. 5 and 6; all wires are $\lambda$-bit long. Let $M$ denote the message to be encrypted,

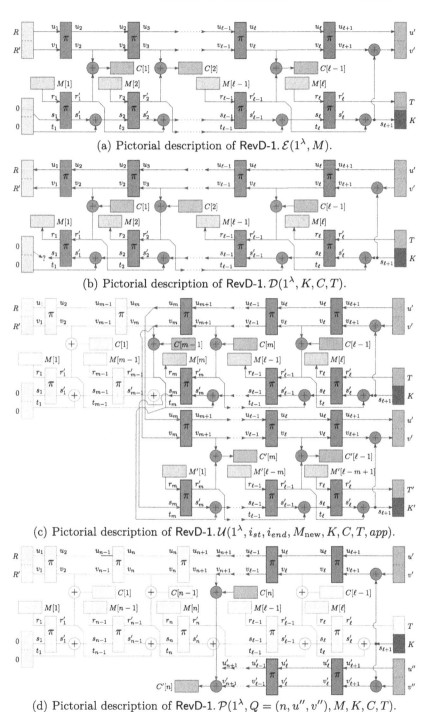

(a) Pictorial description of RevD-1. $\mathcal{E}(1^\lambda, M)$.

(b) Pictorial description of RevD-1. $\mathcal{D}(1^\lambda, K, C, T)$.

(c) Pictorial description of RevD-1. $\mathcal{U}(1^\lambda, i_{st}, i_{end}, M_{\text{new}}, K, C, T, app)$.

(d) Pictorial description of RevD-1. $\mathcal{P}(1^\lambda, Q = (n, u'', v''), M, K, C, T)$.

**Fig. 3.** Diagrammatic description of RevD-1.

RevD-1. $\mathcal{E}(1^\lambda, M)$

$\ell := |M|/\lambda$, $s_1 := 0^\lambda$, $t_1 := 0^\lambda$;
$M[1]||M[2]||\cdots||M[\ell] := M$;
$R \xleftarrow{\$} \{0,1\}^\lambda$, $R' \xleftarrow{\$} \{0,1\}^\lambda$, $u_1 := R$, $v_1 := R'$;
for $(j := 1, 2, \cdots, \ell - 1)$
  $r_j := M[j]$, $r'_j||s'_j := \pi(r_j||s_j)$;
  $u_{j+1}||v_{j+1} := \pi(u_j||v_j)$, $C[j] := v_{j+1} \oplus r'_j$;
  $s_{j+1} := s'_j \oplus t_j$, $t_{j+1} := r'_j$;
$r_\ell := M[\ell]$, $r'_\ell||s'_\ell := \pi(r_\ell||s_\ell)$;
$u_{\ell+1}||v_{\ell+1} := \pi(u_\ell||v_\ell)$, $s_{\ell+1} := s'_\ell \oplus t_\ell$;
$u' := u_{\ell+1}$, $v' := v_{\ell+1} \oplus s_{\ell+1}$;
$K := s_{\ell+1}$, $T := r'_\ell$;
$C := C[1]||C[2]||\cdots||C[\ell-1]||u'||v'$;
return $(K, C, T)$;

RevD-1. $\mathcal{D}(1^\lambda, K, C, T)$

$\ell := |C|/\lambda - 1$, $s_{\ell+1} := K$, $r'_\ell := T$;
$C[1]||C[2]||\cdots||C[\ell-1]||u'||v' := C$;
$u_{\ell+1} := u'$, $v_{\ell+1} := v' \oplus s_{\ell+1}$;
$u_\ell||v_\ell := \pi^{-1}(u_{\ell+1}||v_{\ell+1})$;
if $\ell = 1$, then $t_\ell := 0^\lambda$;
Else $t_\ell := C[\ell-1] \oplus v_\ell$;
$s'_\ell := s_{\ell+1} \oplus t_\ell$, $r_\ell||s_\ell := \pi^{-1}(r'_\ell||s'_\ell)$;
$M[\ell] := r_\ell$;
for $(j := \ell-1, \ell-2, \cdots, 1)$
  $u_j||v_j := \pi^{-1}(u_{j+1}||v_{j+1})$;
  If $j = 1$, then $t_j := 0^\lambda$;
  Else $t_j := C[j-1] \oplus v_j$;
  $r'_j := t_{j+1}$, $s'_j := s_{j+1} \oplus t_j$;
  $(r_j||s_j) := \pi^{-1}(r'_j||s'_j)$, $M[j] := r_j$;
$M := M[1]||M[2]||\cdots||M[\ell]$;
if $s_1 = 0^\lambda$ then return $M$;
else return $\bot$;

RevD-1. $\mathcal{P}(1^\lambda, Q = (n, u'', v''), M, K, C, T)$

$\ell := |C|/\lambda - 1$, $s_{\ell+1} := K$;
$C[1]||C[2]||\cdots||C[\ell-1]||u'||v' := C$;
$u_{\ell+1} := u'$, $v_{\ell+1} := v' \oplus s_{\ell+1}$;
$u'_{\ell+1} := u''$, $v'_{\ell+1} := v'' \oplus s_{\ell+1}$;
for $(j := l, l-1, \cdots, n+1)$
  $u_j||v_j := \pi^{-1}(u_{j+1}||v_{j+1})$;
  $u'_j||v'_j := \pi^{-1}(u'_{j+1}||v'_{j+1})$;
$C'[n] := C[n] \oplus v_{n+1} \oplus v'_{n+1}$;
return $C'[n]$;

RevD-1. $\mathcal{U}(1^\lambda, i_{st}, i_{end}, M_{new}, K, C, T, app)$

$\ell := |C|/\lambda - 1$, $m := \lceil i_{st}/\lambda \rceil$;
$C[1]||C[2]||\cdots||C[\ell-1]||u'||v' := C$;
$s_{\ell+1} := K$, $r'_\ell := T$, $u_{\ell+1} := u'$;
$v_{\ell+1} := v' \oplus s_{\ell+1}$, $u_\ell||v_\ell := \pi^{-1}(u_{\ell+1}||v_{\ell+1})$;
if $\ell = 1$, then $t_\ell := 0^\lambda$;
Else $t_\ell := C[\ell-1] \oplus v_\ell$;
$s'_\ell := s_{\ell+1} \oplus t_\ell$, $r_\ell||s_\ell := \pi^{-1}(r'_\ell||s'_\ell)$;
$M[\ell] := r_\ell$;
for $(j := \ell-1, \ell-2, \cdots, m)$
  $u_j||v_j := \pi^{-1}(u_{j+1}||v_{j+1})$;
  If $j = 1$, then $t_j := 0^\lambda$;
  Else $t_j := C[j-1] \oplus v_j$;
  $r'_j := t_{j+1}$, $s_j := s_{j+1} \oplus t_j$;
  $(r_j||s_j) := \pi^{-1}(r'_j||s'_j)$, $M[j] := r_j$;
$idx_1 := i_{st} \mod \lambda$;
if $idx_1 = 0$, then $idx_1 := \lambda$;
$M' := M[m][1]||M[m][2]||\cdots$
         $\cdots||M[m][idx_1 - 1]||M_{new}$;
if $app = 0$
  $n := \lceil i_{end}/\lambda \rceil$, $idx_2 := i_{end} \mod \lambda$;
  If $idx_2 = 0$, then $idx_2 := \lambda$;
  $M' = M'||M[n][idx_2 + 1]||M[n][idx_2 + 2]$
         $||\cdots||M[n][\lambda]||M[n+1]$
         $||M[n+2]||\cdots||M[\ell]$;
Else $\ell := (m-1) + (|M'|/\lambda)$;
$M'[1]||M'[2]||\cdots||M'[\ell - m + 1] := M'$;
for $(j := m, m+1, \cdots, \ell-1)$
  $r_j := M'[j - m + 1]$, $r'_j||s'_j := \pi(r_j||s_j)$;
  $u_{j+1}||v_{j+1} := \pi(u_j||v_j)$;
  $C'[j] := v_{j+1} \oplus r'_j$;
  $s_{j+1} := s'_j \oplus t_j$, $t_{j+1} := r'_j$;
$r_\ell := M'[\ell - m + 1]$, $r'_\ell||s'_\ell := \pi(r_\ell||s_\ell)$;
$u_{\ell+1}||v_{\ell+1} := \pi(u_\ell||v_\ell)$, $s_{\ell+1} := s'_\ell \oplus t_\ell$;
$u' := u_{\ell+1}$, $v' := v_{\ell+1} \oplus s_{\ell+1}$;
$K' := s_{\ell+1}$, $T' := r'_\ell$;
$C' := C[1]||C[2]||\cdots||C[m-1]||C'[m]$
       $||C'[m+1]||\cdots||C'[\ell-1]||u'||v'$;
return $(K', C', T')$;

RevD-1. $\mathcal{V}(1^\lambda, Q = n, C, T, P)$

if $C[n] = P$, then return TRUE;
Else return FALSE;

**Fig. 4.** Algorithmic description of the *FMLE* scheme RevD-1 for message $M_i$.

$M[i]$ denote the $i$-th block of message, and $M[i][j]$ denote the $j$-th bit of $i$-th block of message. It is worth noting that the decryption is executed in the reverse direction of encryption. The detailed textual description of the 5-tuple of algorithms will appear in the full version of the paper.

**Security of RevD-2.** The details of the proofs for the PRV\$-CDA, TC, CXH and UNC-CDA security of RevD-2 will appear in the full version.

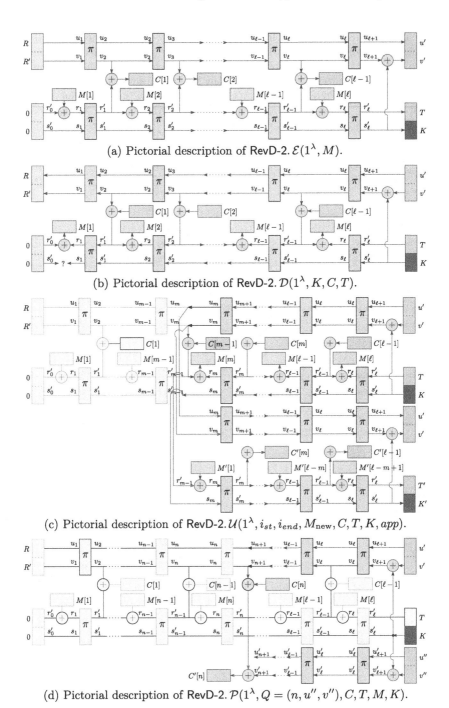

(a) Pictorial description of RevD-2. $\mathcal{E}(1^\lambda, M)$.

(b) Pictorial description of RevD-2. $\mathcal{D}(1^\lambda, K, C, T)$.

(c) Pictorial description of RevD-2. $\mathcal{U}(1^\lambda, i_{st}, i_{end}, M_{new}, C, T, K, app)$.

(d) Pictorial description of RevD-2. $\mathcal{P}(1^\lambda, Q = (n, u'', v''), C, T, M, K)$.

Fig. 5. Diagrammatic description of RevD-2.

**Table 1.** RevD-1 and RevD-2 are compared with the other *FMLE* schemes. Here, $\lambda$ is the security parameter; $F$ is the file to be encrypted; $|F|$ denotes the bit-length of $F$; $B$ is the block-size used in the *UMLE* scheme; $F'$ is the shortest suffix of $F$ containing all modified bits; $k$ is the index of the first bit in the challenge in the PoW protocol; $c_{\mathcal{H}_{|F|}}$, $c_{\mathcal{H}_B}$ and $c_{\mathcal{H}_\lambda}$ are the costs of computing hashes on inputs of lengths $|F|$, $B$ and $\lambda$ respectively; $c_{\mathcal{SE}_{|F|}}$ and $c_{\mathcal{SE}_B}$ are the costs of encryption (in a one-time symmetric encryption) of the messages of lengths $|F|$ and $B$ respectively; $c_{\mathcal{SD}_{|F|}}$ and $c_{\mathcal{SD}_B}$ are the costs of decryption of the messages of lengths $|F|$ and $B$ respectively; $c_{\pi_{2\lambda}}$ and $c_{\pi_{2\lambda}^{-1}}$ are the costs of computing the $2\lambda$-bit permutation and its inverse respectively.

| Const. / Param. | F-CE [8] | F-HCE2 [5] | F-RCE [5] | F-UMLE [13] | RevD-1/RevD-2 This Paper |
|---|---|---|---|---|---|
| **Time of $\mathcal{E}$** | | | | | |
| • Key Gen | $c_{\mathcal{H}_{|F|}}$ | $c_{\mathcal{H}_{|F|}}$ | $c_{\mathcal{H}_{|F|}}$ | $\left(\frac{|F|}{B} + \log_{B/\lambda}|F|\right)c_{\mathcal{H}_B}$ | − |
| • Tag Gen | $c_{\mathcal{H}_{|F|}}$ | $c_{\mathcal{H}_\lambda}$ | $c_{\mathcal{H}_\lambda}$ | $c_{\mathcal{H}_{|F|}} + \left(\frac{|F|}{B} + \log_{B/\lambda}|F|\right)c_{\mathcal{H}_B}$ | − |
| • Cipher | $c_{\mathcal{SE}_{|F|}}$ | $c_{\mathcal{SE}_{|F|}}$ | $c_{\mathcal{SE}_{|F|}}$ | $\left(\frac{|F|}{B} + \log_{B/\lambda}|F|\right)c_{\mathcal{SE}_B}$ | $2 \cdot \frac{|F|}{\lambda}c_{\pi_{2\lambda}}$ |
| # of passes | 3 | 2 | 1 | $1 + \log_{B/\lambda}|F|$ | 1 |
| **Time of $\mathcal{D}$** | | | | | |
| • Plaintext | $c_{\mathcal{SD}_{|F|}}$ | $c_{\mathcal{SD}_{|F|}}$ | $c_{\mathcal{SD}_{|F|}}$ | $\left(\frac{|F|}{B} + \log_{B/\lambda}|F|\right)c_{\mathcal{SD}_B}$ | $2 \cdot \frac{|F|}{\lambda}c_{\pi_{2\lambda}^{-1}}$ |
| • Tag Verif | $c_{\mathcal{H}_{|F|}}$ | $c_{\mathcal{H}_{|F|}} + c_{\mathcal{H}_\lambda}$ | $c_{\mathcal{H}_{|F|}} + c_{\mathcal{H}_\lambda}$ | $\left(\frac{|F|}{B} + \log_{B/\lambda}|F|\right)c_{\mathcal{H}_B}$ | − |
| # of passes | 2 | 2 | 1 | $1 + \log_{B/\lambda}|F|$ | 1 |
| **Time of $\mathcal{U}$** | | | | | |
| • Decryp | $c_{\mathcal{SD}_{|F|}}$ | $c_{\mathcal{SD}_{|F|}}$ | $c_{\mathcal{SD}_{|F|}}$ | $\log_{B/\lambda}|F| \cdot c_{\mathcal{SD}_B}$ | $2 \cdot \frac{|F'|}{\lambda}c_{\pi_{2\lambda}^{-1}}$ |
| • Encryp | $c_{\mathcal{SE}_{|F|}}$ | $c_{\mathcal{SE}_{|F|}}$ | $c_{\mathcal{SE}_{|F|}}$ | $\log_{B/\lambda}|F| \cdot c_{\mathcal{SE}_B}$ | $2 \cdot \frac{|F'|}{\lambda}c_{\pi_{2\lambda}}$ |
| • Key Gen | $c_{\mathcal{H}_{|F|}}$ | $c_{\mathcal{H}_{|F|}}$ | $c_{\mathcal{H}_{|F|}}$ | $\log_{B/\lambda}|F| \cdot c_{\mathcal{H}_B}$ | − |
| • Tag Gen | $c_{\mathcal{H}_{|F|}}$ | $c_{\mathcal{H}_\lambda}$ | $c_{\mathcal{H}_\lambda}$ | $\log_{B/\lambda}|F| \cdot c_{\mathcal{H}_B} + c_{\mathcal{H}_{|F|}}$ | − |
| # of passes | 4 | 3 | 1 | $1 + \frac{\log_{B/\lambda}|F|}{|F|}$ | $2\frac{|F'|}{|F|}$ |
| **Time of $\mathcal{P}$** | | | | | |
| • Gen Proof | *negl.* | *negl.* | $c_{\mathcal{SD}_{|F|}} + c_{\mathcal{SE}_{|F|}}$ | *negl.* | $2\frac{|F| - k}{\lambda}c_{\pi_{2\lambda}^{-1}}$ |
| # of passes | 0 | 0 | 1 | 0 | $1 - \frac{k}{|F|}$ |
| **Storage** | | | | | |
| • Key | $\lambda$ | $\lambda$ | $\lambda$ | $\lambda$ | $\lambda$ |
| • Ciphertext | $|F|$ | $|F|$ | $|F| + \lambda$ | $|F| + \log_{B/\lambda}|F| \cdot B$ | $|F| + \lambda$ |
| • Tag | $\lambda$ | $\lambda$ | $\lambda$ | $\left(\frac{|F|}{B} + \log_{B/\lambda}|F|\right)\lambda$ | $\lambda$ |
| **Security** | | | | | |
| • TC | ✓ | ✓ | ✓ | ✓ | ✓ |
| • STC | ✓ | ✗ | ✗ | ✓ | ✗ |
| • PRV-CDA | ✓ | ✓ | ✓ | ✓ | ✓ |
| • PRV\$-CDA | ✓ | ✓ | ✓ | ✓ | ✓ |
| • CXH | ✓ | ✓ | ✓ | ✓ | ✓ |
| • UNC-CDA | ✓ | ✓ | ✓ | ✓ | ✓ |
| • Dict. Attack | ✗ | ✗ | ✓ | ✗ | ✓ |

**Resistance of RevD-1 and RevD-2 Against Dictionary Attack.** Since, RevD-1 and RevD-2 have randomized encryption algorithms, they are not vulnerable to dictionary attacks (see Sect. 2.2 for a definition of dictionary attack).

RevD-2. $\mathcal{E}(1^\lambda, M)$

$\ell := |M|/\lambda,\ r'_0 := 0^\lambda,\ s'_0 := 0^\lambda;$
$M[1]||M[2]||\cdots||M[\ell] := M;$
$R \xleftarrow{\$} \{0,1\}^\lambda,\ R' \xleftarrow{\$} \{0,1\}^\lambda,\ u_1 := R,\ v_1 := R';$
for $(j := 1, 2, \cdots, \ell - 1)$
$\quad r_j := M[j] \oplus r'_{j-1},\ s_j := s'_{j-1};$
$\quad r'_j||s'_j := \pi(r_j||s_j),\ u_{j+1}||v_{j+1} := \pi(u_j||v_j);$
$\quad C[j] := v_{j+1} \oplus r'_j;$
$r_\ell := M[\ell] \oplus r'_{\ell-1},\ s_\ell := s'_{\ell-1};$
$r'_\ell||s'_\ell := \pi(r_\ell||s_\ell),\ u_{\ell+1}||v_{\ell+1} := \pi(u_\ell||v_\ell);$
$u' := u_{\ell+1},\ v' := v_{\ell+1} \oplus s'_\ell;$
$K := s'_\ell,\ T := r'_\ell;$
$C := C[1]||C[2]||\cdots||C[\ell-1]||u'||v';$
return $(K, C, T);$

RevD-2. $\mathcal{D}(1^\lambda, K, C, T)$

$\ell := |C|/\lambda - 1,\ r'_\ell := T,\ s'_\ell := K;$
$C[1]||C[2]||\cdots||C[\ell-1]||u'||v' := C;$
$u_{\ell+1} := u',\ v_{\ell+1} := v' \oplus s'_\ell;$
$u_\ell||v_\ell := \pi^{-1}(u_{\ell+1}||v_{\ell+1});$
$r_\ell||s_\ell := \pi^{-1}(r'_\ell||s'_\ell);$
If $\ell = 1$, then $r'_{\ell-1} := 0^\lambda;$
Else $r'_{\ell-1} := C[\ell-1] \oplus v_\ell;$
$s'_{\ell-1} := s_\ell,\ M[\ell] := r'_{\ell-1} \oplus r_\ell;$
for $(j := \ell-1, \ell-2, \cdots, 1)$
$\quad r_j||s_j := \pi^{-1}(r'_j||s'_j);$
$\quad u_j||v_j := \pi^{-1}(u_{j+1}||v_{j+1});$
$\quad$ If $j = 1$, then $r'_{j-1} := 0^\lambda;$
$\quad$ Else $r'_{j-1} := C[j-1] \oplus v_j;$
$\quad M[j] := r_j \oplus r'_{j-1},\ s'_{j-1} := s_j;$
$M := M[1]||M[2]||\cdots||M[\ell];$
if $s'_0 = 0^\lambda$, then return $M;$
else return $\perp;$

RevD-2. $\mathcal{P}(1^\lambda, n, u'', v'', C, T, M)$

$\ell := |C|/\lambda - 1,\ s'_\ell := K;$
$C[1]||C[2]||\cdots||C[\ell-1]||u'||v' := C;$
$u_{\ell+1} := u',\ v_{\ell+1} := v' \oplus s'_\ell;$
$u'_{\ell+1} := u'',\ v'_{\ell+1} := v'' \oplus s'_\ell;$
for $(j := l, l-1, \cdots, n+1)$
$\quad u_j||v_j := \pi^{-1}(u_{j+1}||v_{j+1});$
$\quad u'_j||v'_j := \pi^{-1}(u'_{j+1}||v'_{j+1});$
$C'[n] := C[n] \oplus v_{n+1} \oplus v'_{n+1};$
return $C'[n];$

RevD-2. $\mathcal{U}(1^\lambda, i_{st}, i_{end}, M_{new}, C, T, K, app)$

$\ell := |C|/\lambda - 1,\ m := \lceil i_{st}/\lambda \rceil;$
$C[1]||C[2]||\cdots||C[\ell-1]||u'||v' := C;$
$s'_{\ell+1} := K,\ r'_\ell := T,\ u_{\ell+1} := u',\ v_{\ell+1} := v' \oplus s'_\ell;$
$u_\ell||v_\ell := \pi^{-1}(u_{\ell+1}||v_{\ell+1});$
$r_\ell||s_\ell := \pi^{-1}(r'_\ell||s'_\ell);$
If $\ell = 1$, then $r'_{\ell-1} := 0^\lambda;$
Else $r'_{\ell-1} := C[\ell-1] \oplus v_\ell;$
$s'_{\ell-1} := s_\ell,\ M[\ell] := r'_{\ell-1} \oplus r_\ell;$
for $(j := \ell-1, \ell-2, \cdots, m)$
$\quad r_j||s_j := \pi^{-1}(r'_j||s'_j);$
$\quad u_j||v_j := \pi^{-1}(u_{j+1}||v_{j+1});$
$\quad$ If $j = 1$, then $r'_{j-1} := 0^\lambda;$
$\quad$ Else $r'_{j-1} := C[j-1] \oplus v_j;$
$\quad M[j] := r_j \oplus r'_{j-1},\ s'_{j-1} := s_j;$
$idx_1 := i_{st} \bmod \lambda;$
if $idx_1 = 0$, then $idx_1 := \lambda;$
$M' = M[m][1]||M[m][2]||\cdots$
$\quad\quad\quad\quad\cdots||M[m][idx_1 - 1]||M_{new};$
if $app = 0$
$\quad n := \lceil i_{end}/\lambda \rceil,\ idx_2 := i_{end} \bmod \lambda;$
$\quad$ If $idx_2 = 0$, then $idx_2 := \lambda;$
$\quad M' = M'||M[n][idx_2]||M[n][idx_2 + 2]$
$\quad\quad\quad ||\cdots||M[n][\lambda]||M[n+1]$
$\quad\quad\quad ||M[n+2]||\cdots||M[\ell];$
Else $\ell := (m-1) + (|M'|/\lambda);$
$M'[1]||M'[2]||\cdots||M'[\ell-m+1] := M';$
for $(j := m, m+1, \cdots, \ell-1)$
$\quad r_j := M'[j-m+1] \oplus r'_{j-1},\ s_j := s'_{j-1};$
$\quad r'_j||s'_j := \pi(r_j||s_j);$
$\quad u_{j+1}||v_{j+1} := \pi(u_j||v_j);$
$\quad C'[j] := v_{j+1} \oplus r'_j;$
$r_\ell := M'[\ell-m+1] \oplus r'_{\ell-1},\ s_\ell := s'_{\ell-1};$
$r'_\ell||s'_\ell := \pi(r_\ell||s_\ell);$
$u_{\ell+1}||v_{\ell+1} := \pi(u_\ell||v_\ell);$
$u' := u_{\ell+1},\ v' := v_{\ell+1} \oplus s'_\ell;$
$K' := s'_\ell,\ T' := r'_\ell;$
$C' := C[1]||C[2]||\cdots||C[m-1]||C'[m]$
$\quad\quad\quad ||C'[m+1]||\cdots||C'[\ell-1]||u'||v';$
return $(K', C', T');$

RevD-2. $\mathcal{V}(1^\lambda, n, C, T, P)$

if $C[n] = P$, then return TRUE;
Else return FALSE;

**Fig. 6.** Algorithmic description of the *FMLE* scheme RevD-2.

## 6.3 Comparing RevD-1 and RevD-2 with the Other *FMLE* Schemes

In Table 1, we compare the RevD-1 and RevD-2 with the other *FMLE* constructions described in Sect. 5, on the basis of time and space complexities, and the security properties.

In summary, the *FMLE* schemes RevD-1 and RevD-2 possess the randomization property of *MLE* construction RCE, and the efficient update property of *UMLE*. It is also noted that it outperforms all the constructions in terms of the number of passes.

# 7    Conclusion

In this paper, we present a new cryptographic primitive *FMLE* and two new constructions of it: RevD-1 and RevD-2. We showed that these constructions perform better – both with respect to time and memory – than the existing constructions. The high performance is attributed to a unique property named *reverse decryption* of the *FP* hash function and the *APE* authenticated encryption, on which these new constructions are based. The only disadvantage is, perhaps, that these constructions are not STC secure. We leave as an open problem construction of an STC secure efficient *FMLE*.

# References

1. Abadi, M., Boneh, D., Mironov, I., Raghunathan, A., Segev, G.: Message-locked encryption for lock-dependent messages. In: Canetti, R., Garay, J.A. (eds.) CRYPTO 2013. LNCS, vol. 8042, pp. 374–391. Springer, Heidelberg (2013). https://doi.org/10.1007/978-3-642-40041-4_21

2. Andreeva, E., Bilgin, B., Bogdanov, A., Luykx, A., Mennink, B., Mouha, N., Yasuda, K.: APE: authenticated permutation-based encryption for lightweight cryptography. In: Cid, C., Rechberger, C. (eds.) FSE 2014. LNCS, vol. 8540, pp. 168–186. Springer, Heidelberg (2015). https://doi.org/10.1007/978-3-662-46706-0_9

3. Bellare, M., Keelveedhi, S.: Interactive message-locked encryption and secure deduplication. In: Katz, J. (ed.) PKC 2015. LNCS, vol. 9020, pp. 516–538. Springer, Heidelberg (2015). https://doi.org/10.1007/978-3-662-46447-2_23

4. Bellare, M., Keelveedhi, S., Ristenpart, T.: DupLESS: server-aided encryption for deduplicated storage. In: King, S. (ed.) USENIX 2013, pp. 179–194 (2013)

5. Bellare, M., Keelveedhi, S., Ristenpart, T.: Message-locked encryption and secure deduplication. In: Johansson, T., Nguyen, P.Q. (eds.) EUROCRYPT 2013. LNCS, vol. 7881, pp. 296–312. Springer, Heidelberg (2013). https://doi.org/10.1007/978-3-642-38348-9_18

6. Canard, S., Laguillaumie, F., Paindavoine, M.: Verifiable message-locked encryption. In: Foresti, S., Persiano, G. (eds.) CANS 2016. LNCS, vol. 10052, pp. 299–315. Springer, Cham (2016). https://doi.org/10.1007/978-3-319-48965-0_18

7. Chen, R., Mu, Y., Yang, G., Guo, F.: BL-MLE: block-level message-locked encryption for secure large file deduplication. IEEE Trans. Inf. Forensics Secur. **10**(12), 2643–2652 (2015). https://doi.org/10.1109/TIFS.2015.2470221

8. Douceur, J.R., Adya, A., Bolosky, W.J., Simon, D., Theimer, M.: Reclaiming space from duplicate files in a serverless distributed file system. In: ICDCS 2002, pp. 617–624 (2002). https://doi.org/10.1109/ICDCS.2002.1022312

9. Huang, K., Zhang, X., Wang, X.: Block-level message-locked encryption with polynomial commitment for IoT data. J. Inf. Sci. Eng. (JISE), **33**(4), 891–905 (2017). http://jise.iis.sinica.edu.tw/JISESearch/pages/View/PaperView.jsf?keyId=157_2047

10. Jiang, T., Chen, X., Wu, Q., Ma, J., Susilo, W., Lou, W.: Towards efficient fully randomized message-locked encryption. In: Liu, J.K.K., Steinfeld, R. (eds.) ACISP 2016. LNCS, vol. 9722, pp. 361–375. Springer, Cham (2016). https://doi.org/10.1007/978-3-319-40253-6_22

11. Paul, S., Homsirikamol, E., Gaj, K.: A novel permutation-based hash mode of operation FP and the hash function SAMOSA. In: Galbraith, S., Nandi, M. (eds.) INDOCRYPT 2012. LNCS, vol. 7668, pp. 509–527. Springer, Heidelberg (2012). https://doi.org/10.1007/978-3-642-34931-7_29
12. Wang, H., Chen, K., Qin, B., Lai, X., Wen, Y.: A new construction on randomized message-locked encryption in the standard model via UCEs. Sci. China Inf. Sci. **60**(5), 052101 (2017). https://doi.org/10.1007/s11432-015-1037-2
13. Zhao, Y., Chow, S.S.M.: Updatable block-level message-locked encryption. In: Karri, R., Sinanoglu, O., Sadeghi, A., Yi, X. (eds.) Proceedings of the 2017 ACM on Asia Conference on Computer and Communications Security, AsiaCCS 2017, Abu Dhabi, United Arab Emirates, 2–6 April 2017, pp. 449–460. ACM (2017). https://doi.org/10.1145/3052973.3053012

# DogFish: Decentralized Optimistic Game-theoretic FIle SHaring

Seny Kamara[1] and Alptekin Küpçü[2(✉)]

[1] Brown University, Providence, RI, USA
[2] Koç University, İstanbul, Turkey
akupcu@ku.edu.tr

**Abstract.** Peer-to-peer (p2p) file sharing accounts for the most uplink bandwidth use in the Internet. Therefore, in the past few decades, many solutions tried to come up with better proposals to increase the social welfare of the participants. Social welfare in such systems are categorized generally as average download time or uplink bandwidth utilization. One of the most influential proposals was the BitTorrent. Yet, soonafter studies showed that BitTorrent has several problems that incentivize selfish users to game the system and hence decrease social welfare.

Previous work, unfortunately, did not develop a system that maximizes social welfare in a decentralized manner (without a trusted party getting involved in every exchange), while the proposed strategy and honest piece revelation being the only equilibrium for the rational players. This is what we achieve, by modeling a general class of p2p file sharing systems theoretically, then showing honest piece revelation will help achieve social welfare, and then introducing a new cryptographic primitive, called randomized fair exchange, to instantiate our solution.

**Keywords:** Peer-to-peer file sharing · Optimistic fair exchange
Proof of storage · Cryptographic protocol · Game theory

## 1 Introduction

The interaction between parties in peer-to-peer (p2p) file sharing networks is strategic and therefore the study of the incentives behind such networks have become an active area of research. The best known and most successful file sharing network BitTorrent, introduced by Cohen [18], accounts for the most uplink bandwidth use in the Internet [50]. File sharing in BitTorrent can be defined as a two-party game where the peers must decide whether or not to trade a block of the file they are trying to download. It was originally believed that the best strategy for the BitTorrent game was to play tit-for-tat, that is, if a peer provides another peer with a block then the second peer should reciprocate

S. Kamara—Work done while at Microsoft Research.

A. Küpçü—Work partly done while at Microsoft Research.

B. Preneel and F. Vercauteren (Eds.): ACNS 2018, LNCS 10892, pp. 696–714, 2018.
https://doi.org/10.1007/978-3-319-93387-0_36

and provide the first peer with another block. However, the appearance of clients like BitThief [40] and BitTyrant [46], which do not play tit-for-tat, has called this assumption into question. In particular, Levin et al. [37] argued that the BitTorrent game is more properly modeled as an auction.

During a BitTorrent round (roughly 10 s), to whom a peer connects is decided based on others' uploads to the peer at hand and the pieces they advertise to have. The BitTorrent protocol specifies that the peers should report the pieces they own honestly. Yet, they can over- or under-report the pieces they own, to gain strategical advantage, decreasing social welfare [37, 49].

Consider an over-reporting peer. He may be attractive to many other peers since he seems to have something that they do not have; many peers would want to connect to him. But then, during their exchange, they may not be able to obtain anything useful from him, whereas he may obtain many useful blocks. As for an under-reporting peer, as observed before, the peer may gain some strategic advantage against BitTorrent's rarest piece first heuristic [37]. Moreover, if many peers are under-reporting, the system would face starvation [49].

In this paper we address this issue for the first time, as we present a BitTorrent-like p2p file sharing mechanism that incentivizes honest piece revelation, hence increasing social welfare, while working in a decentralized manner without any trusted party involvement per block exchange, and is an equilibrium for rational players. We achieve this goal in a simplified theoretical setting, through the use of novel cryptographic techniques, and a game-theoretic approach to p2p file sharing systems that encompasses different aspects of a protocol such as peer matching and block exchange. We do not claim that our protocol would replace BitTorrent in practice; rather we trust that our theoretical solution insight would help prominent researchers develop both theoretically-sound and practically-applicable protocols for this goal. Our contributions are:

- We propose the first theoretical *decentralized* file sharing protocol (with no trusted party involvement per exchange) that is an *equilibrium* with respect to realistic utility functions (i.e., the number of pieces downloaded).
- To achieve this we introduce and construct a new cryptographic functionality which we refer to as *randomized fair exchange* (RFE). We provide a security definition for RFE and a construction.
- While the use of RFE is enough to disincentivize under-reporting, it does not prevent over-reporting. We then combine RFE with *proofs of storage* to ensure over-reporting is also discouraged.
- Finally, we show that under a simple theoretical model, our solution achieves an equilibrium with the best possible *social welfare* (defined as upload bandwidth utilization) among a large class of protocols that first match peers based on their reported pieces, and then perform pair-wise exchanges.

## 2   Preliminaries

*File Sharing Protocols.* In the BitTorrent protocol files are divided into pieces, and pieces are divided into blocks (see [18] and[1] for details). Exchange takes place in terms of blocks. Only blocks of finished pieces are exchanged. A *torrent* file contains hashes of the pieces so that they can be verified to be the correct ones. There are two types of peers in the system: those who already have all the pieces of the torrent at hand (the **seeders**), and those who do *not* have the complete set of pieces and are still downloading (the **leechers**).

When a new peer joins the system, she obtains a *peerset* (a list of seeders and leechers) from the Tracker (which is a central entity, but does not get involved in exchanges) for the torrent she wants to download, and starts forming peer-to-peer connections with those peers. They announce her the pieces they have. Based on those announcements, she picks a subset of those peers to actually perform block exchanges with. In BitTorrent, usually a peer would pick 4 peers who have given her the most blocks in the previous round (e.g., past 10 s), and 1 more random peer (totaling 5 peers) to give a block to. Those exchanges are not necessarily fair [40,46]. Each time she obtains a new piece, she reports it to her peerset, which may not be done honestly either [37,49].

Throughout the paper, we simplify our discussion by using piece and block interchangeably, since we are describing a BitTorrent-like protocol and not necessarily BitTorrent itself. In our case, we only consider blocks in a torrent, where the hash of each one of them is known from the torrent, and the blocks can be exchanged as soon as they are downloaded.

*Basic Game Theory.* In an $n$-player game, we have players $P_1, \ldots, P_n$, where player $P_i$ has $m$ possible actions $A_i^1, \ldots, A_i^m$ and a real-valued utility function $u_i$. The utility $u_i$ of player $P_i$ is a function of an action profile $A$ such that $A$ specifies one action $A_j^{\ell_j}$ for every player $P_j$. The goal of the players is to obtain the highest possible utility.

Strategy $s_i$ of player $P_i$ is a probability distribution over the possible actions of player $P_i$. Let $s_i(a)$ denote the probability the strategy $s_i$ assigns to the action $a$. Let $s = \{s_1, \ldots, s_n\}$ denote a strategy profile encompassing the strategies of every player. Further denote by $s_{-i} = s - \{s_i\}$ the strategy profile of all players *except* the player $P_i$. Given the strategies of each player, we can define expected utility $U_i$ for player $P_i$ as $U_i(s) = \Sigma_{A \in s} \left( u_i(A) * \Pi_{j=1}^n Pr[s_j(A_j)] \right)$.

A strategy profile $s = \{s_1, \ldots, s_n\}$ is **a Nash equilibrium** if $\forall P_i \quad \forall s_i' \neq s_i \quad U_i(s_i \cup s_{-i}) \geq U_i(s_i' \cup s_{-i})$. A strategy profile $s$ is **a strict Nash equilibrium** if the inequality is strict.

In a **computational setting**, $s$ is considered a **computational Nash equilibrium** if there is a negligible function $neg(k)$ in the security parameter $k$ such that $\forall P_i \quad \forall s_i' \neq s_i \quad U_i(s_i \cup s_{-i}) \geq U_i(s_i' \cup s_{-i}) - neg(k)$. This allows the strategy $s$ to be negligibly worse than the other alternatives. Note that strictness is not important here, since there would be another negligible function that makes

---

[1] http://bittorrent.com.

the inequality strict. Furthermore, we require that the actions of players can be implemented in polynomial time using probabilistic Turing machines (**PPT actions**, in short). $\epsilon$-Nash equilibrium is a generalization where the negligible function is replaced with some other $\epsilon$.

*Proofs of Storage.* Efficient proofs of storage (PoS) were introduced in 2007, independently by Ateniese et al. [4] and Juels and Kaliski [28]. Later on, Ateniese et al. [5] and Dodis et al. [19] generalized these constructions, and Erway et al. [21] and Cash et al. [15] made them work with dynamic data for the first time.

In these constructions, the general idea is that a file is divided into blocks, then cryptographic tags are created for each block. In a regular PoS scenario, the client creates those tags, and outsources the file and the tags to the server for storage. Later, the client or some third party auditor can challenge the server to prove that her file is kept intact. The server sends back a short proof, which is verified using the associated PoS (public) key.

**When Applied to a p2p File Sharing System, We Consider PoS as Follows:** The creator of the torrent creates those tags, and hence each block is associated with a tag in the torrent file. Then, when peers advertise blocks, they can prove to each other that they indeed have the actual blocks they claim to have. Thus, the client role belongs to the torrent creator, and the auditor and the server roles are played by all the peers. Moreover, since the torrent contents are static once created, static proofs of storage with public verifiability (meaning anyone can verify integrity using public information) are enough (e.g., [4,51]).

*Fair Exchange.* In a fair exchange scenario, there are two parties Alice and Bob, where each has an item $e_A$ and $e_B$, respectively, that they want to exchange. At the end of the protocol, it must be the case that either Alice obtains $e_B$ *and* Bob obtains $e_A$, or neither of them obtains anything useful about the other party's item. It is known that fair exchange requires a trusted third party called the *Arbiter* [45], but optimistic protocols employ this Arbiter only when a problem occurs [3]. Previously, two-party fair exchange protocols were used in the BitTorrent setting [10,36], but assuming honest piece revelation.

Multi-party fair exchange protocols achieve similar fairness guarantees for not only two but possibly more parties [31]. When there are multiple parties, we talk about exchange topologies. For example, if we have players $P_1, \ldots, P_n$ in a *ring topology*, this means each $P_i$ will send one item to $P_{(i+1) \bmod n}$. We combine two-party fair exchange protocols with coin tossing to obtain a new primitive called *randomized fair exchange*.

*Notation.* Each player $P_i$ has a set $\mathbf{S}_i$ of blocks she already holds, and a set $\mathbf{R}_i$ of blocks that she reports to have. Note that dishonest reporting means $\mathbf{S}_i \neq \mathbf{R}_i$. The notation $e \xleftarrow{\$} \mathbf{S}_i$ means that an element $e$ is picked randomly from the set $\mathbf{S}_i$. Sets are bold fonted.

We denote by $(\text{OUT}_A; \text{OUT}_B) \leftarrow \Pi_{A,B}(X; Y)$ the execution of a two-party protocol $\Pi$ between parties $A$ and $B$, where $X$ and $Y$ are the inputs provided by and $\text{OUT}_A$ and $\text{OUT}_B$ are the outputs returned to $A$ and $B$, respectively. This notation can be extended to multi-party protocols as well.

# 3   Related Work

*Prisoners' Dilemma.* Prisoners' Dilemma is considered by many as the underlying game of the BitTorrent protocol. Interestingly, even though tit-for-tat (TFT) is *not* a game-theoretic solution to the *finitely-repeated* Prisoners' Dilemma, Axelrod's experiments [6,7] show that it achieves the best results in overall utility gained. Later on, Fader and Hauser [22] published experiments on multi-player version of the Generalized Prisoners' Dilemma, and argued that coalitions of mutually-cooperating players will emerge implicitly, and win the tournaments.

Radner [48] allows $\epsilon$-departures from strict rationality, and shows that as the number of repetitions increase in the finitely-repeated Prisoners' Dilemma, the $\epsilon$-Nash equilibria allow for longer periods of collaboration in the Prisoners' Dilemma. Later, Neyman [43] shows that if the players are limited to polynomial-sized finite state automata, then cooperation in the Prisoners' Dilemma will give a Nash equilibrium. Unfortunately, this result does not hold in the Turing machine model and hence we cannot conclude a computational equilibrium using probabilistic polynomial time players. Halpern [27] argues that if memory has a positive cost, then it acts as a discount factor and rationalizes TFT strategy even for finitely-repeated Prisoners' Dilemma.

If one thinks of BitTorrent as an unboundedly-repeated (or incomplete-information) Prisoners' Dilemma, then TFT can be seen as an equilibrium. Ellison [20] shows this is the case in *anonymous random-matching* scenarios. Feldman et al. [25] use Generalized Prisoners' Dilemma to model p2p networks.

*Honest Piece Reporting.* Levin et al. [37] were the first to describe BitTorrent as an auction rather than a TFT game. They show that under-reporting of pieces constitute a problem and it leads to a tragedy of commons scenario if all peers under-report. Unfortunately, BitTorrent does *not* enforce honest piece reporting. prTorrent [49] also presents, via simulations, that this under-reporting may cause starvation in BitTorrent. They also show that piece rarity, which may be manipulated via under-reporting, can indeed be modeled game-theoretically as a discount parameter in a repeated game such as BitTorrent.

Arteconi et al. [2] consider evolutionary p2p protocols where peers randomly compare their utilities and replicate better actions. They consider honest reporting as the main issue, and analyze effects of dishonest reporting.

Luo et al. [41] define a multi-player game for sharing one piece, rather than a two-player game, to model BitTorrent-like file sharing systems, and propose a utility-based piece selection strategy. They define the concept of the marginal utility of a piece; a concept directly related to the under-reporting strategy described in the papers above. They also argue that as the number of peers increase, each peer is more likely to *not* report the piece that he owns.

Since under-reporting may change the attractiveness of a peer (and rareness of blocks), Guo et al. [26] and Okumuşoğlu et al. [44] argue that not all blocks should be equally valuable, and propose value-based variants of BitTorrent.

*Game-Theoretic File Sharing.* In light of the game-theoretic limitations of Bit-Torrent, alternative p2p file sharing protocols were proposed, including BAR-B

[1], Equicast [30], FOX [38], and Ratfish [8]. Unfortunately, all these works have limitations. For example, BAR-B and FOX only handle static sets of users. The Equicast protocol is only an equilibrium under strong assumptions (e.g., the rate of leechers that join has to equal the rate of leechers that leave) and for restricted utility functions which do not appear to model the real utilities of users. The Ratfish protocol, while being an equilibrium with respect to realistic player utilities, is a partly centralized solution where the trusted Tracker is involved in *every* exchange, which is undesirable in p2p settings. Similarly, Vilaça and Rodrigues [53] assume a trusted mediator. See [17] for a survey.

Another limitation of all these previous works is that none of these works show their solution's performance against a social choice function for p2p file sharing. As such, it is not clear how to evaluate these mechanisms or how to compare them. We also do not compare ourselves against solutions that employ monetary compensation, such as [10,52,54], or social network based reputation solutions [16], whose incentives for honest piece revelation are not clearly analyzed. See [29] for a survey of monetary incentives.

*Theoretical Optimum.* Fan et al. [24] define a performance metric (using the average download time) and a fairness metric (using upload vs. download bandwidth) and compare the original BitTorrent with some parameter-modified versions of it. They prove in their technical report [23] that when fairness is enforced, the average download time *increases*, slowing down the system.

Meng et al. [42] define a theoretical lower-bound for the distribution time of a file using BitTorrent-like systems. They use the *fluid model*, which allows each bit to be shared as soon as it is received, unlike BitTorrent that shares blocks once pieces are received. Yet, interestingly, Kumar and Ross [33] show experimentally that the error between the piece-based model's minimum download time and the fluid model's is less than 1%. Indeed, they claim that the difference between the two models can be safely ignored as long as the number of pieces in the file is much larger than the logarithm of the number of leechers, which is true for medium-sized or large files that we generally encounter in such systems.

# 4   Model

Our goal is to create a system maximizing social welfare in the equilibrium. We assume a homogeneous network, and analyze the protocol in rounds, where **at each round each peer can download at most one piece and upload at most one piece**. This makes our theoretical analysis easier. It also means that there is no bandwidth-based auction as in PropShare [37]. Instead, the matching between pairs will be done based on the mutual attractiveness in terms of the pieces a peer is missing. This allows us to focus on *piece revelation strategies* rather than bandwidth allocation issues.

Also note that **seeders are irrational** and altruistic entities, and there is no piece-revelation strategy for them. In our game-theoretic analysis, therefore, we keep them outside the discussion, since they are irrational. But, we allow seeders to help the system perform better by still distributing blocks.

**Table 1.** Matrix representation of number of pieces received by players at each round. Rows are leechers. Columns are rounds.

|       | 1 | 2 | 3 | ... | m |
|-------|---|---|---|-----|---|
| $P_1$ | 1 | 1 | 1 | 1 | 1 |
| $P_2$ | 1 | 1 | 1 | 1 | 1 |
| $P_3$ | 1 | 1 | 1 | 1 | 1 |
| ...   | 1 | 1 | 1 | 1 | 1 |
| $P_n$ | 1 | 1 | 1 | 1 | 1 |

|       | 1 | 2 | 3 | ... | m | m+1 | m+2 | m+3 | ... | m+n-1 |
|-------|---|---|---|-----|---|-----|-----|-----|-----|-------|
| $P_1$ | 1 | 1 | 1 | 1 | 1 | 0 | 0 | 0 | 0 | 0 |
| $P_2$ | 0 | 1 | 1 | 1 | 1 | 1 | 0 | 0 | 0 | 0 |
| $P_3$ | 0 | 0 | 1 | 1 | 1 | 1 | 1 | 0 | 0 | 0 |
| ...   | 0 | 0 | 0 | 1 | 1 | 1 | 1 | 1 | 1 | 0 |
| $P_n$ | 0 | 0 | 0 | 1 | 1 | 1 | 1 | 1 | 1 | 1 |

A more realistic analysis would model a heterogeneous network, where there are several types of players with different upload/download capabilities (but the protocol may still proceed in rounds). Moreover, our analysis only partly covers malicious irrational entities: while the cryptographic protocols employed prevent malicious actions, our incentive mechanism only works against rational entities. Thus, malicious entities may still over- or under-report the pieces they own.

# 5   Social Welfare for P2P File Sharing

In this section, we first define social welfare, then relate it to honest piece revelation for a general class of p2p file sharing protocols. This general class of protocols we consider incorporates two subprotocols: a peer matching protocol that pairs the peers, and a pair-wise block exchange protocol. This accurately models BitTorrent-like p2p file sharing systems restricted to a round-based exchange model. At each round, first peers are matched in pairs (remember our restriction that within one round only one block can be uploaded or downloaded), and then the exchange takes place. In the upcoming sections, we instantiate those subprotocols and show that they achieve the desired social welfare.

*Social Welfare.* When one considers the social welfare for a p2p file sharing system, there can be several metrics. One of the commonly used metrics in the literature is the *average download time*. Another good measure of an efficient system is indicated as the *utilization of the upload bandwidth* [11], since it ensures the system performs at its best in terms of distributing the file.

Let us denote a protocol as a matrix where *rows* denote the *parties* and the *columns* denote the *rounds*. Each cell $i, t$ denotes the probability that peer $P_i$ obtains some new block at round $t$ (alternatively, it can denote the expected number of blocks downloaded). The socially optimal protocol would be the one where the cells are all 1 until the round $m$ for every peer, where $m$ is the number of blocks in the file. The average download time would then be $m * n/n = m$, which is optimal in our model. Moreover, the upload/download bandwidths will be fully utilized. This corresponds to the left side matrix in Table 1.

Realize that such a protocol may *not* always be achievable. Consider, for example, a **single seeder flash crowd** scenario. In round 1, only one peer can obtain some piece from the seeder, and all other peers will obtain 0 blocks. One socially optimal (and deterministic) protocol here would be the following: The seeder, at round $t$, sends piece number $t$ to peer $P_1$. At the same round, each $P_i$ sends piece $t - i$ to $P_{i+1}$, if she already has that piece, and stays idle otherwise. Thus, peer $P_i$ finishes downloading at round $m + i - 1$.[2] This corresponds to the right side matrix in Table 1. Note that the upload bandwidths are again optimized to the best possible (except $P_n$).

Therefore, when we talk about socially optimal protocols, we cannot just talk about making every entry in the associated matrix 1. Instead, we need the following two properties to optimize the upload bandwidth in our model:

(1) For every peer $P_i$, $P_i$ needs to be matched with some interesting $P_j$ (if such $P_j$ exists). Here, interesting means $P_j$ has some piece $P_i$ does not have.
(2) For every $P_i$, $P_i$ needs to be able to download a new piece (assuming she is matched with some interesting $P_j$ above).

Note that we want protocols that incentivize the behavior above. Observe that (1) needs to hold for *all* peers, and (2) requires $P_j$ to have an incentive to send a new piece to $P_i$. One can create a global incentive mechanism for that, but it would not be very practical. Consider the single seeder flash crowd scenario above. In that deterministic protocol, no peer $P_i$ has an incentive to send a piece to peer $P_{i+1}$. To enforce the protocol, one may employ a ring-topology fair exchange protocol that ensures either the whole ring completes, or no peer can receive a new piece from the previous one (including from the seeder). Unfortunately, this necessitates per round communication complexity that is *quadratic in the number of peers* [31].

*Pairwise Protocols.* Hence, we concentrate on local incentive mechanisms, and in particular, **pair-wise** ones. If we match *mutually interesting* peers and perform a fair exchange between them, then we incentivize the desired behavior using only simple, constant complexity two-party fair exchanges instead of a global multi-party fair exchange mechanism that is costly. Thus, we consider protocols of the following type, where $\mathcal{F}^{MATCH}$ denotes the functionality to match the peers, and $\mathcal{F}^{EXCH}$ denotes the exchange functionality: First peers are matched pair-wise according to their piece revelations, and then pair-wise exchanges take place within the same round. This is depicted in Algorithm 1.

Such protocols assume that the exchanges occur between pairs of peers. Due to our simplification that one piece can be exchanged per round, such a simplified version of BitTorrent would also fit the framework above. As observed before, it may be impossible to reach the social optimum with such a protocol, but on the other hand, global matching and exchange protocols would be impractically inefficient. Therefore, we choose to restrict ourselves to pairwise matching and pairwise exchange protocols. As discussed, we know that to obtain the best possible social welfare (upload bandwidth utilization) in this restricted setting, we

---

[2] For simplicity, representing common behavior, assume each $P_i$ leaves the system the moment she finishes downloading (at the end of round $m + i - 1$). Afterward, at round $m + i$, the seeder sends the last block to peer $P_{i+1}$ (thus every peer receives the last block from the seeder).

---

**Algorithm 1.** Pairwise P2P File Sharing Protocol

---
**while** some peer is still downloading **do**

    $(P_{j_1}; P_{j_2}; ...; P_{j_n}) \leftarrow \mathcal{F}^{MATCH}_{P_1, P_2, ..., P_n}(\mathbf{R}_1; \mathbf{R}_2; ...; \mathbf{R}_n)$

    // *pair-wise such that if the output to $P_i$ is $P_{j_i}$ then the output to $P_{j_i}$ is $P_i$*

    **for** $i = 1$ to $n$ **do**

        $(e_{k_i}; e_{k_{j_i}}) \leftarrow \mathcal{F}^{EXCH}_{P_i, P_{j_i}}(\mathbf{S}_i; \mathbf{S}_{j_i})$

        // *actually, $n/2$ exchanges take place because of pair-wise matching and our round-based model*

    **end for**

**end while**

---

need to incentivize honest piece revelation and maximize the exchanges between the peers to obtain as many 1 values in the corresponding exchange matrix as possible. In the following sections, we first assume that every peer is matched with some interesting peer according to their piece revelations and show how to perform the $\mathcal{F}^{EXCH}$ phase by instantiating it via randomized fair exchange and proofs of storage. This is where our main contribution lies. Then, we finalize our DogFish protocol description by also instantiating the $\mathcal{F}^{MATCH}$ protocol via existing known solutions and finalizing our game-theoretic analysis.

# 6    $\mathcal{F}^{EXCH}$ Instantiation

We instantiate our $\mathcal{F}^{EXCH}$ functionality using randomized fair exchange (a primitive that we introduce and construct) together with proofs of storage. We first define these individual building blocks, and then provide our instantiation and its analysis. Throughout this section, we assume that $\mathcal{F}^{MATCH}$ is already completed matching mutually-interesting peers, and we concentrate on performing pair-wise exchanges during $\mathcal{F}^{EXCH}$. In practice, leechers may also get matched with seeders, but remember that seeder interactions are outside our game-theoretical scope, and hence in our protocols, we only deal with exchanges between two leechers.

## 6.1    Randomized Fair Exchange (RFE)

In regular fair exchange protocols, two parties exchange items such that at the end of the protocol, either both parties obtain each other's item, or neither party obtains anything useful [3]. RFE allows two parties to exchange elements from their sets of items in such a way that each party receives a *new* element *at random*. The RFE functionality is formally described in Fig. 1 and a construction is provided later.

    RFE is a crucial building block of the DogFish protocol, and is used to instantiate the $\mathcal{F}^{EXCH}$ functionality. Intuitively, we want to prevent an adversarial user to strategically pick the pieces to download, hence breaking fairness and deviating the system away from social welfare for the sake of his selfish utility. When blocks to be exchanged are picked randomly by the functionality, as we will

---

**The $\mathcal{F}^{RFE}$ Functionality**

- Upon receiving set $\mathbf{X}_1$ from $P_1$ and set $\mathbf{X}_2$ from $P_2$:
  1. if $\mathbf{X}_2 \setminus \mathbf{X}_1 = \emptyset$ or $\mathbf{X}_1 \setminus \mathbf{X}_2 = \emptyset$, sent $\perp$ to both parties.
  2. else, pick random $e_2 \xleftarrow{\$} \mathbf{X}_2 \setminus \mathbf{X}_1$ and $e_1 \xleftarrow{\$} \mathbf{X}_1 \setminus \mathbf{X}_2$ and send $e_2$ to $P_1$ and $e_1$ to $P_2$.

---

**Fig. 1.** The randomized fair exchange functionality.

show later, the adversary loses any advantage gained by under-reporting. Consider a player who under-reported the pieces he owns. During RFE, it is possible that he will receive a piece that he already owns, hence gaining no utility from the exchange, and in general, decreasing his expected utility. On the contrary, honestly-reporting players, who were matched with mutually-interesting peers, are expected to gain positive utility in RFE (more details later). We instantiate $\mathcal{F}^{RFE}$ using fair exchange and coin tossing protocols in Sect. 7.

## 6.2    Proofs of Storage (PoS)

Another building block for our $\mathcal{F}^{EXCH}$ functionality is a proof of storage protocol. We present the protocol as adapted to the p2p file sharing setting. Remember that the creator of the torrent file constructed the tags and put them in the torrent, together with the public key that will be used for verification purposes (thus, we only consider PoS schemes without secret keys used during challenge verification [34]). Also, we just need static PoS solutions, since torrent contents never change. Thus, such a protocol may be instantiated via, for example, [51] or [4] with only *constant* communication cost.

---

**The $\mathcal{F}^{PoS}$ Functionality**

- Upon receiving the actual blocks $\mathbf{S}_1$ and their tags from $P_1$, and the claimed blocks $\mathbf{R}_1$ and the verification key from $P_2$:
  1. if $\mathbf{S}_1$ does not contain all the claimed blocks in $\mathbf{R}_1$, return REJECT to $P_2$;
  2. else, if all the blocks in $\mathbf{R}_1$ match their corresponding tags and the tags verify using the verification key, send ACCEPT to $P_2$.
  3. else, send REJECT to $P_2$.

---

**Fig. 2.** The proof of storage functionality in the p2p file sharing setting.

Realize that if $P_1$ over-reported during the matching phase, meaning that he does not have all the blocks he claimed in $\mathbf{R}_1$, then $P_2$ will obtain a rejection signal. Similarly, if $P_1$ tries to use fake blocks, $P_2$ will reject. PoS, on the other hand, does not prevent under-reporting, since if one can prove storage of more blocks, he could also prove storage of fewer blocks. Remember though the RFE functionality discouraged under-reporting. PoS functionality discourages over-reporting. In the next section, we combine them to achieve our pair-wise exchange functionality. It is worth noting that $\mathcal{F}^{PoS}$ discourages over-reporting for $P_1$ only. But for our system to be an equilibrium, this must apply to all parties. Hence, we will employ two executions of $\mathcal{F}^{PoS}$ to discourage both parties.

## 6.3   $\mathcal{F}^{EXCH}$ and its Analysis

We first instantiate our pair-wise exchange protocol using the RFE and PoS functionalities described. The $\mathcal{F}^{EXCH}$ functionality instantiation is shown in Fig. 3. The idea is that, to be able to exchange blocks, peers must also prove to each other that they possess the blocks that they claim to own.

---

### The $\mathcal{F}^{EXCH}$ Functionality Instantiation

- $P_1$ provides his blocks $\mathbf{S}_1$ and their PoS tags, the block identifiers $\mathbf{R}_2$ that $P_2$ claimed to know, and the PoS verification key.
- $P_2$ provides her blocks $\mathbf{S}_2$ and their PoS tags, the block identifiers $\mathbf{R}_1$ that $P_1$ claimed to know, and the PoS verification key.
  1. Run $\mathcal{F}^{PoS}$. If $P_2$ receives REJECT at the end, send $\perp$ to both parties and abort.
  2. Run $\mathcal{F}^{PoS}$ again, but with the roles of $P_1$ and $P_2$ reversed. If $P_1$ receives REJECT at the end, send $\perp$ to both parties and abort.
  3. If still not aborted, run $\mathcal{F}^{RFE}$.

---

**Fig. 3.** The pair-wise exchange functionality instantiation.

*Game-Theoretic Analysis.* Since our simplified model only considers exchanging one block per round between peers, the best utility each pair of matched participants can obtain in one round in our analysis is $(1, 1)$ (both peers can obtain 1 block at the end of the exchange). Assuming the matching was done among mutually-interesting peers, the utilities of the matched peers using $\mathcal{F}^{EXCH}$ are described in Table 2. It is impossible assign a number for the "$<1$" parts, since it depends on the runtime values of the sets, and the sheer number of possibilities make the analysis impractical; but it is also unnecessary. **In the exchange game, there is only one strict Nash equilibrium, and that is when both matched peers honestly reported the pieces they own.**[3]

---
[3] More precisely, the zeros in the game should be replaced with negligible utilities (of managing to break PoS security), $<1$ values should be $<1 - 1/m$ (one minus non-negligible, where the file has $m$ blocks), and ones should be one minus negligible (due to the negligible probability of the fair exchange failing). Overall, we chose not to complicate the presentation with these details, but indeed our equilibrium is a *computational Nash equilibrium.*

**Table 2.** Two-player game during $\mathcal{F}^{EXCH}$ assuming peers are matched based on mutual interest. <1 denotes some utility strictly less than one.

| Peer i/j | Honest reporting | Under reporting | Over reporting |
|---|---|---|---|
| Honest reporting | 1, 1 | 1, <1 | 0, 0 |
| Under reporting | <1, 1 | <1, <1 | 0, 0 |
| Over reporting | 0, 0 | 0, 0 | 0, 0 |

---

**The $\mathcal{F}^{COIN}$ Functionality**

- Upon receiving integer $v$ from $P_1$ and integer $v'$ from $P_2$:
    1. if $v \neq v'$ or $v = v' = 0$, return $\bot$ to both parties.
    2. else, pick random integer $r \xleftarrow{\$} [1, v]$ and send it to both parties.

---

**Fig. 4.** The coin tossing functionality.

The intuition is that the **PoS makes it irrational for any rational party to over-report**, because if she does, then it will be detected during the PoS stage and the exchange will be aborted, resulting in zero utility for the over-reporter as well. PoS, however, does not deter under-reporting because it cannot detect that a party has more blocks than it claims to have. But **under-reporting is handled by the RFE protocol**, because if a player under-reports, then she has a non-zero probability of receiving a block she already has, whereas if she reports honestly she will receive a block she does not have with certainty.

## 7   RFE Instantiation

To realize randomized fair exchange, we employ unfair coin tossing protocols together with regular two-party fair exchange protocols.[4]

### 7.1   Coin Tossing

Figure 4 shows the coin tossing (COIN) functionality, where the coin is picked from an agreed-upon range. For our purposes, even though we model the functionality fairly, it is enough to instantiate via an unfair protocol where only one party learns the result, and is supposed to send that to the other party [9, 12].

---

[4] RFE is also related to oblivious transfer [47]. Indeed, at first, we were imagining a randomized oblivious fair exchange would be necessary, but it turns out we do not need obliviousness for the game theoretic analysis to go through.

---

**The $\mathcal{F}^{FEX}$ Functionality**

- Upon receiving item $i_1$ and hash $h_2$ from $P_1$ and item $i_2$ and hash $h_1$ from $P_2$:
    1. if $hash(i_1) \neq h_1$ or $hash(i_2) \neq h_2$, return $\perp$ to both parties.
    2. else, send $i_2$ to $P_1$ and $i_1$ to $P_2$.

---

**Fig. 5.** The fair exchange functionality.

---

**The $\mathcal{F}^{RFE}$ Functionality Instantiation**

- $P_1$ calculates the set $\mathbf{F}_1 = \mathbf{S}_1 - \mathbf{R}_2$ of blocks that he has but $P_2$ claims not to have. Note that if $P_1$ honestly reported, $\mathbf{S}_1 = \mathbf{R}_1$ and hence $\mathbf{F}_1 = \mathbf{R}_1 - \mathbf{R}_2$. Then, $P_1$ sets $v_1 = |\mathbf{F}_1|$.
- $P_1$ also calculates the set $\mathbf{F}_2 = \mathbf{R}_2 - \mathbf{S}_1$ of blocks that he does not have but $P_2$ claims to have. Again if $P_1$ honestly reported, we have $\mathbf{F}_2 = \mathbf{R}_2 - \mathbf{R}_1$. Then, $P_1$ sets $v_2 = |\mathbf{F}_2|$.
- $P_2$ computes the sets $\mathbf{F}'_1 = \mathbf{R}_1 - \mathbf{S}_2$ and $\mathbf{F}'_2 = \mathbf{S}_2 - \mathbf{R}_1$ (similarly, for honest $P_2$ we have $\mathbf{F}'_1 = \mathbf{R}_1 - \mathbf{R}_2$ and $\mathbf{F}'_2 = \mathbf{R}_2 - \mathbf{R}_1$). Then, $P_2$ sets $v'_1 = |\mathbf{F}'_1|$ and $v'_2 = |\mathbf{F}'_2|$.
    1. Run $\mathcal{F}^{COIN}$ where $P_1$ inputs $v_1$ and $P_2$ inputs $v'_1$, and they both obtain $r_1$. If any party obtains $\perp$ instead, abort.
    2. Run $\mathcal{F}^{COIN}$ again where $P_1$ inputs $v_2$ and $P_2$ inputs $v'_2$, and they both obtain $r_2$. If any party obtains $\perp$ instead, abort.
    3. Run $\mathcal{F}^{FEX}$ where the input of $P_1$ is the $r_1^{th}$ element of $\mathbf{F}_1$ together with the hash/tag in the torrent file for the $r_2^{th}$ element of $\mathbf{F}_2$. Similarly, the input of $P_2$ is the $r_2^{th}$ element of $\mathbf{F}'_2$ together with the hash/tag in the torrent file for the $r_1^{th}$ element of $\mathbf{F}'_1$.

---

**Fig. 6.** The randomized fair exchange functionality instantiation.

Note that, coin tossing protocols generally employ commitments, and hence one cannot cheat at the resulting $r$, but can only prevent the other party from learning $r$ (and hence outputting $\perp$).

## 7.2 (Non-randomized) Fair Exchange

As explained before, fair exchange is a simple functionality which requires the existence of a trusted third party [45]. But, in *optimistic* fair exchange scenarios, this trusted Arbiter does not get involved in every exchange [3,35]. This is the main disadvantage of the RatFish protocol, where the trusted Tracker must get involved in every exchange [8]. Figure 5 shows the fair exchange (FEX) functionality.

We focus on fair exchange of blocks, where the hash found in the torrent file enables checking that the block is authentic. In our case PoS tags serve the same purpose as hash values, and hence they can also be employed to check for correctness of the blocks exchanged, using existing instantiations [3,36].

### 7.3   Randomized Fair Exchange Protocol

The idea is similar to our $\mathcal{F}^{EXCH}$ functionality in the sense that we repeat unidirectional protocols both ways. Hence, in $\mathcal{F}^{RFE}$ we execute coin tossing twice, and then perform fair exchange on those random items. Remember that the items' correctness are guaranteed via PoS tags during $\mathcal{F}^{FEX}$. The protocol is depicted in Fig. 6.

Observe that while this functionality checks that the number of different blocks claimed by both parties are the same, this does not immediately prevent under- or over-reporting. For example, a party may under-report one piece and over-report another piece, such that the size of the difference remains the same. In general, we do not even need to ensure the sizes of set differences match, since PoS protocols within $\mathcal{F}^{EXCH}$ ensure that over-reporting is prevented, and randomization in $\mathcal{F}^{RFE}$ ensures that under-reporting is disincentivized. Finally, observe that $\mathcal{F}^{RFE}$ has *constant* communication and round complexity. (Further note that a parallel coin tossing protocol can be employed as well [39].)

## 8   The DogFish Protocol

*Initialization.* As DogFish is a variant of a BitTorrent-like p2p file-sharing protocol, we assume the existence of an external mechanism that enables the parties to find the swarm for a given file **f**. In BitTorrent, this duty is handled by trackers and hence we assume the same. Moreover, to be able to use the PoS, we assume that the owner of the file encodes it with a PoS which yields a set of tags. We assume that the torrent file contains those tags, as well as any public information necessary to verify those tags (i.e., PoS verification key). Finally, we start our description assuming the users already downloaded the torrent file and contacted the tracker, thereby obtaining the list of other peers and the PoS tags and verification key.

*Matching Phase.* DogFish is a peer-to-peer file sharing protocol that is pairwise as in Algorithm 1. At the first phase of the protocol, for the $\mathcal{F}^{MATCH}$ peer matching phase, we need to employ some existing *mutual* matching protocol. The only requirement in the $\mathcal{F}^{MATCH}$ phase is that it matches peers if and only if they both reported some block that the other does not possess. Thus, if $P_i$ and $P_j$ are matched, both $\mathbf{R}_i - \mathbf{R}_j$ and $\mathbf{R}_j - \mathbf{R}_i$ should be non-empty. Remember that we treat irrational seeders separately, and they can get matched even though they are not interested in the other peer. Moreover, as many pairs as possible should be matched for getting closer to the social optimum.

For achieving this, we are faced with two alternatives: Existing BitTorrent papers assume that the $\mathcal{F}^{MATCH}$ protocol of BitTorrent matches mutually interesting peers (both parties have a piece that the other does not possess) through the rarest-first heuristic [11]. Therefore, we can simply employ the BitTorrent

$\mathcal{F}^{MATCH}$ protocol. Alternatively, we can we use a distributed stable matching protocol [13,14,32] where parties share their reported blocks $\mathbf{R}_i$ and jointly compute a mutual matching in a distributed manner. As long as the same $\mathbf{R}_i$ values are used during $\mathcal{F}^{MATCH}$ and $\mathcal{F}^{EXCH}$ phases by rational peers, any cheating attempt during $\mathcal{F}^{MATCH}$ will be penalized during $\mathcal{F}^{EXCH}$. Thus, via one of these alternative methods, we assume DogFish obtains a matching of mutually interesting peers at the end of $\mathcal{F}^{MATCH}$. Observe furthermore that priotization (e.g., via rarest-first heuristic) does not affect our game theoretic analysis, as long as $\mathcal{F}^{MATCH}$ matches as many mutually interested peers as possible.

*Exchange Phase.* Once the matching is done, the round proceeds with the $\mathcal{F}^{EXCH}$ phase where we use the RFE and PoS protocols. Consider the two types of dishonest reporting: over-reporting and under-reporting.

1. If a peer $P_i$ under-reports, her probability of getting a useful block (a block that she does not already possess) goes down (compared to honest reporting) because:
    - While the effect of under-reporting in the matching phase is unclear, she is potentially less likely to be matched. This is because while $\mathbf{R}_j - \mathbf{R}_i$ is now potentially larger due to under-reporting, $\mathbf{R}_i - \mathbf{R}_j$ is getting smaller, and hence $P_i$ is potentially less interesting for other peers. But, this does not affect our analysis, as we show below.
    - Even when $P_i$ gets matched with some $P_j$, because random blocks are picked from $\mathbf{R}_i - \mathbf{R}_j$ and $\mathbf{R}_j - \mathbf{R}_i$ during RFE, it is possible that she gets some block that she under-reported (meaning that she already had the block but reported it as missing). Note that if she honestly reported instead, she was guaranteed to get a useful block after the exchange phase (assuming $P_j$ was honest).
2. If a peer $P_i$ over-reports, her probability of getting a useful block again goes down because:
    - Note that the effect of over-reporting during the matching phase is unclear. While over-reporting may create a larger $\mathbf{R}_i - \mathbf{R}_j$ and hence makes $P_i$ more interesting for $P_j$, the set $\mathbf{R}_j - \mathbf{R}_i$ is potentially getting smaller, decreasing the chance of a mutual matching. A history-based peer selection may help here, by penalizing previous cheating attempts of a peer, but again with random matchings, the effect is unclear. Fortunately, as before, this does not affect our analysis.
    - Regardless of how matching is affected, when $P_i$ gets matched with some $P_j$, over-reporting will be caught during the PoS part of the exchange phase (except with negligible probability), and hence she will not obtain any useful block. Note that if she honestly reported instead, she was guaranteed to get a useful block after $\mathcal{F}^{EXCH}$ (assuming $P_j$ was honest).

The discussion above makes one thing clear: Even when $\mathcal{F}^{MATCH}$ can be gamed, our $\mathcal{F}^{EXCH}$ instantiation ensures honest piece revelation as its equilibrium, as long as $\mathcal{F}^{MATCH}$ always matches all *mutually-interesting* peers. When peers are matched based on mutual interest, our exchange protocol provides enough incentive to act honestly, even during the matching phase. Realize that, as long as all mutually interesting peers are matched, for example via distributed stable matching, we do not need a multi-round analysis. This is because under- or over-reporting in one round does not provide any particular advantage in the matching phase afterward: The main constraint in the matching phase is that each matched peer has at least one block the other peer does not have.

After each exchange, when the new round begins, the peers again advertise their blocks during matching. Since honest piece revelation is the rational thing to do, all rational peers will advertise honestly, including the new piece they obtained in the last round. The protocol proceeds this way for every round, as long as there are at least two leechers. Peers may join or leave the system freely.

In summary, by matching mutually-interesting pairs during $\mathcal{F}^{MATCH}$ (e.g., via the BitTorrent rarest-first mutual matching protocol [11] or via some distributed mutual matching protocol such as stable matching) and making sure both parties obtain the best possible utility during $\mathcal{F}^{EXCH}$ (via RFE and PoS), we maximize the utilization of the upload bandwidth, and hence obtain social welfare. Essentially, we maximized the entries in the matrix representation of the piece exchanges (among pairwise p2p file sharing protocols). Moreover, the DogFish mechanism, and hence honest piece revelation, is the equilibrium in a game where utilities of players are defined as the number of pieces they download in a round. Note that in contrast to RatFish [8], we only need trackers at the beginning, and the rest of the protocol is purely peer-to-peer and decentralized (the Arbiter in our RFE instantiation gets involved *only* if there is a dispute during the fair exchange). This makes DogFish the only known decentralized equilibrium protocol for p2p file sharing achieving social welfare among a large class of protocols under realistic utility functions.

We constructed and analyzed DogFish as a theoretical proposal, hoping that prominent researchers will improve it to be practical. At the current stage, while the cryptographic protocols employed in DogFish are efficient computationally, the round complexity makes the proposal theoretical. For $\mathcal{F}^{MATCH}$, practical solution would be the existing BitTorrent rarest-first mutual matching protocol, since distributed stable matching is costly. For $\mathcal{F}^{EXCH}$, all sub-protocols (coin tossing, fair exchange, and proof of storage) are known to have $O(1)$ computational and communication costs for both parties (usually measured with milliseconds and kilobytes), with $O(1)$ rounds of interaction. But, while $O(1)$, each message passing round increases the total latency, which is another metric to optimize against in practice, and is not considered within our theoretical model. As future work, better $\mathcal{F}^{MATCH}$ protocols should be developed, number of rounds in $\mathcal{F}^{EXCH}$ should be optimized (potentially employing protocols that can be securely parallelized), and an analysis under a heterogeneous model should be conducted.

**Acknowledgements.** The authors acknowledge the support of TÜBİTAK, the Scientific and Technological Research Council of Turkey, under project number 111E019, as well as European Union COST Action IC1306.

# References

1. Aiyer, A.S., Alvisi, L., Clement, A., Dahlin, M., Martin, J.-P., Porth, C.: Bar fault tolerance for cooperative services. ACM SIGOPS Oper. Syst. Rev. **39**(5), 45–58 (2005)

2. Arteconi, S., Hales, D., Babaoglu, O.: Greedy cheating liars and the fools who believe them. In: Brueckner, S.A., Hassas, S., Jelasity, M., Yamins, D. (eds.) ESOA 2006. LNCS (LNAI), vol. 4335, pp. 161–175. Springer, Heidelberg (2007). https:// doi.org/10.1007/978-3-540-69868-5_11

3. Asokan, N., Shoup, V., Waidner, M.: Optimistic fair exchange of digital signatures. IEEE Sel. Areas Commun. **18**, 591–610 (2000)

4. Ateniese, G., Burns, R., Curtmola, R., Herring, J., Khan, O., Kissner, L., Peterson, Z., Song, D.: Remote data checking using provable data possession. ACM Trans. Inf. Syst. Secur. **14**(1), 12:1–12:34 (2011)

5. Ateniese, G., Kamara, S., Katz, J.: Proofs of storage from homomorphic identification protocols. In: Matsui, M. (ed.) ASIACRYPT 2009. LNCS, vol. 5912, pp. 319–333. Springer, Heidelberg (2009). https://doi.org/10.1007/978-3-642-10366-7_19

6. Axelrod, R.: Effective choice in the Prisoner's Dilemma. J. Conflict Resolut. **24**(1), 3–25 (1980)

7. Axelrod, R.: More effective choice in the Prisoner's Dilemma. J. Conflict Resolut. **24**(3), 379–403 (1980)

8. Backes, M., Ciobotaru, O., Krohmer, A.: RatFish: a file sharing protocol provably secure against rational users. In: Gritzalis, D., Preneel, B., Theoharidou, M. (eds.) ESORICS 2010. LNCS, vol. 6345, pp. 607–625. Springer, Heidelberg (2010). https://doi.org/10.1007/978-3-642-15497-3_37

9. Barak, B.: Constant-round coin-tossing with a man in the middle or realizing the shared random string model. In: IEEE FOCS (2002)

10. Belenkiy, M., Chase, M., Erway, C., Jannotti, J., Küpçü, A., Lysyanskaya, A., Rachlin, E.: Making P2P accountable without losing privacy. In: ACM WPES (2007)

11. Berciu, R.M.: Designing incentives in P2P systems. Master's thesis, Baylor University (2013)

12. Blum, M.: Coin flipping by telephone a protocol for solving impossible problems. SIGACT News **15**(1), 23–27 (1983). https://doi.org/10.1145/1008908.1008911

13. Brito, I., Meseguer, P.: Distributed stable matching problems. In: van Beek, P. (ed.) CP 2005. LNCS, vol. 3709, pp. 152–166. Springer, Heidelberg (2005). https://doi.org/10.1007/11564751_14

14. Brito, I., Meseguer, P.: Distributed stable matching problems with ties and incomplete lists. In: Benhamou, F. (ed.) CP 2006. LNCS, vol. 4204, pp. 675–679. Springer, Heidelberg (2006). https://doi.org/10.1007/11889205_49

15. Cash, D., Küpçü, A., Wichs, D.: Dynamic proofs of retrievability via oblivious RAM. J. Cryptol. **30**(1), 22–57 (2017)

16. Chen, K., Shen, H., Sapra, K., Liu, G.: A social network based reputation system for cooperative P2P file sharing. IEEE Trans. Parallel Distrib. Syst. **26**(8), 2140–2153 (2015)

17. Ciccarelli, G., Cigno, R.L.: Collusion in peer-to-peer systems. Comput. Netw. **55**(15), 3517–3532 (2011)

18. Cohen, B.: Incentives build robustness in BitTorrent. In: WEPS (2003)

19. Dodis, Y., Vadhan, S., Wichs, D.: Proofs of retrievability via hardness amplification. In: Reingold, O. (ed.) TCC 2009. LNCS, vol. 5444, pp. 109–127. Springer, Heidelberg (2009). https://doi.org/10.1007/978-3-642-00457-5_8
20. Ellison, G.: Cooperation in the Prisoner's Dilemma with anonymous random matching. Rev. Econ. Stud. **61**(3), 567–588 (1994)
21. Erway, C.C., Küpçü, A., Papamanthou, C., Tamassia, R.: Dynamic provable data possession. ACM Trans. Inf. Syst. Secur. **17**(4), 15:1–15:29 (2015). https://doi.org/10.1145/2699909. Article no. 15
22. Fader, P.S., Hauser, J.R.: Implicit coalitions in a generalized Prisoner's Dilemma. J. Conflict Resolut. **32**(3), 553–582 (1988)
23. Fan, B., Chiu, D., Lui, J.: The delicate tradeoffs in BitTorrent-like file sharing protocol design. Technical report, The Chinese University of Hong Kong (2006)
24. Fan, B., Chiu, D., Lui, J.C.: The delicate tradeoffs in BitTorrent-like file sharing protocol design. In: IEEE ICNP (2006)
25. Feldman, M., Lai, K., Stoica, I., Chuang, J.: Robust incentive techniques for peer-to-peer networks. In: ACM EC (2004)
26. Guo, D., Kwok, Y.-K., Jin, X.: Valuation of information and the associated overpayment problem in peer-to-peer systems. Comput. Commun. **80**, 59–71 (2016)
27. Halpern, J.Y.: Beyond Nash equilibrium: solution concepts for the 21st century. In: ACM PODC (2008)
28. Juels, A., Kaliski, B.S.: PORs: proofs of retrievability for large files. In: ACM CCS (2007)
29. Kash, I.A., Friedman, E.J., Halpern, J.Y.: An equilibrium analysis of scrip systems. ACM Trans. Econ. Comput. **3**(3), 13:1–13:32 (2015)
30. Keidar, I., Melamed, R., Orda, A.: Equicast: scalable multicast with selfish users. Comput. Netw. **53**(13), 2373–2386 (2009)
31. Kılınç, H., Küpçü, A.: Optimally efficient multi-party fair exchange and fair secure multi-party computation. In: Nyberg, K. (ed.) CT-RSA 2015. LNCS, vol. 9048, pp. 330–349. Springer, Cham (2015). https://doi.org/10.1007/978-3-319-16715-2_18
32. Kipnis, A., Patt-Shamir, B.: A note on distributed stable matching. In: IEEE ICDCS (2009)
33. Kumar, R., Ross, K.W.: Peer-assisted file distribution: the minimum distribution time. In: IEEE HOTWEB (2006)
34. Küpçü, A.: Official arbitration with secure cloud storage application. Comput. J. **58**(4), 831–852 (2015)
35. Küpçü, A., Lysyanskaya, A.: Optimistic fair exchange with multiple arbiters. In: Gritzalis, D., Preneel, B., Theoharidou, M. (eds.) ESORICS 2010. LNCS, vol. 6345, pp. 488–507. Springer, Heidelberg (2010). https://doi.org/10.1007/978-3-642-15497-3_30
36. Küpçü, A., Lysyanskaya, A.: Usable optimistic fair exchange. Comput. Netw. **56**, 50–63 (2012)
37. Levin, D., LaCurts, K., Spring, N., Bhattacharjee, B.: BitTorrent is an auction: analyzing and improving BitTorrent's incentives. ACM SIGCOMM Comput. Commun. Rev. **38**(4), 243–254 (2008)
38. Levin, D., Sherwood, R., Bhattacharjee, B.: Fair file swarming with fox. In: IPTPS (2006)
39. Lindell, Y.: Parallel coin-tossing and constant-round secure two-party computation. J. Cryptol. **16**(3), 143–184 (2003)
40. Locher, T., Moor, P., Schmid, S., Wattenhofer, R.: Free riding in BitTorrent is cheap. In: HotNets (2006)

41. Luo, J., Xiao, B., Bu, K., Zhou, S.: Understanding and improving piece-related algorithms in the BitTorrent protocol. IEEE Trans. Parallel Distrib. Syst. **24**(12), 2526–2537 (2013)

42. Meng, X., Tsang, P.-S., Lui, K.-S.: Analysis of distribution time of multiple files in a P2P network. Comput. Netw. **57**(15), 2900–2915 (2013)

43. Neyman, A.: Bounded complexity justifies cooperation in the finitely repeated Prisoners' Dilemma. Econ. Lett. **19**(3), 227–229 (1985)

44. Okumuşoğlu, O., Bayraktar, M.F., Küpçü, A.: JustTorrent: value based-fairer and faster protocols for P2P file sharing. Int. J. Eng. Sci. Appl. **1**(1), 1–10 (2017)

45. Pagnia, H., Gartner, F.C.: On the impossibility of fair exchange without a trusted third party. Technical report, Darmstadt University of Technology TUD-BS-1999-02 (1999)

46. Piatek, M., Isdal, T., Anderson, T., Krishnamurthy, A., Venkataramani, A.: Do incentives build robustness in BitTorrent. In: NSDI (2007)

47. Rabin, M.O.: How to exchange secrets by oblivious transfer. Technical report, Harvard Aiken Computation Laboratory Technical report TR-81 (1981)

48. Radner, R.: Can bounded rationality resolve the Prisoner's Dilemma? In: Essays in Honor of Gerard Debreu, pp. 387–399 (1986)

49. Roy, S.D., Zeng, W.: prTorrent: on establishment of piece rarity in the BitTorrent unchoking algorithm. In: IEEE P2P (2009)

50. Sandvine. Global Internet Phenemona, December 2015

51. Shacham, H., Waters, B.: Compact proofs of retrievability. J. Cryptol. **26**(3), 442–483 (2013)

52. Sirivianos, M., Yang, X., Jarecki, S.: Robust and efficient incentives for cooperative content distribution. IEEE/ACM Trans. Netw. **17**(6), 1766–1779 (2009)

53. Vilaça, X., Rodrigues, L.: On the range of equilibria utilities of a repeated epidemic dissemination game with a mediator. In: ACM ICDCN (2015)

54. Vishnumurthy, V., Chandrakumar, S., Sirer, E.G.: Karma: a secure economic framework for peer-to-peer resource sharing. In: P2PECON (2003)

# Author Index

# Author Index

Printed in the United States
By Bookmasters